C++

Primer Plus

Fourth Edition

Stephen Prata

SAMS

800 East 96th St., Indianapolis, Indiana 46240 USA

C++ Primer Plus
Fourth Edition

International Standard Book Number: 0672322234

Library of Congress Catalog Card Number: 2001089224

Printed in the United States of America

First Printing: November 2001
Second printing with corrections: August 2002
Third printing with corrections: November 2003

05   04   03   6   5   4

ASSOCIATE PUBLISHER
Linda Engelman

ACQUISITIONS EDITOR
Linda Scharp

DEVELOPMENT EDITOR
Karen Wachs

MANAGING EDITOR
Charlotte Clapp

INDEXER
Kelly Castell

PROOFREADERS
Bob LaRoche
Jessica McCarty

TECHNICAL EDITORS
Philippe Bruno
Bill Craun
Michael Maddox
Chris Maunder

TEAM COORDINATOR
Lynne Williams

INTERIOR DESIGNER
Gary Adair

COVER DESIGNER
Gary Adair

PAGE LAYOUT
Ayanna Lacey
Stacey Richwine-DeRome

Trademarks

All terms mentioned in this book that are known to be trademarks or service marks have been appropriately capitalized. Sams Publishing cannot attest to the accuracy of this information. Use of a term in this book should not be regarded as affecting the validity of any trademark or service mark.

Warning and Disclaimer

Every effort has been made to make this book as complete and as accurate as possible, but no warranty or fitness is implied. The information provided is on an "as is" basis. The author and the publisher shall have neither liability nor responsibility to any person or entity with respect to any loss or damages arising from the information contained in this book or from the use of the programs accompanying it.

Bulk Sales

Sams Publishing offers excellent discounts on this book when ordered in quantity for bulk purchases or special sales. For more information, please contact

U.S. Corporate and Government Sales
1-800-382-3419
corpsales@pearsontechgroup.com

For sales outside of the U.S., please contact

International Sales
1-317-428-3341
international@pearsontechgroup.com

CONTENTS AT A GLANCE

TABLE OF CONTENTS

PREFACE

Preface to the Fourth Edition

Learning C++ is an adventure of discovery, particularly because the language accommodates several programming paradigms, including object-oriented programming, generic programming, and the traditional procedural programming. C++ has been a moving target as the language added new features, but now, with the ISO/ANSI C++ Standard of 1998 in place, the language has stabilized. Contemporary compilers support most or all of the features mandated by the standard, and programmers have had time to get used to applying these features. The Fourth Edition of *C++ Primer Plus* reflects the ISO/ANSI standard and describes this matured version of C++.

C++ Primer Plus integrates discussing the basic C language with presenting C++ features, making this book self-contained. It presents C++ fundamentals and illustrates them with short, to-the-point programs that are easy to copy and experiment with. You'll learn about input and output, how to make programs perform repetitive tasks and make choices, the many ways to handle data, and how to use functions. You'll learn about the many features C++ has added to C, including the following:

- Classes and objects

- Inheritance

- Polymorphism, virtual functions, and RTTI (runtime type identification)

- Function overloading

- Reference variables

- Generic, or type-independent programming, as provided by templates and the Standard Template Library (STL)

- The exception mechanism for handling error conditions

- Namespaces for managing names of functions, classes, and variables

C++ Primer Plus brings several virtues to the task of presenting all this material. It builds upon the primer tradition begun by *C Primer Plus* nearly two decades ago and embraces its successful philosophy:

- A primer should be an easy-to-use, friendly guide.

- A primer doesn't assume that you already are familiar with all relevant programming concepts.

- A primer emphasizes hands-on learning with brief, easily typed examples that develop your understanding a concept or two at a time.

- A primer clarifies concepts with illustrations.

- A primer provides questions and exercises to let you test your understanding, making the book suitable for self-learning or for the classroom.

The book helps you understand this rich language and how to use it.

- It provides conceptual guidance about when to use particular features, such as using public inheritance to model what are known as *is-a* relationships.

- It illustrates common C++ programming idioms and techniques.

- It provides a variety of sidebars, including tips, cautions, and real-world notes.

We (the author and editors) do our best to keep the presentation to-the-point, simple, and fun. Our goal is that by the end of the book you'll be able to write solid, effective programs and enjoy yourself doing so.

Like the previous editions, this book practices generic C++ so that it is not tied to any particular kind of computer, operating system, or compiler. All the programs were tested with CodeWarrior Pro 6 (Macintosh and Windows) and Microsoft Visual C++ 6.0, and most were tested with Borland C++ Command-Line Compiler 5.5, Gnu g++ 2.9.5 running under DOS, and Comeau C/C++ 4.42.5 running under Linux. Only a few programs were affected by compiler non-conformance issues.

C++ offers a lot to the programmer; learn and enjoy!

Note to Instructors

One of the goals of the fourth edition is to provide a book that can be used as either a teach-yourself book or a textbook. Here are some of the features that support using *C++ Primer Plus, Fourth Edition* as a textbook:

- This book describes generic C++, so it isn't dependent upon a particular implementation.

- The contents track the ISO/ANSI C++ standards committee's work and include discussions of templates, the Standard Template Library, the **string** class, exceptions, RTTI, and namespaces.

- It doesn't assume prior knowledge of C, so it can be used without a C prerequisite. (Some programming background is desirable, however.)

- Topics are arranged so that the early chapters can be covered rapidly as review chapters for courses that do have a C prerequisite.

- Chapters have review questions and programming exercises.

- The book introduces several topics appropriate for computer science courses, including abstract data types, stacks, queues, simple lists, simulations, generic programming, and using recursion to implement a divide-and-conquer strategy.

- Most chapters are short enough to cover in a week or less.

- The book discusses *when* to use certain features as well as *how* to use them. For example, it links public inheritance to *is-a* relationships and composition and private inheritance to *has-a* relationships, and it discusses when to use virtual functions and when not to.

How This Book Is Organized

This book is divided into 17 chapters and 10 appendixes summarized here.

Chapter 1: Getting Started

This chapter relates how Bjarne Stroustrup created the C++ programming language by adding object-oriented programming support to the C language. You'll learn the distinctions between procedural languages, such as C, and object-oriented languages, such as C++. You'll read about the joint ANSI/ISO work to develop a C++ standard. The chapter discusses the mechanics of creating a C++ program, outlining the approach for several current C++ compilers. Finally, it describes the conventions used in this book.

Chapter 2: Setting Out to C++

Chapter 2 guides you through the process of creating simple C++ programs. You'll learn about the role of the `main()` function and about some of the kinds of statements that C++ programs use. You'll use the predefined `cout` and `cin` objects for program output and input, and you'll learn about creating and using variables. Finally, you'll be introduced to functions, C++'s programming modules.

Chapter 3: Dealing with Data

C++ provides built-in types for storing two kinds of data: integers (numbers with no fractional parts) and floating-point numbers (numbers with fractional parts). To meet the diverse requirements of programmers, C++ offers several types in each category. This chapter discusses these types, including creating variables and writing constants of various types. You'll also learn how C++ handles implicit and explicit conversions from one type to another.

Chapter 4: Compound Types

C++ lets you construct more elaborate types from the basic built-in types. The most advanced form is the class, discussed in Chapters 10, 11, 12, 13 and 14. This chapter discusses other forms, including arrays, which hold several values of a single type; structures, which hold several values of unlike types; and pointers, which identify locations in memory. You'll also learn how to create and store text strings and to handle text input and output. Finally, you'll learn some of the ways C++ handles memory allocation, including the `new` and `delete` operators for managing memory explicitly.

Chapter 5: Loops and Relational Expressions

Programs often must perform repetitive actions, and C++ provides three looping structures for that purpose: the `for` loop, the `while` loop, and the `do while` loop. Such loops must know when they should terminate, and the C++ relational operators enable you to create tests to guide such loops. You'll also learn how to create loops that read and process input character-by-character. Finally, you'll learn how to create two-dimensional arrays and how to use nested loops to process them.

Chapter 6: Branching Statements and Logical Operators

Programs can behave intelligently if they can tailor their behavior to circumstances. In this chapter you'll learn how to control program flow by using the `if`, `if else`, and `switch` statements and the conditional operator. You'll learn how to use logical operators to help express decision-making tests. Also, you'll meet the `cctype` library of functions for evaluating character relations, such as testing whether a character is a digit or a nonprinting character.

Chapter 7: Functions—C++'s Programming Modules

Functions are the basic building blocks of C++ programming. This chapter concentrates on features that C++ functions share with C functions. In particular, you'll review the general format of a function definition and examine how function prototypes increase the reliability of programs. Also, you'll investigate how to write functions to process arrays, character strings, and structures. Next you'll learn about recursion, which is when a function calls itself, and see how it can be used to implement a divide-and-conquer strategy. Finally, you'll meet pointers to functions, which enable you to use a function argument to tell one function to use a second function.

Chapter 8: Adventures in Functions

This chapter explores the new features C++ adds to functions. You'll learn about inline functions, which can speed program execution at the cost of additional program size. You'll work with reference variables, which provide an alternative way to pass information to functions. Default arguments let a function automatically supply values for function arguments that you omit from a function call. Function overloading lets you create functions having the same name but taking different argument lists. All these features have frequent use in class design. Also, you'll learn about function templates, which allow you to specify the design of a family of related functions.

Chapter 9: Memory Models and Namespaces

This chapter discusses putting together multifile programs. It examines your choices in allocating memory, looking at different methods of managing memory and at scope, linkage, and namespaces, which determine what parts of a program know about a variable.

Chapter 10: Objects and Classes

A class is a user-defined type, and an object is an instance of a class, such as a variable. This chapter introduces you to object-oriented programming and to class design. A class declaration describes the information stored in a class object and also the operations (class methods) allowed for class objects. Some parts of an object are visible to the outside world (the public portion), and some are hidden (the private portion). Special class methods (constructors and destructors) come into play when objects are created and destroyed. You will learn about all this and other class details in this chapter, and you'll see how classes can be used to implement abstract data types (ADTs), such as a stack.

Chapter 11: Working with Classes

In this chapter you'll further your understanding of classes. First you'll learn about operator overloading, which lets you define how operators such as + will work with class objects. You'll learn about friend functions, which can access class data that's inaccessible to the world at large. You'll see how certain constructors and overloaded operator member functions can be used to manage conversion to and from class types.

Chapter 12: Classes and Dynamic Memory Allocation

Often it's useful to have a class member point to dynamically allocated memory. If you use new in a class constructor to allocate dynamic memory, you incur the responsibilities of providing an appropriate destructor, of defining an explicit copy constructor, and of defining an explicit assignment operator. This chapter shows you how and discusses the behavior of the member functions generated implicitly if you fail to provide explicit definitions. You'll also expand your experience with classes by using pointers to objects and studying a queue simulation problem.

Chapter 13: Class Inheritance

One of the most powerful features of object-oriented programming is inheritance, by which a derived class inherits the features of a base class, enabling you to reuse the base class code. This chapter discusses public inheritance, which models *is-a* relationships, meaning that a derived object is a special case of a base object. For example, a physicist is a special case of a scientist. Some inheritance relationships are polymorphic, meaning you can write code using a mixture of related classes for which the same method name may invoke behavior that depends upon the object type. Implementing this kind of behavior necessitates using a new kind of member function called a virtual function. Sometimes abstract base classes are the best approach to inheritance relationships. This chapter discusses these matters, pointing out when public inheritance is appropriate and when it is not.

Chapter 14: Reusing Code in C++

Public inheritance is just one way to reuse code. This chapter looks at several other ways. Containment is when one class contains members that are objects of another class. It can be used to model *has-a* relationships, in which one class has components of another class. For example, an automobile has a motor. You also can use private and protected inheritance to model such relationships. This chapter shows you how and points out the differences among the different approaches. Also, you'll learn about class templates, which let you define a class in terms of some unspecified generic type, then use the template to create specific classes in terms of specific types. For example, a stack template enables you to create a stack of integers or a stack of strings. Finally, you'll learn about multiple public inheritance, whereby a class can derive from more than one class.

Chapter 15: Friends, Exceptions, and More

This chapter extends the discussion of friends to include friend classes and friend member functions. Then it presents several new developments in C++, beginning with exceptions, which provide a mechanism for dealing with unusual program occurrences, such an inappropriate function argument values or running out of memory. Then you'll learn about RTTI (runtime type information), a mechanism for identifying object types. Finally, you'll learn about the safer alternatives to unrestricted typecasting.

Chapter 16: The `string` Class and the Standard Template Library

This chapter discusses some useful class libraries recently added to the language. The `string` class is a convenient and powerful alternative to traditional C-style strings. The `auto_ptr` class helps manage dynamically allocated memory. The Standard Template Library (STL) provides several generic containers, including template representations of arrays, queues, lists, sets, and maps. It also provides an efficient library of generic algorithms that can be used with STL containers and also with ordinary arrays.

Chapter 17: Input, Output, and Files

This chapter reviews C++ I/O and discusses how to format output. You'll learn how to use class methods to determine the state of an input or output stream and to see, for example, if there has been a type mismatch on input or if end-of-file has been detected. C++ uses inheritance to derive classes for managing file input and output. You'll learn how to open files for input and output, how to append data to a file, how to use binary files, and how to get random access to a file. Finally, you'll learn how to apply standard I/O methods to read from and write to strings.

Appendix A: Number Bases

This appendix discusses octal, hexadecimal, and binary numbers.

Appendix B: C++ Keywords

This appendix lists C++ keywords.

Appendix C: The ASCII Character Set

This appendix lists the ASCII character set along with decimal, octal, hexadecimal, and binary representations.

Appendix D: Operator Precedence

This appendix lists the C++ operators in order of decreasing precedence.

Appendix E: Other Operators

This appendix summarizes those C++ operators, such as the bitwise operators, not covered in the main body of the text.

Appendix F: The `string` Template Class

This appendix summarizes `string` class methods and functions.

Appendix G: The STL Methods and Functions

This appendix summarizes the STL container methods and the general STL algorithm functions.

Appendix H: Selected Readings

This appendix lists some books that can further your understanding of C++.

Appendix I: Converting to ANSI/ISO Standard C++

This appendix provides guidelines for moving from C and older C++ implementations to Standard C++.

Appendix J: Answers to Review Questions

This appendix contains the answers to the review questions posed at the end of each chapter.

ABOUT THE AUTHOR

Stephen Prata teaches astronomy, physics, and computer science at the College of Marin in Kentfield, California. He received his B.S. from the California Institute of Technology and his Ph.D. from the University of California, Berkeley. Stephen has authored or coauthored over a dozen books for The Waite Group. He wrote The Waite Group's *New C Primer Plus*, which received the Computer Press Association's 1990 Best How-to Computer Book Award and The Waite Group's *C++ Primer Plus*, nominated for the Computer Press Association's Best How-to Computer Book Award in 1991.

DEDICATION

To my colleagues and students at the College of Marin, with whom it is a pleasure to work.

—Stephen Prata

ACKNOWLEDGMENTS

ACKNOWLEDGMENTS TO THE FOURTH EDITION

Several editors from Pearson and from Sams helped originate and maintain this project, so thanks to Linda Sharp, Karen Wachs, and Laurie McGuire. Thanks, too, to Michael Maddox, Bill Craun, Chris Maunder, and Phillipe Bruno for providing technical review and editing. And thanks again to Michael Maddox and Bill Craun for supplying the material for the Real World Notes. Also, thank you Ron Leichty of Metroworks and Greg Comeau of Comeau Computing for your help with the new C99 features and your noteworthy commitment to customer service.

ACKNOWLEDGMENTS TO THE THIRD EDITION

I'd like to thank the editors from Macmillan Press and Waite Group Press for the roles they played in putting this book together: Tracy Dunkelberger, Susan Walton, and Andrea Rosenberg. Thanks, too, to Russ Jacobs for his content and technical editing. From Metrowerks, I'd like to thank Dave Mark, Alex Harper, and especially Ron Liechty, for their help and cooperation.

ACKNOWLEDGMENTS TO THE SECOND EDITION

I'd like to thank Mitchell Waite and Scott Calamar for supporting a second edition and Joel Fugazzotto and Joanne Miller for guiding the project to completion. Thanks to Michael Marcotty of Metrowerks for dealing with my questions about their beta version CodeWarrior compiler. I'd also like to thank the following instructors for taking the time to give us feedback on the first edition: Jeff Buckwalter, Earl Brynner, Mike Holland, Andy Yao, Larry Sanders, Shahin Momtazi, and Don Stephens. Finally, I wish to thank Heidi Brumbaugh for her helpful content editing of new and revised material.

ACKNOWLEDGMENTS TO THE FIRST EDITION

Many people have contributed to this book. In particular, I wish to thank Mitch Waite for his work in developing, shaping, and reshaping this book, and for reviewing the manuscript. I appreciate Harry Henderson's work in reviewing the last few chapters and in testing programs with the Zortech C++ compiler. Thanks to David Gerrold for reviewing the entire manuscript and for championing the needs of less-experienced readers. Also thanks to Hank Shiffman for testing programs using Sun C++ and to Kent Williams for testing programs with AT&T cfront and with G++. Thanks to Nan Borreson of Borland International for her responsive and cheerful assistance with Turbo C++ and Borland C++. Thank you, Ruth Myers and Christine Bush, for handling the relentless paper flow involved with this kind of project. Finally, thanks to Scott Calamar for keeping everything on track.

TELL US WHAT YOU THINK!

As the reader of this book, *you* are our most important critic and commentator. We value your opinion and want to know what we're doing right, what we could do better, what areas you'd like to see us publish in, and any other words of wisdom you're willing to pass our way.

As an associate publisher for Sams, I welcome your comments. You can e-mail or write me directly to let me know what you did or didn't like about this book—as well as what we can do to make our books stronger.

Please note that I cannot help you with technical problems related to the topic of this book, and that due to the high volume of mail I receive, I might not be able to reply to every message.

When you write, please be sure to include this book's title and author as well as your name and phone or fax number. I will carefully review your comments and share them with the author and editors who worked on the book.

E-mail: `feedback@samspublishing.com`

Mail: Michael Stephens
            Sams Publishing
            800 East 96th Street
            Indianapolis, IN 46240 USA

CHAPTER 1

GETTING STARTED

You will learn about the following in this chapter:

- How C++ adds object-oriented concepts to the C language
- How C++ adds generic programming concepts to the C language
- The history and philosophy of C
- Procedural versus object-oriented programming

- The history and philosophy of C++
- Programming language standards
- The mechanics of creating a program
- Conventions used in this book

Welcome to C++! This exciting language, blending the C language with support for object-oriented programming, became one of the most important programming languages of the 1990s and continues strongly into the 2000s. Its C ancestry brings to C++ the tradition of an efficient, compact, fast, and portable language. Its object-oriented heritage brings C++ a fresh programming methodology designed to cope with the escalating complexity of modern programming tasks. Its template features bring yet another new programming methodology, generic programming. This triple heritage is both a blessing and a bane. It makes the language very powerful, but it also means there's more to learn.

In this chapter we'll explore C++'s background further and then go over some of the ground rules for creating C++ programs. The rest of the book teaches you to use the C++ language, going from the modest basics of the language to the glory of object-oriented programming (OOP) and its supporting cast of new jargon—objects, classes, encapsulation, data hiding, polymorphism, and inheritance, then on to its support of generic programming. (Of course, as you learn C++, these terms will be transformed from buzzwords to the necessary vocabulary of cultivated discourse.)

Learning C++

C++ joins three separate programming traditions—the procedural language tradition, represented by C; the object-oriented language tradition, represented by the class enhancements C++ adds to C; and generic programming, supported by C++ templates. This chapter will look into those traditions shortly. But first, let's consider what this heritage implies about learning C++. One reason to use C++ is to avail yourself of its object-oriented features. To do so, you need a sound background in standard C, for that language provides the basic types, operators, control structures, and syntax rules. So, if you already know C, you're poised to learn C++. But it's not just a matter of learning a few more keywords and constructs. Going from C to C++ involves about as much work as learning C in the first place. Also, if you know C, you must unlearn some programming habits as you make the transition to C++. If you don't know C, you have to master the C components, the OOP components, and the generic components to learn C++, but at least you may not have to unlearn programming habits. If you are beginning to think that learning C++ may involve some mind-stretching effort on your part, you're right. This book will guide you through the process in a clear, helpful manner, one step at a time, so the mind-stretching will be sufficiently gentle to leave your brain resilient.

C++ Primer Plus approaches C++ by teaching both its C basis and its new components, so this book assumes you have no prior knowledge of C. You'll start by learning the features C++ shares with C. Even if you know C, you may find this part of the book a good review. Also, it points out concepts that will become important later, and it indicates where C++ differs from C. After you are well-founded in the basics of C, you'll add the C++ superstructure. At this point you'll learn about objects and classes and how C++ implements them. And you will learn about templates.

This book is not intended to be a complete C++ reference; it won't explore every nook and cranny of the language. But you will learn all the major features of the language, including some, like templates, exceptions, and namespaces, that are more recent additions.

Now let's take a brief look at some of C++'s background.

A Little History

Computer technology has evolved at an amazing rate during the last few decades. Today a laptop computer can compute faster and store more information than the mainframe computers of thirty years ago. (Quite a few programmers can recall bearing offerings of decks of punched cards to be submitted to a mighty, room-filling computer system with a majestic 100KB of memory—not enough memory to run a good personal computer game today.) Computer languages have evolved, too. The changes may not be as dramatic, but they are important. Bigger, more powerful computers spawn bigger, more complex programs which, in turn, raise new problems in program management and maintenance.

In the 1970s, languages like C and Pascal helped usher in an era of structured programming, a philosophy that brought some order and discipline to a field badly in need of these qualities. Besides providing the tools for structured programming, C also produced compact, fast-running programs along with the ability to address hardware matters, such as managing communication ports and disk drives. These gifts helped make C the dominant programming language in the 1980s. Meanwhile, the 1980s witnessed the growth of a new programming paradigm: object-oriented programming, or OOP, as embodied in languages such as SmallTalk and C++. Let's examine these two developments (C and OOP) a bit more closely.

The C Language

In the early 1970s, Dennis Ritchie of Bell Laboratories was working on a project to develop the UNIX operating system. (An operating system is a set of programs that manages a computer's resources and handles its interactions with users. For example, it's the operating system that puts the system prompt onscreen and that runs programs for you.) For this work Ritchie needed a language that was concise, that produced compact, fast programs, and that could control hardware efficiently. Traditionally, programmers met these needs by using assembly language, which is closely tied to a computer's internal machine language. However, assembly language is a *low-level* language, that is, it is specific to a particular computer processor. So if you want to move an assembly program to a different kind of computer, you may have to completely rewrite the program using a different assembly language. It was a bit as if each time you bought a new car, you found that the designers decided to change where the controls went and what they did, forcing you to relearn how to drive. But UNIX was intended to work on a variety of computer types (or platforms). That suggested using a high-level language. A *high-level* language is oriented towards problem-solving instead of towards specific hardware. Special programs called *compilers* translate a high-level language to the internal language of a particular computer. Thus, you can use the same high-level language program on different platforms by using a separate compiler for each platform. Ritchie wanted a language that combined low-level efficiency and hardware access with high-level generality and portability. So, building from older languages, he created C.

C Programming Philosophy

Because C++ grafts a new programming philosophy onto C, we should first take a look at the older philosophy that C follows. In general, computer languages deal with two concepts—data and algorithms. The data constitute the information a program uses and processes. The algorithms are the methods the program uses (see Figure 1.1). C, like most mainstream languages to date, is a *procedural* language. That means it emphasizes the algorithm side of programming. Conceptually, procedural programming consists of figuring out the actions a computer should take and then using the programming language to implement those actions. A program prescribes a set of procedures for the computer to follow to produce a particular outcome, much as a recipe prescribes a set of procedures for a cook to follow to produce a cake.

FIGURE 1.1

Data + algorithms = program.

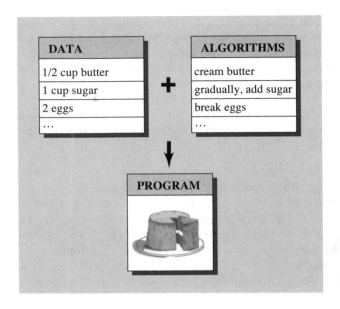

Earlier procedural languages, such as FORTRAN and BASIC, ran into organizational problems as programs grew larger. For example, programs often use branching statements, which route execution to one or another set of instructions depending upon the result of some sort of test. Many older programs had such tangled routing (called "spaghetti programming") that it was virtually impossible to understand a program by reading it, and modifying such a program was an invitation to disaster. In response, computer scientists developed a more disciplined style of programming called *structured programming*. C includes features to facilitate this approach. For example, structured programming limits branching (choosing which instruction to do next) to a small set of well-behaved constructions. C incorporates these constructions (the `for` loop, the `while` loop, the `do while` loop, and the `if else` statement) into its vocabulary.

Top-down design was another of the new principles. The idea is to break a large program into smaller, more manageable tasks. If one of these tasks is still too broad, divide it into yet smaller tasks. Continue with this process until the program is compartmentalized into small, easily programmed modules. (Organize your study. Aargh! Well, organize your desk, your table top, your filing cabinet, and your bookshelves. Aargh! Well, start with the desk and organize each drawer, starting with the middle one. Hmmm, perhaps I can manage that task.) C's design facilitates this approach, encouraging you to develop program units called *functions* to represent individual task modules. As you may have noticed, the structured programming techniques reflect a procedural mind-set, thinking of a program in terms of the actions it performs.

Object-Oriented Programming

Although the principles of structured programming improved the clarity, reliability, and ease of maintenance of programs, large-scale programming still remains a challenge.

Object-oriented programming (OOP) brings a new approach to that challenge. Unlike procedural programming, which emphasizes algorithms, OOP emphasizes the data. Rather than trying to fit a problem to the procedural approach of a language, OOP attempts to fit the language to the problem. The idea is to design data forms that correspond to the essential features of a problem.

In C++, a *class* is a specification describing such a new data form, and an *object* is a particular data structure constructed according to that plan. For example, a class could describe the general properties of a corporation executive (name, title, salary, unusual abilities, for example), while an object would represent a specific executive (Guilford Sheepblat, vice president, $325,000, knows how to use a CONFIG.SYS file). In general, a class defines what data are used to represent an object *and* the operations that can be performed upon that data. For example, suppose you were developing a computer drawing program capable of drawing a rectangle. You could define a class to describe a rectangle. The data part of the specification could include such things as the location of the corners, the height and width, the color and style of the boundary line, and the color and pattern used to fill the rectangle. The operations part of the specification could include methods for moving the rectangle, resizing it, rotating it, changing colors and patterns, and copying the rectangle to another location. If you then use your program to draw a rectangle, it will create an object according to the class specification. That object will hold all the data values describing the rectangle, and you can use the class methods to modify that rectangle. If you draw two rectangles, the program will create two objects, one for each rectangle.

The OOP approach to program design is to first design classes that accurately represent those things with which the program deals. A drawing program, for example, might define classes to represent rectangles, lines, circles, brushes, pens, and the like. The class definitions, recall, include a description of permissible operations for each class, such as moving a circle or rotating a line. Then you proceed to design a program using objects of those classes. The process of going from a lower level of organization, such as classes, to a higher level, such as program design, is called *bottom-up* programming.

There's more to OOP programming than the binding of data and methods into a class definition. OOP, for example, facilitates creating reusable code, and that eventually can save a lot of work. Information hiding safeguards data from improper access. Polymorphism lets you create multiple definitions for operators and functions, with the programming context determining which definition is used. Inheritance lets you derive new classes from old ones. As you can see, object-oriented programming introduces many new ideas and involves a different approach to programming than does procedural programming. Instead of concentrating on tasks, you concentrate on representing concepts. Instead of taking a top-down programming approach, you sometimes take a bottom-up approach. This book will guide you through all these points with plenty of easily grasped examples.

Designing a useful, reliable class can be a difficult task. Fortunately, OOP languages make it simple to incorporate existing classes into your own programming. Vendors provide a variety of useful class libraries, including libraries of classes designed to simplify creating programs for environments such as Windows or the Macintosh. One of the real benefits of C++ is that it lets you easily reuse and adapt existing, well-tested code.

Generic Programming

Generic programming is yet another programming paradigm supported by C++. It shares with OOP the aim of making it simpler to reuse code and the technique of abstracting general concepts. But while OOP emphasizes the data aspect of programming, generic programming emphasizes the algorithmic aspect. And its focus is different. OOP is a tool for managing large projects, while generic programming provides tools for performing common tasks, such as sorting data or merging lists. The term *generic* means to create code that is type-independent. C++ data representations come in many types—integers, numbers with fractional parts, characters, strings of characters, user-defined compound structures of several types. If, for example, you wanted to sort data of these various types, you normally have to create a separate sorting function for each type. Generic programming involves extending the language so that you can write a function for a generic (that is, not specified) type once, and use it for a variety of actual types. C++ templates provide a mechanism for doing that.

C++

Like C, C++ began its life at Bell Labs, where Bjarne Stroustrup developed the language in the early 1980s. In his own words, "C++ was designed primarily so that my friends and I would not have to program in assembler, C, or various modern high-level languages. Its main purpose was to make writing good programs easier and more pleasant for the individual programmer" (Bjarne Stroustrup, *The C++ Programming Language*. Third Edition. Reading, MA: Addison-Wesley Publishing Company, 1997).

Stroustrup was more concerned with making C++ useful than with enforcing particular programming philosophies or styles. Real programming needs are more important than theoretical purity in determining C++ language features. Stroustrup based C++ on C because of C's brevity, its suitability to system programming, its widespread availability, and its close ties to the UNIX operating system. C++'s OOP aspect was inspired by a computer simulation language called Simula67. Stroustrup added OOP features and generic programming support to C without significantly changing the C component. Thus C++ is a superset of C, meaning that any valid C program is a valid C++ program, too. There are some minor discrepancies, but nothing crucial. C++ programs can use existing C software libraries. Libraries are collections of programming modules that you can call up from a program. They provide proven solutions to many common programming problems, thus saving you much time and effort. This has helped the spread of C++.

The name C++ comes from the C increment operator ++, which adds 1 to the value of a variable. The name C++ correctly suggests an augmented version of C.

A computer program translates a real-life problem into a series of actions to be taken by a computer. While the OOP aspect of C++ gives the language the ability to relate to concepts involved in the problem, the C part of C++ gives the language the ability to get close to the hardware (see Figure 1.2). This combination of abilities has helped the spread of C++. It may also involve a mental shift of gears as you turn from one aspect of a program to another. (Indeed, some OOP purists regard adding OOP features to C akin to adding wings to a pig, albeit a lean, efficient pig.) Also, because C++ grafts OOP onto C, you can ignore C++'s object-oriented features. But you'll miss a lot if that's all you do.

FIGURE 1.2
C++ duality.

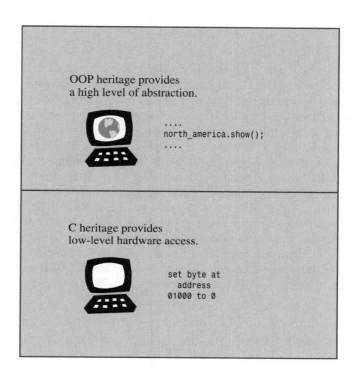

Only after C++ achieved some success did Stroustrup add templates, enabling generic programming. And only after the template feature had been used and enhanced did it become apparent that they were perhaps as significant an addition as OOP—or even more significant, some would argue. The fact that C++ incorporates both OOP and generic programming, as well as the more traditional procedural approach demonstrates that C++ emphasizes the utilitarian over the ideological approach, and that is one of the reasons for the language's success.

Portability and Standards

You've written a handy C++ program for the elderly 286 PC AT computer at work when management decides to replace the machine with a Sun workstation, a computer using a different processor and a different operating system. Can you run your program on the new platform? Of course, you'll have to recompile the program using a C++ compiler designed for the new platform. But will you have to make any changes to the code you wrote? If you can recompile the program without making changes and it runs without a hitch, we say the program is *portable*.

There are a couple of obstacles to portability, the first of which is hardware. A program that is hardware-specific is not likely to be portable. One that takes direct control of an IBM PC VGA video board, for example, will be speaking gibberish as far as a Sun is concerned. (You can minimize portability problems by localizing the hardware-dependent parts in function modules; then you just have to rewrite those specific modules.) We will avoid that sort of programming in this book.

The second obstacle to portability is language divergence. Certainly, that can be a problem with spoken languages. A Yorkshireman's description of the day's events may not be portable to Brooklyn, even though English is spoken in both areas. Computer languages, too, can develop dialects. Is the IBM PC C++ implementation the same as the Sun implementation? Although most implementers would like to make their versions of C++ compatible with others, it's difficult to do so without a published standard describing exactly how the language works. Therefore, the American National Standards Institute (ANSI) created a committee in 1990(ANSI X3J16) to develop a standard for C++. (ANSI already has developed a standard for C.) The International Standardization Organization (ISO) soon joined the process with its own committee (ISO-WG-21), creating a joint ANSI/ISO effort to develop the C++ standard. These committees met jointly three times a year, and we'll simply lump them together notationally as the ANSI/ISO committee. ANSI/ISO's decision to create a standard emphasizes that C++ has become an important and widespread language. It also indicates C++ has reached a certain level of maturity, for it's not productive to introduce standards while a language is developing rapidly. Nonetheless, C++ has undergone significant changes since the committee began its work.

Work on the ANSI/ISO C++ standard began in 1990. The committee issued some interim working papers in the following years. In April 1995 it released a Committee Draft (CD) for public comment. In December 1996 it released a second version (CD2) for further public review. These documents not only refined the description of existing C++ features but also extended the language with exceptions, RTTI, templates, and the Standard Template Library. The final International Standard (ISO/IEC 14882:1998) was adopted in 1998 by the ISO, IEC (International Electrotechnical Committee), and ANSI. This book is based on that standard.

The ANSI/ISO C++ standard additionally draws upon the ANSI C standard, because C++ is supposed to be, as far as possible, a superset of C. That means any valid C program ideally should also be a valid C++ program. There are a few differences between ANSI C and the corresponding rules for C++, but they are minor. Indeed, ANSI C incorporates some features first introduced in C++, such as function prototyping and the **const** type qualifier.

Prior to the emergence of ANSI C, the C community followed a de facto standard based on the book *The C Programming Language*, by Kernighan and Ritchie (Addison-Wesley Publishing Company Reading, MA. 1978). This standard often was termed K&R C; with the emergence of ANSI C, the simpler K&R C now sometimes is called *classic C*.

The ANSI C standard not only defines the C language, it also defines a standard C library that ANSI C implementations must support. C++ also uses that library; this book will refer to it as the standard C library or the standard library. In addition, the ANSI/ISO C++ standard provides a standard library of C++ classes.

More recently, the C standard has been revised; the new standard, sometimes called C99, was adopted by ISO in 1999 and ANSI in 2000. The standard adds some features to C, such as a new integer type, that some C++ compilers support. Although not part of the current C++ standard, these features may become part of the next C++ standard.

Before the ANSI/ISO C++ committee began its work, many people accepted the most recent Bell Labs version of C++ as a standard. For example, a compiler might describe itself as compatible with Release 2.0 or Release 3.0 of C++.

Before getting to the C++ language proper, let's cover some of the groundwork about creating programs and about using this book.

The Mechanics of Creating a Program

Suppose you've written a C++ program. How do you get it running? The exact steps depend upon your computer environment and the particular C++ compiler you use, but they will resemble the following steps (see Figure 1.3):

- Use a text editor of some sort to write the program and save it in a file. This file constitutes the *source code* for your program.

- Compile the source code. This means running a program that translates the source code to the internal language, called *machine language,* used by the host computer. The file containing the translated program is the *object code* for your program.

- Link the object code with additional code. C++ programs, for example, normally use *libraries.* A C++ library contains object code for a collection of computer routines, called *functions,* to perform tasks such as displaying information on the screen or calculating the square root of a number. Linking combines your object code with object code for the functions you use and with some standard startup code to produce a runtime version of your program. The file containing this final product is called the *executable code*.

You will encounter the term source code throughout the book, so be sure to file it away in your personal random-access memory.

The programs in this book are generic and should run in any system supporting modern C++. (However, you may need one of the latest versions to get support for namespaces and the newest template features.) The steps for putting a program together may differ. Let's look a little further at these steps.

Creating the Source Code

Some C++ implementations, such as Microsoft Visual C++, Borland C++ (various versions), Watcom C++, Symantec C++, and Metrowerks CodeWarrior, provide *integrated development environments* (*IDEs*) that let you manage all steps of program development, including editing, from one master program. Other implementations, such as AT&T C++ or GNU C++ on UNIX and Linux, just handle the compilation and linking stages and expect you to type commands on the system command line. In such cases, you can use any available text editor to create and modify source code. On UNIX, for example, you can use `vi` or `ed` or `ex` or `emacs`. On a DOS system, you can use `edlin` or `edit` or any of several available program editors. You can even use a word processor, providing you save the file as a standard DOS ASCII text file instead of in a special word processor format.

FIGURE 1.3
Programming steps.

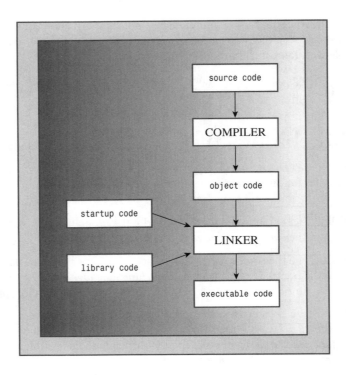

In naming a source file, you must use the proper suffix to identify the file as a C++ file. This not only tells you the file is C++ source code, it tells the compiler that, too. (If a UNIX compiler complains to you about a "bad magic number," that's just its endearingly obscure way of saying that you used the wrong suffix.) The suffix consists of a period followed by a character or group of characters called the extension (see Figure 1.4).

FIGURE 1.4
Source file extension.

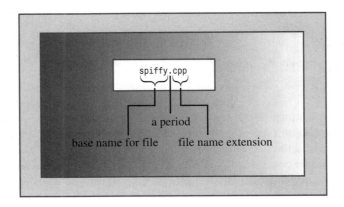

The extension you use depends on the C++ implementation. Table 1.1 shows some common choices. For example, **spiffy.C** is a valid AT&T C++ source code filename. Note that UNIX is case sensitive, meaning you should use an uppercase C character. Actually, a lowercase c extension also works, but standard C uses that extension. So, to avoid confusion on UNIX systems, use **c** with C programs and **C** with C++ programs. If you don't mind typing an extra character or two, you can also use **cc** and **cxx** extensions with some UNIX systems. DOS, being a bit simple-minded compared to UNIX, doesn't distinguish between uppercase and lowercase, so DOS implementations use additional letters, as shown in Table 1.1, to distinguish between C and C++ programs.

TABLE 1.1   Source Code Extensions

C++ Implementation	Source Code Extension
UNIX AT&T	C, cc, cxx, c
GNU C++	C, cc, cxx, cpp
Symantec	cpp, cp
Borland C++	cpp
Watcom	cpp
Microsoft Visual C++	cpp, cxx
Metrowerks CodeWarrior	cp, cpp

Compilation and Linking

Originally, Stroustrup implemented C++ with a C++-to-C compiler program instead of developing a direct C++-to-object code compiler. This program, called **cfront** (for C front end), translated C++ source code to C source code, which could then be compiled by a standard C compiler. This approach simplified introducing C++ to the C community. Other implementations have used this approach to bring C++ to other platforms. As C++ has developed and grown in popularity, more and more implementers have turned to creating C++ compilers that generate object code directly from C++ source code. This direct approach speeds up the compilation process and emphasizes that C++ is a separate, if similar, language.

Often the distinction between a **cfront** translator and compiler is nearly invisible to the user. For example, on a UNIX system the **CC** command may first pass your program to the **cfront** translator and then automatically pass the translator's output on to the C compiler, which is called **cc**. Henceforth, we'll use the term "compiler" to include translate-and-compile combinations. The mechanics of compiling depend upon the implementation, and the following sections outline a few common forms. These summaries outline the basic steps, but they are no substitute for consulting the documentation for your system.

If you have access to the `cfront` translator and know C, you may want to inspect the C translations of your C++ programs and get an inside look at how some C++ features are implemented.

UNIX Compiling and Linking

Suppose, for example, that you are on a UNIX system using AT&T Release 3.0 C++. Use the `CC` command to compile your program. The name is in uppercase letters to distinguish it from the standard UNIX C compiler `cc`. The `CC` compiler is a command-line compiler, meaning you type compilation commands on the UNIX command line.

For example, to compile the C++ source code file `spiffy.C`, you would type this command at the UNIX prompt:

```
CC spiffy.C
```

If, through skill, dedication, or luck, your program has no errors, the compiler generates an object code file with an **o** extension. In this case, the compiler would produce a `spiffy.o` file.

Next, the compiler automatically passes the object code file to the system linker, a program that combines your code with library code to produce the executable file. By default, the executable file is called `a.out`. If you used just one source file, the linker also deletes the `spiffy.o` file, because it's no longer needed. To run the program, just type the name of the executable file:

```
a.out
```

Note that if you compile a new program, the new `a.out` executable file replaces the previous `a.out`. (That's because executable files take a lot of space, so overwriting old executable files helps reduce storage demands.) But if you develop an executable program you want to keep, just use the UNIX `mv` command to change the name of the executable file.

In C++, as in C, you can spread a program over more than one file. (Many of the programs in this book from Chapters 8–16 do this.) In that case, you can compile a program by listing all the files on the command line:

```
CC my.C precious.C
```

If there are multiple source code files, the compiler does not delete the object code files. That way, if you just change the `my.C` file, you can recompile the program with this command:

```
CC my.C precious.o
```

This recompiles the `my.C` file and links it with the previously compiled `precious.o` file.

You might have to identify some libraries explicitly. For example, to access functions defined in the math library, you may have to add the `-lm` flag to the command line.

```
CC usingmath.C -lm
```

Linux Compiling and Linking

Linux systems most commonly use g++, the GNU C++ compiler from the Free Software Foundation. The compiler is included in most Linux distributions, but may not always be installed. The g++ compiler works much like the standard UNIX compiler:

```
g++ spiffy.cxx
```

This produces an executable file call a.out.

Some versions might require that you link in the C++ library:

```
g++ spiffy.cxx -lg++
```

To compile multiple source files, just list them all in the command line:

```
g++ my.cxx precious.cxx
```

This produces an executable file called a.out and two object code files my.o and precious.o. If you subsequently modify just one of the source code files, say my.cxx, you can recompile using my.cxx and the precious.o:

```
g++ my.cxx precious.o
```

The Comeau C++ compiler (www.comeaucomputing.com) is another possibility; it requires the presence of the GNU compiler.

The GNU compiler is available for many platforms, including MS-DOS running on IBM-compatible PCs as well as UNIX systems on a variety of platforms.

Command-Line Compilers for MS-DOS

The most inexpensive route for compiling C++ programs on a Windows PC is to download a free command-line compiler that runs in a Windows MS-DOS window. The MS-DOS version of the GNU C++ is called gpp, and is available at www.delorie.com/djgpp/. Borland provides a free command-line compiler at www.borland.com/bcppbuilder/freecompiler/. For either, you need to read the installation directions, for parts of the installation processes are not automatic.

To use the gpp compiler, first open an MS-DOS window. To compile a source code file named great.cpp, type the following command at the prompt:

```
gpp great.cpp
```

If the program compiles successfully, the resulting executable file is named a.exe.

To use the Borland compiler, first open an MS-DOS window. To compile a source code file named great.cpp, type the following command at the prompt:

```
bcc32 great.cpp
```

If the program compiles successfully, the resulting executable file is named great.exe.

Windows Compilers

Windows products are too abundant and too often revised to make it reasonable to describe them all individually. However, they do share some common features.

Typically, you must create a project for a program and add the file or files constituting your program to the project. Each vendor will supply an IDE (Integrated Development Environment) with menu options and, possibly, automated assistance, in creating a project. One very important matter you have to establish is the kind of program you're creating. Typically, the compiler will offer many choices, such as a Windows application, an MFC Windows application, a dynamic-link library, an ActiveX control, a DOS or character-mode executable, a static library, or a console application. Some of these may be available in both 16-bit and 32-bit versions.

Because the programs in this book are generic, you should avoid choices that require platform-specific code, such as Windows applications. Instead, you want to run in a character-based mode. The choice will depend on the compiler. For Microsoft Visual C++, use the Win32 Console Application option. Metrowerks compilers offer a Win32 Console C++ App option and a Win32 WinSIOUX C++ App option, either of which work. (The former runs the compiled program in a DOS window, the latter runs it in a standard Windows window.) Some Borland versions feature an EasyWin choice that emulates a DOS session; other versions offer a Console option. In general, look to see if there is an option labeled Console, character-mode, or DOS executable, and try that.

After you have the project set up, you'll have to compile and link your program. The IDE typically will give you several choices such as Compile, Build, Make, Build All, Link, Execute, and Run (but not necessarily all these choices in the same IDE!).

- *Compile* typically means compile the code in the file currently open.

- *Build* or *Make* typically means compile the code for all the source code files in the project. This often is an incremental process. That is, if the project has three files, and you change just one, then just that one is recompiled.

- *Build All* typically means compile all the source code files from scratch.

- *Link* means (as described earlier) combine the compiled source code with the necessary library code.

- *Run* or *Execute* means run the program. Typically, if you have not yet done the earlier steps, Run will do them, too, before trying to run a program.

A compiler generates an error message when you violate a language rule and identifies the line with the problem. Unfortunately, when you are new to a language, you may find it difficult to understand the message. Sometimes the actual error may occur before the identified line, and sometimes a single error will generate a chain of error messages.

Tip

When fixing errors, fix the first error first. If you can't find it on the line identified as the line with the error, check the preceding line.

Tip

Occasionally compilers get confused after incompletely building a program and respond by giving meaningless error messages that cannot be fixed. In such cases, you can clear things up by selecting Build All to restart the process from scratch. Unfortunately, it is difficult to distinguish this situation from the more common one in which the error messages merely seem to be meaningless.

Usually, the IDE will let you run the program in an auxiliary window. Some IDEs close the window as soon as the program finishes execution, some leave it open. If your compiler closes the window, you'll have a hard time seeing the output, unless you have quick eyes and a photographic memory. To see the output, you must place some additional code at the end of the program:

```
    cin.get();  // add this statement
    cin.get();  // and maybe this, too
    return 0;
}
```

The `cin.get()` statement reads the next keystroke, so this statement causes the program to wait until you press the Enter key. (No keystrokes get sent to a program until you press Enter, so there's no point in pressing another key.) The second statement is needed if the program otherwise leaves an unprocessed keystroke after its regular input. For example, if you enter a number, you'll type the number and then press Enter. The program will read the number but leave the Enter keystroke unprocessed, and it then will be read by the first `cin.get()`.

The Borland C++Builder compiler departs a bit from more traditional designs. Its primary aim is Windows programming. To use it for generic programs, select New from the File menu. Then select Console App. A window will open that includes a skeleton version of `main()`. Some of the items you can delete, but you should retain the following two nonstandard lines:

```
#include <vcl\condefs.h>
#pragma hdrstop
```

C++ on the Macintosh

The primary Macintosh C++ compiler is Metrowerks CodeWarrior. It provides project-based IDEs similar, in basic concepts, to what you would find in a Windows compiler. Start by selecting New Project from the File menu. You'll be given a choice of project types. For CodeWarrior, choose MacOS:C/C++:ANSI C++ Console in older versions, MacOS:C/C++:Standard Console:Std C++ Console in more recent versions. You also may have to choose between a 68K version (for the Motorola 680X0 series of processors) or a PPC version (for the PowerPC processors).

CodeWarrior supplies a small source code file as part of the initial project. You can try compiling and running that program to see if you have your system set up properly. However, once you provide your own code, you should delete this file from the project. Do so by highlighting the file in the project window and then selecting Remove from the Project menu.

Next, you must add your source code to the project. You can use New from the File menu to create a new file or Open from the File menu to open an existing file. Use a proper suffix, such as `.cp` or `.cpp`. Use the Project menu to add this file to the project list. Some programs in this book require that you add more than one source code file. When you are ready, select Run from the Project menu.

Tip
To save time, you can use just one project for all the sample programs. Delete the previous example source code file from the project list and add the current source code. This saves disk space.

The compiler includes a debugger to help you locate the causes of runtime problems.

Conventions Used in This Book

To help distinguish between different kinds of text, we've used a few typographic conventions. Italic type is used for important words or phrases used for the first time, such as *structured programming*. Monospace type can denote any of the following:

- Names or values used in a program, such as `x`, `starship`, and `3.14`

- Language keywords, such as `int` and `if else`

- Filenames, such as `iostream`

- Functions, such as `main()` and `puts()`

C++ source code is presented as follows:

```
#include <iostream>
using namespace std;
int main()
{
    cout << "What's up, Doc!\n";
    return 0;
}
```

Sample program runs use the same format, except user input appears in boldface:

```
Please enter your name:
Plato
```

Because this book is about object-oriented programming, we've used geometric objects along the way to help you identify various elements of the book. Tips, rules, and notes are marked with light bulbs, pointing hands, and pencils.

You'll find an occasional rule or suggestion in the following format:

Tip

You learn by doing, so try the examples and experiment with them.

By the way, you've just read a real and important suggestion, not just an example of what a rule or suggestion looks like.

Finally, when you enter program input, you normally have to press the Return key or the Enter key to send the input to the program. Some keyboards use one and some the other; this book uses Enter.

Our System

This book describes the ISO/ANSI C++ Standard (ISO/IEC 14882:1998), so the examples should work with any C++ implementation compatible with that standard. (At least, this is the vision and hope of portability.) However, the C++ standard is still new, and you may find a few discrepancies. For example, at the time of this writing, some C++ compilers lack namespaces or the newest template features. Support for the Standard Template Library described in Chapter 16, "The `string` Class and the Standard Template Library," is spotty at the time of this writing. Systems that use the Release 2.0 (or later) `cfront` translator may then pass the translated code to a C compiler that is not fully ANSI-compatible, resulting in some language features being left unimplemented and in some standard ANSI library functions and header files not being supported. Also, some things, such as the number of bytes used to hold an integer, are implementation-dependent.

For the record, the examples in this book were developed using Microsoft Visual C++ 6.0 and Metrowerks CodeWarrior Professional Release 6 on a Pentium PC with a hard disk and running under Windows 98. Most programs were checked using the Borland C++ 5.5 command-line compiler and GNU `gpp` 2.95 on the same system, using Comeau 4.4.45 and GNU g++ 2.95 on an IBM-compatible Pentium running Linux, and using Metrowerks CodeWarrior Professional Release 6 on a Macintosh G3 under System 8.6. The book reports discrepancies stemming from lagging behind the standard generically, as in "older implementations use `ios::fixed` instead of `ios_base::fixed`." The book reports some bugs and idiosyncrasies that would prove troublesome or confusing; however, these may very well be fixed in subsequent releases.

Real World Note: Bjarne Stroustrup's Home Page

Bjarne Stroustrup designed and implemented the C++ programming language and is the author of the definitive reference manuals "The C++ Programming Language" and "The Design and Evolution of C++." His personal Web site at AT&T Labs Research should be the first C++ bookmark, or favorite, you create:

`http://www.research.att.com/~bs/`

This site includes an interesting historical perspective of the how's and why's of the C++ language, Bjarne's biographical material, and C++ FAQs. Believe it, or not, but Bjarne's most frequently asked question is how to pronounce Bjarne Stroustrup. Download the .WAV file to hear for yourself!

CHAPTER 2

SETTING OUT TO C++

In this chapter you learn

- How to create a C++ program
- The general format for a C++ program
- The #include directive
- The main() function
- How to use the cout object for output
- How to place comments in a C++ program
- The newline character \n
- How to declare and use variables
- How to use the cin object for input
- How to define and use simple functions

W hen you construct a simple home, you begin with the foundation and the framework. If you don't have a solid structure from the beginning, you'll have trouble later filling in the details, such as windows, door frames, observatory domes, and parquet ballrooms. Similarly, when you learn a computer language, you should begin by learning the basic structure for a program. Only then can you move on to the details, such as loops and objects. This chapter gives you an overview of the essential structure of a C++ program and previews some topics—notably functions and classes—covered in much greater detail in later chapters. (The idea is to introduce at least some of the basic concepts gradually en route to the great awakenings that come later.)

C++ Initiation

Let's begin with a simple C++ program that displays a message. Listing 2.1 uses the C++ cout (pronounced cee-out) facility to produce character output. The source code includes several comments to the reader; these lines begin with //, and the compiler ignores them. C++ is *case-sensitive*; that is, it discriminates between uppercase characters and lowercase characters. This means you must be careful to use the same case as in the examples. For example, this program uses cout. If you substitute Cout or COUT, the compiler rejects your offering and accuses you of using unknown identifiers. (The compiler also is spelling-sensitive, so don't try kout or coot, either.) The cpp filename extension is a common way to indicate a C++ program; you might need to use a different extension, as described in Chapter 1, "Getting Started."

LISTING 2.1   `myfirst.cpp`

```
// myfirst.cpp--displays a message

#include <iostream>                        // a PREPROCESSOR directive
using namespace std;                       // make definitions visible
int main()                                 // function heading
{                                          // start of function body
    cout << "Come up and C++ me some time.";  // message
    cout << "\n";                          // start a new line
    return 0;                              // terminate main()
}                                          // end of function body
```

Compatibility Note

If you're using an older compiler, you might need to use `#include <iostream.h>` instead of `#include <iostream>`; in this case, you also would omit the `using namespace std;` line. That is, replace

```
#include <iostream>       // the way of the future
using namespace std;      // ditto
```

with

```
#include <iostream.h>  // in case the future has not yet arrived
```

(Some very old compilers use `#include <stream.h>` instead of `#include <iostream.h>`; if you have a compiler that old, you should get either a newer compiler or an older book.) The switch from `iostream.h` to `iostream` is fairly recent, and, at the time of this writing, some vendors haven't implemented it yet.

Some windowing environments run the program in a separate window, and then automatically close the window when the program finishes. As discussed in Chapter 1, you can make the window stay open until you strike a key by adding the following line of code before the return statement:

```
cin.get();
```

For some programs you must add two of these lines. This code causes the program to wait for a key-stroke. You'll learn more about this code in Chapter 4, "Compound Types."

Program Adjustments

You might find that you must alter the examples in this book to run on your system. The two most common changes are those the first Compatibility Note in this chapter mentions. One is a matter of language standards; if your compiler is not up to date, you must include `iostream.h` instead of `iostream` and omit the `namespace` line. The second is a matter of the programming environment; you might need to add one or two `cin.get()` statements to keep the program output visible onscreen. Because these adjustments apply equally to every example in this book, this Compatibility Note is the only alert to them you get. Don't forget them! Future Compatibility Notes alert you to other possible alterations you might have to make.

After you use your editor of choice to copy this program (or else use the source code files from the Sams Publishing Web site at www.samspublishing.com), use your C++ compiler to create the executable code, as Chapter 1 outlined. Here is the output from running the compiled program:

```
Come up and C++ me some time.
```

C Input and Output

If you're used to programming in C, seeing `cout` instead of the `printf()` function might come as a minor shock. C++ can, in fact, use `printf()`, `scanf()`, and all the other standard C input and output functions, provided that you include the usual C `stdio.h` file. But this is a C++ book, so you use C++'s new input facilities, which improve in many ways upon the C versions.

You construct C++ programs from building blocks called *functions*. Typically, you organize a program into major tasks, and then design separate functions to handle those tasks. The example shown in Listing 2.1 is simple enough to consist of a single function named `main()`. The `myfirst.cpp` example has the following elements:

- Comments, indicated by the `//` prefix

- A preprocessor `#include` directive

- A `using namespace` directive

- A function heading: `int main()`

- A function body, delimited by `{` and `}`

- A statement that uses the C++ `cout` facility to display a message

- A return statement to terminate the `main()` function

Let's look at these various elements in greater detail now. The `main()` function is a good place to start because some of the features that precede `main()`, such as the preprocessor directive, are simpler to understand after you see what `main()` does.

The `main()` Function

Stripped of the trimmings, the sample program shown in Listing 2.1 has the following fundamental structure:

```
int main()
{
    statements
    return 0;
}
```

These lines state that you have a function called `main()`, and they describe how the function behaves. Together they constitute a *function definition*. This definition has two parts: the first line, `int main()`, which is called the *function heading*, and the portion enclosed in braces (`{` and `}`), which is the *function body*. Figure 2.1 shows the `main()` function. The function heading is a capsule summary of the function's interface with the rest of the program, and the function body represents your instructions to the computer about what the function should do. In C++ each complete instruction is called a *statement*. You must terminate each statement with a semicolon, so don't omit the semicolons when you type the examples.

FIGURE 2.1

The `main()` function.

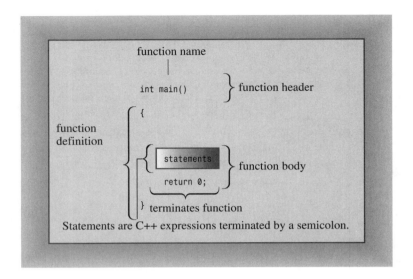

The final statement in `main()`, called a *return statement*, terminates the function. You learn more about the return statement as you read through this chapter.

Statements and Semicolons

A statement represents a complete instruction to a computer. To understand your source code, a compiler needs to know when one statement ends and another begins. Some languages use a statement separator. FORTRAN, for example, uses the end of the line to separate one statement from the next. Pascal uses a semicolon to separate one statement from the next. In Pascal you can omit the semicolon in certain cases, such as after a statement just before an END, when you aren't actually separating two statements. (Pragmatists and minimalists will disagree about whether *can* implies *should*.) But C++, like C, uses a *terminator* rather than a separator. The terminator is the semicolon that marks the end of the statement as part of the statement rather than a marker between statements. The practical upshot is that in C++ you never can omit the semicolon.

The Function Heading as an Interface

Right now the main point to remember is that C++ syntax requires you to begin the definition of the `main()` function with this heading: `int main()`. This chapter discusses the function heading syntax in more detail later when it covers functions in general, but, for those who can't put their curiosity on hold, here's a preview.

In general, a C++ function is activated, or *called*, by another function, and the function heading describes the interface between a function and the function that calls it. The part preceding the function name is called the *function return type*; it describes information flow from a function back to the function that calls it. The part within the parentheses following the function name is called the *argument list* or *parameter list*; it describes information flow from the calling function to the called function. This general format is a bit confusing when you apply it to `main()`, because you normally don't call `main()` from other parts of your program. Typically, however, `main()` is called by startup code that your compiler adds to your program to mediate between the program and the operating system (UNIX, Windows XP, or whatever). In effect, the function header describes the interface between `main()` and the operating system.

Consider the interface for `main()`, beginning with the `int` part. A C++ function called by another function can return a value to the activating (calling) function. That value is called a *return value*. In this case, `main()` can return an integer value, as indicated by the keyword `int`. Next, note the empty parentheses. In general, one C++ function can pass information to another function when it calls that function. The portion of the function heading enclosed in parentheses describes that information. In this case, the empty parentheses mean that the `main()` function takes no information, or, in the usual terminology, `main()` takes no arguments. (To say that `main()` takes no arguments doesn't mean that `main()` is an unreasonable, authoritarian function. Instead, *argument* is the term computer buffs use to refer to information passed from one function to another.)

In short, the heading

```
int main()
```

states that the `main()` function can return an integer value to the function that calls it and that `main()` takes no information from the function that calls it.

Many existing programs use the classic C heading instead:

```
main()       // original C style
```

Under C, omitting the return type is the same as saying that the function is type `int`. However, C++ is phasing this usage out.

You also can use this variant:

```
int main(void)      // very explicit style
```

Using the keyword `void` in the parentheses is an explicit way of saying that the function takes no arguments. Under C++ (but not C), leaving the parentheses empty is the same as using `void` in the parentheses. (In C, leaving the parentheses empty means you are remaining silent about whether or not there are arguments.)

Some programmers use this heading and omit the return statement:

```
void main()
```

This is logically consistent, because a `void` return type means the function doesn't return a value. This variant works on many systems, but, because it isn't mandated as an option under current standards, it does not work on some systems.

Finally, the ANSI/ISO C++ Standard states that a

```
return 0;
```

statement implicitly is understood to come at the end of the `main()` function (but of no other function) if you don't explicitly provide it.

Why `main()` by Any Other Name Is Not the Same

There's an extremely compelling reason to name the function in the `myfirst.cpp` program `main()`: you must do so. Ordinarily, a C++ program requires a function called `main()`. (And not, by the way, `Main()` or `MAIN()` or `mane()`. Remember, case and spelling count.) Because the `myfirst.cpp` program has only one function, that function must bear the responsibility of being `main()`. When you run a C++ program, execution always begins at the beginning of the `main()` function. Therefore, if you don't have `main()`, you don't have a complete program, and the compiler points out that you haven't defined a `main()` function.

There are exceptions. For example, in Windows programming you can write a dynamic link library (`dll`) module. This is code that other Windows programs can use. Because a `dll` module is not a standalone program, it doesn't need a `main()`. Programs for specialized environments, such as for a controller chip in a robot, might not need a `main()`. But your ordinary standalone program does need a `main()`; this books discusses that sort of program.

C++ Comments

The double slash (`//`) introduces a C++ comment. A *comment* is a remark from the programmer to the reader that usually identifies a section of a program or explains some aspect of the code. The compiler ignores comments. After all, it knows C++ at least as well as you do, and, in any case, it's incapable of understanding comments. As far as the compiler is concerned, Listing 2.1 looks as if it were written without comments:

```cpp
#include <iostream>
using namespace std;
int main()
{
    cout << "Come up and C++ me some time.";
    cout << "\n";
    return 0;
}
```

C++ comments run from the `//` to the end of the line. A comment can be on its own line or it can be on the same line as code. Incidentally, note the first line in Listing 2.1:

```cpp
// myfirst.cpp -- displays a message
```

In this book all programs begin with a comment that gives the filename for the source code and a brief program summary. As mentioned in Chapter 1, the filename extension for source code depends on your C++ system. Other systems might use `myfirst.C` or `myfirst.cxx` for names.

Tip
You should use comments to document your programs. The more complex the program, the more valuable comments become. Not only do they help others to understand what you have done, but also they help you understand what you've done, especially if you haven't looked at the program for a while.

C-Style Comments

C++ also recognizes C comments, which are enclosed between /* and */ symbols:

```
#include <iostream> /* a C-style comment */
```

Because the C-style comment is terminated by */ rather than by the end of a line, you can spread it over more than one line. You can use either or both styles in your programs. However, try sticking to the C++ style. Since it doesn't involve remembering to correctly pair an end symbol with a begin symbol, it's less likely to cause problems. Indeed, the new C99 standard has added the // comment to the C language.

The C++ Preprocessor and the `iostream` File

Here's the short version of what you need to know. If your program is to use the usual C++ input or output facilities, provide these two lines:

```
#include <iostream>
using namespace std;
```

If your compiler doesn't like these lines (for example, if it complains that it can't find the file `iostream`), try the following single line instead:

```
#include <iostream.h >    // compatible with older compilers
```

That's all you really must know to make your programs work, but now take a more in-depth look.

C++, like C, uses a *preprocessor*. This is a program that processes a source file before the main compilation takes place. (Some C++ implementations, as you might recall from Chapter 1, use a translator program to convert a C++ program to C. Although the translator also is a form of preprocessor, we're not discussing that preprocessor; instead, we're discussing the one that handles directives whose names begin with #.) You don't have to do anything special to invoke this preprocessor. It automatically operates when you compile the program.

The listing uses the `#include` directive:

```
#include <iostream>    // a PREPROCESSOR directive
```

This directive causes the preprocessor to add the contents of the `iostream` file to your program. This is a typical preprocessor action: adding or replacing text in the source code before it's compiled.

This raises the question of why you should add the contents of the `iostream` file to the program. The answer concerns communication between the program and the outside world. The `io` in `iostream` refers to *input*, which is information brought into the program, and to *output*, which is information sent out from the program. C++'s input/output scheme involves several definitions found in the `iostream` file. Your first program needs these definitions to use the `cout` facility to display a message. The `#include` directive causes the contents of the `iostream` file to be sent along with the contents of your file to the compiler. In essence, the contents of the `iostream` file replace the `#include <iostream>` line in the program. Your original file is not altered, but a composite file formed from your file and `iostream` goes on to the next stage of compilation.

Remember

Programs that use `cin` and `cout` for input and output must include the `iostream` file (or, on some systems, `iostream.h`).

Header Filenames

Files such as `iostream` are called *include files* (because they are included in other files) or *header files* (because they are included at the beginning of a file). C++ compilers come with many header files, each supporting a particular family of facilities. The C tradition has been to use the `h` extension with header files as a simple way to identify the type of file by its name. For example, a `math.h` header file supports various C math functions. Initially, C++ did the same. For example, the header file supporting input and output was named `iostream.h`. More recently, however, C++ usage has changed. Now the `h` extension is reserved for the old C header files (which C++ programs still can use), whereas C++ header files have no extension. There also are C header files that have been converted to C++ header files. These files have been renamed by dropping the `h` extension (making it a C++ style name) and prefixing the filename with a `c` (indicating that it comes from C). For example, the C++ version of `math.h` is the `cmath` header file. Sometimes the C and C++ versions of C header files are identical, whereas in other cases the new version might have a few changes. For purely C++ header files such as `iostream`, dropping the `h` is more than a cosmetic change, for the `h`-free header files also incorporate namespaces, the next topic in this summary. Table 2.1 summarizes the naming conventions for header files.

TABLE 2.1   Header File Naming Conventions

Kind of Header	Convention	Example	Comments
C++ old style	Ends in .h	`iostream.h`	Usable by C++ programs
C old style	Ends in .h	`math.h`	Usable by C, C++ programs
C++ new style	No extension	`iostream`	Usable by C++ programs, uses `namespace std`
Converted C	c prefix, no extension	`cmath`	Usable by C++ programs, might use non-C features such as `namespace std`

In view of the C tradition of using different file extensions to indicate different file types, it appears reasonable to have some special extension to indicate C++ header files. The ANSI/ISO committee felt so, too. The problem was agreeing on which extension to use, so eventually they agreed upon nothing.

Namespaces

If you use `iostream` instead of `iostream.h`, you should use the following namespace directive to make the definitions in `iostream` available to your program:

```
using namespace std;
```

This is called a *using directive*. The simplest thing to do is to accept this for now and worry about it later (for example, in Chapter 9, "Memory Models and Namespaces"). But so that you won't be left completely in the dark, here's an overview of what's happening.

Namespace support is a fairly new C++ feature designed to simplify the writing of programs that combine pre-existing code from several vendors. One potential problem is that you might use two prepackaged products that both have, say, a function called `wanda()`. If you then use the `wanda()` function, the compiler won't know which version you mean. The namespace facility lets a vendor package its wares in a unit called a *namespace* so that you can use the name of a namespace to indicate which vendor's product you want. So Microflop Industries could place its definitions in a namespace called `Microflop`. Then `Microflop::wanda()` would become the full name for its `wanda()` function. Similarly, `Piscine::wanda()` could denote Piscine Corporation's version of `wanda()`. Thus, your program now could use the namespaces to discriminate between various versions:

```
Microflop::wanda("go dancing?");        // use Microflop namespace version
Piscine::wanda("a fish named Desire"); // use Piscine namespace version
```

In this spirit, the classes, functions, and variables that are a standard component of C++ compilers now are placed in a namespace called `std`. This takes place in the h-free header files. This means, for example, that the `cout` variable used for output and defined in `iostream` is really called `std::cout`. However, most users don't feel like converting pre-namespace code, which uses `iostream.h` and `cout`, to namespace code, which uses `iostream` and `std::cout`, unless they can do this without a lot of hassle. This is where the `using` directive comes in. The following line means you can use names defined in the `std` namespace without using the `std::` prefix:

```
using namespace std;
```

This `using` directive makes all the names in the `std` namespace available. Modern practice regards this as a bit lazy. The preferred approach is to make just those names you need available with something called a using declaration:

```
using std::cout; // make cout available
using std::cin;  // make cin available
```

If you put these at the top of the file instead of

```
using namespace std; // lazy approach, all names available
```

you can use `cin` and `cout` without attaching the `std::` to them. But if you need to use other names from `iostream`, you'll have to add them to the `using` list individually. Because you have enough else to do while learning C++, this book will take the lazy approach. But you may want to experiment with these other techniques.

C++ Output with `cout`

Now look at how you display a message. The `myfirst.cpp` program uses the following C++ statement:

```
cout << "Come up and C++ me some time.";
```

The part enclosed within the double quotation marks is the message to print. In C++, any series of characters enclosed in double quotation marks is called a *character string*, presumably because it consists of several characters strung together into a larger unit. The `<<` notation indicates that the statement is sending this string to `cout`; the symbols point the way the information flows. And what is `cout`? It's a predefined object that knows how to display a variety of things, including strings, numbers, and individual characters. (An object, as you might remember from Chapter 1, is a particular instance of a class, and a class defines how data is stored and used.)

Well, this is a bit awkward. You won't be in a position to learn about objects for several more chapters, yet here you have to use one. Actually, this reveals one of the strengths of objects. You don't have to know the innards of an object in order to use it. All you must know is its interface—that is, how to use it. The `cout` object has a simple interface. If `string` represents a string, do the following to display the string:

```
cout << string;
```

This is all you must know to display a string, but now take a look at how the C++ conceptual view represents the process. In this view, the output is a stream—that is, a series of characters flowing from the program. The `cout` object, whose properties are defined in the `iostream` file, represents that stream. The object properties for `cout` include an insertion operator (`<<`) that inserts the information on its right into the stream. So the statement (note the terminating semicolon)

```
cout << "Come up and C++ me some time.";
```

inserts the string "Come up and C++ me some time." into the output stream. Thus, rather than say that your program displays a message, you can say that it inserts a string into the output stream. Somehow, that sounds more impressive. (See Figure 2.2.)

If you're coming to C++ from C, you probably noticed that the insertion operator (`<<`) looks just like the bitwise left-shift operator (`<<`). This is an example of *operator overloading*, by which the same operator symbol can have different meanings. The compiler uses the context to figure out which meaning is intended. C itself has some operator overloading. For example, the `&` symbol represents both the address operator and the bitwise **AND** operator. The `*` symbol represents both multiplication and dereferencing a pointer. The important point here is not the exact function of these operators but that the same symbol can have more than one meaning, with the compiler determining the proper meaning from the context. (You do much the same when you determine the meaning of "shoot" in "shoot the breeze" versus "shoot the piano player.") C++ extends the operator overloading concept by letting you redefine operator meanings for the user-defined types called classes.

FIGURE 2.2

Displaying a string with
`cout`.

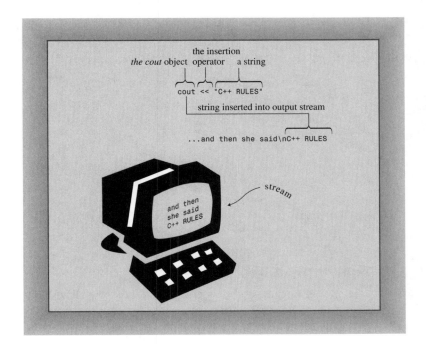

The Newline Character (\n)

Now examine an odd-looking notation that appears in the second output statement:

```
cout << "\n";
```

The \n is a special C++ (and C) notation representing an important concept dubbed the *new-line character*. Although you type the newline character by using two characters (\ and n), these count as a single character. Note that you use the backslash (\), not the regular slash (/). If you display the newline character, the screen cursor moves to the beginning of the next line, and if you send the newline character to a printer, the print head moves to the beginning of the next line. The newline character earns its name.

Note that the **cout** facility does not move automatically to the next line when it prints a string, so the first **cout** statement in Listing 2.1 leaves the cursor positioned just after the period at the end of the output string. To move the cursor to the beginning of the next line, you must send a newline character to the output. Or, to practice C++ lingo, you must insert a newline character into the output stream.

You can use the newline character just like any ordinary character. Listing 2.1 uses it in a separate string, but the listing could have used it in the original string. That is, you can replace the original two output statements with the following:

```
cout << "Come up and C++ me some time.\n";
```

You even can place the newline character in the midst of a string. For example, consider the following statement:

```
cout << "I am a mighty stream\nof lucid\nclarity.\n";
```

Each newline character moves the cursor to the beginning of the next line, making the output as follows:

```
I am a mighty stream
of lucid
clarity.
```

By leaving out newlines, you can make successive **cout** statements print on the same line. For example, the statements

```
cout << "The Good, the";
cout << "Bad, ";
cout << "and the Ukulele\n";
```

produce the following output:

```
The Good, theBad, and the Ukulele
```

Note that the beginning of one string comes immediately after the end of the preceding string. If you want a space where two strings join, you must include it in one of the strings. (Remember that to try out these output examples, you have to place them in a complete program, with a **main()** function heading and opening and closing braces.)

C++ has another way to indicate a newline in output: the word **endl**:

```
cout << "What's next?" << endl;      // endl means start a new line
```

This term is defined in **iostream**. It's a bit easier for most to type than "**\n**", but you only can use it separately, not as part of a string. That is, the string "**What's next?\n**" includes a newline character, but "**What's next?endl**" is just a string ending in the four letters e, n, d, and l.

C++ Source Code Formatting

Some languages, such as FORTRAN, are line-oriented, with one statement to a line. For these languages, the carriage return serves to separate statements. In C++, however, the semicolon marks the end of each statement. This leaves C++ free to treat the carriage return in the same way as a space or a tab. That is, in C++ you normally can use a space where you would use a carriage return, and vice versa. This means you can spread a single statement over several lines or place several statements on one line. For example, you could reformat **myfirst.cpp** as follows:

```
#include <iostream>
   using
    namespace
         std;
      int
main
() { cout
          <<
```

```
"Come up and C++ me some time.";
    cout << "\n"; return 0; }
```

This is visually ugly, but valid, code. You do have to observe some rules. In particular, in C and C++ you can't put a space, tab, or carriage return in the middle of an element such as a name, nor can you place a carriage return in the middle of a string.

```
int ma  in()      // INVALID -- space in name
re
turn 0; // INVALID -- carriage return in word
cout << "Behold the Beans
 of Beauty!"; // INVALID -- carriage return in string
```

The indivisible elements in a line of code are called *tokens*. (See Figure 2.3.) Generally, you must separate one token from the next by a space, tab, or carriage return, which collectively are termed *white space*. Some single characters, such as parentheses and commas, are tokens that need not be set off by white space.

```
return0;        // INVALID, must be return 0;
return(0);      // VALID, white space omitted
return (0);     // VALID, white space used
int main()      // VALID, white space omitted
int main ( )    // ALSO VALID, white space used
```

FIGURE 2.3
Tokens and white space.

C++ Source Code Style

Although C++ gives you much formatting freedom, your programs will be easier to read if you follow a sensible style. Having valid but ugly code should leave you unsatisfied. Most programmers use the style of Listing 2.1, which observes these rules:

- One statement per line

- An opening and a closing brace for a function, each of which is on its own line

- Statements in a function indented from the braces

- No white space around the parentheses associated with a function name

The first three rules have the simple intent to keep the code clean and readable. The fourth helps to differentiate functions from some built-in C++ structures, such as loops, that also use parentheses. The book will alert you to other guidelines as they come up.

More About C++ Statements

A C++ program is a collection of functions, and each function is a collection of statements. C++ has several kinds of statements, so let's look at some of the possibilities. Listing 2.2 provides two new kinds of statements. First, a declaration statement creates a variable. Second, an assignment statement provides a value for that variable. Also, the program shows a new capability for cout.

LISTING 2.2   fleas.cpp

```
// fleas.cpp -- display the value of a variable
#include <iostream>
using namespace std;
int main()
{
    int fleas;              // create an integer variable

    fleas = 38;             // give a value to the variable
    cout << "My cat has ";
    cout << fleas;          // display the value of fleas
    cout << " fleas.\n";
    return 0;
}
```

A blank line separates the declaration from the rest of the program. This practice is the usual C convention, but it's somewhat less common in C++. Here is the program output:

```
My cat has 38 fleas.
```

The next few pages examine this program.

Declaration Statements and Variables

Computers are precise, orderly machines. To store an item of information in a computer, you must identify both the storage location and how much memory storage space the information requires. One relatively painless way to do this in C++ is to use a *declaration statement* to indicate the type of storage and to provide a label for the location. For example, the program has this declaration statement (note the semicolon):

```
int fleas;
```

This statement declares that the program uses enough storage to hold what is called an `int`. The compiler takes care of the details of allocating and labeling memory for that task. C++ can handle several kinds, or types, of data, and the `int` is the most basic data type. It corresponds to an integer, a number with no fractional part. The C++ `int` type can be positive or negative, but the size range depends on the implementation. Chapter 3, "Dealing with Data," provides the details on `int` and the other basic types.

Besides giving the type, the declaration statement declares that henceforth the program will use the name `fleas` to identify the value stored at that location. We call `fleas` a *variable* because you can change its value. In C++ you must declare all variables. If you were to omit the declaration in `fleas.cpp`, the compiler would report an error when the program attempts to use `fleas` further on. (In fact, you might want to try omitting the declaration just to see how your compiler responds. Then, if you see that response in the future, you'll know to check for omitted declarations.)

Why Must Variables Be Declared?

Some languages, notably BASIC, create a new variable whenever you use a new name, without the aid of explicit declarations. That might seem friendlier to the user, and it is—in the short term. The problem is that by misspelling the name of a variable, you inadvertently can create a new variable without realizing it. That is, in BASIC, you can do something like the following:

```
CastleDark = 34
...
CastleDank = CastleDark + MoreGhosts
...
PRINT CastleDark
```

Because `CastleDank` is misspelled (the *r* was typed as an *n*), the changes you make to it leave `CastleDark` unchanged. This kind of error can be hard to trace because it breaks no rules in BASIC. However, in C++ the equivalent code breaks the rule about the need to declare a variable for you to use it, so the compiler catches the error and stomps the potential bug.

In general, then, a declaration indicates the type of data to be stored and the name the program will use for the data that's stored there. In this particular case, the program creates a variable called `fleas` in which it can store an integer. (See Figure 2.4.)

The declaration statement in the program is called a *defining declaration* statement, or *definition*, for short. This means that its presence causes the compiler to allocate memory space for the variable. In more complex situations, you also can have *reference declarations*. These tell the computer to use a variable that already has been defined elsewhere. In general, a declaration need not be a definition, but in this example it is.

FIGURE 2.4
A variable declaration.

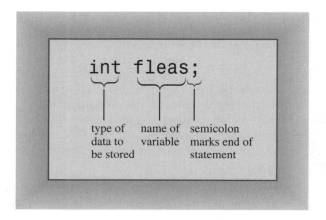

If you're familiar with C or Pascal, you're already familiar with variable declarations. You also might have a modest surprise in store for you. In C and Pascal, all variable declarations normally come at the very beginning of a function or procedure. But C++ has no such restriction. Indeed, the usual C++ style is to declare a variable just before it is first used. That way, you don't have to rummage back through a program to see what the type is. You'll see an example of this later in the chapter. This style does have the disadvantage of not gathering all your variable names in one place; thus, you can't tell at a glance what variables a function uses. (The new C99 standard, incidentally, now makes the rules for C declarations much the same as for C++.)

Tip

The C++ style for declaring variables is to declare a variable as closely as possible to its first use.

The Assignment Statement

An assignment statement assigns a value to a storage location. For example, the statement

```
fleas = 38;
```

assigns the integer 38 to the location represented by the variable `fleas`. The = symbol is called the *assignment operator*. One unusual feature of C++ (and C) is that you can use the assignment operator serially. That is, the following is valid code:

```
int steinway;
int baldwin;
int yamaha;
yamaha = baldwin = steinway = 88;
```

The assignment works from right to left. First, **88** is assigned to `steinway`; then the value of `steinway`, which is now 88, is assigned to `baldwin`; then `baldwin`'s value of 88 is assigned to `yamaha`. (C++ follows C's penchant for allowing weird-appearing code.)

New Trick for cout

Up to now, the examples have given **cout** strings to print. Listing 2.2 additionally gives **cout** a variable whose value is an integer:

```
cout << fleas;
```

The program doesn't print the word **fleas**; instead, it prints the integer value stored in **fleas**, which is 38. Actually, this is two tricks in one. First, **cout** replaces **fleas** with its current numeric value of 38. Second, it translates the value to the proper output characters.

As you see, **cout** works with both strings and integers. This might not seem particularly remarkable to you, but keep in mind that the integer **38** is something quite different from the string **"38"**. The string holds the characters with which you write the number; that is, a 3 character and an 8 character. The program internally stores the code for the 3 character and the 8 character. To print the string, **cout** simply prints each character in the string. But the integer **38** is stored as a numeric value. Rather than store each digit separately, the computer stores 38 as a binary number. (Appendix A, "Number Bases," discusses this representation.) The main point here is that **cout** must translate a number in integer form into character form before it can print it. Furthermore, **cout** is smart enough to recognize that **fleas** is an integer requiring conversion.

Perhaps the contrast with old C will indicate how clever **cout** is. To print the string **"38"** and the integer **38** in C, you could use C's multipurpose output function **printf()**:

```
printf("Printing a string: %s\n", "38");
printf("Printing an integer: %d\n", 38);
```

Without going into the intricacies of **printf()**, note that you must use special codes (**%s** and **%d**) to indicate whether you are going to print a string or an integer. And if you tell **printf()** to print a string but give it an integer by mistake, **printf()** is too unsophisticated to notice your mistake. It just goes ahead and displays garbage.

The intelligent way in which **cout** behaves stems from C++'s object-oriented features. In essence, the C++ insertion operator (<<) adjusts its behavior to fit the type of data that follows it. This is an example of operator overloading. In later chapters, when you take up function overloading and operator overloading, you learn how to implement such smart designs yourself.

cout and printf()

If you are used to C and **printf()**, you might think **cout** looks odd. You might even prefer to cling to your hard-won mastery of **printf()**. But **cout** actually is no stranger in appearance than **printf()** with all of its conversion specifications. More important, **cout** has significant advantages. Its capability to recognize types reflects a more intelligent and foolproof design. Also, it is *extensible*. That is, you can redefine the << operator so that **cout** can recognize and display new data types you develop. And if you relish the fine control **printf()** provides, you can accomplish the same effects with more advanced uses of **cout** (see Chapter 17, "Input, Output, and Files").

More C++ Statements

Look at a couple more examples of statements. The program in Listing 2.3 expands on the preceding example by allowing you to enter a value while the program is running. To do so, it uses cin (pronounced cee-in), the input counterpart to cout. Also, the program shows yet another way to use that master of versatility, the cout object.

LISTING 2.3   yourcat.cpp

```
// yourcat.cpp -- input and output
#include <iostream>
using namespace std;
int main()
{
    int fleas;

    cout << "How many fleas does your cat have?\n";
    cin >> fleas;                 // C++ input
// next line concatenates output
    cout << "Well, that's " << fleas << " fleas too many!\n";

    return 0;
}
```

Here is a sample output:

```
How many fleas does your cat have?
112
Well, that's 112 fleas too many!
```

The program has two new features: using cin to read keyboard input and combining three output statements into one. Let's take a look.

Using cin

As the output demonstrates, the value typed from the keyboard (112) eventually is assigned to the variable fleas. Here is the statement that performs that wonder:

```
cin >> fleas;
```

Looking at this statement, you practically can see information flowing from cin into fleas. Naturally, there is a slightly more formal description of this process. Just as C++ considers output as a stream of characters flowing out of the program, it considers input as a stream of characters flowing into the program. The iostream file defines cin as an object that represents this stream. For output, the << operator inserts characters into the output stream. For input, cin uses the >> operator to extract characters from the input stream. Typically, you provide a variable to the right of the operator to receive the extracted information. (The symbols << and >> were chosen to suggest visually the direction that information flows.)

Like `cout`, `cin` is a smart object. It converts input, which is just a series of characters typed from the keyboard, into a form acceptable to the variable receiving the information. In this case, the program declared `fleas` to be an integer variable, so the input is converted to the numerical form the computer uses to store integers.

More `cout`

The second new feature of `yourcat.cpp` is combining three output statements into one. The `iostream` file defines the `<<` operator so that you can combine (concatenate) output as follows:

```
cout << "Well, that's " << fleas << " fleas too many.\n";
```

This allows you to combine string output and integer output in a single statement. The resulting output is the same as what the following code produces:

```
cout << "Well, that's ";
cout << fleas;
cout << " fleas too many.\n";
```

While you're still in the mood for `cout` advice, you also can rewrite the concatenated version this way, spreading the single statement over three lines:

```
cout    << "Well, that's "
        << fleas
        << " fleas too many.\n";
```

That's because C++'s free format rules treat newlines and spaces between tokens interchangeably. This last technique is convenient when the line width cramps your style.

A Touch of Class

You've seen enough of `cin` and `cout` to justify your exposure to a little object lore. In particular, you learn some more about the notion of classes. Classes are one of the core concepts for object-oriented programming in C++.

A *class* is a data type the user defines. To define a class, you describe what sort of information it can represent and what sort of actions you can perform with that data. A class bears the same relationship to an object that a type does to a variable. That is, a class definition describes a data form and how it can be used, while an object is an entity created according to the data form specification. Or, in noncomputer terms, if a class is analogous to a category such as famous actors, then an object is analogous to a particular example of that category, such as Kermit the Frog. To extend the analogy, a class representation of actors would include definitions of possible actions relating to the class, such as Reading for a Part, Expressing Sorrow, Projecting Menace, Accepting an Award, and the like. If you've been exposed to different OOP terminology, it might help to know that the C++ class corresponds to what some languages term an object type, and the C++ object corresponds to an object instance or instance variable.

Now get a little more specific. Recall this declaration of a variable:

```
int fleas;
```

This creates a particular variable (**fleas**) that has the properties of the **int** type. That is, **fleas** can store an integer and can be used in particular ways—for addition and subtraction, for example. Now consider **cout**. It is an object created to have the properties of the **ostream** class. The **ostream** class definition (another inhabitant of the **iostream** file) describes the sort of data an **ostream** object represents and the operations you can perform with and to it, such as inserting a number or string into an output stream. Similarly, **cin** is an object created with the properties of the **istream** class, also defined in **iostream**.

Remember

The class describes all the properties of a data type, and an object is an entity created according to that description.

You have learned that classes are user-defined types, but as a user you certainly didn't design the **ostream** and **istream** classes. Just as functions can come in function libraries, classes can come in class libraries. That's the case for the **ostream** and **istream** classes. Technically, they are not built in to the C++ language, but are examples of classes that happen to come with the language. The class definitions are laid out in the **iostream** file and are not built in to the compiler. You even can modify these class definitions if you like, although that's not a good idea. (More precisely, it is a truly dreadful idea.) The **iostream** family of classes and the related **fstream** (or file I/O) family are the only sets of class definitions that came with all early implementations of C++. However, the ANSI/ISO C++ committee added a few more class libraries to the standard. Also, most implementations provide additional class definitions as part of the package. Indeed, much of the current appeal of C++ is the existence of extensive and useful class libraries supporting UNIX, Macintosh, and Windows programming.

The class description specifies all the operations that can be performed on objects of that class. To perform such an allowed action on a particular object, you send a message to the object. For example, if you want the **cout** object to display a string, you send it a message that says, in effect, "Object! Display this!" C++ provides a couple of ways to send messages. One way, called using a class method, essentially is a function call like the ones you've seen. The other, which is the one used with **cin** and **cout**, is to redefine an operator. Thus the statement

```
cout << "I am not a crook."
```

uses the redefined **<<** operator to send the "display message" to **cout**. In this case, the message comes with an argument, which is the string to be displayed. (See Figure 2.5.)

FIGURE 2.5

Sending a message to an object.

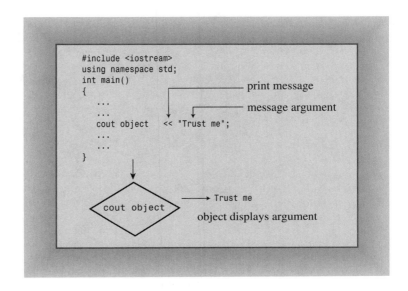

Functions

Because functions are the modules from which C++ programs are built and because they are essential to C++ OOP definitions, you should become thoroughly familiar with them. Because some aspects of functions are advanced topics, the main discussion of functions comes later, in Chapters 7, "Functions—C++'s Programming Modules," and 8, "Adventures in Functions." However, if you deal now with some basic characteristics of functions, you'll be more at ease and more practiced with functions later. The rest of this chapter introduces you to these function basics.

C++ functions come in two varieties: those with return values and those with none. You can find examples of each kind in the standard C++ library of functions, and you can create your own functions of each type. Let's look at a library function that has a return value, and then examine how you can write your own simple functions.

Using a Function with a Return Value

A function that has a return value produces a value that you can assign to a variable. For example, the standard C/C++ library includes a function called `sqrt()` that returns the square root of a number. Suppose you want to calculate the square root of 6.25 and assign it to a variable x. You could use the following statement in your program:

```
x = sqrt(6.25); // returns the value 2.5 and assigns it to x
```

The expression `sqrt(6.25)` invokes, or *calls*, the `sqrt()` function. The expression `sqrt(6.25)` is termed a *function call*, the invoked function is termed the *called function*, and the function containing the function call is termed the *calling function*. (See Figure 2.6.)

FIGURE 2.6

Calling a function.

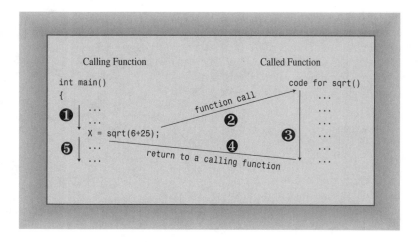

The value in the parentheses (6.25, in this example) is information sent to the function; it is said to be *passed* to the function. A value sent to a function this way is called an ***argument*** or ***parameter***. (See Figure 2.7.) The `sqrt()` function calculates the answer to be 2.5 and sends that value back to the calling function; the value sent back is called the ***return value*** of the function. Think of the return value as what is substituted for the function call in the statement after the function finishes its job. Thus, this example assigns the return value to the variable **x**. In short, an argument is information sent to the function, and the return value is a value sent back from the function.

FIGURE 2.7

Function call syntax.

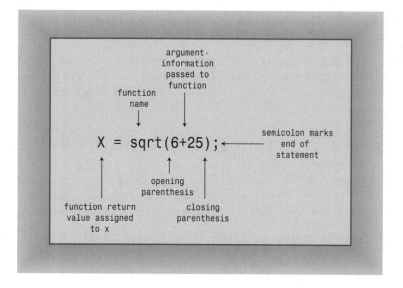

That's practically all there is to it, except that before it uses a function, the C++ compiler must know what kind of arguments the function uses and what kind of return value it has. That is, does the function return an integer? A character? A number with a decimal fraction? A guilty verdict? Or something else? If it lacks this information, the compiler won't know how to interpret the return value. The C++ way for conveying this information is by using a function prototype statement.

Remember

A C++ program should provide a prototype for each function used in the program.

A function prototype does for functions what a variable declaration does for variables—it tells what types are involved. For example, the C++ library defines the `sqrt()` function to take a number with (potentially) a fractional part (like 6.25) as an argument and to return a number of the same type. Some languages refer to such numbers as real numbers, but the name C++ uses for this type is `double`. (You see more of `double` in Chapter 3.) The function prototype for `sqrt()` looks like this:

```
double sqrt(double);    // function prototype
```

The initial `double` means `sqrt()` returns a type `double` value. The `double` in the parentheses means `sqrt()` requires a `double` argument. So this prototype describes `sqrt()` exactly as used in the following code:

```
double x;        // declare x as a type double variable
x = sqrt(6.25);
```

By the way, the terminating semicolon in the prototype identifies it as a statement, and thus makes it a prototype instead of a function heading. If you omit the semicolon, the compiler interprets the line as a function heading and expects you to follow it with a function body that defines the function.

When you use `sqrt()` in a program, you also must provide the prototype. You can do this in either of two ways:

- You can type the function prototype into your source code file yourself.

- You can include the `cmath` (`math.h` on older systems) header file, which has the prototype in it.

The second way is better because the header file is even more likely than you to get the prototype right. Every function in the C++ library has a prototype in one or more header files. Just check the function description in your manual or with online help, if you have it, and the description tells you which header file to use. For example, the description of the `sqrt()` function should tell you to use the `cmath` header file. (Again, you might have to use the older `math.h` header file, which works for both C and C++ programs.)

Don't confuse the function prototype with the function definition. The prototype, as you've seen, only describes the function interface. That is, it describes the information sent to the function and the information sent back. The definition, however, includes the code for the function's workings—for example, the code for calculating the square root of a number. C and C++ divide these two features—prototype and definition—for library functions. The library files contain the compiled code for the functions, whereas the header files contain the prototypes.

You should place a function prototype ahead of where you first use the function. The usual practice is to place prototypes just before the definition of the `main()` function. Listing 2.4 demonstrates the use of the library function `sqrt()`; it provides a prototype by including the `cmath` file.

LISTING 2.4   sqrt.cpp

```cpp
// sqrt.cpp -- use a square root function
#include <iostream>
using namespace std;
#include <cmath>          // or math.h
int main()
{
    double cover;         // use double for real numbers

    cout << "How many square feet of sheets do you have?\n";
    cin >> cover;
    double side;          // create another variable
    side = sqrt(cover); // call function, assign return value
    cout << "You can cover a square with sides of " << side;
    cout << " feet\nwith your sheets.\n";
    return 0;
}
```

Compatibility Note

If you're using an older compiler, you might have to use `#include <math.h>` instead of `#include <cmath>` in Listing 2.4.

Using Library Functions

C++ library functions are stored in library files. When the compiler compiles a program, it must search the library files for the functions you've used. Compilers differ on which library files they search automatically. If you try to run Listing 2.4 and get a message that _sqrt is an undefined external (sounds like a condition to avoid!), chances are that your compiler doesn't automatically search the math library. (Compilers like to add an underscore prefix to function names—another subtle reminder that they have the last say about your program.) If you get such a message, check your compiler documentation to see how to have the compiler search the correct library. The usual UNIX implementations, for example, require that you use a `-lm` option (for *library math*) at the end of the command line:

```
CC sqrt.C -lm
```

Merely including the `cmath` header file provides the prototype but does not necessarily cause the compiler to search the correct library file.

Here's a sample run:

```
How many square feet of sheets do you have?
123.21
You can cover a square with sides of 11.1 feet
with your sheets.
```

Because `sqrt()` works with type `double` values, the example makes the variables that type. Note that you declare a type `double` variable by using the same form, or syntax, as when you declare a type `int` variable:

```
type-name variable-name;
```

Type `double` allows the variables `cover` and `side` to hold values with decimal fractions, such as 123.21 and 1.1. As you see in Chapter 3, type `double` encompasses a much greater range of values than type `int`.

C++ does allow you to declare new variables anywhere in a program, so `sqrt.cpp` didn't declare `side` until just before using it. C++ also allows you to assign a value to a variable when you create it, so you also could have done this:

```
double side = sqrt(cover);
```

You return to this process, called *initialization*, in Chapter 3.

Note that `cin` knows how to convert information from the input stream to type `double`, and `cout` knows how to insert type `double` into the output stream. As noted before, these objects are smart.

Function Variations

Some functions require more than one item of information. These functions use multiple arguments separated by commas. For example, the math function `pow()` takes two arguments and returns a value equal to the first argument raised to the power given by the second argument. It has this prototype:

```
double pow(double, double);  // prototype of a function with two arguments
```

If, say, you wanted to find 5 to 8th power, you would use the function like this:

```
answer = pow(5.0, 8.0);     // function call with a list of arguments
```

Other functions take no arguments. For example, one of the C libraries (the one associated with the `cstdlib` or the `stdlib.h` header file) has a `rand()` function that has no arguments and that returns a random integer. Its prototype looks like this:

```
int rand(void);         // prototype of a function that takes no arguments
```

The keyword `void` explicitly indicates that the function takes no arguments. If you omit `void` and leave the parentheses empty, C++ interprets this as an implicit declaration that there are no arguments. You could use the function this way:

```
myGuess = rand();       // function call with no arguments
```

Note that, unlike some computer languages, you must use the parentheses in the function call even if there are no arguments.

There also are functions that have no return value. For example, suppose you wrote a function that displayed a number in dollar and cents format. You could send it an argument of, say, 23.5, and it would display $23.50 onscreen. Because this function sends a value to the screen instead of to the calling program, it doesn't return a value. You indicate this in the prototype by using the keyword `void` for the return type:

```
void bucks(double);   // prototype for function with no return value
```

Because it doesn't return a value, you can't use the function as part of an assignment statement or of some other expression. Instead, you have a pure function call statement:

```
bucks(1234.56);       // function call, no return value
```

Some languages reserve the term *function* for functions with return values and use the terms *procedure* or *subroutine* for those without return values, but C++, like C, uses the term *function* for both variations.

User-Defined Functions

The standard C library provides over 140 predefined functions. If one fits your needs, by all means use it. But often you have to write your own, particularly when you design classes. Anyway, it's a lot more fun to design your own functions, so now let's examine that process. You've already used several user-defined functions, and they all have been named `main()`. Every C++ program must have a `main()` function, which the user must define. Suppose you want to add a second user-defined function. Just as with a library function, you can call a user-defined function by using its name. And, as with a library function, you must provide a function prototype before using the function, which you typically do by placing the prototype above the `main()` definition. The new element is that you also must provide the source code for the new function. The simplest way is to place the code in the same file after the code for `main()`. Listing 2.5 illustrates these elements.

LISTING 2.5   `ourfunc.cpp`

```
// ourfunc.cpp -- defining your own function
#include <iostream>
using namespace std;
void simon(int);     // function prototype for simon()
int main()
{
    simon(3);          // call the simon() function
    cout << "Pick an integer: ";
    int count;
    cin >> count;
```

LISTING 2.5   Continued

```
    simon(count);    // call it again
    return 0;
}

void simon(int n)    // define the simon() function
{
    cout << "Simon says touch your toes " << n << " times.\n";
}                    // void functions don't need return statements
```

The `main()` function calls the `simon()` function twice, once with an argument of 3 and once with a variable argument `count`. In between, the user enters an integer that's used to set the value of `count`. The example doesn't use a newline character in the `cout` prompting message. This results in the user input appearing on the same line as the prompt. Here is a sample run:

```
Simon says touch your toes 3 times.
Pick an integer: 512
Simon says touch your toes 512 times.
```

Function Form

The definition for the `simon()` function follows the same general form as the definition for `main()`. First, there is a function header. Then, enclosed in braces, comes the function body. You can generalize the form for a function definition as follows:

```
type functionname(argumentlist)
{
    statements
}
```

Note that the source code that defines `simon()` follows the closing brace of `main()`. Like C, and unlike Pascal, C++ does not allow you to embed one function definition inside another. Each function definition stands separately from all others; all functions are created equal. (See Figure 2.8.)

Function Headings

The `simon()` function has this heading:

```
void simon(int n)
```

The initial `void` means that `simon()` has no return value. So calling `simon()` doesn't produce a number that you can assign to a variable in `main()`. Thus, the first function call looks like this:

```
simon(3);            // ok for void functions
```

Because poor `simon()` lacks a return value, you can't use it this way:

```
simple = simon(3);   // not allowed for void functions
```

FIGURE 2.8

Function definitions occur sequentially in a file.

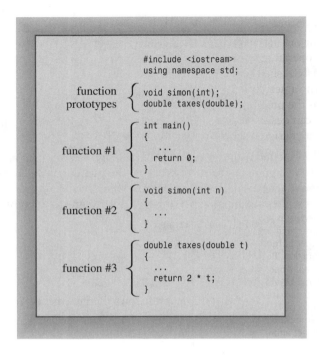

The `int n` within the parentheses means that you are expected to use `simon()` with a single argument of type `int`. The `n` is a new variable assigned the value passed during a function call. Thus, the function call

```
simon(3);
```

assigns the value 3 to the `n` variable defined in the `simon()` heading. When the `cout` statement in the function body uses `n`, it uses the value passed in the function call. That's why `simon(3)` displays a **3** in its output. The call to `simon(count)` in the sample run causes the function to display **512** because that's the value given to `count`. In short, the heading for `simon()` tells you that this function takes a single type `int` argument and that it doesn't have a return value.

Let's review `main()`'s function header:

```
int main()
```

The initial `int` means that `main()` returns an integer value. The empty parentheses (which, optionally, could contain `void`) means that `main()` has no arguments. Functions that have return values should use the keyword `return` to provide the return value and to terminate the function. That's why you've been using the following statement at the end of `main()`:

```
return 0;
```

This is logically consistent: `main()` is supposed to return a type `int` value, and you have it return the integer 0. But, you might wonder, to what are you returning a value? After all, nowhere in any of your programs have you seen anything calling `main()`:

```
squeeze = main();   // absent from our programs
```

The answer is that you can think of your computer's operating system (UNIX, say, or DOS) as calling your program. So `main()`'s return value is returned not to another part of the program but to the operating system. Many operating systems can use the program's return value. For example, UNIX shell scripts and DOS batch files can be designed to run programs and test their return values, usually called exit values. The normal convention is that an exit value of zero means the program ran successfully, whereas a nonzero value means there was a problem. Thus, you can design your C++ program to return a nonzero value if, say, it fails to open a file. You then can design a shell script or batch file to run that program and to take some alternative action if the program signals failure.

Keywords

Keywords are the vocabulary of a computer language. This chapter has used four C++ keywords: `int`, `void`, `return`, and `double`. Because these keywords are special to C++, you can't use them for other purposes. That is, you can't use `return` as the name for a variable or `double` as the name of a function. But you can use them as part of a name, as in `painter` (with its hidden `int`) or `return_aces`. Appendix B, "C++ Keywords," provides a complete list of C++ keywords. Incidentally, `main` is not a keyword because it's not part of the language. Instead, it is the name of a required function. You can use `main` as a variable name. (That can cause a problem in circumstances too esoteric to describe here, and because it is confusing in any case, you'd best not.) Similarly, other function names and object names are not keywords. However, using the same name, say `cout`, for both an object and a variable in a program confuses the compiler. That is, you can use `cout` as a variable name in a function that doesn't use the `cout` object for output, but you can't use `cout` both ways in the same function.

User-Defined Function with a Return Value

Let's go one step further and write a function that uses the return statement. The `main()` function already illustrates the plan for a function with a return value: Give the return type in the function heading and use `return` at the end of the function body. You can use this form to solve a weighty problem for those visiting the United Kingdom. In the U.K., many bathroom scales are calibrated in *stone* instead of in U.S. pounds or international kilograms. The word stone is both singular and plural in this context. (The English language does lack the internal consistency of, say, C++.) One stone is 14 pounds, and the program in Listing 2.6 uses a function to make this conversion.

LISTING 2.6   `convert.cpp`

```
// convert.cpp -- converts stone to pounds
#include <iostream>
using namespace std;
int stonetolb(int);      // function prototype
int main()
{
    int stone;
    cout << "Enter the weight in stone: ";
    cin >> stone;
    int pounds = stonetolb(stone);
```

LISTING 2.6   *Continued*

```
        cout << stone << " stone are ";
        cout << pounds << " pounds.\n";
        return 0;
}

int stonetolb(int sts)
{
        return 14 * sts;
}
```

Here's a sample run:

```
Enter the weight in stone: 14
14 stone are 196 pounds.
```

In `main()`, the program uses `cin` to provide a value for the integer variable `stone`. This value is passed to the `stonetolb()` function as an argument and is assigned to the variable `sts` in that function. `stonetolb()` then uses the `return` keyword to return the value of `14 * sts` to `main()`. This illustrates that you aren't limited to following `return` with a simple number. Here, by using a more complex expression, you avoid the bother of having to create a new variable to which to assign the value before returning it. The program calculates the value of that expression (196 in this example) and returns the resulting value. If returning the value of an expression bothers you, you can take the longer route:

```
int stonetolb(int sts)
{
        int pounds = 14 * sts;
        return pounds;
}
```

Either version produces the same result, but the second version takes slightly longer to do so.

In general, you can use a function with a return value wherever you would use a simple constant of the same type. For example, `stonetolb()` returns a type `int` value. This means you can use the function in the following ways:

```
int aunt = stonetolb(20);
int aunts = aunt + stonetolb(10);
cout << "Ferdie weighs " << stonetolb(16) << " pounds.\n";
```

In each case, the program calculates the return value and then uses that number in these statements.

As these examples show, the function prototype describes the function interface—that is, how the function interacts with the rest of the program. The argument list shows what sort of information goes into the function, and the function type shows the type of value returned. Programmers sometimes describe functions as *black boxes* (a term from electronics) specified by the flow of information into and out of them. The function prototype perfectly portrays that point of view. (See Figure 2.9.)

FIGURE 2.9

The function prototype
and the function as a
black box.

The `stonetolb()` function is short and simple, yet it embodies a full range of functional features:

- It has a heading and a body.

- It accepts an argument.

- It returns a value.

- It requires a prototype.

Consider `stonetolb()` as a standard form for function design. You'll go further into functions in Chapters 7 and 8. In the meantime, the material in this chapter should give you a good feel for how functions work and how they fit into C++.

Real-World Note: Naming Conventions

C++ programmers are blessed (or cursed) with myriad options when naming functions, classes, and variables. Programmers have strong and varied opinions about style, and these often surface as holy wars in public forums. Starting with the same basic idea for a function name, a programmer might select any of the following:

```
MyFunction( )
myfunction( )
myFunction( )
my_function( )
my_funct( )
```

The choice will depend upon the development team, the idiosyncrasies of the technologies or libraries used, as well as the tastes and preferences of the individual programmer. Rest assured that all legal styles are correct, as far as the C++ language is concerned, and can be used based on your own judgment.

Language allowances aside, it is worth noting that a *personal naming style*—one that aids you through consistency and precision—is well worth pursuing. A precise, recognizable personal naming convention is a hallmark of good software engineering, and it will aid you throughout your programming career.

Statement Summary

The following list is a summary of the several kinds of C++ statements you've learned and used in this chapter:

- A declaration statement announces the name and the type of a variable used in a function.

- An assignment statement uses the assignment operator (=) to assign a value to a variable.

- A message statement sends a message to an object, initiating some sort of action.

- A function call activates a function. When the called function terminates, the program returns to the statement in the calling function immediately following the function call.

- A function prototype declares the return type for a function along with the number and type of arguments the function expects.

- A return statement sends a value from a called function back to the calling function.

Summary

A C++ program consists of one or more modules called functions. Programs begin executing at the beginning of the function called `main()` (all lowercase), so you always should have a function by this name. A function, in turn, consists of a heading and a body. The function heading tells you what kind of return value, if any, the function produces and what sort of information it expects to be passed to it by arguments. The function body consists of a series of C++ statements enclosed in paired braces: {}.

C++ statement types include declaration statements, assignment statements, function call statements, object message statements, and return statements. The declaration statement announces the name of a variable and establishes the type of data it can hold. An assignment statement gives a value to a variable. A function call passes program control to the called function. When the function finishes, control returns to the statement in the calling function immediately following the function call. A message instructs an object to perform a particular action. A return statement is the mechanism by which a function returns a value to its calling function.

A class is a user-defined specification for a data type. This specification details how information is to be represented and also the operations that can be performed with the data. An object is an entity created according to a class prescription, just as a simple variable is an entity created according to a data type description.

C++ provides two predefined objects (`cin` and `cout`) for handling input and output. They are examples of the `istream` and `ostream` classes, which are defined in the `iostream` file. These classes view input and output as streams of characters. The insertion operator (`<<`), which is defined for the `ostream` class, lets you insert data into the output stream, and the extraction operator (`>>`), which is defined for the `istream` class, lets you extract information from the input stream. Both `cin` and `cout` are smart objects, capable of automatically converting information from one form to another according to the program context.

C++ can use the extensive set of C library functions. To use a library function, you should include the header file that provides the prototype for the function.

Now that you have an overall view of simple C++ programs, you can go on in the next chapters to fill in details and expand horizons.

Review Questions

You find the answers to these and subsequent review questions in Appendix J, "Answers to Review Questions."

1. What are the modules of C++ programs called?

2. What does the following preprocessor directive do?

   ```
   #include <iostream>
   ```

3. What does the following statement do?

   ```
   using namespace std;
   ```

4. What statement would you use to print the phrase "Hello, world" and then start a new line?

5. What statement would you use to create an integer variable with the name `cheeses`?

6. What statement would you use to assign the value 32 to the variable `cheeses`?

7. What statement would you use to read a value from keyboard input into the variable `cheeses`?

8. What statement would you use to print "We have X varieties of cheese," where the current value of the `cheeses` variable replaces X?

9. What does the following function header tell you about the function?

   ```
   int froop(double t)
   ```

10. When do you not have to use the keyword `return` when you define a function?

Programming Exercises

1. Write a C++ program that displays your name and address.

2. Write a C++ program that asks for a distance in furlongs and converts it to yards (one furlong is 220 yards).

3. Write a C++ program that uses three user-defined functions (counting `main()` as one) and produces the following output:

```
Three blind mice
Three blind mice
See how they run
See how they run
```

One function, called two times, should produce the first two lines, and the remaining function, also called twice, should produce the remaining output.

4. Write a program that has `main()` call a user-defined function that takes a Celsius temperature value as an argument and then returns the equivalent Fahrenheit value. The program should request the Celsius value as input from the user and display the result, as shown in the following code:

```
Please enter a Celsius value: 20
20 degrees Celsius is 68 degrees Fahrenheit.
```

For reference, here is the formula for making the conversion:

Fahrenheit = 1.8 × Celsius + 32.0

5. Write a program that has `main()` call a user-defined function that takes a distance in light years as an argument and then returns the distance in astronomical units. The program should request the light year value as input from the user and display the result, as shown in the following code:

```
Enter the number of light years: 4.2
4.2 light years are 265608 astronomical units.
```

An astronomical unit is the average distance from the Earth to the Sun (about 150,000,000 km or 93,000,000 miles) and a light year is the distance light travels in a year (about 10 trillion kilometers or 6 trillion miles). (The nearest star after the Sun is about 4.2 light years away.) Use type `double` (as in Listing 2.4) and this conversion factor:

1 light year = 63240 astronomical units

CHAPTER 3

DEALING WITH DATA

In this chapter you learn

- Rules for naming C++ variables
- C++'s built-in integer types: `unsigned long`, `long`, `unsigned int`, `int`, `unsigned short`, `short`, `char`, `unsigned char`, `signed char`, and `bool`
- The `climits` file, representing system limits for various integer types
- Numeric constants of various integer types
- Using the `const` qualifier to create symbolic constants
- C++'s built-in floating-point types: `float`, `double`, and `long double`
- The `cfloat` file, representing system limits for various floating-point types
- Numeric constants of various floating-point types
- C++'s arithmetic operators
- Automatic type conversions
- Forced type conversions (type casts)

T he essence of object-oriented programming is designing and extending your own data types. Designed types represent an effort to make a type match the data. If you do this properly, you'll find it much simpler to work with the data later. But before you can create your own types, you must know and understand the types built in to C++ because these types will be your building blocks.

The built-in C++ types come in two groups: fundamental types and compound types. In this chapter you'll meet the fundamental types, which represent integers and floating-point numbers. That might sound like just two types; however, C++ recognizes that no one integer type and no one floating-point type match all programming requirements, so it offers several variants on these two data themes. Next, Chapter 4, "Compound Types," follows up by covering several types built upon the basic types; these additional compound types include arrays, strings, pointers, and structures.

Of course, a program also needs a means to identify stored data. You'll examine one method for doing so—using variables. Next, you'll look at how to do arithmetic in C++. Finally, you'll see how C++ converts values from one type to another.

Simple Variables

Programs typically need to store information—perhaps the current price of IBM stock, the average humidity in New York City in August, the most common letter in the Constitution and its relative frequency, or the number of available Elvis imitators. To store an item of information in a computer, the program must keep track of three fundamental properties:

- Where the information is stored
- What value is kept there
- What kind of information is stored

The strategy the examples have been using so far is to declare a variable. The type used in the declaration describes the kind of information, and the variable name represents the value symbolically. For example, suppose Chief Lab Assistant Igor uses the following statements:

```
int braincount;
braincount = 5;
```

These statements tell the program that it is storing an integer and that the name `braincount` represents the integer's value, 5 in this case. In essence, the program locates a chunk of memory large enough to hold an integer, notes the location, assigns the label `braincount` to the location, and copies the value 5 into the location. These statements don't tell you (or Igor) where in memory the value is stored, but the program does keep track of that information, too. Indeed, you can use the `&` operator to retrieve `braincount`'s address in memory. You'll take up that operator in the next chapter when you investigate a second strategy for identifying data—using pointers.

Names for Variables

C++ encourages you to use meaningful names for variables. If a variable represents the cost of a trip, call it `cost_of_trip` or `costOfTrip`, not just `x` or `cot`. You do have to follow a few simple C++ naming rules:

- The only characters you can use in names are alphabetic characters, digits, and the underscore (_) character.
- The first character in a name cannot be a digit.
- Uppercase characters are considered distinct from lowercase characters.
- You can't use a C++ keyword for a name.

- Names beginning with two underscore characters or with an underscore character followed by an uppercase letter are reserved for use by the implementation. Names beginning with a single underscore character are reserved for use as global identifiers by the implementation.

- C++ places no limits on the length of a name, and all characters in a name are significant.

The next-to-last point is a bit different from the preceding points because using a name like `__time_stop` or `_Donut` doesn't produce a compiler error; instead, it leads to undefined behavior. In other words, there's no telling what the result will be. The reason there is no compiler error is that the names are not illegal but rather are reserved for the implementation to use. The bit about global names refers to where the names are declared; Chapter 4 touches on that topic.

The final point makes C++ different from ANSI C (the recent C99 standard), which guarantees only that the first 63 characters in a name are significant. (In ANSI C, two names that have the same first 63 characters are considered identical, even if the 64th characters differ.)

Here are some valid and invalid C++ names:

```
int poodle;     // valid
int Poodle;     // valid and distinct from poodle
int POODLE;     // valid and even more distinct
Int terrier;    // invalid -- has to be int, not Int
int my_stars3   // valid
int _Mystars3;  // valid but reserved -- starts with underscore
int 4ever;      // invalid because starts with a digit
int double;     // invalid -- double is a C++ keyword
int begin;      // valid -- begin is a Pascal keyword
int __fools;    // valid but reserved -- starts with two underscores
int the_very_best_variable_i_can_be_version_112;  // valid
int honky-tonk;        // invalid -- no hyphens allowed
```

If you want to form a name from two or more words, the usual practice is to separate the words with an underscore character, as in `my_onions`, or to capitalize the initial character of each word after the first, as in `myEyeTooth`. (C veterans tend to use the underscore method in the C tradition, while Pascalians prefer the capitalization approach.) Either form makes it easier to see the individual words and to distinguish between, say, `carDrip` and `cardRip`, or `boat_sport` and `boats_port`.

Real World Note: Variable Names

Schemes for naming variables, like schemes for naming functions, provide fertile ground for fervid discussion. Indeed, this topic produces some of the most strident disagreements in programming. Again, as with function names, the C++ compiler doesn't care about your variable names as long as they are within legal limits, but a consistent, precise personal naming convention will serve you well.

As in function naming, capitalization is a key issue in variable naming (see the Chapter 2 sidebar, "Naming Conventions"), but many programmers may insert an additional level of information in a variable name, a prefix that describes the variable's type or contents. For instance, the integer `myWeight` might be named `nMyWeight`; here, the n prefix is used to represent an integer value, useful when you are reading your code and the definition of the variable isn't immediately at hand. Alternatively, this variable might be named `intMyWeight`, which is more precise and legible, although it does include a couple of extra letters (anathema to many programmers). Other prefixes are commonly used in like fashion: `str` or `sz` represent a null-terminated string of characters, `b` might represent a boolean value, `p` a pointer, `c` a single character.

As you progress into the world of C++, you will find many examples of the prefixed naming style (including the handsome `m_lpctstr` prefix—a class member value which contains a long pointer to a constant, null-terminated string of characters), as well as other, more bizarre and possibly counterintuitive styles which you may or may not adopt as your own. As in all of the stylistic, subjective parts of C++, consistency and precision are best. Use variable names to fit your own needs, preferences, and personal style. (Or, if required, choose names that fit the needs, preferences, and personal style of your employer.)

Integer Types

Integers are numbers with no fractional part, such as 2, 98, –5286, and 0. There are lots of integers, assuming you consider an infinite number to be a lot, so no finite amount of computer memory can represent all possible integers. Thus, a language only can represent a subset of all integers. Some languages, such as Standard Pascal, offer just one integer type (one type fits all!), but C++ provides several choices. This gives you the option of choosing the integer type that best meets a program's particular requirements. This concern with matching type to data presages the designed data types of OOP.

The various C++ integer types differ in the amount of memory they use to hold an integer. A larger block of memory can represent a larger range in integer values. Also, some types (signed types) can represent both positive and negative values, whereas others (unsigned types) can't represent negative values. The usual term for describing the amount of memory used for an integer is *width*. The more memory a value uses, the wider it is. C++'s basic integer types, in order of increasing width, are called `char`, `short`, `int`, and `long`. Each comes in both signed and unsigned versions. That gives you a choice of eight different integer types! Let's look at these integer types in more detail. Because the `char` type has some special properties (it's most often used to represent characters instead of numbers), this chapter will cover the other types first.

The `short`, `int`, and `long` Integer Types

Computer memory consists of units called *bits*. (See the "Bits and Bytes" note.) By using different numbers of bits to store values, the C++ types of `short`, `int`, and `long` can represent up to three different integer widths. It would be convenient if each type were always some particular width for all systems; for example, if `short` were always 16 bits, `int` always 32 bits, and so on. But life is not that simple. The reason is that no one choice is suitable for all computer designs. C++ offers a flexible standard with some guaranteed minimum sizes. Here's what you get:

- A **short** integer is at least 16 bits wide.

- An **int** integer is at least as big as **short**.

- A **long** integer is at least 32 bits wide and at least as big as **int**.

Bits and Bytes

The fundamental unit of computer memory is the *bit*. Think of a bit as an electronic switch that you can set either to off or on. Off represents the value 0, and on represents the value 1. An 8-bit chunk of memory can be set to 256 different combinations. The number 256 comes from the fact that each bit has two possible settings, making the total number of combinations for 8 bits $2 \times 2 \times 2 \times 2 \times 2 \times 2 \times 2 \times 2$, or 256. Thus, an 8-bit unit can represent, say, the values 0 through 255 or the values −128 through 127. Each additional bit doubles the number of combinations. This means you can set a 16-bit unit to 65,536 different values and a 32-bit unit to 4,294,672,296 different values.

A *byte* usually means an 8-bit unit of memory. Byte in this sense is the unit of measurement that describes the amount of memory in a computer, with a kilobyte equal to 1024 bytes and a megabyte equal to 1024 kilobytes. C++, however, defines a byte differently. The C++ *byte* consists of at least enough adjacent bits to accommodate the basic character set for the implementation. That is, the number of possible values must equal or exceed the number of distinct characters. In the U.S., the basic character sets usually are the ASCII and EBCDIC sets, each of which can be accommodated by 8 bits, so the C++ byte typically is 8 bits on systems using these character sets. However, international programming can require much larger character sets, such as Unicode, so some implementations may use a 16-bit byte or even a 32-bit byte.

Many systems currently use the minimum guarantee, making **short** 16 bits and **long** 32 bits. This still leaves several choices open for **int**. It could be 16, 24, or 32 bits in width and meet the standard. Typically, **int** is 16 bits (the same as **short**) for older IBM PC implementations and 32 bits (the same as **long**) for Windows 95, Windows 98, Windows NT, Macintosh, VAX, and many other minicomputer implementations. Some implementations give you a choice of how to handle **int**. (What does your implementation use? The next example shows you how to determine the limits for your system without your having to open a manual.) The differences between implementations for type widths can cause problems when you move a C++ program from one environment to another. But a little care, as discussed later in this chapter, can minimize those problems.

You use these type names to declare variables just as you would use **int**:

```
short score;        // creates a type short integer variable
int temperature;    // creates a type int integer variable
long position;      // creates a type long integer variable
```

Actually, **short** is short for **short int** and **long** is short for **long int**, but hardly anyone uses the longer forms.

The three types, **int**, **short**, and **long**, are signed types, meaning each splits its range approximately equally between positive and negative values. For example, a 16-bit **int** might run from −32768 to +32767.

If you want to know how your system's integers size up, C++ offers tools to let you investigate type sizes with a program. First, the `sizeof` operator returns the size, in bytes, of a type or a variable. (An operator is a built-in language element that operates on one or more items to produce a value. For example, the addition operator, represented by +, adds two values.) Note that the meaning of "byte" is implementation-dependent, so a two-byte `int` could be 16 bits on one system and 32 bits on another. Second, the `climits` header file (or, for older implementations, the `limits.h` header file) contains information about integer type limits. In particular, it defines symbolic names to represent different limits. For example, it defines `INT_MAX` to be the largest possible `int` value and `CHAR_BIT` as the number of bits in a byte. Listing 3.1 demonstrates how to use these facilities. The program also illustrates *initialization*, which is the use of a declaration statement to assign a value to a variable.

LISTING 3.1   `limits.cpp`

```
// limits.cpp -- some integer limits
#include <iostream>
using namespace std;
#include <climits>              // use limits.h for older systems
int main()
{
    int n_int = INT_MAX;        // initialize n_int to max int value
    short n_short = SHRT_MAX;    // symbols defined in limits.h file
    long n_long = LONG_MAX;

    // sizeof operator yields size of type or of variable
    cout << "int is " << sizeof (int) << " bytes.\n";
    cout << "short is " << sizeof n_short << " bytes.\n";
    cout << "long is " << sizeof n_long << " bytes.\n\n";

    cout << "Maximum values:\n";
    cout << "int: " << n_int << '\n';
    cout << "short: " << n_short << '\n';
    cout << "long: " << n_long << "\n\n";

    cout << "Minimum int value = " << INT_MIN << '\n';
    cout << "Bits per byte = " << CHAR_BIT << '\n';
    return 0;
}
```

Compatibility Note

The `climits` header file is the C++ version of the ANSI C `limits.h` header file. Some earlier C++ platforms have neither header file available. If you're using such a system, you must limit yourself to experiencing this example in spirit only.

Here is the output using Microsoft Visual C++ 6.0:

```
int is 4 bytes.
short is 2 bytes.
long is 4 bytes.
```

```
Maximum values:
int: 2147483647
short: 32767
long: 2147483647

Minimum int value = -2147483648
Bits per byte = 8
```

Here is the output for a second system (Borland C++ 3.1 for DOS):

```
int is 2 bytes.
short is 2 bytes.
long is 4 bytes.

Maximum values:
int: 32767
short: 32767
long: 2147483647

Minimum int value = -32768
Bits per byte = 8
```

Program Notes

Let's look at the chief programming features for this program.

The `sizeof` operator reports that `int` is 4 bytes on the base system, which uses an 8-bit byte. You can apply the `sizeof` operator to a type name or to a variable name. When you use the `sizeof` operator with a type name, such as `int`, you enclose the name in parentheses. But if you use the operator with the name of the variable, such as `n_short`, parentheses are optional:

```
cout << "int is " << sizeof (int) << " bytes.\n";
cout << "short is " << sizeof n_short << " bytes.\n";
```

The `climits` header file defines symbolic constants (see the "Symbolic Constants" note) to represent type limits. As mentioned, `INT_MAX` represents the largest value type `int` can hold; this turned out to be 32767 for our DOS system. The compiler manufacturer provides a `climits` file that reflects the values appropriate to that compiler. For example, the `climits` file for a system using a 32-bit `int` would define `INT_MAX` to represent 2147483647. Table 3.1 summarizes the symbolic constants defined in this file; some pertain to types you have not yet learned.

TABLE 3.1   Symbolic Constants from `climits`

Symbolic Constant	Represents
CHAR_BIT	Number of bits in a `char`
CHAR_MAX	Maximum `char` value
CHAR_MIN	Minimum `char` value

TABLE 3.1   Continued

Symbolic Constant	Represents
SCHAR_MAX	Maximum `signed char` value
SCHAR_MIN	Minimum `signed char` value
UCHAR_MAX	Maximum `unsigned char` value
SHRT_MAX	Maximum `short` value
SHRT_MIN	Minimum `short` value
USHRT_MAX	Maximum `unsigned short` value
INT_MAX	Maximum `int` value
INT_MIN	Minimum `int` value
UINT_MAX	Maximum `unsigned int` value
LONG_MAX	Maximum `long` value
LONG_MIN	Minimum `long` value
ULONG_MAX	Maximum `unsigned long` value

Initialization combines assignment with declaration. For example, the statement

```
int n_int = INT_MAX;
```

declares the **n_int** variable and sets it to the largest possible type **int** value. You also can use regular constants to initialize values. You can initialize a variable to another variable, provided that the other variable has been defined first. You even can initialize a variable to an expression, provided that all the values in the expression are known when program execution reaches the declaration:

```
int uncles = 5;                  // initialize uncles to 5
int aunts = uncles;              // initialize aunts to 5
int chairs = aunts + uncles + 4; // initialize chairs to 14
```

Moving the **uncles** declaration to the end of this list of statements would invalidate the other two initializations, for then the value of **uncles** wouldn't be known at the time the program tried to initialize the other variables.

The initialization syntax shown previously comes from C; C++ has a second initialization syntax not shared with C:

```
int owls = 101;  // traditional C initialization
int wrens(432);  // alternative C++ syntax, set wrens to 432
```

Remember

If you don't initialize a variable defined inside a function, the variable's value is *undefined*. That means the value is whatever happened to be sitting at that memory location prior to the creation of the variable.

If you know what the initial value of a variable should be, initialize it. True, separating the declaring of a variable from assigning it a value can create momentary suspense:

```
short year;      // what could it be?
year = 1492;     // oh
```

But initializing the variable when you declare it protects you from forgetting to assign the value later.

Symbolic Constants the Preprocessor Way

The `climits` file contains lines similar to the following:

```
#define INT_MAX 32767
```

The C++ compilation process, recall, first passes the source code through a preprocessor. Here `#define`, like `#include`, is a preprocessor directive. What this particular directive tells the preprocessor is this: Look through the program for instances of `INT_MAX` and replace each occurrence with `32767`. So the `#define` directive works like a global search-and-replace command in a text editor or word processor. The altered program is compiled after these replacements occur. The preprocessor looks for independent tokens (separate words), skipping embedded words. That is, the preprocessor doesn't replace `PINT_MAXIM` with `P32767IM`. You can use `#define` to define your own symbolic constants, too. (See Listing 3.2.) However, the `#define` directive is a C relic. C++ has a better way for creating symbolic constants (the `const` keyword, discussed in a later section), so you won't be using `#define` much. But some header files, particularly those designed to be used with both C and C++, do use it.

Unsigned Types

Each of the three integer types you just learned comes in an unsigned variety that can't hold negative values. This has the advantage of increasing the largest value the variable can hold. For example, if `short` represents the range −32768 to +32767, then the unsigned version can represent the range 0 to 65535. Of course, you should use unsigned types only for quantities that are never negative, such as populations, inventory counts, and happy face manifestations. To create unsigned versions of the basic integer types, just use the keyword `unsigned` to modify the declarations:

```
unsigned short change;    // unsigned short type
unsigned int rovert;      // unsigned int type
unsigned quarterback;     // also unsigned int
unsigned long gone;       // unsigned long type
```

Note that `unsigned` by itself is short for `unsigned int`.

Listing 3.2 illustrates the use of unsigned types. It also shows what might happen if your program tries to go beyond the limits for integer types. Finally, it gives you one last look at the preprocessor #define statement.

LISTING 3.2   exceed.cpp

```cpp
// exceed.cpp -- exceeding some integer limits
#include <iostream>
using namespace std;
#define ZERO 0       // makes ZERO symbol for 0 value
#include <climits>  // defines INT_MAX as largest int value
int main()
{
    short sam = SHRT_MAX;     // initialize a variable to max value
    unsigned short sue = sam;// okay if variable sam already defined

    cout << "Sam has " << sam << " dollars and Sue has " << sue;
    cout << " dollars deposited.\nAdd $1 to each account.\nNow ";
    sam = sam + 1;
    sue = sue + 1;
    cout << "Sam has " << sam << " dollars and Sue has " << sue;
    cout << " dollars deposited.\nPoor Sam!\n";
    sam = ZERO;
    sue = ZERO;
    cout << "Sam has " << sam << " dollars and Sue has " << sue;
    cout << " dollars deposited.\n";
    cout << "Take $1 from each account.\nNow ";
    sam = sam - 1;
    sue = sue - 1;
    cout << "Sam has " << sam << " dollars and Sue has " << sue;
    cout << " dollars deposited.\nLucky Sue!\n";
    return 0;
}
```

Compatibility Note

Listing 3.2, like Listing 3.1, uses the climits file; older compilers might need to use limits.h, and some very old compilers might not have either file available.

Here's the output:

```
Sam has 32767 dollars and Sue has 32767 dollars deposited.
Add $1 to each account.
Now Sam has -32768 dollars and Sue has 32768 dollars deposited.
Poor Sam!
Sam has 0 dollars and Sue has 0 dollars deposited.
Take $1 from each account.
Now Sam has -1 dollars and Sue has 65535 dollars deposited.
Lucky Sue!
```

The program sets a **short** variable (**sam**) and an **unsigned short** variable (**sue**) to the largest **short** value, which is 32767 on our system. Then, it adds 1 to each value. This causes no problems for **sue** because the new value still is much less than the maximum value for an unsigned integer. But **sam** goes from 32767 to –32768! Similarly, subtracting 1 from 0 creates no problems for **sam**, but it makes the unsigned variable **sue** go from 0 to 65535. As you can see, these integers behave much like an odometer or a VCR counter. If you go past the limit, the values just start over at the other end of the range. (See Figure 3.1.) C++ guarantees that unsigned types behave in this fashion. However, C++ doesn't guarantee that signed integer types can exceed their limits (overflow and underflow) without complaint, but that is the most common behavior on current implementations.

FIGURE 3.1

Typical overflow behavior for integers.

Beyond long

The new C99 C standard has added a couple of new types that most likely will be part of the next edition of the C++ standard. Indeed, many C++ compilers already support them. The types are **long long** and **unsigned long long**. Both are guaranteed to be at least 64 bits and to be at least as wide as the **long** and **unsigned long** types.

Which Type?

With this richness of C++ integer types, which should you use? Generally, `int` is set to the most "natural" integer size for the target computer. *Natural size* means the integer form the computer handles most efficiently. If there is no compelling reason to choose another type, use `int`.

Now look at reasons why you might use another type. If a variable represents something that never is negative, such as the number of words in a document, you can use an unsigned type; that way the variable can represent higher values.

If you know that the variable might have to represent integer values too great for a 16-bit integer, use `long`. This is true even if `int` is 32 bits on your system. That way, if you transfer your program to a system with a 16-bit `int`, your program won't embarrass you by suddenly failing to work properly. (See Figure 3.2.)

FIGURE 3.2
For portability, use `long` for big integers.

Using `short` can conserve memory if `short` is smaller than `int`. Most typically, this is important only if you have a large array of integers. (An *array* is a data structure that stores several values of the same type sequentially in memory.) If it is important to conserve space, you should use `short` instead of `int`, even if the two are the same size. Suppose, for example, you move your program from a 16-bit `int` DOS PC system to a 32-bit `int` Windows NT system. That doubles the amount of memory needed to hold an `int` array, but it doesn't affect the requirements for a `short` array. Remember, a bit saved is a bit earned.

If you need only a single byte, you can use `char`. You'll examine that possibility soon.

Integer Constants

An integer constant is one you write out explicitly, such as 212 or 1776. C++, like C, lets you write integers in three different number bases: base 10 (the public favorite), base 8 (the old UNIX favorite), and base 16 (the hardware hacker's favorite). Appendix A, "Number Bases," describes these bases; here we'll look at the C++ representations. C++ uses the first digit or two to identify the base of a number constant. If the first digit is in the range 1–9, the number is base 10 (decimal); thus 93 is base 10. If the first digit is 0 and the second digit is in the range 1–7, the number is base 8 (octal); thus 042 is octal and equal to 34 decimal. If the first two characters are 0x or 0X, the number is base 16 (hexadecimal); thus 0x42 is hex and equal to 66 decimal. For hexadecimal values, the characters a–f and A–F represent the hexadecimal digits corresponding to the values 10–15. 0xF is 15 and 0xA5 is 165 (10 sixteens plus 5 ones). Listing 3.3 is tailor-made to show the three bases.

LISTING 3.3   `hexoct.cpp`

```
// hexoct.cpp -- shows hex and octal constants
#include <iostream>
using namespace std;
int main()
{
    int chest = 42;      // decimal integer constant
    int waist = 0x42;    // hexadecimal integer constant
    int inseam = 042;    // octal integer constant

    cout << "Monsieur cuts a striking figure!\n";
    cout << "chest = " << chest << "\n";
    cout << "waist = " << waist << "\n";
    cout << "inseam = " << inseam << "\n";
    return 0;
}
```

By default, `cout` displays integers in decimal form, regardless of how they are written in a program, as the following output shows:

```
Monsieur cuts a striking figure!
chest = 42
waist = 66
inseam = 34
```

Keep in mind that these notations are merely notational conveniences. For example, if you read that the CGA video memory segment is B000 in hexadecimal, you don't have to convert the value to base 10 45056 before using it in your program. Instead, simply use 0xB000. But whether you write the value ten as 10, 012, or 0xA, it's stored the same way in the computer—as a binary (base two) value.

By the way, if you want to display a value in hexadecimal or octal form, you can use some special features of `cout`. Let's not get into that now, but you can find this information in Chapter 17, "Input, Output, and Files." (You can skim the chapter for that information and ignore the explanations.)

How C++ Decides What Type a Constant Is

A program's declarations tell the C++ compiler the type of a particular integer variable. But what about constants? That is, suppose you represent a number with a constant in a program:

```
cout << "Year = " << 1492 << "\n";
```

Does the program store 1492 as an `int`, a `long`, or some other integer type? The answer is that C++ stores integer constants as type `int` unless there is a reason to do otherwise. Two such reasons are if you use a special suffix to indicate a particular type or if a value is too large to be an `int`.

First, look at the suffixes. These are letters placed at the end of a numeric constant to indicate the type. An `l` or `L` suffix on an integer means the integer is a type `long` constant, a `u` or `U` suffix indicates an `unsigned int` constant, and `ul` (in any combination of orders and uppercase and lowercase) indicates a type `unsigned long` constant. (Because a lowercase `l` can look much like the digit `1`, you should use the uppercase `L` for suffixes.) For example, on a system using a 16-bit `int` and a 32-bit `long`, the number 22022 is stored in 16 bits as an `int`, and the number 22022L is stored in 32 bits as a `long`. Similarly, 22022LU and 22022UL are `unsigned long`.

Next, look at size. C++ has slightly different rules for decimal integers than it has for hexadecimal and octal integers. (Here decimal means base 10, just as hexadecimal means base 16; the term does not necessarily imply a decimal point.) A decimal integer without a suffix is represented by the smallest of the following types that can hold it: `int`, `long`, or `unsigned long`. On a computer system using a 16-bit `int` and a 32-bit `long`, 20000 is represented as type `int`, 40000 is represented as `long`, and 3000000000 is represented as `unsigned long`. A hexadecimal or octal integer without a suffix is represented by the smallest of the following types that can hold it: `int`, `unsigned int`, `long`, `unsigned long`. The same computer system that represents 40000 as `long` represents the hexadecimal equivalent 0x9C40 as an `unsigned int`. That's because hexadecimal frequently is used to express memory addresses, which intrinsically are unsigned. So `unsigned int` is more appropriate than `long` for a 16-bit address.

The `char` Type: Characters and Small Integers

It's time to turn to the final integer type, type `char`. As you probably suspect from its name, the `char` type is designed to store characters, such as letters and digits. Now, whereas storing numbers is no big deal for computers, storing letters is another matter. Programming languages take the easy way out by using a number code for letters. Thus, the char type is another integer type. It's guaranteed to be large enough to represent the entire range of basic symbols—all the letters, digits, punctuation, and the like—for the target computer system. In practice, most systems support fewer than 256 kinds of characters, so a single byte can represent the whole range. Therefore, although char most often is used to handle characters, you also can use it as an integer type typically smaller than short.

The most common symbol set in the United States is the ASCII character set described in Appendix C, "The ASCII Character Set." A numeric code (the ASCII code) represents the characters in the set. For example, 65 is the code for the character A. For convenience, this book assumes ASCII code in its examples. However, a C++ implementation uses whatever code is native to its host system—for example, EBCDIC (pronounced eb-se-dik) on an IBM mainframe. Neither ASCII nor EBCDIC serve international needs that well, and C++ supports a wide-character type that can hold a larger range of values, such as are used by the international Unicode character set. You'll learn about this wchar_t type later in this chapter.

Try the char type in Listing 3.4.

LISTING 3.4   chartype.cpp

```
// chartype.cpp -- the char type
#include <iostream>
using namespace std;
int main( )
{
    char ch;          // declare a char variable

    cout << "Enter a character:\n";
    cin >> ch;
    cout << "Holla! ";
    cout << "Thank you for the " << ch << " character.\n";
    return 0;
}
```

As usual, the \n notation is the C++ representation of the newline character. Here's the output:

```
Enter a character:
M
Holla! Thank you for the M character.
```

The interesting thing is that you type an M, not the corresponding character code of 77. Also, the program prints an M, not a 77. Yet if you peer into memory, you find that 77 is the value stored in the ch variable. The magic, such as it is, lies not in the char type but in cin and cout. These worthy facilities make conversions on your behalf. On input, cin converts the keystroke input M to the value 77. On output, cout converts the value 77 to the displayed character of M; cin and cout are guided by the type of variable. If you place the same value of 77 into an int variable, then cout displays it as 77. (That is, cout displays two 7 characters.) Listing 3.5 illustrates this point. It also shows how to write a character constant in C++: Enclose the character within two single quotation marks, as in 'M'. (Note that the example doesn't use double quotation marks. C++ uses single quotation marks for a character and double quotation marks for a string. The **cout** object can handle either, but, as Chapter 4 discusses, the two are quite different.) Finally, the program introduces a **cout** feature, the **cout.put()** function, which displays a single character.

LISTING 3.5 morechar.cpp

```cpp
// morechar.cpp -- the char type and int type contrasted
#include <iostream>
using namespace std;
int main()
{
    char c = 'M';          // assign ASCII code for M to c
    int i = c;             // store same code in an int
    cout << "The ASCII code for " << c << " is " << i << "\n";

    cout << "Add one to the character code:\n";
    c = c + 1;
    i = c;
    cout << "The ASCII code for " << c << " is " << i << '\n';

    // using the cout.put() member function to display a char
    cout << "Displaying char c using cout.put(c): ";
    cout.put(c);

    // using cout.put() to display a char constant
    cout.put('!');

    cout << "\nDone\n";
    return 0;
}
```

Here is the output:

```
The ASCII code for M is 77
Add one to the character code:
The ASCII code for N is 78
Displaying char c using cout.put(c): N!
Done
```

Program Notes

The notation **'M'** represents the numeric code for the M character, so initializing the **char** variable c to **'M'** sets c to the value **77**. The program then assigns the identical value to the **int** variable i, so both c and i have the value **77**. Next, **cout** displays c as M and i as **77**. As previously stated, a value's type guides **cout** as it chooses how to display that value—just another example of smart objects.

Because c is really an integer, you can apply integer operations to it, such as adding 1. This changes the value of c to 78. The program then resets i to the new value. (Equivalently, you simply can add 1 to i.) Again, **cout** displays the **char** version of that value as a character and the **int** version as a number.

The fact that C++ represents characters as integers is a genuine convenience that makes it easy to manipulate character values. You don't have to use awkward conversion functions to convert characters to ASCII and back.

Finally, the program uses the `cout.put()` function to display both `c` and a character constant.

A Member Function: `cout.put()`

Just what is `cout.put()`, and why does it have a period in its name? The `cout.put()` function is your first example of an important C++ OOP concept, the *member function*. A class, remember, defines how to represent data and how to manipulate it. A member function belongs to a class and describes a method for manipulating class data. The `ostream` class, for example, has a `put()` member function designed to output characters. You can use a member function only with a particular object of that class, such as the `cout` object, in this case. To use a class member function with an object like `cout`, you use a period to combine the object name (`cout`) with the function name (`put()`). The period is called the *membership operator*. The notation `cout.put()` means to use the class member function `put()` with the class object `cout`. Of course, you'll learn about this in greater detail when you reach classes in Chapter 10, "Objects and Classes." Now, the only classes you have are the `istream` and `ostream` classes, and you can experiment with their member functions to get more comfortable with the concept.

The `cout.put()` member function provides an alternative to using the `<<` operator to display a character. At this point you might wonder why there is any need for `cout.put()`. Much of the answer is historical. Before Release 2.0 of C++, `cout` would display character variables as characters but display character constants, such as `'M'` and `'\n'`, as numbers. The problem was that earlier versions of C++, like C, stored character constants as type `int`. That is, the code 77 for `'M'` would be stored in a 16-bit or 32-bit unit. Meanwhile, `char` variables typically occupied 8 bits. A statement like

```
char c = 'M';
```

copied 8 bits (the important 8 bits) from the constant `'M'` to the variable `c`. Unfortunately, this meant that `'M'` and `c` looked quite different to `cout`, even though both held the same value. So a statement like

```
cout << '$';
```

would print the ASCII code for the `$` character rather than simply display `$`. But

```
cout.put('$');
```

would print the character, as desired. Now, after Release 2.0, C++ stores single character constants as type `char`, not type `int`. That means `cout` now correctly handles character constants. C++ always could use the string `"\n"` to start a new line; now it also can use the character constant `'\n'`:

```
cout << "\n"; // using a string
cout << '\n'; // using a character constant
```

A string is enclosed in double quotation marks instead of single quotation marks and can hold more than one character. Strings, even one-character strings, are not the same as type `char`. We'll come back to strings in the next chapter.

The `cin` object has a couple of different ways of reading characters from input. You can more easily explore these by using a program that uses a loop to read several characters, so we'll return to this topic when you cover loops in Chapter 5, "Loops and Relational Expressions."

`char` Constants

You have several options for writing character constants in C++. The simplest choice for ordinary characters, such as letters, punctuation, and digits, is to enclose the character in single quotation marks. This notation stands for the numeric code for the character. For example, an ASCII system has the following correspondences:

```
'A' is 65, the ASCII code for A
'a' is 97, the ASCII code for a
'5' is 53, the ASCII code for the digit 5
' ' is 32, the ASCII code for the space character
'!' is 33, the ASCII code for the exclamation mark
```

Using this notation is better than using the numeric codes explicitly. It's clearer, and it doesn't assume a particular code. If a system uses EBCDIC, then 65 is not the code for A, but `'A'` still represents the character.

You can't enter some characters into a program directly from the keyboard. For example, you can't make the newline character part of a string by pressing the Enter key; instead, the program editor interprets that keystroke as a request for it to start a new line in your source code file. Other characters have difficulties because the C++ language imbues them with special significance. For example, the double quotation mark character delimits strings, so you can't just stick one in the middle of a string. C++ has special notations, called *escape sequences*, for several of these characters, as shown in Table 3.2. For example, \a represents the alert character, which beeps your terminal's speaker or rings its bell. And \" represents the double quotation mark as an ordinary character instead of a string delimiter. You can use these notations in strings or in character constants:

```
char alarm = '\a';
cout << alarm << "Don't do that again!\a\n";
cout << "Ben \"Buggsie\" Hacker was here!\n";
```

The last line produces the following output:

```
Ben "Buggsie" Hacker was here!
```

Note that you treat an escape sequence, such as \a, just as a regular character, such as Q. That is, you enclose it in single quotes to create a character constant and don't use single quotes when including it as part of a string.

TABLE 3.2   C++ Escape Sequence Codes

Character Name	ASCII Symbol	C++ Code	ASCII Decimal Code	ASCII Hex Code
Newline	NL (LF)	\n	10	0xA
Horizontal tab	HT	\t	9	0x9
Vertical tab	VT	\v	11	0xB
Backspace	BS	\b	8	0x8
Carriage return	CR	\r	13	0xD
Alert	BEL	\a	7	0x7
Backslash	\	\\	92	0x5C
Question mark	?	\?	63	0x3F
Single quote	'	\'	39	0x27
Double quote	"	\"	34	0x22

Finally, you can use escape sequences based on the octal or hexadecimal codes for a character. For example, Ctrl+Z has an ASCII code of 26, which is 032 in octal and 0x1a in hexadecimal. You can represent this character by either of the following escape sequences: \032 or \x1a. You can make character constants out of these by enclosing them in single quotes, as in '\032', and you can use them as parts of a string, as in "hi\x1a there".

Tip

When you have a choice between using a numeric escape sequence or a symbolic escape sequence, as in \0x8 versus \b, use the symbolic code. The numeric representation is tied to a particular code, such as ASCII, but the symbolic representation works with all codes and is more readable.

Listing 3.6 demonstrates a few escape sequences. It uses the alert character to get your attention, the newline character to advance the cursor (one small step for a cursor, one giant step for cursorkind), and the backspace character to back the cursor one space to the left. (Houdini once painted a picture of the Hudson River using only escape sequences; he was, of course, a great escape artist.)

LISTING 3.6   bondini.cpp

```cpp
// bondini.cpp -- using escape sequences
#include <iostream>
using namespace std;
int main()
{
```

LISTING 3.6 *Continued*

```
cout << "\aOperation \"HyperHype\" is now activated!\n";
cout << "Enter your agent code:_____\b\b\b\b\b\b\b\b";
long code;
cin >> code;
cout << "\aYou entered " << code << "...\n";
cout << "\aCode verified! Proceed with Plan Z3!\n";
return 0;
}
```

Compatibility Note

Some C++ systems based on pre-ANSI C compilers don't recognize \a. You can substitute \007 for \a on systems that use the ASCII character code. Some systems might behave differently, displaying the \b as a small rectangle rather than backspacing, for example, or perhaps erasing while backspacing.

When you start the program, it puts the following text on the screen:

```
Operation "HyperHype" is now activated!
Enter your agent code:_____
```

After printing the underscore characters, the program uses the backspace character to back up the cursor to the first underscore. You then can enter your secret code and continue. Here's a complete run:

```
Operation "HyperHype" is now activated!
Enter your agent code:42007007
You entered 42007007...
Code verified! Proceed with Plan Z3!
```

Universal Character Names

C++ implementations support a basic source character set, that is, the set of characters you can use to write source code. It consists of the letters (uppercase and lowercase) and digits found on a standard U.S. keyboard, the symbols, such as { and =, used in the C language, and a scattering of other characters, such as newline and space. Then there is a basic execution character set (characters that can be produced by the execution of a program), which adds a few more characters, such as the backspace and alert. The standard additionally allows an implementation to offer extended source character sets and extended execution character sets. Furthermore, those additional characters that qualify as letters can be used as part of the name of an identifier. Thus, a German implementation might allow you to use umlauted vowels and a French implementation might allow accented vowels. C++ has a mechanism for representing such international characters that is independent of any particular keyboard, and that is the use of *universal character names*.

The mechanism is similar to that of escape sequences. A universal character name begins either with \u or \U. The \u form is followed by 8 hexadecimal digits, and the \U form by 16 hexadecimal digits. These digits represent the ISO 10646 code for the character. (ISO 10646 is an international standard under development that provides numeric codes for a wide range of characters. See the box "Unicode and ISO 10646.")

If your implementation supports extended characters, you can use universal character names in identifiers, as character constants, and in strings. For example, consider the following code:

```
int k\u00F6rper;
cout << "Let them eat g\u00E2teau.\n";
```

The ISO 10646 code for ö is 00F6, and the code for â is 00E2. Thus, this C++ code would set the variable name to `körper` and display the following output:

```
Let them eat gâteau.
```

Unicode and ISO 10646

Unicode provides a solution to the representation of various character sets by providing standard numeric codes for a great number of characters and symbols, grouping them by type. For example, the ASCII code is incorporated as a subset of Unicode, so U.S. Latin characters such as A and Z have the same representation under both systems. But Unicode also incorporates other Latin characters, such as are used in European languages; characters from other alphabets, including Greek, Cyrillic, Hebrew, Arabic, Thai, and Bengali; and ideographs, such as those used for Chinese and Japanese. So far Unicode represents over 94,000 symbols, and it still is under development. If you want to know more, you can check the Unicode Consortium's Web site at `www.unicode.org`.

The International Organization for Standardization (ISO) established a working group to develop ISO 10646, also a standard for coding multilingual text. The ISO 10636 group and the Unicode group have worked together since 1991 to keep their standards synchronized with one another.

signed char **and** unsigned char

Unlike `int`, `char` is not signed by default. Nor is it unsigned by default. The choice is left to the C++ implementation in order to allow the compiler developer to best fit the type to the hardware properties. If it is vital to you that `char` has a particular behavior, you can use `signed char` or `unsigned char` explicitly as types:

```
char fodo;            // may be signed, may be unsigned
unsigned char bar;    // definitely unsigned
signed char snark;    // definitely signed
```

These distinctions are particularly important if you use `char` as a numeric type. The `unsigned char` type typically represents the range 0 to 255, and `signed char` typically represents the range –128 to 127. For example, suppose you want to use a `char` variable to hold values as large as 200. That works on some systems but fails on others. You can, however, successfully use `unsigned char` for that purpose on any system. On the other hand, if you use a `char` variable to hold a standard ASCII character, it doesn't really matter whether `char` is signed or unsigned, so you simply can use `char`.

For When You Need More: wchar_t

Programs might have to handle character sets that don't fit within the confines of a single 8-bit byte; for example, the Japanese kanji system. C++ handles this in a couple of ways. First, if a large set of characters is the basic character set for an implementation, a compiler vender can define char as a 16-bit byte or larger. Second, an implementation can support both a small basic character set and a larger extended character set. The usual 8-bit char can represent the basic character set, and a new type, called wchar_t (for *wide character type*), can represent the extended character set. The wchar_t type is an integer type with sufficient space to represent the largest extended character set used on the system. This type has the same size and sign properties as one of the other integer types, which is called the **underlying** type. The choice of underlying type depends on the implementation, so it could be unsigned short on one system and int on another.

The cin and cout family consider input and output as consisting of streams of chars, so they are not suitable for handling the wchar_t type. The latest version of the iostream header file provides parallel facilities in the form of wcin and wcout for handling wchar_t streams. Also, you can indicate a wide-character constant or string by preceding it with an L.

```
wchar_t bob = L'P';         // a wide-character constant
wcout << L"tall" << endl;   // outputting a wide-character string
```

On a system with a two-byte wchar_t, this code stores each character in a two-byte unit of memory. This book won't use the wide-character type, but you should be aware of it, particularly if you become involved in international programming or in using Unicode or ISO 10646.

The New bool Type

The ANSI/ISO C++ Standard has added a new type (new to C++, that is), called bool. It's named in honor of the English mathematician George Boole, who developed a mathematical representation of the laws of logic. In computing, a *Boolean variable* is one whose value can be either true or false. In the past, C++, like C, has not had a Boolean type. Instead, as you'll see in greater detail in Chapters 5 and 6, "Branching Statements and Logical Operators," C++ interprets nonzero values as true and zero values as false. Now, however, you can use the bool type to represent true and false, and the predefined literals true and false represent those values. That is, you can make statements like the following:

```
bool isready = true;
```

The literals true and false can be converted to type int by promotion, with true converting to 1 and false to 0:

```
int ans = true;          // ans assigned 1
int promise = false;     // promise assigned 0
```

Also, any numeric or pointer value can be converted implicitly (that is, without an explicit type cast) to a bool value. Any nonzero value converts to true, whereas a zero value converts to false:

```
bool start = -100;      // start assigned true
bool stop = 0;          // stop assigned false
```

Later chapters illustrate how this type can come in handy.

The const Qualifier

Now let's return to the topic of symbolic names for constants. A symbolic name can suggest what the constant represents. Also, if the program uses the constant in several places and you need to change the value, you can just change the single symbol definition. The note about `#define` statements earlier in this chapter ("Symbolic Constants the Preprocessor Way") promised that C++ has a better way to handle symbolic constants. That way is to use the `const` keyword to modify a variable declaration and initialization. Suppose, for example, that you want a symbolic constant for the number of months in a year. Enter this line in a program:

```
const int MONTHS = 12;   // Months is symbolic constant for 12
```

Now you can use `MONTHS` in a program instead of 12. (A bare 12 in a program might represent the number of inches in a foot or the number of donuts in a dozen, but the name `MONTHS` tells you what it represents.) After you initialize a constant like `MONTHS`, its value is set. The compiler does not let you subsequently change the value `MONTHS`. For example, Borland C++ gives an error message stating that an `lvalue` is required. This is the same message you get if you try, say, to assign the value 4 to 3. (An `lvalue` is a value, such as a variable, that appears on the left side of the assignment operator.) The keyword `const` is termed a *qualifier* because it qualifies the meaning of a declaration.

Capitalize the name to help remind yourself that `MONTHS` is a constant. This is by no means a universal convention, but it helps separate the constants from the variables when you read a program. Another convention is capitalizing just the first character in the name. Yet another convention is to begin constant names with the letter k, as in `kmonths`. And there are yet other conventions. Many organizations have particular coding conventions they expect their programmers to follow.

The general form for creating a constant is this:

```
const type name = value;
```

Note that you initialize a `const` in the declaration. The following sequence is no good:

```
const int toes;     // value of toes undefined at this point
toes = 10;          // too late!
```

If you don't provide a value when you declare the constant, it ends up with an unspecified value that you cannot modify.

If your background is in C, you might feel that the `#define` statement, which was discussed earlier, already does the job adequately. But `const` is better. For one thing, it lets you specify the type explicitly. Second, you can use C++'s scoping rules to limit the definition to particular functions or files. (Scoping rules describe how widely known a name is to different modules; you learn about this in more detail in Chapter 9, "Memory Models and Namespaces.") Third, you can use **const** with more elaborate types, such as the arrays and structures coming up in the next chapter.

Tip
If you are coming to C++ from C and you are about to use #define to define a symbolic constant, use const instead.

ANSI C also uses the **const** qualifier, borrowing it from C++. If you're familiar with the ANSI C version, you should be aware that the C++ version is slightly different. One difference relates to the scope rules, and Chapter 9 covers that point. The other main difference is that in C++ (but not in C) you can use a **const** value to declare the size of an array. You'll see examples in the next chapter.

Floating-Point Numbers

Now that you have seen the complete line of C++ integer types, let's look at the floating-point types, which compose the second major group of fundamental C++ types. These numbers let you represent numbers with fractional parts, such as the gas mileage of an M1 tank (0.56 MPG). They also provide a much greater range in values. If a number is too large to be represented as type **long**, for example, the number of stars in our galaxy (an estimated 400,000,000,000), you can use one of the floating-point types.

With floating-point types, you can represent numbers like 2.5 and 3.14159 and 122442.32—that is, numbers with a fractional part. A computer stores such values in two parts. One part represents a value, and the other part scales that value up or down. Here's an analogy. Consider the two numbers 34.1245 and 34124.5. They're identical except for scale. You can represent the first one as 0.341245 (the base value) and 100 (the scaling factor). You can represent the second as 0.341245 (the same base value) and 100000 (a bigger scaling factor). The scaling factor serves to move the decimal point, hence the term floating-point. C++ uses a similar method to represent floating-point numbers internally, except it's based on binary numbers, so the scaling is by factors of 2 instead of by factors of 10. Fortunately, you don't have to know much about the internal representation. The main points are that floating-point numbers let you represent fractional, very large, and very small values, and they have an internal representation much different from that of integers.

Writing Floating-Point Numbers

C++ has two ways of writing floating-point numbers. The first is to use the standard decimal-point notation you've been using much of your life:

```
12.34               // floating-point
939001.32           // floating-point
0.00023             // floating-point
8.0                 // still floating-point
```

Even if the fractional part is 0, as in 8.0, the decimal point ensures that the number is stored in floating-point format and not as an integer. (The C++ Standard does allow for implementations to represent different locales; for example, providing a mechanism for using the European method of using a comma instead of a period for the decimal point. However, these choices govern how the numbers can appear in input and output, not in code.)

The second method for representing floating-point values is called E notation, and it looks like this: **3.45E6**. This means that the value 3.45 is multiplied by 1,000,000; the E6 means 10 to the 6th power, which is 1 followed by 6 zeros. Thus **3.45E6** means 3,450,000. The 6 is called an *exponent*, and the 3.45 is termed the *mantissa*. Here are more examples:

```
2.52e+8          // can use E or e, + is optional
8.33E-4          // exponent can be negative
7E5              // same as 7.0E+05
-18.32e13        // can have + or - sign in front
2.857e12         // US public debt, 1989
5.98E24          // mass of Earth in kilograms
9.11e-31         // mass of an electron in kilograms
```

As you might have noticed, E notation is most useful for very large and very small numbers.

E notation guarantees that the number is stored in floating-point format, even if no decimal point is used. Note that you can use either **E** or **e**, and the exponent can have a positive or negative sign. (See Figure 3.3.) However, you can't have spaces in the number: **7.2 E6** is invalid.

FIGURE 3.3

E notation.

To use a negative exponent means to divide by a power of 10 instead of multiplying by a power of 10. So 8.33E-4 means 8.33 ÷ 10^4, or 0.000833. Similarly, the electron mass of 9.11e-31 kg means

```
0.000000000000000000000000000000911 kg
```

Take your choice. (Incidentally, note that 911 is the usual emergency telephone number in the United States and that telephone messages are carried by electrons. Coincidence or scientific conspiracy? You be the judge.) Note that –8.33E4 means –83300. A sign in front applies to the number value, while a sign in the exponent applies to the scaling.

Remember

The form `d.dddE+n` means move the decimal point n places to the right, and the form `d.dddE-n` means move the decimal point n places to the left.

Floating-Point Types

Like ANSI C, C++ has three floating-point types: `float`, `double`, and `long double`. These types are described in terms of the number of significant figures they can represent and the minimum allowable range of exponents. *Significant figures* are the meaningful digits in a number. For example, writing the height of Mt. Shasta in California as 14,162 feet uses five significant figures, for it specifies the height to the nearest foot. But writing the height of Mt. Shasta as about 14,000 feet tall uses two significant figures, for the result is rounded to the nearest thousand feet. In this case, the remaining three digits are just placeholders. The number of significant figures doesn't depend on the location of the decimal point. For example, you can write the height as 14.162 thousand feet. Again, this uses five significant digits, because the value is accurate to the fifth digit.

In effect, the C and C++ requirements for significant digits amount to `float` being at least 32 bits, `double` being at least 48 bits and certainly no smaller than `float`, and `long double` being at least as big as `double`. All three can be the same size. Typically, however, `float` is 32 bits, `double` is 64 bits, and `long double` is 80, 96, or 128 bits. Also, the range in exponents for all three types is at least –37 to +37. You can look in the `cfloat` or `float.h` header files to find the limits for your system. (The `cfloat` is the C++ version of the C `float.h` file.) Here, for example, are some annotated entries from the `float.h` file for Borland C++Builder:

```
// the following are the minimum number of significant digits
#define DBL_DIG 15          // double
#define FLT_DIG 6           // float
#define LDBL_DIG 18         // long double

// the following are the number of bits used to represent
// the mantissa
#define DBL_MANT_DIG    53
#define FLT_MANT_DIG    24
#define LDBL_MANT_DIG   64

// the following are the maximum and minimum exponent values
#define DBL_MAX_10_EXP    +308
#define FLT_MAX_10_EXP    +38
#define LDBL_MAX_10_EXP   +4932
```

```
#define DBL_MIN_10_EXP    -307
#define FLT_MIN_10_EXP    -37
#define LDBL_MIN_10_EXP   -4931
```

Compatibility Note

Some C++ implementations have not yet added the `cfloat` header file, and some C++ implementations based on pre-ANSI C compilers don't provide a `float.h` header file.

Listing 3.7 examines types `float` and `double` and how they can differ in the precision to which they represent numbers (that's the significant figure aspect). The program previews an `ostream` method called `setf()` from Chapter 17. This particular call forces output to stay in fixed-point notation so that you better can see the precision. It prevents the program from switching to E notation for large values and causes the program to display six digits to the right of the decimal. The arguments `ios_base::fixed` and `ios_base::floatfield` are constants provided by including `iostream`.

LISTING 3.7   floatnum.cpp

```cpp
// floatnum.cpp -- floating-point types
#include <iostream>
using namespace std;
int main()
{
    cout.setf(ios_base::fixed, ios_base::floatfield); // fixed-point
    float tub = 10.0 / 3.0;     // good to about 6 places
    double mint = 10.0 / 3.0;   // good to about 15 places
    const float million = 1.0e6;

    cout << "tub = " << tub;
    cout << ", a million tubs = " << million * tub;
    cout << ",\nand ten million tubs = ";
    cout << 10 * million * tub << "\n";

    cout << "mint = " << mint << " and a million mints = ";
    cout << million * mint << "\n";
    return 0;
}
```

Here is the output:

```
tub = 3.333333, a million tubs = 3333333.250000,
and ten million tubs = 33333332.000000
mint = 3.333333 and a million mints = 3333333.333333
```

Program Notes

Normally **cout** drops trailing zeros. For example, it would display 3333333.250000 as 3333333.25. The call to **cout.setf()** overrides that behavior, at least in new implementations. The main thing to note here is how **float** has less precision than **double**. Both **tub** and **mint** are initialized to 10.0 / 3.0. That should evaluate to 3.33333333333333333...(etc.). Because **cout** prints six figures to the right of the decimal, you can see that both **tub** and **mint** are accurate that far. But, after the program multiplies each number by a million, you see that **tub** diverges from the proper value after the seventh 3. **tub** is good to seven significant figures. (This system guarantees six significant figures for **float**, but that's the worst-case scenario.) The type **double** variable, however, shows thirteen 3s, so it's good to at least thirteen significant figures. Because the system guarantees fifteen, this shouldn't surprise you. Also, note that multiplying a million **tub**s by ten didn't quite result in the correct answer; this again points out the limitations of **float** precision.

The **ostream** class to which **cout** belongs has class member functions that give you precise control on how the output is formatted—field widths, places to the right of the decimal point, decimal form or E form, and so on. Chapter 17 outlines those choices. This book's examples keep it simple and usually just use the **<<** operator. Occasionally, this practice displays more digits than necessary, but that causes only esthetic harm. If you do mind, you can skim Chapter 17 to see how to use the formatting methods. Don't, however, expect to follow fully the explanations at this point.

source of knowledge and information—in many cases, the best documentation available. Later, as you progress into more complex inclusions and begin to use other, nonstandard libraries in your applications, this habit will serve you well.

Floating-Point Constants

When you write a floating-point constant in a program, in which floating-point type does the program store it? By default, floating-point constants such as 8.24 and 2.4E8 are type `double`. If you want a constant to be type `float`, use an f or F suffix. For type `long double`, use an l or L suffix.

```
1.234f          // a float constant
2.45E20F        // a float constant
2.345324E28     // a double constant
2.2L            // a long double constant
```

Floating-Point Advantages and Disadvantages

Floating-point numbers have two advantages over integers. First, they can represent values between integers. Second, because of the scaling factor, they can represent a much greater range of values. On the other hand, floating-point operations are slower than integer operations, at least on computers without math coprocessors, and you can lose precision. Listing 3.8 illustrates the last point.

LISTING 3.8   fltadd.cpp

```cpp
// fltadd.cpp -- precision problems with float
#include <iostream>
using namespace std;
int main()
{
    float a = 2.34E+22f;
    float b = a + 1.0f;

    cout << "a = " << a << "\n";
    cout << "b - a = " << b - a << "\n";
    return 0;
}
```

Compatibility Note

Some ancient C++ implementations based on pre-ANSI C compilers don't support the f suffix for floating-point constants. If you find yourself facing this problem, you can replace 2.34E+22f with 2.34E+22 and replace 1.0f with (float) 1.0.

The program takes a number, adds 1, and then subtracts the original number. That should result in a value of 1. Does it? Here is the output for one system:

```
a = 2.34e+022
b - a = 0
```

The problem is that 2.34E+22 represents a number with 23 digits to the left of the decimal place. By adding 1, you are attempting to add 1 to the 23rd digit in that number. But type **float** only can represent the first 6 or 7 digits in a number, so trying to change the 23rd digit has no effect on the value.

Classifying the Types

C++ brings some order to its basic types by classifying them into families. Types `signed char`, `short`, `int`, and `long` are termed *signed integer* types. The unsigned versions are termed *unsigned integer* types. The `bool`, `char`, `wchar_t`, signed integer, and unsigned integer types together are termed *integral* types or *integer* types. The `float`, `double`, and `long double` are termed *floating-point* types. Integer and floating-point types collectively are termed *arithmetic* types.

C++ Arithmetic Operators

Perhaps you have warm memories of doing arithmetic drills in grade school. You can give that same pleasure to your computer. C++ uses operators to do arithmetic. It provides operators for five basic arithmetic calculations: addition, subtraction, multiplication, division, and taking the modulus. Each of these operators uses two values (called *operands*) to calculate a final answer. Together, the operator and its operands constitute an *expression*. For example, consider the following statement:

```
int wheels = 4 + 2;
```

The values **4** and **2** are operands, the + symbol is the addition operator, and **4 + 2** is an expression whose value is 6.

Here are C++'s five basic arithmetic operators:

- The + operator adds its operands. For example, **4 + 20** evaluates to **24**.

- The - operator subtracts the second operand from the first. For example, **12 - 3** evaluates to **9**.

- The * operator multiplies its operands. For example, **28 * 4** evaluates to **112**.

- The / operator divides its first operand by the second. For example, **1000 / 5** evaluates to **200**. If both operands are integers, the result is the integer portion of the quotient. For example, **17 / 3** is **5**, with the fractional part discarded.

- The % operator finds the modulus of its first operand with respect to the second. That is, it produces the remainder of dividing the first by the second. For example, **19 % 6** is **1**, because **6** goes into **19** three times with a remainder of **1**. Both operands must be integer types. If one of the operands is negative, the sign of the result depends on the implementation.

Of course, you can use variables as well as constants for operands. Listing 3.9 does just that. Because the % operator works only with integers, we'll leave it for a later example.

LISTING 3.9   arith.cpp

```cpp
// arith.cpp -- some C++ arithmetic
#include <iostream>
using namespace std;
int main()
{
    float hats, heads;

    cout.setf(ios_base::fixed, ios_base::floatfield); // fixed-point
    cout << "Enter a number: ";
    cin >> hats;
    cout << "Enter another number: ";
    cin >> heads;

    cout << "hats = " << hats << "; heads = " << heads << "\n";
    cout << "hats + heads = " << hats + heads << "\n";
    cout << "hats - heads = " << hats - heads << "\n";
    cout << "hats * heads = " << hats * heads << "\n";
    cout << "hats / heads = " << hats / heads << "\n";
    return 0;
}
```

Compatibility Note

If your compiler does not accept the `ios_base` forms in `setf()`, try using the older `ios` forms instead; that is, substitute `ios::fixed` for `ios_base::fixed`, etc.

Here's sample output. As you can see, you can trust C++ to do simple arithmetic:

```
Enter a number: 50.25
Enter another number: 11.17
hats = 50.250000; heads = 11.170000
hats + heads = 61.419998
hats - heads = 39.080002
hats * heads = 561.292480
hats / heads = 4.498657
```

Well, maybe you can't trust it completely. Adding 11.17 to 50.25 should yield 61.42, but the output reports 61.419998. This is not an arithmetic problem; it's a problem with the limited capacity of type `float` to represent significant figures.

Remember, C++ guarantees just six significant figures for `float`. If you round 61.419998 to six figures, you get 61.4200, which is the correct value to the guaranteed precision. The moral is that if you need greater accuracy, use `double` or `long double`.

Which Order: Operator Precedence and Associativity

Can you trust C++ to do complicated arithmetic? Yes, but you must know the rules C++ uses. For example, many expressions involve more than one operator. That can raise questions about which operator gets applied first. For example, consider this statement:

```cpp
int flyingpigs = 3 + 4 * 5;  // 35 or 23?
```

The 4 appears to be an operand for both the + and * operators. When more than one operator can be applied to the same operand, C++ uses *precedence* rules to decide which operator is used first. The arithmetic operators follow the usual algebraic precedence, with multiplication, division, and the taking of the modulus done before addition and subtraction. Thus `3 + 4 * 5` means `3 + (4 * 5)`, not `(3 + 4) * 5`. So the answer is `23`, not `35`. Of course, you can use parentheses to enforce your own priorities. Appendix D, "Operator Precedence," shows precedence for all the C++ operators. In it, note that `*`, `/`, and `%` all are in the same row. That means they have equal precedence. Similarly, addition and subtraction share a lower precedence.

Sometimes the precedence list is not enough. Consider the next statement:

```
float logs = 120 / 4 * 5;      // 150 or 6?
```

Once again 4 is an operand for two operators. But the / and * operators have the same precedence, so precedence alone doesn't tell the program whether first to divide 120 by 4 or to multiply the 4 by 5. Because the first choice leads to a result of 150 and the second to a result of 6, the choice is an important one. When two operators have the same precedence, C++ looks at whether the operators have a left-to-right *associativity* or a right-to-left associativity. Left-to-right associativity means that if two operators acting upon the same operand have the same precedence, apply the left-hand operator first. For right-to-left associativity, apply the right-hand operator first. The associativity information, too, is in Appendix D. There you see that multiplication and division associate left-to-right. That means you use 4 with the leftmost operator first. That is, you divide 120 by 4, get 30 as a result, and then multiply the result by 5 to get 150.

Note that the precedence and associativity rules come into play only when two operators share the same operand. Consider the following expression:

```
int dues = 20 * 5 + 24 * 6;
```

Operator precedence tells you two things: The program must evaluate `20 * 5` before doing addition, and the program must evaluate `24 * 6` before doing addition. But neither precedence nor associativity says which multiplication takes place first. You might think that associativity says to do the leftmost multiplication first, but in this case, the two * operators do not share a common operand, so the rules don't apply. In fact, C++ leaves it to the implementation to decide which order works best on a system. For this example, either order gives the same result, but there are circumstances in which the order can make a difference. You'll see one when Chapter 5 discusses the increment operator.

Division Diversions

You have yet to see the rest of the story about the division operator. The behavior of this operator depends on the type of the operands. If both operands are integers, C++ performs integer division. That means any fractional part of the answer is discarded, making the result an integer. If one or both operands are floating-point values, the fractional part is kept, making the result floating-point. Listing 3.10 illustrates how C++ division works with different types of values. Like Listing 3.9, this invokes the `setf()` member function to modify how the results are displayed.

LISTING 3.10   divide.cpp

```cpp
// divide.cpp -- integer and floating-point division
#include <iostream>
using namespace std;
int main()
{
    cout.setf(ios_base::fixed, ios_base::floatfield);
    cout << "Integer division: 9/5 = " << 9 / 5  << "\n";
    cout << "Floating-point division: 9.0/5.0 = ";
    cout << 9.0 / 5.0 << "\n";
    cout << "Mixed division: 9.0/5 = " << 9.0 / 5  << "\n";
    cout << "double constants: 1e7/9.0 = ";
    cout << 1.e7 / 9.0 <<  "\n";
    cout << "float constants: 1e7f/9.0f = ";
    cout << 1.e7f / 9.0f <<  "\n";
    return 0;
}
```

Compatibility Note

If your compiler does not accept the `ios_base` forms in `setf()`, try using the older `ios` forms instead.

Some C++ implementations based on pre-ANSI C compilers don't support the f̲ suffix for floating-point constants. If you find yourself facing this problem, you can replace `1.e7f` / `9.0f` with `(float) 1.e7 /(float) 9.0`.

Some implementations suppress trailing zeros.

Here is the output for one implementation:

```
Integer division: 9/5 = 1
Floating-point division: 9.0/5.0 = 1.800000
Mixed division: 9.0/5 = 1.800000
double constants: 1e7/9.0 = 1111111.111111
float constants: 1e7f/9.0f = 1111111.125000
```

The first output line shows that dividing the integer 9 by the integer 5 yields the integer 1. The fractional part of 4 / 5 (or 0.8) is discarded. You'll see a practical use for this kind of division when you learn about the modulus operator. The next two lines show that when at least one of the operands is floating-point, you get a floating-point answer of 1.8. Actually, when you try to combine mixed types, C++ converts all the concerned types to the same type. You'll learn about these automatic conversions later in the chapter. The relative precisions of the last two lines show that the result is type **double** if both operands are **double** and that it is **float** if both operands are **float**. Remember, floating-point constants are type **double** by default.

A Glimpse of Operator Overloading

In Listing 3.10, the division operator represents three distinct operations: `int` division, `float` division, and `double` division. C++ uses the context, in this case the type of operands, to determine which operator is meant. The process of using the same symbol for more than one operation is called *operator overloading*. C++ has a few examples of overloading built in to the language. C++ also lets you extend operator overloading to user-defined classes, so what you see here is a precursor of an important OOP property. (See Figure 3.4.)

FIGURE 3.4
Different divisions.

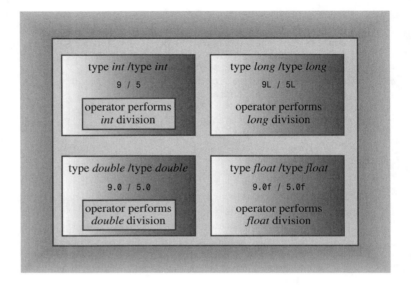

The Modulus Operator

Most people are more familiar with addition, subtraction, multiplication, and division than with the modulus operator, so take a moment to look at this operator in action. The modulus operator returns the remainder of an integer division. In combination with integer division, the modulus operator is particularly useful in problems that require dividing a quantity into different integral units, such as converting inches to feet and inches or converting dollars to quarters, dimes, nickels, and pennies. In Chapter 2, "Setting Out to C++," Listing 2.6 converted weight in British stone to pounds. Listing 3.11 reverses the process, converting weight in pounds to stone. A stone, you remember, is 14 pounds, and most British bathroom scales are calibrated in this unit. The program uses integer division to find the largest number of whole stone in the weight, and it uses the modulus operator to find the number of pounds left over.

LISTING 3.11   modulus.cpp

```
// modulus.cpp -- uses % operator to convert lbs to stone
#include <iostream>
using namespace std;
int main()
{
    const int Lbs_per_stn = 14;
    int lbs;
```

LISTING 3.11   Continued

```
        cout << "Enter your weight in pounds: ";
        cin >> lbs;
        int stone = lbs / Lbs_per_stn;      // whole stone
        int pounds = lbs % Lbs_per_stn;      // remainder in pounds
        cout << lbs << " pounds are " << stone;
        cout << " stone, " << pounds << " pound(s).\n";
        return 0;
    }
```

Here is a sample run:

```
Enter your weight in pounds: 184
184 pounds are 13 stone, 2 pound(s).
```

In the expression `lbs / Lbs_per_stn`, both operands are type `int`, so the computer performs integer division. With a `lbs` value of 184, the expression evaluates to 13. The product of 13 and 14 is 182, so the remainder of dividing 14 into 184 is 2, and that's the value of `lbs % Lbs_per_stn`. Now you are prepared technically, if not emotionally, to respond to questions about your weight when you travel in Great Britain.

Type Conversions

C++'s profusion of types lets you match the type to the need. It also complicates life for the computer. For example, adding two `short` values may involve different hardware instructions than adding two `long` values. With eleven integral types and three floating-point types, the computer can have a lot of different cases to handle, especially if you start mixing types. To help deal with this potential mishmash, C++ makes many type conversions automatically:

- C++ converts values when you assign a value of one arithmetic type to a variable of another arithmetic type.

- C++ converts values when you combine mixed types in expressions.

- C++ converts values when you pass arguments to functions.

If you don't understand what happens in these automatic conversions, you might find some program results baffling, so let's take a more detailed look at the rules.

Conversion on Assignment

C++ is fairly liberal in allowing you to assign a numeric value of one type to a variable of another type. Whenever you do so, the value is converted to the type of the receiving variable. For example, suppose `so_long` is type `long`, `thirty` is type `short`, and you have the following statement in a program:

```
so_long = thirty;               // assigning a short to a long
```

The program takes the value of `thirty` (typically a 16-bit value) and expands it to a `long` value (typically a 32-bit value) upon making this assignment. Note that the expansion creates a new value to place into `so_long`; the contents of `thirty` are unaltered.

Assigning a value to a type with a greater range usually poses no problem. For example, assigning a **short** value to a **long** variable doesn't change the value; it just gives the value a few more bytes in which to laze about. However, assigning a large **long** value like 2111222333 to a **float** variable results in the loss of some precision. Because **float** can have just six significant figures, the value can be rounded to 2.11122E9. Table 3.3 points out some possible conversion problems.

TABLE 3.3   Potential Conversion Problems

Conversion	Potential Problems
Bigger floating-point type to smaller floating-point type, such as **double** to **float**	Loss of precision (significant figures), value might be out of range for target type, in which case result is undefined
Floating-point type to integer type	Loss of fractional part, original value might be out of range for target type, in which case result is undefined
Bigger integer type to smaller integer type, such as **long** to **short**	Original value might be out of range for target type, typically just the low-order bytes are copied

A zero value assigned to a **bool** variable is converted to **false**, and a nonzero value is converted to **true**.

Assigning floating-point values to integer types poses a couple of problems. First, converting floating-point to integer results in truncating the number (discarding the fractional part). Second, a **float** value might be too big to fit in a cramped **int** variable. In that case, C++ doesn't define what the result should be; that means different implementations can respond differently. Listing 3.12 shows a few conversions by assignment.

LISTING 3.12   assign.cpp

```
// assign.cpp -- type changes on assignment
#include <iostream>
using namespace std;
int main()
{
    float tree = 3;     // int converted to float
    int guess = 3.9832; // float converted to int
    int debt = 3.0E12;  // result not defined in C++
    cout << "tree = " << tree << "\n";
    cout << "guess = " << guess << "\n";
```

LISTING 3.12   Continued

```
        cout << "debt = " << debt << "\n";
        return 0;
}
```

Here is the output for one system:

```
tree = 3
guess = 3
debt = 2112827392
```

Here **tree** is assigned the floating-point value 3.0. However, because **cout** drops trailing zeros on output, it displays 3.0 as 3. Assigning 3.9832 to the **int** variable **guess** causes the value to be truncated to 3; C++ uses truncation (discarding the fractional part) and not rounding (finding the closest integer value) when converting floating-point types to integer types. Finally, note that the **int** variable **debt** is unable to hold the value 3.0E12. This creates a situation in which C++ doesn't define the result. On this system, **debt** ends up with the value 2112827392, or about 2.1E09. Well, that's a novel way to reduce massive indebtedness!

Some compilers warn you of possible data loss for those statements that initialize integer variables to floating-point values. Also, the value displayed for **debt** varies from compiler to compiler. For example, running the same program on a second system produced a value of 0.

Conversions in Expressions

Next, consider what happens when you combine two different arithmetic types in one expression. C++ makes two kinds of automatic conversions in that case. First, some types automatically are converted whenever they occur. Second, some types are converted when they are combined with other types in an expression.

First, examine the automatic conversions. When it evaluates expressions, C++ converts **bool**, **char**, **unsigned char**, **signed char**, and **short** values to **int**. In particular, **true** is promoted to 1 and **false** to 0. These conversions are termed *integral promotions*. For example, consider the following fowl statements:

```
short chickens = 20;         // line 1
short ducks = 35;            // line 2
short fowl = chickens + ducks; // line 3
```

To execute the statement on line 3, a C++ program takes the values of **chickens** and **ducks** and converts both to **int**. Then, the program converts the result back to type **short**, because the answer is assigned to a type **short** variable. You might find this a bit roundabout, but it does make sense. The **int** type generally is chosen to be the computer's most natural type, which means the computer probably does calculations fastest for that type.

There's some more integral promotion: the **unsigned short** type is converted to **int** if **short** is smaller than **int**. If the two types are the same size, **unsigned short** is converted to **unsigned int**. This rule ensures that there's no data loss in promoting **unsigned short**.

Similarly, `wchar_t` is promoted to the first of the following types wide enough to accommodate its range: `int`, `unsigned int`, `long`, or `unsigned long`.

Then there are the conversions that take place when you arithmetically combine different types, such as adding an `int` to a `float`. When an operation involves two types, the smaller is converted to the larger. For example, the program in Listing 3.10 divides 9.0 by 5. Because 9.0 is type `double`, the program converts 5 to type `double` before it does the division. More generally, the compiler goes through a checklist to determine which conversions to make in an arithmetic expression. Here's the list—the compiler goes through it in order:

1. If either operand is type `long double`, the other operand is converted to `long double`.

2. Otherwise, if either operand is `double`, the other operand is converted to `double`.

3. Otherwise, if either operand is `float`, the other operand is converted to `float`.

4. Otherwise, the operands are integer types and the integral promotions are made.

5. In that case, if either operand is `unsigned long`, the other operand is converted to `unsigned long`.

6. Otherwise, if one operand is `long int` and the other is `unsigned int`, the conversion depends on the relative sizes of the two types. If `long` can represent possible `unsigned int` values, `unsigned int` is converted to `long`.

7. Otherwise, both operands are converted to `unsigned long`.

8. Otherwise, if either operand is `long`, the other is converted to `long`.

9. Otherwise, if either operand is `unsigned int`, the other is converted to `unsigned int`.

10. If the compiler reaches this point in the list, both operands should be `int`.

ANSI C follows the same rules as C++, but classic K&R C had slightly different rules. For example, classic C always promoted `float` to `double` even if both operands were `float`.

Conversions in Passing Arguments

Normally, C++ function prototyping controls type conversions for the passing of arguments, as you learn in Chapter 7, "Functions—C++'s Programming Modules." However, it is possible, although usually unwise, to waive prototype control for argument passing. In that case, C++ applies the integral promotions to the `char` and `short` types (`signed` and `unsigned`). Also, to preserve compatibility with huge amounts of code in classic C, C++ promotes `float` arguments to `double` when passing them to a function that waives prototyping.

Type Casts

C++ also empowers you to force type conversions explicitly via the type cast mechanism. (C++ recognizes the need for type rules, and it also recognizes the need to occasionally override those rules.) The type cast comes in two forms. For example, to convert an `int` value stored in a variable called `thorn` to type `long`, you can use either of the following expressions:

```
(long) thorn      // makes the value of thorn type long
long (thorn)      // makes the value of thorn type long
```

The type cast doesn't alter the thorn variable itself; instead, it creates a new value of the indicated type, which you then can use in an expression.

More generally, you can do the following:

```
(typeName) value    // converts value to typeName type
typeName (value)    // converts value to typeName type
```

The first form is straight C. The second form is pure C++. The idea behind the new form is to make a type cast look like a function call. This makes type casts for the built-in types look like the type conversions you can design for user-defined classes.

Listing 3.13 gives a short illustration of both forms. Imagine that the first section of this listing is part of a powerful ecological modeling program that does floating-point calculations that are converted to integral numbers of birds and animals. The results you get depend on when you convert. The calculation for auks first adds the floating-point values and then converts the sum to int upon assignment. But the calculations for bats and coots first use type casts to convert the floating-point values to int and then sum the values. The final part of the program shows how you can use a type cast to display the ASCII code for a type char value.

LISTING 3.13 typecast.cpp

```
// typecast.cpp -- forcing type changes
#include <iostream>
using namespace std;
int main()
{
    int auks, bats, coots;

    // the following statement adds the values as double,
    // then converts the result to int
    auks = 19.99 + 11.99;

    // these statements add values as int
    bats = (int) 19.99 + (int) 11.99;   // old C syntax
    coots = int (19.99) + int (11.99);  // new C++ syntax
    cout << "auks = " << auks << ", bats = " << bats;
    cout << ", coots = " << coots << '\n';

    char ch = 'Z';
    cout << "The code for " << ch << " is ";    // print as char
    cout << int(ch) << '\n';                     // print as int
    return 0;
}
```

Here is the result:

```
auks = 31, bats = 30, coots = 30
The code for Z is 90
```

First, adding 19.99 to 11.99 yields 31.98. When this value is assigned to the `int` variable `auks`, it's truncated to 31. But using type casts truncates the same two values to 19 and 11 before addition, making 30 the result for both the `bats` and `coots`. The final `cout` statement uses a type cast to convert a type `char` value to `int` before it displays the result. This causes `cout` to print the value as an integer rather than as a character.

The program illustrates two reasons to use type casting. First, you might have values that are stored as type `double` but are used to calculate a type `int` value. For example, you might be fitting a position to a grid or modeling integer values, such as populations, with floating-point numbers. You might want the calculations to treat the values as `int`. Type casting enables you to do so directly. Notice that you get a different result, at least for these values, when you convert to `int` and add than you do when you add first and then convert to `int`.

The second part of the program shows the most common reason to use a type cast—the capability to compel data in one form to meet a different expectation. In this listing, for example, the `char` variable `ch` holds the code for the letter Z. Using `cout` with `ch` displays the character Z, because `cout` zeros in on the fact that `ch` is type `char`. But by type casting `ch` to type `int`, you get `cout` to shift to `int` mode and print the ASCII code stored in `ch`.

Summary

C++'s basic types fall into two groups. One group consists of values that are stored as integers. The second group consists of values that are stored in a floating-point format. The integer types differ from each other in the amount of memory used to store values and in whether they are signed or unsigned. From smallest to largest, the integer types are `bool`, `char`, `signed char`, `unsigned char`, `short`, `unsigned short`, `int`, `unsigned int`, `long`, and `unsigned long`. There also is a `wchar_t` type whose placement in this sequence of size depends on the implementation. C++ guarantees that `char` is large enough to hold any member of the system's basic character set, `wchar_t` can hold any member of the system's extended character set, `short` is at least 16 bits, `int` is at least as big as `short`, and `long` is at least 32 bits and at least as large as `int`. The exact sizes depend on the implementation.

Characters are represented by their numeric codes. The I/O system determines whether a code is interpreted as a character or as a number.

The floating-point types can represent fractional values and values much larger than integers can represent. The three floating-point types are called `float`, `double`, and `long double`. C++ guarantees that `float` is no larger than `double`, and that `double` is no larger than `long double`. Typically, `float` uses 32 bits of memory, `double` uses 64 bits, and `long double` uses 80 to 128 bits.

By providing a variety of types in different sizes and in both signed and unsigned varieties, C++ lets you match the type to particular data requirements.

C++ uses operators to provide the usual arithmetical support for numeric types: addition, subtraction, multiplication, division, and taking the modulus. When two operators seek to operate on the same value, C++'s precedence and associativity rules determine which operation takes place first.

C++ converts values from one type to another when you assign values to a variable, mix types in arithmetic, and use type casts to force type conversions. Many type conversions are "safe," meaning you can make them with no loss or alteration of data. For example, you can convert an int value to a long value with no problems. Others, such as conversions of floating-point types to integer types, require more care.

At first, you might find the large number of basic C++ types a little excessive, particularly when you take the various conversion rules into account. But most likely you eventually will find occasions when one of the types is just what you need at the time, and you'll thank C++ for having it.

Review Questions

1. Why does C++ have more than one integer type?

2. Declare variables matching the following descriptions:

   a. A short integer with the value 80

   b. An unsigned int integer with the value 42110

   c. An integer with the value 3000000000

3. What safeguards does C++ provide to keep you from exceeding the limits of an integer type?

4. What is the distinction between 33L and 33?

5. Consider the two C++ statements that follow. Are they equivalent?
   ```
   char grade = 65;
   char grade = 'A';
   ```

6. How could you use C++ to find out which character the code 88 represents? Come up with at least two ways.

7. Assigning a long value to a float can result in a round-off error. What about assigning long to double?

8. Evaluate the following expressions as C++ would:

   a. 8 * 9 + 2

   b. 6 * 3 / 4

   c. 3 / 4 * 6

   d. 6.0 * 3 / 4

   e. 15 % 4

9. Suppose **x1** and **x2** are two type **double** variables that you want to add as integers and assign to an integer variable. Construct a C++ statement for doing so.

Programming Exercises

1. Write a short program that asks for your height in integer inches and then converts your height to feet and inches. Have the program use the underscore character to indicate where to type the response. Also, use a **const** symbolic constant to represent the conversion factor.

2. Write a short program that asks for your height in feet and inches and your weight in pounds. (Use three variables to store the information.) Have the program report your BMI (Body Mass Index). To calculate the BMI, first convert your height in feet and inches to your height in inches. Then, convert your height in inches to your height in meters by multiplying by 0.0254. Then, convert your weight in pounds into your mass in kilograms by dividing by 2.2. Finally, compute your BMI by dividing your mass in kilograms by the square of your height in meters. Use symbolic constants to represent the various conversion factors.

3. Write a program that asks how many miles you have driven and how many gallons of gasoline you used and then reports the miles per gallon your car got. Or, if you prefer, the program can request distance in kilometers and petrol in liters and then report the result European style, in liters per 100 kilometers. (Or, perhaps, you can use liters per 100 kilometers.)

4. Write a program that asks you to enter an automobile gasoline consumption figure in the European style (liters per 100 kilometers) and converts to the U.S. style of miles per gallon. Note that in addition to using different units of measurement, the U.S approach (distance / fuel) is the inverse of the European approach (fuel / distance). One hundred kilometers is 62.14 miles miles, and one gallon is 3.875 liters. Thus, 19 mpg is about 12.4 l/100-km, and 27 mpg is about 8.7 l/100-km.

CHAPTER 4

COMPOUND TYPES

In this chapter you learn

- How to create and use arrays

- How to create and use strings

- How to use the `getline()` and `get()` methods for reading strings

- How to mix string and numeric input

- How to create and use structures

- How to create and use unions

- How to create and use enumerations

- How to create and use pointers

- How to manage dynamic memory with `new` and `delete`

- How to create dynamic arrays

- How to create dynamic structures

- About automatic, static, and dynamic storage

Y ou've developed a computer game called User-Hostile in which players match wits with a cryptic and abusive computer interface. Now you must write a program that keeps track of your monthly game sales for a five-year period. Or you want to inventory your accumulation of hacker-hero trading cards. You soon conclude you need something more than C++'s simple basic types to meet these data requirements, and C++ offers something more—compound types. These are types built from the basic integer and floating-point types. The most far-reaching compound type is the class, that bastion of OOP toward which we are progressing. But C++ also supports several more modest compound types taken from C. The array, for example, can hold several values of the same type. A particular kind of array can hold a string, which is a series of characters. Structures can hold several values of differing types. Then there are pointers, which are variables that tell a computer where data is placed. You'll examine all these compound forms (except classes) in this chapter and also take a first look at `new` and `delete` and how you can use them to manage data.

Introducing Arrays

An *array* is a data form that can hold several values all of one type. For example, an array can hold 60 type `int` values that represent five years of game sales data, 12 `short` values that represent the number of days in each month, or 365 `float` values that indicate your food expenses for each day of the year. Each value is stored in a separate array element, and the computer stores all the elements of an array consecutively in memory.

To create an array, you use a declaration statement. An array declaration should indicate three things:

- The type of value to be stored in each element
- The name of the array
- The number of elements in the array

You accomplish this in C++ by modifying the declaration for a simple variable, adding brackets that contain the number of elements. For example, the declaration

```
short months[12];     // creates array of 12 short
```

creates an array named `months` that has 12 elements, each of which can hold a type `short` value. Each element, in essence, is a variable that you can treat as a simple variable.

The general form for declaring an array is this:

```
typeName arrayName[arraySize];
```

The expression *arraySize*, which is the number of elements, must be a constant, such as 10 or a `const` value, or a constant expression, such as `8 * sizeof (int)`, for which all values are known at the time compilation takes place. In particular, *arraySize* cannot be a variable whose value is set while the program is running. However, this chapter shows you later how to use the `new` operator to get around that restriction.

The Array As Compound Type

An array is called a compound type because it is built from some other type. (C uses the term "derived type," but, because C++ uses the term "derived" for class relationships, it had to come up with a new term—"compound type.") You can't simply declare that something is an array; it always has to be an array of some particular type. There is no generalized array type. Instead, there are many specific array types, such as array of *char* or array of `long`. For example, consider this declaration:

```
float loans[20];
```

The type for `loans` is not "array"; rather, it is "array of `float`." This emphasizes that the `loans` array is built from the `float` type.

Much of the usefulness of the array comes from the fact that you can access the array elements individually. The way to do this is to use a *subscript*, or *index*, to number the elements. C++

array numbering starts with 0. (This is nonnegotiable; you have to start at 0. Pascal and BASIC users will have to adjust.) C++ uses a bracket notation with the index to specify an array element. For example, `months[0]` is the first element of the `months` array, and `months[11]` is the last element. Note that the index of the last element is one less than the size of the array. (See Figure 4.1.) Thus, an array declaration enables you to create a lot of variables with a single declaration, and you then can use an index to identify and access individual elements.

Importance of Valid Subscript Values

The compiler does not check to see if you use a valid subscript. For instance, the compiler won't complain if you assign a value to the nonexistent element `months[101]`. But this assignment could cause problems once the program runs, possibly corrupting data or code, possibly causing the program to abort. So it is your responsibility to make sure that your program uses only valid subscript values.

FIGURE 4.1

Creating an array.

The yam analysis program in Listing 4.1 demonstrates a few properties of arrays, including declaring an array, assigning values to array elements, and initializing an array.

LISTING 4.1   `arrayone.cpp`

```
// arrayone.cpp _ small arrays of integers
#include <iostream>
using namespace std;
int main()
{
    int yams[3];      // creates array with three elements
    yams[0] = 7;      // assign value to first element
```

LISTING 4.1   Continued

```
        yams[1] = 8;
        yams[2] = 6;

        int yamcosts[3] = {20, 30, 5}; // create, initialize array
        // NOTE: If your C++ compiler or translator can't initialize
        // this array, use static int yamcosts[3] instead of
        // int yamcosts[3]

        cout << "Total yams = ";
        cout << yams[0] + yams[1] + yams[2] << "\n";
        cout << "The package with " << yams[1] << " yams costs ";
        cout << yamcosts[1] << " cents per yam.\n";
        int total = yams[0] * yamcosts[0] + yams[1] * yamcosts[1];
        total = total + yams[2] * yamcosts[2];
        cout << "The total yam expense is " << total << " cents.\n";

        cout << "\nSize of yams array = " << sizeof yams;
        cout << " bytes.\n";
        cout << "Size of one element = " << sizeof yams[0];
        cout << " bytes.\n";
        return 0;
}
```

Compatibility Note

Current versions of C++, as well as ANSI C, allow you to initialize ordinary arrays defined in a function. However, in some older implementations that use a C++ translator instead of a true compiler, the C++ translator creates C code for a C compiler that is not fully ANSI C-compliant. In that case, you can get an error message like the following example from a Sun C++ 2.0 system:

```
"arrayone.cc", line 10: sorry, not implemented: initialization of
yamcosts (automatic aggregate) Compilation failed
```

The fix is to use the keyword static in the array declaration:

```
// pre-ANSI initialization
static int yamcosts[3] = {20, 30, 5};
```

The keyword static causes the compiler to use a different memory scheme for storing the array, one that allows initialization even under pre-ANSI C. Chapter 9, "Memory Models and Namespaces," discusses this use of static.

Here is the output:

```
Total yams = 21
The package with 8 yams costs 30 cents per yam.
The total yam expense is 410 cents.
Size of yams array = 12 bytes.
Size of one element = 4 bytes.
```

Program Notes

First, the program creates a three-element array called yams. Because yams has three elements, the elements are numbered from 0 through 2, and arrayone.cpp uses index values of 0 through 2 to assign values to the three individual elements. Each individual yam element is an int with all the rights and privileges of an int type, so arrayone.cpp can, and does, assign values to elements, add elements, multiply elements, and display elements.

The program uses the long way to assign values to the yam elements. C++ also lets you initialize array elements within the declaration statement. Listing 4.1 uses this shortcut to assign values to the yamcosts array:

```
int yamcosts[3] = {20, 30, 5};
```

Simply provide a comma-separated list of values (the *initialization list*) enclosed in braces. The spaces in the list are optional. If you don't initialize an array that's defined inside a function, the element values remain undefined. That means the element takes on whatever value previously resided at that location in memory.

Next, the program uses the array values in a few calculations. This part of the program looks cluttered with all the subscripts and brackets. The for loop, coming up in Chapter 5, "Loops and Relational Expressions," provides a powerful way to deal with arrays and eliminates the need to write each index explicitly. Meanwhile, we'll stick to small arrays.

The sizeof operator, you recall, returns the size, in bytes, of a type or data object. Note that if you use the sizeof operator with an array name, you get the number of bytes in the whole array. But if you use sizeof with an array element, you get the size, in bytes, of the element. This illustrates that yams is an array, but yams[1] is just an int.

Initialization Rules for Arrays

C++ has several rules about initializing an array. They restrict when you can do it, and they determine what happens if the number of array elements doesn't match the number of values in the initializer. Let's examine these rules.

You can use the initialization form *only* when defining the array. You cannot use it later, and you cannot assign one array wholesale to another:

```
int cards[4] = {3, 6, 8, 10};     // okay
int hand[4];                      // okay
hand[4] = {5, 6, 7, 9};           // not allowed
hand = cards;                     // not allowed
```

However, you can use subscripts and assign values to the elements of an array individually.

When initializing an array, you can provide fewer values than array elements. For example, the following statement initializes only the first two elements of hotelTips:

```
float hotelTips[5] = {5.0, 2.5};
```

If you partially initialize an array, the compiler sets the remaining elements to zero. Thus, it's easy to initialize all the elements of an array to zero—just initialize the first element explicitly to zero and then let the compiler initialize the remaining elements to zero:

```
long totals[500] = {0};
```

If you leave the square brackets empty when you initialize an array, the C++ compiler counts the elements for you. Suppose, for example, you make this declaration:

```
short things[] = {1, 5, 3, 8};
```

The compiler makes `things` an array of four elements.

Letting the Compiler Do It

Normally, letting the compiler count the number of elements is poor practice, for its count can be different from what you think it is. However, this approach can be safer for initializing a character array to a string, as you'll soon see. And if your main concern is that the program, not you, knows how large an array is, you can do something like this:

```
short things[] = {1, 5, 3, 8};
int num_elements = sizeof things / sizeof (short);
```

Whether this is useful or lazy depends on the circumstances.

Strings

A *string* is a series of characters stored in consecutive bytes of memory. C++ has two ways of dealing with strings. The first, taken from C and often called a *C-style string*, is the method you'll learn here. Chapter 16, "The String Class and the Standard Template Library," takes up an alternative method based on a `string` class library. Meanwhile, the idea of a series of characters stored in consecutive bytes implies that you can store a string in an array of `char`, with each character kept in its own array element. Strings provide a convenient way to store text information, such as messages to the user ("*Please tell me your secret Swiss bank account number:* ") or responses from the user ("*You must be joking*"). C-style strings have a special feature: The last character of every string is the **null character**. This character, written \0, is the character with ASCII code 0, and it serves to mark the string's end. For example, consider the following two declarations:

```
char dog [5] = { 'b', 'e', 'a', 'u', 'x'};     // not a string!
char cat[5] = {'f', 'a', 't', 's', '\0'};      // a string!
```

Both arrays are arrays of `char`, but only the second is a string. The null character plays a fundamental role in C-style strings. For example, C++ has many functions that handle strings, including those used by `cout`. They all work by processing a string character-by-character until they reach the null character. If you ask `cout` to display a nice string like `cat` above, it displays the first four characters, detects the null character, and stops. But if you are ungracious enough to tell `cout` to display the **dog** array above, which is not a string, `cout` prints the five letters in the array and then keeps marching through memory byte-by-byte, interpreting each byte as a character to print, until it reached a null character. Because null characters, which really are bytes set to zero, tend to be common in memory, the damage usually is contained quickly; nonetheless, you should not treat nonstring character arrays as strings.

The `cat` array example makes initializing an array to a string look tedious—all those single quotes and then having to remember the null character. Don't worry. There is a better way to initialize a character array to a string. Just use a quoted string, called a *string constant* or *string literal*, as in the following:

```
char bird[10] = "Mr. Cheeps";    // the \0 is understood
char fish[] = "Bubbles";          // let the compiler count
```

Quoted strings always include the terminating null character implicitly, so you don't have to spell it out. (See Figure 4.2.) Also, the various C++ input facilities for reading a string from keyboard input into a `char` array automatically add the terminating null character for you. (If, when you run the program in Listing 4.1, you discover you have to use the keyword `static` to initialize an array, you have to use it with these `char` arrays, too.)

FIGURE 4.2

Initializing an array to a string.

Of course, you should make sure the array is large enough to hold all the characters of the string, including the null character. Initializing a character array with a string constant is one case where it may be safer to let the compiler count the number of elements for you. There is no harm, other than wasted space, in making an array larger than the string. That's because functions that work with strings are guided by the location of the null character, not by the size of the array. C++ imposes no limits on the length of a string.

Remember

When determining the minimum array size necessary to hold a string, remember to include the terminating null character in your count.

Note that a string constant (double quotes) is not interchangeable with a character constant (single quotes). A character constant, such as `'S'`, is a shorthand notation for the code for a character. On an ASCII system, `'S'` is just another way of writing 83. Thus, the statement

```
char shirt_size = 'S';        // this is fine
```

assigns the value 83 to `shirt_size`. But `"S"` represents the string consisting of two characters, the S and the \0 characters. Even worse, `"S"` actually represents the memory address at which the string is stored. So a statement like

```
char shirt_size = "S";        // illegal type mismatch
```

attempts to assign a memory address to `shirt_size`! Because an address is a separate type in C++, a C++ compiler won't allow this sort of nonsense. (We'll return to this point later, after we've discussed pointers.)

String Concatenation

Sometimes a string may be too long to conveniently fit on one line of code. C++ enables you to concatenate string constants, that is, to combine two quoted strings into one. Indeed, any two string constants separated only by white space (spaces, tabs, and newlines) automatically are joined into one. Thus, all the following output statements are equivalent to each other:

```
cout << "I'd give my right arm to be" " a great violinist.\n";
cout << "I'd give my right arm to be a great violinist.\n";
cout << "I'd give my right ar"
"m to be a great violinist.\n";
```

Note that the join doesn't add any spaces to the joined strings. The first character of the second string immediately follows the last character, not counting \0, of the first string. The \0 character from the first string is replaced by the first character of the second string.

Using Strings in an Array

The two most common ways of getting a string into an array are to initialize an array to a string constant and to read keyboard or file input into an array. Listing 4.2 demonstrates these approaches by initializing one array to a quoted string and using `cin` to place an input string in a second array. The program also uses the standard library function `strlen()` to get the length of a string. The standard `cstring` header file (or `string.h` for older implementations) provides declarations for this and many other string-related functions.

LISTING 4.2   strings.cpp

```
// strings.cpp _ storing strings in an array
#include <iostream>
#include <cstring>  // for the strlen() function
using namespace std;
int main()
{
    const int Size = 15;
```

LISTING 4.2 *Continued*

```
      char name1[Size];                 // empty array
      char name2[Size] = "C++owboy";    // initialized array
      // NOTE: some implementations may require the static keyword
      // to initialize the array name2

      cout << "Howdy! I'm " << name2;
      cout << "! What's your name?\n";
      cin >> name1;
      cout << "Well, " << name1 << ", your name has ";
      cout << strlen(name1) << " letters and is stored\n";
      cout << "in an array of " << sizeof name1 << " bytes.\n";
      cout << "Your initial is " << name1[0] << ".\n";
      name2[3] = '\0';                  // null character
      cout << "Here are the first 3 characters of my name: ";
      cout << name2 << "\n";
      return 0;
}
```

| Compatibility Note |

If your system doesn't provide the `cstring` header file, try the older `string.h` version.

Here is a sample run:

```
Howdy! I'm C++owboy! What's your name?
Basicman
Well, Basicman, your name has 8 letters and is stored
in an array of 15 bytes.
Your initial is B.
Here are the first 3 characters of my name: C++
```

Program Notes

What can you learn from this example? First, note that the `sizeof` operator gives the size of the entire array, 15 bytes, but the `strlen()` function returns the size of the string stored in the array and not the size of the array itself. Also, `strlen()` counts just the visible characters and not the null character. Thus, it returns a value of 8, not 9, for the length of `Basicman`. If `cosmic` is a string, the minimum array size for holding that string is `strlen(cosmic) + 1`.

Because `name1` and `name2` are arrays, you can use an index to access individual characters in the array. For example, the program uses `name1[0]` to find the first character in that array. Also, the program sets `name2[3]` to the null character. That makes the string end after three characters even though more characters remain in the array. (See Figure 4.3.)

Note that the program uses a symbolic constant for the array size. Often, the size of an array appears in several statements in a program. Using a symbolic constant to represent the size of an array simplifies revising the program to use a different array size; you just have to change the value once, where the symbolic constant is defined.

FIGURE 4.3
Shortening a string
with \0.

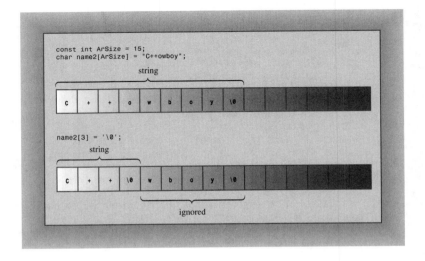

Adventures in String Input

The `strings.cpp` program has a blemish that was concealed through the often useful technique of carefully selected sample input. Listing 4.3 removes the veils and shows that string input can be tricky.

LISTING 4.3 instr1.cpp

```cpp
// instr1.cpp--reading more than one string
#include <iostream>
using namespace std;
int main()
{
    const int ArSize = 20;
    char name[ArSize];
    char dessert[ArSize];

    cout << "Enter your name:\n";
    cin >> name;
    cout << "Enter your favorite dessert:\n";
    cin >> dessert;
    cout << "I have some delicious " << dessert;
    cout << " for you, " << name << ".\n";
    return 0;
}
```

The intent is simple: Read a user's name and favorite dessert from the keyboard and then display the information. Here is a sample run:

```
Enter your name:
Alistair Dreeb
Enter your favorite dessert:
I have some delicious Dreeb for you, Alistair.
```

We didn't even get a chance to respond to the dessert prompt! The program showed it and then immediately moved on to display the final line.

The problem lies with how `cin` determines when you've finished entering a string. You can't enter the null character from the keyboard, so `cin` needs some other means for locating the end of a string. The `cin` technique is to use white space—spaces, tabs, and newlines—to delineate a string. This means `cin` reads just one word when it gets input for a character array. After it reads this word, `cin` automatically adds the terminating null character when it places the string into the array.

The practical result in this example is that `cin` reads `Alistair` as the entire first string and puts it into the name array. This leaves poor `Dreeb` still sitting in the input queue. When `cin` searches the input queue for the response to the favorite dessert question, it finds `Dreeb` still there. Then `cin` gobbles up `Dreeb` and puts it into the dessert array. (See Figure 4.4.)

FIGURE 4.4

The `cin` view of string input.

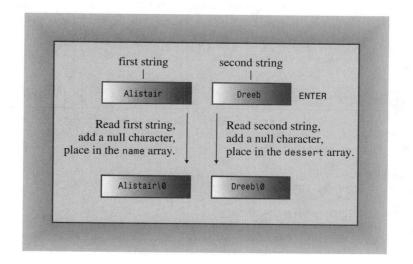

Another problem, which didn't surface in the sample run, is that the input string might turn out to be longer than the destination array. Using `cin` as this example did offers no protection against placing a 30-character string in a 20-character array.

Many programs depend on string input, so it's worthwhile to explore this topic further. We'll have to draw upon some of the more advanced features of `cin`, which are described in Chapter 17, "Input, Output, and Files."

Line-Oriented Input: `getline()` and `get()`

To be able to enter whole phrases instead of single words as a string, you need a different approach to string input. Specifically, you need a line-oriented method instead of a word-oriented method. You are in luck, for the `istream` class, of which `cin` is an example, has some line-oriented class member functions. The `getline()` function, for example, reads a whole line, using the newline character transmitted by the <ENTER> key to mark the end of input. You invoke this method by using `cin.getline()` as a function call. The function takes two arguments. The first argument is the name of the array destined to hold the line of input, and the second argument is a limit on the number of characters to be read. If this limit is, say, 20, the function reads no more than 19 characters, leaving room to automatically add the null character at the end. The `getline()` member function stops reading input when it reaches this numeric limit or when it reads a newline, whichever comes first.

For example, suppose you want to use `getline()` to read a name into the 20-element name array. You would use this call:

```
cin.getline(name,20);
```

This reads the entire line into the **name** array, provided that the line consists of 19 or fewer characters. (The `getline()` member function also has an optional third argument, which Chapter 17 discusses.)

Listing 4.4 modifies Listing 4.3 to use `cin.getline()` instead of a simple `cin`. Otherwise, the program is unchanged.

LISTING 4.4 `instr2.cpp`

```cpp
// instr2.cpp _ reading more than one word with getline
#include <iostream>
using namespace std;
int main()
{
    const int ArSize = 20;
    char name[ArSize];
    char dessert[ArSize];

    cout << "Enter your name:\n";
    cin.getline(name, ArSize);  // reads through newline
    cout << "Enter your favorite dessert:\n";
    cin.getline(dessert, ArSize);
    cout << "I have some delicious " << dessert;
    cout << " for you, " << name << ".\n";
    return 0;
}
```

Compatibility Note

Some early C++ versions don't fully implement all facets of the current C++ I/O package. In particular, the `getline()` member function isn't always available. If this affects you, just read about this example and go on to the next one, which uses a member function that predates `getline()`. Early releases of Turbo C++ implement `getline()` slightly differently so that it does store the newline character in the string. Microsoft Visual C++ 5.0 and 6.0 have a bug in `getline()` as implemented in the `iostream` header file but not in the `ostream.h` version; Service Pack 5 for MSVC++ 6.0, available at the `msdn.microsoft.com/vstdio` Web site, fixes that bug.

Here is some sample output:

```
Enter your name:
Dirk Hammernose
Enter your favorite dessert:
Radish Torte
I have some delicious Radish Torte for you, Dirk Hammernose.
```

The program now reads complete names and delivers the user her just desserts! The `get-line()` function conveniently gets a line at a time. It reads input through the newline character marking the end of the line, but it doesn't save the newline character. Instead, it replaces it with a null character when storing the string. (See Figure 4.5.)

FIGURE 4.5

`getline()` reads and replaces the newline.

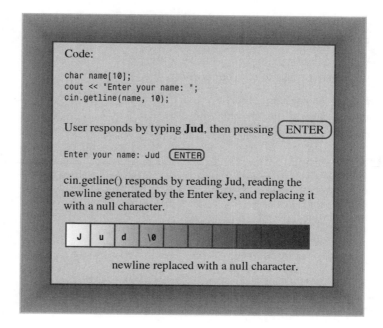

Let's try another approach. The `istream` class has another member function, called `get()`, which comes in several variations. One variant works much like `getline()`. It takes the same arguments, interprets them the same way, and reads to the end of a line. But rather than read and discard the newline character, `get()` leaves that character in the input queue. Suppose we use two calls to `get()` in a row:

```
cin.get(name, ArSize);
cin.get(dessert, Arsize);    // a problem
```

Because the first call leaves the newline in the input queue, that newline is the first character the second call sees. Thus, `get()` concludes that it's reached the end of line without having found anything to read. Without help, `get()` just can't get past that newline.

Fortunately, there is help in the form of a variation of `get()`. The call `cin.get()` (no arguments) reads the single next character, even if it is a newline, so you can use it to dispose of the newline and prepare for the next line of input. That is, this sequence works:

```
cin.get(name, ArSize);     // read first line
cin.get();                 // read newline
cin.get(dessert, Arsize);  // read second line
```

Another way to use `get()` is to *concatenate*, or join, the two class member functions as follows:

```
cin.get(name, ArSize).get(); // concatenate member functions
```

What makes this possible is that `cin.get(name, ArSize)` returns the `cin` object, which then is used as the object that invokes the `get()` function. Similarly, the statement

```
cin.getline(name1, ArSize).getline(name2, ArSize);
```

reads two consecutive input lines into the arrays `name1` and `name2`; it's equivalent to making two separate calls to `cin.getline()`.

Listing 4.5 uses concatenation. In Chapter 11, "Working with Classes," you'll learn how to incorporate this feature into your class definitions.

LISTING 4.5   instr3.cpp

```cpp
// instr3.cpp _ reading more than one word with get() & get()
#include <iostream>
using namespace std;
int main()
{
    const int ArSize = 20;
    char name[ArSize];
    char dessert[ArSize];

    cout << "Enter your name:\n";
    cin.get(name, ArSize).get();    // read string, newline
    cout << "Enter your favorite dessert:\n";
    cin.get(dessert, ArSize).get();
    cout << "I have some delicious " << dessert;
    cout << " for you, " << name << ".\n";
    return 0;
}
```

Compatibility Note

Some older C++ versions don't implement the `get()` variant having no arguments. They do, however, implement yet another `get()` variant, one that takes a single `char` argument. To use it instead of the argument-free `get()`, you need to declare a `char` variable first:

```
char ch;
cin.get(name, ArSize).get(ch);
```

You can use this code instead of what is found in Listing 4.5. Chapters 5, 6, "Branching Statements and Logical Operators," and 17 further discuss the `get()` variants.

Here is a sample run:

```
Enter your name:
Mai Parfait
Enter your favorite dessert:
Chocolate Mousse
I have some delicious Chocolate Mousse for you, Mai Parfait.
```

One thing to note is how C++ allows multiple versions of functions provided that they have different argument lists. If you use, say, `cin.get(name, ArSize)`, the compiler notices you're using the form that puts a string into an array and sets up the appropriate member function. If, instead, you use `cin.get()`, the compiler realizes you want the form that reads one character. Chapter 8, "Adventures in Functions," will explore this feature, called function overloading.

Why use `get()` instead of `getline()` at all? First, older implementations may not have `getline()`. Second, `get()` lets you be a bit more careful. Suppose, for example, you used `get()` to read a line into an array. How can you tell if it read the whole line rather than stopped because the array was filled? Look at the next input character. If it is a newline, then the whole line was read. If it is not a newline, then there is still more input on that line. Chapter 17 investigates this technique. In short, `getline()` is a little simpler to use, but `get()` makes error-checking simpler. You can use either one to read a line of input; just keep the slightly different behaviors in mind.

Empty Lines and Other Problems

What happens after `getline()` or `get()` reads an empty line? The original practice was that the next input statement picked up where the last `getline()` or `get()` left off. However, the current practice is that after `get()` (but not `getline()`) reads an empty line, it sets something called the *failbit*. The implications of this act are that further input is blocked but you can restore input with the following command:

```
cin.clear();
```

Another potential problem is that the input string could be longer than the allocated space. If the input line is longer than the number of characters specified, both `getline()` and `get()` leave the remaining characters in the input queue. However, `getline()` additionally sets the failbit and turns off further input.

Chapters 5, 6, and 17 investigate these properties and how to program around them.

Mixing String and Numeric Input

Mixing numeric input with line-oriented string input can cause problems. Consider the simple program in Listing 4.6.

LISTING 4.6   numstr.cpp

```cpp
// numstr.cpp--following number input with line input
#include <iostream>
using namespace std;
int main()
{
    cout << "What year was your house built?\n";
    int year;
    cin >> year;
    cout << "What is its street address?\n";
    char address[80];
    cin.getline(address, 80);
    cout << "Year built: " << year << "\n";
    cout << "Address: " << address << "\n";
    cout << "Done!\n";
    return 0;
}
```

Running this program would look something like this:

```
What year was your house built?
1966
What is its street address?
Year built: 1966
Address
Done!
```

You never get the opportunity to enter the address. The problem is that when cin reads the year, it leaves the newline generated by the <Enter> key in the input queue. Then, cin.get-line() reads the newline as an empty line and assigns a null string to the address array. The fix is to read and discard the newline before reading the address. This can be done several ways, including using get() with no argument or with a char argument, as described in the preceding example. You can make this call separately:

```
cin >> year;
cin.get();   // or cin.get(ch);
```

Or, you can concatenate the call, making use of the fact that the expression cin >> year returns the cin object:

```
(cin >> year).get();   // or (cin >> year).get(ch);
```

If you make one of these changes to Listing 4.6, it works properly:

```
What year was your house built?
1966
What is its street address?
43821 Unsigned Short Street
Year built: 1966
Address: 43821 Unsigned Short Street
Done!
```

C++ programs frequently use pointers instead of arrays to handle strings. We'll take up that aspect of strings after learning a bit about pointers. Meanwhile, let's take a look at another compound type, the structure.

Introducing Structures

Suppose you want to store information about a basketball player. You might want to store his or her name, salary, height, weight, scoring average, free-throw percentage, assists, and so on. You'd like some sort of data form that could hold all this information in one unit. An array won't do. Although an array can hold several items, each item has to be the same type. That is, one array can hold twenty `int`s and another can hold ten `float`s, but a single array can't store `int`s in some elements and `float`s in other elements.

The answer to your desire (the one about storing information about a basketball player) is the C++ *structure*. The structure is a more versatile data form than an array, for a single structure can hold items of more than one data type. This enables you to unify your data representation by storing all the related basketball information in a single structure variable. If you want to keep track of a whole team, you can use an array of structures. The structure type also is a stepping-stone to that bulwark of C++ OOP, the class. Learning a little about structures now takes us that much closer to the OOP heart of C++.

A structure is a user-definable type, with a structure declaration serving to define the type's data properties. After you define the type, you can create variables of that type. Thus, creating a structure is a two-part process. First, you define a structure description. It describes and labels the different types of data that can be stored in a structure. Then, you can create structure variables, or, more generally, structure data objects, that follow the description's plan.

For example, suppose that Bloataire, Inc., wants to create a type to describe members of its product line of designer inflatables. In particular, the type should hold the name of the item, its volume in cubic feet, and its selling price. Here is a structure description meeting those needs:

```
struct inflatable       // structure description
{
    char name[20];      // an array member
    float volume;       // a float member
    double price;       // a double member
};
```

The keyword `struct` indicates that the code defines the layout for a structure. The identifier `inflatable` is the name, or *tag*, for this form; this makes `inflatable` the name for the new type. Thus, you now can create variables of type `inflatable` just as you create variables of type `char` or `int`. Next, between braces, comes the list of data types to be held in the structure. Each list item is a declaration statement. You can use any of the C++ types here, including arrays and other structures. This example uses an array of `char`, suitable for storing a string, and a `float` and a `double`. Each individual item in the list is called a structure *member*, so the inflatable structure has three members. (See Figure 4.6.)

FIGURE 4.6

Parts of a structure description.

After you have the template, you can create variables of that type:

```
inflatable hat;              // hat is a structure variable of type inflatable
inflatable woopie_cushion;   // type inflatable variable
inflatable mainframe;        // type inflatable variable
```

If you're familiar with C structures, you'll notice (probably with pleasure) that C++ allows you to drop the keyword **struct** when you declare structure variables:

```
struct inflatable goose;   // keyword struct required in C
inflatable vincent;        // keyword struct not required in C++
```

In C++, the structure tag is used just like a fundamental type name. This change emphasizes that a structure declaration defines a new type. It also removes omitting **struct** from the list of curse-inducing errors.

Given that **hat** is type **inflatable**, you use the membership operator (.) to access individual members. For example, **hat.volume** refers to the **volume** member of the structure, and **hat.price** refers to the **price** member. Similarly, **vincent.price** is the **price** member of a **vincent** variable. In short, the member names enable you to access members of a structure much as indices enable you to access elements of an array. Because the **price** member is declared as type **double**, **hat.price** and **vincent.price** both are equivalent to type **double** variables and can be used in any manner an ordinary type **double** variable can. In short, **hat** is a structure, but **hat.price** is a **double**. By the way, the method used to access class member functions like **cin.getline()** has its origins in the method used to access structure member variables like **vincent.price**.

Listing 4.7 illustrates these points about a structure. Also, it shows how to initialize one.

LISTING 4.7   `structur.cpp`

```cpp
// structur.cpp--a simple structure
#include <iostream>
using namespace std;
struct inflatable    // structure template
{
    char name[20];
    float volume;
    double price;
};

int main()
{
    inflatable guest =
    {
        "Glorious Gloria",  // name value
        1.88,               // volume value
        29.99               // price value
    };  // guest is a structure variable of type inflatable
        // It's initialized to the indicated values
    inflatable pal =
    {
        "Audacious Arthur",
        3.12,
        32.99
    };  // pal is a second variable of type inflatable
// NOTE: some implementations require using
// static inflatable guest =

    cout << "Expand your guest list with " << guest.name;
    cout << " and " << pal.name << "!\n";
    // pal.name is the name member of the pal variable
    cout << "You can have both for $";
    cout << guest.price + pal.price << "!\n";
    return 0;
}
```

Compatibility Note

Just as some older versions of C++ do not yet implement the capability to initialize an ordinary array defined in a function, they also do not implement the capability to initialize an ordinary structure defined in a function. Again, the solution is to use the keyword `static` in the declaration.

Here is the output:

```
Expand your guest list with Glorious Gloria and Audacious Arthur!
You can have both for $62.98!
```

Program Notes

One important matter is where to place the structure declaration. There are two choices for `structur.cpp`. You could place the declaration inside the `main()` function, just after the opening brace. The second choice, and the one made here, is to place it outside of and preceding `main()`. When a declaration occurs outside of any function, it's called an *external declaration*. For this program, there is no practical difference between the two choices. But for programs consisting of two or more functions, the difference can be crucial. The external declaration can be used by all the functions following it, whereas the internal declaration can be used only by the function in which the declaration is found. Most often, you want an external structure declaration so that all the functions can use structures of that type. (See Figure 4.7.)

FIGURE 4.7
Local and external structure declarations.

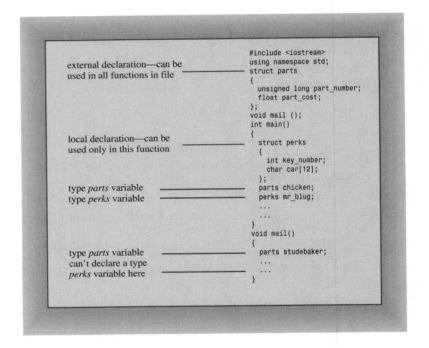

Variables, too, can be defined internally or externally, with external variables shared among functions. (Chapter 9 looks further into that topic.) C++ practices discourage the use of external variables but encourage the use of external structure declarations. Also, it often makes sense to declare symbolic constants externally.

Next, notice the initialization procedure:

```
inflatable guest =
{
"Glorious Gloria",  // name value
     1.88,          // volume value
     29.99          // price value
};
```

As with arrays, you use a comma-separated list of values enclosed within a pair of braces. The program places one value per line, but you can place them all on the same line. Just remember to separate items with a comma:

```
inflatable duck = {"Daphne", 0.12, 9.98};
```

You can initialize each member of the structure to the appropriate kind of datum. For example, the `name` member is a character array, so you can initialize it to a string.

Each structure member is treated as a variable of that type. Thus, `pal.price` is a `double` variable and `pal.name` is an array of `char`. And when the program uses `cout` to display `pal.name`, it displays the member as a string. By the way, because `pal.name` is a character array, we can use subscripts to access individual characters in the array. For example, `pal.name[0]` is the character A. But `pal[0]` is meaningless, because `pal` is a structure, not an array.

Other Structure Properties

C++ makes user-defined types as similar as possible to built-in types. For example, you can pass structures as arguments to a function, and you can have a function use a structure as a return value. Also, you can use the assignment operator (=) to assign one structure to another of the same type. Doing so causes each member of one structure to be set to the value of the corresponding member in the other structure, even if the member is an array. This kind of assignment is called *memberwise assignment*. We'll defer passing and returning structures until we discuss functions in Chapter 7, "Functions—C++'s Programming Modules," but we can take a quick look at structure assignment now. Listing 4.8 provides an example.

LISTING 4.8   `assgn_st.cpp`

```cpp
// assgn_st.cpp--assigning structures
#include <iostream>
using namespace std;
struct inflatable
{
    char name[20];
    float volume;
    double price;
};
int main()
{
    inflatable bouquet =
    {
        "sunflowers",
        0.20,
        12.49
    };
    inflatable choice;
    cout << "bouquet: " << bouquet.name << " for $";
    cout << bouquet.price << "\n";
```

LISTING 4.8   *Continued*

```
       choice = bouquet;   // assign one structure to another
       cout << "choice: " << choice.name << " for $";
       cout << choice.price << "\n";
       return 0;
}
```

Here's the output:

```
bouquet: sunflowers for $12.49
choice: sunflowers for $12.49
```

As you can see, memberwise assignment is at work, for the members of the **choice** structure are assigned the same values stored in the **bouquet** structure.

You can combine the definition of a structure form with the creation of structure variables. To do so, follow the closing brace with the variable name or names:

```
struct perks
{
       int key_number;
       char car[12];
} mr_smith, ms_jones;    // two perks variables
```

You even can initialize a variable you create in this fashion:

```
struct perks
{
       int key_number;
       char car[12];
} mr_glitz =
{
       7,               // value for mr_glitz.key_number member
       "Packard"        // value for mr_glitz.car member
};
```

However, keeping the structure definition separate from the variable declarations usually makes a program easier to read and follow.

Another thing you can do with structures is create a structure with no type name. You do this by omitting a tag name while simultaneously defining a structure form and a variable:

```
struct     // no tag
{
       int x;  // 2 members
       int y;
} position;  // a structure variable
```

This creates one structure variable called **position**. You can access its members with the membership operator, as in **position.x**, but there is no general name for the type. You subsequently can't create other variables of the same type. This book won't be using this limited form of structure.

Aside from the fact a C++ program can use the structure tag as a type name, C structures have all the features we've discussed so far for C++ structures. But C++ structures go further. Unlike

C structures, for example, C++ structures can have member functions in addition to member variables. But these more advanced features most typically are used with classes rather than structures, so we'll discuss them when we cover classes.

Arrays of Structures

The `inflatable` structure contains an array (the `name` array). It's also possible to create arrays whose elements are structures. The technique is exactly the same as for creating arrays of the fundamental types. For example, to create an array of 100 `inflatable` structures, do the following:

```
inflatable gifts[100];  // array of 100 inflatable structures
```

This makes `gifts` an array of `inflatable`s. Hence each element of the array, such as `gifts[0]` or `gifts[99]`, is an `inflatable` object and can be used with the membership operator:

```
cin >> gifts[0].volume;        // use volume member of first struct
cout << gifts[99].price << endl; // display price member of last struct
```

Keep in mind that `gifts` itself is an array, not a structure, so constructions such as `gifts.price` are not valid.

To initialize an array of structures, combine the rule for initializing arrays (a brace-enclosed, comma-separated list of values for each element) with the rule for structures (a brace-enclosed, comma-separated list of values for each member). Because each element of the array is a structure, its value is represented by a structure initialization. Thus, you wind up with a brace-enclosed, comma-separated list of values, each of which itself is a brace-enclosed, comma-separated list of values:

```
inflatable guests[2] =            // initializing an array of structs
    {
        {"Bambi", 0.5, 21.99},      // first structure in array
        {"Godzilla", 2000, 565.99}  // next structure in array
    };
```

As usual, you can format this the way you like. Both initializations can be on the same line, or each separate structure member initialization can get a line of its own, for example.

Bit Fields

C++, like C, enables you to specify structure members that occupy a particular number of bits. This can be handy for creating a data structure that corresponds, say, to a register on some hardware device. The field type should be an integral or enumeration type (enumerations are discussed later in this chapter), and a colon followed by a number indicates the actual number of bits to be used. You can use unnamed fields to provide spacing. Each member is termed a *bit field*. Here's an example:

```
struct torgle_register
{
    int SN : 4;        // 4 bits for SN value
    int : 4;           // 4 bits unused
```

```
    bool goodIn : 1;        // valid input (1 bit)
    bool goodTorgle : 1;   // successful torgling
};
```

You use standard structure notation to access bit fields:

```
torgle_register tr;
...
if (tr.goodIn)
...
```

Bit fields typically are used in low-level programming. Often, using an integral type and the bitwise operators of Appendix E, "Other Operators," provides an alternative approach.

Unions

A *union* is a data format that can hold different data types but only one type at a time. That is, whereas a structure can hold, say, an int *and* a long *and* a double, a union can hold an int *or* a long *or* a double. The syntax is like that for a structure, but the meaning is different. For example, consider the following declaration:

```
union one4all
{
    int int_val;
    long long_val;
    double double_val;
};
```

You can use a one4all variable to hold an int, a long, or a double, just as long as you do so at different times:

```
one4all pail;
pail.int_val = 15;         // store an int
cout << pail.int_val;
pail.double_val = 1.38;    // store a double, int value is lost
cout << pail.double_val;
```

Thus, pail can serve as an int variable on one occasion and as a double variable at another time. The member name identifies the capacity in which the variable is acting. Because a union only holds one value at a time, it has to have space enough to hold its largest member. Hence, the size of the union is the size of its largest member.

One use for the union is to save space when a data item can use two or more formats but never simultaneously. For example, suppose you manage a mixed inventory of widgets, some of which have an integer ID, and some of which have a string ID. Then, you could do the following:

```
struct widget
{
    char brand[20];
    int type;
    union id                    // format depends on widget type
```

```
    {
        long id_num;      // type 1 widgets
        char id_char[20]; // other widgets
    } id_val;
    };
    ...
    widget prize;
    ...
    if (prize.type == 1)                //if statement (Chapter 6)
        cin >> prize.id_val.id_num;    // use member name to indicate mode
    else
        cin >> prize.id_val.id_char;
```

An *anonymous union* has no name; in essence, its members become variables that share the same address. Naturally, only one member can be current at a time:

```
struct widget
{
    char brand[20];
    int type;
    union                   // anonymous union
    {
        long id_num;      // type 1 widgets
        char id_char[20]; // other widgets
    };
};
...
widget prize;
...
if (prize.type == 1)
    cin >> prize.id_num;
else
    cin >> prize.id_char;
```

Because the union is anonymous, `id_num` and `id_char` are treated as two members of `prize` that share the same address. The need for an intermediate identifier *id_val* is eliminated. It is up to the programmer to keep track of which choice is active.

Enumerations

The C++ **enum** facility provides an alternative means to **const** for creating symbolic constants. It also lets you define new types but in a fairly restricted fashion. The syntax for using **enum** resembles structure syntax. For example, consider the following statement:

```
enum spectrum {red, orange, yellow, green, blue, violet, indigo, ultraviolet};
```

This statement does two things:

- It makes **spectrum** the name of a new type; **spectrum** is termed an *enumeration*, much as a **struct** variable is called a structure.

- It establishes **red**, **orange**, **yellow**, and so on, as symbolic constants for the integer values 0—7. These constants are called *enumerators*.

By default, enumerators are assigned integer values starting with 0 for the first enumerator, 1 for the second enumerator, and so forth. You can override the default by explicitly assigning integer values. We'll show you how later.

You can use an enumeration name to declare a variable of that type:

```
spectrum band;
```

An enumeration variable has some special properties, which we'll examine now.

The only valid values that you can assign to an enumeration variable without a type cast are the enumerator values used in defining the type. Thus, we have the following:

```
band = blue;       // valid, blue is an enumerator
band = 2000;       // invalid, 2000 not an enumerator
```

Thus, a spectrum variable is limited to just eight possible values. Some compilers issue a compiler error if you attempt to assign an invalid value, whereas others issue a warning. For maximum portability, you should regard assigning a non-enum value to an enum variable as an error.

Only the assignment operator is defined for enumerations. In particular, arithmetic operations are not defined:

```
band = orange;        // valid
++band;               // not valid
band = orange + red;  // not valid
...
```

However, some implementations do not honor this restriction. That can make it possible to violate the type limits. For example, if band has the value ultraviolet, or 7, then ++band, if valid, increments band to 8, which is not a valid value for a spectrum type. Again, for maximum portability, you should adopt the stricter limitations.

Enumerators are of integer type and can be promoted to type int, but int types are not converted automatically to the enumeration type:

```
int color = blue;   // valid, spectrum type promoted to int
band = 3;           // invalid, int not converted to spectrum
color = 3 + red;    // valid, red converted to int
...
```

Note that even though 3 corresponds to the enumerator green, assigning 3 to band is a type error. But assigning green to band is fine, for they both are type spectrum. Again, some implementations do not enforce this restriction. In the expression 3 + red, addition isn't defined for enumerators. However, red is converted to type int, and the result is type int. Because of the conversion from enumeration to int in this situation, you can use enumerations in arithmetic expressions combining them with ordinary integers even though arithmetic isn't defined for enumerations themselves.

You can assign an int value to an enum provided that the value is valid and that you use an explicit type cast:

```
band = spectrum(3);        // typecast 3 to type spectrum
```

What if you try to type cast an inappropriate value? The result is undefined, meaning that the attempt won't be flagged as an error but that you can't rely upon the value of the result:

```
band = spectrum(40003);    // undefined
```

(See the section "Value Ranges for Enumerations" later in this chapter for a discussion of what values are and are not appropriate.)

As you can see, the rules governing enumerations are fairly restrictive. In practice, enumerations are used more often as a way of defining related symbolic constants than as a means of defining a new type. For example, you might use an enumeration to define symbolic constants for a `switch` statement. (See Chapter 6 for an example.) If you plan to use just the constants and not create variables of the enumeration type, you can omit an enumeration type name:

```
enum {red, orange, yellow, green, blue, violet, indigo, ultraviolet};
```

Setting Enumerator Values

You can set enumerator values explicitly by using the assignment operator:

```
enum bits{one = 1, two = 2, four = 4, eight = 8};
```

The assigned values must be integers. You also can define just some of the enumerators explicitly:

```
enum bigstep{first, second = 100, third};
```

In this case, `first` is 0 by default. Subsequent uninitialized enumerators are larger by one than their predecessors. So, `third` would have the value 101.

Finally, you can create more than one enumerator with the same value:

```
enum {zero, null = 0, one, numero_uno = 1};
```

Here, both `zero` and `null` are 0, and both `one` and `numero_uno` are 1. In earlier versions of C++, you could assign only `int` values (or values that promote to `int`) to enumerators, but that restriction has been removed so that you can use type `long` values.

Value Ranges for Enumerations

Originally, the only valid values for an enumeration were those named in the declaration. However, C++ now supports a refined concept by which you validly can assign values by a type cast to an enumeration variable. Each enumeration has a *range*, and you can assign any integer value in the range, even if it's not an enumerator value, by using a type cast to an enumeration variable. For example, suppose that `bits` and `myflag` are defined this way:

```
enum bits{one = 1, two = 2, four = 4, eight = 8};
bits myflag;
```

Then, the following is valid:

```
myflag = bits(6);    // valid, because 6 is in bits range
```

Here 6 is not one of the enumerations, but it lies in the range the enumerations define.

The range is defined as follows. First, to find the upper limit, take the largest enumerator value. Find the smallest power of two greater than this largest value, subtract one, and that is the upper end of the range. For example, the largest **bigstep** value, as previously defined, is 101. The smallest power of two greater than this is 128, so the upper end of the range is 127. Next, to find the lower limit, find the smallest enumerator value. If it is zero or greater, the lower limit for the range is zero. If the smallest enumerator is negative, use the same approach as for finding the upper limit, but toss in a minus sign. For example, if the smallest enumerator is -6, the next power of two (times a minus sign) is -8, and the lower limit is -7.

The idea is that the compiler can choose how much space to hold an enumeration. It might use one byte or less for an enumeration with a small range and four bytes for an enumeration with type **long** values.

Pointers and the Free Store

The beginning of Chapter 3, "Dealing with Data," mentions three fundamental properties of which a computer program must keep track when it stores data. To save the book the wear and tear of your thumbing back to that chapter, here are those properties again:

- Where the information is stored
- What value is kept there
- What kind of information is stored

You've used one strategy for accomplishing these ends: defining a simple variable. The declaration statement provides the type and a symbolic name for the value. It also causes the program to allocate memory for the value and to keep track of the location internally.

Let's look at a second strategy now, one that becomes particularly important in developing C++ classes. This strategy is based on pointers, which are variables that store addresses of values rather than the values themselves. But before discussing pointers, let's see how to find addresses explicitly for ordinary variables. Just apply the address operator, represented by **&**, to a variable to get its location; for example, if **home** is a variable, **&home** is its address. Listing 4.9 demonstrates this operator.

LISTING 4.9   address.cpp

```
// address.cpp _ using the & operator to find addresses
#include <iostream>
using namespace std;
int main()
{
    int donuts = 6;
    double cups = 4.5;

    cout << "donuts value = " << donuts;
    cout << " and donuts address = " << &donuts << "\n";
```

LISTING 4.9   Continued

```
// NOTE: you may need to use unsigned (&donuts)
//   and unsigned (&cups)
    cout << "cups value = " << cups;
    cout << " and cups address = " << &cups << "\n";
    return 0;
}
```

Compatibility Note

cout is a smart object, but some versions are smarter than others. Thus, some implementations might fail to recognize pointer types. In that case, you have to type cast the address to a recognizable type, such as unsigned int. The appropriate type cast depends on the memory model. The default DOS memory model uses a 2-byte address, hence unsigned int is the proper cast. Some DOS memory models, however, use a 4-byte address, which requires a cast to unsigned long.

Here is the output on one system:

```
donuts value = 6 and donuts address = 0x0065fd40
cups value = 4.5 and cups address = 0x0065fd44
```

When it displays addresses, cout uses hexadecimal notation because that is the usual notation used to describe memory. Our implementation stores donuts at a lower memory location than cups. The difference between the two addresses is 0x0065fd44 - 0x0065fd40, or 4. This makes sense, for donuts is type int, which uses four bytes. Different systems, of course, will give different values for the address. Also, some may store cups first, then donuts, giving a difference of 8 bytes, since cups is double.

Using ordinary variables, then, treats the value as a named quantity and the location as a derived quantity. Now look at the pointer strategy, one that is essential to the C++ programming philosophy of memory management. (See the note on Pointers and the C++ Philosophy.)

Pointers and the C++ Philosophy

Object-oriented programming differs from traditional procedural programming in that OOP emphasizes making decisions during runtime instead of during compile time. *Runtime* means while a program is running, and *compile time* means when the compiler is putting a program together. A runtime decision is like, when on vacation, choosing what sights to see depending on the weather and your mood at the moment, whereas a compile-time decision is more like adhering to a preset schedule regardless of the conditions.

Runtime decisions provide the flexibility to adjust to current circumstances. For example, consider allocating memory for an array. The traditional way is to declare an array. To declare an array in C++, you have to commit yourself to a particular array size. Thus, the array size is set when the program is compiled; it is a compile-time decision. Perhaps you think an array of 20 elements is sufficient 80% of the time, but that occasionally the program will need to handle 200 elements. To be safe, you use an array with 200 elements. This results in your program wasting memory most of the time it's used. OOP tries to make a program more flexible by delaying such decisions until runtime. That way, after the program is running, you can tell it you need only 20 elements one time or that you need 205 elements another time.

In short, you make the array size a runtime decision. To make this approach possible, the language has to allow you to create an array—or the equivalent—while the program runs. The C++ method, as you soon see, involves using the keyword new to request the correct amount of memory and using pointers to keep track of where the newly allocated memory is found.

The new strategy for handling stored data switches things around by treating the location as the named quantity and the value as a derived quantity. A special type of variable—the *pointer*—holds the address of a value. Thus, the name of the pointer represents the location. Applying the * operator, called the *indirect value* or the *dereferencing* operator, yields the value at the location. (Yes, this is the same * symbol used for multiplication; C++ uses the context to determine whether you mean multiplication or dereferencing.) Suppose, for example, that manly is a pointer. Then, manly represents an address, and *manly represents the value at that address. The combination *manly becomes equivalent to an ordinary type int variable. Listing 4.10 demonstrates these points. It also shows how to declare a pointer.

LISTING 4.10   pointer.cpp

```cpp
// pointer.cpp _ our first pointer variable
#include <iostream>
using namespace std;
int main()
{
    int updates = 6;        // declare a variable
    int * p_updates;        // declare pointer to an int

    p_updates = &updates;   // assign address of int to pointer

    // express values two ways
    cout << "Values: updates = " << updates;
    cout << ", *p_updates = " << *p_updates << "\n";

    // express address two ways
    cout << "Addresses: &updates = " << &updates;
    cout << ", p_updates = " << p_updates << "\n";

    // use pointer to change value
    *p_updates = *p_updates + 1;
    cout << "Now updates = " << updates << "\n";
    return 0;
}
```

Here is the output:

```
Values: updates = 6, *p_updates = 6
Addresses: &updates = 0x0065fd48, p_updates = 0x0065fd48
Now updates = 7
```

As you can see, the `int` variable `updates` and the pointer variable `p_updates` are just two sides of the same coin. The `updates` variable represents the value as primary and uses the `&` operator to get the address, whereas the `p_updates` variable represents the address as primary and uses the `*` operator to get the value. (See Figure 4.8.) Because `p_updates` points to `updates`, `*p_updates` and `updates` are completely equivalent. You can use `*p_updates` exactly as you would use a type `int` variable. As the program shows, you even can assign values to `*p_updates`. Doing so changes the value of the pointed-to value, `updates`.

FIGURE 4.8
Two sides of a coin.

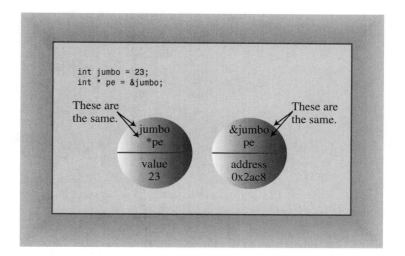

Declaring and Initializing Pointers

Let's examine the process of declaring pointers. A computer needs to keep track of the type of value to which a pointer refers. For example, the address of a `char` typically looks the same as the address of a `double`, but `char` and `double` use different numbers of bytes and different internal formats for storing values. Therefore, a pointer declaration must specify what type of data it is to which the pointer points.

For example, the last example has this declaration:

```
int * p_updates;
```

This states that the combination `* p_updates` is type `int`. Because the `*` operator is used by applying it to a pointer, the `p_updates` variable itself must *be* a pointer. We say that `p_updates` points to type `int`. We also say that the type for `p_updates` is pointer-to-`int` or, more concisely, `int *`. To repeat: `p_updates` is a pointer (an address), and `*p_updates` is an `int` and not a pointer. (See Figure 4.9.)

FIGURE 4.9

Pointers store addresses.

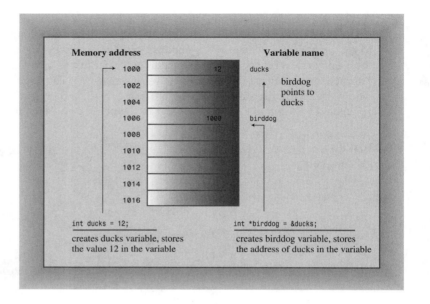

Incidentally, the use of spaces around the * operator are optional. Traditionally, C programmers have used this form:

```
int *ptr;
```

This accentuates the idea that the combination *ptr is a type int value. Many C++ programmers, on the other hand, use this form:

```
int* ptr;
```

This emphasizes the idea that int* is a type, pointer-to-int. Where you put the spaces makes no difference to the compiler. Be aware, however, that the declaration

```
int* p1, p2;
```

creates one pointer (p1) and one ordinary int (p2). You need an * for each pointer variable name.

Remember

In C++, the combination int * is a compound type, pointer-to-int.

You use the same syntax to declare pointers to other types:

```
double * tax_ptr; // tax_ptr points to type double
char * str;       // str points to type char
```

Because you declare `tax_ptr` as a pointer-to-**double**, the compiler knows that `*tax_ptr` is a type **double** value. That is, it knows that `*tax_ptr` represents a number stored in floating-point format that occupies (on most systems) eight bytes. A pointer variable is never simply a pointer. It always is a pointer to a specific type. `tax_ptr` is type pointer-to-**double** (or type **double ***) and `str` is type pointer-to-**char** (or **char ***). Although both are pointers, they are pointers of two different types. Like arrays, pointers are based upon other types.

Note that whereas `tax_ptr` and `str` point to data types of two different sizes, the two variables `tax_ptr` and `str` themselves typically are the same size. That is, the address of a **char** is the same size as the address of a **double**, much as 1016 might be the street address for a department store, whereas 1024 could be the street address of a small cottage. The size or value of an address doesn't really tell you anything about the size or kind of variable or building you find at that address. Usually, addresses require two or four bytes, depending on the computer system. (Some systems might have larger addresses, and a system can use different address sizes for different types.)

You can use a declaration statement to initialize a pointer. In that case, the pointer, not the pointed-to value, is initialized. That is, the statements

```
int higgens = 5;
int * pt = &higgens;
```

set `pt` and not `*pt` to the value `&higgens`.

Listing 4.11 demonstrates how to initialize a pointer to an address.

LISTING 4.11   `init_ptr.cpp`

```
// init_ptr.cpp—initialize a pointer
#include <iostream>
using namespace std;
int main()
{
    int higgens = 5;
    int * pt = &higgens;

    cout << "Value of higgens = " << higgens
         << "; Address of higgens = " << &higgens << "\n";
    cout << "Value of *pt = " << *pi
         << "; Value of pt = " << pi << "\n";
    return 0;
}
```

Here is the output:

```
Value of higgens = 5; Address of higgens = 0068FDF0
Value of *pt = 5; Value of pt = 0068FDF0
```

You can see that the program initializes `pi`, not `*pi`, to the address of **higgens**.

Danger awaits those who incautiously use pointers. One extremely important point is that when you create a pointer in C++, the computer allocates memory to hold an address, but it does not allocate memory to hold the data to which the address points. Creating space for the data involves a separate step. Omitting that step, as in the following, is an invitation to disaster:

```
long * fellow;          // create a pointer-to-long
*fellow = 223323;       // place a value in never-never land
```

Sure, `fellow` is a pointer. But where does it point? The code failed to assign an address to `fellow`. So where is the value 223323 placed? We can't say. Because `fellow` wasn't initialized, it could have any value. Whatever that value is, the program interprets it as the address at which to store 223323. If `fellow` happens to have the value 1200, then the computer attempts to place the data at address 1200, even if that happens to be an address in the middle of your program code. Chances are that wherever `fellow` points, that is not where you want to put the number 223323. This kind of error can produce some of the most insidious and hard-to-trace bugs.

Caution

Pointer Golden Rule: ALWAYS initialize a pointer to a definite and appropriate address before you apply the dereferencing operator (*) to it.

Pointers and Numbers

Pointers are not integer types, even though computers typically handle addresses as integers. Conceptually, pointers are distinct types from integers. Integers are numbers you can add, subtract, divide, and so on. But a pointer describes a location, and it doesn't make sense, for example, to multiply two locations times each other. In terms of the operations you can perform with them, pointers and integers are different from each other. Consequently, you can't simply assign an integer to a pointer:

```
int * pt;
pt = 0xB8000000;  // type mismatch
```

Here, the left side is a pointer to `int`, so you can assign it an address, but the right side is just an integer. You might know that 0xB8000000 is the combined segment-offset address of video memory on your system, but nothing in the statement tells the program that this number is an address. C prior to the new C99 standard let you make assignments like this. But C++ more stringently enforces type agreement, and the compiler will give you an error message saying you have a type mismatch. If you want to use a numeric value as an address, you should use a type cast to convert the number to the appropriate address type:

```
int * pt;
pt = (int *) 0xB8000000; // types now match
```

Now both sides of the assignment statement represent addresses of integers, so the assignment is valid. Note that just because it is the address of a type `int` value doesn't mean that `pi` itself is type `int`. For example, in the large memory model on an IBM PC using DOS, type `int` is a 2-byte value, whereas the addresses are 4-byte values.

Pointers have some other interesting properties that we'll discuss as they become relevant. Meanwhile, let's look at how pointers can be used to manage runtime allocation of memory space.

Allocating Memory with new

Now that you have some feel for how pointers work, let's see how they can implement that important OOP technique of allocating memory as a program runs. So far, we've initialized pointers to the addresses of variables; the variables are *named* memory allocated during compile time, and the pointers merely provide an alias for memory you could access directly by name anyway. The true worth of pointers comes into play when you allocate *unnamed* memory during runtime to hold values. In this case, pointers become the only access to that memory. In C, you could allocate memory with the library function `malloc()`. You still can do so in C++, but C++ also has a better way, the `new` operator.

Let's try out this new technique by creating unnamed, runtime storage for a type `int` value and accessing the value with a pointer. The key is the C++ `new` operator. You tell `new` for what data type you want memory; `new` finds a block of the correct size and returns the address of the block. Assign this address to a pointer, and you're in business. Here's a sample of the technique:

```
int * pn = new int;
```

The `new int` part tells the program you want some `new` storage suitable for holding an `int`. The `new` operator uses the type to figure out how many bytes are needed. Then, it finds the memory and returns the address. Next, assign the address to `pn`, which is declared to be of type pointer-to-`int`. Now `pn` is the address and `*pn` is the value stored there. Compare this with assigning the address of a variable to a pointer:

```
int higgens;
int * pt = &higgens;
```

In both cases (`pn` and `pt`) you assign the address of an `int` to a pointer. In the second case, you also can access the `int` by name: `higgens`. In the first case, your only access is via the pointer. That raises a question: Because the memory to which `pn` points lacks a name, what do you call it? We say that `pn` points to a *data object*. This is not "object" in the sense of "object-oriented programming"; it's just "object" in the sense of "thing." The term "data object" is more general than the term "variable," for it means any block of memory allocated for a data item. Thus, a variable also is a data object, but the memory to which `pn` points is not a variable. The pointer method for handling data objects may seem more awkward at first, but it offers greater control over how your program manages memory.

The general form for obtaining and assigning memory for a single data object, which can be a structure as well as a fundamental type, is this:

```
typeName pointer_name = new typeName;
```

You use the data type twice: once to specify the kind of memory requested and once to declare a suitable pointer. Of course, if you've already declared a pointer of the correct type, you can use it rather than declare a new one. Listing 4.12 illustrates using `new` with two different types.

LISTING 4.12   `use_new.cpp`

```cpp
// use_new.cpp _ using the new operator
#include <iostream>
using namespace std;
int main()
{
    int * pt = new int;          // allocate space for an int
    *pt = 1001;                  // store a value there

    cout << "int ";
    cout << "value = " << *pt << ": location = " << pt << "\n";

    double * pd = new double;    // allocate space for a double
    *pd = 10000001.0;            // store a double there

    cout << "double ";
    cout << "value = " << *pd << ": location = " << pd << "\n";
    cout << "size of pt = " << sizeof pt;
    cout << ": size of *pt = " << sizeof *pt << "\n";
    cout << "size of pd = " << sizeof pd;
    cout << ": size of *pd = " << sizeof *pd << "\n";
    return 0;
}
```

Here is the output:

```
int value = 1001: location = 0x004301a8
double value = 1e+07: location = 0x004301d8
size of pt = 4: size of *pt = 4
size of pd = 4: size of *pd = 8
```

Of course, the exact values for the memory locations differ from system to system.

Program Notes

The program uses **new** to allocate memory for the type **int** and type **double** data objects. This occurs while the program is running. The pointers **pt** and **pd** point to these two data objects. Without them, you cannot access those memory locations. With them, you can use ***pt** and ***pd** just as you would use variables. You assign values to ***pt** and ***pd** to assign values to the new data objects. Similarly, you print ***pt** and ***pd** to display those values.

The program also demonstrates one of the reasons you have to declare the type a pointer points to. An address in itself reveals only the beginning address of the object stored, not its type or the number of bytes used. Look at the addresses of the two values. They are just numbers with no type or size information. Also, note that the size of a pointer-to-**int** is the same as the size of a pointer-to-**double**. Both are just addresses. But because **use_new.cpp** declared the pointer types, the program knows that ***pd** is a **double** value of 8 bytes, whereas ***pt** is an **int** value of 4 bytes. When **use_new.cpp** prints the value of ***pd**, **cout** can tell how many bytes to read and how to interpret them.

Out of Memory?

It's possible that the computer might not have sufficient memory available to satisfy a new request. When that is the case, new returns the value 0. In C++, a pointer with the value 0 is called the *null pointer.* C++ guarantees that the null pointer never points to valid data, so it often is used to indicate failure for operators or functions that otherwise return usable pointers. After you learn about if statements (in Chapter 6), you can check to see if new returns the null pointer and thus protects your program from attempting to exceed its bounds. In addition to returning the null pointer upon failure to allocate memory, new might throw a bad_alloc exception. Chapter 15, "Friends, Exceptions, and More," discusses the exception mechanism.

Freeing Memory with delete

Using new to request memory when you need it is just the more glamorous half of the C++ memory-management package. The other half is the delete operator, which enables you to return memory to the memory pool when you are finished with it. That is an important step toward making the most effective use of memory. Memory that you return, or *free*, then can be reused by other parts of your program. You use delete by following it with a pointer to a block of memory originally allocated with new:

```
int * ps = new int; // allocate memory with new
. . .                // use the memory
delete ps;           // free memory with delete when done
```

This removes the memory to which ps points; it doesn't remove the pointer ps itself. You can reuse ps, for example, to point to another new allocation. You always should balance a use of new with a use of delete; otherwise, you can wind up with a *memory leak*, that is, memory that has been allocated but no longer can be used. If a memory leak grows too large, it can bring a program seeking more memory to a halt.

You should not attempt to free a block of memory that you already have freed. The result of such an attempt is not defined. Also, you cannot use delete to free memory created by declaring variables:

```
int * ps = new int;    // ok
delete ps;............// ok
delete ps;............// not ok now
int jugs = 5;          // ok
int * pi = & jugs;     // ok
delete pi;             // not allowed, memory not allocated by new
```

Caution

Use delete only to free memory allocated with new. However, it is safe to apply delete to a null pointer.

Note that the critical test for using **delete** is that you use it with memory allocated by **new**. This doesn't mean you have to use the same pointer you used with **new**; instead, you have to use the same address:

```
int * ps = new int;    // allocate memory
int * pq = ps;         // set second pointer to same block
delete pq;             // delete with second pointer
```

Ordinarily, you won't create two pointers to the same block of memory, for that raises the possibility you mistakenly will try to delete the same block twice. But, as you soon see, using a second pointer does make sense when you work with a function that returns a pointer.

Using new to Create Dynamic Arrays

If all a program needs is a single value, you might as well declare a simple variable, for that is simpler, if less impressive, than using **new** and a pointer to manage a single small data object. More typically, you use **new** with larger chunks of data, such as arrays, strings, and structures. This is where **new** is useful. Suppose, for example, you're writing a program that might or might not need an array, depending on information given to the program while it is running. If you create an array by declaring it, the space is allocated when the program is compiled. Whether or not the program finally uses the array, the array is there, using up memory. Allocating the array during compile time is called *static binding*, meaning the array is built in to the program at compilation time. But with **new**, you can create an array during runtime if you need it and skip creating the array if you don't need it. Or, you can select an array size after the program is running. This is called *dynamic binding*, meaning that the array is created while the program is running. Such an array is called a *dynamic array*. With static binding, you must specify the array size when you write the program. With dynamic binding, the program can decide upon an array size while the program runs.

For now, we'll look at two basic matters concerning dynamic arrays: how to use C++'s **new** operator to create an array and how to use a pointer to access array elements.

Creating a Dynamic Array with new

It's easy to create a dynamic array in C++; you tell **new** the type of array element and number of elements you want. The syntax requires that you follow the type name with the number of elements in brackets. For example, if you need an array of ten **ints**, do this:

```
int * psome = new int [10]; // get a block of 10 ints
```

The **new** operator returns the address of the first element of the block. In this example, that value is assigned to the pointer **psome**. You should balance the call to **new** with a call to **delete** when the program is finished with using that block of memory.

When you use **new** to create an array, you should use an alternative form of **delete** that indicates that you are freeing an array:

```
delete [] psome;                // free a dynamic array
```

The presence of the brackets tells the program that it should free the whole array, not just the element pointed to by the pointer. Note that the brackets are between `delete` and the pointer. If you use `new` without brackets, use `delete` without brackets. If you use `new` with brackets, use `delete` with brackets. Earlier versions of C++ might not recognize the bracket notation. For the ANSI/ISO Standard, however, the effect of mismatching `new` and `delete` forms is undefined, meaning you can't rely upon some particular behavior.

```
int * pt = new int;
short * ps = new short [500];
delete [] pt;   // effect is undefined, don't do it
delete ps;      // effect is undefined, don't do it
```

In short, observe these rules when you use `new` and `delete`:

- Don't use `delete` to free memory that `new` didn't allocate.
- Don't use `delete` to free the same block of memory twice in succession.
- Use `delete` `[]` if you used `new` `[]` to allocate an array.
- Use `delete` (no brackets) if you used `new` to allocate a single entity.
- It's safe to apply `delete` to the null pointer (nothing happens).

Now let's return to the dynamic array. Note that `psome` is a pointer to a single `int`, the first element of the block. It's your responsibility to keep track of how many elements are in the block. That is, because the compiler doesn't keep track of the fact that `psome` points to the first of ten integers, you have to write your program so that it keeps track of the number of elements.

Actually, the program does keep track of the amount of memory allocated so that it can be correctly freed at a later time when you use the `delete` `[]` operator. But that information isn't publicly available; you can't use the `sizeof` operator, for example, to find the number of bytes in a dynamically allocated array.

The general form for allocating and assigning memory for an array is this:

```
type_name pointer_name = new type_name [num_elements];
```

Invoking the `new` operator secures a block of memory large enough to hold `num_elements` elements of type *type_name*, with `pointer_name` pointing to the first element. As you're about to see, you can use `pointer_name` in many of the same ways you can use an array name.

Using a Dynamic Array

After you create a dynamic array, how do you use it? First, think about the problem conceptually. The statement

```
int * psome = new int [10]; // get a block of 10 ints
```

creates a pointer `psome` that points to the first element of a block of ten `int` values. Think of it as a finger pointing to that element. Suppose an `int` occupies four bytes. Then, by moving your finger four bytes in the correct direction, you can point to the second element. Altogether, there

are ten elements, which is the range over which you can move your finger. Thus, the **new** statement supplies you with all the information you need to identify every element in the block.

Now think about the problem practically. How do you access one of these elements? The first
element is no problem. Because **psome** points to the first element of the array, ***psome** is the
value of the first element. That leaves nine more elements to access. The simplest way may surprise you if you haven't worked with C: Just use the pointer as if it were an array name. That
is, you can use **psome[0]** instead of ***psome** for the first element, **psome[1]** for the second element, and so on. It turns out to be very simple to use a pointer to access a dynamic array, even
if it may not immediately be obvious why the method works. The reason you can do this is
that C and C++ handle arrays internally by using pointers anyway. This near equivalence of
arrays and pointers is one of the beauties of C and C++. We'll elaborate on this equivalence in
a moment. First, Listing 4.13 shows how you can use **new** to create a dynamic array and then
use array notation to access the elements. It also points out a fundamental difference between a
pointer and a true array name.

LISTING 4.13   arraynew.cpp

```
// arraynew.cpp _ using the new operator for arrays
#include <iostream>
using namespace std;
int main()
{
    double * p3 = new double [3]; // space for 3 doubles
    p3[0] = 0.2;                  // treat p3 like an array name
    p3[1] = 0.5;
    p3[2] = 0.8;
    cout << "p3[1] is " << p3[1] << ".\n";
    p3 = p3 + 1;                  // increment the pointer
    cout << "Now p3[0] is " << p3[0] << " and ";
    cout << "p3[1] is " << p3[1] << ".\n";
    p3 = p3 - 1;                  // point back to beginning
    delete [] p3;                 // free the memory
    return 0;
}
```

Here is the output:

```
p3[1] is 0.5.
Now p3[0] is 0.5 and p3[1] is 0.8.
```

As you can see, **arraynew.cpp** uses the pointer **p3** as if it were the name of an array, with
p3[0] as the first element, and so on. The fundamental difference between an array name and
a pointer shows in the following line:

```
p3 = p3 + 1; // okay for pointers, wrong for array names
```

You can't change the value of an array name. But a pointer is a variable, hence you can change its value. Note the effect of adding 1 to **p3**. The expression **p3[0]** now refers to the former second element of the array. Thus adding 1 to **p3** causes it to point to the second element instead of the first. Subtracting one takes the pointer back to its original value so that the program can provide **delete []** with the correct address.

The actual addresses of consecutive **int**s typically differ by two or four bytes, so the fact that adding 1 to **p3** gives the address of the next element suggests that there is something special about pointer arithmetic. There is.

Pointers, Arrays, and Pointer Arithmetic

The near equivalence of pointers and array names stems from *pointer arithmetic* and how C++ handles arrays internally. First, let's check out the arithmetic. Adding 1 to an integer variable increases its value by 1, but adding 1 to a pointer variable increases its value by the number of bytes of the type to which it points. Adding 1 to a pointer to **double** adds 8 to the numerical value on systems with 8-byte **double**, whereas adding 1 to a pointer-to-**short** adds 2 to the pointer value if **short** is 2 bytes. Listing 4.14 demonstrates this amazing point. It also shows a second important point: C++ interprets the array name as an address.

LISTING 4.14   addpntrs.cpp

```
// addpntrs.cpp--pointer addition
#include <iostream>
using namespace std;
int main()
{
    double wages[3] = {10000.0, 20000.0, 30000.0};
    short stacks[3] = {3, 2, 1};

    // Here are two ways to get the address of an array
    double * pw = wages;     // name of an array = address
    short * ps = &stacks[0]; // or use address operator
    // with array element
    cout << "pw = " << pw << ", *pw = " << *pw << "\n";
    pw = pw + 1;
    cout << "add 1 to the pw pointer:\n";
    cout << "pw = " << pw << ", *pw = " << *pw << "\n\n";

    cout << "ps = " << ps << ", *ps = " << *ps << "\n";
    ps = ps + 1;
    cout << "add 1 to the ps pointer:\n";
    cout << "ps = " << ps << ", *ps = " << *ps << "\n\n";

    cout << "access two elements with array notation\n";
    cout << stacks[0] << " " << stacks[1] << "\n";
    cout << "access two elements with pointer notation\n";
    cout << *stacks << " " << *(stacks + 1) << "\n";
```

LISTING 4.14   Continued

```
        cout << sizeof wages << " = size of wages array\n";
        cout << sizeof pw << " = size of pw pointer\n";
        return 0;
}
```

Here is the output:

```
pw = 0x0065fd24, *pw = 10000
add 1 to the pw pointer:
pw = 0x0065fd2c, *pw = 20000

ps = 0x0065fd3c, *ps = 3
add 1 to the ps pointer:
ps = 0x0065fd3e, *ps = 2

access two elements with array notation
3 2
access two elements with pointer notation
3 2
24 = size of wages array
4 = size of pw pointer
```

Program Notes

In most contexts, C++ interprets the name of an array as the address of its first element. Thus, the statement

```
double * pw = wages;
```

makes `pw` a pointer to type `double` and then initializes `pw` to `wages`, which is the address of the first element of the `wages` array. For `wages`, as with any array, we have the following equality:

```
wages = &wages[0] = address of first element of array
```

Just to show that this is no jive, the program explicitly uses the address operator in the expression `&stacks[0]` to initialize the `ps` pointer to the first element of the stacks array.

Next, the program inspects the values of `pw` and `*pw`. The first is an address and the second is the value at that address. Because `pw` points to the first element, the value displayed for `*pw` is that of the first element, 10000. Then, the program adds 1 to `pw`. As promised, this adds 8 (fd24 + 8 = fd2c in hexadecimal) to the numeric address value, because `double` on our system is 8 bytes. This makes `pw` equal to the address of the second element. Thus, `*pw` now is 20000, the value of the second element. (See Figure 4.10.) (The address values in the figure are adjusted to make the figure clearer.)

FIGURE 4.10

Pointer addition.

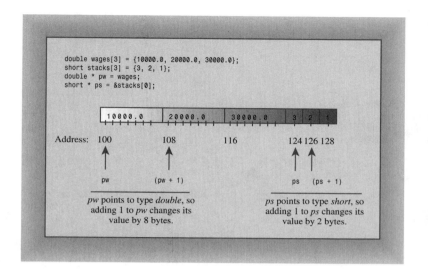

```
double wages[3] = {10000.0, 20000.0, 30000.0};
short stacks[3] = {3, 2, 1};
double * pw = wages;
short * ps = &stacks[0];
```

|10000.0|20000.0|30000.0|3|2|1|

Address: 100   108   116   124 126 128

pw   (pw + 1)   ps   (ps + 1)

pw points to type *double*, so
adding 1 to *pw* changes its
value by 8 bytes.

ps points to type *short*, so
adding 1 to *ps* changes its
value by 2 bytes.

After this, the program goes through similar steps for **ps**. This time, because **ps** points to type **short** and because **short** is 2 bytes, adding 1 to the pointer increases its value by 2. Again, the result is to make the pointer point to the next element of the array.

Remember

Adding 1 to a pointer variable increases its value by the number of bytes of the type to which it points.

Now consider the array expression **stacks[1]**. The C++ compiler treats this expression exactly as if you wrote it as ***(stacks + 1)**. The second expression means calculate the address of the second element of the array and then find the value stored there. The end result is precisely what **stacks[1] means**. (Operator precedence requires that you use the parentheses. Without them, 1 would be added to ***stacks** instead of to **stacks**.)

The program output demonstrates that ***(stacks + 1)** and **stacks[1]** are the same. Similarly, ***(stacks + 2)** is the same as **stacks[2]**. In general, wherever you use array notation, C++ makes the following conversion:

```
arrayname[i] becomes *(arrayname + i)
```

And if you use a pointer instead of an array name, C++ makes the same conversion:

```
pointername[i] becomes *(pointername + i)
```

Thus, in many respects you can use pointer names and array names in the same way. You can use the array brackets notation with either. You can apply the dereferencing operator (*****) to either. In most expressions, each represents an address. One difference is that you can change the value of a pointer while an array name is a constant:

```
pointername = pointername + 1; // valid
arrayname = arrayname + 1;     // not allowed
```

The second difference is that applying the `sizeof` operator to an array name yields the size of the array, but applying `sizeof` to a pointer yields the size of the pointer, even if the pointer points to the array. For example, in Listing 4.15, both `pw` and `wages` refer to the same array. But applying the `sizeof` operator to them produces the following results:

```
24 = size of wages array ® displaying sizeof wages
4 = size of pw pointer   ® displaying sizeof pw
```

This is one case in which C++ doesn't interpret the array name as an address.

In short, using `new` to create an array and using a pointer to access the different elements is a simple matter. Just treat the pointer as an array name. Understanding why this works, however, is an interesting challenge. If you actually want to understand arrays and pointers, you should review their mutual relationships carefully. In fact, you've been exposed to quite a bit of pointer knowledge lately, so let's summarize what's been revealed about pointers and arrays to date.

Summarizing Pointer Points

Declaring Pointers: To declare a pointer to a particular type, use this form:

```
typeName * pointerName;
```

Examples:

```
double * pn;    // pn points to a double value
char * pc;      // pc points to a char value
```

Here `pn` and `pc` are pointers and `double *` and `char *` are the C++ notations for the types pointer-to-`double` and pointer-to-`char`.

Assigning Values to Pointers: You should assign a pointer a memory address. You can apply the `&` operator to a variable name to get an address of named memory, and the `new` operator returns the address of unnamed memory.

Examples:

```
double bubble = 3.2;
pn = &bubble;     // assign address of bubble to pn
pc = new char;    // assign address of newly allocated char memory to pc
```

Dereferencing Pointers: Dereferencing a pointer means referring to the pointed-to value. Apply the dereferencing, or indirect value, operator (`*`) to a pointer to dereference it. Thus, if `pn` is a pointer to `bubble`, as in the last example, then `*pn` is the pointed-to value, or 3.2, in this case.

Examples:

```
cout << *pn; // print the value of bubble
*pc = 'S';   // place 'S' into the memory location whose address is pc
```

Array notation is a second way to dereference a pointer; for instance, pn[0] is the same as *pn. Never dereference a pointer that has not been initialized to a proper address.

Distinguishing Between a Pointer and the Pointed-to Value: Remember, if pt is a pointer-to-int, that *pt is not a pointer-to-int; instead, *pt is the complete equivalent to a type int variable. It is pt that is the pointer.

Examples:

```
int * pt = new int;     // assigns an address to the pointer pt
*pt = 5;                // stores the value 5 at that address
```

Array Names: In most contexts, C++ treats the name of an array as equivalent to the address of the first element of an array.

Example:

```
int tacos[10];          // now tacos is the same as &tacos[0]
```

One exception is when you use the name of an array with the sizeof operator. In that case, sizeof returns the size of the entire array, in bytes.

Pointer Arithmetic: C++ allows you to add an integer to a pointer. The result of adding 1 equals the original address value plus a value equal to the number of bytes in the pointed-to object. You also can subtract an integer from a pointer and take the difference between two pointers. The last operation, which yields an integer, is meaningful only if the two pointers point into the same array (pointing to one position past the end is allowed, too); it then yields the separation between the two elements.

Examples:

```
int tacos[10] = {5,2,8,4,1,2,2,4,6,8};
int * pt = tacos;        // suppose pf and fog are the address 3000
pt = pt + 1;             // now pt is 3004 if a int is four bytes
int *pe = &tacos[9];     // pe is 3036 if an int is four bytes
pe = pe -1;              // now pe is 3032, the address of tacos[8]
int diff = pe - pt;      // diff is 7, the separation between
                         // tacos[8] and tacos[1]
```

Dynamic Binding and Static Binding for Arrays: Use an array declaration to create an array with static binding, that is, an array whose size is set during compilation time:

```
int tacos[10]; // static binding, size fixed at compile time
```

Use the `new [ ]` operator to create an array with dynamic binding (a dynamic array), that is, an array that is allocated and whose size can be set during runtime. Free the memory with `delete [ ]` when you are done:

```
int size;
cin >> size;
int * pz = new int [size];    // dynamic binding, size set at run time
...
delete [] pz;                 // free memory when finished
```

Array Notation and Pointer Notation: Using bracket array notation is equivalent to dereferencing a pointer:

```
tacos[0] means *tacos means the value at address tacos
tacos[3] means *(tacos + 3) means the value at address tacos + 3
```

This is true for both array names and pointer variables, so you can use either pointer notation or array notation with pointers and array names.

Examples:

```
int * pi = new int [10];    // pi points to block of 10 ints
*pi = 5;                    // set zero element to 5
pi[0] = 6;                  // reset zero element to 6
pi[9] = 44;                 // set tenth element to 44
int tacos[10];
*(tacos + 4) = 12;          // set tacos[4] to 12
```

Pointers and Strings

The special relationship between arrays and pointers extends to strings. Consider the following code:

```
char flower[10] = "rose";
cout << flower << "s are red\n";
```

The name of an array is the address of its first element, so `flower` in the `cout` statement is the address of the `char` element containing the character `r`. The `cout` object assumes that the address of a `char` is the address of a string, so it prints the character at that address and then continues printing characters until it runs into the null character (`\0`). In short, if you give `cout` the address of a character, it prints everything from that character to the first null character that follows it.

The crucial element here is not that `flower` is an array name but that `flower` acts as the address of a `char`. This implies that you can use a pointer-to-`char` variable as an argument to `cout`, also, because it, too, is the address of a `char`. Of course, that pointer should point to the beginning of a string. We'll check that out in a moment.

But first, what about the final part of the preceding `cout` statement? If `flower` actually is the address of the first character of a string, what is the expression `"s are red\n"`? To be consistent with `cout`'s handling of string output, this quoted string also should be an address. And it is, for in C++ a quoted string, like an array name, serves as the address of its first element. The preceding code doesn't really send a whole string to `cout`, it just sends the string address. This means strings in an array, quoted string constants, and strings described by pointers all are handled equivalently. Each really is passed along as an address. That's certainly less work than passing each and every character in a string.

Remember

With `cout` and with most C++ expressions, the name of an array of `char`, a pointer-to-char, and a quoted string constant all are interpreted as the address of the first character of a string.

Listing 4.15 illustrates using the different forms of strings. It uses two functions from the string library. The `strlen()` function, which we've used before, returns the length of a string. The `strcpy()` function copies a string from one location to another. Both have function prototypes in the `cstring` header file (or `string.h`, on less up-to-date implementations). The program also showcases, as comments, some pointer misuses that you should try to avoid.

LISTING 4.15   ptrstr.cpp

```
// ptrstr.cpp _ using pointers to strings
#include <iostream>
using namespace std;
#include <cstring>              // declare strlen(), strcpy()
int main()
{
    char animal[20] = "bear";    // animal holds bear
    const char * bird = "wren";  // bird holds address of string
    char * ps;                   // uninitialized

    cout << animal << " and ";   // display bear
    cout << bird << "\n";        // display wren
    // cout << ps << "\n";      may display garbage, may cause a crash

    cout << "Enter a kind of animal: ";
    cin >> animal;               // ok if input < 20 chars
    // cin >> ps; Too horrible a blunder to try; ps doesn't
    //             point to allocated space

    ps = animal;                 // set ps to point to string
    cout << ps << "s!\n";        // ok, same as using animal
    cout << "Before using strcpy():\n";
    cout << animal << " at " << (int *) animal << endl;
    cout << ps << " at " << (int *) ps << endl;

    ps = new char[strlen(animal) + 1];  // get new storage
    strcpy(ps, animal);          // copy string to new storage
    cout << "After using strcpy():\n";
    cout << animal << " at " << (int *) animal << endl;
    cout << ps << " at " << (int *) ps << endl;
    delete [] ps;
    return 0;
}
```

Compatibility Note

If your system doesn't have the `cstring` header file, use the older `string.h` version.

Here is a sample run:

```
bear and wren
Enter a kind of animal: fox
foxs!
Before using strcpy():
fox at 0x0065fd30
fox at 0x0065fd30
After using strcpy():
fox at 0x0065fd30
fox at 0x004301c8
```

Program Notes

The program in Listing 4.15 creates one `char` array (`animal`) and two pointers-to-`char` variables (`bird` and `ps`). The program begins by initializing the `animal` array to the `"bear"` string, just as we've initialized arrays before. Then, the program does something new. It initializes a pointer-to-`char` to a string:

```
const char * bird = "wren"; // bird holds address of string
```

Remember, `"wren"` actually represents the address of the string, so this statement assigns the address of `"wren"` to the `bird` pointer. (Typically, a compiler sets aside an area in memory to hold all the quoted strings used in the program source code, associating each stored string with its address.) This means you can use the pointer `bird` just as you would use the string `"wren"`, as in `cout << "A concerned " << bird << " speaks\n"`. String literals are constants, which is why the code uses the `const` keyword in the declaration. Using `const` in this fashion means you can use `bird` to access the string but not to change it. Chapter 7 takes up the topic of `const` pointers in greater detail. Finally, the pointer `ps` remains uninitialized, so it doesn't point to any string. (This, you recall, usually is a bad idea, and this example is no exception.)

Next, the program illustrates that you can use the array name `animal` and the pointer `bird` equivalently with `cout`. Both, after all, are the addresses of strings, and `cout` displays the two strings (`"bear"` and `"wren"`) stored at those addresses. If you activate the code that makes the error of attempting to display `ps`, you might get a blank line, you might get garbage displayed, and you might get a program crash. Creating an uninitialized pointer is a bit like distributing a blank signed check; you lack control over how it will be used.

For input, the situation is a bit different. It's safe to use the array `animal` for input as long as the input is short enough to fit into the array. It would not be proper to use `bird` for input, however:

- Some compilers treat string literals as read-only constants, leading to a runtime error if you try to write new data over them. That string literals be constant is the mandated behavior in C++, but not all compilers have made that change from older behavior yet.

- Some compilers use just one copy of a string literal to represent all occurrences of that literal in a program.

Let's amplify the second point. C++ doesn't guarantee that string literals are stored uniquely. That is, if you use a string literal "wren" several times in the program, the compiler might store several copies of the string or just one copy. If it does the latter, then setting bird to point to one "wren" makes it point to the only copy of that string. Reading a value into one string could affect what you thought was an independent string elsewhere. In any case, because the bird pointer is declared as const, the compiler prevents any attempt to change the contents of the location pointed to by bird.

Worse yet is trying to read information into the location to which ps points. Because ps is not initialized, you don't know where the information will wind up. It might even overwrite information already in memory. Fortunately, it's easy to avoid these problems—just use a sufficiently large char array to receive input. Don't use string constants to receive input or uninitialized pointers to receive input.

Caution

When you read a string into a program, you always should use the address of previously allocated memory. This address can be in the form of an array name or of a pointer that has been initialized using new.

Next, notice what the following code accomplishes:

```
ps = animal;                    // set ps to point to string
...
cout << animal << " at " << (int *) animal << endl;
cout << ps << " at " << (int *) ps << endl;
```

It produces the following output:

```
fox at 0x0065fd30
fox at 0x0065fd30
```

Normally, if you give cout a pointer, it prints an address. But if the pointer is type char *, cout displays the pointed-to string. If you want to see the address of the string, you have to type cast the pointer to another pointer type, such as int *, which this code does. So, ps displays as the string "fox", but (int *) ps displays as the address where the string is found. Note that assigning animal to ps does not copy the string, it copies the address. This results in two pointers (animal and ps) to the same memory location and string.

To get a copy of a string, you need to do more. First, you need to allocate memory to hold the string. You can do this by declaring a second array or by using **new**. The second approach enables you to custom fit the storage to the string:

```
ps = new char[strlen(animal) + 1]; // get new storage
```

The string `"fox"` doesn't completely fill the `animal` array, so we're wasting space. This bit of code uses `strlen()` to find the length of the string; it adds 1 to get the length including the null character. Then, the program uses **new** to allocate just enough space to hold the string.

Next, you need a way to copy a string from the `animal` array to the newly allocated space. It doesn't work to assign `animal` to `ps`, for that just changes the address stored in `ps` and thus loses the only way the program had to access the newly allocated memory. Instead, you need to use the `strcpy()` library function:

```
strcpy(ps, animal);              // copy string to new storage
```

The `strcpy()` function takes two arguments. The first is the destination address, and the second is the address of the string to be copied. It's up to you to make certain that the destination really is allocated and has sufficient space to hold the copy. That's accomplished here by using `strlen()` to find the correct size and using **new** to get free memory.

Note that by using `strcpy()` and **new**, we get two separate copies of `"fox"`:

```
fox at 0x0065fd30
fox at 0x004301c8
```

Also note that **new** located the new storage at a memory location quite distant from that of the array `animal`.

Often you encounter the need to place a string into an array. Use the = operator when you initialize an array; otherwise, use `strcpy()` or `strncpy()`. You've seen the `strcpy()` function; it works like this:

```
char food[20] = "carrots"; // initialization
strcpy(food, "flan");      // otherwise
```

Note that something like

```
strcpy(food, "a picnic basket filled with many goodies");
```

can cause problems because the **food** array is smaller than the string. In this case, the function copies the rest of the string into the memory bytes immediately following the array, which can overwrite other memory your program is using. To avoid that problem, use `strncpy()` instead. It takes a third argument: the maximum number of characters to be copied. Be aware, however, that if this function runs out of space before it reaches the end of the string, it doesn't add the null character. Thus, you should use the function like this:

```
strncpy(food, "a picnic basket filled with many goodies", 19);
food[19] = '\0';
```

This copies up to 19 characters into the array and then sets the last element to the null character. If the string is shorter than 19 characters, `strncpy()` adds a null character earlier to mark the true end of the string.

Remember

Use `strcpy()` or `strncpy()`, not the assignment operator, to assign a string to an array.

Using new to Create Dynamic Structures

You've seen how it can be advantageous to create arrays during runtime rather than compile time. The same holds true for structures. You need to allocate space for only as many structures as a program needs during a particular run. Again, the **new** operator is the tool to use. With it, you can create dynamic structures. Again, "dynamic" means the memory is allocated during runtime, not during compilation. Incidentally, because classes are much like structures, you are able to use the techniques you learn for structures with classes, too.

Using **new** with structures has two parts: creating the structure and accessing its members. To create a structure, use the structure type with **new**. For example, to create an unnamed structure of the `inflatable` type and assign its address to a suitable pointer, you can do the following:

```
inflatable * ps = new inflatable;
```

This assigns to **ps** the address of a chunk of free memory large enough to hold a structure of the `inflatable` type. Note that the syntax is exactly the same as it is for C++'s built-in types.

The tricky part is accessing members. When you create a dynamic structure, you can't use the dot membership operator with the structure name, because the structure has no name. All you have is its address. C++ provides an operator just for this situation: the arrow membership operator (`->`). This operator, formed by typing a hyphen and then a greater-than symbol, does for pointers to structures what the dot operator does for structure names. For example, if **ps** points to a type `inflatable` structure, then **ps->price** is the **price** member of the pointed-to structure. (See Figure 4.11.)

FIGURE 4.11

Identifying structure members.

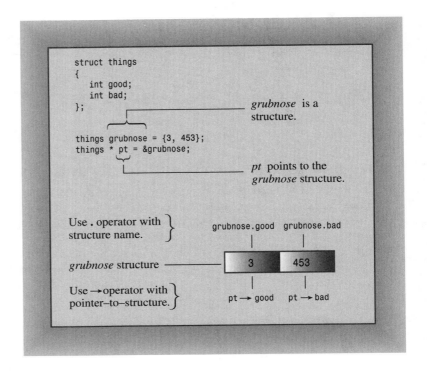

```
struct things
{
    int good;
    int bad;
};                                      grubnose is a
                                        structure.

things grubnose = {3, 453};
things * pt = &grubnose;
                                        pt points to the
                                        grubnose structure.


Use . operator with          grubnose.good  grubnose.bad
structure name.

grubnose structure                        3         453

Use → operator with
pointer–to–structure.          pt → good    pt → bad
```

Remember

Sometimes new users become confused about when to use the dot operator and when to use the arrow operator to specify a structure member. The rule is simple. If the structure identifier is the name of a structure, use the dot operator. If the identifier is a pointer to the structure, use the arrow operator.

A second, uglier approach is to realize that if **ps** is a pointer to a structure, then ***ps** represents the pointed-to value—the structure itself. Then, because ***ps** is a structure, **(*ps).price** is the **price** member of the structure. C++'s operator precedence rules require that you use parentheses in this construction.

Listing 4.16 uses **new** to create an unnamed structure and demonstrates both pointer notations for accessing structure members.

LISTING 4.16   newstrct.cpp

```cpp
// newstrct.cpp _ using new with a structure
#include <iostream>
using namespace std;
struct inflatable   // structure template
{
```

LISTING 4.16 Continued

```
        char name[20];
        float volume;
        double price;
};
int main()
{
        inflatable * ps = new inflatable; // allot structure space
        cout << "Enter name of inflatable item: ";
        cin.get(ps->name, 20);          // method 1 for member access
        cout << "Enter volume in cubic feet: ";
        cin >> (*ps).volume;            // method 2 for member access
        cout << "Enter price: $";
        cin >> ps->price;
        cout << "Name: " << (*ps).name << "\n";   // method 2
        cout << "Volume: " << ps->volume << " cubic feet\n";
        cout << "Price: $" << ps->price << "\n"; // method 1
        delete ps; //free up allocated memory
        return 0;
}
```

Here is a sample run:

```
Enter name of inflatable item: Fabulous Frodo
Enter volume in cubic feet: 1.4
Enter price: $17.99
Name: Fabulous Frodo
Volume: 1.4 cubic feet
Price: $17.99
```

A new and delete Example

Let's look at an example using new and delete to manage storing string input from the keyboard. Listing 4.17 defines a function that returns a pointer to an input string. This function reads the input into a large temporary array and then uses new [] to create a chunk of memory sized to fit to the input string. Then, the function returns the pointer to the block. This approach could conserve a lot of memory for programs that read in a large number of strings.

Suppose your program has to read 1000 strings and that the largest string might be 79 characters long, but most of the strings are much shorter. If you used char arrays to hold the strings, you'd need 1000 arrays of 80 characters each. That's 80,000 bytes, and much of that block of memory would wind up unused. Alternatively, you could create an array of 1000 pointers to char and then use new to allocate only the amount of memory needed for each string. That could save tens of thousands of bytes. Instead of having to use a large array for every string, you fit the memory to the input. Even better, you also could use new to find space to store only as many pointers as needed. Well, that's a little too ambitious for right now. Even using an array of 1000 pointers is a little too ambitious for right now, but Listing 4.17 illustrates some of the technique. Also, just to illustrate how delete works, the program uses it to free memory for reuse.

LISTING 4.17   delete.cpp

```cpp
// delete.cpp _ using the delete operator
#include <iostream>
#include <cstring>        // or string.h
using namespace std;
char * getname(void);    // function prototype
int main()
{
    char * name;         // create pointer but no storage

    name = getname();    // assign address of string to name
    cout << name << " at " << (int *) name << "\n";
    delete [] name;      // memory freed

    name = getname();    // reuse freed memory
    cout << name << " at " << (int *) name << "\n";
    delete [] name;      // memory freed again
    return 0;
}

char * getname()         // return pointer to new string
{
    char temp[80];       // temporary storage
    cout << "Enter last name: ";
    cin >> temp;
    char * pn = new char[strlen(temp) + 1];
    strcpy(pn, temp);    // copy string into smaller space

    return pn;           // temp lost when function ends
}
```

Here is a sample run:

```
Enter last name: Fredeldumpkin
Fredeldumpkin at 0x004326b8
Enter last name: Pook
Pook at 0x004301c8
```

Program Notes

First, consider the function `getname()`. It uses `cin` to place an input word into the `temp` array. Next, it uses `new` to allocate new memory to hold the word. Including the null character, the program needs `strlen(temp) + 1` characters to store the string, so that's the value given to `new`. After the space becomes available, `getname()` uses the standard library function `strcpy()` to copy the string from `temp` to the new block. The function doesn't check to see if the string fits or not, but `getname()` covers that by requesting the right number of bytes with `new`. Finally, the function returns `pn`, the address of the string copy.

In `main()`, the return value (the address) is assigned to the pointer `name`. This pointer is defined in `main()`, but it points to the block of memory allocated in the `getname()` function. The program then prints the string and the address of the string.

Next, after it frees the block pointed to by `name`, `main()` calls `getname()` a second time. C++ doesn't guarantee that newly freed memory is the first to be chosen the next time `new` is used, and in this sample run, it isn't.

Note in this example that `getname()` allocates memory and `main()` frees it. It's usually not a good idea to put `new` and `delete` in separate functions because that makes it easier to forget to use `delete`. But this example does separate `new` from `delete` just to show that it is possible.

To appreciate some of the more subtle aspects of this program, you should know a little more about how C++ handles memory. So let's preview some material that's covered more fully in Chapter 9.

Automatic Storage, Static Storage, and Dynamic Storage

C++ has three ways of managing memory for data, depending on the method used to allocate memory: *automatic storage, static storage*, and *dynamic storage*, sometimes called the *free store* or *heap*. Data objects allocated in these three ways differ from each other in how long they remain in existence. We'll take a quick look at each type.

Automatic Variables

Ordinary variables defined inside a function are called *automatic variables*. They come into existence automatically when the function containing them is invoked, and they expire when the function terminates. For example, the `temp` array in Listing 4.17 exists only while the `getname()` function is active. When program control returns to `main()`, the memory used for `temp` is freed automatically. If `getname()` had returned the address of `temp`, the `name` pointer in `main()` would have been left pointing to a memory location that soon would be reused. That's one reason we had to use `new` in `getname()`.

Actually, automatic values are local to the block containing them. A block is a section of code enclosed between braces. So far, all our blocks have been entire functions. But, as you'll see in the next chapter, you can have blocks within a function. If you define a variable inside one of those blocks, it exists only while the program is executing statements inside the block.

Static Storage

Static storage is storage that exists throughout the execution of an entire program. There are two ways to make a variable static. One is to define it externally, outside a function. The other is to use the keyword `static` when declaring a variable:

```
static double fee = 56.50;
```

Under K&R C, you only can initialize static arrays and structures, whereas C++ Release 2.0 (and later) and ANSI C allow you to initialize automatic arrays and structures, too. However, as some of you may have discovered, some C++ implementations do not yet implement initialization for automatic arrays and structures.

Chapter 9 takes up static storage in more detail. The main point here about automatic and static storage is that these methods rigidly define the lifetime of a variable. Either the variable exists for the entire duration of a program (the static variable) or else it exists only while a particular function is being executed (the automatic variable).

Dynamic Storage

The `new` and `delete` operators, however, provide a more flexible approach. They manage a pool of memory, which C++ refers to as the free store. This pool is separate from the memory used for static and automatic variables. As Listing 4.17 shows, `new` and `delete` enable you to allocate memory in one function and free it in another. Thus, the lifetime of the data is not tied arbitrarily to the life of the program or the life of a function. Using `new` and `delete` together gives you much more control over how a program uses memory than does using ordinary variables.

Real World Note: Stacks, Heaps, and Memory Leaks

What happens if you *don't* call `delete` after creating a variable on the free store (or heap) with the `new` operator? The variable or construct dynamically allocated on the free store continues to persist if `delete` is not called, even though the memory that contains your pointer has been freed due to rules of scope and object lifetime. In essence, you have no way to access your construct on the free store, because the pointer to the memory that contains it is gone. You have now created a *memory leak*. Memory that has been leaked remains unusable through the life of your program; it's been allocated but can't be de-allocated. In extreme (though not uncommon) cases, memory leaks can be so severe they use up all the memory available to the application, causing it to crash with an out-of-memory error. Additionally, these leaks may negatively affect some operating systems or other applications running in the same memory space, causing them, in turn, to fail.

Memory leaks are created by even the best programmers and software companies. To avoid them, it's best to get into the habit of joining your new and delete operators immediately, planning for and entering the deletion of your construct as soon as you dynamically allocate it on the free store.

Note

Pointers are among the most powerful of C++ tools. They also are the most dangerous, for they permit computer-unfriendly actions, such as using an uninitialized pointer to access memory or attempting to free the same memory block twice. Furthermore, until practice makes you used to pointer notation and pointer concepts, pointers can be confusing. This book returns to pointers several more times in the hopes that each exposure will make you more comfortable with them.

Summary

The array, the structure, and the pointer are three C++ compound types. The array can hold several values all of the same type in a single data object. By using an index, or subscript, you can access the individual elements in an array.

The structure can hold several values of different types in a single data object, and you can use the membership operator (.) to access individual members. The first step in using structures is creating a structure template defining what members the structure holds. The name, or tag, for this template then becomes a new type identifier. You then can declare structure variables of that type.

A union can hold a single value, but it can be of a variety of types, with the member name indicating which mode is being used.

Pointers are variables designed to hold addresses. We say a pointer points to the address it holds. The pointer declaration always states to what type of object a pointer points. Applying the dereferencing operator (*) to a pointer yields the value at the location to which the pointer points.

A string is a series of characters terminated by a null character. A string can be represented by a quoted string constant, in which case the null character is implicitly understood. You can store a string in an array of `char`, and you can represent a string by a pointer-to-`char` that is initialized to point to the string. The `strlen()` function returns the length of a string, not counting the null character. The `strcpy()` function copies a string from one location to another. When using these functions, include the `cstring` or the `string.h` header file.

The `new` operator lets you request memory for a data object while a program is running. The operator returns the address of the memory it obtains, and you can assign that address to a pointer. The only means to access that memory is to use the pointer. If the data object is a simple variable, you can use the dereferencing operator (*) to indicate a value. If the data object is an array, you can use the pointer as if it were an array name to access the elements. If the data object is a structure, you can use the pointer dereferencing operator (->) to access structure members.

Pointers and arrays are closely connected. If `ar` is an array name, then the expression `ar[i]` is interpreted as `*(ar + i)`, with the array name interpreted as the address of the first element of the array. Thus, the array name plays the same role as a pointer. In turn, you can use a pointer name with array notation to access elements in an array allocated by `new`.

The `new` and `delete` operators let you explicitly control when data objects are allocated and when they are returned to the memory pool. Automatic variables, which are those declared within a function, and static variables, which are defined outside a function or with the keyword static, are less flexible. An automatic variable comes into being when the block containing it (typically a function definition) is entered, and it expires when the block is left. A static variable persists for the duration of a program.

Review Questions

1. How would you declare each of the following?

    a. `actors` is an array of 30 `char`.

    b. `betsie` is an array of 100 `short`.

     c. `chuck` is an array of 13 `float`.

     d. `dipsea` is an array of 64 `long double`.

2. Declare an array of five `int`s and initialize it to the first five odd positive integers.

3. Write a statement that assigns the sum of the first and last elements of the array in question 2 to the variable `even`.

4. Write a statement that displays the value of the second element in the `float` array `ideas`.

5. Declare an array of `char` and initialize it to the string `"cheeseburger"`.

6. Devise a structure declaration that describes a fish. The structure should include the kind, the weight in whole ounces, and the length in fractional inches.

7. Declare a variable of the type defined in question 6 and initialize it.

8. Use `enum` to define a type called `Response` with the possible values of `Yes`, `No`, and `Maybe`. `Yes` should be 1, `No` should be 0, and `Maybe` should be 2.

9. Suppose `ted` is a `double` variable. Declare a pointer that points to `ted` and use the pointer to display `ted`'s value.

10. Suppose `treacle` is an array of 10 `float`s. Declare a pointer that points to the first element of `treacle` and use the pointer to display the first and last elements of the array.

11. Write a code fragment that asks the user to enter a positive integer and then creates a dynamic array of that many `int`s.

12. Is the following valid code? If so, what does it print?

```
cout << (int *) "Home of the jolly bytes";
```

13. Write a code fragment that dynamically allocates a structure of the type described in question 6 and then reads a value for the kind member of the structure.

14. Listing 4.6 illustrates a problem with the following numeric input with line-oriented string input. How would replacing

```
cin.getline(address,80);
```

with

```
cin >> address;
```

affect the working of this program?

Programming Exercises

1. Write a C++ program that requests and displays information as shown in the following example of output. Note that the program should be able to accept first names of more than one word. Also note that the program adjusts the grade downward, that is, up one

letter. Assume the user requests an A, B, or C so that you don't have to worry about the gap between a D and an F.

```
What is your first name? Betty Sue
What is your last name? Yew
What letter grade do you deserve? B
What is your age? 22
Name: Yew, Betty Sue
Grade: C
Age: 22
```

2. The `CandyBar` structure contains three members. The first member holds the brand name of a candy bar. The second member holds the weight (which may have a fractional part) of the candy bar, and the third member holds the number of calories (an integer value) in the candy bar. Write a program that declares such a structure and creates a `CandyBar` variable called `snack`, initializing its members to `"Mocha Munch"`, `2.3`, and `350`, respectively. The initialization should be part of the declaration for `snack`. Finally, the program should display the contents of the `snack` variable.

3. The `CandyBar` structure contains three members, as described in Programming Exercise 2. Write a program that creates an array of three `CandyBar` structures, initializes them to values of your choice, and then displays the contents of each structure.

4. William Wingate runs a pizza-analysis service. For each pizza, he needs to record the following information:

    • The name of the pizza company, which can consist of more than one word

    • The diameter of the pizza

    • The weight of the pizza

   Devise a structure that can hold this information and write a program using a structure variable of that type. The program should ask the user to enter each of the preceding items of information, and then the program should display that information. Use `cin` (or its methods) and `cout`.

5. Do programming exercise 4, but use `new` to allocate a structure instead of declaring a structure variable. Also, have the program request the pizza diameter before it requests the pizza company name.

6. Do programming exercise 3, but, instead of declaring an array of three `CandyBar` structures, use `new` to allocate the array dynamically.

CHAPTER 5

LOOPS AND RELATIONAL EXPRESSIONS

In this chapter you learn

- The `for` loop
- Expressions and statements
- The increment and decrement operators: `++` and `--`
- Combination assignment operators
- Compound statements (blocks)
- The comma operator
- Relational operators: `>`, `>=`, `==`, `<=`, `<`, and `!=`

- The `while` loop
- The `typedef` facility
- The `do while` loop
- The `get()` character input method
- The end-of-file condition
- Nested loops and two-dimensional arrays

Computers do more than store data. They analyze, consolidate, rearrange, extract, modify, extrapolate, synthesize, and otherwise manipulate data. Sometimes they even distort and trash data, but we'll try to steer clear of that kind of behavior. To perform their manipulative miracles, programs need tools for performing repetitive actions and for making decisions. C++, of course, provides such tools. Indeed, it uses the same `for` loops, `while` loops, `do while` loops, `if` statements, and `switch` statements that regular C employs, so if you know C, you can zip through this and the next chapter. (But don't zip too fast—you don't want to miss how `cin` handles character input!) These various program control statements often use relational expressions and logical expressions to govern their behavior. This chapter discusses loops and relational expressions, and the next chapter follows up with branching statements and logical expressions.

Introducing the `for` Loop

Circumstances often call upon a program to perform repetitive tasks, such as adding together the elements of an array one by one or printing some paean to productivity twenty times. The C++ `for` loop makes such tasks easy to do. Let's look at a loop in Listing 5.1, see what it does, and then discuss how it works.

LISTING 5.1   `forloop.cpp`

```cpp
// forloop.cpp -- introducing the for loop
#include <iostream>
using namespace std;
int main()
{
    int i;  // create a counter
    //   initialize; test ; update
    for (i = 0; i < 5; i++)
        cout << "C++ knows loops.\n";
    cout << "C++ knows when to stop.\n";
    return 0;
}
```

Here is the output:

```
C++ knows loops.
C++ knows loops.
C++ knows loops.
C++ knows loops.
C++ knows loops.
C++ knows when to stop.
```

This loop begins by setting the integer `i` to 0:

```
i = 0
```

This is the *loop initialization* part of the loop. Then, in the *loop test*, the program tests to see if `i` is less than 5:

```
i < 5
```

If so, the program executes the following statement, which is termed the *loop body*:

```
cout << "C++ knows loops.\n";
```

Then, the program uses the *loop update* part of the loop to increase `i` by 1:

```
i++
```

This uses the `++` operator, called the *increment operator*. It increments the value of its operand by 1. (The increment operator is not restricted to `for` loops. For example, you can use

```
i++;
```

instead of

```
i = i + 1;
```

as a statement in a program.) Incrementing `i` completes the first cycle of the loop.

Next, the loop begins a new cycle by comparing the new `i` value with 5. Because the new value (1) also is less than 5, the loop prints another line and then finishes by incrementing `i` again. That sets the stage for a fresh cycle of testing, executing a statement, and updating the value of `i`. The process continues until the loop updates `i` to 5. Then, the next test fails, and the program moves on to the next statement after the loop.

`for` Loop Parts

A `for` loop, then, provides a step-by-step recipe for performing repeated actions. Let's take a more detailed look at how it's set up. The usual parts of a `for` loop handle these steps:

- Setting a value initially

- Performing a test to see whether the loop should continue

- Executing the loop actions

- Updating value(s) used for the test

The C++ loop design positions these elements so that you can spot them at a glance. The initialization, test, and update actions constitute a three-part control section enclosed in parentheses. Each part is an expression, and semicolons separate the expressions from each other. The statement following the control section is called the *body* of the loop, and it is executed as long as the test expression remains true:

```
for (initialization; test-expression; update-expression)
    body
```

C++ syntax counts a complete `for` statement as a single statement, even though it can incorporate one or more statements in the body portion. (Having more than one statement requires using a compound statement, or block, as discussed later in this chapter.)

The loop performs initialization just once. Typically, programs use this expression to set a variable to a starting value and then use the variable to count loop cycles.

The *test-expression* determines whether the loop body gets executed. Typically, this expression is a relational expression, that is, one that compares two values. Our example compares the value of `i` to 5, checking to see if `i` is less than 5. If the comparison is true, the program executes the loop body. Actually, C++ doesn't limit *test-expression* to true-false comparisons. You can use any expression, and C++ will typecast it to type `bool`. Thus, an expression with a value of 0 is converted to the `bool` value `false`, and the loop terminates. If the expression evaluates to nonzero, it is typecast to the `bool` value `true`, and the loop continues. Listing 5.2 demonstrates this by using the expression `i` as the test condition. (In the update section, `i--` is similar to `i++` except that it decreases the value of `i` by 1 each time it's used.)

LISTING 5.2   num_test.cpp

```
// num_test.cpp -- use numeric test in for loop
#include <iostream>
using namespace std;
int main()
{
    cout << "Enter the starting countdown value: ";
    int limit;
    cin >> limit;
    int i;
    for (i = limit; i; i--)      // quits when i is 0
        cout << "i = " << i << "\n";
    cout << "Done now that i = " << i << "\n";
    return 0;
}
```

Here is the output:

```
Enter the starting countdown value: 4
i = 4
i = 3
i = 2
i = 1
Done now that i = 0
```

Note that the loop terminates when i reaches 0.

How do relational expressions, such as i < 5, fit into this framework of terminating a loop with a 0 value? Before the **bool** type was introduced, relational expressions evaluated to 1 if true and 0 if false. Thus, the value of the expression 3 < 5 was 1 and the value of 5 < 5 was 0. Now that C++ has added the **bool** type, however, relational expressions evaluate to the **bool** literals **true** and **false** instead of 1 and 0. This change doesn't lead to incompatibilities, however, for a C++ program converts **true** and **false** to 1 and 0 where integer values are expected, and it converts 0 to **false** and nonzero to **true** where **bool** values are expected.

The **for** loop is an entry-condition loop. This means the test expression is evaluated *before* each loop cycle. The loop never executes the loop body when the test expression is false. For example, suppose you rerun the program in Listing 5.2 but give 0 as a starting value. Because the test condition fails the very first time it's evaluated, the loop body never gets executed:

```
Enter the starting countdown value: 0
Done now that i = 0
```

This look-before-you-loop attitude can help keep a program out of trouble.

The *update-expression* is evaluated at the end of the loop, after the body has been executed. Typically, it's used to increase or decrease the value of the variable keeping track of the number of loop cycles. However, it can be any valid C++ expression, as can the other control expressions. This makes the **for** loop capable of much more than simply counting from 0 to 5, the way the first loop example did. You'll see some examples later.

The **for** loop body consists of a single statement, but you'll soon learn how to stretch that rule. Figure 5.1 summarizes the **for** loop design.

FIGURE 5.1

The **for** loop.

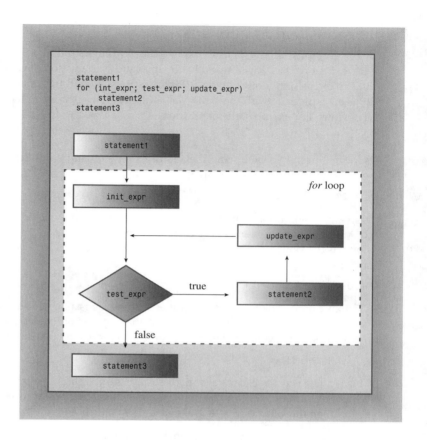

```
statement1
for (int_expr; test_expr; update_expr)
    statement2
statement3
```

A **for** statement looks something like a function call because it uses a name followed by paired parentheses. However, **for**'s status as a C++ keyword prevents the compiler from thinking **for** is a function. It also prevents you from naming a function **for**.

Tip

Common C++ style is to place a space between **for** and the following parentheses and to omit space between a function name and the following parentheses:

```
for (int i = 6; i < 10; i++)
    smart_function(i);
```

Other control statements, such as **if** and **while**, are treated similarly to **for**. This serves to reinforce visually the distinction between a control statement and a function call. Also, common practice is to indent the body of a **for** statement to make it stand out visually.

Expressions and Statements

A `for` control section uses three expressions. Within its self-imposed limits of syntax, C++ is a very expressive language. Any value or any valid combination of values and operators constitute an expression. For example, 10 is an expression with the value 10 (no surprise), and 28 * 20 is an expression with the value 560. In C++, every expression has a value. Often the value is obvious. For example, the expression

```
22 + 27
```

is formed from two values and the addition operator, and it has the value 49. Sometimes the value is less obvious. For example,

```
x = 20
```

is an expression because it's formed from two values and the assignment operator. C++ defines the value of an assignment expression to be the value of the member on the left, so the expression has the value 20. The fact that assignment expressions have values permits statements such as the following:

```
maids = (cooks = 4) + 3;
```

The expression `cooks = 4` has the value 4, so `maids` is assigned the value 7. However, just because C++ permits this behavior doesn't mean you should encourage it. But the same rule that makes this peculiar statement possible also makes the following useful statement possible:

```
x = y = z = 0;
```

This is a fast way to set several variables to the same value. The precedence table (Appendix D, "Operator Precedence") reveals that assignment associates right-to-left, so first 0 is assigned to `z`, and then the value of `z = 0` is assigned to `y`, and so on.

Finally, as mentioned before, relational expressions such as `x < y` evaluate to the `bool` values `true` or `false`. The short program in Listing 5.3 illustrates some points about expression values. The `<<` operator has higher precedence than the operators used in the expressions, so the code uses parentheses to enforce the correct order.

LISTING 5.3   express.cpp

```cpp
// express.cpp -- values of expressions
#include <iostream>
using namespace std;
int main()
{
    int x;

    cout << "The expression x = 100 has the value ";
    cout << (x = 100) << "\n";
    cout << "Now x = " << x << "\n";
    cout << "The expression x < 3 has the value ";
    cout << (x < 3) << "\n";
    cout << "The expression x > 3 has the value ";
```

LISTING 5.3   Continued

```
    cout << (x > 3) << "\n";
    cout.setf(ios_base::boolalpha);    //a newer C++ feature
    cout << "The expression x < 3 has the value ";
    cout << (x < 3) << "\n";
    cout << "The expression x > 3 has the value ";
    cout << (x > 3) << "\n";
    return 0;
}
```

Compatibility Note

Older implementations of C++ may require using `ios::boolalpha` instead of `ios_base::boolalpha` as the argument for `cout.setf()`. Yet older implementations might not recognize either form.

Here is the output:

```
The expression x = 100 has the value 100
Now x = 100
The expression x < 3 has the value 0
The expression x > 3 has the value 1
The expression x < 3 has the value false
The expression x > 3 has the value true
```

Normally, `cout` converts `bool` values to `int` before displaying them, but the `cout.setf(ios::boolalpha)` function call sets a flag that instructs `cout` to display the words `true` and `false` instead of `1` and `0`.

Remember

A C++ expression is a value or a combination of values and operators, and every C++ expression has a value.

To evaluate the expression `x = 100`, C++ must assign the value 100 to `x`. When the very act of evaluating an expression changes the value of data in memory, we say the evaluation has a *side effect*. Thus, evaluating an assignment expression has the side effect of changing the assignee's value. You might think of assignment as the intended effect, but from the standpoint of how C++ is constructed, evaluating the expression is the primary effect. Not all expressions have side effects. For example, evaluating `x + 15` calculates a new value, but it doesn't change the value of `x`. But evaluating `++x + 15` does have a side effect, because it involves incrementing `x`.

From expression to statement is a short step; just add a semicolon. Thus

```
age = 100
```

is an expression, whereas

```
age = 100;
```

is a statement. Any expression can become a statement if you add a semicolon, but the result might not make programming sense. For example, if `rodents` is a variable, then

```
rodents + 6;      // valid, but useless, statement
```

is a valid C++ statement. The compiler allows it, but the statement doesn't accomplish anything useful. The program merely calculates the sum, does nothing with it, and goes on to the next statement. (A smart compiler might even skip the statement.)

Nonexpressions and Statements

Some concepts, such as knowing the structure of a `for` loop, are crucial to understanding C++. But there also are relatively minor aspects of syntax that suddenly can bedevil you just when you think you understand the language. We'll look at a couple of them now.

Although it is true that adding a semicolon to any expression makes it a statement, the reverse is not true. That is, removing a semicolon from a statement does not necessarily convert it to an expression. Of the kinds of statements we've used so far, return statements, declaration statements, and `for` statements don't fit the *statement = expression + semicolon* mold. For example, although

```
int toad;
```

is a statement, the fragment `int toad` is not an expression and does not have a value. This makes code such as the following invalid:

```
eggs = int toad * 1000;   // invalid, not an expression
cin >> int toad;          // can't combine declaration with cin
```

Similarly, you can't assign a `for` loop to a variable:

```
int fx = for (int i = 0; i< 4; i++)
    cout >> i;   // not possible
```

Here the `for` loop is not an expression, so it has no value and you can't assign it.

Bending the Rules

C++ adds a feature to C loops that requires some artful adjustments to the `for` loop syntax. This was the original syntax:

```
for (expression; expression; expression)
    statement
```

In particular, the control section of a `for` structure consisted of three expressions, as defined earlier, separated by semicolons. C++ loops allow you do to things like the following, however:

```
for (int i = 0; i < 5; i++)
```

That is, you can declare a variable in the initialization area of a `for` loop. This can be convenient, but it doesn't fit the original syntax because a declaration is not an expression. This lawless behavior originally was accommodated by defining a new kind of expression, the *declaration-statement expression*, which was a declaration stripped of the semicolon, and which could appear only in a `for` statement. That adjustment has been dropped, however. Instead, the syntax for the `for` statement has been modified to the following:

```
for (for-init-statement condition; expression)
    statement
```

At first glance, this looks odd because there is just one semicolon instead of two. But that's okay because the *for-init-statement* is identified as a statement, and a statement has its own semicolon. As for the *for-init-statement*, it's identified as either an expression-statement or a declaration. This syntax rule replaces an expression followed by a semicolon with a statement, which has its own semicolon. What this boils down to is that C++ program-mers want to be able to declare and initialize a variable in a `for` loop initialization, and they'll do whatever is necessary to C++ syntax and to the English language to make it possible.

There's a practical aspect to declaring a variable in a *for-init-statement* about which you should know. Such a variable exists only within the `for` statement. That is, after the program leaves the loop, the variable is eliminated:

```
for (int i = 0; i < 5; i++)
    cout << "C++ knows loops.\n";
cout << i << endl;  // oops! i no longer defined
```

Another thing you should know is that some C++ implementations follow an earlier rule and treat the preceding loop as if `i` were declared *before* the loop, thus making it available after the loop terminates. Use of this new option for declaring a variable in a `for` loop initialization results, at least at this time, in different behaviors on different systems.

Caution

At the time of writing, not all compilers have caught up with the current rule that a variable declared in a `for` loop control section expires when the loop terminates.

Back to the `for` Loop

Let's be a bit more ambitious with loops. Listing 5.4 uses a loop to calculate and store the first 16 factorials. Factorials, which are handy for computing odds, are calculated the following way. Zero factorial, written as 0!, is defined to be 1. Then, 1! is 1 * 0!, or 1. Next, 2! is 2 * 1!, or 2. Then, 3! is 3 * 2!, or 6, and so on, with the factorial of each integer being the product of that integer with the preceding factorial. (One of the pianist Victor Borge's best-known mono-logues features phonetic punctuation, in which the exclamation mark is pronounced some-thing like phffft pptz, with a moist accent. However, in this case, "!" is pronounced "factorial.") The program uses one loop to calculate the values of successive factorials, storing them in an array. Then, it uses a second loop to display the results. Also, the program introduces the use of external declarations for values.

LISTING 5.4   formore.cpp

```cpp
// formore.cpp -- more looping with for
#include <iostream>
using namespace std;
const int ArSize = 16;      // example of external declaration
int main()
{
    double factorials[ArSize];
    factorials[1] = factorials[0] = 1.0;
    int i;
    for (i = 2; i < ArSize; i++)
        factorials[i] = i * factorials[i-1];
    for (i = 0; i < ArSize; i++)
        cout << i << "! = " << factorials[i] << "\n";
    return 0;
}
```

Here is the output:

```
0! = 1
1! = 1
2! = 2
3! = 6
4! = 24
5! = 120
6! = 720
7! = 5040
8! = 40320
9! = 362880
10! = 3.6288e+006
11! = 3.99168e+007
12! = 4.79002e+008
13! = 6.22702e+009
14! = 8.71783e+010
15! = 1.30767e+012
```

Factorials get big fast!

Program Notes

The program creates an array to hold the factorial values. Element 0 is 0!, element 1 is 1!, and so on. Because the first two factorials equal 1, the program sets the first two elements of the **factorials** array to 1.0. (Remember, the first element of an array has an index value of 0.) After that, the program uses a loop to set each factorial to the product of the index with the previous factorial. The loop illustrates that you can use the loop counter as a variable in the body of the loop.

The program demonstrates how the **for** loop works hand in hand with arrays by providing a convenient means to access each array member in turn. Also, formore.cpp uses **const** to create a symbolic representation (**ArSize**) for the array size. Then, it uses **ArSize** wherever the array size comes into play, such as in the array definition and in the limits for the loops handling the array. Now, if you wish to extend the program to, say, 20 factorials, you just have to set ArSize to 20 in the program and recompile. By using a symbolic constant, you avoid having to change every occurrence of 16 to 20 individually.

Tip
It's usually a good idea to define a const value to represent the number of elements in an array. Use the const value in the array declaration and in all other references to the array size, such as in a for loop.

The limit i < ArSize expression reflects the fact that subscripts for an array with ArSize elements run from 0 to ArSize - 1, so the array index should stop 1 short of ArSize. You could use the test i <= ArSize - 1 instead, but it looks awkward in comparison.

One program sidelight is that it declares the const int variable ArSize outside the body of main(). As the end of Chapter 4, "Compound Types," mentions, this makes ArSize external data. The two consequences of declaring ArSize in this fashion are that ArSize exists for the duration of the program and that all functions in the program file can use it. In this particular case, the program has just one function, so declaring ArSize externally has little practical effect. But multifunction programs often benefit from sharing external constants, so we'll practice using them now.

Changing the Step Size

So far the loop examples have increased or decreased the loop counter by 1 each cycle. You can change that by changing the update expression. The program in Listing 5.5, for example, increases the loop counter by a user-selected step size. Rather than use i++ as the update expression, it uses the expression i = i + by, where by is the user-selected step size.

LISTING 5.5   bigstep.cpp

```
// bigstep.cpp -- count as directed
#include <iostream>
using namespace std;
int main()
{
    cout << "Enter an integer: ";
    int by;
    cin >> by;
    cout << "Counting by " << by << "s:\n";
    for (int i = 0; i < 100; i = i + by)
        cout << i << "\n";
    return 0;
}
```

Here is a sample run:

```
Enter an integer: 17
Counting by 17s:
```

```
0
17
34
51
68
85
```

When i reaches the value 102, the loop quits. The main point here is that the update expression can be any valid expression. For example, if you want to square i and add **10** each cycle, you can use i = i * i + **10**.

Inside Strings with the `for` Loop

The `for` loop provides a direct way to access each character in a string in turn. Listing 5.6, for example, enables you to enter a string and then displays the string character-by-character in reverse order. The `strlen()` yields the number of characters in the string; the loop uses that value in its initializing expression to set i to the index of the last character in the string, not counting the null character. To count backward, the program uses the decrement operator (--) to decrease the array subscript by 1 each loop. Also, Listing 5.6 uses the greater-than or equal-to relational operator (>=) to test whether the loop has reached the first element. We'll summarize all the relational operators soon.

LISTING 5.6   forstr1.cpp

```cpp
// forstr1.cpp -- using for with a string
#include <iostream>
#include <cstring>
using namespace std;
const int ArSize = 20;
int main()
{
    cout << "Enter a word: ";
    char word[ArSize];
    cin >> word;

    // display letters in reverse order
    for (int i = strlen(word) - 1; i >= 0; i—)
        cout << word[i];
    cout << "\nBye.\n";
    return 0;
}
```

Compatibility Note

You might have to use `string.h` instead of `cstring` if your implementation has not yet added the new header files.

Here is a sample run:

```
Enter a word: animal
lamina
Bye.
```

Yes, the program succeeds in printing animal backward; choosing animal as a test word more clearly illustrates the effect of this program than choosing, say, redder or stats.

The Increment (++) and Decrement (- -) Operators

C++ features several operators that frequently are used in loops, so let's take a little time to examine them now. You've already seen two: the increment operator (++), which inspired the name C++, and the decrement operator (- -). These perform two exceedingly common loop operations: increasing or decreasing a loop counter by 1. However, there's more to their story than you've seen to date. Each operator comes in two varieties. The *prefix* version comes before the operand, as in ++x. The *postfix* version comes after the operand, as in x++. The two versions have the same effect upon the operand, but they differ in when they take place. It's like getting paid for mowing the lawn in advance or afterward; both methods have the same final effect on your wallet, but they differ in when the money gets added. Listing 5.7 demonstrates this difference for the increment operator.

LISTING 5.7   plus_one.cpp

```cpp
// plus_one.cpp -- the increment operator
#include <iostream>
using namespace std;
int main()
{
    int a = 20;
    int b = 20;

    cout << "a   = " << a << ":    b = " << b << "\n";
    cout << "a++ = " << a++ << ": ++b = " << ++b << "\n";
    cout << "a   = " << a << ":    b = " << b << "\n";
    return 0;
}
```

Here is the output:

```
a     = 20:    b = 20
a++   = 20: ++b = 21
a     = 21:    b = 21
```

Roughly speaking, the notation a++ means "use the current value of a in evaluating an expression, and then increment the value of a." Similarly, the notation ++b means "first increment the value of b, and then use the new value in evaluating the expression." For example, we have the following relationships:

```cpp
int x = 5;
int y = ++x;      // change x, then assign to y
                  // y is 6, x is 6
```

```
int z = 5;
int y = z++;        // assign to y, then change z
                    // y is 5, z is 6
```

The increment and decrement operators are a concise, convenient way to handle the common task of increasing or decreasing values by 1. You can use them with pointers as well as with basic variables. Recall that adding 1 to a pointer increases its value by the number of bytes in the type it points to. The same rule holds for incrementing and decrementing pointers.

Remember

Incrementing and decrementing pointers follow pointer arithmetic rules. Thus, if pt points to the first member of an array, then ++pt changes pt so that it points to the second member.

The increment and decrement operators are nifty little operators, but don't get carried away and increment or decrement the same value more than once in the same statement. The problem is that the use-then-change and change-then-use rules can become ambiguous. That is, a statement such as

```
x = 2 * x++ * (3 - ++x);    // don't do it
```

can produce quite different results on different systems. C++ does not define correct behavior for this sort of statement.

Combination Assignment Operators

Listing 5.5 uses the following expression to update a loop counter:

```
i = i + by
```

C++ has a combined addition and assignment operator that accomplishes the same result more concisely:

```
i += by
```

The += operator adds the values of its two operands and assigns the result to the operand on the left. This implies that the left operand must be something to which you can assign a value, such as a variable, an array element, a structure member, or data you identify by dereferencing a pointer:

```
int k = 5;
k += 3;                 // ok, k set to 8
int *pa = new int[10];  // pa points to pa[0]
pa[4] = 12;
pa[4] += 6;             // ok, pa[4] set to 18
*(pa + 4) += 7;         // ok, pa[4] set to 25
pa += 2;                // ok, pa points to the former pa[2]
34 += 10;               // quite wrong
```

Each arithmetic operator has a corresponding assignment operator, as summarized in Table 5.1. Each operator works analogously to +=. Thus, the statement

```
k *= 10;
```

replaces the current value of k with a value 10 times greater.

TABLE 5.1   Combined Assignment Operators

Operator	Effect (L=left operand, R=right operand)
+=	Assigns L + R to L
—=	Assigns L – R to L
*=	Assigns L * R to L
/=	Assigns L / R to L
%=	Assigns L % R to L

Compound Statements, or Blocks

The format, or syntax, for writing a C++ `for` statement might seem restrictive to you because the body of the loop must be a single statement. That's awkward if you want the loop body to contain several statements. Fortunately, C++ provides a syntax loophole through which you may stuff as many statements as you like into a loop body. The trick is to use paired braces to construct a *compound statement*, or *block*. The block consists of paired braces and the statements they enclose and, for the purposes of syntax, counts as a single statement. For example, the program in Listing 5.8 uses braces to combine three separate statements into a single block. This enables the body of the loop to prompt the user, read input, and do a calculation. The program calculates the running sum of the numbers you enter, and this provides a natural occasion for using the += operator.

LISTING 5.8   block.cpp

```
// block.cpp -- use a block statement
#include <iostream>
using namespace std;
int main()
{
    cout << "The Amazing Accounto will sum and average ";
    cout << "five numbers for you.\n";
    cout << "Please enter five values:\n";
    double number;
    double sum = 0.0;
    for (int i = 1; i <= 5; i++)
    {                                      // block starts here
        cout << "Value " << i << ": ";
```

LISTING 5.8   Continued

```
        cin >> number;
        sum += number;
    }                           // block ends here
    cout << "Five exquisite choices indeed! ";
    cout << "They sum to " << sum << "\n";
    cout << "and average to " << sum / 5 << ".\n";
    cout << "The Amazing Accounto bids you adieu!\n";
    return 0;
}
```

Here is a sample run:

```
The Amazing Accounto will sum and average five numbers for you.
Please enter five values:
Value 1: 1942
Value 2: 1948
Value 3: 1957
Value 4: 1974
Value 5: 1980
Five exquisite choices indeed! They sum to 9801
and average to 1960.2.
The Amazing Accounto bids you adieu!
```

Suppose you leave in the indentation but omit the braces:

```
for (int i = 1; i <= 5; i++)
        cout << "Value " << i << ": ";      // loop ends here
        cin >> number;                       // after the loop
        sum += number;
cout << "Five exquisite choices indeed! ";
```

The compiler ignores indentation, so only the first statement would be in the loop. Thus, the loop would print the five prompts and do nothing more. After the loop completed, the program would move to the following lines, reading and summing just one number.

Compound statements have another interesting property. If you define a new variable inside a block, the variable persists only as long as the program is executing statements within the block. When execution leaves the block, the variable is deallocated. That means the variable is known only within the block:

```
#include  <iostream>
using namespace std;
int main()
{
    int x = 20;
    {                         // block starts
        int y = 100;
        cout << x << "\n";     // ok
        cout << y << "\n";     // ok
    }                         // block ends
```

```
   cout << x << "\n";   // ok
   cout << y << "\n";            // invalid, won't compile
   return 0;
}
```

Note that a variable defined in an outer block still is defined in the inner block.

What happens if you declare a variable in a block that has the same name as one outside the block? The new variable hides the old one from its point of appearance until the end of the block. Then, the old one becomes visible again.

```
int main()
{
   int x = 20;             // original x
   {                       // block starts
      cout << x << "\n";   // use original x
      int x = 100;         // new x
      cout << x << "\n";   // use new x
   }                       // block ends
   cout << x << "\n";      // use original x
   return 0;
}
```

The Comma Operator (or More Syntax Tricks)

The block, as you saw, enables you to sneak two or more statements into a place where C++ syntax allows just one statement. The comma operator does the same for expressions, enabling you to sneak two expressions into a place where C++ syntax allows only one expression. For example, suppose you have a loop in which one variable increases by 1 each cycle and a second variable decreases by 1 each cycle. Doing both in the update part of a **for** loop control section would be convenient, but the loop syntax allows just one expression there. The solution is to use the comma operator to combine the two expressions into one:

```
j++, i--   // two expressions count as one for syntax purposes
```

The comma is not always a comma operator. For example, the comma in the declaration

```
int i, j;  // comma is a separator here, not an operator
```

serves to separate adjacent names in a list of variables.

Listing 5.9 uses the comma operator twice in a program that reverses the contents of a character array. Note that Listing 5.6 displays the contents of an array in reverse order, but Listing 5.9 actually moves characters around in the array. The program also uses a block to group several statements into one.

LISTING 5.9   forstr2.cpp
_____

```
// forstr2.cpp -- reversing an array
#include <iostream>
#include <cstring>
using namespace std;
```

LISTING 5.9   *Continued*

```
const int ArSize = 20;
int main()
{
    cout << "Enter a word: ";
    char word[ArSize];
    cin >> word;

    // physically modify array
    char temp;
    int i, j;
    for (j = 0, i = strlen(word) - 1; j < i; i--, j++)
    {                        // start block
        temp = word[i];
        word[i] = word[j];
        word[j] = temp;
    }                        // end block
    cout << word << "\nDone\n";
    return 0;
}
```

Here is a sample run:

```
Enter a word: parts
strap
Done
```

Program Notes

Look at the `for` control section:

```
for (j = 0, i = strlen(word) - 1; j < i; i--, j++)
```

First, it uses the comma operator to squeeze two initializations into one expression for the first part of the control section. Then, it uses the comma operator again to combine two updates into a single expression for the last part of the control section.

Next, look at the body. The program uses braces to combine several statements into a single unit. In the body, the program reverses the word by switching the first element of the array with the last element. Then, it increments `j` and decrements `i` so that they now refer to the next-to-the-first element and the next-to-the-last element. After this is done, the program swaps those elements. Note that the test condition `j<i` makes the loop stop when it reaches the center of the array. If it were to continue past this point, it would begin swapping the switched elements back to their original positions. (See Figure 5.2.)

Another thing to note is the location for declaring the variables `temp`, `i`, and `j`. The code declares `i` and `j` before the loop, because you can't combine two declarations with a comma operator. That's because declarations already use the comma for another purpose—separating items in a list. You can use a single declaration-statement expression to create and initialize two variables, but it's a bit confusing visually:

```
int j = 0, i = strlen(word) - 1;
```

FIGURE 5.2

Reversing a string.

In this case the comma is just a list separator, not the comma operator, so the expression declares and initializes both j and i. However, it looks as if it declares only j.

Incidentally, you can declare `temp` inside the `for` loop:

```
int temp = word[i];
```

This results in `temp` being allocated and deallocated each loop cycle. This might be a bit slower than declaring `temp` once before the loop. On the other hand, after the loop is finished, `temp` is discarded if it's declared inside the loop.

Comma Operator Tidbits

By far the most common use for the comma operator is to fit two or more expressions into a single `for` loop expression. But C++ does provide the operator with two additional properties. First, it guarantees that the first expression is evaluated before the second expression. Expressions such as the following are safe:

```
i = 20, j = 2 * i       // i set to 20, j set to 40
```

Second, C++ states that the value of a comma expression is the value of the second part. The value of the preceding expression, for example, is 40, because that is the value of j = 2 * i.

The comma operator has the lowest precedence of any operator. For example, the statement

```
cata = 17,240;
```

gets read as

```
(cats = 17), 240;
```

That is, `cats` is set to 17, and 240 does nothing. But, because parentheses have high precedence,

```
cats = (17,240);
```

results in `cats` being set to 240, the value of the expression on the right.

Relational Expressions

Computers are more than relentless number crunchers. They have the capability to compare values, and this capability is the foundation of computer decision-making. In C++, relational operators embody this ability. C++ provides six relational operators to compare numbers. Because characters are represented by their ASCII code, you can use these operators with characters, too, but they don't work with C-style strings. Each relational expression reduces to the `bool` value `true` if the comparison is true and to the `bool` value `false` if the comparison is false, so they are well suited for use in a loop test expression. (Older implementations evaluate true relational expressions to `1` and false relational expressions to `0`.) Table 5.2 summarizes these operators.

TABLE 5.2   Relational Operators

Operator	Meaning
<	Is less than
<=	Is less than or equal to
==	Is equal to
>	Is greater than
>=	Is greater than or equal to
!=	Is not equal to

The six relational operators exhaust the comparisons C++ enables you to make for numbers. If you want to compare two values to see which is the more beautiful or the luckier, you must look elsewhere.

Here are some sample tests:

```
for (x = 20; x > 5; x--) // continue while x is greater than 5
for (x = 1; y != x; x++) // continue while y is not equal to x
for (cin >> x; x == 0; cin >> x))    // continue while x is 0
```

The relational operators have a lower precedence than the arithmetic operators. That means the expression

```
x + 3 > y - 2                 // expression 1
```

corresponds to

```
(x + 3) > (y - 2)             // expression 2
```

and not the following:

```
x + (3 > y) - 2               // expression 3
```

Because the expression (3 > y) is either 1 or 0 after the **bool** value is promoted to **int**, expressions 2 and 3 both are valid. But most of us would want expression 1 to mean expression 2, and that is what C++ does.

The Mistake You'll Probably Make

Don't confuse testing the is-equal-to operator (==) with the assignment operator (=). The expression

```
musicians == 4    // comparison
```

asks the musical question, is **musicians** equal to 4? The expression has the value **true** or **false**. The expression

```
musicians = 4     // assignment
```

assigns the value 4 to **musicians**. The whole expression, in this case, has the value 4, because that's the value of the left side.

The flexible design of the **for** loop creates an interesting opportunity for error. If you accidentally drop an equal sign (=) from the == operator and use an assignment expression instead of a relational expression for the test part of a **for** loop, you still produce valid code. That's because you can use any valid C++ expression for a **for** loop test condition. Remember, nonzero values test as **true** and zero tests as **false**. An expression that assigns 4 to **musicians** has the value 4 and is treated as **true**. If you come from a language, such as Pascal or BASIC, that uses = to test for equality, you might be particularly prone to this slip.

Listing 5.10 shows a situation in which you can make this sort of error. The program attempts to examine an array of quiz scores and stop when it reaches the first score that's not a 20. It shows a loop that correctly uses comparison and then one that mistakenly uses assignment in the test condition. The program also has another egregious design error that you'll see how to fix later. (You learn from your mistakes, and Listing 5.10 is happy to help in that respect.)

LISTING 5.10   equal.cpp

```cpp
// equal.cpp -- equality vs assignment
#include <iostream>
using namespace std;
int main()
{
    int quizscores[10] =
        { 20, 20, 20, 20, 20, 19, 20, 18, 20, 20};

    cout << "Doing it right:\n";
    int i;
    for (i = 0; quizscores[i] == 20; i++)
        cout << "quiz " << i << " is a 20\n";

    cout << "Doing it dangerously wrong:\n";
    for (i = 0; quizscores[i] = 20; i++)
        cout << "quiz " << i << " is a 20\n";

    return 0;
}
```

Because this program has a serious problem, you might prefer reading about it to actually running it. Here is some sample output:

```
Doing it right:
quiz 0 is a 20
quiz 1 is a 20
quiz 2 is a 20
quiz 3 is a 20
quiz 4 is a 20
Doing it dangerously wrong:
quiz 0 is a 20
quiz 1 is a 20
quiz 2 is a 20
quiz 3 is a 20
quiz 4 is a 20
quiz 5 is a 20
quiz 6 is a 20
quiz 7 is a 20
quiz 8 is a 20
quiz 9 is a 20
quiz 10 is a 20
quiz 11 is a 20
quiz 12 is a 20
quiz 13 is a 20
...
```

The first loop correctly halts after displaying the first five quiz scores. But the second starts by displaying the whole array. Worse than that, it says every value is 20. Worse than that, it doesn't stop at the end of the array!

Where things go wrong, of course, is with the following test expression:

```
quizscores[i] = 20
```

First, simply because it assigns a nonzero value to the array element, the expression always is nonzero, hence always true. Second, because the expression assigns values to the array elements, it actually changes the data. Third, because the test expression remains true, the program continues changing data beyond the end of the array. It just keeps putting more and more 20s into memory! This is not good.

The difficulty with this kind of error is that the code is syntactically correct, so the compiler won't tag it as an error. (However, years and years of C and C++ programmers making this error eventually has led many compilers to issue a warning asking if that's what you really meant to do.)

 Caution

Don't use = to compare for equality; use ==.

Like C, C++ grants you more freedom than most programming languages. This comes at the cost of requiring greater responsibility on your part. Nothing but your own good planning prevents a program from going beyond the bounds of a standard C++ array. However, with C++ classes, you can design a protected array type that prevents this sort of nonsense. Chapter 13, "Class Inheritance," provides an example. In the meantime, you should build the protection into your programs when you need it. For example, the loop should have included a test that kept it from going past the last member. That's true even for the "good" loop. If all the scores had been 20s, it, too, would have exceeded the array bounds. In short, the loop needed to test the values of the array and the array index. Chapter 6, "Branching Statements and Logical Operators," shows you how to use logical operators to combine two such tests into a single condition.

Comparing Strings

Suppose you want to see if a string in a character array is the word **mate**. If **word** is the array name, the following test might not do what you think:

```
word == "mate"
```

Remember that the name of an array is a synonym for its address. Similarly, a quoted string constant is a synonym for its address. Thus, the preceding relational expression doesn't test to see whether the strings are the same—it checks to see whether they are stored at the same address. The answer to that is no, even if the two strings have the same characters.

Because C++ handles strings as addresses, you get little satisfaction if you try to use the relational operators to compare strings. Instead, you can go to the C-style string library and use the **strcmp()** function to compare strings. This function takes two string addresses as arguments. That means the arguments can be pointers, string constants, or character array names.

If the two strings are identical, the function returns the value zero. If the first string precedes the second alphabetically, strcmp() returns a negative value, and if the first string follows the second alphabetically, strcmp() returns a positive value. Actually, "in the system collating sequence" is more accurate than "alphabetically." This means that characters are compared according to the system code for characters. For example, in ASCII code, all uppercase letters have smaller codes than the lowercase letters, so uppercase precedes lowercase in the collating sequence. Therefore, the string "Zoo" precedes the string "aviary". The fact that comparisons are based on code values also means that uppercase and lowercase letters differ, so the string "FOO" is different from the "foo" string.

In some languages, such as BASIC and standard Pascal, strings stored in differently sized arrays are necessarily unequal to each other. But C-style strings are defined by the terminating null character, not by the size of the containing array. This means that two strings can be identical even if they are contained in differently sized arrays:

```
char big[80] = "Daffy";        // 5 letters plus \0
char little[6] = "Daffy";      // 5 letters plus \0
```

By the way, although you can't use relational operators to compare strings, you can use them to compare characters, because characters actually are integer types. So,

```
for (ch = 'a'; ch <= 'z'; ch++)
    cout << ch;
```

is valid code, at least for the ASCII character set, for displaying the characters of the alphabet.

Listing 5.11 uses strcmp() in the test condition of a for loop. The program displays a word, changes its first letter, displays the word again, and keeps going until strcmp() determines the word is the same as the string "mate". Note that the listing includes the cstring file because it provides a function prototype for strcmp().

LISTING 5.11   compstr.cpp

```
// compstr.cpp -- comparing strings
#include <iostream>
#include <cstring>      // prototype for strcmp()
using namespace std;
int main()
{
    char word[5] = "?ate";

    for (char ch = 'a'; strcmp(word, "mate"); ch++)
    {
        cout << word << "\n";
        word[0] = ch;
    }
    cout << "After loop ends, word is " << word << "\n";
    return 0;
}
```

Compatibility Note

You might have to use `string.h` instead of `cstring`. Also, the code assumes the system uses the ASCII character code set. In this set, the codes for the letters a through z are consecutive, and the code for the ? character immediately precedes the code for a.

Here is the output:

```
?ate
aate
bate
cate
date
eate
fate
gate
hate
iate
jate
kate
late
After loop ends, word is mate
```

Program Notes

The program has some interesting points. One, of course, is the test. We want the loop to continue as long as `word` is not `mate`. That is, we want the test to continue as long as `strcmp()` says the two strings are not the same. The most obvious test for that is this:

```
strcmp(word, "mate") != 0     // strings are not the same
```

This statement has the value 1 (true) if the strings are unequal and the value 0 (false) if they are equal. But what about `strcmp(word, "mate")` by itself? It has a nonzero value (true) if the strings are unequal and the value 0 (false) if the strings are equal. In essence, the function returns **true** if the strings are different and **false** if they are the same. You can use just the function instead of the whole relational expression. This produces the same behavior and involves less typing. Also, it's the way C and C++ programmers traditionally have used `strcmp()`.

Remember

Use `strcmp()` to test strings for equality or order. The expression

```
strcmp(str1,str2) == 0
```

is true if `str1` and `str2` are identical; the expressions

```
strcmp(str1, str2) != 0
```

and

```
strcmp(str1, str2)
```

are true if `str1` and `str2` are not identical; the expression

```
strcmp(str1,str2) < 0
```

is true if `str1` precedes `str2`; and the expression

```
strcmp(str1, str2) > 0
```

is true if `str1` follows `str2`. Thus, the `strcmp()` function can play the role of the `==`, `!=`, `<`, and `>` operators, depending upon how you set up a test condition.

Next, `compstr.cpp` uses the increment operator to march the variable `ch` through the alphabet:

```
ch++
```

You can use the increment and decrement operators with character variables, because type `char` really is an integer type, so the operation actually changes the integer code stored in the variable. Also, note that using an array index makes it simple to change individual characters in a string:

```
word[0] = ch;
```

Finally, unlike most of the `for` loops to date, this loop isn't a counting loop. That is, it doesn't execute a block of statements a specified number of times. Instead, the loop watches for a particular circumstance (`word` being `"mate"`) to signal that it's time to stop. More typically, C++ programs use `while` loops for this second kind of test, so let's examine that form now.

The `while` Loop

The `while` loop is a `for` loop stripped of the initialization and update parts; it has just a test condition and a body:

```
while (test-condition)
        body
```

First, a program evaluates the *test-condition* expression. If the expression evaluates to `true`, the program executes the statement(s) in the body. As with a `for` loop, the body consists of a single statement or a block defined by paired braces. After it finishes with the body, the program returns to the test-condition and reevaluates it. If the condition is nonzero, the program executes the body again. This cycle of testing and execution continues until the test-condition evaluates to `false`. (See Figure 5.3.) Clearly, if you want the loop to terminate eventually, something within the loop body must do something to affect the test-condition expression. For example, the loop can increment a variable used in the test condition or read a new value from keyboard input. Like the `for` loop, the `while` loop is an entry-condition loop. Thus, if the test-condition evaluates to `false` at the beginning, the program never executes the body of the loop.

FIGURE 5.3

The while loop.

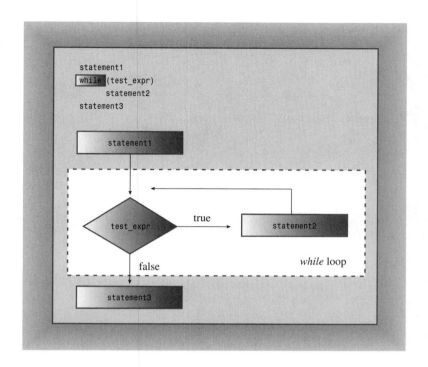

Listing 5.12 puts the while loop to work. The loop cycles through each character in a string and displays the character and its ASCII code. The loop quits when it reaches the null character. This technique of stepping through a string character-by-character until reaching the null character is a standard C++ method for processing strings. Because a string contains its own termination marker, programs often don't need explicit information about how long a string is.

LISTING 5.12   while.cpp

```cpp
// while.cpp -- introducing the while loop
#include <iostream>
using namespace std;
const int ArSize = 20;
int main()
{
    char name[ArSize];

    cout << "Your first name, please: ";
    cin >> name;
    cout << "Here is your name, verticalized and ASCIIized:\n";
    int i = 0;                  // start at beginning of string
    while (name[i] != '\0')     // process to end of string
    {
        cout << name[i] << ": " << int(name[i]) << '\n';
        i++;                    // don't forget this step
```

LISTING 5.12 Continued

```
        }
        return 0;
}
```

Here is a sample run:

```
Your first name, please: Muffy
Here is your name, verticalized and ASCIIized:
M: 77
u: 117
f: 102
f: 102
y: 121
```

(No, verticalized and ASCIIized are not real words or even good would-be words. But they do add an endearing technoid tone to the output.)

Program Notes

The `while` condition looks like this:

```
while (name[i] != '\0')
```

It tests whether a particular character in the array is the null character. For this test eventually to succeed, the loop body needs to change the value of `i`. It does so by incrementing `i` at the end of the loop body. Omitting this step keeps the loop stuck on the same array element, printing the character and its code until you manage to kill the program. Such an infinite loop is one of the most common problems with loops. Often you can cause it when you forget to update some value within the loop body.

You can rewrite the `while` line this way:

```
while (name[i])
```

With this change, the program works just as it did before. That's because when `name[i]` is an ordinary character, its value is the character code, which is nonzero, or true. But when `name[i]` is the null character, its character-code value is 0, or false. This notation is more concise (and more commonly used) but less clear than what we used. Dumb compilers might produce faster code for the second version, but smart compilers will produce the same code for both.

To get the program to print the ASCII code for a character, the program uses a type cast to convert `name[i]` to an integer type. Then, `cout` prints the value as an integer rather than interprets it as a character code.

for Versus while

In C++ the `for` and `while` loops essentially are equivalent. For example, the `for` loop

```
for (init-expression; test-expression; update-expression)
{
```

```
        statement(s)
}
```

could be rewritten this way:

```
init-expression;
while (test-expression)
{
    statement(s)
    update-expression;
}
```

Similarly, the `while` loop

```
while (test-expression)
    body
```

could be rewritten this way:

```
for ( ;test-expression;)
    body
```

The `for` loop requires three expressions (or, more technically, one statement followed by two expressions), but they can be empty expressions (or statements). Only the two semicolons are mandatory. Incidentally, a missing test expression in a `for` loop is construed as true, so the loop

```
for ( ; ; )
    body
```

runs forever.

Because the `for` loop and `while` loop are nearly equivalent, the one you use is a matter of style. (There is a slight difference if the body includes a `continue` statement, which is discussed in Chapter 6. Typically, programmers use the `for` loop for counting loops because the `for` loop format enables you to place all the relevant information—initial value, terminating value, and method of updating the counter—in one place. Programmers most often use the `while` loop when they don't know in advance precisely how many times the loop will execute.

Keep in mind the following guidelines when you design a loop:

1. Identify the condition that terminates loop execution.

2. Initialize that condition before the first test.

3. Update the condition each loop cycle before the condition is tested again.

One nice thing about the `for` loop is that its structure provides a place to implement these three guidelines, thus helping you to remember to do so.

Bad Punctuation

Both the `for` loop and the `while` loop have bodies consisting of the single statement following the parenthesized expressions. As you've seen, that single statement can be a block, which can contain several statements. Keep in mind that braces, not indentation, define a block. Consider the following loop, for example:

```
i = 0;
while (name[i] != '\0')
        cout << name[i] << "\n";
        i++;
cout << "Done\n";
```

The indentation tells us the program author intended the `i++;` statement to be part of the loop body. The absence of braces, however, tells the compiler that the body consists solely of the first `cout` statement. Thus, the loop keeps printing the first character of the array indefinitely. The program never reaches the `i++;` statement because it is outside the loop.

The next example shows another potential pitfall:

```
i = 0;
while (name[i] != '\0');      // problem semicolon
{
        cout << name[i] << "\n";
        i++;
}
cout << "Done\n";
```

This time the code got the braces right, but it also inserted an extra semicolon. Remember, a semicolon terminates a statement, so this semicolon terminates the `while` loop. In other words, the body of the loop is a *null statement*, that is, nothing followed by a semicolon. All the material in braces now comes *after* the loop. It never is reached. Instead, the loop cycles doing nothing forever. Beware the straggling semicolon.

Just a Moment

Sometimes it's useful to build a time delay into a program. For example, you might have encountered programs that flash a message onscreen and then go on to something else before you can read it. You're left with the fear that you've missed irretrievable information of vital importance. It would be so much nicer if the program paused five seconds before moving on. The `while` loop is handy for producing this effect. One of the earlier techniques was to make the computer count for a while to use up time:

```
long wait = 0;
while (wait < 10000)
    wait++;              // counting silently
```

The problem with this approach is that you have to change the counting limit when you change computer processor speed. Several games written for the original IBM PC, for example, became unmanageably fast when run on its faster successors. A better approach is to let the system clock do the timing for you.

The ANSI C and the C++ libraries have a function to help you do this. The function is called `clock()`, and it returns the system time elapsed since a program started execution. There are a couple of complications. First, `clock()` doesn't necessarily return the time in seconds. Second, the function's return type might be `long` on some systems, `unsigned long` on others, or perhaps some other type.

But the `ctime` header file (`time.h` on less current implementations) provides solutions to these problems. First, it defines a symbolic constant, `CLOCKS_PER_SEC`, that equals the number of system time units per second. So dividing the system time by this value yields seconds. Or, you can multiply seconds by `CLOCKS_PER_SEC` to get time in the system units. Second, `ctime` establishes `clock_t` as an alias for the `clock()` return type. (See the note about Type Aliases.) This means you can declare a variable as type `clock_t` and the compiler then converts that to `long` or `unsigned int` or whatever the proper type is for your system.

Compatibility Notes

Systems that haven't added the `ctime` header file can use `time.h` instead. Some C++ implementations might have problems with `waiting.cpp` if the implementation's library component is not fully ANSI C-compliant. That's because the `clock()` function is an ANSI addition to the traditional C library. Also, some premature implementations of ANSI C used `CLK_TCK` or `TCK_CLK` instead of the longer `CLOCKS_PER_SEC`. Some older versions of g++ don't recognize any of these defined constants. Some environments (such as MSVC++ 1.0 but not MSVC++ 6.0) have problems with the alarm character `\a` and coordinating the display with the time delay.

Listing 5.13 shows how to use `clock()` and the `ctime` header to create a time-delay loop.

LISTING 5.13   waiting.cpp

```
// waiting.cpp -- using clock() in a time-delay loop
#include <iostream>
#include <ctime> // describes clock() function, clock_t type
using namespace std;
int main()
{
    cout << "Enter the delay time, in seconds: ";
    float secs;
    cin >> secs;
    clock_t delay = secs * CLOCKS_PER_SEC;  // convert to clock ticks
    cout << "starting\a\n";
    clock_t start = clock();
    while (clock() - start < delay )        // wait until time elapses
        ;                                   // note the semicolon
    cout << "done \a\n";
    return 0;
}
```

By calculating the delay time in system units instead of in seconds, the program avoids having to convert system time to seconds each loop cycle.

Type Aliases

C++ has two ways to establish a new name as an alias for a type. One is to use the preprocessor:

```
#define BYTE char // preprocessor replaces BYTE with char
```

The preprocessor then replaces all occurrences of BYTE with char when you compile a program, thus making BYTE an alias for char.

The second method is to use the C++ (and C) keyword typedef to create an alias. For example, to make byte an alias for char, do this:

```
typedef char byte;    // makes byte an alias for char
```

Here's the general form:

```
typedef typeName aliasName;
```

In other words, if you want aliasName to be an alias for a particular type, declare aliasName as if it were a variable of that type and then prefix the declaration with the typedef keyword. For example, to make byte_pointer an alias for pointer-to-char, declare byte_pointer as a pointer-to-char and then stick typedef in front:

```
typedef char * byte_pointer; // pointer to char type
```

You could try something similar with #define, but that won't work if you declare a list of variables. For example, consider the following:

```
#define FLOAT_POINTER float *
FLOAT_POINTER pa, pb;
```

Preprocessor substitution converts the declaration to this:

```
float * pa, pb;  // pa a pointer to float, pb just a float
```

The typedef approach doesn't have that problem.

Notice that typedef doesn't create a new type. It just creates a new name for an old type. If you make word an alias for int, cout treats a type word value as the int it really is.

The do while Loop

You've now seen the for loop and the while loop. The third C++ loop is the do while. It's different from the other two because it's an *exit-condition* loop. That means this devil-may-care loop first executes the body of the loop and only then evaluates the test expression to see whether it should continue looping. If the condition evaluates to false, the loop terminates; otherwise, a new cycle of execution and testing begins. Such a loop always executes at least once because its program flow must pass through the body of the loop before reaching the test. Here's the syntax:

```
do
      body
while (test-expression);
```

The body portion can be a single statement or a brace-delimited statement block. Figure 5.4 summarizes the program flow for the do while loop.

FIGURE 5.4
The do while loop.

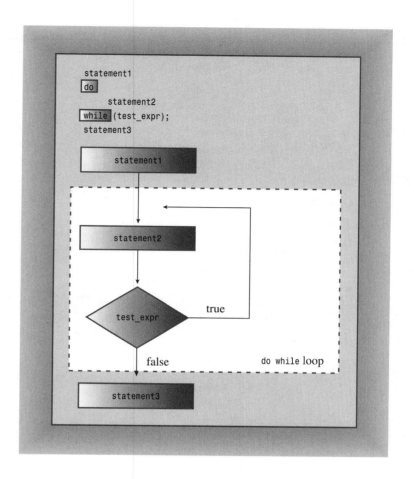

Usually, an entry-condition loop is a better choice than an exit-condition loop because the entry-condition loop checks before looping. For example, suppose Listing 5.12 had used **do while** instead of **while**. Then, the loop would have printed the null character and its code before it found it already had reached the end of the string. But sometimes a **do while** test does make sense. For example, if you're requesting user input, the program has to obtain the input before testing it. Listing 5.14 shows how to use **do while** in that situation.

LISTING 5.14   dowhile.cpp

```
// dowhile.cpp -- exit-condition loop
#include <iostream>
using namespace std;
int main()
{
    int n;
```

LISTING 5.14   *Continued*

```
    cout << "Enter numbers in the range 1-10 to find ";
    cout << "my favorite number\n";
    do
    {
        cin >> n;          // execute body
    } while (n != 7);      // then test
    cout << "Yes, 7 is my favorite.\n" ;
    return 0;
}
```

Here's a sample run:

```
Enter numbers in the range 1-10 to find my favorite number
9
4
7
Yes, 7 is my favorite.
```

Real World Note: Strange for Loops

It's not terribly common, but you may occasionally see code that resembles the following:

```
for(;;)   // sometimes called a "forever loop"
{
    I++;
    // do something ...
    if (30 >= I) break;
}
```

or another variation:

```
for(;;I++)
{
    if (30 >= I) break;
        // do something ...
}
```

The code relies upon the fact that an empty test condition in a `for` loop is treated as being true. Neither of these examples is easy to read, and neither should be used as a general model of writing a loop. The functionality of the first example is more clearly expressed in a `do while` loop:

```
do {
    I++;
    // do something;
while (30 < I);
```

Similarly, the second example can be expressed more clearly as a `while` loop:

```
while (I < 30)
{
    // do something
    I++;
}
```

In general, writing clear, easily understood code is a more useful goal than the demonstration of the ability to exploit obscure features of the language.

Loops and Text Input

Now that you've seen how loops work, let's look at one of the most common and important tasks assigned to loops: reading text character-by-character from a file or from the keyboard. For example, you might want to write a program that counts the number of characters, lines, and words in the input. Traditionally, C++, like C, uses the `while` loop for this sort of task. We'll investigate now how that is done. If you already know C, don't skim through this part too fast. Although the C++ `while` loop is the same as C's, C++'s I/O facilities are different. This can give the C++ loop a somewhat different look. In fact, the `cin` object supports three distinct modes of single-character input, each with a different user interface. Look at how to use these choices with `while` loops.

Using Unadorned `cin` for Input

If a program is going to use a loop to read text input from the keyboard, it has to have some way of knowing when to stop. How can it know when to stop? One way is to choose some special character, sometimes called a *sentinel character*, to act as a stop sign. For example, Listing 5.15 stops reading input when the program encounters a # character. The program counts the number of characters it reads and it echoes them. That is, it redisplays the characters that have been read. (Pressing a keyboard key doesn't automatically place a character on the screen; programs have to do that drudge work by echoing the input character. Typically, the operating system handles that task. In this case, both the operating system and the test program echo the input.) When finished, it reports the total number of characters processed. Listing 5.15 shows the program.

LISTING 5.15   `textin1.cpp`

```cpp
// textin1.cpp -- reading chars with a while loop
#include <iostream>
using namespace std;
int main()
{
    char ch;
    int count = 0;      // use basic input

    cin >> ch;          // get a character
    while (ch != '#')   // test the character
    {
        cout << ch;     // echo the character
        count++;        // count the character
        cin >> ch;      // get the next character
    }
    cout << "\n" << count << " characters read\n";
    return 0;
}
```

Here's a sample run:

see ken run#really fast
seekenrun
9 characters read

Apparently Ken runs so fast, he obliterates space itself—or at least the space characters in the input.

Program Notes

First, note the structure. The program reads the first input character before it reaches the loop. That way, the first character can be tested when the program reaches the loop statement. This is important, for the first character might be #. Because textin1.cpp uses an entry-condition loop, the program correctly skips the entire loop in that case. And because the variable count previously was set to zero, count has the correct value.

Suppose the first character read is not a #. Then, the program enters the loop, displays the character, increments the count, and reads the next character. This last step is vital. Without it, the loop repeatedly processes the first input character forever. With it, the program advances to the next character.

Note the loop design follows the guidelines mentioned earlier. The condition that terminates the loop is if the last character read is #. The condition is initialized by reading a character before the loop starts. The condition is updated by reading a new character at the end of the loop.

This all sounds reasonable. So why does the program omit the spaces on output? Blame cin. When reading type char values, just as when reading other basic types, cin skips over spaces and newlines. The spaces in the input are not echoed, and so they are not counted.

To further complicate things, the input to cin is buffered. That means the characters you type don't get sent to the program until you press Enter. This is why we were able to type characters after the #. After we pressed Enter, the whole sequence of characters was sent to the program, but the program quit processing the input after it reached the # character.

cin.get(char) to the Rescue

Usually, programs that read input character-by-character need to examine every character, including spaces, tabs, and newlines. The istream class (defined in iostream), to which cin belongs, includes member functions that meet this need. In particular, the member function cin.get(ch) reads the next character, even if it is a space, from the input and assigns it to the variable ch. By replacing cin>>ch with this function call, you can fix Listing 5.15. Listing 5.16 shows the result.

LISTING 5.16   textin2.cpp

```
// textin2.cpp -- using cin.get(char)
#include <iostream>
using namespace std;
```

LISTING 5.16   Continued

```cpp
int main()
{
    char ch;
    int count = 0;

    cin.get(ch);          // use the cin.get(ch) function
    while (ch != '#')
    {
        cout << ch;
        count++;
        cin.get(ch);    // use it again
    }
    cout << "\n" << count << " characters read\n";
    return 0;
}
```

Here is a sample run:

Did you use a #2 pencil?
Did you use a
14 characters read

Now the program echoes and counts every character, including the spaces. Input still is buffered, so it still is possible to type more input than what eventually reaches the program.

If you are familiar with C, this program may strike you as terribly wrong! The `cin.get(ch)` call places a value in the `ch` variable, which means it alters the value of the variable. In C, you must pass the address of a variable to a function if you want to change the value of that variable. But the call to `cin.get()` in Listing 5.16 passes `ch`, not `&ch`. In C, code like this won't work. In C++ it can, provided that the function declares the argument as a *reference*. This is a feature type new to C++. The `iostream` header file declares the argument to `cin.get(ch)` as a reference type, so this function can alter the value of its argument. We get to the details in Chapter 8, "Adventures in Functions." Meanwhile, the C mavens among you can relax—ordinarily, argument passing in C++ works just as it does in C. For `cin.get(ch)`, however, it doesn't.

Which `cin.get()`?

Chapter 4 uses this code:

```cpp
char name[ArSize];
...

cout << "Enter your name:\n";
cin.get(name, ArSize).get();
```

The last line is equivalent to two consecutive function calls:

```cpp
cin.get(name, ArSize);
cin.get();
```

One version of `cin.get()` takes two arguments: the array name, which is the address of the string (technically, type `char*`), and `ArSize`, which is an integer of type `int`. (Recall that the name of an array is the address of its first element, so the name of a character array is type `char*`.) Then, the program uses `cin.get()` with no arguments. And, most recently, we've used `cin.get()` this way:

```
char ch;
cin.get(ch);
```

This time `cin.get()` has one argument, and it is type `char`.

Once again it is time for those of you familiar with C to get excited or confused. In C, if a function takes a pointer-to-`char` and an `int` as arguments, you can't successfully use the same function with a single argument of a different type. But you can do so in C++ because the language supports an OOP feature called *function overloading*. Function overloading allows you to create different functions that have the same name provided that they have different argument lists. If, for example, you use `cin.get(name, ArSize)` in C++, the compiler finds the version of `cin.get()` that uses a `char*` and an `int` as arguments. But if you use `cin.get(ch)`, the compiler fetches the version that uses a single type `char` argument. And if the code provides no arguments, the compiler uses the version of `cin.get()` that takes no arguments. Function overloading enables you to use the same name for related functions that perform the same basic task in different ways or for different types. This is another topic awaiting you in Chapter 8. Meanwhile, you can get accustomed to function overloading by using the examples that come with the `istream` class. To distinguish between the different function versions, we'll include the argument list when referring to them. Thus, `cin.get()` means the version that takes no arguments and `cin.get(char)` means the version that takes one argument.

The End-of-File Condition

As Listing 5.16 shows, using a symbol such as `#` to signal the end of input is not always satisfactory, because such a symbol might be part of legitimate input. The same is true of other arbitrarily chosen symbols, such as `@` or `%`. If the input comes from a file, you can employ a much more powerful technique—detecting the end-of-file (EOF). C++ input facilities cooperate with the operating system to detect when input reaches the end of a file and report that information back to a program.

At first glance, reading information from files seems to have little to do with `cin` and keyboard input, but there are two connections. First, many operating systems, including UNIX and MS-DOS, support *redirection*, which enables you to substitute a file for keyboard input. For example, suppose in MS-DOS that you have an executable program called `gofish.exe` and a text file called `fishtale`. Then, you can give this command line at the DOS prompt:

```
gofish <fishtale
```

This causes the program to take input from the `fishtale` file instead of from the keyboard. The `<` symbol is the redirection operator for both UNIX and DOS. Second, many operating systems allow you to simulate the end-of-file condition from the keyboard. In UNIX you do so by pressing Ctrl+D at the beginning of a line. In DOS, you press Ctrl+Z, Enter anywhere on the line. Some implementations support similar behavior even though the underlying operating system doesn't. The end-of-file concept for keyboard entry actually is a legacy of command-line environments. However, Symantec C++ for the Mac imitates UNIX and recognizes Ctrl+D as a simulated EOF. Metrowerks Codewarrior recognizes Ctrl+Z in the Macintosh and the Windows environments. The Microsoft Visual C++ 6.0 and the Borland C++Builder Windows environments support a console mode in which Ctrl+Z works without an Enter. However, after Ctrl+Z is detected, these last two environments fail to display any output prior to the first newline displayed, so eof emulation is not perfect.

If your programming environment can test for the end of a file, you can use the program with redirected files and you can use it for keyboard input in which you simulate end-of-file. That sounds useful, so let's see how it's done.

When `cin` detects the end-of-file (EOF), it sets two bits (the *eofbit* and the *failbit*) to 1. You can use a member function named `eof()` to see whether the eofbit has been set; the call `cin.eof()` returns the `bool` value `true` if EOF has been detected and `false` otherwise. Similarly, the `fail()` member function returns `true` if either the *eofbit* or the *failbit* has been set to 1 and `false` otherwise. Note that the `eof()` and `fail()` methods report the result of the most recent attempt to read; that is, they report on the past rather than look ahead. So a `cin.eof()` or `cin.fail()` test always should follow an attempt to read. The design of Listing 5.17 reflects this fact. It uses `fail()` instead of `eof()` because the former method appears to work with a broader range of implementations.

Compatibility Note

Some systems do not support simulated EOF from the keyboard. Other systems, including Microsoft Visual C++ 6.0, Metrowerks Codewarrior, and Borland C++Builder, support it imperfectly. If you have been using `cin.get()` to freeze the screen until you can read it, that won't work here because detecting EOF turns off further attempts to read input. However, you can use a timing loop like that in Listing 5.13 to keep the screen visible for a while.

LISTING 5.17   textin3.cpp

```cpp
// textin3.cpp -- reading chars to end of file
#include <iostream>
using namespace std;
int main()
{
    char ch;
    int count = 0;
    cin.get(ch);         // attempt to read a char
    while (cin.fail() == false)  // test for EOF
    {
        cout << ch;       // echo character
        count++;
        cin.get(ch);     // attempt to read another char
    }
```

LISTING 5.17 *Continued*

```
        cout << "\n" << count << " characters read\n";
        return 0;
}
```

Here is sample output. Because we ran the program on a Windows 98 system, we pressed
Ctrl+Z to simulate the end-of-file condition. DOS users would press Ctrl+Z, Enter instead.
UNIX and Symantec C++ for the Mac users would press Ctrl+D instead.

```
The green bird sings in the winter.<ENTER>
The green bird sings in the winter.
Yes, but the crow flies in the dawn.<ENTER>
Yes, but the crow flies in the dawn.
<CTRL><Z>
73 characters read
```

By using redirection, you can use this program to display a text file and report how many characters it has. This time, we have a program read, echo, and count a two-line file on a UNIX
system (the $ is a UNIX prompt):

```
$ textin3 < stuff
I am a UNIX file. I am proud
to be a UNIX file.
49 characters read
$
```

End-of-File Ends Input

When a `cin` method detects end-of-file, recall, it sets a flag in the `cin` object indicating the
end-of-file condition. When this flag is set, `cin` does not read any more input, and further calls
to `cin` have no effect. For file input, this makes sense because you shouldn't read past the end
of a file. For keyboard input, however, you might use a simulated end-of-file to terminate a
loop but then want to read more input later. The `cin.clear()` method clears the end-of-file
flag and lets input proceed again. Chapter 17, "Input, Output, and Files," discusses this further. Keep in mind, however, that in a Windows 98 console emulation mode, typing Ctrl+Z
effectively terminates both input and output beyond the powers of `cin.clear()` to restore
them.

Common Idioms

The essential design of the input loop is this:

```
cin.get(ch);          // attempt to read a char
while (cin.fail() == false)  // test for EOF
{
    ...               // do stuff
    cin.get(ch);      // attempt to read another char
}
```

There are some shortcuts you can make. Chapter 6 introduces the ! operator, which toggles true to false, and vice versa. You can use it to rewrite the while test to look like this:

```
while (!cin.fail())    // while input has not failed
```

The return value for the cin.get(char) method is cin, an object. However, the istream class provides a function that can convert an istream object such as cin to a bool value; this conversion function is called when cin occurs in a location where a bool is expected, such as in the test condition of a while loop. Furthermore, the bool value for the conversion is true if the last attempted read was successful and false otherwise. This means you can rewrite the while test to look like this:

```
while (cin)     // while input is successful
```

This is a bit more general than using !cin.fail() or !cin.eof(), for it detects other possible causes of failure, such as disk failure.

Finally, because the return value of cin.get(char) is cin, you can condense the loop to this format:

```
while (cin.get(ch))  // while input is successful
{
    ...                // do stuff
}
```

To evaluate the loop test, the program first has to execute the call to cin.get(ch), which, if successful, places a value into ch. Then, the program obtains the return value from the function call, which is cin. Then, it applies the bool conversion to cin, which yields true if input worked, false otherwise. The three guidelines (identifying the termination condition, initializing the condition, and updating the condition) all are compressed into one loop test condition.

Yet Another cin.get()

The more nostalgic of the C users among you might yearn for C's character I/O functions, getchar() and putchar(). They still are available if you want them. Just use the stdio.h header file as you would in C (or use the more current cstdio). Or, you can use member functions from the istream and ostream classes that work in much the same way. We look at that approach now.

Compatibility Note

Some older implementations don't support the cin.get() member function (no arguments) discussed here.

The cin.get() member function with no arguments returns the next character from the input. That is, you use it in this way:

```
ch = cin.get();
```

(Recall that cin.get(ch) returns an object, not the character read.) This function works much the same as C's getchar(), returning the character code as a type int value. Similarly, you can use the cout.put() function (see Chapter 3, "Dealing with Data") to display the character:

```
cout.put(ch);
```

It works much like C's putchar(), except that its argument should be type char instead of type int.

Compatibility Note

Originally, the put() member had a single prototype of put(char). You could pass it an int argument, which then would be type cast to char. The Standard also calls for a single prototype. However, many current implementations provide three prototypes: put(char), put(signed char), and put(unsigned char). Using put() with an int argument in these implementations generates an error message because there is more than one choice for converting the int. An explicit type cast, such as cin.put(char(c)), works for int types.

To use cin.get() successfully, you need to know how it handles the end-of-file condition. When the function reaches the end of a file, there are no more characters to be returned. Instead, cin.get() returns a special value represented by the symbolic constant EOF. This constant is defined in the iostream header file. The EOF value must be different from any valid character value so that the program won't confuse EOF with a regular character. Typically, EOF is defined as the value -1, because no character has an ASCII code of -1, but you don't need to know the actual value. Just use EOF in the program. For example, the heart of Listing 5.15 looked like this:

```
cin >> ch;
while (ch != '#')
{
    cout << ch;
    count++;
    cin >> ch;
}
```

You can use an int ch, replace cin with cin.get(), cout with cout.put(), and '#' with EOF:

```
int ch;        /// for compatibility with EOF value
ch = cin.get();
while (ch != EOF)
{
    cout.put(ch);    // cout.put(char(ch)) for some implementations
    count++;
    ch = cin.get();
}
```

If ch is a character, the loop displays it. If ch is EOF, the loop terminates.

Tip

You should realize that EOF does not represent a character in the input. Instead, it's a signal that there are no more characters.

There's a subtle but important point about using `cin.get()` beyond the changes made so far. Because EOF represents a value outside the valid character codes, it's possible that it might not be compatible with the `char` type. For example, on some systems type `char` is unsigned, so a `char` variable could never have the usual EOF value of −1. For this reason, if you use `cin.get()` (no argument) and test for EOF, you must assign the return value to type `int` instead of type `char`. Also, if you make `ch` type `int` instead of type `char`, you might have to do a type cast to `char` when displaying `ch`.

Listing 5.18 incorporates the `cin.get()` approach into a new version of Listing 5.15. It also condenses the code by combining character input with the `while` loop test.

LISTING 5.18   textin4.cpp

```cpp
// textin4.cpp -- reading chars with cin.get()
#include <iostream.h>
int main(void)
{
    int ch;                      // should be int, not char
    int count = 0;

    while ((ch = cin.get()) != EOF) // test for end-of-file
    {
        cout.put(char(ch));
        count++;
    }
    cout << "\n" << count << " characters read\n";
     return 0;
}
```

Compatibility Note

Some systems either do not support simulated EOF from the keyboard or support it imperfectly, and that may prevent this example from running as described. If you have been using `cin.get()` to freeze the screen until you can read it, that won't work here because detecting EOF turns off further attempts to read input. However, you can use a timing loop like that in Listing 5.13 to keep the screen visible for awhile.

Here's a sample run:

The sullen mackerel sulks in the shadowy shallows.<ENTER>
The sullen mackerel sulks in the shadowy shallows.

```
Yes, but the blue bird of happiness harbors secrets.<ENTER>
Yes, but the blue bird of happiness harbors secrets.
^Z
104 characters read
```

Let's analyze the loop condition:

```
while ((ch = cin.get()) != EOF)
```

The parentheses that enclose the subexpression `ch=cin.get()` cause the program to evaluate that expression first. To do the evaluation, the program first has to call the `cin.get()` function. Next, it assigns the function return value to `ch`. Because the value of an assignment statement is the value of the left operand, the whole subexpression reduces to the value of `ch`. If this value is EOF, the loop terminates; otherwise, it continues. The test condition needs all the parentheses. Suppose we leave some out:

```
while (ch = cin.get() != EOF)
```

The `!=` operator has higher precedence than `=`, so first the program compares `cin.get()`'s return value to EOF. A comparison produces a `false` or `true` result; that `bool` value is converted to 0 or 1, and that's the value that gets assigned to `ch`.

Using `cin.get(ch)` (with an argument) for input, on the other hand, doesn't create any type problems. The `cin.get(char)` function, recall, doesn't assign a special value to `ch` on end-of-file. In fact it doesn't assign anything to `ch` in that case. `ch` is never called upon to hold a non-`char` value. Table 5.3 summarizes the differences between `cin.get(char)` and `cin.get()`.

So which should you use, `cin.get()` or `cin.get(char)`? The form with the character argument is integrated more fully into the object approach because its return value is an `istream` object. This means, for example, that you can chain uses. For example, the following code means read the next input character into `ch1` and the following input character into `ch2`:

```
cin.get(ch1).get(ch2);
```

This works because the function call `cin.get(ch1)` returns the `cin` object, which then acts as the object to which `get(ch2)` is attached.

Probably the main use for the `get()` form is to let you make quick-and-dirty conversions from the `getchar()` and `putchar()` functions of `stdio.h` to the `cin.get()` and `cout.put()` methods of `iostream`. Just replace one header file with the other and globally replace `getchar()` and `putchar()` with their act-alike method equivalents. (If the old code uses a type `int` variable for input, you have to make further adjustments if your implementation has multiple prototypes for `put()`.)

TABLE 5.3   `cin.get(ch)` versus `cin.get()`

Property	cin.get(ch)	ch=cin.get()
Method for conveying input character	Assign to argument ch	Use function return value to assign to ch

TABLE 5.3   Continued

Property	cin.get(ch)	ch=cin.get()
Function return value for character input	A class istream object (true after bool conversion)	Code for character as type int value
Function return value at end-of-file	A class istream object (false after bool conversion)	EOF

Nested Loops and Two-Dimensional Arrays

Earlier you saw how the `for` loop is a natural tool for processing arrays. Let's go a step further and look at how a `for` loop within a `for` loop (nested loops) serves to handle two-dimensional arrays.

First, let's examine what a two-dimensional array is. The arrays used so far are termed one-dimensional arrays because you can visualize each array as a single row of data. You can visualize a two-dimensional array as being more like a table, having both rows and columns of data. You can use a two-dimensional array, for example, to represent quarterly sales figures for six separate districts, with one row of data for each district. Or, you can use a two-dimensional array to represent the position of RoboDork on a computerized game board.

C++ doesn't provide a special two-dimensional array type. Instead, you create an array for which each element is itself an array. For example, suppose you want to store maximum temperature data for five cities over a four-year period. In that case, you can declare an array as follows:

```
int maxtemps[4][5];
```

This declaration means that `maxtemps` is an array with four elements. Each of these elements is an array of five integers. (See Figure 5.5.) You can think of the `maxtemps` array as representing four rows of five temperature values each.

The expression `maxtemps[0]` is the first element of the `maxtemps` array, hence `maxtemps[0]` is itself an array of five `int`s. The first element of the `maxtemps[0]` array is `maxtemps[0][0]`, and this element is a single `int`. Thus, you need to use two subscripts to access the `int` elements. You can think of the first subscript as representing the row and the second subscript as representing the column. (See Figure 5.6.)

FIGURE 5.5
An array of arrays.

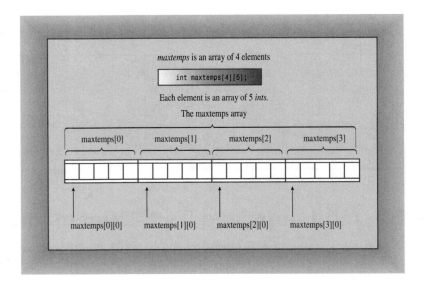

FIGURE 5.6
Accessing array elements
with subscripts.

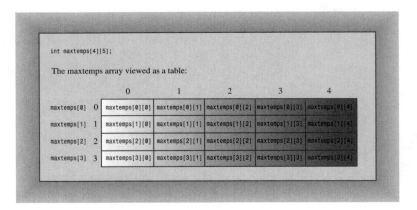

Suppose you want to print all the array contents. Then, you can use one **for** loop to change rows and a second, nested **for** loop to change columns:

```cpp
for (int row = 0; row < 4; row++)
{
    for (int col = 0; col < 5; col++)
        cout << maxtemps[row][col] << "\t";
    cout << "\n";
}
```

For each value of row, the inner **for** loop cycles through all the **col** values. This example prints a tab character (**\t** in C++ notation) after each value and a newline character after each complete row.

Initializing a Two-Dimensional Array

When you create a two-dimensional array, you have the option of initializing each element. The technique is based on that for initializing a one-dimensional array. That method, you remember, is to provide a comma-separated list of values enclosed in braces:

```
// initializing a one-dimensional array
int btus[5] = { 23, 26, 24, 31, 28};
```

For a two-dimensional array, each element is itself an array, so you can initialize each element by using a form like that in the previous code example. Thus, the initialization consists of a comma-separated series of one-dimensional initializations all enclosed in a set of braces:

```
int maxtemps[4][5] =            // 2-D array
{
    {94, 98, 87, 103, 101},     // values for maxtemps[0]
    {98, 99, 91, 107, 105},     // values for maxtemps[1]
    {93, 91, 90, 101, 104},     // values for maxtemps[2]
    {95, 100, 88, 105, 103}     // values for maxtemps[3]
};
```

The term `{94, 98, 87, 103, 101}` initializes the first row, represented by `maxtemps[0]`. As a matter of style, placing each row of data on its own line, if possible, makes the data easier to read.

Listing 5.19 incorporates an initialized two-dimensional array and a nested loop into a program. This time the program reverses the order of the loops, placing the column loop (city index) on the outside and the row loop (year index) on the inside. Also, it uses a common C++ practice of initializing an array of pointers to a set of string constants. That is, `cities` is declared as an array of pointers-to-`char`. That makes each element, such as `cities[0]`, a pointer-to-`char` that can be initialized to the address of a string. The program initializes `cities[0]` to the address of the `"Gribble City"` string, and so on. Thus, this array of pointers behaves like an array of strings.

LISTING 5.19   nested.cpp

```
// nested.cpp -- nested loops and 2-D array
#include <iostream>
using namespace std;
const int Cities = 5;
const int Years = 4;
int main()
{
    const char * cities[Cities] =   // array of pointers
    {                               // to 5 strings
        "Gribble City",
        "Gribbletown",
        "New Gribble",
        "San Gribble",
        "Gribble Vista"
    };
```

LISTING 5.19   Continued

```cpp
int maxtemps[Years][Cities] =    // 2-D array
{
    {95, 99, 86, 100, 104},   // values for maxtemps[0]
    {95, 97, 90, 106, 102},   // values for maxtemps[1]
    {96, 100, 940, 107, 105}, // values for maxtemps[2]
    {97, 102, 89, 108, 104}   // values for maxtemps[3]
};

cout << "Maximum temperatures for 1999 - 2002\n\n";
for (int city = 0; city < Cities; city++)
{
    cout << cities[city] << ":\t";
    for (int year = 0; year < Years; year++)
        cout << maxtemps[year][city] << "\t";
    cout << "\n";
}

return 0;
}
```

Here is the program output:

```
Maximum temperatures for 1999 - 2002

Gribble City:   95  95  96  97
Gribbletown:    99  97  100 102
New Gribble:    86  90  940 89
San Gribble:    100 106 107 108
Gribble Vista:  104 102 105 104
```

Using tabs in the output spaces the data more regularly than using spaces would. However, different tab settings can cause the output to vary in appearance from one system to another. Chapter 17 presents more precise, but more complex, methods for formatting output.

Summary

C++ offers three varieties of loops: the `for` loop, the `while` loop, and the `do while` loop. A loop cycles through the same set of instructions repetitively as long as the loop test condition evaluates to `true` or nonzero, and the loop terminates execution when the test condition evaluates to `false` or zero. The `for` loop and the `while` loop are entry-condition loops, meaning they examine the test condition before executing the statements in the body of the loop. The `do while` loop is an exit-condition loop, meaning it examines the test condition after executing the statements in the body of the loop.

The syntax for each loop calls for the loop body to consist of a single statement. However, that statement can be a compound statement, or block, formed by enclosing several statements within paired curly braces.

Relational expressions, which compare two values, are often used as loop test conditions. Relational expressions are formed by using one of the six relational operators: <, <=, ==, >=, >, or !=. Relational expressions evaluate to the type `bool` values `true` and `false`.

Many programs read text input or text files character-by-character. The `istream` class provides several ways to do this. If `ch` is a type `char` variable, the statement

```
cin >> ch;
```

reads the next input character into `ch`. However, it skips over spaces, newlines, and tabs. The member function call

```
cin.get(ch);
```

reads the next input character, regardless of its value, and places it in `ch`. The member function call `cin.get()` returns the next input character, including spaces, newlines, and tabs, so it can be used as follows:

```
ch = cin.get();
```

The `cin.get(char)` member function call reports encountering the end-of-file condition by returning a value with the `bool` conversion of `false`, whereas the `cin.get()` member function call reports end-of-file by returning the value `EOF`, which is defined in the `iostream` file.

A nested loop is a loop within a loop. Nested loops provide a natural way to process two-dimensional arrays.

Review Questions

1. What's the difference between an entry-condition loop and an exit-condition loop? Which kind is each of the C++ loops?

2. What would the following code fragment print if it were part of a valid program?

```
int i;
for (i = 0; i < 5; i++)
        cout << i;
        cout << "\n";
```

3. What would the following code fragment print if it were part of a valid program?

```
int j;
for (j = 0; j < 11; j += 3)
        cout << j;
cout << "\n" << j << "\n";
```

4. What would the following code fragment print if it were part of a valid program?

```
int j = 5;
while ( ++j < 9)
        cout << j++ << "\n";
```

5. What would the following code fragment print if it were part of a valid program?

```
int k = 8;
do
        cout <<" k = " << k << "\n";
while (k++ < 5);
```

6. Write a `for` loop that prints the values 1 2 4 8 16 32 64 by increasing the value of a counting variable by a factor of 2 each cycle.

7. How do you make a loop body include more than one statement?

8. Is the following statement valid? If not, why not? If so, what does it do?

```
int x = (1,024);
```

What about the following?

```
int y;
y = 1,024;
```

9. How does `cin>>ch` differ from `cin.get(ch)` and `ch=cin.get()` in how it views input?

Programming Exercises

1. Write a program that requests the user to enter two integers. The program then should calculate and report the sum of all the integers between and including the two integers. At this point, assume that the smaller integer is entered first. For example, if the user enters 2 and 9, the program reports that the sum of all the integers from 2 through 9 is 44.

2. Write a program that asks you to type in numbers. After each entry, the number reports the cumulative sum of the entries to date. The program terminates when you enter a zero.

3. Daphne invests $100 at 10% simple interest. That is, every year, the investment earns 10% of the original investment, or $10 each and every year:

   interest = 0.10 × original balance

   At the same time, Cleo invests $100 at 5% compound interest. That is, interest is 5% of the current balance, including previous additions of interest:

   interest = 0.05 × current balance

   Cleo earns 5% of $100 the first year, giving her $105. The next year she earns 5% of $105, or $5.25, and so on. Write a program that finds how many years it takes for the value of Cleo's investment to exceed the value of Daphne's investment and then displays the value of both investments at that time.

4. You sell *C++ For Fools*. Write a program that has you enter a year's worth of monthly sales (in terms of number of books, not of money). The program should use a loop to

prompt you by month, using an array of char * initialized to the month strings and storing the input data in an array of int. Then, the program should find the sum of the array contents and report the total sales for the year.

5. Do Programming Exercise 4 but use a two-dimensional array to store input for three years of monthly sales. Report the total sales for each individual year and for the combined years.

6. Design a structure called car that holds the following information about an automobile: its make as a string in a character array and the year it was built as an integer. Write a program that asks the user how many cars to catalog. The program then should use new to create a dynamic array of that many car structures. Next, it should prompt the user to input the make (which might consist of more than one word) and year information for each structure. Note that this requires some care, for it alternates reading strings with numeric data (see Chapter 4). Finally, it should display the contents of each structure. A sample run should look something like the following:

```
How many cars do you wish to catalog? 2
Car #1:
Please enter the make: Hudson Hornet
Please enter the year made: 1952
Car #2:
Please enter the make: Kaiser
Please enter the year made: 1951
Here is your collection:
1952 Hudson Hornet
1951 Kaiser
```

7. Write a program using nested loops that asks the user to enter a value for the number of rows to display. It then displays that many rows of asterisks, with one asterisk in the first row, two in the second row, and so on. For each row, the asterisks are preceded by the number of periods needed to make all the rows display a total number of characters equal to the number of rows. A sample run would look like this:

```
Enter number of rows: 5
....*
...**
..***
.****
*****
```

CHAPTER 6

BRANCHING STATEMENTS AND LOGICAL OPERATORS

In this chapter you learn

- The `if` statement

- The `if else` statement

- Logical operators: `&&`, `||`, and `!`

- The `cctype` library of character functions

- The conditional operator: `?:`

- The `switch` statement

- The `continue` and `break` statements

- Number-reading loops

One of the keys to designing intelligent programs is to give them the ability to make decisions. Chapter 5, "Loops and Relational Expressions," shows you one kind of decision making—looping—in which a program decides whether or not to continue looping. Now you investigate how C++ lets you use branching statements to decide among alternative actions. Which vampire-protection scheme (garlic or cross) should the program use? What menu choice has the user selected? Did the user enter a zero? C++ provides the `if` and `switch` statements to implement decisions, and they are this chapter's main topics. You also look at the conditional operator, which provides another way to make a choice, and the logical operators, which let you combine two tests into one.

The `if` Statement

When a C++ program must choose whether or not to take a particular action, you usually implement the choice with an `if` statement. The `if` comes in two forms: `if` and `if else`. Let's investigate the simple `if` first. It's modeled after ordinary English, as in "If you have a Captain Cookie card, you get a free cookie." The `if` statement directs a program to execute a statement or statement block if a test condition is true and to skip that statement or block if the condition is false. Thus, an `if` statement lets a program decide whether a particular statement should be executed.

The syntax is similar to the `while` syntax:

```
if (test-condition)
    statement
```

A true *test-condition* causes the program to execute *statement*, which can be a single statement or a block. A false *test-condition* causes the program to skip *statement*. (See Figure 6.1.) As with loop test conditions, an `if` test condition is typecast to a `bool` value, so zero becomes `false` and nonzero becomes `true`. The entire `if` construction counts as a single statement.

FIGURE 6.1

The `if` statement.

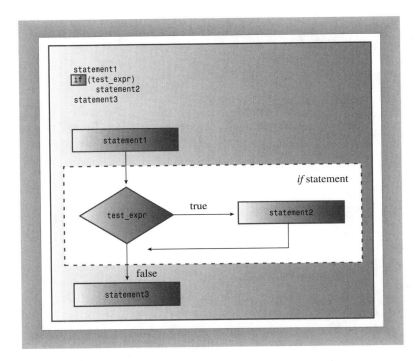

Most often, *test-condition* is a relational expression such as those used to control loops. Suppose, for example, you want a program that counts the spaces in the input as well as the total number of characters. You can use `cin.get(char)` in a `while` loop to read the characters and then use an `if` statement to identify and count the space characters. Listing 6.1 does just that, using the period to recognize the end of a sentence.

LISTING 6.1   if.cpp

```
// if.cpp -- using the if statement
#include <iostream>
using namespace std;
int main()
{
    char ch;
```

LISTING 6.1 Continued

```
    int spaces = 0;
    int total = 0;
    cin.get(ch);
    while (ch != '.')   // quit at end of sentence
    {
        if (ch == ' ')  // check if ch is a space
            spaces++;
        total++;        // done every time
        cin.get(ch);
    }
    cout << spaces << " spaces, " << total;
    cout << " characters total in sentence\n";
    return 0;
}
```

Here's some sample output:

The balloonist was an airhead
with lofty goals.
6 spaces, 46 characters total in sentence

As the comments indicate, the **spaces++;** statement is executed only when **ch** is a space. Because it is outside the **if** statement, the **total++;** statement is executed every loop cycle. Note that the total count includes the newline character generated by pressing Enter.

The `if else` Statement

While the **if** statement lets a program decide whether a *particular* statement or block is executed, the **if else** statement lets a program decide which of *two* statements or blocks is executed. It's an invaluable statement for creating alternative courses of action. The C++ **if else** is modeled after simple English, as in "If you have a Captain Cookie card, you get a Cookie Plus Plus, else you just get a Cookie d'Ordinaire." The **if else** statement has this general form:

```
if (test-condition)
    statement1
else
    statement2
```

If *test-condition* is true or nonzero, the program executes *statement1* and skips over *statement2*. Otherwise, when *test-condition* is false or zero, the program skips *statement1* and executes *statement2* instead. So the code fragment

```
if (answer == 1492)
    cout << "That's right!\n";
else
    cout << "You'd better review Chapter 1 again.\n";
```

prints the first message if **answer** is 1492 and prints the second message otherwise. Each statement can be either a single statement or a statement block delimited by braces. (See Figure 6.2.) The entire **if else** construct counts syntactically as a single statement.

FIGURE 6.2
The if else statement.

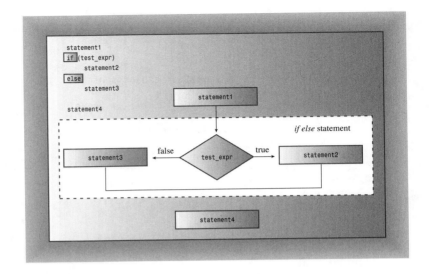

For example, suppose you want to alter incoming text by scrambling the letters while keeping the newline character intact. That way, each line of input is converted to an output line of equal length. This means you want the program to take one course of action for newline characters and a different course of action for all other characters. As Listing 6.2 shows, if else makes this task easy.

LISTING 6.2 ifelse.cpp

```cpp
// ifelse.cpp -- using the if else statement
#include <iostream>
using namespace std;
int main()
{
    char ch;

    cout << "Type, and I shall repeat.\n";
    cin.get(ch);
    while (ch != '.')
    {
        if (ch == '\n')
            cout << ch;      // done if newline
        else
            cout << ++ch;    // done otherwise
        cin.get(ch);
    }
// try ch + 1 instead of ++ch for interesting effect
    cout << "\nPlease excuse the slight confusion.\n";
    return 0;
}
```

Here's some sample output:

```
Type, and I shall repeat.
I am extraordinarily pleased
J!bn!fyusbpsejobsjmz!qmfbtfe
to use such a powerful computer.
up!vtf!tvdi!b!qpxfsgvm!dpnqvufs
Please excuse the slight confusion.
```

Note that one of the program comments suggests that changing ++ch to ch+1 has an interesting effect. Can you deduce what it will be? If not, try it out and then see if you can explain what's happening. (Hint: Think about how cout handles different types.)

Formatting Your if else Statements

Keep in mind that the two if else alternatives must be single statements. If you need more than one statement, use braces to collect them into a single block statement. Unlike some languages, such as BASIC or FORTRAN, C++ does not automatically consider everything between if and else a block, so you have to use braces to make the statements a block. The following code, for example, produces a compiler error. The compiler sees it as a simple if statement that ends with the zorro++; statement. Then there is a cout statement. So far, so good. But then there is what the compiler perceives as an unattached else, and that is flagged as a syntax error.

```
if (ch == 'Z')
    zorro++;        // if ends here
    cout << "Another Zorro candidate\n";
else                // wrong
    dull++;
    cout << "Not a Zorro candidate\n";
```

Add the braces to convert the code to what you want:

```
if (ch == 'Z')
{                           // if true block
    zorro++;
    cout << "Another Zorro candidate\n";
}
else
{                           // if false block
    dull++;
    cout << "Not a Zorro candidate\n";
}
```

Because C++ is a free-form language, you can arrange the braces as you like, as long as they enclose the statements. The preceding code shows one popular format. Here's another:

```
if (ch == 'Z') {
    zorro++;
    cout << "Another Zorro candidate\n";
    }
```

```
else {
    dull++;
    cout << "Not a Zorro candidate\n";
    }
```

The first form emphasizes the block structure for the statements, whereas the second form more closely ties the blocks to the keywords if and else. Either style is clear and consistent and should serve you well; however, you may encounter an instructor or employer with strong and specific views on the matter.

The if else if else Construction

Computer programs, like life, might present you with a choice of more than two selections. You can extend the C++ if else statement to meet that need. The else, you've seen, should be followed by a single statement, which can be a block. Because an if else statement itself is a single statement, it can follow an else:

```
if (ch == 'A')
    a_grade++;           // alternative # 1
else
    if (ch == 'B')       // alternative # 2
        b_grade++;       // subalternative # 2a
    else
        soso++;          // subalternative # 2b
```

If ch is not 'A', the program goes to the else. There, a second if else subdivides that alternative into two more choices. C++'s free formatting enables you to arrange these elements into an easier-to-read format:

```
if (ch == 'A')
    a_grade++;           // alternative # 1
else if (ch == 'B')
    b_grade++;           // alternative # 2
else
    soso++;              // alternative # 3
```

This looks like a new control structure—an if else if else structure. But actually it is one if else contained within a second. This revised format looks much cleaner, and it enables you to skim through the code to pick out the different alternatives. This entire construction still counts as one statement.

Listing 6.3 uses this preferred formatting to construct a modest quiz program.

LISTING 6.3   ifelseif.cpp
_____

```
// ifelseif.cpp -- using if else if else
#include <iostream>
using namespace std;
const int Fave = 27;
int main()
{
    int n;
```

LISTING 6.3   Continued

```
    cout << "Enter a number in the range 1-100 to find ";
    cout << "my favorite number: ";
    do
    {
        cin >> n;
        if (n < Fave)
            cout << "Too low -- guess again: ";
        else if (n > Fave)
            cout << "Too high -- guess again: ";
        else
            cout << Fave << " is right!\n";
    } while (n != Fave);
    return 0;
}
```

Here's some sample output:

```
Enter a number in the range 1-100 to find my favorite number: 50
Too high -- guess again: 25
Too low -- guess again: 37
Too high -- guess again: 31
Too high -- guess again: 28
Too high -- guess again: 27
27 is right!
```

Real World Note: Conditional Operators and Bug Prevention

Many programmers reverse the more intuitive expression *variable* == *value* to *value* == *variable* in order to catch errors where the equality is mistyped as an assignment operator. For example, entering the conditional as

```
if (3 == myNumber)
```

is valid and will work properly. However, if you happen to mistype

```
if (3 = myNumber)
```

the compiler will generate an error message, as it believes you are attempting to assign a value to a literal (3 always equals 3, and can't be assigned another value). Suppose you made a similar mistake made using the former notation:

```
if (myNumber = 3)
```

The compiler will simply assign the value 3 to myNumber, and the block within the if will run— a very common error, and a difficult error to find. As a general rule, writing code that allows the compiler to find errors is much easier than repairing the causes of mysterious faulty results.

Logical Expressions

Often you must test for more than one condition. For example, for a character to be a lower-case letter, its value must be greater than or equal to 'a' and less than or equal to 'z'. Or, if you ask a user to respond with a y or an n, you want to accept uppercase (Y and N) as well as lowercase. To meet this kind of need, C++ provides three logical operators to combine or modify existing expressions. The operators are logical OR, written ||; logical AND, written &&; and logical NOT, written !. Examine them now.

The Logical OR Operator: ||

In English, the word *or* can indicate when one or both of two conditions satisfy a requirement. For example, you can go to the MegaMicro company picnic if you *or* your spouse work for MegaMicro, Inc. The C++ equivalent is the logical OR operator, written ||. This operator combines two expressions into one. If either or both of the original expressions are **true**, or nonzero, the resulting expression has the value **true**. Otherwise the expression has the value **false**. Here are some examples:

```
5 ==5 || 5 == 9     // true because first expression is true
5 > 3 || 5 > 10     // true because first expression is true
5 > 8 || 5 < 10     // true because second expression is true
5 < 8 || 5 > 2      // true because both expressions are true
5 > 8 || 5 < 2      // false because both expressions are false
```

Because the || has a lower precedence than the relational operators, you don't need to use parentheses in these expressions. Table 6.1 summarizes how the || operator works.

C++ provides that the || operator is a *sequence point*. That is, any value changes indicated in the left side take place before the right side is evaluated. For example, consider the following expression:

```
i++ < 6 || i == j
```

Suppose i originally has the value 10. By the time the comparison with j takes place, i has the value 11. Also, C++ won't bother evaluating the expression on the right if the expression on the left is true, for it only takes one true expression to make the whole logical expression true. (The semicolon and the comma operator also are sequence points.)

Listing 6.4 uses the || operator in an if statement to check for both uppercase and lowercase versions of a character. Also, it uses C++'s string concatenation feature (see Chapter 4, "Compound Types") to spread a single string over three lines.

TABLE 6.1   The || Operator

	The Value of expr1 || expr2	
	expr1 == true	expr1 == false
expr2 == true	true	true
expr2 == false	true	false

LISTING 6.4   or.cpp

```
// or.cpp -- use logical OR operator
#include <iostream>
using namespace std;
int main()
{
    cout << "This program may reformat your hard disk\n"
            "and destroy all your data.\n"
            "Do you wish to continue? <y/n> ";
    char ch;
    cin >> ch;
    if (ch == 'y' || ch == 'Y')           // y or Y
        cout << "You were warned!\a\a\n";
    else if (ch == 'n' || ch == 'N')      // n or N
        cout << "A wise choice ... bye\n";
    else
        cout << "That wasn't a y or an n, so I guess I'll "
                "trash your disk anyway.\n";
    return 0;
}
```

Here is a sample run:

```
This program may reformat your hard disk
and destroy all your data.
Do you wish to continue? <y/n> N
A wise choice ... bye
```

The program reads just one character, so only the first character in the response matters. That means the user could have replied NO! instead of N. The program would just read the N. But if the program tried to read more input later, it would start at the O.

The Logical AND Operator: &&

The logical AND operator, written **&&**, also combines two expressions into one. The resulting expression has the value **true** only if both of the original expressions are **true**. Here are some examples:

```
5 == 5 && 4 == 4     // true because both expressions are true
5 == 3 && 4 == 4     // false because first expression is false
5 > 3 && 5 > 10      // false because second expression is false
5 > 8 && 5 < 10      // false because first expression is false
5 < 8 && 5 > 2       // true because both expressions are true
5 > 8 && 5 < 2       // false because both expressions are false
```

Because the **&&** has a lower precedence than the relational operators, you don't need to use parentheses in these expressions. Like the **||** operator, the **&&** operator acts as a sequence point, so the left side is evaluated and any side effects are carried out before the right side is evaluated. If the left side is false, the whole logical expression must be false, so C++ doesn't bother evaluating the right side in that case. Table 6.2 summarizes how the **&&** operator works.

TABLE 6.2   The && Operator

	The Value of expr1 && expr2	
	expr1 == true	expr1 == false
expr2 == true	true	false
expr2 == false	false	false

Listing 6.5 shows how to use **&&** to cope with a common situation, terminating a **while** loop, for two different reasons. In the listing, a **while** loop reads values into an array. One test (**i < ArSize**) terminates the loop when the array is full. The second test (**temp >= 0**) gives the user the option of quitting early by entering a negative number. The **&&** operator lets you combine the two tests into a single condition. The program also uses two **if** statements, an **if else** statement, and a **for** loop, so it demonstrates several topics from this and the preceding chapter.

LISTING 6.5   and.cpp

```cpp
// and.cpp -- use logical AND operator
#include <iostream>
using namespace std;
const int ArSize = 6;
int main()
{
    float naaq[ArSize];
    cout << "Enter the NAAQs (New Age Awareness Quotients) "
        << "of\nyour neighbors. Program terminates "
        << "when you make\n" << ArSize << " entries "
        << "or enter a negative value.\n";

    int i = 0;
    float temp;
    cin >> temp;
    while (i < ArSize && temp >= 0) // 2 quitting criteria
    {
        naaq[i++] = temp;
        if (i < ArSize)              // room left in the array,
            cin >> temp;             // so get next value
    }
    if (i == 0)
        cout << "No data--bye\n";
    else
    {
        cout << "Enter your NAAQ: ";
        float you;
        cin >> you;
        int count = 0;
        for (int j = 0; j < i; j++)
            if (naaq[j] > you)
```

LISTING 6.5 *Continued*

```
                    count++;
          cout << count;
          cout << " of your neighbors have greater awareness of\n"
               << "the New Age than you do.\n";
     }
     return 0;
}
```

Note that the program places input into a temporary variable `temp`. Only after it verifies that the input is valid does the program assign the value to the array.

Here are a couple of sample runs. One terminates after six entries, and the second terminates after a negative value is entered:

```
Enter the NAAQs (New Age Awareness Quotients) of
your neighbors. Program terminates when you make
6 entries or enter a negative value.
28 72 19
6
130 145
Enter your NAAQ: 50
3 of your neighbors have greater awareness of
the New Age than you do.

Enter the NAAQs (New Age Awareness Quotients) of
your neighbors. Program terminates when you make
6 entries or enter a negative value.
123 119
4
89
-1
Enter your NAAQ: 123.027
0 of your neighbors have greater awareness of
the New Age than you do.
```

Program Notes

Look at the input part of the program:

```
cin >> temp;
while (i < ArSize && temp >= 0)      // 2 quitting criteria
{
     naaq[i++] = temp;
     if (i < ArSize)                 // room left in the array,
          cin >> temp;               // so read next value
}
```

The program begins by reading the first input value into a temporary variable called `temp`. Then, the `while` test condition checks to see if there still is room left in the array (`i < ArSize`) and if the input value is nonnegative (`temp >= 0`). If so, it copies the `temp` value to the array and increases the array index by 1. At this point, because array numbering starts at 0, `i` equals the total number of entries to date. That is, if `i` starts out at 0, the first cycle through the loop assigns a value to `naaq[0]` and then sets `i` to 1.

The loop terminates when the array is filled or when the user enters a negative number. Note that the loop reads another value into `temp` only if `i` is less than `ArSize`, that is, only if there still is room left in the array.

After it gets data, the program uses an `if else` statement to comment if no data were entered (that is, if the first entry was a negative number) and to process the data if any is present.

Setting Up Ranges with &&

The `&&` operator also lets you set up a series of `if else if else` statements with each choice corresponding to a particular range of values. Listing 6.6 illustrates the approach. It also shows a useful technique for handling a series of messages. Just as a pointer-to-`char` variable can identify a single string by pointing to its beginning, an array of pointers-to-`char` can identify a series of strings. Simply assign the address of each string to a different array element. Listing 6.6 uses the `qualify` array to hold the addresses of four strings. For example, `qualify[1]` holds the address of the string `"mud tug-of-war\n"`. The program then can use `qualify[1]` like any other pointer to a string—for example, with `cout` or with `strlen()` or `strcmp()`. Using the `const` qualifier protects these strings from accidental alterations.

LISTING 6.6   `more_and.cpp`

```
// more_and.cpp -- use logical AND operator
#include <iostream>
using namespace std;
const char * qualify[4] =        // an array of pointers
{                                // to strings
    "10,000-meter race.\n",
    "mud tug-of-war.\n",
    "masters canoe jousting.\n",
    "pie-throwing festival.\n"
};
int main()
{
    int age;
    cout << "Enter your age in years: ";
    cin >> age;
    int index;

    if (age > 17 && age < 35)
        index = 0;
    else if (age >= 35 && age < 50)
        index = 1;
    else if (age >= 50 && age < 65)
        index = 2;
    else
        index = 3;
```

LISTING 6.6   Continued

```
    cout << "You qualify for the " << qualify[index];
    return 0;
}
```

Compatibility Note

You might recall that some C++ implementations require that you use the keyword `static` in an array declaration in order to make it possible to initialize that array. That restriction, as Chapter 9, "Memory Models and Namespaces," discusses, applies to arrays declared inside a function body. When an array is declared outside a function body, as is `qualify` in Listing 6.6, it's termed an *external* array and can be initialized even in pre-ANSI C implementations.

Here is a sample run:

```
Enter your age in years: 87
You qualify for the pie-throwing festival.
```

The entered age didn't match any of the test ranges, so the program set index to 3 and then printed the corresponding string.

Program Notes

The expression `age > 17 && age < 35` tests for ages between the two values, that is, ages in the range 18–34. The expression `age >= 35 && age < 50` uses the `<=` operator to include 35 in its range, which is 35–49. If the program had used `age > 35 && age < 50`, the value 35 would have been missed by all the tests. When you use range tests, you should check that the ranges don't have holes between them and that they don't overlap. Also, be sure to set up each range correctly; see the note on Range Tests.

The `if else` statement serves to select an array index, which, in turn, identifies a particular string.

Range Tests

Note that each part of a range test should use the AND operator to join two complete relational expressions:

```
if (age > 17 && age < 35)    // OK
```

Don't borrow from mathematics and use the following notation:

```
if (17 < age < 35)           // Don't do this!
```

If you make this error, the compiler won't catch it, for it still is valid C++ syntax. The `<` operator associates from left to right, so the previous expression means the following:

```
if ( (17 < age) < 35)
```

But `17 < age` is either `true`, or 1, or else `false`, or 0. In either case, the expression `17 < age` is less than `35`, so the entire test is always `true`!

The Logical NOT Operator: !

The ! operator negates, or reverses the truth value of, the expression that follows it. That is, if expression is true, then !expression is false, and vice versa. More precisely, if expression is true or nonzero, then !expression is false. Incidentally, many people call the exclamation point *bang*, making !x bang-exe and !!x bang-bang-exe.

Usually you more clearly can express a relationship without using this operator:

```
if (!(x > 5))           // if (x <= 5) is clearer
```

But the ! operator can be useful with functions that return true-false values or values that can be interpreted that way. For example, strcmp(s1,s2) returns a nonzero (true) value if the two strings s1 and s2 are different from each other and a zero value if they are the same. This implies that !strcmp(s1,s2) is true if the two strings are equal.

Listing 6.7 uses this technique (applying the ! operator to a function return value) to screen numeric input for suitability to be assigned to type int. The user-defined function is_int(), which we discuss further in a moment, returns true if its argument is within the range of values assignable to type int. The program then uses the test while(!is_int(num)) to reject values that don't fit in the range.

LISTING 6.7   not.cpp

```cpp
// not.cpp -- using the not operator
#include <iostream>
#include <climits>
using namespace std;
bool is_int(double);
int main()
{
    double num;

    cout << "Yo, dude! Enter an integer value: ";
    cin >> num;
    while (!is_int(num))     // continue while num is not int-able
    {
        cout << "Out of range -- please try again: ";
        cin >> num;
    }
    int val = num;
    cout << "You've entered the integer " << val << "\nBye\n";
    return 0;
}

bool is_int(double x)
{
    if (x <= INT_MAX && x >= INT_MIN)     // use climits values
        return true;
    else
        return false;
}
```

Compatibility Note

If your system doesn't provide `climits`, use `limits.h`.

Here is a sample run on a system with a 32-bit `int`:

```
Yo, dude! Enter an integer value: 6234128679
Out of range -- please try again: -8000222333
Out of range -- please try again: 99999
You've entered the integer 99999
Bye
```

Program Notes

If you enter a too-large value to a program reading a type `int`, many implementations simply truncate the value to fit without informing you that data was lost. This program avoids that by first reading the potential `int` as a `double`. The `double` type has more than enough precision to hold a typical `int` value, and its range is much greater.

The Boolean function `is_int()` uses the two symbolic constants (`INT_MAX` and `INT_MIN`) defined in the `climits` file (discussed in Chapter 3, "Dealing with Data") to determine whether its argument is within the proper limits. If so, the program returns a value of `true`; otherwise, it returns `false`.

The `main()` program uses a `while` loop to reject invalid input until the user gets it right. You could make the program friendlier by displaying the `int` limits when the input is out of range. Once the input has been validated, the program assigns it to an `int` variable.

Logical Operator Facts

As we mentioned, the C++ logical OR and logical AND operators have a lower precedence than relational operators. That means an expression such as

```
x > 5 && x < 10
```

is read this way:

```
(x > 5) && (x < 10)
```

The `!` operator, on the other hand, has a higher precedence than any of the relational or arithmetic operators. Therefore, to negate an expression, you should enclose the expression in parentheses:

```
!(x > 5)      // is it false that x is greater than 5
!x > 5        // is !x greater than 5
```

The second expression, incidentally, is always false, for `!x` only can have the values `true` or `false`, which get converted to 1 or 0.

The logical AND operator has a higher precedence than the logical OR operator. Thus the expression

```
age > 30 && age < 45 || weight > 300
```

means the following:

```
(age > 30 && age < 45) || weight > 300
```

That is, one condition is that **age** be in the range 31 to 44, and the second condition is that **weight** be greater than 300. The entire expression is **true** if one or the other or both of these conditions are true.

You can, of course, use parentheses to tell the program the interpretation you want. For example, suppose you want to use **&&** to combine the condition that **age** be greater than 50 or **weight** be greater than 300 with the condition that **donation** be greater than 1000. You have to enclose the OR part within parentheses:

```
(age > 50 || weight > 300) && donation > 1000
```

Otherwise, the compiler combines the **weight** condition with the **donation** condition instead of with the **age** condition.

Although the C++ operator precedence rules often make it possible to write compound comparisons without using parentheses, the simplest course of action is to use parentheses to group the tests, whether or not the parentheses are needed. It makes the code easier to read, it doesn't force someone else to look up some of the less commonly used precedence rules, and it reduces the chance of making errors because you don't quite remember the exact rule that applies.

C++ guarantees that when a program evaluates a logical expression, it evaluates it from left to right and stops evaluation as soon as it knows what the answer is. Suppose, for example, you have this condition:

```
x != 0  && 1.0 / x > 100.0
```

If the first condition is false, then the whole expression must be false. That's because for this expression to be true, each individual condition must be true. Knowing the first condition is false, the program doesn't bother evaluating the second condition. That's fortunate in this example, for evaluating the second condition would result in dividing by 0, which is not in a computer's realm of possible actions.

Alternative Representations

Not all keyboards provide all the symbols used for the logical operators, so the C++ standard provides alternative representations, as shown in Table 6.3. The identifiers **and**, **or**, and **not** are C++ reserved words, meaning you can't use them as names for variables, etc. They are not considered keywords because they are alternative representations of existing language features. Incidentally, these are not reserved words in C, but a C program can use them as operators providing it includes the **iso646.h** header file. C++ does not require using a header file.

TABLE 6.3 Logical Operators: Alternative Representations

Operator	Alternative Representation	
&&	and	
||	or	
!	not	

The `cctype` Library of Character Functions

C++ has inherited from C a handy package of character-related functions, prototyped in the `cctype` header file (`ctype.h`, in the older style), that simplify such tasks as determining whether a character is an uppercase letter or a digit or punctuation, and the like. For example, the `isalpha(ch)` function returns a nonzero value if `ch` is a letter and a zero value otherwise. Similarly, the `ispunct(ch)` returns a true value only if `ch` is a punctuation character, such as a comma or period. (These functions have return type `int` rather than `bool`, but the usual `bool` conversions allow you to treat them as type `bool`.)

Using these functions is more convenient than using the AND and OR operators. For example, here's how you might use AND and OR to test if a character `ch` is an alphabetic character:

```
if ((ch >= 'a' && ch <= 'z') || (ch >= 'A' && ch <= 'Z'))
```

Compare that to using `isalpha()`:

```
if (isalpha(ch))
```

Not only is `isalpha()` easier to use, it is more general. The AND, OR form assumes that character codes for A through Z are in sequence, with no other characters having codes in that range. This assumption is true for the ASCII code, but it need not be true in general.

Listing 6.8 demonstrates some functions from this family. In particular, it uses `isalpha()`, which tests for alphabetic characters; `isdigits()`, which tests for digit characters, such as 3; `isspace()`, which tests for white-space characters, such as newlines, spaces, and tabs; and `ispunct()`, which tests for punctuation characters. The program also reviews the `if else if` structure and using a `while` loop with `cin.get(char)`.

LISTING 6.8 `cctypes.cpp`

```
// cctypes.cpp--use ctype.h library
#include <iostream>
#include <cctype>                    // prototypes for character functions
using namespace std;
int main()
{
    cout << "Enter text for analysis, and type @"
            " to terminate input.\n";
```

LISTING 6.8   Continued

```
        char ch;
        int whitespace = 0;
        int digits = 0;
        int chars = 0;
        int punct = 0;
        int others = 0;

        cin.get(ch);              // get first character
        while(ch != '@')          // test for sentinal
        {
            if(isalpha(ch))       // is it an alphabetic character?
                chars++;
            else if(isspace(ch))  // is it a whitespace character?
                whitespace++;
            else if(isdigit(ch))  // is it a digit?
                digits++;
            else if(ispunct(ch))  // is it punctuation?
                punct++;
            else
                others++;
            cin.get(ch);          // get next character
        }
        cout << chars << " letters, "
             << whitespace << " whitespace, "
             << digits << " digits, "
             << punct << " punctuations, "
             << others << " others.\n";
        return 0;
}
```

Here is a sample run; note that the white-space count includes newlines:

```
Enter text for analysis, and type @ to terminate input.
Jody "Java-Java" Joystone, noted restaurant critic,
celebrated her 39th birthday with a carafe of 1982
Chateau Panda.@
89 letters, 16 whitespace, 6 digits, 6 punctuations, 0 others.
```

Table 6.4 summarizes the functions available in the **cctype** package. Some systems may lack some of these functions or have additional ones.

TABLE 6.4   The **cctype** Character Functions

Function name	Return value
isalnum()	True if argument is alphanumeric, i.e., a letter or a digit
isalpha()	True if argument is alphabetic
iscntrl()	True if argument is a control character
isdigit()	True if argument is a decimal digit (0–9)

TABLE 6.4   Continued

Function name	Return value
isgraph()	True if argument is any printing character other than a space
islower()	True if argument is a lowercase letter
isprint()	True if argument is any printing character, including a space
ispunct()	True if argument is a punctuation character
isspace()	True if argument is a standard white-space character, i.e., a space, formfeed, newline, carriage return, horizontal tab, or vertical tab
isupper()	True if argument is an uppercase letter
isxdigit()	True if argument is a hexadecimal digit character, i.e., 0–9, a–f, or A–F
tolower()	If the argument is an uppercase character, tolower() returns the lowercase version of that character; otherwise, it returns the argument unaltered
toupper()	If the argument is a lowercase character, toupper() returns the uppercase version of that character; otherwise, it returns the argument unaltered

The ?: Operator

C++ has an operator that often can be used instead of the **if else** statement. This operator is called the *conditional operator*, written **?:**, and, for you trivia buffs, it is the only C++ operator that requires three operands. The general form looks like this:

expression1 ? *expression2* : *expression3*

If *expression1* is true, then the value of the whole conditional expression is the value of *expression2*. Otherwise, the value of the whole expression is the value of *expression3*. Here are two examples showing how the operator works:

```
5 > 3 ? 10 : 12   // 5 > 3 is true, so expression value is 10
3 == 9? 25 : 18   // 3 == 9 is false, so expression value is 18
```

We can paraphrase the first example this way: If 5 is greater than 3, the expression evaluates to 10; otherwise, it evaluates to 12. In real programming situations, of course, the expressions would involve variables.

Listing 6.9 uses the conditional operator to determine the larger of two values.

LISTING 6.9 condit.cpp

```
// condit.cpp -- using the conditional operator
#include <iostream>
using namespace std;
int main()
{
    int a, b;
    cout << "Enter two integers: ";
    cin >> a >> b;
    cout << "The larger of " << a << " and " << b;
    int c = a > b ? a : b;   // c = a if a > b, else c = b
    cout << " is " << c << "\n";
    return 0;
}
```

Here is a sample run:

```
Enter two numbers: 25 27
The larger of 25 and 27 is 27
```

The key part of the program is this statement:

```
int c = a > b ? a : b;
```

It produces the same result as the following statements:

```
int c;
if (a > b)
    c = a;
else
    c = b;
```

Compared to the if else sequence, the conditional operator is more concise but, at first, less obvious. One difference between the two approaches is that the conditional operator produces an expression and hence a single value that can be assigned or be incorporated into a larger expression, as the program did when it assigned the value of the conditional expression to the variable c. The conditional operator's concise form, unusual syntax, and overall weird appearance make it a great favorite among programmers who appreciate those qualities. One favorite trick for the reprehensible goal of concealing the purpose of code is to nest conditional expressions within one another, as the following mild example shows:

```
const char x[2] [20] = {"Jason ","at your service\n"};
const char * y = "Quillstone ";

for (int i = 0; i < 3; i++)
    cout << ((i < 2)? !i ? x [i] : y : x[1]);
```

This is merely an obscure (but, by no means, maximally obscure) way to print the three strings in the following order:

```
Jason Quillstone at your service
```

In terms of readability, the conditional operator is best suited for simple relationships and simple expression values:

```
x = (x > y) ? x : y;
```

If the code becomes more involved, it probably can be expressed more clearly as an `if else` statement.

The `switch` Statement

Suppose you create a screen menu that asks the user to select one of five choices, for example, Cheap, Moderate, Expensive, Extravagant, and Excessive. You can extend an `if else if else` sequence to handle five alternatives, but the C++ `switch` statement more easily handles selecting a choice from an extended list. Here's the general form for a `switch` statement:

```
switch (integer-expression)
{
    case label1 : statement(s)
    case label2 : statement(s)
    ...
    default     : statement(s)
}
```

A C++ `switch` statement acts as a routing device that tells the computer which line of code to execute next. On reaching a `switch`, the program jumps to the line labeled with the value corresponding to the value of *integer-expression*. For example, if *integer-expression* has the value 4, the program goes to the line having a `case 4:` label. The value *integer-expression*, as the name suggests, must be an expression that reduces to an integer value. Also, each label must be an integer constant expression. Most often, labels are simple `int` or `char` constants, such as `1` or `'q'`, or enumerators. If *integer-expression* doesn't match any of the labels, the program jumps to the line labeled `default`. The `default` label is optional. If you omit it and there is no match, the program jumps to the next statement following the `switch`. (See Figure 6.3.)

The `switch` statement is different from similar statements in languages such as Pascal in a very important way. Each C++ case label functions only as a line label, not as a boundary between choices. That is, after a program jumps to a particular line in a `switch`, it then sequentially executes all the statements following that line in the switch unless you explicitly direct it otherwise. Execution does NOT automatically stop at the next case. To make execution stop at the end of a particular group of statements, you must use the `break` statement. This causes execution to jump to the statement following the `switch`.

Listing 6.10 shows how to use `switch` and `break` together to implement a simple menu for executives. The program uses a `showmenu()` function to display a set of choices. A `switch` statement then selects an action based on the user's response.

FIGURE 6.3

The switch statement.

Compatibility Note

Some implementations treat the \a escape sequence (used in **case** 1 in Listing 6.10) as silent.

LISTING 6.10   switch.cpp

```cpp
// switch.cpp -- use the switch statement
#include <iostream>
using namespace std;
void showmenu();   // function prototypes
void report();
void comfort();
int main()
{
    showmenu();
    int choice;
    cin >> choice;
    while (choice != 5)
    {
        switch(choice)
        {
            case 1  :   cout << "\a\n";
                        break;
            case 2  :   report();
                        break;
            case 3  :   cout << "The boss was in all day.\n";
                        break;
            case 4  :   comfort();
                        break;
            default :   cout << "That's not a choice.\n";
        }
        showmenu();
        cin >> choice;
    }
    cout << "Bye!\n";
```

LISTING 6.10   Continued

```
        return 0;
    }

    void showmenu()
    {
        cout << "Please enter 1, 2, 3, 4, or 5:\n"
                "1) alarm            2) report\n"
                "3) alibi            4) comfort\n"
                "5) quit\n";
    }
    void report()
    {
        cout << "It's been an excellent week for business.\n"
            "Sales are up 120%. Expenses are down 35%.\n";
    }
    void comfort()
    {
        cout << "Your employees think you are the finest CEO\n"
            "in the industry. The board of directors think\n"
            "you are the finest CEO in the industry.\n";
    }
```

Here is a sample run of the executive menu program:

```
Please enter 1, 2, 3, 4, or 5:
1) alarm            2) report
3) alibi            4) comfort
5) quit
4
Your employees think you are the finest CEO
in the industry. The board of directors think
you are the finest CEO in the industry.
Please enter 1, 2, 3, 4, or 5:
1) alarm            2) report
3) alibi            4) comfort
5) quit
2
It's been an excellent week for business.
Sales are up 120%. Expenses are down 35%.
Please enter 1, 2, 3, 4, or 5:
1) alarm            2) report
3) alibi            4) comfort
5) quit
6
That's not a choice.
Please enter 1, 2, 3, 4, or 5:
1) alarm            2) report
3) alibi            4) comfort
5) quit
5
Bye!
```

The `while` loop terminates when the user enters a 5. Entering 1 through 4 activates the corresponding choice from the `switch` list, and entering 6 triggers the default statements.

As noted before, this program needs the **break** statements to confine execution to a particular portion of a switch. To see that this is so, you can remove the **break** statements from Listing 6.10 and see how it works afterwards. You'll find, for example, that entering 2 causes the program to execute *all* the statements associated with case labels 2, 3, 4, and the default. C++ works this way because that sort of behavior can be useful. For one thing, it makes it simple to use multiple labels. For example, suppose you rewrote Listing 6.10 using characters instead of integers as menu choices and switch labels. Then, you could use both an uppercase and a lowercase label for the same statements:

```cpp
char choice;
cin >> choice;
while (choice != 'Q' && choice != 'q')
{
    switch(choice)
    {
        case 'a':
        case 'A': cout << "\a\n";
                  break;
        case 'r':
        case 'R': report();
                  break;
        case 'l':
        case 'L': cout << "The boss was in all day.\n";
                  break;
        case 'c'
        case 'C': comfort();
                  break;
        default : cout << "That's not a choice.\n";
    }
    showmenu();
    cin >> choice;
}
```

Because there is no **break** immediately following `case 'a'`, program execution passes on to the next line, which is the statement following `case 'A'`.

Using Enumerators as Labels

Listing 6.11 illustrates using **enum** to define a set of related constants and then using the constants in a `switch`. In general, `cin` doesn't recognize enumerated types (it can't know how you will define them), so the program reads the choice as an `int`. When the `switch` statement compares the `int` value to an enumerator case label, it promotes the enumerator to `int`. Also, the enumerators are promoted to type `int` in the `while` loop test condition.

LISTING 6.11   enum.cpp

```cpp
// enum.cpp -- use enum
#include <iostream>
using namespace std;
// create named constants for 0 - 6
enum {red, orange, yellow, green, blue, violet, indigo};

int main()
{
    cout << "Enter color code (0-6): ";
    int code;
    cin >> code;
    while (code >= red && code <= indigo)
    {
        switch (code)
        {
            case red    : cout << "Her lips were red.\n"; break;
            case orange : cout << "Her hair was orange.\n"; break;
            case yellow : cout << "Her shoes were yellow.\n"; break;
            case green  : cout << "Her nails were green.\n"; break;
            case blue   : cout << "Her sweatsuit was blue.\n"; break;
            case violet : cout << "Her eyes were violet.\n"; break;
            case indigo : cout << "Her mood was indigo.\n"; break;
        }
        cout << "Enter color code (0-6): ";
        cin >> code;
    }
    cout << "Bye\n";
    return 0;
}
```

Here's a sample output:

```
Enter color code (0-6): 3
Her nails were green.
Enter color code (0-6): 5
Her eyes were violet.
Enter color code (0-6): 2
Her shoes were yellow.
Enter color code (0-6): 8
Bye
```

switch **and** if else

Both the `switch` statement and the `if else` statement let a program select from a list of alternatives. The `if else` is the more versatile of the two. For example, it can handle ranges, as in the following:

```cpp
if (age > 17 && age < 35)
    index = 0;
else if (age >= 35 && age < 50)
    index = 1;
```

```
else if (age >= 50 && age < 65)
    index = 2;
else
    index = 3;
```

The switch, however, isn't designed to handle ranges. Each switch case label must be a single value. Also, that value must be an integer (which includes char), so a switch won't handle floating-point tests. And the case label value must be a constant. If your alternatives involve ranges or floating-point tests or comparing two variables, use if else.

If, however, all the alternatives can be identified with integer constants, you can use a switch or an if else statement. Because that's precisely the situation that the switch statement is designed to process, the switch statement usually is the more efficient choice in terms of code size and execution speed, unless there are only a couple of alternatives from which to choose.

Tip

If you can use either an if else if sequence or a switch statement, the usual rule is to use a switch if you have three or more alternatives.

The break and continue Statements

The break and continue statements enable a program to skip over parts of the code. You can use the break statement in a switch statement and in any of the loops. It causes program execution to pass to the next statement following the switch or the loop. The continue statement is used in loops and causes a program to skip the rest of the body of the loop and then start a new loop cycle. (See Figure 6.4.)

Listing 6.12 shows how the two statements work. The program lets you enter a line of text. The loop echoes each character and uses break to terminate the loop if the character is a period. This shows how you can use break to terminate a loop from within when some condition becomes true. Next the program counts spaces, but not other characters. The loop uses continue to skip over the counting part of the loop when the character isn't a space.

LISTING 6.12   jump.cpp

```
// jump.cpp -- using continue and break
#include <iostream>
using namespace std;
const int ArSize = 80;
int main()
{
    char line[ArSize];
    int spaces = 0;

    cout << "Enter a line of text:\n";
    cin.get(line, ArSize);
    for (int i = 0; line[i] != '\0'; i++)
    {
```

LISTING 6.12   *Continued*

```
            cout << line[i];    // display character
            if (line[i] == '.') // quit if it's a period
                break;
            if (line[i] != ' ') // skip rest of loop
                continue;
            spaces++;
        }
        cout << "\n" << spaces << " spaces\n";
        cout << "Done.\n";
        return 0;
    }
```

Here's a sample run:

Let's do lunch today. You can pay!
Let's do lunch today.
3 spaces
Done.

FIGURE 6.4

The `break` and `continue` statements.

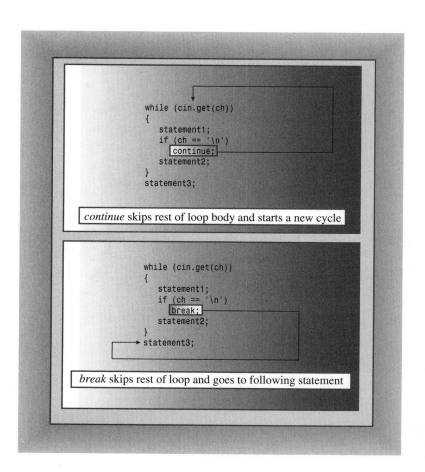

```
while (cin.get(ch))
{
    statement1;
    if (ch == '\n')
        continue;
    statement2;
}
statement3;
```

continue skips rest of loop body and starts a new cycle

```
while (cin.get(ch))
{
    statement1;
    if (ch == '\n')
        break;
    statement2;
}
statement3;
```

break skips rest of loop and goes to following statement

Program Notes

Note that whereas the `continue` statement causes the program to skip the rest of the loop body, it doesn't skip the loop update expression. In a `for` loop, the `continue` statement makes the program skip directly to the update expression and then to the test expression. For a `while` loop, however, `continue` makes the program go directly to the test expression. So any update expression in a `while` loop body following the `continue` would be skipped. In some cases, that could be a problem.

This program didn't have to use `continue`. Instead, it could have used this code:

```
if (line[i] == ' ')
    spaces++;
```

However, the `continue` statement can make the program more readable when several statements follow the `continue`. That way, you don't need to make all those statements part of an `if` statement.

C++, like C, also has a `goto` statement. A statement like

```
goto paris
```

means to jump to the location bearing `paris:` as a label. That is, you can have code like this:

```
char ch;
cin >> ch;
if (ch == 'P')
    goto paris;
cout << ...
...
paris: cout << "You've just arrived at Paris.\n";
```

In most circumstances, using a `goto` is a bad hack, and you should use structured controls, such as `if else`, `switch`, `continue`, and the like, to control program flow.

Number-Reading Loops

You're preparing a program to read a series of numbers into an array. You want to give the user the option to terminate input before filling the array. One way is utilize how `cin` behaves. Consider the following code:

```
int n;
cin >> n;
```

What happens if the user responds by entering a word instead of a number? Four things occur in such a mismatch:

- The value of `n` is left unchanged.
- The mismatched input is left in the input queue.

- An error flag is set in the `cin` object.

- The call to the `cin` method, if converted to type `bool`, returns `false`.

The fact that the method returns `false` means that you can use non-numeric input to terminate a number-reading loop. The fact that non-numeric input sets an error flag means that you have to reset the flag before the program can read more input. The `clear()` method, which also resets the end-of-file condition (see Chapter 5), resets the bad input flag. (Either bad input or end-of-file can cause `cin` to return `false`. Chapter 17, "Input, Output, and Files," discusses how to distinguish between the two cases.) Let's look at a couple of examples illustrating these techniques.

You want to write a program to calculate the average weight of your day's catch of fish. There's a five-fish limit, so a five-element array can hold all the data, but it's possible that you could catch fewer fish. Listing 6.13 uses a loop that terminates if the array is full or if you enter non-numeric input.

LISTING 6.13   cinfish.cpp

```cpp
// cinfish.cpp -- non-numeric input terminates loop
#include <iostream>
using namespace std;
const int Max = 5;
int main()
{
// get data
    double fish[Max];
    cout << "Please enter the weights of your fish.\n";
    cout << "You may enter up to " << Max
            << " fish <q to terminate>.\n";
    cout << "fish #1: ";
    int i = 0;
    while (i < Max && cin >> fish[i]) {
        if (++i < Max)
            cout << "fish #" << i+1 << ": ";
    }
// calculate average
    double total = 0.0;
    for (int j = 0; j < i; j++)
        total += fish[j];
// report results
    if (i == 0)
        cout << "No fish\n";
    else
        cout << total / i << " = average weight of "
            << i << " fish\n";
    cout << "Done.\n";
    return 0;
}
```

Compatibility Note

Some older Borland compilers give a warning about

```
cout << "fish #" << i+1 << ": ";
```

to the effect that ambiguous operators need parentheses. Don't worry. They're just warning about a possible grouping error if << is used in its original meaning as a left-shift operator.

The expression `cin >> fish[i]` really is a `cin` method function call, and the function returns `cin`. If `cin` is part of a test condition, it's converted to type `bool`. The conversion value is `true` if input succeeds and `false` otherwise. A `false` value for the expression terminates the loop. By the way, here's a sample run:

```
Please enter the weights of your fish.
You may enter up to 5 fish <q to terminate>.
fish #1: 30
fish #2: 35
fish #3: 25
fish #4: 40
fish #5: q
32.5 = average weight of 4 fish
Done.
```

Note the following line of code:

```
while (i < Max && cin >> fish[i]) {
```

Recall that C++ doesn't evaluate the right side of a logical AND expression if the left side is false. In this case, evaluating the right side means using `cin` to place input into the array. If `i` does equal `Max`, the loop terminates without trying to read a value into a location past the end of the array.

The last example didn't attempt to read any input after non-numeric input. Let's look at a case that does. Suppose you are required to submit exactly five golf scores to a C++ program to establish your average. If a user enters non-numeric input, the program should object, insisting on numeric input. As you've seen, you can use the value of a `cin` input expression to test for non-numeric input. Suppose you find the user did enter the wrong stuff. You need to take three steps:

- Reset `cin` to accept new input.

- Get rid of the bad input.

- Prompt the user to try again.

Note that you have to reset `cin` before getting rid of the bad input. Listing 6.14 shows how these tasks can be accomplished.

LISTING 6.14   `cingolf.cpp`

```cpp
// cingolf.cpp -- non-numeric input skipped
#include <iostream>
using namespace std;
const int Max = 5;
int main()
{
// get data
    int golf[Max];
    cout << "Please enter your golf scores.\n";
    cout << "You must enter " << Max << " rounds.\n";
    int i;
    for (i = 0; i < Max; i++)
    {
        cout << "round #" << i+1 << ": ";
        while (!(cin >> golf[i])) {
            cin.clear();        // reset input
            while (cin.get() != '\n')
                continue;       // get rid of bad input
            cout << "Please enter a number: ";
        }
    }
// calculate average
    double total = 0.0;
    for (i = 0; i < Max; i++)
        total += golf[i];
// report results
    cout << total / Max << " = average score "
            << Max << " rounds\n";
    return 0;
}
```

Compatibility Note

Some older Borland compilers give a warning about

```cpp
cout << "round #" << i+1 << ": ";
```

to the effect that ambiguous operators need parentheses. Don't worry. They're just warning about a possible grouping error if << is used in its original meaning as a left-shift operator.

Here is a sample run:

```
Please enter your golf scores.
You must enter 5 rounds.
round #1: 88
round #2: 87
round #3: must i?
Please enter a number: 103
round #4: 94
round #5: 86
91.6 = average score 5 rounds
```

Program Notes

The heart of the error-handling code is the following:

```
while (!(cin >> golf[i])) {
    cin.clear();      // reset input
    while (cin.get() != '\n')
        continue; // get rid of bad input
    cout << "Please enter a number: ";
}
```

If the user enters 88, the `cin` expression is `true`, a value is placed in the array, the expression `!(cin >> golf[i])` is `false`, and this inner loop terminates. But if the user enters `must i?`, the `cin` expression is `false`, nothing is placed into the array, the expression `!(cin >> golf[i])` is `true`, and the program enters the inner `while` loop. The first statement in the loop uses the `clear()` method to reset input. If you omit this statement, the program refuses to read any more input. Next, the program uses `cin.get()` in a `while` loop to read the remaining input through the end of the line. This gets rid of the bad input along with anything else on the line. Another approach is to read to the next white space, which would get rid of bad input one word at a time instead of one line at a time. Finally, the program tells the user to enter a number.

Summary

Programs and programming become more interesting when you introduce statements that guide the program through alternative actions. (Whether this also makes the programmer more interesting is a point we've not fully researched.) C++ provides the `if` statement, the `if else` statement, and the `switch` statements as means for managing choices. The C++ `if` statement lets a program execute a statement or statement block conditionally. That is, the program executes the statement or block if a particular condition is met. The C++ `if else` statement lets a program select from two choices which statement or statement block to execute. You can append additional `if else`s to the statement to present a series of choices. The C++ `switch` statement directs the program to a particular case in a list of choices.

C++ also provides operators to help in decision making. Chapter 5 discusses the relational expressions, which compare two values. The `if` and `if else` statements typically use relational expressions as test conditions. By using C++'s logical operators (`&&`, `||`, and `!`), you can combine or modify relational expressions, constructing more elaborate tests. The conditional operator (`?:`) provides a compact way to choose from two values.

The `cctype` library of character functions provides a convenient and powerful set of tools for analyzing character input.

With C++'s loops and decision-making statements, you have the tools for writing interesting, intelligent, and powerful programs. But we've only begun to investigate the real powers of C++. Next, we look at functions.

Review Questions

1. Consider the following two code fragments for counting spaces and newlines:

```
// Version 1
while (cin.get(ch))      // quit on eof
{
    if (ch == ' ')
            spaces++;
    if (ch == '\n')
          newlines++;
}
// Version 2
while (cin.get(ch))      // quit on eof
{
    if (ch == ' ')
            spaces++;
    else if (ch == '\n')
          newlines++;
}
```

What advantages, if any, does the second form have over the first?

2. In Listing 6.2, what is the effect of replacing ++ch with ch+1?

3. Consider carefully the following program:

```
#include <iostream>
using namespace std;
int main()
{
    char ch;
    int ct1, ct2;

    ct1 = ct2 = 0;
    while ((ch = cin.get()) != '$')
    {
        cout << ch;
        ct1++;
        if (ch = '$')
              ct2++;
        cout << ch;
    }
    cout <<"ct1 = " << ct1 << ", ct2 = " << ct2 << "\n";
    return 0;
}
```

Suppose we provide the following input, where ➡ represents pressing Enter:

```
Hi!➡
Send $10 or $20 now! ➡
```

What is the output? (Recall that input is buffered.)

4. Construct logical expressions to represent the following conditions:

    a. `weight` is greater than or equal to 115 but less than 125.

    b. `ch` is q or Q.

    c. `x` is even but is not **26**.

    d. `x` is even but is not a multiple of **26**.

    e. `donation` is in the range 1000–2000 or `guest` is **1**.

    f. `ch` is a lowercase letter or an uppercase letter (assume the lowercase letters are coded sequentially and that the uppercase letters are coded sequentially but that there is a gap in the code between uppercase and lowercase).

5. In English the statement "I will not not speak" means the same as "I will speak." In C++, is `!!x` the same as `x`?

6. Construct a conditional expression that is equal to the absolute value of a variable. That is, if a variable `x` is positive, the value of the expression is just `x`, but if `x` is negative, the value of the expression is `-x`, which is positive.

7. Rewrite the following fragment using `switch`:

```
if (ch == 'A')
    a_grade++;
else if (ch == 'B')
    b_grade++;
else if (ch == 'C')
    c_grade++;
else if (ch == 'D')
    d_grade++;
else
    f_grade++;
```

8. In Listing 6.10, what advantage would there be in using character labels, such as **a** and **c**, instead of numbers for the menu choices and switch cases? (Hint: Think about what happens if the user types **q** in either case and what happens if the user types **5** in either case.)

9. Consider the following code fragment:

```
int line = 0;
char ch;
while (cin.get(ch))
{
    if (ch == 'Q')
        break;
    if (ch != '\n')
        continue;
    line++;
}
```

Rewrite this code without using **break** or **continue**.

Programming Exercises

1. Write a program that reads keyboard input to the @ symbol and that echoes the input except for digits, converting each uppercase character to lowercase, and vice versa. (Don't forget the **cctype** family.)

2. Write a program that reads up to ten donation values into an array of **double**. The program should terminate input on non-numeric input. It should report the average of the numbers and also report how many numbers in the array are larger than the average.

3. Write a precursor to a menu-driven program. The program should display a menu offering four choices, each labeled with a letter. If the user responds with a letter other than one of the four valid choices, the program should prompt the user to enter a valid response until the user complies. Then, the program should use a switch to select a simple action based on the user's selection. A program run could look something like this:

```
Please enter one of the following choices:
c) carnivore            p) pianist
t) tree                 g) game
f
Please enter a c, p, t, or g: q
Please enter a c, p, t, or g: t
A maple is a tree.
```

4. When you join the Benevolent Order of Programmers, you can be known at BOP meetings by your real name, your job title, or by your secret BOP name. Write a program that can list members by real name, by job title, by secret name, or by a member's preference. Base the program on the following structure:

```
// Benevolent Order of Programmers name structure
struct bop {
    char fullname[strsize];  // real name
    char title[strsize];     // job title
    char bopname[strsize];   // secret BOP name
    int preference;          // 0 = fullname, 1 = title, 2 = bopname
};
```

In the program, create a small array of such structures and initialize it to suitable values. Have the program run a loop that lets the user select from different alternatives:

```
a. display by name      b. display by title
c. display by bopname   d. display by preference
q. quit
```

Note that "display by preference" does not mean display the preference member; it means display the member corresponding to the preference number. For instance, if preference is 1, choice d would display the programmer's job title. A sample run may look something like the following:

```
Benevolent Order of Programmers Report
a. display by name      b. display by title
c. display by bopname   d. display by preference
```

```
q. quit
Enter your choice: a
Wimp Macho
Raki Rhodes
Celia Laiter
Hoppy Hipman
Pat Hand
Next choice: d
Wimp Macho
Junior Programmer
MIPS
Analyst Trainee
LOOPY
Next choice: q
Bye!
```

5. The Kingdom of Neutronia, where the unit of currency is the tvarp, has the following income tax code:

first 5000 tvarps: 0% tax

next 10000 tvarps: 10% tax

next 20000 tvarps: 15% tax

tvarps after 35000: 20% tax

For example, someone earning 38000 tvarps would owe $5000 \times 0.00 + 10000 \times 0.10 + 20000 \times 0.15 + 3000 \times 0.20$, or 4600 tvarps. Write a program that uses a loop to solicit incomes and to report tax owed. The loop terminates when the user enters a negative number or nonnumeric input.

6. Your task is to put together a program that keeps track of monetary contributions to the Society for the Preservation of Rightful Influence. It should ask the user to enter the number of contributors, then solicit the user to enter the name and contribution of each contributor. The information should be stored in a dynamically allocated array of structures. Each structure should have two members: a character array to store the name and a double member to hold the amount of the contribution. After reading all the data, the program should then display the names and amounts donated for all donors who contributed $10,000 or more. This list should be headed by a label indicating that the following donors are Grand Patrons. After that, the program should list the remaining donors. That list should be headed Patrons. If there are no donors in one of the categories, the program should print the word "none." Aside from displaying two categories, the program need do no sorting.

CHAPTER 7

FUNCTIONS—C++'S PROGRAMMING MODULES

In this chapter you learn

- Function basics (review)
- Function prototypes
- How to pass function arguments by value
- How to design functions to process arrays
- How to use const pointer parameters
- How to design functions to process text strings
- How to design functions to process structures
- Functions that call themselves (recursion)
- Pointers to functions

Fun is where you find it. Look closely, and you can find it in functions. C++ comes with a large library of useful functions (the standard ANSI C library plus several C++ classes), but real programming pleasure comes with writing your own. In this and the next chapter you'll examine how to define functions, convey information to them, and retrieve information from them. After reviewing how functions work, this chapter concentrates on how to use functions in conjunction with arrays, strings, and structures. Finally, it touches on recursion and pointers to functions. If you've paid your C dues, you'll find much of this chapter familiar. But don't be lulled into a false sense of expertise. C++ has made several additions to what C functions can do, and the next chapter deals primarily with those. Meanwhile, let's attend to the fundamentals.

Function Review

First, let's review what you've already seen about functions. To use a C++ function, you must do the following:

- Provide a function definition.
- Provide a function prototype.
- Call the function.

If you're using a library function, the function already has been defined and compiled for you. Also, you can use a standard library header file to provide the prototype. All that's left to do is call the function properly. The examples in this book have done that several times. For example, the standard C library includes the `strlen()` function for finding the length of the string. The associated standard header file `cstring` contains the function prototype for `strlen()` and several other string-related functions. This advance work allows you to use the `strlen()` function in programs without further worries.

But when you create your own functions, you have to handle all three aspects—defining, prototyping, and calling—yourself. Listing 7.1 shows these steps in a short example.

LISTING 7.1   `calling.cpp`

```cpp
// calling.cpp -- defining, prototyping, and calling a function
#include <iostream>
using namespace std;

void simple();     // function prototype

int main()
{
    cout << "main() will call the simple() function:\n";
    simple();      // function call
    return 0;
}

// function definition
void simple()
{
    cout << "I'm but a simple function.\n";
}
```

Here's the output:

```
main() will call the simple() function:
I'm but a simple function.
```

Let's take a more detailed look at these steps now.

Defining a Function

You can group functions into two categories: those that don't have return values and those that do. Functions without return values are termed type **void** functions and have the following general form:

```
void functionName(parameterList)
{
    statement(s)
    return;          // optional
}
```

Here *parameterList* specifies the types and number of arguments (parameters) passed to the function. This chapter more fully investigates this list later. The optional return statement marks the end of the function. Otherwise, the function terminates at the closing brace. Type void functions correspond to Pascal procedures, FORTRAN subroutines, and modern BASIC subprogram procedures. Typically, you use a void function to perform some sort of action. For example, a function to print Cheers! a given number (n) of times can look like this:

```
void cheers(int n)             // no return value
{
    for (int i = 0; i < n; i++)
        cout << "Cheers! ";
    cout << "\n";
}
```

The int n parameter list means that cheers() expects to be passed an int value as an argument when you call this function.

A function with a return value produces a value that it returns to the function that called it. In other words, if the function returns the square root of 9.0 (sqrt(9.0)), then the function call has the value 3.0. Such a function is declared as having the same type as the value it returns. Here is the general form:

```
typeName functionName(parameterList)
{
    statements
    return value;    // value is of type typename
}
```

Functions with return values require that you use a return statement so that the value is returned to the calling function. The value itself can be a constant, a variable, or a more general expression. The only requirement is that the expression reduce to a value that has, or is convertible to, the *typeName* type. (If the declared return type is, say, double, and the function returns an int expression, the int value is typecast to type double.) The function then returns the final value to the function that called it. C++ does place a restriction on what types you can use for a return value: The return value cannot be an array. Everything else is possible— integers, floating-point numbers, pointers, even structures and objects! (Interestingly, even though a C++ function can't return an array directly, it can return an array that's part of a structure or object.)

As a programmer, you don't need to know how a function returns a value, but knowing the method might clarify the concept for you. (Also, it gives you something to talk about with your friends and family.) Typically, a function returns a value by copying the return value to a specified CPU register or memory location. Then, the calling program examines that location. Both the returning function and the calling function have to agree on the type of data at that location. The function prototype tells the calling program what to expect, and the function definition tells the called program what to return (see Figure 7.1). Providing the same information in the prototype as in the definition might seem like extra work, but it does make good sense. Certainly, if you want a courier to pick up something from your desk at the office, you enhance the odds of the task being done right if you provide a description of what you want both to the courier and to someone at the office.

FIGURE 7.1
A typical return value mechanism.

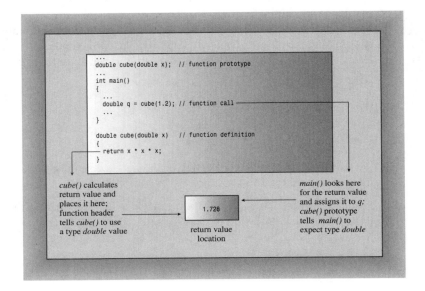

A function terminates after executing a return statement. If a function has more than one return statement—for example, as alternatives to different **if else** selections—the function terminates after it executes the first return statement it reaches:

```
int bigger(int a, int b)
{
    if (a > b )
        return a;  // if a > b, function terminates here
    else
        return b;  // otherwise, function terminates here
}
```

Here the **else** isn't needed, but it does help the casual reader understand the intent.

Functions with return values are much like functions in Pascal, FORTRAN, and BASIC. They return a value to the calling program, which then can assign that value to a variable, display the value, or otherwise use it. Here's a simple example that returns the cube of a type **double** value:

```
double cube(double x)    // x times x times x
{
```

```
        return x * x * x; // a type double value
}
```

For example, the function call `cube(1.2)` returns the value `1.728`. Note that this return statement uses an expression. The function computes the value of the expression (`1.728`, in this case) and returns the value.

Function Prototyping and Function Calls

By now you are familiar with making function calls, but you may be less comfortable with function prototyping because that's often been hidden in the `include` files. Let's use the `cheers()` and `cube()` functions in a program (see Listing 7.2); notice the function prototypes.

LISTING 7.2   protos.cpp

```
// protos.cpp -- use prototypes and function calls
#include <iostream>
using namespace std;
void cheers(int);       // prototype: no return value
double cube(double x);  // prototype: returns a double
int main(void)
{
    cheers(5);          // function call
    cout << "Give me a number: ";
    double side;
    cin >> side;
    double volume = cube(side);    // function call
    cout << "A " << side <<"-foot cube has a volume of ";
    cout << volume << " cubic feet.\n";
    cheers(cube(2));    // prototype protection at work
    return 0;
}

void cheers(int n)
{
    for (int i = 0; i < n; i++)
        cout << "Cheers! ";
    cout << "\n";
}

double cube(double x)
{
    return x * x * x;
}
```

Here's a sample run:

```
Cheers! Cheers! Cheers! Cheers! Cheers!
Give me a number: 5
A 5-foot cube has a volume of 125 cubic feet.
Cheers! Cheers! Cheers! Cheers! Cheers! Cheers! Cheers! Cheers!
```

Note that `main()` calls the type `void` function `cheers()` by using the function name and arguments followed by a semicolon: `cheers(5);`. That's an example of a function call statement. But because `cube()` has a return value, `main()` can use it as part of an assignment statement:

```
double volume = cube(side);
```

But we said you should concentrate on the prototypes. What should you know about prototypes? First, you should understand why C++ requires prototypes. Then, because C++ requires prototypes, you should know the proper syntax. Finally, you should appreciate what the prototype does for you. Let's look at these points in turn, using Listing 7.2 as a basis for discussion.

Why Prototypes?

The prototype describes the function interface to the compiler. That is, it tells the compiler what type of return value, if any, the function has, and it tells the compiler the number and type of function arguments. Consider, for example, how a prototype affects this function call from Listing 7.2:

```
double volume = cube(side);
```

First, the prototype tells the compiler that `cube()` should have one type `double` argument. If the program fails to provide one, prototyping allows the compiler to catch the error. Second, when the `cube()` function finishes its calculation, it places its return value at some specified location—perhaps in a CPU register, perhaps in memory. Then, the calling function, `main()` in this case, retrieves the value from that location. Because the prototype states that `cube()` is type `double`, the compiler knows how many bytes to retrieve and how to interpret them. Without that information, the compiler could only guess, and that is something compilers won't do.

Still, you might wonder, why does the compiler need a prototype? Can't it just look further in the file and see how the functions are defined? One problem with that approach is that it is less efficient. The compiler would have to put compiling `main()` on hold while searching the rest of the file. An even more serious problem is the fact that the function might not even be in the file. C++ allows you to spread a program over several files, which you can compile independently and then combine later. If that's the case, the compiler might not have access to the function code when it's compiling `main()`. The same is true if the function is part of a library. The only way to avoid using a function prototype is to place the function definition before its first use. That is not always possible. Also, the C++ programming style is to put `main()` first because it generally provides the structure for the whole program.

Prototype Syntax

A function prototype is a statement, so it must have a terminating semicolon. The simplest way to get a prototype is to copy the function heading from the function definition and add a semicolon. That's what the program does for `cube()`:

```
double cube(double x); // add ; to heading to get prototype
```

However, the function prototype does not require that you provide names for the variables; a list of types is enough. The program prototypes `cheers()` by using only the argument type:

```
void cheers(int); // okay to drop variable names in prototype
```

In general, you either can include or exclude variable names in the argument lists for prototypes. The variable names in the prototype just act as placeholders, so if you do use names, they don't have to match the names in the function definition.

C++ Versus ANSI C Prototyping

ANSI C borrowed prototyping from C++, but the two languages do have some differences. The most important is that ANSI C, to preserve compatibility with classic C, made prototyping optional, whereas C++ makes prototyping mandatory. For example, consider the following function declaration:

```
void say_hi();
```

In C++, leaving the parentheses empty is the same as using the keyword `void` within the parentheses. It means the function has no arguments. In ANSI C, leaving the parentheses empty means that you are declining to state what the arguments are. That is, it means you're foregoing prototyping the argument list. The C++ equivalent for not identifying the argument list is to use ellipsis:

```
void say_bye(...);   // C++ abdication of resposibility
```

Normally this is needed only for interfacing with C functions having a variable number of arguments, such as `printf()`.

What Prototypes Do for You

You've seen that prototypes help the compiler. But what do they do for you? They greatly reduce the chances for program errors. In particular, prototypes ensure the following:

- The compiler correctly handles the function return value.

- The compiler checks that you use the correct number of function arguments.

- The compiler checks that you use the correct type of arguments. If not, it converts the arguments to the correct type, if possible.

We've already discussed how to handle correctly the return value. Let's look now at what happens when you use the wrong number of arguments. For example, suppose you made the following call:

```
double z = cube();
```

Without function prototyping, the compiler lets this go by. When the function is called, it looks where the call to `cube()` should have placed a number and uses whatever value happens to be there. This, for example, is how C worked before ANSI C borrowed prototyping from C++. Because prototyping is optional for ANSI C, this still is how some C programs work. But in C++ prototyping is not optional, so you are guaranteed protection from that sort of error.

Next, suppose you provide an argument but it is the wrong type. In C, this could create weird errors. For example, if a function expects a type `int` value (assume that's 16 bits) and you pass a `double` (assume that's 64 bits), the function looks at just the first 16 bits of the 64 and tries to interpret them as an `int` value. C++, however, automatically converts the value you pass to the type specified in the prototype, provided that both are arithmetic types. For example, Listing 7.2 manages to get two type mismatches in one statement:

```
cheers(cube(2));
```

First, the program passes the `int` value of 2 to `cube()`, which expects type `double`. The compiler, noting that the `cube()` prototype specifies a type `double` argument, converts 2 to 2.0, a type `double` value. Then, `cube()` returns a type `double` value (8.0) to be used as an argument to `cheers()`. Again, the compiler checks the prototypes and notes that `cheers()` requires an `int`. It converts the return value to the integer 8. In general, prototyping produces automatic type casts to the expected types. (Function overloading, discussed in Chapter 8, "Adventures in Functions," can create ambiguous situations, however, that prevent some automatic type casts.)

Automatic type conversion doesn't head off all possible errors. For example, if you pass a value of 8.33E27 to a function that expects an `int`, such a large value cannot be converted correctly to a mere `int`. Some compilers warn you of possible data loss when there is an automatic conversion from a larger type to a smaller.

Also, prototyping results in type conversion only when it makes sense. It won't, for example, convert an integer to a structure or pointer.

Prototyping takes place during compile time and is termed *static type checking*. Static type checking, as we've just seen, catches many errors that are much more difficult to catch during runtime.

Function Arguments and Passing by Value

It's time to take a closer look at function arguments. C++ normally passes arguments *by value*. That means the numeric value of the argument is passed to the function, where it is assigned to a new variable. For example, Listing 7.2 has this function call:

```
double volume = cube(side);
```

Here `side` is a variable that, in the sample run, had the value 5. The function heading for `cube()`, recall, was this:

```
double cube(double x)
```

When this function is called, it creates a new type `double` variable called `x` and assigns the value 5 to it. This insulates data in `main()` from actions that take place in `cube()`, for `cube()` works with a copy of `side` rather than with the original data. You'll see an example of this protection soon. A variable that's used to receive passed values is called a *formal argument* or *formal parameter*. The value passed to the function is called the *actual argument* or *actual parameter*. To simplify matters a bit, the C++ standard uses the word *argument* by itself to denote an actual argument or parameter and the word *parameter* by itself to denote a formal argument or parameter. Using this terminology, argument passing assigns the argument to the parameter. (See Figure 7.2.)

FIGURE 7.2

Passing by value.

Variables, including parameters, declared within a function are private to the function. When a function is called, the computer allocates the memory needed for these variables. When the function terminates, the computer frees the memory that was used for those variables. (Some C++ literature refers to this allocating and freeing of memory as creating and destroying variables. That does make it sound much more exciting.) Such variables are called *local variables* because they are localized to the function. As we mentioned, this helps preserve data integrity. It also means that if you declare a variable called x in `main()` and another variable called x in some other function, these are two distinct, unrelated variables, much as the Albany in California is distinct from the Albany in New York. (See Figure 7.3.) Such variables also are termed *automatic variables* because they are allocated and deallocated automatically during program execution.

Multiple Arguments

Functions can have more than one argument. In the function call, just separate the arguments with commas:

```
n_chars('R', 25);
```

This passes two arguments to the function `n_chars()`, which will be defined shortly.

Similarly, when you define the function, you use a comma-separated list of parameter declarations in the function heading:

```
void n_chars(char c, int n)  // two arguments
```

FIGURE 7.3

Local variables.

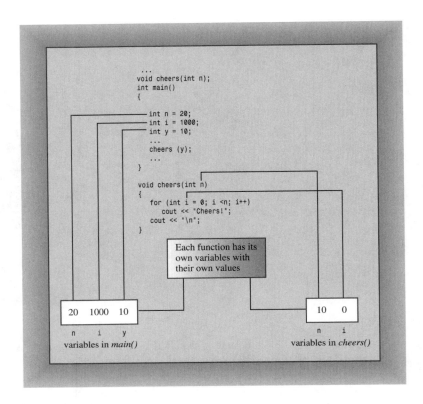

This function heading states that the function `n_chars()` takes one type `char` argument and one type `int` argument. The parameters `c` and `n` are assigned the values passed to the function. If a function has two parameters of the same type, you have to give the type of each parameter separately. You can't combine declarations the way you can when you declare regular variables:

```
void fifi(float a, float b) // declare each variable separately
void fufu(float a, b)       // NOT acceptable
```

As with other functions, just add a semicolon to get a prototype:

```
void n_chars(char c, int n); // prototype, style 1
```

As with single arguments, you don't have to use the same variable names in the prototype as in the definition, and you can omit the variable names in the prototype:

```
void n_chars(char, int);    // prototype, style 2
```

However, providing variable names can make the prototype more understandable, particularly if two parameters are the same type. Then, the names can remind you which argument is which:

```
double melon_density(double weight, double volume);
```

Listing 7.3 shows an example of a function with two arguments. It also illustrates how changing the value of a formal parameter in a function has no effect on the data in the calling program.

LISTING 7.3   twoarg.cpp

```
// twoarg.cpp -- a function with 2 arguments
#include <iostream>
using namespace std;
void n_chars(char, int);
int main()
{
    int times;
    char ch;

    cout << "Enter a character: ";
    cin >> ch;
    while (ch != 'q')          // q to quit
    {
        cout << "Enter an integer: ";
        cin >> times;
        n_chars(ch, times); // function with two arguments
        cout << "\nEnter another character or press the"
                " q-key to quit: ";
            cin >> ch;
    }
    cout << "The value of times is " << times << ".\n";
    cout << "Bye\n";
    return 0;
}

void n_chars(char c, int n) // displays c n times
{
    while (n-- > 0)            // continue until n reaches 0
        cout << c;
}
```

Here is a sample run:

```
Enter a character: W
Enter an integer: 50
WWWWWWWWWWWWWWWWWWWWWWWWWWWWWWWWWWWWWWWWWWWWWWWWWWWW
Enter another character or press the q-key to quit: a
Enter an integer: 20
aaaaaaaaaaaaaaaaaaaa
Enter another character or press the q-key to quit: q
The value of times is 20.
Bye
```

Program Notes

The `main()` function uses a `while` loop to provide repeated input (and to keep your loop skills fresh). Note that it uses `cin >> ch` to read a character rather than `cin.get(ch)` or `ch = cin.get()`. There's a good reason for doing so. The `cin.get()` pair of functions, you recall, read all input characters, including spaces and newlines, whereas `cin >>` skips spaces and newlines. When you respond to the program prompt, you have to press Enter at the end of each line, thus generating a newline character. The `cin >> ch` approach conveniently skips over these newlines, but the `cin.get()` siblings read the newline following each number entered as the next character to display. You can program around this nuisance, but it's simpler to use `cin` as the program does.

The `n_chars()` function takes two arguments: a character `c` and an integer `n`. It then uses a loop to display the character the number of times the integer specifies:

```
while (n-- > 0)          // continue until n reaches 0
     cout << c;
```

Notice that the program keeps count by decrementing the `n` variable, where `n` is the formal parameter from the argument list. This variable is assigned the value of the `times` variable in `main()`. The `while` loop then decreases `n` to zero, but, as the sample run demonstrates, changing the value of `n` has no effect on `times`.

Another Two-Argument Function

Let's create a more ambitious function, one that performs a nontrivial calculation. Also, the function will illustrate the use of local variables other than the function's formal arguments.

Many states in the United States now sponsor a lottery with some form of Lotto game. Lotto lets you pick a certain number of choices from a card. For example, you might get to pick six numbers from a card having 51 numbers. Then, the Lotto managers pick six numbers at random. If your choice exactly matches theirs, you win a few million dollars or so. Our function will calculate the probability that you have a winning pick. (Yes, a function that successfully predicts the winning picks themselves would be more useful, but C++, although powerful, has yet to implement psychic faculties.)

First, we need a formula. Suppose you have to pick six values out of 51. Then, mathematics says you have one chance in `R` of winning, where the following formula gives `R`:

$$R = \frac{51 \times 50 \times 49 \times 48 \times 47 \times 46}{6 \times 5 \times 4 \times 3 \times 2 \times 1}$$

For six choices the denominator is the product of the first six integers, or six factorial. The numerator also is the product of six consecutive numbers, this time starting with 51 and going down. More generally, if you pick `picks` values out of `numbers` numbers, the denominator is `picks` factorial and the numerator is the product of `picks` integers starting with the value `numbers` and working down. You can use a `for` loop to make that calculation:

```
long double result = 1.0;
for (n = numbers, p = picks; p > 0; n--, p--)
    result = result * n / p ;
```

Rather than multiplying all the numerator terms first, the loop begins by multiplying 1.0 by the first numerator term and then dividing by the first denominator term. Then, in the next cycle, the loop multiplies and divides by the second numerator and denominator terms. This keeps the running product smaller than if you did all the multiplication first. For example, compare

```
(10 * 9) / (2 * 1)
```

with the following:

```
(10 / 2) * (9 / 1)
```

The first evaluates to 90 / 2 and then to 45, whereas the second evaluates to 5 * 9 and then to 45. Both give the same answer, but the first method produces a larger intermediate value (90) than does the second. The more factors you have, the bigger the difference gets. For large numbers, this strategy of alternating multiplication with division can keep the calculation from overflowing the maximum possible floating-point value.

Listing 7.4 incorporates this formula into an `odds()` function. Because the number of picks and the total number of choices should be positive values, the program uses the `unsigned int` type (`unsigned`, for short) for those quantities. Multiplying several integers together can produce pretty large results, so `lotto.cpp` uses the `long double` type for the function's return value. Also, terms such as 49 / 6 produce a truncation error for integer types.

Compatibility Note

Some C++ implementations don't support type `long double`. If your implementation falls into that category, try ordinary `double` instead.

LISTING 7.4   `lotto.cpp`

```cpp
// lotto.cpp -- odds against winning
#include <iostream>
using namespace std;
// Note: some implementations require double instead of long double
long double odds(unsigned numbers, unsigned picks);
int main()
{
    double total, choices;
    cout << "Enter total number of game card choices and\n"
            "number of picks allowed:\n";
    while ((cin >> total >> choices) && choices <= total)
    {
        cout << "You have one chance in ";
        cout << odds(total, choices);      // compute the odds
        cout << " of winning.\n";
```

LISTING 7.4 Continued

```
            cout << "Next two numbers (q to quit): ";
        }
        cout << "bye\n";
        return 0;
    }

    // the following function calculates the odds of picking picks
    // numbers correctly from numbers choices
    long double odds(unsigned numbers, unsigned picks)
    {
        long double result = 1.0;  // here come some local variables
        long double n;
        unsigned p;

        for (n = numbers, p = picks; p > 0; n--, p--)
            result = result * n / p ;
        return result;
    }
```

Here's a sample run. Notice that increasing the number of choices on the game card greatly increases the odds against winning.

```
Enter total number of game card choices and
number of picks allowed:
49 6
You have one chance in 1.39838e+007 of winning.
Next two numbers (q to quit): 51 6
You have one chance in 1.80095e+007 of winning.
Next two numbers (q to quit): 38 6
You have one chance in 2.76068e+006 of winning.
Next two numbers (q to quit): q
bye
```

Program Notes

The `odds()` function illustrates two kinds of local variables you can have in a function. First, there are the formal parameters (`numbers` and `picks`), which are declared in the function heading before the opening brace. Then come the other local variables (`result`, n, and p). They are declared in between the braces bounding the function definition. The main difference between the formal parameters and the other local variables is that the formal parameters get their values from the function that calls `odds()`, whereas the other variables get values from within the function.

Functions and Arrays

So far the example functions have been simple, using only the basic types for arguments and return values. But functions can be the key to handling more involved types, such as arrays and structures. Let's take a look now at how arrays and functions get along with each other.

Suppose you use an array to keep track of how many cookies each person has eaten at the family picnic. (Each array index corresponds to a person, and the value of the element corresponds to the number of cookies that person ate.) Now you want the total. That's easy to do; just use a loop to add all the array elements. But adding array elements is such a common task that it makes sense to design a function to do the job. Then, you won't have to write a new loop every time you have to sum an array.

Let's consider what the function interface involves. Because the function calculates a sum, it should return the answer. If you keep your cookies intact, you can use a function with a type int return value. So that the function knows what array to sum, you want to pass the array name as an argument. And to make the function general so that it is not restricted to an array of a particular size, you pass the size of the array. The only new ingredient here is that you have to declare that one of the formal arguments is an array name. Let's see what that and the rest of the function heading look like:

```
int sum_arr(int arr[], int n) // arr = array name, n = size
```

This looks plausible. The brackets seem to indicate that arr is an array, and the fact that the brackets are empty seems to indicate you can use the function with an array of any size. But things are not always what they seem: arr is not really an array; it's a pointer! The good news is that you can write the rest of the function just as if arr were an array. First, let's see that this approach works, and then let's look into why it works.

Listing 7.5 illustrates using a pointer as if it were an array name. The program initializes the array to some values and uses the sum_arr() function to calculate the sum. Note that the sum_arr() function uses arr as if it were an array name.

LISTING 7.5   arrfun1.cpp

```
// arrfun1.cpp -- functions with an array argument
#include <iostream>
using namespace std;
const int ArSize = 8;
int sum_arr(int arr[], int n);          // prototype
int main()
{
    int cookies[ArSize] = {1,2,4,8,16,32,64,128};
// some systems require preceding int with static to
// enable array initialization

    int sum = sum_arr(cookies, ArSize);
    cout << "Total cookies eaten: " << sum <<  "\n";
    return 0;
}

// return the sum of an integer array
int sum_arr(int arr[], int n)
{
    int total = 0;
```

LISTING 7.5   _Continued_

```
    for (int i = 0; i < n; i++)
        total = total + arr[i];
    return total;
}
```

Here is the program output:

```
Total cookies eaten: 255
```

As you can see, the program works. Now let's look at why it works.

How Pointers Enable Array-Processing Functions

The key is that C++, like C, in most contexts treats the name of an array as if it were a pointer. Recall from Chapter 4, "Compound Types," that C++ interprets an array name as the address of its first element:

```
cookies == &cookies[0]   // array name is address of first element
```

(There are two exceptions to this rule. First, the array declaration uses the array name to label the storage. Second, applying `sizeof` to an array name yields the size of the whole array, in bytes.)

Listing 7.5 makes the following function call:

```
int sum = sum_arr(cookies, ArSize);
```

Here `cookies` is the name of an array, hence by C++ rules `cookies` is the address of its first element. The function passes an address. Because the array has type `int` elements, `cookies` must be type pointer-to-`int`, or `int *`. That suggests that the correct function heading should be this:

```
int sum_arr(int * arr, int n) // arr = array name, n = size
```

Here `int *arr` has replaced `int arr[]`. It turns out that both headings are correct, for in C++ the notations `int *arr` and `int arr[]` have the identical meaning when (and _only_ when) used in a function heading or function prototype. Both mean that `arr` is a pointer-to-`int`. However, the array notation version (`int arr[]`) symbolically reminds us that `arr` not only points to an `int`, it points to the first `int` in an array of `int`s. We'll use the array notation when the pointer is to the first element of an array, and we'll use the pointer notation when the pointer is to an isolated value. Don't forget that the notations `int *arr` and `int arr[]` are not synonymous in any other context. For example, you can't use the notation `int tip[]` to declare a pointer in the body of a function.

Given that the variable `arr` actually is a pointer, the rest of the function makes sense. As you might recall from the discussion of dynamic arrays in Chapter 4, you can use the bracket array notation equally well with array names or with pointers to access elements of an array. Whether `arr` is a pointer or an array name, the expression `arr[3]` means the fourth element of the array. And it probably will do no harm at this point to remind you of the following two identities:

```
arr[i] == *(arr + i)     // values in two notations
&arr[i] == arr + i       // addresses in two notations
```

Remember, adding 1 to a pointer, including an array name, actually adds a value equal to the size, in bytes, of the type to which the pointer points. Pointer addition and array subscription are two equivalent ways of counting elements from the beginning of an array.

Implications of Using Arrays As Arguments

Let's look at the implications of Listing 7.5. The function call sum_arr(cookies, ArSize) passes the address of the first element of the cookies array and the number of elements of the array to the sum_arr() function. The sum_arr() function assigns the cookies address to the pointer variable arr and assigns ArSize to the int variable n. This means Listing 7.5 doesn't really pass the array contents to the function. Instead, it tells the function where the array is (the address), what kind of elements it has (the type), and how many elements it has (the n variable). (See Figure 7.4.) Armed with this information, the function then uses the original array. Pass an ordinary variable, and the function works with a copy. But pass an array, and the function works with the original. Actually, this difference doesn't violate C++'s pass-by-value approach. The sum_arr() function still passes a value that's assigned to a new variable. But that value is a single address, not the contents of an array.

FIGURE 7.4

Telling a function about an array.

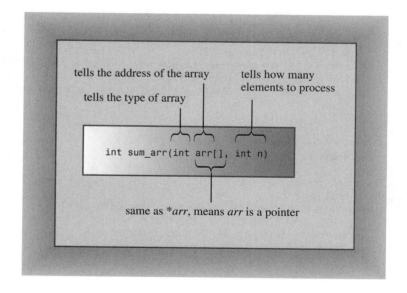

Is the correspondence between array names and pointers a good thing? Indeed, it is. The design decision to use array addresses as arguments saves the time and memory needed to copy an entire array. The overhead for using copies can be prohibitive if you're working with large arrays. Not only does a program need more computer memory, but it has to spend time copying large blocks of data. On the other hand, working with the original data raises the possibility of inadvertent data corruption. That's a real problem in classic C, but ANSI C and C++'s const modifier provides a remedy. We'll soon show an example. But first, let's alter Listing 7.5 to illustrate some points about how array functions operate. Listing 7.6 demonstrates that cookies and arr have the same value. It also shows how the pointer concept makes the sum_arr function more versatile than it may have appeared at first.

LISTING 7.6   arrfun2.cpp

```
// arrfun2.cpp -- functions with an array argument
#include <iostream>
using namespace std;
const int ArSize = 8;
int sum_arr(int arr[], int n);
int main()
{
    int cookies[ArSize] = {1,2,4,8,16,32,64,128};
//  some systems require preceding int with static to
//  enable array initialization

    cout << cookies << " = array address, ";
//  some systems require a type cast: unsigned (cookies)

    cout << sizeof cookies << " = sizeof cookies\n";
    int sum = sum_arr(cookies, ArSize);
    cout << "Total cookies eaten: " << sum <<  "\n";
    sum = sum_arr(cookies, 3);          // a lie
    cout << "First three eaters ate " << sum << " cookies.\n";
    sum = sum_arr(cookies + 4, 4);      // another lie
    cout << "Last four eaters ate " << sum << " cookies.\n";
    return 0;
}

// return the sum of an integer array
int sum_arr(int arr[], int n)
{
    int total = 0;
    cout << arr << " = arr, ";
// some systems require a type cast: unsigned (arr)

    cout << sizeof arr << " = sizeof arr\n";
    for (int i = 0; i < n; i++)
        total = total + arr[i];
    return total;
}
```

Here's the output (the address values and the array and integer sizes will vary from system to system):

```
0x0065fd24 = array address, 32 = sizeof cookies
0x0065fd24 = arr, 4 = sizeof arr
Total cookies eaten: 255
0x0065fd24 = arr, 4 = sizeof arr
```

```
First three eaters ate 7 cookies.
0x0065fd34 = arr, 4 = sizeof arr
Last four eaters ate 240 cookies.
```

Program Notes

Listing 7.6 illustrates some very interesting points about array functions. First, note that `cookies` and `arr` both evaluate to the same address, exactly as claimed. But `sizeof cookies` is 32, whereas `sizeof arr` is only 4. That's because `sizeof cookies` is the size of the whole array, whereas `sizeof arr` is the size of the pointer variable. (This program execution takes place on a system using 4-byte addresses.) By the way, that's why you have to pass explicitly the size of the array rather than use `sizeof arr` in `sum_arr()`.

Because the only way `sum_arr()` knows the number of elements in the array is through what you tell it with the second argument, you can lie to the function. For example, the second time the program uses the function, it makes this call:

```
sum = sum_arr(cookies, 3);
```

By telling the function that `cookies` has but three elements, you get the function to calculate the sum of the first three elements.

Why stop there? You also can lie about where the array starts:

```
sum = sum_arr(cookies + 4, 4);
```

Because `cookies` acts as the address of the first element, `cookies + 4` acts as the address of the fifth element. This statement sums the fifth, sixth, seventh, and eighth elements of the array. Note in the output how the third call to the function assigns a different address to `arr` than the first two calls did. And yes, you can use `&cookies[4]` instead of `cookies + 4` as the argument; both mean the same thing.

Remember

To indicate the kind of array and the number of elements to an array-processing function, pass the information as two separate arguments:

```
void fillArray(int arr[], int size);   // prototype
```

Don't try to pass the array size by using brackets notation:

```
void fillArray(int arr[size]);          // NO -- bad prototype
```

More Array Function Examples

When you choose to use an array to represent data, you are making a design decision. But design decisions should go beyond how data is stored; they also should involve how the data is used. Often, you'll find it profitable to write specific functions to handle specific data operations. (The profits here are increased program reliability, ease of modification, and ease of debugging.) Also, when you begin integrating storage properties with operations when you think about a program, you are taking an important step toward the OOP mind-set; that, too, might prove profitable in the future.

Let's examine a simple case. Suppose you want to use an array to keep track of the dollar values of your real estate. (If necessary, suppose you have real estate.) You have to decide what type to use. Certainly, **double** is less restrictive in its range than **int** or **long**, and it provides enough significant digits to represent the values precisely. Next, you have to decide on the number of array elements. (With dynamic arrays created with **new**, you can put off that decision, but let's keep things simple.) Let's say that you have no more than five properties, so you can use an array of five **doubles**.

Now consider the possible operations you might want to execute with the real estate array. Two very basic ones are reading values into the array and displaying the array contents. Let's add one more operation to the list: reassessing the value of the properties. For simplicity, assume that all your properties increase or decrease in value at the same rate. (Remember, this is a book on C++, not on real estate management.) Next, fit a function to each operation and then write the code accordingly. We go through these steps next.

Filling the Array

Because a function with an array name argument accesses the original array, not a copy, you can use a function call to assign values to array elements. One argument to the function will be the name of the array to be filled. In general, a program might manage more than one person's investments, hence more than one array, so you won't want to build the array size into the function. Instead, pass the array size as a second argument, as in the previous example. Also, it's possible that you might want to quit reading data before filling the array, so you want to build that feature into the function. Because you might enter fewer than the maximum number of elements, it makes sense to have the function return the actual number of values entered. These considerations suggest the following function prototype:

```cpp
int fill_array(double ar[], int limit);
```

The function takes an array name argument and an argument specifying the maximum number of items to be read, and the function returns the actual number of items read. For example, if you use this function with an array of five elements, you pass 5 as the second argument. If you enter only three values, the function returns 3.

You can use a loop to read successive values into the array, but how can you terminate the loop early? One way is to use a special value to indicate the end of input. Because no property should have a negative value, you can use a negative number to indicate the end of input. Also, the function should do something about bad input, such as terminating further input. Given this, you can code the function as follows:

```cpp
int fill_array(double ar[], int limit)
{
    double temp;
    int i;
    for (i = 0; i < limit; i++)
    {
        cout << "Enter value #" << (i + 1) << ": ";
        cin >> temp;
        if (!cin)    // bad input
```

```
          {
              cin.clear();
              while (cin.get() != '\n')
                  continue;
              cout << "Bad input; input process terminated.\n";
              break;
          }
          else if (temp < 0)       // signal to terminate
              break;
          ar[i] = temp;
      }
      return i;
  }
```

Note that the code includes a prompt to the user in the program. If the user enters a non-negative value, the value is assigned to the array. Otherwise, the loop terminates. If the user enters only valid values, the loop terminates after it reads limit values. The last thing the loop does is increment i, so after the loop terminates, i is 1 greater than the last array index, hence it's equal to the number of filled elements. The function then returns that value.

Showing the Array and Protecting It with const

Building a function to display the array contents is simple. You pass the name of the array and the number of filled elements to the function, which then uses a loop to display each element. But there is another consideration—guaranteeing that the display function doesn't alter the original array. Unless the purpose of a function is to alter data passed to it, you should safeguard it from doing so. That protection comes automatically with ordinary arguments, because C++ passes them by value and the function works with a copy. But functions that use an array work with the original. After all, that's why the fill_array() function is able to do its job. To keep a function from accidentally altering the contents of an array argument, you can use the keyword const (discussed in Chapter 3, "Dealing with Data") when you declare the formal argument:

```
void show_array(const double ar[], int n);
```

The declaration states that the pointer ar points to constant data. This means that you can't use ar to change the data. That is, you can use a value such as ar[0], but you can't change that value. Note that this doesn't mean that the original array need be constant; it just means that you can't use ar in the show_array() function to change the data. Thus, show_array() treats the array as read-only data. Suppose you accidentally violate this restriction by doing something like the following in the show_array() function:

```
ar[0] += 10;
```

Then, the compiler will put a stop to your wrongful ways. Borland C++, for example, gives an error message like this (edited slightly):

```
Cannot modify a const object in function
        show_array(const double *,int)
```

The message reminds us that C++ interprets the declaration `const double ar[]` to mean `const double *ar`. Thus, the declaration really says that `ar` points to a constant value. We'll discuss this in detail when we finish with the current example. Meanwhile, here is the code for the `show_array()` function:

```
void show_array(const double ar[], int n)
{
    for (int i = 0; i < n; i++)
    {
        cout << "Property #" << (i + 1) << ": $";
        cout << ar[i] << "\n";
    }
}
```

Modifying the Array

The third operation for our array is multiplying each element by the same revaluation factor. You need to pass three arguments to the function: the factor, the array, and the number of elements. No return value is needed, so the function can look like this:

```
void revalue(double r, double ar[], int n)
{
    for (int i = 0; i < n; i++)
        ar[i] *= r;
}
```

Because this function is supposed to alter the array values, you don't use `const` when you declare `ar`.

Putting the Pieces Together

Now that we've defined the data type in terms of how it's stored (an array) and how it's used (three functions), we can put together a program that uses the design. Because we've already built all the array-handling tools, we've greatly simplified programming `main()`. Most of the remaining programming work consists of having `main()` call the functions we've just developed. Listing 7.7 shows the result.

LISTING 7.7   arrfun3.cpp

```
// arrfun3.cpp -- array functions and const
#include <iostream>
using namespace std;
const int Max = 5;

// function prototypes
int fill_array(double ar[], int limit);
void show_array(const double ar[], int n);   // don't change data
void revalue(double r, double ar[], int n);

int main()
{
    double properties[Max];
```

LISTING 7.7   *Continued*

```cpp
    int size = fill_array(properties, Max);
    show_array(properties, size);
    cout << "Enter revaluation factor: ";
    double factor;
    cin >> factor;
    revalue(factor, properties, size);
    show_array(properties, size);
    cout << "Done.\n";
    return 0;
}

int fill_array(double ar[], int limit)
{
    double temp;
    int i;
    for (i = 0; i < limit; i++)
    {
        cout << "Enter value #" << (i + 1) << ": ";
        cin >> temp;
        if (!cin)      // bad input
        {
            cin.clear();
            while (cin.get() != '\n')
                continue;
            cout << "Bad input; input process terminated.\n";
            break;
        }
        else if (temp < 0)      // signal to terminate
            break;
        ar[i] = temp;
    }
    return i;
}

// the following function can use, but not alter,
// the array whose address is ar
void show_array(const double ar[], int n)
{
    for (int i = 0; i < n; i++)
    {
        cout << "Property #" << (i + 1) << ": $";
        cout << ar[i] << "\n";
    }
}

// multiplies each element of ar[] by r
void revalue(double r, double ar[], int n)
{
    for (int i = 0; i < n; i++)
        ar[i] *= r;
}
```

Here are two sample runs. Recall that input should quit when the user enters five properties or enters a negative number, whichever comes first. The first example illustrates reaching the five-property limit, and the second example illustrates entering a negative value.

```
Enter value #1: 100000
Enter value #2: 80000
Enter value #3: 222000
Enter value #4: 240000
Enter value #5: 118000
Property #1: $100000
Property #2: $80000
Property #3: $222000
Property #4: $240000
Property #5: $118000
Enter reassessment rate: 1.10
Property #1: $110000
Property #2: $88000
Property #3: $244200
Property #4: $264000
Property #5: $129800
Done.

Enter value #1: 200000
Enter value #2: 84000
Enter value #3: 160000
Enter value #4: -2
Property #1: $200000
Property #2: $84000
Property #3: $160000
Enter reassessment rate: 1.20
Property #1: $240000
Property #2: $100800
Property #3: $192000
Done.
```

Program Notes

We've already discussed the important programming details, so let's reflect on the process. We began by thinking about the data type and designed appropriate functions to handle the data. Then, we assembled these functions into a program. This sometimes is called bottom-up programming, because the design process moves from the component parts to the whole. This approach is well suited to OOP, which concentrates on data representation and manipulation first. Traditional procedural programming, on the other hand, leans toward top-down programming, in which you develop a modular grand design first and then turn your attention to the details. Both methods are useful, and both lead to modular programs.

Functions Using Array Ranges

As you've seen, C++ functions that process arrays need to be informed about the kind of data in the array, the location of the beginning of the array, and the number of elements in it. The traditional C/C++ approach to functions that process arrays is to pass a pointer to the start of the array as one argument and to pass the size of the array as a second argument. (The pointer tells the function both where to find the array and the kind of data in it.) That gives the function the information it needs to find all the data.

There is another approach to giving the function the information it needs, and that is to specify a *range* of elements. This can be done by passing two pointers: one identifying the start of the array and one identifying the end of the array. The C++ Standard Template Library (presented in Chapter 16, "The String Class and the Standard Template Library"), for example, generalizes the range approach. The STL approach uses the concept of "one past the end" to indicate the extent. That is, in the case of an array, the argument identifying the end of the array would be a pointer to the location just after the last element. For example, suppose we have this declaration:

```
double elbuod[20];
```

Then the two pointers `elboud` and `elboud + 20` define the range. First, `elboub`, being the name of the array, points to the first element. The expression `elboud + 19` points to the last element (that is, `elboud[19]`), so `elboud + 20` points to one past the end of the array. Passing a range to a function tells it which elements to process. Listing 7.8 modifies Listing 7.6 to use two pointers to specify a range.

LISTING 7.8 `arrfun4.cpp`

```cpp
// arrfun4.cpp -- functions with an array range
#include <iostream>
using namespace std;
const int ArSize = 8;
int sum_arr(const int * begin, const int * end);
int main()
{
    int cookies[ArSize] = {1,2,4,8,16,32,64,128};
//  some systems require preceding int with static to
//  enable array initialization

    int sum = sum_arr(cookies, cookies + ArSize);
    cout << "Total cookies eaten: " << sum <<  "\n";
    sum = sum_arr(cookies, cookies + 3);        // first 3 elements
    cout << "First three eaters ate " << sum << " cookies.\n";
    sum = sum_arr(cookies + 4, cookies + 8);    // last 4 elements
    cout << "Last four eaters ate " << sum << " cookies.\n";
    return 0;
}

// return the sum of an integer array
int sum_arr(const int * begin, const int * end)
{
    const int * pt;
    int total = 0;
```

LISTING 7.8   Continued

```
    for (pt = begin; pt != end; pt++)
        total = total + *pt;
    return total;
}
```

Here's the output:

```
Total cookies eaten: 255
First three eaters ate 7 cookies.
Last four eaters ate 240 cookies.
```

Program Notes

First, notice the `for` loop in the `sum_array()` function:

```
for (pt = begin; pt != end; pt++)
    total = total + *pt;
```

It sets `pt` to point to the first element to be processed (the one pointed to by `begin`) and adds `*pt` (the value of the element) to `total`. Then the loop updates `pt` to point to the next element. The process continues as long as `pt != end`. When `pt` finally equals `end`, it's pointing to the location following the last element of the range, so the loop halts.

Second, notice how the different function calls specify different ranges within the array:

```
int sum = sum_arr(cookies, cookies + ArSize);
...
sum = sum_arr(cookies, cookies + 3);        // first 3 elements
...
sum = sum_arr(cookies + 4, cookies + 8);    // last 4 elements
```

The pointer value `cookies + ArSize` points the location following the last element. (The array has `ArSize` elements, so `cookies[ArSize - 1]` is the last element, and its address is `cookies + ArSize - 1`.) So the range `cookies, cookies + ArSize` specifies the entire array. Similarly, `cookies, cookies + 3` specifies the first three elements, and so on.

Note, by the way, that the rules for pointer subtraction imply that, in `sum_arr()`, the expression `end - begin` is an integer value equal to the number of elements in the range.

Pointers and const

Using `const` with pointers has some subtle aspects (pointers always seem to have subtle aspects), so let's take a closer look. You can use the `const` keyword two different ways with pointers. The first way is to make a pointer point to a constant object, and that prevents you from using the pointer to change the pointed-to value. The second way is to make the pointer itself constant, and that prevents you from changing where the pointer points. Now for the details.

First, let's declare a pointer `pt` that points to a constant:

```
int age = 39;
const int * pt = &age;
```

This declaration states that pt points to a const int (39, in this case). Therefore, you can't use pt to change that value. In other words, the value *pt is const and cannot be modified:

```
*pt += 1;           // INVALID because pt points to a const int
cin >> *pt;         // INVALID for the same reason
```

Now for a subtle point. Our declaration for pt doesn't necessarily mean that the value it points to is really a constant; it just means the value is a constant insofar as pt is concerned. For example, pt points to age, and age is not const. You can change the value of age directly by using the age variable, but you can't change the value indirectly via the pt pointer:

```
*pt = 20;           // INVALID because pt points to a const int
age = 20;           // VALID because age is not declared to be const
```

In the past, we've assigned the address of a regular variable to a regular pointer. Now we've assigned the address of a regular variable to a pointer-to-const. That leaves two other possibilities: assigning the address of a const variable to a pointer-to-const and assigning the address of a const to a regular pointer. Are they both possible? The first is, and the second isn't:

```
const float g_earth = 9.80;
const float * pe = &g_earth;    // VALID

const float g_moon = 1.63;
float * pm = &g_moon;           // INVALID
```

For the first case, you can use neither g_earth nor pe to change the value 9.80. C++ doesn't allow the second case for a simple reason—if you can assign the address of g_moon to pm, then you can cheat and use pm to alter the value of g_moon. That makes a mockery of g_moon's const status, so C++ prohibits you from assigning the address of a const to a non-const pointer.

The situation becomes a bit more complex if you have pointers to pointers. As you saw earlier, assigning a non-const pointer to a const pointer is okay, provided that we're dealing with just one level of indirection:

```
int age = 39;           // age++ is a valid operation
int * pd = &age;        // *pd = 41 is a valid operation
const int * pt = pd;    // *pt = 42 is an invalid operation
```

But pointer assignments that mix const and non-const in this manner no longer are safe when you go to two levels of indirection. If it were allowed, you could do something like this:

```
const int **pp2;
int *p1;
const int n = 13;
pp2 = &p1; // not allowed, but suppose it were
*pp2 = &n; // valid, both const, but sets p1 to point at n
*p1 = 10; // valid, but changes const n
```

Here the code assigns a non-const address (&p1) to a const pointer (pp2), and that allows p1 to be used to alter const data. So the rule that you can assign a non-const address or pointer to a const pointer only works if there is just one level of indirection, for example, if the pointer points to a fundamental data type.

Suppose you have an array of **const** data:

```
const int months[12] = {31,28,31,30,31,30, 31, 31,30,31,30,31};
```

The prohibition against assigning the address of a constant array means that you cannot pass the array name as an argument to a function using a non-constant formal argument:

```
int sum(int arr[], int n);  // should have been const int arr[]
...
int j = sum(months, 12);    // not allowed
```

The function call attempts to assign a **const** pointer (**months**) to a non-**const** pointer (**arr**), and the compiler disallows the function call.

Now another subtle point: the declarations

```
int age = 39;
const int * pt = &age;
```

only prevent you from changing the value to which **pt** points, which is 39. It doesn't prevent you from changing the value of **pt** itself. That is, you can assign a new address to **pt**:

```
int sage = 80;
pt = &sage; // okay to point to another location
```

But you still can't use **pt** to change the value to which it points (now 80).

The second way to use **const** makes it impossible to change the value of the pointer itself:

```
int sloth = 3;
const int * ps = &sloth;      // a pointer to const int
int * const finger = &sloth;  // a const pointer to int
```

Note that the last declaration has repositioned the keyword **const**. This form of declaration constrains **finger** to point only to **sloth**. However, it does allow you to use **finger** to alter the value of sloth. The middle declaration does not allow you to use ps to alter the value of sloth, but it does permit you to have ps point to another location. In short, finger and *ps are both const, and *finger and ps are not const. (See Figure 7.5.)

FIGURE 7.5

Pointers-to-const and const pointers.

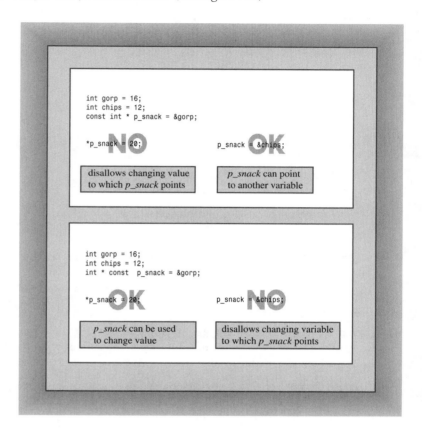

If you like, you can declare a const pointer to a const object:

```
double trouble = 2.0E30;
const double * const stick = &trouble;
```

Here stick can point only to trouble, and stick cannot be used to change the value of trouble. In short, both stick and *stick are const.

Typically you use the pointer-to-const form to protect data when you pass pointers as function arguments. For example, recall the show_array() prototype from Listing 7.7:

```
void show_array(const double ar[], int n);
```

Using const in that declaration means that show_array() cannot alter the values in any array passed to it. This technique works as long as there is just one level of indirection. Here, for example, the array elements are a fundamental type. But if they were pointers or pointers-to-pointers, you wouldn't use const.

Functions and Two-Dimensional Arrays

To write a function that has a two-dimensional array as an argument, you need to remember that the name of an array is treated as its address, so the corresponding formal parameter is a pointer, just as for one-dimensional arrays. The tricky part is declaring the pointer correctly. Suppose, for example, we start with this code:

```
int data[3][4] = {{1,2,3,4}, {9,8,7,6}, {2,4,6 8}};
int total = sum(data, 3);
```

What should the prototype for `sum()` look like? And why does the function pass the number of rows (3) as an argument and not also the number of columns (4)?

Well, `data` is the name of an array with three elements. The first element is, itself, an array of 4 `int` values. Thus, the type of `data` is pointer-to-array-of-4-`int`, so an appropriate prototype would be this:

```
int sum(int (*ar2)[4], int size);
```

The parentheses are needed, for the declaration

```
int *ar2[4]
```

would declare an array of four pointers-to-`int` instead of a single pointer-to-array-of-4-`int`, and a function parameter cannot be an array. There's an alternative format that means exactly the same thing as the correct prototype, but, perhaps, is easier to read:

```
int sum(int ar2[][4], int size);
```

Either prototype states that `ar2` is a pointer, not an array. Also note that pointer type specifically says it points to an array of 4 `int`. Thus, the pointer type specifies the number of columns, which is why the number of columns is not passed as a separate function argument.

Because the pointer type specifies the number of columns, the `sum()` function only works with arrays with four columns. But the number of rows is specified by the variable size, so `sum()` can work with a varying number of rows:

```
int a[100][4];
int b[6][4];
...
int total1 = sum(a, 100);    // sum all of a
int total2 = sum(b, 6);      // sum all of b
int total3 = sum(a, 10);     // sum first 10 rows of a
int total4 = sum(a+10, 20);  // sum next 20 rows of a
```

Given that the parameter `ar2` is a pointer to an array, how do we use it in the function definition? The simplest way is to use `ar2` as if it were the name of a two-dimensional array. Here's a possible function definition:

```
int sum(int ar2[][4], int size)
{
    int total = 0;
    for (int row = 0; row < size; row++)
        for (col = 0; col < 4; col++)
```

```
            total += ar2[row][col];
    return total;
}
```

Again, note that the number of rows is whatever is passed to the `size` parameter, but the number of columns is fixed at 4, both in the parameter declaration for `ar2` and in the inner `for` loop.

Here's why you can use array notation. Because `ar2` points to the first element (element 0) of an array whose elements are array-of-4-`int`, the expression `ar2 + row` points to element number `row`. Therefore `ar2[row]` is element number `row`. That element is itself an array-of-4-`int`, so `ar2[row]` is the name of that array-of-4-`int`. Applying a subscript to an array name gives an array element, so `ar2[row][col]` is an element of the array-of-4-`int`, hence is a single `int` value. The pointer `ar2` has to be dereferenced twice to get to the data. The simplest way is to use brackets twice.

Incidentally, the code for `sum()` doesn't use `const` in declaring the parameter `ar2` because that technique is for pointers to fundamental types, whereas `ar2` is a pointer to a pointer.

Functions and C-Style Strings

A C-style string, you recall, consists of a series of characters terminated by the null character. Much of what you've learned about designing array functions applies to string functions, too. But there are a few special twists to strings that we unravel now.

Suppose you want to pass a string as an argument to a function. You have three choices for representing a string:

- An array of `char`

- A quoted string constant (also called a string literal)

- A pointer-to-`char` set to the address of a string

All three choices, however, are type pointer-to-`char` (more concisely, type `char *`), so you can use all three as arguments to string-processing functions:

```
char ghost[15] = "galloping";
char * str = "galumphing";
int n1 = strlen(ghost);         // ghost is &ghost[0]
int n2 = strlen(str);           // pointer to char
int n3 = strlen("gamboling");   // address of string
```

Informally, you can say you're passing a string as an argument, but you're really passing the address of the first character in the string. This implies that a string function prototype should use type `char *` as the type for the formal parameter representing a string.

One important difference between a string and a regular array is that the string has a built-in terminating character. (Recall that a `char` array containing characters but no null character is just an array and not a string.) That means you don't have to pass the size of the string as an argument. Instead, the function can use a loop to examine each character in the string in turn until the loop reaches the terminating null character. Listing 7.9 illustrates that approach with a function that counts the number of times a given character appears in a string.

LISTING 7.9   strgfun.cpp

```cpp
// strgfun.cpp -- functions with a string argument
#include <iostream>
using namespace std;
int c_in_str(const char * str, char ch);
int main()
{
    char mmm[15] = "minimum";     // string in an array
// some systems require preceding char with static to
// enable array initialization

    char *wail = "ululate";    // wail points to string

    int ms = c_in_str(mmm, 'm');
    int us = c_in_str(wail, 'u');
    cout << ms << " m characters in " << mmm << "\n";
    cout << us << " u characters in " << wail << "\n";
    return 0;
}

// this function counts the number of ch characters
// in the string str
int c_in_str(const char * str, char ch)
{
    int count = 0;

    while (*str)         // quit when *str is '\0'
    {
        if (*str == ch)
            count++;
        str++;           // move pointer to next char
    }
    return count;
}
```

Here's the output:

```
3 m characters in minimum
2 u characters in ululate
```

Program Notes

Because the `c_int_str()` function shouldn't alter the original string, it uses the **const** modifier when it declares the formal parameter **str**. Then, if you mistakenly let the function alter part of the string, the compiler catches your error. Of course, you can use array notation instead to declare **str** in the function heading:

```cpp
int c_in_str(const char str[], char ch) // also okay
```

However, using pointer notation reminds you that the argument doesn't have to be the name of an array but can be some other form of pointer.

The function itself demonstrates a standard way to process the characters in a string:

```
while (*str)
{
    statements
    str++;
}
```

Initially, `str` points to the first character in the string, so `*str` represents the first character itself. For example, immediately after the first function call, `*str` has the value m, the first character in minimum. As long as the character is not the null character (\0), `*str` is nonzero, so the loop continues. At the end of each loop the expression `str++` increments the pointer by one byte so that it points to the next character in the string. Eventually, `str` points to the terminating null character, making `*str` equal to 0, which is the numeric code for the null character. That condition terminates the loop. (Why are string-processing functions ruthless? Because they stop at nothing.)

Functions That Return Strings

Now suppose you want to write a function that returns a string. Well, a function can't do that. But it can return the address of a string, and that's even better. Listing 7.10, for example, defines a function called `buildstr()` that returns a pointer. This function takes two arguments: a character and a number. Using `new`, the function creates a string whose length equals the number, and then it initializes each element to the character. Then, it returns a pointer to the new string.

LISTING 7.10   strgback.cpp

```cpp
// strgback.cpp -- a function returning a pointer to char
#include <iostream>
using namespace std;
char * buildstr(char c, int n);      // prototype
int main()
{
    int times;
    char ch;

    cout << "Enter a character: ";
    cin >> ch;
    cout << "Enter an integer: ";
    cin >> times;
    char *ps = buildstr(ch, times);
    cout << ps << "\n";
    delete [] ps;                    // free memory
    ps = buildstr('+', 20);          // reuse pointer
    cout << ps << "-DONE-" << ps << "\n";
    delete [] ps;                    // free memory
```

LISTING 7.10   Continued

```
        return 0;
}

// builds string made of n c characters
char * buildstr(char c, int n)
{
    char * pstr = new char[n + 1];
    pstr[n] = '\0';          // terminate string
    while (n-- > 0)
        pstr[n] = c;         // fill rest of string
    return pstr;
}
```

Here's a sample run:

```
Enter a character: V
Enter an integer: 46
VVVVVVVVVVVVVVVVVVVVVVVVVVVVVVVVVVVVVVVVVVVVVVVV
+++++++++++++++++++++-DONE-+++++++++++++++++++++
```

Program Notes

To create a string of n visible characters, you need storage for n + 1 characters in order to have space for the null character. So the function asks for n + 1 bytes to hold the string. Next, it sets the final byte to the null character. Then, it fills in the rest of the array from back to front. The loop

```
while (n-- > 0)
    pstr[n] = c;
```

cycles n times as n decreases to zero, filling n elements. At the start of the final cycle, n has the value 1. Because n-- means use the value and then decrement it, the while loop test condition compares 1 to 0, finds the test to be true, and continues. But after making the test, the function decrements n to 0, so pstr[0] is the last element set to c. The reason for filling the string from back to front instead of front to back is to avoid using an additional variable. Using the other order would involve something like this:

```
int i = 0;
while (i < n)
    pstr[i++] = c;
```

Note that the variable pstr is local to the buildstr function, so when that function terminates, the memory used for pstr (but not for the string) is freed. But because the function returns the value of pstr, the program is able to access the new string through the ps pointer in main().

The program uses delete to free memory used for the string after the string is no longer needed. Then, it reuses ps to point to the new block of memory obtained for the next string and frees that memory. The disadvantage to this kind of design (having a function return a pointer to memory allocated by `new`) is that it makes it the programmer's responsibility to remember to use `delete`. The `auto_ptr` template, discussed in Chapter 16, can help automate the process.

Functions and Structures

Let's move from arrays to structures. It's easier to write functions for structures than for arrays. Although structure variables resemble arrays in that both can hold several data items, structure variables behave like basic, single-valued variables when it comes to functions. That is, unlike an array, a structure ties its data into a single entity that will be treated as a unit. Recall that you can assign one structure to another. Similarly, you can pass structures by value, just as you do with ordinary variables. In that case, the function works with a copy of the original structure. Also, a function can return a structure. There's no funny business like the name of an array being the address of its first element. The name of a structure is simply the name of the structure, and if you want its address, you have to use the `&` address operator.

The most direct way to program by using structures is to treat them as you would treat the basic types; that is, pass them as arguments and use them, if necessary, as return values. However, there is one disadvantage to passing structures by value. If the structure is large, the space and effort involved in making a copy of a structure can increase memory requirements and slow the system down. For those reasons (and because, at first, C didn't allow the passing of structures by value), many C programmers prefer passing the address of a structure and then using a pointer to access the structure contents. C++ provides a third alternative, called passing by reference, that we discuss in Chapter 8. We examine the other two choices now, beginning with passing and returning entire structures.

Passing and Returning Structures

Passing structures by value makes the most sense when the structure is relatively compact, so let's develop a couple of examples along those lines. The first example deals with travel time (not to be confused with time travel). Some maps will tell you that it is three hours, 50 minutes, from Thunder Falls to Bingo City and one hour, 25 minutes, from Bingo City to Grotesquo. You can use a structure to represent such times, using one member for the hour value and a second member for the minute value. Adding two times is a little tricky because you might have to transfer some of the minutes to the hours part. For example, the two preceding times sum to four hours, 75 minutes, which should be converted to five hours, 15 minutes. Let's develop a structure to represent a time value and then a function that takes two such structures as arguments and returns a structure that represents their sum.

Defining the structure is simple:

```
struct travel_time
{
    int hours;
    int mins;
};
```

Next, consider the prototype for a `sum()` function that returns the sum of two such structures. The return value should be type `travel_time`, and so should the two arguments. Thus, the prototype should look like this:

```
travel_time sum(travel_time t1, travel_time t2);
```

To add two times, first add the minute members. Integer division by 60 yields the number of hours to carry over, and the modulus operator (%) yields the number of minutes left. Listing 7.11 incorporates this approach into the `sum()` function and adds a `show_time()` function to display the contents of a `travel_time` structure.

LISTING 7.11   travel.cpp

```cpp
// travel.cpp -- using structures with functions
#include <iostream>
using namespace std;
struct travel_time
{
    int hours;
    int mins;
};
const int Mins_per_hr = 60;

travel_time sum(travel_time t1, travel_time t2);
void show_time(travel_time t);

int main()
{
    travel_time day1 = {5, 45};    // 5 hrs, 45 min
    travel_time day2 = {4, 55};    // 4 hrs, 55 min

    travel_time trip = sum(day1, day2);
    cout << "Two-day total: ";
    show_time(trip);

    travel_time day3= {4, 32};
    cout << "Three-day total: ";
    show_time(sum(trip, day3));

    return 0;
}

travel_time sum(travel_time t1, travel_time t2)
{
    travel_time total;

    total.mins = (t1.mins + t2.mins) % Mins_per_hr;
    total.hours = t1.hours + t2.hours +
                    (t1.mins + t2.mins) / Mins_per_hr;
    return total;
}
```

LISTING 7.11 Continued

```
void show_time(travel_time t)
{
    cout << t.hours << " hours, "
         << t.mins << " minutes\n";
}
```

Here `travel_time` acts just like a standard type name; you can use it to declare variables, function return types, and function argument types. Because variables like `total` and `t1` are `travel_time` structures, you can apply the dot membership operator to them. Note that because the `sum()` function returns a `travel_time` structure, you can use it as an argument for the `show_time()` function. Because C++ functions, by default, pass arguments by value, the `show_time(sum(trip, day3))` function call first evaluates the `sum(trip, day3)` function call in order to find its return value. The `show_time()` call then passes `sum()`'s return value, not the function itself, to `show_time()`. Here's the program output:

```
Two-day total: 10 hours, 40 minutes
Three-day total: 15 hours, 12 minutes
```

Another Example

Much of what you learn about functions and C++ structures carries over to C++ classes, so it's worth looking at a second example. This time we deal with space instead of time. In particular, the example defines two structures representing two different ways of describing positions and then develops functions to convert one form to the other and show the result. This example is a bit more mathematical than the last, but you don't have to follow the mathematics to follow the C++.

Suppose you want to describe the position of a point on the screen or a location on a map relative to some origin. One way is to state the horizontal offset and the vertical offset of the point from the origin. Traditionally, mathematicians use the symbol x to represent the horizontal offset and y to represent the vertical offset. (See Figure 7.6.) Together, x and y constitute *rectangular coordinates*. You can define a structure consisting of two coordinates to represent a position:

```
struct rect
{
    double x;        // horizontal distance from origin
    double y;        // vertical distance from origin
};
```

A second way to describe the position of a point is to state how far it is from the origin and in what direction it is (for example, 40 degrees north of east). Traditionally, mathematicians measure the angle counterclockwise from the positive horizontal axis. (See Figure 7.7.) The distance and angle together constitute *polar coordinates*. You can define a second structure to represent this view of a position:

```
struct polar
{
    double distance;   // distance from origin
```

```
    double angle;        // direction from origin
};
```

FIGURE 7.6
Rectangular coordinates.

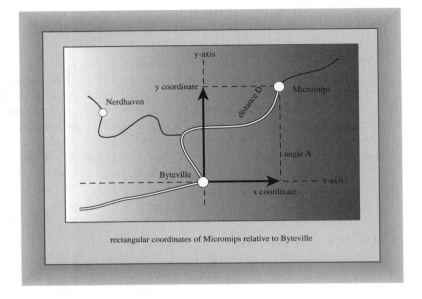

rectangular coordinates of Micromips relative to Byteville

FIGURE 7.7
Polar coordinates.

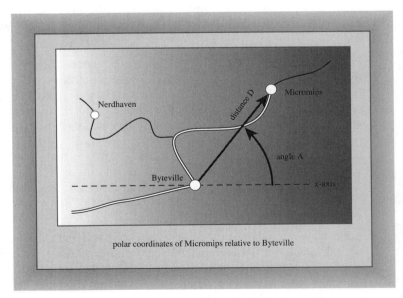

polar coordinates of Micromips relative to Byteville

Let's construct a function that displays the contents of a type **polar** structure. The math functions in the C++ library assume angles are in radians, so we measure angles in that unit. But for display purposes, we convert radian measure to degrees. That means multiplying by $180/\pi$, which is approximately 57.29577951. Here's the function:

```
// show polar coordinates, converting angle to degrees
void show_polar (polar dapos)
{
    const double Rad_to_deg = 57.29577951;

    cout << "distance = " << dapos.distance;
    cout << ", angle = " << dapos.angle * Rad_to_deg;
    cout << " degrees\n";
}
```

Notice that the formal variable is type **polar**. When you pass a **polar** structure to this function, the structure contents are copied into the **dapos** structure, and the function then uses that copy in its work. Because **dapos** is a structure, the function uses the membership (dot) operator (see Chapter 4) to identify structure members.

Next, let's try something more ambitious and write a function that converts rectangular coordinates to polar coordinates. We'll have the function accept a **rect** structure as its argument and return a **polar** structure to the calling function. This involves using functions from the math library, so the program has to include the **math.h** header file. Also, on some systems you have to tell the compiler to load the math library (see Chapter 1, "Getting Started"). You can use the Pythagorean theorem to get the distance from the horizontal and vertical components:

```
distance = sqrt( x * x + y * y)
```

The **atan2()** function from the math library calculates the angle from the **x** and **y** values:

```
angle = atan2(y, x)
```

(There's also an **atan()** function, but it doesn't distinguish between angles 180 degrees apart. That uncertainty is no more desirable in a math function than it is in a wilderness guide.)

Given these formulas, you can write the function as follows:

```
// convert rectangular to polar coordinates
polar rect_to_polar(rect xypos)    // type polar
{
    polar answer;

    answer.distance =
        sqrt( xypos.x * xypos.x + xypos.y * xypos.y);
    answer.angle = atan2(xypos.y, xypos.x);
    return answer;       // returns a polar structure
}
```

Now that the functions are ready, writing the rest of the program is straightforward. Listing 7.12 presents the result.

LISTING 7.12 strctfun.cpp

```
// strctfun.cpp -- functions with a structure argument
#include <iostream>
#include <cmath>
using namespace std;
```

LISTING 7.12   Continued

```cpp
// structure templates
struct polar
{
    double distance;// distance from origin
    double angle;    // direction from origin
};
struct rect
{
    double x;        // horizontal distance from origin
    double y;        // vertical distance from origin
};

// prototypes
polar rect_to_polar(rect xypos);
void show_polar(polar dapos);

int main()
{
    rect rplace;
    polar pplace;

    cout << "Enter the x and y values: ";
    while (cin >> rplace.x >> rplace.y)  // slick use of cin
    {
        pplace = rect_to_polar(rplace);
        show_polar(pplace);
        cout << "Next two numbers (q to quit): ";
    }
    cout << "Done.\n";
    return 0;
}

// convert rectangular to polar coordinates
polar rect_to_polar(rect xypos)
{
    polar answer;

    answer.distance =
        sqrt( xypos.x * xypos.x + xypos.y * xypos.y);
    answer.angle = atan2(xypos.y, xypos.x);
    return answer;       // returns a polar structure
}

// show polar coordinates, converting angle to degrees
void show_polar (polar dapos)
{
    const double Rad_to_deg = 57.29577951;

    cout << "distance = " << dapos.distance;
    cout << ", angle = " << dapos.angle * Rad_to_deg;
    cout << " degrees\n";
}
```

Compatibility Note

Some implementations still use `math.h` instead of the newer `cmath` header file. Some compilers require explicit instructions to search the math library. For example, older versions of g++ uses this command line:

```
g++ structfun.C -lm
```

Here is a sample run:

```
Enter the x and y values: 30 40
distance = 50, angle = 53.1301 degrees
Next two numbers (q to quit): -100 100
distance = 141.421, angle = 135 degrees
Next two numbers (q to quit): q
```

Program Notes

We've already discussed the two functions, so let's review how the program uses `cin` to control a `while` loop:

```
while (cin >> rplace.x >> rplace.y)
```

Recall that `cin` is an object of the `istream` class. The extraction operator (`>>`) is designed in such a way that `cin >> rplace.x` also is an object of that type. As you'll see in Chapter 11, "Working with Classes," class operators are implemented with functions. What really happens when you use `cin >> rplace.x` is that the program calls a function that returns a type `istream` value. Apply the extraction operator to the `cin >> rplace.x` object (as in `cin >> rplace.x >> rplace.y`), and you again get an object of the `istream` class. Thus, the entire `while` loop test expression eventually evaluates to `cin`, which, as you may recall, when used in the context of a test expression is converted to a `bool` value of `true` or `false`, depending on whether input succeeded or not. In this loop, for example, `cin` expects the user to enter two numbers. If, instead, you enter `q`, as we did, `cin >>` recognizes that `q` is not a number. It leaves the `q` in the input queue and returns a value that's converted to `false`, terminating the loop.

Compare this approach for reading numbers to this simpler one:

```
for (int i = 0; i < limit; i++)
{
   cout << "Enter value #" << (i + 1) << ": ";
   cin >> temp;
   if (temp < 0)
      break;
   ar[i] = temp;
}
```

To terminate that loop early, you enter a negative number. That restricts input to non-negative values. That restriction fits the needs of some programs, but more typically you would want a means of terminating a loop that didn't exclude certain numeric values. Using `cin >>` as the test condition eliminates such restrictions, for it accepts all valid numeric input. Keep this trick in mind when you need an input loop for numbers. Also, keep in mind that non-numeric input sets an error condition that prevents the reading of any more input. If your program needs input subsequent to the input loop, you must use `cin.clear()` to reset input, and you might then need to get rid of the offending input by reading it. Listing 7.7 illustrated those techniques.

Passing Structure Addresses

Suppose you want to save time and space by passing the address of a structure instead of passing the entire structure. This requires rewriting the functions so that they use pointers to structures. First, let's see how to rewrite the `show_polar()` function. You need to make three changes:

- When calling the function, pass it the address of the structure (`&pplace`) rather than the structure itself (`pplace`).

- Declare the formal parameter to be a pointer-to-`polar`, that is, type `polar *`. Because the function shouldn't modify the structure, use the `const` modifier.

- Because the formal parameter is a pointer instead of a structure, use the indirect membership operator (`->`) rather than the membership operator (dot).

After the changes, the function looks like this:

```
// show polar coordinates, converting angle to degrees
void show_polar (const polar * pda)
{
    const double Rad_to_deg = 57.29577951;

    cout << "distance = " << pda->distance;
    cout << ", angle = " << pda->angle * Rad_to_deg;
    cout << " degrees\n";
}
```

Next, let's alter `rect_to_polar`. This is more involved because the original `rect_to_polar` function returns a structure. To take full advantage of pointer efficiency, you should use a pointer instead of a return value. The way to do this is to pass two pointers to the function. The first points to the structure to be converted, and the second points to the structure that's to hold the conversion. Instead of *returning* a new structure, the function *modifies* an existing structure in the calling function. Hence, although the first argument is `const` pointer, the second is not `const`. Otherwise, apply the same principles used to convert `show_polar()` to pointer arguments. Listing 7.13 shows the reworked program.

LISTING 7.13   strctptr.cpp

```
// strctptr.cpp -- functions with pointer to structure arguments
#include <iostream>
#include <cmath>
using namespace std;
```

LISTING 7.13 *Continued*

```cpp
// structure templates
struct polar
{
    double distance;    // distance from origin
    double angle;       // direction from origin
};
struct rect
{
    double x;           // horizontal distance from origin
    double y;           // vertical distance from origin
};

// prototypes
void rect_to_polar(const rect * pxy, polar * pda);
void show_polar (const polar * pda);

int main()
{
    rect rplace;
    polar pplace;

    cout << "Enter the x and y values: ";
    while (cin >> rplace.x >> rplace.y)
    {
        rect_to_polar(&rplace, &pplace);    // pass addresses
        show_polar(&pplace);          // pass address
        cout << "Next two numbers (q to quit): ";
    }
    cout << "Done.\n";
    return 0;
}

// show polar coordinates, converting angle to degrees
void show_polar (const polar * pda)
{
    const double Rad_to_deg = 57.29577951;

    cout << "distance = " << pda->distance;
    cout << ", angle = " << pda->angle * Rad_to_deg;
    cout << " degrees\n";
}

// convert rectangular to polar coordinates
void rect_to_polar(const rect * pxy, polar * pda)
{
    pda->distance =
        sqrt(pxy->x * pxy->x + pxy->y * pxy->y);
    pda->angle = atan2(pxy->y, pxy->x); ]
}
```

Compatibility Note

Some implementations still use `math.h` instead of the newer `cmath` header file. Some compilers require explicit instructions to search the math library.

From the user's standpoint, the program in Listing 7.13 behaves like that in Listing 7.12. The hidden difference is that 7.12 works with copies of structures, whereas 7.13 uses pointers to the original structures.

Recursion

And now for something completely different. A C++ function has the interesting characteristic that it can call itself. (Unlike C, however, C++ does not let `main()` call itself.) This ability is termed *recursion*. Recursion is an important tool in certain types of programming, such as artificial intelligence, but we'll just take a superficial look (artificial shallowness) at how it works.

If a recursive function calls itself, then the newly called function calls itself, and so on, ad infinitum unless the code includes something to terminate the chain of calls. The usual method is to make the recursive call part of an `if` statement. For example, a type `void` recursive function called `recurs()` can have a form like this:

```
void recurs(argumentlist)
{
    statements1
    if (test)
        recurs(arguments)
    statements2
}
```

With luck or foresight, *test* eventually becomes false, and the chain of calls is broken.

Recursive calls produce an intriguing chain of events. As long as the `if` statement remains true, each call to `recurs()` executes *statements1* and then invokes a new incarnation of `recurs()` without reaching *statements2*. When the `if` statement becomes false, the current call then proceeds to *statements2*. Then, when the current call terminates, program control returns to the previous version of `recurs()` that called it. Then, that version of `recurs()` completes executing its *statements2* section and terminates, returning control to the prior call, and so on. Thus, if `recurs()` undergoes five recursive calls, first the *statements1* section is executed five times in the order in which the functions were called, and then the *statements2* section is executed five times in the opposite order in which the functions were called. After going in five levels of recursion, the program then has to back out through the same five levels. Listing 7.14 illustrates this behavior.

LISTING 7.14   recur.cpp

```cpp
// recur.cpp -- use recursion
#include <iostream>
using namespace std;
void countdown(int n);

int main()
{
    countdown(4);            // call the recursive function
    return 0;
}

void countdown(int n)
{
    cout << "Counting down ... " << n << "\n";
    if (n > 0)
        countdown(n-1);      // function calls itself
    cout << n << ": Kaboom!\n";
}
```

Here's the output:

```
Counting down ... 4    [la]level 1; adding levels of recursion
Counting down ... 3    [la]level 2
Counting down ... 2    [la]level 3
Counting down ... 1    [la]level 4
Counting down ... 0    [la]level 5; final recursive call
0: Kaboom!    [la]level 5; beginning to back out
1: Kaboom!    [la]level 4
2: Kaboom!    [la]level 3
3: Kaboom!    [la]level 2
4: Kaboom!    [la]level 1
```

Note that each recursive call creates its own set of variables, so by the time the program reaches the fifth call, it has five separate variables called n, each with a different value.

Recursion is particularly useful for situations that call for repeatedly subdividing a task into two smaller, similar tasks. For example, consider this approach to drawing a ruler. Mark the two ends, locate the midpoint and mark it. Then, apply this same procedure to the left half of the ruler and then to the right half. If you want more subdivisions, apply the same procedure to each of the current subdivisions. This recursive approach sometimes is called the *divide-and-conquer strategy*. Listing 7.15 illustrates this approach with the recursive function subdivide(). It uses a string initially filled with spaces except for a | character at each end. The main program uses a loop to call the **subdivide()** function six times, each time increasing the number of recursion levels and printing the resulting string. Thus, each line of output represents an additional level of recursion.

LISTING 7.15   ruler.cpp

```cpp
// ruler.cpp - use recursion to subdivide a ruler
#include <iostream>
using namespace std;
const int Len = 66;
const int Divs = 6;
void subdivide(char ar[], int low, int high, int level);
int main()
{
    char ruler[Len];
    int i;
    for (i = 1; i < Len - 2; i++)
        ruler[i] = ' ';
    ruler[Len - 1] = '\0';
    int max = Len - 2;
    int min = 0;
    ruler[min] = ruler[max] = '|';
    cout << ruler << "\n";
    for (i = 1; i <= Divs; i++)
    {
        subdivide(ruler,min,max, i);
        cout << ruler << "\n";
        for (int j = 1; j < Len - 2; j++)
            ruler[j] = ' ';   // reset to blank ruler
    }

    return 0;
}
void subdivide(char ar[], int low, int high, int level)
{
    if (level == 0)
        return;
    int mid = (high + low) / 2;
    ar[mid] = '|';
    subdivide(ar, low, mid, level - 1);
    subdivide(ar, mid, high, level - 1);
}
```

Here is the program's output:

```
|                                                              |
|                              |                               |
|              |               |               |               |
|      |       |       |       |       |       |       |       |
|  |   |   |   |   |   |   |   |   |   |   |   |   |   |   |    |
| | | | | | | | | | | | | | | | | | | | | | | | | | | | | | | |
||||||||||||||||||||||||||||||||||||||||||||||||||||||||||||||||
```

Program Notes

The subdivide() function uses a variable called level to control the recursion level. When the function calls itself, it reduces level by 1, and the function with a level of 0 terminates. Note that subdivide() calls itself twice, once for the left subdivision and once for the right subdivision. The original midpoint becomes the right end for one call and the left end for the other call. Notice that the number of calls grows geometrically. That is, one call generates two, which generate four calls, which generate eight, and so on. That's why the level 6 call is able to fill in 64 elements $(2^6 = 64)$.

Pointers to Functions

No discussion of C or C++ functions would be complete without mention of pointers to functions. We'll take a quick look at this topic and leave the full exposition of the possibilities to more advanced texts.

Functions, like data items, have addresses. A function's address is the memory address at which the stored machine language code for the function begins. Normally, it's neither important nor useful for us or the user to know that address, but it can be useful to a program. For example, it's possible to write a function that takes the address of another function as an argument. That enables the first function to find the second function and run it. This approach is more awkward than simply having the first function call the second one directly, but it leaves open the possibility of passing different function addresses at different times. That means the first function can use different functions at different times.

Function Pointer Basics

Let's clarify this process with an example. Suppose you want to design an `estimate()` function that estimates the amount of time necessary to write a given number of lines of code, and you want different programmers to use the function. Part of the code for `estimate()` will be the same for all users, but the function will allow each programmer to provide his or her own algorithm for estimating time. The mechanism for that will be to pass to `estimate()` the address of the particular algorithm function the programmer wants to use. To implement this plan, you need to be able to do the following:

- Take the address of a function.

- Declare a pointer to a function.

- Use a pointer to a function to invoke the function.

Obtaining the Address of a Function

Taking the address of a function is simple: just use the function name without trailing parentheses. That is, if `think()` is a function, then `think` is the address of the function. To pass a function as an argument, pass the function name. Be sure you distinguish between passing the *address* of a function and passing the *return value* of a function:

```
process(think);     // passes address of think() to process()
thought(think());   // passes return value of think() to thought()
```

The `process()` call enables the `process()` function to invoke the `think()` function from within `process()`. The `thought()` call first invokes the `think()` function and then passes the return value of `think()` to the `thought()` function.

Declaring a Pointer to a Function

When you've declared pointers to data types, the declaration has had to specify exactly to what type the pointer points. Similarly, a pointer to a function has to specify to what type of function the pointer points. This means the declaration should identify the function's return type and the function's signature (its argument list). That is, the declaration should tell us the same things about a function that a function prototype does. For example, suppose Pam LeCoder has written a time-estimating function with the following prototype:

```
double pam(int);   // prototype
```

Here's what a declaration of an appropriate pointer type looks like:

```
double (*pf)(int);    // pf points to a function that takes
                      // one int argument and that
                      // returns type double
```

Note that this looks just like the `pam()` declaration, with `(*pf)` playing the part of `pam`. Because `pam` is a function, so is `(*pf)`. And if `(*pf)` is a function, then `pf` is a pointer to a function.

Tip

In general, to declare a pointer to a particular kind of function, you first can write a prototype for a regular function of the desired kind and then replace the function name by an expression in the form of `(*pf)`. That makes `pf` a pointer to a function of that type.

The declaration requires the parentheses around `*pf` to provide the proper operator precedence. Parentheses have a higher precedence than the `*` operator, so `*pf(int)` means `pf()` is a function that returns a pointer, whereas `(*pf)(int)` means `pf` is a pointer to a function:

```
double (*pf)(int); // pf points to a function that returns double
double *pf(int);    // pf() a function that returns a pointer-to-double
```

After you've declared `pf` properly, you can assign it the address of a matching function:

```
double pam(int);
double (*pf)(int);
pf = pam;           // pf now points to the pam() function
```

Note that `pam()` has to match `pf` in both signature and return type. The compiler rejects non-matching assignments:

```
double ned(double);
int ted(int);
double (*pf)(int);
pf = ned;          // invalid -- mismatched signature
pf = ted;          // invalid -- mismatched return types
```

Let's return to the `estimate()` function we mentioned earlier. Suppose you want to pass it the number of lines of code to be written and the address of an estimating algorithm, such as the `pam()` function. Then, it could have the following prototype:

```
void estimate(int lines, double (*pf)(int));
```

This declaration says the second argument is a pointer to a function that has an `int` argument and a `double` return value. To have `estimate()` use the `pam()` function, pass it `pam()`'s address:

```
estimate(50, pam); // function call telling estimate() to use pam()
```

Clearly, the tricky part about using pointers to functions is writing the prototypes, whereas passing the address is very simple.

Using a Pointer to Invoke a Function

Now we get to the final part of the technique, which is using a pointer to call the pointed-to function. The clue comes in the pointer declaration. There, recall, `(*pf)` played the same role as a function name. Thus, all we have to do is use `(*pf)` as if it were a function name:

```
double pam(int);
double (*pf)(int);
pf = pam;             // pf now points to the pam() function
double x = pam(4);    // call pam() using the function name
double y = (*pf)(5);  // call pam() using the pointer pf
```

Actually, C++ also allows you to use `pf` as if it were a function name:

```
double y = pf(5);     // also call pam() using the pointer pf
```

We'll use the first form. It is uglier, but it provides a strong visual reminder that the code is using a function pointer.

History Versus Logic

Holy syntax! How can `pf` and `(*pf)` be equivalent? Historically, one school of thought maintains that because `pf` is a pointer to a function, `*pf` is a function; hence, you should use `(*pf)()` as a function call. A second school maintains that because the name of a function is a pointer to that function, a pointer to that function should act like the name of a function; hence, you should use `pf()` as a function call. C++ takes the compromise view that both forms are correct, or at least can be allowed, even though they are logically inconsistent with each other. Before you judge that compromise too harshly, reflect that the ability to hold views that are not logically self-consistent is a hallmark of the human mental process.

Listing 7.16 demonstrates using function pointers in a program. It calls the `estimate()` function twice, once passing the `betsy()` function address and once passing the `pam()` function address. In the first case, `estimate()` uses `betsy()` to calculate the number of hours necessary, and in the second case, `estimate()` uses `pam()` for the calculation. This design facilitates future program development. When Ralph develops his own algorithm for estimating time, he doesn't have to rewrite `estimate()`. Instead, he merely needs to supply his own `ralph()` function, making sure it has the correct signature and return type. Of course, rewriting `estimate()`

isn't a difficult task, but the same principle applies to more complex code. Also, the function pointer method allows Ralph to modify the behavior of `estimate()` even if he doesn't have access to the source code for `estimate()`.

LISTING 7.16   fun_ptr.cpp

```
// fun_ptr.cpp -- pointers to functions
#include <iostream>
using namespace std;
double betsy(int);
double pam(int);

// second argument is pointer to a type double function that
// takes a type int argument
void estimate(int lines, double (*pf)(int));

int main()
{
    int code;

    cout << "How many lines of code do you need? ";
    cin >> code;
    cout << "Here's Betsy's estimate:\n";
    estimate(code, betsy);
    cout << "Here's Pam's estimate:\n";
    estimate(code, pam);
    return 0;
}

double betsy(int lns)
{
    return 0.05 * lns;
}

double pam(int lns)
{
    return 0.03 * lns + 0.0004 * lns * lns;
}

void estimate(int lines, double (*pf)(int))
{
    cout << lines << " lines will take ";
    cout << (*pf)(lines) << " hour(s)\n";
}
```

Here are two sample runs:

```
How many lines of code do you need? 30
Here's Betsy's estimate:
30 lines will take 1.5 hour(s)
Here's Pam's estimate:
30 lines will take 1.26 hour(s)
```

```
How many lines of code do you need? 100
Here's Betsy's estimate:
100 lines will take 5 hour(s)
Here's Pam's estimate:
100 lines will take 7 hour(s)
```

Summary

Functions are the C++ programming modules. To use a function, you need to provide a definition and a prototype, and you have to use a function call. The function definition is the code that implements what the function does. The function prototype describes the function interface: how many and what kinds of values to pass to the function and what sort of return type, if any, to get from it. The function call causes the program to pass the function arguments to the function and to transfer program execution to the function code.

By default, C++ functions pass arguments by value. This means that the formal parameters in the function definition are new variables that are initialized to the values provided by the function call. Thus, C++ functions protect the integrity of the original data by working with copies.

C++ treats an array name argument as the address of the first element of the array. Technically, this still is passing by value, for the pointer is a copy of the original address, but the function uses the pointer to access the contents of the original array. When declaring formal parameters for a function (and only then), the following two declarations are equivalent:

```
typeName arr[];
typeName * arr;
```

Both mean arr is a pointer to *typeName*. When you write the function code, however, you can use arr as if it were an array name in order to access elements: arr[i]. Even when passing pointers, you can preserve the integrity of the original data by declaring the formal argument to be a pointer to a const type. Because passing the address of an array conveys no information about the size of the array, you normally would pass the array size as a separate argument.

C++ provides three ways to represent C-style strings: a character array, a string constant, and a pointer to a string. All are type char* (pointer-to-char), so they are passed to a function as a type char* argument. C++ uses the null character (\0) to terminate strings, and string functions test for the null character to determine the end of any string they are processing.

C++ treats structures the same as basic types, meaning that you can pass them by value and use them as function return types. However, if the structure is large, it might be more efficient to pass a pointer to the structure and let the function work with the original data.

A C++ function can be recursive; that is, the code for a particular function can include a call of itself.

The name of a C++ function acts as the address of the function. By using a function argument that is a pointer to a function, you can pass to a function the name of a second function that you want the first function to evoke.

Review Questions

1. What are the three steps in using a function?

2. Construct function prototypes that match the following descriptions:

   a. `igor()` takes no arguments and has no return value.

   b. `tofu()` takes an `int` argument and returns a `float`.

   c. `mpg()` takes two type `double` arguments and returns a `double`.

   d. `summation()` takes the name of a `long` array and an array size as values and returns a `long` value.

   e. `doctor()` takes a string argument (the string is not to be modified) and returns a `double` value.

   f. `ofcourse()` takes a `boss` structure as an argument and returns nothing.

   g. `plot()` takes a pointer to a `map` structure as an argument and returns a string.

3. Write a function that takes three arguments: the name of an `int` array, the array size, and an `int` value. Have the function set each element of the array to the `int` value.

4. Write a function that takes three arguments: a pointer to the first element of a range in an array, a pointer to the element following the end of a range in an array,, and an `int` value. Have the function set each element of the array to the `int` value.

5. Write a function that takes a `double` array name and an array size as arguments and returns the largest value in that array. Note that this function shouldn't alter the contents of the array.

6. Why don't we use the `const` qualifier for function arguments that are one of the fundamental types?

7. What are the three forms a C-style string can take in a C++ program?

8. Write a function that has this prototype:

   ```
   int replace(char * str, char c1, char c2);
   ```

   Have the function replace every occurrence of `c1` in the string `str` with `c2`, and have the function return the number of replacements it makes.

9. What does the expression `*"pizza"` mean? What about `"taco"[2]`?

10. C++ enables you to pass a structure by value and it lets you pass the address of a structure. If `glitz` is a structure variable, how would you pass it by value? How would you pass its address? What are the trade-offs of the two approaches?

11. The function `judge()` has a type `int` return value. As an argument, it takes the address of a function that takes a pointer to a `const char` as an argument and that also returns an `int`. Write the function prototype.

Programming Exercises

1. Write a program that repeatedly asks you to enter pairs of numbers until at least one of the pair is zero. For each pair, the program should use a function to calculate the harmonic mean of the numbers. The function should return the answer to `main()`, which reports the result. The harmonic mean of the numbers is the inverse of the average of the inverses and can be calculated as follows:

   harmonic mean = 2.0 * x * y / (x + y)

2. Write a program that asks you to enter up to ten golf scores, which are to be stored in an array. You should provide a means for the user to terminate input prior to entering ten scores. The program should display all the scores on one line and report the average score. Handle input, display, and the average calculation with three separate array-processing functions.

3. Here is a structure template:

   ```
   struct box
   {
        char maker[40];
        float height;
        float width;
        float length;
        float volume;
   };
   ```

   a. Write a function that passes a **box** structure by value and that displays the value of each member.

   b. Write a function that passes the address of a **box** structure and that sets the **volume** member to the product of the other three dimensions.

   c. Write a simple program that uses these two functions.

4. Many state lotteries use a variation of the simple lottery portrayed by Listing 7.4. In these variations you choose several numbers from one set and call them the field numbers. For example, you might select 5 numbers from the field 1–47). You also pick a single number (called a mega number or a power ball, etc.) from a second range, such as 1–27. To win the grand prize, you have to guess all the picks correctly. The chance of winning is the product of the probability of picking all the field numbers times the probability of picking the mega number. For instance, the odds of winning the example described here is the product of the odds of picking 5 out of 47 correctly times the odds of picking 1 out of 27 correctly. Modify Listing 7.4 to calculate the odds of winning this kind of lottery.

5. Define a recursive function that takes an integer argument and returns the factorial of that argument. Recall that 3 factorial, written 3!, equals $3 \times 2!$, and so on, with 0! defined as 1. In general, n! = n * (n − 1)!. Test it in a program that uses a loop to allow the user to enter various values for which the program reports the factorial.

6. Write a program that uses the following functions:

   Fill_array() takes as arguments the name of an array of **double** and an array size. It prompts the user to enter **double** values to be entered in the array. It ceases taking input when the array is full or when the user enters non-numeric input, and it returns the actual number of entries.

   Show_array() takes as arguments the name of an array of **double** and an array size and displays the contents of the array.

   Reverse_array() takes as arguments the name of an array of **double** and an array size and reverses the order of the values stored in the array.

   The program should fill an array, show the array, reverse the array, show the array, reverse all but the first and last elements of the array, and then show the array.

7. Redo Listing 7.7, modifying the three array-handling functions to each use two pointer parameters to represent a range. The fill_array() function, instead of returning the actual number of items read, should return a pointer to the location after the last location filled; the other functions can use this pointer as the second argument to identify the end of the data.

8. This exercise provides practice in writing functions dealing with arrays and structures. The following is a program skeleton. Complete it by providing the described functions.

```
#include <iostream>
using namespace std;

const int SLEN = 30;
struct student {
    char fullname[SLEN];
    char hobby[SLEN];
    int ooplevel;
};
// getinfo() has two arguments: a pointer to the first element of
// an array of student structures and an int representing the
// number of elements of the array. The function solicits and
// stores data about students. It terminates input upon filling
// the array or upon encountering a blank line for the student
// name. The function returns the actual number of array elements
// filled.
int getinfo(student pa[], int n);

// display1() takes a student structure as an argument
// and displays its contents
void display1(student st);

// display2() takes the address of student structure as an
// argument and displays the structure's contents
void display2(const student * ps);

// display3() takes the address of the first element of an array
// of student structures and the number of array elements as
```

```
// arguments and displays the contents of the structures
void display3(const student pa[], int n);

int main()
{
    cout << "Enter class size: ";
    int class_size;
    cin >> class_size;
    while (cin.get() != '\n')
        continue;

    student * ptr_stu = new student[class_size];
    int entered = getinfo(ptr_stu, class_size);
    for (int i = 0; i < entered; i++)
    {
        display1(ptr_stu[i]);
        display2(&ptr_stu[i]);
    }
    display3(ptr_stu, entered);
    delete [] ptr_stu;
    cout << "Done\n";
    return 0;
}
```

9. Design a function `calculate()` that takes two type `double` values and a pointer to a function that takes two `double` arguments and returns a `double`. The `calculate()` function also should be type `double`, and it should return the value that the pointed-to function calculates using the double arguments to `calculate()`. For example, suppose we have this definition for the `add()` function:

```
double add(double x, double y)
{
    return x + y;
}
```

Then, the function call in

```
double q = calculate(2.5, 10.4, add);
```

would cause `calculate()` to pass the values `2.5` and `10.4` to the `add()` function and then return the `add()` return value (12.9).

Use these functions and at least one additional function in the `add()` mold in a program. The program should use a loop that allows the user to enter pairs of numbers. For each pair, use `calculate()` to invoke `add()` and at least one other function. If you are feeling adventurous, try creating an array of pointers to `add()`-style functions and use a loop to successively apply `calculate()` to a series of functions by using these pointers. Hint: Here's how to declare such an array of three pointers:

```
double (*pf[3])(double, double);
```

You can initialize such an array by using the usual array initialization syntax and function names as addresses.

CHAPTER 8

ADVENTURES IN FUNCTIONS

With the last chapter under your belt, you now know a lot about C++ functions, but there's much more to come. C++ provides many new function features that separate C++ from its C heritage. The new features include inline functions, passing variables by reference, default argument values, function overloading (polymorphism), and template functions. This chapter, more than any other you've read so far, explores features found in C++ but not C, so it marks your first major foray into plus-plussedness.

Inline Functions

Let's begin by examining inline functions, a C++ enhancement designed to speed up programs. The primary distinction between normal functions and inline functions is not in how you code them but in how the C++ compiler incorporates them into a program. To understand the distinction between inline functions and normal functions, you need to peer more deeply into a program's innards than we have so far. Let's do that now.

The final product of the compilation process is an executable program, which consists of a set of machine language instructions. When you start a program, the operating system loads these instructions into the computer's memory, so each instruction has a particular memory address. The computer then goes through these instructions step-by-step. Sometimes, as when you have a loop or a branching statement, program execution will skip over instructions, jumping back or forward to a particular address. Normal function calls also involve having a program jump to another address (the function's address) and then jump back when the function terminates. Let's look at a typical implementation of that process in a little more detail. When the program reaches the function call instruction, the program stores the memory address of the instruction immediately following the function call, copies function arguments to the stack (a block of memory reserved for that purpose), jumps to the memory location that marks the beginning of the function, executes the function code (perhaps placing a return value in a register), and then jumps back to the instruction whose address it saved.[1] Jumping back and forth and keeping track of where to jump means that there is an overhead in elapsed time to using functions.

The C++ inline function provides an alternative. This is a function whose compiled code is "in line" with the other code in the program. That is, the compiler replaces the function call with the corresponding function code. With inline code, the program doesn't have to jump to another location to execute the code and then jump back. Inline functions thus run a little faster than regular functions, but there is a memory penalty. If a program calls an inline function at 10 separate locations, then the program winds up with ten copies of the function inserted into the code. (See Figure 8.1.)

FIGURE 8.1
Inline functions versus regular functions.

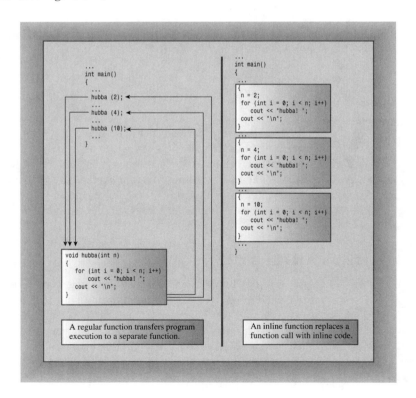

It's a bit like having to leave off reading some text to find out what a footnote says and then, upon finishing the footnote, returning to where you were reading in the text.

You should be selective about using inline functions. If the time needed to execute the function code is long compared to the time needed to handle the function call mechanism, then the time saved is a relatively small fraction of the entire process. If the code execution time is short, then an inline call can save a large fraction of the time used by the non-inline call. On the other hand, you are now saving a large fraction of a relatively quick process, so the absolute time savings may not be that great unless the function is called frequently.

To use this feature, you must take at least one of two actions:

- Preface the function declaration with the keyword `inline`.
- Preface the function definition with the keyword `inline`.

A common practice is to omit the prototype and to place the entire definition (meaning the function header and all the function code) where the prototype normally would go.

The compiler does not have to honor your request to make a function inline. It might decide the function is too large or notice that it calls itself (recursion is not allowed or indeed possible for inline functions), or the feature might not be implemented for your particular compiler.

Listing 8.1 illustrates the inline technique with an inline `square()` function that squares its argument. Note that we've placed the entire definition on one line. That's not required, but if the definition doesn't fit on one line, the function probably is a poor candidate for an inline function.

LISTING 8.1   inline.cpp

```cpp
// inline.cpp -- use an inline function
#include <iostream>
using namespace std;

// an inline function definition
inline double square(double x) { return x * x; }

int main()
{
    double a, b;
    double c = 13.0;

    a = square(5.0);
    b = square(4.5 + 7.5);   // can pass expressions
    cout << "a = " << a << ", b = " << b << "\n";
    cout << "c = " << c;
    cout << ", c squared = " << square(c++) << "\n";
    cout << "Now c = " << c << "\n";
    return 0;
}
```

Here's the output:

```
a = 25, b = 144
c = 13, c squared = 169
Now c = 14
```

The output illustrates that inline functions pass arguments by value just like regular functions do. If the argument is an expression, such as 4.5 + 7.5, the function passes the value of the expression, 12 in this case. This makes C++'s inline facility far superior to C's macro definitions. See the "Inline Versus Macros" sidebar.

Even though the program doesn't provide a separate prototype, C++'s prototyping features still are in play. That's because the entire definition, which comes before the function's first use, serves as a prototype. This means you can use `square()` with an `int` argument or a `long` argument, and the program automatically type casts the value to type `double` before passing it to the function.

Inline Versus Macros

The `inline` facility is a C++ addition. C uses the preprocessor `#define` statement to provide *macros*, a crude implementation of inline code. For example, here's a macro for squaring a number:

```
#define SQUARE(X) X*X
```

This works not by passing arguments but by text substitution, with the X acting as a symbolic label for the "argument":

```
a = SQUARE(5.0); is replaced by a = 5.0*5.0;
b = SQUARE(4.5 + 7.5); is replaced by b = 4.5 + 7.5 * 4.5 + 7.5;
d = SQUARE(c++); is replaced by d = c++*c++;
```

Only the first example works properly. You can improve matters with a liberal application of parentheses:

```
#define SQUARE(X) ((X)*(X))
```

Still, the problem remains that macros don't pass by value. Even with this new definition, `SQUARE(c++)` increments c twice, but the inline `square()` function in Listing 8.1 evaluates c, passes that value to be squared, and then increments c once.

The intent here is not to show you how to write C macros. Rather, it is to suggest that if you have been using C macros to perform function-like services, consider converting them to C++ inline functions.

Reference Variables

C++ adds a new compound type to the language—the reference variable. A *reference* is a name that acts as an alias, or alternative name, for a previously defined variable. For example, if you make `twain` a reference to the `clemens` variable, you can use `twain` and `clemens` interchangeably to represent that variable. Of what use is such an alias? Is it to help people who are embarrassed by their choice of variable names? Maybe, but the main use for a reference is as a formal argument to a function. By using a reference as an argument, the function works with the original data instead of with a copy. References provide a convenient alternative to pointers for processing large structures with a function, and they are essential for designing classes. Before you see how to use references with functions, however, let's examine the basics of defining and using a reference. Keep in mind that the purpose of the following discussion is to illustrate how references work, not how they typically are used.

Creating a Reference Variable

You might recall that C and C++ use the & symbol to indicate the address of a variable. C++ assigns an additional meaning to the & symbol and presses it into service for declaring references. For example, to make `rodents` an alternative name for the variable `rats`, do the following:

```
int rats;
int & rodents = rats;    // makes rodents an alias for rats
```

In this context, & is not the address operator. Instead, it serves as part of the type identifier. Just as `char *` in a declaration means pointer-to-`char`, `int &` means reference-to-`int`. The reference declaration allows you to use `rats` and `rodents` interchangeably; both refer to the same value and the same memory location. Listing 8.2 illustrates the truth of this claim.

LISTING 8.2   `firstref.cpp`

```cpp
// firstref.cpp -- defining and using a reference
#include <iostream>
using namespace std;
int main()
{
    int rats = 101;
    int & rodents = rats;    // rodents is a reference

    cout << "rats = " << rats;
    cout << ", rodents = " << rodents << "\n";
    rodents++;
    cout << "rats = " << rats;
    cout << ", rodents = " << rodents << "\n";

// some implementations require type casting the following
// addresses to type unsigned
    cout << "rats address = " << &rats;
    cout << ", rodents address = " << &rodents << "\n";
    return 0;
}
```

Note that the & operator in the statement

```
int & rodents = rats;
```

is not the address operator but declares that `rodents` is of type `int &`, that is, a reference to an `int` variable. But the & operator in the statement

```
cout<<", rodents address ="<< &rodents << "\n";
```

is the address operator, with `&rodents` representing the address of the variable to which `rodents` refers. Here is the program's output:

```
rats = 101, rodents = 101
rats = 102, rodents = 102
rats address = 0x0065fd48, rodents address = 0x0065fd48
```

As you can see, both `rats` and `rodents` have the same value and the same address. Incrementing `rodents` by 1 affects both variables. More precisely, the `rodents++` operation increments a single variable for which we have two names. (Again, keep in mind that although this example shows you how a reference works, it doesn't represent the typical use for a reference, which is as a function parameter, particularly for structure and object arguments. We look into these uses pretty soon.)

References tend to be a bit confusing at first to C veterans coming to C++ because they are tantalizingly reminiscent of pointers, yet somehow different. For example, you can create both a reference and a pointer to refer to `rats`:

```
int rats = 101;
int & rodents = rats;    // rodents a reference
int * prats = &rats;     // prats a pointer
```

Then, you could use the expressions `rodents` and `*prats` interchangeably with `rats` and use the expressions `&rodents` and `prats` interchangeably with `&rats`. From this standpoint, a reference looks a lot like a pointer in disguised notation in which the `*` dereferencing operator is understood implicitly. And, in fact, that's more or less what a reference is. But there are differences besides those of notation. For one, it is necessary to initialize the reference when you declare it; you can't declare the reference and then assign it a value later the way you can with a pointer:

```
int rat;
int & rodent;
rodent = rat;    // No, you can't do this.
```

Remember

You should initialize a reference variable when you declare it.

A reference is more like a `const` pointer; you have to initialize it when you create it, and once a reference pledges its allegiance to a particular variable, it sticks to its pledge. That is,

```
int & rodents = rats;
```

is, in essence, a disguised notation for something like this:

```
int * const pr = &rats;
```

Here, the reference `rodents` plays the same role as the expression `*pr`.

Listing 8.3 shows what happens if you try to make a reference change allegiance from a `rats` variable to a `bunnies` variable.

LISTING 8.3   `secref.cpp`

```
// secref.cpp -- defining and using a reference
#include <iostream>
using namespace std;
```

LISTING 8.3   Continued

```
int main()
{
    int rats = 101;
    int & rodents = rats;    // rodents is a reference

    cout << "rats = " << rats;
    cout << ", rodents = " << rodents << "\n";

    cout << "rats address = " << &rats;
    cout << ", rodents address = " << &rodents << "\n";

    int bunnies = 50;
    rodents = bunnies;        // can we change the reference?
    cout << "bunnies = " << bunnies;
    cout << ", rats = " << rats;
    cout << ", rodents = " << rodents << "\n";

    cout << "bunnies address = " << &bunnies;
    cout << ", rodents address = " << &rodents << "\n";
    return 0;
}
```

Here's the output:

```
rats = 101, rodents = 101
rats address = 0x0065fd44, rodents address = 0x0065fd44
bunnies = 50, rats = 50, rodents = 50
bunnies address = 0x0065fd48, rodents address = 0x0065fd4
```

Initially, `rodents` refers to `rats`, but then the program apparently attempts to make `rodents` a reference to `bunnies`:

```
rodents = bunnies;
```

For a moment, it looks as if this attempt has succeeded, for the value of `rodents` changes from 101 to 50. But closer inspection reveals that `rats` also has changed to 50 and that `rats` and `rodents` still share the same address, which differs from the `bunnies` address. Because `rodents` is an alias for `rats`, the assignment statement really means the same as the following:

```
rats = bunnies;
```

That is, it means "assign the value of the `bunnies` variable to the `rat` variable." In short, you can set a reference by an initializing declaration, not by assignment.

Suppose you tried the following:

```
int rats = 101;
int * pi = &rats;
int & rodents = *pt;
int bunnies = 50;
pt = &bunnies;
```

Initializing `rodents` to `*pt` makes `rodents` refer to `rats`. Subsequently altering `pt` to point to `bunnies` does not alter the fact that `rodents` refers to `rats`.

References As Function Parameters

Most often, references are used as function parameters, making a variable name in the function an alias for a variable in the calling program. This method of passing arguments is called *passing by reference*. Passing by reference allows a called function to access variables in the calling function. C++'s addition of the feature is a break from C, which only passes by value. Passing by value, recall, results in the called function working with copies of values from the calling program. (See Figure 8.2.) Of course, C lets you get around the passing by value limitation by using pointers.

FIGURE 8.2

Passing by value and passing by reference.

Let's compare using references and using pointers in a common computer problem: swapping the values of two variables. A swapping function has to be able to alter values of variables in the calling program. That means the usual approach of passing variables by value won't work, because the function will end up swapping the contents of copies of the original variables instead of the variables themselves. If you pass references, however, the function can work with the original data. Alternatively, you can pass pointers in order to access the original data. Listing 8.4 shows all three methods, including the one that doesn't work, so that you can compare them.

LISTING 8.4   swaps.cpp

```cpp
// swaps.cpp -- swapping with references and with pointers
#include <iostream>
using namespace std;
void swapr(int & a, int & b);   // a, b are aliases for ints
void swapp(int * p, int * q);   // p, q are addresses of ints
void swapv(int a, int b);       // a, b are new variables
int main()
{
    int wallet1 = 300;
    int wallet2 = 350;

    cout << "wallet1 = $" << wallet1;
    cout << " wallet2 = $" << wallet2 << "\n";

    cout << "Using references to swap contents:\n";
    swapr(wallet1, wallet2);   // pass variables
    cout << "wallet1 = $" << wallet1;
    cout << " wallet2 = $" << wallet2 << "\n";

    cout << "Using pointers to swap contents:\n";
    swapp(&wallet1, &wallet2); // pass addresses of variables
    cout << "wallet1 = $" << wallet1;
    cout << " wallet2 = $" << wallet2 << "\n";

    cout << "Trying to use passing by value:\n";
    swapv(wallet1, wallet2);   // pass values of variables
    cout << "wallet1 = $" << wallet1;
    cout << " wallet2 = $" << wallet2 << "\n";
    return 0;
}

void swapr(int & a, int & b)    // use references{
    int temp;

    temp = a;       // use a, b for values of variables
    a = b;
    b = temp;
}

void swapp(int * p, int * q)    // use pointers
{
    int temp;

    temp = *p;      // use *p, *q for values of variables
    *p = *q;
    *q = temp;
}

void swapv(int a, int b)        // try using values
{
    int temp;
```

LISTING 8.4   Continued

```
        temp = a;      // use a, b for values of variables
        a = b;
        b = temp;
}
```

Here's the output:

```
wallet1 = $300 wallet2 = $350        " original values
Using references to swap contents:
wallet1 = $350 wallet2 = $300        " values swapped
Using pointers to swap contents:
wallet1 = $300 wallet2 = $350        " values swapped again
Trying to use passing by value:
wallet1 = $300 wallet2 = $350        " swap failed
```

As we expected, the reference and pointer methods both successfully swap the contents of the two wallets, whereas the passing by value method fails.

Program Notes

First, note how each function is called:

```
swapr(wallet1, wallet2);       // pass variables
swapp(&wallet1, &wallet2);     // pass addresses of variables
swapv(wallet1, wallet2);       // pass values of variables
```

Passing by reference (swapr(wallet1, wallet2)) and passing by value (swapv(wallet1, wallet2)) look identical. The only way you can tell that swapr() passes by reference is by looking at the prototype or the function definition. However, the presence of the address operator (&) makes it obvious when a function passes by address ((swapp(&wallet1, &wallet2)). (Recall that the type declaration int *p means that p is a pointer to an int and therefore the argument corresponding to p should be an address, such as &wallet1.)

Next, compare the code for the functions swapr() (passing by reference) and swapv() (passing by value). The only outward difference between the two is how the function parameters are declared:

```
void swapr(int & a, int & b)
void swapv(int a, int b)
```

The internal difference, of course, is that in swapr() the variables a and b serve as aliases for wallet1 and wallet2, so swapping a and b swaps wallet1 and wallet2. But in swapv(), the variables a and b are new variables that copy the values of wallet1 and wallet2, so swapping a and b has no effect on wallet1 and wallet2.

Finally, compare the functions swapr() (passing a reference) and swapp() (passing a pointer). The first difference is in how the function parameters are declared:

```
void swapr(int & a, int & b)
void swapp(int * p, int * q)
```

The second difference is that the pointer version requires using the * dereferencing operator throughout when the function uses p and q.

Earlier, we said you should initialize a reference variable when you define it. You can consider reference function arguments as being initialized to the argument passed by the function call. That is, the function call

```
swapr(wallet1, wallet2);
```

initializes the formal parameter a to wallet1 and the formal parameter b to wallet2.

Reference Properties and Oddities

Using reference arguments has several twists about which you need to know. First, consider Listing 8.5. It uses two functions to cube an argument. One takes a type double argument, whereas the other takes a reference to double. The actual code for cubing is purposefully a bit odd to illustrate a point.

LISTING 8.5   cubes.cpp

```cpp
// cubes.cpp -- regular and reference arguments
#include <iostream>
using namespace std;
double cube(double a);
double refcube(double &ra);
int main ()
{
    double x = 3.0;

    cout << cube(x);
    cout << " = cube of " << x << "\n";
    cout << refcube(x);
    cout << " = cube of " << x << "\n";
    return 0;
}

double cube(double a)
{
    a *= a * a;
    return a;
}

double refcube(double &ra)
{
    ra *= ra * ra;
    return ra;
}
```

Here is the output:

```
27 = cube of 3
27 = cube of 27
```

Note that the `refcube()` function modifies the value of x in `main()` whereas `cube()` doesn't, which reminds us of why passing by value is the norm. The variable a is local to `cube()`. It is initialized to the value of x, but changing a has no effect on x. But because `refcube()` uses a reference argument, the changes it makes to `ra` actually are made to x. If your intent is that a function use the information passed to it without modifying the information, and if you're using a reference, you should use a constant reference. Here, for example, we should have used `const` in the function prototype and function heading:

```
double refcube(const double &ra);
```

Had we done this, the compiler would have generated an error message when it found code altering the value of `ra`.

Incidentally, if you need to write a function along the lines of this example, use passing by value rather than the more exotic passing by reference. Reference arguments become useful with larger data units, such as structures and classes, as you soon see.

Functions that pass by value, such as the `cube()` function in Listing 8.5, can use many kinds of actual arguments. For example, all the following calls are valid:

```
double z = cube(x + 2.0);     // evaluate x + 2.0, pass value
z = cube(8.0);                // pass the value 8.0
int k = 10;
z = cube(k);       // convert value of k to double, pass value
double yo[3] = { 2.2, 3.3, 4.4};
z = cube (yo[2]);             // pass the value 4.4
```

Suppose you try similar arguments for a function with a reference parameter. It would seem that passing a reference should be more restrictive. After all, if `ra` is the alternative name for a variable, then the actual argument should be that variable. Something like

```
double z = refcube(x + 3.0);  // may not compile
```

doesn't appear to make sense because the expression x + 3.0 is not a variable. For example, you can't assign a value to such an expression:

```
x + 3.0 = 5.0;  // nonsensical
```

What happens if you try a function call like `refcube(x + 3.0)`? In contemporary C++, that's an error, and some compilers will tell you so. Others give you a warning along the following lines:

```
Warning: Temporary used for parameter 'ra' in call to refcube(double &)
```

The reason for this milder response is that C++, in its early years, did allow you to pass expressions to a reference variable. In some cases, it still does. What happens is this: Because x + 3.0 is not a type `double` variable, the program creates a temporary, nameless variable, initializing it to the value of the expression x + 3.0. Then, `ra` becomes a reference to that temporary variable. Let's take a closer look at temporary variables and see when they are and are not created.

Temporary Variables, Reference Arguments, and const

C++ can generate a temporary variable if the actual argument doesn't match a reference argument. Currently, C++ permits this only if the argument is a const reference, but this is a new restriction. Let's look at the cases in which C++ does generate temporary variables and see why the restriction to a const reference makes sense.

First, when is a temporary variable created? Provided that the reference parameter is a const, the compiler generates a temporary variable in two kinds of situations:

- The actual argument is the correct type, but isn't an Lvalue

- The actual argument is of the wrong type, but of a type that can be converted to the correct type

An argument that's an *Lvalue* is a data object that can be referenced. For example, a variable, an array element, a structure member, a reference, and a dereferenced pointer are Lvalues. Non-Lvalues include literal constants and expressions with multiple terms. For example, suppose we redefine refcube() so that it has a constant reference argument:

```
double refcube(const double &ra)
{
    return ra * ra * ra;
}
```

Now consider the following code:

```
double side = 3.0;
double * pd = &side;
double & rd = side;
long edge = 5L;
double lens[4] = { 2.0, 5.0, 10.0, 12.0};
double c1 = refcube(side);          // ra is side
double c2 = refcube(lens[2]);       // ra is lens[2]
double c3 = refcube(rd);            // ra is rd is side
double c4 = refcube(*pd);           // ra is *pd is side
double c5 = refcube(edge);          // ra is temporary variable
double c6 = refcube(7.0);           // ra is temporary variable
double c7 = refcube(side + 10.0);   // ra is temporary variable
```

The arguments side, lens[2], rd, and *pd are type double data objects with names, so it is possible to generate a reference for them, and no temporary variables are needed. (Recall that an element of an array behaves like a variable of the same type as the element.) But edge, although a variable, is of the wrong type. A reference to a double can't refer to a long. The arguments 7.0 and side + 10.0, on the other hand, are the right type, but are not named data objects. In each of these cases, the compiler generates a temporary, anonymous variable and makes ra refer to it. These temporary variables last for the duration of the function call, but then the compiler is free to dump them.

So why is this behavior okay for constant references but not otherwise? Recall the swapr() function of Listing 8.4:

```
void swapr(int & a, int & b)   // use references
{
    int temp;

    temp = a;       // use a, b for values of variables
    a = b;
    b = temp;
}
```

What would happen if we did the following under the freer rules of early C++?

```
long a = 3, b = 5;
swapr(a, b);
```

Here there is a type mismatch, so the compiler would create two temporary int variables, initialize them to 3 and 5, and then swap the contents of the temporary variables, leaving a and b unaltered.

In short, if the intent of a function with reference arguments is to modify variables passed as arguments, situations that create temporary variables thwart that purpose. The solution is to prohibit creating temporary variables in these situations, and that is what the C++ standard now does. (However, some compilers still, by default, issue warnings instead of error messages, so if you do see a warning about temporary variables, don't ignore it.)

Now think about the `refcube()` function. Its intent is merely to use passed values, not to modify them, so temporary variables cause no harm and make the function more general in the sorts of arguments that it can handle. Therefore, if the declaration states that a reference is const, C++ generates temporary variables when necessary. In essence, a C++ function with a const reference formal argument and a nonmatching actual argument mimics the traditional passing by value behavior, guaranteeing that the original data is unaltered and using a temporary variable to hold the value.

Remember

If a function call argument isn't an Lvalue or does not match the type of the corresponding const reference parameter, C++ creates an anonymous variable of the correct type, assigns the value of the function call argument to the anonymous variable, and has the parameter refer to that variable.

Use const When You Can

There are three strong reasons to declare reference arguments as references to constant data:

- Using const protects you against programming errors that inadvertently alter data.
- Using const allows a function to process both const and non-const actual arguments, while a function omitting const in the prototype only can accept non-const data.
- Using a const reference allows the function to generate and use a temporary variable appropriately.

You should declare formal reference arguments as const whenever it's appropriate to do so.

Using References with a Structure

References work wonderfully with structures and classes, C++'s user-defined types. Indeed references were introduced primarily for use with these types, not for use with the basic built-in types.

The method for using a reference to a structure is the same as the method for using a reference to a basic variable; just use the **&** reference operator when declaring a structure parameter. The program in Listing 8.6 does exactly that. It also adds an interesting twist by having a function return a reference. This makes it possible to use a function invocation as an argument to a function. Well, that's true of any function with a return value. But it also makes it possible to assign a value to a function invocation, and that's possible only with a reference return type. We'll explain these points after showing the program's output. The program has a **use()** function that displays two members of a structure and increments a third member. Thus, the third member can keep track of how many times a particular structure has been handled by the **use()** function.

LISTING 8.6 strtref.cpp

```cpp
// strtref.cpp -- using structure references
#include <iostream>
using namespace std;
struct sysop
{
    char name[26];
    char quote[64];
    int used;
};

sysop & use(sysop & sysopref);   // function with a reference return type

int main()
{
// NOTE: some implementations require using the keyword static
// in the two structure declarations to enable initialization
    sysop looper =
    {
        "Rick \"Fortran\" Looper",
        "I'm a goto kind of guy.",
        0
    };

    use(looper);            // looper is type sysop
    cout << looper.used << " use(s)\n";

    use (use(looper));      // use(looper) is type sysop
    cout << looper.used << " use(s)\n";

    sysop morf =
    {
```

LISTING 8.6   *Continued*

```
                "Polly Morf",
                "Polly's not a hacker.",
                0
        };
        use(looper) = morf;      // can assign to function!
        cout << looper.name << " says:\n" << looper.quote << '\n';
        return 0;
}

// use() returns the reference passed to it
sysop & use(sysop & sysopref)
{
        cout << sysopref.name << " says:\n";
        cout << sysopref.quote << "\n";
        sysopref.used++;
        return sysopref;
}
```

Here's the output:

```
Rick "Fortran" Looper says:
I'm a goto kind of guy.
1 use(s)
Rick "Fortran" Looper says:
I'm a goto kind of guy.
Rick "Fortran" Looper says:
I'm a goto kind of guy.
3 use(s)
Rick "Fortran" Looper says:
I'm a goto kind of guy.
Polly Morf says:
Polly's not a hacker.
```

Program Notes

The program ventures into three new areas. The first is using a reference to a structure, illustrated by the first function call:

```
use(looper);
```

It passes the structure **looper** by reference to the **use()** function, making **sysopref** a synonym for **looper**. When the **use()** function displays the **name** and **quote** members of **sysopref**, it really displays the members of **looper**. Also, when the function increments **sysopref.used** to 1, it really increments **looper.used**, as the program output shows:

```
Rick "Fortran" Looper says:
I'm a goto kind of guy.
1 use(s)
```

The second new area is using a reference as a return value. Normally, the return mechanism copies the returned value to a temporary storage area, which the calling program then accesses. Returning a reference, however, means that the calling program accesses the return value directly without there being a copy. Typically, the reference refers to a reference passed to the function in the first place, so the calling function actually winds up directly accessing one of its own variables. Here, for example, `sysopref` is a reference to `looper`, so the return value is the original `looper` variable in `main()`.

Because `use()` returns a type `sysop` reference, it can be used as an argument to any function expecting either a `sysop` argument or a reference-to-`sysop` argument, such as `use()` itself. Thus, the next function call in Listing 8.6 is really two function calls, with one function's return value serving as the argument for the second:

```
use(use(looper));
```

The inner function call prints the `name` and `quote` members and increments the `used` member to 2. The function returns `sysopref`, reducing what's left to the following:

```
use(sysopref);
```

Because `sysopref` is a reference to `looper`, this function call is equivalent to the following:

```
use(looper);
```

So `use()` displays the two string members again and increments the `used` member to 3.

| Remember |

A function that returns a reference is actually an alias for the referred-to variable.

The third new area the program explores is that you can assign a value to a function if that function has a reference type return value:

```
use(looper) = morf;
```

For nonreference return values, this assignment is a syntax error, but it's okay for `use()`. This is the order of events. First, the `use()` function is evaluated. That means `looper` is passed by reference to `use()`. As usual, the function displays two members and increments the `used` member to 4. Then, the function returns the reference. Because the return value refers to `looper`, this makes the final step equivalent to the following:

```
looper = morf;
```

C++ allows you to assign one structure to another, so this copies the contents of the `morf` structure into `looper`, as is shown when displaying `looper.name` produces Morf's name and not Looper's. In short, the statement

```
use(looper) = morf;  // return value a reference to looper
```

is equivalent to the following:

```
use(looper);
looper = morf;
```

You may have noticed that assigning to a reference return value produces confusing-looking code. The main reason for returning a reference is efficiency, *not* to enable this peculiar assignment mechanism. However, the assignment property occasionally is handy for some forms of operator redefinition. You can use it, for example, to redefine the array subscript operator [ ] for a class that defines a string or a more powerful version of an array.

Considerations When Returning a Reference or a Pointer

When a function returns a reference or a pointer to a data object, that object had better continue to exist once the function terminates. The simplest way to do that is to have the function return a reference or pointer that was passed to it as an argument. That way, the reference or pointer already refers to something in the calling program. The **use()** function in Listing 8.6 uses this technique.

A second method is to use **new** to create new storage. You've already seen examples in which **new** creates space for a string and the function returns a pointer to that space. Here's how you could do something similar with a reference:

```
sysop & clone(sysop & sysopref)
{
    sysop * psysop = new sysop;
    *psysop = sysopref;   // copy info
    return *psysop;       // return reference to copy
}
```

The first statement creates a nameless **sysop** structure. The pointer **psysop** points to the structure, so ***psysop** is the structure. The code appears to return the structure, but the function declaration indicates the function really returns a reference to this structure. You then could use the function this way:

```
sysop & jolly = clone(looper);
```

This makes **jolly** a reference to the new structure. There is a problem with this approach, which is that you should use **delete** to free memory allocated by **new** when the memory is no longer needed. A call to **clone()** hides the call to **new**, making it simpler to forget to use **delete** later. The **auto_ptr** template discussed in Chapter 16, "The String Class and the Standard Template Library," can help automate the deletion process.

What you want to avoid is code along these lines:

```
sysop & clone2(sysop & sysopref)
{
```

```
        sysop newguy;           // first step to big error
        newguy = sysopref;      // copy info
        return newguy;          // return reference to copy
}
```

This has the unfortunate effect of returning a reference to a temporary variable (`newguy`) that passes from existence as soon as the function terminates. (This chapter discusses the persistence of various kinds of variables later, in the section on storage classes.) Similarly, you should avoid returning pointers to such temporary variables.

When to Use Reference Arguments

There are two main reasons for using reference arguments:

- To allow you to alter a data object in the calling function

- To speed up a program by passing a reference instead of an entire data object

The second reason is most important for larger data objects, such as structures and class objects. These two reasons are the same reasons one might have for using a pointer argument. This makes sense, for reference arguments are really just a different interface for pointer-based code. So, when should you use a reference? Use a pointer? Pass by value? Here are some guidelines.

A function uses passed data without modifying it:

- If the data object is small, such as a built-in data type or a small structure, pass it by value.

- If the data object is an array, use a pointer because that's your only choice. Make the pointer a pointer to `const`.

- If the data object is a good-sized structure, use a `const` pointer or a `const` reference to increase program efficiency. You save the time and space needed to copy a structure or a class design. Make the pointer or reference `const`.

- If the data object is a class object, use a `const` reference. The semantics of class design often require using a reference, which is the main reason why C++ added this feature. Thus, the standard way to pass class object arguments is by reference.

A function modifies data in the calling function:

- If the data object is a built-in data type, use a pointer. If you spot code like `fixit(&x)`, where `x` is an `int`, it's pretty clear that this function intends to modify `x`.

- If the data object is an array, use your only choice, a pointer.

- If the data object is a structure, use a reference or a pointer.

- If the data object is a class object, use a reference.

Of course, these are just guidelines, and there might be reasons for making different choices. For example, `cin` uses references for basic types so that you can use `cin >> n` instead of `cin >> &n`.

Default Arguments

Let's look at another topic from C++'s bag of new tricks—the *default argument*. A default argument is a value that's used automatically if you omit the corresponding actual argument from a function call. For example, if you set up `void wow(int n)` so that n has a default value of 1, then the function call `wow()` is the same as `wow(1)`. This gives you greater flexibility in how you use a function. Suppose you have a function called `left()` that returns the first n characters of a string, with the string and n as arguments. More precisely, the function returns a pointer to a new string consisting of the selected portion of the original string. For example, the call `left("theory", 3)` constructs a new string "the" and returns a pointer to it. Now suppose you establish a default value of 1 for the second argument. The call `left("theory", 3)` would work as before, with your choice of 3 overriding the default. But the call `left("theory")`, instead of being an error, would assume a second argument of 1 and return a pointer to the string "t". This kind of default is helpful if your program often needs to extract a one-character string but occasionally needs to extract longer strings.

How do you establish a default value? You must use the function prototype. Because the compiler looks at the prototype to see how many arguments a function uses, the function prototype also has to alert the program to the possibility of default arguments. The method is to assign a value to the argument in the prototype. For example, here's the prototype fitting this description of `left()`:

```
char * left(const char * str, int n = 1);
```

We want the function to return a new string, so its type is `char*`, or pointer-to-`char`. We want to leave the original string unaltered, so we use the `const` qualifier for the first argument. We want n to have a default value of 1, so we assign that value to n. A default argument value is an initialization value. Thus, the prototype above initializes n to the value 1. If you leave n alone, it has the value 1, but if you pass an argument, the new value overwrites the 1.

When you use a function with an argument list, you must add defaults from right to left. That is, you can't provide a default value for a particular argument unless you also provide defaults for all the arguments to its right:

```
int harpo(int n, int m = 4, int j = 5);      // VALID
int chico(int n, int m = 6, int j);          // INVALID
int groucho(int k = 1, int m = 2, int n = 3); // VALID
```

The `harpo()` prototype, for example, permits calls with one, two, or three arguments:

```
beeps = harpo(2);       // same as harpo(2,4,5)
beeps = harpo(1,8);     // same as harpo(1,8,5)
beeps = harpo (8,7,6);  // no default arguments used
```

The actual arguments are assigned to the corresponding formal arguments from left to right; you can't skip over arguments. Thus, the following isn't allowed:

```
beeps = harpo(3, ,8);   // invalid, doesn't set m to 4
```

Default arguments aren't a major programming breakthrough; rather, they are a convenience. When you get to class design, you'll find they can reduce the number of constructors, methods, and method overloads you have to define.

Listing 8.7 puts default arguments to use. Note that only the prototype indicates the default. The function definition is the same as it would have been without default arguments.

LISTING 8.7 `left.cpp`

```
// left.cpp -- string function with a default argument
#include <iostream>
using namespace std;
const int ArSize = 80;
char * left(const char * str, int n = 1);
int main()
{
    char sample[ArSize];
    cout << "Enter a string:\n";
    cin.get(sample,ArSize);
    char *ps = left(sample, 4);
    cout << ps << "\n";
    delete [] ps;        // free old string
    ps = left(sample);
    cout << ps << "\n";
    delete [] ps;        // free new string
    return 0;
}

// This function returns a pointer to a new string
// consisting of the first n characters in the str string.
char * left(const char * str, int n)
{
    if(n < 0)
        n = 0;
    char * p = new char[n+1];
    int i;
    for (i = 0; i < n && str[i]; i++)
        p[i] = str[i];  // copy characters
    while (i <= n)
        p[i++] = '\0';  // set rest of string to '\0'
    return p;
}
```

Here's a sample run:

```
Enter a string:
forthcoming
fort
f
```

Program Notes

The program uses **new** to create a new string for holding the selected characters. One awkward possibility is that an uncooperative user requests a negative number of characters. In that case, the function sets the character count to zero and eventually returns the null string. Another awkward possibility is that an irresponsible user requests more characters than the string contains. The function protects against this by using a combined test:

```
i < n && str[i]
```

The **i < n** test stops the loop after n characters have been copied. The second part of the test, the expression **str[i]**, is the code for the character about to be copied. If the loop reaches the null character, the code is zero, and the loop terminates. The final **while** loop terminates the string with the null character and then sets the rest of the allocated space, if any, to null characters.

Another approach for setting the size of the new string is to set **n** to the smaller of the passed value and the string length:

```
int len = strlen(str);
n = (n < len) ? n : len;     // the lesser of n and len
char * p = new char[n+1];
```

This ensures that **new** doesn't allocate more space than what's needed to hold the string. That can be useful if you make a call like **left("Hi!", 32767)**. The first approach copies the "Hi!" into an array of 32767 characters, setting all but the first three characters to the null character. The second approach copies "Hi!" into an array of four characters. But, by adding another function call (**strlen()**), it increases the program size, slows the process, and requires that you remember to include the **cstring** (or **string.h**) header file. C programmers have tended to opt for faster running, more compact code and leave a greater burden on the programmer to use functions correctly. The C++ tradition, however, places greater weight on reliability. After all, a slower program working correctly is better than a fast program that works incorrectly. If the time taken to call **strlen()** turns out to be a problem, you can let **left()** determine the lesser of n and the string length directly. For example, the following loop quits when m reaches n or the end of the string, whichever comes first:

```
int m = 0;
while ( m <= n && str[m] != '\0')
     m++;
char * p = new char[m+1]:
// use m instead of n in rest of code
```

Function Polymorphism (Function Overloading)

Function polymorphism is a neat C++ addition to C's capabilities. While default arguments let you call the same function using varying numbers of arguments, *function polymorphism*, also called *function overloading*, lets you use multiple functions sharing the same name. The word "polymorphism" means having many forms, so function polymorphism lets a function have many forms. Similarly, the expression "function overloading" means you can attach more than one function to the same name, thus overloading the name. Both expressions boil down to the same thing, but we'll usually use the expression function overloading—it sounds harder-working. You can use function overloading to design a family of functions that do essentially the same thing, but using different argument lists.

Overloaded functions are analogous to verbs having more than one meaning. For example, Miss Piggy can root at the ball park for the home team, and or she can root in the soil for truffles. The context (one hopes) tells you which meaning of root is intended in each case. Similarly, C++ uses the context to decide which version of an overloaded function is intended.

The key to function overloading is a function's argument list, also called the *function signature*. If two functions use the same number and types of arguments in the same order, they have the same signature; the variable names don't matter. C++ enables you to define two functions by the same name provided that the functions have different signatures. The signature can differ in the number of arguments or in the type of arguments, or both. For example, you can define a set of `print()` functions with the following prototypes:

```
void print(const char * str, int width);   // #1
void print(double d, int width);           // #2
void print(long l, int width);             // #3
void print(int i, int width);              // #4
void print(const char *str);               // #5
```

When you then use a `print()` function, the compiler matches your use to the prototype that has the same signature:

```
print("Pancakes", 15);        // use #1
print("Syrup");               // use #5
print(1999.0, 10);            // use #2
print(1999, 12);              // use #4
print(1999L, 15);             // use #3
```

For example, `print("Pancakes", 15)` uses a string and an integer as arguments, and that matches prototype #1.

When you use overloaded functions, be sure you use the proper argument types in the function call. For example, consider the following statements:

```
unsigned int year = 3210;
print(year, 6);               // ambiguous call
```

Which prototype does the `print()` call match here? It doesn't match any of them! A lack of a matching prototype doesn't automatically rule out using one of the functions, for C++ will try to use standard type conversions to force a match. If, say, the *only* `print()` prototype were #2, the function call `print(year, 6)` would convert the `year` value to type `double`. But in the code above there are three prototypes that take a number as the first argument, providing three different choices for converting `year`. Faced with this ambiguous situation, C++ rejects the function call as an error.

Some signatures that appear different from each other can't coexist. For example, consider these two prototypes:

```
double cube(double x);
double cube(double & x);
```

You might think this is a place you could use function overloading, for the function signatures appear to be different. But consider things from the compiler's standpoint. Suppose you have code like this:

```
cout << cube(x);
```

The x argument matches both the double x prototype and the double &x prototype. Thus, the compiler has no way of knowing which function to use. Therefore, to avoid such confusion, when it checks function signatures, the compiler considers a reference to a type and the type itself to be the same signature.

The function matching process does discriminate between const and non-const variables. Consider the following prototypes:

```
void dribble(char * bits);        // overloaded
void dribble (const char *cbits); // overloaded
void dabble(char * bits);         // not overloaded
void drivel(const char * bits);   // not overloaded
```

Here's what various function calls would match:

```
const char p1[20] = "How's the weather?";
char p2[20] = "How's business?";
dribble(p1);    // dribble(const char *);
dribble(p2);    // dribble(char *);
dabble(p1);     // no match
dabble(p2);     // dabble(char *);
drivel(p1);     // drivel(const char *);
drivel(p2);     // drivel(const char *);
```

The dribble() function has two prototypes, one for const pointers and one for regular pointers, and the compiler selects one or the other depending on whether or not the actual argument is const. The dabble() function only matches a call with a non-const argument, but the drivel() function matches calls with either const or non-const arguments. The reason for this difference in behavior between drivel() and dabble() is that it's valid to assign a non-const value to a const variable, but not vice versa.

Keep in mind that it's the signature, not the function type, that enables function overloading. For example, the following two declarations are incompatible:

```
long gronk(int n, float m);      // same signatures,
double gronk(int n, float m);    // hence not allowed
```

Therefore, C++ won't permit you to overload gronk() in this fashion. You can have different return types, but only if the signatures also are different:

```
long gronk(int n, float m);      // different signatures,
double gronk(float n, float m);  // hence allowed
```

After we discuss templates later in this chapter, we'll further discuss function matching.

An Overloading Example

We've already developed a `left()` function that returns a pointer to the first n characters in a string. Let's add a second `left()` function, one that returns the first n digits in an integer. You can use it, for example, to examine the first three digits of a U.S. postal ZIP code stored as an integer, a useful act if you want to sort for urban areas.

The integer function is a bit more difficult to program than the string version, because we don't have the benefit of each digit being stored in its own array element. One approach is first to compute the number of digits in the number. Dividing a number by 10 lops off one digit, so you can use division to count digits. More precisely, you can do so with a loop like this:

```
unsigned digits = 1;
while (n /= 10)
    digits++;
```

This loop counts how many times you can remove a digit from n until none are left. Recall that `n /= 10` is short for `n = n / 10`. If n is 8, for example, the test condition assigns to n the value 8 / 10, or 0, because it's integer division. That terminates the loop, and `digits` remains at 1. But if n is 238, the first loop test sets n to 238 / 10, or 23. That's nonzero, so the loop increases `digits` to 2. The next cycle sets n to 23 / 10, or 2. Again, that's nonzero, so `digits` grows to 3. The next cycle sets n to 2 / 10, or 0, and the loop quits, leaving `digits` set to the correct value, 3.

Now suppose you know the number has five digits, and you want to return the first three digits. You can get that value by dividing the number by 10 and then dividing the answer by 10 again. Each division by 10 lops one more digit off the right end. To calculate the number of digits to lop, just subtract the number of digits to be shown from the total number of digits. For example, to show four digits of a nine-digit number, lop off the last five digits. You can code this approach as follows:

```
ct = digits - ct;
while (ct--)
    num /= 10;
return num;
```

Listing 8.8 incorporates this code into a new `left()` function. The function includes some additional code to handle special cases, such as asking for zero digits or asking for more digits than the number possesses. Because the signature of the new `left()` differs from that of the old `left()`, we can, and do, use both functions in the same program.

LISTING 8.8   leftover.cpp

```
// leftover.cpp -- overloading the left() function
#include <iostream>
using namespace std;
unsigned long left(unsigned long num, unsigned ct);
char * left(const char * str, int n = 1);
```

LISTING 8.8   Continued

```cpp
int main()
{
    char * trip = "Hawaii!!";   // test value
    unsigned long n = 12345678; // test value
    int i;
    char * temp;

    for (i = 1; i < 10; i++)
    {
        cout << left(n, i) << "\n";
        temp = left(trip,i);
        cout << temp << "\n";
        delete [] temp; // point to temporary storage
    }
    return 0;

}

// This function returns the first ct digits of the number num.
unsigned long left(unsigned long num, unsigned ct)
{
    unsigned digits = 1;
    unsigned long n = num;

    if (ct == 0 || num == 0)
        return 0;       // return 0 if no digits
    while (n /= 10)
        digits++;
    if (digits > ct)
    {
    ct = digits - ct;
    while (ct--)
        num /= 10;
    return num;          // return left ct digits
    }
    else                 // if ct >= number of digits
        return num;      // return the whole number
}

// This function returns a pointer to a new string
// consisting of the first n characters in the str string.
char * left(const char * str, int n)
{
    if(n < 0)
        n = 0;
    char * p = new char[n+1];
    int i;
    for (i = 0; i < n && str[i]; i++)
        p[i] = str[i];  // copy characters
    while (i <= n)
        p[i++] = '\0';  // set rest of string to '\0'
    return p;
}
```

Here's the output:

```
1
H
12
Ha
123
Haw
1234
Hawa
12345
Hawai
123456
Hawaii
1234567
Hawaii!
12345678
Hawaii!!
12345678
Hawaii!!
```

When to Use Function Overloading

You might find function overloading fascinating, but don't overuse the facility. You should reserve function overloading for functions that perform basically the same task but with different forms of data. Also, you might want to check whether you can accomplish the same end with default arguments. For example, you could replace the single, string-oriented `left()` function with two overloaded functions:

```
char * left(const char * str, unsigned n);    // two arguments
char * left(const char * str);                 // one argument
```

But using the single function with a default argument is simpler. There's just one function to write, instead of two, and the program requires memory for just one function, instead of two. If you decide to modify the function, there's only one you have to edit. However, if you require different types of arguments, default arguments are of no avail, so then you should use function overloading.

What Is Name Decoration?

How does C++ keep track of which overloaded function is which? It assigns these functions a secret identity. When you use the editor of your C++ development tool to write and compile programs, your C++ compiler performs a bit of magic on your behalf—known as *name decoration* or *name mangling*—through which each function name is encrypted based on the formal parameter types specified in the function's prototype. Consider the following undecorated function prototype:

```
long MyFunctionFoo(int, float);
```

This format is fine for us humans; we know that the function accepts two arguments of type `int` and `float`, and returns a value of type `long`. For its own use, the compiler documents this interface by transforming the name into an internal representation of a more unsightly appearance, perhaps something like this:

```
?MyFunctionFoo@@YAXH@Z
```

The apparent gibberish decorating the original name (or mangling it, depending upon your attitude) encodes the number and types of parameters. A different function signature would have resulted in a different set of symbols being added, and different compilers would use different conventions for their efforts at decorating.

Function Templates

Contemporary C++ compilers implement one of the newer C++ additions, *function templates*. Function templates are a generic function description; that is, they define a function in terms of a generic type for which a specific type, such as `int` or `double`, can be substituted. By passing a type as a parameter to a template, you cause the compiler to generate a function for that particular type. Because templates let you program in terms of a generic type instead of a specific type, the process is sometimes termed *generic programming*. Because types are represented by parameters, the template feature is sometimes referred to as *parameterized types*. Let's see why such a feature is useful and how it works.

Earlier we defined a function that swapped two `int` values. Suppose you want to swap two `double` values instead. One approach is to duplicate the original code but replace each `int` with `double`. If you need to swap two `char` values, you can use the same technique again. Still, it's wasteful of your valuable time to have to make these petty changes, and there's always the possibility of making an error. If you make the changes by hand, you might overlook an `int`. If you do a global search-and-replace to substitute, say, `double` for `int`, you might do something such as converting

```
int x;
short interval;
```

to the following:

```
double x;           // intended change of type
short doubleerval;  // unintended change of variable namee
```

C++'s function template capability automates the process, saving you time and providing greater reliability.

Function templates enable you to define a function in terms of some arbitrary type. For example, you can set up a swapping template like this:

```
template <class Any>
void Swap(Any &a, Any &b)
{
    Any temp;
    temp = a;
    a = b;
    b = temp;
}
```

The first line specifies that you are setting up a template and that you're naming the arbitrary type Any. The keywords **template** and **class** are obligatory, except that you can use the keyword **typename** instead of **class**. Also, you must use the angle brackets. The type name (Any in the example) is your choice, as long as you follow the usual C++ naming rules; many programmers use simple names like T. The rest of the code describes the algorithm for swapping two values of type Any. The template does not create any functions. Instead, it provides the compiler with directions about how to define a function. If you want a function to swap ints, then the compiler creates a function following the template pattern, substituting int for Any. Similarly, if you need a function to swap **doubles**, the compiler follows the template, substituting the **double** type for Any.

The keyword **typename** is a recent addition to C++. You can use instead of the keyword **class** in this particular context. That is, you can write the template definition this way:

```
template <typename Any>
void Swap(Any &a, Any &b)
{
    Any temp;
    temp = a;
    a = b;
    b = temp;
}
```

The **typename** keyword makes it a bit more obvious that the parameter Any represents a type; however, large libraries of code already have been developed by using the older keyword **class**. The C++ Standard treats the two keywords identically when they are used in this context.

Tip

Use templates if you need functions that apply the same algorithm to a variety of types. If you aren't concerned with backward compatibility and can put up with the effort of typing a longer word, use the keyword **typename** rather than **class** when you declare type parameters.

To let the compiler know that you need a particular form of swap function, just use a function called Swap() in your program. The compiler checks the argument types you use and then generates the corresponding function. Listing 8.9 shows how this works. The program layout follows the usual pattern for ordinary functions with a template function prototype near the top of the file and the template function definition following main().

Compatibility Note

Noncurrent versions of C++ compilers might not support templates. New versions accept the keyword **typename** as an alternative to **class**. Older versions of g++ require that both the template prototype and the template definition appear before the template is used, but this has been fixed in newer releases.

LISTING 8.9   funtemp.cpp

```cpp
// funtemp.cpp -- using a function template
#include <iostream>
using namespace std;
// function template prototype
template <class Any>  // or typename Any
void Swap(Any &a, Any &b);

int main()
{
    int i = 10;
    int j = 20;
    cout << "i, j = " << i << ", " << j << ".\n";
    cout << "Using compiler-generated int swapper:\n";
    Swap(i,j);  // generates void Swap(int &, int &)
    cout << "Now i, j = " << i << ", " << j << ".\n";

    double x = 24.5;
    double y = 81.7;
    cout << "x, y = " << x << ", " << y << ".\n";
    cout << "Using compiler-generated double swapper:\n";
    Swap(x,y);  // generates void Swap(double &, double &)
    cout << "Now x, y = " << x << ", " << y << ".\n";

    return 0;
}

// function template definition
template <class Any>  // or typename Any
void Swap(Any &a, Any &b)
{
    Any temp;    // temp a variable of type Any
    temp = a;
    a = b;
    b = temp;
}
```

The first `Swap()` function has two `int` arguments, so the compiler generates an `int` version of the function. That is, it replaces each use of `Any` with `int`, producing a definition that looks like this:

```cpp
void Swap(int &a, int &b)
{
    int temp;
    temp = a;
    a = b;
    b = temp;
}
```

You don't see this code, but the compiler generates, then uses it in the program. The second `Swap()` function has two `double` arguments, so the compiler generates a `double` version. That is, it replaces `Any` with `double`, generating this code:

```
void Swap(double &a, double &b)
{
    double temp;
    temp = a;
    a = b;
    b = temp;
}
```

Here's the program output; you can see the process has worked:

```
i, j = 10, 20.
Using compiler-generated int swapper:
Now i, j = 20, 10.
x, y = 24.5, 81.7.
Using compiler-generated double swapper:
Now x, y = 81.7, 24.5.
```

Note that function templates don't make your executable programs any shorter. In Listing 8.9, you still wind up with two separate function definitions, just as if you had defined each function manually. And the final code doesn't contain any templates; it just contains the actual functions generated for your program. The benefits of templates are that they make generating multiple function definitions simpler and more reliable.

Overloaded Templates

You use templates when you need functions that apply the same algorithm to a variety of types, as in Listing 8.8. It might be, however, that not all types would use the same algorithm. To meet this possibility, you can overload template definitions, just as you overload regular function definitions. As with ordinary overloading, overloaded templates need distinct function signatures. For example, Listing 8.10 adds a new swapping template, one for swapping elements of two arrays. The original template has the signature (`Any &, Any &`), whereas the new template has the signature (`Any [], Any [], int`). Note that the final argument in this case happens to be a specific type (`int`) rather than a generic type. Not all template arguments have to be template parameter types.

When, in `twotemps.cpp`, the compiler encounters the first use of `Swap()`, it notices that it has two `int` arguments and matches it to the original template. The second use, however, has two `int` arrays and an `int` value as arguments, and this matches the new template.

LISTING 8.10   twotemps.cpp

```cpp
// twotemps.cpp -- using overloaded template functions
#include <iostream>
using namespace std;
template <class Any>     // original template
void Swap(Any &a, Any &b);

template <class Any>     // new template
void Swap(Any *a, Any *b, int n);
```

LISTING 8.10   Continued

```cpp
void Show(int a[]);
const int Lim = 8;
int main()
{
    int i = 10, j = 20;
    cout << "i, j = " << i << ", " << j << ".\n";
    cout << "Using compiler-generated int swapper:\n";
    Swap(i,j);                  // matches original template
    cout << "Now i, j = " << i << ", " << j << ".\n";

    int d1[Lim] = {0,7,0,4,1,7,7,6};
    int d2[Lim] = {0,6,2,0,1,9,6,9};
    cout << "Original arrays:\n";
    Show(d1);
    Show(d2);
    Swap(d1,d2,Lim);            // matches new template
    cout << "Swapped arrays:\n";
    Show(d1);
    Show(d2);

    return 0;
}

template <class Any>
void Swap(Any &a, Any &b)
{
    Any temp;
    temp = a;
    a = b;
    b = temp;
}

template <class Any>
void Swap(Any a[], Any b[], int n)
{
    Any temp;
    for (int i = 0; i < n; i++)
    {
        temp = a[i];
        a[i] = b[i];
        b[i] = temp;
    }
}

void Show(int a[])
{
    cout << a[0] << a[1] << "/";
    cout << a[2] << a[3] << "/";
    for (int i = 4; i < Lim; i++)
        cout << a[i];
    cout << "\n";
}
```

Compatibility Note

Noncurrent versions of C++ compilers might not support templates. New versions might accept the keyword `typename` instead of `class`. Older versions of C++ are more picky about type matching and require the following code to make the `const int Lim` match the template requirement for an ordinary `int`:

```
Swap(xd1,d2, int (Lim));        // typecast Lim to non-const int
```

Older versions of g++ requires that the template definitions be placed ahead of `main()`.

Here is the program's output:

```
i, j = 10, 20.
Using compiler-generated int swapper:
Now i, j = 20, 10.
Original arrays:
07/04/1776
07/20/1969
Swapped arrays:
07/20/1969
07/04/1776
```

Explicit Specializations

Suppose you define a structure like the following:

```
struct job
{
        char name[40];
        double salary;
        int floor;
};
```

Also, suppose you want to be able to swap the contents of two such structures. The original template uses the following code to effect a swap:

```
temp = a;
a = b;
b = temp;
```

Because C++ allows you to assign one structure to another, this works fine, even if type `Any` is a `job` structure. But suppose you only want to swap the `salary` and `floor` members, keeping the `name` members unchanged. This requires different code, but the arguments to `Swap()` would be the same as for the first case (references to two `job` structures), so you can't use template overloading to supply the alternative code.

However, you can supply a specialized function definition, called an *explicit specialization*, with the required code. If the compiler finds a specialized definition that exactly matches a function call, it uses that definition without looking for templates.

The specialization mechanism has changed with the evolution of the language. We look at the current form as mandated by the C++ Standard, then look at two older forms supported by older compilers.

Third Generation Specialization (ISO/ANSI C++ Standard)

After C++ experimented with the approaches described later, the C++ Standard settled upon this approach:

1. For a given function name, you can have a non-template function, a template function, and an explicit specialization template function.

2. The prototype and definition for an explicit specialization should be preceded by `template <>` and should mention the specialized type by name.

3. A specialization overrides the regular template, and a non-template function overrides both.

Here's how prototypes for swapping type `job` structures would look for these three forms:

```
// non-template function prototype
void Swap(job &, job &);

// template prototype
template <class Any>
void Swap(Any &, Any &);

// explicit specialization for the job type
template <> void Swap<job>(job &, job &);
```

As mentioned previously, if more than one of these prototypes is present, the compiler chooses the non-template version over explicit specializations and template versions, and it chooses an explicit specialization over a version generated from a template.

```
...
template <class Any>              // template
void Swap(Any &, Any &);

// explicit specialization for the job type
template <> void Swap<job>(job &, job &);
int main()
{
    double u, v;
    ...
    Swap(u,v);  // use template
    job a, b;
    ...
    Swap(a,b);  // use void Swap<job>(job &, job &)
}
```

The `<job>` in `Swap<job>` is optional, for the function argument types indicate that this is a specialization for `job`. Thus, the prototype also can be written this way:

```
template <> void Swap(job &, job &);    // simpler form
```

The template function heading also can be simplified by omitting the `<int>` part.

In case you have to work with an older compiler, we'll come back to pre-Standard usage soon, but first, let's see how explicit specializations are supposed to work.

An Example

Listing 8.11 illustrates how explicit specialization works. It's set up to follow the C++ Standard.

LISTING 8.11   `twoswap.cpp`

```cpp
// twoswap.cpp -- specialization overrides a template
#include <iostream>
using namespace std;
template <class Any>
void Swap(Any &a, Any &b);

struct job
{
    char name[40];
    double salary;
    int floor;
};

// explicit specialization
template <> void Swap<job>(job &j1, job &j2);
void Show(job &j);

int main()
{
    cout.precision(2);
    cout.setf(ios::fixed, ios::floatfield);
    int i = 10, j = 20;
    cout << "i, j = " << i << ", " << j << ".\n";
    cout << "Using compiler-generated int swapper:\n";
    Swap(i,j);    // generates void Swap(int &, int &)
    cout << "Now i, j = " << i << ", " << j << ".\n";

    job sue = {"Susan Yaffee", 63000.60, 7};
    job sidney = {"Sidney Taffee", 66060.72, 9};
    cout << "Before job swapping:\n";
    Show(sue);
    Show(sidney);
    Swap(sue, sidney); // uses void Swap(job &, job &)
    cout << "After job swapping:\n";
    Show(sue);
    Show(sidney);

    return 0;
}
```

LISTING 8.11   Continued

```
template <class Any>
void Swap(Any &a, Any &b)      // general version
{
    Any temp;
    temp = a;
    a = b;
    b = temp;
}

// swaps just the salary and floor fields of a job structure

template <> void Swap<job>(job &j1, job &j2)   // specialization
{
    double t1;
    int t2;
    t1 = j1.salary;
    j1.salary = j2.salary;
    j2.salary = t1;
    t2 = j1.floor;
    j1.floor = j2.floor;
    j2.floor = t2;
}

void Show(job &j)
{
    cout << j.name << ": $" << j.salary
         << " on floor " << j.floor << "\n";
}
```

Compatibility Note

This version of the program requires ISO/ANSI C++ support.

Here's the program output:

```
i, j = 10, 20.
Using compiler-generated int swapper:
Now i, j = 20, 10.
Before job swapping:
Susan Yaffee: $63000.60 on floor 7
Sidney Taffee: $66060.72 on floor 9
After job swapping:
Susan Yaffee: $66060.72 on floor 9
Sidney Taffee: $63000.60 on floor 7
```

Earlier Approaches to Specialization

If Listing 8.11 didn't work with your compiler, you may have to revert to earlier usage. The simplest is to provide an ordinary function defined for the particular type you wish to process. That is, in Listing 8.11, you would replace

```
template <> void Swap<job>(job &j1, job &j2);
```

with

```
void Swap(int & n, int & m);    // regular prototype
```

and replace

```
template <> void Swap<job>(job &j1, job &j2)  // specialization
{
...
}
```

with

```
void Swap(job &j1, job &j2)    // regular function
{
...// code unchanged
}
```

When the compiler reaches the `Swap(sue, sidney)` function call , it has the choice of generating a function definition using the template or of using the nontemplate `Swap(job &, job &)` function. The original template facility (as well as the current standard) has the compiler use the non-template version.

If this approach doesn't work for you, you may be using a compiler that installed a non-official predraft version of templates in which templates were chosen *ahead* of ordinary functions. With this rule in effect, the compiler would use the template `Swap()` instead of the `job` version. So to get the desired effect, you'd have to use an explicit specialization that didn't quite have the modern form. That is, instead of using

```
template <> void Swap<job>(job &j1, job &j2);  // ISO/ANSI C++
```

you would use the following form:

```
void Swap<job>(job &, job &);    // earlier form of specialization
```

Notice that it is missing the `template <>` preface. You'd make the same adjustment in the function heading. That is,

```
template <> void Swap<job>(job &j1, job &j2)  // specialization
{
...
}
```

becomes

```
void Swap<job>(job &j1, job &j2)  // old form  of specialization
{
...// code unchanged
}
```

If you're using a contemporary C++ compiler (and we hope you are), you won't have to deal with these adjustments.

Instantiations and Specializations

To extend our understanding of templates, we need to investigate the terms instantiation and specicalization. Keep in mind that including a function template in your code does not in itself generate a function definition. It's merely a plan for generating a function definition. When the compiler uses the template to generate a function definition for a particular type, the result is termed an *instantiation* of the template. For example, in Listing 8.11, the function call `Swap(i,j)` causes the compiler to generate an instantiation of the `Swap()` using `int` as the type. The template *is not* a function definition, but the specific instantiation using `int` *is* a function definition. This type of instantiation is termed an *implicit instantiation*, because the compiler deduces the necessity for making the definition by noting that the program uses a `Swap()` function with `int` parameters.

Originally, implicit instantiation was the only way the compiler generated function definitions from templates, but now C++ allows for *explicit instantiation*. That means you can instruct the compiler to create a particular instantiation, for example, `Swap<int>()`, directly. The syntax is to declare the particular variety you want, using the `<>` notation to indicate the type and pre- fixing the declaration with the keyword `template`:

```
template void Swap<int>(int, int);  // explicit instantiation
```

A compiler that implements this feature will, upon seeing this declaration, use the `Swap()` template to generate an instantiation using the `int` type. That is, this declaration means "Use the `Swap()` template to generate a function definition for the `int` type."

Contrast the explicit instantiation with the explicit specialization, which uses one or the other of these equivalent declarations:

```
template <> void Swap<int>(int &, int &);  // explicit specialization
template <> void Swap(int &, int &);       // explicit specialization
```

The difference is that these declarations mean "Don't use the `Swap()` template to generate a function definition. Instead, use a separate, specialized function definition explicitly defined for the `int` type." These prototypes have to be coupled with their own function definitions.

Caution
It is an error to try to use both an explicit instantiation and an explicit specialization for the same type(s) in the same programming unit.

Implicit instantiations, explicit instantiations, and explicit specializations collectively are termed *specializations*. What they all have in common is that they represent a function defini- tion using specific types rather than one that is a generic description.

The addition of the explicit instantiation led to the new syntax of using **template** and **template <>** prefixes in declarations to distinguish between the explicit instantiation and the explicit specialization. Often, the cost of doing more is more syntax rules. The following frag- ment summarizes these concepts:

```
...
template <class Any>
void Swap (Any &, Any &);  // template prototype

template <> void Swap<int>(job &, job &);  // explicit specialization for job
int main(void)
{
  template void Swap<char>(char &, char &);  // explicit instantiation for char
  short a, b;
  ...
  Swap(a,b);   // implicit template instantiation for short
  job n, m;
  ...
  Swap(n, m); // use explicit specialization for job
  char g, h;
  ...
   Swap(g, h);  // use explicit template instantiation for char
   ...
}
```

When the compiler reaches the explicit instantiation for `char`, it uses the template definition to generate a `char` version of `Swap()`. When the compiler reaches the function call `Swap(a,b)`, it generates a `short` version of `Swap()`. When the compiler reaches `Swap(n,m)`, it uses the separate definition (the explicit specialization) provided for the `job` type. When the compiler reaches `Swap(g,h)`, it uses the template specialization it already generated when it processed the explicit instantiation.

Which Function?

What with function overloading, function templates, and function template overloading, C++ needs, and has, a well-defined strategy for deciding which function definition to use for a function call, particularly when there are multiple arguments. The process is called *overload resolution*. Detailing the complete strategy would take a small chapter, so let's take an overview of how the process works:

- Phase 1: Assemble a list of candidate functions. These are functions and template functions with the same name as the called function.

- Phase 2: From the candidate functions, assemble a list of viable functions. These are functions with the correct number of arguments and for which there is an implicit conversion sequence, which includes the case of an exact match for each type of actual argument to the type of the corresponding formal argument. For example, a function call with a type `float` argument could have that value converted to a `double` to match a type `double` formal parameter, and a template could generate an instantiation for `float`.

- Phase 3: Determine if there is a best viable function. If so, use that function. Otherwise, the function call is an error.

Consider a case with just one function argument, for example, the following call:

```
may('B');    // actual argument is type char
```

First, the compiler rounds up the suspects, which are functions and function templates having the name may(). Then, it finds those that can be called with one argument. For example, the following will pass muster because they have the same name:

```
void may(int);                          // #1
float may(float, float = 3);            // #2
void may(char);                         // #3
char * may(const char *);               // #4
char may(const char &);                 // #5
template<class T> void may(const T &);  // #6
template<class T. void may(T *);        // #7
```

Note that just the signatures and not the return types are considered. Two of these candidates(#4 and #7), however, are not viable because an integral type cannot be converted implicitly (i.e., without an explicit type cast) to a pointer type. The remaining template will be used to generate a specialization with T taken as type char. That leaves five viable functions, each of which could be used if it were the only function declared.

Next, the compiler has to determine which of the viable functions is best. It looks at the conversion required to make the function call argument match the viable candidate's argument. In general, the ranking from best to worst is this:

1. Exact match, with regular functions outranking templates.

2. Conversion by promotion (the automatic conversions of char and short to int and of float to double, for example)

3. Conversion by standard conversion (converting int to char or long to double, for example)

4. User-defined conversions, such as those defined in class declarations

For example, function #1 is better than function #2 because char-to-int is a promotion (Chapter 3, "Dealing with Data"), whereas char-to-float is a standard conversion (Chapter 3). Functions #3, #5, and #6 are better than either #1 or #2, because they are exact matches. Both #3 and #5 are better than #6 because #6 is a template. This analysis raises a couple of questions. What is an exact match, and what happens if you get two of them?

Exact Matches and Best Matches

C++ allows some "trivial conversions" when making an exact match. Table 8.1 lists them, with *Type* standing for some arbitrary type. For example, an int actual argument is an exact match to an int & formal parameter. Note that *Type* can be something like char &, so these rules include converting char & to const char &. The *Type (argument-list)* entry means that a function name as an actual argument matches a function pointer as a formal parameter as long as both have the same return type and argument list. (Remember function pointers from Chapter 7, "Functions—C++'s Programming Modules," and how you can pass the name of a function as an argument to a function expecting a pointer to a function.) We discuss the volatile keyword later in this chapter.

TABLE 8.1   Trivial Conversions Allowed for an Exact Match

From an actual argument	To a formal argument
Type	*Type &*
Type &	*Type*
Type [ ]	** Type*
Type (argument-list)	*Type (*)(argument-list)*
Type	const *Type*
Type	volatile *Type*
Type *	const *Type **
Type *	volatile *Type **

Anyway, suppose you have the following function code:

```
struct blot {int a; char b[10];};
blot ink = {25, "spots"};
...
recycle(ink);
```

Then, all the following prototypes would be exact matches:

```
void recycle(blot);        // #1  blot-to-blot
void recycle(const blot);  // #2  blot-to-(const blot)
void recycle(blot &);      // #3  blot-to-(blot &)
void recycle(const blot &); // #4  blot-to-(const blot &)
```

As you might expect, the result of having several matching prototypes is that the compiler cannot complete the overload resolution process. There is no best viable function, and the compiler generates an error message, probably using words like "ambiguous."

However, sometimes there can be overload resolution even if two functions are an exact match. First, pointers and references to non-`const` data preferentially are matched to non-`const` pointer and reference parameters. That is, if only functions #3 and #4 were available in the `recycle()` example, #3 would be chosen because `ink` wasn't declared as `const`. However, this discrimination between `const` and non-`const` applies just to data referred to by pointers and references. That is, if only #1 and #2 were available, you would get an ambiguity error.

Another case where one exact match is better than another is when one function is a non-template function and the other isn't. In that case, the non-template is considered better than a template, including explicit specializations.

If you wind up with two exact matches that both happen to be template functions, the template function that is the more specialized, if either, is the better function. That means, for example, that an explicit specialization is chosen over one generated implicitly from the template pattern:

```
struct blot {int a; char b[10];};
template <class Type> void recycle (Type t); // template
template <> void recycle<blot> (blot & t);    // specialization for blot
...
blot ink = {25, "spots"};
...
recycle(ink);  // use specialization
```

The term "most specialized" doesn't necessarily imply an explicit specialization; more generally, it indicates that fewer conversions take place when the compiler deduces what type to
use. For example, consider the following two templates:

```
template <class Type> void recycle (Type t);     #1
template <class Type> void recycle (Type * t);..#2
```

Suppose the program that contains these templates also contains the following code:

```
struct blot {int a; char b[10];};
blot ink = {25, "spots"};
...
recycle(&ink);  // address of a structure
```

The `recycle(&ink)` call matches template #1 with `Type` interpreted as `blot *`. The `recy-
cle(&ink)` function call also matches template #2, this time with `Type` being `ink`. This combi-
nation sends two implicit instantiations, `recycle<blot *>(blot *)` and
`recycle<blot>(blot *)`, to the viable function pool.

Of these two template functions, `recycle<blot *>(blot *)` is considered the more specialized because it underwent fewer conversions in being generated. That is, template #2 already
explicitly said the function argument was pointer-to-*Type* so *Type* could be directly identified
with `blot`. Template #1, however, had *Type* as the function argument, so *Type* had to be interpreted as pointer-to-`blot`. That is, in template #2, *Type* already was specialized as a pointer,
hence the term "more specialized."

The rules for finding the most specialized template are called the *partial ordering rules* for function templates. Like explicit instantiations, they are new additions to the language.

A Partial Ordering Rules Example

Let's examine a complete program that uses the partial ordering rules for identifying which
template definition to use. Listing 8.12 has two template definitions for displaying the contents
of an array. The first definition (template A) assumes that the array passed as an argument contains the data to be displayed. The second definition (template B) assumes that the array argument contains pointers to the data to be displayed.

LISTING 8.12   temptempover.cpp
_____

```
// tempover.cpp --- template overloading
#include <iostream>
using namespace std;
```

LISTING 8.12   Continued

```
template <typename T>              // template A
void ShowArray(T arr[], int n);

template <typename T>              // template B
void ShowArray(T * arr[], int n);

struct debts
{
    char name[50];
    double amount;
};

int main(void)
{
    int things[6] = {13, 31, 103, 301, 310, 130};
    struct debts mr_E[3] =
    {
        {"Ima Wolfe", 2400.0},
        {"Ura Foxe ", 1300.0},
        {"Iby Stout", 1800.0}
    };
    double * pd[3];

    for (int i = 0; i < 3; i++)
        pd[i] = &mr_E[i].amount;

    cout << "Listing Mr. E's counts of things:\n";
    ShowArray(things, 6);  // uses template A
    cout << "Listing Mr. E's debts:\n";
    ShowArray(pd, 3);        // uses template B (more specialized)
    return 0;
}

template <typename T>
void ShowArray(T arr[], int n)
{
    cout << "template A\n";
    for (int i = 0; i < n; i++)
        cout << arr[i] << ' ';
    cout << endl;
}

template <typename T>
void ShowArray(T * arr[], int n)
{
    cout << "template B\n";
    for (int i = 0; i < n; i++)
        cout << *arr[i] << ' ';
    cout << endl;
}
```

First, consider this function call:

```
ShowArray(things, 6);
```

The identifier `things` is the name of an array of `int`, so it matches the template

```
template <typename T>           // template A
void ShowArray(T arr[], int n);
```

with `T` taken to be type `int`.

Next, consider this function call:

```
ShowArray(pd, 3);
```

Here, `pd` is the name of an array of `double *`. This could be matched by template A:

```
template <typename T>           // template A
void ShowArray(T arr[], int n);
```

Here, `T` would be taken to be type `double *`. In this case, the template function would display the contents of the `pd` array, namely, three addresses. The function call also could be matched by template B:

```
template <typename T>           // template B
void ShowArray(T * arr[], int n);
```

In this case, `T` would be type `double`, and the function displays the dereferenced elements `*arr[i]`, that is, the `double` values pointed to by the array contents. Of the two templates, template B is the more specialized because it makes the specific assumption that the array contents are pointers, so it is the template that gets used.

Here's the output:

```
Listing Mr. E's counts of things:
template A
13 31 103 301 310 130
Listing Mr. E's debts:
template B
2400 1300 1800
```

If you remove template B from the program, the compiler will then use template A for listing the contents of `pd`, so it will list the addresses instead of the values.

In short, the overload resolution process looks for a function that's the best match. If there's just one, that function is chosen. If there are more than one otherwise tied, but only one is a non-template function, that's chosen. If there are more than one candidates otherwise tied, and all are template functions, but one template is more specialized than the rest, that is chosen. If there are two or more equally good non-template functions, or if there are two or more equally good template functions, none of which is more specialized than the rest, the function call is ambiguous and an error. If there are no matching calls, of course, that also is an error.

Functions with Multiple Arguments

Where matters really get involved is when a function call with multiple arguments is matched to prototypes with multiple arguments. The compiler must look at matches for all the arguments. If it can find a function that is better than all the other viable functions, it's the chosen one. For one function to be better than another function, it has to provide at least as good a match for all arguments and a better match for at least one argument.

This book does not intend to challenge the matching process with complex examples. The rules are there so that there is a well-defined result for any possible set of function prototypes and templates.

Summary

C++ has expanded C function capabilities. By using the inline keyword with a function definition and by placing that definition ahead of the first call to that function, you suggest to the C++ compiler that it make the function inline. That is, instead of having the program jump to a separate section of code to execute the function, the compiler replaces the function call with the corresponding code inline. An inline facility should be used only when the function is short.

A reference variable is a kind of disguised pointer that lets you create an alias (a second name) for a variable. Reference variables primarily are used as arguments to functions processing structures and class objects.

C++ prototypes enable you to define default values for arguments. If a function call omits the corresponding argument, the program uses the default value. If the function includes an argument value, the program uses that value instead of the default. Default arguments can be provided only from right to left in the argument list. Thus, if you provide a default value for a particular argument, you also must provide default values for all arguments to the right of that argument.

A function's signature is its argument list. You can define two functions having the same name provided that they have different signatures. This is called function polymorphism, or function overloading. Typically, you overload functions to provide essentially the same service to different data types.

Function templates automate the process of overloading functions. You define a function using a generic type and a particular algorithm, and the compiler generates appropriate function definitions for the particular argument types you use in a program.

Review Questions

1. What kinds of functions are good candidates for inline status?

2. Suppose the `song()` function has this prototype:

```
void song(char * name, int times);
```

      a. How would you modify the prototype so that the default value for **times** is 1?

      b. What changes would you make in the function definition?

      c. Can you provide a default value of "O, My Papa" for **name**?

3. Write overloaded versions of **iquote()**, a function that displays its argument enclosed in double quotation marks. Write three versions: one for an **int** argument, one for a **double** argument, and one for a **string** argument.

4. Here is a structure template:

```
struct box
{
    char maker[40];
    float height;
    float width;
    float length;
    float volume;
};
```

      a. Write a function that has a reference to a **box** structure as its formal argument and displays the value of each member.

      b. Write a function that has a reference to a **box** structure as its formal argument and sets the **volume** member to the product of the other three dimensions.

5. Here are some desired effects. Indicate whether each can be accomplished with default arguments, function overloading, both, or neither. Provide appropriate prototypes.

      a. **mass(density, volume)** returns the mass of an object having a density of **density** and a volume of **volume**, whereas **mass(density)** returns the mass having a density of **density** and a volume of 1.0 cubic meters. All quantities are type **double**.

      b. **repeat(10, "I'm OK")** displays the indicated string ten times, whereas **repeat("But you're kind of stupid")** displays the indicated string five times.

      c. **average(3,6)** returns the **int** average of two **int** arguments, whereas **average(3.0, 6.0)** returns the **double** average of two **double** values.

      d. **mangle("I'm glad to meet you")** returns the character **I** or a pointer to the string "I'm mad to gleet you" depending on whether you assign the return value to a **char** variable or to a **char*** variable.

6. Write a function template that returns the larger of its two arguments.

7. Given the template of Review Question 6 and the **box** structure of Review Question 4, provide a template specialization that takes two **box** arguments and returns the one with the larger volume.

Programming Exercises

1. Write a function that normally takes one argument, the address of a string, and prints that string once. However, if a second, type int argument is provided and is nonzero, the function prints the string a number of times equal to the number of times that function has been called to at that point. (Note that the number of times the string is printed is not equal to the value of the second argument; it's equal to the number of times the function has been called.) Yes, this is a silly function, but it makes you use some of the techniques discussed in this chapter. Use the function in a simple program that demonstrates how the function works.

2. The CandyBar structure contains three members. The first member holds the brand name of a candy bar. The second member holds the weight (which may have a fractional part) of the candy bar, and the third member holds the number of calories (an integer value) in the candy bar. Write a program that uses a function that takes as arguments a reference to a CandyBar, a pointer-to-char, a double, and an int and uses the last three values to set the corresponding members of the structure. The last three arguments should have default values of "Millennium Munch," 2.85, and 350. Also, the program should use a function taking a reference to a CandyBar as an argument and display the contents of the structure. Use const where appropriate.

3. Following is a program skeleton. Complete it by providing the described functions and prototypes. Note that there should be two show() functions, each using default arguments. Use const arguments when appropriate. Note that set() should use new to allocate sufficient space to hold the designated string. The techniques used here are similar to those used in designing and implementing classes. (You might have to alter the header file names and delete the using-directive, depending upon your compiler.)

```
#include <iostream>
using namespace std;
#include <cstring>        // for strlen(), strcpy()
struct stringy {
    char * str;           // points to a string
    int ct;               // length of string (not counting '\0')
    };

// prototypes for set(), show(), and show() go here
int main()
{
    stringy beany;
    char testing[] = "Reality isn't what it used to be.";

    set(beany, testing);    // first argument is a reference,
                // allocates space to hold copy of testing,
                // sets str member of beany to point to the
                // new block, copies testing to new block,
                // and sets ct member of beany
    show(beany);        // prints member string once
    show(beany, 2);     // prints member string twice
    testing[0] = 'D';
```

```
        testing[1] = 'u';
        show(testing);    // prints testing string once
        show(testing, 3); // prints testing string thrice
        show("Done!");
        return 0;
    }
```

4. Write a template function `max5()` that takes as its argument an array of five items of type T and returns the largest item in the array. (Because the size is fixed, it can be hard-coded into the loop instead of passed as an argument.) Test it in a program that uses the function with an array of 5 `int` value and an array of 5 `double` values.

5. Write a template function `maxn()` that takes as its arguments an array of items of type T and an integer representing the number of elements in the array and which returns the largest item in the array. Test it in a program that uses the function template with an array of 6 `int` value and an array of 4 `double` values. The program also should include a specialization that takes an array of pointers-to-`char` as an argument and the number of pointers as a second argument and which returns the address of the longest string. If there are more than one string having the longest length, the function returns the address of the first one tied for longest. Test the specialization with an array of 5 string pointers.

6. Modify Listing 8.12 so that the template functions return the sum of the array contents instead of displaying the contents. The program now should report the total number of things and the sum of all the debts.

CHAPTER 9

MEMORY MODELS AND NAMESPACES

In this chapter you learn

- Separate compilation

- Storage duration, scope, and linkage

- Namespaces

C++ offers many choices for storing data in memory. You have choices for how long data remains in memory (storage duration) and choices for which parts of a program have access to data (scope and linkage). The C++ namespace facility provides additional control over access. Larger programs typically consist of several source code files that may share some data in common. Such programs involve the separate compilation of the program files, so this chapter will begin with that topic.

Separate Compilation

C++, like C, allows and even encourages you to locate the component functions of a program in separate files. As Chapter 1, "Getting Started," describes, you can compile the files separately and then link them into the final executable program. (A C++ compiler typically compiles programs and also manages the linker program.) If you modify just one file, you can recompile just that one file and then link it to the previously compiled versions of the other files. This facility makes it easier to manage large programs. Furthermore, most C++ environments provide additional facilities to help with the management. Unix and Linux systems, for example, have the **make** program; it keeps track of which files a program depends upon and when they were last modified. If you run **make** and it detects you've changed one or more source files since the last compilation, **make** remembers the proper steps needed to reconstitute the program. The Borland C++, Microsoft Visual C++, and Metrowerks CodeWarrior IDEs (integrated development environments) provide similar facilities with their Project menus.

Let's look at a simple example. Instead of looking at compilation details, which depend on the implementation, let's concentrate on more general aspects, such as design.

Suppose, for example, you decide to break up the program in Listing 7.11 by placing the functions in a separate file. That listing, recall, converted rectangular coordinates to polar coordinates and then displayed the result. You can't simply cut the original file on a dotted line after the end of `main()`. The problem is that `main()` and the other two functions all use the same structure declarations, so you need to put the declarations in both files. Simply typing them in is an invitation to err. Even if you copy the structure declarations correctly, you have to remember to modify both sets of declarations if you make changes later. In short, spreading a program over multiple files creates new problems.

Who wants more problems? The developers of C and C++ didn't, so they've provided the `#include` facility to deal with this situation. Instead of placing the structure declarations in each file, you can place them in a header file and then include that header file in each source code file. That way, if you modify the structure declaration, you can do so just once, in the header file. Also, you can place the function prototypes in the header file. Thus, you can divide the original program into three parts:

- A header file that contains the structure declarations and prototypes for functions using those structures
- A source code file that contains the code for the structure-related functions
- A source code file that contains the code that calls upon those functions

This is a useful strategy for organizing a program. If, for example, you write another program that uses those same functions, just include the header file and add the function file to the project or `make` list. Also, this organization reflects the OOP approach. One file, the header file, contains the definition of the user-defined types. A second file contains the function code for manipulating the user-defined types. Together, they form a package you can use for a variety of programs.

Don't put function definitions or variable declarations into a header file. It might work for a simple setup, but usually it leads to trouble. For example, if you had a function definition in a header file and then included the header file in two other files that are part of a single program, you'd wind up with two definitions of the same function in a single program, which is an error, unless the function is inline. Here are some things commonly found in header files:

- Function prototypes
- Symbolic constants defined using `#define` or `const`
- Structure declarations
- Class declarations
- Template declarations
- Inline functions

It's okay to put structure declarations in a header file, for they don't create variables; they just tell the compiler how to create a structure variable when you declare one in a source code file.

Similarly, template declarations aren't code to be compiled; they are instructions to the compiler on how to generate function definitions to match function calls found in the source code. Data declared `const` and inline functions have special linkage properties (coming up soon) that allow them to be placed in header files without causing problems.

Listings 9.1, 9.2, and 9.3 show the result of dividing Listing 7.11 into separate parts. Note that we use `"coordin.h"` instead of `<coordin.h>` when including the header file. If the filename is enclosed in angle brackets, the C++ compiler looks at the part of the host system's file system that holds the standard header files. But if the filename is enclosed in double quotation marks, the compiler first looks at the current working directory or at the source code directory (or some such choice, depending upon the compiler). If it doesn't find the header file there, it then looks in the standard location. So use quotation marks, not angle brackets, when including your own header files.

Figure 9.1 outlines the steps for putting this program together on a Unix system. Note that you just give the CC compile command and the other steps follow automatically. The g++ command-line compiler and the Borland C++ command-line compiler (`bcc32.exe`) also behave that way. Symantec C++, Borland C++, Turbo C++, Metrowerks CodeWarrior, Watcom C++, and Microsoft Visual C++ go through essentially the same steps, but, as outlined in Chapter 1, you initiate the process differently, using menus that let you create a project and associate source code files with it. Note that you only add source code files, not header files to projects. That's because the `#include` directive manages the header files. Also, don't use `#include` to include source code files, as that can lead to multiple declarations.

Caution

In Integrated Development Environments, don't add header files to the project list, and don't use `#include` to include source code files in other source code files.

LISTING 9.1   coordin.h

```
// coordin.h -- structure templates and function prototypes
// structure templates
#ifndef COORDIN_H_
#define COORDIN_H_

struct polar
{
    double distance;      // distance from origin
    double angle;          // direction from origin
};
struct rect
{
    double x;          // horizontal distance from origin
    double y;          // vertical distance from origin
};
```

LISTING 9.1   Continued

```
// prototypes
polar rect_to_polar(rect xypos);
void show_polar(polar dapos);

#endif
```

FIGURE 9.1
Compiling a multifile
C++ program on a Unix
system.

Header File Management

You should include a header file just once in a file. That might seem to be an easy thing to remember, but it's possible to include a header file several times without knowing you did so. For example, you might use a header file that includes another header file. There's a standard C/C++ technique for avoiding multiple inclusions of header files. It's based on the preprocessor #ifndef (for *if not defined*) directive. A code segment like

```
#ifndef COORDIN_H_
...
#endif
```

means process the statements between the `#ifndef` and `#endif` only if the name `COORDIN_H_` has not been defined previously by the preprocessor `#define` directive.

Normally, you use the `#define` statement to create symbolic constants, as in the following:

```
#define MAXIMUM 4096
```

But simply using `#define` with a name is enough to establish that a name is defined, as in the following:

```
#define COORDIN_H_
```

The technique, which Listing 9.1 uses, is to wrap the file contents in an `#ifndef`:

```
#ifndef COORDIN_H_
#define COORDIN_H_
// place include file contents here
#endif
```

The first time the compiler encounters the file, the name `COORDIN_H_` should be undefined. (We chose a name based on the `include` filename with a few underscore characters tossed in so as to create a name unlikely to be defined elsewhere.) That being the case, the compiler looks at the material between the `#ifndef` and the `#endif`, which is what we want. In the process of looking at the material, the compiler reads the line defining `COORDIN_H_`. If it then encounters a second inclusion of `coordin.h` in the same file, the compiler notes that `COORDIN_H_` is defined and skips to the line following the `#endif`. Note that this method doesn't keep the compiler from including a file twice. Instead, it makes it ignore the contents of all but the first inclusion. Most of the standard C and C++ header files use this scheme.

LISTING 9.2   `file1.cpp`

```
// file1.cpp -- example of a two-file program
#include <iostream>
#include "coordin.h" // structure templates, function prototypes
using namespace std;
int main()
{
    rect rplace;
    polar pplace;

    cout << "Enter the x and y values: ";
    while (cin >> rplace.x >> rplace.y)  // slick use of cin
    {
        pplace = rect_to_polar(rplace);
        show_polar(pplace);
        cout << "Next two numbers (q to quit): ";
    }
    cout << "Bye!\n";
    return 0;
}
```

LISTING 9.3   `file2.cpp`

```
// file2.cpp -- contains functions called in file1.cpp
#include <iostream>
```

LISTING 9.3 Continued

```
#include <cmath>
#include "coordin.h" // structure templates, function prototypes
using namespace std;

// convert rectangular to polar coordinates
polar rect_to_polar(rect xypos)
{
    polar answer;

    answer.distance =
        sqrt( xypos.x * xypos.x + xypos.y * xypos.y);
    answer.angle = atan2(xypos.y, xypos.x);
    return answer;       // returns a polar structure
}

// show polar coordinates, converting angle to degrees
void show_polar (polar dapos)
{
    const double Rad_to_deg = 57.29577951;

    cout << "distance = " << dapos.distance;
    cout << ", angle = " << dapos.angle * Rad_to_deg;
    cout << " degrees\n";
}
```

By the way, although we've discussed separate compilation in terms of files, the language description uses the term *translation unit* instead of file in order to preserve greater generality; the file metaphor is not the only possible way to organize information for a computer.

Real World Note: Multiple Library Linking

The C++ Standard allows each compiler designer the latitude to implement name decoration or mangling (see the Real World Note on name decoration in Chapter 8, "Adventures in Functions") as it sees fit, so you should be aware that binary modules (object-code files) created with different compilers will, most likely, not link properly. That is, the two compilers will generate different decorated names for the same function. This name difference will prevent the linker from matching the function call generated by one compiler with the function definition generated by a second compiler. When attempting to link compiled modules, make sure that each object file or library was generated with the same compiler. If you are provided with the source code, you can usually resolve link errors by recompiling the source with your compiler.

Storage Duration, Scope, and Linkage

Now that you've seen a multifile program, it's a good time to extend the discussion of memory schemes in Chapter 4, "Compound Types," for storage categories affect how information can be shared across files. It might have been awhile since you last read Chapter 4, so let's review what it said about memory. C++ uses three separate schemes for storing data, and the schemes differ in how long they preserve data in memory.

- Variables declared inside a function definition have *automatic storage duration*; that includes function parameters. They are created when program execution enters the function or block in which they are defined, and the memory used for them is freed when execution leaves the function or block. C++ has two kinds of automatic storage duration variables.

- Variables defined outside of a function definition or else by using the keyword `static` have *static storage duration*. They persist for the entire time a program is running. C++ has three kinds of static storage duration variables.

- Memory allocated by the `new` operator persists until freed with the `delete` operator or until the program ends, whichever comes first. This memory has *dynamic storage duration* and sometimes is termed the *free store*.

We get the rest of the story now, including fascinating details about when variables of different types are in scope, or visible (usable by the program), and about linkage, which determines what information is shared across files.

Scope and Linkage

Scope describes how widely visible a name is in a file (translation unit). For example, a variable defined in a function can be used in that function, but not in another, whereas a variable defined in a file above the function definitions can be used in all the functions. *Linkage* describes how a name can be shared in different units. A name with *external linkage* can be shared across files, and a name with *internal linkage* can be shared by functions within a single file. Names of automatic variables have no linkage, for they are not shared.

A C++ variable can have one of several scopes. A variable having *local scope* (also termed *block scope*) is known only within the block in which it is defined. A block, remember, is a series of statements enclosed in braces. A function body, for example, is a block, but you can have other blocks nested within the function body. A variable having *global scope* (also termed *file scope*) is known throughout the file after the point where it is defined. Automatic variables have local scope, and a static variable can have either scope, depending on how it is defined. Names used in a *function prototype scope* are known just within the parentheses enclosing the argument list. (That's why it doesn't really matter what they are or if they are even present.) Members declared in a class have *class scope* (see Chapter 10, "Objects and Classes"). Variables declared in a namespace have *namespace scope*. (Now that namespaces have been added to the language, the global scope has become a special case of namespace scope.)

C++ functions can have class scope or namespace scope, including global scope, but they can't have local scope. (Because a function can't be defined inside a block, if a function were to have local scope, it could only be known to itself, and hence couldn't be called by another function. Such a function couldn't function.)

The various C++ storage choices are characterized by their storage duration, their scope, and their linkage. Let's look at C++'s storage classes in terms of these properties. We begin by examining the situation before namespaces were added to the mix, and then see how namespaces modify the picture.

Automatic Storage Duration

Function parameters and variables declared inside a function have, by default, automatic storage duration. They also have local scope and no linkage. That is, if you declare a variable called `texas` in `main()` and declare another variable with the same name in a function called `oil()`, you've created two independent variables, each known only in the function in which it's defined. Anything you do to the `texas` in `oil()` has no effect on the `texas` in `main()`, and vice versa. Also, each variable is allocated when program execution enters the innermost block containing the definition, and each fades from existence when its function terminates. (Note that the variable is allocated when execution enters the block, but the scope begins only after the point of declaration.)

If you define a variable inside of a block, the variable's persistence and scope are confined to that block. Suppose, for example, you define a variable called `teledeli` at the beginning of `main()`. Now suppose you start a new block within `main()` and define a new variable, called `websight` in the block. Then, `teledeli` is visible in both the outer and inner blocks, whereas `websight` exists only in the inner block and is in scope only from its point of definition until program execution passes the end of the block:

```cpp
int main()
{
    int teledeli = 5;
    {                              // websight allocated
        cout << "Hello\n";
        int websight = -2;         // websight scope begins
        cout << websight << ' ' << teledeli << endl;
    }                              // websight expires
    cout << teledeli << endl;
    ...
}
```

But what if you name the variable in the inner block `teledeli` instead of `websight` so that you have two variables of the same name, with one in the outer block and one in the inner block? In this case, the program interprets the `teledeli` name to mean the local block variable while the program executes statements within the block. We say the new definition *hides* the prior definition. The new definition is in scope, and the old definition temporarily is out of scope. When the program leaves the block, the original definition comes back into scope. (See Figure 9.2.)

FIGURE 9.2

Blocks and scope.

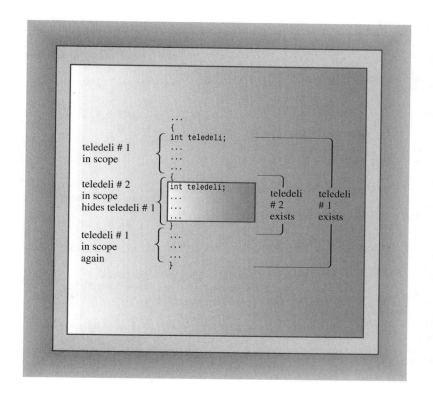

Listing 9.4 illustrates how automatic variables are localized to the function or block that contains them.

LISTING 9.4   auto.cpp

```
// auto.cpp -- illustrating scope of automatic variables
#include <iostream>
using namespace std;
void oil(int x);
int main()
{
// NOTE: some implementations require that you type cast the
// addresses in this program to type unsigned

    int texas = 31;
    int year = 1999;
    cout << "In main(), texas = " << texas << ", &texas =";
    cout << &texas << "\n";
    cout << "In main(), year = " << year << ", &year =";
    cout << &year << "\n";
```

LISTING 9.4   *Continued*

```cpp
    oil(texas);
    cout << "In main(), texas = " << texas << ", &texas =";
    cout << &texas << "\n";
    cout << "In main(), year = " << year << ", &year =";
    cout << &year << "\n";
    return 0;
}

void oil(int x)
{
    int texas = 5;

    cout << "In oil(), texas = " << texas << ", &texas =";
    cout << &texas << "\n";
    cout << "In oil(), x = " << x << ", &x =";
    cout << &x << "\n";
    {                               // start a block
        int texas = 113;
        cout << "In block, texas = " << texas;
        cout << ", &texas = " << &texas << "\n";
                cout << "In block, x = " << x << ", &x =";
        cout << &x << "\n";
    }                               // end a block
    cout << "Post-block texas = " << texas;
    cout << ", &texas = " << &texas << "\n";
}
```

Here is the output:

```
In main(), texas = 31, &texas =0x0065fd54
In main(), year = 1999, &year =0x0065fd58
In oil(), texas = 5, &texas =0x0065fd40
In oil(), x = 31, &x =0x0065fd50
In block, texas = 113, &texas = 0x0065fd44
In block, x = 31, &x =0x0065fd50
Post-block texas = 5, &texas = 0x0065fd40
In main(), texas = 31, &texas =0x0065fd54
In main(), year = 1999, &year =0x0065fd58
```

Notice how each of the three **texas** variables has its own distinct address and how the program uses only the particular variable in scope at the moment, so assigning the value 113 to the **texas** in the inner block in **oil()** has no effect on the other variables of the same name.

Let's summarize the sequence of events. When **main()** starts, the program allocates space for **texas** and **year**, and these variables come into scope. When the program calls **oil()**, these variables remain in memory but pass out of scope. Two new variables, **x** and **texas**, are allocated and come into scope. When program execution reaches the inner block in **oil()**, the new **texas** passes out of scope as it is superseded by an even newer definition. The variable **x**, however, stays in scope because the block doesn't define a new **x**. When execution exits the block, the memory for the newest `texas` is freed, and `texas` number 2 comes back into scope. When the `oil()` function terminates, that `texas` and `x` expire, and the original `texas` and `year` come back into scope.

Incidentally, you can use the C++ (and C) keyword `auto` to indicate the storage class explicitly:

```
int froob(int n)
{
    auto float ford;
    ...
}
```

Because you can use the `auto` keyword only with variables that already are automatic by default, programmers rarely bother using it. Occasionally, it's used to clarify code to the reader. For example, you can use it to indicate that you purposely are creating an automatic variable that overrides a global definition, such as those we discuss shortly.

Initialization of Automatic Variables

You can initialize an automatic variable with any expression whose value will be known when the declaration is reached:

```
int w;          // value of w is indeterminate
int x = 5;      // initialized with a constant expression
int y = 2 * x;  // use previously determined value of x
cin >> w;
int z = 3 * w;  // use new value of w
```

Automatic Variables and the Stack

You might gain a better understanding of automatic variables by seeing how a typical C++ compiler implements them. Because the number of automatic variables grows and shrinks as functions start and terminate, the program has to manage automatic variables as it runs. The usual means is to set aside a section of memory and treat it as a stack for managing the flow and ebb of variables. It's called a stack because new data figuratively is stacked atop old data (that is, at an adjacent location, not at the same location) and then removed from the stack when a program is finished with it. The default size of the stack depends on the implementation, but a compiler generally provides the option of changing the size. The program keeps track of the stack by using two pointers. One points to the base of the stack, where the memory set aside for the stack begins, and one points to the top of the stack, which is the next free memory location. When a function is called, its automatic variables are added to the stack, and the pointer to the top points to the next available free space following the variables. When the function terminates, the top pointer is reset to the value it had before the function was called, effectively freeing the memory that had been used for the new variables.

A stack is a LIFO (last-in, first-out) design, meaning the last variables added to the stack are the first to go. The design simplifies argument passing. The function call places the values of its arguments on top of the stack and resets the top pointer. The called function uses the description of its formal parameters to determine the addresses of each argument. Figure 9.3, for example, shows a `fib()` function that, when called, passes a 2-byte `int` and a 4-byte `long`.

These values go on the stack. When `fib()` begins execution, it associates the names `real` and `tell` with the two values. When `fib()` terminates, the top-of-stack pointer is relocated to its former position. The new values aren't erased, but they no longer are labeled, and the space they occupy will be used by the next process that places values on the stack. (The figure is somewhat simplified, for function calls may pass additional information, such as a return address.)

FIGURE 9.3

Passing arguments with a stack.

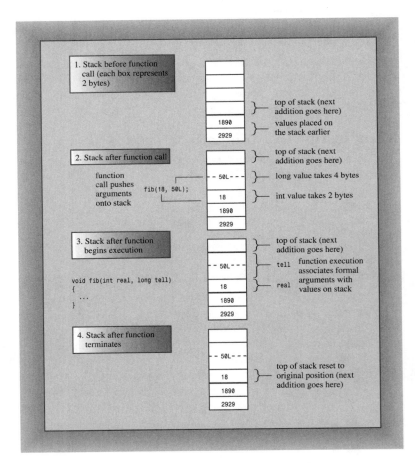

Register Variables

C++, like C, supports the `register` keyword for declaring local variables. A register variable is another form of automatic variable, so it has automatic storage duration, local scope, and no linkage. The `register` keyword is a hint to the compiler that you want it to provide fast access to the variable, perhaps by using a CPU register instead of the stack to handle a particular variable. The idea is that the CPU can access a value in one of its registers more rapidly than it can access memory in the stack. To declare a register variable, preface the type with the keyword `register`:

```
register int count_fast;   // request for a register variable
```

You've probably noticed the qualifying words "hint" and "request." The compiler doesn't have to honor the request. For example, the registers may already be occupied, or you might request a type that doesn't fit in a register. Many programmers feel that modern compilers are often smart enough not to need the hint. If you write a `for` loop, for example, the compiler might take it upon itself to use a register for the loop index.

If a variable is stored in a register, it doesn't have a memory address; therefore you can't apply the address operator to a register variable:

```
void gromb(int *);
...
int x;
register int y;
gromb(&x);        // ok
gromb(&y);        // not allowed
```

Using `register` in the declaration is enough to invoke this restriction, even if the compiler doesn't actually use a register for the variable.

In short, an ordinary local variable, a local variable declared using `auto`, and a local variable declared using `register` all have automatic storage duration, local scope, and no linkage.

```
short waffles;           // auto variable by default
auto short pancakes;     // explicitly auto
register int muffins;    // register variable
```

Declaring a local variable without a specifier is the same as declaring it with `auto`, and such a variable is typically handled by being placed on a memory stack. Using the `register` specifier is a hint that the variable will be heavily used, and the compiler may choose to use something other than the memory stack to hold it; for example, a CPU register.

Static Duration Variables

C++, like C, provides static storage duration variables with three kinds of linkage: external linkage, internal linkage, and no linkage. All three last for the duration of the program; they are less ephemeral than automatic variables. Because the number of static variables doesn't change as the program runs, the program doesn't need a special device like a stack to manage them. Instead, the compiler allocates a fixed block of memory to hold all the static variables, and those variables stay present as long as the program executes. Also, if you don't explicitly initialize a static variable, the compiler sets it to zero. Static arrays and structures have all the bits of each element or member set to zero by default.

Let's see how to create the three different kinds of static duration variables; then we can go on to examine their properties. To create a static duration variable with external linkage, declare it outside of any block. To create a static duration variable with internal linkage, declare it outside of any block and use the **static** storage class modifier. To create a static duration variable with no linkage, declare it inside a block using the **static** modifier. The following code fragment shows these three variations:

```
...
int global = 1000;          // static duration, external linkage
static int one_file = 50;   // static duration, internal linkage
int main()
{
...
}
void funct1(int n)
{
    static int count = 0;   // static duration, no linkage
    int llama = 0;
...
}
void funct2(int q)
{
...
}
```

As already stated, all the static duration variables (**global**, **one_file**, and **count**) persist from the time the program begins execution until it terminates. The variable **count**, which is declared inside of **funct1()**, has local scope and no linkage, which means it can be used only inside the **funct1()** function, just like the automatic variable **llama**. But, unlike **llama**, **count** remains in memory even when the **funct1()** function is not being executed. Both **global** and **one_file** have file scope, meaning they can be used from the point of declaration until the end of the file. In particular, both can be used in **main()**, **funct1()**, and **funct2()**. Because **one_file** has internal linkage, it can be used only in the file containing this code. Because **global** has external linkage, it also can be used in other files that are part of the program.

All static duration variables share the following two initialization features:

1. An uninitialized static variable has all its bits set to 0.

2. A static variable can be initialized only with a constant expression.

A constant expression can use literal constants, **const** and **enum** constants, and the **sizeof** operator. The following code fragment illustrates these points:

```
int x;                      // x set to 0
int y = 49;                 // 49 is a constant expression
int z = 2 * sizeof(int) + 1; // also a constant expression
int m = 2 * z;              // invalid, z not a constant
int main() {...}
```

Table 9.1 summarizes the storage class features as used in the pre-namespace era. Next, let's examine the static duration varieties in more detail.

TABLE 9.1   The Five Kinds of Variable Storage

Storage Description	Duration	Scope	Linkage	How Declared
automatic	automatic	block	none	in a block (optionally with the keyword auto)
register	automatic	block	none	in a block with the keyword register
static with no linkage	static	block	none	in a block with the keyword static
static with external linkage	static	file	external	outside of all functions
static with internal linkage	static	file	internal	outside of all functions with the keyword static

Static Duration, External Linkage

Variables with external linkage often are simply called external variables. They necessarily have static storage duration and file scope. External variables are defined outside of, and hence external to, any function. For example, they could be declared above the `main()` function. You can use an external variable in any function that follows the external variable's definition in the file. Thus, external variables also are termed global variables in contrast to automatic variables, which are local variables. However, if you define an automatic variable having the same name as an external variable, the automatic variable is the one in scope when the program executes that particular function. Listing 9.5 illustrates these points. It also shows how you can use the keyword `extern` to redeclare an external variable defined earlier and how you can use C++'s scope resolution operator to access an otherwise hidden external variable. Because the example is a one-file program, it doesn't illustrate the external linkage property; a later example will do that.

LISTING 9.5   `external.cpp`

```cpp
// external.cpp -- external variables
#include <iostream>
using namespace std;
// external variable
double warming = 0.3;

// function prototypes
void update(double dt);
void local();

int main()                   // uses global variable
{
    cout << "Global warming is " << warming << " degrees.\n";
    update(0.1);             // call function to change warming
    cout << "Global warming is " << warming << " degrees.\n";
    local();                 // call function with local warming
    cout << "Global warming is " << warming << " degrees.\n";
    return 0;
}

void update(double dt)       // modifies global variable
{
    extern double warming;   // optional redeclaration
    warming += dt;
    cout << "Updating global warming to " << warming;
    cout << " degrees.\n";
}

void local()                 // uses local variable
{
    double warming = 0.8;    // new variable hides external one

    cout << "Local warming = " << warming << " degrees.\n";
        // Access global variable with the
        // scope resolution operator
    cout << "But global warming = " << ::warming;
    cout << " degrees.\n";
}
```

Here is the output:

```
Global warming is 0.3 degrees.
Updating global warming to 0.4 degrees.
Global warming is 0.4 degrees.
Local warming = 0.8 degrees.
But global warming = 0.4 degrees.
Global warming is 0.4 degrees.
```

Program Notes

The program output illustrates that both `main()` and `update()` can access the external variable `warming`. Note that the change that `update()` makes to `warming` shows up in subsequent uses of the variable.

The `update()` function redeclares the `warming` variable by using the keyword `extern`. This keyword means "use the variable by this name previously defined externally." Because that is what `update()` would do anyway if you omitted the entire declaration, this declaration is optional. It serves to document that the function is designed to use the external variable. The original declaration

```
double warming = 0.3;
```

is called a *defining declaration*, or, simply, a *definition*. It causes storage for the variable to be allocated. The redeclaration

```
extern double warming;
```

is called a *referencing declaration* , or, simply, a *declaration*. It does not cause storage to be allocated, for it refers to an existing variable. You can use the *extern* keyword only in declarations referring to variables defined elsewhere (or functions—more on that later). Also, you cannot initialize a variable in a referencing declaration:

```
extern double warming = 0.5;   // INVALID
```

You can initialize a variable in a declaration only if the declaration allocates the variable, that is, only in a defining declaration. After all, the term initialization means assigning a value to a memory location when that location is allocated.

The `local()` function demonstrates that when you define a local variable having the same name as a global variable, the local version hides the global version. The `local()` function, for example, uses the local definition of `warming` when it displays `warming`'s value.

C++ takes a step beyond C by offering the *scope resolution operator* (`::`). When prefixed to the name of a variable, this operator means to use the global version of that variable. Thus, `local()` displays `warming` as 0.8, but it displays `::warming` as 0.4. You'll encounter this operator again in namespaces and classes.

Global or Local?

Now that you have a choice of using global or local variables, which should you use? At first, global variables have a seductive appeal—because all functions have access to a global variable, you don't have to bother passing arguments. But this easy access has a heavy price—unreliable programs. Computing experience has shown that the better job your program does of isolating data from unnecessary access, the better job the program does in preserving the integrity of the data. Most often, you should use local variables and pass data to functions on a need-to-know basis rather than make data available indiscriminately with global variables. As you will see, OOP takes this data isolation a step further.

Global variables do have their uses, however. For example, you might have a block of data that's to be used by several functions, such as an array of month names or the atomic weights of the elements. The external storage class is particularly suited to representing constant data, for then you can use the keyword `const` to protect the data from change.

```
const char * const months[12] =
{
    "January", "February", "March", "April", "May",
    "June", "July", "August", "September", "October",
    "November", "December"
};
```

The first `const` protects the strings from change, and the second `const` makes sure that each pointer in the array remains pointing to the same string to which it pointed initially.

Static Duration, Internal Linkage

Applying the `static` modifier to file-scope variable gives it internal linkage. The difference between internal linkage and external linkage becomes meaningful in multifile programs. In that context, a variable with internal linkage is local to the file containing it. But a regular external variable has external linkage, meaning it can be used in different files. For external linkage, one and only one file can contain the external definition for the variable. Other files that want to use that variable must use the keyword `extern` in a reference declaration. (See Figure 9.4.)

FIGURE 9.4
Defining declaration and referencing declaration.

```
// file1.cpp
#include <iostream>
using namespace std;

// function prototypes
#include "mystuff.h"

// defining an external variable
int process_status = 0;

void promise ();
int main()
{
    ...
}

void promise ()
{
    ...
}
```

```
// file2.cpp
#include <iostream>
using namespace std;

// function prototypes
#include "mystuff.h"

// referencing an external variable
extern int process_status;

int manipulate(int n)
{
    ...
}

char * remark(char * str)
{
    ...
}
```

This file defines the variable process_status, causing the compiler to allocate space for it.

This file uses extern to instruct the program to use the variable process_status that was defined in another file.

If a file doesn't provide the `extern` declaration of a variable, it can't use an external variable defined elsewhere:

```
// file1
int errors = 20;       // global declaration
```

```
...
------------------------------------------------
// file 2
...                        // missing an extern int errors declaration
void froobish()
{
    cout << errors;  // doomed attempt to use errors
..
```

If a file attempts to define a second external variable by the same name, that's an error:

```
// file1
int errors = 20;          // external declaration
...
------------------------------------------------
// file 2
int errors;               // invalid declaration
void froobish()
{
    cout << errors;      // doomed attempt to use errors
..
```

The correct approach is to use the keyword **extern** in the second file:

```
// file1
int errors = 20;          // external declaration
...
------------------------------------------------
// file 2
extern int errors;        // refers to errors from file1
void froobish()
{
    cout << errors;      // uses errors defined in file1
..
```

But if a file declares a static external variable having the same name as an ordinary external variable declared in another file, the static version is the one in scope for that file:

```
// file1
int errors = 20;          // external declaration
...
------------------------------------------------
// file2
static int errors = 5;  // known to file2 only
void froobish()
{
    cout << errors;      // uses errors defined in file2
    ...
```

Remember

In a multifile program, you can define an external variable in one and only one file. All other files using that variable have to declare that variable with the **extern** keyword.

Use an external variable to share data among different parts of a multifile program. Use a static variable with internal linkage to share data among functions found in just one file. (Namespaces offer an alternative method for this, and the standard indicates that using `static` to create internal linkage will be phased out in the future.) Also, if you make a file-scope variable static, you needn't worry about its name conflicting with file-scope variables found in other files.

Listings 9.6 and 9.7 show how C++ handles variables with external and internal linkage. Listing 9.6 (`twofile1.cpp`) defines the external variables `tom` and `dick` and the static external variable `harry`. The `main()` function in that file displays the addresses of the three variables and then calls the `remote_access()` function, which is defined in a second file. Listing 9.7 (`twofile2.cpp`) shows that file. In addition to defining `remote_access()`, the file uses the `extern` keyword to share `tom` with the first file. Next, the file defines a static variable called `dick`. The `static` modifier makes this variable local to the file and overrides the global definition. Then, the file defines an external variable called `harry`. It can do so without conflicting with the `harry` of the first file because the first `harry` has internal linkage only. Then, the `remote_access()` function displays the addresses of these three variables so that you can compare them with the addresses of the corresponding variables in the first file. Remember to compile both files and link them to get the complete program.

LISTING 9.6   `twofile1.cpp`

```
// twofile1.cpp -- variables with external and internal linkage
#include <iostream>      // to be compiled with two file2.cpp
using namespace std;
int tom = 3;             // external variable definition
int dick = 30;           // external variable definition
static int harry = 300; // static, internal linkage

// function prototype
void remote_access();

int main()
{
    cout << "main() reports the following addresses:\n";
    cout << &tom << " = &tom, " << &dick << " = &dick, ";
    cout << &harry << " = &harry\n";
    remote_access();
    return 0;
}
```

LISTING 9.7   `twofile2.cpp`

```
// twofile2.cpp -- variables with internal and external linkage
#include <iostream>
using namespace std;
extern int tom;          // tom defined elsewhere
static int dick = 10;    // overrides external dick
```

LISTING 9.7   Continued

```
    int harry = 200;          // external variable definition,
                              // no conflict with twofile1 harry

    void remote_access()
    {
        cout << "remote_access() reports the following addresses:\n";
        cout << &tom << " = &tom, " << &dick << " = &dick, ";
        cout << &harry << " = &harry\n";
    }
```

Here is the output:

```
main() reports the following addresses:
0x0041a020 = &tom, 0x0041a024 = &dick, 0x0041a028 = &harry
remote_access() reports the following addresses:
0x0041a020 = &tom, 0x0041a450 = &dick, 0x0041a454 = &harry
```

As you can see, both files use the same **tom** variable but different **dick** and **harry** variables.

Static Storage Duration, No Linkage

So far, we've looked at a file-scope variable with external linkage and a file-scope variable with internal linkage. Now let's look at the third member of the static duration family, a local variable with no linkage. Such a variable is created by applying the **static** modifier to a variable defined inside a block. When you use it inside a block, **static** makes a local variable have static storage duration. That means that even though the variable is known within that block, it exists even while the block is inactive. Thus, a static local variable can preserve its value between function calls. (Static variables would be useful for reincarnation—you could use them to pass secret account numbers for a Swiss bank to your next appearance.) Also, if you initialize a static local variable, the program initializes the variable once, when the program starts up. Subsequent calls to the function don't reinitialize the variable the way they do for automatic variables. Listing 9.8 illustrates these points.

Incidentally, the program shows one way to deal with line input that may exceed the size of the destination array. The **cin.get(input,ArSize)** input method, recall, reads up to the end of the line or up to **ArSize - 1** characters, whichever comes first. It leaves the newline character in the input queue. This program reads the character that follows the line input. If it is a newline character, then the whole line was read. If it isn't a newline character, there are more characters left on the line. This program then uses a loop to reject the rest of the line, but you can modify the code to use the rest of the line for the next input cycle. The program also uses the fact that attempting to read an empty line with **get(char *, int)** causes **cin** to test as **false**.

LISTING 9.8   static.cpp

```
// static.cpp -- using a static local variable
#include <iostream>
using namespace std;
```

LISTING 9.8   *Continued*

```cpp
// constants
const int ArSize = 10;

// function prototype
void strcount(const char * str);

int main()
{
    char input[ArSize];
    char next;

    cout << "Enter a line:\n";
    cin.get(input, ArSize);
    while (cin)
    {
        cin.get(next);
        while (next != '\n')      // string didn't fit!
            cin.get(next);
        strcount(input);
        cout << "Enter next line (empty line to quit):\n";
        cin.get(input, ArSize);
    }
    cout << "Bye\n";
    return 0;
}

void strcount(const char * str)
{
    static int total = 0;         // static local variable
    int count = 0;                // automatic local variable

    cout << "\"" << str <<"\" contains ";
    while (*str++)                // go to end of string
        count++;
    total += count;
    cout << count << " characters\n";
    cout << total << " characters total\n";
}
```

Compatibility Note

Some older compilers don't implement the requirement that when `cin.get(char *,int)` reads an empty line, it sets the failbit error flag, causing `cin` to test as `false`. In that case, you can replace the test

```cpp
while (cin)
```

with this:

```cpp
while (input[0])
```

Or, for a test that works for both old and new implementations, do this:

```cpp
while (cin && input[0])
```

Here is the program's output:

```
Enter a line:
nice pants
"nice pant" contains 9 characters
9 characters total
Enter next line (empty line to quit):
thanks
"thanks" contains 6 characters
15 characters total
Enter next line (empty line to quit):
parting is such sweet sorrow
"parting i" contains 9 characters
24 characters total
Enter next line (empty line to quit):
ok
"ok" contains 2 characters
26 characters total
Enter next line (empty line to quit):

Bye
```

Note that because the array size is 10, the program does not read more than 9 characters per line. Also note that the automatic variable `count` is reset to 0 each time the function is called. However, the static variable `total` is set to 0 once, at the beginning. After that, `total` retains its value between function calls, so it's able to maintain a running total.

Specifiers and Qualifiers

Certain C++ keywords, called *storage class specifiers* and *cv-qualifiers*, provide additional information about storage. Here's a list of the storage class specifiers:

```
auto

register

static

extern

mutable
```

You've already seen most of these, and you can use no more than one of them in a single declaration. To review, the keyword `auto` can be used in a declaration to document that variable is an automatic variable. The keyword `register` is used in a declaration to indicate the register storage class. The keyword `static`, when used with a file-scope declaration, indicates internal linkage. When used with a local declaration, it indicates static storage duration for a local variable. The keyword `extern` indicates a reference declaration, that is, that the declaration refers to a variable defined elsewhere. The keyword `mutable` is explained in terms of `const`, so let's look at the cv-qualifiers first before returning to mutable.

Here are the cv-qualifiers:

```
const

volatile
```

The most commonly used is `const`, and you've already seen its purpose. It indicates that memory, once initialized, should not be altered by a program. We come back to `const` in a moment.

The `volatile` keyword indicates that the value in a memory location can be altered even though nothing in the program code modifies the contents. This is less mysterious than it sounds. For example, you could have a pointer to a hardware location that contains the time or information from a serial port. Here the hardware, not the program, changes the contents. Or two programs may interact, sharing data. The intent of this keyword is to improve the optimization abilities of compilers. For example, suppose the compiler notices that a program uses the value of a particular variable twice within a few statements. Rather than have the program look up the value twice, the compiler might cache the value in a register. This optimization assumes that the value of the variable doesn't change between the two uses. If you don't declare a variable to be `volatile`, then the compiler can feel free to make this optimization. If you do declare the variable to be `volatile`, you're telling the compiler not to make that sort of optimization.

Now let's return to `mutable`. You can use it to indicate that a particular member of a structure (or class) can be altered even if a particular structure (or class) variable is a `const`. For example, consider the following code:

```
struct data
{
    char name[30];
    mutable int accesses;
    ...
};
const data veep = {"Claybourne Clodde", 0, ... };
strcpy(veep.name, "Joye Joux");    // not allowed
veep.accesses++;                   // allowed
```

The `const` qualifier to `veep` prevents a program from changing `veep`'s members, but the `mutable` specifier to the `accesses` member shields `accesses` from that restriction.

This book won't be using `volatile` or `mutable`, but there is more to learn about `const`.

More About `const`

In C++ (but not C), the `const` modifier alters the default storage classes slightly. Whereas a global variable has external linkage by default, a `const` global variable has internal linkage by default. That is, C++ treats a global `const` definition as if the `static` specifier had been used.

```
const int fingers = 10;    // same as static const int fingers;
int main(void)
```

```
{
    ...
```

C++ altered the rules for constant types to make life easier for you. Suppose, for example, you have a set of constants that you'd like to place in a header file and that you use this header file in several files in the same program. After the preprocessor includes the header file contents in each source file, each source file will contain definitions like this:

```
const int fingers = 10;
const char * warning = "Wak!";
```

If global **const** declarations had external linkage like regular variables, this would be an error, for you can define a global variable in one file only. That is, only one file can contain the preceding declaration, whereas the other files have to provide reference declarations using the **extern** keyword. Moreover, only the declarations without the **extern** keyword can initialize values:

```
// extern would be required if const had external linkage
extern const int fingers;        // can't be initialized
extern const char * warning;
```

So, you need one set of definitions for one file and a different set of declarations for the other files. But, because externally defined **const** data have internal linkage, you can use the same declarations in all files.

Internal linkage also means that each file gets its own set of constants rather than sharing them. Each definition is private to the file containing it. This is why it's a good idea to put constant definitions in a header file. That way, as long as you include the same header file in two source code files, they receive the same set of constants.

If, for some reason, you want to make a constant have external linkage, you can use the **extern** keyword to override the default internal linkage:

```
extern const int states = 50;    // external linkage
```

You must use the **extern** keyword to declare the constant in all files using the constant. This differs from regular external variables, in which you don't use the keyword **extern** when you define a variable, but use **extern** in other files using that variable. Also, unlike regular variables, you can initialize an **extern const** value. Indeed, you have to, for **const** data requires initialization.

When you declare a **const** within a function or block, it has block scope, meaning the constant is usable only when the program is executing code within the block. This means that you can create constants within a function or block and not have to worry about the name conflicting with constants defined elsewhere.

Functions and Linkage

Functions, too, have linkage propertieslinllinl, although the selection is more limited than for variables. C++, like C, does not allow you to define one function inside another, so all functions automatically have a static storage duration, meaning they are all present as long as the program is running. By default, functions have external linkage, meaning they can be shared across files. You can, in fact, use the keyword **extern** in a function prototype to indicate the function is defined in another file, but that is optional. (For the program to find the function in another file, that file must be one of the files being compiled as part of the program or a library file searched by the linker.) You also can use the keyword **static** to give a function internal linkage, confining its use to a single file. You would apply this keyword to the prototype and to the function definition:

```
static int private(double x);
...
static int private(double x)
{
    ...
}
```

That means the function is known only in that file. It also means you can use the same name for another function in a different file. As with variables, a static function overrides an external definition for the file containing the static declaration, so a file containing a static function definition will use that version of the function even if there is an external definition of a function with the same name.

C++ has a "one definition rule" that states that every program shall contain exactly one definition of every non-inline function. For functions with external linkage, this means that only one file of a multifile program can contain the function definition. However, each file that uses the function should have the function prototype.

Inline functions are excepted from this rule to allow you to place inline function definitions in a header file. Thus, each file that includes the header file ends up having the inline function definition. However, C++ does require that all the inline definitions for a particular function be identical.

Where C++ Finds Functions

Suppose you call a function in a particular file in a program. Where does C++ look for the function definition? If the function prototype in that file indicates that function is static, the compiler looks only in that file for the function. Otherwise, the compiler (including the linker, too) looks in all the program files. If it finds two definitions, the compiler sends you an error message, for you can have only one definition for an external function. If it fails to find any definition in your files, the function then searches the libraries. This implies that if you define a function having the same name as a library function, the compiler uses your version rather than the library version. (However, C++ reserves the names of the standard library functions, meaning you shouldn't reuse them.) Some compiler-linkers need explicit instructions to identify which libraries to search.

Language Linking

There is another form of linking, called *language linking*, that affects functions. First, a little background. A linker needs a different symbolic name for each distinct function. In C, this was simple to implement because there could only be one C function by a given name. So, for internal purposes, a C compiler might translate a C function name such as **spiff** to **_spiff**.

The C approach is termed *C language linkage*. C++, however, can have several functions with the same C++ name that have to be translated to separate symbolic names. Thus, the C++ compiler indulged in the process of name mangling or name decoration (as discussed in Chapter 8) to generate different symbolic names for overloaded functions. For example, it could convert `spiff(int)` to, say, `_spiff_i`, and `spiff(double, double)` to `_spiff_d_d`. The C++ approach is *C++ language linkage*.

When the linker looks for a function to match a C++ function call, it uses a different look-up method than it does to match a C function call. But suppose you want to use a precompiled function from a C library in a C++ program? For example, suppose you have this code:

```
spiff(22); // want spiff(int) from a C library
```

Its symbolic name in the C library file is **_spiff**, but, for our hypothetical linker, the C++ look-up convention is to look for the symbolic name **_spiff_i**. To get around this problem, you can use the function prototype to indicate which protocol to use:

```
extern "C" void spiff(int);    // use C protocol for name look-up
extern void spoff(int);        // use C++ protocol for name look-up
extern "C++" void spaff(int); // use C++ protocol for name look-up
```

The first uses C language linkage. The second and third use C++ language linkage. The second does so by default, and the third explicitly.

Storage Schemes and Dynamic Allocation

You've seen the five schemes C++ uses to allocate memory for variables (including arrays and structures). They don't apply to memory allocated by using the C++ `new` operator (or by the older C `malloc()` function). We call that kind of memory *dynamic memory*. As you saw in Chapter 4, dynamic memory is controlled by the `new` and `delete` operators, not by scope and linkage rules. Thus, dynamic memory can be allocated from one function and freed from another function. Unlike automatic memory, dynamic memory is not LIFO; the order of allocation and freeing depends upon when and how `new` and `delete` are used. Typically, the compiler uses three separate memory chunks: one for static variables (this chunk might be subdivided), one for automatic variables, and one for dynamic storage.

Although the storage scheme concepts don't apply to dynamic memory, they do apply to pointer variables used to keep track of dynamic memory. For example, suppose you have the following statement inside a function:

```
float * p_fees = new float [20];
```

The 80 bytes (assuming a `float` is four bytes) of memory allocated by `new` remains in memory until the `delete` operator frees it. But the **p_fees** pointer passes from existence when the function containing this declaration terminates. If you want to have the 80 bytes of allocated memory available to another function, you need to pass or return its address to that function. On the other hand, if you declare **p_fees** with external linkage, then the **p_fees** pointer will be available to all the functions following that declaration in the file. And by using

```
extern float * p_fees;
```

in a second file, you make that same pointer available in the second file. Note, however, that a statement using **new** to set **p_fees** has to be in a function because static storage variables can only be initialized with constant expressions:

```
float * p_fees;  // = new float[20] not allowed here
int main()
{
    p_fees = new float [20];
...
```

Compatibility Note

Memory allocated by new typically is freed when the program terminates. However, this is not always true. Under DOS, for example, in some circumstances a request for a large block of memory can result in a block that is not deleted automatically when the program terminates.

Namespaces

Names in C++ can refer to variables, functions, structures, enumerations, classes, and class and structure members. When programming projects grow large, the potential for name conflicts increases. When you use class libraries from more than one source, you can get name conflicts. For example, two libraries might both define classes named **List**, **Tree**, and **Node**, but in incompatible ways. You might want the **List** class from one library and the **Tree** from the other, and each might expect its own version of **Node**. Such conflicts are termed namespace problems.

The C++ Standard provides namespace facilities to provide greater control over the scope of names. It has taken a while for compilers to incorporate namespaces, but, by now, support has become common.

Traditional C++ Namespaces

Before looking at the new facilities, let's review the namespace properties that already exist in C++ and introduce some terminology. This can help make the idea of namespaces seem more familiar.

The first term is *declarative region*. A declarative region is a region in which declarations can be made. For example, you can declare a global variable outside of any function. The declarative region for that variable is the file in which it is declared. If you declare a variable inside a function, its declarative region is the innermost block in which it is declared.

The second term is *potential scope*. The potential scope for a variable begins at its point of declaration and extends to the end of its declarative region. So the potential scope is more limited than the declarative region because you can't use a variable above the point it is first defined.

A variable, however, might not be visible everywhere in its potential scope. For example, it can be hidden by another variable of the same name declared in a nested declarative region. For example, a local variable declared in a function (the declarative region is the function) hides a global variable declared in the same file (the declarative region is the file). The portion of the program that actually can see the variable is termed the *scope*, which is the way we've been using the term all along. Figures 9.5 and 9.6 illustrate the terms declarative region, potential scope, and scope.

FIGURE 9.5

Declarative regions.

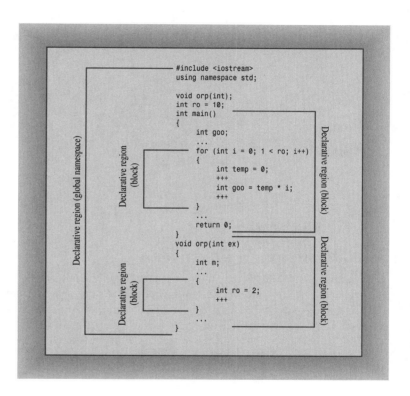

C++'s rules about global and local variables define a kind of namespace hierarchy. Each declarative region can declare names that are independent of names declared in other declarative regions. A local variable declared in one function doesn't conflict with a local variable declared in a second function.

FIGURE 9.6
Potential scope and
scope.

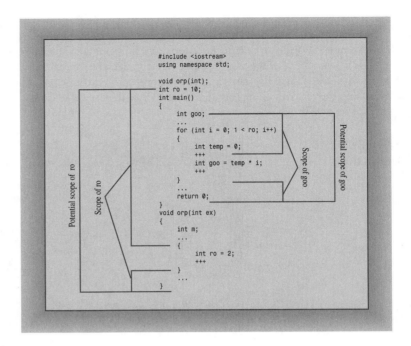

New Namespace Features

What C++ now adds is the ability to create named namespaces by defining a new kind of
declarative region, one whose main purpose is to provide an area in which to declare names.
The names in one namespace don't conflict with the same names declared in other namespaces, and there are mechanisms for letting other parts of a program use items declared in a
namespace. The following code, for example, uses the new keyword `namespace` to create two
namespaces, `Jack` and `Jill`.

```
namespace Jack {
    double pail;
    void fetch();
    int pal;
    struct Well { ... };
}
namespace Jill {
    double bucket(double n) { ... }
    double fetch;
    int pal;
    struct Hill { ... };
}
```

Namespaces can be located at the global level or inside other namespaces, but they cannot be
placed in a block. Thus, a name declared in a namespace has external linkage by default
(unless it refers to a constant).

In addition to user-defined namespaces, there is one more namespace, the *global namespace*. This corresponds to the file-level declarative region, so what used to be termed global variables are now described as being part of the global namespace.

The names in any one namespace can't conflict with names in another namespace. Thus, the `fetch` in `Jack` can coexist with the `fetch` in `Jill`, and the `Hill` in `Jill` can coexist with an external `Hill`. The rules governing declarations and definitions in a namespace are the same as the rules for global declarations and definitions.

Namespaces are *open*, meaning you can add names to existing namespaces. For example, the statement

```
namespace Jill {
    char * goose(const char *);
}
```

adds the name `goose` to the existing list of names in `Jill`.

Similarly, the original `Jack` namespace provided a prototype for a `fetch()` function. You can provide the code for the function later in the file (or in another file) by using the `Jack` namespace again:

```
namespace Jack {
    void fetch()
    {
        ...
    }
}
```

Of course, you need a way to access names in a given namespace. The simplest way is to use `::`, the scope resolution operator, to *qualify* a name with its namespace:

```
Jack::pail = 12.34;   // use a variable
Jill::Hill mole;      // create a type Hill structure
Jack::fetch();        // use a function
```

An unadorned name, such as `pail`, is termed the *unqualified name*, whereas a name with the namespace, as in `Jack::pail`, is termed a *qualified name*.

Using-Declarations and Using-Directives

Having to qualify names every time they are used is not an appealing prospect, so C++ provides two mechanisms—the *using-declaration* and the *using-directive*—to simplify using namespace names. The using-declaration lets you make particular identifiers available, and the using-directive makes the entire namespace accessible.

The using-declaration consists of preceding a qualified name with the new keyword `using`:

```
using Jill::fetch;    // a using-declaration
```

A using-declaration adds a particular name to the declarative region in which it occurs. For example, a using-declaration of `Jill::fetch` in `main()` adds `fetch` to the declarative region defined by `main()`. After making this declaration, you can use the name `fetch` instead of `Jill::fetch`.

```
namespace Jill {
    double bucket(double n) { ... }
    double fetch;
    struct Hill { ... };
}
char fetch;
int main()
{
    using Jill::fetch;      // put fetch into local namespace
    double fetch;           // Error! Already have a local fetch
    cin >> fetch;           // read a value into Jill::fetch
    cin >> ::fetch;         // read a value into global fetch
    ...
}
```

Because a using-declaration adds the name to the local declarative region, this example precludes creating another local variable by the name of `fetch`. Also, like any other local variable, `fetch` would override a global variable by the same name.

Placing a using-declaration at the external level adds the name to the global namespace:

```
void other();
namespace Jill {
    double bucket(double n) { ... }
    double fetch;
    struct Hill { ... };
}
using Jill::fetch;    // put fetch into global namespace
int main()
{
    cin >> fetch;         // read a value into Jill::fetch
    other()
...
}

void other()
{
    cout << fetch;  // display Jill::fetch
...
}
```

A using-declaration, then, makes a single name available. In contrast, the using-directive makes all the names available. A using-directive consists of preceding a namespace name with the keywords **using namespace**, and it makes *all* the names in the namespace available without using the scope resolution operator:

```
using namespace Jack;  // make all the names in Jack available
```

Placing a using-directive at the global level makes the namespace names available globally. You've seen this in action many a time:

```
#include <iostream>    // places names in namespace std
using namespace std;   // make names available globally
```

Placing a using-directive in a particular function makes the names available just in that function.

```
int vorn(int m)
{
    using namespace jack; // make names available in vorn()
...
}
```

Using-Directive Versus Using-Declaration

Using a using-directive to import all the names wholesale is *not* the same as using multiple using-declarations. It's more like the mass application of a scope resolution operator. When you use a using-declaration, it is as if the name is declared at the location of the using-declaration. If a particular name already is declared in a function, you can't import the same name with a using-declaration. When you use a using-directive, however, name resolution takes place as if you declared the names in the smallest declarative region containing both the using-declaration and the namespace itself. For the following example, that would be the global namespace. If you use a using-directive to import a name that already is declared in a function, the local name will hide the namespace name, just as it would hide a global variable of the same name. However, you still can use the scope resolution operator:

```
namespace Jill {
    double bucket(double n) { ... }
    double fetch;
    struct Hill { ... };
}
char fetch;                     // global namespace
int main()
{
    using namespace Jill;       // import all namespace names
    Hill Thrill;                // create a type Jill::Hill structure
    double water = bucket(2);   // use Jill::bucket();
    double fetch;               // not an error; hides Jill::fetch
    cin >> fetch;               // read a value into the local fetch
    cin >> ::fetch;             // read a value into global fetch
    cin >> Jill::fetch;         // read a value into Jill::fetch
    ...
}

int foom()
{
    Hill top;                   // ERROR
    Jill::Hill crest;           // valid
}
```

Here, in `main()`, the name `Jill::fetch` is placed in the local namespace. It doesn't have local scope, so it doesn't override the global `fetch`. But the locally declared `fetch` hides both `Jill::fetch` and the global `fetch`. However, both of the last two `fetch` variables are available if you use the scope resolution operator. You might want to compare this example to the preceding one, which used a using-declaration.

One other point of note is that although a using-directive in a function treats the namespace names as being declared outside the function, it doesn't make those names available to other functions in the file. Hence in the preceding example, the `foom()` function can't use the unqualified `Hill` identifier.

Remember

Suppose a namespace and a declarative region both define the same name. If you attempt to use a using-declaration to bring the namespace name into the declarative region, the two names conflict, and you get an error. If you use a using-directive to bring the namespace name into the declarative region, the local version of the name hides the namespace version.

Generally speaking, the using-declaration is safer to use because it shows exactly what names you are making available. And if the name conflicts with a local name, the compiler lets you know. The using-directive adds all names, even ones you might not need. If a local name conflicts, it overrides the namespace version, and you won't be warned. Also, the open nature of namespaces means that the complete list of names in a namespace might be spread over several locations, making it difficult to know exactly which names you are adding.

What about the approach used for this book's examples?

```
#include <iostream>
using namespace std;
```

First, the `iostream` header file puts everything in the `std` namespace. Then, the next line exports everything in that namespace into the global namespace. Thus, this approach merely reproduces the pre-namespace era. The main rationale for this approach is expediency. It's easy to do, and if your system doesn't have namespaces, you can replace the preceding two lines with the original form:

```
#include <iostream.h>
```

However, the hope of namespace proponents is that you will be more selective and use either the resolution operator or the using-declaration. That is, don't use the following:

```
using namespace std;   // avoid as too indiscriminate
```

Instead, do this:

```
int x;
std::cin >> x;
std::cout << x << std::endl;
```

Or else do this:

```
using std::cin;
using std::cout;
using std::endl;
int x;
cin >> x;
cout << x << endl;
```

You can use nested namespaces, as described next, to create a namespace holding the using-declarations you commonly use.

More Namespace Features

You can nest namespace declarations:

```
namespace elements
{
    namespace fire
    {
        int flame;
        ...
    }
    float water;
}
```

In this case, you refer to the `flame` variable as `elements::fire::flame`. Similarly, you can make the inner names available with this using-directive:

```
using namespace elements::fire;
```

Also, you can use using-directives and using-declarations inside namespaces:

```
namespace myth
{
    using Jill::fetch;
    using namespace elements;
    using std::cout;
    using std::cin;
}
```

Suppose you want to access `Jill::fetch`. Because `Jill::fetch` is now part of the `myth` namespace, where it can be called `fetch`, you can access it this way:

```
std::cin >> myth::fetch;
```

Of course, because it also is part of the `Jill` namespace, you still can call it `Jill::fetch`:

```
std::cout << Jill::fetch;  // display value read into myth::fetch
```

Or you can do this, providing no local variables conflict:

```
using namespace myth;
cin >> fetch;      // really std::cin and Jill::fetch
```

Now consider applying a using-directive to the *myth* namespace. The using-directive is *transitive*. We say an operation *op* is transitive if A *op* B and B *op* C implies A *op* C. For example, the > operator is transitive. (That is, A bigger than B and B bigger than C implies A bigger than C.) In this context, the upshot is that the statement

```
using namespace myth;
```

results in the `elements` namespace being added via a using-directive also, so it's the same as the following:

```
using namespace myth;
using namespace elements;
```

You can create an alias for a namespace. For example, suppose you have a namespace defined as follows:

```
namespace my_very_favorite_things { ... };
```

You can make `mvft` an alias for `my_very_favorite_things` with the following statement:

```
namespace mvft = my_very_favorite_things;
```

You can use this technique to simplify using nested namespaces:

```
namespace MEF = myth::elements::fire;
using MEF::flame;
```

Unnamed Namespaces

You can create an `unnamed namespace` by omitting the namespace name:

```
namespace          // unnamed namespace
{
    int ice;
    int bandycoot;
}
```

This behaves as if it were followed by a using-directive; that is, the names declared in this namespace are in potential scope until the end of the declarative region containing the unnamed namespace. In this respect, they are like global variables. However, because the namespace has no name, you can't explicitly use a using-directive or using-declaration to make the names available elsewhere. In particular, you can't use names from an unnamed namespace in a file other than the one containing the namespace declaration. This provides an alternative to using static variables with internal linkage. Indeed, the C++ standard deprecates the use of the keyword **static** in namespaces and global scope. ("Deprecate" is a term the standard uses to indicate practices that currently are valid but most likely will be rendered invalid by future revisions of the standard.) Suppose, for example, you have this code:

```
static int counts;   // static storage, internal linkage
int other();
int main()
{
}
int other()
{
}
```

The intent of the standard is that you should do this instead:

```
namespace
{
    int counts;   // static storage, internal linkage
}
int other();
int main()
```

```
{
}
int other()
{
}
```

A Namespace Example

Let's take a look at a multifile example that demonstrates some of the namespace features. The first file is a header file that contains some items normally found in header files—constants, structure definitions, and function prototypes. In this case the items are placed in two namespaces. The first namespace, called **pers**, contains a definition of a **Person** structure, plus prototypes for a function that fills a structure with a person's name and a function that displays the structure contents. The second namespace, called **debts**, defines a structure for storing the name of a person and the amount of money owed to that person. This structure uses the **Person** structure, so, the **debts** namespace has a using-directive to make the names in the **pers** available in the **debts** namespace. The **debts** namespace also contains some prototypes. Listing 9.9 shows this header file.

LISTING 9.9   namesp.h

```
// namesp.h
namespace pers
{
    const int LEN = 40;
    struct Person
    {
        char fname[LEN];
        char lname[LEN];
    };
    void getPerson(Person &);
    void showPerson(const Person &);
}

namespace debts
{
    using namespace pers;
    struct Debt
    {
        Person name;
        double amount;
    };

    void getDebt(Debt &);
    void showDebt(const Debt &);
    double sumDebts(const Debt ar[], int n);
}
```

The next file follows the usual pattern of having a source code file provide definitions for functions prototyped in a header file. The function names, being declared in a namespace, have namespace scope so the definitions need to be in the same namespace as the declarations. This is where the open nature of namespaces comes in handy. The original namespaces are brought in by including **namesp.h** (Listing 9.9). The file then adds the function definitions to the two namespaces, as shown in Listing 9.10.

LISTING 9.10   namesp.cpp

```cpp
// namesp.cpp -- namespaces
#include <iostream>
using namespace std;
#include "namesp.h"

namespace pers
{
    void getPerson(Person & rp)
    {
        cout << "Enter first name: ";
        cin >> rp.fname;
        cout << "Enter last name: ";
        cin >> rp.lname;
    }

    void showPerson(const Person & rp)
    {
        cout << rp.lname << ", " << rp.fname;
    }
}

namespace debts
{
    void getDebt(Debt & rd)
    {
        getPerson(rd.name);
        cout << "Enter debt: ";
        cin >> rd.amount;
    }

    void showDebt(const Debt & rd)
    {
        showPerson(rd.name);
        cout <<": $" << rd.amount << endl;
    }

    double sumDebts(const Debt ar[], int n)
    {
        double total = 0;
        for (int i = 0; i < n; i++)
            total += ar[i].amount;
        return total;
    }
}
```

Finally, the third file of the program is a source code file using the structures and functions declared and defined in the namespaces. Listing 9.11 shows several methods of making the namespace identifiers available.

LISTING 9.11   namesp.cpp

```
// usenmsp.cpp -- using namespaces
#include <iostream>
using namespace std;
#include "namesp.h"

void other(void);
void another(void);
int main(void)
{
    using debts::Debt;
    using debts::showDebt;
    Debt golf = { {"Benny", "Goatsniff"}, 120.0 };
    showDebt(golf);
    other();
    another();

    return 0;
}

void other(void)
{
    using namespace debts;
    Person dg = {"Doodles", "Glister"};
    showPerson(dg);
    cout << endl;
    Debt zippy[3];
    int i;

    for (i = 0; i < 3; i++)
        getDebt(zippy[i]);

    for (i = 0; i < 3; i++)
        showDebt(zippy[i]);
    cout << "Total debt: $" << sumDebts(zippy, 3) << endl;

    return;
}

void another(void)
{
    using pers::Person;;

    Person collector = { "Milo", "Rightshift" };
    pers::showPerson(collector);
    cout << endl;
}
```

First, `main()` using two using-declarations:

```
using debts::Debt;       // makes the Debt structure definition available
using debts::showDebt;   // makes the showDebt function available
```

Note that using-declarations just use the name; for example, the second one doesn't describe the return type or function signature for `showDebt`; it just gives the name. (Thus, if a function were overloaded, a single using-declaration would import all the versions.) Also, although both `Debt` and `showDebt()` use the `Person` type, it isn't necessary to import any of the `Person` names because the `debt` namespace already has a using-directive including the `pers` namespace.

Next, the `other()` function takes the less desirable approach of importing the entire namespace with a using-directive:

```
using namespace debts;   // make all debts and pers names available to other()
```

Because the using-directive in `debts` imports the `pers` namespace, the `other()` function can use the `Person` type and the `showPerson()` function.

Finally, the `another()` function uses a using-declaration and the scope resolution operator to access specific names:

```
using pers::Person;;
pers::showPerson(collector);
```

Here is a sample run of the program:

```
Goatsniff, Benny: $120
Glister, Doodles
Enter first name: Arabella
Enter last name: Binx
Enter debt: 100
Enter first name: Cleve
Enter last name: Delaproux
Enter debt: 120
Enter first name: Eddie
Enter last name: Fiotox
Enter debt: 200
Binx, Arabella: $100
Delaproux, Cleve: $120
Fiotox, Eddie: $200
Total debt: $420
Rightshift, Milo
```

Namespaces and the Future

As programmers become familiar with namespaces, common programming idioms will emerge. In particular, many hope that use of the global namespace will wither away and that class libraries will be designed by using the namespace mechanisms. Indeed, current C++ already calls for placing standard library functions in a namespace called `std`.

As mentioned before, changes in the header filenames reflect these changes. The older style header files, such as `iostream.h`, do not use namespaces, but the newer `iostream` header file should use the `std` namespace.

Summary

C++ encourages you to use multiple files in developing programs. An effective organizational strategy is to use a header file to define user types and provide function prototypes for functions to manipulate the user types. Use a separate source code file for the function definitions. Together, the header file and the source file define and implement the user-defined type and how it can be used. Then, `main()` and other functions using those functions can go into a third file.

C++'s storage schemes determine how long variables remain in memory (storage duration) and what parts of a program have access to them (scope and linkage). Automatic variables are those defined within a block, such as a function body or a block within the body. They exist and are known only while the program executes statements in the block that contains the definition. Automatic variables may be declared using the storage class specifiers `auto` or `register` or with no specifier at all, which is the same as using `auto`. The `register` specifier is a hint to the compiler that the variable is heavily used.

Static variables exist for the duration of the program. A variable defined outside of any function is known to all functions in the file following its definition (file scope) and is made available to other files in the program (external linkage). For another file to use such a variable, that file must declare it by using the `extern` keyword. A variable shared across files should have a defining declaration in one file (`extern` not used) and reference declarations in the other files (`extern` used). A variable defined outside any function but qualified with the keyword `static` has file scope but is not made available to other files (internal linkage). A variable defined inside a block but qualified with the keyword `static` is local to that block (local scope, no linkage) but retains its value for the duration of the program.

C++ functions, by default, have external storage class, so they can be shared across files. But functions qualified with the keyword `static` have internal linkage and are confined to the defining file.

Namespaces let you define named regions in which you can declare identifiers. The intent is to reduce name conflicts, particularly in large programs using code from several vendors. Identifiers in a namespace can be made available by using the scope resolution operator, by using a using-declaration, or by using a using-directive.

Review Questions

1. What storage scheme would you use for the following situations?

    a. `homer` is a formal argument (parameter) to a function.

    b. The `secret` variable is to be shared by two files.

c. The `topsecret` variable is to be shared by the functions in one file but hidden from other files.

d. `beencalled` keeps track of how many times the function containing it has been called.

2. Discuss the differences between a using-declaration and a using-directive.

3. Rewrite the following so that it doesn't use using-declarations or using-directives.

```
#include <iostream>
using namespace std;
int main()
{
    double x;
    cout << "Enter value: ";
    while (! (cin >> x) )
    {
        cout << "Bad input. Please enter a number: ";
        cin.clear();
        while (cin.get() != '\n')
            continue;
    }
    cout << "Value = " << x << endl;
    return 0;
}
```

4. Rewrite the following so that it uses using-declarations instead of the using-directive.

```
#include <iostream>
using namespace std;
int main()
{
    double x;
    cout << "Enter value: ";
    while (! (cin >> x) )
    {
        cout << "Bad input. Please enter a number: ";
        cin.clear();
        while (cin.get() != '\n')
            continue;
    }
    cout << "Value = " << x << endl;
    return 0;
}
```

5. The `average(3,6)` function returns an `int` average of the two `int` arguments when called in one file, and it returns a `double` average of the two `int` arguments when called in a second file in the same program. How could you set this up?

6. What will the following two-file program display?

```
// file1.cpp
#include <iostream>
using namespace std;
```

```cpp
void other();
void another();
int x = 10;
int y;

int main()
{
    cout << x << endl;
    {
        int x = 4;
        cout << x << endl;
        cout << y << endl;
    }
    other();
    another();
    return 0;
}

void other()
{
    int y = 1;
    cout << "Other: " << x << ", " << y << endl;
}

// file 2.cpp
#include <iostream>
using namespace std;
extern int x;
namespace
{
    int y = -4;
}

void another()
{
    cout << "another(): " << x << ", " << y << endl;
}
```

7. What will the following program display?

```cpp
#include <iostream>
using namespace std;
void other();
namespace n1
{
    int x = 1;
}

namespace n2
{
    int x = 2;
}
```

```
int main()
{
    using namespace n1;
    cout << x << endl;
     {
         int x = 4;
         cout << x << ", " << n1::x << ", " << n2::x << endl;
     }
    using n2::x;
    cout << x << endl;

    other();
    return 0;
}

void other()
{
    using namespace n2;
    cout << x << endl;
    {
        int x = 4;
        cout << x << ", " << n1::x << ", " << n2::x << endl;
    }
    using n2::x;
    cout << x << endl;
}
```

Programming Exercises

1. Here is a header file:

```
// golf.h -- for pe8-3.cpp

const int Len = 40;
struct golf
{
    char fullname[Len];
    int handicap;
};

// non-interactive version:
//  function sets golf structure to provided name, handicap
//  using values passed as arguments to the function
void setgolf(golf & g, const char * name, int hc);

// interactive version:
//  function solicits name and handicap from user
//  and sets the members of g to the values entered
//  returns 1 if name is entered, 0 if name is empty string
int setgolf(golf & g);
```

```
// function resets handicap to new value
void handicap(golf & g, int hc);

// function displays contents of golf structure
void showgolf(const golf & g);
```

Note that `setgolf()` is overloaded. Using the first version would look like this:

```
golf ann;
setgolf(ann, "Ann Birdfree", 24);
```

The function call provides the information that's stored in the **ann** structure. Using the second version would look like this:

```
golf andy;
setgolf(andy);
```

The function would prompt the user to enter the name and handicap and store them in the **andy** structure. This function could (but doesn't need to) use the first version internally.

Put together a multifile program based on this header. One file, named `golf.cpp`, should provide suitable function definitions to match the prototypes in the header file. A second file should contain **main()** and demonstrate all the features of the prototyped functions. For example, a loop should solicit input for an array of golf structures and terminate when the array is full or the user enters an empty string for the golfer's name. The **main()** function should use only the prototyped functions to access the golf structures.

2. Here is a namespace:

```
namespace SALES
{
    const int QUARTERS = 4;
    struct Sales
    {
        double sales[QUARTERS];
        double average;
        double max;
        double min;
    };

    // copies the lesser of 4 or n items from the array ar
    // to the sales member of s and computes and stores the
    // average, maximum, and minimum values of the entered items;
    // remaining elements of sales, if any, set to 0
    void setSales(Sales & s, const double ar[], int n);

    // gathers sales for 4 quarters interactively, stores them
    // in the sales member of s and computes and stores the
    // average, maximum, and minumum values
    void setSales(Sales & s);
```

```
        // display all information in structure s
        void showSales(const Sales & s);
}
```

Write a three-file program based on this namespace. The first file should be a header file containing the namespace. The second file should be a source code file extending the namespace to provide definitions for the three prototyped functions. The third file should declare two **Sales** objects. It should use the interactive version of **setSales()** to provide values for one structure and the non-interactive version of **setSales()** to provide values for the second structure. It should display the contents of both structures by using **showSales()**.

CHAPTER 10

OBJECTS AND CLASSES

In this chapter you learn

- Procedural and object-oriented programming
- The class concept
- How to define and implement a class
- Public and private class access
- Class data members
- Class methods (class function members)

- Creating and using class objects
- Class constructors and destructors
- const member functions
- The this pointer
- Creating arrays of objects
- Class scope
- Abstract data types (ADTs)

O bject-oriented programming (OOP) is a particular conceptual approach to designing programs, and C++ has enhanced C with features that ease the way to applying that approach. The most important OOP features are these:

- Abstraction
- Encapsulation and data hiding
- Polymorphism
- Inheritance
- Reusable code

The class is the single most important C++ enhancement for implementing these features and tying them together. This chapter begins our examination of classes. It explains abstraction, encapsulation, and data hiding, and shows how classes implement these features. It discusses how to define a class, provide a class with public and private sections, and create member functions that work with the class data. Also, the chapter acquaints you with constructors and destructors, which are special member functions for creating and disposing of objects belonging to a class. Finally, you meet the `this` pointer, an important component of some class programming. The following chapters extend the discussion to operator overloading (another variety of polymorphism) and inheritance, the basis for reusing code.

Procedural and Object-Oriented Programming

Although we have occasionally explored the OOP perspective on programming, we've usually stuck pretty close to the standard procedural approach of languages such as C, Pascal, and BASIC. Let's look at an example that clarifies how the OOP outlook differs from that of procedural programming.

As the newest member of the Genre Giants softball team, you've been asked to keep the team statistics. Naturally, you turn to your computer for help. If you were a procedural programmer, you might think along these lines:

> Let's see, I want to enter the name, times at bat, number of hits, batting averages (for those who don't follow baseball or softball, the batting average is the number of hits divided by the player's official number of times at bat; an at bat terminates when a player gets on base or makes an out, but certain events, such as getting a walk, don't count as official times at bat), and all those other great basic statistics for each player. Wait, the computer is supposed to make life easier for me, so let's have it figure out some of that stuff, such as the batting average. Also, I want the program to report the results. How should I organize this? I guess I should do things right and use functions. Yeah, I'll make `main()` call a function to get the input, call a function to make the calculations, and then call a function to report the results. Hmmm, what happens when I get data from the next game? I don't want to start from scratch again. Okay, I can add a function to update the statistics. Golly, maybe I'll need a menu in `main()` to select between entering, calculating, updating, and showing the data. Hmmm—how am I going to represent the data? I could use an array of strings to hold the players' names, another array to hold the at bats for each player, yet another array to hold the hits, and so on. No, that's dumb. I can design a structure to hold all the information for a single player and then use an array of those structures to represent the whole team.

In short, you first concentrate on the procedures you will follow and then think about how to represent the data. (Note: So that you don't have to keep the program running the whole season, you probably also want to be able to save data to a file and read data from a file. But as we haven't covered files yet, we ignore that complication for now.)

Now let's see how your perspective changes when you don your OOP hat (an attractive polymorphic design). You begin by thinking about the data. Furthermore, you think about the data not only in terms of how to represent it, but in terms of how it's to be used:

Let's see—what am I keeping track of? A ball player, of course. So, I want an object that represents the whole player, not just her batting average or times at bat. Yeah, that'll be my fundamental data unit, an object representing the name and statistics for a player. I'll need some methods to handle this object. Hmmm, I guess I need a method to get basic information into this unit. The computer should calculate some of the stuff, like the batting averages—I can add methods to do calculations. And the program should do those calculations automatically, without the user having to remember to ask to have them done. Also, I'll need methods for updating and displaying the information. So, the user gets three ways to interact with the data: initialization, updating, and reporting. That's the user interface.

In short, you concentrate on the object as the user perceives it, thinking about the data you need to describe the object and the operations that will describe the user's interaction with the data. After you develop a description of that interface, you move on to decide how to implement the interface and data storage. Finally, you put together a program to use your new design.

Abstraction and Classes

Life is full of complexities, and one way we cope with complexity is to frame simplifying abstractions. You are a collection of over an octillion atoms. Some students of the mind would say your mind is a collection of semiautonomous agents. But it's much simpler to think of yourself as a single entity. In computing, abstraction is the crucial step of representing information in terms of its interface with the user. That is, you abstract the essential operational features of a problem and express a solution in those terms. In the softball statistics example, the interface describes how the user initializes, updates, and displays the data. From abstraction, it is a short step to the user-defined type, which in C++ is a class design that implements that interface.

What's a Type?

Let's think a little more about what constitutes a type. For example, what is a nerd? If you subscribe to the popular stereotype, you may think of a nerd in visual terms—thick, black-rimmed glasses, pocket protector full of pens, and so on. After a little reflection, you might conclude that a nerd is better defined operationally, for example, in how he or she responds to an awkward social situation. We have a similar situation, if you don't mind stretched analogies, with a procedural language like C. At first, you tend to think of a data type in terms of its appearance—how it is stored in memory. A `char`, for example, is one byte of memory, and a `double` often is eight bytes of memory. But a little reflection leads us to conclude that a data type also is defined in terms of the operations that can be performed upon it. For example, the `int` type can use all the arithmetic operations. You can add, subtract, multiply, and divide integers. You also can use the modulus operator (`%`) with them.

On the other hand, consider pointers. A pointer might very well require the same amount of memory as an `int`. It might even be represented internally as an integer. But a pointer doesn't allow the same operations that an integer does. You can't, for example, multiply two pointers by each other. The concept makes no sense, so C++ doesn't implement it. Thus, when you declare a variable as an `int` or as a pointer-to-`float`, you're not just allocating memory—you also are establishing which operations can be performed with the variable. In short, specifying a basic type does two things:

- It determines how much memory is needed for a data object.

- It determines what operations, or methods, can be performed using the data object.

For built-in types, this information is built in to the compiler. But when you define a user-defined type in C++, you have to provide the same kind of information yourself. In exchange for this extra work, you gain the power and flexibility to custom fit new data types to match real-world requirements.

The Class

The *class* is the C++ vehicle for translating an abstraction to a user-defined type. It combines data representation and methods for manipulating that data into one neat package. Let's look at a class that represents stocks.

First, we have to think a bit about how to represent stocks. We could take one share of stock as the basic unit and define a class to represent a share. However, that implies that you would need 100 objects to represent 100 shares, and that's not practical. Instead, let's represent a person's current holdings in a particular stock as a basic unit. The number of shares owned would be part of the data representation. A realistic approach would have to maintain records of such things as initial purchase price and date of purchase, for tax purposes. Also, it would have to manage events such as stock splits. That seems a bit ambitious for our first effort at defining a class, so let's take an idealized, simplified view of matters. In particular, let's limit the operations we can perform to the following:

- Acquire stock in a company.

- Buy more shares of the same stock.

- Sell stock.

- Update the per-share value of a stock.

- Display information about the holdings.

We can use this list to define the public interface for the stock class, leaving additional features as exercises for the interested. To support this interface, we need to store some information. Again, we use a simplified approach. For example, we won't worry about the standard U.S. practice of evaluating stocks in multiples of eighths of a dollar. (Apparently the New York Stock Exchange must have seen this simplification in a previous edition of the book, for it has decided to change over to the system used here.) We will store the following information:

- Name of company

- Number of stocks owned

- Value of each share

- Total value of all shares

Next, let's define the class. Generally, a class specification has two parts:

- A *class declaration*, which describes the data component, in terms of data members, and the public interface, in terms of member functions

- The *class method definitions*, which describe how certain class member functions are implemented

Roughly speaking, the class declaration provides a class overview, whereas the method definitions supply the details.

Listing 10.1 presents a tentative class declaration for a `Stock` class. (To help identify classes, we follow a common, but not universal, convention of capitalizing class names.) You'll notice it looks like a structure declaration with a few additional wrinkles, such as member functions and public and private sections. We'll improve on this declaration shortly (so don't use it as a model), but first let's see how this definition works.

LISTING 10.1   The First Part of `stocks.cpp`

```
// beginning of stocks.cpp file
class Stock  // class declaration
{
private:
    char company[30];
    int shares;
    double share_val;
    double total_val;
    void set_tot() { total_val = shares * share_val; }
public:
    void acquire(const char * co, int n, double pr);
    void buy(int num, double price);
    void sell(int num, double price);
    void update(double price);
    void show();
};    // note semicolon at the end
```

You'll get a closer look at the class details later, but first let's examine the more general features. To begin, the C++ keyword `class` identifies this code as defining the design of a class. The syntax identifies `Stock` as the type name for this new class. This declaration enables us to declare variables, called *objects*, or *instances*, of the `Stock` type. Each individual object represents a single holding. For example, the declarations

```
Stock sally;
Stock solly;
```

create two `Stock` objects called `sally` and `solly`. The `sally` object, for example, could represent Sally's stock holdings in a particular company.

Next, notice that the information we decided to store appears in the form of class data members, such as `company` and `shares`. The `company` member of `sally`, for example, holds the name of the company, the `share` member holds the number of shares Sally owns, the `share_val` member holds the value of each share, and the `total_val` member holds the total value of all the shares. Similarly, the operations we want appear as class function members, such as `sell()` and `update()`. Class member functions also are termed *class methods*. A member function can be defined in place, like `set_tot()`, or it can be represented by a prototype, like the other member functions in this class. The full definitions for the other member functions come later, but the prototypes suffice to describe the function interfaces. The binding of data and methods into a single unit is the most striking feature of the class. Because of this design, creating a `Stock` object automatically establishes the rules governing how that object can be used.

You've already seen how the `istream` and `ostream` classes have member functions, such as `get()` and `getline()`. The function prototypes in the `Stock` class declaration demonstrate how member functions are established. The `iostream` header file, for example, has a `getline()` prototype in the `istream` class declaration.

Also new are the keywords `private` and `public`. These labels describe *access control* for class members. Any program that uses an object of a particular class can access the public portions directly. A program can access the private members of an object *only* by using the public member functions (or, as you see in Chapter 11, "Working with Classes," via a friend function). For example, the only way to alter the `shares` member of the `Stock` class is to use one of the `Stock` member functions. Thus, the public member functions act as go-betweens between a program and an object's private members; they provide the interface between object and program. This insulation of data from direct access by a program is called *data hiding*. (C++ provides a third access-control keyword, *protected*, which we discuss when we cover class inheritance in Chapter 13, "Class Inheritance.") (See Figure 10.1.) Whereas data hiding may be an unscrupulous act in, say, a stock fund prospectus, it's a good practice in computing because it preserves the integrity of the data.

A class design attempts to separate the public interface from the specifics of the implementation. The public interface represents the abstraction component of the design. Gathering the implementation details together and separating them from the abstraction is called *encapsulation*. *Data hiding* (putting data into the private section of a class) is an instance of encapsulation and so is hiding functional details of an implementation in the private section, as the `Stock` class does with `set_tot()`. Another example of encapsulation is the usual practice of placing class function definitions in a separate file from the class declaration.

FIGURE 10.1

The Stock class.

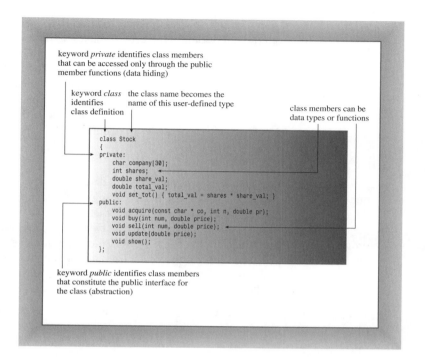

keyword *private* identifies class members
that can be accessed only through the public
member functions (data hiding)

keyword *class*   the class name becomes the
identifies   name of this user-defined type
class definition

class members can be
data types or functions

```
class Stock
{
private:
    char company[30];
    int shares;
    double share_val;
    double total_val;
    void set_tot() { total_val = shares * share_val; }
public:
    void acquire(const char * co, int n, double pr);
    void buy(int num, double price);
    void sell(int num, double price);
    void update(double price);
    void show();
};
```

keyword *public* identifies class members
that constitute the public interface for
the class (abstraction)

OOP and C++

Object-oriented programming is a programming style that you can use to some degree with any language. Certainly, you can incorporate many OOP ideas into ordinary C programs. For example, Chapter 9, "Memory Models and Namespaces," provides an example (Listings 9.1, 9.2, 9.3) in which a header file contains a structure prototype along with the prototypes for functions to manipulate that structure. Thus, the `main()` function simply defines variables of that structure type and uses the associated functions to handle those variables; `main()` does not directly access structure members. In essence, that example defines an abstract type that places the storage format and the function prototypes in a header file, hiding the actual data representation from `main()`. C++, however, includes features specifically intended to implement the OOP approach, so it enables you to take the process a few steps further than you can with C. First, placing the data representation and the function prototypes into a single class declaration instead of into a file unifies the description by placing everything in one class declaration. Second, making the data representation private enforces the stricture that data only is accessed by authorized functions. If, in the C example, `main()` directly accesses a structure member, it violates the spirit of OOP, but it doesn't break any C language rules. But trying to access directly, say, the `shares` member of a `Stock` object does break a C++ language rule, and the compiler will catch it.

Note that data hiding not only prevents you from accessing the data directly, but it also absolves you (in the roll as a user of the class) from needing to know how the data is represented. For example, the `show()` member displays, among other things, the total value of a holding. This value can be stored as part of an object, as this code does, or it can be calculated when needed. From the standpoint of the user, it makes no difference which approach is used. What you do need to know is what the different member functions accomplish; that is, you need to know what kinds of arguments a member function takes and what kind of return value it has. The principle is to separate the details of the implementation from the design of the interface. If you later find a better way to implement the data representation or the details of the member functions, you can change those details without changing the program interface, and that makes programs much easier to maintain.

Public or Private?

You can declare class members, whether they are data items or member functions, either in the public or the private section of a class. But because one of the main OOP precepts is to hide the data, data items normally go into the private section. The member functions that constitute the class interface go into the public section; otherwise, you can't call those functions from a program. As the `Stock` declaration shows, you also can put member functions in the private section. You can't call such functions directly from a program, but the public methods can use them. Typically, you use private member functions to handle implementation details that don't form part of the public interface.

You don't have to use the keyword `private` in class declarations, for that is the default access control for class objects:

```
class World
{
    float mass;         // private by default
    char name[20];      // private by default
public:
    void tellall(void);
    ...
};
```

However, we'll explicitly use the `private` label in order to emphasize the concept of data hiding.

Classes and Structures

Class descriptions look much like structure declarations with the addition of member functions and the `public` and `private` visibility labels. In fact, C++ extends to structures the same features classes have. The only difference is that the default access type for a structure is `public`, whereas the default type for the class is `private`. C++ programmers commonly use classes to implement class descriptions while restricting structures to representing pure data objects or, occasionally, classes with no private component.

Implementing Class Member Functions

We still have the second part of the class specification to do: providing code for those member functions represented by a prototype in the class declaration. Let's look at that next. Member function definitions are much like regular function definitions. They have a function heading and a function body. They can have return types and arguments. But they also have two special characteristics:

- When you define a member function, you use the scope operator (::) to identify the class to which the function belongs.
- Class methods can access the private components of the class.

Let's look at these points now.

First, the function heading for a member function uses the scope operator (::) to indicate to which class the function belongs. For example, the heading for the update() member function looks like this:

```
void Stock::update(double price)
```

This notation means we are defining the update() function that is a member of the Stock class. Not only does this identify update() as a member function, it means we can use the same name for a member function for a different class. For example, an update() function for a Buffoon class would have this function heading:

```
void Buffoon::update()
```

Thus, the scope resolution operator resolves the identity of the class to which a method definition applies. We say that the identifier update() has *class scope*. Other member functions of the Stock class can, if necessary, use the update() method without using the scope resolution operator. That's because they belong to the same class, making update() in scope. Using update() outside of the class declaration and method definitions, however, requires special measures, which we get to soon.

One way of looking at method names is that the complete name of a class method includes the class name. We say that Stock::update() is the *qualified name* of the function. A simple update(), on the other hand, is an abbreviation (the *unqualified name*) for the full name, one that can be used just in class scope.

The second special characteristic of methods is that a method can access the private members of a class. For example, the show() method can use code like this:

```
cout << "Company: " << company
     << "  Shares: " << shares << '\n'
     << "  Share Price: $" << share_val
     << "  Total Worth: $" << total_val << '\n';
```

Here company, shares, and so on, are private data members of the Stock class. If you try to use a nonmember function to access these data members, the compiler stops you cold in your tracks. (However, friend functions, which Chapter 11 discusses, provide an exception.)

With these two points in mind, we can implement the class methods as shown in Listing 10.2. These method definitions can go in a separate file or in the same file with the class declaration. Because we are beginning simply, we assume that these definitions follow the class declaration in the same file. This is the easiest, although not the best, way to make the class declaration available to the method definitions. (The best way, which we apply later in this chapter, is to use a header file for the class declaration and a separate source code file for the class member function definitions.)

LISTING 10.2 stocks.cpp *Continued*

```
//more stocks.cpp -- implementing the class member functions
#include <iostream>
using namespace std;
#include <cstring>  // --or string.h--for strncpy()

void Stock::acquire(const char * co, int n, double pr)
{
    strncpy(company, co, 29); // truncate co to fit if needed
    company[29] = '\0';
    if (n < 0)
    {
        cerr << "Number of shares can't be negative; "
            << "shares set to 0.\n";
        shares = 0;
    }
    else
        shares = n;
    share_val = pr;
    set_tot();
}

void Stock::buy(int num, double price)
{
    if (num < 0)
    {
        cerr << "Number of shares purchased can't be negative. "
            << "Transaction is aborted.\n";
    }
    else
    {
        shares += num;
        share_val = price;
        set_tot();
    }
}

void Stock::sell(int num, double price)
{
    if (num < 0)
    {
        cerr << "Number of shares sold can't be negative. "
            << "Transaction is aborted.\n";
    }
    else if (num > shares)
    {
        cerr << "You can't sell more than you have! "
```

LISTING 10.2   Continued

```
                    << "Transaction is aborted.\n";
        }
        else
        {
            shares -= num;
            share_val = price;
            set_tot();
        }
}

void Stock::update(double price)
{
    share_val = price;
    set_tot();
}

void Stock::show()
{
    cout << "Company: " << company
         << "  Shares: " << shares << '\n'
         << "  Share Price: $" << share_val
         << "  Total Worth: $" << total_val << '\n';
}
```

Member Function Notes

The `acquire()` function manages the first acquisition of stock for a given company, whereas `buy()` and `sell()` manage adding to or subtracting from an existing holding. The last two methods make sure that the number of shares bought or sold is not a negative number. Also, if the user attempts to sell more shares than he or she has, the `sell()` function terminates the transaction. The technique of making the data private and limiting access to public functions gives us control over how the data can be used; in this case, it allows us to insert these safe-guards against faulty transactions.

Four of the member functions set or reset the `total_val` member value. Rather than write this calculation four times, the class has each function call the `set_tot()` function. Because this function is merely the means of implementing the code and not part of the public interface, the class makes `set_tot()` a private member function. If the calculation were lengthy, this could save some typing and code space. Here, however, the main value is that by using a function call instead of retyping the calculation each time, you ensure that the exact same calculation gets done. Also, if you have to revise the calculation (not likely in this particular case), you have to revise it in just one location.

The `acquire()` method uses `strncpy()` to copy the string. In case you've forgotten, the call `strncpy(s2, s1, n)` copies `s1` to `s2` or else up to `n` characters from `s1` to `s2`, whichever comes first. If `s1` contains fewer characters than `n`, the `strncpy()` function pads `s2` with null characters. That is, `strncpy(firstname,"Tim", 6)` copies the characters T, i, and m to `firstname` and then adds three null characters to bring the total to six characters. But if `s1` is longer than n, no null characters are appended. That is, `strncpy(firstname, "Priscilla", 4)` just copies the characters P, r, i, and s to `firstname`, making it a character array but, because it lacks a terminating null character, not a string. Therefore, `acquire()` places a null character at the end of the array to guarantee that it is a string.

cerr

The `cerr` object, like `cout`, is an `ostream` object. The difference is that operating system redirection affects `cout` but not `cerr`. The `cerr` object is used for error messages. Thus, if you redirect program output to a file and there is an error, you still get the error message onscreen.

Inline Methods

Any function with a definition in the class declaration automatically becomes an inline function. Thus, `Stock::set_tot()` is an inline function. Class declarations often use inline functions for short member functions, and `set_tot()` qualifies on that account.

You can, if you like, define a member function outside the class declaration and still make it inline. To do so, just use the `inline` qualifier when you define the function in the class implementation section:

```
class Stock
{
private:
    ...
    void set_tot();  // definition kept separate
public:
    ...
};

inline void Stock::set_tot()  // use inline in definition
{
    total_val = shares * share_val;
}
```

The special rules for inline functions require that they be defined in each file in which they are used. The easiest way to make sure that inline definitions are available to all files in a multifile program is to include the inline definition in the same header file in which the corresponding class is defined. (Some development systems may have smart linkers that allow the inline definitions to go into a separate implementation file.)

Incidentally, according to the *rewrite rule*, defining a method in a class declaration is equivalent to replacing the method definition with a prototype and then rewriting the definition as an inline function immediately after the class declaration. That is, the original inline definition of `set_tot()` in Listing 10.2 is equivalent to the one just shown, with the definition following the class declaration.

Which Object?

Now we come to one of the most important aspects of using objects: how you apply a class method to an object. Code such as

```
shares += num;
```

uses the `shares` member of an object. But which object? That's an excellent question! To answer it, first consider how you create an object. The simplest way is to declare class variables:

```
Stock kate, joe;
```

This creates two objects of the `Stock` class, one named `kate` and one named `joe`.

Next, consider how to use a member function with one of these objects. The answer, as with structures and structure members, is to use the membership operator:

```
kate.show();    // the kate object calls the member function
joe.show();     // the joe object calls the member function
```

The first call invokes `show()` as a member of the `kate` object. This means the method interprets shares as `kate.shares` and share_val as `kate.share_val`. Similarly, the call `joe.show()` makes the `show()` method interpret `shares` and `share_val` as `joe.shares` and `joe.share_val`, respectively.

Remember

When you call a member function, it uses the data members of the particular object used to invoke the member function.

Similarly, the function call `kate.sell()` invokes the `set_tot()` function as if it were `kate.set_tot()`, causing that function to get its data from the `kate` object.

Each new object you create contains storage for its own internal variables, the class members. But all objects of the same class share the same set of class methods, with just one copy of each method. Suppose, for example, that `kate` and `joe` are `Stock` objects. Then, `kate.shares` occupies one chunk of memory and `joe.shares` occupies a second chunk of memory. But `kate.show()` and `joe.show()` both invoke the same method, that is, both execute the same block of code. They just apply the code to different data. Calling a member function is what some OOP languages term *sending a message*. Thus, sending the same message to two different objects invokes the same method but applies it to two different objects. (See Figure 10.2.)

FIGURE 10.2

Objects, data, and member functions.

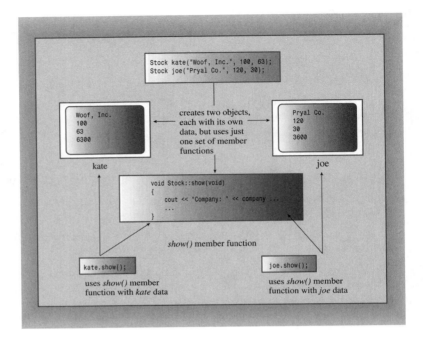

Using a Class

Now you've seen how to define a class and its class methods. The next step is to produce a program that creates and uses objects of a class. The C++ goal is to make using classes as similar as possible to using the basic, built-in types, such as int and char. You can create a class object by declaring a class variable or using new to allocate an object of a class type. You can pass objects as arguments, return them as function return values, and assign one object to another. C++ provides facilities for initializing objects, teaching cin and cout to recognize objects, and even providing automatic type conversions between objects of similar classes. It will be a while before you can do all these things, but let's start now with the simpler properties. Indeed, you've already seen how to declare a class object and call a member function. Listing 10.3 combines those techniques with the class declaration and the member function definitions to form a complete program. It creates a Stock object named stock1. The program is simple, but it does test the features we built in to the class.

LISTING 10.3   The Full stocks.cpp Program

```
// stocks.cpp -- the whole program
#include <iostream>
#include <cstring>  // --or string.h--for strncpy()
using namespace std;

class Stock  // class declaration
{
```

LISTING 10.3 Continued

```cpp
private:
    char company[30];
    int shares;
    double share_val;
    double total_val;
    void set_tot() { total_val = shares * share_val; }
public:
    void acquire(const char * co, int n, double pr);
    void buy(int num, double price);
    void sell(int num, double price);
    void update(double price);
    void show();
};    // note semicolon at the end

void Stock::acquire(const char * co, int n, double pr)
{
    strncpy(company, co, 29); // truncate co to fit if needed
    company[29] = '\0';
    if (n < 0)
    {
        cerr << "Number of shares can't be negative; "
             << "shares set to 0.\n";
        shares = 0;
    }
    else
        shares = n;
    share_val = pr;
    set_tot();
}

void Stock::buy(int num, double price)
{
     if (num < 0)
    {
        cerr << "Number of shares purchased can't be negative. "
             << "Transaction is aborted.\n";
    }
    else
    {
        shares += num;
        share_val = price;
        set_tot();
    }
}

void Stock::sell(int num, double price)
{
    if (num < 0)
    {
        cerr << "Number of shares sold can't be negative. "
             << "Transaction is aborted.\n";
    }
```

LISTING 10.3   Continued

```
        else if (num > shares)
        {
            cerr << "You can't sell more than you have! "
                 << "Transaction is aborted.\n";
        }
        else
        {
            shares -= num;
            share_val = price;
            set_tot();
        }
}

void Stock::update(double price)
{
    share_val = price;
    set_tot();
}

void Stock::show()
{
    cout << "Company: " << company
         << "  Shares: " << shares << '\n'
         << "  Share Price: $" << share_val
         << "  Total Worth: $" << total_val << '\n';
}

int main()
{
    Stock stock1;

    stock1.acquire("NanoSmart", 20, 12.50);
    cout.setf(ios_base::fixed);        // #.## format
    cout.precision(2);                 // #.## format
    cout.setf(ios_base::showpoint);    // #.## format
    stock1.show();
    stock1.buy(15, 18.25);
    stock1.show();
    stock1.sell(400, 20.00);
    stock1.show();
    return 0;
}
```

The program uses three formatting commands:

```
cout.setf(ios_base::fixed);       // use fixed decimal point format
cout.precision(2);                // two places to right of decimal
cout.setf(ios_base::showpoint);   // show trailing zeros
```

The net effect is to display two digits to the right of the decimal, including trailing zeros. Actually, only the first two are needed according to current practices, and older implementations just need the first and third. Using all three produces the same output for both implementations. See Chapter 17, "Input, Output, and Files," for the details. Meanwhile, here is the program output:

```
Company: NanoSmart  Shares: 20
  Share Price: $12.50  Total Worth: $250.00
Company: NanoSmart  Shares: 35
  Share Price: $18.25  Total Worth: $638.75
You can't sell more than you have! Transaction is aborted.
Company: NanoSmart  Shares: 35
  Share Price: $18.25  Total Worth: $638.75
```

Note that `main()` is just a vehicle for testing the design of the `Stock` class. Given that the class works as we like, we now can use the `Stock` class as a user-defined type in other programs. The critical point in using the new type is understanding what the member functions do; you shouldn't have to think about the implementation details. See the "The Client/Server Model" sidebar.

The Client/Server Model

OOP programmers often discuss program design in terms of a client/server model. In this conceptualization, the *client* is a program that uses the class. The class declaration, including the class methods, constitute the *server*, which is a resource available to the programs that need it. The client uses the server through the publicly defined interface only. This means the client's only responsibility, and, by extension, the client's programmer's only responsibility, is to know that interface. The server's responsibility, and, by extension, the server's designer's responsibility, is to see that the server reliably and accurately performs according to that interface. Any changes the server designer makes to the class design should be to details of implementation, not to the interface. This allows programmers to improve the client and the server independently of each other, without changes in the server having unforeseen repercussions in the client's behavior.

Our Story to Date

The first step in specifying a class design is providing a class declaration. The class declaration is modeled after a structure declaration and can include data members and function members. The declaration has a private section, and members declared in that section can be accessed only through the member functions. The declaration also has a public section, and members declared there can be accessed directly by a program using class objects. Typically, data members go into the private section and member functions go into the public section, so a typical class declaration has this form:

```
class className
{
private:
    data member declarations
public:
    member function prototypes
};
```

The contents of the public section constitute the abstract part of the design, the public interface. Encapsulating data in the private section protects the integrity of the data and is called data hiding. Thus, the class is the C++ way of making it easy to implement the OOP goals of abstraction, data hiding, and encapsulation.

The second step in specifying the class design is to implement the class member functions. You can use a complete function definition instead of a function prototype in the class declaration, but the usual practice, except for very brief functions, is to provide the function definitions separately. In that case, you need to use the scope operator to indicate to which class a member function belongs. For example, suppose the `Bozo` class has a member function called `Retort()` that returns a pointer to a `char`. Then, the function heading would look like this:

```
char * Bozo::Retort()
```

In other words, `Retort()` is not just a type `char *` function; it is a type `char *` function that belongs to the `Bozo` class. The full, or qualified, name of the function is `Bozo::Retort()`. The name `Retort()`, on the other hand, is an abbreviation of the qualified name, and it can be used only in certain circumstances, such as in the code for the class methods.

Another way of describing this situation is to say the name `Retort` has class scope, so the scope resolution operator is needed to qualify the name when it is used outside the class declaration and a class method.

To create an object, which is a particular example of a class, use the class name as if it were a type name:

```
Bozo bozetta;
```

This works because a class *is* a user-defined type.

A class member function, or method, is invoked by a class object. You do so by using the dot membership operator:

```
cout << Bozetta.Retort();
```

This invokes the `Retort()` member function, and whenever the code for that function refers to a particular data member, the function uses the value that member has in the `bozetta` object.

Class Constructors and Destructors

Meanwhile, there's more to be done with the `Stock` class. There are certain standard functions, called *constructors* and *destructors*, that you should normally provide for a class. Let's see why they are needed and how to write them.

One of C++'s aims is to make using class objects similar to using standard types. However, you can't yet initialize a `Stock` object the way you can an ordinary `int` or `struct`:

```
int year = 2001;                          // okay
struct thing
{
    char * pn;
```

```
     int m;
};
thing amabob = {"wodget", -23};                   //okay
Stock hot = {"Sukie's Autos, Inc.", 200, 50.25};   // NO!
```

The reason you can't initialize a Stock object this way is because the data parts have private access status, which means a program cannot access the data members directly. As you've seen, the only way a program can access the data members is through a member function. Therefore, you need to devise an appropriate member function if you're to succeed in initializing an object. (You could initialize a class object as just shown if you made the data members public instead of private, but making the data public goes against one of the main justifications for classes; that is, data hiding.)

In general, it's best that all objects be initialized when they are created. For example, consider the following code:

```
Stock gift;
gift.buy(10, 24.75);
```

With the current implementation of the Stock class, the gift object has no value for the company member. The class design assumes that the user calls acquire() before calling any other member functions, but there is no way to enforce that assumption. One way around this difficulty is to have objects initialized automatically when they are created. To accomplish this, C++ provides for special member functions, called *class constructors*, especially for constructing new objects and assigning values to their data members. More precisely, C++ provides a name for these member functions and a syntax for using them, and you provide the method definition. The name is the same as the class name. For example, a possible constructor for the Stock class is a member function called Stock(). The constructor prototype and heading have an interesting property—although the constructor has no return value, it's not declared type void. In fact, a constructor has no declared type.

Declaring and Defining Constructors

Let's build a Stock constructor. Because a Stock object has three values to be provided from the outside world, you should give the constructor three arguments. (The fourth value, the total_val member, is calculated from shares and share_val, so you don't have to provide it to the constructor.) Possibly, you just want to set the company member and set the other values to zero; this can be done with default arguments (see Chapter 8, "Adventures in Functions."). Thus, the prototype would look like this:

```
// constructor prototype with some default arguments
Stock(const char * co, int n = 0, double pr = 0.0);
```

The first argument is a pointer to the string that is used to initialize the company character array class members. The n and pr arguments provide values for the shares and share_val members. Note that there is no return type. The prototype goes in the public section of the class declaration.

Next, here's one possible definition for the constructor:

```
// constructor definition
Stock::Stock(const char * co, int n, double pr)
{
    strncpy(company, co, 29);
    company[29] = '\0';
    shares = n;
    share_val = pr;
    set_tot();
}
```

This is the same code that we used for the **acquire()** function. The difference is that a program automatically invokes the constructor when it declares an object.

	Caution

Often those new to constructors try to use the class member names as arguments to the constructor:

```
// NO!
Stock::Stock(const char * company, int shares, double share_val)
{
...
}
```

This is wrong. The constructor arguments don't represent the class members, they represent values that are assigned to the class members. Thus, they must have distinct names; otherwise you end up confusing code like this:

```
shares = shares;
```

One common coding practice to help avoid such confusion is to use an m_ prefix to identify data member names:

```
class Stock
{
private:
    char m_company[30];
    int m_shares;
    ....
```

Using a Constructor

C++ provides two ways to initialize an object by using the constructor. The first is to call the constructor explicitly:

```
Stock food = Stock("World Cabbage", 250, 1.25);
```

This sets the **company** member of the **food** object to the string **"World Cabbage"**, the **shares** member to **250**, and so on.

The second way is to call the constructor implicitly:

```
Stock garment("Furry Mason", 50, 2.5);
```

This more compact form is equivalent to the following explicit call:

```
Stock garment = Stock("Furry Mason", 50, 2.5));
```

C++ uses a class constructor whenever you create an object of that class, even when you use **new** for dynamic memory allocation. Here's how to use the constructor with **new**:

```
Stock *pstock = new Stock("Electroshock Games", 18, 19.0);
```

This statement creates a **Stock** object, initializes it to the values provided by the arguments, and assigns the address of the object to the **pstock** pointer. In this case, the object doesn't have a name, but you can use the pointer to manage the object. We put off further discussion of pointers to objects until Chapter 11.

Constructors are used differently from the other class methods. Normally, you use an object to invoke a method:

```
stock1.show();  // stock1 object invokes show() method
```

However, you can't use an object to invoke a constructor because, until the constructor finishes its work of making the object, there is no object. Rather than being invoked by an object, the constructor is used to create the object.

The Default Constructor

The *default constructor* is the constructor used to create an object when you don't provide explicit initialization values. That is, it's the constructor used for declarations like this:

```
Stock stock1;  // uses the default constructor
```

Hey, Listing 10.3 already did that! The reason this statement works is that if you fail to provide any constructors, C++ automatically supplies a default constructor. It's a default version of a default constructor, and it does nothing. For the **Stock** class, it would look like this:

```
Stock::Stock() { }
```

The net result is that the **stock1** object is created with its members uninitialized, just as

```
int x;
```

creates **x** without providing it a value. The fact that the default constructor has no arguments reflects the fact that no values appear in the declaration.

A curious fact about the default constructor is that the compiler provides one only if you don't define any constructors. Once you define any constructor for a class, the responsibility for providing a default constructor for that class passes from the compiler to you. If you provide a nondefault constructor, such as **Stock(const char * co, int n, double pr)** and don't provide your own version of a default constructor, then a declaration like

```
Stock stock1;  // not possible with current constructor
```

becomes an error. The reason for this behavior is that you might want to make it impossible to create uninitialized objects. If, however, you wish to create objects without explicit initialization, you must define your own default constructor. This is a constructor that takes no arguments. You can define a default constructor two ways. One is to provide default values for all the arguments to the existing constructor:

```
Stock(const char * co = "Error", int n = 0, double pr = 0.0);
```

The second is to use function overloading to define a second constructor, one that has no arguments:

```
Stock();
```

You can have only one default constructor, so be sure that you don't do both. (With early versions of C++, you could use only the second method for creating a default constructor.)

Actually, you usually should initialize objects in order to ensure that all members begin with known, reasonable values. Thus, the default constructor typically provides implicit initialization for all member values. Here, for example, is how you might define one for the **Stock** class:

```
Stock::Stock()
{
    strcpy(company, "no name");
    shares = 0;
    share_val = 0.0;
    total_val = 0.0;
}
```

Tip

When you design a class, you usually should provide a default constructor that implicitly initializes all class members.

After you've used either method (no arguments or default values for all arguments) to create the default constructor, you can declare object variables without initializing them explicitly:

```
Stock first;              // calls default constructor implicitly
Stock first = Stock();    // calls it explicitly
Stock *prelief = new Stock; // calls it implicitly
```

However, don't be misled by the implicit form of the nondefault constructor:

```
Stock first("Concrete Conglomerate");    // calls constructor
Stock second();                          // declares a function
Stock third;                             // calls default constructor
```

The first declaration calls the nondefault constructor, that is, the one that takes arguments. The second declaration states that **second()** is a function that returns a **Stock** object. When you implicitly call the default constructor, don't use parentheses.

Destructors

When you use a constructor to create an object, the program undertakes the responsibility of tracking that object until it expires. At that time, the program automatically calls a special member function bearing the formidable title of *destructor*. The destructor should clean up any debris, so it actually serves a constructive purpose. For example, if your constructor uses `new` to allocate memory, the destructor should use `delete` to free that memory. The `Stock` constructor doesn't do anything fancy like using `new`, so it doesn't really need a destructor. But it's a good idea to provide one anyway in case a future class revision needs one.

Like a constructor, the destructor has a special name: the class name preceded by a tilde (~). Thus, the destructor for the `Stock` class is called `~Stock()`. Also, like a constructor, a destructor can have no return value and has no declared type. Unlike the constructor, the destructor must have no arguments. Thus, the prototype for a `Stock` destructor must be this:

```
~Stock();
```

Because a `Stock` destructor has no vital duties, we can code it as a do-nothing function:

```
Stock::~Stock()
{
}
```

However, just so that you can see when the destructor is called, we'll code it this way:

```
Stock::~Stock()      // class destructor
{
    cout << "Bye, " << company << "!\n";
}
```

When should a destructor be called? This is a decision handled by the compiler; normally your code shouldn't explicitly call the destructor. If you create a static storage class object, its destructor is called automatically when the program terminates. If you create an automatic storage class object, as we have been doing, its destructor is called automatically when the program exits the block of code in which the object is defined. If the object is created by using `new`, it resides in heap memory, or the free store, and its destructor is called automatically when you use `delete` to free the memory. Finally, a program can create temporary objects to carry out certain operations; in that case, the program automatically calls the destructor for the object when it has finished using it.

Because the destructor is called automatically when a class object expires, there has to be a destructor. If you don't provide one, the compiler provides a default destructor that does nothing.

Improving the `Stock` Class

The next step is to incorporate the constructors and the destructor into the class and method definitions. This time we follow the usual C++ practice and organize the program into separate files. We place the class declaration in a header file called `stock1.h`. (As the name suggests, we have future revisions in mind.) The class methods go into a file called `stock1.cpp`. In general, the header file containing the class declaration and the source code file containing the methods definitions should have the same base name so that you can keep track of which files belong together. Using separate files for the class declaration and the member functions separates the abstract definition of the interface (the class declaration) from the details of implementation (the member function definitions). You could, for example, distribute the class declaration as a text header file but distribute the function definitions as compiled code. Finally, we place the program using these resources in a third file, which we call usestok1.cpp.

The Header File

Listing 10.4 shows the header file. It adds prototypes for the constructor and destructor functions to the original class declaration. Also, it dispenses with the acquire() function, which no longer is necessary now that the class has constructors. The file also uses the #ifndef technique of Chapter 9 to protect against multiple inclusion of this file.

LISTING 10.4   stock1.h

```
// stock1.h
#ifndef STOCK1_H_
#define STOCK1_H_

class Stock
{
private:
    char company[30];
    int shares;
    double share_val;
    double total_val;
    void set_tot() { total_val = shares * share_val; }
public:
    Stock();          // default constructor
    Stock(const char * co, int n = 0, double pr = 0.0);
    ~Stock();         // noisy destructor
    void buy(int num, double price);
    void sell(int num, double price);
    void update(double price);
    void show();
};

#endif
```

The Implementation File

Listing 10.5 provides the method definitions. It includes the stock1.h file in order to provide the class declaration. (Recall that enclosing the filename in double quotation marks instead of in brackets means the compiler searches for it at the same location your source files are found.) Also, the listing includes the system iostream and cstring files, because the methods use cin, cout, and strncpy(). This file adds the constructor and destructor method definitions to the prior methods. To help you see when these methods are called, they each display a message. This is not a usual feature of constructors and destructors, but it can help you better visualize how classes use them.

LISTING 10.5   stock1.cpp

```cpp
// stock1.cpp
#include <iostream>
#include <cstring>
using namespace std;
#include "stock1.h"

// constructors
Stock::Stock()          // default constructor
{
    cout << "Default constructor called\n";
    strcpy(company, "no name");
    shares = 0;
    share_val = 0.0;
    total_val = 0.0;
}

Stock::Stock(const char * co, int n, double pr)
{
    cout << "Constructor using " << co << " called\n";
    strncpy(company, co, 29);
    company[29] = '\0';
    shares = n;
    share_val = pr;
    set_tot();
}
// class destructor
Stock::~Stock()          // verbose class destructor
{
    cout << "Bye, " << company << "!\n";
}

// other methods
void Stock::buy(int num, double price)
{
    if (num < 0)
    {
        cerr << "Number of shares purchased can't be negative. "
             << "Transaction is aborted.\n";
    }
    else
    {
        shares += num;
        share_val = price;
        set_tot();
    }
}

void Stock::sell(int num, double price)
{
    if (num < 0)
    {
        cerr << "Number of shares sold can't be negative. "
```

LISTING 10.5 Continued

```
                    << "Transaction is aborted.\n";
    }
    else if (num > shares)
    {
        cerr << "You can't sell more than you have! "
             << "Transaction is aborted.\n";
    }
    else
    {
        shares -= num;
        share_val = price;
        set_tot();
    }
}

void Stock::update(double price)
{
    share_val = price;
    set_tot();
}

void Stock::show()
{
    cout << "Company: " << company
         << "  Shares: " << shares << '\n'
         << "  Share Price: $" << share_val
         << "  Total Worth: $" << total_val << '\n';
}
```

Compatibility Note

You might have to use string.h rather than cstring.

A Client File

Listing 10.6 provides a short program for testing the new methods. Like stock1.cpp, it includes the stock1.h file to provide the class declaration. The program demonstrates constructors and destructors. It also uses the same formatting commands invoked by Listing 10.3. To compile the complete program, use the techniques for multifile programs described in Chapters 1, "Getting Started," and 8.

LISTING 10.6 usestok1.cpp

```
// usestok1.cpp -- use the Stock class
#include <iostream>
using namespace std;
#include "stock1.h"
```

LISTING 10.6   Continued

```
int main()
{
    cout.precision(2);                               // #.## format
    cout.setf(ios_base::fixed, ios_base::floatfield);// #.## format
    cout.setf(ios_base::showpoint);                  // #.## format

    cout << "Using constructors to create new objects\n";
    Stock stock1("NanoSmart", 12, 20.0);             // syntax 1
    stock1.show();
    Stock stock2 = Stock ("Boffo Objects", 2, 2.0); // syntax 2
    stock2.show();

    cout << "Assigning stock1 to stock2:\n";
    stock2 = stock1;
    cout << "Listing stock1 and stock2:\n";
    stock1.show();
    stock2.show();

    cout << "Using a constructor to reset an object\n";
    stock1 = Stock("Nifty Foods", 10, 50.0);    // temp object
    cout << "Revised stock1:\n";
    stock1.show();
    cout << "Done\n";
    return 0;
}
```

Compatibility Note

You might have to use the older `ios::` instead of `ios_base::`.

Here's the output from one version of the compiled program:

```
Using constructors to create new objects
Constructor using NanoSmart called
Company: NanoSmart  Shares: 12
  Share Price: $20.00  Total Worth: $240.00
Constructor using Boffo Objects called
Company: Boffo Objects  Shares: 2
  Share Price: $2.00  Total Worth: $4.00
Assigning stock1 to stock2:
Listing stock1 and stock2:
Company: NanoSmart  Shares: 12
  Share Price: $20.00  Total Worth: $240.00
Company: NanoSmart  Shares: 12
  Share Price: $20.00  Total Worth: $240.00
Using a constructor to reset an object
Constructor using Nifty Foods called
Bye, Nifty Foods!
Revised stock1:
Company: Nifty Foods  Shares: 10
```

```
  Share Price: $50.00   Total Worth: $500.00
Done
Bye, NanoSmart!
Bye, Nifty Foods!
```

Some compilers may produce a program with this initial output, which has one additional line:

```
Using constructors to create new objects
Constructor using NanoSmart called
Company: NanoSmart  Shares: 12
  Share Price: $20.00  Total Worth: $240.00
Constructor using Boffo Objects called
Bye, Boffo Objects!                          [1a]additional line
Company: Boffo Objects  Shares: 2
  Share Price: $2.00  Total Worth: $4.00
...
```

The next section will explain the "Bye, Boffo Objects!" line.

Program Notes

The statement

```
Stock stock1("NanoSmart", 12, 20.0);
```

creates a Stock object called stock1 and initializes its data members to the indicated values:

```
Constructor using NanoSmart called
Company: NanoSmart  Shares: 12
```

The statement

```
Stock stock2 = Stock ("Boffo Objects", 2, 2.0);
```

uses the second variety of syntax to create and initialize an object called stock2. The C++ standard allows a compiler a couple of ways to execute this second syntax. One is to make it behave exactly like the first one:

```
Constructor using Boffo Objects called
Company: Boffo Objects  Shares: 2
```

The second way is to allow the call to the constructor to create a temporary object that is then copied to stock2. Then the temporary object is discarded. If the compiler uses this option, the destructor is called for the temporary object, producing this output instead:

```
Constructor using Boffo Objects called
Bye, Boffo Objects!
Company: Boffo Objects  Shares: 2
```

The compiler that produced this output disposed of the temporary object immediately, but it's possible a compiler might wait longer, in which case the destructor message would be displayed later.

The statement

```
stock2 = stock1;     // object assignment
```

illustrates that you can assign one object to another of the same type. As with structure assignment, class object assignment, by default, copies the members of one object to the other. In this case, the original contents of stock2 are overwritten.

Remember

When you assign one object to another of the same class, C++, by default, copies the contents of each data member of the source object to the corresponding data member of the target object.

You can use the constructor for more than initializing a new object. For example, the program has this statement in main():

```
stock1 = Stock("Nifty Foods", 10, 50.0);
```

The stock1 object already exists. Thus, instead of initializing stock1, this statement assigns new values to the object. It does so by having the constructor create a new, temporary object and then copy the contents of the new object to stock1. Then the program disposes of the temporary object, invoking the destructor as it does so.

```
Using a constructor to reset an object
Constructor using Nifty Foods called [1a]temporary object created
Bye, Nifty Foods!                    [1a]temporary object destroyed
Revised stock1:
Company: Nifty Foods   Shares: 10    [1a]data now copied to stock1
  Share Price: $50.00  Total Worth: $500.00
```

Some compilers might dispose of the temporary object later, delaying the destructor call.

Finally, at the end, the program displays this:

```
Done
Bye, NanoSmart!
Bye, Nifty Foods!
```

When the main() terminates, its local variables (stock1 and stock2) pass from our plane of existence. Because such automatic variables go on the stack, the last object created is the first deleted, and the first created is the last deleted. (Recall that "NanoSmart" originally was in stock1 but later was transferred to stock2, and stock1 was reset to "Nifty Foods".)

The output points out that there is a fundamental difference between the following two statements:

```
Stock stock2 = Stock ("Boffo Objects", 2, 2.0);
stock1 = Stock("Nifty Foods", 10, 50.0); // temporary object
```

The first statement is initialization; it creates an object with the indicated value; it may or may not create a temporary object. The second statement is assignment. It always creates a temporary object and then copies it to an existing object.

Tip

If you can set object values either by initialization or by assignment, choose initialization. It usually is more efficient.

const Member Functions

Consider the following code snippets:

```
const Stock land = Stock("Kludgehorn Properties");
land.show();
```

With current C++, the compiler should object to the second line. Why? Because the code for `show()` fails to guarantee that it won't modify the invoking object, which, as it is `const`, should not be altered. We've solved this kind of problem before by declaring a function's argument to be a `const` reference or a pointer to `const`. But here we have a syntax problem: The `show()` method doesn't have any arguments. Instead, the object it uses is provided implicitly by the method invocation. What's needed is a new syntax, one that says a function promises not to modify the invoking object. The C++ solution is to place the `const` keyword after the function parentheses. That is, the `show()` declaration should look like this:

```
void show() const;        // promises not to change invoking object
```

Similarly, the beginning of the function definition should look like this:

```
void stock::show() const   // promises not to change invoking object
```

Class functions declared and defined this way are called `const` member functions. Just as you should use `const` references and pointers as formal function arguments whenever appropriate, you should make class methods `const` whenever they don't modify the invoking object. We'll follow this rule from here on out.

Constructors and Destructors in Review

Now that we've gone through a few examples of constructors and destructors, you might want to pause and assimilate what has passed. To help you, here is a summary of these methods.

A constructor is a special class member function that's called whenever an object of that class is created. A class constructor has the same name as its class, but, through the miracle of function overloading, you can have more than one constructor with the same name, provided that each has its own signature, or argument list. Also, a constructor has no declared type. Usually, the constructor is used to initialize members of a class object. Your initialization should match the constructor's argument list. For example, suppose the `Bozo` class has the following prototype for a class constructor:

```
Bozo(char * fname, char * lname);    // constructor prototype
```

Then, you would use it to initialize new objects as follows:

```
Bozo bozetta = bozo("Bozetta", "Biggens");    // primary form
Bozo fufu("Fufu", "O'Dweeb");                  // short form
Bozo *pc = new Bozo("Popo", "Le Peu");         // dynamic object
```

If a constructor has just one argument, that constructor is invoked if you initialize an object to a value that has the same type as the constructor argument. For example, suppose you have this constructor prototype:

```
Bozo(int age);
```

Then, you can use any of the following forms to initialize an object:

```
Bozo dribble = bozo(44);    // primary form
Bozo roon(66);              // secondary form
Bozo tubby = 32;            // special form for one-argument constructors
```

Actually, the third example is a new point, not a review point, but it seemed like a nice time to tell you about it. Chapter 11 mentions a way to turn off this feature.

Remember

A constructor that you can use with a single argument allows you to use assignment syntax to initialize an object to a value:

```
Classname object = value;
```

The default constructor has no arguments, and it is used if you create an object without explicitly initializing it. If you fail to provide any constructors, the compiler defines a default constructor for you. Otherwise, you have to supply your own default constructor. It can have no arguments or else have default values for all arguments:

```
Bozo();        // default constructor prototype
Bistro(const char * s = "Chez Zero");    // default for Bistro class
```

The program uses the default constructor for uninitialized objects:

```
Bozo bubi;              // use default
Bozo *pb = new Bozo;    // use default
```

Just as a program invokes a constructor when an object is created, it invokes a destructor when an object is destroyed. You can have only one destructor per class. It has no return type, not even **void**; it has no arguments; and its name is the class name preceded by a tilde. The **Bozo** class destructor, for example, has the following prototype:

```
~Bozo();    // class destructor
```

Class destructors become necessary when class constructors use **new**.

Knowing Your Objects: The this Pointer

There's still more to be done with the **Stock** class. So far each class member function has dealt with but a single object, which has been the object that invokes it. Sometimes, however, a method might need to deal with two objects, and doing so may involve a curious C++ pointer called **this**. Let's see how this need can unfold.

Although the `Stock` class declaration displays data, it's deficient in analytic power. For example, by looking at the `show()` output you can tell which of your holdings has the greatest value, but the program can't tell because it can't access `total_val` directly. The most direct way of letting a program know about stored data is to provide methods to return values. Typically, you use inline code for this:

```
class Stock
{
private:
    ...
    double total_val;
    ...
public:
    double total() const { return total_val; }
    ...
};
```

This definition, in effect, makes `total_val` read-only memory as far as a direct program access is concerned.

By adding this function to the class declaration, you can let a program investigate a series of stocks to find the one with the greatest value. However, let's take a different approach, mainly so you can learn about the `this` pointer. The approach is to define a member function that looks at two `Stock` objects and returns a reference to the larger of the two. Attempting to implement this approach raises some interesting questions, and we look into them now.

First, how do you provide the member function with two objects to compare? Suppose, for example, you decide to name the method `topval()`. Then, the function call `stock1.topval()` accesses the data of the `stock1` object, whereas the message `stock2.topval()` accesses the data of the `stock2` object. If you want the method to compare two objects, you have to pass the second object as an argument. For efficiency, pass the argument by reference. That is, have the `topval()` method use a type `const Stock &` argument.

Second, how do you communicate the method's answer back to the calling program? The most direct way is to have the method return a reference to the object that has the larger total value. Thus, the comparison method should have the following prototype:

```
const Stock & topval(const Stock & s) const;
```

This function accesses one object implicitly and one object explicitly, and it returns a reference to one of those two objects. The `const` in the parentheses states that the function won't modify the explicitly accessed object, and the `const` that follows the parentheses states that the function won't modify the implicitly accessed object. Because the function returns a reference to one of the two `const` objects, the return type also has to be a `const` reference.

Suppose, then, that you want to compare `Stock` objects `stock1` and `stock2` and assign the one with the greater total value to the object `top`. You can use either of the following statements:

```
top = stock1.topval(stock2);
top = stock2.topval(stock1);
```

The first form accesses **stock1** implicitly and **stock2** explicitly, whereas the second accesses **stock1** explicitly and **stock2** implicitly. (See Figure 10.3.) Either way, the method compares the two objects and returns a reference to the one with the higher total value.

FIGURE 10.3

Accessing two objects with a member function.

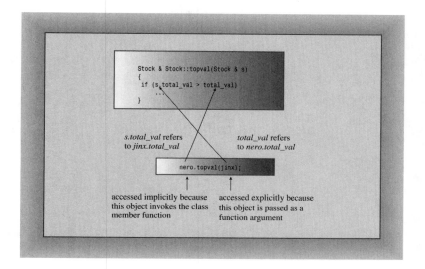

Actually, this notation is a bit confusing. It would be clearer if you could somehow use the relational operator > to compare the two objects. You can do so with operator overloading, which Chapter 11 discusses.

Meanwhile, there's still the implementation of **topval()** to attend to. That raises a slight problem. Here's a partial implementation that highlights the problem:

```
const Stock & Stock::topval(const Stock & s) const
{
    if (s.total_val > total_val)
        return s;                    // argument object
    else
        return ?????;                // invoking object
}
```

Here **s.total_val** is the total value for the object passed as an argument, and **total_val** is the total value for the object to which the message is sent. If **s.total_val** is greater than **total_val**, the function returns **s**. Otherwise, it returns the object used to evoke the method. (In OOP talk, that is the object to which the **topval** message is sent.) The problem is, what do you call that object? If you make the call **stock1.topval(stock2)**, then **s** is a reference for **stock2** (that is, an alias for **stock2**), but there is no alias for **stock1**.

The C++ solution to this problem is a special pointer called **this**. The **this** pointer points to the object used to invoke a member function. (Basically, **this** is passed as a hidden argument to the method.) Thus, the function call **stock1.topval(stock2)** sets **this** to the address of the **stock1** object and makes that pointer available to the **topval()** method. Similarly, the function call **stock2.topval(stock1)** sets **this** to the address of the **stock2** object. In general, all class methods have a **this** pointer set to the address of the object invoking the method. Indeed, **total_val** in **topval()** is just shorthand notation for **this->total_val**. (Recall from Chapter 4, "Compound Types," that you use the **->** operator to access structure members via a pointer. The same is true for class members.) (See Figure 10.4.)

FIGURE 10.4

this points to the invoking object.

The **this** pointer

Each member function, including constructors and destructors, has a **this** pointer. The special property of the **this** pointer is that it points to the invoking object. If a method needs to refer to the invoking object as a whole, it can use the expression ***this**. Using the **const** qualifier after the function argument parentheses qualifies **this** as being **const**; in that case, you can't use **this** to change the object's value.

What you want to return, however, is not **this**, because **this** is the address of the object. You want to return the object itself, and that is symbolized by ***this**. (Recall that applying the dereferencing operator ***** to a pointer yields the value to which the pointer points.) Now you can complete the method definition by using ***this** as an alias for the invoking object.

```
const Stock & Stock::topval(const Stock & s) const
{
    if (s.total_val > total_val)
        return s;              // argument object
```

```
        else
            return *this;        // invoking object
    }
```

The fact that the return type is a reference means the returned object is the invoking object itself rather than a copy passed by the return mechanism. Listing 10.7 shows the new header file.

LISTING 10.7   stock2.h

```
// stock2.h -- improved version
#ifndef STOCK2_H_
#define STOCK2_H_

class Stock
{
private:
    char company[30];
    int shares;
    double share_val;
    double total_val;
    void set_tot() { total_val = shares * share_val; }
public:
    Stock();         // default constructor
    Stock(const char * co, int n, double pr);
    ~Stock() {}      // do-nothing destructor
    void buy(int num, double price);
    void sell(int num, double price);
    void update(double price);
    void show() const;
    const Stock & topval(const Stock & s) const;
};

#endif
```

Listing 10.8 presents the revised class methods file. It includes the new **topval()** method. Also, now that you've seen how the constructors and destructors work, let's replace them with silent versions.

LISTING 10.8   stock2.cpp

```
// stock2.cpp -- improved version
#include <iostream>
#include <cstring>
using namespace std;
#include "stock2.h"

// constructors
Stock::Stock()           // default constructor
{
    strcpy(company, "no name");
```

LISTING 10.8   Continued

```cpp
    shares = 0;
    share_val = 0.0;
    total_val = 0.0;
}

Stock::Stock(const char * co, int n, double pr)
{
    strncpy(company, co, 29);
    company[29] = '\0';
    shares = n;
    share_val = pr;
    set_tot();
}

// other methods
void Stock::buy(int num, double price)
{
     if (num < 0)
     {
        cerr << "Number of shares purchased can't be negative. "
             << "Transaction is aborted.\n";
     }
     else
     {
        shares += num;
        share_val = price;
        set_tot();
     }
}

void Stock::sell(int num, double price)
{
    if (num < 0)
    {
        cerr << "Number of shares sold can't be negative. "
             << "Transaction is aborted.\n";
    }
    else if (num > shares)
    {
        cerr << "You can't sell more than you have! "
             << "Transaction is aborted.\n";
    }
    else
    {
        shares -= num;
        share_val = price;
        set_tot();
    }
}

void Stock::update(double price)
{
```

LISTING 10.8   Continued

```
        share_val = price;
        set_tot();
    }

    void Stock::show() const
    {
        cout << "Company: " << company
             << "  Shares: " << shares << '\n'
             << "  Share Price: $" << share_val
             << "  Total Worth: $" << total_val << '\n';
    }

    const Stock & Stock::topval(const Stock & s) const
    {
        if (s.total_val > total_val)
            return s;
        else
            return *this;
    }
```

Of course, we want to see if the **this** pointer works, and a natural place to use the new method is in a program with an array of objects, which leads us to the next topic.

An Array of Objects

Often, as with the **Stock** examples, you want to create several objects of the same class. You can create separate object variables, as the examples have done so far, but it might make more sense to create an array of objects. That might sound like a major leap into the unknown, but, in fact, you declare an array of objects the same way you would an array of any of the standard types:

```
Stock mystuff[4]; // creates an array of 4 Stock objects
```

Recall that a program always calls the default class constructor when it creates class objects that aren't explicitly initialized. This declaration requires either that the class explicitly defines no constructors at all, in which case the implicit do-nothing default constructor is used, or, as in this case, that an explicit default constructor is defined. Each element—**mystuff[0]**, **mystuff[1]**, and so on—is a **Stock** object and thus can be used with the **Stock** methods:

```
mystuff[0].update();       // apply update() to 1st element
mystuff[3].show();         // apply show() to 4th element
Stock tops = mystuff[2].topval(mystuff[1]);
                           // compare 3rd and 2nd elements
```

You can use a constructor to initialize the array elements. In that case, you have to call the constructor for each individual element:

```
const int STKS = 4;
Stock stocks[STKS] = {
    Stock("NanoSmart", 12.5, 20),
```

```
        Stock("Boffo Objects", 200, 2.0),
        Stock("Monolithic Obelisks", 130, 3.25),
        Stock("Fleep Enterprises", 60, 6.5)
        };
```

Here the code uses the standard form for initializing an array: a comma-separated list of values enclosed in braces. In this case, a call to the constructor method represents each value. If the class has more than one constructor, you can use different constructors for different elements:

```
const int STKS = 10;
Stock stocks[STKS] = {
        Stock("NanoSmart", 12.5, 20),
        Stock(),
        Stock("Monolithic Obelisks", 130, 3.25),
};
```

This initializes `stocks[0]` and `stocks[2]` using the `Stock(const char * co, int n, double pr)` constructor and `stocks[1]` using the `Stock()` constructor. Because this declaration only partially initializes the array, the remaining seven members are initialized using the default constructor.

The scheme for initializing an array of objects still initially uses the default constructor to create the array elements. Then, the constructors in the braces create temporary objects whose contents are copied to the vector. Thus, a class must have a default constructor if you want to create arrays of class objects.

Caution

If you want to create an array of class objects, the class must have a default constructor.

Listing 10.9 applies these principles to a short program that initializes four array elements, displays their contents, and tests the elements to find the one with the highest total value. Because `topval()` examines just two objects at a time, the program uses a `for` loop to examine the whole array. Use the header file and methods file shown in Listings 10.7 and 10.8, respectively.

LISTING 10.9   usestok2.cpp

```
// usestok2.cpp -- use the Stock class
// compile with stock2.cpp
#include <iostream>
using namespace std;
#include "stock2.h"

const int STKS = 4;
int main()
{
// create an array of initialized objects
    Stock stocks[STKS] = {
```

LISTING 10.9   Continued

```
        Stock("NanoSmart", 12, 20.0),
        Stock("Boffo Objects", 200, 2.0),
        Stock("Monolithic Obelisks", 130, 3.25),
        Stock("Fleep Enterprises", 60, 6.5)
        };

    cout.setf(ios_base::fixed, ios_base::floatfield);// #.## format
    cout.precision(2);                               // #.## format
    cout.setf(ios_base::showpoint);                  // #.## format

    cout << "Stock holdings:\n";
    int st;
    for (st = 0; st < STKS; st++)
        stocks[st].show();

    Stock top = stocks[0];
    for (st = 1; st < STKS; st++)
        top = top.topval(stocks[st]);
    cout << "\nMost valuable holding:\n";
    top.show();

    return 0;
}
```

Compatibility Note

You might have to use `stdlib.h` and `string.h` rather than `cstdlib` and `cstring`. Also, you might have to use the older `ios::` instead of `ios_base::`.

Here is the output:

```
Stock holdings:
Company: NanoSmart  Shares: 12
  Share Price: $20.00  Total Worth: $240.00
Company: Boffo Objects  Shares: 200
  Share Price: $2.00  Total Worth: $400.00
Company: Monolithic Obelisks  Shares: 130
  Share Price: $3.25  Total Worth: $422.50
Company: Fleep Enterprises  Shares: 60
  Share Price: $6.50  Total Worth: $390.00

Most valuable holding:
Company: Monolithic Obelisks  Shares: 130
  Share Price: $3.25  Total Worth: $422.50
```

One thing to note is how most of the work goes into designing the class. Once that's done, writing the program itself is rather simple.

Incidentally, knowing about the `this` pointer makes it easier to see how C++ works under the skin. For example, the C++ front end `cfront` converts C++ programs to C programs. To handle method definitions, all it has to do is convert a C++ method definition like

```
void Stock::show() const
{
    cout << "Company: " << company
         << "   Shares: " << shares << '\n'
         << "   Share Price: $" << share_val
         << "   Total Worth: $" << total_val << '\n';
}
```

to the following C-style definition:

```
void show(const Stock * this)
{
    cout << "Company: " << this->company
         << "   Shares: " << this->shares << '\n'
         << "   Share Price: $" << this->share_val
         << "   Total Worth: $" << this->total_val << '\n';
}
```

That is, it converts a `Stock::` qualifier to a function argument that is a pointer to `Stock` and then uses the pointer to access class members.

Similarly, the front end converts function calls like

```
top.show();
```

to:

```
show(&top);
```

In this fashion, the `this` pointer is assigned the address of the invoking object. (The actual details might be more involved.)

Class Scope

Chapter 9 discusses global, or file, scope and local, or block, scope. You can use a variable with global scope, recall, anywhere in the file that contains its definition, whereas a variable with local scope is local to the block that contains its definition. Function names, too, can have global scope, but they never have local scope. C++ classes introduce a new kind of scope: *class scope*. Class scope applies to names defined in a class, such as the names of class data members and class member functions. Items that have class scope are known within the class but not outside the class. Thus, you can use the same class member names in different classes without conflict: The `shares` member of the `Stock` class is a variable distinct from the `shares` member of a `JobRide` class. Also, class scope means you can't directly access members of a class from the outside world. This is true even for public function members. That is, to invoke a public member function, you have to use an object:

```
Stock sleeper("Exclusive Ore", 100, 0.25);  // create object
sleeper.show();        // use object to invoke a member function
show();                // invalid -- can't call method directly
```

Similarly, you have to use the scope resolution operator when you define member functions:

```
void Stock::update(double price)
{
    ...
}
```

In short, within a class declaration or a member function definition you can use an unadorned member name (the unqualified name), as when `sell()` calls the `set_tot()` member function. A constructor name is recognized when called because its name is the same as the class name. Otherwise, you must use the direct membership operator (.), the indirect membership operator (->), or the scope resolution operator (::), depending on the context, when you use a class member name. The following code fragment illustrates how identifiers with class scope can be accessed:

```
class Ik
{
private:
    int fuss;       // fuss has class scope
public:
    Ik(int f  = 9) {fuss = f; }  // fuss is in scope
    void ViewIk() const;         // ViewIk has class scope
};

void Ik::ViewIk() const    //Ik:: places ViewIk into scope
{
    cout << fuss << endl;  // fuss in scope within class methods
}
...
int main()
{
    Ik * pik = new Ik;
    Ik ee = Ik(8); // constructor in scope because has class name
    ee.ViewIk();    // class object brings ViewIk into scope
    pik->ViewIk(); // pointer-to-Ik brings ViewIk into scope
...
```

Class Scope Constants

Sometimes it would be nice to have symbolic constants of class scope. For example, the `Stock` class declaration used a literal 30 to specify the array size for `company`. Also, because the constant is the same for all objects, it would be nice to create a single constant shared by all objects. You might think the following would be a solution:

```
class Stock
{
private:
    const int Len = 30;    // declare a constant? FAILS
    char company[Len];
    ...
```

But this won't work because declaring a class describes what an object looks like but doesn't create an object. Hence, until you create an object, there's no place to store a value. There are, however, a couple of ways to achieve essentially the same desired effect.

First, you can declare an enumeration within a class. An enumeration given in a class declaration has class scope, so you can use enumerations to provide class scope symbolic names for integer constants. That is, you can start off the `Stock` declaration this way:

```
class Stock
{
private:
    enum {Len = 30};  // class-specific constant
    char company[Len];
    ...
```

Note that declaring an enumeration in this fashion does not create a class data member. That is, each individual object does not carry an enumeration in it. Rather, `Len` is just a symbolic name that the compiler replaces with **30** when it encounters it in code in class scope.

Because this uses the enumeration merely to create a symbolic constant with no intent of creating variables of the enumeration type, you needn't provide an enumeration tag. Incidentally, for many implementations, the `ios_base` class does something similar in its public section; that's the source of identifiers such as `ios_base::fixed`. Here **fixed** is typically an enumerator defined in the `ios_base` class.

More recently, C++ has introduced a second way of defining a constant within a class—using the keyword `static`:

```
class Stock
{
private:
    static const int Len = 30;    // declare a constant! WORKS
    char company[Len];
    ...
```

This creates a single constant called `Len` that is stored with other static variables rather than in an object. Thus, there is only one `Len` constant shared by all `Stock` objects. Chapter 12, "Classes and Dynamic Memory Allocation," looks further into static class members. You only can use this technique for declaring static constants with integral and enumeration values. You can't store a **double** constant this way.

An Abstract Data Type

The `Stock` class is pretty specific. Often, however, programmers define classes to represent more general concepts. For example, classes are a good way to implement what computer scientists describe as *abstract data types*, or ADTs, for short. As the name suggests, an ADT describes a data type in a general fashion, without bringing in language or implementation details. Consider, for example, the stack. The stack is a way of storing data in which data is always added to or deleted from the top of the stack. C++ programs, for example, use a stack to manage automatic variables. As new automatic variables are generated, they are added to the top of the stack. When they expire, they are removed from a stack.

Let's describe the properties of a stack in a general, abstract way. First, a stack holds several items. (That property makes it a *container*, an even more general abstraction.) Next, a stack is characterized by the operations you can perform on one.

- You can create an empty stack.
- You can add an item to the top of a stack (*push* an item).
- You can remove an item from the top (*pop* an item).
- You can check to see if the stack is full.
- You can check to see if the stack is empty.

You can match this description with a class declaration in which the public member functions provide an interface that represents the stack operations. The private data members take care of storing the stack data. The class concept is a nice match to the ADT approach.

The private section has to commit itself to how to hold the data. For example, you can use an ordinary array, a dynamically allocated array, or some more advanced data structure, such as a linked list. The public interface, however, should hide the exact representation. Instead, it should be expressed in general terms, such as creating a stack, pushing an item, and so on. Listing 10.10 shows one approach. It assumes that the `bool` type has been implemented. If it hasn't been on your system, you can use `int`, `0`, and `1` rather than `bool`, `false`, and `true`.

LISTING 10.10   stack.h

```
// stack.h -- class definition for the stack ADT
#ifndef STACK_H_
#define STACK_H_
typedef unsigned long Item;

class Stack
{
private:
    enum {MAX = 10};     // constant specific to class
    Item items[MAX];     // holds stack items
    int top;             // index for top stack item
public:
    Stack();
    bool isempty() const;
    bool isfull() const;
    // push() returns false if stack already is full, true otherwise
    bool push(const Item & item);   // add item to stack
    // pop() returns false if stack already is empty, true otherwise
    bool pop(Item & item);          // pop top into item
};
#endif
```

Compatibility Note

If your system hasn't implemented the `bool` type, you can use `int`, `0`, and `1` rather than `bool`, `false`, and `true`. Alternatively, your system might support an earlier, non-standard form, such as `boolean` or `Boolean`.

In this example, the private section shows that the stack is implemented by using an array, but the public section doesn't reveal that fact. Thus, you can replace the array with, say, a dynamic array without changing the class interface. That means changing the stack implementation doesn't require that you recode programs using the stack. You just recompile the stack code and link it with existing program code.

The interface is redundant in that `pop()` and `push()` return information about the stack status (full or empty) instead of being type `void`. This provides the programmer with a couple of options as to how to handle exceeding the stack limit or emptying the stack. He or she can use `isempty()` and `isfull()` to check before attempting to modify the stack, or else use the return value of `push()` and `pop()` to determine if the operation is successful.

Rather than define the stack in terms of some particular type, the class describes it in terms of a general `Item` type. In this case, the header file uses `typedef` to make `Item` the same as `unsigned long`. If you want, say, a stack of `double` or of a structure type, you can change the `typedef` and leave the class declaration and method definitions unaltered. Class templates (see Chapter 14, "Reusing Code in C++") provide a more powerful method for isolating the type of data stored from the class design.

Next, let's implement the class methods. Listing 10.11 shows one possibility.

LISTING 10.11   stack.cpp

```
// stack.cpp -- Stack member functions
#include "stack.h"
Stack::Stack()    // create an empty stack
{
    top = 0;
}

bool Stack::isempty() const
{
    return top == 0;
}

bool Stack::isfull() const
{
    return top == MAX;
}

bool Stack::push(const Item & item)
{
    if (top < MAX)
```

LISTING 10.11 Continued

```
        {
            items[top++] = item;
            return true;
        }
        else
            return false;
    }

    bool Stack::pop(Item & item)
    {
        if (top > 0)
        {
            item = items[--top];
            return true;
        }
        else
            return false;
    }
```

The default constructor guarantees that all stacks are created empty. The code for `pop()` and `push()` guarantees that the top of the stack is managed properly. Guarantees like this are one of the things that make object-oriented programming more reliable. Suppose, instead, you create a separate array to represent the stack and an independent variable to represent the index of the top. Then, it is your responsibility to get the code right each time you create a new stack. Without the protection that private data offers, there's always the possibility of making some program blunder that alters data unintentionally.

Let's test this stack. Listing 10.12 models the life of a clerk who processes purchase orders from the top of his in-basket, using the *LIFO* (last-in, first-out) approach of a stack.

LISTING 10.12 `stacker.cpp`

```
// stacker.cpp -- test Stack class
#include <iostream>
using namespace std;
#include <cctype>  // or ctype.h
#include "stack.h"
int main()
{
    Stack st; // create an empty stack
    char c;
    unsigned long po;
    cout << "Please enter A to add a purchase order,\n"
        << "P to process a PO, or Q to quit.\n";
    while (cin >> c && toupper(c) != 'Q')
    {
        while (cin.get() != '\n')
            continue;
        if (!isalpha(c))
        {
```

LISTING 10.12 *Continued*

```
            cout << '\a';
            continue;
        }
        switch(c)
        {
            case 'A':
            case 'a': cout << "Enter a PO number to add: ";
                      cin >> po;
                      if (st.isfull())
                          cout << "stack already full\n";
                      else
                          st.push(po);
                      break;
            case 'P':
            case 'p': if (st.isempty())
                          cout << "stack already empty\n";
                      else {
                          st.pop(po);
                          cout << "PO #" << po << " popped\n";
                      }
                      break;
        }
        cout << "Please enter A to add a purchase order,\n"
             << "P to process a PO, or Q to quit.\n";
    }
    cout << "Bye\n";
    return 0;
}
```

The little `while` loop that gets rid of the rest of the line isn't absolutely necessary here, but it will come in handy in a modification of this program in Chapter 14. Here's a sample run:

```
Please enter A to add a purchase order,
P to process a PO, or Q to quit.
A
Enter a PO number to add: 17885
Please enter A to add a purchase order,
P to process a PO, or Q to quit.
P
PO #17885 popped
Please enter A to add a purchase order,
P to process a PO, or Q to quit.
A
Enter a PO number to add: 17965
Please enter A to add a purchase order,
P to process a PO, or Q to quit.
A
Enter a PO number to add: 18002
Please enter A to add a purchase order,
P to process a PO, or Q to quit.
P
PO #18002 popped
```

```
Please enter A to add a purchase order,
P to process a PO, or Q to quit.
P
PO #17965 popped
Please enter A to add a purchase order,
P to process a PO, or Q to quit.
P
stack already empty
Please enter A to add a purchase order,
P to process a PO, or Q to quit.
Q
Bye
```

Real World Note: Minimizing Class Size with Selective Data Typing

When designing your classes, give careful thought to the data types used for your class members. Imprudent use of nonstandard or platform-dependent data types will inflate the size of your classes, thereby increasing the memory footprint, or working set, of your programs. This is both inefficient and considered bad form.

A classic example, which demonstrates this point, involves using a nonstandard BOOL typedef instead of the standard *bool* data type. Consider these simple classes:

```cpp
typedef int BOOL;
class BadClassDesign
{
  BOOL m_b1;
  BOOL m_b2;
  BOOL m_b3;
  BOOL m_b4;
  BOOL m_b5;
  BOOL m_b6;
};

class GoodClassDesign
{
  bool m_b1;
  bool m_b2;
  bool m_b3;
  bool m_b4;
  bool m_b5;
  bool m_b6;
};
```

Unlike bool, which usually occupies only one byte on most platforms, each BOOL typically will occupy four bytes. If the intent for the class members is to manage a true Boolean value of true or false, only one byte is actually required. For the typical Intel platform machine, class BadClassDesign occupies 24 bytes while class ClassGoodDesign uses only 6 bytes. That's a 400% savings!

You should always strive to use appropriate data types that minimize the amount of memory your program requires.

Summary

Object-oriented programming emphasizes how a program represents data. The first step toward solving a programming problem by using the OOP approach is describing the data in terms of its interface with the program, specifying how the data is used. Next, design a class that implements the interface. Typically, private data members store the information, whereas public member functions, also called methods, provide the only access to the data. The class combines data and methods into one unit, and the private aspect accomplishes data hiding.

Usually, you separate the class declaration into two parts, typically kept in separate files. The class declaration proper goes into a header file, with the methods represented by function prototypes. The source code that defines the member functions goes into a methods file. This approach separates the description of the interface from the details of the implementation. In principle, you only need to know the public class interface to use the class. Of course, you can look at the implementation (unless it's been supplied to you in compiled form only), but your program shouldn't rely on details of the implementation, such as knowing a particular value is stored as an `int`. As long as a program and a class communicate only through methods defining the interface, you are free to improve either part separately without worrying about unforeseen interactions.

A class is a user-defined type, and an object is an instance of a class. That means an object is a variable of that type or the equivalent of a variable, such as memory allocated by **new** according to the class specification. C++ tries to make user-defined types as similar as possible to standard types, so you can declare objects, pointers to objects, and arrays of objects. You can pass objects as arguments, return them as function return values, and assign one object to another of the same type. If you provide a constructor method, you can initialize objects when they are created. If you provide a destructor method, the program executes that method when the object expires.

Each object holds its own copies of the data portion of a class declaration, but they share the class methods. If `mr_object` is the name of a particular object and `try_me()` is a member function, you invoke the member function by using the dot membership operator: `mr_object.try_me()`. OOP terminology describes this function call as sending a `try_me` message to the `mr_object` object. Any reference to class data members in the `try_me()` method then applies to the data members of the `mr_object` object. Similarly, the function call `i_object.try_me()` accesses the data members of the `i_object` object.

If you want a member function to act on more than one object, you can pass additional objects to the method as arguments. If a method needs to refer explicitly to the object that evoked it, it can use the **this** pointer. The **this** pointer is set to the address of the evoking object, so ***this** is an alias for the object itself.

Classes are well matched to describing abstract data types (ADTs). The public member function interface provides the services described by an ADT, and the class's private section and the code for the class methods provide an implementation hidden from clients of the class.

Review Questions

1. What is a class?

2. How does a class accomplish abstraction, encapsulation, and data hiding?

3. What is the relationship between an object and a class?

4. In what way, aside from being functions, are class function members different from class data members?

5. Define a class to represent a bank account. Data members should include the depositor's name, the account number (use a string), and the balance. Member functions should allow the following:

   • Creating an object and initializing it.

   • Displaying the depositor's name, account number, and balance

   • Depositing an amount of money given by an argument

   • Withdrawing an amount of money given by an argument

   Just show the class declaration, not the method implementations. (Programming Exercise 1 provides you with an opportunity to write the implementation.)

6. When are class constructors called? When are class destructors called?

7. Provide code for a constructor for the bank account class of question 5.

8. What is a default constructor and what's the advantage of having one?

9. Modify the `Stock` class (the version in `stock2.h`) so that it has member functions that return the values of the individual data members. Note: A member that returns the company name should not provide a weapon for altering the array. That is, it can't simply return a `char *`. It could return a `const` pointer, or it could return a pointer to a copy of the array, manufactured by using `new`.

10. What are `this` and `*this`?

Programming Exercises

1. Provide method definitions for the class described in review question 5 and write a short program illustrating all the features.

2. Do programming exercise 1 from Chapter 9, but replace the code shown there with an appropriate `golf` class declaration. Replace `setgolf(golf &, const char *, int)` with a constructor with the appropriate argument for providing initial values. Retain the interactive version of `setgolf()`, but implement it using the constructor. (For example, for the code for `setgolf()`, obtain the data, pass the data to the constructor to create a temporary object, and assign the temporary object to the invoking object, which would be `*this`.)

3. Do programming exercise 2 from Chapter 9, but convert the **Sales** structure and its associated functions to a class and its methods. Replace the **setSales(Sales &, double [], int)** function with a constructor. Implement the interactive **setSales(Sales &)** method using the constructor. Keep the class within the namespace **SALES**.

4. Consider the following structure declaration:

```
struct customer {
    char fullname[35];
    double payment;
};
```

Write a program that adds and removes customer structures from a stack, represented by a class declaration. Each time a customer is removed, his payment is added to a running total and the running total is reported. Note: You should be able to use the **Stack** class unaltered; just change the **typedef** declaration so that **Item** is type **customer** instead of **unsigned long**.

5. Here's a class declaration:

```
class Move
{
private:
    double x;
    double y;
public:
    Move(double a = 0, double b = 0);    // sets x, y to a, b
    showmove() const;                    // shows current x, y values
    Move add(const Move & m) const;
// this function adds x of m to x of invoking object to get new x,
// adds y of m to y of invoking object to get new y, creates a new
// move object initialized to new x, y values and returns it
    reset(double a = 0, double b = 0);   // resets x,y to a, b
};
```

Supply member function definitions and a program that exercises the class.

6. A Betelgeusean plorg has these properties:

Data

A plorg has a name of no more than 19 letters.

A plorg has a contentment index (CI), which is an integer.

Operations

A new plorg starts out with a name and a CI value of 50.

A plorg's CI can change.

A plorg can report its name and CI.

The default plorg has a name of **"Plorga"**.

Write a `Plorg` class declaration (data members and member function prototypes) that represents a plorg. Write the function definitions for the member functions. Write a short program that demonstrates all the features of the `Plorg` class.

7. We can describe a simple list as follows:

- A simple list can hold zero or more items of some particular type.
- You can create an empty list.
- You can add items to a list.
- You can determine if the list is empty.
- You can determine if the list is full.
- You can visit each item in a list and perform some action upon it.

As you can see, this list really is simple, not allowing insertion or deletion, for example. The main use of such a list is to provide a simplified programming project. In this case, create a class matching this description. You can implement the list as an array or, if you're familiar with the data type, as a linked list. But the public interface should not depend on your choice. That is, the public interface should not have array indices, pointers to nodes, and so on. It should be expressed in the general concepts of creating a list, adding an item to the list, and so on. The usual way to handle visiting each item and performing an action is to use a function that takes a function pointer as an argument:

```
void visit(void (*pf)(Item &));
```

Here `pf` points to a function (not a member function) that takes a reference to `Item` argument, where `Item` is the type for items in the list. The `visit()` function applies this function to each item in the list.

You also should provide a short program utilizing your design.

CHAPTER 11

WORKING WITH CLASSES

You will learn about the following in this chapter:

- Operator overloading
- Friend functions
- Overloading the << operator for output
- State members

- Using rand() to generate random values
- Automatic conversions and type casts for classes
- Class conversion functions

C++ classes are feature-rich, complex, and powerful. In Chapter 9, "Memory Models and Namespaces," you began a journey toward object-oriented programming by learning to define and use a simple class. You saw how a class defines a data type by defining the type of data to be used to represent an object and by also defining, through member functions, the operations that can be performed with that data. And you learned about two special member functions, the constructor and the destructor, that manage creating and discarding objects made to a class specification. This chapter will take you a few steps further in the exploration of class properties, concentrating on class design techniques rather than on general principles. You'll probably find some of the features covered here straightforward, some a bit more subtle. To best understand these new features, you should try the examples and experiment with them. What happens if I use a regular argument instead of a reference argument for this function? What happens if I leave something out of a destructor? Don't be afraid to make mistakes; usually you can learn more from unraveling an error than by doing something correctly, but by rote. (However, don't assume that a maelstrom of mistakes inevitably leads to incredible insight.) In the end, you'll be rewarded with a fuller understanding of how C++ works and of what C++ can do for you.

This chapter starts with operator overloading, which lets you use standard C++ operators such as = and + with class objects. Then it examines friends, the C++ mechanism for letting non-member functions access private data. Finally, it looks at how you can instruct C++ to perform automatic type conversions with classes. As you go through this and the next chapter, you'll gain a greater appreciation of the roles class constructors and class destructors play. Also, you'll see some of the stages you may go through as you develop and improve a class design.

One difficulty with learning C++, at least by the time you've gotten this far into the subject, is that there is an awful lot to remember. And it's unreasonable to expect to remember it all until you've logged enough experience on which to hang your memories. Learning C++, in this respect, is like learning a feature-laden word processor or spreadsheet program. No one feature is that daunting, but, in practice, most people really know well only those features they use regularly, such as searching for text or italicizing. You may recall having read somewhere how to generate alternative characters or create a table of contents, but those skills probably won't be part of your daily repertoire until you find yourself in a situation in which you need them frequently. Probably the best approach to absorbing the wealth of material in this chapter is to begin incorporating just some of these new features into your own C++ programming. As your experiences enhance your understanding and appreciation of these features, begin adding other C++ features. As Bjarne Stroustrup, the creator of C++, suggested at a C++ conference for professional programmers: "Ease yourself into the language. Don't feel you have to use all of the features, and don't try to use them all on the first day."

Operator Overloading

Let's look at a technique for giving object operations a prettier look. *Operator overloading* is another example of C++ polymorphism. In Chapter 8, "Adventures in Functions," you saw how C++ enables you to define several functions having the same name as long as they have different signatures (argument lists). That was function overloading, or functional polymorphism. Its purpose is to let you use the same function name for the same basic operation even though you apply the operation to different data types. (Imagine how awkward English would be if you had to use a different verb form for each different type of object—lift_lft your left foot, but lift_sp your spoon.) Operator overloading extends the overloading concept to operators, letting you assign multiple meanings to C++ operators. Actually, many C++ (and C) operators already are overloaded. For example, the * operator, when applied to an address, yields the value stored at that address. But applying * to two numbers yields the product of the values. C++ uses the number and type of operands to decide which action to take.

C++ lets you extend operator overloading to user-defined types, permitting you, say, to use the + symbol to add two objects. Again, the compiler will use the number and type of operands to determine which definition of addition to use. Overloaded operators often can make code look more natural. For example, a common computing task is adding two arrays. Usually, this winds up looking like the following `for` loop:

```
for (int i = 0; i < 20; i++)
    evening[i] = sam[i] + janet[i];  // add element by element
```

But in C++, you can define a class that represents arrays and that overloads the + operator so that you can do this:

```
evening = sam + janet;                  // add two array objects
```

This simple addition notation conceals the mechanics and emphasizes what is essential, and that is another OOP goal.

To overload an operator, you use a special function form called an *operator function*. An operator function has the form:

```
operatorop(argument-list)
```

where *op* is the symbol for the operator being overloaded. That is, **operator+()** overloads the + operator (*op* is +) and **operator*()** overloads the * operator (*op* is *). The *op* has to be a valid C++ operator; you can't just make up a new symbol. For example, you can't have an **operator@()** function because C++ has no @ operator. But the **operator[]()** function would overload the [] operator because [] is the array-indexing operator. Suppose, for example, that you have a **Salesperson** class for which you define an **operator+()** member function to overload the + operator so that it adds sales figures of one salesperson object to another. Then, if **district2**, **sid**, and **sara** all are objects of the **Salesperson** class, you can write this equation:

```
district2 = sid + sara;
```

The compiler, recognizing the operands as belonging to the **Salesperson** class, will replace the operator with the corresponding operator function:

```
district2 = sid.operator+(sara);
```

The function will then use the **sid** object implicitly (because it invoked the method) and the **sara** object explicitly (because it's passed as an argument) to calculate the sum, which it then returns. Of course, the nice part is that you can use the nifty + operator notation instead of the clunky function notation.

C++ imposes some restrictions on operator overloading, but they're easier to understand after you've seen how overloading works. So let's develop a few examples first to clarify the process and then discuss the limitations.

Time on Our Hands

If you worked on the Priggs account 2 hours 35 minutes in the morning and 2 hours 40 minutes in the afternoon, how long did you work altogether on the account? Here's an example where the concept of addition makes sense, but the units that you are adding (a mixture of hours and minutes) doesn't match a built-in type. Chapter 7, "Functions—C++'s Programming Modules," handled a similar case by defining a **travel_time** structure and a **sum()** function for adding such structures. Now we can generalize that to a **Time** class using a method to handle addition. Let's begin with an ordinary method, called **Sum()**, then see how to convert it to an overloaded operator. Listing 11.1 shows the class declaration.

LISTING 11.1 mytime0.h

```
// mytime0.h -- Time class before operator overloading
#ifndef MYTIME0_H_
#define MYTIME0_H_
#include <iostream>
using namespace std;
```

LISTING 11.1   Continued

```
class Time
{
private:
    int hours;
    int minutes;
public:
    Time();
    Time(int h, int m = 0);
    void AddMin(int m);
    void AddHr(int h);
    void Reset(int h = 0, int m = 0);
    Time Sum(const Time & t) const;
    void Show() const;
};
#endif
```

The class provides methods for adjusting and resetting times, for displaying time values, and for adding two times. Listing 11.2 shows the methods definitions; note how the `AddMin()` and `Sum()` methods use integer division and the modulus operator to adjust the `minutes` and `hours` values when the total number of minutes exceeds 59.

LISTING 11.2   `mytime0.cpp`

```
// mytime0.cpp  -- implement Time methods
#include "mytime0.h"

Time::Time()
{
    hours = minutes = 0;
}

Time::Time(int h, int m )
{
    hours = h;
    minutes = m;
}

void Time::AddMin(int m)
{
    minutes += m;
    hours += minutes / 60;
    minutes %= 60;
}
void Time::AddHr(int h)
{
    hours += h;
}

void Time::Reset(int h, int m)
{
```

LISTING 11.2   Continued

```
        hours = h;
        minutes = m;
}

Time Time::Sum(const Time & t) const
{
        Time sum;
        sum.minutes = minutes + t.minutes;
        sum.hours = hours + t.hours + sum.minutes / 60;
        sum.minutes %= 60;
        return sum;
}

void Time::Show() const
{
        cout << hours << " hours, " << minutes << " minutes";
        cout << '\n';
}
```

Consider the code for the `Sum()` function. Note that the argument is a reference but that the return type is not a reference. The reason for making the argument a reference is efficiency. The code would produce the same results if the `Time` object were passed by value, but it's usually faster and more memory-efficient to just pass a reference.

The return value, however, cannot be a reference. The reason is that the function creates a new `Time` object (`sum`) representing the sum of the other two `Time` objects. Returning the object, as this code does, creates a copy of the object that the calling function can use. If the return type were `Time &`, however, the reference would be to the `sum` object. But the `sum` object is a local variable and is destroyed when the function terminates, so the reference would be a reference to a nonexistent object. Using a `Time` return type, however, means the program constructs a *copy* of `sum` before destroying it, and the calling function gets the copy.

Caution

Don't return a reference to a local variable or other temporary object.

Finally, Listing 11.3 tests the time summation part of the class.

LISTING 11.3   usetime0.cpp

```
// usetime0.cpp -- use first draft of Time class
// compile usetime0.cpp and mytime0.cpp together
#include <iostream>
#include "mytime0.h"
using namespace std;

int main()
{
```

LISTING 11.3   Continued

```
        Time A;
        Time B(5, 40);
        Time C(2, 55);

        cout << "A = ";
        A.Show();
        cout << "B = ";
        B.Show();
        cout << "C = ";
        C.Show();

        A = B.Sum(C);
        cout << "B.Sum(C) = ";
        A.Show();
        return 0;
    }
```

Here is the output:

```
A = 0 hours, 0 minutes
B = 5 hours, 40 minutes
C = 2 hours, 55 minutes
B.Sum(C) = 8 hours, 35 minutes
```

Adding an Addition Operator

It's a simple matter to convert the Time class to using an overloaded addition operator. Just change the name of Sum() to the odder-looking name operator+(). That's right; just append the operator symbol (+, in this case) to end of operator and use the result as a method name. This is one place where you can use a character other than a letter, digit, or underscore in an identifier name. Listings 11.4 and 11.5 reflect this small change.

LISTING 11.4   mytime1.h

```
// mytime1.h -- Time class after operator overloading
#ifndef MYTIME1_H_
#define MYTIME1_H_
#include <iostream>
using namespace std;

class Time
{
private:
    int hours;
    int minutes;
public:
    Time();
    Time(int h, int m = 0);
    void AddMin(int m);
    void AddHr(int h);
```

LISTING 11.4   Continued

```
        void Reset(int h = 0, int m = 0);
        Time operator+(const Time & t) const;
        void Show() const;
};
#endif
```

LISTING 11.5   mytime1.cpp

```
// mytime1.cpp  -- implement Time methods
#include "mytime1.h"

Time::Time()
{
    hours = minutes = 0;
}

Time::Time(int h, int m )
{
    hours = h;
    minutes = m;
}

void Time::AddMin(int m)
{
    minutes += m;
    hours += minutes / 60;
    minutes %= 60;
}
void Time::AddHr(int h)
{
    hours += h;
}

void Time::Reset(int h, int m)
{
    hours = h;
    minutes = m;
}

Time Time::operator+(const Time & t) const
{
    Time sum;
    sum.minutes = minutes + t.minutes;
    sum.hours = hours + t.hours + sum.minutes / 60;
    sum.minutes %= 60;
    return sum;
}

void Time::Show() const
{
```

LISTING 11.5   Continued

```
            cout << hours << " hours, " << minutes << " minutes";
            cout << '\n';
}
```

Like Sum(), operator+() is invoked by a Time object, takes a second Time object as an argument, and returns a Time object. Thus, you can invoke the operator+() method using the same syntax that Sum() used:

```
A = B.operator+(C);    // function notation
```

But naming the method operator+() also lets you use operator notation:

```
A = B + C;                 // operator notation
```

Either notation invokes the operator+() method. Note that with the operator notation, the object to the left of the operator (B, in this case) is the invoking object, and the object to the right (C, in this case) is the one passed as an argument. Listing 11.6 illustrates this point.

LISTING 11.6   usetime1.cpp

```
// usetime1.cpp -- use second draft of Time class
// compile usetime1.cpp and mytime1.cpp together
#include <iostream>
#include "mytime1.h"
using namespace std;

int main()
{
    Time A;
    Time B(5, 40);
    Time C(2, 55);

    cout << "A = ";
    A.Show();
    cout << "B = ";
    B.Show();
    cout << "C = ";
    C.Show();

    A = B.operator+(C);  // function notation
    cout << "A = B.operator+(C) = ";
    A.Show();
    B = A + C;                  // operator notation
    cout << "A + C = ";
    B.Show();       return 0;
}
```

Here is the output:

```
A = 0 hours, 0 minutes
B = 5 hours, 40 minutes
C = 2 hours, 55 minutes
```

```
A = B.operator+(C) = 8 hours, 35 minutes
A + C = 11 hours, 30 minutes
```

In short, the name of the `operator+()` function allows it to be invoked using either function notation or operator notation. The compiler uses the operand types to figure out what to do:

```
int a, b, c;
Time A, B, C;
c = a + b;      // use int addition
C = A + B;      // use addition as defined for Time objects
```

Overloading Restrictions

Most C++ operators (see Table 11.1) can be overloaded in the same manner. Overloaded operators (with some exceptions) don't necessarily have to be member functions. However, at least one of the operands has to be a user-defined type. Let's take a closer look at the limits C++ imposes on user-defined operator overloading:

1. The overloaded operator must have at least one operand that is a user-defined type. This prevents you from overloading operators for the standard types. Thus, you can't redefine the minus operator (-) so that it yields the sum of two **double** values instead of their difference. This restriction preserves program sanity, although it may hinder creative accounting.

2. You can't use an operator in a manner that violates the syntax rules for the original operator. For example, you can't overload the modulus operator (%) so that it can be used with a single operand:

```
int x;
Time shiva;
% x;        // invalid for modulus operator
% shiva;    // invalid for overloaded operator
```

Similarly, you can't alter operator precedence. So if you overload the addition operator to let you add two classes, the new operator has the same precedence as ordinary addition.

3. You can't create new operator symbols. For example, you can't define an `operator**()` function to denote exponentiation.

4. You cannot overload the following operators:

sizeof	The sizeof operator
.	Membership operator
.*	Pointer-to-member operator
::	Scope resolution operator
?:	Conditional operator
typeid	An RTTI operator

sizeof	The sizeof operator
const_cast	A type cast operator
dynamic_cast	A type cast operator
reinterpret_cast	A type cast operator
static_cast	A type cast operator

This still leaves all the operators in Table 11.1 available for overloading.

5. Most of the operators in Table 11.1 can be overloaded by using either member or non-member functions. However, you can use *only* member functions to overload the following operators:

=	Assignment operator
()	Function call operator
[]	Subscripting operator
->	Class member access by pointer operator

Note

We have not covered, nor will we cover, every operator mentioned in the list of restrictions or in Table 11.1. However, Appendix E, "Other Operators," does summarize those operators not covered in the main body of this text.

TABLE 11.1 Operators That Can Be Overloaded

+	-	*	/	%	^ &	|
~= *=	!	=	<	>	+=	-=
/= >>=	%=	^=	&=	|=	<<	>>
<<= ++	==	!=	<=	>=	&&	||
— delete	,	->*	->	()	[]	new
new []	delete []					

In addition to these formal restrictions, you should use sensible restraint in overloading operators. For example, don't overload the * operator so that it swaps the data members of two Time
objects. Nothing in the notation would suggest what the operator did, so it would be better to
define a class method with an explanatory name like Swap().

More Overloaded Operators

Some other operations make sense for the Time class. For example, you might want to subtract
one time from another or multiply a time by a factor. This suggests overloading the subtraction
and multiplication operators. The technique is the same as for the addition operator—create
operator-() and operator*() methods. That is, add the following prototypes to the class
declaration:

```
Time operator-(const Time & t) const;
Time operator*(double n) const;
```

Listing 11.7 shows the new header file.

LISTING 11.7   mytime2.h

```
// mytime2.h -- Time class after operator overloading
#ifndef MYTIME2_H_
#define MYTIME2_H_
#include <iostream>
using namespace std;

class Time
{
private:
    int hours;
    int minutes;
public:
    Time();
    Time(int h, int m = 0);
    void AddMin(int m);
    void AddHr(int h);
    void Reset(int h = 0, int m = 0);
    Time operator+(const Time & t) const;
    Time operator-(const Time & t) const;
    Time operator*(double n) const;
    void Show() const;
};
#endif.
```

Then add definitions for the new methods to the implementation file, as shown in
Listing 11.8.

LISTING 11.8   `mytime2.cpp`

```cpp
// mytime2.cpp  -- implement Time methods
#include "mytime2.h"

Time::Time()
{
    hours = minutes = 0;
}

Time::Time(int h, int m )
{
    hours = h;
    minutes = m;
}

void Time::AddMin(int m)
{
    minutes += m;
    hours += minutes / 60;
    minutes %= 60;
}
void Time::AddHr(int h)
{
    hours += h;
}

void Time::Reset(int h, int m)
{
    hours = h;
    minutes = m;
}

Time Time::operator+(const Time & t) const
{
    Time sum;
    sum.minutes = minutes + t.minutes;
    sum.hours = hours + t.hours + sum.minutes / 60;
    sum.minutes %= 60;
    return sum;
}

Time Time::operator-(const Time & t) const
{
    Time diff;
    int tot1, tot2;
    tot1 = t.minutes + 60 * t.hours;
    tot2 = minutes + 60 * hours;
    diff.minutes = (tot2 - tot1) % 60;
    diff.hours = (tot2 - tot1) / 60;
    return diff;
}
```

LISTING 11.8   Continued

```cpp
Time Time::operator*(double mult) const
{
    Time result;
    long totalminutes = hours * mult * 60 + minutes * mult;
    result.hours = totalminutes / 60;
    result.minutes = totalminutes % 60;
    return result;
}

void Time::Show() const
{
    cout << hours << " hours, " << minutes << " minutes";
    cout << '\n';
}
```

With these changes made, you can test the new definitions with the code shown in Listing 11.9.

LISTING 11.9   usetime2.cpp

```cpp
// usetime2.cpp -- use third draft of Time class
// compile usetime2.cpp and mytime2.cpp together
#include <iostream>
#include "mytime2.h"
using namespace std;

int main()
{
    Time A;
    Time B(5, 40);
    Time C(2, 55);

    cout << "A = ";
    A.Show();
    cout << "B = ";
    B.Show();
    cout << "C = ";
    C.Show();

    A = B + C;      // operator+()
    cout << "B + C = ";
    A.Show();
    A = B - C;      // operator-()
    cout << "B - C = ";
    A.Show();
    A = B * 2.75;   // operator*()
    cout << "B * 2.75 = ";
    A.Show();
    return 0;
}
```

Here is the output:

```
A = 0 hours, 0 minutes
B = 5 hours, 40 minutes
C = 2 hours, 55 minutes
B + C = 8 hours, 35 minutes
B - C = 2 hours, 45 minutes
B * 2.75 = 15 hours, 35 minutes
```

Introducing Friends

As you've seen, C++ controls access to the private portions of a class object. Usually public class methods serve as the only access, but sometimes this restriction is too rigid to fit particular programming problems. In such cases, C++ provides another form of access, the *friend*. Friends come in three varieties:

- Friend functions

- Friend classes

- Friend member functions

By making a function a friend to a class, you allow the function the same access privileges that a member function of the class has. We'll look into friend functions now, leaving the other two varieties to Chapter 15, "Friends, Exceptions, and More."

Before seeing how to make friends, let's look into why they might be needed. Often, overloading a binary operator (one with two arguments) for a class generates a need for friends. Multiplying a `Time` object by a real number provides just such a situation, so let's study that case.

In the `Time` class example, the overloaded multiplication operator is different from the other two overloaded operators in that it combines two different types. That is, the addition and subtraction operators each combine two `Time` values, but the multiplication operator combines a `Time` value with a `double` value. This restricts how the operator can be used. Remember, the left operand is the invoking object. That is,

```
A = B * 2.75;
```

translates to the following member function call:

```
A = B.operator*(2.75);
```

But what about the following statement?

```
A = 2.75 * B;     // cannot correspond to a member function
```

Conceptually, `2.75 * B` should be the same as `B * 2.75`, but the first expression cannot correspond to a member function because `2.75` is not a type `Time` object. Remember, the left operand is the invoking object, but `2.75` is not an object. So the compiler cannot replace the expression with a member function call.

One way around this difficulty is to tell everyone (and to remember yourself) that you can only write `B * 2.75` but never write `2.75 * B`. This is a programmer-friendly, user-beware solution, and that's not what OOP is about.

However, there is another possibility—a nonmember function. (Remember, most operators can be overloaded using either member or nonmember functions.) A nonmember function is not invoked by an object; instead, any values it uses, including objects, are explicit arguments. Thus, the compiler could match the expression

```
A = 2.75 * B;       // cannot correspond to a member function
```

to the following nonmember function call:

```
A = operator*(2.75, B);
```

The function would have this prototype:

```
Time operator*(double m, const Time & t);
```

With the nonmember overloaded operator function, the left operand of an operator expression corresponds to the first argument of the operator function, and the right operand corresponds to the second argument. Meanwhile, the original member function will handle operands in the opposite order, that is, a `Time` value times a `double` value.

Using a nonmember function solves the problem of getting the operands in the desired order (first `double`, then `Time`), but it raises a new problem: Nonmember functions can't directly access private data in a class. Well, at least ordinary nonmember functions lack access. But there is a special category of nonmember function called a *friend* that can access private members of a class.

Creating Friends

The first step toward creating a friend function is to place a prototype in the class declaration, prefixing the declaration with the keyword `friend`:

```
friend Time operator*(double m, const Time & t);  // goes in class declaration
```

This prototype has two implications:

- Although the `operator*()` function is declared in the class declaration, it is not a member function.

- Although the `operator*()` function is not a member function, it has the same access rights as a member function.

The second step is to write the function definition. Since it is not a member function, don't use the `Time::` qualifier. Also, don't use the `friend` keyword in the definition:

```
Time operator*(double m, const Time & t)  // friend not used in definition
{
    Time result;
    long totalminutes = t.hours * mult * 60 +t. minutes * mult;
    result.hours = totalminutes / 60;
```

```
    result.minutes = totalminutes % 60;
    return result;
}
```

With this declaration and definition, the statement

```
A = 2.75 * B;
```

translates to

```
A = operator*(2.75, B);
```

and invokes the nonmember friend function we just defined.

In short, a friend function to a class is a nonmember function that has the same access rights as a member function.

Are Friends Unfaithful to OOP?

At first glance, it might seem that friends violate the OOP principle of data hiding, for the friend mechanism allows nonmember functions to access private data. However, that's an overly narrow view. Instead, think of friend functions as part of an extended interface for a class. For example, from a conceptual point of view, multiplying a `double` times a `Time` value is pretty much the same as multiplying a `Time` value times a `double`. That the first requires a friend function whereas the second can be done with a member function is the result of C++ syntax, not of a deep conceptual difference. By using both a friend function and a class method, you can express either operation with the same user interface. Also, keep in mind that only a class declaration can decide which functions are friends, so the class declaration still controls which functions access private data. In short, class methods and friends are just two different mechanisms for expressing a class interface.

Actually, this particular friend function can be written as non-friend by altering the definition as follows:

```
Time operator*(double m, const Time & t)
{
    return t * m;     // use a member function
}
```

The original version accessed `t.minutes` and `t.hours` explicitly, so it had to be a friend. This version only uses the `Time` object `t` as a whole, letting a member function handle the private values, so this version doesn't have to be a friend. Nonetheless, it's still a good idea to make this version a friend, too. Most importantly, it ties the function in as part of the official class interface. Second, if you later find a need for the function to access private data directly, you only have to change the function definition and not the class prototype.

Tip

If you want to overload an operator for a class and you want to use the operator with a nonclass term as the first operand, you can use a friend function to reverse the operand order.

A Common Kind of Friend: Overloading the << Operator

One of the more useful features of classes is that you can overload the << operator so that you can use it with **cout** to display an object's contents. In some ways, this overloading is a bit trickier than the earlier examples, so we'll develop it in two steps instead of in one.

Suppose **trip** is a **Time** object. To display **Time** values, we've been using **Show ()**. Wouldn't it be nice, however, if you could do the following?

```
cout << trip;  // make cout recognize Time class?
```

You can, because << is one of the C++ operators that can be overloaded. In fact, it already is heavily overloaded. In its most basic incarnation, the << operator is one of C and C++'s bit manipulation operators; it shifts bits left in a value (see Appendix E). But the **ostream** class overloads the operator, converting it into an output tool. Recall that **cout** is an **ostream** object and that it is smart enough to recognize all the basic C++ types. That's because the **ostream** class declaration includes an overloaded **operator<<()** definition for each of the basic types. That is, one definition uses an **int** argument, one uses a **double** argument, and so on. So, one way to teach **cout** to recognize a **Time** object is to add a new function operator definition to the **ostream** class declaration. But it's not a good idea to alter the **iostream** file and mess around with a standard interface. It's better to use the **Time** class declaration to teach the **Time** class how to use **cout**.

First Version of Overloading <<

To teach the **Time** class to use **cout**, you'll have to use a friend function. Why? Because a statement like

```
cout << trip;
```

uses two objects, with the **ostream** class object (**cout**) first. If you use a **Time** member function to overload <<, the **Time** object would come first, as it did when we overloaded the * operator with a member function. That means you would have to use the << operator this way:

```
trip << cout;  // if operator<<() were a Time member function
```

That would be confusing. But by using a friend function, you can overload the operator this way:

```
void operator<<(ostream & os, const Time & t)
{
    os << t.hours << " hours, " << t.minutes << " minutes";
}
```

This lets you use

```
cout << trip;
```

to print data in the following format:

```
4 hours, 23 minutes
```

Friend or No Friend?

The new `Time` class declaration makes the `operator<<()` function a friend function to the `Time` class. But this function, although not inimical to the `ostream` class, is not a friend to it. The `operator<<()` function takes an `ostream` argument and a `Time` argument, so it might seem this function has to be friends to both classes. If you look at the code for the function, however, you'll notice that the function accesses individual members of the `Time` object but only uses the `ostream` object as a whole. Because `operator<<()` accesses private `Time` object members directly, it has to be a friend to the `Time` class. But because it does not directly access private `ostream` object members, the function does not have to be a friend to the `ostream` class. That's nice, for it means you don't have to tinker with the `ostream` definition.

Note that the new `operator<<()` definition uses an `ostream` reference `os` as its first argument. Normally, `os` will refer to the `cout` object, as it does in the expression `cout << trip`. But you could use the operator with other `ostream` objects, in which case `os` would refer to those objects. (What? You don't know of any other `ostream` objects? Don't forget `cerr`, introduced in Chapter 10, "Objects and Classes." Also, in Chapter 17, "Input, Output, and Files," you'll learn how to create new objects to manage output to files, and these objects can use `ostream` methods. You then can use the `operator<<()` definition to write `Time` data to files as well as to the screen.) Furthermore, the call `cout << trip` should use the `cout` object itself, not a copy, so the function passes the object as a reference instead of by value. Thus, the expression `cout << trip` causes `os` to be an alias for `cout`, and the expression `cerr << trip` causes `os` to be an alias for `cerr`. The `Time` object can be passed by value or by reference, because either form makes the object values available to the function. Again, passing by reference uses less memory and time than passing by value.

Second Version of Overloading <<

The implementation we just presented has a problem. Statements such as

```
cout << trip;
```

work fine, but the implementation doesn't allow you to combine the redefined << operator with the ones `cout` normally uses:

```
cout << "Trip time: " << trip << " (Tuesday)\n"; // can't do
```

To understand why this doesn't work and what must be done to make it work, you first need to know a bit more about how `cout` operates. Consider the following statements:

```
int x = 5;
int y = 8;
cout << x << y;
```

C++ reads the output statement from left to right, meaning it is equivalent to the following:

```
(cout << x) << y;
```

The << operator, as defined in **iostream**, takes an `ostream` object to its left. Clearly, the expression `cout << x` satisfies that requirement because `cout` is an `ostream` object. But the output statement also requires that the whole expression `(cout << x)` be a type `ostream` object, because that expression is to the left of `<< y`. Therefore, the `ostream` class implements the `operator<<()` function so that it returns an `ostream` object. In particular, it returns the invoking object, `cout`, in this case. Thus, the expression (`cout << x`) is itself an `ostream` object, and it can be used to the left of the `<<` operator.

You can take the same approach with the friend function. Just revise the `operator<<()` function so that it returns a reference to an `ostream` object:

```
ostream & operator<<(ostream & os, const Time & t)
{
    os << t.hours << " hours, " << t.minutes << " minutes";
    return os;
}
```

Note that the return type is `ostream &`. That means, recall, that the function returns a reference to an `ostream` object. Because a program passes an object reference to the function to begin with, the net effect is that the function's return value is just the object passed to it. That is, the statement

```
cout << trip;
```

becomes the following function call:

```
operator<<(cout, trip);
```

And that call returns the `cout` object. So now the following statement does work:

```
cout << "Trip time: " << trip << " (Tuesday)\n"; // can do
```

Let's break this into separate steps to see how it works. First,

```
cout << "Trip time: "
```

invokes the particular `ostream` definition of `<<` that displays a string and returns the `cout` object, so the expression `cout << "Trip time: "` displays the string and then is replaced by its return value, `cout`. This reduces the original statement to the following one:

```
cout << trip << " (Tuesday)\n";
```

Next, the program uses the `Time` declaration of `<<` to display the trip values and to return the `cout` object again. This reduces the statement to the following:

```
cout << " (Tuesday)\n";
```

The program now finishes up by using the `ostream` definition of `<<` for strings to display the final string.

Tip

In general, to overload the `<<` operator to display an object of class *c_name*, use a friend function with a definition of this form:

```
ostream & operator<<(ostream & os, const c_name & obj)
{
    os << ... ;  // display object contents
    return os;
}
```

Listing 11.10 shows the class definition as modified to include the two friend functions oper-ator*() and operator<<(). It implements the first as an inline function because the code is so short. (When the definition also is the prototype, as in this case, you do use the friend pre-fix.)

Remember

You use the friend keyword only in the prototype found in the class declaration. You don't use it in the function definition, unless the definition also is the prototype.

LISTING 11.10   mytime3.h

```
// mytime3.h -- Time class with friends
#ifndef MYTIME3_H_
#define MYTIME3_H_
#include <iostream>
using namespace std;

class Time
{
private:
    int hours;
    int minutes;
public:
    Time();
    Time(int h, int m = 0);
    void AddMin(int m);
    void AddHr(int h);
    void Reset(int h = 0, int m = 0);
    Time operator+(const Time & t) const;
    Time operator-(const Time & t) const;
    Time operator*(double n) const;
    friend Time operator*(double m, const Time & t)
            { return t * m; }   // inline definition
    friend ostream & operator<<(ostream & os, const Time & t);
};
#endif
```

Listing 11.11 shows the revised set of definitions. Note again that the methods use the Time:: qualifier while the friend function does not.

LISTING 11.11   mytime3.cpp

```
// mytime3.cpp  -- implement Time methods
#include "mytime3.h"

Time::Time()
{
```

LISTING 11.11   Continued

```
    hours = minutes = 0;
}

Time::Time(int h, int m )
{
    hours = h;
    minutes = m;
}

void Time::AddMin(int m)
{
    minutes += m;
    hours += minutes / 60;
    minutes %= 60;
}
void Time::AddHr(int h)
{
    hours += h;
}

void Time::Reset(int h, int m)
{
    hours = h;
    minutes = m;
}

Time Time::operator+(const Time & t) const
{
    Time sum;
    sum.minutes = minutes + t.minutes;
    sum.hours = hours + t.hours + sum.minutes / 60;
    sum.minutes %= 60;
    return sum;
}

Time Time::operator-(const Time & t) const
{
    Time diff;
    int tot1, tot2;
    tot1 = t.minutes + 60 * t.hours;
    tot2 = minutes + 60 * hours;
    diff.minutes = (tot2 - tot1) % 60;
    diff.hours = (tot2 - tot1) / 60;
    return diff;
}

Time Time::operator*(double mult) const
{
    Time result;
    long totalminutes = hours * mult * 60 + minutes * mult;
    result.hours = totalminutes / 60;
    result.minutes = totalminutes % 60;
```

LISTING 11.11   Continued

```
        return result;
}

ostream & operator<<(ostream & os, const Time & t)
{
    os << t.hours << " hours, " << t.minutes << " minutes";
    return os;
}
```

Listing 11.12 shows a sample program.

LISTING 11.12   usetime3.cpp

```
// usetime3.cpp -- use fourth draft of Time class
// compile usetime3.cpp and mytime3.cpp together
#include <iostream>
#include "mytime3.h"
using namespace std;

int main()
{
    Time A;
    Time B(5, 40);
    Time C(2, 55);

    cout << "A, B, and C:\n";
    cout << A <<"; " << B << ": " << C << endl;
    A = B + C;      // operator+()
    cout << "B + C: " << A << endl;
    A = B * 2.75;   // member operator*()
    cout << "B * 2.75: " << A << endl;
    cout << "10 * B: " << 10 * B << endl;
    return 0;
}
```

Here is the output:

```
A, B, and C:
0 hours, 0 minutes; 5 hours, 40 minutes: 2 hours, 55 minutes
B + C: 8 hours, 35 minutes
B * 2.75: 15 hours, 35 minutes
10 * B: 56 hours, 40 minutes
```

Overloaded Operators: Member Versus Nonmember Functions

For many operators, you have a choice between using member functions or nonmember functions to implement operator overloading. Typically, the nonmember version would be a friend function so that it can access directly the private data for a class. For example, consider the addition operator for the `Time` class. It had this prototype in the `Time` class declaration:

```
Time operator+(const Time & t) const;                    // member version
```

Instead, the class could have used the following prototype:

```
friend Time operator+(const Time & t1, const Time & t2);   // non-member version
```

The addition operator requires two operands. For the member function version, one is passed implicitly via the `this` pointer and the second is passed explicitly as a function argument. For the friend version, both are passed as arguments.

> ### Remember
>
> A nonmember version of an overloaded operator function requires as many formal parameters as the operator has operands. A member version of the same operator requires one parameter less because one operand is passed implicitly as the invoking object.

Either of these two prototypes matches the expression `B + C`, where `B` and `C` are type `Time` objects. That is, the compiler can convert the statement

```
A = B + C;
```

to either of the following:

```
A = B.operator+(C);      // member function
A = operator+(B, C);     // non-member function
```

Keep in mind that you must choose one or the other form when defining a given operator, but not both. Because both forms match the same expression, defining both forms is considered an ambiguity error.

Which form, then, is it best to use? For some operators, as mentioned earlier, the member function is the only valid choice. Otherwise, it often doesn't make much difference. Sometimes, depending upon the class design, the nonmember version may have an advantage, particularly if you have defined type conversions for the class. This chapter will show an example later.

More Overloading: A Vector Class

Let's look at another class design that uses operator overloading and friends, a class representing vectors. The class will also illustrate further aspects of class design, such as incorporating two different ways of describing the same thing into an object. Even if you don't care for vectors, you can use many of the new techniques in other contexts. A *vector*, as the term is used in engineering and physics, is a quantity having both a magnitude (size) and a direction. For example, if you push something, the effect depends on how hard you push (the magnitude) and in what direction you push. A push in one direction can save a tottering vase, whereas a push in the opposite direction can hasten its rush to doom. To fully describe the motion of your car, you should give both the speed (the magnitude) and the direction; arguing with the highway patrol that you were driving under the speed limit carries little weight if you were traveling in the wrong direction. (Immunologists and computer scientists may use the term vector differently; ignore them, at least until Chapter 16, "The **string** Class and the Standard Template Library," which looks at the computer science version.) The following note tells you more about vectors, but understanding them completely isn't necessary for following the C++ aspects of the examples.

Vectors

You're a worker bee that has discovered a marvelous nectar cache. You rush back to the hive and announce you've found nectar 120 yards away. "Not enough information," buzz the other bees. "You have to tell us the direction, too!" You answer, "It's 30 degrees north of the sun direction." Knowing both the distance (magnitude) and the direction, the other bees rush to the sweet site. Bees know vectors.

Many quantities involve both a magnitude and a direction. The effect of a push, for example, depends on both its strength and direction. Moving an object on a computer screen involves a distance and a direction. You can describe such things using vectors. For example, you can describe moving (displacing) an object on the screen with a vector, which you can visualize as an arrow drawn from the starting position to the final position. The length of the vector is its magnitude, and that describes how far the point has been displaced. The orientation of the arrow describes the direction (see Figure 11.1). A vector representing such a change in position is called a *displacement vector*.

Now you're Lhanappa, the great mammoth hunter. Scouts report a mammoth herd 14.1 kilometers to the northwest. But, because of a southeast wind, you don't want to approach from the southeast. So you go 10 kilometers west, then 10 kilometers north, approaching the herd from the south. You know these two displacement vectors bring you to the same location as the single 14.1-kilometer vector pointing northwest. Lhanappa, the great mammoth hunter, also knows how to add vectors.

Adding two vectors has a simple geometric interpretation. First, draw one vector. Then draw the second vector starting from the arrow-end of the first vector. Finally, draw a vector from the starting point of the first vector to the end point of the second vector. This third vector represents the sum of the first two (see Figure 11.2). Note that the length of the sum can be less than the sum of the individual lengths.

Vectors make a natural choice for operator overloading. First, you can't represent a vector with a single number, so it makes sense to create a class to represent vectors. Second, vectors have analogs to ordinary arithmetic operations such as addition and subtraction. This parallel suggests overloading the corresponding operators so you can use them with vectors.

To keep things simple, we'll implement a two-dimensional vector, such as a screen displacement, instead of a three-dimensional vector, such as might represent movement of a helicopter or a gymnast. You need just two numbers to describe a two-dimensional vector, but you have a choice of what set of two numbers:

- You can describe a vector by its magnitude (length) and direction (an angle).

- You can represent the vector by its x and y components.

FIGURE 11.1
Describing a displacement with a vector.

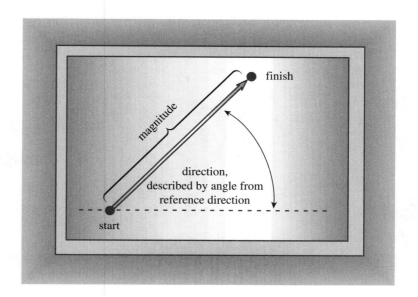

FIGURE 11.2
Adding two vectors.

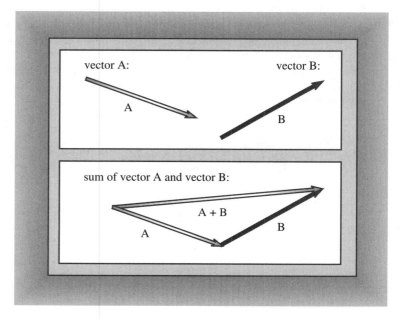

The components are a horizontal vector (the x component) and a vertical vector (the y component), which add up to the final vector. For example, you can describe a motion as moving a point 30 units to the right and 40 units up (see Figure 11.3). That motion puts the point at the same spot as moving 50 units at an angle of 53.1° from the horizontal. Therefore, a vector with a magnitude of 50 and an angle of 53.1° is equivalent to a vector having a horizontal component of 30 and a vertical component of 40. What counts with displacement vectors is where you start and where you end up, not the exact route taken to get there. This choice of representation is basically the same thing we covered with the Chapter 7 program that converted between rectangular and polar coordinates.

FIGURE 11.3
x and y components of a vector.

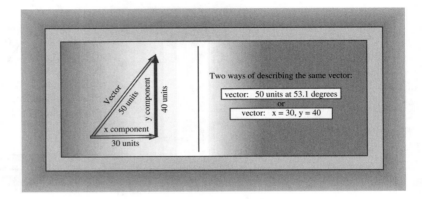

Sometimes one form is more convenient, sometimes the other, so we'll incorporate both representations into the class description. See the note on Multiple Representations and Classes coming up shortly. Also, we'll design the class so that if you alter one representation of a vector, the object automatically updates the other representation. The ability to build such intelligence into an object is another C++ class virtue. Listing 11.13 presents a class declaration. To refresh your memory about namespaces, the listing places the class declaration inside the VECTOR namespace.

Compatibility Note

If your system does not support namespaces, you can remove the following lines:

```
namespace VECTOR
{
```

and

```
}    // end namespace VECTOR
```

LISTING 11.13   vector.h

```
// vect.h -- Vector class with <<, mode state
#ifndef VECTOR_H_
#define VECTOR_H_
namespace VECTOR
{

    class Vector
    {
    private:
```

LISTING 11.13 Continued

```
        double x;          // horizontal value
        double y;          // vertical value
        double mag;        // length of vector
        double ang;        // direction of vector
        char mode;         // 'r' = rectangular, 'p' = polar
    // private methods for setting values
        void set_mag();
        void set_ang();
        void set_x();
        void set_y();
    public:
        Vector();
        Vector(double n1, double n2, char form = 'r');
        void set(double n1, double n2, char form = 'r');
        ~Vector();
        double xval() const {return x;}       // report x value
        double yval() const {return y;}       // report y value
        double magval() const {return mag;}   // report magnitude
        double angval() const {return ang;}   // report angle
        void polar_mode();                     // set mode to 'p'
        void rect_mode();                      // set mode to 'r'
    // operator overloading
        Vector operator+(const Vector & b) const;
        Vector operator-(const Vector & b) const;
        Vector operator-() const;
        Vector operator*(double n) const;
    // friends
        friend Vector operator*(double n, const Vector & a);
        friend ostream & operator<<(ostream & os, const Vector & v);
    };

}   // end namespace VECTOR
#endif
```

Notice that the four functions that report component values are defined in the class declaration. This automatically makes them inline functions. The fact that these functions are so short makes them excellent candidates for inlining. None of them should alter object data, so they are declared using the **const** modifier. As you may recall from Chapter 10, this is the syntax for declaring a function that doesn't modify the object it implicitly accesses.

Listing 11.14 shows all the methods and friend functions declared in Listing 11.13. The listing uses the open nature of namespaces to add the method definitions to the **VECTOR** namespace. Note how the constructor functions and the **set()** function each set both the rectangular and the polar representations of the vector. Thus, either set of values is available immediately without further calculation should you need them. Also, as mentioned in Chapters 4, "Compound Types," and 7, C++'s built-in math functions use angles in radians, so the functions built conversion to and from degrees into the methods. The implementation hides such things as converting from polar coordinates to rectangular coordinates or converting radians to degrees from the user. All the user needs to know is that the class uses angles in degrees and that it makes a vector available in two equivalent representations.

These design decisions follow the OOP tradition of having the class interface concentrate on the essentials (the abstract model) while hiding the details. Thus, when you use the **Vector** class, you can think about a vector's general features, such as that they can represent displacements and that you can add two vectors. Whether you express a vector in component notation or in magnitude, direction notation becomes secondary, for you can set a vector's values and display them in whichever format is most convenient at the time.

We'll look at some of the features in more detail next.

Compatibility Note

Some systems may still use `math.h` instead of `cmath`. Also, some C++ systems don't automatically search the math library. For example, some UNIX systems require that you do the following:

```
$ CC source_file(s) -lm
```

The `-lm` option instructs the linker to search the math library. So, when you eventually compile programs using the `Vector` class, if you get a message about undefined externals, try the `-lm` option or check to see if your system requires something similar.

As with the header file, if your system does not support namespaces, you can remove the following lines:

```
namespace VECTOR
{
```

and

```
}    // end namespace VECTOR
```

LISTING 11.14 vector.cpp

```cpp
// vect.cpp -- methods for Vector class
#include <iostream>
#include <cmath>
using namespace std;
#include "vect.h"

namespace VECTOR
{

    const double Rad_to_deg = 57.2957795130823;

    // private methods
    // calculates magnitude from x and y
    void Vector::set_mag()
    {
        mag = sqrt(x * x + y * y);
    }

    void Vector::set_ang()
    {
        if (x == 0.0 && y == 0.0)
            ang = 0.0;
```

LISTING 11.14   Continued

```cpp
        else
            ang = atan2(y, x);
    }
    // set x from polar coordinate
    void Vector::set_x()
    {
        x = mag * cos(ang);
    }

    // set y from polar coordinate
    void Vector::set_y()
    {
        y = mag * sin(ang);
    }

    // public methods
    Vector::Vector()                // default constructor
    {
        x = y = mag = ang = 0.0;
        mode = 'r';
    }

    // construct vector from rectangular coordinates if form is r
    // (the default) or else from polar coordinates if form is p
    Vector::Vector(double n1, double n2, char form)
    {
        mode = form;
        if (form == 'r')
          {
            x = n1;
            y = n2;
            set_mag();
            set_ang();
          }
        else if (form == 'p')
          {
            mag = n1;
            ang = n2 / Rad_to_deg;
            set_x();
            set_y();
          }
        else
          {
            cout << "Incorrect 3rd argument to Vector() -- ";
            cout << "vector set to 0\n";
            x = y = mag = ang = 0.0;
            mode = 'r';
          }
    }

    // set vector from rectangular coordinates if form is r (the
    // default) or else from polar coordinates if form is p
```

LISTING 11.14   Continued

```cpp
void Vector:: set(double n1, double n2, char form)
{
    mode = form;
    if (form == 'r')
     {
        x = n1;
        y = n2;
        set_mag();
        set_ang();
    }
    else if (form == 'p')
    {
        mag = n1;
        ang = n2 / Rad_to_deg;
        set_x();
        set_y();
    }
    else
    {
        cout << "Incorrect 3rd argument to Vector() -- ";
        cout << "vector set to 0\n";
        x = y = mag = ang = 0.0;
        mode = 'r';
    }
}

Vector::~Vector()     // destructor
{
}

void Vector::polar_mode()    // set to polar mode
{
    mode = 'p';
}

void Vector::rect_mode()     // set to rectangular mode
{
    mode = 'r';
}

// operator overloading
// add two Vectors
Vector Vector::operator+(const Vector & b) const
{
    return Vector(x + b.x, y + b.y);
}

// subtract Vector b from a
Vector Vector::operator-(const Vector & b) const
{
    return Vector(x - b.x, y - b.y);
}
```

LISTING 11.14   Continued

```
    // reverse sign of Vector
    Vector Vector::operator-() const
    {
        return Vector(-x, -y);
    }

    // multiple vector by n
    Vector Vector::operator*(double n) const
    {
        return Vector(n * x, n * y);
    }

    // friend methods
    // multiply n by Vector a
    Vector operator*(double n, const Vector & a)
    {
        return a * n;
    }

    // display rectangular coordinates if mode is r,
    // else display polar coordinates if mode is p
    ostream & operator<<(ostream & os, const Vector & v)
    {
        if (v.mode == 'r')
            os << "(x,y) = (" << v.x << ", " << v.y << ")";
        else if (v.mode == 'p')
        {
            os << "(m,a) = (" << v.mag << ", "
                << v.ang * Rad_to_deg << ")";
        }
        else
            os << "Vector object mode is invalid";
        return os;
    }

}  // end namespace VECTOR
```

Using a State Member

The class stores both the rectangular coordinates and the polar coordinates for a vector. It uses a member called **mode** to control which form the constructor, the **set()** method, and the overloaded **operator<<()** function use, with 'r' representing the rectangular mode (the default) and 'p' the polar mode. Such a member is termed a *state member* because it describes the state an object is in. To see what this means, look at the code for the constructor:

```
Vector::Vector(double n1, double n2, char form)
{
    mode = form;
    if (form == 'r')
     {
```

```
            x = n1;
            y = n2;
            set_mag();
            set_ang();
    }
    else if (form == 'p')
    {
            mag = n1;
            ang = n2 / Rad_to_deg;
            set_x();
            set_y();
    }
    else
    {
            cout << "Incorrect 3rd argument to Vector() -- ";
            cout << "vector set to 0\n";
            x = y = mag = ang = 0.0;
            mode = 'r';
    }
}
```

If the third argument is 'r' or if it is omitted (the prototype assigns a default value of 'r'), the inputs are interpreted as rectangular coordinates, whereas a value of 'p' causes them to be interpreted as polar coordinates:

```
Vector folly(3.0, 4.0);              // set x = 3, y = 4
Vector foolery(20.0, 30.0, 'p');     // set mag = 20, ang = 30
```

Note that the constructor uses the private methods set_mag() and set_ang() to set the magnitude and angle values if you provide x and y values, and it uses the private set_x() and set_y() methods to set x and y values if you provide magnitude and angle values. Also note that the constructor delivers a warning message and sets the state to 'r' if something other than 'r' or 'p' is specified.

Similarly, the operator<<() function uses the mode to determine how values are displayed:

```
// display rectangular coordinates if mode is r,
// else display polar coordinates if mode is p
ostream & operator<<(ostream & os, const Vector & v)
{
    if (v.mode == 'r')
        os << "(x,y) = (" << v.x << ", " << v.y << ")";
    else if (v.mode == 'p')
    {
        os << "(m,a) = (" << v.mag << ", "
            << v.ang * Rad_to_deg << ")";
    }
    else
        os << "Vector object mode is invalid";
    return os;
}
```

The various methods that can set the mode are careful to accept only 'r' and 'p' as valid values, so the final else in this function never should be reached. Still, it's often a good idea to check; such a check can help catch an otherwise obscure programming error.

Multiple Representations and Classes

Quantities having different, but equivalent, representations are common. For example, you can measure gasoline consumption in miles per gallon, as done in the United States, or in liters per 100 kilometers, as done in Europe. You can represent a number in string form or numeric form, and you can represent intelligence as an IQ or in kiloturkeys. Classes lend themselves nicely to encompassing different aspects and representations of an entity in a single object. First, you can store multiple representations in one object. Second, you can write the class functions so that assigning values for one representation automatically assigns values for the other representation(s). For example, the set_by_polar() method for the Vector class sets the mag and ang members to the function arguments, but it also sets the x and y members. By handling conversions internally, a class can help you think of a quantity in terms of its essential nature rather than in terms of its representation.

More Overloading

Adding two vectors is very simple when you use x,y coordinates. Just add the two x components to get the x component of the answer and add the two y components to get the y component of the answer. From this description, you might be tempted to use this code:

```
Vector Vector::operator+(const Vector & b) const
{
    Vector sum;
    sum.x = x + b.x;
    sum.y = y + b.y;
    return sum;
}
```

And this would be fine if the object stored only the x and y components. Unfortunately, this version of the code fails to set the polar values. This could be fixed by adding more code:

```
Vector Vector::operator+(const Vector & b) const
{
    Vector sum;
    sum.x = x + b.x;
    sum.y = y + b.y;
    sum.set_ang(sum.x, sum.y);
    sum.set_mag(sum.x, sum.y);
    return sum;
}
```

But it is much simpler and more reliable to let a constructor do the work:

```
Vector Vector::operator+(const Vector & b) const
{
    return Vector(x + b.x, y + b.y);       // return the constructed Vector
}
```

Here, the code hands the `Vector` constructor the two new values for the x and y components. The constructor then creates a nameless new object using these values, and the function returns a copy of that object. This way, you guarantee that the new `Vector` object is created according to the standard rules you lay down in the constructor.

Tip
If a method needs to compute a new class object, see if you can use a class constructor to do the work. Not only does that save you trouble, it ensures that the new object is constructed in the proper fashion.

Multiplication

In visual terms, multiplying a vector by a number makes the vector longer or shorter by that factor. So multiplying a vector by 3 produces a vector with three times the length, but still pointed in the same direction. It's easy to translate that image into how the class represents a vector. In polar terms, multiply the magnitude and leave the angle alone. In rectangular terms, you multiply a vector by a number by multiplying its x and y components separately by the number. That is, if a vector has components of 5 and 12, multiplying by 3 makes the components 15 and 36. And that is what the overloaded multiplication operator does:

```
Vector Vector::operator*(double n) const
{
    return Vector(n * x, n * y);
}
```

As with overloaded addition, the code lets a constructor create the correct `Vector` from the new x and y components. This handles multiplying a `Vector` value times a `double` value. Just as in the `Time` example, we can use an inline friend function to handle `double` times `Vector`:

```
Vector operator*(double n, const Vector & a)  // friend function
{
    return a * n;   // convert double times Vector to Vector times double
}
```

More Refinement: Overloading an Overloaded Operator

In ordinary C++, the - operator already has two meanings. First, when used with two operands, it's the subtraction operator. The subtraction operator is termed a *binary operator* because it has exactly two operands. Second, when used with one operand, as in `-x`, it's a minus sign operator. This form is termed a *unary operator*, meaning it has exactly one operand. Both operations—subtraction and sign reversal—make sense for vectors, too, so the `Vector` class has both.

To subtract vector B from vector A, you simply subtract components, so the definition for overloading subtraction is quite similar to the one for addition:

```
Vector operator-(const Vector & b) const;        // prototype
Vector Vector::operator-(const Vector & b) const // definition
```

```
{
    return Vector(x - b.x, y - b.y);  // return the constructed Vector
}
```

Here, it's important to get the correct order. Consider the following statement:

```
diff = v1 - v2;
```

It's converted to a member function call:

```
diff = v1.operator-(v2);
```

This means the vector passed as the explicit argument is subtracted from the implicit vector argument, so we should use `x - b.x` and not `b.x - x`.

Next, consider the unary minus operator, which takes just one operand. Applying this operator to a regular number, as in -x, changes the sign of the value. Thus, applying this operator to a vector reverses the sign of each component. More precisely, the function should return a new vector that is the reverse of the original. (In polar terms, negation leaves the magnitude unchanged, but reverses the direction. Many politicians with little or no mathematical training, nonetheless, have an intuitive mastery of this operation.) Here are the prototype and definition for overloading negation:

```
Vector operator-() const;
Vector Vector::operator-() const
{
    return Vector (-x, -y);
}
```

Note that now there are two separate definitions for `operator-()`. That's fine, because the two definitions have different signatures. You can define both binary and unary versions of the - operator because C++ provides both binary and unary versions of that operator to begin with. An operator having only a binary form, such as division (/), can only be overloaded as a binary operator.

Remember

Because operator overloading is implemented with functions, you can overload the same operator many times, as long as each operator function has a distinct signature and as long as each operator function has the same number of operands as the corresponding built-in C++ operator.

An Implementation Comment

This implementation stores both rectangular and polar coordinates for a vector in the object. However, the public interface doesn't depend upon this fact. All the interface calls for is that both representations can be displayed and that individual values can be returned. The internal implementation could be quite different. For example, the object could store just the x and y components. Then, say, the `magval()` method, which returns the value of the magnitude of the vector, could calculate the magnitude from the x and y values instead of just looking up the value as stored in the object. Such an approach changes the implementation, but leaves the user interface unchanged. This separation of interface from implementation is one of the goals of OOP. It lets you fine-tune an implementation without changing the code in programs that use the class.

Both of these implementations have advantages and disadvantages. Storing the data means the object occupies more memory and that code has to be careful to update both rectangular and polar representations each time a `Vector` object is changed. But data look-up is faster. If an application often had need to access both representations of a vector, the implementation used in this example would be preferable; if polar data were needed only infrequently, the other implementation would be better. You could choose to use one implementation in one program and the second implementation in another, yet retain the same user interface for both.

Taking the Vector Class on a Random Walk

Listing 11.15 provides a short program using the revised class. It simulates the famous Drunkard's Walk problem. Actually, now that the drunk is recognized as someone with a serious health problem rather than as a source of amusement, it's usually called the Random Walk problem. The idea is that you place someone at a lamp post. The subject begins walking, but the direction of each step varies randomly from the preceding step. One way of phrasing the problem is, how many steps does it take the random walker to travel, say, 50 feet away from the post. In terms of vectors, this amounts to adding a bunch of randomly oriented vectors until the sum exceeds 50 feet.

Listing 11.15 lets you select the target distance to be traveled and the length of the wanderer's step. It maintains a running total representing the position after each step (represented as a vector), and reports the number of steps needed to reach the target distance along with the walker's location (in both formats). As you'll see, the walker's progress is quite inefficient. A journey of a thousand steps, each two feet long, may carry the walker only 50 feet from the starting point. The program divides the net distance traveled (50 feet in this case) by the number of steps to provide a measure of the walker's inefficiency. All the random direction changes make this average much smaller than the length of a single step. To select directions randomly, the program uses the standard library functions `rand()`, `srand()`, and `time()`, described in the Program Notes. Remember to compile Listing 11.14 along with Listing 11.15.

LISTING 11.15   randwalk.cpp

```
// randwalk.cpp -- use the Vector class
// compile with the vect.cpp file
#include <iostream>
#include <cstdlib>        // rand(), srand() prototypes
#include <ctime>          // time() prototype
using namespace std;
#include "vect.h"
int main()
{
    using VECTOR::Vector;
```

LISTING 11.15   Continued

```cpp
    srand(time(0));      // seed random-number generator
    double direction;
    Vector step;
    Vector result(0.0, 0.0);
    unsigned long steps = 0;
    double target;
    double dstep;
    cout << "Enter target distance (q to quit): ";
    while (cin >> target)
    {
        cout << "Enter step length: ";
        if (!(cin >> dstep))
            break;

        while (result.magval() < target)
        {
            direction = rand() % 360;
            step.set(dstep, direction, 'p');
            result = result + step;
            steps++;
        }
        cout << "After " << steps << " steps, the subject "
            "has the following location:\n";
        cout << result << "\n";
        result.polar_mode();
        cout << " or\n" << result << "\n";
        cout << "Average outward distance per step = "
            << result.magval()/steps << "\n";
        steps = 0;
        result.set(0.0, 0.0);
        cout << "Enter target distance (q to quit): ";
    }
    cout << "Bye!\n";

    return 0;
}
```

Compatibility Note

You might have to use `stdlib.h` instead of `cstdlib` and `time.h` instead of `ctime`. If you system doesn't support namespaces, omit the following line:

```cpp
using VECTOR::Vector;
```

Here is a sample run:

```
Enter target distance (q to quit): 50
Enter step length: 2
After 253 steps, the subject has the following location:
(x,y) = (46.1512, 20.4902)
 or
```

```
(m,a) = (50.495, 23.9402)
Average outward distance per step = 0.199587
Enter target distance (q to quit): 50
Enter step length: 2
After 951 steps, the subject has the following location:
(x,y) = (-21.9577, 45.3019)
  or
(m,a) = (50.3429, 115.8593)
Average outward distance per step = 0.0529362
Enter target distance (q to quit): 50
Enter step length: 1
After 1716 steps, the subject has the following location:
(x,y) = (40.0164, 31.1244)
  or
(m,a) = (50.6956, 37.8755)
Average outward distance per step = 0.0295429
Enter target distance (q to quit): q
Bye!
```

The random nature of the process produces considerable variation from trial to trial, even if the initial conditions are the same. On the average, however, halving the step size quadruples the number of steps needed to cover a given distance. Probability theory suggests that, on the average, the number of steps (N) of length s needed to reach a net distance of D is given by the following equation:

$$N = (D/s)^2$$

This is just an average, but there will be considerable variations from trial to trial. For example, a thousand trials of attempting to travel 50 feet in 2-foot steps yielded an average of 636 steps (close to the theoretical value of 625) to travel that far, but the range was from 91 to 3951. Similarly, a thousand trials of traveling 50 feet in 1-foot steps averaged 2557 steps (close to the theoretical value of 2500) with a range of 345 to 10882. So if you find yourself walking randomly, be confident and take long steps. You still won't have any control over the direction you wind up going, but at least you'll get farther.

Program Notes

First, let's note how painless it was to use the VECTOR namespace. The using-declaration

```
using VECTOR::Vector;
```

placed the name of the Vector class in scope. Because all the Vector class methods have class scope, importing the class name also made the Vector methods available without the need of any further using-declarations.

Next, let's talk about random numbers. The standard ANSI C library, which also comes with C++, includes a rand() function that returns a random integer in the range from 0 to some implementation-dependent value. Our program uses the modulus operator to get an angle value in the range 0–359. The rand() function works by applying an algorithm to an initial seed value to get a random value. That value is used as the seed for the next function call, and so on. The numbers are really *pseudorandom*, for ten consecutive calls normally produce the same set of ten random numbers. (The exact values will depend on the implementation.) However, the `srand()` function lets you override the default seed value and initiate a different sequence of random numbers. This program uses the return value of `time(0)` to set the seed. The `time(0)` function returns the current calendar time, often implemented as the number of seconds since some specific date. (More generally, `time()` takes the address of a type `time_t` variable and puts the time into that variable and also returns it. Using 0 for the address argument obviates the need for an otherwise unneeded `time_t` variable.) Thus, the statement

```
srand(time(0));
```

sets a different seed each time you run the program, making the random output appear even more random. The `cstdlib` header file (formerly `stdlib.h`) contains the prototypes for `srand()` and `rand()`, whereas `ctime` (formerly `time.h`) contains the `time()` prototype.

The program uses the `result` vector to keep track of the walker's progress. Each cycle of the inner loop, the program sets the `step` vector to a new direction and adds it to the current `result` vector. When the magnitude of `result` exceeds the target distance, the loop terminates.

By setting the vector mode, the program displays the final position in rectangular terms and in polar terms.

Incidentally, the statement

```
result = result + step;
```

has the effect of placing `result` in the `'r'` mode regardless of the initial modes of `result` and `step`. Here's why. First, the addition operator function creates and returns a new vector holding the sum of the two arguments. The function creates that vector using the default constructor, which creates vectors in the `'r'` mode. Thus, the vector being assigned to `result` is in the `'r'` mode. By default, assignment assigns each member variable individually, so `'r'` is assigned to `result.mode`. If you would prefer some other behavior, such as `result` retaining its original mode, you can override default assignment by defining an assignment operator for the class. The next chapter shows examples of this.

Automatic Conversions and Type Casts for Classes

The next topic on the class menu is type conversion. We'll look into how C++ handles conversions to and from user-defined types. To set the stage, let's first review how C++ handles conversions for its built-in types. When you make a statement assigning a value of one standard type to a variable of another standard type, C++ automatically will convert the value to the same type as the receiving variable, providing the two types are compatible. For example, the following statements all generate numeric type conversions:

```
long count = 8;       // int value 8 converted to type long
double time = 11;     // int value 11 converted to type double
int side = 3.33;      // double value 3.33 converted to type int 3
```

These assignments work because C++ recognizes that the diverse numeric types all represent the same basic thing, a number, and because C++ incorporates built-in rules for making the conversions. Recall, however (from your reading of Chapter 3, "Dealing with Data"), that you can lose some precision in these conversions. For example, assigning 3.33 to the int variable that side results in that side getting the value 3, losing the 0.33 part.

The C++ language does not automatically convert types that are not compatible. For example, the statement

```
int * p = 10;   // type clash
```

fails because the left-hand side is a pointer-type, whereas the right-hand side is a number. And even though a computer may represent an address internally with an integer, integers and pointers conceptually are quite different. For example, you wouldn't square a pointer. However, when automatic conversions fail, you may use a type cast:

```
int * p = (int *) 10;   // ok, p and (int *) 10 both pointers
```

This sets a pointer to the address 10 by type casting 10 to type pointer-to-int (that is, type int *).

You may define a class sufficiently related to a basic type or to another class that it makes sense to convert from one form to another. In that case, you can instruct C++ how to make such conversions automatically or, perhaps, via a type cast. To show how that works, let's recast the pounds-to-stone program from Chapter 3 into class form. First, design an appropriate type. Fundamentally, we're representing one thing (a weight) two ways (pounds and stone). A class provides an excellent way to incorporate two representations of one concept into a single entity. Therefore, it makes sense to place both representations of weight into the same class and then to provide class methods for expressing the weight in different forms. Listing 11.16 provides the class header.

LISTING 11.16   stonewt.h

```
// stonewt.h -- definition for Stonewt class
#ifndef STONEWT_H_
#define STONEWT_H_
class Stonewt
{
private:
    enum {Lbs_per_stn = 14};     // pounds per stone
    int stone;                   // whole stones
    double pds_left;             // fractional pounds
    double pounds;               // entire weight in pounds
public:
    Stonewt(double lbs);         // constructor for double pounds
    Stonewt(int stn, double lbs); // constructor for stone, lbs
    Stonewt();                   // default constructor
    ~Stonewt();
```

LISTING 11.16   Continued

```
        void show_lbs() const;      // show weight in pounds format
        void show_stn() const;      // show weight in stone format
};
#endif
```

As mentioned in Chapter 10, **enum** provides a convenient way to define class-specific constants, providing that they are integers. New compilers allow the following alternative:

```
static const int Lbs_per_stn = 14;
```

Note that the class has three constructors. They allow you to initialize a **Stonewt** object to a floating-point number of pounds, or to a stone and pound combination. Or you can create a **Stonewt** object without initializing it:

```
Stonewt kindy(118);   // weight = 118 pounds
Stonewt kandy(8, 2);  // weight = 8 stone, 2 pounds
Stonewt kendy;        // weight = default value
```

Also, the class provides two display functions. One displays the weight in pounds, and the other displays the weight in stone and pounds. Listing 11.17 shows the class methods implementation. Note that each constructor assigns values to all three private members. Thus, creating a **Stonewt** object automatically sets both representations of weight.

LISTING 11.17   stonewt.cpp

```
// stonewt.cpp -- Stonewt methods
#include <iostream>
using namespace std;
#include "stonewt.h"

// construct Stonewt object from double value
Stonewt::Stonewt(double lbs)
{
    stone = int (lbs) / Lbs_per_stn;    // integer division
    pds_left = int (lbs) % Lbs_per_stn + lbs - int(lbs);
    pounds = lbs;
}

// construct Stonewt object from stone, double values
Stonewt::Stonewt(int stn, double lbs)
{
    stone = stn;
    pds_left = lbs;
    pounds =  stn * Lbs_per_stn +lbs;
}

Stonewt::Stonewt()            // default constructor, wt = 0
{
    stone = pounds = pds_left = 0;
}
```

LISTING 11.17   *Continued*

```
Stonewt::~Stonewt()            // destructor
{
}

// show weight in stones
void Stonewt::show_stn() const
{
    cout << stone << " stone, " << pds_left << " pounds\n";
}

// show weight in pounds
void Stonewt::show_lbs() const
{
    cout << pounds << " pounds\n";
}
```

Because a `Stonewt` object represents a single weight, it makes sense to provide ways to convert an integer or a floating-point value to a `Stonewt` object. And we have already done so! In C++, any constructor taking a single argument acts as a blueprint for converting a value of that argument type to the class type. Thus the constructor

```
Stonewt(double lbs);    // template for double-to-Stonewt conversion
```

serves as instructions for converting a type `double` value to a type `Stonewt` value. That is, you can write code like the following:

```
Stonewt myCat;          // create a Stonewt object
myCat = 19.6;           // use Stonewt(double) to convert 19.6 to Stonewt
```

The program will use the `Stonewt(double)` constructor to construct a temporary `Stonewt` object, using 19.6 as the initialization value. Then memberwise assignment will copy the contents of the temporary object into `myCat`. This process is termed an implicit conversion because it happens automatically without the need of an explicit type cast.

Only a constructor that can be used with just one argument works as a conversion function. The constructor

```
Stonewt(int stn, double lbs);
```

has two arguments, so it cannot be used to convert types.

Having a constructor work as an automatic type-conversion function seems like a nice feature. As programmers acquired more experience working with C++, however, they found that the automatic aspect isn't always desirable, for it can lead to unexpected conversions. So recent C++ implementations have a new keyword, **explicit**, to turn off the automatic aspect. That is, you can declare the constructor this way:

```
explicit Stonewt(double lbs);    // no implicit conversions allowed
```

This turns off implicit conversions such as the example above but still allows explicit conversions; that is, conversions using explicit type casts:

```
Stonewt myCat;          // create a Stonewt object
myCat = 19.6;           // not valid if Stonewt(double) is declared as explicit
mycat = Stonewt(19.6);  // ok, an explicit conversion
mycat = (Stonewt) 19.6; // ok, old form for explicit typecast
```

Remember

A C++ constructor containing one argument defines a type conversion from the argument type to the class type. If the constructor is qualified with the keyword `explicit`, the constructor is used for explicit conversions only; otherwise, it also is used for implicit conversions.

When will the compiler use the `Stonewt(double)` function? If the keyword `explicit` is used in the declaration, `Stonewt(double)` will be used only for an explicit type cast; otherwise, it also will be used for the following implicit conversions.

- When you initialize a `Stonewt` object to a type `double` value

- When you assign a type `double` value to a `Stonewt` object

- When you pass a type `double` value to a function expecting a `Stonewt` argument

- When a function that's declared to return a `Stonewt` value tries to return a `double` value

- When any of the situations above uses a built-in type that unambiguously can be converted to type `double`

Let's look at the last point in more detail. The argument-matching process provided by function prototyping will let the `Stonewt(double)` constructor act as conversions for other numerical types. That is, both of the following statements work by first converting `int` to `double` and then using the `Stonewt(double)` constructor.

```
Stonewt Jumbo(7000);    // uses Stonewt(double), converting int to double
Jumbo = 7300;           // uses Stonewt(double), converting int to double
```

However, this two-step conversion process works only if there is an unambiguous choice. That is, if the class also defined a `Stonewt(long)` constructor, the compiler would reject these statements, probably pointing out that an `int` can be converted to either a `long` or a `double`, so the call is ambiguous.

Listing 11.18 uses the class constructors to initialize some `Stonewt` objects and to handle type conversions. Remember to compile Listing 11.17 along with Listing 11.18.

LISTING 11.18   stone.cpp

```
// stone.cpp -- user-defined conversions
// compile with stonewt.cpp
#include <iostream>
using namespace std;
#include "stonewt.h"
void display(Stonewt st, int n);
int main()
```

LISTING 11.18   *Continued*

```
    {
        Stonewt pavarotti = 260;  // uses constructor to initialize
        Stonewt wolfe(285.7);     // same as Stonewt wolfe = 285.7;
        Stonewt taft(21, 8);

        cout << "The tenor weighed ";
        pavarotti.show_stn();
        cout << "The detective weighed ";
        wolfe.show_stn();
        cout << "The President weighed ";
        taft.show_lbs();
        pavarotti = 265.8;        // uses constructor for conversion
        taft = 325;               // same as taft = Stonewt(325);
        cout << "After dinner, t he tenor weighed ";
        pavarotti.show_stn();
        cout << "After dinner, the President weighed ";
        taft.show_lbs();
        display(taft, 2);
        cout << "The wrestler weighed even more.\n";
        display(422, 2);
        cout << "No stone left unearned\n";
        return 0;
    }

    void display(Stonewt st, int n)
    {
        for (int i = 0; i < n; i++)
        {
            cout << "Wow! ";
            st.show_stn();
        }
    }
```

Here is the output:

```
The tenor weighed 18 stone, 8 pounds
The detective weighed 20 stone, 5.7 pounds
The President weighed 302 pounds
After dinner, the tenor weighed 18 stone, 13.8 pounds
After dinner, the President weighed 325 pounds
Wow! 23 stone, 3 pounds
Wow! 23 stone, 3 pounds
The wrestler weighed even more.
Wow! 30 stone, 2 pounds
Wow! 30 stone, 2 pounds
No stone left unearned
```

Program Notes

First, note that when a constructor has a single argument, you can use the following form when initializing a class object:

```
// a syntax for initializing a class object when
// using a constructor with one argument
Stonewt pavarotti = 260;
```

This is equivalent to the other two forms we've used:

```
// standard syntax forms for initializing class objects
Stonewt pavarotti(260);
Stonewt pavarotti = Stonewt(260);
```

However, the last two forms can also be used with constructors having multiple arguments.

Next, note the following two assignments from Listing 11.18:

```
pavarotti = 265.8;
taft = 325;
```

The first assignment uses the constructor with a type `double` argument to convert 265.8 to a type `Stonewt` value. This sets the `pounds` member of `pavarotti` to 265.8. Because it uses the constructor, this assignment also sets the `stone` and `pds_left` members of the class. Similarly, the second assignment converts a type `int` value to type `double` and then uses `Stonewt(double)` to set all three member values in the process.

Finally, note the following function call:

```
display(422, 2);    // convert 422 to double, then to Stonewt
```

The prototype for `display()` indicates that its first argument should be the `Stonewt` object. Confronted with an `int` argument, the compiler looks for a `Stonewt(int)` constructor to convert the `int` to the desired `Stonewt` type. Failing to find that constructor, the compiler looks for a constructor with some other built-in type to which an `int` can be converted. The `Stonewt(double)` constructor fits the bill. So the compiler converts `int` to `double` and then uses `Stonewt(double)` to convert the result to a `Stonewt` object.

Conversion Functions

Listing 11.18 converts a number to a `Stonewt` object. Can you do the reverse? That is, can you convert a `Stonewt` object to a `double` value, as in the following?

```
Stonewt wolfe(285.7);
double host = wolfe;  // ?? possible ??
```

The answer is that you can do this, but not by using constructors. Constructors only provide for converting another type *to* the class type. To do the reverse, you have to use a special form of C++ operator function called a *conversion function*.

Conversion functions are user-defined type casts, and you can use them the way you would use a type cast. For example, if you define a `Stonewt`-to-`double` conversion function, you can use the following conversions:

```
Stonewt wolfe(285.7);
double host = double (wolfe);     // syntax #1
double thinker = (double) wolfe;  // syntax #2
```

Or you can let the compiler figure out what to do:

```
Stonewt wells(20, 3);
double star = wells;   // implicit use of conversion function
```

The compiler, noting that the right-hand side is type `Stonewt` and the left-hand side is type `double`, looks to see if you've defined a conversion function matching that description. (If it can't find such a definition, the compiler generates an error message to the effect that it can't assign a `Stonewt` to a `double`.)

So how do you create a conversion function? To convert to type *typeName*, use a conversion function of this form:

```
operator typeName();
```

Note the following points:

- The conversion function must be a class method.
- The conversion function must not specify a return type.
- The conversion function must have no arguments.

For example, a function to convert to type `double` would have this prototype:

```
operator double();
```

The *typeName* part tells the conversion the type to which to convert, so no return type is needed. The fact that the function is a class method means it has to be invoked by a particular class object, and that tells the function which value to convert. Thus, the function doesn't need arguments.

To add functions converting `stone_wt` objects to type `int` and to type `double`, then, requires adding the following prototypes to the class declaration:

```
operator int();
operator double();
```

Listing 11.19 shows the modified class declaration.

LISTING 11.19   stonewt1.h

```
// stonewt1.h -- revised definition for Stonewt class
#ifndef STONEWT1_H_
#define STONEWT1_H_
class Stonewt
{
private:
    enum {Lbs_per_stn = 14};       // pounds per stone
int stone;                         // whole stones
    double pds_left;               // fractional pounds
    double pounds;                 // entire weight in pounds
public:
    Stonewt(double lbs);           // construct from double pounds
```

LISTING 11.19   Continued

```
        Stonewt(int stn, double lbs);  // construct from stone, lbs
        Stonewt();                      // default constructor
        ~Stonewt();
        void show_lbs() const;          // show weight in pounds format
        void show_stn() const;          // show weight in stone format
    // conversion functions
        operator int() const;
        operator double() const;
};
#endif
```

Next, Listing 11.20 shows the definitions for these two conversion functions; these definitions should be added to the class member function file. Note that each function does return the desired value even though there is no declared return type. Also note the int conversion definition rounds to the nearest integer rather than truncating. For example, if **pounds** is 114.4, then **pounds + 0.5** is 114.9, and int **(114.9)** is 114. But if **pounds** is 114.6, then **pounds + 0.5** is 115.1, and int **(115.1)** is 115.

LISTING 11.20   stonewt1.cpp

```
// stonewt1.cpp -- Stonewt class methods + conversion functions
#include <iostream>
using namespace std;
#include "stonewt1.h"

// previous definitions go here

// conversion functions
Stonewt::operator int() const
{

    return int (pounds + 0.5);

}

Stonewt::operator double()const
{
    return pounds;
}
```

Listing 11.21 tests the new conversion functions. The assignment statement in the program uses an implicit conversion, whereas the final **cout** statement uses an explicit type cast. Remember to compile Listing 11.20 along with Listing 11.21.

LISTING 11.21   stone1.cpp

```
// stone1.cpp -- user-defined conversion functions
// compile with stonewt1.cpp
#include <iostream>
```

LISTING 11.21   Continued

```
using namespace std;
#include "stonewt1.h"

int main()
{
    Stonewt poppins(9,2.8);      // 9 stone, 2.8 pounds
    double p_wt = poppins;       // implicit conversion
    cout << "Convert to double => ";
    cout << "Poppins: " << p_wt << " pounds.\n";
    cout << "Convert to int => ";
    cout << "Poppins: " << int (poppins) << " pounds.\n";
    return 0;
}
```

Here's the program output; it shows the result of converting the type Stonewt object to type double and to type int:

```
Convert to double => Poppins: 128.8 pounds.
Convert to int => Poppins: 129 pounds.
```

Applying Type Conversions Automatically

The last example used int (poppins) with cout. Suppose, instead, it omitted the explicit type cast:

```
cout << "Poppins: " << poppins << " pounds.\n";
```

Would the program use an implicit conversion, as it did in the following statement?

```
double p_wt = poppins;
```

The answer is no. In the p_wt example, the context indicates that poppins should be converted to type double. But in the cout example, nothing indicates whether the conversion should be to int or to double. Facing this lack of information, the compiler would complain that you were using an ambiguous conversion. Nothing in the statement indicates what type to use.

Interestingly, if the class had defined only the double conversion function, the compiler would accept our statement. That's because with only one conversion possible, there is no ambiguity.

You can have a similar situation with assignment. With the current class declarations, the compiler rejects the following statement as ambiguous.

```
long gone = poppins;   // ambiguous
```

In C++, you can assign both int and double values to a long variable, so the compiler legitimately can use either conversion function. The compiler doesn't want the responsibility of choosing which. But if you eliminate one of the two conversion functions, the compiler accepts the statement. For example, suppose you omit the double definition. Then the compiler will use the int conversion to convert poppins to a type int value. Then it converts the int value to type long when assigning it to gone.

When the class defines two or more conversions, you can still use an explicit type cast to indicate which conversion function to use. You can use either type cast notation:

```
long gone = (double) poppins;   // use double conversion
long gone = int (poppins);      // use int conversion
```

The first statement converts `poppins` weight to a `double` value, and then assignment converts the `double` value to type `long`. Similarly, the second statement converts `poppins` first to type `int`, and then to `long`.

Like conversion constructors, conversion functions can be a mixed blessing. The problem with providing functions that make automatic, implicit conversions is that they may make conversions when you don't expect them. Suppose, for example, you happen to write the following sleep-deprived code:

```
int ar[20];
...
Stonewt temp(14, 4);
...
int Temp = 1;
...
cout << ar[temp] << "!\n";  // used temp instead of Temp
```

Normally, you'd expect the compiler to catch a blunder such as using an object instead of an integer as an array index. But the `Stonewt` class defines an `operator int()`, so the `Stonewt` object `temp` will be converted to the `int` 200 and be used as an array index. The moral is that often it's better to use explicit conversions and exclude the possibility of implicit conversions. The keyword `explicit` doesn't work with conversion functions, but all you have to do is replace a conversion function with a nonconversion function that does the same task, but only if called explicitly. That is, you can replace

```
Stonewt::operator int() { return int (pounds + 0.5); }
```

with

```
int Stonewt::Stone_to_Int() { return int (pounds + 0.5); }
```

This will disallow

```
int plb = poppins;
```

but, if you really need a conversion, allow the following:

```
int plb = poppins.Stone_to_Int();
```

Caution

Use implicit conversion functions with care. Often a function that can only be invoked explicitly is the better choice.

In summary, then, C++ provides the following type conversions for classes:

- A class constructor that has but a single argument serves as an instruction for converting a value of the argument type to the class type. For example, the `Stonewt` class constructor with a type `int` argument is invoked automatically when you assign a type `int` value to a `Stonewt` object. Using `explicit` in the constructor declaration, however, eliminates implicit conversions, allowing only explicit conversions.

- A special class member operator function called a conversion function serves as an instruction for converting a class object to some other type. The conversion function is a class member, has no declared return type, has no arguments, and is called `operator` *typeName*`()`, where *typeName* is the type to which the object is to be converted. This conversion function is invoked automatically when you assign a class object to a variable of that type or use the type cast operator to that type.

Conversions and Friends

Let's bring addition to the `Stonewt` class. As we mentioned when discussing the `Time` class, you can use either a member function or a friend function to overload addition. (To simplify matters, assume that no conversion functions of the `operator double()` form are defined.) You can implement addition with the following member function:

```
Stonewt Stonewt::operator+(const Stonewt & st) const
{
    double pds = pounds + st.pounds;
    Stonewt sum(pds);
    return sum;
}
```

Or you can implement addition as a friend function this way:

```
Stonewt operator+(const Stonewt & st1, const Stonewt & st2)
{
    double pds = st1.pounds + st2.pounds;
    Stonewt sum(pds);
    return sum;
}
```

Either form lets you do the following:

```
Stonewt jennySt(9, 12);
Stonewt bennySt(12, 8);
Stonewt total;
total = jennySt + bennySt;
```

Also, given the `Stonewt(double)` constructor, each form lets you do the following:

```
Stonewt jennySt(9, 12);
double kennyD = 176.0;
Stonewt total;
total = jennySt + kennyD;
```

But only the friend function lets you do this:

```
Stonewt jennySt(9, 12);
double pennyD = 146.0;
Stonewt total;
total = pennyD + jennySt;
```

To see why, translate each addition into the corresponding function calls. First,

```
total = jennySt + bennySt;
```

becomes

```
total = jennySt.operator+(bennySt);    // member function
```

or else

```
total = operator+(jennySt, bennySt);   // friend function
```

In either case, the actual argument types match the formal arguments. Also, the member function is invoked, as required, by a `Stonewt` object.

Next,

```
total = jennySt + kennyD;
```

becomes

```
total = jennySt.operator+(kennyD);    // member function
```

or else

```
total = operator+(jennySt, kennyD);   // friend function
```

Again, the member function is invoked, as required, by a `Stonewt` object. This time, in each case, one argument is type `double`, which invokes the `Stonewt(double)` constructor to convert the argument to a `Stonewt` object.

By the way, having an `operator double()` member function defined would create confusion at this point, for that would create another option for interpretation. Instead of converting `kennyD` to `double` and performing `Stonewt` addition, the compiler could convert `jennySt` to `double` and perform `double` addition. Too many conversion functions create ambiguities.

Finally,

```
total = pennyD + jennySt;
```

becomes

```
total = operator+(pennyD, jennySt);   // friend function
```

Here, both arguments are type `double`, which invokes the `Stonewt(double)` constructor to convert them to `Stonewt` objects. The member function cannot be invoked, however.

```
total = pennyD.operator+(jennySt);   // not meaningful
```

The reason is that only a class object can invoke a member function. C++ will not attempt to convert `pennyD` to a `Stonewt` object. Conversion takes place for member function arguments, not for member function invokers.

The lesson here is that defining addition as a friend makes it easier for a program to accommodate automatic type conversions. The reason is that both operands become function arguments, so function prototyping comes into play for both operands.

A Choice

Given that you want to add `double` quantities to `Stonewt` quantities, you have a couple of choices. The first, which we just outlined, is to define `operator+(const Stonewt &, const Stonewt &)` as a friend function and have the `Stonewt(double)` constructor handle conversions of type `double` arguments to type `Stonewt` arguments.

The second choice is to further overload the addition operator with functions that explicitly use one type `double` argument:

```
Stonewt operator+(double x);  // member function
friend Stonewt operator+(double x, Stonewt & s);
```

That way, the statement

```
total = jennySt + kennyD; // Stonewt + double
```

exactly matches the `operator+(double x)` member function, and the statement

```
total = pennyD + jennySt; // double + Stonewt
```

exactly matches the `operator+(double x, Stonewt &s)` friend function. Earlier, we did something similar for `Vector` multiplication.

Each choice has its advantages. The first choice (relying upon implicit conversions) results in a shorter program because you define fewer functions. That also implies less work for you and fewer chances to mess up. The disadvantage is the added overhead in time and memory needed to invoke the conversion constructor whenever a conversion is needed. The second choice (additional functions explicitly matching the types), however, is the mirror image. It makes for a longer program and more work on your part, but it runs a bit faster.

If your program makes intensive use of adding `double` values to `Stonewt` objects, it may pay to overload addition to handle such cases directly. If the program just uses such addition occasionally, it's simpler to rely on automatic conversions, or, if you want to be more careful, upon explicit conversions.

Real World Note: Calling Bootstrap Functions Before `main()`

The first function called in any executable is always its `main()` entry point. While this is true, there are a few tricks you can perform to alter this behavior. For example, consider a scheduling program that coordinates the production of golf clubs. Normally, when the program is started, information from a variety of sources is required to accurately schedule the daily production run of golf clubs. So you might want some "bootstrap" functions called first to prepare the ground for `main()`.

A *global object* (i.e., an object with file scope) is precisely what you're looking for because global objects are guaranteed to be constructed before a program's `main()` function is called. What you can do is create a class with a default constructor that invokes all of your bootstrap functions. These could, for example, initialize various data components of the object. Then you can create a global object. The following code illustrates this technique.

```
class CompileRequirements
{
  private:
    // essential information
  public:
    CompileRequirements()    // default constructor
    {
      GetDataFromSales();          // various
      GetDataFromManufacturing();  // bootstrap
      GetDataFromFinance();        // functions
    }
};

//Instance of Req class has global scope
CompileRequirements Req;      // uses default constructor

int main(void)
{
  // Read Req and build schedule
  BuildScheduleFromReq();

  //
  // rest of program code
  //
}
```

Summary

This chapter covers many important aspects of defining and using classes. Some of the material in this chapter may seem vague to you until your own experiences enrich your understanding. Meanwhile, let's summarize the chapter.

Normally, the only way you can access private class members is by using a class method. C++ alleviates that restriction with friend functions. To make a function a friend function, declare the function in the class declaration and preface the declaration with the keyword `friend`.

C++ extends overloading to operators by letting you define special operator functions that describe how particular operators relate to a particular class. An operator function can be a class member function or a friend function. (A few operators can only be class member functions.) C++ lets you invoke an operator function either by calling the function or by using the overloaded operator with its usual syntax. An operator function for the operator *op* has this form:

`operatorop(argument-list)`

The *argument-list* represents operands for the operator. If the operator function is a class member function, then the first operand is the invoking object and isn't part of the *argument-list*. For example, we overloaded addition by defining an `operator+()` member function for the `Vector` class. If `up`, `right`, and `result` are three vectors, you can use either of the following statements to invoke vector addition:

```
result = up.operator+(right);
result = up + right;
```

For the second version, the fact that the operands **up** and **right** are type **Vector** tells C++ to use the **Vector** definition of addition.

When an operator function is a member function, the first operand is the object invoking the function. In the preceding statements, for example, the **up** object is the invoking object. If you want to define an operator function so that the first operand is not a class object, you must use a friend function. Then you can pass the operands to the function definition in whichever order you want.

One of the most common tasks for operator overloading is defining the **<<** operator so that it can be used in conjunction with the **cout** object to display an object's contents. To allow an **ostream** object to be the first operand, define the operator function as a friend. To allow the redefined operator to be concatenated with itself, make the return type **ostream &**. Here's a general form satisfying those requirements:

```
ostream & operator<<(ostream & os, const c_name & obj)
{
    os << ... ;   // display object contents
    return os;
}
```

If, however, the class has methods that return values for the data members you want to display, you can use those methods instead of direct access in **operator<<()**. In that case, the function needn't (and shouldn't) be a friend.

C++ lets you establish conversions to and from class types. First, any class constructor taking a single argument acts as a conversion function, converting values of the argument type to the class type. C++ invokes the constructor automatically if you assign a value of the argument type to an object. For example, suppose you have a **String** class with a constructor that takes **char *** value as its sole argument. Then, if **bean** is a **String** object, you can use the following statement:

```
bean = "pinto";    // converts type char * to type String
```

If, however, you precede the constructor declaration with the keyword **explicit**, then the constructor can be used only for explicit conversions:

```
bean = String("pinto");    // converts type char * to type String explicitly
```

To convert from a class to another type, you must define a conversion function providing instruction about how to make the conversion. A conversion function must be a member function. If it is to convert to type *typeName*, it should have the following prototype:

```
operator typeName();
```

Note that it must have no declared return type, must have no arguments, and must (despite having no declared return type) return the converted value. For example, a function to convert type **Vector** to type **double** would have this function form:

```
Vector::operator double()
{
    ...
    return a_double_value;
}
```

Experience has shown that often it is better not to rely upon such implicit conversion functions.

As you might have noticed, classes require much more care and attention to detail than do simple C-style structures. In return, they do much more for you.

Review Questions

1. Use a member function to overload the multiplication operator for the Stonewt class; have the operator multiply the data members by a type double value. Note that this will require carryover for the stone-pound representation. That is, twice 10 stone 8 pounds is 21 stone 2 pounds.

2. What are the differences between a friend function and a member function?

3. Does a nonmember function have to be a friend to access a class's members?

4. Use a friend function to overload the multiplication operator for the Stonewt class; have the operator multiply the double value by the Stone value.

5. Which operators cannot be overloaded?

6. What restriction applies to overloading the following operators? = () [] ->

7. Define a conversion function for the Vector class that converts a Vector to a type double value representing the vector's magnitude.

Programming Exercises

1. Modify Listing 11.15 so that instead of reporting the results of a single trial for a particular target-step combination, it reports the highest, lowest, and average number of steps for N trials, where N is an integer entered by the user.

2. Rewrite the final Time class example (Listings 11.10, 11.11, and 11.12) so that all the overloaded operators are implemented using friend functions.

3. Rewrite the Stonewt class (Listings 11.16 and 11.17) so that it has a state member governing whether the object is interpreted in stone form, integer pounds form, or floating-point pounds form. Overload the << operator to replace the show_stn() and show_lbs() methods. Overload the addition, subtraction, and multiplication operators so that one can add, subtract, and multiply Stonewt values. Test your class with a short program that uses all the class methods and friends.

4. Rewrite the `Stonewt` class (Listings 11.16 and 11.17) so that it overloads all six relational operators. The operators should compare the **pounds** members and return a type **bool** value. Write a program that declares an array of six `Stonewt` objects and initializes the first three objects in the array declaration. Then it should use a loop to read in values used to set the remaining three array elements. Then it should report the smallest element, the largest element, and how many elements are greater or equal to 11 stone. (The simplest approach is to create a `Stonewt` object initialized to 11 stone and to compare the other objects with that object.)

5. A complex number has two parts: a real part and an imaginary part. One way to write an imaginary number is this: (3.0, 4.0). Here 3.0 is the real part and 4.0 is the imaginary part. Suppose a = (A,Bi) and c = (C,Di). Here are some complex operations:

   - Addition: a + c = (A + C, (B + D)i)

   - Subtraction: a − c = (A − C, (B − D)i)

   - Multiplication: a * c = (A * C − B*D, (A*D + B*C)i)

   - Multiplication: (x a real number): x * c = (x*C,x*Di)

   - Conjugation: ~a = (A, − Bi)

   Define a complex class so that the following program can use it with correct results. Note that you have to overload the << and >> operators. Many systems already have complex support in a `complex.h` header file, so use `complex0.h` to avoid conflicts. Use `const` whenever warranted.

```cpp
#include <iostream>
using namespace std;
#include "complex0.h"   // to avoid confusion with complex.h
int main()
{
    complex a(3.0, 4.0);    // initialize to (3,4i)
    complex c;
    cout << "Enter a complex number (q to quit):\n";
    while (cin >> c)
    {
        cout << "c is " << c << '\n';
        cout << "complex conjugate is " << ~c << '\n';
        cout << "a is " << a << '\n';
        cout << "a + c is " << a + c << '\n';
        cout << "a - c is " << a - c << '\n';
        cout << "a * c is " << a * c << '\n';
        cout << "2 * c is " << 2 * c << '\n';
        cout << "Enter a complex number (q to quit):\n";
    }
    cout << "Done!\n";
    return 0;
}
```

Here is a sample run. Note that `cin >> c`, through overloading, now prompts for real and imaginary parts:

```
Enter a complex number (q to quit):
real: 10
imaginary: 12
c is (10,12i)
complex conjugate is (10,-12i)
a is (3,4i)
a + c is (13,16i)
a - c is (-7,-8i)
a * c is (-18,76i)
2 * c is (20,24i)
Enter a complex number (q to quit):
real: q
Done!
```

CHAPTER 12

CLASSES AND DYNAMIC MEMORY ALLOCATION

You will learn about the following in this chapter:

- Using dynamic memory allocation for class members

- Implicit and explicit copy constructors

- Implicit and explicit overloaded assignment operators

- What you must do if you use new in a constructor

- Using static class members

- Using pointers to objects

- Implementing a queue ADT

T his chapter looks at how to use new and **delete** with classes and how to deal with some of the subtle problems that using dynamic memory can cause. This may sound like a short list of topics, but these topics affect constructor design, destructor design, and operator overloading.

Let's look at a specific example of how C++ can add to your memory load. Suppose you want to create a class with a member representing someone's last name. The simplest way is to use a character array member to hold the name. But this has some drawbacks. You might use a 14-character array and then run into Bartholomew Smeadsbury-Crafthovingham. Or, to be safer, you may use a 40-character array. But, if you then create an array of 2000 such objects, you'll waste a lot of memory with character arrays that are only partly filled. (At this point, we're adding to the computer's memory load.) There is an alternative.

Often it is much better to decide many matters, such as how much storage to use, when a program runs than when it's compiled. The usual C++ approach to storing a name in an object is to use the new operator in a class constructor to allocate the correct amount of memory while the program is running. But introducing new to a class constructor raises several new problems unless you remember to take a series of additional steps, such as expanding the class destructor, bringing all constructors into harmony with the new destructor, and writing additional class methods to facilitate correct initialization and assignment. (This chapter, of course, will explain all these steps.) If you're just learning C++, you may be better off sticking initially to the simple, if inferior, character array approach. Then, when a class design works well, you can return to your OOP workbench and enhance the class declaration by using new. In short, grow gradually into C++.

Dynamic Memory and Classes

What would you like for breakfast, lunch, and dinner for the next month? How many ounces of milk for dinner on the third day? How many raisins in your cereal for breakfast on the fifteenth day? If you're like most people, you'd rather postpone some of those decisions until the actual mealtimes. Part of C++ strategy is to take the same attitude toward memory allocation, letting the program decide about memory during runtime rather than during compile time. That way, memory use can depend on the needs of a program instead of upon a rigid set of storage-class rules. To gain dynamic control of memory, you remember, C++ utilizes the new and delete operators. Unhappily, using these operators with classes can pose some new programming problems. As you'll see, destructors can become necessary instead of merely ornamental. And sometimes, you have to overload the assignment operator to get programs to behave properly. We'll look into these matters now.

Review Example and Static Class Members

We haven't used new and delete for a while, so let's review them with a short program. While we're at it, we'll introduce a new storage class: the static class member. The vehicle will be a StringBad class, later to be superseded by the slightly more able String class. (C++ now comes with a string class library, supported by the string header file, and Chapter 16, "The String Class and the Standard Template Library," discusses that class. Meanwhile, the humble StringBad and String classes in this chapter will provide some insight into what underlies such a class.) StringBad and String class objects will hold a pointer to a string and a value representing the string length. We'll use the StringBad and String classes primarily to give an inside look at how new, delete, and static class members operate. For that reason, the constructors and destructors will display messages when called so that you can follow the action. Also, we'll omit several useful member and friend functions, such as overloaded ++ and >> operators and a conversion function, in order to simplify the class interface. (But rejoice! The review questions for this chapter give you the opportunity to add those useful support functions.) Listing 12.1 shows the class declaration.

Why call the class StringBad? This is to remind you that StringBad is an example under development. It's the first stage of developing a class using dynamic memory allocation, and it does the obvious things correctly; for example, it uses new and delete correctly in the constructors and destructor. It doesn't really do bad things, but the design omits doing some additional good things that are necessary but not at all obvious. Seeing the problems the class does have should help you understand and remember the non-obvious changes we will make later, when we convert it to the more functional String class.

LISTING 12.1   strngbad.h

```
// strngbad.h -- flawed string class definition
#include <iostream>
using namespace std;
#ifndef STRNGBAD_H_
#define STRNGBAD_H_
class StringBad
{
private:
    char * str;             // pointer to string
    int len;                // length of string
    static int num_strings; // number of objects
public:
    StringBad(const char * s); // constructor
    StringBad();               // default constructor
    ~StringBad();              // destructor
// friend function
    friend ostream & operator<<(ostream & os,
                        const StringBad & st);
};
#endif
```

You should note two points about this declaration. First, it uses a pointer-to-**char** instead of a **char** array to represent a name. This means that the class declaration does not allocate storage space for the string itself. Instead, it will use **new** in the constructors to allocate space for the string. This arrangement avoids straitjacketing the class declaration with a predefined limit to the string size.

Second, the definition declares the **num_strings** member as belonging to the **static** storage class. A *static class member* has a special property: A program creates only one copy of a static class variable regardless of the number of objects created. That is, a static member is shared among all objects of that class, much as a phone number might be shared among all members of a family. If, say, you create 10 **StringBad** objects, there would be 10 **str** members and 10 **len** members, but just one shared **num_strings** member (see Figure 12.1). This is convenient for data that should be private to a class but that should have the same value for all class objects. The **num_strings** member, for example, is intended to keep track of the number of objects created.

By the way, we've used the **num_strings** member as a convenient means of illustrating static data members and as a device to point out potential programming problems. In general, a string class doesn't need such a member.

Let's look at the implementation of the class methods in Listing 12.2. There, you'll see how these two points (using a pointer and using a static member) are handled.

FIGURE 12.1
The static data member.

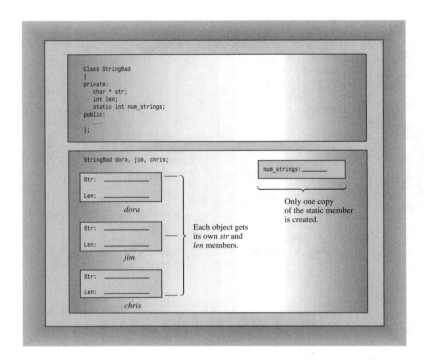

LISTING 12.2   strngbad.cpp

```
// strngbad.cpp -- StringBad class methods
#include <iostream>
#include <cstring>                // string.h for some
#include "strngbad.h"
using namespace std;

// initializing static class member
int StringBad::num_strings = 0;

// class methods

// construct StringBad from C string
StringBad::StringBad(const char * s)
{
    len = strlen(s);             // set size
    str = new char[len + 1];     // allot storage
    strcpy(str, s);              // initialize pointer
    num_strings++;               // set object count
    cout << num_strings << ": \"" << str
         << "\" object created\n"; // For Your Information
}

StringBad::StringBad()           // default constructor
{
    len = 4;
```

LISTING 12.2   Continued

```
    str = new char[4];
    strcpy(str, "C++");              // default string
    num_strings++;
    cout << num_strings << ": \"" << str
        << "\" default object created\n";  // FYI
}

StringBad::~StringBad()              // necessary destructor
{
    cout << "\"" << str << "\" object deleted, ";   // FYI
    --num_strings;                   // required
    cout << num_strings << " left\n"; // FYI
    delete [] str;                   // required
}

ostream & operator<<(ostream & os, const StringBad & st)
{
    os << st.str;
    return os;
}
```

First, notice the following statement from Listing 12.2:

```
int StringBad::num_strings = 0;
```

This statement initializes the static num_strings member to zero. Note that you cannot initialize a static member variable inside the class declaration. That's because the declaration is a description of how memory is to be allocated, but it doesn't allocate memory. You allocate and initialize memory by creating an object using that format. In the case of a static class member, you initialize the static member independently with a separate statement outside the class declaration. That's because the static class member is stored separately rather than as part of an object. Note that the initialization statement gives the type and uses the scope operator.

```
int StringBad::num_strings = 0;
```

This initialization goes in the methods file, not in the class declaration file. That's because the class declaration is in a header file, and a program may include a header file in several other files. That would result in multiple copies of the initialization statement, which is an error.

The exception (Chapter 10, "Objects and Classes") to the noninitialization of a static data member inside the class declaration is if the static data member is a **const** of integral or enumeration type.

Remember

A static data member is declared in the class declaration and is initialized in the file containing the class methods. The scope operator is used in the initialization to indicate to which class the static member belongs. However, if the static member is a **const** integral type or an enumeration type, it can be initialized in the class declaration itself.

Next, notice that each constructor contains the expression num_strings++. This ensures that each time a program creates a new object, the shared variable num_strings increases by one, keeping track of the total number of String objects. Also, the destructor contains the expression --num_strings. Thus, the String class also keeps track of deleted objects, keeping the value of the num_strings member current.

Now look at the first constructor, which initializes a String object with a regular C string:

```
StringBad::StringBad(const char * s)
{
    len = strlen(s);                // set size
    str = new char[len + 1];        // allot storage
    strcpy(str, s);                 // initialize pointer
    num_strings++;                  // set object count
    cout << num_strings << ": \"" << str
         << "\" object created\n";  // For Your Information
}
```

The class str member, recall, is just a pointer, so the constructor has to provide the memory for holding a string. You can pass a string pointer to the constructor when you initialize an object:

```
String boston("Boston");
```

The constructor then must allocate enough memory to hold the string, and then copy the string to that location. Let's go through the process step-by-step.

First, the function initializes the len member, using the strlen() function to compute the length of the string. Next, it uses new to allocate sufficient space to hold the string, and then assigns the address of the new memory to the str member. (Recall that strlen() returns the length of a string not counting the terminating null character, so the constructor adds 1 to len to allow space for the string including the null character.)

Next, the constructor uses strcpy() to copy the passed string into the new memory. Then it updates the object count. Finally, to help us monitor what's going on, the constructor displays the current number of objects and the string stored in the object. This feature will come in handy later, when we deliberately lead the String class into trouble.

To understand this approach, you should realize that the string is not stored in the object. The string is stored separately, in heap memory, and the object merely stores information saying where to find the string.

Note that you do not do this:

```
str = s;  // not the way to go
```

This merely stores the address without making a copy of the string.

The default constructor behaves similarly, except that it provides a default string of "C++".

The destructor contains the example's most important addition to our handling of classes:

```
StringBad::~StringBad()                 // necessary destructor
{
```

```
    cout << "\"" << str << "\" object deleted, ";    // FYI
    --num_strings;                          // required
    cout << num_strings << " left\n"; // FYI
    delete [] str;                          // required
}
```

The destructor begins by announcing when the destructor gets called. This part is informative, but not essential. The `delete` statement, however, is vital. Recall that the `str` member points to memory allocated with `new`. When a `StringBad` object expires, the `str` pointer expires. But the memory `str` pointed to remains allocated unless you use `delete` to free it. Deleting an object frees the memory occupied by the object itself, but it does not automatically free memory pointed to by pointers that were object members. For that, you must use the destructor. By placing the `delete` statement in the destructor, you ensure that the memory allocated with `new` by a constructor is freed when the object expires.

Remember

Whenever you use `new` in a constructor to allocate memory, you should use `delete` in the corresponding destructor to free that memory. If you use `new []` (with brackets), then you should use `delete []` (with brackets).

Listing 12.3, taken from a program under development at *The Daily Vegetable*, illustrates when and how the `Stringbad` constructors and destructors work. Remember to compile Listing 12.2 along with Listing 12.3.

LISTING 12.3   vegnews.cpp

```
// vegnews.cpp -- using new and delete with classes
// compile with strngbad.cpp
#include <iostream>
using namespace std;
#include "strngbad.h"

void callme1(StringBad &);  // pass by reference
void callme2(StringBad);    // pass by value

int main()
{
    StringBad headline1("Celery Stalks at Midnight");
    StringBad headline2("Lettuce Prey");
    StringBad sports("Spinach Leaves Bowl for Dollars");
    cout << "headline1: " << headline1 << endl;
    cout << "headline2: " << headline2 << endl;
    cout << "sports: " << sports << endl;
    callme1(headline1);
    cout << "headline1: " << headline1 << endl;
    callme2(headline2);
    cout << "headline2: " << headline2 << endl;
    cout << "Initialize one object to another:\n";
```

LISTING 12.3   *Continued*

```
    StringBad sailor = sports;
    cout << "sailor: " << sailor << endl;
    cout << "Assign one object to another:\n";
    StringBad knot;
    knot = headline1;
    cout << "knot: " << knot << endl;
    cout << "End of main()\n";

    return 0;
}

void callme1(StringBad & rsb)
{
    cout << "String passed by reference:\n";
    cout << "     \"" << rsb << "\"\n";
}

void callme2(StringBad sb)
{
    cout << "String passed by value:\n";
    cout << "     \"" << sb << "\"\n";
}
```

Compatibility Note

This first draft of a design for StringBad has some deliberate flaws that make the exact output undefined. Several compilers, for example, produced versions that aborted before completing. However, although the output details may differ, the basic problems and solutions are the same.

Here is the output produced after compiling the program with the Borland C++ 5.5 command-line compiler:

```
1: "Celery Stalks at Midnight" object created
2: "Lettuce Prey" object created
3: "Spinach Leaves Bowl for Dollars" object created
headline1: Celery Stalks at Midnight
headline2: Lettuce Prey
sports: Spinach Leaves Bowl for Dollars
String passed by reference:
    "Celery Stalks at Midnight"
headline1: Celery Stalks at Midnight
String passed by value:
    "Lettuce Prey"
"Lettuce Prey" object deleted, 2 left
headline2: Dûº
Initialize one object to another:
sailor: Spinach Leaves Bowl for Dollars
Assign one object to another:
3: "C++" default object created
knot: Celery Stalks at Midnight
```

```
End of main()
"Celery Stalks at Midnight" object deleted, 2 left
"Spinach Leaves Bowl for Dollars" object deleted, 1 left
"Spinach Leaves Bowl for Doll8" object deleted, 0 left
"@g" object deleted, -1 left
"-|" object deleted, -2 left
```

Program Notes

The program starts out fine, but it staggers to a strange and ultimately disastrous conclusion. Let's begin by looking at the good parts. The constructor announces it has created three StringBad objects, numbering them, and the program lists them using the overloaded >> operator:

```
1: "Celery Stalks at Midnight" object created
2: "Lettuce Prey" object created
3: "Spinach Leaves Bowl for Dollars" object created
headline1: Celery Stalks at Midnight
headline2: Lettuce Prey
sports: Spinach Leaves Bowl for Dollars
```

Then the program passes headline1 to the callme1() function and redisplays headline1 after the call. Here's the code:

```
callme1(headline1);
cout << "headline1: " << headline1 << endl;
```

And here's the result:

```
String passed by reference:
    "Celery Stalks at Midnight"
headline1: Celery Stalks at Midnight
```

This section of code seems to have worked fine, too.

But then the program executes the following code:

```
callme2(headline2);
cout << "headline2: " << headline2 << endl;
```

Here, callme2() passes headline2 by value instead of by reference, and the result indicates a serious problem!

```
String passed by value:
    "Lettuce Prey"
"Lettuce Prey" object deleted, 2 left
headline2: Dûº
```

First, somehow passing headline2 as a function argument caused the destructor to be called. Second, although passing by value is supposed to protect the original argument from change, the function seems to have messed up the original string beyond recognition.

Even worse, look at the end of the output, when the destructor gets called automatically for each of the objects created earlier:

```
End of main()
```

```
"Celery Stalks at Midnight" object deleted, 2 left
"Spinach Leaves Bowl for Dollars" object deleted, 1 left
"Spinach Leaves Bowl for Doll8" object deleted, 0 left
"@g" object deleted, -1 left
"-|" object deleted, -2 left
```

Because automatic storage objects are deleted in an order opposite to that in which they are created, the first three objects deleted are knots, sailor, and sport. The knots and sailor deletions look okay, but for sport, Dollars has become Doll8. The only thing the program did with sport was use it to initialize sailor, but that act appears to have altered sport. And the last two objects deleted, headline2 and headline1, are unrecognizable. Something has messed up these strings before they were deleted. Also, the counting is bizarre. How can there be -2 objects left?

Actually, the peculiar counting is a clue. Every object is constructed once and destroyed once, so the number of constructor calls should equal the number of destructor calls. Since the object count (num_strings) was decremented two extra times more than it was incremented, two objects must have been created using a constructor that didn't increment num_strings. The class definition declared and defined two constructors (both of which increment num_strings), but it turns out that the program used three. For example, consider this line:

```
StringBad sailor = sports;
```

What constructor is used here? Not the default constructor, and not the constructor with a const char * parameter. Remember, initialization using this form is another syntax for the following:

```
StringBad sailor = StringBad(sports); //constructor using sports
```

Because sports is type StringBad, a matching constructor could have this prototype:

```
StringBad(const StringBad &);
```

And it turns out the compiler automatically generates this constructor (called a *copy constructor* because it makes a copy of an object) if you initialize one object to another. The automatic version would not know about updating the num_strings static variable, so it would mess up the counting scheme. Indeed, all the problems exhibited by this example stem from member functions that the compiler generates automatically, so let's look at that topic now.

Implicit Member Functions

The problems with the StringBad class stem from implicit member functions that are defined automatically and whose behavior is inappropriate to this particular class design. In particular, C++ automatically provides the following member functions:

- A default constructor if you define no constructors

- A copy constructor if you don't define one

- An assignment operator if you don't define one

- A default destructor if you don't define one

- An address operator if you don't define one

It turns out that the implicit copy constructor and the implicit assignment operator caused the `StringBad` class problems.

The implicit address operator returns the address of the invoking object (that is, the value of the `this` pointer). That's fine for our purposes, and we won't discuss this member function further. The default destructor does nothing, and we won't discuss it, either, other than pointing out the class already has provided a substitute for it. But the others do warrant more discussion.

The Default Constructor

If you fail to provide any constructors at all, C++ provides you with a default constructor. For example, suppose you define a `Klunk` class and omit any constructors. Then the compiler will supply the following default:

```
Klunk::Klunk() { }  // implicit default constructor
```

That is, it supplies a constructor that takes no arguments and that does nothing. It's needed because creating an object always invokes a constructor:

```
Klunk lunk;  // invokes default constructor
```

The default constructor makes `lunk` like an ordinary automatic variable; that is, its value at initialization is unknown.

After you define any constructor, C++ doesn't bother to define a default constructor. If you want to create objects that aren't initialized explicitly, or if you want to create an array of objects, you then have to define a default constructor explicitly. It's the constructor with no arguments, but you can use it to set particular values:

```
Klunk::Klunk()  // explicit default constructor
{
    klunk_ct = 0;
    ...
}
```

A constructor with arguments still can be a default constructor if all its arguments have default values. For example, the `Klunk` class could have the following inline constructor:

```
Klunk(int n = 0) { klunk_ct = n; }
```

However, you can have only one default constructor. That is, you can't do this:

```
Klunk() { klunk_ct = 0 }
Klunk(int n = 0) { klunk_ct = n; }    // ambiguous
```

The Copy Constructor

The copy constructor is used to copy an object to a newly created object. That is, it's used during initialization, not during ordinary assignment. The copy constructor for a class has this prototype:

```
Class_name(const Class_name &);
```

Note that it takes a constant reference to a class object as its argument. For example, the copy constructor for the `String` class would have this prototype:

```
StringBad(const StringBad &);
```

You must know two things about the copy constructor: when it's used and what it does.

When the Copy Constructor Is Used

The copy constructor is invoked whenever a new object is created and initialized to an existing object of the same kind. This happens in several situations. The most obvious situation is when you explicitly initialize a new object to an existing object. For example, given that `motto` is a `StringBad` object, the following four defining declarations invoke the copy constructor:

```
StringBad ditto(motto);  // calls StringBad(const StringBad &)
StringBad metoo = motto; // calls StringBad(const StringBad &)
StringBad also = StringBad(motto);
                         // calls StringBad(const StringBad &)
StringBad * pStringBad = new StringBad(motto);
                         // calls StringBad(const StringBad &)
```

Depending upon the implementation, the middle two declarations may use the copy constructor directly to create `metoo` and `also`, or they may use the copy constructor to generate temporary objects whose contents are then assigned to `metoo` and `also`. The last example initializes an anonymous object to `motto` and assigns the address of the new object to the `pstring` pointer.

Less obviously, the compiler uses the copy constructor whenever a program generates copies of an object. In particular, it's used when a function passes an object by value (like `callme2()` does in Listing 12.3) or when a function returns an object. Remember, passing by value means creating a copy of the original variable. The compiler also uses the copy constructor whenever it generates temporary objects. For example, a compiler might generate a temporary `Vector` object to hold an intermediate result when adding three `Vector` objects. Compilers will vary as to when they generate temporary objects, but all will invoke the copy constructor when passing objects by value and when returning them. In particular, the function call in Listing 12.3 invoked the copy constructor:

```
callme2(headline2);
```

The program uses the copy constructor to initialize `sb`, the formal `StringBad`-type parameter for the `callme2()` function.

By the way, the fact that passing an object by value involves invoking a copy constructor is a good reason for passing by reference instead. That saves the time of invoking the constructor and the space for storing the new object.

What the Copy Constructor Does

The default copy constructor performs a member-by-member copy of the nonstatic members (memberwise copying, also sometimes called shallow copying). Each member is copied by value. In Listing 12.3, the statement

```
StringBad sailor = sports;
```

amounts to the following (aside from the fact that it wouldn't compile because access to private members is not allowed):

```
StringBad sailor;
sailor.str = sports.str;
sailor.len = sports.len;
```

If a member is itself a class object, the copy constructor for that class is used to copy one member object to another. Static members, such as `num_strings`, are unaffected, for they belong to the class as a whole instead of to individual objects. Figure 12.2 illustrates the action of the implicit copy constructor.

FIGURE 12.2

Memberwise copying.

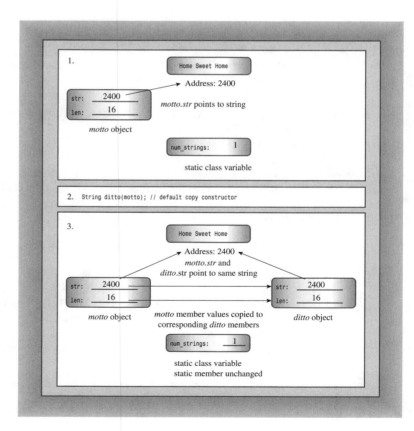

Where We Went Wrong

We are now in a position to understand the twofold weirdness of Listing 12.3. The first weirdness is that the program output indicates two more objects destroyed than constructed. The explanation is that the program did create two additional objects using the default copy constructor. The copy constructor was used to initialize the formal parameter of `callme2()` when that function was called, and it was used to initialize the object `sailor` to `sports`. The default copy constructor doesn't vocalize its activities, so it didn't announce its creations, and it didn't increment the `num_strings` counter. The destructor, however, does update the count, and it's invoked upon the demise of all objects, regardless of how they were constructed. This weirdness is a problem, for it means the program doesn't keep an accurate object count. The solution is to provide an explicit copy constructor that does update the count:

```
String::String(const String & s)
{
    num_strings++;
    ...// important stuff to go here
}
```

Tip

If your class has a static data member whose value changes when new objects are created, provide an explicit copy constructor that handles the accounting.

The second weirdness is the most subtle and dangerous of the bunch. One symptom is the garbled string contents:

```
headline2: Dûº
```

Another system is that many compiled versions of the program abort. CodeWarrior 6.0, for example, issues an "Unhandled exception" message. Microsoft Visual C++ 6.0 (debug mode) displayed an error message window saying that a Debug Assertion failed. Other systems might provide different messages or even no message, but the same evil lurks within the programs.

The cause is that the implicit copy constructor copies by value. Consider Listing 12.3, for example. The effect, recall, is this:

```
sailor.str = sport.str;
```

This does not copy the string; it copies the pointer to a string. That is, after `sailor` is initialized to `sports`, you wind up with two pointers to the same string. That's not a problem when the `operator<<()` function uses the pointer to display the string. It *is* a problem when the destructor is called. The `StringBad` destructor, recall, frees the memory pointed to by the `str` pointer. The effect of destroying `sailor` is this:

```
delete [] sailor.str;    // delete the string that ditto.str points to
```

The `sailor.str` pointer points to `"Spinach Leaves Bowl for Dollars"` because it was assigned the value of `sports.str`, which pointed to that string. So the `delete` statement frees the memory occupied by the string `"Spinach Leaves Bowl for Dollars"`.

Next, the effect of destroying `sports` is this:

```
delete [] sports.str;    // effect is undefined
```

Here, `sports.str` points to the same memory location that has already been freed by the destructor for `sailor`, and this results in undefined, possibly harmful, behavior. In our case, the program produces mangled strings, which usually is a sign of memory mismanagement.

Fixing the Problem with an Explicit Copy Constructor

The cure is to make a *deep copy*. That is, rather than just copying the address of the string, the copy constructor should duplicate the string and assign the address of the duplicate to the `str` member. That way, each object gets its own string rather than referring to another object's string. And each call of the destructor frees a different string rather than having duplicate attempts at freeing the same string. Here's how you can code the `String` copy constructor:

```
StringBad::StringBad(const StringBad & st)
{
    num_strings++;              // handle static member update
    len = st.len;               // same length
    str = new char [len + 1];   // allot space
    strcpy(str, st.str);        // copy string to new location
    cout << num_strings << ": \"" << str
         << "\" object created\n"; // For Your Information
}
```

What makes defining the copy constructor necessary is the fact that some class members were new-initialized pointers to data rather than the data themselves. Figure 12.3 illustrates deep copying.

Caution

If a class contains members that are pointers initialized by new, then you should define a copy constructor that copies the pointed-to data instead of copying the pointers themselves. This is termed deep copying. The alternative form of copying (memberwise, or shallow, copying) just copies pointer values. A shallow copy is just that—the shallow "scraping off" of pointer information for copying, rather than the deeper "mining" required to copy the constructs referred to by the pointers.

FIGURE 12.3

Deep copying.

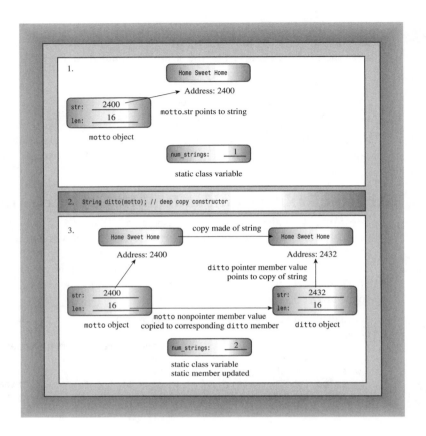

The Assignment Operator

Not all the problems in Listing 12.3 can be blamed on the default copy constructor; we have to look at the default assignment operator, too. Just as ANSI C allows structure assignment, C++ allows class object assignment. It does so by automatically overloading the assignment operator for a class. This operator has the following prototype:

```
Class_name & Class_name::operator=(const Class_name &);
```

That is, it takes and returns a reference to an object of the class. For example, here's the prototype for the **StringBad** class:

```
StringBad & StringBad::operator=(const StringBad &);
```

When the Assignment Operator Is Used

The overloaded assignment operator is used when you assign one object to another existing object:

```
StringBad headline1("Celery Stalks at Midnight");
...
```

```
StringBad knot;
knot = headline1;    // assignment operator invoked
```

The assignment operator is not necessarily used when initializing an object:

```
StringBad metoo = knot; // use copy constructor
```

Here metoo is a newly created object being initialized to knot's values; hence, the copy constructor is used. However, as mentioned before, implementations have the option of handling this statement in two steps: using the copy constructor to create a temporary object, and then using assignment to copy the values to the new object. That is, initialization always invokes the copy constructor, and forms using the = operator may also invoke the assignment operator.

What the Assignment Operator Does

Like the copy constructor, the implicit implementation of the assignment operator performs a member-to-member copy. If a member is itself an object of some class, the program uses the assignment operator defined for that class to do the copying for that particular member. Static data members are unaffected.

Where We Went Wrong

Listing 12.3 assigned headline1 to knot:

```
knot = headline1;
```

When the destructor was called for knot, it displayed this message:

```
"Celery Stalks at Midnight" object deleted, 2 left
```

When the destructor was called for headline1, it displayed this message:

```
"-|" object deleted, -2 left
```

(Some implementations abort before getting this far.)

We see the same problem that the implicit copy constructor caused: corrupted data. Once again, the problem is memberwise-copying, which causes both headline1.str and knot.str to point to the same address. Thus, when the destructor is called for knot, it deletes the string "Celery Stalks at Midnight", and when it's called for headline1, it attempts to delete the previously deleted string. As mentioned earlier, the effect of attempting to delete previously deleted data is undefined, so it may change the memory contents, and it may cause a program to abort. As some like to point out, if the effect of a particular operation is undefined, your compiler can do anything it wants, including displaying the Declaration of Independence or freeing your hard disk of unsightly files.

Fixing Assignment

The solution for the problems created by an inappropriate default assignment operator is to provide your own assignment operator definition, one that makes a deep copy. The implementation is similar to that of the copy constructor, but there are some differences.

1. Because the target object may already refer to previously allocated data, the function should use `delete[]` to free former obligations.

2. The function should protect against assigning an object to itself; otherwise, the freeing of memory described previously could erase the object's contents before they are reassigned.

3. The function returns a reference to the invoking object.

By returning an object, the function can emulate the way ordinary assignment for built-in types can be chained. That is, if A, B, and C are `StringBad` objects, you can write the following:

```
A = B = C;
```

In function notation, this becomes the following:

```
A.operator=(B.operator=(C));
```

Thus, the return value of `B.operator=(C)` becomes the argument of the `A.operator=()` function. Because the return value is a reference to a `String` object, it is the correct argument type.

Here's how you could write an assignment operator for the `StringBad` class:

```
StringBad & StringBad::operator=(const StringBad & st)
{
    if (this == &st)            // object assigned to itself
        return *this;           // all done
    delete [] str;              // free old string
    len = st.len;
    str = new char [len + 1];   // get space for new string
    strcpy(str, st.str);        // copy the string
    return *this;               // return reference to invoking object
}
```

First, the code checks for self-assignment. It does so by seeing if the address of the right-hand side of the assignment (`&s`) is the same as the address of the receiving object (`this`). If so, the program returns `*this` and terminates. You may recall from Chapter 10 that the assignment operator is one of the operators that can be overloaded only by a class member function.

Otherwise, the function proceeds to free the memory that `str` pointed to. The reason for this is that shortly thereafter `str` will be assigned the address of a new string. If you don't first apply the `delete` operator, the previous string would remain in memory. Because the program no longer has a pointer to the old string, that memory would be wasted.

Next, the program proceeds like the copy constructor, allocating enough space for the new string, then copying the string from the right-hand object to the new location.

When it is finished, the program returns `*this` and terminates.

Assignment does not create a new object, so you don't have to adjust the value of the static data member `num_strings`.

If you add the copy constructor and the assignment operator described previously to the `StringBad` class, you'll find it clears up all the problems. Here, for example, are the last few lines of output after these changes have been made:

```
End of main()
"Celery Stalks at Midnight" object deleted, 4 left
"Spinach Leaves Bowl for Dollars" object deleted, 3 left
"Spinach Leaves Bowl for Dollars" object deleted, 2 left
"Lettuce Prey" object deleted, 1 left
"Celery Stalks at Midnight" object deleted, 0 left
```

The object counting is correct now, and none of the strings have been mangled.

The New, Improved String Class

Now that we are a bit wiser, let's revise the `StringBad` class, renaming it `String`. First, we'll add the copy constructor and the assignment operator we just discussed so that the class correctly manages the memory used by class objects. Next, now that we've seen when objects are constructed and destroyed, we can mute the class constructors and destructors so that they no longer announce each time they are used. Also, now that we're no longer watching the constructors at work, let's simplify the default constructor so that it constructs an empty string instead of "C++".

Next, let's add a few capabilities to the class. A useful `String` class would incorporate all the functionality of the standard `cstring` library of string functions, but we'll add only enough to show the way. (Keep in mind that this `String` class is an illustrative example and that the C++ standard string class is much more extensive.) In particular, we'll add the following methods:

```cpp
int length () const { return len; }
friend bool operator<(const String &st, const String &st2);
friend bool operator>(const String &st1, const String &st2);
friend bool operator==(const String &st, const String &st2);
friend operator>>(istream & is, String & st);
char & operator[](int i);
const char & operator[](int i) const;
static int HowMany();
```

The first new method returns the length of the stored string. The next three friend functions allow you to compare strings. The `operator>>()` function provides simple input capabilities. The two `operator[]()` functions provide array-notation access to individual characters in a string. The static class method `HowMany()` will complement the static class data member `num_strings`. Let's look at some details.

Revised Default Constructor

The new default constructor merits notice. It will look like this:

```cpp
String::String()
{
    len = 0;
    str = new char[1];
```

```
    str[0] = '\0';                      // default string
}
```

You might wonder why the code does this:

```
str = new char[1];
```

and not this:

```
str = new char;
```

Both forms allocate the same amount of memory. The difference is that the first form is compatible with the class destructor and the second is not. The destructor, recall, contains this code:

```
delete [] str;
```

Using **delete** with brackets is compatible with pointers initialized by using **new** with brackets and with the null pointer. So another possibility would have been to replace

```
str = new char[1];
str[0] = '\0';                      // default string
```

with this:

```
str = 0; // sets str to the null pointer
```

The effect of using **delete []** with any pointers initialized any other way is undefined:

```
char words[15] = "bad idea";
char * p1= words;
char * p2 = new char;
char * p3;
delete [] p1; // undefined, so don't do it
delete [] p2; // undefined, so don't do it
delete [] p3; // undefined, so don't do it
```

Comparison Members

Three of the methods perform comparisons. The **operator<()** function returns **true** if the first string comes before the second string alphabetically (or, more precisely, in the machine collating sequence). The simplest way to implement the string comparison functions is to use the standard **strcmp()** function, which returns a negative value if its first argument precedes the second alphabetically, zero if the strings are the same, and a positive value if the first follows the second alphabetically. So, you can use **strcmp()** like this:

```
bool operator<(const String &st1, const String &st2)
{
    if (strcmp(st1.str, st2.str) > 0)
        return true;
    else
        return false;
}
```

Since the built-in > operator already returns a type **bool** value, you can simplify the code further to this:

```
bool operator<(const String &st1, const String &st2)
{
    return (strcmp(st1.str, st2.str) < 0);
}
```

Similarly, you can code the other two comparison functions like this:

```
bool operator>(const String &st1, const String &st2)
{
    return st2.str < st1.str;
}

bool operator==(const String &st1, const String &st2)
{
    return (strcmp(st1.str, st2.str) == 0);
}
```

The first definition expresses the > operator in terms of the < operator and would be a good choice for an inline function.

Making the comparison functions friends facilitates comparisons between String objects and regular C strings. For example, suppose answer is a String object and that you have the following code:

```
if ("love" == answer)
```

This gets translated to the following:

```
if (operator==("love", answer))
```

The compiler then uses one of the constructors to convert the code, in effect, to this:

```
if (operator==(String("love"), answer))
```

And this matches the prototype.

Accessing Characters with Bracket Notation

With a standard C-style string, you can use brackets to access individual characters:

```
char city[40] = "Amsterdam";
cout << city[0] << endl; // display the letter A
```

In C++ the two bracket symbols constitute a single operator, the bracket operator, and you can overload this operator with a method called operator[](). Typically, a binary C++ operator (one with two operands) puts the operator between the two operands, as in 2 + 5. But the bracket operator places one operand in front of the first bracket and the other operand between the two brackets. Thus, in the expression city[0], city is the first operand, [] is the operator, and 0 is the second operand.

Suppose that opera is a String object:

```
String opera("The Magic Flute");
```

If you use the expression opera[4], C++ will look for a method with this name and signature:

```
operator[](int i)
```

If it finds a matching prototype, the compiler will replace the expression `opera[4]` with this function call:

```
opera.operator[](4)
```

The `opera` object invokes the method, and the array subscript **4** becomes the function argument.

Here's a simple implementation:

```
char & String::operator[](int i)
{
    return str[i];
}
```

With this definition, the statement

```
cout << opera[4];
```

becomes this:

```
cout << opera.operator[4];
```

The return value is `opera.str[4]`, or the character `'M'`. So the public method gives access to private data.

Declaring the return type as type `char &` allows you to assign values to a particular element. For example, you can do the following:

```
String means("might");
means[0] = 'r';
```

The second statement is converted to an overloaded operator function call:

```
means.operator[][0] = 'r';
```

This assigns `'r'` to the method's return value. But the function returns a reference to `means.str[0]`, making the code equivalent to

```
means.str[0] = 'r';
```

This last line of code violates private access, but, because `operator[]()` is a class method, it is allowed to alter the array contents. The net effect is that `"might"` becomes `"right"`.

Suppose you have a constant object:

```
const String answer("futile");
```

Then, if the only definition for `operator[]()` available is the one you've just seen, the following code will be labeled an error:

```
cout << answer[1];   // compile-time error
```

The reason is that `answer` is `const` and the method doesn't promise not to alter data. (In fact, sometimes the method's job is to alter data, so it can't promise not to.)

However, C++ distinguishes between `const` and non-`const` function signatures when overloading, so we can provide a second version of `operator[]()` that is used just by `const` `String` objects:

```
// for use with const String objects
const char & String::operator[](int i) const
{
    return str[i];
}
```

With the definitions you have read-write access to regular `String` objects and read-only access to `const String` data:

```
String text("Once upon a time");
const String answer("futile");
cout << text[1];      // ok, uses non-const version of operator[]()
cout << answer[1];    // ok, uses const version of operator[]()
cout >> text[1];      // ok, uses non-const version of operator[]()
cin >> answer[1];     // compile-time error
```

Static Class Member Functions

It's also possible to declare a member function as being static. (The keyword `static` should appear in the function declaration but not in the function definition, if the latter is separate.) This has two important consequences.

First, a static member function doesn't have to be invoked by an object; in fact, it doesn't even get a `this` pointer to play with. If the static member function is declared in the public section, it can be invoked using the class name and the scope resolution operator. We can give the `String` class a static member function called `HowMany()` with the following prototype/definition in the class declaration:

```
static int HowMany() { return num_strings; }
```

It could be invoked like this:

```
int count = String::HowMany();  // invoking a static member function
```

The second consequence is that, because a static member function is not associated with a particular object, the only data members it can use are the static data members. For example, the `HowMany()` static method can access the `num_strings` static member, but not `str` or `len`.

Similarly, a static member function can be used to set a class-wide flag that controls how some aspect of the class interface behaves. For example, it controls the formatting used by a method that displays class contents.

Further Assignment Operator Overloading

Before looking at the new listings, let's consider another matter. Suppose you want to copy an ordinary string to a `String` object. For example, suppose you use `getline()` to read a string and you want to place it in a `String` object. The class methods already allow you to do the following:

```
String name;
char temp[40];
cin.getline(temp, 40);
name = temp;  // use constructor to convert type
```

However, this might not be a satisfactory solution if you have to do it often. To see why, let's review how the final statement works:

1. The program uses the `String(const char *)` constructor to construct a temporary `String` object containing a copy of the string stored in `temp`. Remember (Chapter 11, "Working with Classes") that a constructor with a single argument serves as a conversion function.

2. The program uses the `String & String::operator=(const String &)` function to copy information from the temporary object to the name object.

3. The program calls the `~String()` destructor to delete the temporary object.

The simplest way to make the process more efficient is to overload the assignment operator so that it works directly with ordinary strings. This removes the extra steps of creating and destroying a temporary object. Here's one possible implementation:

```
String & String::operator=(const char * s)
{
    delete [] str;
    len = strlen(s);
    str = new char[len + 1];
    strcpy(str, s);
    return *this;
}
```

As usual, you must deallocate memory formerly managed by `str` and allocate enough memory for the new string.

Listing 12.4 shows the revised class declaration. In addition to the changes already mentioned, it defines a constant `CINLIM` that will be used in implementing `operator>>()`.

LISTING 12.4   string1.h

```
// string1.h -- fixed and augmented string class definition
#include <iostream>
using namespace std;
#ifndef STRING1_H_
#define STRING1_H_
class String
{
private:
    char * str;              // pointer to string
    int len;                 // length of string
    static int num_strings;  // number of objects
    static const int CINLIM = 80;  // cin input limit
public:
// constructors and other methods
    String(const char * s); // constructor
```

LISTING 12.4   Continued

```
        String();                   // default constructor
        String(const String &);  // copy constructor
        ~String();                  // destructor
        int length () const { return len; }
    // overloaded operator methods
        String & operator=(const String &);
        String & operator=(const char *);
        char & operator[](int i);
        const char & operator[](int i) const;
    // overloaded operator friends
        friend bool operator<(const String &st, const String &st2);
        friend bool operator>(const String &st1, const String &st2);
        friend bool operator==(const String &st, const String &st2);
        friend ostream & operator<<(ostream & os, const String & st);
        friend istream & operator>>(istream & is, String & st);
    // static function
        static int HowMany();
    };
    #endif
```

Compatibility Note

You might have a compiler that has not implemented `bool`. In that case, you can use `int` instead of `bool`, `0` instead of `false`, and `1` instead of `true`. If your compiler doesn't support static class constants, you can define CINLIM with an enumeration:

```
enum {CINLIM = 90};
```

Next, Listing 12.5 presents the revised method definitions.

LISTING 12.5   string1.cpp

```
// string1.cpp -- String class methods
#include <iostream>
#include <cstring>                      // string.h for some
#include "string1.h"
using namespace std;

// initializing static class member

int String::num_strings = 0;

// static method
int String::HowMany()
{
    return num_strings;
}

// class methods
String::String(const char * s)        // construct String from C string
{
```

LISTING 12.5   Continued

```
    len = strlen(s);              // set size
    str = new char[len + 1];      // allot storage
    strcpy(str, s);               // initialize pointer
    num_strings++;                // set object count
}

String::String()                 // default constructor
{
    len = 4;
    str = new char[1];
    str[0] = '\0';                // default string
    num_strings++;
}

String::String(const String & st)
{
    num_strings++;                // handle static member update
    len = st.len;                 // same length
    str = new char [len + 1];     // allot space
    strcpy(str, st.str);          // copy string to new location
}

String::~String()                    // necessary destructor
{
    --num_strings;                   // required
    delete [] str;                   // required
}

// overloaded operator methods

    // assign a String to a String
String & String::operator=(const String & st)
{
    if (this == &st)
        return *this;
    delete [] str;
    len = st.len;
    str = new char[len + 1];
    strcpy(str, st.str);
    return *this;
}

    // assign a C string to a String
String & String::operator=(const char * s)
{
    delete [] str;
    len = strlen(s);
    str = new char[len + 1];
    strcpy(str, s);
    return *this;
}
```

LISTING 12.5   Continued

```
    // read-write char access for non-const String
char & String::operator[](int i)
{
    return str[i];
}

    // read-only char access for const String
const char & String::operator[](int i) const
{
    return str[i];
}

// overloaded operator friends

bool operator<(const String &st1, const String &st2)
{
    return (strcmp(st1.str, st2.str) < 0);
}

bool operator>(const String &st1, const String &st2)
{
    return st2.str < st1.str;
}

bool operator==(const String &st1, const String &st2)
{
    return (strcmp(st1.str, st2.str) == 0);
}

    // simple String output
ostream & operator<<(ostream & os, const String & st)
{
    os << st.str;
    return os;
}

    // quick and dirty String input
istream & operator>>(istream & is, String & st)
{
    char temp[String::CINLIM];
    is.get(temp, String::CINLIM);
    if (is)
        st = temp;
    while (is && is.get() != '\n')
        continue;
    return is;
}
```

The overloaded >> operator provides a simple way to read a line of keyboard input into a
String object. It assumes an input line of String::CINLIM characters or fewer and discards
any characters beyond that limit. Keep in mind that the value of an istream object in an if

condition evaluates to `false` if input fails for some reason, such as encountering an end-of-file condition, or, in the case of `get(char *, int)`, reading an empty line.

Let's exercise the class with a short program that lets you enter a few strings. The program has the user enter sayings, puts the strings into `String` objects, displays them, and reports which string is the shortest and which comes first alphabetically. Listing 12.6 shows the program.

LISTING 12.6   sayings1.cpp

```
// sayings1.cpp -- uses expanded string class
// compile with string1.cpp
#include <iostream>
using namespace std;
#include "string1.h"
const int ArSize = 10;
const int MaxLen =81;
int main()
{
    String name;
    cout <<"Hi, what's your name?\n>> ";
    cin >> name;

    cout << name << ", please enter up to " << ArSize
         << " short sayings <empty line to quit>:\n";
    String sayings[ArSize];     // array of objects
    char temp[MaxLen];          // temporary string storage
    int i;
    for (i = 0; i < ArSize; i++)
    {
        cout << i+1 << ": ";
        cin.get(temp, MaxLen);
        while (cin && cin.get() != '\n')
            continue;
        if (!cin || temp[0] == '\0')     // empty line?
            break;                       // i not incremented
        else
            sayings[i] = temp;  // overloaded assignment
    }
    int total = i;                       // total # of lines read

    cout << "Here are your sayings:\n";
    for (i = 0; i < total; i++)
        cout << sayings[i][0] << ": " << sayings[i] << "\n";

    int shortest = 0;
    int first = 0;
    for (i = 1; i < total; i++)
    {
        if (sayings[i].length() < sayings[shortest].length())
            shortest = i;
        if (sayings[i] < sayings[first])
            first = i;
```

LISTING 12.6   Continued

```
    }
    cout << "Shortest saying:\n" << sayings[shortest] << "\n";
    cout << "First alphabetically:\n" << sayings[first] << "\n";
    cout << "This program used "<< String::HowMany()
         << " String objects. Bye.\n";

    return 0;
}
```

Compatibility Note

Older versions of get(char *, int) don't evaluate to false upon reading an empty line. For those versions, however, the first character in the string will be a null if an empty line is entered. This example uses the following code:

```
if (!cin || temp[0] == '\0')    // empty line?
    break;                       // i not incremented
```

If the implementation follows the current standard, the first test in the if statement will detect an empty line, whereas the second test will detect the empty line for older implementations.

The program asks the user to enter up to ten sayings. Each saying is read into a temporary character array and then copied to a String object. If the user enters a blank line, a break statement terminates the input loop. After echoing the input, the program uses the length() and operator<() member functions to locate the shortest string and the alphabetically earliest string. The program also uses the subscript operator ([]) to preface each saying with its initial character. Here's a sample run:

```
Hi, what's your name?
>> Misty Gutz
Misty Gutz, please enter up to 10 short sayings <empty line to quit>:
1: a fool and his money are soon parted
2: penny wise, pound foolish
3: the love of money is the root of much evil
4: out of sight, out of mind
5: absence makes the heart grow fonder
6: absinthe makes the hart grow fonder
7:
a: a fool and his money are soon parted
p: penny wise, pound foolish
t: the love of money is the root of much evil
o: out of sight, out of mind
a: absence makes the heart grow fonder
a: absinthe makes the hart grow fonder
Shortest saying:
penny wise, pound foolish
First alphabetically:
a fool and his money are soon parted
This program used 11 String objects. Bye.
```

Things to Remember When Using new in Constructors

By now you've noticed that you must take special care when using **new** to initialize pointer members of an object. In particular, you should do the following:

- If you use **new** to initialize a pointer member in a constructor, you should use **delete** in the destructor.

- The uses of **new** and **delete** should be compatible. Pair **new** with **delete** and **new [ ]** with **delete [ ]**.

- If there are multiple constructors, all should use **new** the same way, either all with brackets or all without brackets. There's only one destructor, so all constructors have to be compatible to that destructor. It is, however, permissible to initialize a pointer with **new** in one constructor and with the null pointer (**NULL** or 0) in another constructor because it's okay to apply the **delete** operation (with or without brackets) to the null pointer.

NULL or 0?

The null pointer can be represented by **0** or by **NULL**, a symbolic constant defined as **0** in several header files. C programmers often use **NULL** instead of **0** as a visual reminder that the value is pointer value, just as they use '\0' instead of **0** for the null character as a visual reminder that this value is a character. The C++ tradition, however, seems to favor using a simple **0** instead of the equivalent **NULL**.

- You should define a copy constructor that initializes one object to another by doing deep copying. Typically, the constructor would emulate the following example:

```
String::String(const String & st)
{
    num_strings++;              // handle static member update if necessary
    len = st.len;               // same length
    str = new char [len + 1];   // allot space
    strcpy(str, st.str);        // copy string to new location
}
```

- In particular, the copy constructor should allocate space to hold the copied data, and it should copy the data, not just the address of the data. Also, it should update any static class members whose value would be affected by the process.

- You should define an assignment operator that copies one object to another by doing deep copying. Typically, the class method would emulate the following example:

```
String & String::operator=(const String & st)
{
    if (this == &st)            // object assigned to itself
        return *this;           // all done
    delete [] str;              // free old string
    len = st.len;
    str = new char [len + 1];   // get space for new string
    strcpy(str, st.str);        // copy the string
    return *this;               // return reference to invoking object
}
```

• In particular, the method should check for self-assignment; it should free memory formerly pointed to by the member pointer; it should copy the data, not just the address of the data; and it should return a reference to the invoking object.

The following excerpt contains two examples of what not to do and one example of a good constructor:

```
String::String()
{
    str = "default string";     // oops, no new []
    len = strlen(str);
}

String::String(const char * s)
{
    len = strlen(s);
    str = new char;             // oops, no []
    strcpy(str, s);             // oops, no room
}

String::String(const String & st)
{
        len = st.len;
        str = new char[len + 1];     // good, allocate space
        strcpy(str, st.str);         // good, copy value
}
```

The first constructor fails to use **new** to initialize `str`. The destructor, when called for a default object, will apply **delete** to `str`. The result of applying **delete** to a pointer not initialized by **new** is undefined, but probably bad. Any of the following would be okay:

```
String::String()
{
    len = 0;
    str = new char[1];   // uses new with []
    str[0] = '\0';
}

String::String()
{
    len = 0;
    str = NULL;   // or the equivalent str = 0;
}

String::String()
{
    static const char * s = "C++";       // initialized just once
    len = strlen(s);
    str = new char[len + 1];             // uses new with []
    strcpy(str, s);
}
```

The second constructor in the original excerpt applies **new**, but it fails to request the correct amount of memory; hence, **new** will return a block containing space for but one character.

Attempting to copy a longer string to that location is asking for memory problems. Also, the use of **new** without brackets is inconsistent with the correct form of the other constructors.

The third constructor is fine.

Finally, here's a destructor that *won't* work correctly with the previous constructors.

```
String::~String()
{
    delete str;       // oops, should be delete [] str;
}
```

The destructor uses **delete** incorrectly. Because the constructors request arrays of characters, the destructor should delete an array.

Using Pointers to Objects

C++ programs often use pointers to objects, so let's get in a bit of practice. Listing 12.6 used array index values to keep track of the shortest string and of the first string alphabetically. Another approach is to use pointers to point to the current leaders in these categories. Listing 12.7 implements this approach, using two pointers to **String**. Initially, the **shortest** pointer points to the first object in the array. Each time the program finds an object with a shorter string, it resets **shortest** to point to that object. Similarly, a **first** pointer tracks the alphabetically earliest string. Note that these two pointers do not create new objects; they merely point to existing objects. Hence they don't require using **new** to allocate additional memory.

For variety, the program uses a pointer that does keep track of a new object:

```
String * favorite = new String(sayings[choice]);
```

Here the pointer **favorite** provides the only access to the nameless object created by **new**. This particular syntax means to initialize the new **String** object by using the object **sayings[choice]**. That invokes the copy constructor because the argument type for the copy constructor (**const String &**) matches the initialization value (**sayings[choice]**). The program uses **srand()**, **rand()**, and **time()** to select a value for choice at random.

Object Initialization with new

In general, if *Class_name* is a class and if *value* is of type *Type_name*, the statement

```
Class_name * pclass = new Class_name(value);
```

invokes the

```
Class_name(Type_name);
```

constructor. There may be trivial conversions, such as to:

```
Class_name(const Type_name &);
```

Also, the usual conversions invoked by prototype matching, such as from **int** to **double**, will take place as long as there is no ambiguity. An initialization of the form

```
Class_name * ptr = new Class_name;
```

invokes the default constructor.

LISTING 12.7   sayings2.cpp

```
// sayings2.cpp -- uses pointers to objects
// compile with string1.cpp
#include <iostream>
using namespace std;
#include <cstdlib>        // (or stdlib.h) for rand(), srand()
#include <ctime>          // (or time.h) for time()
#include "string1.h"
const int ArSize = 10;
const int MaxLen = 81;
int main()
{
    String name;
    cout <<"Hi, what's your name?\n>> ";
    cin >> name;

    cout << name << ", please enter up to " << ArSize
         << " short sayings <empty line to quit>:\n";
    String sayings[ArSize];
    char temp[MaxLen];                  // temporary string storage
    int i;
    for (i = 0; i < ArSize; i++)
    {
        cout << i+1 << ": ";
        cin.get(temp, MaxLen);
        while (cin && cin.get() != '\n')
            continue;
        if (!cin || temp[0] == '\0')  // empty line?
            break;                    // i not incremented
        else
            sayings[i] = temp;        // overloaded assignment
    }
    int total = i;                      // total # of lines read

    cout << "Here are your sayings:\n";
    for (i = 0; i < total; i++)
        cout << sayings[i] << "\n";

// use pointers to keep track of shortest, first strings
    String * shortest = &sayings[0]; // initialize to first object
    String * first = &sayings[0];
    for (i = 1; i < total; i++)
    {
        if (sayings[i].length() < shortest->length())
            shortest = &sayings[i];
        if (sayings[i] < *first)      // compare values
            first = &sayings[i];      // assign address
    }
    cout << "Shortest saying:\n" << * shortest << "\n";
    cout << "First alphabetically:\n" << * first << "\n";

    srand(time(0));
    int choice = rand() % total;     // pick index at random
```

LISTING 12.7   Continued

```
// use new to create, initialize new String object
    String * favorite = new String(sayings[choice]);
    cout << "My favorite saying:\n" << *favorite << "\n";
    delete favorite;
    cout << "Bye.\n";
    return 0;
}
```

Compatibility Note

Older implementations might require including `stdlib.h` instead of `cstdlib` and `time.h` instead of `ctime`.

Here's a sample run:

```
Hi, what's your name?
>> Kirt Rood
Kirt Rood, please enter up to 10 short sayings <empty line to quit>:
1: a friend in need is a friend indeed
2: neither a borrower nor a lender be
3: a stitch in time saves nine
4: a niche in time saves stine
5: it takes a crook to catch a crook
6: cold hands, warm heart
7:
Here are your sayings:
a friend in need is a friend indeed
neither a borrower nor a lender be
a stitch in time saves nine
a niche in time saves stine
it takes a crook to catch a crook
cold hands, warm heart
Shortest saying:
cold hands, warm heart
First alphabetically:
a friend in need is a friend indeed
My favorite saying:
a stitch in time saves nine
Bye
```

Looking Again at `new` and `delete`

Note that the program uses **new** and `delete` on two levels. First, it uses **new** to allocate storage space for the name strings for each object that is created. This happens in the constructor functions, so the destructor function uses `delete` to free that memory. Because each string is an array of characters, the destructor uses `delete` with brackets. Thus, memory used to store the string contents is freed automatically when an object is destroyed. Second, the program uses `new` to allocate an entire object:

```
String * favorite = new String(sayings[choice]);
```

This allocates space not for the name string but for the object, that is, for the `str` pointer that holds the address of the string and for the `len` member. (It does not allocate space for the `num_strings` member because that is a static member stored separately from the objects.) Creating the object, in turn, calls the constructor, which allocates space for storing the string and assigns the string's address to `str`. The program then used `delete` to delete this object when it was finished with it. The object is a single object, so the program uses `delete` without brackets. Again, this frees only the space used to hold the `str` pointer and the `len` member. It doesn't free the memory used to hold the string `str` points to, but the destructor takes care of that final task. (See Figure 12.4.)

FIGURE 12.4

When destructors are called.

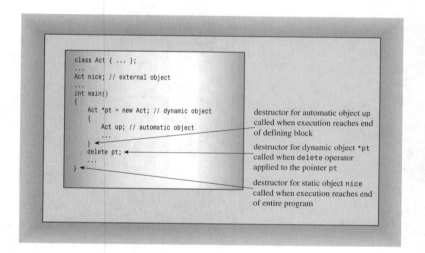

Let's emphasize again when destructors get called. (Also see Figure 12.4.)

1. If an object is an automatic variable, the object's destructor is called when the program exits the block in which the object is defined. Thus, the destructor is called for `headlines[0]` and `headlines[1]` when the program exits `main()`, and the destructor for `grub` is called when the program exits `callme1()`.

2. If an object is a static variable (external, static, static external, or from a namespace), its destructor is called when the program terminates. This is what happened for the `sports` object.

3. If an object is created by `new`, its destructor is called only when you explicitly `delete` the object.

Pointers and Objects Summary

You should note several points about using pointers to objects. (Also see Figure 12.5.)

- You declare a pointer to an object using the usual notation:

```
String * glamour;
```

- You can initialize a pointer to point to an existing object:

```
String * first = &sayings[0];
```

FIGURE 12.5

Pointers and objects.

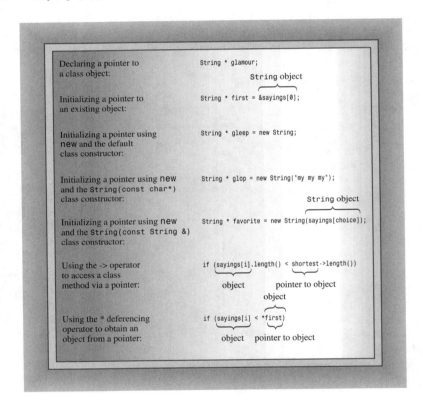

- You can initialize a pointer using new; this creates a new object:

```
String * favorite = new String(sayings[choice]);
```

Also see Figure 12.6.

- Using new with a class invokes the appropriate class constructor to initialize the newly created object:

```
// invokes default constructor
String * gleep = new String;
```

```
// invokes the String(const char *) constructor
String * glop = new String("my my my");

// invokes the String(const String &) constructor
String * favorite = new String(sayings[choice]);
```

- You use the `->` operator to access a class method via a pointer:

```
if (sayings[i].length() < shortest->length())
```

- You apply the dereferencing operator (`*`) to a pointer to an object to obtain an object:

```
if (sayings[i] < *first)      // compare object values
        first = &sayings[i];   // assign object address
```

Figure 12.6 summarizes the statement.

FIGURE 12.6

Creating an object with **new**.

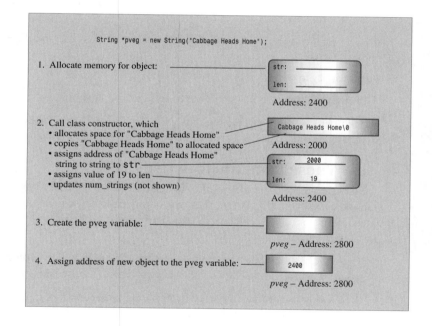

Reviewing Techniques

By now, you've encountered several programming techniques for dealing with various class-related problems, and you may be having trouble keeping track of all of them. So let's summarize several techniques and when they are used.

Overloading the << Operator

To redefine the `<<` operator so that you use it with **cout** to display an object's contents, define a friend operator function of the following form:

```
ostream & operator<<(ostream & os, const c_name & obj)
{
```

```
os << ... ;   // display object contents
    return os;
}
```

Here *c_name* represents the name of the class. If the class provides public methods that return the required contents, you can use those methods in the operator function and dispense with the friend status.

Conversion Functions

To convert a single value to a class type, create a class constructor of the following form of prototype:

```
c_name(type_name value);
```

Here *c_name* represents the class name, and **type_name** represents the name of the type that you want to convert.

To convert a class type to some other type, create a class member function having the following prototype:

```
operator type_name();
```

Although the function has no declared return type, it should return a value of the desired type.

Remember, use conversion functions with care. You can use the keyword **explicit** when declaring a constructor to prevent it from being used for implicit conversions.

Classes Whose Constructors Use new

Classes that use the **new** operator to allocate memory pointed to by a class member require several precautions in the design. (Yes, we summarized these precautions recently, but the rules are very important to remember, particularly because the compiler does not know them and, thus, won't catch your mistakes.)

1. Any class member pointing to memory allocated by **new** should have the **delete** operator applied to it in the class destructor. This frees the allocated memory.

2. If a destructor frees memory by applying **delete** to a pointer that is a class member, then every constructor for that class should initialize that pointer either by using **new** or by setting the pointer to the null pointer.

3. Constructors should settle on using either **new** [] or **new**, but not a mixture of both. The destructor should use **delete** [] if the constructors use **new** [], and it should use **delete** if the constructors use **new**.

4. You should define a copy constructor that allocates new memory rather than copying a pointer to existing memory. This enables a program to initialize one class object to another. The constructor normally should have the following form of prototype:

```
className(const className &)
```

5. You should define a class member function overloading the assignment operator and having the following form of function definition (here `c_pointer` is a member of the `c_name` class and has the type pointer-to-*type_name*):

```
c_name & c_name::operator=(const c_name & cn)
{
    if (this == & cn_)
        return *this;       // done if self-assignment
    delete c_pointer;
    c_pointer = new type_name[size];
    // then copy data pointed to by cn.c_pointer to
    // location pointed to by c_pointer
    ...
    return *this;
}
```

A Queue Simulation

Let's apply our improved understanding of classes to a programming problem. The Bank of Heather wants to open an automatic teller in the Food Heap supermarket. The Food Heap management is concerned about lines at the automatic teller interfering with traffic flow in the market and may want to impose a limit on the number of people allowed to line up at the teller machine. The Bank of Heather people want estimates of how long customers will have to wait in line. Your task is to prepare a program to simulate the situation so that management can see what the effect of the automatic teller might be.

A rather natural way of representing the problem is to use a queue of customers. A queue is an abstract data type (ADT) that holds an ordered sequence of items. New items are added to the rear of the queue, and items can be removed from the front. A queue is a bit like a stack, except that a stack has additions and removals at the same end. This makes a stack a LIFO (last-in, first-out) structure, whereas the queue is a FIFO (first in, first out) structure. Conceptually, a queue is like a line at a checkout stand or automatic teller, so it's ideally suited to the task. So, one part of your project will be to define a Queue class. (In Chapter 16, you'll read about the Standard Template Library queue class, but you'll learn more developing your own.)

The items in the queue will be customers. A Bank of Heather representative tells you that, on the average, a third of the customers will take one minute to be processed, a third will take two minutes, and a third will take three minutes. Furthermore, customers arrive at random intervals, but the average number of customers per hour is fairly constant. Two more parts of your project will be to design a class representing customers and to put together a program simulating the interactions between customers and the queue (see Figure 12.7).

FIGURE 12.7
A queue.

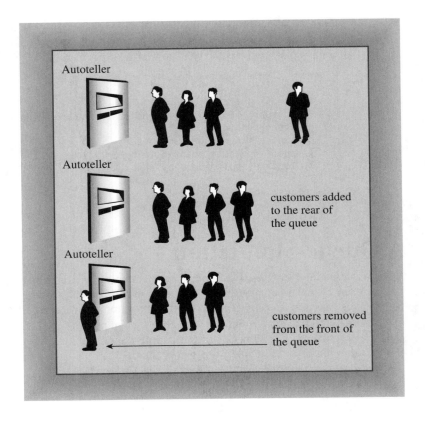

A Queue Class

The first order of business is designing a `Queue` class. First, let's list the attributes of the kind of queue we'll need:

- A queue holds an ordered sequence of items.
- A queue has a limit to the number of items it can hold.
- You should be able to create an empty queue.
- You should be able to check if a queue is empty.
- You should be able to check if a queue is full.
- You should be able to add an item to the end of a queue.
- You should be able to remove an item from the front of the queue.
- You should be able to determine the number of items in the queue.

As usual when designing a class, you'll need to develop a public interface and a private implementation.

The Interface

The queue attributes suggest the following public interface for a queue class:

```
class Queue
{
    enum {Q_SIZE = 10};
private:
// private representation to be developed later
public:
    Queue(int qs = Q_SIZE); // create queue with a qs limit
    ~Queue();
    bool isempty() const;
    bool isfull() const;
    int queuecount() const;
    bool enqueue(const Item &item); // add item to end
    bool dequeue(Item &item);       // remove item from front
};
```

The constructor creates an empty queue. By default, the queue can hold up to 10 items, but that can be overridden with an explicit initialization argument:

```
Queue line1;               // queue with 10-item limit
Queue line2(20);           // queue with 20-item limit
```

When using the queue, you can use a **typedef** to define **Item**. (In Chapter 14, "Reusing Code in C++," you'll learn how to use class templates instead.)

The Implementation

Next, let's implement the interface. First, you have to decide how to represent the queue data. One approach is to use **new** to dynamically allocate an array with the required number of elements. However, arrays aren't a good match to queue operations. For example, removing an item from the front of the array should be followed up by shifting every remaining element one unit closer to the front. Or else you'll need to do something more elaborate, such as treating the array as circular. The *linked list*, however, is a reasonable fit to the requirements of a queue. A linked list consists of a sequence of *nodes*. Each node contains the information to be held in the list plus a pointer to the next node in the list. For this queue, each data part will be a type **Item** value, and you can use a structure to represent a node:

```
struct Node
{
    Item item;              // data stored in the node
    struct Node * next;     // pointer to next node
};
```

Figure 12.8 illustrates a linked list.

The example shown in Figure 12.8 is called a *singly linked list* because each node has a single link, or pointer, to another node. If you have the address of the first node, you can follow the pointers to each subsequent node in the list. Commonly, the pointer in the last node in the list is set to **NULL** (or, equivalently, to **0**) to indicate that there are no further nodes. To keep track of a linked list, you must know the address of the first node. You can use a data member of the

Queue class to point to the beginning of the list. In principle, that's all the information you need, for you can trace down the chain of nodes to find any other node. However, because a queue always adds a new item to the end of the queue, it will be convenient to have a data member pointing to the last node, too (see Figure 12.9). In addition, you can use data members to keep track of the maximum number of items allowed in the queue and of the current number of items. Thus, the private part of the class declaration can look like this:

```
class Queue
{
// class scope definitions
    // Node is a nested structure definition local to this class
    struct Node { Item item; struct Node * next;};
    enum {Q_SIZE = 10};
private:
    Node * front;      // pointer to front of Queue
    Node * rear;       // pointer to rear of Queue
    int items;         // current number of items in Queue
    const int qsize;   // maximum number of items in Queue
    ...
public:
//...
};
```

FIGURE 12.8

A linked list.

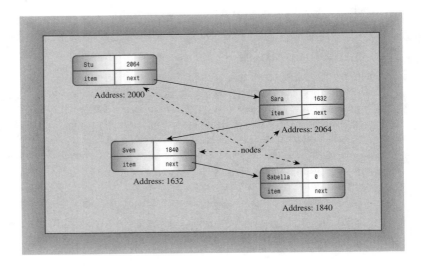

The declaration uses a new C++ feature: the ability to nest a structure or class declaration inside a class. By placing the **Node** declaration inside the **Queue** class, you give it class scope. That is, **Node** is a type that you can use to declare class members and as a type name in class methods, but the type is restricted to the class. That way, you don't have to worry about this declaration of **Node** conflicting with some global declaration or with a **Node** declared inside some other class. Not all compilers currently support nested structures and classes. If yours doesn't, then you'll have to define a **Node** structure globally, giving it file scope.

FIGURE 12.9

A `Queue` object.

Nested Structures and Classes

A structure, class, or enumeration declared within a class declaration is said to be nested in the class. It has class scope. Such a declaration doesn't create a data object. Rather, it specifies a type that can be used internally within the class. If the declaration is made in the private section of the class, then the declared type can be used only within the class. If the declaration is made in the public section, then the declared type also can be used out of the class by using the scope resolution operator. For example, if `Node` were declared in the public section of the `Queue` class, then you could declare variables of type `Queue::Node` outside the class.

After you settle upon a data representation, the next step is to code the class methods.

The Class Methods

The class constructor should provide values for the class members. Because the queue begins in an empty state, you should set the front and rear pointers to `NULL` (or `0`) and `items` to `0`. Also, you should set the maximum queue size `qsize` to the constructor argument `qs`. Here's an implementation that does not work:

```
Queue::Queue(int qs)
{
    front = rear = NULL;
    items = 0;
    qsize = qs;    // not acceptable!
}
```

The problem is that `qsize` is a `const`, so it can be *initialized* to a value, but it can't be *assigned* a value. Conceptually, calling a constructor creates an object before the code within the brackets is executed. Thus, calling the `Queue(int qs)` constructor causes the program to first allocate space for the four member variables. Then program flow enters the brackets and uses ordinary assignment to place values into the allocated space. Therefore, if you want to initialize a **const** data member, you have to do so when the object is created, before execution reaches the body of the constructor. C++ provides a special syntax for doing just that. It's called a *member initializer list*. The member initializer list consists of a comma-separated list of initializers preceded by a colon. It's placed after the closing parenthesis of the argument list and before the opening bracket of the function body. If a data member is named `mdata` and if it's to be initialized to value `val`, the initializer has the form `mdata(val)`. Using this notation, you can write the `Queue` constructor like this:

```
Queue::Queue(int qs) : qsize(qs)    // initialize qsize to qs
{
    front = rear = NULL;
    items = 0;
}
```

In general, the initial value can involve constants and arguments from the constructor's argument list. The technique is not limited to initializing constants; you also can write the `Queue` constructor like this:

```
Queue::Queue(int qs) : qsize(qs), front(NULL), rear(NULL), items(0)
{
}
```

Only constructors can use this initializer-list syntax. As you've seen, you have to use this syntax for **const** class members. You also have to use it for class members that are declared as references:

```
class Agency {...};
class Agent
{
private:
    Agency & belong;    // must use initializer list to initialize
    ...
};
Agent::Agent(Agency & a) : belong(a) {...}
```

That's because references, like **const** data, can be initialized only when created. For simple data members, such as `front` and `items`, it doesn't make much difference whether you use a member initializer list or use assignment in the function body. As you'll see in Chapter 14, however, it's more efficient to use the member initializer list for members that are themselves class objects.

The Member Initializer List Syntax

If `Classy` is a class and if `mem1`, `mem2`, and `mem3` are class data members, a class constructor can use the following syntax to initialize the data members:

```
Classy::Classy(int n, int m) :mem1(n), mem2(0), mem3(n*m + 2)
{
```

```
//...
}
```

This initializes mem1 to n, mem2 to 0, and mem3 to n*m + 2. Conceptually, these initializations take place when the object is created and before any code within the brackets is executed. Note the following:

- This form can be used only with constructors.
- You must use this form to initialize a nonstatic **const** data member.
- You must use this form to initialize a reference data member.

Data members get initialized in the order in which they appear in the class declaration, not in the order in which initializers are listed.

Caution

You can't use the member initializer list syntax with class methods other than constructors.

Incidentally, the parenthesized form used in the member initializer list can be used in ordinary initializations, too. That is, if you like, you can replace code like

```
int games = 162;
double talk = 2.71828;
```

with

```
int games(162);
double talk(2.71828);
```

This lets initializing built-in types look like initializing class objects.

The code for isempty(), isfull(), and queuecount() is simple. If items is 0, the queue is empty. If items is qsize, the queue is full. Returning the value of items answers the question of how many items are in the queue. We'll show the code in a header file later.

Adding an item to the rear of the queue (enqueuing) is more involved. Here is one approach:

```
bool Queue::enqueue(const Item & item)
{
    if (isfull())
        return false;
    Node * add = new Node;  // create node
    if (add == NULL)
        return false;        // quit if none available
    add->item = item;        // set node pointers
    add->next = NULL;
    items++;
    if (front == NULL)       // if queue is empty,
        front = add;         // place item at front
    else
        rear->next = add;    // else place at rear
    rear = add;              // have rear point to new node
    return true;
}
```

In brief, the method goes through the following phases (also see Figure 12.10):

1. Terminate if the queue is already full.

2. Create a new node, terminating if it can't do so, for example, if the request for more memory fails.

3. Place proper values into the node. In this case, the code copies an **Item** value into the data part of the node and sets the node's next pointer to **NULL**. This prepares the node to be the last item in the queue.

4. Increase the item count (**items**) by one.

5. Attach the node to the rear of the queue. There are two parts to this process. The first is linking the node to the other nodes in the list. This is done by having the **next** pointer of the currently rear node point to the new rear node. The second part is to set the **Queue** member pointer **rear** to point to the new node so that the queue can access the last node directly. If the queue is empty, you also must set the **front** pointer to point to the new node. (If there's just one node, it's both the front and the rear node.)

FIGURE 12.10

Enqueuing an item.

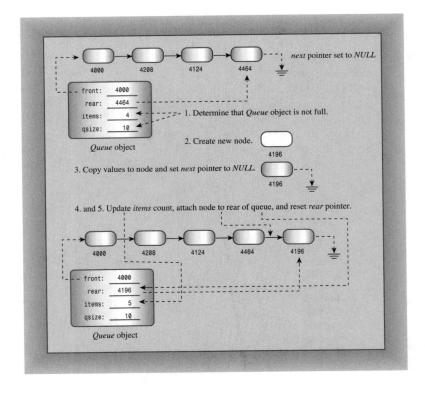

Removing an item from the front of the queue (dequeuing) also has several steps.

```
bool Queue::dequeue(Item & item)
{
    if (front == NULL)
        return false;
    item = front->item;    // set item to first item in queue
    items--;
    Node * temp = front;    // save location of first item
    front = front->next;    // reset front to next item
    delete temp;            // delete former first item
    if (items == 0)
        rear = NULL;
    return true;
}
```

In brief, the method goes through the following phases (also see Figure 12.11):

FIGURE 12.11

Dequeuing an item.

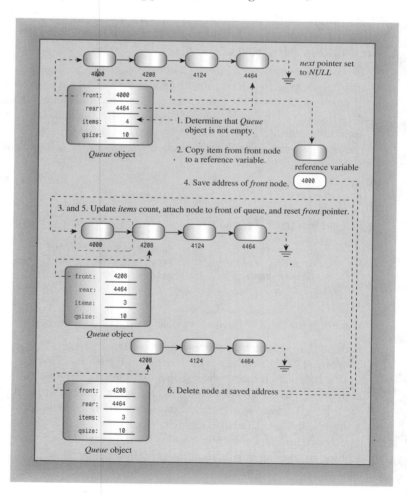

1. Terminate if the queue is already empty.

2. Provide the first item in the queue to the calling function. This is accomplished by copying the data portion of the current **front** node into the reference variable passed to the method.

3. Decrease the item count (**items**) by one.

4. Save the location of the front node for later deletion.

5. Take the node off the queue. This is accomplished by setting the **Queue** member pointer **front** to point to the next node, whose address is provided by **front->next**.

6. To conserve memory, delete the former first node.

7. If the list is now empty, set rear to **NULL**. (The front pointer already would be **NULL** in this case after being set to **front->next**.)

Step 4 is necessary because step 5 erases the queue's memory of where the former first node is.

Other Class Methods?

Do you need any more methods? The class constructor doesn't use **new**, so, at first glance, it may appear you don't have to worry about the special requirements of classes that do use **new** in the constructors. Of course, that first glance is misleading, for adding objects to a queue does invoke **new** to create new nodes. It's true that the **dequeue()** method cleans up by deleting nodes, but there's no guarantee that a queue will be empty when it expires. Therefore, the class does require an explicit destructor, one that deletes all remaining nodes. Here's an implementation:

```
Queue::~Queue()
{
    Node * temp;
    while (front != NULL)    // while queue is not yet empty
    {
        temp = front;        // save address of front item
        front = front->next;// reset pointer to next item
        delete temp;         // delete former front
    }
}
```

It starts at the front of the list and deletes each node in turn.

Hmmm. You've seen that classes using **new** usually require explicit copy constructors and assignment operators that do deep copying. Is that the case here? The first question to answer is, does the default memberwise copying do the right thing? The answer is no. Memberwise copying of a **Queue** object would produce a new object that pointed to the front and rear of the same linked list as the original. Thus, adding an item to the copy **Queue** object changes the shared linked list. That's bad enough. What's worse is that only the copy's rear pointer gets updated, essentially corrupting the list from the standpoint of the original object. Clearly, then, cloning or copying queues requires providing a copy constructor and an assignment constructor that do deep copying.

Of course, that raises the question of why you would want to copy a queue. Well, perhaps you would want to save snapshots of a queue during different stages of a simulation. Or you would like to provide identical input to two different strategies. Actually, it might be useful to have operations that split a queue, the way supermarkets sometimes do when opening an additional checkout stand. Similarly, you might want to combine two queues into one or truncate a queue.

But we don't want to do any of these things in this simulation. Can't you simply ignore those concerns and use the methods you already have? Of course you can. However, at some time in the future, you may need to use a queue again, this time with copying. And you might forget that you failed to provide proper code for copying. Your programs will compile and run, but will generate puzzling results and crashes. So it would seem that it's best to provide a copy constructor and an assignment operator, even though you don't need them now.

Fortunately, there is a sneaky way to avoid doing this extra work while still protecting yourself from future program crashes. The idea is to define the required methods as dummy private methods:

```
class Queue
{
private:
    Queue(const Queue & q) : qsize(0) { }   // preemptive definition
    Queue & operator=(const Queue & q) { return *this;}
//...
};
```

This has two effects. First, it overrides the default method definitions that otherwise would be generated automatically. Second, because these methods are private, they can't be used by the world at large. That is, if **nip** and **tuck** are **Queue** objects, the compiler won't allow the following:

```
Queue snick(nip);    // not allowed
tuck = nip;          // not allowed
```

Therefore, instead of being faced with mysterious runtime malfunctions in the future, you'll get an easier-to-trace compiler error stating that these methods aren't accessible. Also, this trick is useful when you define a class whose objects should not be copied.

Are there any other effects to note? Yes. Recall that the copy constructor is invoked when objects are passed (or returned) by value. However, this is no problem if you follow the preferred practice of passing objects as references. Also, the copy constructor is used to create other temporary objects. But the **Queue** definition lacks operations that lead to temporary objects, such as overloading the addition operator.

The Customer Class

Next, you must design a customer class. In general, a teller machine customer has many properties, such as a name, account numbers, and account balances. However, the only properties you need for the simulation are when a customer joins the queue and the time required for the customer's transaction. When the simulation produces a new customer, the program will create a new customer object, storing in it the customer's time of arrival and a randomly generated value for the transaction time. When the customer reaches the front of the queue, the program will note the time and subtract the queue-joining time to get the customer's waiting time. Here's how you can define and implement the `Customer` class:

```
class Customer
{
private:
    long arrive;          // arrival time for customer
    int processtime;      // processing time for customer
public:
    Customer() { arrive = processtime = 0; }
    void set(long when);
    long when() const { return arrive; }
    int ptime() const { return processtime; }
};
void Customer::set(long when)
{
    processtime = rand() % 3 + 1;
    arrive = when;
}
```

The default constructor creates a null customer. The `set()` member function sets the arrival time to its argument and randomly picks a value from 1 through 3 for the processing time.

Listing 12.8 gathers together the `Queue` and `Customer` class declarations, and Listing 12.9 provides the methods.

LISTING 12.8   queue.h

```
// queue.h -- interface for a queue
#ifndef QUEUE_H_
#define QUEUE_H_
// This queue will contain Customer items
class Customer
{
private:
    long arrive;          // arrival time for customer
    int processtime;      // processing time for customer
public:
    Customer() { arrive = processtime = 0; }
    void set(long when);
    long when() const { return arrive; }
    int ptime() const { return processtime; }
};

typedef Customer Item;

class Queue
{
// class scope definitions
    // Node is a nested structure definition local to this class
```

LISTING 12.8 Continued

```
        struct Node { Item item; struct Node * next;};
        enum {Q_SIZE = 10};
private:
    Node * front;          // pointer to front of Queue
    Node * rear;           // pointer to rear of Queue
    int items;             // current number of items in Queue
    const int qsize;       // maximum number of items in Queue
    // preemptive definitions to prevent public copying
    Queue(const Queue & q) : qsize(0) { }
    Queue & operator=(const Queue & q) { return *this;}
public:
    Queue(int qs = Q_SIZE); // create queue with a qs limit
    ~Queue();
    bool isempty() const;
    bool isfull() const;
    int queuecount() const;
    bool enqueue(const Item &item); // add item to end
    bool dequeue(Item &item);       // remove item from front
};
#endif
```

LISTING 12.9 queue.cpp

```
// queue.cpp -- Queue and Customer methods
#include "queue.h"
#include <cstdlib>            // (or stdlib.h) for rand()
using namespace std;

// Queue methods
Queue::Queue(int qs) : qsize(qs)
{
    front = rear = NULL;
    items = 0;
}

Queue::~Queue()
{
    Node * temp;
    while (front != NULL)    // while queue is not yet empty
    {
        temp = front;        // save address of front item
        front = front->next;// reset pointer to next item
        delete temp;         // delete former front
    }
}

bool Queue::isempty() const
{
    return items == 0;
}
```

LISTING 12.9 *Continued*

```cpp
bool Queue::isfull() const
{
    return items == qsize;
}

int Queue::queuecount() const
{
    return items;
}

// Add item to queue
bool Queue::enqueue(const Item & item)
{
    if (isfull())
        return false;
    Node * add = new Node;   // create node
    if (add == NULL)
        return false;        // quit if none available
    add->item = item;        // set node pointers
    add->next = NULL;
    items++;
    if (front == NULL)       // if queue is empty,
        front = add;         // place item at front
    else
        rear->next = add;    // else place at rear
    rear = add;              // have rear point to new node
    return true;
}

// Place front item into item variable and remove from queue
bool Queue::dequeue(Item & item)
{
    if (front == NULL)
        return false;
    item = front->item;      // set item to first item in queue
    items--;
    Node * temp = front;     // save location of first item
    front = front->next;     // reset front to next item
    delete temp;             // delete former first item
    if (items == 0)
        rear = NULL;
    return true;
}

// customer method

// when is the time at which the customer arrives
// the arrival time is set to when and the processing
// time set to a random value in the range 1 - 3
```

LISTING 12.9   Continued

```
void Customer::set(long when)
{
    processtime = rand() % 3 + 1;
    arrive = when;
}
```

	Compatibility Note

You might have a compiler that has not implemented `bool`. In that case, you can use `int` instead of `bool`, `0` instead of `false`, and `1` instead of `true`. You may have to use `stdlib.h` instead of the newer `cstdlib`.

The Simulation

We now have the tools needed for the automatic teller simulation. The program will allow the user to enter three quantities: the maximum queue size, the number of hours the program will simulate, and the average number of customers per hour. The program will use a loop in which each cycle represents one minute. During each minute cycle, the program will do the following:

1. Determine whether a new customer has arrived. If so, add the customer to the queue if there is room, otherwise turn the customer away.

2. If no one is being processed, take the first person from the queue. Determine how long the person has been waiting, and set a `wait_time` counter to the processing time that the new customer will need.

3. If a customer is being processed, decrement the `wait_time` counter one minute.

4. Track various quantities, such as the number of customers served, customers turned away, cumulative time spent waiting in line, and cumulative queue length.

When the simulation cycle is finished, the program will report various statistical findings.

An interesting matter is how the program determines whether a new customer has arrived. Suppose, on the average, 10 customers arrive an hour. That amounts to a customer every 6 minutes. The program computes and stores that value in the variable `min_per_cust`. However, having a customer show up exactly every 6 minutes is unrealistic. What we really want (at least most of the time) is a more random process that averages to a customer every 6 minutes. The program uses this function to determine if a customer shows up during a cycle:

```
bool newcustomer(double x)
{
    return (rand() * x / RAND_MAX < 1);
}
```

Here's how it works. The value `RAND_MAX` is defined in the `cstdlib` file (formerly `stdlib.h`) and represents the largest value the `rand()` function can return (0 is the lowest value). Suppose that `x`, the average time between customers, is 6. Then the value of `rand() * x /`

RAND_MAX will be somewhere between 0 and 6. In particular, it will be less than 1 a sixth of the time, on the average. However, it's possible that this function might yield two customers spaced 1 minute apart one time, or 20 minutes apart another time. This behavior leads to the clumpiness that often distinguishes real processes from the clocklike regularity of exactly one customer every 6 minutes. This particular method breaks down if the average time between arrivals drops below 1 minute, but the simulation is not intended to handle that scenario. If you did need to deal with such a case, you'd use a finer time resolution, perhaps letting each cycle represent 10 seconds.

Compatibility Note

Some compilers don't define RAND_MAX. If you face that situation, you can define a value for RAND_MAX yourself by using #define or else a const int. If you can't find the correct value documented, try using the largest possible int value, given by INT_MAX in the climits or the limits.h header file.

Listing 12.10 presents the details of the simulation. Running the simulation for a long time period provides insight into long-term averages, and running it for short times provides insight into short-term variations.

LISTING 12.10   bank.cpp

```cpp
// bank.cpp -- use the Queue interface
#include <iostream>
using namespace std;
#include <cstdlib> // for rand() and srand()
#include <ctime>   // for time()
#include "queue.h"
const int MIN_PER_HR = 60;

bool newcustomer(double x); // is there a new customer?

int main()
{
// setting things up
    srand(time(0));          // random initializing of rand()

    cout << "Case Study: Bank of Heather Automatic Teller\n";
    cout << "Enter maximum size of queue: ";
    int qs;
    cin >> qs;
    Queue line(qs);          // line queue holds up to qs people

    cout << "Enter the number of simulation hours: ";
    int hours;               // hours of simulation
    cin >> hours;
    // simulation will run 1 cycle per minute
    long cyclelimit = MIN_PER_HR * hours; // # of cycles
```

LISTING 12.10   Continued

```
    cout << "Enter the average number of customers per hour: ";
    double perhour;              // average # of arrival per hour
    cin >> perhour;
    double min_per_cust;     // average time between arrivals
    min_per_cust = MIN_PER_HR / perhour;

    Item temp;                   // new customer data
    long turnaways = 0;      // turned away by full queue
    long customers = 0;      // joined the queue
    long served = 0;         // served during the simulation
    long sum_line = 0;       // cumulative line length
    int wait_time = 0;       // time until autoteller is free
    long line_wait = 0;      // cumulative time in line


// running the simulation
    for (int cycle = 0; cycle < cyclelimit; cycle++)
    {
        if (newcustomer(min_per_cust))  // have newcomer
        {
            if (line.isfull())
                turnaways++;
            else
            {
                customers++;
                temp.set(cycle);     // cycle = time of arrival
                line.enqueue(temp); // add newcomer to line
            }
        }
        if (wait_time <= 0 && !line.isempty())
        {
            line.dequeue (temp);      // attend next customer
            wait_time = temp.ptime(); // for wait_time minutes
            line_wait += cycle - temp.when();
            served++;
        }
        if (wait_time > 0)
            wait_time--;
        sum_line += line.queuecount();
    }

// reporting results
    if (customers > 0)
    {
        cout << "customers accepted: " << customers << '\n';
        cout << "  customers served: " << served << '\n';
        cout << "          turnaways: " << turnaways << '\n';
        cout << "average queue size: ";
        cout.precision(2);
        cout.setf(ios_base::fixed, ios_base::floatfield);
        cout.setf(ios_base::showpoint);
        cout << (double) sum_line / cyclelimit << '\n';
```

LISTING 12.10   Continued

```
            cout << " average wait time: "
                 << (double) line_wait / served << " minutes\n";
    }
    else
        cout << "No customers!\n";

    return 0;
}

//  x = average time, in minutes, between customers
//  return value is true if customer shows up this minute
bool newcustomer(double x)
{
    return (rand() * x / RAND_MAX < 1);
}
```

Compatibility Note

You might have a compiler that has not implemented `bool`. In that case, you can use `int` instead of `bool`, `0` instead of `false`, and `1` instead of `true`. You may have to use `stdlib.h` and `time.h` instead of the newer `cstdlib` and `ctime`. You may have to define `RAND_MAX` yourself.

Here are a few sample runs for a longer time period:

```
Case Study: Bank of Heather Automatic Teller
Enter maximum size of queue: 10
Enter the number of simulation hours: 100
Enter the average number of customers per hour: 15
customers accepted: 1485
  customers served: 1485
         turnaways: 0
average queue size: 0.15
 average wait time: 0.63 minutes

Case Study: Bank of Heather Automatic Teller
Enter maximum size of queue: 10
Enter the number of simulation hours: 100
Enter the average number of customers per hour: 30
customers accepted: 2896
  customers served: 2888
         turnaways: 101
average queue size: 4.64
 average wait time: 9.63 minutes

Case Study: Bank of Heather Automatic Teller
Enter maximum size of queue: 20
Enter the number of simulation hours: 100
Enter the average number of customers per hour: 30
customers accepted: 2943
  customers served: 2943
         turnaways: 93
```

```
average queue size: 13.06
 average wait time: 26.63 minutes
```

Note that going from 15 customers an hour to 30 customers an hour doesn't double the average wait time, it increases it by about a factor of 15. Allowing a longer queue just makes matters worse. However, the simulation doesn't allow for the fact that many customers, frustrated with a long wait, would simply leave the queue.

Here are a few more sample runs. These illustrate the short-term variations one might see, even though the average number of customers per hour is kept constant.

```
Case Study: Bank of Heather Automatic Teller
Enter maximum size of queue: 10
Enter the number of simulation hours: 4
Enter the average number of customers per hour: 30
customers accepted: 114
  customers served: 110
        turnaways: 0
average queue size: 2.15
 average wait time: 4.52 minutes

Case Study: Bank of Heather Automatic Teller
Enter maximum size of queue: 10
Enter the number of simulation hours: 4
Enter the average number of customers per hour: 30
customers accepted: 121
  customers served: 116
        turnaways: 5
average queue size: 5.28
 average wait time: 10.72 minutes

Case Study: Bank of Heather Automatic Teller
Enter maximum size of queue: 10
Enter the number of simulation hours: 4
Enter the average number of customers per hour: 30
customers accepted: 112
  customers served: 109
        turnaways: 0
average queue size: 2.41
 average wait time: 5.16 minutes
```

Real World Note: The Singleton Design Pattern

Often you can find a single general pattern that solves a variety of problems. This is true in human interactions; there's the recipe "take a deep breath and count to ten before responding." In programming, too, common patterns emerge when you study software design problems. A design pattern is the software equivalent of a particular cooking style, in which the same approach can be applied to different selections of ingredients. You can apply a design pattern to create an elegant and consistent solution to your recurring problem domains. For example, you can use the Singleton pattern when you want exactly one and only one instance of your class to be returned to a caller. Here's how such a class might be declared:

```
class TheOnlyInstance
{
  public:
    static TheOnlyInstance* GetTheOnlyInstance();
    // other methods
  protected:
    TheOnlyInstance() {}
  private:
    // private data
};
```

By declaring the `TheOnlyInstance` constructor as `protected` and omitting any public constructor, you can ensure that no local instances can be created:

```
int main()
{
    TheOnlyInstance noCanDo;   // not allowed
```

The public static method `GetTheOnlyInstance` serves as the sole access point for the class during its lifetime. When called, it returns an instance of class `TheOnlyInstance`.

```
TheOnlyInstance* TheOnlyInstance::GetTheOnlyInstance()
{
    static TheOnlyInstance objTheOnlyInstance;
    return &objTheOnlyInstance;
}
```

The `GetTheOnlyInstance` method simply creates a static instance of class `TheOnlyInstance` the first time the static `GetTheOnlyInstance` method is called. A static object constructed in this manner remains valid until the program terminates at which point it is automatically destroyed. To retrieve a pointer to the only instance of this class, a program can simply call the static method `GetTheOnlyInstance`, which returns the address of the singleton object.

```
TheOnlyInstance* pTheOnlyInstance = TheOnlyInstance::GetTheOnlyInstance();
```

Because a static variable remains in memory between function calls, subsequent calls of `GetTheOnlyInstance` return the address of the same static object.

Summary

This chapter covers many important aspects of defining and using classes. Several of these aspects are subtle, even difficult, concepts. If some of them seem obscure or unusually complex to you, don't feel bad—they affect most newcomers to C++ that way. Often, the way you come to really appreciate concepts like copy constructors is through getting into trouble by ignoring them. So some of the material in this chapter may seem vague to you until your own experiences enrich your understanding. Meanwhile, let's summarize the chapter.

You can use **new** in a class constructor to allocate memory for data and then assign the address of the memory to a class member. This enables a class, for example, to handle strings of various sizes without committing the class design in advance to a fixed array size. Using **new** in class constructors also raises potential problems when an object expires. If an object has member pointers pointing to memory allocated by **new**, freeing the memory used to hold the object does not automatically free the memory pointed to by the object member pointers. Therefore, if you use **new** in a class constructor to allocate memory, you should use **delete** in the class destructor to free that memory. That way, the demise of an object automatically triggers the deletion of pointed-to memory.

Objects having members pointing to memory allocated by **new** also have problems with initializing one object to another or assigning one object to another. By default, C++ uses memberwise initialization and assignment, which means that the initialized or the assigned-to object winds up with exact copies of the original object's members. If an original member points to a block of data, the copy member points to the same block. When the program eventually deletes the two objects, the class destructor will attempt to delete the same block of memory twice, which is an error. The solution is to define a special copy constructor that redefines initialization and to overload the assignment operator. In each case, the new definition should create duplicates of any pointed-to data and have the new object point to the copies. That way, both the old and the new object refer to separate, but identical, data with no overlap. The same reasoning applies to defining an assignment operator. In each case, the goal is making a deep copy, that is, copying the real data and not just pointers to them.

C++ allows you to place structure, class, and enumeration definitions inside a class. Such nested types have class scope, meaning that they are local to the class and don't conflict with structures, classes, and enumerations of the same name defined elsewhere.

C++ provides a special syntax for class constructors that can be used to initialize data members. This syntax consists of a colon followed by a comma-separated list of initializers. This is placed after the closing parenthesis of the constructor arguments and before the opening brace of the function body. Each initializer consists of the name of the member being initialized followed by parentheses containing the initialization value. Conceptually, these initializations take place when the object is created and before any statements in the function body are executed. The syntax looks like this:

```
queue(int qs) : qsize(qs), items(0), front(NULL), rear(NULL) { }
```

This form is obligatory if the data member is a nonstatic **const** member or a reference.

As you might have noticed, classes require much more care and attention to detail than do simple C-style structures. In return, they do much more for you.

Review Questions

1. Suppose a **String** class has the following private members:

```
class String
{
private:
    char * str;     // points to string allocated by new
    int len;        // holds length of string
//...
};
```

a. What's wrong with this default constructor?

```
String::String() {}
```

b. What's wrong with this constructor?

```
String::String(const char * s)
{
    str = s;
    len = strlen(s);
}
```

c. What's wrong with this constructor?

```
String::String(const char * s)
{
    strcpy(str, s);
    len = strlen(s);
}
```

2. Name three problems that may arise if you define a class in which a pointer member is initialized using **new** and indicate how they can be remedied.

3. What class methods does the compiler generate automatically if you don't provide them explicitly? Describe how these implicitly generated functions behave.

4. Identify and correct errors in the following class declaration:

```
class nifty
{
// data
    char personality[];
    int talents;
// methods
    nifty();
    nifty(char * s);
    ostream & operator<<(ostream & os, nifty & n);
}

nifty:nifty()
{
    personality = NULL;
    talents = 0;
}

nifty:nifty(char * s)
{
    personality = new char [strlen(s)];
    personality = s;
    talents = 0;
}

ostream & nifty:operator<<(ostream & os, nifty & n)
{
    os << n;
}
```

5. Consider the following class declaration:

```
class Golfer
{
private:
    char * fullname;      // points to string containing golfer's name
    int games;            // holds number of golf games played
    int * scores;         // points to first element of array of golf scores
public:
    Golfer();
    Golfer(const char * name, int g= 0);
    // creates empty dynamic array of g elements if g > 0
    Golfer(const Golfer & g);
    ~Golfer();
};
```

a. What class methods would be invoked by each of the following statements?

```
Golfer nancy;                              // #1
Golfer lulu("Little Lulu");                // #2
Golfer roy("Roy Hobbs", 12);               // #3
Golfer * par = new Golfer;                 // #4
Golfer next = lulu;                        // #5
Golfer hazzard = "Weed Thwacker";          // #6
*par = nancy;                              // #7
nancy = "Nancy Putter";                    // #8
```

b. Clearly, the class requires several more methods to make it useful, but what additional method does it require to protect against data corruption?

Programming Exercises

1. Consider the following class declaration:

```
class Cow {
    char name[20];
    char * hobby;
    double weight;
public:
    Cow();
    Cow(const char * nm, const char * ho, double wt);
    Cow(const Cow(constCow&c);
    ~Cow();
    Cow & operator=(const Cow & c);
    void ShowCow() const;  // display all cow data
};
```

Provide the implementation for this class and write a short program that uses all the member functions.

2. Enhance the **String** class declaration (that is, upgrade **string1.h** to **string2.h**) by doing the following:

   a. Overload the + operator to allow you to join two strings into one.

   b. Provide a **stringlow()** member function that converts all alphabetic characters in a string to lowercase. (Don't forget the **cctype** family of character functions.)

   c. Provide a **stringup()** member function that converts all alphabetic characters in a string to uppercase.

   d. Provide a member function that takes a **char** argument and returns the number of times that character appears in the string.

Test your work in the following program:

```
// pe12_2.cpp
#include <iostream>
using namespace std;
#include "string2.h"
int main()
{
    String s1(" and I am a C++ student.");
    String s2 = "Please enter your name: ";
    String s3;
    cout << s2;                    // overloaded << operator
    cin >> s3;                     // overloaded >> operator
    s2 = "My name is " + s3;       // overloaded =, + operators
    cout << s2 << ".\n";
    s2 = s2 + s1;
    s2.stringup();                 // converts string to uppercase
    cout << "The string\n" << s2 << "\ncontains " << s2.has('A')
         << " 'A' characters in it.\n";
    s1 = "red";      // String(const char *),
                     // then String & operator=(const String&)
    String rgb[3] = { String(s1), String("green"), String("blue")};
    cout << "Enter the name of a primary color for mixing light: ";
    String ans;
    bool success = false;
    while (cin >> ans)
    {
        ans.stringlow();         // converts string to lowercase
        for (int i = 0; i < 3; i++)
        {
            if (ans == rgb[i])   // overloaded == operator
            {
                cout << "That's right!\n";
                success = true;
                break;
            }
        }
        if (success)
            break;
        else
```

```
            cout << "Try again!\n";
        }
        cout << "Bye\n";
        return 0;
    }
```

Your output should look like this sample run:

```
Please enter your name: Fretta Farbo
My name is Fretta Farbo.
The string
MY NAME IS FRETTA FARBO AND I AM A C++ STUDENT.
contains 6 'A' characters in it.
Enter the name of a primary color for mixing light: yellow
Try again!
BLUE
That's right!
Bye
```

3. Rewrite the **Stock** class, as described in Listings 10.7 and 10.8, so that it uses dynamically allocated memory instead of fixed arrays to hold the stock names. Also, replace the **show()** member function with an overloaded **operator<<()** definition. Test the new definition program in Listing 10.9.

4. Consider the following variation of the **Stack** class defined in Listing 10.10.

```
// stack.h — class declaration for the stack ADT
typedef unsigned long Item;

class Stack
{
private:
    enum {MAX = 10};        // constant specific to class
    Item * pitems;          // holds stack items
    int size;               // number of elements in stack
    int top;                // index for top stack item
public:
    Stack(int n = 10);      // creates stack with n elements
    Stack(const Stack & st);
    ~Stack();
    bool isempty() const;
    bool isfull() const;
    // push() returns false if stack already is full, true otherwise
    bool push(const Item & item); // add item to stack
    // pop() returns false if stack already is empty, true otherwise
    bool pop(Item & item);  // pop top into item
    Stack & operator=(const Stack & st);
};
```

As the private members suggest, this class uses a dynamically allocated array to hold the stack items. Rewrite the methods to fit this new representation, and write a program that demonstrates all the methods, including the copy constructor and assignment operator.

5. The Bank of Heather has performed a study showing that autoteller customers won't wait more than one minute in line. Using the simulation of Listing 12.10, find a value for number of customers per hour that leads to an average wait time of one minute. (Use at least a 100-hour trial period.)

6. The Bank of Heather would like to know what would happen if they added a second automatic teller. Modify the simulation so that it has two queues. Assume a customer will join the first queue if it has fewer people in it than the second queue and that he will join the second queue otherwise. Again, find a value for number of customers per hour that leads to an average wait time of one minute. (Note: This is a nonlinear problem in that doubling the number of machines doesn't double the number of customers that can be handled per hour with a one-minute wait maximum.)

CHAPTER 13

CLASS INHERITANCE

You will learn about the following in this chapter:

- Inheritance as an is-a relationship
- How to publicly derive one class from another
- Protected access
- Constructor member initializer lists
- Upcasting and downcasting
- Virtual member functions

- Early (static) binding and late (dynamic) binding
- Abstract base classes
- Pure virtual functions
- When and how to use public inheritance

One of the main goals of object-oriented programming is providing reusable code. When you develop a new project, particularly if the project is large, it's nice to be able to reuse proven code rather than to reinvent it. Employing old code saves time and, because it has already been used and tested, can help suppress the introduction of bugs into a program. Also, the less you have to concern yourself with details, the better you can concentrate upon overall program strategy.

Traditional C function libraries provide reusability through predefined, precompiled functions, such as `strlen()` and `rand()`, that you can use in your programs. Many vendors furnish specialized C libraries providing functions beyond those of the standard C library. For example, you can purchase libraries of database management functions and of screen control functions. However, function libraries have a limitation. Unless the vendor supplies the source code for its library functions (and often it doesn't), you can't extend or modify the functions to meet your particular needs. Instead, you have to shape your program to meet the workings of the library. Even if the vendor does supply the source code, you run the risk of unintentionally modifying how part of a function works or of altering the relationships among library functions as you add your changes.

C++ classes bring you a higher level of reusability. Many vendors now offer class libraries, which consist of class declarations and implementations. Because a class combines data representation with class methods, it provides a more integrated package than does a function library. A single class, for example, may provide all the resources for managing a dialog box. Often, class libraries are available in source code, meaning that you can modify them to meet your needs. But C++ has a better method than code modification for extending and modifying classes. This method, called *class inheritance*, lets you derive new classes from old ones, with the derived class inheriting the properties, including the methods, of the old class, called a base class. Just as inheriting a fortune is usually easier than earning one from scratch, deriving a class through inheritance is usually easier than designing a new one. Here are some things you can do with inheritance:

- You can add functionality to an existing class. For example, given a basic array class, you could add arithmetic operations.

- You can add to the data that a class represents. For example, given a basic string class, you could derive a class that adds a data member representing a color to be used when displaying the string.

- You can modify how a class method behaves. For example, given a `Passenger` class that represents the services provided to an airline passenger, you can derive a `FirstClassPassenger` class that provides a higher level of services.

Of course, you could accomplish the same aims by duplicating the original class code and modifying it, but the inheritance mechanism allows you to proceed by just providing the new features. You don't even need access to the source code to derive a class. Thus, if you purchase a class library that provides only the header files and the compiled code for class methods, you still can derive new classes based upon the library classes. Conversely, you can distribute your own classes to others, keeping parts of your implementation secret, yet still giving your clients the option of adding features to your classes.

Inheritance is a splendid concept, and its basic implementation is quite simple. But managing inheritance so that it works properly in all situations requires some adjustments. This chapter looks at both the simple and the subtle aspects of inheritance.

Beginning with a Simple Base Class

When one class inherits from another, the original class is called a *base class* and the inheriting class is called a *derived class*. So, to illustrate inheritance, we need to begin with a base class. The Webtown Social Club has decided to keep track of those members who play table tennis. As head programmer for the club, you have designed the simple `TableTennisPlayer` class defined by Listings 13.1 and 13.2.

LISTING 13.1 `tabtenn0.h`

```
// tabtenn0.h
#ifndef TABTENN0_H_
#define TABTENN0_H_
```

LISTING 13.1   Continued

```cpp
// simple base class
class TableTennisPlayer
{
private:
    enum {LIM = 20};
    char firstname[LIM];
    char lastname[LIM];
    bool hasTable;
public:
    TableTennisPlayer (const char * fn = "none",
                       const char * ln = "none", bool ht = false);
    void Name() const;
    bool HasTable() const { return hasTable; };
    void ResetTable(bool v) { hasTable = v; };
};
#endif
```

LISTING 13.2   tabtenn0.cpp

```cpp
//tabtenn0.cpp -- simple base class methods
#include "tabtenn0.h"
#include <iostream>
#include <cstring>
using namespace std;

TableTennisPlayer::TableTennisPlayer (const char * fn, const char * ln,
                bool ht)
{
    strncpy(firstname, fn, LIM - 1);
    firstname[LIM - 1] = '\0';
    strncpy(lastname, ln, LIM - 1);
    lastname[LIM - 1] = '\0';
    hasTable = ht;
}

void TableTennisPlayer::Name() const
{
    cout << lastname << ", " << firstname;
}
```

All the class does is keep track of a player's name and whether he or she has a table. Listing 13.3 shows this modest class in action.

LISTING 13.3   usett0.cpp

```cpp
// usett0.cpp -- use base class
#include <iostream>
#include "tabtenn0.h"
using namespace std; //introduces namespace std
```

LISTING 13.3   Continued

```
int main ( void )
{
    TableTennisPlayer player1("Chuck", "Blizzard", true);
    TableTennisPlayer player2("Tara", "Boomdea", false);
    player1.Name();
    if (player1.HasTable())
        cout << ": has a table.\n";
    else
        cout << ": hasn't a table.\n";
    player2.Name();
    if (player2.HasTable())
        cout << ": has a table";
    else
        cout << ": hasn't a table.\n";

    return 0;
}
```

And here's the output:

```
Blizzard, Chuck: has a table.
Boomdea, Tara: hasn't a table.
```

Deriving a Class

Some members of the Webtown Social Club have played in local table tennis tournaments, and they demand a class that includes the point ratings they've earned through their play. Rather than start from scratch, you can derive a class from the `TableTennisClass`. The first step is to have the `RatedPlayer` class declaration show that it derives from the `TableTennisClass` class:

```
// RatedPlayer derives from the TableTennisPlayer base class
class RatedPlayer : public TableTennisPlayer
{
...
};
```

The colon indicates the `RatedPlayer` class is based upon the `TableTennisPlayer` class. This particular heading indicates that `TableTennisPlayer` is a public base class; this is termed *public derivation*. An object of a derived class incorporates a base-class object. With public derivation, the public members of the base class become public members of the derived class. The private portions of a base class become part of the derived class, but they can be accessed only through public and protected methods of the base class. (We'll get to protected members in a bit.)

What does this accomplish? If you declare a `RatedPlayer` object, it has the following special properties:

- An object of the derived type has stored within it the data members of the base type. (The derived class inherits the base class implementation.)

- An object of the derived type can use the methods of the base type. (The derived class inherits the base class interface.)

Thus, a `RatedPlayer` object can store the first name and last name of a player and whether or not the player has a table. Also, a `RatedPlayer` object can use the `Name()`, `HasTable()`, and `ResetTable()` methods from the `TableTennisPlayer` class. Also see Figure 13.1.

FIGURE 13.1

Base class and derived class objects.

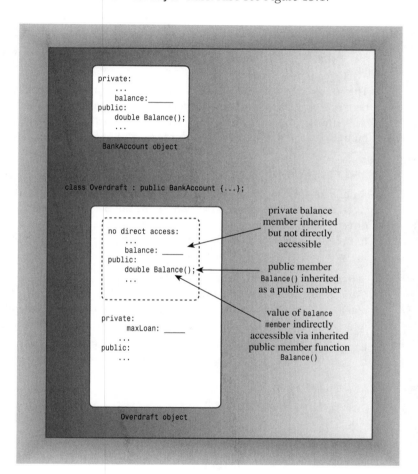

What needs to be added to these inherited features?

- A derived class needs its own constructors.

- A derived class can add additional data members and member functions as needed.

In this particular case, the class needs one more data member to hold the ratings value. It also should have a method for retrieving the rating and a method for resetting the rating. So the class declaration could look like this:

```
// simple derived class
class RatedPlayer : public TableTennisPlayer
{
private:
    unsigned int rating;      // add a data member
public:
    RatedPlayer (unsigned int r = 0, const char * fn = "none",
                    const char * ln = "none", bool ht = false);
    RatedPlayer(unsigned int r, const TableTennisPlayer & tp);
    unsigned int Rating() { return rating; }        // add a method
    void ResetRating (unsigned int r) {rating = r;} // add a method
};
```

The constructors have to provide data for the new members, if any, and for the inherited members. The first **RatedPlayer** constructor uses a separate formal parameter for each member, while the second **RatedPlayer** constructor uses a **TableTennisPlayer** parameter, which will bundle three items (**firstname**, **lastname**, and **hasTable**) into a single unit.

Constructors: Access Considerations

A derived class does not have direct access to the private members of the base class; it has to work through the base class methods. For example, the **RatedPlayer** constructors cannot directly set the inherited members (**firstname**, **lastname**, and **hasTable**). Instead, they have to use public base class methods to access private base class members. In particular, the derived class constructors have to use the base class constructors.

When a program constructs a derived class object, it first constructs the base class object. Conceptually, that means the base class object should be constructed before the program enters the body of the derived class constructor. C++ uses the member initializer list syntax to accomplish this. Here, for instance, is the code for the first **RatedPlayer** constructor:

```
RatedPlayer::RatedPlayer(unsigned int r, const char * fn,
    const char * ln, bool ht) : TableTennisPlayer(fn, ln, ht)
{
    rating = r;
}
```

The

```
: TableTennisPlayer(fn, ln, ht)
```

part is the member initializer list. It's executable code, and it calls the **TableTennisPlayer** constructor. Suppose, for example, a program has the following declaration:

```
RatedPlayer rplayer1(1140, "Mallory", "Duck", true);
```

The **RealPlayer** constructor assigns the actual arguments "**Mallory**", "**Duck**", and **true** to the formal parameters **fn**, **ln**, and **ht**. It then passes these parameters on as actual arguments to the **TableTennisPlayer** constructor. This constructor, in turn, creates the embedded **TableTennisPlayer** object and stores the data "**Mallory**", "**Duck**", and **true** in it. Then program enters the body of the **RealPlayer** constructor, completes the construction of the **RealPlayer** object, and assigns the value of the parameter r (i.e., **1140**) to the **rating** member. See Figure 13.2.

FIGURE 13.2

Passing arguments through to a base-class constructor.

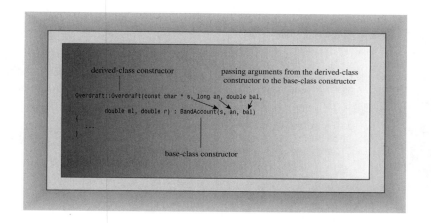

What if you omit the member initializer list?

```
RatedPlayer::RatedPlayer(unsigned int r, const char * fn,
    const char * ln, bool ht) // what if no initializer list?
{
    rating = r;
}
```

The base class object must be created first, so if you omit calling a base class constructor, the program will use the default base class constructor, so the previous code is the same as if you had written this:

```
RatedPlayer::RatedPlayer(unsigned int r, const char * fn,
    const char * ln, bool ht) // : TableTennisPlayer()
{
    rating = r;
}
```

Unless you want the default constructor to be used, you should explicitly provide the correct base class constructor call.

Now let's look at code for the second constructor:

```
RatedPlayer::RatedPlayer(unsigned int r, const TableTennisPlayer & tp)
    : TableTennisPlayer(tp)
{
    rating = r;
}
```

Again, the `TableTennisPlayer` information is passed on to a `TableTennisPlayer` constructor:

```
TableTennisPlayer(tp)
```

Because `tp` is type `const TableTennisPlayer &`, this call invokes the base class copy constructor. The base class didn't define a copy constructor, but recall (Chapter 12, "Classes and Dynamic Memory Allocation") that the compiler automatically generates a copy constructor if one is needed and you haven't defined one already. In this case, the implicit copy constructor, which does member-wise copying, is fine, because the class doesn't use dynamic memory allocation.

You may, if you like, also use member initializer list syntax for members of the derived class. In this case, you use the member name instead of the class name in the list. Thus, the second constructor also can be written in this manner:

```
// alternative version
RatedPlayer::RatedPlayer(unsigned int r, const TableTennisPlayer & tp)
    : TableTennisPlayer(tp), rating(r)
{
}
```

The key points about constructors for derived classes are these:

- The base class object is constructed first.
- The derived class constructor should pass base class information to a base class constructor via a member initializer list.
- The derived class constructor should initialize those data members that were added to the derived class.

This example doesn't provide explicit destructors, so the implicit destructors are used. Destroying an object reverses the order used to construct an object. That is, the body of the derived class destructor is executed first, then the base class destructor is called automatically.

Remember

When creating an object of a derived class, a program first calls the base-class constructor and then the derived-class constructor. The base-class constructor is responsible for initializing the inherited data members. The derived-class constructor is responsible for initializing any added data members. You can use the initializer-list syntax to indicate which base-class constructor to use. Otherwise, the default base-class constructor is used.

When an object of a derived class expires, the program first calls the derived-class destructor and then the base-class destructor.

Member Initializer Lists

A constructor for a derived class can use the initializer-list mechanism to pass values along to a base-class constructor.

```
derived::derived(type1 x, type2 y) : base(x,y) // initializer list
{
    ...
}
```

Here, `derived` is the derived class, `base` is the base class, and `x` and `y` are variables used by the base-class constructor. If, say, the derived constructor receives the arguments 10 and 12, this mechanism then passes 10 and 12 on to the base constructor defined as taking arguments of these types.

Except for the case of virtual base classes (Chapter 14, "Reusing Code in C++"), a class can pass values back only to its immediate base class. However, that class can use the same mechanism to pass back information to its immediate base class, and so on. If you don't supply a base-class constructor in a member initializer list, the program will use the default base-class constructor. The member initializer list can be used *only* with constructors.

Using the Derived Class

To use the derived class, a program needs access to the base class declarations. Listing 13.4 places both class declarations in the same header file. You could give each class its own header file, but because the two classes are related, it makes more organizational sense to keep the class declarations together.

LISTING 13.4   tabtenn1.h

```
// tabtenn1.h  -- simple inheritance
#ifndef TABTENN1_H_
#define TABTENN1_H_
// simple base class
class TableTennisPlayer
{
private:
    enum {LIM = 20};
    char firstname[LIM];
    char lastname[LIM];
    bool hasTable;
public:
    TableTennisPlayer (const char * fn = "none",
                       const char * ln = "none", bool ht = false);
    void Name() const;
    bool HasTable() const { return hasTable; } ;
    void ResetTable(bool v) { hasTable = v; };
};

// simple derived class
class RatedPlayer : public TableTennisPlayer
{
private:
    unsigned int rating;
public:
    RatedPlayer (unsigned int r = 0, const char * fn = "none",
                       const char * ln = "none", bool ht = false);
    RatedPlayer(unsigned int r, const TableTennisPlayer & tp);
    unsigned int Rating() { return rating; }
    void ResetRating (unsigned int r) {rating = r;}
};

#endif
```

Listing 13.5 provides the method definitions for both classes. Again, you could use separate files, but it's simpler to keep the definitions together.

LISTING 13.5   tabtenn1.cpp

```cpp
// tabtenn1.cpp -- simple base class methods
#include "tabtenn1.h"
#include <iostream>
#include <cstring>
using namespace std;

// TableTennisPlayer methods
TableTennisPlayer::TableTennisPlayer (const char * fn, const char * ln,
                bool ht)
{
    strncpy(firstname, fn, LIM - 1);
    firstname[LIM - 1] = '\0';
    strncpy(lastname, ln, LIM - 1);
    lastname[LIM - 1] = '\0';
    hasTable = ht;
}

void TableTennisPlayer::Name() const
{
    cout << lastname << ", " << firstname;
}

// RatedPlayer methods
RatedPlayer::RatedPlayer(unsigned int r, const char * fn,
     const char * ln, bool ht) : TableTennisPlayer(fn, ln, ht)
{
    rating = r;
}

RatedPlayer::RatedPlayer(unsigned int r, const TableTennisPlayer & tp)
    : TableTennisPlayer(tp), rating(r)
{
}
```

Listing 13.6 creates objects of both the **TableTennisPlayer** class and the **RatedPlayer** class. Notice how objects of both classes can use the **TableTennisPlayer** **Name()** and **HasTable()** methods.

LISTING 13.6   usett1.cpp

```cpp
// usett1.cpp -- use base class
#include <iostream>
#include "tabtenn1.h"
using namespace std; //introduces namespace std

int main ( void )
{
```

LISTING 13.6   Continued

```
        TableTennisPlayer player1("Tara", "Boomdea", false);
        RatedPlayer rplayer1(1140, "Mallory", "Duck", true);
        rplayer1.Name();              // derived object uses base method
        if (rplayer1.HasTable())
            cout << ": has a table.\n";
        else
            cout << ": hasn't a table.\n";
        player1.Name();               // base object uses base method
        if (player1.HasTable())
            cout << ": has a table";
        else
            cout << ": hasn't a table.\n";
        cout << "Name: ";
        rplayer1.Name();
        cout << "; Rating: " << rplayer1.Rating() << endl;
        RatedPlayer rplayer2(1212, player1);
        cout << "Name: ";
        rplayer2.Name();
        cout << "; Rating: " << rplayer2.Rating() << endl;

        return 0;
}
```

Here is the output:

```
Duck, Mallory: has a table.
Boomdea, Tara: hasn't a table.
Name: Duck, Mallory; Rating: 1140
Name: Boomdea, Tara; Rating: 1212
```

Special Relationships

A derived class has some special relationships with the base class. One, which you've just seen, is that a derived class object can use base class methods:

```
RatedPlayer rplayer1(1140, "Mallory", "Duck", true);
rplayer1.Name();  // derived object uses base method
```

Two other important relationships are that a base class pointer can point to a derived class object without an explicit type cast and that a base class reference can refer to a derived class object without an explicit type cast:

```
RatedPlayer rplayer1(1140, "Mallory", "Duck", true);
TableTennisPlayer & rt = rplayer;
TableTennisPlayer * pt = &rplayer;
rt.Name();   // invoke Name() with reference
pt->Name();  // invoke Name() with pointer
```

However, a base class pointer or reference can invoke just base class methods, so you couldn't use rt or pt to invoke, say, the derived class ResetRanking() method.

Ordinarily, C++ requires that references and pointer types match the assigned types, but this rule is relaxed for inheritance. However, the rule relaxation is just in one direction. You can't assign base class objects and addresses to derived class references and pointers:

```
TableTennisPlary player("Betsy", "Bloop", true);
RatedPlayer & rr = player;      // NOT ALLOWED
RatedPlayer * pr = player;      // NOT ALLOWED
```

Both these sets of rules make sense. For example, consider the implications of having a base class reference refer to a derived object. Then you can use the base class reference to invoke base class methods for the derived class object. Because the derived class inherits the base class methods, this causes no problems. Now consider what would happen if you could assign a base class object to a derived class reference. The derived class reference would be able to invoke derived class methods for the base object, and that can be a problem. For example, applying the `RatedPlayer::Rating()` method to a `TableTennisPlayer` object makes no sense because the `TableTennisPlayer` object doesn't have a `rating` member.

That base class references and pointers can refer to derived objects has some interesting consequences. One is that functions defined with base class reference or pointer arguments can be used with either base class or derived class objects. For instance, consider this function:

```
void Show(const TableTennisPlayer & rt)
{
    cout << "Name: ";
    rt.Name();
    cout << "\nTable: ";
    if (rt.HasTable())
        cout << "yes\n";
    else
        cout << "no\n";
}
```

The formal parameter `rt` is a reference to a base class, so it can refer to a base class object or to a derived object. Thus, you can use `Show()` with either a `TableTennis` argument or a `RatedPlayer` argument:

```
TableTennisPlayer player1("Tara", "Boomdea", false);
RatedPlayer rplayer1(1140, "Mallory", "Duck", true);
Show(player1);   // works with TableTennisPlayer argument
Show(rplayer1);  // works with RatedPlayer argument
```

A similar relationship would hold for a function with a pointer-to-base-class formal parameter; it could be used with either the address of a base class object or the address of a derived class object as an actual argument.

The reference compatibility property also allows you to initialize a base class object to a derived object, although somewhat indirectly. Suppose you have this code:

```
RatedPlayer olaf1(1840, "Olaf", "Loaf", true);
TableTennisPlayer olaf2(olaf1);
```

The exact match for initializing `olaf2` would be a constructor with this prototype:

```
TableTennisPlayer(const RatedPlayer &);        // doesn't exist
```

The class definitions don't include this constructor, but there is the implicit copy constructor:

```
// implicit copy constructor
TableTennisPlayer(const TableTennisPlayer &);
```

The formal parameter is a reference to the base type, so it can refer to a derived type. Thus, the attempt to initialize olaf2 to olaf1 uses this constructor, which copies the firstname, last-name, and hasTable members. In other words, it initializes olaf2 to the TableTennisPlayer object embedded in the RatedPlayer object olaf1.

Similarly, you can assign a derived object to a base class object:

```
RatedPlayer olaf1(1840, "Olaf", "Loaf", true);
TableTennisPlayer winner;
winner = olaf1; // assign derived to base object
```

In this case, the program will use the implicit overloaded assignment operator:

```
TableTennisPlayer & operator=(const TableTennisPlayer &) const;
```

Again, a base class reference refers to a derived class object, and the base class portion of olaf1 is copied to winner.

Inheritance—An *Is-a* Relationship

The special relationship between a derived class and base class is based upon an underlying model for C++ inheritance. Actually, C++ has three varieties of inheritance: public, protected, and private. Public inheritance is the most common form, and it models an *is-a* relationship. This is shorthand for saying that an object of a derived class should also be an object of the base class. Anything you do with a base-class object, you should be able to do with a derived-class object. Suppose, for example, you have a Fruit class. It could store, say, the weight and caloric content of a fruit. Because a banana is a particular kind of fruit, you could derive a Banana class from the Fruit class. The new class would inherit all the data members of the original class, so a Banana object would have members representing the weight and caloric content of a banana. The new Banana class also might add members that apply particularly to bananas and not to fruit in general, such as the Banana Institute Peel Index. Because the derived class can add features, it's probably more accurate to describe the relationship as an *is-a-kind-of* relationship, but *is-a* is the usual term.

To clarify the *is-a* relationship, let's look at some examples that don't match that model. Public inheritance doesn't model a *has-a* relationship. A lunch, for example, might contain a fruit. But a lunch, in general, is not a fruit. Therefore, you should not derive a Lunch class from the Fruit class in an attempt to place fruit in a lunch. The correct way to handle putting fruit into a lunch is to consider the matter as a *has-a* relationship: A lunch has a fruit. As you'll see in Chapter 14, that's most easily modeled by including a Fruit object as a data member of a Lunch class (see Figure 13.3).

FIGURE 13.3

Is-a and has-a relationships.

A banana *is a* fruit,
but
a lunch *has a* banana.

Public inheritance doesn't model an *is-like-a* relationship, that is, it doesn't do similes. It's often pointed out that lawyers are like sharks. But it is not literally true that a lawyer is a shark. For example, sharks can live underwater. Therefore, you shouldn't derive a `Lawyer` class from a `Shark` class. Inheritance can add properties to a base class; it doesn't remove properties from a base class. In some cases, shared characteristics can be handled by designing a class encompassing those characteristics and then using that class, either in an *is-a* or *has-a* relationship, to define the related classes.

Public inheritance doesn't model an *is-implemented-as-a* relationship. For example, you could implement a stack using an array. However, it wouldn't be proper to derive a `Stack` class from an `Array` class. A stack is not an array. For example, array indexing is not a stack property. Also, a stack could be implemented in some other way, such as by using a linked list. A proper approach would be to hide the array implementation by giving the stack a private `Array` object member.

Public inheritance doesn't model a *uses-a* relationship. For example, a computer can use a laser printer, but it doesn't make sense to derive a `Printer` class from a `Computer` class, or vice versa. One might, however, devise friend functions or classes to handle communication between `Printer` objects and `Computer` objects.

Nothing in the C++ language prevents you from using public inheritance to model *has-a*, *is-implemented-as-a*, or *uses-a* relationships. However, doing so usually leads to programming problems. So let's stick to the *is-a* relationships.

Polymorphic Public Inheritance

The `RatedPlayer` example of inheritance is a simple one. Objects of the derived class use the base class methods without change. But you can encounter situations in which you want a method to behave differently for the derived class than it does for the base class. That is, the way a particular method behaves will depend upon the object that invokes it. This more sophisticated behavior is termed *polymorphic* ("having many forms") because you can have multiple behaviors for a method, depending upon the context. There are two key mechanisms for implementing polymorphic public inheritance:

- Redefining base class methods in a derived class

- Using virtual methods

It's time for another example. You have leveraged your experience with the Webtown Social Club to become head programmer for the Pontoon National Bank. The first thing they ask you to do is develop two classes. One class will represent its basic checking plan, the Brass Account, and the second class will represent the Brass Plus checking account, which adds an overdraft protection feature. That is, if you write a check larger (but not too much larger) than your balance, the bank will cover the check, charging you for the excess payment and adding a surcharge. We can characterize the two accounts in terms of data to be stored and operations to be allowed.

First, here is the information for a Brass Account checking plan.

- Client name

- Account number

- Current balance

And here are the operations to be represented:

- Creating an account

- Depositing money into the account

- Withdrawing money from the account

- Displaying the account information

For the Brass Plus Account checking plan, the Pontoon National Bank wants all the features of the Brass Account plus the following additional items of information:

- An upper limit to the overdraft protection
- An interest rate charged for overdraft loans
- The overdraft amount currently owed to the bank

No additional operations are needed, but two operations need to be implemented differently:

- The withdrawing money operation has to incorporate overdraft protection
- The display operation has to show the additional information required by the Brass Plus Account

Suppose we call one class `Brass` and the second class `BrassPlus`. Should you derive `BrassPlus` publicly from `Brass`? To answer this question, first answer another: Does the `BrassPlus` class meet the *is-a* test? Sure. Everything that is true of a `Brass` object will be true for a `BrassPlus` object. Both store a client name, an account number, and a balance. With both, you can make deposits and withdrawals and display account information. Note that the *is-a* relationship is not, in general, reversible. A fruit, in general, is not a banana. A `Brass` object won't have all the capabilities of a `BrassPlus` object.

Developing the Two Classes

The Brass Account class information is pretty straightforward, but the bank hasn't told you enough details about how the overdraft system works. In response to your request for further information, the friendly Pontoon National Bank representative tells you the following:

- A Brass Plus account limits how much money the bank will lend you to cover overdrafts. The default value is $500, but some customers may start with a different limit.
- The bank may change a customer's overdraft limit.
- A Brass Plus account charges interest on the loan. The default value is 10%, but some customers may start with a different rate.
- The bank may change a customer's interest rate.
- The account keeps track of how much the customer owes the bank (overdraft loans plus interest). The user cannot pay off this amount by a regular deposit or by a transfer from another account. Instead, he must pay in cash to a special bank officer, who will, if necessary, seek out the customer. Once the debt is paid, the account can reset the amount owed to 0.

The last feature is an unusual way for a bank to do business, but it has the fortunate side effect of keeping the programming problem simpler.

This list suggests the new class needs constructors that provide account information and that include a debt limit with a default value of $500 and an interest rate with a default value of

10%. Also, there should be methods for resetting the debt limit, interest rate, and current debt. These are all things to be added to the **Brass** class, and they will be declared in the **BrassPlus** class declaration.

The information about the two classes suggests class declarations like those in Listing 13.7.

LISTING 13.7   brass.h

```
// brass.h  -- bank account classes
#ifndef BRASS_H_
#define BRASS_H_

// Brass Account Class
class Brass
{
private:
    enum {MAX = 35};
    char fullName[MAX];
    long acctNum;
    double balance;
public:
    Brass(const char *s = "Nullbody", long an = -1,
                double bal = 0.0);
    void Deposit(double amt);
    virtual void Withdraw(double amt);
    double Balance() const;
    virtual void ViewAcct() const;
    virtual ~Brass() {}
};

//Brass Plus Account Class
class BrassPlus : public Brass
{
private:
    double maxLoan;
    double rate;
    double owesBank;
public:
    BrassPlus(const char *s = "Nullbody", long an = -1,
            double bal = 0.0, double ml = 500,
            double r = 0.10);
    BrassPlus(const Brass & ba, double ml = 500, double r = 0.1);
    virtual void ViewAcct()const;
    virtual void Withdraw(double amt);
    void ResetMax(double m) { maxLoan = m; }
    void ResetRate(double r) { rate = r; }
    void ResetOwes() { owesBank = 0; }
};

#endif
```

There are several points to notice.

- The **BrassPlus** class adds three new private data members and three new public member functions to the **Brass** class.

- Both the **Brass** class and the **BrassPlus** class declare the **ViewAcct()** and **Withdraw()** methods; these are the methods that will behave differently for a **BrassPlus** object than they do with a **Brass** object.

- The **Brass** class uses the new keyword **virtual** in declaring **ViewAcct()** and **Withdraw()**. These methods are now termed *virtual methods*.

- The **Brass** class also declares a virtual destructor, even though the destructor does nothing.

The first point is nothing new. The **RatedPlayer** class did something similar when it added a new data member and two new methods to the **TableTennisPlayer** class.

The second point is how the declarations specify that methods are to behave differently for the derived class. The two **ViewAcct()** prototypes indicate that there will be two separate method definitions. The qualified name for the base class version is **Brass::ViewAcct()**, and the qualified name for the derived class version is **BrassPlus::ViewAcct()**. A program will use the object type to determine which version to use:

```
Brass dom("Dominic Banker", 11224, 4183.45);
BrassPlus dot("Dorothy Banker", 12118, 2592.00);
dom.ViewAcct();        // use Brass::ViewAcct()
dot.ViewAcct();        // use BrassPlus::ViewAcct()
```

Similarly, there will be two versions of **Withdraw()**, one that's used by **Brass** objects and one that's used by **BrassPlus** objects. Methods that behave the same for both classes, such as **Deposit()** and **Balance()**, are declared only in the base class.

The third point (the use of **virtual**) is more involved. It determines which method is used if the method is invoked by a reference or a pointer instead of by an object. If you don't use the keyword **virtual**, the program chooses a method based on the reference type or pointer type. If you do use the keyword **virtual**, the program chooses a method based on the type of object the reference or pointer refers to. Here is how a program behaves if **ViewAcct()** is not virtual:

```
// behavior with non-virtual ViewAcct()
// method chosen according to reference type
Brass dom("Dominic Banker", 11224, 4183.45);
BrassPlus dot("Dorothy Banker", 12118, 2592.00);
Brass & b1_ref = dom;
Brass & b2_ref = dot;
b1_ref.ViewAcct();     // use Brass::ViewAcct()
b2_ref.ViewAcct();     // use Brass::ViewAcct()
```

The reference variables are type **Brass**, so **Brass::ViewAccount()** is chosen. Using pointers to **Brass** instead of references results in similar behavior.

In contrast, here is the behavior if `ViewAcct()` is virtual:

```
// behavior with virtual ViewAcct()
// method chosen according to object type
Brass dom("Dominic Banker", 11224, 4183.45);
BrassPlus dot("Dorothy Banker", 12118, 2592.00);
Brass & b1_ref = dom;
Brass & b2_ref = dot;
b1_ref.ViewAcct();      // use Brass::ViewAcct()
b2_ref.ViewAcct();      // use BrassPlus::ViewAcct()
```

Here both references are type `Brass`, but `b2_ref` refers to a `BrassPlus` object, so `BrassPlus::ViewAcct()` is used for it. Using pointers to `Brass` instead of references results in similar behavior.

It turns out, as you'll see in a bit, that this behavior of virtual functions is very handy. Therefore, it is the common practice to declare as virtual in the base class those methods that might be redefined in a derived class. Once a method is declared virtual in a base class, it automatically is virtual in the derived class, but it is a good idea to document which functions are virtual by using the keyword `virtual` in the derived class declarations, too.

The fourth point was that the base class declared a virtual destructor. This is to make sure that the correct sequence of destructors is called when a derived object is destroyed. We'll discuss this point in more detail later in this chapter.

Remember

If you redefine a base class method in a derived class, the usual practice is to declare the base class method as virtual. This makes the program choose the method version based on object type instead of the type of a reference or pointer. It's also the usual practice to declare a virtual destructor for the base class.

Class Implementations

The next step is to prepare the class implementation. Part of this has been done already by the inline function definitions in the header file. Listing 13.8 provides the remaining method definitions. Note that the keyword `virtual` is used just in the method prototypes in the class declaration, not in the method definitions in Listing 13.8.

LISTING 13.8   `brass.cpp`

```
// brass.cpp -- bank account class methods
#include <iostream>
#include <cstring>
using namespace std;

#include "brass.h"
```

LISTING 13.8   Continued

```cpp
// Brass methods

Brass::Brass(const char *s, long an, double bal)
{
    strncpy(fullName, s, MAX - 1);
    fullName[MAX - 1] = '\0';
    acctNum = an;
    balance = bal;
}

void Brass::Deposit(double amt)
{
    if (amt < 0)
        cout << "Negative deposit not allowed; "
             << "deposit is cancelled.\n";
    else
        balance += amt;
}

void Brass::Withdraw(double amt)
{
    if (amt < 0)
        cout << "Negative deposit not allowed; "
             << "withdrawal canceled.\n";
    else if (amt <= balance)
        balance -= amt;
    else
        cout << "Withdrawal amount of $" << amt
             << " exceeds your balance.\n"
             << "Withdrawal canceled.\n";
}
double Brass::Balance() const
{
    return balance;
}

void Brass::ViewAcct() const
{
    // set up ###.## format
    ios_base::fmtflags initialState =
        cout.setf(ios_base::fixed, ios_base::floatfield);
    cout.setf(ios_base::showpoint);
    cout.precision(2);
    cout << "Client: " << fullName << endl;
    cout << "Account Number: " << acctNum << endl;
    cout << "Balance: $" << balance << endl;
    cout.setf(initialState); // restore original format
}

// BrassPlus Methods
BrassPlus::BrassPlus(const char *s, long an, double bal,
```

LISTING 13.8   *Continued*

```
                  double ml, double r) : Brass(s, an, bal)
{
    maxLoan = ml;
    owesBank = 0.0;
    rate = r;
}

BrassPlus::BrassPlus(const Brass & ba, double ml, double r)
           : Brass(ba)    // uses implicit copy constructor
{
    maxLoan = ml;
    owesBank = 0.0;
    rate = r;
}

// redefine how ViewAcct() works
void BrassPlus::ViewAcct() const
{
    // set up ###.## format
    ios_base::fmtflags initialState =
        cout.setf(ios_base::fixed, ios_base::floatfield);
    cout.setf(ios_base::showpoint);
    cout.precision(2);

    Brass::ViewAcct();    // display base portion
    cout << "Maximum loan: $" << maxLoan << endl;
    cout << "Owed to bank: $" << owesBank << endl;
    cout << "Loan Rate: " << 100 * rate << "%\n";
    cout.setf(initialState);
}

// redefine how Withdraw() works
void BrassPlus::Withdraw(double amt)
{
    // set up ###.## format
    ios_base::fmtflags initialState =
        cout.setf(ios_base::fixed, ios_base::floatfield);
    cout.setf(ios_base::showpoint);
    cout.precision(2);

    double bal = Balance();
    if (amt <= bal)
        Brass::Withdraw(amt);
    else if ( amt <= bal + maxLoan - owesBank)
    {
        double advance = amt - bal;
        owesBank += advance * (1.0 + rate);
        cout << "Bank advance: $" << advance << endl;
        cout << "Finance charge: $" << advance * rate << endl;
        Deposit(advance);
        Brass::Withdraw(amt);
    }
```

LISTING 13.8   *Continued*

```
        else
            cout << "Credit limit exceeded. Transaction cancelled.\n";
        cout.setf(initialState);
}
```

Before looking at details such as handling of formatting in some of the methods, let's examine the aspects that relate directly to inheritance. Keep in mind that the derived class does not have direct access to private base class data; the derived class has to use base class public methods to access that data. The means of access depends upon the method. Constructors use one technique, and other member functions use a different technique.

The technique that derived class constructors use to initialize base class private data is the member initializer list syntax. The **RatedPlayer** class constructors use that technique, and so do the **BrassPlus** constructors:

```
BrassPlus::BrassPlus(const char *s, long an, double bal,
        double ml, double r) : Brass(s, an, bal)
{
    maxLoan = ml;
    owesBank = 0.0;
    rate = r;
}

BrassPlus::BrassPlus(const Brass & ba, double ml, double r)
        : Brass(ba)    // uses implicit copy constructor
{
    maxLoan = ml;
    owesBank = 0.0;
    rate = r;
}
```

Each of these constructors uses the member initializer list syntax to pass base class information to a base class constructor and then uses the constructor body to initialize the new data items added by **BrassPlus** class.

Non-constructors can't use the member initializer list syntax. But a derived class method can call a public base class method. For instance, ignoring the formatting aspect, the core of the **BrassPlus** version of **ViewAcct()** is this:

```
// redefine how ViewAcct() works
void BrassPlus::ViewAcct() const
{
...
    Brass::ViewAcct();    // display base portion
    cout << "Maximum loan: $" << maxLoan << endl;
    cout << "Owed to bank: $" << owesBank << endl;
    cout << "Loan Rate: " << 100 * rate << "%\n";
...
}
```

In other words, `BrassPlus::ViewAcct()` displays the added `BrassPlus` data members and calls upon the base class method `Brass::ViewAcct()` to display the base class data members. Using the scope resolution operator in a derived class method to invoke a base class method is a standard technique.

It's vital that the code use the scope resolution operator. Suppose, instead, you wrote the code this way:

```
// redefine how ViewAcct() works
void BrassPlus::ViewAcct() const
{
...
    ViewAcct();    // oops! recursive call
...
}
```

If code doesn't use the scope resolution operator, the compiler assumes that `ViewAcct()` is `BrassPlus::ViewAcct()`, and this creates a recursive function that has no termination—not a good thing.

Next, consider the `BrassPlus::Withdraw()` method. If the client withdraws an amount larger than the balance, the method should arrange for a loan. It can use `Brass::Withdraw()` to access the balance member, but `Brass::Withdraw()` issues an error message if the withdrawal amount exceeds the balance. This implementation avoids the message by using the `Deposit()` method to make the loan and then calling `Brass::Withdraw()` once sufficient funds are available:

```
// redefine how Withdraw() works
void BrassPlus::Withdraw(double amt)
{
...
    double bal = Balance();
    if (amt <= bal)
        Brass::Withdraw(amt);
    else if ( amt <= bal + maxLoan - owesBank)
    {
        double advance = amt - bal;
        owesBank += advance * (1.0 + rate);
        cout << "Bank advance: $" << advance << endl;
        cout << "Finance charge: $" << advance * rate << endl;
        Deposit(advance);
        Brass::Withdraw(amt);
    }
    else
        cout << "Credit limit exceeded. Transaction cancelled.\n";
...
}
```

Note that the method uses the base class `Balance()` function to determine the original balance. The code doesn't have to use the scope resolution operator for `Balance()` because this method has not been redefined in the derived class.

The ViewAcct() methods use formatting commands to set the output mode for floating-point values to fixed-point, two places to the right of the decimal. Once these modes are set, output stays in that mode, so the polite thing for these methods to do is to reset the formatting mode to its state prior to calling the methods. Therefore, these methods capture the original format state with this code:

```
ios_base::fmtflags initialState =
    cout.setf(ios_base::fixed, ios_base::floatfield);
```

The setf() method returns a value representing the format state before the function was called. New C++ implementations define the ios_base::fmtflags type as the type for this value, and this statement saves the state in a variable (initialState) of that type. (Older versions might use unsigned int instead for the type.) When ViewAcct() finishes, it passes initialState to setf() as an argument, and that restores the original format settings:

```
cout.setf(initialState);
```

Using the Classes

First, let's try the class definitions with a Brass object and a BrassPlus object, as shown in Listing 13.9.

LISTING 13.9   usebrass1.cpp

```cpp
// usebrass1.cpp -- test bank account classes
// compile with brass.cpp
#include <iostream>
using namespace std;
#include "brass.h"

int main()
{
    Brass Porky("Porcelot Pigg", 381299, 4000.00);
    BrassPlus Hoggy("Horatio Hogg", 382288, 3000.00);
    Porky.ViewAcct();
    cout << endl;
    Hoggy.ViewAcct();
    cout << endl;
    cout << "Depositing $1000 into the Hogg Account:\n";
    Hoggy.Deposit(1000.00);
    cout << "New balance: $" << Hoggy.Balance() << endl;
    cout << "Withdrawing $4200 from the Porky Account:\n";
    Porky.Withdraw(4200.00);
    cout << "Pigg account balance: $" << Porky.Balance() << endl;
    cout << "Withdrawing $4200 from the Hoggy Account:\n";
    Hoggy.Withdraw(4200.00);
    Hoggy.ViewAcct();

    return 0;
}
```

Here's the output; note how Hogg gets overdraft protection and Pigg does not:

```
Client: Porcelot Pigg
Account Number: 381299
Balance: $4000.00

Client: Horatio Hogg
Account Number: 382288
Balance: $3000.00
Maximum loan: $500.00
Owed to bank: $0.00
Loan Rate: 10.00%

Depositing $1000 into the Hogg Account:
New balance: $4000.00
Withdrawing $4200 from the Porky Account:
Withdrawal amount of $4200.00 exceeds your balance.
Withdrawal canceled.
Pigg account balance: $4000.00
Withdrawing $4200 from the Hoggy Account:
Bank advance: $200.00
Finance charge: $20.00
Client: Horatio Hogg
Account Number: 382288
Balance: $0.00
Maximum loan: $500.00
Owed to bank: $220.00
Loan Rate: 10.00%
```

Showing Virtual Method Behavior

Because the methods were invoked by objects, this last example didn't make use of the virtual method feature. Let's look at an example for which the virtual methods do come into play. Suppose you would like to manage a mixture of Brass and BrassPlus accounts. It would be nice if you could have a single array holding a mixture of Brass and BrassPlus objects, but that's not possible. Every item in an array has to be of the same type, and Brass and BrassPlus are two separate types. However, you can create an array of pointers-to-Brass. In that case, every element is of the same type, but because of the public inheritance model, a pointer-to-Brass can point to either a Brass or a BrassPlus object. Thus, in effect, you have a way of representing a collection of more than one type of object with a single array. This is polymorphism, and Listing 13.10 shows a simple example.

LISTING 13.10   usebrass2.cpp

```cpp
// usebrass2.cpp -- polymorphic example
// compile with brass.cpp
#include <iostream>
using namespace std;
#include "brass.h"
const int CLIENTS = 4;
const int LEN = 40;
```

LISTING 13.10   Continued

```cpp
int main()
{
   Brass * p_clients[CLIENTS];

   int i;
   for (i = 0; i < CLIENTS; i++)
   {
       char temp[LEN];
       long tempnum;
       double tempbal;
       char kind;
       cout << "Enter client's name: ";
       cin.getline(temp, LEN);
       cout << "Enter client's account number: ";
       cin >> tempnum;
       cout << "Enter opening balance: $";
       cin >> tempbal;
       cout << "Enter 1 for Brass Account or "
            << "2 for BrassPlus Account: ";
       while (cin >> kind && (kind != '1' && kind != '2'))
           cout <<"Enter either 1 or 2: ";
       if (kind == '1')
           p_clients[i] = new Brass(temp, tempnum, tempbal);
       else
       {
           double tmax, trate;
           cout << "Enter the overdraft limit: $";
           cin >> tmax;
           cout << "Enter the interest rate "
                << "as a decimal fraction: ";
           cin >> trate;
           p_clients[i] = new BrassPlus(temp, tempnum, tempbal,
                                          tmax, trate);

        }
         while (cin.get() != '\n')
             continue;
   }
   cout << endl;
   for (i = 0; i < CLIENTS; i++)
   {
       p_clients[i]->ViewAcct();
       cout << endl;
   }

   for (i = 0; i < CLIENTS; i++)
   {
       delete p_clients[i];   // free memory
   }
   cout << "Done.\n";

   return 0;
}
```

The program lets user input determine the type of account to be added, then uses new to create and initialize an object of the proper type.

Here is a sample run:

```
Enter client's name: Harry Fishsong
Enter client's account number: 112233
Enter opening balance: $1500
Enter 1 for Brass Account or 2 for BrassPlus Account: 1
Enter client's name: Dinah Otternoe
Enter client's account number: 121213
Enter opening balance: $1800
Enter 1 for Brass Account or 2 for BrassPlus Account: 2
Enter the overdraft limit: $350
Enter the interest rate as a decimal fraction: 0.12
Enter client's name: Brenda Birdherd
Enter client's account number: 212118
Enter opening balance: $5200
Enter 1 for Brass Account or 2 for BrassPlus Account: 2
Enter the overdraft limit: $800
Enter the interest rate as a decimal fraction: 0.10
Enter client's name: Tim Turtletop
Enter client's account number: 233255
Enter opening balance: $688
Enter 1 for Brass Account or 2 for BrassPlus Account: 1

Client: Harry Fishsong
Account Number: 112233
Balance: $1500.00

Client: Dinah Otternoe
Account Number: 121213
Balance: $1800.00
Maximum loan: $350.00
Owed to bank: $0.00
Loan Rate: 12.00%

Client: Brenda Birdherd
Account Number: 212118
Balance: $5200.00
Maximum loan: $800.00
Owed to bank: $0.00
Loan Rate: 10.00%

Client: Tim Turtletop
Account Number: 233255
Balance: $688.00

Done.
```

The polymorphic aspect is provided by the following code:

```
for (i = 0; i < CLIENTS; i++)
{
    p_clients[i]->ViewAcct();
    cout << endl;
}
```

If the array member points to a `Brass` object, `Brass::ViewAcct()` is invoked; if the array member points to a `BrassPlus` object, `BrassPlus::ViewAcct()` is invoked. If `Brass::ViewAcct()` had not been declared virtual, then `Brass:ViewAcct()`would be invoked in all cases.

The Need for Virtual Destructors

The code using `delete` to free the objects allocated by `new` illustrates why the base class should have a virtual destructor, even if no destructor appears to be needed. If the destructors are not virtual, then just the destructor corresponding to the pointer type is called. In Listing 13.10, this means that only the `Brass` destructor would be called, even in the pointer points to a `BrassPlus` object. If the destructors are virtual, the destructor corresponding to the object type is called. So if a pointer points to a `BrassPlus` object, the `BrassPlus` destructor is called. And once a `BrassPlus` destructor finishes, it automatically calls the base class constructor. Thus, using virtual destructors ensures that the correct sequence of destructors is called. In Listing 13.10, this correct behavior wasn't essential because the destructors did nothing. But if, say, `BrassPlus` had a do-something destructor, it would be vital for `Brass` to have a virtual destructor, even if it did nothing.

Static and Dynamic Binding

Which block of executable code gets used when a program calls a function? The compiler has the responsibility of answering this question. Interpreting a function call in the source code as executing a particular block of function code is termed *binding* the function name. With C, the task was simple, for each function name corresponded to a distinct function. With C++, the task became more complex because of function overloading. The compiler has to look at the function arguments as well as the function name to figure out which function to use. Nonetheless, this kind of binding was a task the compiler could perform during the compiling process; binding that takes place during compilation is called *static binding* (or *early binding*). Virtual functions, however, make the job more difficult yet. As you saw in Listing 13.10, the decision of which function to use can't be made at compile time because the compiler doesn't know which kind of object the user is going to choose to make. Therefore, the compiler has to generate code that allows the correct virtual method to be selected as the program runs; this is called *dynamic binding* (or *late binding*). Now that you've seen virtual methods at work, let's look at this process in greater depth, beginning with how C++ handles pointer and reference type compatibility.

Pointer and Reference Type Compatibility

Dynamic binding in C++ is associated with methods invoked by pointers and references, and this is governed, in part, by the inheritance process. One way public inheritance models the *is-a* relationship is in how it handles pointers and references to objects. Normally, C++ does not allow you to assign an address of one type to a pointer of another type. Nor does it let a reference to one type refer to another type:

```
double x = 2.5;
int * pi = &x;    // invalid assignment, mismatched pointer types
long & rl = x;    // invalid assignment, mismatched reference type
```

However, as you've seen, a reference or a pointer to a base class can refer to a derived-class object without using an explicit type cast. For example, the following initializations are allowed:

```
BrassPlus dilly ("Annie Dill", 493222, 2000);
Brass * pb = &dilly;    // ok
Brass & rb = dilly;     // ok
```

Converting a derived-class reference or pointer to a base-class reference or pointer is called *upcasting*, and it is always allowed for public inheritance without the need for an explicit type cast. This rule is part of expressing the *is-a* relationship. A `BrassPlus` object is a `Brass` object in that it inherits all the data members and member functions of a `Brass` object. Therefore, anything that you can do to a `Brass` object, you can do to a `BrassPlus` object. So a function designed to handle a `Brass` reference can, without fear of creating problems, perform the same acts upon a `BrassPlus` object. The same idea applies if you pass a pointer to an object as a function argument. Upcasting is transitive. That is, if you derive a `BrassPlusPlus` class from `BrassPlus`, then a `Brass` pointer or reference can refer to a `Brass` object, a `BrassPlus` object, or a `BrassPlusPlus` object.

The opposite process, converting a base-class pointer or reference to a derived-class pointer or reference, is called *downcasting*, and it is not allowed without an explicit type cast. The reason for this restriction is that the *is-a* relationship is not, in general, reversible. A derived class could add new data members, and the class member functions that used these data members wouldn't apply to the base class. For example, suppose you derive a `Singer` class from an `Employee` class, adding a data member representing a singer's vocal range and a member function, called `range()`, that reports the value for the vocal range. It wouldn't make sense to apply the `range()` method to an `Employee` object. But if implicit downcasting were allowed, you could accidentally set a pointer-to-`Singer` to the address of an `Employee` object and use the pointer to invoke the `range()` method (see Figure 13.4).

Implicit upcasting makes it possible for a base class pointer or reference to refer to either a base class object or a derived object, and that produces the need for dynamic binding. The virtual member function is the C++ answer to that need.

FIGURE 13.4
Upcasting and
downcasting.

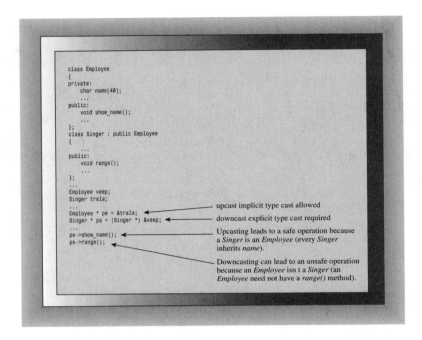

```
class Employee
{
private:
    char name[40];
    ...
public:
    void show_name();
    ...
};
class Singer : public Employee
{
    ...
public:
    void range();
    ...
};
...
Employee veep;
Singer trala;
...
Employee * pe = &trala;        ◄──── upcast implicit type cast allowed
Singer * ps = (Singer *) &veep;  ◄──── downcast explicit type cast required
...
pe->show_name();    ◄──── Upcasting leads to a safe operation because
ps->range();                  a Singer is an Employee (every Singer
                              inherits name).

                    ◄──── Downcasting can lead to an unsafe operation
                          because an Employee isn t a Singer (an
                          Employee need not have a range() method).
```

Virtual Member Functions and Dynamic Binding

Let's revisit the process of invoking a method with a reference or pointer. Consider the following code:

```
BrassPlus ophelia;    // derived-class object
Brass * bp;           // base-class pointer
bp = &ophelia;        // Brass pointer to BrassPlus object
bp->ViewAcct();       // which version?
```

As discussed before, if `ViewAcct()` is not declared as virtual in the base class, `bp->ViewAcct()` goes by the pointer type (`Brass *`) and invokes `Brass::ViewAcct()`. The pointer type is known at compile time, so the compiler can bind `ViewAcct()` to `Brass::ViewAcct()` at compile time. In short, the compiler uses static binding for non-virtual methods.

But if `ViewAcct()` is declared as virtual in the base class, `bp->ViewAcct()` goes by the object type (`BrassPlus`) and invokes `BrassPlus::ViewAcct()`. In this example, you can see the object type is `BrassPlus`, but, in general, (as in Listing 13.10) the object type might only be determined when the program is running. Therefore, the compiler generates code that binds `ViewAcct()` to `Brass::ViewAcct()` or `BrassPlus::ViewAcct()`, depending on the object type, while the program executes. In short, the compiler uses dynamic binding for virtual methods.

In most cases, dynamic binding is a good thing, for it allows a program to choose the method designed for a particular type. Given this fact, you might be wondering about the following:

- Why have two kinds of binding?
- If dynamic binding is so good, why isn't it the default?
- How does it work?

We'll look at answers to these questions next.

Why Two Kinds of Binding?

Because dynamic binding allows you to redefine class methods while static binding makes a partial botch of it, why have static binding at all? There are two reasons: efficiency and a conceptual model.

First, consider efficiency. For a program to be able to make a runtime decision, it has to have some way to keep track of what sort of object a base-class pointer or reference refers to, and that entails some extra processing overhead. (We'll describe one method of dynamic binding later.) If, for example, you design a class that won't be used as a base class for inheritance, you don't need dynamic binding. Similarly, if you have a derived class, such as the `RatedPlayer` example, that does not redefine any methods, you don't need dynamic binding. In these cases, it makes more sense to use static binding and gain a little efficiency. The fact that static binding is more efficient is why it is the default choice for C++. Stroustrup says one of the guiding principles of C++ is that you shouldn't have to pay (in memory usage or processing time) for those features you don't use. Go to virtual functions only if your program design needs them.

Next, consider the conceptual model. When you design a class, you may have member functions that you don't want redefined in derived classes. For example, the `Brass::Balance()` function, which returns the account balance, seems like a function that shouldn't be redefined. By making this function nonvirtual, you accomplish two things. First, you make it more efficient. Second, you announce that it is your intention that this function not be redefined. That suggests the following rule of thumb.

Tip
If a method in a base class will be redefined in a derived class, make it virtual. If the method should not be redefined, make it nonvirtual.

Of course, when you design a class, it's not always obvious into which category a method falls. Like many aspects of real life, class design is not a linear process.

How Virtual Functions Work

C++ specifies how virtual functions should behave, but it leaves the implementation up to the compiler writer. You don't need to know the implementation method to use virtual functions, but seeing how it is done may help you understand the concepts better, so let's take a look.

The usual way compilers handle virtual functions is to add a hidden member to each object. The hidden member holds a pointer to an array of function addresses. Such an array usually is termed a *virtual function table*, or *vtbl*. The table holds the addresses of the virtual functions declared for objects of that class. For example, an object of a base class will contain a pointer to a table of addresses of all the virtual functions for that class. An object of a derived class will contain a pointer to a separate table of addresses. If the derived class provides a new definition of a virtual function, the table holds the address of the new function. If the derived class doesn't redefine the virtual function, the table holds the address of the original version of the function. If the derived class defines a new function and makes it virtual, its address is added to the table (see Figure 13.5). Note that whether you define one or ten virtual functions for a class, you add just one address member to an object; it's the table size that varies.

FIGURE 13.5

A virtual function mechanism.

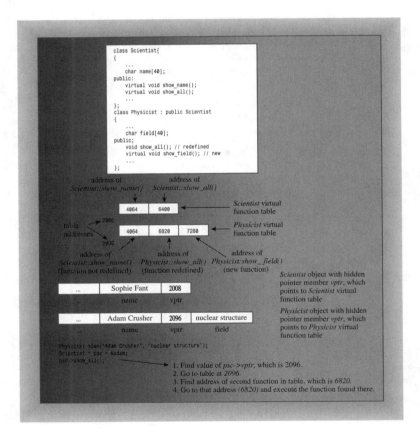

When you call a virtual function, the program looks at the table address stored in an object and goes to the corresponding table of function addresses. If you use the first virtual function defined in the class declaration, the program will use the first function address in the array and execute the function having that address. If you use the third virtual function in the class declaration, the program will use the function whose address is in the third element of the array.

In short, using virtual functions has the following modest costs in memory and execution speed:

- Each object has its size increased by the amount needed to hold an address.

- For each class, the compiler creates a table (an array) of addresses of virtual functions.

- For each function call, there's an extra step of going to a table to look up an address.

Keep in mind that although nonvirtual functions are slightly more efficient than virtual functions, they don't provide dynamic binding.

Virtual Things to Know

We've already discussed the main points about virtual functions:

- Beginning a class method declaration with the keyword `virtual` in a base class makes the function virtual for the base class and all classes derived from the base class, including classes derived from the derived classes, and so on.

- If a virtual method is invoked by using a reference to an object or by a pointer to an object, the program will use the method defined for the object type rather than the method defined for the reference or pointer type. This is called dynamic, or late, binding. This behavior is important, for it's always valid for a base class pointer or reference to refer to an object of a derived type.

- If you're defining a class that will be used as a base class for inheritance, declare as virtual functions those class methods that may have to be redefined in derived classes.

There are several other things you may need to know about virtual functions, some of which have been mentioned in passing already. Let's look at them next.

Constructors

Constructors can't be virtual. A derived class doesn't inherit the base class constructors, so usually there's not much point to making them virtual, anyway.

Destructors

Destructors should be virtual unless a class isn't to be used as a base class. For example, suppose `Employee` is a base class and `Singer` is a derived class that adds a `char *` member that points to memory allocated by `new`. Then, when a `Singer` object expires, it's vital that the `~Singer()` destructor be called to free that memory.

Now consider the following code:

```
Employee * pe = new Singer; // legal because Employee is base for Singer
...
delete pe;                  // ~Employee() or ~Singer()?
```

If the default static binding applies, the `delete` statement will invoke the `~Employee()` destructor. This will free memory pointed to by the `Employee` components of the `Singer` object but not memory pointed to by the new class members. However, if the destructors are virtual, the same code invokes the `~Singer()` destructor, which frees memory pointed to by the Singer component, and then calls the `~Employee()` destructor to free memory pointed to by the `Employee` component.

Note that this implies that even if a base class doesn't require the services of an explicit destructor, you shouldn't rely upon the default constructor. Instead, provide a virtual destructor, even if it has nothing to do:

```
virtual ~BaseClass() { }
```

Tip
Normally, you should provide a base class with a virtual destructor, even if the class doesn't need a destructor.

Friends

Friends can't be virtual functions because friends are not class members, and only members can be virtual functions. If this poses a problem for a design, you may be able to sidestep it by having the friend function use virtual member functions internally.

No Redefinition

If a derived class fails to redefine a virtual function, the class will use the base class version of the function. If a derived class is part of a long chain of derivations, it will use the most recently defined version of the virtual function. The exception is if the base versions are hidden, as described next.

Redefinition Hides Methods

Suppose you create something like the following:

```
class Dwelling
{
public:
    virtual void showperks(int a) const;
...
};
class Hovel : public Dwelling
{
{
public:
    void showperks();
...
};
```

This causes a problem. You may get a compiler warning similar to the following:

```
Warning: Hovel::showperks(void) hides Dwelling::showperks(int)
```

Or perhaps you won't get a warning. Either way, the code has the following implications:

```
Hovel trump;
trump.showperks();      // valid
trump.showperks(5);     // invalid
```

The new definition defines a `showperks()` that takes no arguments. Rather than resulting in two overloaded versions of the function, this redefinition *hides* the base class version that takes an `int` argument. In short, redefining inherited methods is not a variation of overloading. If you redefine a function in a derived class, it doesn't just override the base class declaration with the same function signature. Instead, it hides *all* base class methods of the same name, regardless of the argument signatures.

This fact of life leads to a couple of rules of thumb. First, if you redefine an inherited method, make sure you match the original prototype exactly. One exception is that a return type that is a reference or pointer to a base class can be replaced by a reference or pointer to the derived class. (This exception is new, and not all compilers recognize it yet. Also, note that this exception applies only to return values, not to arguments.) Second, if the base class declaration is overloaded, redefine all the base class versions in the derived class:

```
class Dwelling
{
public:
// three overloaded showperks()
    virtual void showperks(int a) const;
    virtual void showperks(double x) const;
    virtual void showperks() const;
    ...
};
class Hovel : public Dwelling
{
public:
// three redefined showperks()
    void showperks(int a) const;
    void showperks(double x) const;
    void showperks() const;
    ...
};
```

If you redefine just one version, the other two become hidden and cannot be used by objects of the derived class. Note that if no change is needed, the redefinition can simply call the base-class version.

Access Control-protected

So far the class examples have used the keywords `public` and `private` to control access to class members. There is one more access category, denoted with the keyword `protected`. The `protected` keyword is like `private` in that the outside world can access class members in a `protected` section only by using public class members. The difference between `private` and `protected` comes into play only within classes derived from the base class. Members of a derived class can access protected members of a base class directly, but they cannot directly access private members of the base class. So members in the protected category behave like private members as far as the outside world is concerned but behave like public members as far as derived classes are concerned.

For example, suppose the `Brass` class declared the `balance` member as protected:

```
class Brass
{
protected:
    double balance;
...
};
```

Then the `BrassPlus` class could access `balance` directly without using `Brass` methods. For example, the core of `BrassPlus::Withdraw()` could be written this way:

```
void BrassPlus::Withdraw(double amt)
{
    if (amt < 0)
        cout << "Negative deposit not allowed; "
             << "withdrawal canceled.\n";
    else if (amt <= balance)       // access balance directly
        balance -= amt;
    else if ( amt <= balance + maxLoan - owesBank)
    {
        double advance = amt - balance;
        owesBank += advance * (1.0 + rate);
        cout << "Bank advance: $" << advance << endl;
        cout << "Finance charge: $" << advance * rate << endl;
        Deposit(advance);
        balance -= amt;
    }
    else
        cout << "Credit limit exceeded. Transaction cancelled.\n";
}
```

Using protected data members may simplify writing the code, but it has a design defect. For example, continuing with the `BrassPlus` example, if `balance` were protected, you could write code like this:

```
void BrassPlus::Reset(double amt)
{
    balance = amt;
}
```

The `Brass` class was designed so that the `Deposit()` and `Withdraw()` interface provided the only means for altering `balance`. But the `Reset()` method essentially makes `balance` a public variable as far as `BrassPlus` objects are concerned, ignoring, for example, the safeguards found in `Withdraw()`.

Caution

Prefer private to protected access control for class data members, and use base-class methods to provide derived classes access to base-class data.

However, protected access control can be quite useful for member functions, giving derived classes access to internal functions that are not available publicly.

Abstract Base Classes

So far you've seen simple inheritance and the more intricate polymorphic inheritance. The next step in increasing sophistication is the *abstract base class*, or ABC. Let's look at some programming situations that provide the background for the ABC.

Sometimes the application of the *is-a* rule is not as simple as it might appear. Suppose, for example, you are developing a graphics program that is supposed to represent, among other things, circles and ellipses. A circle is a special case of an ellipse; it's an ellipse whose long axis is the same as its short axis. Therefore, all circles are ellipses, and it is tempting to derive a `Circle` class from an `Ellipse` class. But once you get to the details, you may find problems.

To see this, first consider what you might include as part of an `Ellipse` class. Data members could include the coordinates of the center of the ellipse, the semimajor axis (half the long diameter), the semiminor axis (half the short diameter), and an orientation angle giving the angle from the horizontal coordinate axis to the semimajor axis. Also, the class could include methods to move the ellipse, to return the area of the ellipse, to rotate the ellipse, and to scale the semimajor and semiminor axes:

```
class Ellipse
{
private:
    double x;      // x-coordinate of the ellipse's center
    double y;      // y-coordinate of the ellipse's center
    double a;      // semimajor axis
    double b;      // semiminor axis
    double angle;  // orientation angle in degrees
    ...
public:
    ...
    void Move(int nx, ny) { x = nx; y = ny; }
    virtual double Area() const { return 3.14159 * a * b; }
    virtual void Rotate(double nang) { angle = nang; }
    virtual void Scale(double sa, double sb)  { a *= sa; b *= sb; }
    ...
};
```

Now suppose you derive a `Circle` class:

```
class Circle : public Ellipse
{
    ...
};
```

Although a circle is an ellipse, this derivation is awkward. For example, a circle only needs a single value, its radius, to describe its size and shape instead of having a semimajor axis (**a**) and semiminor axis (**b**). The `Circle` constructors can take care of that by assigning the same value to the **a** and **b** members, but then you have redundant representation of the same information. The `angle` parameter and the `Rotate()` method don't really make sense for a circle, and the `Scale()` method, as it stands, can change a circle to a noncircle by scaling the two axes differently. You can try fixing things with tricks, such as putting a redefined `Rotate()` method in the private section of the `Circle` class so that `Rotate()` can't be used publicly with a circle, but, on the whole, it seems simpler to define a `Circle` class without using inheritance:

```
class Circle      // no inheritance
{
private:
    double x;     // x-coordinate of the circle's center
    double y;     // y-coordinate of the circle's center
    double r;     // radius
    ...
public:
    ...
    void Move(int nx, ny) { x = nx; y = ny; }
    double Area() const { return 3.14159 * r * r; }
    void Scale(double sr)  { r *= sr; }
    ...
};
```

Now the class has only the members it needs. Yet this solution also seems weak. The `Circle` and `Ellipse` classes have a lot in common, but defining them separately ignores that fact.

There is another solution, and that is to abstract from the `Ellipse` and `Circle` classes what they have in common and place those features in an abstract base class. Next, derive both the `Circle` and `Ellipse` classes from the ABC. Then, for example, you can use an array of base-class pointers to manage a mixture of `Ellipse` and `Circle` objects (that is, you can use a polymorphic approach). In this case, what the two classes have in common are the coordinates of the center of the shape, a `Move()` method, which is the same for both, and an `Area()` method, which works differently for the two classes. Indeed, the `Area()` method can't even be implemented for the ABC because it doesn't have the necessary data members. C++ has a way to provide an unimplemented function by using a *pure virtual function*. A pure virtual function has = **0** at the end of its declaration, as shown for the `Area()` method:

```
class BaseEllipse  // abstract base class
{
private:
    double x;     // x-coordinate of center
    double y;     // y-coordinate of center
```

```
    ...
public:
    BaseEllipse(double x0 = 0, double y0 = 0) : x(x0),y(y0) {}
    virtual ~BaseEllipse() {}
    void Move(int nx, ny) { x = nx; y = ny; }
    virtual double Area() const = 0; // a pure virtual function
    ...
}
```

When a class declaration contains a pure virtual function, you can't create an object of that class. The idea is that classes with pure virtual functions exist solely to serve as base classes. For a class to be a genuine abstract base class, it has to have at least one pure virtual function. It is the = **0** in the prototype that makes a virtual function a pure virtual function. In this case the function had no definition, but C++ does allow even a pure virtual function to have a definition.

Now you can derive the **Ellipse** class and **Circle** class from the **BaseEllipse** class, adding the members needed to complete each class. One point to note is that the **Circle** class always represents circles, while the **Ellipse** class represents ellipses that also can be circles. However, an **Ellipse** class circle can be rescaled to a noncircle, while a **Circle** class circle must remain a circle.

A program using these classes will be able to create **Ellipse** objects and **Circle** objects, but no **BaseEllipse** objects. Because **Circle** and **Ellipse** objects have the same base class, a collection of such objects can be managed with an array of **BaseEllipse** pointers. Classes like **Circle** and **Ellipse** sometimes are termed *concrete* classes to indicate that you can create objects of those types.

In short, an ABC describes an interface using a least one pure virtual function, and classes derived from an ABC use regular virtual functions to implement the interface in terms of the properties of the particular derived class.

Applying the ABC Concept

You'd probably like to see a complete example of an ABC, so let's apply the concept to representing the **Brass** and **BrassPlus** accounts, starting with an abstract base class called **AcctABC**. This class should contain all methods and data members that are common to both the **Brass** and the **BrassPlus** classes. Those methods that are to work differently for the **BrassPlus** class than they do for the **Brass** class should be declared as virtual functions. At least one virtual function should be a pure virtual function in order to make the **AcctABC** class abstract.

Listing 13.11 is a header file declaring the **AcctABC** class (an abstract base class), the **Brass** class, and the **BrassPlus** class (both concrete classes). To facilitate derived class access to base class data, the **AcctABC** provides some protected methods. These, recall, are methods that derived class methods can call but which are not part of the public interface for derived class objects. It also provides a protected member function to handle the formatting previously performed in several methods. Also, the **AcctABC** class has two pure virtual functions, so it is, indeed, an abstract class.

LISTING 13.11   acctabc.h

```cpp
// acctabc.h  -- bank account classes
#ifndef ACCTABC_H_
#define ACCTABC_H_

// Abstract Base Class
class AcctABC
{
private:
    enum {MAX = 35};
    char fullName[MAX];
    long acctNum;
    double balance;
protected:
    const char * FullName() const {return fullName;}
    long AcctNum() const {return acctNum;}
    ios_base::fmtflags SetFormat() const;
public:
    AcctABC(const char *s = "Nullbody", long an = -1,
                double bal = 0.0);
    void Deposit(double amt) ;
    virtual void Withdraw(double amt) = 0; // pure virtual function
    double Balance() const {return balance;};
    virtual void ViewAcct() const = 0;    // pure virtual function
    virtual ~AcctABC() {}
};

// Brass Account Class
class Brass :public AcctABC
{
public:
    Brass(const char *s = "Nullbody", long an = -1,
            double bal = 0.0) : AcctABC(s, an, bal) { }
    virtual void Withdraw(double amt);
    virtual void ViewAcct() const;
    virtual ~Brass() {}
};

//Brass Plus Account Class
class BrassPlus : public AcctABC
{
private:
    double maxLoan;
    double rate;
    double owesBank;
public:
    BrassPlus(const char *s = "Nullbody", long an = -1,
            double bal = 0.0, double ml = 500,
            double r = 0.10);
    BrassPlus(const Brass & ba, double ml = 500, double r = 0.1);
    virtual void ViewAcct()const;
    virtual void Withdraw(double amt);
    void ResetMax(double m) { maxLoan = m; }
```

LISTING 13.11   Continued

```
         void ResetRate(double r) { rate = r; };
         void ResetOwes() { owesBank = 0; }
};

#endif
```

The next step is to implement those methods that don't already have inline definitions. Listing 13.12 does that.

LISTING 13.12   acctABC.cpp

```cpp
// acctabc.cpp -- bank account class methods
#include <iostream>
#include <cstring>
using namespace std;

#include "acctabc.h"

// Abstract Base Class
AcctABC::AcctABC(const char *s, long an, double bal)
{
    strncpy(fullName, s, MAX - 1);
    fullName[MAX - 1] = '\0';
    acctNum = an;
    balance = bal;
}

void AcctABC::Deposit(double amt)
{
    if (amt < 0)
        cout << "Negative deposit not allowed; "
             << "deposit is cancelled.\n";
    else
        balance += amt;
}

void AcctABC::Withdraw(double amt)
{
    balance -= amt;
}

// protected method
ios_base::fmtflags AcctABC::SetFormat() const
{
 // set up ###.## format
    ios_base::fmtflags initialState =
        cout.setf(ios_base::fixed, ios_base::floatfield);
    cout.setf(ios_base::showpoint);
    cout.precision(2);
    return initialState;
}
```

LISTING 13.12   *Continued*

```cpp
// Brass methods
void Brass::Withdraw(double amt)
{
    if (amt < 0)
        cout << "Negative deposit not allowed; "
             << "withdrawal canceled.\n";
    else if (amt <= Balance())
        AcctABC::Withdraw(amt);
    else
        cout << "Withdrawal amount of $" << amt
             << " exceeds your balance.\n"
             << "Withdrawal canceled.\n";
}

void Brass::ViewAcct() const
{

    ios_base::fmtflags initialState = SetFormat();
    cout << "Brass Client: " << FullName() << endl;
    cout << "Account Number: " << AcctNum() << endl;
    cout << "Balance: $" << Balance() << endl;
    cout.setf(initialState);
}

// BrassPlus Methods
BrassPlus::BrassPlus(const char *s, long an, double bal,
           double ml, double r) : AcctABC(s, an, bal)
{
    maxLoan = ml;
    owesBank = 0.0;
    rate = r;
}

BrassPlus::BrassPlus(const Brass & ba, double ml, double r)
           : AcctABC(ba)    // uses implicit copy constructor
{
    maxLoan = ml;
    owesBank = 0.0;
    rate = r;
}

void BrassPlus::ViewAcct() const
{
    ios_base::fmtflags initialState = SetFormat();

    cout << "BrassPlus Client: " << FullName() << endl;
    cout << "Account Number: " << AcctNum() << endl;
    cout << "Balance: $" << Balance() << endl;
    cout << "Maximum loan: $" << maxLoan << endl;
    cout << "Owed to bank: $" << owesBank << endl;
    cout << "Loan Rate: " << 100 * rate << "%\n";
    cout.setf(initialState);
```

LISTING 13.12 Continued

```
    }

void BrassPlus::Withdraw(double amt)
{
    ios_base::fmtflags initialState = SetFormat();

    double bal = Balance();
    if (amt <= bal)
        AcctABC::Withdraw(amt);
    else if ( amt <= bal + maxLoan - owesBank)
    {
        double advance = amt - bal;
        owesBank += advance * (1.0 + rate);
        cout << "Bank advance: $" << advance << endl;
        cout << "Finance charge: $" << advance * rate << endl;
        Deposit(advance);
        AcctABC::Withdraw(amt);
    }
    else
        cout << "Credit limit exceeded. Transaction cancelled.\n";
    cout.setf(initialState);
}
```

The `FullName()` and `AcctNum()` protected methods provide read-only access to the `fullName` and `acctNum` data members and make it possible to customize `ViewAcct()` a little more individually for each derived class.

This new implementation of the `Brass` and `BrassPlus` accounts can be used in the same manner as the old one, for the class methods have the same names and interfaces as before. For example, to convert Listing 13.10 to use the new implementation, you just need to take these steps:

- Link `usebrass2.cpp` with `acctabc.cpp` instead of with `brass.cpp`.

- Include `acctabc.h` instead of `brass.h`.

- Replace

  `Brass * p_clients[CLIENTS];`

  with

  `AcctABC * p_clients[CLIENTS];`

Comments

The abstract base class methodology is a much more systematic, disciplined way to approach inheritance than the more ad hoc, spur of the moment approach used by the `RatedPlayer` example. Before designing an abstract base class, you first have to develop a model of what classes are needed to represent a programming problem and how they relate to one another. One school of thought holds that if you design an inheritance hierarchy of classes, the only concrete classes should be those that never serve as a base class. This approach does tend to produce cleaner designs with fewer complications.

Real World Note: Enforcing Interface Rules with Abstract Base Classes

One way of thinking about abstract base classes is to consider them an enforcement of interface. The abstract base class demands that its pure virtual functions be overridden in any derived classes—forcing the derived class to obey the rules of interface the ABC has set. This model is common in component-based programming paradigms, where the use of ABCs allows the component designer to create an "interface contract" where all components derived from the ABC are guaranteed to uphold *at least* the common functionality specified by the ABC.

Inheritance and Dynamic Memory Allocation

How does inheritance interact with dynamic memory allocation (the use of `new` and `delete`)? For example, if a base class uses dynamic memory allocation and redefines assignment and a copy constructor, how does that affect the implementation of derived class? The answer depends on the nature of derived class. If the derived class does not itself use dynamic memory allocation, you needn't take any special steps. If the derived class does also use dynamic memory allocation, then there are a couple of new tricks to learn. Let's look at these two cases.

Case 1—Derived Class Doesn't Use `new`

Suppose we begin with the following base class that uses dynamic memory allocation:

```
//  Base Class Using DMA
class baseDMA
{
private:
    char * label;
    int rating;

public:
    baseDMA(const char * l = "null", int r = 0);
    baseDMA(const baseDMA & rs);
    virtual ~baseDMA();
    baseDMA & operator=(const baseDMA & rs);
...
};
```

The declaration contains those special methods required when constructors use `new`: a destructor, a copy constructor, and an overloaded assignment operator.

Now suppose you derive a `lackDMA` class from `baseDMA` and that `lackDMA` does not use `new` or have other unusual design features that require special treatment:

```
// derived class without DMA
class lacksDMA :public baseDMA
{
private:
```

```
      char color[40];
public:
...
};
```

Do you now have to define an explicit destructor, copy constructor, and assignment operator for the `lackDMA` class? The answer is no.

First, consider the need for a destructor. If you don't define one, the compiler will define a default constructor that does nothing. Actually, the default constructor for a derived class always does something; it calls the base-class destructor after executing its own code. Because the `lackDMA` members, we assume, don't require any special action, the default destructor is fine.

Next, consider the copy constructor. You've seen (Chapter 12) that the default copy constructor does memberwise copying, which is inappropriate for dynamic memory allocation. However, memberwise copying is fine for the new `lacksDMA` member. That leaves the matter of the inherited `baseDMA` object. What you need to know is that memberwise copying uses the form of copying that is defined for the data type in question. So copying a `long` to a `long` is done using ordinary assignment. But copying a class member or an inherited class component is done using the copy constructor for that class. Thus, the default copy constructor for the `lacksDMA` class uses the explicit `baseDMA` copy constructor to copy the `baseDMA` portion of a `lacksDMA` object. So the default copy constructor is fine for the new `lacksDMA` member, and it's also fine for the inherited `baseDMA` object.

Essentially the same situation holds for assignment. The default assignment operator for a class automatically uses the base-class assignment operator for the base-class component. So it, too, is fine.

Case 2—Derived Class Does Use new

Suppose, however, that the derived class does use `new`:

```
// derived class with DMA
class hasDMA :public baseDMA
{
private:
    char * style;   // use new in constructors
public:
...
};
```

Then, of course, you do have to define an explicit destructor, copy constructor, and assignment operator for the derived class. Let's consider these methods in turn.

A derived class destructor automatically calls the base class constructor, so its own responsibility is to clean up after what the derived class constructors do. Thus, the `hasDMA` destructor has to free the memory managed by the `style` pointer, and can rely upon the `baseDMA` destructor to free the memory managed by the `label` pointer:

```
baseDMA::~baseDMA()  // takes care of baseDMA stuff
{
    delete [] label;
}

hasDMA::~hasDMA()        // takes care of hasDMA stuff
{
    delete [] style;
}
```

Next, consider copy constructors. The **baseDMA** copy constructor follows the usual pattern:

```
baseDMA::baseDMA(const baseDMA & rs)
{
    label = new char[strlen(rs.label) + 1];
    strcpy(label, rs.label);
    rating = rs.rating;
}
```

The **hasDMA** copy constructor only has access to **hasDMA** data, so it must invoke the **baseDMA** copy constructor to handle the **baseDMA** share of the data:

```
hasDMA::hasDMA(const hasDMA & hs)
        : baseDMA(hs)
{
    style = new char[strlen(hs.style) + 1];
    strcpy(style, hs.style);
}
```

The point to note is that the member initializer list passes a **hasDMA** reference to a **baseDMA** constructor. There is no **baseDMA** constructor with a type **hasDMA** reference parameter, but none is needed. That's because the **baseDMA** copy constructor has a **baseDMA** reference parameter, and a base class reference can refer to a derived type. Thus, the **baseDMA** copy constructor uses the **baseDMA** portion of the **hasDMA** argument to construct the **baseDMA** portion of the new object.

Next, consider assignment operators. The **baseDMA** assignment operator follows the usual pattern:

```
baseDMA & baseDMA::operator=(const baseDMA & rs)
{
    if (this == &rs)
        return *this;
    delete [] label;
    label = new char[strlen(rs.label) + 1];
    strcpy(label, rs.label);
    rating = rs.rating;
    return *this;
}
```

Because **hasDMA** also uses dynamic memory allocation, it, too, needs an explicit assignment operator. Being a **hasDMA** method, it only has direct access to **hasDMA** data. Nonetheless, an explicit assignment operator for a derived class also has to take care of assignment for the inherited base class `baseDMA` object. You can do this by explicitly calling the base class assignment operator, as shown here:

```
hasDMA & hasDMA::operator=(const hasDMA & hs)
{
    if (this == &hs)
        return *this;
    baseDMA::operator=(hs);   // copy base portion
    style = new char[strlen(hs.style) + 1];
    strcpy(style, hs.style);
    return *this;
}
```

The statement

```
baseDMA::operator=(hs);   // copy base portion
```

may look a little odd. But using function notation instead of operator notation lets one use the scope resolution operator. In effect, the statement means the following:

```
*this = hs;   // use baseDMA::operator=()
```

But, of course, the compiler ignores comments, so if you used the latter code, it would use `hasDMA::operator=()` instead and create a recursive call. Using the function notation gets the correct assignment operator called.

An Inheritance Example with Dynamic Memory Allocation and Friends

To illustrate the ideas just discussed, let's integrate the `baseDMA`, `lacksDMA`, and `hasDMA` classes just discussed into a single example. Listing 13.13 is a header file for these classes. To what we've already discussed, it adds a friend function to illustrate how derived classes can access friends to a base class.

LISTING 13.13   dma.h

```
// dma.h  -- inheritance and dynamic memory allocation
#ifndef DMA_H_
#define DMA_H_
#include <iostream>
using namespace std;

//  Base Class Using DMA
class baseDMA
{
private:
    char * label;
    int rating;

public:
    baseDMA(const char * l = "null", int r = 0);
    baseDMA(const baseDMA & rs);
```

LISTING 13.13 *Continued*

```
        virtual ~baseDMA();
        baseDMA & operator=(const baseDMA & rs);
        friend ostream & operator<<(ostream & os, const baseDMA & rs);
    };


    // derived class without DMA
    // no destructor needed
    // uses implicit copy constructor
    // uses implicit assignment operator
    class lacksDMA :public baseDMA
    {
    private:
        char color[40];
    public:
        lacksDMA(const char * c = "blank", const char * l = "null",
                    int r = 0);
        lacksDMA(const char * c, const baseDMA & rs);
        friend ostream & operator<<(ostream & os,
                                    const lacksDMA & rs);
    };

    // derived class with DMA
    class hasDMA :public baseDMA
    {
    private:
        char * style;
    public:
        hasDMA(const char * s = "none", const char * l = "null",
                    int r = 0);
        hasDMA(const char * s, const baseDMA & rs);
        hasDMA(const hasDMA & hs);
        ~hasDMA();
        hasDMA & operator=(const hasDMA & rs);
        friend ostream & operator<<(ostream & os,
                                    const hasDMA & rs);
    };

    #endif
```

Listing 13.14 provides the method definitions for these three classes:

LISTING 13.14 dma.cpp

```
// dma.cpp --dma class methods

#include "dma.h"
#include <cstring>

// baseDMA methods
baseDMA::baseDMA(const char * l, int r)
{
```

LISTING 13.14 *Continued*

```
        label = new char[strlen(l) + 1];
        strcpy(label, l);
        rating = r;
    }

    baseDMA::baseDMA(const baseDMA & rs)
    {
        label = new char[strlen(rs.label) + 1];
        strcpy(label, rs.label);
        rating = rs.rating;
    }

    baseDMA::~baseDMA()
    {
        delete [] label;
    }

    baseDMA & baseDMA::operator=(const baseDMA & rs)
    {
        if (this == &rs)
            return *this;
        delete [] label;
        label = new char[strlen(rs.label) + 1];
        strcpy(label, rs.label);
        rating = rs.rating;
        return *this;
    }

    ostream & operator<<(ostream & os, const baseDMA & rs)
    {
        os << "Label: " << rs.label << endl;
        os << "Rating: " << rs.rating << endl;
        return os;
    }

    // lacksDMA methods
    lacksDMA::lacksDMA(const char * c, const char * l, int r)
        : baseDMA(l, r)
    {
        strncpy(color, c, 39);
        color[39] = '\0';
    }

    lacksDMA::lacksDMA(const char * c, const baseDMA & rs)
        : baseDMA(rs)
    {
        strncpy(color, c, 39);
        color[39] = '\0';
    }

    ostream & operator<<(ostream & os, const lacksDMA & ls)
    {
```

LISTING 13.14   Continued

```cpp
    os << (const baseDMA &) ls;
    os << "Color: " << ls.color << endl;
    return os;
}

// hasDMA methods
hasDMA::hasDMA(const char * s, const char * l, int r)
        : baseDMA(l, r)
{
    style = new char[strlen(s) + 1];
    strcpy(style, s);
}

hasDMA::hasDMA(const char * s, const baseDMA & rs)
        : baseDMA(rs)
{
    style = new char[strlen(s) + 1];
    strcpy(style, s);
}

hasDMA::hasDMA(const hasDMA & hs)
        : baseDMA(hs)  // invoke base class copy constructor
{
    style = new char[strlen(hs.style) + 1];
    strcpy(style, hs.style);
}

hasDMA::~hasDMA()
{
    delete [] style;
}

hasDMA & hasDMA::operator=(const hasDMA & hs)
{
    if (this == &hs)
        return *this;
    baseDMA::operator=(hs);  // copy base portion
    style = new char[strlen(hs.style) + 1];
    strcpy(style, hs.style);
    return *this;
}

ostream & operator<<(ostream & os, const hasDMA & hs)
{
    os << (const baseDMA &) hs;
    os << "Style: " << hs.style << endl;
    return os;
}
```

The new feature to note is how derived classes can make use of a friend to a base class.
Consider, for example, the following friend to the hasDMA class:

```cpp
friend ostream & operator<<(ostream & os, const hasDMA & rs);
```

Being a friend to the `hasDMA` class gives this function access to the `style` member. But there's a problem: This function is not a friend to the `baseDMA` class, so how can it access the `label` and `rating` members? The answer is to use the `operator<<()` function that is a friend to the `baseDMA` class. The next problem is that because friends are not member functions, you can't use the scope resolution operator to indicate which function to use. The answer to this problem is to use a type cast so that prototype matching will select the correct function. Thus, the code type casts the type `const hasDMA &` parameter to a type `const baseDMA &` argument:

```
ostream & operator<<(ostream & os, const hasDMA & hs)
{
//  typecast to match operator<<(ostream & , const baseDMA &)
    os << (const baseDMA &) hs;
    os << "Style: " << hs.style << endl;
    return os;
}
```

Listing 13.15 tests the classes in a short program.

LISTING 13.15   usedma.cpp

```
// usedma.cpp -- inheritance, friends, and DMA
// compile with dma.cpp
#include <iostream>
using namespace std;
#include "dma.h"
int main()
{
    baseDMA shirt("Portabelly", 8);
    lacksDMA balloon("red", "Blimpo", 4);
    hasDMA map("Mercator", "Buffalo Keys", 5);
    cout << shirt << endl;
    cout << balloon << endl;
    cout << map << endl;
    lacksDMA balloon2(balloon);
    hasDMA map2;
    map2 = map;
    cout << balloon2 << endl;
    cout << map2 << endl;
    return 0;
}
```

Here's the output:

```
Label: Portabelly
Rating: 8

Label: Blimpo
Rating: 4
Color: red

Label: Buffalo Keys
Rating: 5
Style: Mercator
```

LISTING 13.15   Continued

```
Label: Blimpo
Rating: 4
Color: red

Label: Buffalo Keys
Rating: 5
Style: Mercator
```

Class Design Review

C++ can be applied to a wide variety of programming problems, and you can't reduce class design to some paint-by-the-numbers routine. However, there are some guidelines that often apply, and this is as good a time as any to go over them, by reviewing and amplifying earlier discussions.

Member Functions That the Compiler Generates for You

As first discussed in Chapter 13, "Class Inheritance," the compiler automatically generates certain public member functions. The fact that it does suggests that these member functions are particularly important. Let's look again at some of them now.

The Default Constructor

A default constructor is one with no arguments, or else one for which all the arguments have default arguments. If you don't define any constructors, the compiler defines a default constructor for you. It doesn't do anything, but it must exist for you to do certain things. For example, suppose `Star` is a class. You need a default constructor to do the following:

```
Star rigel;        // create an object without explicit initialization
Star pleiades[6];  // create an array of objects
```

Also, if you write a derived class constructor without explicitly invoking a base class constructor in the member initializer list, the compiler will use the base class default constructor to construct the base class portion of the new object.

If you do define a constructor of any kind, the compiler will not define a default constructor for you. In that case, it's up to you to provide a default constructor if one is needed.

Note that one of the motivations for having constructors is to ensure that objects always are properly initialized. Also, if your class has any pointer members, they certainly should be initialized. Thus, it's a good idea to supply an explicit default constructor that initializes all class data members to reasonable values.

The Copy Constructor

The copy constructor is a constructor that takes a constant reference to the class type as its argument. For example, the copy constructor for a **Star** class would have this prototype:

```
Star(const Star &);
```

The class copy constructor is used in the following situations:

- When a new object is initialized to an object of the same class
- When an object is passed to a function by value
- When a function returns an object by value
- When the compiler generates a temporary object

If your program doesn't use a copy constructor (explicitly or implicitly), the compiler provides a prototype, but not a function definition. Otherwise, the program defines a copy constructor that performs memberwise initialization. That is, each member of the new object is initialized to the value of the corresponding member of the original object.

In some cases, memberwise initialization is undesirable. For example, member pointers initialized with **new** generally require that you institute deep copying, as with the **baseDMA** class example. Or a class may have a static variable that needs to be modified. In such cases, you need to define your own copy constructor.

The Assignment Operator

The default assignment operator handles assigning one object to another of the same class. Don't confuse assignment with initialization. If the statement creates a new object, it's using initialization, and if it alters the value of an existing object, it's assignment:

```
Star sirius;
Star alpha = sirius;     // initialization (one notation)
Star dogstar;
dogstar = sirius;        // assignment
```

If you need to define the copy constructor explicitly, you also need, for the same reasons, to define the assignment operator explicitly. The prototype for a **Star** class assignment operator is this:

```
Star & Star::operator=(const Star &);
```

Note that the assignment operator function returns a reference to a **Star** object. The **baseDMA** class shows a typical example of an explicit assignment operator function.

The compiler doesn't generate assignment operators for assigning one type to another. Suppose you want to be able to assign a string to a **Star** object. One approach is to define such an operator explicitly:

```
Star & Star::operator=(const char *) {...}
```

A second approach is to rely upon a conversion function (see "Conversions" in the next section) to convert a string to a **Star** object and use the **Star**-to-**Star** assignment function. The first approach runs more quickly, but requires more code. The conversion function approach can lead to compiler-befuddling situations.

Other Class Method Considerations

There are several other points to keep in mind as you define a class. The following sections list some of these.

Constructors

Constructors are different from other class methods in that they create new objects, while other methods are invoked by existing objects.

Destructors

Remember to define an explicit destructor that deletes any memory allocated by **new** in the class constructors and takes care of any other special bookkeeping that destroying a class object requires. If the class is to be used as a base class, provide a virtual destructor even if the class doesn't require a constructor.

Conversions

Any constructor that can be invoked with exactly one argument defines conversion from the argument type to the class type. For example, consider the following constructor prototypes for a **Star** class:

```
Star(const char *);                        // converts char * to Star
Star(const Spectral &, int members = 1); // converts Spectral to Star
```

Conversion constructors get used, for example, when a convertible type is passed to a function defined as taking a class argument. For example, suppose you have the following:

```
Star north;
north = "polaris";
```

The second statement would invoke the **Star::operator=(const Star &)** function, using **Star::Star(const char *)** to generate a **Star** object to be used as an argument for the assignment operator function. This assumes that you haven't defined a **(char *)**-to-**Star** assignment operator.

Using **explicit** in the prototype for a one-argument constructor disables implicit conversions, but still allows explicit conversions:

```
class Star
{
...
public:
    explicit Star(const char *);
...
};
```

```
Star north;
north = "polaris";        // not allowed
north = Star("polaris");  // allowed
```

To convert from a class object to some other type, define a conversion function (Chapter 11, "Working with Classes"). A conversion function is a class member function with no arguments or declared return type that has the name of the type to be converted to. Despite having no declared return type, the function should return the desired conversion value. Here are some samples:

```
Star::Star double() {...}           // converts star to double
Star::Star const char * () {...}    // converts to const char
```

You should be judicious with such functions, only using them if they make good sense. Also, with some class designs, having conversion functions increases the likelihood of writing ambiguous code. For example, suppose you had defined a **double** conversion for the **vector** type of Chapter 11, and suppose you had the following code:

```
vector ius(6.0, 0.0);
vector lux = ius + 20.2;         // ambiguous
```

The compiler could convert **ius** to **double** and use **double** addition, or else convert **20.2** to **vector** (using one of the constructors) and use **vector** addition. Instead, it would do neither and inform you of an ambiguous construction.

Passing an Object by Value Versus Passing a Reference

In general, if you write a function using an object argument, you should pass the object by reference rather than by value. One reason for this is efficiency. Passing an object by value involves generating a temporary copy, which means calling the copy constructor and then later calling the destructor. Calling these functions takes time, and copying a large object can be quite a bit slower than passing a reference. If the function doesn't modify the object, declare the argument as a **const** reference.

Another reason for passing objects by reference is that, in the case of inheritance using virtual functions, a function defined as accepting a base class reference argument can also be used successfully with derived classes, as you saw earlier in this chapter. Also see the discussion of virtual methods later this chapter.

Returning an Object Versus Returning a Reference

Some class methods return objects. You've probably noticed that some of these members return objects directly while others return references. Sometimes a method must return an object, but if it isn't necessary, you should use a reference instead. Let's look at this more closely.

First, the only coding difference between returning an object directly and returning a reference is in the function prototype and header:

```
Star nova1(const Star &);    // returns a Star object
Star & nova2(const Star &);  // returns a reference to a Star
```

Next, the reason that you should return a reference rather than an object is that returning an object involves generating a temporary copy of the returned object. It's the copy that's made available to the calling program. Thus, returning an object involves the time cost of calling a copy constructor to generate the copy and of calling the destructor to get rid of the copy. Returning a reference saves time and memory use. Returning an object directly is analogous to passing an object by value: Both processes generate temporary copies. Similarly, returning a reference is analogous to passing an object by reference: Both the calling and the called function operate upon the same object.

However, it's not always possible to return a reference. A function shouldn't return a reference to a temporary object created in the function, for the reference becomes invalid when the function terminates and the object disappears. In this case, the code should return an object in order to generate a copy that will be available to the calling program.

As a rule of thumb, if a function returns a temporary object created in the function, don't use a reference. For example, the following method uses a constructor to create a new object, and it then returns a copy of that object:

```cpp
Vector Vector::operator+(const Vector & b) const
{
    return Vector(x + b.x, y + b.y);
}
```

If a function returns an object that was passed to it via a reference or pointer, return the object by reference. For example, the following code returns, by reference, either the object that invokes the function or else the object passed as an argument:

```cpp
const Stock & Stock::topval(const Stock & s) const
{
    if (s.total_val > total_val)
        return s;           // argument object
    else
        return *this;       // invoking object
}
```

Using const

Be alert to opportunities to use const. You can use it to guarantee that a method doesn't modify an argument:

```cpp
Star::Star(const char * s) {...} // won't change the string to which s points
```

You can use const to guarantee that a method won't modify the object that invokes it:

```cpp
void Star::show() const {...} // won't change invoking object
```

Here const means const Star * this, where this points to the invoking object.

Normally, a function that returns a reference can be on the left side of an assignment statement, which really means you can assign a value to the object referred to. But you can use const to ensure that a reference or pointer return value can't be used to modify data in an object:

```
const Stock & Stock::topval(const Stock & s) const
{
    if (s.total_val > total_val)
        return s;              // argument object
    else
        return *this;          // invoking object
}
```

Here the method returns a reference either to `this` or to `s`. Because `this` and `s` are both declared `const`, the function is not allowed to change them, which means the returned reference also must be declared `const`.

Note that if a function declares an argument as a reference or pointer to a `const`, it cannot pass along that argument to another function unless that function also guarantees not to change the argument.

Public Inheritance Considerations

Naturally, adding inheritance to a program brings in more things to keep in mind. Let's look at a few.

The *is-a* Relationship

Be guided by the *is-a* relationship. If your proposed derived class is not a particular kind of the base class, don't use public derivation. For example, don't derive a `Brain` class from a `Programmer` class. If you want to represent the belief that a programmer has a brain, use a `Brain` class object as a member of the `Programmer` class.

In some cases the best approach may be to create an abstract data class with pure virtual functions and to derive other classes from it.

Remember that one expression of the *is-a* relationship is that a base class pointer can point to a derived class object and that a base class reference can refer to a derived class object without an explicit type cast. Also remember that the reverse is not true; thus, you cannot have a derived class pointer or reference refer to a base class object without an explicit type cast. Depending upon the class declarations, such an explicit type cast (a downcast) may or may not make sense. (You might want to review Figure 13.4.)

What's Not Inherited

Constructors are not inherited. However, derived class constructors typically use the member-initializer-list syntax to call upon base class constructors to construct the base class portion of a derived object. If the derived class constructor doesn't explicitly call a base constructor by using the member-initializer-list syntax, it will use the base class's default constructor. In an inheritance chain, each class can use a member initializer list to pass back information to its immediate base class.

Destructors are not inherited. However, when an object is destroyed, the program first calls the derived destructor, and then the base destructor. If there is a default base class destructor, the compiler generates a default derived class destructor. Generally speaking, if a class serves as a base class, its destructor should be virtual.

The Assignment Operator

The assignment operator is not inherited. The reason is simple. An inherited method has the same function signature in a derived class as it does in the base class. However, the assignment operator has a function signature that changes from class to class because it has a formal parameter that is the class type. The assignment operator does have some interesting properties that we'll look at next.

The compiler automatically supplies every class with an assignment operator for assigning one object to another of the same class. The default, or implicit, version of this operator uses memberwise assignment, with each member of the target object being assigned the value of the corresponding member of the source object. However, if the object belongs to a derived class, the compiler uses the base class assignment operator to handle assignment for the base class portion of the derived object. If you've explicitly provided an assignment operator for the base class, that operator is used. Similarly, if a class contains a member that is an object of another class, the assignment operator for that class is used for that member.

As you've seen several times, you need to provide an explicit assignment operator if class constructors use new to initialize pointers. Because C++ uses the base class assignment operator for the base part of derived objects, you don't need to redefine the assignment operator for a derived class *unless* it adds data members that require special care. For example, the baseDMA class defined assignment explicitly, but the derived lacksDMA class uses the implicit assignment operator generated for that class.

Suppose, however, that a derived class does use new, and you have to provide an explicit assignment operator. The operator must provide for every member of the class, not just the new members. The hasDMA class illustrates how this can be done:

```
hasDMA & hasDMA::operator=(const hasDMA & hs)
{
    if (this == &hs)
        return *this;
    baseDMA::operator=(hs);  // copy base portion
    style = new char[strlen(hs.style) + 1];
    strcpy(style, hs.style);
    return *this;
}
```

What about assigning a derived object to a base object? (Note: This is not the same as initializing a base class reference to a derived object.)

```
Brass blips;                                             // base class
BrassPlus snips("Rafe Plosh", 91191,3993.19, 600.0, 0.12); // derived class
blips = snips;                          // assign derived object to base object
```

Which assignment operator is used? Remember that the assignment statement is translated into a method invoked by the left-hand object:

```
blips.operator=(snips);
```

Here the left-hand object is a `Brass` object, so it invokes the `Brass::operator=(const Brass &)` function. The *is-a* relationship allows the `Brass` reference to refer to a derived class object, such as `snips`. The assignment operator only deals with base class members, so the `maxLoan` member and other `BrassPlus` members of `snips` are ignored in the assignment. In short, you can assign a derived object to a base object, and only the base class members are involved.

What about the reverse? Can you assign a base class object to a derived object?

```
Brass gp("Griff Hexbait", 21234, 1200);    // base class
BrassPlus temp;                             // derived class
temp = gp;    // possible?
```

Here the assignment statement would be translated as follows:

```
temp.operator=(gp);
```

The left-hand object is a `BrassPlus` object, so it invokes the `BrassPlus::operator=(const BrassPlus &)` function. However, a derived class reference cannot automatically refer to a base object, so this code *won't* run unless there *also* is a conversion constructor:

```
BrassPlus(const Brass &);
```

(It could be, as is the case for the `BrassPlus` class, that there is a constructor with additional arguments, provided they have default values.) In that case, the program will use this constructor to create a temporary `BrassPlus` object from `gp`, which will then be used as an argument to the assignment operator.

Alternatively, you could define an assignment operator for assigning a base class to a derived class:

```
BrassPlus & BrassPlus ::operator=(const Brass &) {...}
```

Here the types match the assignment statement exactly, and no type conversions are needed.

In short, the answer to the question "Can you assign a base class object to a derived object?" is "Maybe." You can if the derived class has a constructor that defines the conversion of a base class object to a derived class object. And you can if the derived class defines an assignment operator for assigning a base class object to a derived object. If neither of these two conditions holds, then you can't make the assignment.

Private Versus Protected

Remember that protected members act like public members as far as a derived class is concerned, but like private members for the world at large. A derived class can access protected members of a base class directly, but can access private members only via base class member functions. Thus, making base class members private offers more security, while making them protected simplifies coding and speeds up access. Stroustrup feels that it's better to use private data members than protected data members, but that protected methods are useful. (Bjarne Stroustrup, *The Design and Evolution of C++*. Reading, MA: Addison-Wesley Publishing Company, 1994.)

Virtual Methods

When you design a base class, you have to decide whether to make class methods virtual or not. If you want a derived class to be able to redefine a method, define the method as virtual in the base class. This enables late, or dynamic, binding. If you don't want the method redefined, don't make it virtual. This doesn't prevent someone from redefining the method, but it should be interpreted as meaning that you don't want it redefined.

Note that inappropriate code can circumvent dynamic binding. Consider, for example, the following two functions:

```
void show(const Brass & rba)
{
    rba.ViewAcct();
    cout << endl;
}

void inadequate(Brass ba)
{
    ba.ViewAcct();
    cout << endl;
}
```

The first passes an object by reference, and the second passes an object by value.

Now suppose you use each with a derived class argument:

```
BrassPlus buzz("Buzz Parsec", 00001111, 4300);
show(buzz);
inadequate(buzz);
```

The `show()` function call results in the `rba` argument being a reference to the `BrassPlus` object `buzz`, so `rba.ViewAcct()` is interpreted as the `BrassPlus` version, as it should be. But in the `inadequate()` function, which passes an object by value, `ba` is a `Brass` object constructed by the `Brass(const Brass &)` constructor. (Automatic upcasting allows the constructor argument to refer to a `BrassPlus` object.) Thus, in `inadequate()`, `ba.ViewAcct()` is the `Brass` version, so only the `Brass` component of `buzz` is displayed.

Destructors

As mentioned before, a base class destructor should be virtual. That way, when you delete a derived object via a base class pointer or reference to the object, the program uses the derived class destructor followed by the base class destructor rather than using only the base class destructor.

Class Function Summary

C++ class functions come in many variations. Some can be inherited, some can't. Some operator functions can be either member functions or friends, while others can only be member functions. Table 13.1, based on a similar table from the ARM (*Annotated Reference Manual*), summarizes these properties. In it, the notation *op=* stands for assignment operators of the form +=, *=, and so on. Note that the properties for the *op=* operators are no different from those of the "other operators" category. The reason for listing *op=* separately is to point out that these operators don't behave like the = operator.

TABLE 13.1   Member Function Properties

Function	Inherited	Member or friend	Generated by default	Can be virtual	Can have a return type
Constructor	No	Member	Yes	No	No
Destructor	No	Member	Yes	Yes	No
=	No	Member	Yes	Yes	Yes
&	Yes	Either	Yes	Yes	Yes
Conversion	Yes	Member	No	Yes	No
()	Yes	Member	No	Yes	Yes
[]	Yes	Member	No	Yes	Yes
->	Yes	Member	No	Yes	Yes
op=	Yes	Either	No	Yes	Yes
new	Yes	Static member	No	No	void *
delete	Yes	Static member	No	No	void
Other operators	Yes	Either	No	Yes	Yes
Other members	Yes	Member	No	Yes	Yes
Friends	No	Friend	No	No	Yes

Summary

Inheritance enables you to adapt programming code to your particular needs by defining a new class (a derived class) from an existing class (the base class). Public inheritance models an *is-a* relationship, meaning a derived-class object also should be a kind of base-class object. As part of the *is-a* model, a derived class inherits the data members and most methods of the base class. However, a derived class doesn't inherit the base class constructors, destructors, and assignment operators. A derived class can access the public and protected members of the base class directly and the private base class members via the public and protected base-class methods. You then can add new data members and methods to the class, and you can use the derived class as a base class for further development. Each derived class requires its own constructors. When a program creates a derived class object, it first calls a base class constructor and then the derived class constructor. When a program deletes an object, it first calls the derived class destructor and then the base class destructor.

If a class is meant to be a base class, you may choose to use protected members instead of private members so that derived classes can access those members directly. However, using private members will, in general, reduce the scope for programming bugs. If you intend that a derived class can redefine a base class method, make it a virtual function by declaring it with the keyword `virtual`. This enables objects accessed by pointers or references to be handled on the basis of the object type rather than on the basis of the reference type or pointer type. In particular, the destructor for a base class normally should be virtual.

You might want to define an ABC (abstract base class) that defines an interface without getting into implementation matters. For example, you could define an abstract `Shape` class from which particular shape classes, such as `Circle` and `Square`, will be derived. An abstract base class must include at least one pure virtual method. You can declare a pure virtual method by placing `= 0` before the closing semicolon of the declaration.

```
virtual double area() const = 0;
```

You don't have to define pure virtual methods, and you can't create an object of a class containing pure virtual members. Instead, they serve to define a common interface to be used by derived classes.

Review Questions

1. What does a derived class inherit from a base class?

2. What doesn't a derived class inherit from a base class?

3. Suppose the return type for the `baseDMA::operator=()` function were defined as `void` instead of `baseDMA &`. What effect, if any, would that have? What if the return type were `baseDMA` instead of `baseDMA &`?

4. In what order are class constructors and class destructors called when a derived class object is created and deleted?

5. If a derived class doesn't add any data members to the base class, does the derived class require constructors?

6. Suppose a base class and a derived class both define a method of the same name and a derived class object invokes the method. What method is called?

7. When should a derived class define an assignment operator?

8. Can you assign the address of an object of a derived class to a pointer to the base class? Can you assign the address of an object of a base class to a pointer to the derived class?

9. Can you assign an object of a derived class to an object of the base class? Can you assign an object of a base class to an object of the derived class?

10. Suppose you define a function that takes a reference to a base class object as an argument. Why can this function also use a derived class object as an argument?

11. Suppose you define a function that takes a base class object as an argument (that is, the function passes a base class object by value). Why can this function also use a derived class object as an argument?

12. Why is it usually better to pass objects by reference than by value?

13. Suppose `Corporation` is a base class and `PublicCorporation` is a derived class. Also suppose that each class defines a `head()` member function, that `ph` is a pointer to the `Corporation` type, and that `ph` is assigned the address of a `PublicCorporation` object. How is `ph->head()` interpreted if the base class defines `head()` as a

    a. Regular nonvirtual method

    b. Virtual method

14. What's wrong, if anything, with the following code?

```
class Kitchen
{
private:
    double kit_sq_ft;
public:
    Kitchen() {kit_sq_ft = 0.0; }
    virtual double area() { return kit_sq_ft * kit_sq_ft; }
};
class House : public Kitchen
{
private:
    double all_sq_ft;
public:
    House() {all_sq_ft += kit_sq_ft;}
    double area(const char *s) { cout << s; return all_sq_ft; }
};
```

Programming Exercises

1. Start with the following class declaration:

```
// base class
class Cd {  // represents a CD disk
private:
    char performers[50];
    char label[20];
    int selections;   // number of selections
    double playtime;  // playing time in minutes
public:
```

```
        Cd(char * s1, char * s2, int n, double x);
        Cd(const Cd & d);
        Cd();
        ~Cd();
        void Report() const;  // reports all CD data
        Cd & operator=(const Cd & d);
    };
```

Derive a **Classic** class that adds an array of **char** members that will hold a string identifying the primary work on the CD. If the base class requires that any functions be virtual, modify the base class declaration to make it so. If a declared method is not needed, remove it from the definition. Test your product with the following program:

```cpp
#include <iostream>
using namespace std;
#include "classic.h"    // which will contain #include cd.h
void Bravo(const Cd & disk);
int main()
{
    Cd c1("Beatles", "Capitol", 14, 35.5);
    Classic c2 = Classic("Piano Sonata in B flat, Fantasia in C",
                    "Alfred Brendel", "Philips", 2, 57.17);
    Cd *pcd = &c1;

    cout << "Using object directly:\n";
    c1.Report();     // use Cd method
    c2.Report();     // use Classic method

    cout << "Using type cd * pointer to objects:\n";
    pcd->Report();   // use Cd method for cd object
    pcd = &c2;
    pcd->Report();   // use Classic method for classic object

    cout << "Calling a function with a Cd reference argument:\n";
    Bravo(c1);
    Bravo(c2);

    cout << "Testing assignment: ";
    Classic copy;
    copy = c2;
    copy.Report()

    return 0;
}

void Bravo(const Cd & disk)
{
    disk.Report();
}
```

2. Repeat exercise 1, but this time use dynamic memory allocation instead of fixed-size arrays for the various strings tracked by the two classes.

3. Revise the `baseDMA-lacksDMA-hasDMA` class hierarchy so that all three classes are derived from an abstract base class. Test the result with a program similar to the one in Listing 13.10. That is, it should feature an array of pointers to the abstract base class and allow the user to make runtime decisions as to what types of objects are created. Add virtual `View()` methods to the class definitions to handle displaying the data.

4. The Benevolent Order of Programmers maintains a collection of bottled port. To describe it, the BOP Portmaster has devised a `Port` class as declared below:

```cpp
#include <iostream>
using namespace std;
class Port
{
private:
    char * brand;
    char style[20]; // i.e., tawny, ruby, vintage
    int bottles;
public:
    Port(const char * br = "none", const char * st = "none", int b = 0);
    Port(const Port & p);              // copy constructor
    virtual ~Port() { delete [] brand; }
    Port & operator=(const Port & p);
    Port & operator+=(int b);          // adds b to bottles
    Port & operator-=(int b);          // subtracts b from bottles, if
                                       //available
    int BottleCount() const { return bottles; }
    virtual void Show() const;
    friend ostream & operator<<(ostream & os, const Port & p);
};
```

The `Show()` method presents information in the following format:

```
Brand: Gallo
Kind: tawny
Bottles: 20
```

The `operator<<()` function presents information in the following format (no newline at the end):

```
Gallo, tawny, 20
```

The Portmaster completed the method definitions for the `Port` class and then derived the `VintagePort` class as follows before being relieved of his position for accidentally routing a bottle of '45 Cockburn to someone preparing an experimental barbecue sauce.

```cpp
class VintagePort : public Port // style necessarily = "vintage"
{
private:
    char * nickname;           // i.e., "The Noble" or "Old Velvet", etc.
    int year;                  // vintage year
public:
    VintagePort();
    VintagePort(const char * br, int b, const char * nn, int y);
    VintagePort(const VintagePort & vp);
    ~VintagePort() { delete [] nickname; }
```

```
        VintagePort & operator=(const VintagePort & vp);
        void Show() const;
        friend ostream & operator<<(ostream & os, const VintagePort & vp);
};
```

You get the job of completing the `VintagePort` work.

   a. Your first task is to re-create the `Port` method definitions, for the former Portmaster immolated his upon being relieved.

   b. Your second task is to explain why certain methods are redefined and others are not.

   c. Your third task is to explain why `operator=()` and `operator<<()` are not virtual.

   d. Your fourth task is to provide definitions for the `VintagePort` methods.

CHAPTER 14

REUSING CODE IN C++

> **You will learn about the following in this chapter:**
>
> - *Has-a* relationships
> - Classes with member objects (containment)
> - Private and protected inheritance
> - Multiple inheritance
>
> - Virtual base classes
> - Creating class templates
> - Using class templates
> - Template specializations

One of the main goals of C++ is to facilitate the reuse of code. Public inheritance is one mechanism for achieving this goal, but not the only one. This chapter will investigate other choices. One technique is using class members that are themselves objects of another class. This is referred to as *containment* or *composition* or *layering*. Another option is using private or protected inheritance. Containment, private inheritance, and protected inheritance typically are used to implement *has-a* relationships, that is, relationships for which the new class has an object of another class. For example, a `Stereo` class might have a `CdPlayer` object. Multiple inheritance lets you create classes that inherit from two or more base classes, combining their functionality.

Chapter 10, "Objects and Classes," introduced function templates. Now we'll look at class templates, which provide another way of reusing code. Class templates let you define a class in generic terms. Then you can use the template to create specific classes defined for specific types. For example, you could define a general stack template and then use the template to create one class representing a stack of `int` values and another class representing a stack of `double` values. You could even generate a class representing a stack of stacks.

Classes with Object Members

Let's begin with classes that include class objects as members. Some classes, such as the `String` class of Chapter 12, "Classes and Dynamic Memory Allocation," or the standard C++ classes and templates of Chapter 16, "The `string` Class and the Standard Template Library," offer convenient ways of representing components of a more extensive class. We'll look at a particular example now.

What is a student? Someone enrolled in a school? Someone engaged in thoughtful investiga-tion? A refugee from the harsh exigencies of the real world? Someone with an identifying name and a set of quiz scores? Clearly, the last definition is a totally inadequate characterization of a person, but it is well-suited for a simple computer representation. So let's develop a **Student** class based on that definition.

Simplifying a student to a name and a set of quiz scores suggests using a **String** class object (Chapter 12) to hold the name and an array class object (coming up soon) to hold the scores (assumed to be type **double**). (Once you learn about the library classes discussed in Chapter 16, you probably would use the standard **string** and **vector** classes.) You might be tempted to publicly derive a **Student** class from these two classes. That would be an example of multi-ple public inheritance, which C++ allows, but it would be inappropriate here. The reason is that the relationship of a student to these classes doesn't fit the *is-a* model. A student is not a name. A student is not an array of quiz scores. What we have here is a *has-a* relationship. A student has a name, and a student has an array of quiz scores. The usual C++ technique for modeling *has-a* relationships is to use composition or containment; that is, to create a class composed of, or containing, members that are objects of another class. For example, we can begin a **Student** class declaration like this:

```
class Student
{
private:
      String name;       // use a String object for name
      ArrayDb scores;    // use an ArrayDb object for scores
      ......
};
```

As usual, the class makes the data members private. This implies that the **Student** class mem-ber functions can use the public interfaces of the **String** and **ArrayDb** (for *array* of *double*) classes to access and modify the **name** and **scores** objects, but that the outside world cannot do so. The only access the outside world will have to **name** and **scores** is through the public interface defined for the **Student** class (see Figure 14.1). A common way of describing this is saying that the **Student** class acquires the implementation of its member objects, but doesn't inherit the interface. For example a **Student** object uses the **String** implementation rather than a **char * name** or a **char name[26]** implementation for holding the name. But a **Student** object does not innately have the ability to use the **String operator==()** function.

Interfaces and Implementations

With public inheritance, a class inherits an interface, and, perhaps, an implementation. (Pure virtual functions in a base class can provide an interface without an implementation.) Acquiring the inter-face is part of the *is-a* relationship. With composition, on the other hand, a class acquires the imple-mentation without the interface. Not inheriting the interface is part of the *has-a* relationship.

FIGURE 14.1
Containment.

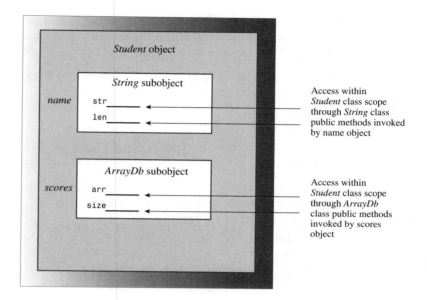

The fact that a class object doesn't automatically acquire the interface of a contained object is a good thing for a *has-a* relationship. For example, one could extend the `String` class to overload the + operator to allow concatenating two strings, but, conceptually, it doesn't make sense to concatenate two `Student` objects. That's one reason not to use public inheritance in this case. On the other hand, parts of the interface for the contained class may make sense for the new class. For example, you might want to use the `operator<()` method from the `String` interface to sort `Student` objects by name. You can do so by defining a `Student::Operator<()` member function that, internally, uses the `String::Operator<()` function. Let's move on to some details.

The `ArrayDb` Class

The first detail is developing the `ArrayDb` class so that the `Student` class can use it. This class will be quite similar to the `String` class because the latter is an array, too, in this case, of `char`. First, let's list some necessary and/or desirable features for the `ArrayDb` class.

- It should be able to store several **double** values.

- It should provide random access to individual values using bracket notation with an index.

- One can assign one array to another.

- The class will perform bounds checking to ensure that array indices are valid.

The first two features are the essence of an array. The third feature is not true of built-in arrays but is true for class objects, so creating an array class will provide that feature. The final feature, again, is not true for built-in arrays, but can be added as part of the second feature.

At this point, much of the design can ape the `String` declaration, replacing type `char` with type `double`. That is, you can do this:

```
class ArrayDb
{
private:
    unsigned int size;            // number of array elements
    double * arr;                 // address of first element
public:
    ArrayDb();                    // default constructor
    // create an ArrayDb of n elements, set each to val
    ArrayDb(unsigned int n, double val = 0.0);
    // create an ArrayDb of n elements, initialize to array pn
    ArrayDb(const double * pn, unsigned int n);
    ArrayDb(const ArrayDb & a);   // copy constructor
    virtual ~ArrayDb();           // destructor
    double & operator[](int i); // array indexing
    const double & operator[](int i) const; // array indexing
        // other stuff to be added here
    ArrayDb & operator=(const ArrayDb & a);
    friend ostream & operator<<(ostream & os, const ArrayDb & a);
};
```

The class will use dynamic memory allocation to create an array of the desired size. Therefore, it also will provide a destructor, a copy constructor, and an assignment operator. For convenience, it will have a few more constructors.

Tweaking `operator[]()`

To provide random access using array notation, the class has to overload the `[]` operator, just as the `String` class did. This will allow code like the following:

```
ArrayDb scores(5, 20.0); // 5 elements, each set to 20.0
double temp = scores[3];
scores[3] = 16.5:
```

Clients of the `ArrayDB` class can access array elements individually only through the overloaded `[]` operator. This gives you the opportunity to build in some safety checks. In particular, the method can check to see if the proposed array index is in bounds. That is, you can write the operator this way:

```
double & ArrayDb::operator[](int i)
{
    // check index before continuing
    if (i < 0 || i >= size)
    {
        cerr << "Error in array limits: "
            << i << " is a bad index\n";
        exit(1);
```

```
    }
    return arr[i];
}
```

This slows down a program, for it requires evaluating an `if` statement every time the program accesses an array element. But it adds safety, preventing a program from placing a value in the 2000th element of a 5-element array.

As with the `String` class, we need a `const` version of the `[]` operator to allow read-only access for constant `ArrayDb` objects:

```cpp
const double & ArrayDb::operator[](int i) const
{
    // check index before continuing
    if (i < 0 || i >= size)
    {
        cerr << "Error in array limits: "
            << i << " is a bad index\n";
        exit(1);
    }
    return arr[i];
}
```

The compiler will select the `const` version of `operator[]()` for use with `const ArrayDb` objects and use the other version for non-`const ArrayDb` objects.

Listing 14.1 shows the header file for the `ArrayDb` class. For extra convenience, the class definition includes an `Average()` method that returns the average of the array elements.

LISTING 14.1   `arraydb.h`

```cpp
// arraydb.h -- array class
#ifndef ARRAYDB_H_
#define ARRAYDB_H_
#include <iostream>
using namespace std;

class ArrayDb
{
private:
    unsigned int size;              // number of array elements
    double * arr;                   // address of first element
public:
    ArrayDb();                      // default constructor
    // create an ArrayDb of n elements, set each to val
    explicit ArrayDb(unsigned int n, double val = 0.0);
    // create an ArrayDb of n elements, initialize to array pn
    ArrayDb(const double * pn, unsigned int n);
    ArrayDb(const ArrayDb & a);     // copy constructor
    virtual ~ArrayDb();             // destructor
    unsigned int ArSize() const {return size;}// returns array size
    double Average() const;         // return array average
```

LISTING 14.1   *Continued*

```
// overloaded operators
    double & operator[](int i); // array indexing
    const double & operator[](int i) const; // array indexing
    ArrayDb & operator=(const ArrayDb & a);
    friend ostream & operator<<(ostream & os, const ArrayDb & a);
};

#endif
```

Compatibility Note

Older implementations don't support the `explicit` keyword.

One point of interest is that one of the constructors uses `explicit`:

```
explicit ArrayDb(unsigned int n, double val = 0.0);
```

A constructor that can be called with one argument, recall, serves as an implicit conversion function from the argument type to the class type. In this case, the first argument represents the number of elements in the array rather than a value for the array, so having the constructor serve as an `int`-to-`ArrayDb` conversion function does not make sense. Using `explicit` turns off implicit conversions. If this keyword were omitted, then code like the following would be possible:

```
ArrayDb doh(20,100);  // array of 20 elements, each set to 100
doh = 5;   // set doh to an array of 5 elements, each set to 0
```

Here, the inattentive programmer typed `doh` instead of `doh[0]`. If the constructor omitted `explicit`, 5 would be converted to a temporary `ArrayDb` object using the constructor call `ArrayDb(5)`, with the default value of 0 being used for the second argument. Then assignment would replace the original `doh` with the temporary object. With `explicit` in place, the compiler will catch the assignment operator as an error.

Real World Note: C++ and Constraints

C++ is full of features that allow the programmer to constrain programmatic constructs to certain limits—`explicit` to remove the implicit conversion of single-argument constructors, **const** to constrain the use of methods to modify data, and more. The underlying motive is simply this: *compile-time errors are better than run-time errors*.

Consider an admittedly horrible example of a runtime error: a key value, responsible for the reported height of an aircraft is mangled (programmer-speak for *altered*), quite accidentally, by a maintenance programmer who modifies the value using a method of his own, derived from your original `Airplane::reportHeight()` method, which uses the value properly and doesn't misreport it). Avoiding this error is as simple as creating the `reportHeight()` method as **const** in the first place; the maintenance programmer can't derive a method to mangle the data, because you've protected him. If he tries, his compiler stops him, and forces him to create his method as **const** also.

Use of the C++ language to prevent disaster by generating compiler errors is a sure sign of an expe-rienced, thoughtful programmer. The features exist to help, and using them to their utmost is, in the long run, sure to result in better software.

Listing 14.2 shows the implementation.

LISTING 14.2   `arraydb.cpp`

```cpp
// arraydb.cpp -- ArrayDb class methods
#include <iostream>
using namespace std;
#include <cstdlib>    // exit() prototype
#include "arraydb.h"

// default constructor -- no arguments
ArrayDb::ArrayDb()
{
    arr = NULL;
    size = 0;
}

// constructs array of n elements, each set to val
ArrayDb::ArrayDb(unsigned int n, double val)
{
    arr = new double[n];
    size = n;
    for (int i = 0; i < size; i++)
        arr[i] = val;
}

// initialize ArrayDb object to a non-class array
ArrayDb::ArrayDb(const double *pn, unsigned int n)
{
    arr = new double[n];
    size = n;
    for (int i = 0; i < size; i++)
        arr[i] = pn[i];
}

// initialize ArrayDb object to another ArrayDb object
ArrayDb::ArrayDb(const ArrayDb & a)
{
    size = a.size;
    arr = new double[size];
    for (int i = 0; i < size; i++)
        arr[i] = a.arr[i];
}

ArrayDb::~ArrayDb()
{
    delete [] arr;
}
```

LISTING 14.2 Continued

```cpp
double ArrayDb::Average() const
{
    double sum = 0;
    int i;
    int lim = ArSize();
    for (i = 0; i < lim; i++)
        sum += arr[i];
    if (i > 0)
        return sum / i;
    else
    {
        cerr << "No entries in score array\n";
        return 0;
    }
}

// let user access elements by index (assignment allowed)
double & ArrayDb::operator[](int i)
{
    // check index before continuing
    if (i < 0 || i >= size)
    {
        cerr << "Error in array limits: "
            << i << " is a bad index\n";
        exit(1);
    }
    return arr[i];
}

// let user access elements by index (assignment disallowed)
const double & ArrayDb::operator[](int i) const
{
    // check index before continuing
    if (i < 0 || i >= size)
    {
        cerr << "Error in array limits: "
            << i << " is a bad index\n";
        exit(1);
    }
    return arr[i];
}

// define class assignment
ArrayDb & ArrayDb::operator=(const ArrayDb & a)
{
    if (this == &a)        // if object assigned to self,
        return *this;      // don't change anything
    delete [] arr;
    size = a.size;
    arr = new double[size];
    for (int i = 0; i < size; i++)
        arr[i] = a.arr[i];
```

LISTING 14.2   Continued

```
        return *this;
    }

// quick output, 5 values to a line
ostream & operator<<(ostream & os, const ArrayDb & a)
{
    int i;
    for (i = 0; i < a.size; i++)
    {
        os << a.arr[i] << " ";
        if (i % 5 == 4)
            os << "\n";
    }
    if (i % 5 != 0)
        os << "\n";
    return os;
}
```

The Student Class Example

With the `ArrayDb` class now in hand, let's proceed to provide the `Student` class declaration. It should, of course, include constructors and at least a few functions to provide an interface for the `Student` class. Listing 14.3 does this, defining all the constructors inline.

LISTING 14.3   studentc.h

```
// studentc.h -- defining a Student class using containment
#ifndef STUDNTC_H_
#define STUDENTC_H_

#include <iostream>
using namespace std;
#include "arraydb.h"
#include "string1.h"    // from Chapter 12

class Student
{
private:
    String name;        // contained object
    ArrayDb scores;     // contained object
public:
    Student() : name("Null Student"), scores() {}
    Student(const String & s)
        : name(s), scores() {}
    Student(int n) : name("Nully"), scores(n) {}
    Student(const String & s, int n)
        : name(s), scores(n) {}
    Student(const String & s, const ArrayDb & a)
        : name(s), scores(a) {}
    Student(const char * str, const double * pd, int n)
```

LISTING 14.3   Continued

```
            : name(str), scores(pd, n) {}
        ~Student() {}
        double & operator[](int i);
        const double & operator[](int i) const;
        double Average() const;

// friends
        friend ostream & operator<<(ostream & os, const Student & stu);
        friend istream & operator>>(istream & is, Student & stu);
};

#endif
```

Initializing Contained Objects

Note that constructors all use the by-now-familiar member-initializer-list syntax to initialize the `name` and `scores` member objects. In some past cases, the constructors used it to initialize members that were built-in types:

```
Queue::Queue(int qs) : qsize(qs)  {...} // initialize qsize to qs
```

This code uses the name of the data member (`qsize`) in a member initializer list. Also, constructors from previous examples have used a member initializer list to initialize the base class portion of a derived object:

```
hasDMA::hasDMA(const hasDMA & hs) : baseDMA(hs) {...}
```

For inherited objects, constructors used the class name in the member initializer list to invoke a specific base class constructor. For member objects, constructors use the member name. For example, look at the last constructor in Listing 14.3:

```
Student(const char * str, const double * pd, int n)
        : name(str), scores(pd, n) {}
```

Because it initializes member objects, not inherited objects, it uses the member names, not the class names, in the initialization list. Each item in this initialization list invokes the matching constructor. That is, `name(str)` invokes the `String(const char *)` constructor, and `scores(pd, n)` invokes the `ArrayDb(const double *, int)` constructor.

What happens if you don't use the initialization-list syntax? As with inherited components, C++ requires that all member objects be constructed before the rest of an object is constructed. So if you omit the initialization list, C++ will use the default constructors defined for the member objects classes.

Initialization Order

When you have a member initializer list that initializes more than one item, the items are initialized in the order they were declared, not in the order in which they appear in the initializer list. For example, suppose we wrote a `Student` constructor this way:

```
Student(const char * str, const double * pd, int n)
        : scores(pd, n),  name(str) {}
```

The name member would still be initialized first because it is declared first in the class definition. The exact initialization order is not important for this example, but it would be important if the code used the value of one member as part of the initialization expression for a second member.

Using an Interface for a Contained Object

The interface for a contained object isn't public, but it can be used within the class methods. For example, here is how you can define a function that returns the average of a student's scores:

```cpp
double Student::Average() const
{
    return scores.Average();
}
```

This defines a method that can be invoked by a Student object. Internally, it uses the ArrayDb::Average() function. That's because scores is an ArrayDb object, so it can invoke the member functions of the ArrayDb class. In short, the Student object invokes a Student method, and the Student method uses the contained ArrayDB object to invoke an ArrayDb method.

Similarly, you can define a friend function that uses both the String and the ArrayDb versions of the << operator:

```cpp
ostream & operator<<(ostream & os, const Student & stu)
{
    os << "Scores for " << stu.name << ":\n";
    os << stu.scores;
    return os;
}
```

Because stu.name is a String object, it invokes the operator<<(ostream &, const String &) function. Similarly, the ArrayDb object stu.scores invokes the operator<<(ostream &, const ArrayDb &) function. Note that the new function has to be a friend to the Student class so that it can access the name and scores member of a Student object.

Listing 14.4 shows the class methods file for the Student class. It includes methods that allow you to use the [] operator to access individual scores in a Student object.

LISTING 14.4   studentc.cpp

```cpp
// studentc.cpp -- Student class using containment
#include "studentc.h"

double Student::Average() const
{
    return scores.Average();  // use ArrayDb::Average()
}

double & Student::operator[](int i)
{
```

LISTING 14.4   Continued

```
      return scores[i];        // use ArrayDb::operator[]()
}

const double & Student::operator[](int i) const
{
    return scores[i];
}

// friends

// use String and ArrayDb versions
ostream & operator<<(ostream & os, const Student & stu)
{
    os << "Scores for " << stu.name << ":\n";
    os << stu.scores;
    return os;
}

// use String version
istream & operator>>(istream & is, Student & stu)
{
    is >> stu.name;
    return is;
}
```

This hasn't required much new code. Using containment allows you to take advantage of the code you've already written.

Using the New Class

Let's put together a small program to test the new class. To keep things simple, it will use an array of just three **Student** objects, each holding five quiz scores. And it'll use an unsophisticated input cycle that doesn't verify input and that doesn't let you cut the input process short. Listing 14.5 presents the test program. Compile it along with **studentc.cpp**, **string1.cpp**, and **arrayDb.cpp**.

LISTING 14.5   use_stuc.cpp

```
// use_stuc.cpp -- use a composite class
// compile with studentc.cpp, string1.cpp, arraydb.cpp
#include <iostream>
using namespace std;
#include "studentc.h"

void set(Student & sa, int n);

const int pupils = 3;
const int quizzes = 5;

int main()
```

LISTING 14.5   Continued

```cpp
{
    Student ada[pupils] = {quizzes, quizzes, quizzes};

    int i;
    for (i = 0; i < pupils; i++)
        set(ada[i], quizzes);
    for (i = 0; i < pupils; i++)
    {
        cout << "\n" << ada[i];
        cout << "average: " << ada[i].Average() << "\n";
    }
    cout << "Done.\n";
    return 0;
}

void set(Student & sa, int n)
{
    cout << "Please enter the student's name: ";
    cin >> sa;
    cout << "Please enter " << n << " quiz scores:\n";
    for (int i = 0; i < n; i++)
        cin >> sa[i];
    while (cin.get() != '\n')
        continue;
}
```

Here is a sample run:

```
Please enter the student's name: Gil Bayts
Please enter 5 quiz scores:
92 94 96 93 95
Please enter the student's name: Pat Roone
Please enter 5 quiz scores:
83 89 72 78 95
Please enter the student's name: Fleur O'Day
Please enter 5 quiz scores:
92 89 96 78 64

Scores for Gil Bayts:
92 94 96 93 95
average: 94

Scores for Pat Roone:
83 89 72 78 95
average: 83.4

Scores for Fleur O'Day
92 89 96 78 64
average: 83.8
```

Private Inheritance

C++ has a second means of implementing the *has-a* relationship—*private inheritance*. With private inheritance, public and protected members of the base class become private members of the derived class. This means the methods of the base class do not become part of the public interface of the derived object. They can be used, however, inside the member functions of the derived class.

Let's look at the interface topic more closely. With public inheritance, the public methods of the base class become public methods of the derived class. In short, the derived class inherits the base class interface. This is part of the *is-a* relationship. With private inheritance, the public methods of the base class become private methods of the derived class. In short, the derived class does not inherit the base class interface. As you saw with contained objects, this lack of inheritance is part of the *has-a* relationship.

With private inheritance, a class does inherit the implementation. That is, if you base a `Student` class on a `String` class, the `Student` class winds up with an inherited `String` class component that can be used to store a string. Furthermore, the `Student` methods can use the `String` methods internally to access the String component.

Containment adds an object to a class as a named member object, while private inheritance adds an object to a class as an unnamed inherited object. We'll use the term `subobject` to denote an object added by inheritance or by containment.

Private inheritance, then, provides the same features as containment: Acquire the implementation, don't acquire the interface. Therefore it, too, can be used to implement a *has-a* relationship. Let's see how you can use private inheritance to redesign the `Student` class.

The `Student` Class Example (New Version)

To get private inheritance, use the keyword `private` instead of `public` when defining the class. (Actually, `private` is the default, so omitting an access qualifier also leads to private inheritance.) The `Student` class should inherit from two classes, so the declaration will list both:

```
class Student : private String, private ArrayDb
{
public:
    ......
};
```

Having more than one base class is called *multiple inheritance*, or MI. In general, multiple inheritance, particularly public multiple inheritance, can lead to problems that have to be resolved with additional syntax rules. We'll talk about such matters later in this chapter. But in this particular case, MI causes no problems.

Note that the new class won't need a private section. That's because the two inherited base classes already provide all the needed data members. Containment provided two explicitly named objects as members. Private inheritance, however, provides two nameless subobjects as inherited members. This is the first of the main differences in the two approaches.

Initializing Base Class Components

Having implicitly inherited components instead of member objects will affect the coding, for you no longer can use **name** and **scores** to describe the objects. Instead, you have to go back to the techniques you used for public inheritance. For example, consider constructors. Containment used this constructor:

```
Student(const char * str, const double * pd, int n)
  : name(str), scores(pd, n) {}       // use object names for containment
```

The new version will use the member-initializer-list syntax for inherited classes, which uses the *class* name instead of a *member* name to identify constructors:

```
Student(const char * str, const double * pd, int n)
  : String(str), ArrayDb(pd, n) {}  // use class names for inheritance
```

That is, the member initializer list uses terms like **String(str)** instead of **name(str)**. This is the second main difference in the two approaches

Listing 14.6 shows the new class declaration. The only changes are the omission of explicit object names and the use of class names instead of member names in the inline constructors.

LISTING 14.6   studenti.h

```
// studenti.h -- defining a Student class using private inheritance
#ifndef STUDNTI_H_
#define STUDENTI_H_

#include <iostream>
using namespace std;
#include "arraydb.h"
#include "string1.h"

class Student : private String, private ArrayDb  // inherited objects
{
public:
    Student() : String("Null Student"), ArrayDb() {}
    Student(const String & s)
        : String(s), ArrayDb() {}
    Student(int n) : String("Nully"), ArrayDb(n) {}
    Student(const String & s, int n)
        : String(s), ArrayDb(n) {}
    Student(const String & s, const ArrayDb & a)
        : String(s), ArrayDb(a) {}
    Student(const char * str, const double * pd, int n)
        : String(str), ArrayDb(pd, n) {}
    ~Student() {}
    double & operator[](int i);
    const double & operator[](int i) const;
```

LISTING 14.6   Continued

```
        double Average() const;
// friends
        friend ostream & operator<<(ostream & os, const Student & stu);
        friend istream & operator>>(istream & is, Student & stu);
};

#endif
```

Using Base Class Methods

Private inheritance limits the use of base class methods to within derived class methods. Sometimes, however, you might like to make a base class facility available publicly. For example, the class declaration suggests the ability to use an **Average()** function. As with containment, the technique for doing this is to use the private **ArrayDb::Average()** function within a public **Student::average()** function (see Figure 14.2). Containment invoked the method with an object:

```
double Student::Average() const
{
    return scores.Average();  // use ArrayDb::Average()
}
```

FIGURE 14.2
Private inheritance.

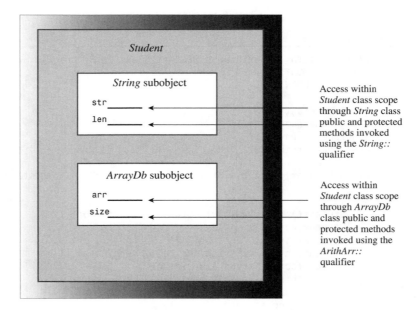

Student

String subobject

str _____◄

len _____◄

Access within *Student* class scope through *String* class public and protected methods invoked using the *String::* qualifier

ArrayDb subobject

arr _____◄

size _____◄

Access within *Student* class scope through *ArrayDb* class public and protected methods invoked using the *ArithArr::* qualifier

Here, however, inheritance lets you use the class name and the scope resolution operator to invoke a base-class function:

```
double Student::Average() const
{
```

```
        return ArrayDb::Average();
}
```

Omitting the `ArrayDb::` qualifier would have caused the compiler to interpret the `Average()` function call as `Student::Average()`, leading to a highly undesirable recursive function definition. In short, the containment approach used object names to invoke a method, while private inheritance uses the class name and the scope resolution operator instead.

This technique of explicitly qualifying a function name with its class name doesn't work for friend functions because they don't belong to a class. However, you can use an explicit type cast to the base class to invoke the correct functions. For example, consider the following friend function definition:

```
ostream & operator<<(ostream & os, const Student & stu)
{
    os << "Scores for " << (const String &) stu << ":\n";
    os << (const ArrayDb &) stu;
    return os;
}
```

If `plato` is a `Student` object, then the statement

```
cout << plato;
```

will invoke this function, with `stu` being a reference to `plato` and `os` being a reference to `cout`. Within the code, the type cast in

```
os << "Scores for " << (const String &) stu << ":\n";
```

explicitly converts `stu` to a reference to a type `String` object, and that matches the `operator<<(ostream &, const String &)` function. Similarly, the type cast in

```
os << (const ArrayDb &) stu;
```

invokes the `operator<<(ostream &, const ArrayDb &)` function.

The reference `stu` doesn't get converted automatically to a `String` or `ArrayDb` reference. The fundamental reason is this: With private inheritance, a reference or pointer to a base class cannot be assigned a reference or pointer to a derived class without an explicit type cast.

However, even if the example had used public inheritance, it would have had to use explicit type casts. One reason is that without a type cast, code like

```
os << stu;
```

would match the friend function prototype, leading to a recursive call. A second reason is that because the class uses multiple inheritance, the compiler couldn't tell which base class to convert to in this case, for both possible conversions match existing `operator<<()` functions.

Listing 14.7 shows all the class methods, other than those defined inline in the class declaration.

LISTING 14.7 studenti.cpp

```
// studenti.cpp -- Student class using private inheritance
#include "studenti.h"
double Student::Average() const
{
    return ArrayDb::Average();
}

double & Student::operator[](int i)
{
    return  ArrayDb::operator[](i);
}

const double & Student::operator[](int i) const
{
    return ArrayDb::operator[](i);
}

// friends
ostream & operator<<(ostream & os, const Student & stu)
{
    os << "Scores for " << (const String &) stu << ":\n";
    os << (const ArrayDb &) stu;
    return os;
}

istream & operator>>(istream & is, Student & stu)
{
    is >> (String &) stu;
    return is;
}
```

Again, because the example reuses the `String` and `ArrayDb` code, relatively little new code is needed.

Using the Revised `Student` Class

Once again it's time to test a new class. Note that the two versions of the `Student` class have exactly the same public interface, so you can test it with exactly the same program. The only difference is that you have to include `studenti.h` instead of `studentc.h`, and you have to link the program with `studenti.cpp` instead of with `studentc.cpp`. Listing 14.8 shows the program. Compile it along with `studenti.cpp`, `string1.cpp`, and `arrayDb.cpp`.

LISTING 14.8 use_stui.cpp

```
// use_stui.cpp -- use a class with private derivation
// compile with studenti.cpp, string1.cpp, arraydb.cpp
#include <iostream>
using namespace std;
#include "studenti.h"
```

LISTING 14.8 Continued

```cpp
void set(Student & sa, int n);

const int pupils = 3;
const int quizzes = 5;

int main()
{
    Student ada[pupils] = {quizzes, quizzes, quizzes};

    int i;
    for (i = 0; i < pupils; i++)
        set(ada[i], quizzes);
    for (i = 0; i < pupils; i++)
    {
        cout << "\n" << ada[i];
        cout << "average: " << ada[i].Average() << "\n";
    }
    return 0;
}

void set(Student & sa, int n)
{
    cout << "Please enter the student's name: ";
    cin >> sa;
    cout << "Please enter " << n << " quiz scores:\n";
    for (int i = 0; i < n; i++)
        cin >> sa[i];
    while (cin.get() != '\n')
        continue;
}
```

Here is a sample run:

```
Please enter the student's name: Gil Bayts
Please enter 5 quiz scores:
92 94 96 93 95
Please enter the student's name: Pat Roone
Please enter 5 quiz scores:
83 89 72 78 95
Please enter the student's name: Fleur O'Day
Please enter 5 quiz scores:
92 89 96 78 64

Scores for Gil Bayts:
92 94 96 93 95
average: 94

Scores for Pat Roone:
83 89 72 78 95
average: 83.4
```

```
Scores for Fleur O'Day
92 89 96 78 64
average: 83.8
```

The same input as before leads to the same output as before.

Containment or Private Inheritance?

Given that you can model a *has-a* relationship either with containment or with private inheritance, which should you use? Most C++ programmers prefer containment. First, it's easier to follow. When you look at the class declaration, you see explicitly named objects representing the contained classes, and your code can refer to these objects by name. Using inheritance makes the relationship appear more abstract. Second, inheritance can raise problems, particularly if a class inherits from more than one base class. You may have to deal with issues such as separate base classes having methods of the same name or of separate base classes sharing a common ancestor. All in all, you're less likely to run into trouble using containment. Also, containment allows you to include more than one subobject of the same class. If a class needs three **String** objects, you can declare three separate **String** members using the containment approach. But inheritance limits you to a single object. (It is difficult to tell objects apart when they all are nameless.)

However, private inheritance does offer features beyond those provided by containment. Suppose, for example, that a class has protected members, which could either be data members or member functions. Such members are available to derived classes, but not to the world at large. If you include such a class in another class using composition, the new class is part of the world at large, not a derived class. Hence it can't access protected members. But using inheritance makes the new class a derived class, so it can access protected members.

Another situation that calls for using private inheritance is if you want to redefine virtual functions. Again, this is a privilege accorded to a derived class but not to a containing class. With private inheritance, the redefined functions would be usable just within the class, not publicly.

Tip
In general, use containment to model a *has-a* relationship. Use private inheritance if the new class needs to access protected members in the original class or if it needs to redefine virtual functions.

Protected Inheritance

Protected inheritance is a variation on private inheritance. It uses the keyword **protected** when listing a base class:

```
class Student : protected String, protected ArrayDb {...};
```

With protected inheritance, public and protected members of a base class become protected members of the derived class. As with private inheritance, the interface for the base class is available to the derived class, but not to the outside world. The main difference between private and protected inheritance occurs when you derive another class from the derived class.

With private inheritance, this third-generation class doesn't get the internal use of the base class interface. That's because the public base class methods become private in the derived class, and private members and methods can't be directly accessed by the next level of derivation. With protected inheritance, public base methods become protected in the second generation and so are available internally to the next level of derivation.

Table 14.1 summarizes public, private, and protected inheritance. The term *implicit upcasting* means that you can have a base class pointer or reference refer to a derived class object without using an explicit type cast.

TABLE 14.1   Varieties of Inheritance

Property	Public Inheritance	Protected Inheritance	Private Inheritance
Public members become	Public members of the derived class	Protected members of the derived class	Private members of the derived class
Protected members become	Protected members of the derived class	Protected members of the derived class	Private members of the derived class
Private members become	Accessible only through the base class interface	Accessible only through the base class interface	Accessible only through the base class interface
Implicit upcasting	Yes	Yes (but only within the derived class)	No

Redefining Access with `using`

Public members of a base class become protected or private when you use protected or private derivation. The last example showed how the derived class can make a base class method available by having a derived class method use the base class method:

```
double Student::Average() const
{
    return ArrayDb::Average();
}
```

There is an alternative to wrapping one function call in another, and that is to use a using-declaration (like those used with namespaces) to announce a particular base class member can be used by the derived class, even though the derivation is private. For example, in `studenti.h`, you can omit the declaration for `Student::Average()` and replace it with a using-declaration:

```
class Student : private String, private ArrayDb
{
public:
    using ArrayDb::Average;
```

```
    ...
};
```

The using-declaration makes the `ArrayDb::Average()` method available as if it were a public `Student` method. That means you can drop the `Student::Average()` definition from `studenti.cpp` and still use `Average()` as before:

```
cout << "average: " << ada[i].Average() << "\n";
```

The difference is that now `ArrayDb::Average()` is called directly rather than through an intermediate call to `Student::Average()`.

Note that the using-declaration just uses the member name—no parentheses, no function signatures, no return types. For example, to make the `ArrayDB operator[]()` method available to the `Student` class, you'd place the following using-declaration in the public section of the `Student` class declaration:

```
using ArrayDb::operator[];
```

This would make both versions (`const` and non-`const`) available. The using-declaration approach works only for inheritance and not for containment.

There is an older way for redeclaring base-class methods in a privately derived class, and that's to place the method name in the public section of the derived class. Here's how that would be done:

```
class Student : private String, private ArrayDb
{
public:
    ArrayDb::operator[];  // redeclare as public, just use name
    ...
};
```

It looks like a using-declaration without the `using` keyword. This approach is *deprecated*, meaning that the intention is to phase it out. So if your compiler supports the using-declaration, use it to make a method from a private base class available to the derived class.

Multiple Inheritance

Multiple inheritance (MI) describes a class that has more than one immediate base class. As with single inheritance, public multiple inheritance should express an *is-a* relationship. For example, if you have a `Waiter` class and a `Singer` class, you could derive a `SingingWaiter` class from the two:

```
class SingingWaiter : public Waiter, public Singer {...};
```

Note that you must qualify each base class with the keyword `public`. That's because the compiler assumes private derivation unless instructed otherwise:

```
class SingingWaiter : public Waiter, Singer {...}; // Singer is a private base
```

As discussed earlier in this chapter, private and protected MI can express a *has-a* relationship; the studenti.h implementation of the Student class is an example. We'll concentrate on public inheritance now.

Multiple inheritance can introduce new problems for the programmer. The two chief problems are inheriting different methods of the same name from two different base classes and inheriting multiple instances of a class via two or more related immediate base classes. Meeting these problems involves introducing a few new rules and syntax variations. Thus, using multiple inheritance can be more difficult and problem-prone than using single inheritance. For this reason, many in the C++ community object strongly to MI; some want it removed from the language. Others love MI and argue that it's very useful, even necessary, for particular projects. Still others suggest using MI cautiously and in moderation.

Let's explore a particular example and see what the problems and solutions are. We need several classes to create a multiple inheritance situation. We'll define an abstract Worker base class and derive a Waiter class and a Singer class from it. Then we can use MI to derive a SingingWaiter class from the Waiter and Singer classes (see Figure 14.3). This is a case in which a base class (Worker) is inherited via two separate derivations, which is the circumstance that causes the most difficulties with MI. We'll start with declarations for the Worker, Waiter, and Singer classes, as shown in Listing 14.9.

FIGURE 14.3
Multiple inheritance with a shared ancestor.

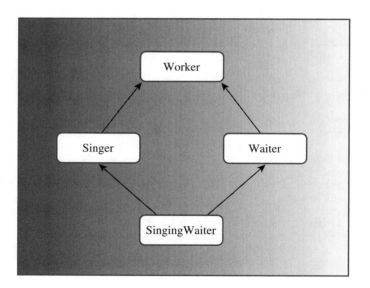

LISTING 14.9 Worker.h

```
// worker0.h  -- working classes
#ifndef WORKER0_H_
#define WORKER0_H_

#include "string1.h"
```

LISTING 14.9   Continued

```
class Worker    // an abstract base class
{
private:
    String fullname;
    long id;
public:
    Worker() : fullname("no one"), id(0L) {}
    Worker(const String & s, long n)
            : fullname(s), id(n) {}
    virtual ~Worker() = 0;   // pure virtual destructor
    virtual void Set();
    virtual void Show() const;
};

class Waiter : public Worker
{
private:
    int panache;
public:
    Waiter() : Worker(), panache(0) {}
    Waiter(const String & s, long n, int p = 0)
            : Worker(s, n), panache(p) {}
    Waiter(const Worker & wk, int p = 0)
            : Worker(wk), panache(p) {}
    void Set();
    void Show() const;
};

class Singer : public Worker
{
protected:
    enum {other, alto, contralto, soprano,
                    bass, baritone, tenor};
    enum {Vtypes = 7};
private:
    static char *pv[Vtypes];    // string equivs of voice types
    int voice;
public:
    Singer() : Worker(), voice(other) {}
    Singer(const String & s, long n, int v = other)
            : Worker(s, n), voice(v) {}
    Singer(const Worker & wk, int v = other)
            : Worker(wk), voice(v) {}
    void Set();
    void Show() const;
};

#endif
```

Next comes the implementation file, as shown in Listing 14.10.

LISTING 14.10   worker0.cpp

```cpp
// worker0.cpp -- working class methods
#include "worker.h"
#include <iostream>
using namespace std;
// Worker methods

   // must implement virtual destructor, even if pure
Worker::~Worker() {}

void Worker::Set()
{
    cout << "Enter worker's name: ";
    cin >> fullname;
    cout << "Enter worker's ID: ";
    cin >> id;
    while (cin.get() != '\n')
        continue;
}

void Worker::Show() const
{
    cout << "Name: " << fullname << "\n";
    cout << "Employee ID: " << id << "\n";
}

// Waiter methods
void Waiter::Set()
{
    Worker::Set();
    cout << "Enter waiter's panache rating: ";
    cin >> panache;
    while (cin.get() != '\n')
        continue;
}

void Waiter::Show() const
{
    cout << "Category: waiter\n";
    Worker::Show();
    cout << "Panache rating: " << panache << "\n";
}

// Singer methods

char * Singer::pv[] = {"other", "alto", "contralto",
            "soprano", "bass", "baritone", "tenor"};

void Singer::Set()
{
    Worker::Set();
    cout << "Enter number for singer's vocal range:\n";
    int i;
```

LISTING 14.10   Continued

```
        for (i = 0; i < Vtypes; i++)
        {
            cout << i << ": " << pv[i] << "    ";
            if ( i % 4 == 3)
                cout << '\n';
        }
        if (i % 4 != 0)
            cout << '\n';
        cin >> voice;
        while (cin.get() != '\n')
            continue;
}

void Singer::Show() const
{
    cout << "Category: singer\n";
    Worker::Show();
    cout << "Vocal range: " << pv[voice] << "\n";
}
```

With these two files, you can write a program using these classes. However, they lead to some
problems if we add a `SingingWaiter` class derived from both the `Singer` class and `Waiter`
class. In particular, we'll need to face the following questions:

- How many workers?

- Which method?

How Many Workers?

Suppose you begin by publicly deriving `SingingWaiter` from `Singer` and `Waiter`:

```
class SingingWaiter: public Singer, public  Waiter {...};
```

Because both `Singer` and `Waiter` inherit a `Worker` component, a `SingingWaiter` winds up
with two `Worker` components (see Figure 14.4).

As you might expect, this raises problems. For example, ordinarily you can assign the address
of a derived class object to a base class pointer, but this becomes ambiguous now:

```
SingingWaiter ed;
Worker * pw = &ed;    // ambiguous
```

Normally, such an assignment sets a base class pointer to the address of the base class object
within the derived object. But `ed` contains two `Worker` objects, hence there are two addresses
from which to choose. You could specify which object by using a type cast:

```
Worker * pw1 = (Waiter *) &ed;    // the Worker in Waiter
Worker * pw2 = (Singer *) &ed;    // the Worker in Singer
```

FIGURE 14.4

Inheriting two base objects.

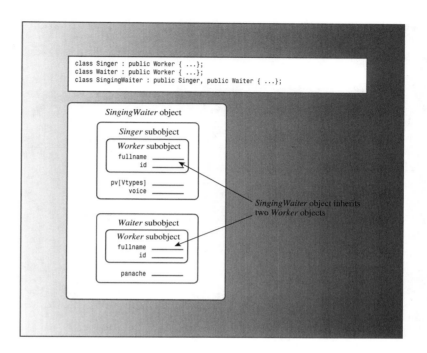

```
class Singer : public Worker { ...};
class Waiter : public Worker { ...};
class SingingWaiter : public Singer, public Waiter { ...};
```

SingingWaiter object

Singer subobject

Worker subobject

fullname _____

id _____

pv[Vtypes] _____

voice _____

Waiter subobject

Worker subobject

fullname _____

id _____

panache _____

SingingWaiter object inherits two *Worker* objects

This certainly complicates the technique of using an array of base class pointers to refer to a variety of objects (polymorphism).

Having two copies of a `Worker` object causes other problems, too. However, the real issue is why should you have two copies of a `Worker` object at all? A singing waiter, like any other worker, should have just one name and one ID. When C++ added multiple inheritance to its bag of tricks, it added a new technique, the *virtual base class*, to make this possible.

Virtual Base Classes

Virtual base classes allow an object derived from multiple bases that themselves share a common base to inherit just one object of that shared base class. For this example, you would make `Worker` a virtual base class to `Singer` and `Waiter` by using the keyword `virtual` in the class declarations (`virtual` and `public` can appear in either order):

```
class Singer : virtual public Worker {...};
class Waiter : public virtual Worker {...};
```

Then you would define `SingingWaiter` as before:

```
class SingingWaiter: public Singer, public  Waiter {...};
```

Now a `SingingWaiter` object will contain a single copy of a `Worker` object. In essence, the inherited `Singer` and `Waiter` objects share a common `Worker` object instead of each bringing in its own copy (see Figure 14.5). Because `SingingWaiter` now contains but one `Worker` subobject, you can use polymorphism again.

FIGURE 14.5

Inheritance with a virtual base class.

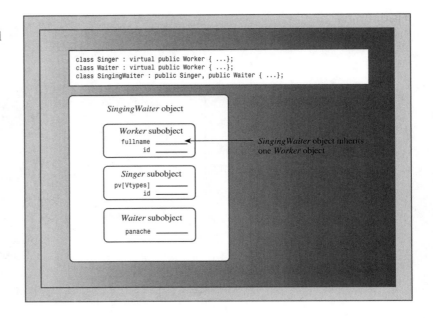

```
class Singer : virtual public Worker { ...};
class Waiter : virtual public Worker { ...};
class SingingWaiter : public Singer, public Waiter { ...};
```

SingingWaiter object

Worker subobject
fullname _____
id _____

Singer subobject
pv[Vtypes] _____
id _____

Waiter subobject
panache _____

SingingWaiter object inherits one *Worker* object

Let's look at some questions you may have:

- Why the term virtual?
- Why not dispense with declaring base classes virtual and make virtual behavior the norm for multiple inheritance?
- Are there any catches?

First, why the term virtual? After all, there doesn't seem to be an obvious connection between the concepts of virtual functions and virtual base classes. It turns out that there is strong pressure from the C++ community to resist the introduction of new keywords. It would be awkward, for example, if a new keyword corresponded to the name of some important function or variable in a major program. So C++ merely recycled the keyword **virtual** for the new facility—a bit of keyword overloading.

Next, why not dispense with declaring base classes virtual and make virtual behavior the norm for multiple inheritance? First, there are cases for which one might want multiple copies of a base. Second, making a base class virtual requires that a program do some additional accounting, and you shouldn't have to pay for that facility if you don't need it. Third, there are the disadvantages presented in the next paragraph.

Finally, are there catches? Yes. Making virtual base classes work requires adjustments to C++ rules, and you have to code some things differently. Also, using virtual base classes may involve changing existing code. For example, adding the **SingingWaiter** class to the **Worker** hierarchy required that you go back and add the **virtual** keyword to the **Singer** and **Waiter** classes.

New Constructor Rules

Having virtual base classes requires a new approach to class constructors. With nonvirtual base classes, the *only* constructors that can appear in an initialization list are constructors for the immediate base classes. But these constructors can, in turn, pass information on to their bases. For example, you can have the following organization of constructors:

```
class A
{
    int a;
public:
    A(int n = 0) { a = n; }
    ...
};
class B: public A
{
    int b;
public:
    B(int m = 0, int n = 0) : A(n) { b = m; }
    ...
};
class C : public B
{
    int c;
public:
    C(int q = 0, int m = 0, int n = 0) : B(m, n) { c = q; }
    ...
};
```

A C constructor can invoke only constructors from the B class, and a B constructor can invoke only constructors from the A class. Here the C constructor uses the q value and passes the values of m and n back to the B constructor. The B constructor uses the value of m and passes the value of n back to the A constructor.

This automatic passing of information doesn't work if Worker is a virtual base class. For example, consider the following possible constructor for the multiple inheritance example:

```
SingingWaiter(const Worker & wk, int p = 0, int v = Singer::other)
                : Waiter(wk,p), Singer(wk,v) {}  // flawed
```

The problem is that automatic passing of information would pass wk to the Worker object via two separate paths (Waiter and Singer). To avoid this potential conflict, C++ disables the automatic passing of information through an intermediate class to a base class *if* the base class is virtual. Thus, the previous constructor will initialize the **panache** and **voice** members, but the information in the wk argument *won't* get to the Waiter subobject. However, the compiler must construct a base object component before constructing derived objects; in the previous case, it will use the default Worker constructor.

If you want to use something other than the default constructor for a virtual base class, you need to invoke the appropriate base constructor explicitly. Thus, the constructor should look like this:

```
SingingWaiter(const Worker & wk, int p = 0, int v = Singer::other)
             : Worker(wk), Waiter(wk,p), Singer(wk,v) {}
```

Here the code explicitly invokes the `Worker(const Worker &)` constructor. Note that this usage is legal and often necessary for virtual base classes and illegal for nonvirtual base classes.

Caution

If a class has an indirect virtual base class, a constructor for that class should explicitly invoke a constructor for the virtual base class unless all that is needed is the default constructor for the virtual base class.

Which Method?

In addition to introducing changes in class constructor rules, MI often requires other coding adjustments. Consider the problem of extending the `Show()` method to the `SingingWaiter` class. Because a `SingingWaiter` object has no new data members, you might think the class could just use the inherited methods. This brings up the first problem. Suppose you do omit a new version of `Show()` and try to use a `SingingWaiter` object to invoke an inherited `Show()` method:

```
SingingWaiter newhire("Elise Hawks", 2005, 6, soprano);
newhire.Show();  // ambiguous
```

With single inheritance, failing to redefine `Show()` results in using the most recent ancestral definition. In this case, each direct ancestor has a `Show()` function, making this call ambiguous.

Caution

Multiple inheritance can result in ambiguous function calls. For example, a `BadDude` class could inherit two quite different `Draw()` methods from a `Gunslinger` class and a `PokerPlayer` class.

You can use the scope resolution operator to clarify what you mean:

```
SingingWaiter newhire("Elise Hawks", 2005, 6, soprano);
newhire.Singer::Show();  // use Singer version
```

However, a better approach is to redefine `Show()` for `SingingWaiter` and to have it specify which `Show()` to use. For example, if you want a `SingingWaiter` object to use the `Singer` version, do this:

```
void SingingWaiter::Show()
{
    Singer::Show();
}
```

This method of having the derived method call the base method works well enough for single inheritance. For example, suppose the `HeadWaiter` class derives from the `Waiter` class. You could use a sequence of definitions like this, with each derived class adding to the information displayed by its base class:

```cpp
void Worker::Show() const
{
    cout << "Name: " << fullname << "\n";
    cout << "Employee ID: " << id << "\n";
}

void Waiter::Show() const
{
    Worker::Show();
    cout << "Panache rating: " << panache << "\n";
}
void HeadWaiter::Show() const
{
    Waiter::Show();
    cout << "Presence rating: " << presence << "\n";
}
```

This incremental approach fails for the `SingingWaiter` case, however. The method

```cpp
void SingingWaiter::Show()
{
    Singer::Show();
}
```

fails because it ignores the `Waiter` component. You can remedy that by called the `Waiter` version also:

```cpp
void SingingWaiter::Show()
{
    Singer::Show();
    Waiter::Show();
}
```

This displays a person's name and ID twice, for `Singer::Show()` and with `Waiter::Show()` both call `Worker::Show()`.

How can this be fixed? One way is to use a modular approach instead of an incremental approach. That is, provide a method that displays only `Worker` components, another method that displays only `Waiter` components (instead of `Waiter` plus `Worker` components), and another that displays only `Singer` components. Then the `SingingWaiter::Show()` method can put those components together. For example, you can do this:

```cpp
void Worker::Data() const
{
    cout << "Name: " << fullname << "\n";
    cout << "Employee ID: " << id << "\n";
}

void Waiter::Data() const
{
    cout << "Panache rating: " << panache << "\n";
```

```
}

void Singer::Data() const
{
    cout << "Vocal range: " << pv[voice] << "\n";
}

void SingingWaiter::Data() const
{
    Singer::Data();
    Waiter::Data();
}

void SingingWaiter::Show() const
{
    cout << "Category: singing waiter\n";
    Worker::Data();
    Data();
}
```

Similarly, the other `Show()` methods would be built from the appropriate `Data()` components.

With this approach, objects would still use the `Show()` method publicly. The `Data()` methods, on the other hand, should be internal to the classes, helper methods used to facilitate the public interface. However, making the `Data()` methods private would prevent, say, `Waiter` code from using `Worker::Data()`. Here is just the kind of situation for which the protected access class is useful. If the `Data()` methods are protected, they can by used internally by all the classes in the hierarchy while being kept hidden from the outside world.

Another approach would have been to make all the data components protected instead of private, but using protected methods instead of protected data puts tighter control on the allowable access to the data.

The `Set()` methods, which solicit data for setting object values, present a similar problem. `SingingWaiter::Set()`, for example, should ask for `Worker` information once, not twice. The same solution works. You can provide protected `Get()` methods that solicit information for just a single class, then put together `Set()` methods that use the `Get()` methods as building blocks.

In short, introducing multiple inheritance with a shared ancestor requires introducing virtual base classes, altering the rules for constructor initialization lists, and possibly recoding the classes if they had not been written with MI in mind. Listing 14.11 shows the modified class declarations instituting these changes, and Listing 14.12 shows the implementation.

LISTING 14.11 workermi.h

```
// workermi.h  -- working classes with MI
#ifndef WORKERMI_H_
#define WORKERMI_H_

#include "string1.h"
```

LISTING 14.11 Continued

```
class Worker    // an abstract base class
{
private:
    String fullname;
    long id;
protected:
    virtual void Data() const;
    virtual void Get();
public:
    Worker() : fullname("no one"), id(0L) {}
    Worker(const String & s, long n)
            : fullname(s), id(n) {}
    virtual ~Worker() = 0; // pure virtual function
    virtual void Set() = 0;
    virtual void Show() const = 0;
};

class Waiter : virtual public Worker
{
private:
    int panache;
protected:
    void Data() const;
    void Get();
public:
    Waiter() : Worker(), panache(0) {}
    Waiter(const String & s, long n, int p = 0)
            : Worker(s, n), panache(p) {}
    Waiter(const Worker & wk, int p = 0)
            : Worker(wk), panache(p) {}
    void Set();
    void Show() const;
};

class Singer : virtual public Worker
{
protected:
enum {other, alto, contralto, soprano,
                    bass, baritone, tenor};
    enum {Vtypes = 7};
    void Data() const;
    void Get();
private:
    static char *pv[Vtypes];    // string equivs of voice types
    int voice;
public:
    Singer() : Worker(), voice(other) {}
    Singer(const String & s, long n, int v = other)
            : Worker(s, n), voice(v) {}
    Singer(const Worker & wk, int v = other)
            : Worker(wk), voice(v) {}
    void Set();
```

LISTING 14.11 Continued

```cpp
    void Show() const;
};


// multiple inheritance
class SingingWaiter : public Singer, public Waiter
{
protected:
    void Data() const;
    void Get();
public:
    SingingWaiter()  {}
    SingingWaiter(const String & s, long n, int p = 0,
                            int v = Singer::other)
            : Worker(s,n), Waiter(s, n, p), Singer(s, n, v) {}
    SingingWaiter(const Worker & wk, int p = 0, int v = Singer::other)
            : Worker(wk), Waiter(wk,p), Singer(wk,v) {}
    SingingWaiter(const Waiter & wt, int v = other)
            : Worker(wt),Waiter(wt), Singer(wt,v) {}
    SingingWaiter(const Singer & wt, int p = 0)
            : Worker(wt),Waiter(wt,p), Singer(wt) {}
    void Set();
    void Show() const;
};

#endif
```

LISTING 14.12 workermi.cpp

```cpp
// workermi.cpp -- working class methods with MI
#include "workermi.h"
#include <iostream>
using namespace std;
// Worker methods
Worker::~Worker() { }

// protected methods
void Worker::Data() const
{
    cout << "Name: " << fullname << "\n";
    cout << "Employee ID: " << id << "\n";
}

void Worker::Get()
{
    cin >> fullname;
    cout << "Enter worker's ID: ";
    cin >> id;
    while (cin.get() != '\n')
        continue;
}
```

LISTING 14.12 Continued

```cpp
// Waiter methods
void Waiter::Set()
{
    cout << "Enter waiter's name: ";
    Worker::Get();
    Get();
}

void Waiter::Show() const
{
    cout << "Category: waiter\n";
    Worker::Data();
    Data();
}

// protected methods
void Waiter::Data() const
{
    cout << "Panache rating: " << panache << "\n";
}

void Waiter::Get()
{
    cout << "Enter waiter's panache rating: ";
    cin >> panache;
    while (cin.get() != '\n')
        continue;
}

// Singer methods

char * Singer::pv[Singer::Vtypes] = {"other", "alto", "contralto",
            "soprano", "bass", "baritone", "tenor"};

void Singer::Set()
{
    cout << "Enter singer's name: ";
    Worker::Get();
    Get();
}

void Singer::Show() const
{
    cout << "Category: singer\n";
    Worker::Data();
    Data();
}

// protected methods
void Singer::Data() const
{
```

LISTING 14.12 Continued

```
        cout << "Vocal range: " << pv[voice] << "\n";
}

void Singer::Get()
{
    cout << "Enter number for singer's vocal range:\n";
    int i;
    for (i = 0; i < Vtypes; i++)
    {
        cout << i << ": " << pv[i] << "    ";
        if ( i % 4 == 3)
            cout << '\n';
    }
    if (i % 4 != 0)
        cout << '\n';
    cin >> voice;
    while (cin.get() != '\n')
        continue;
}

// SingingWaiter methods
void SingingWaiter::Data() const
{
    Singer::Data();
    Waiter::Data();
}

void SingingWaiter::Get()
{
    Waiter::Get();
    Singer::Get();
}

void SingingWaiter::Set()
{
    cout << "Enter singing waiter's name: ";
    Worker::Get();
    Get();
}

void SingingWaiter::Show() const
{
    cout << "Category: singing waiter\n";
    Worker::Data();
    Data();
}
```

Of course, curiosity demands we test these classes, and Listing 14.13 provides code to do so. Note that the program makes use of the polymorphic property by assigning the addresses of various kinds of classes to base class pointers. Compile it along with `workermi.cpp` and `string1.cpp`.

LISTING 14.13 workmi.cpp

```cpp
// workmi.cpp -- multiple inheritance
// compile with workermi.cpp, string1.cpp
#include <iostream>
using namespace std;
#include <cstring>
#include "workermi.h"
const int SIZE = 5;
int main()
{
    Worker * lolas[SIZE];

    int ct;
    for (ct = 0; ct < SIZE; ct++)
    {
        char choice;
        cout << "Enter the employee category:\n"
            << "w: waiter  s: singer  "
            << "t: singing waiter  q: quit\n";
        cin >> choice;
        while (strchr("ewstq", choice) == NULL)
        {
            cout << "Please enter a w, s, t, or q: ";
            cin >> choice;
        }
        if (choice == 'q')
            break;
        switch(choice)
        {
            case 'w':  lolas[ct] = new Waiter;
                       break;
            case 's':  lolas[ct] = new Singer;
                       break;
            case 't':  lolas[ct] = new SingingWaiter;
                       break;
        }
        cin.get();
        lolas[ct]->Set();
    }

    cout << "\nHere is your staff:\n";
    int i;
    for (i = 0; i < ct; i++)
    {
        cout << '\n';
        lolas[i]->Show();
    }
    for (i = 0; i < ct; i++)
        delete lolas[i];
    cout << "Bye.\n";
    return 0;
}
```

Here is a sample run:

```
Enter the employee category:
w: waiter  s: singer  t: singing waiter  q: quit
w
Enter waiter's name: Wally Slipshod
Enter worker's ID: 1040
Enter waiter's panache rating: 4
Enter the employee category:
w: waiter  s: singer  t: singing waiter  q: quit
s
Enter singer's name: Sinclair Parma
Enter worker's ID: 1044
Enter number for singer's vocal range:
0: other   1: alto   2: contralto   3: soprano
4: bass   5: baritone   6: tenor
5
Enter the employee category:
w: waiter  s: singer  t: singing waiter  q: quit
t
Enter singing waiter's name: Natasha Gargalova
Enter worker's ID: 1021
Enter waiter's panache rating: 6
Enter number for singer's vocal range:
0: other   1: alto   2: contralto   3: soprano
4: bass   5: baritone   6: tenor
3
Enter the employee category:
w: waiter  s: singer  t: singing waiter  q: quit
q

Here is your staff:

Category: waiter
Name: Wally Slipshod
Employee ID: 1040
Panache rating: 4

Category: singer
Name: Sinclair Parma
Employee ID: 1044
Vocal range: baritone

Category: singing waiter
Name: Natasha Gargalova
Employee ID: 1021
Vocal range: soprano
Panache rating: 6
Bye.
```

Let's look at a few more matters concerning multiple inheritance.

Mixed Virtual and Nonvirtual Bases

Consider again the case of a derived class that inherits a base class by more than one route. If the base class is virtual, the derived class contains one subobject of the base class. If the base class is not virtual, the derived class contains multiple subobjects. What if there is a mixture? Suppose, for example, that class B is a virtual base class to classes C and D and a nonvirtual base class to classes X and Y. Furthermore, suppose class M is derived from C, D, X, and Y. In this case, class M contains one class B subobject for all the virtually derived ancestors (that is, classes C and D) and a separate class B subobject for each nonvirtual ancestor (that is, classes X and Y). So, all told, it would contain three class B subobjects. When a class inherits a particular base class through several virtual paths and several nonvirtual paths, the class has one base-class subobject to represent all the virtual paths and a separate base-class subobject to represent each nonvirtual path.

Virtual Base Classes and Dominance

Using virtual base classes alters how C++ resolves ambiguities. With nonvirtual base classes the rules are simple. If a class inherits two or more members (data or methods) of the same name from different classes, using that name without qualifying it with a class name is ambiguous. If virtual base classes are involved, however, such a use may or may not be ambiguous. In this case, if one name *dominates* all others, it can be used unambiguously without a qualifier.

So how does one member name dominate another? A name in a derived class dominates the same name in any ancestor class, direct or indirect. For example, consider the following definitions:

```
class B
{
public:
     short q();
     ...
};

class C : virtual public B
{
public:
     long q();
     int omb()
     ...
};

class D : public C
{
     ...
};

class E : virtual public B
{
private:
     int omb();
     ...
```

```
};

class F:  public D, public E
{
    ...
};
```

Here the definition of q() in class C dominates the definition in class B because C is derived from B. Thus, methods in F can use q() to denote C::q(). On the other hand, neither definition of omb() dominates the other because neither C nor E is a base class to the other. Therefore, an attempt by F to use an unqualified omb() would be ambiguous.

The virtual ambiguity rules pay no attention to access rules. That is, even though E::omb() is private and hence not directly accessible to class F, using omb() is ambiguous. Similarly, even if C::q() were private, it would dominate D::q(). In that case, you could call B::q() in class F, but an unqualified q() for that would refer to the inaccessible C::q().

Multiple Inheritance Synopsis

First, let's review multiple inheritance without virtual base classes. This form of MI imposes no new rules. However, if a class inherits two members of the same name but from different classes, you need to use class qualifiers in the derived class to distinguish between the two members. That is, methods in the BadDude class, derived from Gunslinger and PokerPlayer, would use Gunslinger::draw() and PokerPlayer::draw() to distinguish between draw() methods inherited from the two classes. Otherwise the compiler should complain about ambiguous usage.

If one class inherits from a nonvirtual base class by more than one route, then the class inherits one base class object for each nonvirtual instance of the base class. In some cases this may be what you want, but more often multiple instances of a base class are a problem.

Next, let's look at MI with virtual base classes. A class becomes a virtual base class when a derived class uses the keyword virtual when indicating derivation:

```
class marketing : public virtual reality { ... };
```

The main change, and the reason for virtual base classes, is that a class that inherits from one or more instances of a virtual base class inherits just one base class object. Implementing this feature entails other requirements:

- A derived class with an indirect virtual base class should have its constructors invoke the indirect base class constructors directly, something which is illegal for indirect nonvirtual base classes.

- Name ambiguity is resolved by the dominance rule.

As you can see, multiple inheritance can introduce programming complexities. However, most of these complexities arise when a derived class inherits from the same base class by more than one route. If you avoid that situation, about the only thing you need to watch for is qualifying inherited names when necessary.

Class Templates

Inheritance (public, private, or protected) and containment aren't always the answer to a desire to reuse code. Consider, for example, the `Stack` class (Chapter 10), the `Queue` class (Chapter 12), and the `ArrayDb` class (this chapter). These are all examples of *container classes*, which are classes designed to hold other objects or data types. The `Stack` class, for example, stored `unsigned long` values. You could just as easily define a stack class for storing `double` values or `String` objects. The code would be identical other than for the type of object stored. However, rather than writing new class declarations, it would be nice if you could define a stack in a generic (that is, type-independent) fashion and then provide a specific type as a parameter to the class. Then you could use the same generic code to produce stacks of different kinds of values. In Chapter 10, the `Stack` example used `typedef` as a first pass at dealing with this desire. However, that approach has a couple of drawbacks. First, you have to edit the header file each time you change the type. Second, you can use the technique to generate just one kind of stack per program. That is, you can't have a `typedef` represent two different types simultaneously, so you can't use the method to define a stack of `int`s and a stack of `String`s in the same program.

C++'s class templates provide a better way to generate generic class declarations. (C++ originally did not support templates, and, since their introduction, templates have continued to evolve, so it is possible that your compiler may not support all the features presented here.) Templates provide *parameterized* types, that is, the capability of passing a type name as an argument to a recipe for building a class or a function. By feeding the type name `int` to a `Queue` template, for example, you can get the compiler to construct a `Queue` class for queuing `int`s.

C++'s Standard Template Library (STL), which Chapter 16 discusses in part, provides powerful and flexible template implementations of several container classes. This chapter will explore designs of a more elementary nature.

Defining a Class Template

Let's use the `Stack` class from Chapter 10 as the basis from which to build a template. Here's the original class declaration:

```
typedef unsigned long Item;

class Stack
{
private:
    enum {MAX = 10};    // constant specific to class
    Item items[MAX];    // holds stack items
    int top;            // index for top stack item
public:
    Stack();
    bool isempty() const;
    bool isfull() const;
    // push() returns false if stack already is full, true otherwise
```

```
        bool push(const Item & item);   // add item to stack
        // pop() returns false if stack already is empty, true otherwise
        bool pop(Item & item);          // pop top into item
};
```

The template approach will replace the **Stack** definition with a template definition and the **Stack** member functions with template member functions. As with template functions, you preface a template class with code of the following form:

```
template <class Type>
```

The keyword **template** informs the compiler that you're about to define a template. The part in angle brackets is analogous to an argument list to a function. You can think of the keyword **class** as serving as a type name for a variable that accepts a type as a value, and of **Type** representing a name for this variable.

Using **class** here doesn't mean that **Type** must be a class; it just means that **Type** serves as a generic type specifier for which a real type will be substituted when the template is used. Newer implementations allow you to use the less confusing keyword **typename** instead of **class** in this context:

```
template <typename Type>  // newer choice
```

You can use your choice of generic typename in the **Type** position; the name rules are the same as those for any other identifier. Popular choices include **T** and **Type**; we'll use the latter. When a template is invoked, **Type** will be replaced with a specific type value, such as **int** or **String**. Within the template definition, use the generic typename to identify the type to be stored in the stack. For the **Stack** case, that would mean using **Type** wherever the old declaration formerly used the **typedef** identifier **Item**. For example,

```
Item items[MAX];  // holds stack items
```

becomes the following:

```
Type items[MAX];  // holds stack items
```

Similarly, you can replace the class methods of the original class with template member functions. Each function heading will be prefaced with the same template announcement:

```
template <class Type>
```

Again, replace the **typedef** identifier **Item** with the generic typename **Type**. One more change is that you need to change the class qualifier from **Stack::** to **Stack<Type>::**. For example,

```
bool Stack::push(const Item & item)
{
...
}
```

becomes the following:

```
template <class Type>                         // or template <typename Type>
bool Stack<Type>::push(const Type & item)
{
...
}
```

If you define a method within the class declaration (an inline definition), you can omit the template preface and the class qualifier.

Listing 14.14 shows the combined class and member function templates. It's important to realize that these templates are not class and member function definitions. Rather, they are instructions to the C++ compiler about how to generate class and member function definitions. A particular actualization of a template, such as a stack class for handling String objects, is called an *instantiation* or *specialization*. Unless you have a compiler that has implemented the new export keyword, placing the template member functions in a separate implementation file won't work. Because the templates aren't functions, they can't be compiled separately. Templates have to be used in conjunction with requests for particular instantiations of templates. The simplest way to make this work is to place all the template information in a header file and to include the header file in the file that will use the templates.

LISTING 14.14   stacktp.h

```
// stacktp.h -- a stack template
#ifndef STACKTP_H_
#define STACKTP_H_
template <class Type>
class Stack
{
private:
    enum {MAX = 10};      // constant specific to class
    Type items[MAX];      // holds stack items
    int top;              // index for top stack item
public:
    Stack();
    bool isempty();
    bool isfull();
    bool push(const Type & item); // add item to stack
    bool pop(Type & item);        // pop top into item
};

template <class Type>
Stack<Type>::Stack()
{
    top = 0;
}

template <class Type>
bool Stack<Type>::isempty()
{
    return top == 0;
}

template <class Type>
bool Stack<Type>::isfull()
{
    return top == MAX;
}
```

LISTING 14.14   Continued

```
template <class Type>
bool Stack<Type>::push(const Type & item)
{
    if (top < MAX)
    {
        items[top++] = item;
        return true;
    }
    else
        return false;
}

template <class Type>
bool Stack<Type>::pop(Type & item)
{
    if (top > 0)
    {
        item = items[--top];
        return true;
    }
    else
        return false;
}

#endif
```

If your compiler does implement the new **export** keyword, you can place the template method definitions in a separate file providing you preface each definition with **export**:

```
export template <class Type>
Stack<Type>::Stack()
{
    top = 0;
}
```

Then you could follow the same convention used for ordinary classes:

1. Place the template class declaration in a header file and use the **#include** directive to make the declaration available to a program.

2. Place the template class method definitions in a source code file and use a project file or equivalent to make the definitions available to a program.

Using a Template Class

Merely including a template in a program doesn't generate a template class. You have to ask for an instantiation. To do this, declare an object of the template class type, replacing the generic typename with the particular type you want. For example, here's how you would create two stacks, one for stacking **ints** and one for stacking **String** objects:

```
Stack<int> kernels;      // create a stack of ints
Stack<String> colonels;  // create a stack of String objects
```

Seeing these two declarations, the compiler will follow the `Stack<Type>` template to generate two separate class declarations and two separate sets of class methods. The `Stack<int>` class declaration will replace `Type` throughout with `int`, while the `Stack<String>` class declaration will replace `Type` throughout with `String`. Of course, the algorithms you use have to be consistent with the types. The stack class, for example, assumes that you can assign one item to another. This assumption is true for basic types, structures, and classes (unless you make the assignment operator private), but not for arrays.

Generic type identifiers such as `Type` in the example are called *type parameters*, meaning that they act something like a variable, but instead of assigning a numeric value to them, you assign a type to them. So in the `kernel` declaration, the type parameter `Type` has the value `int`.

Notice that you have to provide the desired type explicitly. This is different from ordinary function templates, for which the compiler can use the argument types to a function to figure out what kind of function to generate:

```
Template <class T>
void simple(T t) { cout << t << '\n';}
...
simple(2);          // generate void simple(int)
simple("two")       // generate void simple(char *)
```

Listing 14.15 modifies the original stack-testing program (Listing 11.13) to use string purchase order IDs instead of `unsigned long` values. Because it uses our `String` class, compile it with `string1.cpp`.

LISTING 14.15   `stacktem.cpp`

```cpp
// stacktem.cpp -- test template stack class
// compiler with string1.cpp
#include <iostream>
using namespace std;
#include <cctype>
#include "stacktp.h"
#include "string1.h"
int main()
{
    Stack<String> st;   // create an empty stack
    char c;
    String po;
    cout << "Please enter A to add a purchase order,\n"
         << "P to process a PO, or Q to quit.\n";
    while (cin >> c && toupper (c) != 'Q')
    {
        while (cin.get() != '\n')
            continue;
        if (!isalpha(c))
        {
            cout << '\a';
            continue;
        }
```

LISTING 14.15   Continued

```
        switch(c)
        {
            case 'A':
            case 'a': cout << "Enter a PO number to add: ";
                      cin >> po;
                      if (st.isfull())
                          cout << "stack already full\n";
                      else
                          st.push(po);
                      break;
            case 'P':
            case 'p': if (st.isempty())
                          cout << "stack already empty\n";
                      else {
                          st.pop(po);
                          cout << "PO #" << po << " popped\n";
                          break;
                      }
        }
        cout << "Please enter A to add a purchase order,\n"
             << "P to process a PO, or Q to quit.\n";
    }
    cout << "Bye\n";
    return 0;
}
```

Compatibility Note

Use the older `ctype.h` header file if your implementation doesn't provide `cctype`.

Here's a sample run:

```
Please enter A to add a purchase order,
P to process a PO, or Q to quit.
A
Enter a PO number to add: red911porsche
Please enter A to add a purchase order,
P to process a PO, or Q to quit.
A
Enter a PO number to add: greenS8audi
Please enter A to add a purchase order,
P to process a PO, or Q to quit.
A
Enter a PO number to add: silver747boing
Please enter A to add a purchase order,
P to process a PO, or Q to quit.
P
PO #silver747boing popped
Please enter A to add a purchase order,
P to process a PO, or Q to quit.
```

```
P
PO #greenS8audi popped
Please enter A to add a purchase order,
P to process a PO, or Q to quit.
P
PO #red911porsche popped
Please enter A to add a purchase order,
P to process a PO, or Q to quit.
P
stack already empty
Please enter A to add a purchase order,
P to process a PO, or Q to quit.
Q
Bye
```

A Closer Look at the Template Class

You can use a built-in type or a class object as the type for the `Stack<Type>` class template. What about a pointer? For example, can you use a pointer to a `char` instead of a `String` object in Listing 14.15? After all, such pointers are the built-in way for handling C++ strings. The answer is that you can create a stack of pointers, but it won't work very well without major modifications in the program. The compiler can create the class, but it's your task to see that it's used sensibly. Let's see why such a stack of pointers doesn't work very well with Listing 14.11, then let's look at an example where a stack of pointers is useful.

Using a Stack of Pointers Incorrectly

We'll quickly look at three simple, but flawed, attempts to adapt Listing 14.15 to use a stack of pointers. These attempts illustrate the lesson that you should keep the design of a template in mind and not just use it blindly. All three begin with this perfectly valid invocation of the `Stack<Type>` template:

```
Stack<char *> st; // create a stack for pointers-to-char
```

Version 1 then replaces

```
String po;
```

with

```
char * po;
```

The idea is to use a `char` pointer instead of a `String` object to receive the keyboard input. This approach fails immediately because merely creating a pointer doesn't create space to hold the input strings. (The program would compile, but quite possibly would crash after `cin` tried to store input in some inappropriate location.)

Version 2 replaces

```
String po;
```

with

```
char po[40];
```

This allocates space for an input string. Furthermore, **po** is of type **char** *, so it can be placed on the stack. But an array is fundamentally at odds with the assumptions made for the **pop()** method:

```
template <class Type>
bool Stack<Type>::pop(Type & item)
{
    if (top > 0)
    {
        item = items[--top];
        return true;
    }
    else
        return false;
}
```

First, the reference variable **item** has to refer to an Lvalue of some sort, not to an array name. Second, the code assumes that you can assign to **item**. Even if **item** could refer to an array, you can't assign to an array name. So this approach fails, too.

Version 3 replaces

```
String po;
```

with

```
char * po = new char[40];
```

This allocates space for an input string. Furthermore, **po** is a variable and hence compatible with the code for **pop()**. Here, however, we come up against the most fundamental problem. There is only one **po** variable, and it always points to the same memory location. True, the contents of the memory change each time a new string is read, but every push operation puts exactly the same address onto the stack. So when you pop the stack, you always get the same address back, and it always refers to the last string read into memory. In particular, the stack is not storing each new string as it comes in, and it serves no useful purpose.

Using a Stack of Pointers Correctly

One way to use a stack of pointers is to have the calling program provide an array of pointers, with each pointer pointing to a different string. Putting these pointers on a stack then makes sense, for each pointer will refer to a different string. Note that it is the responsibility of the calling program, not the stack, to create the separate pointers. The stack's job is to manage the pointers, not create them.

For example, suppose we have to simulate the following situation. Someone has delivered a cart of folders to Plodson. If Plodson's in-basket is empty, he removes the top folder from the cart and places it in his in-basket. If his in-basket is full, Plodson removes the top file from the basket, processes it, and places it in his out-basket. If the in-basket is neither empty nor full, Plodson may process the top file in the in-basket, or he may take the next file from the cart and put it into his in-basket. In what he secretly regards as a bit of madcap self-expression, he flips a coin to decide which of these actions to take. We'd like to investigate the effects of his method on the original file order.

We can model this with an array of pointers to strings representing the files on the cart. Each string will contain the name of the person described by the file. We can use a stack to represent the in-basket, and we can use a second array of pointers to represent the out-basket. Adding a file to the in-basket is represented by pushing a pointer from the input array onto the stack, and processing a file is represented by popping an item from the stack, and adding it to the out-basket.

Given the importance of examining all aspects of this problem, it would be useful to be able to try different stack sizes. Listing 14.16 redefines the `Stack<Type>` class slightly so that the `Stack` constructor accepts an optional size argument. This involves using a dynamic array internally, so the class now needs a destructor, a copy constructor, and an assignment operator. Also, the definition shortens the code by making several of the methods inline.

LISTING 14.16   stcktp1.h

```
// stcktp1.h -- modified Stack template
#ifndef STCKTP1_H_
#define STCKTP1_H_

template <class Type>
class Stack
{
private:
    enum {SIZE = 10};    // default size
    int stacksize;
    Type * items;        // holds stack items
    int top;             // index for top stack item
public:
    explicit Stack(int ss = SIZE);
    Stack(const Stack & st);
    ~Stack() { delete [] items; }
    bool isempty() { return top == 0; }
    bool isfull() { return top == stacksize; }
    bool push(const Type & item);    // add item to stack
    bool pop(Type & item);           // pop top into item
    Stack & operator=(const Stack & st);
};

template <class Type>
Stack<Type>::Stack(int ss) : stacksize(ss), top(0)
{
    items = new Type [stacksize];
}

template <class Type>
Stack<Type>::Stack(const Stack & st)
{
    stacksize = st.stacksize;
    top = st.top;
    items = new Type [stacksize];
    for (int i = 0; i < top; i++)
```

LISTING 14.16 Continued

```cpp
        items[i] = st.items[i];
}

template <class Type>
bool Stack<Type>::push(const Type & item)
{
    if (top < stacksize)
    {
        items[top++] = item;
        return true;
    }
    else
        return false;
}

template <class Type>
bool Stack<Type>::pop(Type & item)
{
    if (top > 0)
    {
        item = items[--top];
        return true;
    }
    else
        return false;
}

template <class Type>
Stack<Type> & Stack<Type>::operator=(const Stack<Type> & st)
{
    if (this == &st)
        return *this;
    delete [] items;
    stacksize = st.stacksize;
    top = st.top;
    items = new Type [stacksize];
    for (int i = 0; i < top; i++)
        items[i] = st.items[i];
    return *this;
}

#endif
```

Compatibility Note

Some implementations might not recognize `explicit`.

Notice that the prototype declares the return type for the assignment operator function to be a reference to `Stack` while the actual template function definition identifies the type as

Stack<Type>. The former is an abbreviation for the latter, but it can be used only within the class scope. That is, you can use Stack inside the template declaration and inside the template function definitions, but outside the class, as when identifying return types and when using the scope resolution operator, you need to use the full Stack<Type> form.

The program in Listing 14.17 uses the new stack template to implement the Plodson simulation. It uses rand(), srand(), and time() in the same way previous simulations have to generate random numbers. Here, randomly generating a 0 or a 1 simulates the coin toss.

LISTING 14.17   stkoptr1.cpp

```
// stkoptr1.cpp -- test stack of pointers
#include <iostream>
using namespace std;
#include <cstdlib>       // for rand(), srand()
#include <ctime>         // for time()
#include "stcktp1.h"
const int Stacksize = 4;
const int Num = 10;
int main()
{
    srand(time(0)); // randomize rand()
    cout << "Please enter stack size: ";
    int stacksize;
    cin >> stacksize;
    Stack<const char *> st(stacksize); // create an empty stack with 4 slots


    const char * in[Num] = {
            " 1: Hank Gilgamesh", " 2: Kiki Ishtar",
            " 3: Betty Rocker", " 4: Ian Flagranti",
            " 5: Wolfgang Kibble", " 6: Portia Koop",
            " 7: Joy Almondo", " 8: Xaverie Paprika",
            " 9: Juan Moore", "10: Misha Mache"
            };
    const char * out[Num];

    int processed = 0;
    int nextin = 0;
    while (processed < Num)
    {
        if (st.isempty())
            st.push(in[nextin++]);
        else if (st.isfull())
            st.pop(out[processed++]);
        else if (rand() % 2  && nextin < Num)    // 50-50 chance
            st.push(in[nextin++]);
        else
            st.pop(out[processed++]);
    }
```

LISTING 14.17   *Continued*

```
    for (int i = 0; i < Num; i++)
        cout << out[i] << "\n";

    cout << "Bye\n";
    return 0;
}
```

Compatibility Note

Some implementations require `stdlib.h` instead of `cstdlib` and `time.h` instead of `ctime`.

Two sample runs follow. Note that the final file ordering can differ quite a bit from one trial to the next, even when the stack size is kept unaltered.

```
Please enter stack size: 5
 2: Kiki Ishtar
 1: Hank Gilgamesh
 3: Betty Rocker
 5: Wolfgang Kibble
 4: Ian Flagranti
 7: Joy Almondo
 9: Juan Moore
 8: Xaverie Paprika
 6: Portia Koop
10: Misha Mache
Bye

Please enter stack size: 5
 3: Betty Rocker
 5: Wolfgang Kibble
 6: Portia Koop
 4: Ian Flagranti
 8: Xaverie Paprika
 9: Juan Moore
10: Misha Mache
 7: Joy Almondo
 2: Kiki Ishtar
 1: Hank Gilgamesh
Bye
```

Program Notes

The strings themselves never move. Pushing a string onto the stack really creates a new pointer to an existing string. That is, it creates a pointer whose value is the address of an existing string. And popping a string off the stack copies that address value into the **out** array.

The program uses `const char *` as a type because the array of pointers is initialized to a set of string constants.

What effect does the stack destructor have upon the strings? None. The class constructor uses new to create an array for holding pointers. The class destructor eliminates that array, not the strings to which the array elements pointed.

An Array Template Example and Non-Type Arguments

Templates frequently are used for container classes, for the idea of type parameters matches well with the need to apply a common storage plan to a variety of types. Indeed, the desire to provide reusable code for container classes was the main motivation for introducing templates, so let's look at another example, exploring a few more facets of template design and use. In particular, we'll look at non-type, or expression, arguments and at using an array to handle an inheritance family.

Let's begin with a simple array template that lets you specify an array size. One technique, which the last version of the Stack template used, is using a dynamic array within the class and a constructor argument to provide the number of elements. Another approach is using a template argument to provide the size for a regular array. Listing 14.18 shows how this can be done.

LISTING 14.18 arraytp.h

```
//arraytp.h  -- Array Template
#ifndef ARRAYTP_H_
#define ARRAYTP_H_

#include <iostream>
using namespace std;
#include <cstdlib>

template <class T, int n>
class ArrayTP
{
private:
    T ar[n];
public:
    ArrayTP() {};
    explicit ArrayTP(const T & v);
    virtual T & operator[](int i);
    virtual const T & operator[](int i) const;
};

template <class T, int n>
ArrayTP<T,n>::ArrayTP(const T & v)
{
    for (int i = 0; i < n; i++)
        ar[i] = v;
}

template <class T, int n>
T & ArrayTP<T,n>::operator[](int i)
```

LISTING 14.18 Continued

```
{
    if (i < 0 || i >= n)
    {
        cerr << "Error in array limits: " << i
            << " is out of range\n";
        exit(1);
    }
    return ar[i];
}

template <class T, int n>
const T & ArrayTP<T,n>::operator[](int i) const
{
    if (i < 0 || i >= n)
    {
        cerr << "Error in array limits: " << i
            << " is out of range\n";
        exit(1);
    }
    return ar[i];
}

#endif
```

Note the template heading:

```
template <class T, int n>
```

The keyword `class` (or, equivalently in this context, `typename`) identifies T as a type parameter, or type argument. The `int` identifies n as being an `int` type. This second kind of parameter, one which specifies a particular type instead of acting as a generic name for a type, is called a *non-type* or *expression argument*. Suppose you have the following declaration:

```
ArrayTP<double, 12> eggweights;
```

This causes the compiler to define a class called `ArrayTP<double,12>` and to create an `eggweights` object of that class. When defining the class, the compiler replaces T with `double` and n with `12`.

Expression arguments have some restrictions. An expression argument can be an integral type, an enumeration type, a reference, or a pointer. Thus, `double m` is ruled out, but `double & rm` and `double * pm` are allowed. Also, the template code can't alter the value of the argument or take its address. Thus, in the `ArrayTP` template, expressions such as `n++` or `&n` would not be allowed. Also, when you instantiate a template, the value used for the expression argument should be a constant expression.

This approach for sizing an array has one advantage over the constructor approach used in `Stack`. The constructor approach uses heap memory managed by `new` and `delete`, while the expression argument approach uses the memory stack maintained for automatic variables. This provides faster execution time, particularly if you have a lot of small arrays.

The main drawback to the expression argument approach is that each array size generates its own template. That is, the declarations

```
ArrayTP<double, 12> eggweights;
ArrayTP(double, 13> donuts;
```

generate two separate class declarations. But the declarations

```
Stack<int> eggs(12);
Stack<int> dunkers(13);
```

generate just one class declaration, and the size information is passed to the constructor for that class.

Another difference is that the constructor approach is more versatile because the array size is stored as a class member rather than being hard-coded into the definition. This makes it possible, for example, to define assignment from an array of one size to an array of another size or to build a class that allows resizable arrays.

Template Versatility

You can apply the same techniques to template classes as you do to regular classes. Template classes can serve as base classes, and they can be component classes. They can themselves be type arguments to other templates. For example, you can implement a stack template using an array template. Or you can have an array template used to construct an array whose elements are stacks based on a stack template. That is, you can have code along the following lines:

```
template <class T>
class Array
{
private:
    T entry;
    ...
};

template <class Type>
class GrowArray : public Array<Type> {...};  // inheritance

template <class Tp>
class Stack
{
    Array<Tp> ar;        // use an Array<> as a component
    ...
};
...
Array < Stack<int> > asi;  // an array of stacks of int
```

In the last statement, you must separate the two > symbols by at least one whitespace character in order to avoid confusion with the >> operator.

Using a Template Recursively

Another example of template versatility is that you can use templates recursively. For example, given the earlier definition of an array template, you can use it as follows:

```
ArrayTP< ArrayTP<int,5>, 10> twodee;
```

This makes `twodee` an array of 10 elements, each of which is an array of 5 `ints`. The equivalent ordinary array would have this declaration:

```
int twodee[10][5];
```

Note the syntax for templates presents the dimensions in the opposite order from that of the equivalent ordinary two-dimensional array. The program in Listing 14.19 tries this idea. It also uses the `ArrayTP` template to create one-dimensional arrays to hold the sum and average value of each of the ten sets of five numbers. The method call `cout.width(2)` causes the next item to be displayed to use a field width of 2 characters, unless a larger width is needed to show the whole number.

LISTING 14.19   twod.cpp

```cpp
// twod.cpp -- making a 2-d array
#include <iostream>
using namespace std;
#include "arraytp.h"
int main(void)
{
    ArrayTP<int, 10> sums;
    ArrayTP<double, 10> aves;
    ArrayTP< ArrayTP<int,5>, 10> twodee;

    int i, j;

    for (i = 0; i < 10; i++)
    {
        sums[i] = 0;
        for (j = 0; j < 5; j++)
        {
            twodee[i][j] = (i + 1) * (j + 1);
            sums[i] += twodee[i][j];
        }
        aves[i] = (double) sums[i] / 10;
    }
    for (i = 0; i < 10; i++)
    {
        for (j = 0; j < 5; j++)
        {
            cout.width(2);
            cout << twodee[i][j] << ' ';
        }
        cout << ": sum = ";
```

LISTING 14.19 Continued

```
            cout.width(3);
            cout  << sums[i] << ", average = " << aves[i] << endl;
        }

    cout << "Done.\n";

    return 0;
}
```

Here's the output:

```
 1  2  3  4  5 : sum =  15, average = 1.5
 2  4  6  8 10 : sum =  30, average = 3
 3  6  9 12 15 : sum =  45, average = 4.5
 4  8 12 16 20 : sum =  60, average = 6
 5 10 15 20 25 : sum =  75, average = 7.5
 6 12 18 24 30 : sum =  90, average = 9
 7 14 21 28 35 : sum = 105, average = 10.5
 8 16 24 32 40 : sum = 120, average = 12
 9 18 27 36 45 : sum = 135, average = 13.5
10 20 30 40 50 : sum = 150, average = 15
Done.
```

Using More Than One Type Parameter

You can have templates with more than one type parameter. For example, suppose you want a class that holds two kinds of values. You can create and use a `Pair` template class for holding two disparate values. (Incidentally, the Standard Template Library provides a similar template called `pair`.) The short program in Listing 14.20 shows an example.

LISTING 14.20 pairs.cpp

```
// pairs.cpp -- define and use a Pair template
#include <iostream>
using namespace std;

template <class T1, class T2>
class Pair
{
private:
    T1 a;
    T2 b;
public:
    T1 & first(const T1 & f);
    T2 & second(const T2 & s);
    T1 first() const { return a; }
    T2 second() const { return b; }
    Pair(const T1 & f, const T2 & s) : a(f), b(s) { }
    Pair (){}
};
```

LISTING 14.20   Continued

```cpp
template<class T1, class T2>
T1 & Pair<T1,T2>::first(const T1 & f)
{
    a = f;
    return a;
}
template<class T1, class T2>
T2 & Pair<T1,T2>::second(const T2 & s)
{
    b = s;
    return b;
}

int main()
{
    Pair<char *, int> ratings[4] =
    {
        Pair<char *, int>("The Purple Duke", 5),
        Pair<char *, int>("Jake's Frisco Cafe", 4),
        Pair<char *, int>("Mont Souffle", 5),
        Pair<char *, int>("Gertie's Eats", 3)
    };

    int joints = sizeof(ratings) / sizeof (Pair<char *, int>);
    cout << "Rating:\t Eatery\n";
    for (int i = 0; i < joints; i++)
        cout << ratings[i].second() << ":\t "
            << ratings[i].first() << "\n";

    ratings[3].second(6);
    cout << "Oops! Revised rating:\n";
    cout << ratings[3].second() << ":\t "
        << ratings[3].first() << "\n";

    return 0;;
}
```

One thing to note is that in `main()`, you have to use `Pair<char *,int>` to invoke the constructors and as an argument for `sizeof`. That's because `Pair<char *,int>` and not `Pair` is the class name. Also, `Pair<String,ArrayDb>` would be the name of an entirely different class.

Here's the program output:

```
Rating:  Eatery
5:       The Purple Duke
4:       Jake's Frisco Cafe
5:       Mont Souffle
3:       Gertie's Eats
Oops! Revised rating:
6:       Gertie's Eats
```

Default Type Template Parameters

Another new class template feature is that you can provide default values for type parameters:

```
template <class T1, class T2 = int> class Topo {...};
```

This causes the compiler to use `int` for the type `T2` if a value for `T2` is omitted:

```
Topo<double, double> m1; // T1 is double, T2 is double
Topo<double> m2;         // T1 is double, T2 is int
```

The Standard Template Library (Chapter 16) often uses this feature, with the default type being a class.

Although you can provide default values for class template type parameters, you can't do so for function template parameters. However, you can provide default values for non-type parameters for both class and function templates.

Template Specializations

Class templates are like function templates in that you can have implicit instantiations, explicit instantiations, and explicit specializations, collectively known as *specializations*. That is, a template describes a class in terms of a general type, while a specialization is a class declaration generated using a specific type.

Implicit Instantiations

The examples that you have seen so far used *implicit instantiations*. That is, they declare one or more objects indicating the desired type, and the compiler generates a specialized class definition using the recipe provided by the general template:

```
ArrayTb<int, 100> stuff; // implicit instantiation
```

The compiler doesn't generate an implicit instantiation of the class until it needs an object:

```
ArrayTb<double, 30> * pt;     // a pointer, no object needed yet
pt = new ArrayTb<double, 30>; // now an object is needed
```

The second statement causes the compiler to generate a class definition and also an object created according to that definition.

Explicit Instantiations

The compiler generates an *explicit instantiation* of a class declaration when you declare a class using the keyword `template` and indicating the desired type or types. The declaration should be in the same namespace as the template definition. For example, the declaration

```
template class ArrayTb<String, 100>; // generate ArrayTB<String, 100> class
```

declares `ArrayTb<String, 100>` to be a class. In this case the compiler generates the class definition, including method definitions, even though no object of the class has yet been created or mentioned. Just as with the implicit instantiation, the general template is used as a guide to generate the specialization.

Explicit Specializations

The *explicit specialization* is a definition for a particular type or types that is to be used instead of the general template. Sometimes you may need or want to modify a template to behave differently when instantiated for a particular type; in that case you can create an explicit specialization. Suppose, for example, that you've defined a template for a class representing a sorted array for which items are sorted as they are added to the array:

```
template <class T>
class SortedArray
{
    ...// details omitted
};
```

Also, suppose the template uses the > operator to compare values. This works well for numbers. It will work if T represents a class type, too, provided that you've defined a T::operator>() method. But it won't work if T is a string represented by type char *. Actually, the template will work, but the strings will wind up sorted by address rather than alphabetically. What is needed is a class definition that uses strcmp() instead of >. In such a case, you can provide an explicit template specialization. This takes the form of a template defined for one specific type instead of for a general type. When faced with the choice of a specialized template and a general template that both match an instantiation request, the compiler will use the specialized version.

A specialized class template definition has the following form:

```
template <> class Classname<specialized-type-name> { ... };
```

Older compilers may only recognize the older form, which dispenses with the template <>:

```
class Classname<specialized-type-name> { ... };
```

To provide a SortedArray template specialized for the char * type using the new notation, you would use code like the following:

```
template <> class SortedArray<char *>
{
    ...// details omitted
};
```

Here the implementation code would use strcmp() instead of > to compare array values. Now, requests for a SortedArray of char * will use this specialized definition instead of the more general template definition:

```
SortedArray<int> scores;     // use general definition
SortedArray<char *> dates;   // use specialized definition
```

Partial Specializations

C++ also allows for *partial specializations*, which partially restrict the generality of a template. A partial specialization, for example, can provide a specific type for one of the type parameters:

```
// general template
    template <class T1, class T2> class Pair {...};
```

```
// specialization with T2 set to int
   template <class T1> class Pair<T1, int> {...};
```

The <> following the keyword **template** declares the type parameters that are still unspecialized. So the second declaration specializes T2 to **int** but leaves T1 open. Note that specifying all the types leads to an empty bracket pair and a complete explicit specialization:

```
// specialization with T1 and T2 set to int
   template <> class Pair<int, int> {...};
```

The compiler uses the most specialized template if there is a choice:

```
Pair<double, double> p1; // use general Pair template
Pair<double, int> p2;    // use Pair<T1, int> partial specialization
Pair<int, int> p3;       // use Pair<int, int> explicit specialization
```

Or you can partially specialize an existing template by providing a special version for pointers:

```
template<class T>        // general version
class Feeb { ... };
template<class T*>       // pointer partial specialization
class Feeb { ... };      // modified code
```

If you provide a non-pointer type, the compiler will use the general version; if you provide a pointer, the compiler will use the pointer specialization:

```
Feeb<char> fb1;          // use general Feeb template, T is char
Feeb<char *> fb2;        // use Feeb T* specialization, T is char
```

Without the partial specialization, the second declaration would have used the general template, interpreting T as type **char ***. With the partial specialization, it uses the specialized template, interpreting T as **char**.

The partial specialization feature allows for making a variety of restrictions. For example, you can do the following:

```
// general template
   template <class T1, class T2, class T3> class Trio{...};
// specialization with T3 set to T2
   template <class T1, class T2> class Trio<T1, T2, T2> {...};
// specialization with T3 and T2 set to T1*
   template <class T1> class Trio<T1, T1*, T1*> {...};
```

Given these declarations, the compiler would make the following choices:

```
Trio<int, short, char *> t1; // use general template
Trio<int, short> t2; // use Trio<T1, T2, T2>
Trio<char, char *, char *> t3; use Trio<T1, T1*, T1*>
```

Member Templates

Another of the more recent additions to C++ template support is that a template can be a member of a structure, class, or template class. The Standard Template Library requires this feature to fully implement its design. Listing 14.21 provides a short example of a template class with a nested template class and a template function as members.

LISTING 14.21   tempmemb.cpp

```cpp
// tempmemb.cpp -- template members
#include <iostream>
using namespace std;

template <typename T>
class beta
{
private:
    template <typename V>  // nested template class member
    class hold
    {
    private:
        V val;
    public:
        hold(V v  = 0) : val(v) {}
        void show() const { cout << val << endl; }
        V Value() const { return val; }
    };
    hold<T> q;              // template object
    hold<int> n;            // template object
public:
    beta( T t, int i) : q(t), n(i) {}
    template<typename U>    // template method
    U blab(U u, T t) { return (n.Value() + q.Value()) * u / t; }
    void Show() const { q.show(); n.show();}
};
int main()
{
    beta<double> guy(3.5, 3);

    guy.Show();
    cout << guy.blab(10, 2.3) << endl;
    cout << "Done\n";
    return 0;
}
```

The hold template is declared in the private section, so it is accessible only within the beta class scope. The beta class uses the hold template to declare two data members:

```cpp
hold<T> q;              // template object
hold<int> n;            // template object
```

The n is a hold object based on the int type, while the q member is a hold object based on the T type (the beta template parameter). In main(), the declaration

```cpp
beta<double> guy(3.5, 3);
```

makes T represent double, making q type hold<double>.

The blab() method has one type (U) that is determined implicitly by the argument value when the method is called and one type (T) that is determined by the instantiation type of the object.

In this example, the declaration for **guy** sets **T** to type **double**, and the first argument in the method call in

```
cout << guy.blab(10, 2.5) << endl;
```

sets **U** to type **int**. Thus, although the automatic type conversions brought about by mixed types cause the calculation in **blab()** to be done as type **double**, the return value, being type **U**, is an **int**, as the following program output shows:

```
3.5
3
28
Done
```

If you replace the **10** with **10.0** in the call to **guy.blab()**, **U** is set to **double**, making the return type **double**, and you get this output instead:

```
3.5
3
28.2609
Done
```

As mentioned, the type of the second parameter is set to **double** by the declaration of the **guy** object. Unlike the first parameter, then, the type of the second parameter is not set by the function call. For instance, the statement

```
cout << guy.blab(10, 3) << endl;
```

would still implement **blah()** as **blah(int, double)**, and the **3** would be converted to type **double** by the usual function prototype rules.

You can declare the **hold** class and **blah** method in the **beta** template and define them outside the **beta** template. However, because implementing templates is still a new process, it may be more difficult to get the compiler to accept these forms. Some compilers may not accept template members at all, and others that accept them as shown in Listing 14.21 don't accept definitions outside the class. However, if your compiler is willing and able, here's how defining the template methods outside the **beta** template would look:

```
template <typename T>
class beta
{
private:
    template <typename V>  // declaration
    class hold;
    hold<T> q;
    hold<int> n;
public:
    beta( T t, int i) : q(t), n(i) {}
    template<typename U>   // declaration
    U blab(U u, T t);
    void Show() const { q.show(); n.show();}
};
```

```
// member definition
template <typename T>
  template<typename V>
    class beta<T>::hold
    {
    private:
        V val;
    public:
        hold(V v  = 0) : val(v) {}
        void show() const { cout << val << endl; }
        V Value() const { return val; }
    };

// member definition
template <typename T>
  template <typename U>
    U beta<T>::blab(U u, T t)
    {
        return (n.Value() + q.Value()) * u / t;
    }
```

The definitions have to identify T, V, and U as template parameters. Because the templates are nested, you have to use the

```
template <typename T>
  template <typename V>
```

syntax instead of the

```
template<typename T, typename V>
```

syntax. The definitions also must indicate that hold and blab are members of the beta<T> class, and they use the scope resolution operator to do so.

Templates As Parameters

You've seen that a template can have type parameters, such as typename T, and non-type parameters, such as int n. A template also can have a parameter that is itself a template. Such parameters are yet another recent addition to templates that is used to implement the Standard Template Library.

Listing 14.22 shows an example for which the template parameter is template <typename T> class Thing. Here template <typename T> class is the type and Thing is the parameter. What does this imply? Suppose you have this declaration:

```
Crab<King> legs;
```

For this to be accepted, the template argument King has to be a template class whose declaration matches that of the template parameter Thing:

```
template <typename T>
class King {...};
```

The Crab declaration declares two objects:

```
Thing<int> s1;
Thing<double> s2;
```

The previous declaration for legs would then result in substituting King<int> for Thing<int> and King<double> for Thing<double>. Listing 14.22, however, has this declaration:

```
Crab<Stack> nebula;
```

Hence, in this case, Thing<int> is instantiated as Stack<int> and Thing<double> is instantiated as Stack<double>. In short, the template parameter Thing is replaced by whatever template type is used as a template argument in declaring a Crab object.

The Crab class declaration makes three further assumptions about the template class represented by Thing. The class should have a push() method, the class should have a pop() method, and these methods should have a particular interface. The Crab class can use any template class that matches the Thing type declaration and which has the prerequisite push() and pop() methods. This chapter happens to have one such class, the Stack template defined in stacktp.h, so the example uses that class.

LISTING 14.22   tempparm.cpp

```
// tempparm.cpp -- template template parameters
#include <iostream>
using namespace std;
#include "stacktp.h"

template <template <typename T> class Thing>
class Crab
{
private:
    Thing<int> s1;
    Thing<double> s2;
public:
    Crab() {};
    // assumes the thing class has push() and pop() members
    bool push(int a, double x) { return s1.push(a) && s2.push(x); }
    bool pop(int & a, double & x){ return s1.pop(a) && s2.pop(x); }
};

int main()
{
    Crab<Stack> nebula;
// Stack must match template <typename T> class thing
    int ni;
    double nb;

    while (cin>> ni >> nb && ni > 0 && nb > 0)
    {
        if (!nebula.push(ni, nb))
```

LISTING 14.22 *Continued*

```
                break;
        }

        while (nebula.pop(ni, nb))
                cout << ni << ", " << nb << endl;
        cout << "Done.\n";

        return 0;
}
```

Here is a sample run:

```
50 11.23
14 91.82
88 17.91
0 0
88, 17.91
14, 91.82
50, 11.23
Done.
```

Template Classes and Friends

Template class declarations can have friends, too. We can classify friends of templates into three categories:

- Nontemplate friends

- Bound template friends, meaning the type of the friend is determined by the type of the class when a class is instantiated

- Unbound template friends, meaning that all specializations of the friend are friends to each specialization of the class

We'll look at examples of each.

Nontemplate Friend Functions to Template Classes

Let's declare an ordinary function in a template class as a friend:

```
template <class T>
class HasFriend
{
        friend void counts();       // friend to all HasFriend instantiations
        ...
};
```

This declaration makes the `counts()` function a friend to all possible instantiations of the template. For example, it would be a friend to the `HasFriend<int>` class and the `HasFriend<String>` class.

The `counts()` function is not invoked by an object (it's a friend, not a member function) and it has no object parameters, so how does it access a `HasFriend` object? There are several possibilities. It could access a global object; it could access nonglobal objects by using a global pointer; it could create its own objects; it could access static data members of a template class, which exist separate from an object.

Suppose you want to provide a template class argument to a friend function. Can you have a friend declaration like this, for example:

```
friend void report(HasFriend &);    // possible?
```

The answer is no. The reason is that there is no such thing as a `HasFriend` object. There are only particular specializations, such as `HasFriend<short>`. To provide a template class argument, then, you have to indicate a specialization. For example, you can do this:

```
template <class T>
class HasFriend
{
    friend void report(HasFriend<T> &); // bound template friend
    ...
};
```

To understand what this does, imagine the specialization produced if you declare an object of a particular type:

```
HasFriend<int> hf;
```

The compiler would replace the template parameter `T` with `int`, giving the friend declaration this form:

```
class HasFriend<int>
{
    friend void report(HasFriend<int> &); // bound template friend
    ...
};
```

That is, `report()` with a `HasFriend<int>` parameter becomes a friend to the `HasFriend<int>` class. Similarly, `report()` with a `HasFriend<double>` parameter would be an overloaded version of `report()` that is friend to the `HasFriend<double>` class.

Note that `report()` is not itself a template function; it just has a parameter that is a template. This means that you have to define explicit specializations for those friends you plan to use:

```
void report(HasFriend<short> &) { ... };  // explicit specialization for short
void report(HasFriend<int> &) { ... };    // explicit specialization for int
```

Listing 14.23 illustrates these points. The `HasFriend` template has a static member `ct`. Note that this means that each particular specialization of the class has its own static member. The `counts()` method, which is a friend to all `HasFriend` specializations, reports the value of `ct` for two particular specializations: `HasFriend<int>` and `HasFriend<double>`. The program also provides two `report()` functions, each of which is a friend to one particular `HasFriend` specialization.

LISTING 14.23   frnd2tmp.cpp

```cpp
// frnd2tmp.cpp -- template class with non-template friends
#include <iostream>
using namespace std;

template <typename T>
class HasFriend
{
private:
    T item;
    static int ct;
public:
    HasFriend(const T & i) : item(i) {ct++;}
    ~HasFriend()  {ct--; }
    friend void counts();
    friend void reports(HasFriend<T> &); // template parameter
};

// each specialization has its own static data member
template <typename T>
int HasFriend<T>::ct = 0;

// non-template friend to all HasFriend<T> classes
void counts()
{
    cout << "int count: " << HasFriend<int>::ct << endl;
    cout << "double count: " << HasFriend<double>::ct << endl;
}

// non-template friend to the HasFriend<int> class
void reports(HasFriend<int> & hf)
{
    cout <<"HasFriend<int>: " << hf.item << endl;
}

// non-template friend to the HasFriend<double> class
void reports(HasFriend<double> & hf)
{
    cout <<"HasFriend<double>: " << hf.item << endl;
}

int main()
{
    counts();
    HasFriend<int> hfi1(10);
    HasFriend<int> hfi2(20);
    HasFriend<double> hfd(10.5);
    reports(hfi2);
    reports(hfd);
    counts();

    return 0;
}
```

Here is the program output:

```
int count: 0
double count: 0
HasFriend<int>: 20
HasFriend<double>: 10.5
int count: 2
double count: 1
```

Bound Template Friend Functions to Template Classes

We can modify the last example by making the friend functions templates themselves. In particular, we'll set things up for bound template friends, so each specialization of a class gets a matching specialization for a friend. The technique is a bit more complex than for non-template friends and involves three steps.

For the first step, declare each template function before the class definition.

```
template <typename T> void counts();
template <typename T> void report(T &);
```

Next, declare the templates again as friends inside the function. These statements declare specializations based on the class template parameter type:

```
template <typename TT>
class HasFriendT
{
...
    friend void counts<TT>();
    friend void report<>(HasFriendT<TT> &);
};
```

The <> in the declarations identifies these as template specializations. In the case of `report()`, the <> can be left empty because the template type argument (`HasFriendT<TT>`) can be deduced from the function argument. You could, however, use `report<HasFriendT<TT>>(HasFriendT<TT> &)` instead. The `counts()` function, however, has no parameters, so you have to use the template argument syntax (`<TT>`) to indicate its specialization. Note, too, that TT is the parameter type for the `HasFriendT` class.

Again, the best way to understand these declarations is to imagine what they become when you declare an object of a particular specialization. For example, suppose you declare this object:

```
HasFriendT<int> squack;
```

Then the compiler substitutes int for TT and generates the following class definition:

```
class HasFriendT<int>
{
...
    friend void counts<int>();
    friend void report<>(HasFriendT<int> &);
};
```

One specialization is based on TT, which becomes int, and the other on HasFriendT<TT>, which becomes HasFriendT<int>. Thus, the template specializations counts<int>() and report<HasFriendT<int> >() are declared as friends to the HasFriendT<int> class.

The third requirement the program must meet is to provide template definitions for the friends. Listing 14.24 illustrates these three aspects. Note that Listing 14.23 had one count() function that was a friend to all HasFriend classes, while Listing 14.24 has two count() functions, one a friend to each of the instantiated class types. Because the count() function calls have no function parameter from which the compiler can deduce the desired specialization, these calls use the count<int>() and count<double>() forms to indicate the specialization. For the calls to report(), however, the compiler can use the argument type to deduce the specialization. You could use the <> form to the same effect:

```
report<HasFriendT<int> >(hfi2);   // same as report(hfi2);
```

LISTING 14.24   tmp2tmp.cpp

```cpp
// tmp2tmp.cpp -- template friends to a template class
#include <iostream>
using namespace std;

// template prototypes
template <typename T> void counts();
template <typename T> void report(T &);

// template class
template <typename TT>
class HasFriendT
{
private:
    TT item;
    static int ct;
public:
    HasFriendT(const TT & i) : item(i) {ct++;}
    ~HasFriendT() { ct--; }
    friend void counts<TT>();
    friend void report<>(HasFriendT<TT> &);
};

template <typename T>
int HasFriendT<T>::ct = 0;

// template friend functions definitions
template <typename T>
void counts()
{
    cout << "template counts(): " << HasFriendT<T>::ct << endl;
}

template <typename T>
void report(T & hf)
```

LISTING 14.24 Continued

```
{
    cout << hf.item << endl;
}

int main()
{
    counts<int>();
    HasFriendT<int> hfi1(10);
    HasFriendT<int> hfi2(20);
    HasFriendT<double> hfd(10.5);
    report(hfi2);  // generate report(HasFriendT<int> &)
    report(hfd);   // generate report(HasFriendT<double> &)
    counts<double>();
    counts<int>();

    return 0;
}
```

Here is the output:

```
template counts(): 0
20
10.5
template counts(): 1
template counts(): 2
```

Unbound Template Friend Functions to Template Classes

The bound template friend functions were template specializations of a template declared outside of a class. An `int` class specialization got an `int` function specialization, and so on. By declaring a template inside a class, you can create unbound friend functions for which every function specialization is a friend to every class specialization. For unbound friends, the friend template type parameters are different from the template class type parameters:

```
template <typename T>
class ManyFriend
{
...
    template <typename C, typename D> friend void show2(C &, D &);
};
```

Listing 14.25 shows an example using an unbound friend. In it, the function call `show2(hfi1, hfi2)` gets matched to the following specialization:

```
void show2<ManyFriend<int> &, ManyFriend<int> &>
        (ManyFriend<int> & c, ManyFriend<int> & d);
```

Because it is a friend to all specializations of `ManyFriend`, this function has access to the `item` members of all specializations. But it only uses access to `ManyFriend<int>` objects.

Similarly, `show2(hfd, hfi2)` gets matched to this specialization:

```
void show2<ManyFriend<double> &, ManyFriend<int> &>
          (ManyFriend<double> & c, ManyFriend<int> & d);
```

It, too, is a friend to all `ManyFriend` specializations, and it uses its access to the `item` member of a `ManyFriend<int>` object and to the `item` member of a `ManyFriend<double>` object.

LISTING 14.25   `manyfrnd.cpp`

```cpp
// manyfrnd.cpp -- unbound template friend to a template class
#include <iostream>
using namespace std;

template <typename T>
class ManyFriend
{
private:
    T item;
public:
    ManyFriend(const T & i) : item(i) {}
    template <typename C, typename D> friend void show2(C &, D &);
};

template <typename C, typename D> void show2(C & c, D & d)
{
    cout << c.item << ", " << d.item << endl;
}

int main()
{
    ManyFriend<int> hfi1(10);
    ManyFriend<int> hfi2(20);
    ManyFriend<double> hfd(10.5);
    show2(hfi1, hfi2);
    show2(hfd, hfi2);

    return 0;
}
```

Here's the output:

```
10, 20
10.5, 20
```

Summary

C++ provides several means for reusing code. Public inheritance, described in Chapter 13, "Class Inheritance," enables you to model *is-a* relationships, with derived classes being able to reuse the code of base classes. Private and protected inheritance also let you reuse base class code, this time modeling *has-a* relationships. With private inheritance, public and protected members of the base class become private members of the derived class. With protected inheritance, public and protected members of the base class become protected members of the derived class. Thus, in either case, the public interface of the base class becomes an internal interface for the derived class. This sometimes is described as inheriting the implementation but not the interface, for a derived object can't explicitly use the base class interface. Thus, you can't view a derived object as a kind of base object. Because of this, a base class pointer or reference is not allowed to refer to a derived object without an explicit type cast.

You also can reuse class code by developing a class with members that are themselves objects. This approach, called containment, layering, or composition, also models the *has-a* relationship. Containment is simpler to implement and use than private or protected inheritance, so it usually is preferred. However, private and protected inheritance have slightly different capabilities. For example, inheritance allows a derived class access to protected members of a base class. Also, it allows a derived class to redefine a virtual function inherited from the base class. Because containment is not a form of inheritance, neither of these capabilities are options when you reuse class code by containment. On the other hand, containment is more suitable if you need several objects of a given class. For example, a **State** class could contain an array of **County** objects.

Multiple inheritance (MI) allows you to reuse code for more than one class in a class design. Private or protected MI models the *has-a* relationship, while public MI models the *is-a* relationship. Multiple inheritance can create problems with multi-defined names and multi-inherited bases. You can use class qualifiers to resolve name ambiguities and virtual base classes to avoid multi-inherited bases. However, using virtual base classes introduces new rules for writing initialization lists for constructors and for resolving ambiguities.

Class templates let you create a generic class design in which a type, usually a member type, is represented by a type parameter. A typical template looks like this:

```
template <class T>
class Ic
{
     T v;
     ...
public:
     Ic(const T & val) : v(val) { }
     ...
};
```

Here the T is the type parameter and acts as a stand-in for a real type to be specified at a later time. (This parameter can have any valid C++ name, but T and Type are common choices.) You also can use **typename** instead of **class** in this context:

```
template <typename T>  // same as template <class T>
class Rev {...} ;
```

Class definitions (instantiations) are generated when you declare a class object, specifying a particular type. For example, the declaration

```
class Ic<short> sic;    // implicit instantiation
```

causes the compiler to generate a class declaration in which every occurrence of the type parameter T in the template is replaced by the actual type **short** in the class declaration. In this case the class name is `Ic<short>`, not `Ic`. `Ic<short>` is termed a specialization of the template. In particular, it is an implicit instantiation.

An explicit instantiation occurs when you declare a specific specialization of the class using the keyword **template**:

```
template class IC<int>;  // explicit instantiation
```

In this situation, the compiler uses the general template to generate an **int** specialization `Ic<int>` even though no objects have yet been requested of that class.

You can provide explicit specializations which are specialized class declarations that override a template definition. Just define the class, starting with **template<>**, then the template class name followed by angle brackets containing the type for which you want a specialization. For example, you could provide a specialized **Ic** class for character pointers as follows:

```
template <> class Ic<char *>.
{
      char * str;
      ...
public:
      Ic(const char * s) : str(s) { }
      ...
};
```

Then a declaration of the form

```
class Ic<char *> chic;
```

would use the specialized definition for **chic** rather than using the general template.

A class template can specify more than one generic type and can also have non-type parameters:

```
template <class T, class TT, int n>
class Pals {...};
```

A class template also can have parameters that are templates:

```
template < template <typename T> class CL, typename U, int z>
class Trophy {...};
```

Here z stand for an **int** value, U stands for the name of a type, and CL stands for a class template declared using **template <typename T>**.

The declaration

```
Pals<double, String, 6> mix;
```

would generate an implicit instantiation using **double** for T, **String** for TT, and **6** for n.

Class templates can be partially specialized:

```
template <class T> Pals<T, T, 10> {...};
```

```
template <class T, class TT> Pals<T, TT, 100> {...};
template <class T, int n> Pals <T, T*, n> {...};
```

The first creates a specialization in which both types are the same and n has the value 6. Similarly, the second creates a specialization for n equal to 100, and the third creates a specialization for which the second type is a pointer to the first type.

Template classes can be members of other classes, structures, and templates

The goal of all these methods is to allow you to reuse tested code without having to copy it manually. This simplifies the programming task and makes programs more reliable.

Review Questions

1. For each of the following sets of classes, indicate whether public or private derivation is more appropriate for the second column:

class Bear	class PolarBear
class Kitchen	class Home
class Person	class Programmer
class Person	class HorseAndJockey
class Person, class Automobile	class Driver

2. Suppose we have the following definitions:

   ```
   class Frabjous {
   private:
           char fab[20];
   public:
           Frabjous(const char * s = "C++") : fab(s) { }
           virtual void tell() { cout << fab; }
   };

   class Gloam {
   private:
           int glip;
           Frabjous fb;
   public:
           Gloam(int g = 0, const char * s = "C++");
           Gloam(int g, const Frabjous & f);
           void tell();
   };
   ```

   Given that the Gloam version of tell() should display the values of glip and fb, provide definitions for the three Gloam methods.

3. Suppose we have the following definitions:

```
class Frabjous {
private:
      char fab[20];
public:
      Frabjous(const char * s = "C++") : fab(s) { }
      virtual void tell() { cout << fab; }
};

class Gloam : private Frabjous{
private:
      int glip;
public:
      Gloam(int g = 0, const char * s = "C++");
      Gloam(int g, const Frabjous & f);
      void tell();
};
```

Given that the `Gloam` version of `tell()` should display the values of `glip` and `fab`, provide definitions for the three `Gloam` methods.

4. Suppose we have the following definition, based on the `Stack` template of Listing 14.14 and the `Worker` class of Listing 14.11:

```
Stack<Worker *> sw;
```

Write out the class declaration that will be generated. Just do the class declaration, not the non-inline class methods.

5. Use the template definitions in this chapter to define the following:

   - An array of `String` objects

   - A stack of arrays of `double`

   - An array of stacks of pointers to `Worker` objects

How many template class definitions are produced in Listing 14.19?

6. Describe the differences between virtual and nonvirtual base classes.

Programming Exercises

1. The `Wine` class has a `String` class object member (Chapter 12) holding the name of a wine and a `Pair` object (this chapter) holding two `ArrayDb` objects (this chapter). The first `ArrayDb` object holds a list of vintage years and the second `ArrayDb` object holds the number of bottles owned for the corresponding vintage year. For example, the first `ArrayDb` object of the `Pair` might hold the years 1988, 1992, and 1996, while the second `ArrayDb` object of the `Pair` might hold the bottle counts 24, 36, and 48. It may be convenient for `Wine` to have an int member storing the number of years (3 in the above example). The program should prompt you to enter a wine name, the number of elements of the array, and the year and bottle count information for each array element.

The program should use this data to construct a `Wine` object, then display the information stored in the object.

2. The `Wine` class has a `String` class object member (Chapter 12) holding the name of a wine and a `Pair` object (this chapter) holding two `ArrayDb` objects (this chapter). The first `ArrayDb` object holds a list of vintage years and the second `ArrayDb` object holds the number of bottles owned for the corresponding vintage year. For example, the first `ArrayDb` object of the `Pair` might hold the years 1988, 1992, and 1996, while the second `ArrayDb` object of the `Pair` might hold the bottle counts 24, 36, and 48. It may be convenient for `Wine` to have an int member storing the number of years (3 in the above example).

3. Define a `QueueTp` template. Test it by creating a queue of pointers-to-`Worker` (as defined in Listing 14.11) and using the queue in a program similar to that of Listing 14.13.

4. A `Person` class holds the first name and the last name of a person. In addition to its constructors, it has a `Show()` method that displays both names. A `Gunslinger` class derives virtually from the `Person` class. It has a `Draw()` member that returns a type `double` value representing a gunslinger's draw time. The class also has an `int` member representing the number of notches on a gunslinger's gun. Finally, it has a `Show()` function that displays all this information.

   A `PokerPlayer` class derives virtually from the `Person` class. It has a `Draw()` member that returns a random number in the range 1 through 52 representing a card value. (Optionally, you could define a `Card` class with suit and face value members and use a `Card` return value for `Draw()`). The `PokerPlayer` class uses the `Person show()` function. The `BadDude` class derives publicly from the `Gunslinger` and `PokerPlayer` classes. It has a `Gdraw()` member that returns a bad dude's draw time and a `Cdraw()` member that returns the next card drawn. It has an appropriate `Show()` function. Define all these classes and methods, along with any other necessary methods (such as methods for setting object values), and test them in a simple program similar to that of Listing 14.11.

5. Here are some class declarations:

```
// emp.h -- header file for employee class and children
#include <cstring>
#include <iostream>
using namespace std;

const int SLEN = 20;
class employee
{
protected:
    char fname[SLEN];
    char lname[SLEN];
    char job[SLEN];
public:
    employee();
    employee(char * fn, char * ln, char * j);
    employee(const employee & e);
    virtual void ShowAll() const;
    virtual void SetAll();  // prompts user for values
    friend ostream & operator<<(ostream & os, const employee & e);
```

```
};

class manager:  virtual public employee
{
protected:
    int inchargeof;
public:
    manager();
    manager(char * fn, char * ln, char * j, int ico = 0);
    manager(const employee & e, int ico);
    manager(const manager & m);
    void ShowAll() const;
    void SetAll();
};

class fink: virtual public employee
{
protected:
    char reportsto[SLEN];
public:
    fink();
    fink(char * fn, char * ln, char * j, char * rpo);
    fink(const employee & e, char * rpo);
    fink(const fink & e);
    void ShowAll() const;
    void SetAll();
};


class highfink: public manager, public fink
{
public:
    highfink();
    highfink(char * fn, char * ln, char * j, char * rpo, int ico);
    highfink(const employee & e, char * rpo, int ico);
    highfink(const fink & f, int ico);
    highfink(const manager & m, char * rpo);
    highfink(const highfink & h);
    void ShowAll() const;
    void SetAll();
};
```

Note that the class hierarchy uses multiple inheritance with a virtual base class, so keep in mind the special rules for constructor initialization lists for that case. Also note that the data members are declared protected instead of private. This simplifies the code for some of the highfink methods. (Note, for example, if highfink::ShowAll() simply calls fink::ShowAll() and manager::ShowAll(), it winds up calling employee::ShowAll() twice.) However, you may want to use private data and provide additional protected methods in the manner of the Worker class with MI. Provide the class method implementations and test the classes in a program. Here is a minimal test program. You should add at least one test of a SetAll() member function.

```
// useemp1.cpp -- use employee classes
#include <iostream>
using namespace std;
#include "emp.h"

int main()
{
    employee th("Trip", "Harris", "Thumper");
    cout << th << '\n';
    th.ShowAll();


    manager db("Debbie", "Bolt", "Twigger", 5);
    cout << db << '\n';
    db.ShowAll();

    cout << "Press a key for next batch of output:\n";
    cin.get();

    fink mo("Matt", "Oggs", "Oiler", "Debbie Bolt");
    cout << mo << '\n';
    mo.ShowAll();
    highfink hf(db, "Curly Kew");
    hf.ShowAll();

    cout << "Using an employee * pointer:\n";
    employee  * tri[4] = { &th, &db, &mo, &hf };
    for (int i = 0; i < 4; i++)
        tri[i]->ShowAll();

    return 0;;
}
```

Why is no assignment operator defined?

Why are showall() and setall() virtual?

Why is employee a virtual base class?

Why does the highfink class have no data section?

Why is only one version of operator<<() needed?

What would happen if the end of the program were replaced with this code?

```
employee  tri[4] = {th, db, mo, hf};
for (int i = 0; i < 4; i++)
    tri[i].showall();
```

CHAPTER 15

FRIENDS, EXCEPTIONS, AND MORE

You will learn about the following in this chapter:
- Friend classes
- Friend class methods
- Nested classes
- Throwing exceptions, try blocks, and catch blocks

- Exception classes
- RTTI (runtime type information)
- `dynamic_cast` and `typeid`
- `static_cast`, `const_cast`, and `reinterpret_cast`

*T*his chapter ties up some loose ends, then ventures into some of the most recent additions to the C++ language. The loose ends include friend classes, friend member functions, and nested classes, which are classes declared within other classes. The recent additions discussed here are exceptions, RTTI, and improved type cast control. C++ exception handling provides a mechanism for dealing with unusual occurrences that otherwise would bring a program to a halt. RTTI, or runtime type information, is a mechanism for identifying object types. The new type cast operators improve the safety of type casts. These last three facilities are fairly new to C++, and older compilers do not support them.

Friends

Several examples in this book have used friend functions as part of the extended interface for a class. Such functions are not the only kinds of friends a class can have. A class also can be a friend. In that case, any method of the friend class can access private and protected members of the original class. Also, you can be more restrictive and designate just particular member functions of a class to be friends to another class. A class defines which functions, member functions, or classes are friends; friendship cannot be imposed from the outside. Thus, although friends do grant outside access to a class's private portion, they don't really violate the spirit of object-oriented programming. Instead, they provide more flexibility to the public interface.

Friend Classes

When might you want to make one class a friend to another? Let's look at an example. Suppose you must program a simple simulation of a television and a remote control. You decide to define a `Tv` class representing a television and a `Remote` class representing a remote control. Clearly, there should be some sort of relationship between these classes, but what kind? A remote control is not a television and vice versa, so the *is-a* relationship of public inheritance doesn't apply. Nor is either a component of the other, so the *has-a* relationship of containment or of private or protected inheritance doesn't apply. What is true is that a remote control can modify the state of a television, and this suggests making the `Remote` class a friend to the `Tv` class.

First, let's define the `Tv` class. You can represent a television with a set of state members, that is, variables that describe various aspects of the television. Here are some of the possible states:

- On-off
- Channel setting
- Volume setting
- Cable or antenna tuning mode
- TV tuner or VCR input

The tuning mode reflects the fact that, in the U.S., the spacing between channels for channels 14 and up is different for cable reception than it is for UHF broadcast reception. The input selection chooses between TV, which could be either cable or broadcast TV, and a VCR. Some sets may offer more choices, but this list is enough for our purposes.

Also, a television has some parameters that aren't state variables. For example, televisions vary in the number of channels they can receive, and you can include a member to track that value.

Next, you must provide the class with methods for altering these settings. Many television sets these days hide their controls behind panels, but it's still possible with most televisions to change channels, and so on, without a remote control. However, often you can go up or down one channel at a time but can't select a channel at random. Similarly, there's usually a button for increasing the volume and one for decreasing the volume.

A remote control should duplicate the controls built in to the television. Many of its methods can be implemented by using `Tv` methods. In addition, a remote control typically provides random access channel selection. That is, you can go directly from channel 2 to channel 20 without going through all the intervening channels. Also, many remotes can work in two modes—as a television controller and as a VCR controller.

These considerations suggest a definition like that shown in Listing 15.1. The definition includes several constants defined as enumerations. The statement making `Remote` a friend class is this:

```
friend class Remote;
```

A friend declaration can appear in a public, private, or protected section; the location makes no difference. Because the Remote class mentions the Tv class, the compiler has to know about the Tv class before it can handle the Remote class. The simplest way to accomplish this is to define the Tv class first. Alternatively, you can use a forward declaration; we'll discuss that option soon.

Compatibility Note

If your compiler doesn't support the bool type, use int, 0, and 1 instead of bool, false, and true.

LISTING 15.1   tv.h

```cpp
// tv.h -- Tv and Remote classes
#ifndef TV_H_
#define TV_H_

class Tv
{
public:
    friend class Remote;    // Remote can access Tv private parts
    enum {Off, On};
    enum {MinVal,MaxVal = 20};
    enum {Antenna, Cable};
    enum {TV, VCR};

    Tv(int s = Off, int mc = 100) : state(s), volume(5),
        maxchannel(mc), channel(2), mode(Cable), input(TV) {}
    void onoff() {state = (state == On)? Off : On;}
    bool ison() const {return state == On;}
    bool volup();
    bool voldown();
    void chanup();
    void chandown();
    void set_mode() {mode = (mode == Antenna)? Cable : Antenna;}
    void set_input() {input = (input == TV)? VCR : TV;}
    void settings() const; // display all settings
private:
    int state;              // on or off
    int volume;             // assumed to be digitized
    int maxchannel;         // maximum number of channels
    int channel;            // current channel setting
    int mode;               // broadcast or cable
    int input;              // TV or VCR
};

class Remote
{
private:
    int mode;               // controls TV or VCR
public:
    Remote(int m = Tv::TV) : mode(m) {}
```

LISTING 15.1 Continued

```
        bool volup(Tv & t) { return t.volup();}
        bool voldown(Tv & t) { return t.voldown();}
        void onoff(Tv & t) { t.onoff(); }
        void chanup(Tv & t) {t.chanup();}
        void chandown(Tv & t) {t.chandown();}
        void set_chan(Tv & t, int c) {t.channel = c;}
        void set_mode(Tv & t) {t.set_mode();}
        void set_input(Tv & t) {t.set_input();}
};
#endif
```

Most of the class methods are defined inline. Note that each **Remote** method other than the constructor takes a reference to a **Tv** object as an argument. That reflects that a remote has to be aimed at a particular TV. Listing 15.2 shows the remaining definitions. The volume-setting functions change the volume member by one unit unless the sound has reached its minimum or maximum setting. The channel selection functions use wraparound, with the lowest channel setting, taken to be 1, immediately following the highest channel setting, maxchannel.

Many of the methods use the conditional operator to toggle a state between two settings:

```
void onoff() {state = (state == On)? Off : On;}
```

Provided that the two state values are 0 and 1, this can be done more compactly using the combined bitwise exclusive OR and assignment operator (^=) discussed in Appendix E, "Other Operators:"

```
void onoff() {state ^= 1;}
```

In fact, you could store up to eight bivalent state settings in a single unsigned **char** variable and toggle them individually, but that's another story, one made possible by the bitwise operators discussed in Appendix E.

LISTING 15.2 tv.cpp

```
// tv.cpp -- methods for the Tv class (Remote methods are inline)
#include <iostream>
using namespace std;
#include "tv.h"

bool Tv::volup()
{
    if (volume < MaxVal)
    {
        volume++;
        return true;
    }
    else
        return false;
}
bool Tv::voldown()
{
```

LISTING 15.2   Continued

```
        if (volume > MinVal)
        {
            volume--;
            return true;
        }
        else
            return false;
    }

    void Tv::chanup()
    {
        if (channel < maxchannel)
            channel++;
        else
            channel = 1;
    }

    void Tv::chandown()
    {
        if (channel > 1)
            channel--;
        else
            channel = maxchannel;
    }

    void Tv::settings() const
    {
        cout << "TV is " << (state == Off? "Off" : "On") << '\n';
        if (state == On)
        {
            cout << "Volume setting = " << volume << '\n';
            cout << "Channel setting = " << channel << '\n';
            cout << "Mode = "
                 << (mode == Antenna? "antenna" : "cable") << '\n';
            cout << "Input = "
                 << (input == TV? "TV" : "VCR") << '\n';
        }
    }
```

Next, Listing 15.3 is a short program that tests some of the features. The same controller is used to control two separate televisions.

LISTING 15.3   use_tv.cpp

```
//use_tv.cpp
#include <iostream>
using namespace std;
#include "tv.h"

int main()
{
```

LISTING 15.3   Continued

```
    Tv s20;
    cout << "Initial settings for 20\" TV:\n";
    s20.settings();
    s20.onoff();
    s20.chanup();
    cout << "\nAdjusted settings for 20\" TV:\n";
    s20.settings();

    Remote grey;

    grey.set_chan(s20, 10);
    grey.volup(s20);
    grey.volup(s20);
    cout << "\n20\" settings after using remote:\n";
    s20.settings();

    Tv s27(Tv::On);
    s27.set_mode();
    grey.set_chan(s27,28);
    cout << "\n27\" settings:\n";
    s27.settings();

    return 0;
}
```

Here is the program output:

```
Initial settings for 27" TV:
TV is Off

Adjusted settings for 27" TV:
TV is On
Volume setting = 5
Channel setting = 3
Mode = cable
Input = TV

27" settings after using remote:
TV is On
Volume setting = 7
Channel setting = 10
Mode = cable
Input = TV

34" settings:
TV is On
Volume setting = 5
Channel setting = 2
Mode = antenna
Input = TV
```

The main point to this exercise is that class friendship is a natural idiom in which to express some relationships. Without some form of friendship you would either have to make the private parts of the Tv class public or else construct some awkward, larger class that encompasses both a television and a remote control. And that solution wouldn't reflect the fact that a single remote control can be used with several televisions.

Friend Member Functions

Looking at the code for the last example, you may notice that most of the Remote methods are implemented using the public interface for the Tv class. This means that those methods don't really need friend status. Indeed, the only Remote method that accesses a private Tv member directly is Remote::set_chan(), so that's the only method that needs to be a friend. You do have the option of making just selected class members friends to another class rather than making the entire class a friend, but it's a bit more awkward. You need to be careful about the order in which you arrange the various declarations and definitions. Let's see why.

The way to make Remote::set_chan() a friend to the Tv class is to declare it as a friend in the Tv class declaration:

```
class Tv
{
    friend void Remote::set_chan(Tv & t, int c);
    ...
};
```

However, for the compiler to process this statement, it needs to have already seen the Remote definition. Otherwise, it won't know that Remote is a class and that set_chan() is a method of that class. That suggests putting the Remote definition above the Tv definition. But the fact that Remote methods mention Tv objects means that the Tv definition should come above the Remote definition. Part of the way around the circular dependence is to use a *forward declaration*. That means inserting the statement

```
class Tv;                // forward declaration
```

above the Remote definition. This provides the following arrangement:

```
class Tv;  // forward declaration
class Remote { ... };
class Tv { ... };
```

Could you use the following arrangement instead?

```
class Remote;            // forward declaration
class Tv { ... };
class Remote { ... };
```

The answer is no. The reason, as mentioned earlier, is that when the compiler sees that a Remote method is declared as a friend in the Tv class declaration, the compiler needs to have already viewed the declaration of the Remote class in general and of the set_chan() method in particular.

Another difficulty remains. In Listing 15.1, the `Remote` declaration contained inline code such as the following:

```
void onoff(Tv & t) { t.onoff(); }
```

Because this calls a `Tv` method, the compiler needs to have seen the `Tv` class declaration at this point so that it knows what methods `Tv` has. But, as you've seen, that declaration necessarily follows the `Remote` declaration. The solution to this problem is to restrict `Remote` to method *declarations* and to place the actual *definitions* after the `Tv` class. This leads to the following ordering:

```
class Tv;                 // forward declaration
class Remote { ... };       // Tv-using methods as prototypes only
class Tv { ... };
// put Remote method definitions here
```

The `Remote` prototypes look like this:

```
void onoff(Tv & t);
```

All the compiler needs to know when inspecting this prototype is that `Tv` is a class, and the forward declaration supplies that information. By the time the compiler reaches the actual method definitions, it has already read the `Tv` class declaration and has the added information needed to compile those methods. By using the `inline` keyword in the method definitions, you still can make the methods inline methods. Listing 15.4 shows the revised header file.

LISTING 15.4   tvfm.h

```
// tvfm.h -- Tv and Remote classes using a friend member
#ifndef TVFM_H_
#define TVFM_H_

class Tv;                        // forward declaration

class Remote
{
public:
    enum State{Off, On};
    enum {MinVal,MaxVal = 20};
    enum {Antenna, Cable};
    enum {TV, VCR};
private:
    int mode;
public:
    Remote(int m = TV) : mode(m) {}
    bool volup(Tv & t);          // prototype only
    bool voldown(Tv & t);
    void onoff(Tv & t) ;
    void chanup(Tv & t) ;
    void chandown(Tv & t) ;
    void set_mode(Tv & t) ;
```

LISTING 15.4 *Continued*

```
        void set_input(Tv & t);
        void set_chan(Tv & t, int c);

};

class Tv
{
public:
        friend void Remote::set_chan(Tv & t, int c);
        enum State{Off, On};
        enum {MinVal,MaxVal = 20};
        enum {Antenna, Cable};
        enum {TV, VCR};

        Tv(int s = Off, int mc = 100) : state(s), volume(5),
            maxchannel(mc), channel(2), mode(Cable), input(TV) {}
        void onoff() {state = (state == On)? Off : On;}
        bool ison() const {return state == On;}
        bool volup();
        bool voldown();
        void chanup();
        void chandown();
        void set_mode() {mode = (mode == Antenna)? Cable : Antenna;}
        void set_input() {input = (input == TV)? VCR : TV;}
        void settings() const;
private:
        int state;
        int volume;
        int maxchannel;
        int channel;
        int mode;
        int input;
};

// Remote methods as inline functions
inline bool Remote::volup(Tv & t) { return t.volup();}
inline bool Remote::voldown(Tv & t) { return t.voldown();}
inline void Remote::onoff(Tv & t) { t.onoff(); }
inline void Remote::chanup(Tv & t) {t.chanup();}
inline void Remote::chandown(Tv & t) {t.chandown();}
inline void Remote::set_mode(Tv & t) {t.set_mode();}
inline void Remote::set_input(Tv & t) {t.set_input();}
inline void Remote::set_chan(Tv & t, int c) {t.channel = c;}
#endif
```

This version behaves the same as the original. The difference is that just one **Remote** method is a friend to the **Tv** class instead of all the **Remote** methods. Figure 15.1 illustrates this difference.

FIGURE 15.1
Class friends versus class member friends.

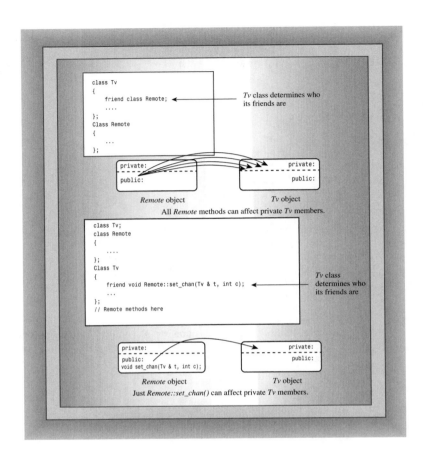

By the way, making the entire `Remote` class a friend doesn't need a forward declaration because the friend statement itself identifies `Remote` as a class:

```
friend class Remote;
```

Other Friendly Relationships

Other combinations of friends and classes are possible. Let's take a brief look at some of them now. Suppose the advance of technology brings interactive remote controllers. For example, an interactive remote control unit might let you enter a response to some question posed on a television program, and the television might activate a buzzer in your controller if your response were wrong. Ignoring the possibility of television using such facilities to program the viewers, let's just look at the C++ programming aspects. The new setup would benefit from mutual friendship, with some `Remote` methods being able to affect a `Tv` object, as before, and with some `Tv` methods being able to affect a `Remote` object. This can be accomplished by making the classes friends to each other. That is, `Tv` will be a friend to `Remote` in addition to

Remote being a friend to Tv. One point to keep in mind is that a Tv method that uses a Remote object can be prototyped *before* the Remote class declaration but must be defined *after* the declaration so that the compiler will have enough information to compile the method. The setup would look like this:

```
class Tv
{
friend class Remote;
public:
    void buzz(Remote & r);
    ...
};
class Remote
{
friend class Tv;
public:
    void Bool volup(Tv & t) { t.volup(); }
    ...
};
inline void Tv::buzz(Remote & r)
{
    ...
}
```

Because the Remote declaration follows the Tv declaration, Remote::volup() can be defined in the class declaration. The Tv::buzz() method, however, has to be defined outside the Tv declaration so that the definition can follow the Remote declaration. If you don't want buzz() to be inline, define it in a separate method definitions file.

Shared Friends

Another use for friends is when a function needs to access private data in two separate classes. Logically, such a function should be a member function of each class, but that's impossible. It could be a member of one class and a friend to the other, but sometimes it's more reasonable to make the function friends to both. Suppose, for example, that you have a Probe class representing some sort of programmable measuring device and an Analyzer class representing some sort of programmable analyzing device. Each has an internal clock, and you would like to be able to synchronize the two clocks. You could do something along the following lines:

```
class Analyzer;  // forward declaration
class Probe
{
    friend void sync(Analyzer & a, const Probe & p);  // sync a to p
    friend void sync(Probe & p, const Analyzer & a);  // sync p to a
    ...
};
class Analyzer
{
    friend void sync(Analyzer & a, const Probe & p);  // sync a to p
    friend void sync(Probe & p, const Analyzer & a);  // sync p to a
    ...
};
```

```
// define the friend functions
inline void sync(Analyzer & a, const Probe & p)
{
    ...
}
inline void sync(Probe & p, const Analyzer & a)
{
    ...
}
```

The forward declaration enables the compiler to know that **Analyzer** is a type when it reaches the friend declarations in the **Probe** class declaration.

Nested Classes

In C++, you can place a class declaration inside another class. The class declared within another is called a *nested class*, and it helps avoid name clutter by giving the new type class scope. Member functions of the class containing the declaration can create and use objects of the nested class. The outside world can use the nested class only if the declaration is in the public section and if you use the scope resolution operator. (Older versions of C++, however, don't allow nested classes or else implement the concept incompletely.)

Nesting classes is not the same as containment. Containment, recall, means having a class object as a member of another class. Nesting a class, on the other hand, does not create a class member. Instead, it defines a type that is known just locally to the class containing the nested class declaration.

The usual reasons for nesting a class are to assist the implementation of another class and to avoid name conflicts. The **Queue** class example (Chapter 12, "Classes and Dynamic Memory Allocation," Listing 12.8) provided a disguised case of nested classes by nesting a structure definition:

```
class Queue
{
// class scope definitions
    // Node is a nested structure definition local to this class
    struct Node {Item item; struct Node * next;};
    ...
};
```

Because a structure is a class whose members are public by default, **Node** really is a nested class. However, this definition doesn't take advantage of class abilities. In particular, it lacks an explicit constructor. Let's remedy that now.

First, let's find where **Node** objects are created in the **Queue** example. Examining the class declaration (Listing 11.12) and the methods definitions (Listing 12.9) reveals that the only place in which **Node** objects are created is in the **enqueue()** method:

```
bool Queue::enqueue(const Item & item)
{
```

```
        if (isfull())
            return false;
        Node * add = new Node;   // create node
        if (add == NULL)
            return false;        // quit if none available
        add->item = item;          // set node pointers
        add->next = NULL;
        ...
    }
```

Here the code explicitly assigns values to the `Node` members after creating a `Node`. This is the sort of work that more properly is done by a constructor.

Knowing now where and how a constructor should be used, you can provide an appropriate constructor definition:

```
class Queue
{
// class scope definitions
    // Node is a nested class definition local to this class
    class Node
    {
    public:
        Item item;
        Node * next;
        Node(const Item & i) : item(i), next(0) { }
    };
    ...
};
```

This constructor initializes the node's `item` member to `i` and sets the `next` pointer to `0`, which is one way of writing the null pointer in C++. (Using `NULL` would require including a header file that defines `NULL`.) Because all nodes created by the `Queue` class have `next` initially set to the null pointer, this is the only constructor the class needs.

Next, rewrite `enqueue()` using the constructor:

```
bool Queue::enqueue(const Item & item)
{
    if (isfull())
        return false;
    Node * add = new Node(item);   // create, initialize node
    if (add == 0)
        return fFalse;             // quit if none available
    ...
}
```

This makes the code for `enqueue()` a bit shorter and a bit safer, for it automates initialization rather than requiring that the programmer remember correctly what should be done.

This example defined the constructor in the class declaration. Suppose you wanted to define it in a methods file, instead. The definition must reflect that the *Node* class is defined within the `Queue` class. This is accomplished by using the scope resolution operator twice:

```
Queue::Node::Node(const Item & i) : item(i), next(0) { }
```

Nested Classes and Access

Two kinds of access pertain to nested classes. First, where a nested class is declared controls the scope of the nested class; that is, it establishes which parts of a program can create objects of that class. Second, as with any class, the public, protected, and private sections of a nested class provide access control to class members. Where and how a nested class can be used depends upon both scope and access control. Let's examine these points further.

Scope

If the nested class is declared in a private section of a second class, it is known only to that second class. This applies, for example, to the **Node** class nested in the **Queue** declaration in the last example. (It may appear that **Node** was defined before the private section, but remember that private is the default access for classes.) Hence, **Queue** members can use **Node** objects and pointers to **Node** objects, but other parts of a program won't even know that the **Node** class exists. If you were to derive a class from **Queue**, **Node** would be invisible to that class, too, because a derived class can't directly access the private parts of a base class.

If the nested class is declared in a protected section of a second class, it is visible to that class but invisible to the outside world. However, in this case, a derived class would know about the nested class and could directly create objects of that type.

If a nested class is declared in a public section of a second class, it is available to the second class, to classes derived from the second class, and, because it's public, to the outside world. However, because the nested class has class scope, it has to be used with a class qualifier in the outside world. For example, suppose you have this declaration:

```
class Team
{
public:
        class Coach { ... };
        ...
};
```

Now suppose you have an unemployed coach, one who belongs to no team. To create a **Coach** object outside of the **Team** class, you can do this:

```
Team::Coach forhire;  // create a Coach object outside the Team class
```

These same scope considerations apply to nested structures and enumerations, too. Indeed, many programmers use public enumerations to provide class constants that can be used by client programmers. For example, the many implementations of classes defined to support the **iostream** facility use this technique to provide various formatting options, as we've touched upon earlier and will explore more fully in Chapter 17, "Input, Output, and Files." Table 15.1 summarizes scope properties for nested classes, structures, and enumerations.

TABLE 15.1   Scope Properties for Nested Classes, Structures, and Enumerations

Where Declared in Nesting Class	Available to Nesting Class	Available to Classes Derived from the Nesting Class	Available to the Outside World
Private section	Yes	No	No
Protected section	Yes	Yes	No
Public section	Yes	Yes	Yes, with class qualifier

Access Control

After a class is in scope, access control comes into play. The same rules govern access to a nested class that govern access to a regular class. Declaring the Node class in the Queue class declaration does not grant the Queue class any special access privileges to the Node class, nor does it grant the Node class any special access privileges to the Queue class. Thus, a Queue class object can access only the public members of a Node object explicitly. For that reason, the Queue example made all the members of the Node class public. This violates the usual practice of making data members private, but the Node class is an internal implementation feature of the Queue class and is not visible to the outside world. That's because the Node class is declared in the private section of the Queue class. Thus, although Queue methods can access Node members directly, a client using the Queue class cannot do so.

In short, the location of a class declaration determines the scope or visibility of a class. Given that a particular class is in scope, the usual access control rules (public, protected, private, friend) determine the access a program has to members of the nested class.

Nesting in a Template

You've seen that templates are a good choice for implementing container classes such as the Queue class. You may be wondering if having a nested class poses any problems to converting the Queue class definition to a template. The answer is no. Listing 15.5 shows how this conversion can be made. As is common for class templates, the header file includes the class template along with method function templates.

LISTING 15.5   queuetp.h

```
// queuetp.h -- queue template with a nested class
#ifndef QUEUETP_H_
#define QUEUETP_H_
```

LISTING 15.5   *Continued*

```cpp
template <class Item>
class QueueTP
{
private:
    enum {Q_SIZE = 10};
    // Node is a nested class definition
    class Node
    {
    public:
        Item item;
        Node * next;
        Node(const Item & i):item(i), next(0){ }
    };
    Node * front;         // pointer to front of Queue
    Node * rear;          // pointer to rear of Queue
    int items;            // current number of items in Queue
    const int qsize;      // maximum number of items in Queue
    QueueTP(const QueueTP & q) : qsize(0) {}
    QueueTP & operator=(const QueueTP & q) { return *this; }
public:
    QueueTP(int qs = Q_SIZE);
    ~QueueTP();
    bool isempty() const
    {
        return items == 0;
    }
    bool isfull() const
    {
        return items == qsize;
    }
    int queuecount() const
    {
        return items;
    }
    bool enqueue(const Item &item); // add item to end
    bool dequeue(Item &item);        // remove item from front
};

// QueueTP methods
template <class Item>
QueueTP<Item>::QueueTP(int qs) : qsize(qs)
{
    front = rear = 0;
    items = 0;
}

template <class Item>
QueueTP<Item>::~QueueTP()
{
    Node * temp;
    while (front != 0)     // while queue is not yet empty
    {
```

LISTING 15.5 *Continued*

```
            temp = front;      // save address of front item
            front = front->next;// reset pointer to next item
            delete temp;       // delete former front
        }
    }

    // Add item to queue
    template <class Item>
    bool QueueTP<Item>::enqueue(const Item & item)
    {
        if (isfull())
            return false;
        Node * add = new Node(item);   // create node
        if (add == NULL)
            return false;      // quit if none available
        items++;
        if (front == 0)        // if queue is empty,
            front = add;       // place item at front
        else
            rear->next = add;  // else place at rear
        rear = add;            // have rear point to new node
        return true;
    }

    // Place front item into item variable and remove from queue
    template <class Item>
    bool QueueTP<Item>::dequeue(Item & item)
    {
        if (front == 0)
            return false;
        item = front->item;    // set item to first item in queue
        items--;
        Node * temp = front;   // save location of first item
        front = front->next;   // reset front to next item
        delete temp;           // delete former first item
        if (items == 0)
            rear = 0;
        return true;
    }

    #endif
```

One interesting thing about this template is that **Node** is defined in terms of the generic type **Item**. Thus, a declaration like

```
QueueTp<double> dq;
```

leads to a **Node** defined to hold type **double** values, while

```
QueueTp<char> cq;
```

leads to a `Node` defined to hold type `char` values. These two `Node` classes are defined in two separate `QueueTP` classes, so there is no name conflict between the two. That is, one node is type `QueueTP<double>::Node` and the other is type `QueueTP<char>::Node`.

Listing 15.6 offers a short program for testing the new class. It creates a queue of `String` objects, so it should be compiled in conjunction with `string1.cpp` (Chapter 12).

LISTING 15.6   nested.cpp

```
// nested.cpp -- use queue having a nested class
// compile along with string1.cpp
#include <iostream>
using namespace std;
#include "string1.h"
#include "queuetp.h"

int main()
{
    QueueTP<String> cs(5);
    String temp;

    while(!cs.isfull())
    {
        cout << "Please enter your name. You will be "
                "served in the order of arrival.\n"
                "name: ";
        cin >> temp;
        cs.enqueue(temp);
    }
    cout << "The queue is full. Processing begins!\n";

    while (!cs.isempty())
    {
        cs.dequeue(temp);
        cout << "Now processing " << temp << "...\n";
    }
    return 0;
}
```

Here is a sample run:

```
Please enter your name. You will be served in the order of arrival.
name: Kinsey Millhone
Please enter your name. You will be served in the order of arrival.
name: Adam Dalgliesh
Please enter your name. You will be served in the order of arrival.
name: Andrew Dalziel
Please enter your name. You will be served in the order of arrival.
name: Kay Scarpetta
Please enter your name. You will be served in the order of arrival.
name: Richard Jury
The queue is full. Processing begins!
Now processing Kinsey Millhone...
```

```
Now processing Adam Dalgliesh...
Now processing Andrew Dalziel...
Now processing Kay Scarpetta...
Now processing Richard Jury...
```

Exceptions

Programs sometimes encounter runtime problems that prevent the program from continuing normally. For example, a program may try to open an unavailable file, or it may request more memory than is available, or it may encounter values it cannot abide. Usually, programmers try to anticipate such calamities. C++ exceptions provide a powerful and flexible tool for dealing with these situations. Exceptions were added to C++ recently, and not all compilers have implemented them yet.

Before examining exceptions, let's look at some of the more rudimentary options available to the programmer. As a test case, take a function that calculates the harmonic mean of two numbers. The harmonic mean of two numbers is defined as the inverse of the average of the inverses. This can be reduced to the following expression:

```
2.0 * x * y / (x + y)
```

Note that if y is the negative of x, this formula results in division by zero, a rather undesirable operation. One way to handle this is to have the function call the `abort()` function if one argument is the negative of the other. The `abort()` function has its prototype in the `cstdlib` (or `stdlib.h`) header file. A typical implementation, if called, sends a message like "abnormal program termination" to the standard error stream (the same as the one used by `cerr`) and terminates the program. It also returns an implementation-dependent value indicating failure to the operating system or, if the program was initiated by another program, to the parent process. Whether `abort()` flushes file buffers (memory areas used to store material for transfers to and from files) depends upon the implementation. If you prefer, you can use `exit()`, which does flush file buffers, but without displaying a message. Listing 15.7 shows a short program using `abort()`.

LISTING 15.7   error1.cpp

```cpp
//error1.cpp -- use the abort() function
#include <iostream>
using namespace std;
#include <cstdlib>
double hmean(double a, double b);

int main()
{
    double x, y, z;
```

LISTING 15.7 *Continued*

```
    cout << "Enter two numbers: ";
    while (cin >> x >> y)
    {
        z = hmean(x,y);
        cout << "Harmonic mean of " << x << " and " << y
             << " is " << z << "\n";
        cout << "Enter next set of numbers <q to quit>: ";
    }
    cout << "Bye!\n";
    return 0;
}

double hmean(double a, double b)
{
    if (a == -b)
    {
        cout << "untenable arguments to hmean()\n";
        abort();
    }
    return 2.0 * a * b / (a + b);
}
```

Here's a sample run:

```
Enter two numbers: 3 6
Harmonic mean of 3 and 6 is 4
Enter next set of numbers <q to quit>: 10 -10
untenable arguments to hmean()
abnormal program termination
```

Note that calling the `abort()` function from `hmean()` terminates the program directly without returning first to `main()`.

The program could avoid aborting by checking the values of x and y before calling the `hmean()` function. However, it's not safe to rely upon a programmer to know (or care) enough to perform such a check.

A more flexible approach than aborting is to use a function's return value to indicate a problem. For example, the `get(void)` member of the `ostream` class ordinarily returns the ASCII code for the next input character, but it returns the special value `EOF` if it encounters the end of a file. This approach doesn't work for `hmean()`. Any numeric value could be a valid return value, so there's no special value available to indicate a problem. In this kind of situation, you can use a pointer argument or reference argument to get a value back to the calling program and use the function return value to indicate success or failure. The `istream` family of overloaded `>>` operators uses a variant of this technique. By informing the calling program of the success or failure, you give the program the option of taking actions other than aborting. Listing 15.8 shows an example of this approach. It redefines `hmean()` as a `bool` function whose return value indicates success or failure. It adds a third argument for obtaining the answer.

LISTING 15.8   error2.cpp

```
//error2.cpp __ return an error code
#include <iostream>
using namespace std;
#include <cfloat>  // (or float.h) for DBL_MAX

bool hmean(double a, double b, double * ans);

int main()
{
    double x, y, z;

    cout << "Enter two numbers: ";
    while (cin >> x >> y)
    {
        if (hmean(x,y,&z))
            cout << "Harmonic mean of " << x << " and " << y
                << " is " << z << "\n";
        else
            cout << "One value should not be the negative "
                << "of the other - try again.\n";
        cout << "Enter next set of numbers <q to quit>: ";
    }
    cout << "Bye!\n";
    return 0;
}

bool hmean(double a, double b, double * ans)
{
    if (a == -b)
    {
        *ans = DBL_MAX;
        return false;
    }
    else
    {
        *ans = 2.0 * a * b / (a + b);
        return true;
    }
}
```

Here's a sample run:

```
Enter two numbers: 3 6
Harmonic mean of 3 and 6 is 4
Enter next set of numbers <q to quit>: 10 -10
One value should not be the negative of the other - try again.
Enter next set of numbers <q to quit>: 1 19
Harmonic mean of 1 and 19 is 1.9
Enter next set of numbers <q to quit>: q
Bye!
```

Program Notes

Here, the program design allowed the user to continue, bypassing the effects of bad input. Of course, the design does rely upon the user to check the function return value, something that programmers don't always do. For example, to keep the sample programs short, most of the listings in this book don't check to see if `new` returns the null pointer or if `cout` was successful in handling output.

You could use either a pointer or a reference for the third arguments. Many programmers prefer using pointers for arguments of the built-in types, for it makes it obvious which argument is being used for the answer.

The Exception Mechanism

Now let's see how you can handle problems with the exception mechanism. A C++ *exception* is a response to an exceptional circumstance that arises while a program is running, such as an attempt to divide by zero. Exceptions provide a way to transfer control from one part of a program to another. Handling an exception has three components:

- Throwing an exception
- Catching an exception with a handler
- Using a try block

A program throws an exception when a problem shows up. For example, you can modify `hmean()` in Listing 15.7 to throw an exception instead of calling the `abort()` function. A throw statement, in essence, is a jump; that is, it tells a program to jump to statements at another location. The `throw` keyword indicates the throwing of an exception. It's followed by a value, such as a character string or an object, indicating the nature of the exception.

A program catches an exception with an *exception handler* at the place in a program where you want to handle the problem. The `catch` keyword indicates the catching of an exception. A handler begins with the keyword `catch` followed, in parentheses, by a type declaration indicating the type of exception to which it responds. That, in turn, is followed by a brace-enclosed block of code indicating the actions to take. The `catch` keyword, along with the exception type, serves as a label identifying the point in a program to which execution should jump when an exception is thrown. An exception handler also is called a *catch block*.

A *try block* identifies a block of code for which particular exceptions will be activated. It's followed by one or more catch blocks. The try block itself is indicated by the keyword `try` followed by a brace-enclosed block of code indicating the code for which exceptions will be noticed.

The easiest way to see how these three elements fit together is to look at a short example, such as that provided in Listing 15.9.

LISTING 15.9   error3.cpp

```
//error3.cpp
#include <iostream>
using namespace std;
double hmean(double a, double b);

int main()
{
    double x, y, z;

    cout << "Enter two numbers: ";
    while (cin >> x >> y)
    {
        try {                       // start of try block
            z = hmean(x,y);
        }                           // end of try block
        catch (const char * s)  // start of exception handler
        {
            cout << s << "\n";
            cout << "Enter a new pair of numbers: ";
            continue;
        }                           // end of handler
        cout << "Harmonic mean of " << x << " and " << y
            << " is " << z << "\n";
        cout << "Enter next set of numbers <q to quit>: ";
    }
    cout << "Bye!\n";
    return 0;
}

double hmean(double a, double b)
{
    if (a == -b)
        throw "bad hmean() arguments: a = -b not allowed";
    return 2.0 * a * b / (a + b);
}
```

Here's a sample run:

```
Enter two numbers: 3 6
Harmonic mean of 3 and 6 is 4
Enter next set of numbers <q to quit>: 10 -10
bad hmean() arguments: a = -b not allowed
Enter a new pair of numbers: 1 19
Harmonic mean of 1 and 19 is 1.9
Enter next set of numbers <q to quit>: q
Bye!
```

Program Notes

The try block looks like this:

```
try {                     // start of try block
    z = hmean(x,y);
}                         // end of try block
```

If any statement in this block leads to an exception being thrown, the catch blocks after this block will handle the exception. If the program called `hmean()` somewhere else outside this (and any other) try block, it wouldn't have the opportunity to handle an exception.

Throwing an exception looks like this:

```
if (a == -b)
    throw "bad hmean() arguments: a = -b not allowed";
```

In this case, the thrown exception is the string `"bad hmean() arguments: a = -b not allowed"`. Executing the throw is a bit like executing a return statement in that it terminates function execution. However, instead of returning control to the calling program, a throw causes a program to back up through the sequence of current function calls until it finds the function containing the try block. In Listing 15.9, that function is the same as the calling function. Soon you'll see an example involving backing up more than one function. Meanwhile, in this case, the throw passes program control back to `main()`. There, the program looks for an exception handler (following the try block) that matches the type of exception thrown.

The handler, or catch block, looks like this:

```
catch (char * s)  // start of exception handler
{
    cout << s << "\n";
    cout << "Enter a new pair of numbers: ";
    continue;
}                         // end of handler
```

It looks a bit like a function definition, but it's not. The keyword `catch` identifies this as a handler, and the `char * s` means that this handler matches a thrown exception that is a string. This declaration of `s` acts much like a function argument definition in that a matching thrown exception is assigned to `s`. Also, if an exception does match this handler, the program executes the code within the braces.

If a program completes executing statements in a try block without any exceptions being thrown, it skips the catch block or blocks after the try block and goes to the first statement following the handlers. So when the sample run processed the values 3 and 6, program execution went directly to the output statement reporting the result.

Let's trace through the events in the sample run after the values 10 and -10 are passed to the `hmean()` function. The `if` test causes `hmean()` to throw an exception. This terminates execution of `hmean()`. Searching back, the program determines that `hmean()` was called from within a try block in `main()`. It then looks for a catch block with a type matching the exception type. The single catch block present has a `char *` parameter, so it does match. Detecting the match, the program assigns the string `"bad hmean() arguments: a = -b not allowed"` to the variable **s**. Next, the program executes the code in the handler. First, it prints **s**, which is the caught exception. Then it prints instructions to the user to enter new data. Finally, it executes a `continue` statement, which causes the program to skip the rest of the `while` loop and jump to its beginning again. The fact that the `continue` takes the program to the beginning of the loop illustrates the fact that handler statements are part of the loop and that the catch line acts like a label directing program flow (see Figure 15.2).

FIGURE 15.2
Program flow with exceptions.

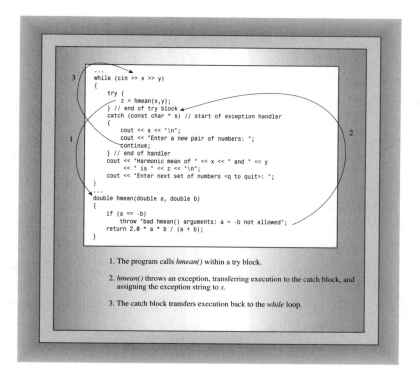

1. The program calls *hmean()* within a try block.

2. *hmean()* throws an exception, transferring execution to the catch block, and assigning the exception string to *s*.

3. The catch block transfers execution back to the *while* loop.

You might be wondering what happens if a function throws an exception and there's no try block or else no matching handler. By default, the program eventually calls the `abort()` function, but you can modify that behavior. We'll return to this topic later.

Exception Versatility

C++ exceptions offer versatility, for the try block lets you select which code gets checked for exceptions and the handlers let you specify what gets done. For example, in Listing 15.9, the try block was inside the loop, so program execution continued inside the loop after the exception was handled. By placing the loop inside the try block, you can make an exception transfer execution to outside the loop, thus terminating the loop. Listing 15.10 illustrates that. It also demonstrates two more points:

- You can qualify a function definition with an exception specification to indicate which kinds of exceptions it throws.

- A catch block can handle more than one source of exceptions.

To qualify a function prototype to indicate the kinds of exceptions it throws, append an exception specification, which consists of the keyword **throw** followed by a comma-separated list of exception types enclosed in parentheses:

```
double hmean(double a, double b) throw(const char *);
```

This accomplishes two things. First, it tells the compiler what sort of exception or exceptions a function throws. If the function then throws some other type of exception, the program will react to the faux pas by calling (eventually) the **abort()** function. (We'll examine this behavior and how it can be modified in more detail later.) Second, using an exception specification alerts anyone who reads the prototype that this particular function throws an exception, reminding the reader that he or she may want to provide a try block and a handler. Functions that throw more than one kind of exception can provide a comma-separated list of exception types; the syntax imitates that of an argument list for a function prototype. For example, the following prototype indicates a function that can throw either a **char *** exception or a **double** exception:

```
double multi_err(double z) throw(const char *, double);
```

The same information that appears in a prototype, as you can see in Listing 15.10, also should appear in the function definition.

Using empty parentheses in the exception specification indicates that the function does not throw exceptions:

```
double simple(double z) throw(); // doesn't throw an exception
```

Listing 15.10, as mentioned earlier, places the entire **while** loop inside the try block. It also adds a second exception-throwing function, **gmean()**. This function returns the geometric mean of two numbers, which is defined as the square root of their product. This function isn't defined for negative arguments, which provides grounds for throwing an exception. Like **hmean()**, **gmean()** throws a string-type exception, so the same catch block will catch exceptions from either of these two functions.

LISTING 15.10   error4.cpp

```
//error4.cpp
#include <iostream>
using namespace std;
#include <cmath> // or math.h, unix users may need -lm flag
double hmean(double a, double b) throw(const char *);
double gmean(double a, double b) throw(const char *);

int main()
{
    double x, y, z;
```

LISTING 15.10   *Continued*

```
    cout << "Enter two numbers: ";
    try {                    // start of try block
        while (cin >> x >> y)
        {
            z = hmean(x,y);
            cout << "Harmonic mean of " << x << " and " << y
                << " is " << z << "\n";
            cout << "Geometric mean of " << x << " and " << y
                << " is " << gmean(x,y) << "\n";
            cout << "Enter next set of numbers <q to quit>: ";
        }
    }                        // end of try block
    catch (const char * s)      // start of catch block
    {
        cout << s << "\n";
        cout << "Sorry, you don't get to play any more. ";
    }                        // end of catch block
    cout << "Bye!\n";
    return 0;
}

double hmean(double a, double b) throw(const char *)
{
    if (a == -b)
        throw "bad hmean() arguments: a = -b not allowed";
    return 2.0 * a * b / (a + b);
}

double gmean(double a, double b) throw(const char *)
{
    if (a < 0 || b < 0)
        throw "bad gmean() arguments: negative values not allowed";
    return sqrt(a * b);
}
```

Here's a sample run that gets terminated by bad input for the `hmean()` function:

```
Enter two numbers: 1 100
Harmonic mean of 1 and 100 is 1.9802
Geometric mean of 1 and 100 is 10
Enter next set of numbers <q to quit>: 10 -10
bad hmean() arguments: a = -b not allowed
Sorry, you don't get to play any more. Bye!
```

Because the exception handler is outside the loop, bad input terminates the loop. After the program finishes the code in the handler, it proceeds to the next line in the program, which prints Bye!.

For comparison, here's a sample run that gets terminated by bad input for the `gmean()` function:

```
Enter two numbers: 1 100
Harmonic mean of 1 and 100 is 1.9802
```

```
Geometric mean of 1 and 100 is 10
Enter next set of numbers <q to quit>: 3 -15
Harmonic mean of 3 and -15 is 7.5
bad gmean() arguments: negative values not allowed
Sorry, you don't get to play any more. Bye!
```

The message reveals which exception was handled.

Multiple Try Blocks

You have many choices about setting up try blocks. For example, you could handle the two function calls individually, placing each within its own try block. That allows you to program a different response for the two possible exceptions, as the following code shows:

```
while (cin >> x >> y)
{
    try {                      // try block #1
        z = hmean(x,y);
    }                          // end of try block #1
    catch (const char * s)    // start of catch block #1
    {
        cout << s << "\n";
        out << "Enter a new pair of numbers: ";
        ontinue;
    }                          // end of catch block #1
    cout << "Harmonic mean of " << x << " and " << y
        << " is " << z << "\n";
    try {                      // try block #2
        z = gmean(x,y);
    }                          // end of try block #2
    catch (const char * s)    // start of catch block #2
    {
        cout << s << "\n";
        cout << "Data entry terminated!\n";
        break;
    }                          // end of catch block #2
    cout << "Enter next set of numbers <q to quit>: ";
}
```

Another possibility is to nest try blocks, as the next example shows:

```
try {                          // outer try block
    while (cin >> x >> y)
    {
    try {                      // inner try block
        z = hmean(x,y);
    }                          // end of inner try block
    catch (const char * s)    // inner catch block
    {
    cout << s << "\n";
        cout << "Enter a new pair of numbers: ";
        continue;
    }                          // end of inner catch block
        cout << "Harmonic mean of " << x << " and " << y
```

```
                   << " is " << z << "\n";
         cout << "Geometric mean of " << x << " and " << y
                   << " is " << gmean(x,y) << "\n";
         cout << "Enter next set of numbers <q to quit>: ";
     }
}                                // end of outer try block
catch (const char * s)           // outer catch block
{
     cout << s << "\n";
     cout << "Sorry, you don't get to play any more. ";
}                                // end of outer catch block
```

Here an exception thrown by hmean() gets caught by the inner exception handler, which allows the loop to continue. But an exception thrown by gmean() gets caught by the outer exception handler, which terminates the loop.

Unwinding the Stack

Suppose a try block doesn't contain a direct call to a function throwing an exception but that it calls a function that calls a function that throws an exception. Execution still jumps from the function in which the exception is thrown to the function containing the try block and handlers. Doing so involves *unwinding the stack*, which we'll discuss now.

First, let's look at how C++ normally handles function calls and returns. C++ typically handles function calls by placing information on a stack (Chapter 9, "Memory Models and Namespaces"). In particular, a program places the address of a calling function instruction (a *return address*) on the stack. When the called function completes, the program uses this address to determine where to continue with program execution. Also, the function call places any function arguments on the stack, where they are treated as automatic variables. If the called function creates any new automatic variables, they, too, are added to the stack. If a called function calls another function, its information is added to the stack, and so on. When a function terminates, program execution passes to the address stored when the function was called, and the top of the stack is freed. Thus a function normally returns to the function that called it, and so on, with each function liberating its automatic variables as it terminates. If an automatic variable is a class object, then the class destructor, if any, is called.

Now suppose a function terminates via an exception throw instead of via a return call. Again, the program frees memory from the stack. But instead of stopping at the first return address on the stack, the program continues freeing the stack until it reaches a return address that resides in a try block (see Figure 15.3). Control then passes to the exception handlers at the end of the block rather than to the first statement following the function call. This is the process called *unwinding the stack*. One very important feature of the throw mechanism is that, just as with function returns, the class destructors are called for any automatic class objects on the stack. However, a function return just processes objects put on the stack by that function, while the throw statement processes objects put on the stack by the entire sequence of function calls between the try block and the throw. Without the unwinding-the-stack feature, a throw would leave destructors uncalled for automatic class objects placed on the stack by intermediate function calls.

FIGURE 15.3

throw versus return.

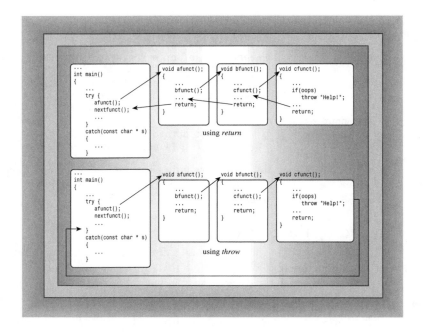

Listing 15.11 provides an example of unwinding the stack. In it, `main()` calls `details()`, and `details()` calls `hmean()`. When `hmean()` throws an exception, control returns all the way to `main()`, where it is caught. In the process, the automatic variables representing the arguments to `hmean()` and `details()` are freed.

LISTING 15.11 error5.cpp

```cpp
//error5.cpp
#include <iostream>
using namespace std;
double hmean(double a, double b) throw(const char *);
void details(double a, double b) throw(const char *);
int main()
{
    double x, y;

    cout << "Enter two numbers: ";
    try {
        while (cin >> x >> y)
            details(x,y);
    }
    catch (const char * s)
    {
        cout << s << "\n";
        cout << "Sorry, you can't play anymore. ";
    }
```

LISTING 15.11 *Continued*

```
        cout << "Bye!\n";
        return 0;
}

void details(double a, double b) throw(const char *){
    cout << "Harmonic mean of " << a << " and " << b
        << " is " << hmean(a,b) << "\n";
    cout << "Enter next set of numbers <q to quit>: ";
}

double hmean(double a, double b) throw(const char *)
{
    if (a == -b)
        throw "bad hmean() arguments: a = -b not allowed";
    return 2.0 * a * b / (a + b);
}
```

Here's a sample run; note that throwing the exception skips directly to `main()`, keeping `details()` from displaying the text that otherwise would have been displayed had `hmean()` terminated normally.

```
Enter two numbers: 3 15
Harmonic mean of 3 and 15 is 5
Enter next set of numbers <q to quit>: 20 -20
bad hmean() arguments: a = -b not allowed
Sorry, you don't get to play any more. Bye!
```

More Options

You can set up a handler to catch any kind of exception. Also, if a try block is nested, you can have its handlers pass control on up to the handlers for the containing try block.

To catch any exception, use the ellipses for the exception type:

```
catch (...) { // statements }
```

To pass control to a containing try block, use `throw` without a following exception:

```
catch (const char * s)
{
        cout << "Exception caught in inner loop.\n";
        throw;  // send to containing try block
}
```

This sample, for example, prints a message, then passes control to the containing try block, where the program once again will look for a handler matching the original thrown exception.

Note that there is more than one way for one try block to contain another. One way is to nest one within another, as discussed earlier. Another way is for one try block to contain a function call that invokes a function containing a try block. In the first case, the preceding sample code would pass control to the outer try block. In the second case, the sample code would cause the program to unwind the stack to find the next try block.

Exceptions and Classes

Exceptions aren't just for handling error conditions in regular functions. They also can be part of a class design. For example, a constructor could throw an exception if a call to the **new** operator fails. Or the overloaded [ ] operator for an array class can throw an exception if an index is out of range. Often it's useful if the exception can carry information with it, such as the value of an invalid index. One could use, say, a type **int** exception in that case, but it's more useful to throw an exception that's an object. The type of object will help identify the source of the exception. The earlier example with **hmean()** and **qmean()** had the problem that both went through the same type (**char char ***) of exception, making it cumbersome to set up catch blocks that discriminate between the two. By using objects, you can design a different type object for each exception you wish to catch. And the object itself can carry the needful information.

Tip

If you have a function throw an exception, define an exception class to be used as the type of exception thrown.

In fact, the usual practice in using exceptions is to throw objects as exceptions and to catch them by reference:

```
class problem {...};
...
void super() throw (problem &)
{
    ...
    if (oh_no)
    {
        problem oops(); // construct object
        throw oops;     // throw it
    ...
}
...
try {
    super();
}
catch(problem & p)
{
...
}
```

Incidentally, while the throw-catch mechanism is much like function argument passing, there are a few differences. For example, the compiler always creates a temporary copy when throwing an exception, so in the preceding sample code, **p** would refer to a copy of **oops** rather than **oops**. That's a good thing, because **oops** no longer exists after **super()** terminates. Often it is simpler to combine construction with the throw:

```
throw problem();     // construct and throw type problem object
```

When exceptions refer to class processes, it's often useful if the exception type is defined as a nested class. Not only does this make the exception type indicate the class originating an exception, it helps prevent name conflicts. For example, suppose you have a class called `ArrayDbE` in which you publicly declare another class called `BadIndex`. If the `[]` operator finds a bad index value, it can throw an exception of type `BadIndex`. Then a handler for this exception would look like this:

```
catch (ArrayDbE::BadIndex &) { ...}
```

The `ArrayDbE::` qualifier identifies `BadIndex` as being declared in the `ArrayDbE` class. It also informs a reader that this handler is intended for exceptions generated by `ArrayDbE` objects. The `BadIndex` name gives the reader a pretty good idea as to the nature of the exception. This sounds rather attractive, so let's develop the idea. In particular, let's add exceptions to the `ArrayDb` class first developed in Chapter 14, "Reusing Code in C++."

To the header file, add an exception `BadIndex` class, that is, a class defining objects to be thrown as exceptions. As outlined earlier, it will be used for bad index values, and it will hold the value of the bad index. Note that the nested class declaration just describes the class; it doesn't create objects. The class methods will create objects of this class if they throw exceptions of the `BadIndex` type. Also note that the nested class is public. This allows the catch blocks to have access to the type. Listing 15.12 shows the new header file. The rest of the definition, aside from changing the class name, is the same as the definition of `ArrayDb` in Chapter 14, except that it qualifies the method prototypes to indicate which exceptions they can throw. That is, it replaces

```
virtual double & operator[](int i);
```

with

```
virtual double & operator[](int i) throw(ArrayDbe::BadIndex &);
```

and so on. (As with ordinary function arguments, it's usually better to pass references instead of objects when throwing exceptions.)

LISTING 15.12   arraydbe.h

```
// arraydbe.h -- define array class with exceptions
#ifndef ARRAYDBE_H_
#define ARRAYDBE_H_
#include <iostream>
using namespace std;

class ArrayDbE
{
private:
    unsigned int size;  // number of array elements
protected:
    double * arr;       // address of first element
public:
    class BadIndex      // exception class for indexing problems
    {
```

LISTING 15.12   Continued

```
     private:
         int badindex;    // problematic index value
      public:
         BadIndex(int i) : badindex(i) {}
         virtual void Report() const;
    };
    ArrayDbE();                             // default constructor
    // create an ArrayDbE of n elements, set each to val
    ArrayDbE(unsigned int n, double val = 0.0);
    // create an ArrayDbE of n elements, initialize to array pn
    ArrayDbE(const double * pn, unsigned int n);
    // copy constructor
    ArrayDbE(const ArrayDbE & a);
    virtual ~ArrayDbE();                    // destructor
    unsigned int ArSize() const;            // returns array size
    double Average() const;                 // return array average
// overloaded operators
        // array indexing, allowing assignment
    virtual double & operator[](int i) throw(ArrayDbE::BadIndex &);
        // array indexing (no =)
    virtual const double & operator[](int i) const throw(ArrayDbE::BadIndex &);
    ArrayDbE & operator=(const ArrayDbE & a);
    friend ostream & operator<<(ostream & os, const ArrayDbE & a);
};

#endif
```

Next, you must provide the class methods. These are the same methods used in Chapter 12 with the addition of some exception throwing. Because the overloaded [] operators throw exceptions instead of calling the exit() function, the program no longer needs to include the cstdlib file. Listing 15.13 shows the result.

LISTING 15.13   arraydbe.cpp

```
// arraydbe.cpp -- ArrayDbE class methods
#include <iostream>
using namespace std;
#include "arraydbe.h"

// BadIndex method
void ArrayDbE::BadIndex::Report() const
{
    cerr << "Out of bounds index value: " << badindex << endl;
}

// ArrayDbE methods
// default constructor -- no arguments
ArrayDbE::ArrayDbE()
{
    arr = NULL;
```

LISTING 15.13 Continued

```
      size = 0;
}

// constructs array of n elements, each set to val
ArrayDbE::ArrayDbE(unsigned int n, double val)
{
    arr = new double[n];
    size = n;
    for (int i = 0; i < size; i++)
        arr[i] = val;
}

// initialize ArrayDbE object to a non-class array
ArrayDbE::ArrayDbE(const double *pn, unsigned int n)
{
    arr = new double[n];
    size = n;
    for (int i = 0; i < size; i++)
        arr[i] = pn[i];
}

// initialize ArrayDbE object to another ArrayDbE object
ArrayDbE::ArrayDbE(const ArrayDbE & a)
{
    size = a.size;
    arr = new double[size];
    for (int i = 0; i < size; i++)
        arr[i] = a.arr[i];
}

ArrayDbE::~ArrayDbE()
{
    delete [] arr;
}

double ArrayDbE::Average() const
{
    double sum = 0;
    int i;
    int lim = ArSize();
    for (i = 0; i < lim; i++)
        sum += arr[i];
    if (i > 0)
        return sum / i;
    else
    {
        cerr << "No entries in score array\n";
        return 0;
    }
}
```

LISTING 15.13 *Continued*

```cpp
// return array size
unsigned int ArrayDbE::ArSize() const
{
    return size;
}

// let user access elements by index (assignment allowed)
double & ArrayDbE::operator[](int i) throw(ArrayDbE::BadIndex &)
{
    // check index before continuing
    if (i < 0 || i >= size)
        throw BadIndex(i);
    return arr[i];
}

// let user access elements by index (assignment disallowed)
const double & ArrayDbE::operator[](int i)const throw(ArrayDbE::BadIndex &)
{
    // check index before continuing
    if (i < 0 || i >= size)
        throw BadIndex(i);
    return arr[i];
}

// define class assignment
ArrayDbE & ArrayDbE::operator=(const ArrayDbE & a)
{
    if (this == &a)       // if object assigned to self,
        return *this;     // don't change anything
    delete arr;
    size = a.size;
    arr = new double[size];
    for (int i = 0; i < size; i++)
        arr[i] = a.arr[i];
    return *this;
}

// quick output, 5 values to a line
ostream & operator<<(ostream & os, const ArrayDbE & a)
{
    int i;
    for (i = 0; i < a.size; i++)
    {
        os << a.arr[i] << " ";
        if (i % 5 == 4)
            os << "\n";
    }
    if (i % 5 != 0)
        os << "\n";
    return os;
}
```

Note that the exceptions now are objects instead of strings. Also note that these exception throws use the exception class constructor to create and initialize the exception objects:

```
if (i < 0 || i >= size)
        throw BadIndex(i);     // create, initialize a BadIndex object
```

What about catching this kind of exception? The exceptions are objects, not character strings, so the catch block has to reflect that fact. Also, because the exception is a nested type, the code needs to use the scope resolution operator.

```
try {
    ...
}
catch(ArrayDbE::BadIndex &) {
    ...
}
```

Listing 15.14 provides a short program demonstrating the process.

LISTING 15.14   exceptar.cpp

```
// exceptar.cpp -- use the ArrayDbE class
// Compile with arraydbe.cpp
#include <iostream>
using namespace std;
#include "arraydbe.h"

const int Players = 5;
int main()
{
    try {
        ArrayDbE Team(Players);
        cout << "Enter free-throw percentages for your 5 "
                "top players as a decimal fraction:\n";
        int player;
        for (player = 0; player < Players; player++)
        {
            cout << "Player " << (player + 1) << ": % = ";
            cin >> Team[player];
        }
        cout.precision(1);
        cout.setf(ios_base::showpoint);
        cout.setf(ios_base::fixed,ios_base::floatfield);
        cout << "Recapitulating, here are the percentages:\n";
        for (player = 0; player <= Players; player++)
            cout << "Player #" << (player + 1) << ": "
                    << 100.0 * Team[player] << "%\n";
    }                                      // end of try block
    catch (ArrayDbE::BadIndex & bi)        // start of handler
    {
        cout << "ArrayDbE exception:\n";
        bi.Report();
    }                                      // end of handler
```

LISTING 15.14   Continued

```
      cout << "Bye!\n";
      return 0;
}
```

Compatibility Note

Some compilers may not recognize the new form `ios_base::` and will require `ios::` instead.

Note the second `for` loop deliberately exceeds the array bounds, triggering an exception. Here is a sample run:

```
Enter free-throw percentages for your 5 top players as a decimal fraction:
Player 1: % = 0.923
Player 2: % = 0.858
Player 3: % = 0.821
Player 4: % = 0.744
Player 5: % = 0.697
Recapitulating, here are the percentages:
Player #1: 92.3%
Player #2: 85.8%
Player #3: 82.1%
Player #4: 74.4%
Player #5: 69.7%
ArrayDbE exception:
Out of bounds index value: 5
Bye!
```

Because the loop is inside the try block, throwing the exception terminates the loop as control passes to the second catch block following the try block.

By the way, remember that variables defined in a block, including a try block, are local to the block. For example, the variable `player` is undefined once program control passes beyond the try block in Listing 15.15.

Exceptions and Inheritance

Inheritance interacts with exceptions in a couple of ways. First, if a class has publicly nested exception classes, a derived class inherits those exception classes. Second, you can derive new exception classes from existing ones. We'll look at both these possibilities in the next example.

First, derive a `LimitArE` class from the `ArrayDbE` class. The `LimitArE` class will allow for array indexing to begin with values other than 0. This can be accomplished by storing a value representing the starting index and by redefining the functions. Internally, the array indexing still will begin with 0. But if, say, you specify 1900 as the starting index, the `operator[]()` method will translate an external index of 1908 to an internal index 1908—1900, or 8. Listing 15.15 shows the details.

The `BadIndex` exception declared in the `ArrayDbE` class stored the offending index value. With variable index limits, it would be nice if the exception also stored the correct range for indices. You can accomplish this by deriving a new exception class from `BadIndex`:

```
class SonOfBad : public ArrayDbE::BadIndex
{
private:
    int l_lim;
    int u_lim;
public:
    SonOfBad(int i, int l, int u) : BadIndex(i),
            l_lim(l), u_lim(u) {}
    void Report() const;   // redefines Report()
};
```

You can nest the `SonOfBad` declaration in the `LimitArE` declaration. Listing 15.15 shows the result.

LISTING 15.15   `limarre.h`

```
// limarre.h -- LimitArE class with exceptions

#ifndef LIMARRE_H_
#define LIMARRE_H_

#include "arraydbe.h"

class LimitArE : public ArrayDbE
{
public:
    class SonOfBad : public ArrayDbE::BadIndex
    {
    private:
        int l_lim;
        int u_lim;
    public:
        SonOfBad(int i, int l, int u) : BadIndex(i),
                l_lim(l), u_lim(u) {}
        void Report() const;
    };
private:
    unsigned int low_bnd;            // new data member
protected:
    // handle bounds checking
    virtual void ok(int i) const throw(ArrayDbE::BadIndex &);
public:
// constructors
    LimitArE() : ArrayDbE(), low_bnd(0) {}
    LimitArE(unsigned int n, double val = 0.0)
                : ArrayDbE(n,val), low_bnd(0) {}
    LimitArE(unsigned int n, int lb, double val = 0.0)
                : ArrayDbE(n, val), low_bnd(lb) {}
```

LISTING 15.15   Continued

```
        LimitArE(const double * pn, unsigned int n)
                    : ArrayDbE(pn, n), low_bnd(0) {}
        LimitArE(const ArrayDbE & a) : ArrayDbE(a), low_bnd(0) {}
// new methods
        void new_lb(int lb) {low_bnd = lb;}      // reset lower bound
        int lbound() {return low_bnd;}           // return lower bound
        int ubound() {return ArSize() + low_bnd - 1;} // upper bound
// redefined operators
        double & operator[](int i) throw(ArrayDbE::BadIndex &);
        const double & operator[](int i) const throw(ArrayDbE::BadIndex &);
};
#endif
```

This design moves index checking from the overloaded [] methods to an ok() method that's called by the overloaded [] methods. C++ requires that the throw specification for virtual method redefined in the derived class match the throw specification in the base class. However, a base class reference can refer to a derived object. Therefore, although the LimitArE::ok() method throws a SonOfBad exception, the throw specifiers can list the ArrayDbe::BadIndex class. Listing 15.16 shows the class methods.

LISTING 15.16   limarre.cpp

```
// limarre.cpp
#include "limarre.h"
#include <iostream>
using namespace std;

// BadIndex method
void LimitArE::SonOfBad::Report() const
{
    ArrayDbE::BadIndex::Report();
    cerr << "Index should be in the range " << l_lim
         << " through " << u_lim << endl;
}

//limarre methods
// private method
    // lower bound for array index is now low_bnd, and
    // upper bound is now low_bnd + size - 1
void LimitArE::ok(int i) const throw(ArrayDbE::BadIndex &)
{
    unsigned long size = ArSize();
    if (i < low_bnd || i >= size + low_bnd)
        throw SonOfBad(i, low_bnd, low_bnd + size - 1);
}

// redefined operators
double & LimitArE::operator[](int i) throw(ArrayDbE::BadIndex &)
{
    ok(i);
```

LISTING 15.16   Continued

```
        return arr[i - low_bnd];
    }

    const double & LimitArE::operator[](int i) const throw(ArrayDbE::BadIndex &)
    {
        ok(i);
        return arr[i - low_bnd];
    }
}
```

Suppose you have a program with both **ArrayDbE** and **LimitArE** objects. Then you would want a try block that catches the two possible exceptions: **BadIndex** and **SonOfBad**. You can do that by following the try block with two consecutive catch blocks:

```
try {
    LimitArE income(Years, FirstYear);
    ArrayDbE busywork(Years);
    ...
}   // end of try block
catch (LimitArE::SonOfBad & bi)    // 1st handler
{
    ...
}
catch (ArrayDbE::BadIndex & bi)    // 2nd handler
{
    ...
}
```

When there is a sequence of catch blocks, a program attempts to match a thrown exception to the first catch block, then the second catch block, and so on. As soon as there's a match, the program executes that catch block. Providing the code in the catch block doesn't terminate the program or generate another throw; the program jumps to the statement following the final catch block after completing any one catch block in the sequence.

This particular sequence of catch blocks has an interesting property—a catch block with a **BadIndex** reference can catch either a **BadIndex** exception or a **SonOfBad** exception. That's because a base class reference can refer to a derived object. However, a catch block with a **SonOfBad** reference can't catch a **BadIndex** object. That's because a derived object reference can't refer to a base class object without an explicit type cast. This state of affairs suggests placing the **SonOfBad** catch block above the **BadIndex** catch block. That way, the **SonOfBad** catch block will catch a **SonOfBad** exception while passing a **BadIndex** exception on to the next catch block. The program in Listing 15.17 illustrates this approach.

LISTING 15.17   excptinh.cpp

```
// excptinh.cpp -- use the ArrayDbE and LimitArE classes
// Compile with arraydbe.cpp, limarre.cpp
#include <iostream>
using namespace std;
```

LISTING 15.17 *Continued*

```cpp
#include "arraydbe.h"
#include "limarre.h"

const int Years = 4;
const int FirstYear = 2001;
int main()
{
    int year;
    double total = 0;
    try {
        LimitArE income(Years, FirstYear);
        ArrayDbE busywork(Years);
        cout << "Enter your income for the last " << Years
             << " years:\n";
        for (year = FirstYear; year < FirstYear + Years; year++)
        {
            cout << "Year " << year << ": $";
            cin >> income[year];
            busywork[year - FirstYear] = 0.2 * income[year];
        }
        cout.precision(2);
        cout.setf(ios::showpoint);
        cout.setf(ios::fixed,ios::floatfield);
        cout << "Recapitulating, here are the figures:\n";
        for (year = FirstYear; year <= FirstYear + Years; year++)
        {
            cout << year << ": $" << income[year] << "\n";
            total += income[year];
        }
        cout << "busywork values: " << busywork;
    }   // end of try block
    catch (LimitArE::SonOfBad & bi)    // 1st handler
    {
        cout << "LimitArE exception:\n";
        bi.Report();
    }
    catch (ArrayDbE::BadIndex & bi)    // 2nd handler
    {
        cout << "ArrayDbE exception:\n";
        bi.Report();
    }
    cout << "Total income for " << (year - FirstYear)
         << " years is $" << total << ".\n";
    cout << "Bye!\n";
    return 0;
}
```

Compatibility Note

Some compilers may not recognize the new form `ios_base::` and will require `ios::` instead.

Here is a sample run:

```
Enter your income for the last 4 years:
Year 2001: $54000
Year 2002: $28000
Year 2003: $92000
Year 2004: $37000
Recapitulating, here are the figures:
2001: $54000.00
2002: $28000.00
2003: $92000.00
2004: $37000.00
LimitArE exception:
Out of bounds index value: 2005
Index should be in the range 2001 through 2004
Total income for 4 years is $211000.00.Bye!
```

The **SonOfBad** exception terminated execution of the try block and transferred execution to the second catch block. Once the program finished processing the catch block, it jumped to the first statement following the catch blocks.

The following tip summarizes this example's main lesson.

Tip

If you have an inheritance hierarchy of exception classes, arrange the order of the catch blocks so the most derived class exception is caught first and the base class exception is caught last.

The exception Class

The main intent for C++ exceptions is to provide language-level support for designing fault-tolerant programs. That is, exceptions make it easier to incorporate error handling into a program design rather than tacking on some more rigid form of error handling as an afterthought. The flexibility and relative convenience of exceptions should encourage programmers to integrate fault handling into the program design process, if appropriate. In short, exceptions are the kind of feature that, like classes, can modify your approach to programming.

Newer C++ compilers are incorporating exceptions into the language. For example, the **exception** header file (formerly **exception.h** or **except.h**) defines an **exception** class that C++ uses as a base class for other exception classes used to support the language. Your code, too, can throw an **exception** object or use the **exception** class as a base class. One virtual member function is named **what()**, and it returns a string, the nature of which is implementation-dependent. But if you derive a class, you then can choose what string you want returned. For example, you could replace the **BadIndex** declaration with one based on the **exception** class. Because the contents of the **exception** header file are part of the **std** namespace, you can make them available with a using directive:

```
#include <exception>
using namespace std;
```

```
class ArrayDbE
{
private:
    unsigned int size;   // number of array elements
protected:
    double * arr;        // address of first element
public:
    class OutOfBounds : public exception
    {
    public:
        OutOfBounds() : exception() {};
        const char * what() {return "Array limit out of bounds\n";}
    };
    ...
};
```

Then you could have the overloaded [] methods throw an `OutOfBounds` exception, have a program using the class catch that type of exception, and use the `what()` method to identify the problem:

```
catch (ArrayDbE::OutOfBounds & ob)    //  handler
{
    cout << "ArrayDbE exception: "
            << ob.what() << endl;
}
```

By the way, instead of making all the exception class declarations available with a using directive, you could use the scope resolution operator:

```
class OutOfBounds : public std::exception
```

The `bad_alloc` Exception and new

C++ gives implementations two choices for handling memory allocation problems when using new. The first choice, and once the only choice, is to have new return the null pointer if it can't satisfy a memory request. The second choice is to have new throw a `bad_alloc` exception. The new header (formerly new.h) includes a declaration for the `bad_alloc` class, which is publicly derived from the `exception` class. An implementation may offer just one choice or, perhaps by using a compiler switch or some other method, let you choose the approach you prefer.

Listing 15.18 straddles the issue by trying both approaches. If the exception is caught, the program displays the implementation-dependent message returned by the inherited `what()` method and terminates early. Otherwise, it proceeds to see if the return value was the null pointer. (The purpose here is to show the two ways to check for memory allocation errors, not to suggest that a typical program would actually use both methods.)

LISTING 15.18   newexcp.cpp

```
// newexcp.cpp -- the bad_alloc exception
#include <iostream>
using namespace std;
```

LISTING 15.18   *Continued*

```
#include <new>
#include <cstdlib>

struct Big
{
    double stuff[2000];
};

int main()
{
    Big * pb;
    try {
        cout << "Trying to get a big block of memory:\n";
        pb = new Big[10000];
        cout << "Got past the new request:\n";
    }
    catch (bad_alloc & ba)
    {
        cout << "Caught the exception!\n";
        cout << ba.what() << endl;
        exit(1);
    }
    if (pb != 0)
    {
        pb[0].stuff[0] = 4;
        cout << pb[0].stuff[0] << endl;
    }
    else
        cout << "pb is null pointer\n";
    delete [] pb;
    return 0;
}
```

When Exceptions Go Astray

After an exception has been thrown, it has two opportunities to cause problems. First, if it is thrown in a function having an exception specification, it has to match one of the types in the specification list. If it doesn't, the unmatched exception is branded an *unexpected exception*, and, by default, it causes the program to abort. If the exception passes this first hurdle (or avoids it because the function lacks an exception specification), it then has to be caught. If it isn't, which can happen if there is no containing try block or no matching catch block, the exception is branded an *uncaught exception*, and, by default, it causes the program to abort. However, you can alter a program's response to unexpected and uncaught exceptions. Let's see how, beginning with uncaught exceptions.

An uncaught exception doesn't initiate an immediate abort. Instead, the program first calls a function called `terminate()`. By default, `terminate()` calls the `abort()` function. You can modify the behavior of `terminate()` by *registering* a function that `terminate()` should call instead of `abort()`. To do this, call the `set_terminate()` function. Both `set_terminate()` and `terminate()` are declared in the `exception` header file:

```
typedef void (*terminate_handler)();
terminate_handler set_terminate(terminate_handler f) throw();
void terminate();
```

The `set_terminate()` function takes, as its argument, the name of a function (that is, its address) having no arguments and the `void` return type. It returns the address of the previously registered function. If you call the `set_terminate()` function more than once, `terminate()` calls the function set by the most recent call to `set_terminate()`.

Let's look at an example. Suppose you want an uncaught exception to cause a program to print a message to that effect and then call the `exit()` function, providing an exit status value of 5. First, include the `exception` header file. You can make its declarations available with a using directive or appropriate using declarations, or you can use the `std::` qualifier.

```
#include <exception>
using namespace std;
```

Next, design a function that does the two required actions and has the proper prototype:

```
void myQuit()
{
    cout << "Terminating due to uncaught exception\n";
    exit(5);
}
```

Finally, at the start of your program, designate this function as your chosen termination action:

```
set_terminate(myQuit);
```

Next, let's look at unexpected exceptions. By using exception specifications for a function, you provide the means for users of the functions to know which exceptions to catch. That is, suppose you have the following prototype:

```
double Argh(double, double) throw(exception &);
```

Then you might use the function this way:

```
try {
    x = Argh(a, b);
}
catch(exception & ex)
{
    ...
}
```

It's good to know which exceptions to catch; recall that an uncaught exception, by default, aborts the program.

However, there's a bit more to the story. In principle, the exception specification should include exceptions thrown by functions called by the function in question. For example, if `Argh()` calls a `Duh()` function that can throw a `retort` object exception, then `retort` should appear in the `Argh()` exception specification as well as in the `Duh()` exception specification.

Unless you write all the functions yourself and are careful, there's no guarantee this will get done correctly. You might, for example, use an older commercial library whose functions don't have exception specifications. This suggests looking more closely at what happens if a function does throw an exception not in its exception specification.

The behavior is much like that for uncaught exceptions. If there is an unexpected exception, the program calls the `unexpected()` function. (You didn't expect the `unexpected()` function? No one expects the `unexpected()` function!) This function, in turn, calls `terminate()`, which, by default, calls `abort()`. Just as there is a `set_terminate()` function that modifies the behavior of `terminate()`, there is a `set_unexpected()` function that modifies the behavior of `unexpected()`; these new functions also are declared in the exception header file:

```
typedef void (*unexpected_handler)();
unexpected_handler set_unexpected(unexpected_handler f) throw();
void unexpected();
```

However, the behavior of the function you supply `set_unexpected()` is more regulated than that of a function for `set_terminate()`. In particular, the `unexpected_handler` function has the following choices:

- It can end the program by calling `terminate()` (the default behavior), `abort()`, or `exit()`.

- It can throw an exception.

The result of throwing an exception (the second choice above) depends upon the exception thrown by the replacement `unexpected_handler` function and the original exception specification for the function that threw the unexpected type:

- If the newly thrown exception matches the original exception specification, then the program proceeds normally from there; that is, it will look for a catch block matching the newly thrown exception. Basically, this approach replaces an exception of an unexpected type to an exception of an expected type.

- If the newly thrown exception does not match the original exception specification and if the exception specification *does not* include the `std::bad_exception` type, the program calls `terminate()`. The `bad_exception` type derives from the `exception` type and is declared in the `exception` header file.

- If the newly thrown exception does not match the original exception specification and if the original exception specification *does* include the `std::bad_exception` type, the unmatched exception is replaced with an exception of the `std::bad_exception` type.

In short, if you'd like to catch all exceptions, expected or otherwise, you can do something along these lines:

First, make sure the exception header file declarations are available:

```
#include <exception>
using namespace std;
```

Next, design a replacement function that converts unexpected exceptions to the **bad_exception** type and that has the proper prototype:

```
void myUnexpected()
{
    throw std::bad_exception();   //or just throw;
}
```

Just using **throw** without an exception rethrows the original exception. However, it will be replaced with a **bad_exception** object if the exception specification includes that type.

Next, at the start of your program, designate this function as your chosen unexpected exception action:

```
set_unexpected(myUnexpeced);
```

Finally, include the **bad_exception** type in exception specifications and catch block sequences:

```
double Argh(double, double) throw(exception &, bad_exception &);
...
try {
    x = Argh(a, b);
}
catch(exception & ex)
{
    ...
}
catch(bad_exception & ex)
{
    ...
}
```

Exception Cautions

From the preceding discussion of using exceptions, you might gather (and gather correctly) that exception handling should be designed into a program rather than tacked on. It has some disadvantages. For example, using exceptions adds to the size and subtracts from the speed of a program. Exception specifications don't work well with templates, because template functions might throw different kinds of exceptions depending upon the particular specialization used. Exceptions and dynamic memory allocation don't always work that well together.

Let's look a little further at dynamic memory allocation and exceptions. First, consider the following function:

```
void test1(int n)
{
    String mesg("I'm trapped in an endless loop");
    ...
    if (oh_no)
        throw exception();
    ...
    return;
}
```

The `String` class, recall, used dynamic memory allocation. Normally, the `String` destructor for `mesg` would be called when the function reached return and terminated. Thanks to stack unwinding, the throw statement, even though it terminates the function prematurely, still allows the destructor to be called. So here memory is managed properly.

Now consider this function:

```
void test2(int n)
{
    double * ar = new double[n];
    ...
    if (oh_no)
        throw exception();
    ...
    delete [] ar;
    return;
}
```

Here there is a problem. Unwinding the stack removes the variable `ar` from the stack. But the premature termination of the function means the `delete [ ]` statement at the end of the function is skipped. The pointer is gone, but the memory block it pointed to is still intact and inaccessible. In short, there is a memory leak.

The leak can be avoided. For example, you can catch the exception in the same function that throws it, put some cleanup code into the catch block, then rethrow the exception:

```
void test3(int n)
{
    double * ar = new double[n];
    ...
    try {
        if (oh_no)
            throw exception();
    }
    catch(exception & ex)
    {
        delete [] ar;
        throw;
    }
    ...
    delete [] ar;
    return;
}
```

However, this clearly enhances the opportunities for oversights and other errors. Another solution is to use the `auto_ptr` template discussed in Chapter 16, "The String Class and the Standard Template Library."

In short, while exception handling is extremely important for some projects, it does have costs in programming effort, program size, and program speed. Also, compiler exception support and user experience have not yet reached the mature level. So you might want to use this feature with moderation.

Real World Note: Exception Handling

In modern libraries, exception handling can appear to reach new levels of complexity—much of it due to undocumented or poorly documented exception handling routines. Anyone familiar with the use of a modern operating system has surely seen the errors and problems caused by unhandled exceptions. The programmers behind these errors often face an uphill battle, learning the complexity that lies within the libraries: what exceptions are thrown, why and when they occur, and how to handle them.

The novice programmer quickly finds the research battle to understand exception handling in a library is as difficult as the struggle to learn the language itself; modern libraries can contain routines and paradigms as alien and difficult as any C++ syntax detail. Exposure to and understanding the intricacies of your libraries and classes is, for good software, as necessary as the time you spend learning C++ itself. The exception and error-handling details you decipher from your libraries' documentation and source code will always serve you, and your software, in good stead.

RTTI

RTTI is short for runtime type information. It's one of the more recent additions to C++ and isn't supported by many older implementations. Other implementations may have compiler settings for turning RTTI on and off. The intent of RTTI is to provide a standard way for a program to determine the type of object during runtime. Many class libraries have already provided ways to do so for their own class objects, but in the absence of built-in support in C++, each vendor's mechanism typically is incompatible with those of other vendors. Creating a language standard for RTTI should allow future libraries to be compatible with each other.

What's It For?

Suppose you have a hierarchy of classes descended from a common base. You can set a base class pointer to point to an object of any of the classes in this hierarchy. Next, you call a function that, after processing some information, selects one of these classes, creates an object of that type, and returns its address, which gets assigned to a base class pointer. How can you tell what kind of object it points to?

Before answering this question, let's think about why you would want to know the type. Perhaps you want to invoke the correct version of a class method. If that's the case, you don't really need to know the object type as long as that function is a virtual function possessed by all members of the class hierarchy. But it could be that a derived object has an uninherited method. In that case, only some objects could use the method. Or maybe, for debugging purposes, you would like to keep track of which kinds of objects were generated. For these last two cases, RTTI provides an answer.

How Does It Work?

C++ has three components supporting RTTI:

- The `dynamic_cast` operator generates a pointer to a derived type from a pointer to a base type, if possible. Otherwise, the operator returns 0, the null pointer.

- The `typeid` operator returns a value identifying the exact type of an object.

- A `type_info` structure holds information about a particular type.

You can use RTTI only with a class hierarchy having virtual functions. The reason for this is that these are the only class hierarchies for which you should be assigning the addresses of derived objects to base class pointers.

Caution

RTTI works only for classes with virtual functions.

Let's examine the three components of RTTI.

The `dynamic_cast` Operator

The `dynamic_cast` operator is intended to be the most heavily used RTTI component. It doesn't answer the question of what type of object a pointer points to. Instead, it answers the question of whether you can safely assign the address of the object to a pointer of a particular type. Let's see what that means. Suppose you have the following hierarchy:

```
class Grand { // has virtual methods};
class Superb : public Grand { ... };
class Magnificent : public Superb { ... };
```

Next, suppose you have the following pointers:

```
Grand * pg = new Grand;
Grand * ps = new Superb;
Grand * pm = new Magnificent;
```

Finally, consider the following type casts:

```
Magnificent * p1 = (Magnificent *) pm;      // #1
Magnificent * p2 = (Magnificent *) pg;      // #2
Superb * p3 = (Magnificent *) pm;           // #3
```

Which of the previous type casts are safe? Depending upon the class declarations, all of them could be safe, but the only ones guaranteed to be safe are the ones in which the pointer is the same type as the object or else a direct or indirect base type for the object. For example, type cast #1 is safe because it sets a type `Magnificent` pointer to point to a type `Magnificent` object. Type cast #2 is not safe because it assigns the address of a base object (`Grand`) to a derived class (`Magnificent`) pointer. Thus, the program would expect the base class object to have derived class properties, and that, in general, is false. A `Magnificent` object, for example, might have data members that a `Grand` object would lack. Type cast #3, however, is safe, because it assigns the address of a derived object to a base class pointer. That is, public derivation promises that a `Magnificent` object also is a `Superb` object (direct base) and a `Grand` object (indirect base). Thus, it's safe to assign its address to pointers of all three types. Virtual functions ensure that using pointers of any of the three types to a `Magnificent` object will invoke `Magnificent` methods.

Note that the question of whether a type conversion is safe is both more general and more useful than the question of what kind of object is pointed to. The usual reason for wanting to know the type is so that you can know if it's safe to invoke a particular method. You don't necessarily need an exact type match to invoke a method. The type can be a base type for which a virtual version of the method is defined. The next example will illustrate this point.

First, however, let's look at the **dynamic_cast** syntax. The operator is used like this, where **pg** points to an object:

```
Superb * pm = dynamic_cast<Superb *>(pg);
```

This asks the question, can the pointer **pg** be type cast safely (as described previously) to the type **Superb** *? If it can, the operator returns the address of the object. Otherwise it returns 0, the null pointer.

Remember

In general, the expression

```
dynamic_cast<Type *>(pt)
```

converts the pointer **pt** to a pointer of type **Type** * if the pointed-to object (***pt**) is of type **Type** or else derived directly or indirectly from type **Type**. Otherwise, the expression evaluates to 0, the null pointer.

Listing 15.19 illustrates the process. First, it defines three classes, coincidentally named **Grand**, **Superb**, and **Magnificent**. The **Grand** class defines a virtual **Speak()** function, which each of the other classes redefines. The **Superb** class defines a virtual **Say()** function, which **Magnificent** redefines (see Figure 15.4). The program defines a **GetOne()** function that randomly creates and initializes an object of one of these three types, then returns the address as a type **Grand** * pointer. (The **GetOne()** function simulates an interactive user making decisions.) A loop assigns this pointer to a type **Grand** * variable called **pg**, then uses **pg** to invoke the **Speak()** function. Because this function is virtual, the code correctly invokes the **Speak()** version appropriate to the pointed-to object:

```
for (int i = 0; i < 5; i++)
{
    pg = GetOne();
    pg->Speak();
    ...
}
```

However, you can't use this exact approach to invoke the **Say()** function; it's not defined for the **Grand** class. However, you can use the **dynamic_cast** operator to see if **pg** can be type cast to a pointer to **Superb**. This will be true if the object is either type **Superb** or **Magnificent**. In either case, you can invoke the **Say()** function safely:

```
if (ps = dynamic_cast<Superb *>(pg))
    ps->Say();
```

FIGURE 15.4

The Grand family of classes.

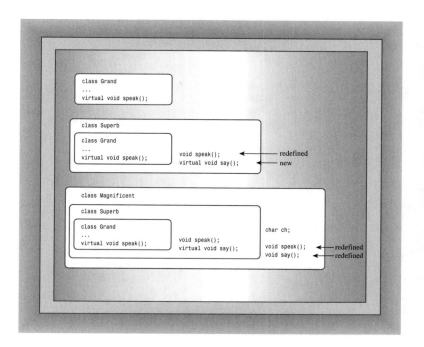

Recall that the value of an assignment expression is the value of its left-hand side. Thus, the value of the `if` condition is `ps`. If the type cast succeeds, `ps` is nonzero, or true. If the type cast fails, which it will if `pg` points to a Grand object, `ps` is zero, or false. Listing 15.19 shows the full code. (By the way, some compilers, noting that usually one uses the == operator in an `if` statement condition, may issue a warning about unintended assignment.)

LISTING 15.19   `rtti1.cpp`

```
// rtti1.cpp -- use the RTTI dynamic_cast operator
#include <iostream>
using namespace std;
#include <cstdlib>
#include <ctime>

class Grand
{
private:
    int hold;
public:
    Grand(int h = 0) : hold(h) {}
    virtual void Speak() const { cout << "I am a grand class!\n";}
    virtual int Value() const { return hold; }
};
```

LISTING 15.19 Continued

```cpp
class Superb : public Grand
{
public:
    Superb(int h = 0) : Grand(h) {}
    void Speak() const {cout << "I am a superb class!!\n"; }
    virtual void Say() const
        { cout << "I hold the superb value of " << Value() << "!\n";}
};

class Magnificent : public Superb
{
private:
    char ch;
public:
    Magnificent(int h = 0, char c = 'A') : Superb(h), ch(c) {}
    void Speak() const {cout << "I am a magnificent class!!!\n";}
    void Say() const {cout << "I hold the character " << ch <<
                " and the integer "  << Value() << "!\n"; }
};

Grand * GetOne();
int main()
{
    srand(time(0));
    Grand * pg;
    Superb * ps;
    for (int i = 0; i < 5; i++)
    {
        pg = GetOne();
        pg->Speak();
        if( ps = dynamic_cast<Superb *>(pg))
            ps->Say();
    }
    return 0;
}

Grand * GetOne()     // generate one of three kinds of objects randomly
{
    Grand * p;
    switch( rand() % 3)
    {
        case 0: p = new Grand(rand() % 100);
                break;
        case 1: p = new Superb(rand() % 100);
                break;
        case 2: p = new Magnificent(rand() % 100, 'A' + rand() % 26);
                break;
    }
    return p;
}
```

This program illustrates an important point. You should use virtual functions when possible and RTTI only when necessary. Here is a sample output:

```
I am a superb class!!
I hold the superb value of 68!
I am a magnificent class!!!
I hold the character R and the integer 68!
I am a magnificent class!!!
I hold the character D and the integer 12!
I am a magnificent class!!!
I hold the character V and the integer 59!
I am a grand class!
```

As you can see, the `Say()` methods were invoked just for the `Superb` and the `Magnificent` classes.

You can use `dynamic_cast` with references, too. The usage is slightly different; there is no reference value corresponding to the null-pointer type, hence there's no special reference value that can be used to indicate failure. Instead, when goaded by an improper request, `dynamic_cast` throws a type `bad_cast` exception, which is derived from the `exception` class and defined in the `typeinfo` header file. Thus, the operator can be used as follows, where `rg` is a reference to a `Grand` object:

```
#include <typeinfo> // for bad_cast
...
try {
    Superb & rs = dynamic_cast<Superb &>(rg);
    ...
}
catch(bad_cast &){
    ...
};
```

The `typeid` Operator and `type_info` Class

The `typeid` operator lets you determine if two objects are the same type. Somewhat like `sizeof`, it accepts two kinds of arguments:

- The name of a class

- An expression that evaluates to an object

The `typeid` operator returns a reference to a `type_info` object, where `type_info` is a class defined in the `typeinfo` header file (formerly `typeinfo.h`). The `type_info` class overloads the `==` and `!=` operators so that you can use these operators to compare types. For example, the expression

```
typeid(Magnificent) == typeid(*pg)
```

evaluates to the bool value true if pg points to a Magnificent object and to false otherwise. If pg happens to be a null pointer, the program will throw a bad_typeid exception. This exception type is derived from the exception class and is declared in the typeinfo header file.

The implementation of the type_info class will vary among vendors, but it will include a name() member that returns an implementation-dependent string that typically would be the name of the class. For example, the statement

```
cout << "Now processing type " << typeid(*pg).name() << ".\n";
```

displays the string defined for the class of the object to which the pointer pg points.

Listing 15.20 modifies Listing 15.19 so that it uses the typeid operator and the name() member function. Note that they are used for situations that dynamic_cast and virtual functions don't handle. The typeid test is used to select an action that isn't even a class method, so it can't be invoked by a class pointer. The name() method statement shows how the method can be used in debugging. Note that the program includes the typeinfo header file.

LISTING 15.20 rtti2.cpp

```
// rtti2.cpp  -- use dynamic_cast, typeid, and type_info
#include <iostream>
using namespace std;
#include <cstdlib>
#include <ctime>
#include <typeinfo>

class Grand
{
private:
    int hold;
public:
    Grand(int h = 0) : hold(h) {}
    virtual void Speak() const { cout << "I am a grand class!\n";}
    virtual int Value() const { return hold; }
};

class Superb : public Grand
{
public:
    Superb(int h = 0) : Grand(h) {}
    void Speak() const {cout << "I am a superb class!!\n"; }
    virtual void Say() const
        { cout << "I hold the superb value of " << Value() << "!\n";}
};

class Magnificent : public Superb
{
private:
    char ch;
public:
    Magnificent(int h = 0, char c = 'A') : Superb(h), ch(c) {}
```

LISTING 15.20   *Continued*

```
        void Speak() const {cout << "I am a magnificent class!!!\n";}
        void Say() const {cout << "I hold the character " << ch <<
                    " and the integer "  << Value() << "!\n"; }
};

Grand * GetOne();
int main()
{
    srand(time(0));
    Grand * pg;
    Superb * ps;
    for (int i = 0; i < 5; i++)
    {
        pg = GetOne();
        cout << "Now processing type " << typeid(*pg).name() << ".\n";
        pg->Speak();
        if( ps = dynamic_cast<Superb *>(pg))
            ps->Say();
        if (typeid(Magnificent) == typeid(*pg))
            cout << "Yes, you're really magnificent.\n";
    }
    return 0;
}

Grand * GetOne()
{
    Grand * p;

    switch( rand() % 3)
    {
        case 0: p = new Grand(rand() % 100);
                    break;
        case 1: p = new Superb(rand() % 100);
                    break;
        case 2: p = new Magnificent(rand() % 100, 'A' + rand() % 26);
                    break;
    }
    return p;
}
```

Here's a sample run:

```
Now processing type Magnificent.
I am a magnificent class!!!
I hold the character P and the integer 52!
Yes, you're really magnificent.
Now processing type Superb.
I am a superb class!!
I hold the superb value of 37!
Now processing type Grand.
I am a grand class!
Now processing type Superb.
```

```
I am a superb class!!
I hold the superb value of 18!
Now processing type Grand.
I am a grand class!
```

Misusing RTTI

RTTI has many vocal critics within the C++ community. They view RTTI as unnecessary, a potential source of program inefficiency, and as a possible contributor to bad programming practices. Without delving into the debate over RTTI, let's look at the sort of programming that you should avoid.

Consider the core of Listing 15.19:

```
Grand * pg;
Superb * ps;
for (int i = 0; i < 5; i++)
{
    pg = GetOne();
    pg->Speak();
    if( ps = dynamic_cast<Superb *>(pg))
        ps->Say();
}
```

By using `typeid` and ignoring `dynamic_cast` and virtual functions, you can rewrite this code as follows:

```
Grand * pg;
Superb * ps;
Magnificent * pm;
for (int i = 0; i < 5; i++)
{
    pg = GetOne();
    if (typeid(Magnificent) == typeid(*pg))
    {
        pm = (Magnificent *) pg;
        pm->Speak();
        pm->Say();
    }
    else if (typeid(Superb) == typeid(*pg))
    {
        ps = (Superb *) pg;
        ps->Speak();
        ps->Say();
    }
    else
        pg->Speak();
}
```

Not only is this uglier and longer than the original, it has the serious flaw of naming each class explicitly. Suppose, for example, that you find it necessary to derive an `Insufferable` class from the `Magnificent` class. The new class redefines `Speak()` and `Say()`. With the version that uses `typeid` to test explicitly for each type, you would have to modify the `for` loop code, adding a new `else if` section. The original version, however, requires no changes at all. The

```
pg->Speak();
```

statement works for all classes derived from `Grand`, and the

```
if( ps = dynamic_cast<Superb *>(pg))
    ps->Say();
```

statement works for all classes derived from `Superb`.

Tip

If you find yourself using `typeid` in an extended series of `if else` statements, check to see whether you should have been using virtual functions and `dynamic_cast`.

Type Cast Operators

The C cast operator, in Bjarne Stroustrup's view, is too lax. For example, consider the following:

```
struct Data
{
    double data[200];
};

struct Junk
{
    int junk[100];
};
Data d = {2.5e33, 3.5e-19, 20.2e32};
char * pch = (char *) (&d);   // typecast #1 - convert to string
char ch = char (&d);          // typecast #2 - convert address to a char
Junk * pj = (Junk *) (&d);    // typecast #3 - convert to Junk pointer
```

First, which of these three type casts makes any sense? Unless you resort to the implausible, none of them make much sense. Second, which of these three type casts are allowed? All of them are.

Stroustrup's response to this laxity was to add four type cast operators that provide more discipline for the casting process:

```
dynamic_cast
const_cast
static_cast
reinterpret_cast
```

Instead of using a general type cast, you can select an operator suited to a particular purpose. This documents the intended reason for the type cast and gives the compiler a chance to check that you did what you thought you did.

You've already seen the **dynamic_cast** operator. To summarize, suppose **High** and **Low** are two classes, that ph is type **High** * and pl is type **Low** *. Then the statement

```
pl = dynamic_cast<Low *> ph;
```

assigns a **Low** * pointer to pl only if **Low** is an accessible base class (direct or indirect) to **High**. Otherwise, the statement assigns the null pointer to pl. In general, the operator has this syntax:

```
dynamic_cast < type-name > (expression)
```

The purpose of this operator is to allow upcasts within a class hierarchy (such type casts being safe because of the *is-a* relationship) and to disallow other casts.

The **const_cast** operator is for making a type cast with the sole purpose of changing whether a value is **const** or **volatile** or not. It has the same syntax as the **dynamic_cast** operator:

```
const_cast < type-name > (expression)
```

The result making such a cast is an error if any other aspect of the type is altered. That is, *type_name* and *expression* must be of the same type except they can differ in the presence or absence of **const** or **volatile**. Again, suppose **High** and **Low** are two classes:

```
High bar;
const High * pbar;
    ...
High * pb = const_cast<High *> (pbar);    // valid
Low * pl = const_cast<Low *> (pbar);      // invalid
```

The first type cast makes *pb a pointer that can be used to alter the value of the bar object; it removes the **const** label. The second type cast is invalid, because it also attempts to change the type from **High** * to **Low** *.

The reason for this operator is that occasionally you may have a need for a value that is constant most of the time but which can be changed occasionally. Then you can declare the value as **const** and use **const_cast** when you need to alter the value. This could be done using the general cast, but the general cast can also simultaneously change the type:

```
High bar;
const High * pbar;
    ...
High * pb = (const High *) (pbar);    // valid
Low * pl = (const Low *) (pbar);      // also valid
```

Because the simultaneous change of type and constantness may be an unintentional programming slip, using the **const_cast** operator is safer.

The **const_cast** is not all powerful. It can change the pointer access to a quantity, but the effect of attempting to change a quantity that is declared **const** is undefined. Let's clarify this statement with the short example shown in Listing 15.21.

LISTING 15.21 constcast.cpp

```
// constcast.cpp
#include <iostream>
using std::cout;

void change(const int * pt, int n);

int main()
{
    int pop1 = 38383;
    const int pop2 = 2000;

    cout << "pop1, pop2: " << pop1 << ", " << pop2 << '\n';
    change(&pop1, -1);
    change(&pop2, -1);
    cout << "pop1, pop2: " << pop1 << ", " << pop2 << '\n';

    return 0;
}

void change(const int * pt, int n)
{
    int * pc;
    if (n < 0)
    {
        pc = const_cast<int *>(pt);
        *pc = 100;
    }
}
```

The `const_cast` operator can remove the `const` from `const int * pt`, thus allowing the compiler to accept the following statement in `change()`:

```
*pc = 100;
```

However, because `pop2` is declared as `const`, the compiler may protect it from any change, as is shown by the following sample output:

```
pop1, pop2: 38383, 2000
pop1, pop2: 100, 2000
```

As you can see, the calls to `change()` altered `pop1` but not `pop2`. (The particular compiler used here generated a temporary copy of `pop2` and assigned that address to `pc`, but, as mentioned, the standard says the behavior in this situation is undefined.)

The `static_cast` operator has the same syntax as the others:

```
static_cast < type-name > (expression)
```

It's valid only if *type_name* can be converted implicitly to the same type *expression* has, or vice versa. Otherwise, the cast is an error. Suppose `High` is a base class to `Low` and that `Pond` is an unrelated class. Then conversions from `High` to `Low` and `Low` to `High` are valid, but a conversion from `Low` to `Pond` is disallowed:

```
High bar;
Low blow;
...
High * pb = static_cast<High *> (&blow);      // valid upcast
Low * pl = static_cast<Low *> (&bar);         // valid downcast
Pond * pmer = static_cast<Pond *> (&blow);    // invalid, Pond unrelated
```

The first conversion is valid because an upcast can be done explicitly. The second conversion, from a base-class pointer to a derived-class pointer can't be done without an explicit type conversion. But because the type cast in the other direction can be made without a type cast, it's valid to use a `static_cast` for a downcast.

Similarly, because an enumeration value can be converted to an integral type without a type cast, an integral type can be converted to an enumeration value with `static_cast`. Similarly, you can use `static_cast` to convert `double` to `int`, `float` to `long`, and the various other numeric conversions.

The `reinterpret_cast` operator is for inherently risky type-casts. It won't let you cast away `const`, but it will do other unsavory things. Sometimes a programmer has to do implementation-dependent, unsavory things, and using the `reinterpret_cast` operator makes it simpler to keep track of such acts. It has the same syntax as the other three:

```
reinterpret_cast < type-name > (expression)
```

Here is a sample use:

```
struct dat {short a; short b};
long value = 0xA224B118;
dat * pd = reinterpret_cast< dat *) (&value);
cout << pd->a;    // display first 2 bytes of value
```

Typically, such casts would be used for low-level, implementation-dependent programming and would not be portable. For example, this code sample produces different output on an IBM-compatible than it does on a Macintosh because the two systems store the bytes in multi-byte integer types in opposite orders.

Summary

Friends allow you to develop a more flexible interface for classes. A class can have other functions, other classes, and member functions of other classes as friends. In some cases, you may need to use forward declarations and to exert care in the ordering of class declarations and methods in order to get friends to mesh properly.

Nested classes are classes declared within other classes. Nested classes facilitate the design of helper classes that implement other classes but needn't be part of a public interface.

The C++ exception mechanism provides a flexible way to deal with awkward programming events such as inappropriate values, failed I/O attempts, and the like. Throwing an exception terminates the function currently executing and transfers control to a matching catch block. Catch blocks immediately follow a try block, and for an exception to be caught, the function call that directly or indirectly led to the exception must be in the try block. The program then executes the code in the catch block. This code may attempt to fix the problem or it can terminate the program. A class can be designed with nested exception classes that can be thrown when problems specific to the class are detected. A function can include an exception specification identifying those exceptions that can be thrown in that function. Uncaught exceptions (those with no matching catch block) by default, terminate a program. So do unexpected exceptions (those not matching an exception specification.)

The RTTI (runtime type information) features allow a program to detect the type of an object. The `dynamic_cast` operator is used to cast a derived class pointer to a base class pointer; its main purpose is to ensure that it's okay to invoke a virtual function call. The `typeid` operator returns a `type_info` object. Two `typeid` return values can be compared to determine if an object is of a specific type, and the returned `type_info` object can be used to obtain information about an object.

The `dynamic_cast` operator, along with `static_cast`, `const_cast`, and `reinterpret_cast`, provide safer, better-documented type casts than the general cast mechanism.

Review Questions

1. What's wrong with the following attempts at establishing friends?

   a.

   ```
   class snap {
       friend clasp;
       ...
   };
   class clasp { ... };
   ```

   b.

   ```
   class cuff {
   public:
         void snip(muff &) { ... }
       ...
   };
   class muff {
       friend void cuff::snip(muff &);
       ...
   };
   ```

   c.

   ```
   class muff {
         friend void cuff::snip(muff &);
       ...
   };
   class cuff {
   public:
         void snip(muff &) { ... }
       ...
   };
   ```

2. You've seen how to create mutual class friends. Can you create a more restricted form of friendship in which only some members of class B are friends to class A and some members of A are friends to B? Explain.

3. What problems might the following nested class declaration have?

```
class Ribs
{
private:
    class Sauce
    {
        int soy;
        int sugar;
    public:
        Sauce(int s1, int s2) : soy(s1), sugar(s2) { }
    };
    ...
};
```

4. How does `throw` differ from `return`?

5. Suppose you have a hierarchy of exception classes derived from a base exception class. In what order should you place catch blocks?

6. Consider the `Grand`, `Superb`, and `Magnificent` classes defined in this chapter. Suppose `pg` is a type `Grand *` pointer assigned the address of an object of one of these three classes and that `ps` is a type `Superb *` pointer. What is the difference in how the following two code samples behave?

```
if (ps = dynamic_cast<Superb *>(pg))
    ps->say();   // sample #1

if (typeid(*pg) == typeid(Superb))
    (Superb *) pg)->say();  // sample #2
```

7. How is the `static_cast` operator different from the `dynamic_cast` operator?

Programming Exercises

1. Modify the `Tv` and `Remote` classes as follows:

   a. Make them mutual friends.

   b. Add a state variable member to the `Remote` class that describes whether the remote control is in normal or interactive mode.

   c. Add a `Remote` method that displays the mode.

   d. Provide the `Tv` class with a method for toggling the new `Remote` member. This method should work only if the `Tv` is in the on state.

   Write a short program testing these new features.

2. Modify Listing 15.10 so that `hmean()` throws an exception of type `hmeanexcp` and `gmean()` throws an exception of type `gmeanexcp`. Both of these exception types are to be classes derived from the `exception` class provided by the `<exception>` header file, and you should overload the `what()` method for each new class so that the message displayed by `what()` reports the function name and the nature of the problem. Also, upon catching an `hmeanexcp` exception, the program should prompt for a new data pair and continue with the loop, while upon catching a `gmeanexcp` exception, the program should break out of the loop and continue with the code following the loop.

THE string CLASS AND THE STANDARD TEMPLATE LIBRARY

You will learn about the following in this chapter:

- The standard C++ string class
- The auto_ptr template
- The Standard Template Library (STL)
- Container classes
- Iterators
- Function objects (functors)
- STL algorithms

By now you are familiar with the C++ goal of reusable code. One of the big payoffs is when you can reuse code written by others. That's where class libraries come in. There are many commercially available C++ class libraries, and there also are the libraries that come as part of the C++ package. For example, you've been using the input/output classes supported by the ostream header file. This chapter will look at other reusable code available for your programming pleasure. First, the chapter examines the string class, which simplifies programming with strings. Then it looks at auto_ptr, a "smart pointer" template class that makes managing dynamic memory a bit easier. Finally, it looks at the Standard Template Library (or STL), a collection of useful templates for handling various kinds of container objects. STL exemplifies a recent programming paradigm called generic programming.

The string Class

Many programming applications need to process strings. C provides some support with its string.h (cstring in C++) family of string functions, and many early C++ implementations provided home-grown classes to handle strings. Chapter 12, "Classes and Dynamic Memory Allocation," introduced a modest String class to illustrate some aspects of class design. ANSI/ISO C++ itself provides a more powerful version called the string class. It is supported by the string header file.(Note that the string.h and cstring header files support the C library string functions for C-style strings, not the string class.) The key to using a class is knowing its public interface, and the `string` class has an extensive set of methods, including several constructors, overloaded operators for assigning strings, concatenating strings, comparing strings, and accessing individual elements, as well as utilities for finding characters and substrings in a string, and more. In short, the `string` class has lots of stuff.

Constructing a String

Let's begin with looking at the `string` constructors. After all, one of the most important things to know about a class is what your options are when creating objects of that class. Listing 16.1 uses all six of the `string` constructors (labeled *ctor*, the traditional C++ abbreviation for constructor). Table 16.1 briefly describes the constructors in the order used in the program. The constructor representations are simplified in that they conceal the fact that `string` really is a `typedef` for a template specialization `basic_string<char>` and that they omit an optional argument relating to memory management. (This aspect is discussed later this chapter and in Appendix F, "The `String` Template Class.") The type `size_type` is an implementation-dependent integral type defined in the `string` header file. The class defines `string::npos` as the maximum possible length of the string. Typically, this would equal the maximum value of an `unsigned int`. Also, the table uses the common abbreviation NBTS for null-byte-terminated string, that is, the traditional C string, which is terminated with a null character.

TABLE 16.1   `string` Class Constructors

Constructor	Description
`string(const char * s)`	Initializes `string` object to NBTS pointed to by *s*.
`string(size_type n, char c)`	Creates a `string` object of *n* elements, each initialized to the character *c*.
`string(const string & str, string size_type pos = 0, size_type n = npos)`	Initializes `string` object to the object *str*, starting at position *pos* in *str* and going to end of *str* or using *n* characters, whichever comes first.
`string()`	Creates a default `string` object of 0 size.
`string(const char * s, size_type n)`	Initializes `string` object to NBTS pointed to by *s* and continues for *n* characters even if that exceeds the size of the NBTS.
`template<class Iter> string(Iter begin, Iter end)`	Initializes `string` object to the values in the range [*begin*, *end*), where *begin* and *end* act like pointers and specify locations; the range includes *begin* and is up to but not including *end*.

The program also uses the overloaded += operator, which appends one string to another, the overloaded = operator for assigning one string to another, the overloaded << operator for displaying a **string** object, and the overloaded [ ] operator for accessing an individual character in a string.

LISTING 16.1   str1.cpp

```
// str1.cpp -- introducing the string class
#include <iostream>
#include <string>
using namespace std;
// using string constructors

int main()
{
    string one("Lottery Winner!");      // ctor #1
    cout << one << endl;                 // overloaded <<
    string two(20, '$');                 // ctor #2
    cout << two << endl;
    string three(one);                   // ctor #3
    cout << three << endl;
    one += " Oops!";                     // overloaded +=
    cout << one << endl;
    two = "Sorry! That was ";
    three[0] = 'P';
    string four;                         // ctor #4
    four = two + three;                  // overloaded +, =
    cout << four << endl;
    char alls[] = "All's well that ends well";
    string five(alls,20);                // ctor #5
    cout << five << "!\n";
    string six(alls+6, alls + 10);       // ctor #6
    cout << six  << ", ";
    string seven(&five[6], &five[10]);// ctor #6 again
    cout << seven << "...\n";

    return 0;
}
```

	Compatibility Note

Some older **string** implementations do not support *ctor* #6.

Here is the program's output:

```
Lottery Winner!
$$$$$$$$$$$$$$$$$$$$
Lottery Winner!
Lottery Winner! Oops!
Sorry! That was Pottery Winner!
All's well that ends!
well, well...
```

Program Notes

The start of the program illustrates that you can initialize a **string** object to a regular C-style string and display it using the overloaded << operator:

```
string one("Lottery Winner!");    // ctor #1
cout << one << endl;              // overloaded <<
```

The next constructor initializes the **string** object **two** to a string consisting of 20 $ characters:

```
string two(20, '$');              // ctor #2
```

The copy constructor initializes the **string** object **three** to the **string** object **one**:

```
string three(one);                // ctor #3
```

The overloaded += operator appends the string " Oops!" to the string **one**:

```
one += " Oops!";                  // overloaded +=
```

This particular example appends a C-style string to a **string** object. However, the += operator is multiply overloaded so that you also can append **string** objects and single characters:

```
one += two;    // append a string object (not in program)
one += '!';    // append a type char value (not in program)
```

Similarly, the = operator is overloaded so that you can assign a **string** object to a **string** object, a C-style string to a **string** object, or a simple **char** value to a **string** object:

```
two = "Sorry! That was ";  // assign a C-style string
two = one;                 // assign a string object (not in program)
two = '?';                 // assign a char value (not in program)
```

Overloading the [ ] operator, as the **String** example in Chapter 13, "Class Inheritance," did, permits access to individual characters in a **string** object by using array notation:

```
three[0] = 'P';
```

A default constructor creates an empty string that later can be given a value:

```
string four;                      // ctor #4
four = two + three;               // overloaded +, =
```

The second line uses the overloaded + operator to create a temporary **string** object which is then assigned, using the overloaded = operator, to the **four** object. As you might expect, the + operator concatenates its two operands into a single **string** object. The operator is multiply overloaded so the second operand can be a **string** object or a C-style string or a **char** value.

The fifth constructor takes a C-style string and an integer as arguments, with the integer indicating how many characters to copy:

```
char alls[] = "All's well that ends well";
string five(alls,20);             // ctor #5
```

Here, as the output shows, just the first 20 characters ("All's well that ends") are used to initialize the **five** object. As Table 16.1 notes, if the character count exceeds the length of the C-style string, the requested number of characters are still copied. So replacing 20 with 40 in the above example would result in 15 junk characters being copied at the end of `five`. (That is, the constructor would interpret the contents in memory following the string "All's well that ends well" as character codes.)

The sixth constructor has a template argument:

```
template<class Iter> string(Iter begin, Iter end);
```

The intent is that *begin* and *end* act like pointers pointing to two locations in memory. (In general, *begin* and *end* can be iterators, generalizations of pointers extensively used in the STL.) The constructor then uses the values between the locations pointed to by *begin* and *end* to initialize the `string` object it constructs. The notation `[begin,end)`, borrowed from mathematics, means the range includes *begin* but doesn't include *end*. That is, *end* points to a location one past the last value to be used. Consider the following statement:

```
string six(alls+6, alls + 10);    // ctor #6
```

Because the name of an array is a pointer, both `alls + 6` and `alls + 10` are type `char *`, so the template is used with `Iter` replaced by type `char *`. The first argument points to the first `w` in the `alls` array, and the second argument points to the space following the first `well`. Thus, `six` is initialized to the string `"well"`. Figure 16.1 shows how the constructor works.

FIGURE 16.1

`string` constructor using a range.

Now suppose you want to use this constructor to initialize an object to part of another `string` object, say, the object `five`. The following does not work:

```
string seven(five + 6, five + 10);
```

The reason is that the name of an object, unlike the name of an array, is not treated as the address of an object, hence `five` is not a pointer and `five + 6` is meaningless. However, `five[6]` is a `char` value, so `&five[6]` is an address and can be used as an argument to the constructor:

```
string seven(&five[6], &five[10]);// ctor #6 again
```

`string` Class Input

Another useful thing to know about a class is what input options are available. For C-style strings, recall, you have three options:

```
char info[100];
cin >> info;                // read a word
cin.getline(info, 100);     // read a line, discard \n
cin.get(info, 100);         // read a line, leave \n in queue
```

So what are the input options for a `string` object? First, the `string` class overloads the `>>` operator, much as the `String` class did in Chapter 12. Because the first operand is not a `string` object, the overloaded `>>` operator function is not a class method. Instead, it is a general function taking an `istream` object as its first argument and a `string` object as its second argument. To be consistent with how the `>>` operator treats C-strings, the `string` version also reads a single word, terminating input upon reaching a whitespace character, detecting end of file, or reaching the maximum allowable number of characters that can be stored in a `string` object. The function works by first erasing the contents of the target string and then reading and appending one character at a time. As long as the input sequence is shorter than the maximum allowable number of characters for a `string` object, the `operator>>(istream &, string &)` function automatically dimensions the `string` object to fit the input string. The upshot is that you can use `>>` with `string` objects just as you do with C-style strings, but without worrying about overrunning the array size:

```
char fname[10];
cin >> fname;        // could be a problem if input size > 9 characters
string lname;
cin >> lname;        // can read a very, very long word
```

Providing a `getline()` equivalent is a bit less transparent because `getline()`, unlike `operator>>()`, can't be used with operator notation. Instead, it uses membership notation:

```
cin.getline(fname, 10);
```

To get the same syntax to work with a `string` object would require adding a new member function to the `istream` class, which would not be wise. Instead, the string library defines a non-member function `getline()` that takes an `istream` object as its first argument and a `string` object as its second argument. Thus, it's used as follows to read a line of input into a `string` object:

```
string fullName;
getline(cin, fullName);  // instead of cin.getline(fname, 10);
```

The `getline()` function first erases the contents of the destination string and then reads one character at a time from the input queue, appending it to the string. This continues until the function reaches the end of the line, detects the end of file, or reaches maximum capacity of a `string` object. The newline character, if detected, is read but not stored in the string. Note that unlike the `istream` version, the `string` version doesn't have a size parameter indicating the maximum number of characters to read. That's because it dimensions the `string` object automatically to fit the input. Listing 16.2 illustrates using the two input options.

LISTING 16.2   str2.cpp

```
// str2.cpp -- string input
#include <iostream>
#include <string>
using namespace std;

int main()
{
    string word;
    cout << "Enter a line: ";
    cin >> word;
    while (cin.get() != '\n')
        continue;
    cout << word << " is all I wanted.\n";

    string line;
    cout << "Enter a line (really!): ";
    getline(cin, line);
    cout << "Line: " << line << endl;
    return 0;
}
```

Compatibility Note

Microsoft Visual C++ 5.0 and 6.0 have a bug in the getline() implementation that causes output following getline() not to appear until something is entered again.

Here is a sample run:

```
Enter a line: Time and tide wait for no one.
Time is all I wanted.
Enter a line (really!): All things come to he who waits.
Line: All things come to he who waits.
```

Working with Strings

So far, you've learned that you can create **string** objects in a variety of ways, display the contents of a **string** object, read data into a **string** object, append to a **string** object, assign to a **string** object, and concatenate two **string** objects. What else can you do?

You can compare strings. All six relational operators are overloaded for **string** objects, with one object being considered less than another if it occurs earlier in the machine collating sequence. If the machine collating sequence is the ASCII code, that implies that digits are less than uppercase characters and uppercase characters are less than lowercase characters. Each relational operator is overloaded three ways so that you can compare a **string** object with another **string** object, compare a **string** object with a C-style string, and compare a C-style string with a **string** object:

```
string snake1("cobra");
string snake2("coral");
```

```
char snake3[20] = "anaconda";
if (snake1 < snake 2)           // operator<(const string &, const string &)
    ...
if (snake1 == snake3)           // operator==(const string &, const char *)
    ...
if (snake3 != snake2)           // operator!=(const char *, const string &)
    ...
```

You can determine the size of a string. Both the `size()` and `length()` member functions return the number of characters in a string:

```
if (snake1.length() == snake2.size())
    cout << "Both strings have the same length.\n"
```

Why two functions that do the same thing? The `length()` member comes from earlier versions of the `string` class, while `size()` was added for STL compatibility.

You can search a string for a given substring or character in a variety of ways. Table 16.2 provides a short description of four variations of a `find()` method. Recall that `string::npos` is the maximum possible number of characters in a string, typically the largest `unsigned int` or `unsigned long value`.

TABLE 16.2 The Overloaded `find()` Method

Method Prototype	Description
`size_type find(const string & str, size_type pos = 0) const`	Finds the first occurrence of the substring str, starting the search at location pos in the invoking string. Returns the index of the first character of the substring if found, and returns string::npos otherwise.
`size_type find(const char * s, size_type pos = 0) const`	Finds the first occurrence of the substring s, starting the search at location pos in the invoking string. Returns the index of the first character of the substring if found, and returns string::npos otherwise.
`size_type find(const char * s, size_type pos = 0, size_type n)`	Finds the first occurrence of the substring consisting of the first n characters in s, starting the search at location pos in the invoking string. Returns the index of the first character of the substring if found, and returns string::npos otherwise.

TABLE 16.2   Continued

Method Prototype	Description
`size_type find(char ch,` `size_type pos = 0) const`	Finds the first occurrence of the character *ch*, starting the search at location *pos* in the invoking string. Returns the index of the character if found, and returns `string::npos` otherwise.

The library also provides the related methods `rfind()`, `find_first_of()`, `find_last_of()`, `find_first_not_of()`, and `find_last_not_of()`, each with the same set of overloaded function signatures as the `find()` method. The `rfind()` finds the last occurrence of a substring or character. The `find_first_of()` finds the first occurrence in the invoking string of any of the characters in the argument. For example, the statement:

```
int where = snake1.find_first_of("hark");
```

would return the location of the **r** in `"cobra"` (i.e., the index 3) because that's the first occurrence of any of the letters in `"hark"` in `"cobra"`. The `find_last_of()` method works the same, except it finds the last occurrence. Thus, the statement:

```
int where = snake1.last_first_of("hark");
```

would return the location of the **a** in `"cobra"`. The `find_first_not_of()` method finds the first character in the invoking string that is not a character in the argument. So

```
int where = snake1.find_first_not_of("hark");
```

would return the location of the **c** in `cobra`, for **c** is not found in `hark`. We leave the description of `find_last_not_of()` as an exercise for the reader.

There are many more methods, but these are enough to put together a sample program that's a graphically impaired version of the word game Hangman. It stores a list of words in an array of `string` objects, picks a word at random, and lets you guess letters in the word. Six wrong guesses, and you lose. The program uses the `find()` function to check your guesses and the `+=` operator to build a `string` object to keep track of your wrong guesses. To keep track of your good guesses, the program creates a word the same length as the mystery word but consisting of hyphens. The hyphens are then replaced by correct guesses. Listing 16.3 shows the program.

LISTING 16.3   `str3.cpp`

```cpp
// str3.cpp -- some string methods
#include <iostream>
#include <string>
#include <cstdlib>
#include <ctime>
#include <cctype>
using namespace std;
```

LISTING 16.3 Continued

```cpp
const int NUM = 26;
const string wordlist[NUM] = {"apiary", "beetle", "cereal",
    "danger", "ensign", "florid", "garage", "health", "insult",
    "jackal", "keeper", "loaner", "manage", "nonce", "onset",
    "plaid", "quilt", "remote", "stolid", "train", "useful",
    "valid", "whence", "xenon", "yearn", "zippy"};

int main()
{
    srand(time(0));
    char play;
    cout << "Will you play a word game? <y/n> ";
    cin >> play;
    play = tolower(play);
    while (play == 'y')
    {
        string target = wordlist[rand() % NUM];
        int length = target.length();
        string attempt(length, '-');
        string badchars;
        int guesses = 6;
        cout << "Guess my secret word. It has " << length
             << " letters, and you guess\n"
             << "one letter at a time. You get " << guesses
             << " wrong guesses.\n";
        cout << "Your word: " << attempt << endl;
        while (guesses > 0 && attempt != target)
        {
            char letter;
            cout << "Guess a letter: ";
            cin >> letter;
            if (badchars.find(letter) != string::npos
                || attempt.find(letter) != string::npos)
            {
                cout << "You already guessed that. Try again.\n";
                    continue;
            }
            int loc = target.find(letter);
            if (loc == string::npos)
            {
                cout << "Oh, bad guess!\n";
                --guesses;
                badchars += letter; // add to string
            }
            else
            {
                cout << "Good guess!\n";
                attempt[loc]=letter;
                // check if letter appears again
                loc = target.find(letter, loc + 1);
                while (loc != string::npos)
                {
```

LISTING 16.3   Continued

```
                    attempt[loc]=letter;
                    loc = target.find(letter, loc + 1);
                }
            }
            cout << "Your word: " << attempt << endl;
            if (attempt != target)
            {
                if (badchars.length() > 0)
                    cout << "Bad choices: " << badchars << endl;
                cout << guesses << " bad guesses left\n";
            }
        }
        if (guesses > 0)
            cout << "That's right!\n";
        else
            cout << "Sorry, the word is " << target << ".\n";

        cout << "Will you play another? <y/n> ";
        cin >> play;
        play = tolower(play);
    }

    cout << "Bye\n";

    return 0;
}
```

Here's a sample run:

```
Will you play a word game? <y/n> y
Guess my secret word. It has 6 letters, and you guess
one letter at a time. You get 6 wrong guesses.
Your word: ------
Guess a letter: e
Oh, bad guess!
Your word: ------
Bad choices: e
5 bad guesses left
Guess a letter: a
Good guess!
Your word: a--a--
Bad choices: e
5 bad guesses left
Guess a letter: t
Oh, bad guess!
Your word: a--a--
Bad choices: et
4 bad guesses left
Guess a letter: r
Good guess!
Your word: a--ar-
Bad choices: et
4 bad guesses left
```

```
Guess a letter: y
Good guess!
Your word: a--ary
Bad choices: et
4 bad guesses left
Guess a letter: i
Good guess!
Your word: a-iary
Bad choices: et
4 bad guesses left
Guess a letter: p
Good guess!
Your word: apiary
That's right!
Will you play another? <y/n> n
Bye
```

Program Notes

The fact that the relational operators are overloaded lets you treat strings in the same fashion you would treat numeric variables:

```
while (guesses > 0 && attempt != target)
```

This is easier to follow than, say, using `strcmp()` with C-style strings.

The program uses `find()` to check if a character has been selected earlier; if it has been selected, it will be found in either the `badchars` string (bad guesses) or in the `attempt` string (good guesses):

```
if (badchars.find(letter) != string::npos
    || attempt.find(letter) != string::npos)
```

The `npos` variable is a static member of the `string` class. Its value, recall, is the maximum allowable number of characters for a `string` object. Therefore, because indexing begins at 0, it is 1 greater than the largest possible index and can be used to indicate failure to find a character or a string.

The program makes use of the fact that one of the overloaded versions of the `+=` operator lets you append individual characters to a string:

```
badchars += letter;   // append a char to a string object
```

The heart of the program begins by checking if the chosen letter is in the mystery word:

```
int loc = target.find(letter);
```

If `loc` is a valid value, the letter can be placed in the corresponding location in the answer string:

```
attempt[loc]=letter;
```

However, a given letter may occur more than once in the mystery word, so the program has to keep checking. Here the program uses the optional second argument to `find()`, which lets you specify a starting place in the string from which to begin the search. Because the letter was found at location `loc`, the next search should begin at `loc + 1`. A `while` loop keeps the search going until no more occurrences of that character are found. Note that `find()` indicates failure if `loc` is after the end of the string:

```
// check if letter appears again
loc = target.find(letter, loc + 1);
while (loc != string::npos)
{
    attempt[loc]=letter;
    loc = target.find(letter, loc + 1);
}
```

Real World Note: Overloading C Functions to Use string Objects

You can use the overloaded `==` operator to compare `string` objects. However, the case-sensitive nature in which the `==` operator performs its equality comparison can be a problem in some cases. Often, two strings need to be compared for equality without respect to their case. For example, a program may compare input from a user with a constant value, and the user may not use the same case. Consider the following sample:

```
#include <string>        //  string object

...

string strA;
cin >> strA;   // assume user enters Maplesyrup
string strB = "mapleSyrup";  // stored constand

if( strA == strB )
{
  cout << "The strings are equal.\n";
}
else
{
  cout << "The strings are not equal.\n";
}
```

Because `'M'` is different from `'m'` and `'s'` is different from `'S'`, the output is this:

```
The strings are not equal.
```

What if your program needed to perform a case-insensitive comparison on `strA` and `strB`? Many C libraries provide a `stricmp()` or `_stricmp()` function that does a case-insensitive test. (However, this function isn't listed in the C standard, so it's not universally available.) By creating your own overloaded version of this function, you can cobble together a simple workaround.

```
#include <string.h>  // for stricmp() on many systems
#include <string>    // string object

string strA;
cin >> strA;   // assume user enters Maplesyrup
string strB = "mapleSyrup";  // stored constant
```

```
inline bool stricmp( const std::string& strA,
                     const std::string& strB )  // overloaded function
{
  return stricmp( strA.c_str(), strB.c_str() ) == 0;    // C function
}

bool bStringsAreEqual = stricmp( strA, strB );
```

Using simplified syntax, you can now compare two strings for equality without regard to case.

What Else?

The string library supplies many other facilities. There are functions for erasing part or all of a string, for replacing part or all of one string with part or all of another string, for inserting material into a string or removing material from a string, for comparing part or all of one string with part or all of another string, and for extracting a substring from a string. There's a function for copying part of one string to another string, and a function for swapping the contents of two strings. Most of these functions are overloaded so that they can work with C-style strings as well as with **string** objects. Appendix F describes the string library function briefly.

This section has treated the **string** class as if it were based on the **char** type. In fact, as mentioned earlier, the string library really is based on a template class:

```
template<class charT, class traits = char _traits<charT>,
        class Allocator = allocator<charT> >
basic_string {...};
```

The class includes the following two **typedef**s:

```
typedef basic_string<char> string;
typedef basic_string<wchar_t> wstring;
```

This allows you to use strings based on the **wchar_t** as well as the **char** type. You even could develop some sort of character-like class and use the **basic_string** class template with it, providing your class met certain requirements. The **traits** class is a class that describes specific facts about the chosen character type, such as how to compare values. There are predefined specializations of the **char_traits** template for the **char** and **wchar_t** types, and these are the default values for **traits**. The **Allocator** class represents a class to manage memory allocation. There are predefined specializations of the **allocator** template for the **char** and **wchar_t** types, and these are the defaults. They use **new** and **delete** in the usual fashion, but you could reserve a chunk of memory and provide your own allocation methods.

The auto_ptr Class

The **auto_ptr** class is a template class for managing the use of dynamic memory allocation. Let's take a look at what might be needed and how it can be accomplished. Consider the following function:

```
void remodel(string & str)
{
    string * ps = new string(str);
    ...
    str = ps;
    return;
}
```

You probably see its flaw. Each time the function is called, it allocates memory from the heap but never returns it, creating a memory leak. You also know the solution—just remember to free the allocated memory by adding the following statement just before the **return** statement:

```
delete ps;
```

However, a solution involving the phrase "just remember to" seldom is the best solution. Sometimes you won't remember. Or you will remember but accidentally remove or comment out the code. And even if you do remember, there still can be problems. Consider the following variation:

```
void remodel(string & str)
{
    string * ps = new string(str);
    ...
    if (weird_thing())
        throw exception();
    str = *ps;
    delete ps;
    return;
}
```

If the exception is thrown, the **delete** statement isn't reached, and again there is a memory leak.

You can fix that oversight, as illustrated in Chapter 14, "Reusing Code in C++," but it would be nice if there were a neater solution. Let's think about what is needed. When a function like **remodel()** terminates, either normally or by throwing an exception, local variables are removed from the stack memory—so the memory occupied by the pointer **ps** is freed. What would be nice is if the memory pointed to by **ps** were also freed. That means that you would want the program to take an additional action when **ps** expires. That extra service is not provided for basic types, but it can be provided for classes via the destructor mechanism. Thus, the problem with **ps** is that it is just an ordinary pointer and not a class object. If it were an object, you could have its destructor delete the pointed-to memory when the object expires. And that is the idea behind **auto_ptr**.

Using an auto_ptr

The **auto_ptr** template defines a pointer-like object intended to be assigned an address obtained (directly or indirectly) by **new**. When an **auto_ptr** object expires, its destructor uses **delete** to free the memory. Thus, if you assign an address returned by **new** to an **auto_ptr** object, you don't have to remember to free the memory later; it will be freed automatically when the **auto_ptr** object expires. Figure 16.2 illustrates the behavioral difference between an **auto_ptr** and a regular pointer.

FIGURE 16.2

Regular pointer versus
`auto_ptr`.

To create an `auto_ptr` object, include the `memory` header file, which includes the `auto_ptr` template. Then use the usual template syntax to instantiate the kind of pointer you require. The template includes the following:

```
template<class X> class auto_ptr {
public:
    explicit auto_ptr(X* p =0) throw();
...};
```

(The throw() notation, recall, means this constructor doesn't throw an exception.) Thus, asking for an auto_ptr of type X gives you an auto_ptr pointing to type X:

```
auto_ptr<double> pd(new double);   // an auto_ptr to double
                                   // (use in place of double *)
auto_ptr<string> ps(new string);   // an auto_ptr to string
                                   // (use in place of string *)
```

Here new double is a pointer returned by new to a newly allocated chunk of memory. It is the argument to the auto_ptr<double> constructor; that is, it is the actual argument corresponding to the formal parameter p in the prototype. Similarly, new string also is an actual argument for a constructor.

Thus, to convert the remodel() function, you would follow these three steps:

1. Include the memory header file.

2. Replace the pointer-to-string with an auto_ptr to string.

3. Remove the delete statement.

Here's the function with those changes made:

```
#include <memory>
void remodel(string & str)
{
    auto_ptr<string> ps (new string(str));
    ...
    if (weird_thing())
        throw exception();
    str = *ps;
    // delete ps;  NO LONGER NEEDED
    return;
}
```

Note that auto_ptr constructor is explicit, meaning there is no implicit type cast from a pointer to an auto_ptr:

```
auto_ptr<double> pd;
double *p_reg = new double;
pd = p_reg;                    // not allowed (implicit conversion)
pd = auto_ptr<double>(p_reg); // allowed (explicit conversion
auto_ptr<double> pauto = pd;  // not allowed (implicit conversion)
auto_ptr<double> pauto(pd);   // allowed (explicit conversion
```

The auto_ptr is an example of a *smart pointer*, an object that acts like a pointer, but with additional features. The auto_ptr class is defined so that, in most respects, it acts like a regular pointer. For example, given that ps is an auto_ptr, you can dereference it (*ps), increment it (++ps), use it to access structure members (ps->puffIndex), and assign it to a regular pointer that points to the same type. You also can assign one auto_ptr to another of the same type, but that raises an issue that the next section will face.

The template allows you to initialize an auto_ptr object to an ordinary pointer via a constructor:

auto_ptr Considerations

The `auto_ptr` is not a panacea. For example, consider the following code:

```
auto_ptr<int> pi(new int [200]);   // NO!
```

Remember, you must pair `delete` with `new` and `delete` `[]` with `new` `[]`. The `auto_ptr` template uses `delete`, not `delete` `[]`, so it only can be used with `new`, not `new` `[]`. There is no `auto_ptr` equivalent for use with dynamic arrays. You could copy the `auto_ptr` template from the `memory` header file, rename it `auto_arr_ptr`, and convert the copy to use `delete` `[]` instead of `delete`. In that case, you would want to add support for the `[]` operator.

What about this?

```
string vacation("I wandered lonely as a cloud.");
auto_ptr<string> pvac(&vacation);   // NO!
```

This would apply the `delete` operator to non-heap memory, which is wrong.

Caution

Use an `auto_ptr` object only for memory allocated by `new`, not for memory allocated by `new` `[]` or by simply declaring a variable.

Now consider assignment:

```
auto_ptr<string> ps (new string("I reigned lonely as a cloud."));
auto_ptr<string> vocation;
vocation = ps;
```

What should the assignment statement accomplish? If `ps` and `vocation` were ordinary pointers, the result would be two pointers pointing to the same `string` object. That is not acceptable here, for then the program would wind up attempting to delete the same object twice, once when `ps` expires, and once when `vocation` expires. There are ways to avoid this problem:

- Define the assignment operator so that it makes a deep copy. This results in two pointers pointing to two distinct objects, one of which is a copy of the other.

- Institute the concept of *ownership*, with only one smart pointer allowed to own a particular object. Only if the smart pointer owns the object will its constructor delete the object. Then have assignment transfer ownership. This is the strategy used for `auto_ptr`.

- Create an even smarter pointer that keeps track of how many smart pointers refer to a particular object. This is called *reference counting*. Assignment, for example, would increase the count by one, and the expiration of a pointer would decrease the count by one. Only when the final pointer expires would `delete` be invoked.

The same strategies, of course, would also be applied to the copy constructors.

Each approach has its uses. Here's a situation, for example, that may not work properly using `auto_ptr` objects:

```
auto_ptr<string> films[5] =
{
    auto_ptr<string> (new string("Fowl Balls")),
    auto_ptr<string> (new string("Duck Walks")),
    auto_ptr<string> (new string("Chicken Runs")),
    auto_ptr<string> (new string("Turkey Errors")),
    auto_ptr<string> (new string("Goose Eggs"))
};
auto_ptr<string> pwin(films[2]);
int i;
cout << "The nominees for best avian baseball film are\n";
for (i = 0; i < 5; i++)
    cout << *films[i] << endl;
cout << "The winner is " << *pwin << "!\n";
```

The problem is that transferring ownership from `films[2]` to `pwin` may cause `films[2]` to no longer refer to the string. That is, after an `auto_ptr` object gives up ownership, it may no longer be usable. Whether it's usable or not is an implementation choice.

Smart Pointers

The C++ library `auto_ptr` is an example of a *smart pointer*. A smart pointer is a class designed so that objects of that class have pointer-like properties. For example, a smart pointer can store the address of memory allocated by `new` and can be dereferenced. Because a smart pointer is a class object, it can modify and augment the behavior of a simple pointer. For instance, a smart pointer can institute reference counting. This allows several objects to share a single representation of a value tracked by a smart pointer. When the number of objects using the value drops to zero, the smart pointer can then delete the value. Smart pointers can allow for more efficient use of memory and help prevent memory leaks, but they do require the user to become familiar with new programming techniques.

The Standard Template Library

The Standard Template Library, or STL, provides a collection of templates representing *containers*, *iterators*, *function objects*, and *algorithms*. A container is a unit, like an array, that can hold several values. STL containers are homogeneous, that is, they hold values all of the same kind. Algorithms are recipes for accomplishing particular tasks, such as sorting an array or finding a particular value in a list. Iterators are objects that let you move through a container much as pointers let you move through an array; they are generalizations of pointers. Function objects are objects that act like functions; they can be class objects or function pointers (which includes function names because a function name acts as a pointer). The STL lets you construct a variety of containers, including arrays, queues, and lists, and lets you perform a variety of operations, including searching, sorting, and randomizing.

Alex Stepanov and Meng Lee developed STL at Hewlett-Laboratories, releasing the implementation in 1994. The ISO/ANSI C++ committee voted to incorporate it as a part of the C++ standard. The STL is not an example of object-oriented programming. Instead, it represents a different programming paradigm called *generic programming*. This makes STL interesting both in terms of what it does and in its approach. There's too much information about the STL to present in a single chapter, so we'll look at some representative examples and examine the spirit of the approach. We'll begin by looking at a few specific examples. Then, once you have a hands-on appreciation for containers, iterators, and algorithms, we'll look at the underlying design philosophy, and then take an overview of whole STL. Appendix G, "The STL Methods and Functions," summarizes the various STL methods and functions.

The `vector` **Template Class**

In computing, the term *vector* corresponds to an array rather than to the mathematical vector discussed in Chapter 11, "Working with Classes." (Mathematically, an N-dimensional mathematical vector can be represented by a set of N components, so, in that aspect, a mathematical vector is like an N-dimensional array. However, a mathematical vector has additional properties, such as inner and outer products, that a computer vector doesn't necessarily have.) A computing-style vector holds a set of like values that can be accessed randomly. That is, you can use, say, an index to directly access the tenth element of a vector without having to access the preceding nine elements first. So a `vector` class would provide operations similar to that of the `ArrayDb` class of Chapter 14. That is, you could create a `vector` object, assign one `vector` object to another, and use the `[ ]` operator to access `vector` elements. To make the class generic, make it a template class. That's what the STL does, defining a `vector` template in the `vector` (formerly `vector.h`) header file.

To create a `vector` template object, you use the usual `<type>` notation to indicate the type to be used. Also, the `vector` template uses dynamic memory allocation, and you can use an initialization argument to indicate how many vector elements you want:

```
#include vector
using namespace std;
vector<int> ratings(5);      // a vector of 5 ints
int n;
cin >> n;
vector<double> scores(n);    // a vector of n doubles
```

After you create a `vector` object, operator overloading for `[ ]` makes it possible to use the usual array notation for accessing individual elements:

```
ratings[0] = 9;
for (int i = 0; i < n; i++)
    cout << scores[i] << endl;
```

Allocators Again

Like the string class, the various STL container templates take an optional template argument specifying what allocator object to use to manage memory. For example, the vector template begins like this:

```
template <class T, class Allocator = allocator<T> >
    class vector {...
```

If you omit a value for this template argument, the container template uses the allocator<T> class by default. This class uses new and delete in the standard ways.

Listing 16.4 uses this class in an undemanding application. This particular program creates two vector objects, one an int specialization and one a string specialization; each has five elements.

LISTING 16.4   vect1.cpp

```cpp
// vect1.cpp -- introducing the vector template
#include <iostream>
#include <string>
#include <vector>
using namespace std;

const int NUM = 5;
int main()
{
    vector<int> ratings(NUM);
    vector<string> titles(NUM);
    cout << "You will do exactly as told. You will enter\n"
        << NUM << " book titles and your ratings (0-10).\n";
    int i;
    for (i = 0; i < NUM; i++)
    {
        cout << "Enter title #" << i + 1 << ": ";
        getline(cin,titles[i]);
        cout << "Enter your rating (0-10): ";
        cin >> ratings[i];
        cin.get();
    }
    cout << "Thank you. You entered the following:\n"
        << "Rating\tBook\n";
    for (i = 0; i < NUM; i++)
    {
        cout << ratings[i] << "\t" << titles[i] << endl;
    }

    return 0;
}
```

Here's a sample run:

```
You will do exactly as told. You will enter
5 book titles and your ratings (0-10).
Enter title #1: The Cat Who Knew C++
Enter your rating (0-10): 6
Enter title #2: Felonious Felines
Enter your rating (0-10): 4
Enter title #3: Warlords of Wonk
Enter your rating (0-10): 3
Enter title #4: Don't Touch That Metaphor
Enter your rating (0-10): 5
Enter title #5: Panic Oriented Programming
Enter your rating (0-10): 8
Thank you. You entered the following:
Rating  Book
6       The Cat Who Knew C++
4       Felonious Felines
3       Warlords of Wonk
5       Don't Touch That Metaphor
8       Panic Oriented Programming
```

All this program does is use the `vector` template as a convenient way to create a dynamically allocated array. Let's see an example that uses more of the class methods.

Things to Do to Your Vectors

What else can the `vector` template do for you? All the STL containers provide certain basic methods, including `size()`, which returns the number of elements in a container, `swap()`, which exchanges the contents of two containers, `begin()`, which returns an iterator referring to the first element in a container, and `end()`, which returns an iterator representing *past-the-end* for the container.

What's an iterator? It's a generalization of a pointer. In fact, it can be a pointer. Or it can be an object for which pointer-like operations such as dereferencing (`operator*()`) and incrementing (`operator++()`) have been defined. As you'll see later, generalizing pointers to iterators allows the STL to provide a uniform interface for a variety of container classes, including ones for which simple pointers wouldn't work. Each container class defines a suitable iterator. The type name for this iterator is a class scope `typedef` called `iterator`. For example, to declare an iterator for a type `double` specialization of `vector`, you would do this:

```
vector<double>::iterator pd;   // pd an iterator
```

Suppose `scores` is a `vector<double>` object:

```
vector<double> scores;
```

Then you can use the iterator `pd` do things like the following:

```
pd = scores.begin();   // have pd point to the first element
*pd = 22.3;            // dereference pd and assign value to first element
++pd;                  // make pd point to the next element
```

As you can see, an iterator behaves like a pointer.

What's *past-the-end*? It is an iterator referring to an element one past the last element in a container. The idea is similar to the null character being one element past the last actual character in a C-style string, except that null character is the value in the element and past-the-end is a pointer (or iterator) to the element. The `end()` member function identifies the past-the-end location. If you set an iterator to the first element in a container and keep incrementing it, eventually it will reach past-the-end, and you will have traversed the entire contents of the container. Thus, if `scores` and `pd` are defined as above, you can display the contents with this code:

```
for (pd = scores.begin(); pd != scores.end(); pd++)
    cout << *pd << endl;;
```

All containers have the methods just discussed. The `vector` template class also has some methods that only some STL containers have. One handy method, called `push_back()` adds an element to the end of a vector. While doing so, it attends to memory management so that the vector size increases to accommodate added members. This means you can write code like the following:

```
vector<double> scores;  // create an empty vector
double temp;
while (cin >> temp && temp >= 0)
    scores.push_back(temp);
cout << "You entered " << scores.size() << " scores.\n";
```

Each loop cycle adds one more element to the `scores` vector. You don't have to pick the number of element when you write the program or when you run the program. As long as the program has access to sufficient memory, it will expand the size of `scores` as necessary.

There is an `erase()` method that removes a given range of a vector. It takes two iterator arguments defining the range to be removed. It's important to understand how the STL defines ranges using two iterators. The first iterator refers to the beginning of the range, and the second iterator is one beyond the end of the range. For example:

```
scores.erase(scores.begin(), scores.begin() + 2);
```

erases the first and second elements, that is, those referred to by `begin()` and `begin() + 1`. (Because `vector` provides random access, operations like `begin() + 2` are defined for the `vector` class iterators.) If `it1` and `it2` are two iterators, the STL literature uses the notation [p1,p2) to indicate a range starting with `p1` and going up to, but not including, `p2`. Thus, the range [`begin()`, `end()`) encompasses the entire contents of a collection (see Figure 16.3). Also, the range [p1,p1) is an empty range. The [) notation is not part of C++, so it doesn't appear in code; it just appears in documentation.

FIGURE 16.3

The STL range concept.

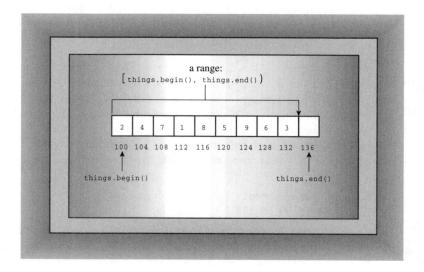

An `insert()` method complements `erase()`. It takes three iterator arguments. The first gives the position ahead of which new elements are to be inserted. The second and third iterator parameters define the range to be inserted. This range typically is part of another object. For example, the code

```
vector<int> old;
vector<int> new;
...
old.insert(old.begin(), new.begin() + 1, new.end());
```

inserts all but the first element of the **new** vector ahead of the first element of the **old** vector. Incidentally, this is a case where having a past-the-end element is handy, for it makes it simple to append something to the end of a vector:

```
old.insert(old.end(), new.begin() + 1, new.end());
```

Here the new material is inserted ahead of `old.end()`, meaning it's placed *after* the last element in the vector.

Listing 16.5 illustrates the use of `size()`, `begin()`, `end()`, `push_back()`, `erase()`, and `insert()`. To simplify data-handling, the `rating` and `title` components of Listing 16.4 are incorporated into a single `Review` structure, and `FillReview()` and `ShowReview()` functions provide input and output facilities for `Review` objects.

LISTING 16.5   vect2.cpp

```cpp
// vect2.cpp -- methods and iterators
#include <iostream>
#include <string>
#include <vector>
using namespace std;

struct Review {
    string title;
    int rating;
};
bool FillReview(Review & rr);
void ShowReview(const Review & rr);
int main()
{
    vector<Review> books;
    Review temp;
    while (FillReview(temp))
        books.push_back(temp);
    cout << "Thank you. You entered the following:\n"
         << "Rating\tBook\n";
    int num = books.size();
    for (int i = 0; i < num; i++)
        ShowReview(books[i]);
    cout << "Reprising:\n"
         << "Rating\tBook\n";
    vector<Review>::iterator pr;
    for (pr = books.begin(); pr != books.end(); pr++)
        ShowReview(*pr);
    vector <Review> oldlist(books);     // copy constructor used
    if (num > 3)
    {
        // remove 2 items
        books.erase(books.begin() + 1, books.begin() + 3);
        cout << "After erasure:\n";
        for (pr = books.begin(); pr != books.end(); pr++)
            ShowReview(*pr);
        // insert 1 item
        books.insert(books.begin(), oldlist.begin() + 1,
                     oldlist.begin() + 2);
        cout << "After insertion:\n";
        for (pr = books.begin(); pr != books.end(); pr++)
            ShowReview(*pr);
    }
    books.swap(oldlist);
    cout << "Swapping oldlist with books:\n";
    for (pr = books.begin(); pr != books.end(); pr++)
        ShowReview(*pr);
    return 0;
}
```

LISTING 16.5   Continued

```
bool FillReview(Review & rr)
{
    cout << "Enter book title (quit to quit): ";
    getline(cin,rr.title);
    if (rr.title == "quit")
        return false;
    cout << "Enter book rating: ";
    cin >> rr.rating;
    if (!cin)
        return false;
    cin.get();
    return true;
}

void ShowReview(const Review & rr)
{
    cout << rr.rating << "\t" << rr.title << endl;
}
```

 Compatibility Note

Older implementations use vector.h instead of the vector header file. Although the order of include files shouldn't matter, some older versions of g++ require the string header file to appear before STL header files. Microsoft Visual C++ 6.0 has a bug in its getline() implementation such that the following output doesn't appear until something is entered again. (In this example, the bug requires you hit Enter twice after entering a title.)

Here is a sample program run:

```
Enter book title (quit to quit): The Cat Who Knew Vectors
Enter book rating: 5
Enter book title (quit to quit): Candid Canines
Enter book rating: 7
Enter book title (quit to quit): Warriors of Wonk
Enter book rating: 4
Enter book title (quit to quit): Quantum Manners
Enter book rating: 8
Enter book title (quit to quit): quit
Thank you. You entered the following:
Rating  Book
5       The Cat Who Knew Vectors
7       Candid Canines
4       Warriors of Wonk
8       Quantum Manners
Reprising:
Rating  Book
5       The Cat Who Knew Vectors
7       Candid Canines
4       Warriors of Wonk
8       Quantum Manners
```

```
After erasure:
5        The Cat Who Knew Vectors
8        Quantum Manners
After insertion:
7        Candid Canines
5        The Cat Who Knew Vectors
8        Quantum Manners
Swapping oldlist with books:
5        The Cat Who Knew Vectors
7        Candid Canines
4        Warriors of Wonk
8        Quantum Manners
```

More Things to Do to Your Vectors

There are many things programmers commonly do with arrays, such as search them, sort them, randomize the order, and so on. Does the vector template class have methods for these common operations? No! The STL takes a broader view, defining *non-member* functions for these operations. Thus, instead of defining a separate `find()` member function for each container class, it defines a single `find()` non-member function that can be used for all container classes. This design philosophy saves a lot of duplicate work. For example, suppose you had 8 container classes and 10 operations to support. If each class had its own member function, you'd need 8*10 or 80 separate member function definitions. But with the STL approach, you'd need just 10 separate non-member function definitions. And if you defined a new container class, providing you followed the proper guidelines, it, too, could use the existing 10 non-member functions to find, sort, and so on.

Let's examine three representative STL functions: `for_each()`, `random_shuffle()`, and `sort()`. The `for_each()` function can be used with any container class. It takes three arguments. The first two are iterators defining a range in the container, and the last is a pointer to a function. (More generally, the last argument is a function object; you'll learn about them presently.) The `for_each()` function then applies the pointed-to function to each container element in the range. The pointed-to function must not alter the value of the container elements. You can use the `for_each()` function instead of a `for` loop. For example, you can replace the code:

```
vector<Review>::iterator pr;
for (pr = books.begin(); pr != books.end(); pr++)
    ShowReview(*pr);
```

with the following:

```
for_each(books.begin(), books.end(), ShowReview);
```

This enables you to avoid dirtying your hands (and code) with explicit use of iterator variables.

The `random_shuffle()` function takes two iterators specifying a range and rearranges the elements in that range in random order. For example, the statement

```
random_shuffle(books.begin(), books.end());
```

randomly rearranges the order of all the elements in the **books** vector. Unlike **for_each**, which works with any container class, this function requires that the container class allow random access, which the **vector** class does.

The **sort()** function, too, requires that the container support random access. It comes in two versions. The first version takes two iterators defining a range, and it sorts that range using the < operator defined for the type element stored in the container. For example,

```
vector<int> coolstuff;
...
sort(coolstuff.begin(), coolstuff.end());
```

sorts the contents of **coolstuff** in ascending order, using the built-in < operator to compare values.

If the container elements are user-defined objects, then there has to be an **operator<()** function defined that works with that type object in order to use **sort()**. For example, you could sort a vector containing **Review** objects if you provided either a **Review** member function or a non-member function for **operator<()**. Because **Review** is a structure, its members are public, and a non-member function like this would serve:

```
bool operator<(const Review & r1, const Review & r2)
{
    if (r1.title < r2.title)
        return true;
    else if (r1.title == r2.title && r1.rating < r2.rating)
        return true;
    else
        return false;
}
```

With a function like this in place, you then could sort a vector of **Review** objects (such as **books**):

```
sort(books.begin(), books.end());
```

This version of the **operator<()** function sorts in lexicographic order of the title members. If two objects have the same title members, they then are sorted in ratings order. But suppose you want to sort in decreasing order or in order of ratings instead of titles? Then you can use the second form of **sort()**. It takes three arguments. The first two, again, are iterators indicating the range. The final argument is a pointer to function (more generally, a function object) to be used instead of **operator<()** for making the comparison. The return value should be convertible to **bool**, with **false** meaning the two arguments are in the wrong order. Here's an example of such a function:

```
bool WorseThan(const Review & r1, const Review & r2)
{
    if (r1.rating < r2.rating)
        return true;
    else
        return false;
}
```

With this function in place, you can use the following statement to sort the **books** vector of **Review** objects in order of increasing rating values:

```
sort(books.begin(), books.end(), WorseThan);
```

Note that the **WorseThan()** function does a less complete job than **operator<()** of ordering **Review** objects. If two objects have the same title member, the **operator<()** function sorts using the rating member. But if two objects have the same rating member, **WorseThan()** treats them as equivalent. The first kind of ordering is called *total ordering*, and the second kind is called *strict weak ordering*. With total ordering, if both $a < b$ and $b < a$ are false, then a and b must be identical. With strict weak ordering, that's not so. They might be identical, or they might just have one aspect that is the same, such as the **rating** member in the **WorseThan()** example. So instead of saying the two objects are identical, the best you can say for strict weak ordering is that they are *equivalent*.

Listing 16.6 illustrates the use of these STL functions.

LISTING 16.6 vect3.cpp

```cpp
// vect3.cpp -- using STL functions
#include <iostream>
#include <string>
#include <vector>
#include <algorithm>
using namespace std;

struct Review {
    string title;
    int rating;
};

bool operator<(const Review & r1, const Review & r2);
bool worseThan(const Review & r1, const Review & r2);
bool FillReview(Review & rr);
void ShowReview(const Review & rr);
int main()
{
    vector<Review> books;
    Review temp;
    while (FillReview(temp))
        books.push_back(temp);
    cout << "Thank you. You entered the following "
         << books.size() << " ratings:\n"
          << "Rating\tBook\n";
    for_each(books.begin(), books.end(), ShowReview);

    sort(books.begin(), books.end());
    cout << "Sorted by title:\nRating\tBook\n";
    for_each(books.begin(), books.end(), ShowReview);
```

LISTING 16.6 *Continued*

```cpp
    sort(books.begin(), books.end(), worseThan);
    cout << "Sorted by rating:\nRating\tBook\n";
    for_each(books.begin(), books.end(), ShowReview);

    random_shuffle(books.begin(), books.end());
    cout << "After shuffling:\nRating\tBook\n";
    for_each(books.begin(), books.end(), ShowReview);
    cout << "Bye.\n";
    return 0;
}

bool operator<(const Review & r1, const Review & r2)
{
    if (r1.title < r2.title)
        return true;
    else if (r1.title == r2.title && r1.rating < r2.rating)
        return true;
    else
        return false;
}

bool worseThan(const Review & r1, const Review & r2)
{
    if (r1.rating < r2.rating)
        return true;
    else
        return false;
}

bool FillReview(Review & rr)
{
    cout << "Enter book title (quit to quit): ";
    getline(cin,rr.title);
    if (rr.title == "quit")
        return false;
    cout << "Enter book rating: ";
    cin >> rr.rating;
    if (!cin)
        return false;
    cin.get();
    return true;
}

void ShowReview(const Review & rr)
{
    cout << rr.rating << "\t" << rr.title << endl;
}
```

Compatibility Notes

Older implementations use vector.h instead of the vector header file and algo.h instead of the algorithm header file. Although the order of include files shouldn't matter, g++ 2.7.1 required the string header file to appear before STL header files. The Microsoft Visual C++ 5.0 getline() has a bug that delays the next output line appearing until after the next input. Also, Microsoft Visual C++ 5.0 requires you to define operator==() in addition to operator<(). The Borland C++Builder 1.0 getline() requires an explicit delimiter argument.

Here's a sample run:

```
Enter book title (quit to quit): The Cat Who Can Teach You Weight Loss
Enter book rating: 8
Enter book title (quit to quit): The Dogs of Dharma
Enter book rating: 6
Enter book title (quit to quit): The Wimps of Wonk
Enter book rating: 3
Enter book title (quit to quit): Farewell and Delete
Enter book rating: 7
Enter book title (quit to quit): quit
Thank you. You entered the following 4 ratings:
Rating  Book
8       The Cat Who Can Teach You Weight Loss
6       The Dogs of Dharma
3       The Wimps of Wonk
7       Farewell and Delete
Sorted by title:
Rating  Book
7       Farewell and Delete
8       The Cat Who Can Teach You Weight Loss
6       The Dogs of Dharma
3       The Wimps of Wonk
Sorted by rating:
Rating  Book
3       The Wimps of Wonk
6       The Dogs of Dharma
7       Farewell and Delete
8       The Cat Who Can Teach You Weight Loss
After shuffling:
Rating  Book
7       Farewell and Delete
3       The Wimps of Wonk
6       The Dogs of Dharma
8       The Cat Who Can Teach You Weight Loss
Bye.
```

Generic Programming

Now that you have some experience using the STL, let's look at the underlying philosophy. The STL is an example of *generic programming*. Object-oriented programming concentrates on the data aspect of programming, while generic programming concentrates on algorithms. The main things the two approaches have in common are abstraction and the creation of reusable code, but the philosophies are quite different

A goal of generic programming is to write code that is independent of data types. Templates are the C++ tools for doing generic programs. Templates, of course, let you define a function or class in terms of a generic type. The STL goes further by providing a generic representation of algorithms. Templates make this possible, but not without the added element of careful and conscious design. To see how this mixture of templates and design works, let's see why iterators are needed.

Why Iterators?

Understanding iterators is perhaps the key to understanding the STL. Just as templates make the algorithms independent of the type of data stored, iterators make the algorithms independent of the type of container used. Thus, they are an essential component of the STL's generic approach.

To see why iterators are needed, let's look at how you might implement a `find` function for two different data representations and then see how you could generalize the approach. First, consider a function that searches an ordinary array of `double` for a particular value. You could write the function like this:

```
double * find_ar(double * ar, int n, const double & val)
{
    for (int i = 0; i < n; i++)
        if (ar[i] == val)
            return &ar[i];
    return 0;
}
```

If the function finds the value in the array, it returns the address in the array where the value is found; otherwise it returns the null pointer. It uses subscript notation to move through the array. You could use a template to generalize to arrays of any type having an == operator. Nonetheless, this algorithm is still tied to one particular data structure—the array.

So let's look at searching another kind of data structure, the linked list. (Chapter 12 used a linked list to implement a `Queue` class.) The list consists of linked `Node` structures:

```
struct Node
{
    double item;
    Node * next;
};
```

Suppose you have a pointer pointing to the first node in the list. The **p_next** pointer in each node points to the next node, and the **p_next** pointer for the last node in the list is set to 0. You could write a **find_ll()** function this way:

```
Node* find_ll(Node * head, const double & val)
{
    Node * start;
    for (start = head; start!= 0; start = start->next)
        if (start->item == val)
            return start;
    return 0;
}
```

Again, you could use a template to generalize this to lists of any data type supporting the == operator. Nonetheless, this algorithm is still tied to one particular data structure—the linked list.

If you consider details of implementation, the two **find** functions use different algorithms: One uses array indexing to move through a list of items, the other resets **start** to **start->next**. But broadly, the two algorithms are the same: Compare the value with each value in the container in sequence until you find a match.

The goal of generic programming would be to have a single **find** function that would work with arrays or linked lists or any other container type. That is, not only should the function be independent of the data type stored in the container, it should be independent of the data structure of the container itself. Templates provide a generic representation for the data type stored in a container. What's needed is a generic representation of the process of moving through the values in a container. The iterator is that generalized representation.

What properties should an iterator have in order to implement a **find** function? Here's a short list:

- You should be able to dereference an iterator in order to access the value to which it refers. That is, if **p** is an iterator, ***p** should be defined.

- You should be able to assign one iterator to another. That is, if **p** and **q** are iterators, the expression **p = q** should be defined.

- You should be able to compare one iterator to another for equality. That is, if **p** and **q** are iterators, the expressions **p == q** and **p != q** should be defined.

- You should be able to move an iterator through all the elements of a container. This can be satisfied by defining **++p** and **p++** for an iterator **p**.

There are more things an iterator could do, but nothing more it need do, at least, not for the purposes of a **find** function. Actually, the STL defines several levels of iterators of increasing capabilities, and we'll return to that matter later. Note, by the way, that an ordinary pointer meets the requirements of an iterator. Hence, you can rewrite the **find_arr()** function like this:

```
typedef double * iterator;
iterator find_ar(iterator ar, int n, const double & val)
{
    for (int i = 0; i < n; i++, ar++)
        if (*ar == val)
            return ar;
    return 0;
}
```

Then you can alter the function parameter list so that it takes a pointer to the beginning of the array and a pointer to one past the end of the array as arguments to indicate a range. (Listing 7.8 did something similar.) And the function can return the end pointer as a sign the value was not found.

```
typedef double * iterator;
iterator find_ar(iterator begin, iterator end, const double & val)
{
    iterator ar;
    for (ar = begin; ar != end; ar++)
        if (*ar == val)
            return ar;
    return end;    // indicates val not found
}
```

For the find_ll() function, you can define an iterator class that defines the * and ++ operators:

```
struct Node
{
    double item;
    Node * p_next;
};

class iterator
{
    Node * pt;
public:
    iterator() : pt(0) {}
    iterator (Node * pn) : pt(pn) {}
    double operator*() { return pt->item;}
    iterator& operator++()      // for ++it
    {
        pt = pt->next;
        return *this;
    }
    iterator operator++(int)  // for it++
    {
        iterator tmp = *this;
        pt = pt->next;
        return tmp;
    }
// ... operator==(), operator!=(), etc.
};
```

(To distinguish between the prefix and postfix versions of the ++ operator, C++ adopted the convention of letting operator++() be the prefix version and operator++(int) be the postsuffix version; the argument is never used, hence needn't be given a name.)

The main point here is not how, in detail, to define the iterator class, but that with such a class, the second find function can be written like this:

```
iterator find_ll(iterator head, const double & val)
{
    iterator start;
    for (start = head; start!= 0; ++start)
        if (*start == val)
            return start;
    return 0;
}
```

This is very nearly the same as find_ar(). The point of difference is in how the two functions determine if they've reached the end of the values being searched. The find_ar() function uses an iterator to one-past-the-end, while find_ll() uses a null value stored in the final node. Remove that difference, and you can make the two functions identical. For example, you could require that the linked list have one additional element after the last official element. That is, have both the array and the linked list have a past-the-end element, and end the search when the iterator reaches the past-the-end position. Then find_ar() and find_ll() will have the same way of detecting the end of data and become identical algorithms. Note that requiring a past-the-end element moves from making requirements upon iterators to making requirements upon the container class.

The STL follows the approach just outlined. First, each container class (vector, list, deque, and so on) defines an iterator type appropriate to the class. For one class, the iterator might be a pointer; for another, it might be an object. Whatever the implementation, the iterator will provide the needed operations, such as * and ++. (Some classes may need more operations than others.) Next, each container class will have a past-the-end marker, which is the value assigned to an iterator when it has been incremented one past the last value in the container. Have begin() and end() methods that return iterators to the first element in a container and to the past-the-end position. Have the ++ operation take an iterator from the first element to past-the-end, visiting every container element en route.

To use a container class, you don't need to know how its iterators are implemented nor how past-the-end is implemented. It's enough to know it does have iterators, that begin() returns an iterator to the first element and that end() returns an iterator to past-the-end. For example, suppose you want to print the values in a vector<double> object. Then you can do this:

```
vector<double>::iterator pr;
for (pr = scores.begin(); pr != scores.end(); pr++)
    cout << *pr << endl;
```

Here the line

```
vector<double>::iterator pr;
```

identifies `pr` as the iterator type defined for the `vector<double>` class. If you used the `list<double>` class template instead to store scores, you could use this code:

```
list<double>::iterator pr;
for (pr = scores.begin(); pr != scores.end(); pr++)
    cout << *pr << endl;
```

The only change is in the type declared for `pr`. Thus, by having each class define appropriate iterators and designing the classes in a uniform fashion, the STL lets you write the same code for containers having quite dissimilar internal representations.

Actually, as a matter of style, it's better to avoid using the iterators directly; instead, if possible, use an STL function, such as `for_each()`, that takes care of the details for you.

Let's summarize the STL approach. Start with an algorithm for processing a container. Express it in as general terms as possible, making it independent of data type and container type. To make the general algorithm work with specific cases, define iterators that meet the needs of the algorithm and place requirements on the container design. That is, basic iterator properties and container properties stem from requirements placed upon them by the algorithm.

Kinds of Iterators

Different algorithms have different requirements for iterators. For example, a find algorithm needs the `++` operator to be defined so the iterator can step through the entire container. It needs read access to data but not write access. (It just looks at data and doesn't change it.) A sort algorithm, however, requires random access so that it can swap the two non-adjacent elements. If `iter` is an iterator, you can get random access by defining the `+` operator so that you can use expressions like `iter + 10`. Also, a sort algorithm needs to be able both to read and to write data.

The STL defines five kinds of iterators and describes its algorithms in terms of which kinds of iterators it needs. The five kinds are the *input iterator*, *output iterator*, *forward iterator*, *bidirectional iterator*, and *random access iterator*. For example, the `find()` prototype looks like this:

```
template<class InputIterator, class T>
InputIterator find(InputIterator first, InputIterator last, const T& value);
```

This tells you that this algorithm requires an input iterator. Similarly, the prototype

```
template<class RandomAccessIterator>
void sort(RandomAccessIterator first, RandomAccessIterator last);
```

tells you that the sort algorithm requires a random access iterator.

All five kinds of iterators can be dereferenced (that is, the * operator is defined for them) and can be compared for equality (using the == operator, possibly overloaded) and inequality (using the != operator, possibly overloaded.) If two iterators test as equal, then dereferencing one should produce the same value as dereferencing the second. That is, if:

```
iter1 == iter2
```

is true, then the following also is true:

```
*iter1 == *iter2
```

Of course these properties hold true for built-in operators and pointers, so these requirements are guides for what you must do when overloading these operators for an iterator class. Now let's look at other iterator properties.

Input Iterator

The term "input" is used from the viewpoint of a program. That is, information going from the container to the program is considered input, just as information from a keyboard to the program is considered input. So an input iterator is one that can be used by a program to read values from a container. In particular, dereferencing an input iterator must allow a program to read a value from a container, but it needn't allow a program to alter that value. So algorithms that require an input iterator are algorithms that don't change values held in a container.

An input iterator has to allow you to access all the values in a container. It does so by supporting the ++ operator, both in prefix and suffix form. If you set an input operator to the first element in a container and increment it until reaching past-the-end, it will point to every container item once en route. Incidentally, there is no guarantee that traversing a container a second time with an input iterator will move through the values in the same order. Also, after an input iterator has been incremented, there is no guarantee that its prior value can still be dereferenced. Any algorithm based on an input iterator, then, should be a single-pass algorithm that doesn't rely upon iterator values from a previous pass or upon earlier iterator values from the same pass.

Note that an input iterator is a one-way iterator; it can increment, but it can't back up.

Output Iterator

Here the term "output" indicates that the iterator is used for transferring information from a program to a container. The output iterator is similar to the input iterator, except that dereferencing is guaranteed to allow a program to alter a container value, but not to read it. If the ability to write without reading seems strange, keep in mind that property also applies to output sent to your display; cout can modify the stream of characters sent to the display, but it can't read what's on the screen. The STL is general enough that its containers can represent output devices, so you can run into the same situation with containers. Also, if an algorithm modifies the contents of a container (for example, by generating new values to be stored) without reading the contents, there's no reason to require that it use an iterator that can read the contents.

In short, you can use an input iterator for single-pass, read-only algorithms and an output operator for single-pass, write-only algorithms.

Forward Iterator

Like the input and output iterators, the forward iterator uses only the ++ operators for navigating through a container. So it can only go forward through a container one element at a time. However, unlike input and output iterators, it always goes through a sequence of values in the same order. Also, after you increment a forward iterator, you still can dereference the prior iterator value, if you've saved it, and get the same value. These properties make multiple-pass algorithms possible.

A forward iterator can allow you to both read and modify data, or it can allow you just to read it:

```
int * pirw;       // read-write iterator
const int * pir;  // read-only iterator
```

Bidirectional Iterator

Suppose you have an algorithm that needs to be able to traverse a container in both directions? For example, a reverse function could swap the first and last elements, increment the pointer to the first element, decrement the pointer to a second element, and repeat the process. A bidirectional iterator has all the features of a forward iterator and adds support for the two decrement operators (prefix and postfix).

Random Access Iterator

Some algorithms, such as sort and binary search, require the ability to jump directly to an arbitrary element of a container. This is termed random access and requires a random access iterator. It has all the features of a bidirectional iterator, plus it adds operations (like pointer addition) supporting random access and relational operators for ordering the elements. Table 16.3 lists the operations a random access iterator has beyond those of the bidirectional iterator. In this table, X represents a random iterator type, T represents the type pointed to, a and b are iterator values, n is an integer, and r is random iterator variable or reference.

TABLE 16.3   Random Access Iterator Operations

Expression	Comments
a + n	Points to the nth element after the one a points to
n + a	Same as a + n
a - n	Points to the nth element before the one a points to
r += n	Equivalent to r = r + n
r -= n	Equivalent to r = r - n
a[n]	Equivalent to *(a + n)
b - a	The value of n such that b = a + n

TABLE 16.3   Continued

Expression	Comments
a < b	True of b - a > 0
a > b	True if b < a
a >= b	True if !(a < b)
a <= b	True if !(a > b)

Expressions like a + n are valid only if both a and a + n lie within the range of the container (including past-the-end).

Iterator Hierarchy

You probably noticed that the iterator kinds form a hierarchy. A forward iterator has all the capabilities of an input iterator and of an output iterator plus its own capabilities. A bidirectional iterator has all the capabilities of a forward iterator plus its own capabilities. And a random access iterator has all the capabilities of a forward iterator plus its own capabilities. Table 16.4 summarizes the main iterator capabilities. In it, i is an iterator, n is an integer.

TABLE 16.4   Iterator Capabilities

Iterator Capability	Input	Output	Forward	Bidirectional	Random Access
Dereferencing read	yes	no	yes	yes	yes
Dereferencing write	no	yes	yes	yes	yes
Fixed and repeatable order	no	no	yes	yes	yes
++i i++	yes	yes	yes	yes	yes
--i i--	no	no	no	yes	yes
i[n]	no	no	no	no	yes
i + n	no	no	no	no	yes
i - n	no	no	no	no	yes

TABLE 16.4   Continued

Iterator Capability	Input	Output	Forward	Bidirectional	Random Access
i += n	no	no	no	no	yes
i -=n	no	no	no	no	yes

An algorithm written in terms of a particular kind of iterator can use that kind of iterator or any other iterator that has the required capabilities. So a container with, say, a random access iterator can use an algorithm written for an input iterator.

Why all these different kinds of iterators? The idea is to write an algorithm using the iterator with the fewest requirements possible, allowing it to be used with the largest range of containers. Thus, the `find()` function, by using a lowly input iterator, can be used with any container containing readable values. The `sort()` function, however, by requiring a random access iterator, can be used just with containers that support that kind of iterator.

Note that the various iterator kinds are not defined types; rather, they are conceptual characterizations. As mentioned earlier, each container class defines a class scope `typedef` name called `iterator`. So the `vector<int>` class has iterators of type `vector<int>::iterator`. But the documentation for this class would tell you that vector iterators are random access iterators. That, in turn, allows you to use algorithms based upon any iterator type because a random access iterator has all the iterator capabilities. Similarly, a `list<int>` class has iterators of type `list<int>::iterator`. The STL implements a doubly linked list, so it uses a bidirectional iterator. Thus, it can't use algorithms based on random access iterators, but it can use algorithms based on less demanding iterators.

Concepts, Refinements, and Models

The STL has several features, such as kinds of iterators, that aren't expressible in the C++ language. That is, although you can design, say, a class having the properties of a forward iterator, you can't have the compiler restrict an algorithm to only using that class. The reason is that the forward iterator is a set of requirements, not a type. The requirements could be satisfied by an iterator class you've designed, but it also can be satisfied by an ordinary pointer. An STL algorithm works with any iterator implementation that meets its requirements. STL literature uses the word *concept* to describe a set of requirements. Thus, there is an input iterator concept, a forward iterator concept, and so on. By the way, if you do need iterators for, say, a container class you're designing, the STL does include iterator templates for the standard varieties.

Concepts can have an inheritance-like relationship. For example, a bidirectional iterator inherits the capabilities of a forward iterator. However, you can't apply the C++ inheritance mechanism to iterators. For example, you might implement a forward iterator as a class and a bidirectional iterator as a regular pointer. So, in terms of the C++ language, this particular bidirectional iterator, being a built-in type, couldn't be derived from a class. Conceptually, however, it does inherit. Some STL literature uses the term *refinement* to indicate this conceptual inheritance. Thus, a bidirectional iterator is a refinement of the forward iterator concept.

A particular implementation of a concept is termed a *model*. Thus, an ordinary pointer-to-int is a model of the concept random access iterator. It's also a model of forward iterator, for it satisfies all the requirements of that concept.

The Pointer As Iterator

Iterators are generalizations of pointers, and a pointer satisfies all the iterator requirements. Iterators form the interface for STL algorithms, and pointers are iterators, so STL algorithms can use pointers to operate upon non-STL containers. For example, you can use STL algorithms with arrays. Suppose `Receipts` is an array of `double` values, and you would like to sort in ascending order:

```
const int SIZE = 100;
double Receipts[SIZE];
```

The STL `sort()` function, recall, takes as arguments an iterator pointing to the first element in a container and an iterator pointing to past-the-end. Well, `&Receipts[0]` (or just `Receipts`) is the address of the first element, and `&Receipts[SIZE]` (or just `Receipts + SIZE`) is the address of the element following the last element in the array. Thus, the function call:

```
sort(Receipts, Receipts + SIZE);
```

sorts the array. C++, by the way, does guarantee that the expression `Receipts + n` is defined as long as the result lies in the array or one past the end.

Thus, the fact that pointers are iterators and that algorithms are iterator-based makes it possible to apply STL algorithms to ordinary arrays. Similarly, you can apply STL algorithms to data forms of your own design, providing you supply suitable iterators (which may be pointers or objects) and past-the-end indicators.

copy(), ostream_iterator, and istream_iterator

The STL provides some predefined iterators. To see why, let's establish some background. There is an algorithm (`copy()`) for copying data from one container to another. This algorithm is expressed in terms of iterators, so it can copy from one kind of container to another or even from or to an array, because you can use pointers into an array as iterators. For example, the following copies an array into a vector:

```
int casts[10] = {6, 7, 2, 9 ,4 , 11, 8, 7, 10, 5};
vector<int> dice[10];
copy(casts, casts + 10, dice.begin());   // copy array to vector
```

The first two iterator arguments to `copy()` represent a range to be copied, and the final iterator argument represents the location to which the first item is copied. The first two arguments must be input iterators (or better), and the final argument must be an output iterator (or better). The `copy()` function overwrites existing data in the destination container, and the container has to be large enough to hold the copied elements. So you can't use `copy()` to place data in an empty vector, at least not without resorting to a trick to be revealed later.

Now suppose you wanted to copy information to the display. You could use `copy()` providing there was an iterator representing the output stream. The STL provides such an iterator with the `ostream_iterator` template. Using STL terminology, this template is a model of the output iterator concept. It is also an example of an *adapter*, a class or function that converts some other interface to an interface used by the STL. You can create an iterator of this kind by including the `iterator` (formerly `iterator.h`) header file and making a declaration:

```
#include <iterator>
...
ostream_iterator<int, char> out_iter(cout, " ");
```

The `out_iter` iterator now becomes an interface allowing you to use `cout` to display information. The first template argument (`int`, in this case) indicates the data type being sent to the output stream. The second template argument (`char`, in this case) indicates the character type used by the output stream. (Another possible value would be `wchar_t`.) The first constructor argument (`cout`, in this case), identifies the output stream being used. It also could be a stream used for file output, as discussed in Chapter 17, "Input, Output, and Files." The final character string argument is a separator to be displayed after each item sent to the output stream.

Caution

Older implementations use just the first template argument for the `ostream_iterator`:

```
ostream_iterator<int> out_iter(cout, " "); // older implementation
```

You could use the iterator like this:

```
*out_iter++ = 15;    // works like cout << 15 << " ";
```

For a regular pointer, this would mean assigning the value 15 to the pointed-to location, and then incrementing the pointer. For this `ostream_iterator`, however, the statement means send 15 and then a string consisting of a space to the output stream managed by `cout`. Then get ready for the next output operation. You can use the iterator with `copy()` as follows:

```
copy(dice.begin(), dice.end(), out_iter);    // copy vector to output stream
```

This would mean to copy the entire range of the `dice` container to the output stream, that is, to display the contents of the container.

Or, you can skip creating a named iterator and construct an anonymous iterator instead. That is, you can use the adapter like this:

```
copy(dice.begin(), dice.end(), ostream_iterator<int, char>(cout, " ") );
```

Similarly, the `iterator` header file defines an `istream_iterator` template for adapting `istream` input to the iterator interface. It is a model of input iterator. You can use two `istream_iterator` objects to define an input range for `copy()`:

```
copy(istream_iterator<int, char>(cin),
    istream_iterator<int, char>(), dice.begin());
```

Like `ostream_iterator`, `istream_iterator` uses two template arguments. The first indicates the data type to be read, and the second indicates the character type used by the input stream. Using a constructor argument of `cin` means to use the input stream managed by `cin`. Omitting the constructor argument indicates input failure, so the previous code means to read from the input stream until end-of-file, type mismatch, or some other input failure.

Other Useful Iterators

The iterator header file provides some other special-purpose predefined iterator types in addition to `ostream_iterator` and `istream_iterator`. They are `reverse_iterator`, `back_insert_iterator`, `front_insert_iterator`, and `insert_iterator`.

Let's start with seeing what a `reverse iterator` does. In essence, incrementing a `reverse iterator` causes it to decrement. Why not just decrement a regular iterator? The main reason is to simplify using existing functions. Suppose you want to display the contents of the `dice` container. As you just saw, you can use `copy()` and an `ostream_iterator` to copy the contents to the output stream:

```
ostream_iterator<int, char> out_iter(cout, " ");
copy(dice.begin(), dice.end(), out_iter);  // display in forward order
```

Now suppose you want to print the contents in reverse order. (Perhaps you are performing time-reversal studies.) There are several approaches that don't work, but rather than wallow in them, let's go to one that does. The `vector` class has a member function called `rbegin()` that returns a `reverse_iterator` pointing to past-the-end and a member `rend()` that returns a `reverse_iterator` pointing to the first element. Because incrementing a `reverse_iterator` makes it decrement, you can use the statement:

```
copy(dice.rbegin(), dice.rend(), out_iter); // display in reverse order
```

to display the contents backward. You don't even have to declare a `reverse_iterator`.

Remember

Both `rbegin()` and `end()` return the same value (past-the-end), but as a different type (`reverse_iterator` versus `iterator`). Similarly, both `rend()` and `begin()` return the same value (an iterator to the first element), but as a different type.

There is a special compensation reverse pointers have to make. Suppose `rp` is a reverse pointer initialized to `dice.rbegin()`. What should `*rp` be? Since `rbegin()` returns past-the-end, you shouldn't try to dereference that address. Similarly, if `rend()` is really the location of the first element, `copy()` would stop one location earlier because the end of the range is not in a range. Reverse pointers solve both problems by decrementing first, then dereferencing. That is, `*rp` dereferences the iterator value immediately preceding the current value of `*rp`. If `rp` points to position six, `*rp` is the value of position five, and so on. Listing 16.7 illustrates using `copy()`, an `istream` iterator and a reverse iterator.

LISTING 16.7   copyit.cpp

```cpp
// copyit.cpp -- copy() and iterators
#include <iostream>
#include <iterator>
#include <vector>
using namespace std;

int main()
{
    int casts[10] = {6, 7, 2, 9 ,4 , 11, 8, 7, 10, 5};
    vector<int> dice(10);
    // copy from array to vector
    copy(casts, casts + 10, dice.begin());
    cout << "Let the dice be cast!\n";
    // create an ostream iterator
    ostream_iterator<int, char> out_iter(cout, " ");
    // copy from vector to output
    copy(dice.begin(), dice.end(), out_iter);
    cout << endl;
    cout <<"Implicit use of reverse iterator.\n";
    copy(dice.rbegin(), dice.rend(), out_iter);
    cout << endl;
    cout <<"Explicit use of reverse iterator.\n";
    vector<int>::reverse_iterator ri;
    for (ri = dice.rbegin(); ri != dice.rend(); ++ri)
        cout << *ri << ' ';
    cout << endl;

    return 0;
}
```

Compatibility Notes

Older implementations may use the `iterator.h` and `vector.h` header files instead. Also, some implementations use `ostream_iterator<int>` instead of `ostream_iterator<int, char>`.

Here is the output:

```
Let the dice be cast!
6 7 2 9 4 11 8 7 10 5
Implicit use of reverse iterator.
5 10 7 8 11 4 9 2 7 6
Explicit use of reverse iterator.
5 10 7 8 11 4 9 2 7 6
```

If you have the choice of explicitly declaring iterators or using STL functions to handle the matter internally, for example, by passing an `rbegin()` return value to a function, take the latter course. It's one less thing to do and one less opportunity to experience human fallibility.

The other three iterators (`back_insert_iterator`, `front_insert_iterator`, and `insert_iterator`) also increase the generality of the STL algorithms. Many STL functions are like `copy()` in that they send their results to a location indicated by an output iterator. Recall that

```
copy(casts, casts + 10, dice.begin());
```

copies values to the location beginning at `dice.begin()`. These values overwrite the prior contents in `dice`, and the function assumes that `dice` has enough room to hold the values. That is, `copy()` does not automatically adjust the size of the destination to fit the information sent to it. Listing 16.7 took care of that situation by declaring `dice` to have 10 elements, but suppose you don't know in advance how big `dice` should be? Or suppose you want to add elements to `dice` rather than overwrite existing ones?

The three insert iterators solve these problems by converting the copying process to an insertion process. Insertion adds new elements without overwriting existing data and uses automatic memory allocation to ensure the new information fits. A `back_insert_iterator` inserts items at the end of the container, while a `front_insert_iterator` inserts items at the front. Finally, the `insert_iterator` inserts items in front of the location specified as an argument to the `insert_iterator` constructor. All three are models of the output container concept.

There are restrictions. A back insertion iterator can be used only with container types that allow rapid insertion at the end. (Rapid means a constant time algorithm; the section on containers discusses this concept further.) The `vector` class qualifies. A front insertion iterator can be used only with container types allowing constant time insertion at the beginning. Here the `vector` class doesn't qualify but the `queue` class does. The insertion iterator doesn't have these restrictions. Thus, you can use it to insert material at the front of a vector. However, a front insertion iterator will do so faster for those container types that support it.

Tip

You can use an insert iterator to convert an algorithm that copies data to one that inserts data.

These iterators take the container type as a template argument and the actual container identifier as a constructor argument. That is, to create a back insertion iterator for a `vector<int>` container called `dice`, you do this:

```
back_insert_iterator<vector<int> > back_iter(dice);
```

Declaring a front insertion iterator has the same form. An insertion iterator declaration has an additional constructor argument to identify the insertion location:

```
insert_iterator<vector<int> > insert_iter(dice, dice.begin() );
```

Listing 16.8 illustrates using two of these iterators.

LISTING 16.8   inserts.cpp

```cpp
// inserts.cpp -- copy() and insert iterators
#include <iostream>
#include <string>
#include <iterator>
#include <vector>
using namespace std;

int main()
{
    string s1[4] = {"fine", "fish", "fashion", "fate"};
    string s2[2] = {"busy", "bats"};
    string s3[2] = {"silly", "singers"};
    vector<string> words(4);
    copy(s1, s1 + 4, words.begin());
    ostream_iterator<string, char> out(cout, " ");
    copy (words.begin(), words.end(), out);
    cout << endl;

// construct anonymous back_insert_iterator object
    copy(s2, s2 + 2, back_insert_iterator<vector<string> >(words));
    copy (words.begin(), words.end(), out);
    cout << endl;

// construct anonymous insert_iterator object
    copy(s3, s3 + 2, insert_iterator<vector<string> >(words, words.begin()));
    copy (words.begin(), words.end(), out);
    cout << endl;

    return 0;
}
```

Compatibility Note

Older compilers may use list.h and iterator.h. Also, some compilers may use ostream_itera-tor<int> instead of ostream_iterator<int,char>.

Here is the output:

```
fine fish fashion fate
fine fish fashion fate busy bats
silly singers fine fish fashion fate busy bats
```

If you're feeling overwhelmed by all the iterator varieties, keep in mind that using them will make them familiar. Also keep in mind that these predefined iterators expand the generality of the STL algorithms. Thus, not only can **copy()** copy information from one container to another, it can copy information from a container to the output stream and from the input stream to a container. And you also can use **copy()** to insert material into another container. So you wind up with a single function doing the work of many. And because **copy()** is just one of several STL functions that use an output iterator, these predefined iterators multiply the capabilities of those functions, too.

Kinds of Containers

The STL has both container concepts and container types. The concepts are general categories with names like container, sequence container, associative container, and so on. The container types are templates you can use to create specific container objects. The eleven container types are deque, list, queue, priority_queue, stack, vector, map, multimap, set, multiset, and bitset. (This chapter won't discuss bitset, which is a container for dealing with data at the bit level.) Because the concepts categorize the types, let's start with them.

The Container Concept

There is no type corresponding to the basic container concept, but the concept describes elements common to all the container classes. It's sort of a conceptual abstract base class— conceptual because the container classes don't actually use the inheritance mechanism. Or putting it another way, the container concept lays down a set of requirements that all STL container classes must satisfy.

A container is an object that stores other objects, which are all of a single type. The stored objects may be objects in the OOP sense, or they may be values of built-in types. Data stored in a container are *owned* by the container. That means when a container expires, so do the data stored in the container. (However, if the data are pointers, the pointed-to data does not necessarily expire.)

You can't store just any kind of object in a container. In particular, the type has to be *copy constructable* and *assignable*. Basic types satisfy these requirements as do class types unless the class definition makes one or both of the copy constructor and the assignment operator private or protected.

The basic container doesn't guarantee that its elements are stored in any particular order or that the order doesn't change, but refinements to the concept may add such guarantees. All containers do provide certain features and operations. Table 16.5 summarizes several of these common features. In the table, X represents a container type, such as vector, T represents the type of object stored in the container, a and b represent values of type X, and u represents an identifier of type X.

TABLE 16.5   Some Basic Container Properties

Expression	Return type	Comment	Complexity
X::iterator	Iterator type pointing to T	Any iterator category except output iterator	Compile time
X::value_type	T	The type for T	Compile time
X u;		Creates 0-size container called u	Constant

TABLE 16.5   Continued

Expression	Return type	Comment	Complexity
X();		Creates 0-size anonymous container	Constant
X u(a);		Copy constructor	Linear
X u = a;		Same effect as X u(a);	
(&a)->~X();	void	Apply destructor to every element of a container	Linear
a.begin()	iterator	Returns an iterator referring to first element of container	Constant
a.end()	iterator	Returns an iterator that is a past-the-end value	Constant
a.size()	unsigned integral type	Number of elements, equal to a.end() - a.begin()	Constant
a.swap(b)	void	Swap contents of a and b	Constant
a == b	convertible to bool	True if a and b have the same size and each element in a is equivalent to (== is true) the corresponding element in b	Linear
a != b	convertible to bool	same as !(a == b)	Linear

The complexity column describes the time needed to perform an operator. This table lists three possibilities, which, from fastest to slowest, are as follows:

- compile time
- constant time
- linear time

If the complexity is compile time, the action is performed during compilation and uses no execution time. A constant complexity means the operation takes place during runtime but doesn't depend upon the number of elements in an object. A linear complexity means the time is proportional to the number of elements. Thus, if a and b are containers, a == b has linear complexity because the == operation may have to be applied to each element of the container. Actually, that is a worst-case scenario. If two containers have different sizes, no individual comparisons need be made.

Constant Time and Linear Time Complexity

Consider a long narrow box filled with large packages arranged in a line, and suppose the box is open at just one end. Suppose my task is to unload the package at the open end. This is a constant time task. Whether there are 10 packages or a 1000 packages behind the one at the end makes no difference.

Now suppose my task is to fetch the package at the closed end of the box. This is a linear time task. If there are 10 packages altogether, I have to unload 10 packages to get the one at the closed end. If there are 100 packages, I have to unload 100 packages at the end. Assuming I'm a tireless worker who can move only one package at a time, that will take ten times longer.

Now suppose my task is to fetch an arbitrary package. It might happen that the package I'm supposed to get is the first one at hand. However, on the average, the number of packages I have to move is still proportional to the number of packages in the container, so the task still has linear time complexity.

Replacing the long narrow box with a similar box having open sides would change the task to constant time complexity, for then I could move directly to the desired package and remove it without moving the others.

The idea of time complexity describes the effect of container size on execution time but ignores other factors. If a superhero can unload packages from a box with one open end 1000 times faster than me, the task as executed by her still has linear time complexity. In this case, her linear time performance with a closed box (open end) would be faster than my constant time performance with an open box as long as the boxes didn't have too many packages.

Complexity requirements are characteristic of the STL. While the details of an implementation may be hidden, the performance specifications should be public so that you know the computing cost of doing a particular operation.

Sequences

You can refine the basic container concept by adding requirements. The *sequence* is an important refinement, for six of the STL container types (deque, list, queue, priority_queue, stack, and vector) are sequences. (Recall that a queue allows elements to be added at the rear end and removed from the front. A double-ended queue, represented by **deque**, allows addition and removal at both ends.) The sequence concept adds the requirement that the iterator be at least a forward iterator. This, in turn, guarantees that the elements are arranged in a definite order that doesn't change from one cycle of iteration to the next.

The sequence also requires that its elements be arranged in strict linear order. That is, there is a first element, a last element, and each element but the first and last has exactly one element immediately ahead of it and one element immediately after it. An array and a linked list are examples of a sequence, while a branching structure (in which each node points to two daughter nodes) would not be.

Because elements in sequence have a definite order, operations such as inserting values at a particular location and erasing a particular range become possible. Table 16.6 lists these and other operations required of a sequence. The table uses the same notation as Table 16.5, with the addition of **t** representing a value of type **T**, that is, the type of value stored in the container, of **n**, an integer, and of **p**, **q**, **i** and **j**, representing iterators.

TABLE 16.6   Sequence Requirements

Expression	Return Type	Comments
`X a(n,t);`		Declares a sequence a of n copies of value t
`X(n, t)`		Creates an anonymous sequence of n copies of value t
`X a(i, j)`		Declares a sequence a initialized to the contents of range [i,j)
`X(i, j)`		Creates an anonymous sequence initialized to the contents of range [i,j)
`a.insert(p,t)`	iterator	Inserts a copy of t before p
`a.insert(p,n,t)`	void	Inserts n copies of t before p
`a.insert(p,i,j)`	void	Insert copies of elements in the range [i,j) before p
`a.erase(p)`	iterator	Erases the element pointed to by p
`a.erase(p,q)`	iterator	Erases the elements in the range [p,q)
`a.clear()`	void	Same as `erase(begin(), end())`

Because the **deque**, **list**, **queue**, **stack**, and **vector** template classes all are models of the sequence concept, they all support the operators of Table 16.6. In addition there are operations that are available to some of these five models. When allowed, they have constant time complexity. Table 16.7 lists these additional operations.

TABLE 16.7 Optional Sequence Requirements

Expression	Return Type	Meaning	Container
a.front()	T&	*a.begin()	vector, list, deque
a.back()	T&	*--a.end()	vector, list, deque
a.push_front(t)	void	a.insert(a.begin(), t)	list, deque
a.push_back(t)	void	a.insert(a.end(), t)	vector, list, deque
a.pop_front(t)	void	a.erase(a.begin())	list, deque
a.pop_back(t)	void	a.erase(--a.end())	vector, list, deque
a[n]	T&	*(a.begin() + n)	vector, deque
a.at(n)	T&	*(a.begin() + n)	vector, deque

Table 16.7 does merit a comment or two. First, you'll notice that **a[n]** and **a.at(n)** both return a reference to the nth element (numbering from 0) in a container. The difference is that **a.at(n)** does bounds checking and throws an **out_of_range** exception if n is outside the valid range for the container. Next, you might wonder why, say, **push_front()** is defined for **list** and **deque** and not **vector**. Suppose you want to insert a new value at the front of a vector of 100 elements. To make room, you have to move element 99 to position 100, and then move element 98 to position 99, and so on. This is an operation with linear time complexity because moving 100 elements would take 100 times as long as moving a single element. But the operations in Table 16.7 are supposed to be implemented only if they can be performed with constant time complexity. The design for lists and double-ended queues, however, allows an element to be added to the front without moving the other elements to new locations, so they can implement **push_front()** with constant time complexity. Figure 16.4 illustrates **push_front()** and **push_back()**.

Let's take a closer look at the six sequence container types.

vector

You've already seen several examples using the **vector** template, which is declared in the **vector** header file. In brief, **vector** is a class representation of an array. The class provides automatic memory management that allows the size of a **vector** object to vary dynamically, growing and shrinking as elements are added or removed. It provides random access to elements. Elements can be added to or removed from the end in constant time, but insertion and removal from the beginning and the middle are linear-time operations.

FIGURE 16.4

push_front() and
push_back().

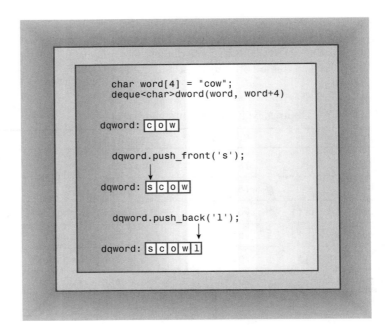

```
char word[4] = "cow";
deque<char>dword(word, word+4)
```

dqword: `c o w`

`dqword.push_front('s');`

dqword: `s c o w`

`dqword.push_back('l');`

dqword: `s c o w l`

In addition to being a sequence, a **vector** also is a model of the *reversible container* concept. This adds two more class methods: **rbegin()** returns an iterator to the first element of the reversed sequence, and **rend()** returns a past-the-end iterator for the reversed sequence. So if **dice** is a **vector<int>** container and **Show(int)** is a function that displays an integer, the following code will first display the contents of **dice** in forward order and then in reverse order:

```
for_each(dice.begin(), dice.end(), Show);    // display in order
cout << endl;
for_each(dice.rbegin(), dice.rend(), Show);  // display in reversed order
cout << endl;
```

The iterator returned by the two methods is of a class scope type **reverse_iterator**. Incrementing such an iterator, recall, causes it to move through a reversible container in reverse order.

The **vector** template class is the simplest of the sequence types and is considered the type that should be used by default unless the program requirements are better satisfied by the particular virtues of the other types.

deque

The **deque** template class (declared in the **deque** header file) represents a double-ended queue, a type often called a *deque* (sounds like deck), for short. As implemented in the STL, it's a lot like a **vector**, supporting random access. The main difference is that inserting and removing items from the beginning of a **deque** object are constant-time operations instead of being linear-time operations the way they are for **vector**. So if most operations take place at the beginning and ends of a sequence, consider using a **deque** data structure.

The goal of constant-time insertion and removal at both ends of a deque make the design of a deque more complex than that of a vector. Thus, while both offer random access to elements and linear-time insertion and removal from the middle of a sequence, the vector should allow faster execution of these operations.

list

The list template class (declared in the list header file) represents a doubly linked list. Each element, other than the first and last, is linked to the item before it and the item following it, implying that a list can be traversed in both directions. The crucial difference between list and vector is that list provides for constant-time insertion and removal of elements at any location in the list. (The vector template, recall, provides linear-time insertion and removal except at the end, where it provides constant-time insertion and removal.) Thus, vector emphasizes rapid access via random access, while a list emphasizes rapid insertion and removal of elements.

Like vector, list is a reversible container. Unlike vector, list does not support array notation and random access. Unlike a vector iterator, a list iterator remains pointing to the same element even after items are inserted into or removed from a container. Let's clarify this statement. Suppose you have an iterator pointing to the fifth element of a vector container. Then suppose you insert an element at the beginning of the container. All the other elements have to be moved to make room, so after the insertion, the fifth element now contains the value that used to be in the fourth element. Thus, the iterator points to the same location but different data. Inserting a new element into a list, however, doesn't move the existing elements; it just alters the link information. An iterator pointing to a certain item still points to the same item, but it may be linked to different items than before.

The list template class has some list-oriented member functions in addition to those that come with sequences and reversible containers. Table 16.8 lists many of them. (For a complete list of STL methods and functions, see Appendix G.) The Alloc template parameter is one you normally don't have to worry about because it has a default value.

TABLE 16.8   Some list Member Functions

Function	Description
void merge(list<T, Alloc>& x)	Merges list x with the invoking list. Both lists must be sorted. The resulting sorted list is in the invoking list, and x is left empty. This function has linear time complexity.
void remove(const T & val)	Removes all instances of val from the list. This function has linear time complexity.
void sort()	Sorts the list using the < operator; the complexity is N log N for N elements.

TABLE 16.8   Continued

Function	Description
void splice(iterator pos, list<T, Alloc> x)	Inserts the contents of list x in front of position **pos**, and x is left empty. This function has constant-time complexity.
void unique()	Collapses each consecutive group of equal elements to a single element. This function has linear-time complexity.

Listing 16.9 illustrates these methods along with the insert() method.

LISTING 16.9   list.cpp

```
// list.cpp -- using a list
#include <iostream>
#include <list>
#include <iterator>
using namespace std;

int main()
{
    list<int> one(5, 2); // list of 5 2s
    int stuff[5] = {1,2,4,8, 6};
    list<int> two;
    two.insert(two.begin(),stuff, stuff + 5 );
    int more[6] = {6, 4, 2, 4, 6, 5};
    list<int> three(two);
    three.insert(three.end(), more, more + 6);

    cout << "List one: ";
    ostream_iterator<int,char> out(cout, " ");
    copy(one.begin(), one.end(), out);
    cout << endl << "List two: ";
    copy(two.begin(), two.end(), out);
    cout << endl << "List three: ";
    copy(three.begin(), three.end(), out);
    three.remove(2);
    cout << endl << "List three minus 2s: ";
    copy(three.begin(), three.end(), out);
    three.splice(three.begin(), one);
    cout << endl << "List three after splice: ";
    copy(three.begin(), three.end(), out);
    cout << endl << "List one: ";
    copy(one.begin(), one.end(), out);
    three.unique();
    cout << endl << "List three after unique: ";
    copy(three.begin(), three.end(), out);
    three.sort();
    three.unique();
```

LISTING 16.9   Continued

```
    cout << endl << "List three after sort & unique: ";
    copy(three.begin(), three.end(), out);
    two.sort();
    three.merge(two);
    cout << endl << "Sorted two merged into three: ";
    copy(three.begin(), three.end(), out);
    cout << endl;

    return 0;
}
```

Compatibility Note

Older versions may use `list.h` and `iterator.h`. Also, older versions may use `ostream_iterator<int>` instead of `ostream_iterator<int,char>`.

Here is the output:

```
List one: 2 2 2 2
List two: 1 2 4 8 6
List three: 1 2 4 8 6 6 4 2 4 6 5
List three minus 2s: 1 4 8 6 6 4 4 6 5
List three after splice: 2 2 2 2 1 4 8 6 6 4 4 6 5
List one:
List three after unique: 2 1 4 8 6 4 6 5
List three after sort & unique: 1 2 4 5 6 8
Sorted two merged into three: 1 1 2 2 4 4 5 6 6 8 8
```

Program Notes

The program uses the technique discussed earlier for using the general STL `copy()` function and an `ostream_iterator` object to display the contents of a container.

The main difference between `insert()` and `splice()` is that `insert()` inserts a copy of the original range into the destination, while `splice()` moves the original range into the destination. Thus, after the contents of `one` are spliced to `three`, `one` is left empty. (The `splice()` method has additional prototypes for moving single elements and a range of elements.) The `splice()` method leaves iterators valid. That is, if you set a particular iterator to point to an element in `one`, that iterator would still point to the same element after `splice()` relocated it in `three`.

Notice that `unique()` only reduces adjacent equal values to a single value. After the program executes `three.unique()`, `three` still contains two 4s and two 6s that weren't adjacent. But applying `sort()` and then `unique()` does limit each value to a single appearance.

There is a non-member `sort()` function (Listing 16.6), but it requires random access iterators. Because the trade-off for rapid insertion was giving up random access, you can't use the non-member `sort()` with a list. Therefore, the class includes a member version that works within the restrictions of the class.

The list *Toolbox*

The list methods form a handy toolbox. Suppose, for example, that you have two mailing lists to organize. You could sort each list, merge them, and then use unique() to remove multiple entries.

The sort(), merge(), and unique() methods also each have a version accepting an additional argument to specify an alternative function to be used for comparing elements. Similarly, the remove() method has a version with an additional argument specifying a function used to determine whether or not an element is removed. These arguments are examples of predicate functions, a topic to which we'll return later.

queue

The queue template class (declared in the queue (formerly queue.h header file) is an adapter class. Recall that the ostream_iterator template is an adapter that allows an output stream to use the iterator interface. Similarly, the queue template allows an underlying class (deque, by default) to exhibit the typical queue interface.

The queue template is more restrictive than deque. Not only doesn't it permit random access to elements of a queue, the queue class doesn't even allow you to iterate through a queue. Instead, it limits you to the basic operations that define a queue. You can add an element to the rear of queue, remove an element from the front of a queue, view the values of the front and rear elements, check the number of elements, and test to see if the queue is empty. Table 16.9 lists these operations.

TABLE 16.9   queue Operations

Method	Description
bool empty() const	Returns true if the queue is empty, and false otherwise.
size_type size() const	Returns the number of elements in the queue.
T& front()	Returns a reference to the element at the front of the queue.
T& back()	Returns a reference to the element at the back of the queue.
void push(const T& x)	Inserts x at the back of the queue.
void pop()	Removes the element at the front of the queue.

Note that pop() is a data removal method, not a data retrieval method. If you want to use a value from a queue, first use front() to retrieve the value, and then pop() to remove it from the queue.

priority_queue

The `priority_queue` template class (also declared in the `queue` header file) is another adapter class. It supports the same operations as `queue`. The main difference is that the largest item gets moved to the front of the queue. (Life is not always fair, and neither are queues.) An internal difference is that the default underlying class is `vector`. You can alter the comparison used to determine what gets to the head of the queue by providing an optional constructor argument:

```
priority_queue<int> pq1;                 // default version
priority_queue<int> pq2(greater<int>);   // use greater<int> to order
```

The `greater<>()` function is a predefined function object discussed later in this chapter.

stack

Like `queue`, `stack` (declared in the `stack`—formerly `stack.h`—header file) is an adapter class. It gives an underlying class (`vector`, by default) the typical stack interface.

The `stack` template is more restrictive than `vector`. Not only doesn't it permit random access to elements of a stack, the `stack` class doesn't even allow you to iterate through a stack. Instead, it limits you to the basic operations that define a stack. You can push a value onto the top of a stack, pop an element from the top of a stack, view the value at the top of the stack, check the number of elements, and test to see if the stack is empty. Table 16.10 lists these operations.

TABLE 16.10   stack Operations

Method	Description
bool empty() const	Returns `true` if the stack is empty, and `false` otherwise.
size_type size() const	Returns the number of elements in the stack.
T& top()	Returns a reference to the element at the top of the stack.
void push(const T& x)	Inserts x at the top of the stack.
void pop()	Removes the element at the top of the stack.

Much as with `queue`, if you want to use a value from a stack, first use `top()` to retrieve the value, then use `pop()` to remove it from the queue.

Associative Containers

The *associative container* is another refinement of the container concept. An associative container associates a value with a *key* and uses the key to find the value. For example, the values could be structures representing employee information, such as name, address, office number, home and work phones, health plan, and so on, and the key could be a unique employee number. To fetch the employee information, a program would use the key to locate the employee structure. Recall that for a container `X`, in general, the expression `X::value_type` indicates the type of value stored in the container. For an associative container, the expression `X::key_type` indicates the type used for the key.

The strength of an associative container is that it provides rapid access to its elements. Like a sequence, an associative container allows you to insert new elements; however, you can't specify a particular location for the inserted elements. The reason is that an associative container usually has a particular algorithm for determining where to place data so that it can retrieve information quickly.

The STL provides four associative containers: `set`, `multiset`, `map`, and `multimap`. The first two types are defined in the `set` header file (formerly separately in `set.h` and `multiset.h`), and the second two types are defined in the `map` header file (formerly separately in `map.h` and `multimap.h`).

The simplest of the bunch is `set`; the value type is the same as the key type, and the keys are unique, meaning there is no more than one instance of a key in a set. Indeed, for `set`, the value is the key. The `multiset` type is like the `set` type except that it can have more than one value with the same key. For example, if the key and value type are `int`, a `multiset` object could hold, say 1,2,2,2,3,5,7,7.

For the `map` type, the value type is different from the key type, and the keys are unique, with only one value per key. The `multimap` type is similar to `map`, except one key can be associated with multiple values.

There's too much information about these types to cover in this chapter (but Appendix G does list the methods), so let's just look at a simple example using `set` and a simple example using `multimap`.

A set Example

The STL `set` models several concepts. It is an associative set, it is reversible, it is sorted, and the keys are unique, so it can hold no more than one of any given value. Like `vector` and `list`, `set` uses a template parameter to provide the type stored:

```
set<string> A;   // a set of string objects
```

An optional second template argument can be used to indicate a comparison function or object to be used to order the key. By default, the `less<>` template (discussed later) is used. Older implementations may not provide a default value and thus require an explicit template parameter:

```
set<string, less<string> > A;   // older implementation
```

Consider the following code:

```
const int N = 6;
string s1[N] = {"buffoon", "thinkers", "for", "heavy", "can", "for"};
set<string> A(s1, s1 + N);        // initialize set A using a range from array
ostream_iterator<string, char> out(cout, " ");
copy(A.begin(), A.end(), out);
```

Like other containers, set has a constructor (see Table 16.6) that takes a range of iterators as arguments. This provides a simple way to initialize a set to the contents of an array. Remember, the last element of a range is one past the end, and s1 + N points to one position past the end of array s1. The output for this code fragment illustrates that keys are unique (the string "for" appears twice in the array but once in the set) and that the set is sorted:

```
buffoon can for heavy thinkers
```

Mathematics defines some standard operations for sets. The union of two sets is a set that combines the contents of the two sets. If a particular value is common to both sets, it appears just once in the union because of the unique key feature. The intersection of two sets is a set consisting of those elements common to both sets. The difference between two sets is the first set minus the elements common to both sets.

The STL provides algorithms supporting these operations. They are general functions rather than methods, so they aren't restricted to set objects. However, all set objects automatically satisfy the precondition for using these algorithms, namely, that the container be sorted. The set_union() function takes five iterators as arguments. The first two define a range in one set, the second two a range in a second set, and the final iterator is an output iterator identifying a location to copy the resultant set. For example, to display the union of sets A and B, you can do this:

```
set_union(A.begin(), A.end(), B.begin(), B.end(),
        ostream_iterator<string, char> out(cout, " "));
```

Suppose you want to place the result into a set C instead of displaying it. Then you would want the last argument to be an iterator into C. The obvious choice is C.begin(), but it doesn't work for two reasons. The first reason is that associative sets treat keys as constant values, so the iterator returned by C.begin() is a constant iterator and can't be used as an output iterator. The second reason not to use C.begin() directly is that set_union(), like copy(), overwrites existing data in a container and requires the container to have sufficient space to hold the new information. C, being empty, does not satisfy that requirement. But the insert_iterator template discussed earlier solves both problems. Earlier you saw that it converts copying to insertion. Also, it models the output iterator concept, so you can use it to write to a container. So you can construct an anonymous insert_iterator to copy information to C. The constructor, recall, takes the name of the container and an iterator as arguments:

```
set_union(A.begin(), A.end(), B.begin(), B.end(),
        insert_iterator<set<string> >(C, C.begin()));
```

The set_intersection() and set_difference() functions find the set intersection and set difference of two sets, and they have the same interface as set_union().

Two useful set methods are lower_bound() and upper_bound(). The lower_bound() method takes a key as its argument and returns an iterator pointing to the first member of the set that is not less than the key argument. Similarly, the upper_bound() method takes a key as its argument and returns an iterator pointing to the first member of the set that is greater than the key argument. For example, if you had a set of strings, you could use these methods to identify a range encompassing all strings from "b" up to "f" in the set.

Because sorting determines where additions to a set go, the class has insertion methods that just specify the material to be inserted without specifying a position. If A and B are sets of strings, for example, you can do this:

```
string s("tennis");
A.insert(s);                    // insert a value
B.insert(A.begin(), A.end());   // insert a range
```

Listing 16.10 illustrates these uses of sets.

LISTING 16.10   setops.cpp
_____

```
// setops.cpp -- some set operations
#include <iostream>
#include <string>
#include <set>
#include <algorithm>
#include <iterator>
using namespace std;

int main()
{
    const int N = 6;
    string s1[N] = {"buffoon", "thinkers", "for", "heavy", "can", "for"};
    string s2[N] = {"metal", "any", "food", "elegant", "deliver","for"};

    set<string> A(s1, s1 + N);
    set<string> B(s2, s2 + N);

    ostream_iterator<string, char> out(cout, " ");
    cout << "Set A: ";
    copy(A.begin(), A.end(), out);
    cout << endl;
    cout << "Set B: ";
    copy(B.begin(), B.end(), out);
    cout << endl;

    cout << "Union of A and B:\n";
    set_union(A.begin(), A.end(), B.begin(), B.end(), out);
    cout << endl;

    cout << "Intersection of A and B:\n";
    set_intersection(A.begin(), A.end(), B.begin(), B.end(), out);
    cout << endl;

    cout << "Difference of A and B:\n";
    set_difference(A.begin(), A.end(), B.begin(), B.end(), out);
    cout << endl;

    set<string> C;
    cout << "Set C:\n";
```

LISTING 16.10   Continued

```
    set_union(A.begin(), A.end(), B.begin(), B.end(),
        insert_iterator<set<string> >(C, C.begin()));
    copy(C.begin(), C.end(), out);
    cout << endl;

    string s3("grungy");
    C.insert(s3);
    cout << "Set C after insertion:\n";
    copy(C.begin(), C.end(),out);
    cout << endl;

    cout << "Showing a range:\n";
    copy(C.lower_bound("ghost"),C.upper_bound("spook"), out);
    cout << endl;

    return 0;
}
```

<table>
<tr><td></td><td style="background:#ccc">Compatibility Note</td></tr>
</table>

Older implementations may use `set.h`, `iterator.h`, and `algo.h`. Older implementations may require `less<string>` as a second template argument for `set`. Also, older versions may use `ostream_iterator<string>` instead of `ostream_iterator<string,char>`.

Here is the output:

```
Set A: buffoon can for heavy thinkers
Set B: any deliver elegant food for metal
Union of A and B:
any buffoon can deliver elegant food for heavy metal thinkers
Intersection of A and B:
for
Difference of A and B:
buffoon can heavy thinkers
Set C:
any buffoon can deliver elegant food for heavy metal thinkers
Set C after insertion:
any buffoon can deliver elegant food for grungy heavy metal thinkers
Showing a range:
grungy heavy metal
```

A multimap **Example**

Like `set`, `multimap` is a reversible, sorted, associative container. However, the key type is different from the value type, and a `multimap` object can have more than one value associated with a particular key.

The basic `multimap` declaration specifies the key type and the type of value stored as template arguments. For example, the following declaration creates a `multimap` object using `int` as the key type and `string` as the type of value stored:

```
multimap<int,string> codes;
```

An optional third template argument can be used to indicate a comparison function or object to be used to order the key. By default, the `less<>` template (discussed later) is used with the key type as its parameter. Older implementations may require this template parameter explicitly.

To keep information together, the actual value type combines the key type and the data type into a single pair. To do this, the STL uses a `pair<class T, class U>` template class for storing two kinds of values in a single object. If `keytype` is the key type and `datatype` is the type of the stored data, then the value type is `pair<const keytype, datatype>`. For example, the value type for the `codes` object declared earlier is `pair<const int, string>`.

Suppose, for example, you wanted to store city names using the area code as a key. This happens to fit the `codes` declaration, which uses an `int` for a key and a `string` as a data type. One approach is to create a pair and then insert it:

```
pair<const int, string> item(213, "Los Angeles");
codes.insert(item);
```

Or you can create an anonymous `pair` object and insert it in a single statement:

```
codes.insert(pair<const int, string> (213, "Los Angeles"));
```

Because items are sorted by key, there's no need to identify an insertion location.

Given a `pair` object, you can access the two components by using the `first` and `second` members:

```
pair<const int, string> item(213, "Los Angeles");
cout << item.first << ' ' << item.second << endl;
```

What about getting information about a `multimap` object? The `count()` member function takes a key as its argument and returns the number of items having that key. There are `lower_bound()` and `upper_bound()` member functions that take a key and work as they did for `set`. There's an `equal_range()` member function that takes a key as its argument and returns iterators representing the range matching that key. In order to return two values, the method packages them into a `pair` object, this time with both template arguments being the iterator type. For example, the following would print a list of cities in the `codes` object with area code 718:

```
pair<multimap<KeyType, string>::iterator,
    multimap<KeyType, string>::iterator> range
                        = codes.equal_range(718);
cout << "Cities with area code 718:\n";
for (it = range.first; it != range.second; ++it)
    cout <<  (*it).second    << endl;
```

Listing 16.11 demonstrates most of these techniques. It also uses `typedef` to simplify some of the code writing.

LISTING 16.11   multmap.cpp

```cpp
// multmap.cpp -- use a multimap
#include <iostream>
using namespace std;
#include <string>
#include <map>
#include <algorithm>

typedef int KeyType;
typedef pair<const KeyType, string> Pair;
typedef multimap<KeyType, string> MapCode;

int main()
{
    MapCode codes;

    codes.insert(Pair(415, "San Francisco"));
    codes.insert(Pair(510, "Oakland"));
    codes.insert(Pair(718, "Brooklyn"));
    codes.insert(Pair(718, "Staten Island"));
    codes.insert(Pair(415, "San Rafael"));
    codes.insert(Pair(510, "Berkeley"));

    cout << "Number of cities with area code 415: "
        << codes.count(415) << endl;
    cout << "Number of cities with area code 718: "
        << codes.count(718) << endl;
    cout << "Number of cities with area code 510: "
        << codes.count(510) << endl;
    cout << "Area Code   City\n";
    MapCode::iterator it;
    for (it = codes.begin(); it != codes.end(); ++it)
        cout << "     " << (*it).first << "     "
            << (*it).second    << endl;

    pair<MapCode::iterator, MapCode::iterator> range
        = codes.equal_range(718);
    cout << "Cities with area code 718:\n";
    for (it = range.first; it != range.second; ++it)
        cout <<  (*it).second    << endl;

    return 0;
}
```

Compatibility Note

Older implementations may use `multimap.h` and `algo.h`. Older implementations may require `less<Pair>` as a third template argument for `multimap`. Also, older versions may use `ostream_iterator<string>` instead of `ostream_iterator<string,char>`. Borland's C++Builder 1.0 wants the `const` omitted from the `Pair` typedef.

Here is the output:

```
Number of cities with area code 415: 2
Number of cities with area code 718: 2
Number of cities with area code 510: 2
Area Code   City
    415     San Francisco
    415     San Rafael
    510     Oakland
    510     Berkeley
    718     Brooklyn
    718     Staten Island
Cities with area code 718:
Brooklyn
Staten Island
```

Function Objects (aka Functors)

Many STL algorithms use *function objects*, also known as *functors*. A functor is any object that can be used with () in the manner of a function. This includes normal function names, pointers to functions, and class objects for which the () operator is overloaded, that is, classes for which the peculiar-looking function `operator()()` is defined. For example, you could define a class like this:

```cpp
class Linear
{
private:
    double slope;
    double y0;
public:
    Linear(double _sl = 1, double _y = 0)
        : slope(_sl), y0(_y) {}
    double operator()(double x) {return y0 + slope * x; }
};
```

The overloaded () operator then allows you to use `Linear` objects like functions:

```cpp
Linear f1;
Linear f2(2.5, 10.0);
double y1 = f1(12.5);    // rhs is f1.operator()(12.5)
double y2 = f2(0.4);
```

Remember the `for_each` function? It applied a specified function to each member of a range:

```cpp
for_each(books.begin(), books.end(), ShowReview);
```

In general, the third argument could be a functor, not just a regular function. Actually, this raises a question. How do you declare the third argument? You can't declare it as a function pointer, for a function pointer specifies the argument type. Because a container can contain about any type, you don't know in advance what particular argument type should be used. The STL solves that problem by using templates. The `for_each` prototype looks like this:

```cpp
template<class InputIterator, class Function>
Function for_each(InputIterator first, InputIterator last, Function f);
```

The `ShowReview()` prototype was this:

```
void ShowReview(const Review &);
```

This makes the identifier `ShowReview` have the type `void (*)(const Review &)`, so that is the type assigned to the template argument `Function`. With a different function call, the `Function` argument could represent a class type having an overloaded `()` operator. Ultimately, the `for_each()` code will have an expression using `f(...)`. In the `ShowReview()` example, `f` is a pointer to a function, and `f(...)` invokes the function. If the final `for_each()` argument is an object, then `f(...)` becomes the object invoking its overloaded `()` operator.

Functor Concepts

Just as the STL defines concepts for containers and iterators, it defines functor concepts:

- A *generator* is a functor that can be called with no arguments.
- A *unary function* is a functor that can be called with one argument.
- A *binary function* is a functor that can be called with two arguments.

For example, the functor supplied to `for_each()` should be a unary function because it is applied to one container element at a time.

Of course, these concepts come with refinements:

- A unary function that returns a `bool` value is a *predicate*.
- A binary function that returns a `bool` value is a *binary predicate*.

Several STL functions require predicate or binary predicate arguments. For example, Listing 16.6 uses a version of `sort()` that took a binary predicate as its third argument:

```
bool WorseThan(const Review & r1, const Review & r2);
...
sort(books.begin(), books.end(), WorseThan);
```

The `list` template has a `remove_if()` member that takes a predicate as an argument. It applies the predicate to each member in the indicated range, removing those elements for which the predicate returns `true`. For example, the following code would remove all elements greater than 100 from the list `three`:

```
bool tooBig(int n){ return n > 100; }
list<int> scores;
...
scores.remove_if(tooBig);
```

Incidentally, this last example shows where a class functor might be useful. Suppose you wanted to remove every value greater than 200 from a second list. It would be nice if you could pass the cut-off value to `tooBig()` as a second argument so you could use the function with different values, but a predicate can have but one argument. If, however, you design a `TooBig` class, you can use class members instead of function arguments to convey additional information:

```
template<class T>
class TooBig
{
private:
    T cutoff;
public:
    TooBig(const T & t) : cutoff(t) {}
    bool operator()(const T & v) { return v > cutoff; }
};
```

Here one value (v) is passed as a function argument while the second argument (cutoff) is set by the class constructor. Given this definition, you can initialize different TooBig objects to different cut-off values:

```
TooBig<int> f100(100);
list<int> froobies;
list<int> scores;
...
froobies.remove_if(f100);              // use a named function object
scores.remove_if(TooBig<int>(200));    // construct a function object
```

Compatibility Note

The remove_if() method is a template method of a template class. Template methods are a recent extension to C++ template facilities (mainly because the STL needs them), and most compilers at the time of this writing haven't implemented them yet. However, there also is a non-member remove_if() function that takes a range (two iterators) and a predicate as arguments.

Suppose that you already had a template function with two arguments:

```
template <class T>
bool tooBig(const T & val, const T & lim)
{
    return val > lim;
}
```

You can use a class to convert it to a one-argument function object:

```
template<class T>
class TooBig2
{
private:
    T cutoff;
public:
    TooBig2(const T & t) : cutoff(t) {}
    bool operator()(const T & v) { return tooBig<T>(v, cutoff); }
};
```

That is, you can do the following:

```
TooBig2<int> tB100(100);
int x;
cin >> x;
if (tB100(x))    // same as if (tooBig(x,100))
    ...
```

So the call `tB100(x)` is the same as `tooBig(x,100)`, but the two-argument function is converted to a one-argument function object, with the second argument being used to construct the function object. In short, the class functor `TooBig2` is a function adapter, adapting a function to meet a different interface.

Predefined Functors

The STL defines several elementary function objects. They perform actions such as adding two values, comparing two values for equality, and so on. They are provided to help support STL functions that take functions as arguments. For example, consider the `transform()` function. It has two versions. The first version takes four arguments. The first two are iterators specifying a range in a container. (By now you must be familiar with that approach.) The third is an iterator specifying where to copy the result. The final is a functor which is applied to each element in the range to produce each new element in the result. For example, consider the following:

```
const int LIM = 5;
double arr1[LIM] = {36, 39, 42, 45, 48};
vector<double> gr8(arr1, arr1 + LIM);
ostream_iterator<double, char> out(cout, " ");
transform(gr8.begin(), gr8.end(), out, sqrt);
```

This code would calculate the square root of each element and send the resulting values to the output stream. The destination iterator can be in the original range. For example, replacing `out` in the above example with `gr8.begin()` would copy the new values over the old values. Clearly, the functor used must be one that works with a single argument.

The second version uses a function that takes two arguments, applying it to one element from each of two ranges. It takes an additional argument, which comes third in order, identifying the start of the second range. For example, if `m8` were a second `vector<double>` object and if `mean(double, double)` returned the mean of two values, the following would output the average of each pair of values from `gr8` and `m8`:

```
transform(gr8.begin(), gr8.end(), m8.begin(), out, mean);
```

Now suppose you want to add the two arrays. You can't use `+` as an argument because, for type `double`, `+` is a built-in operator, not a function. You could define a function to add two numbers and use it:

```
double add(double x, double y) { return x + y; }
...
transform(gr8.begin(), gr8.end(), m8.begin(), out, add);
```

But then you'd have to define a separate function for each type. It would be better to define a template, except you don't have to, because the STL already has. The `functional` (formerly `function.h`) header defines several template class function objects including one called `plus<>()`.

Using the `plus<>` class for ordinary addition is possible, if awkward:

```
#include <functional>
...
plus<double> add;  // create a plus<double> object
double y = add(2.2, 3.4); // using plus<double>::operator()()
```

But it makes it easy to provide a function object as an argument:

```
transform(gr8.begin(), gr8.end(), m8.begin(), out, plus<double>() );
```

Here, rather than create a named object, the code uses the **plus<double>** constructor to construct a function object to do the adding. (The parentheses indicate calling the default constructor; what's passed to **transform()** is the constructed function object.)

The STL provides function object equivalents for all the built-in arithmetic, relational, and logical operators. Table 16.11 shows the names for these functor equivalents. They can be used with the C++ built-in types or with any user-defined type that overloads the corresponding operator.

Caution

Older implementations use the name **times** instead of **multiplies**.

TABLE 16.11   Operators and Function Object Equivalents

Operator	Function Object Equivalent
+	plus
-	minus
*	multiplies
/	divides
%	modulus
-	negate
==	equal_to
!=	not_equal_to
>	greater
<	less
>=	greater_equal
<=	less_equal
&&	logical_and
||	logical_or
!	logical_not

Adaptable Functors and Function Adapters

The predefined functors of Table 16.11 are all *adaptable*. Actually, the STL has five related concepts: the *adaptable generator*, the *adaptable unary function*, the *adaptable binary function*, the *adaptable predicate*, and the *adaptable binary predicate*.

What makes a functor object adaptable is that it carries `typedef` members identifying its argument types and return type. The members are called `result_type`, `first_argument_type`, and `second_argument_type`, and they represent what they sound like. For example, the return type of a `plus<int>` object is identified as `plus<int>::result_type`, and this would be a `typedef` for `int`.

The significance of a function object being adaptable is that it then can be used by function adapter objects which assume the existence of these `typedef` members. For example, a function with an argument that is an adaptable functor can use the `result_type` member to declare a variable that matches the function's return type.

Indeed, the STL provides function adapter classes that use these facilities. For example, suppose you want to multiply each element of the vector `gr8` by 2.5. That calls for using the `transform()` version with a unary function argument, like the

```
transform(gr8.begin(), gr8.end(), out, sqrt);
```

example shown earlier. The `multiplies()` functor can do the multiplication, but it's a binary function. So you need a function adapter that converts a functor with two arguments to one with one argument. The `TooBig2` example earlier showed one way, but the STL has automated the process with the `binder1st` and `binder2nd` classes, which convert adaptable binary functions to adaptable unary functions.

Let's look at `binder1st`. Suppose you have an adaptable binary function object `f2()`. You can create a `binder1st` object that binds a particular value, call it `val`, to be used as the first argument to `f2()`:

```
binder1st(f2, val) f1;
```

Then, invoking `f1(x)` with its single argument returns the same value as invoking `f2()` with `val` as its first argument and `f1()`'s argument as its second argument. That is, `f1(x)` is equivalent to `f2(val, x)` except that it is a unary function instead of a binary function. The `f2()` function has been adapted. Again, this is possible only if `f2()` is an adaptable function.

This might seem a bit awkward. However, the STL provides the `bind1st()` function to simplify using the `binder1st` class. You give it the function name and value used to construct a `binder1st` object, and it returns an object of that type. For example, let's convert the binary function `multiplies()` to a unary function that multiplies its argument by 2.5. Just do this:

```
bind1st(multiplies<double>(), 2.5)
```

Thus, the solution to multiplying every element in `gr8` by 2.5 and displaying the results is this:

```
transform(gr8.begin(), gr8.end(), out,
        bind1st(multiplies<double>(), 2.5));
```

The **binder2nd** class is similar, except that it assigns the constant to the second argument instead of the first. It has a helper function called **bind2nd** that works analogously to **bind1st**.

Listing 16.12 incorporates some of the recent examples into a short program.

LISTING 16.12   funadap.cpp

```cpp
// funadap.cpp -- using function adapters
#include <iostream>
using namespace std;
#include <vector>
#include <iterator>
#include <algorithm>
#include <functional>

void Show(double);
const int LIM = 5;
int main()
{
    double arr1[LIM] = {36, 39, 42, 45, 48};
    double arr2[LIM] = {25, 27, 29, 31, 33};
    vector<double> gr8(arr1, arr1 + LIM);
    vector<double> m8(arr2, arr2 + LIM);

    cout << "gr8:\t";
    for_each(gr8.begin(), gr8.end(), Show);
    cout << endl;
    cout << "m8: \t";
    for_each(m8.begin(), m8.end(), Show);
    cout << endl;

    vector<double> sum(LIM);
    transform(gr8.begin(), gr8.end(), m8.begin(), sum.begin(),
            plus<double>());
    cout << "sum:\t";
    for_each(sum.begin(), sum.end(), Show);
    cout << endl;

    vector<double> prod(LIM);
    transform(gr8.begin(), gr8.end(), prod.begin(),
            bind1st(multiplies<double>(), 2.5));
    cout << "prod:\t";
    for_each(prod.begin(), prod.end(), Show);
    cout << endl;

    return 0;
```

LISTING 16.12   Continued

```
}

void Show(double v)
{
    cout << v << ' ';
}
```

Compatibility Note

Older implementations may use vector.h, iterator.h, algo.h, and function.h. Older implementations may use times instead of multiplies.

Here is the output:

```
gr8:    36 39 42 45 48
m8:     25 27 29 31 33
sum:    61 66 71 76 81
prod:   90 97.5 105 112.5 120
```

Algorithms

The STL contains many non-member functions for working with containers. You've seen a few of them already: sort(), copy(), find(), for_each(), random_shuffle(), set_union(), set_intersection(), set_difference(), and transform(). You've probably noticed they feature the same overall design, using iterators to identify data ranges to be processed and to identify where results are to go. Some also take a function object argument to be used as part of the data processing.

There are two main generic components to the algorithm function designs. First, they use templates to provide generic types. Second, they use iterators to provide a generic representation for accessing data in a container. Thus, the copy() function can work with a container holding type double values in an array, with a container holding string values in a linked list, or with a container storing user-defined objects in a tree structure, such as used by set. Because pointers are a special case of iterators, STL functions such as copy() can be used with ordinary arrays.

The uniform container design allows there to be meaningful relations between containers of different kinds. For example, you can use copy() to copy values from an ordinary array to a vector object, from a vector object to a list object, and from a list object to a set object. You can use == to compare different kinds of containers, for example, deque and vector. This is possible because the overloaded == operator for containers uses iterators to compare contents, so a deque object and a vector object test as equal if they have the same content in the same order.

Algorithm Groups

The STL divides the algorithm library into four groups:

- Non-modifying sequence operations
- Mutating sequence operations
- Sorting and related operations
- Generalized numeric operations

The first three groups are described in the `algorithm` (formerly `algo.h`) header file, while the fourth group, being specifically oriented towards numeric data, gets its own header file, called `numeric`. (Formerly, they, too, were in `algol.h`.)

Non-modifying sequence operations operate on each element in a range. These operations leave a container unchanged. For example, `find()` and `for_each()` belong to this category.

Mutating sequence operations also operate on each element in a range. As the name suggests, however, they can change the contents of a container. The change could be in values or in the order in which the values are stored. For example, `transform()`, `random_shuffle()`, and `copy()` fall into this category.

Sorting and related operations include several sorting functions (including `sort()`) and a variety of other functions, including the set operations.

The numeric operations include functions to sum the contents of a range, calculate the inner product of two containers, calculate partial sums, and calculate adjacent differences. Typically, these are operations characteristic of arrays, so `vector` is the container most likely to be used with them.

Appendix G provides a complete summary of these functions.

General Properties

As you've seen again and again, STL functions work with iterators and iterator ranges. The function prototype indicates the assumptions made about the iterators. For example, the `copy()` function has this prototype:

```
template<class InputIterator, class OutputIterator>
OutputIterator copy(InputIterator first, InputIterator last,
                    OutputIterator result);
```

Because the identifiers `InputIterator` and `OutputIterator` are template parameters, they just as easily could have been `T` and `U`. However, the STL documentation uses the template parameter names to indicate the concept that the parameter models. So this declaration tells us that the range parameters must be input iterators or better and that the iterator indicating where the result goes must be an output parameter or better.

One way of classifying algorithms is on the basis of where the result of the algorithm is placed. Some algorithms do their work in place, others create copies. For example, when the `sort()`

function is finished, the result occupies the same location that the original data did. So `sort()` is an *in-place algorithm*. The `copy()` function, however, sends the result of its work to another location, so it is a *copying algorithm*. The `transform()` function can do both. Like `copy()`, it uses an output iterator to indicate where the results go. Unlike `copy()`, `transform()` allows the output iterator to point to a location in the input range, so it can copy the transformed values over the original values.

Some algorithms come in two versions: an in-place version and a copying version. The STL convention is to append `_copy` to the name of the copying version. The latter version will take an additional output iterator parameter to specify the location to which to copy the outcome. For example, there is a `replace()` function with this prototype:

```
template<class ForwardIterator, class T>
void replace(ForwardIterator first, ForwardIterator last,
             const T& old_value, const T& new_value);
```

It replaces each instance of `old_value` with `new_value`. This occurs in place. Because this algorithm both reads from and writes to container elements, the iterator type has to be `ForwardIterator` or better. The copying version has this prototype:

```
template<class InputIterator, class OutputIterator, class T>
OutputIterator replace_copy(InputIterator first, InputIterator last,
             OutputIterator result,
             const T& old_value, const T& new_value);
```

This time the resulting data is copied to a new location given by `result`, so the read-only input iterator is sufficient for specifying the range.

Note that `replace_copy()` has an `OutputIterator` return type. The convention for copying algorithms is that they return an iterator pointing to the location one past that last value copied.

Another common variation is that some functions have a version that performs an action conditionally, depending upon the result of applying a function to a container element. These versions typically append `_if` to the function name. For example, `replace_if()` replaces an old value with a new value if applying a function to the old value returns a value of `true`. Here's the prototype:

```
template<class ForwardIterator, class Predicate class T>
void replace_if(ForwardIterator first, ForwardIterator last,
             Predicate pred, const T& new_value);
```

A predicate, recall, is the name of a unary function returning a `bool` value. There's also a version called `replace_copy_if()`. You probably can figure out what it does and what its prototype is like.

As with `InputIterator`, `Predicate` is a template parameter name and could just as easily be called `T` or `U`. However, the STL chooses to use `Predicate` to remind the user that the actual argument should be a model of the `Predicate` concept. Similarly, the STL uses terms like `Generator` and `BinaryPredicate` to identify arguments that should model other function object concepts.

The STL and the `string` Class

The `string` class, although not part of the STL, is designed with the STL in mind. For example, it has `begin()`, `end()`, `rbegin()`, and `rend()` members. Thus, it can use the STL interface. Listing 16.13 uses the STL to show all the permutations you can form from the letters in a word. A permutation is a rearrangement of the order of the elements in a container. The `next_permutation()` algorithm transforms the contents of a range to the next permutation; in the case of a string, the permutations are arranged in increasing alphabetical order. The algorithm returns `true` if it succeeds and `false` if the range already is in the final sequence. To get all the permutations of a range, you should start with the elements in the earliest possible order, and the program uses the STL `sort()` algorithm for that purpose.

LISTING 16.13   strgstl.cpp

```cpp
// strgstl.cpp -- applying the STL to a string
#include <iostream>
#include <string>
#include <algorithm>
using namespace std;

int main()
{
    string letters;

    cout << "Enter the letter grouping (quit to quit): ";
    while (cin >> letters && letters != "quit")
    {
        cout << "Permutations of " << letters << endl;
        sort(letters.begin(), letters.end());
        cout << letters << endl;
        while (next_permutation(letters.begin(), letters.end()))
            cout << letters << endl;
        cout << "Enter next sequence (quit to quit): ";
    }
    cout << "Done.\n";

    return 0;
}
```

Here's a sample run:

```
Enter the letter grouping (quit to quit): wed
Permutations of wed
dew
dwe
edw
ewd
wde
wed
Enter next sequence (quit to quit): wee
Permutations of wee
```

```
eew
ewe
wee
Enter next sequence (quit to quit): quit
Done.
```

Note that the `next_permutation()` algorithm automatically provides only unique permutations, which is why the output shows more permutations for the word "wed" than for the word "wee", which has duplicate letters.

Functions Versus Container Methods

Sometimes you have a choice between using an STL method and an STL function. Usually, the method is the better choice. First, it should be better optimized for a particular container. Second, being a member function, it can use a template class's memory management facilities and resize a container when needed.

Suppose, for example, that you have a list of numbers and you want to remove all instances of a certain value, say 4, from the list. If `la` is a `list<int>` object, you can use the list `remove()` method:

```
la.remove(4);   // remove all 4s from the list
```

After this method call, all elements with the value 4 are removed from the list, and the list is automatically resized.

There also is an STL algorithm called `remove()` (see Appendix G). Instead of being invoked by an object, it takes range arguments. So, if `lb` is a `list<int>` object, a call to the function could look like this:

```
remove(lb.begin(), lb.end(), 4);
```

However, because this `remove()` is not a member, it can't adjust the size of the list. Instead, it makes sure all the non-removed items are at the beginning of the list, and it returns an iterator to the new past-the-end value. You then can use this iterator to fix the list size. For example, you can use the list `erase()` method to remove a range describing the part of the list that no longer is needed. Listing 16.14 shows how this process works.

LISTING 16.14   `listrmv.cpp`

```cpp
// listrmv.cpp -- applying the STL to a string
#include <iostream>
#include <list>
#include <algorithm>
using namespace std;

void Show(int);
const int LIM = 10;
int main()
```

LISTING 16.14   *Continued*

```cpp
{
    int ar[LIM] = {4, 5, 4, 2, 2, 3, 4, 8, 1, 4};
    list<int> la(ar, ar + LIM);
    list<int> lb(la);

    cout << "Original list contents:\n\t";
    for_each(la.begin(), la.end(), Show);
    cout << endl;
    la.remove(4);
    cout << "After using the remove() method:\n";
    cout << "la:\t";
    for_each(la.begin(), la.end(), Show);
    cout << endl;
    list<int>::iterator last;
    last = remove(lb.begin(), lb.end(), 4);
    cout << "After using the remove() function:\n";
    cout << "lb:\t";
    for_each(lb.begin(), lb.end(), Show);
    cout << endl;
    lb.erase(last, lb.end());
    cout << "After using the erase() method:\n";
    cout << "lb:\t";
    for_each(lb.begin(), lb.end(), Show);
    cout << endl;

    return 0;
}

void Show(int v)
{
    cout << v << ' ';
}
```

Here's the output:

```
Original list contents:
    4 5 4 2 2 3 4 8 1 4
After using the remove() method:
la: 5 2 2 3 8 1
After using the remove() function:
lb: 5 2 2 3 8 1 4 8 1 4
After using the erase() method:
lb: 5 2 2 3 8 1
```

As you can see, the `remove()` method reduced the list `la` from 10 elements to 6 elements. However, list `lb` still contained 10 elements after the `remove()` function was applied to it.

Although the methods are usually better suited, the non-method functions are more general. As you've seen, you can use them on arrays and `string` objects as well as STL containers, and you can use them with mixed container types, for example, saving data from a vector container in a list or a set.

Using the STL

The STL is a library whose parts are designed to work together. The STL components are tools, but they also are building blocks to create other tools. Let's illustrate that with an example. Suppose you want to write a program that lets the user enter words. At the end, you'd like a record of the words as they were entered, an alphabetical list of the words used (capitalization differences ignored), and a record of how many times each word was entered. To keep things simple, assume the input contains no numbers or punctuation.

Entering and saving the list of words is simple enough. Following the example of Listing 16.5, you can create a **vector<string>** object and use **push_back()** to add input words to the vector:

```
vector<string> words;
string input;
while (cin >> input && input != "quit")
    words.push_back(input);
```

What about getting the alphabetic word list? You can use **sort()** followed by **unique()**, but that approach overwrites the original data because **sort()** is an in-place algorithm. There is an easier way that avoids this problem. Create a **set<string>** object, and copy (using an insert iterator) the words from the vector to the set. A set automatically sorts its contents, taking the place of calling **sort()**, and a set only allows one copy of a key, so that takes the place of calling **unique()**. Wait! The specification called for ignoring the case differences. One way to handle that is to use **transform()** instead of **copy()** to copy data from the vector to the set. For the transformation function, use one that converts a string to lowercase.

```
set<string> wordset;
transform(words.begin(), words.end(),
    insert_iterator<set<string> > (wordset, wordset.begin()), ToLower);
```

The **ToLower()** function is easy to write. Just use **transform()** to apply the **tolower()** function to each element in the string, using the string both as source and destination. Remember, **string** objects, too, can use the STL functions. Passing and returning the string as a reference means the algorithm works on the original string without having to make copies.

```
string & ToLower(string & st)
{
    transform(st.begin(), st.end(), st.begin(), tolower);
    return st;
}
```

One possible problem is that the **tolower()** function is defined as **int tolower(int)**, and some compilers want the function to match the element type, which is **char**. One solution is to replace **tolower** with **toLower** and to provide the following definition:

```
char toLower(char ch) { return tolower(ch); }
```

To get the number of times each word appeared in the input, you can use the **count()** function. It takes a range and a value as arguments and returns the number of times the value appears in the range. You can use the **vector** object to provide the range and the **set** object to provide the list of words to count. That is, for each word in the set, count how many times it appears in the vector. To keep the resulting count associated with the correct word, store the word and the count as a `pair<const string, int>` object in a `map` object. The word will be the key (just one copy), and the count will be the value. This can be done in a single loop:

```
map<string, int> wordmap;
set<string>::iterator  si;
for (si = wordset.begin(); si != wordset.end(); si++)
    wordmap.insert(pair<string, int>(*si, count(words.begin(),
    words.end(), *si)));
```

> **Caution**
>
> Older STL implementations declare `count()` as type `void`. Instead of using a return value, you pro-vide a fourth argument passed as a reference, and the number of items is added to that argument:
>
> ```
> int ct = 0;
> count(words.begin(), words.end(), *si), ct));    count added to ct
> ```

The map class has an interesting feature—you can use array notation with keys serving as indices to access the stored values. For example, `wordmap["the"]` would represent the value associated with the key `"the"`, which in this case is the number of occurrences of the string `"the"`. Because the `wordset` container holds all the keys used by `wordmap`, you can use the fol-lowing code as an alternative and more attractive way of storing results:

```
for (si = wordset.begin(); si != wordset.end(); si++)
    wordmap[*si] = count(words.begin(), words.end(), *si);
```

Because `si` points to a string in the `wordset` container, `*si` is a string and can serve as a key for `wordmap`. This code places both keys and values into the `wordmap` map.

Similarly, you can use the array notation to report results:

```
for (si = wordset.begin(); si != wordset.end(); si++)
    cout << *si << ": " << wordmap[*si] << endl;
```

If a key is invalid, the corresponding value is 0.

Listing 16.15 puts these ideas together and includes code to display the contents of the three containers (a vector with the input, a set with a word list, and a map with a word count).

LISTING 16.15   usealgo.cpp

```
//usealgo.cpp
#include <iostream>
#include <string>
#include <vector>
#include <set>
#include <map>
#include <iterator>
#include <algorithm>
#include <cctype>
```

LISTING 16.15   Continued

```cpp
using namespace std;

char toLower(char ch) { return tolower(ch); }
string & ToLower(string & st);
void display(const string & s);

int main()
{
    vector<string> words;
    cout << "Enter words (enter quit to quit):\n";
    string input;
    while (cin >> input && input != "quit")
        words.push_back(input);

    cout << "You entered the following words:\n";
    for_each(words.begin(), words.end(), display);
    cout << endl;

    // place words in set, converting to lowercase
    set<string> wordset;
    transform(words.begin(), words.end(),
        insert_iterator<set<string> > (wordset, wordset.begin()),
        ToLower);
    cout << "\nAlphabetic list of words:\n";
    for_each(wordset.begin(), wordset.end(), display);
    cout << endl;

    // place word and frequency in map
    map<string, int> wordmap;
    set<string>::iterator si;
    for (si = wordset.begin(); si != wordset.end(); si++)
        wordmap[*si] = count(words.begin(), words.end(), *si);

    // display map contents
    cout << "\nWord frequency:\n";
    for (si = wordset.begin(); si != wordset.end(); si++)
        cout << *si << ": " << wordmap[*si] << endl;

    return 0;
}

string & ToLower(string & st)
{
    transform(st.begin(), st.end(), st.begin(), toLower);
    return st;
}

void display(const string & s)
{
    cout << s << " ";
}
```

Compatibility Note

Older implementations may use `vector.h`, `set.h`, `map.h`, `iterator.h`, `algo.h`, and `ctype.h`. Older implementations may require the `set` and `map` templates to use an additional `less<string>` template parameter. Older versions use the type `void count()` function mentioned earlier.

Here is a sample run:

```
Enter words (enter quit to quit):
The dog saw the cat and thought the cat fat
The cat thought the cat perfect
quit
You entered the following words:
The dog saw the cat and thought the cat fat The cat thought the cat perfect

Alphabetic list of words:
and cat dog fat perfect saw that the thought

Word frequency:
and: 1
cat: 4
dog: 1
fat: 1
perfect: 1
saw: 1
that: 1
the: 4
thought: 2
```

The moral here is that your attitude when using the STL should be, how much code can I avoid writing myself? STL's generic and flexible design should save you lots of work. Also, the STL designers are algorithm people very much concerned with efficiency. So the algorithms are well-chosen and inline.

Other Libraries

C++ provides some other class libraries that are more specialized than the examples covered in this chapter. The `complex` header file provides a `complex` class template for complex numbers, with specializations for `float`, `long`, and `long double`. The class provides standard complex number operations along with standard functions that can be used with complex numbers.

The `valarray` header file provides a `valarray` template class. This class template is designed to represent numeric arrays and provides support for a variety of numeric array operations, such as adding the contents of one array to another, applying math functions to each element of an array, and applying linear algebra operations to arrays.

Summary

C++ provides a powerful set of libraries that provide solutions to many common programming problems and the tools to simplify many more problems. The string class provides a convenient means to handle strings as objects. The class provides automatic memory management and a host of methods and functions for working with strings. For example, they allow you to concatenate strings, insert one string into another, reverse a string, search a string for characters or substrings, and perform input and output operations.

The auto_ptr template makes it easier to manage memory allocated by new. If you use an auto_ptr object instead of a regular pointer to hold the address returned by new, you don't have to remember to use the delete operator later. When the auto_ptr object expires, its destructor will call the delete operator automatically.

The Standard Template Library, or STL, is a collection of container class templates, iterator class templates, function object templates, and algorithm function templates that feature a unified design based on generic programming principles. The algorithms use templates to make them generic in terms of type of stored object and an iterator interface to make them generic in terms of the type of container. Iterators are generalizations of pointers.

The STL uses the term "concept" to denote a set of requirements. For example, the concept of forward iterator includes the requirements that a forward iterator object can be dereferenced for reading and writing, and that it can be incremented. Actual implementations of the concept are said to "model" the concept. For example, the forward iterator concept could be modeled by an ordinary pointer or by an object designed to navigate a linked list. Concepts based on other concepts are termed "refinements". For example, the bidirectional iterator is refinement of the forward iterator concept.

Container classes, such as vector and set, are models of container concepts, such as container, sequence, and associative container. The STL defines several container class templates: vector, deque, list, set, multiset, map, multimap, and bitset. It also defines adapter class templates queue, priority_queue, and stack; these classes adapt an underlying container class to give it the characteristic interface suggested by the adapter class template name. Thus, stack, although based, in default, on vector, allows insertion and removal only at the top of the stack.

Some algorithms are expressed as container class methods, but the bulk are expressed as general, non-member functions. This is made possible by using iterators as the interface between containers and algorithms. One advantage to this approach is that there need be just one for_each() or copy() function, and so on, instead of a separate version for each container. A second advantage is that STL algorithms can be used with non-STL containers, such as ordinary arrays, string objects, and any classes you design consistent with the STL iterator and container idiom.

Both containers and algorithms are characterized by the type of iterator they provide or need. You should check that the container features an iterator concept that supports the algorithm's needs. For example, the for_each() algorithm uses an input iterator, whose minimal requirements are met by all the STL container class types. But sort() requires random access iterators, which not all container classes support. A container class may offer a specialized method as an option if it doesn't meet the requirements for a particular algorithm. For example, the `list` class has a `sort()` method based on bidirectional iterators, so it can use that method instead of the general function.

The STL also provides function objects, or functors, that are classes for which the `()` operator is overloaded; that is, for which the `operator()()` method is defined. Objects of such classes can be invoked using function notation but can carry additional information. Adaptable function objects, for example, have `typedef` statements identifying the argument types and the return value type for the function object. This information can be used by other components, such as function adapters.

The STL, by representing common container types and providing a variety of common operations implemented with efficient algorithms, all done in a generic manner, provides an excellent source of reusable code. You may be able to solve a programming problem directly with the STL tools, or you may be able to use them as building blocks to construct the solution you need.

The `complex` and `valarray` template classes support numerical operations for complex numbers and arrays.

Review Questions

1. Consider the following class declaration:

```
class RQ1
{
private:
    char * st;       // points to C-style string
public:
    RQ1() { st = new char [1]; strcpy(st,""); }
    RQ1(const char * s)
    {st = new char [strlen(s) + 1]; strcpy(st, s); }
    RQ1(const RQ1 & rq)
    {st = new char [strlen(rq.st) + 1]; strcpy(st, rq.st); }
    ~RQ1() {delete [] st};
    RQ & operator=(const RQ & rq);
    // more stuff
};
```

Convert this to a declaration using a `string` object instead. What methods no longer need an explicit definition?

2. Name at least two advantages `string` objects have over C-style strings in terms of ease-of-use.

3. Write a function that takes a reference to a `string` as an argument and which converts the `string` to all uppercase.

4. Which of the following are not examples of correct usage (conceptually or syntactically) of `auto_ptr`? (Assume the needed header files have been included.)

```
auto_ptr<int> pia(new int[20]);
auto_ptr<str> (new string);
int rigue = 7;
auto_ptr<int>pr(&rigue);
auto_ptr dbl (new double);
```

5. If you could make the mechanical equivalent of a stack that held golf clubs instead of numbers, why would it (conceptually) be a bad golf bag?

6. Why would a `set` container be a poor choice for storing a hole-by-hole record of your golf scores?

7. Because a pointer is an iterator, why didn't the STL designers simply use pointers instead of iterators?

8. Why didn't the STL designers simply define a base iterator class, use inheritance to derive classes for the other iterator types, and express the algorithms in terms of those iterator classes?

9. Give at least three examples of convenience advantages that a `vector` object has over an ordinary array.

10. If Listing 16.6 were implemented with `list` instead of `vector`, what parts of the program would become invalid? Could the invalid part be fixed easily? If so, how?

Programming Exercises

1. A palindrome is a string that is the same backwards as it is forwards. For example, "tot" and "otto" are rather short palindromes. Write a program that lets a user enter a string and which passes a reference to the string to a `bool` function. The function should return `true` if the string is a palindrome and `false` otherwise. At this point, don't worry about complications such as capitalization, spaces, and punctuation. That is, this simple version will reject "Otto" and "Madam, I'm Adam". Feel free to scan the list of string methods in Appendix F for methods to simplify the task.

2. Do the same problem as given in programming exercise 1, but do worry about complications such as capitalization, spaces, and punctuation. That is, "Madam, I'm Adam" should test as a palindrome. For example, the testing function could reduce the string to "madamimadam" and then test if the reverse is the same. Don't forget the useful `cctype` library. You may find an STL function or two useful, although not necessary.

3. You must write a function with an old-style interface. It has this prototype:

```
int reduce(long ar[], int n);
```

The arguments are the name of an array and the number of elements in the array. The function sorts an array, removes duplicate values, and returns a value equal to the number of elements in the reduced array. Write the function using STL functions. (If you decide to use the general `unique()` function, note that it returns the end of the resulting range.) Test the function in a short program.

4. Do the same problem as described in programming exercise 3, except make it a template function:

```
template <class T>
int reduce(T ar[], int n);
```

Test the function in a short program using both a `long` instantiation and a `string` instantiation.

5. Redo the example shown in Listing 12.13 using the STL `queue` template class instead of the `Queue` class of Chapter 12.

6. A common game is the lottery card. The card has numbered spots of which a certain number are selected at random. Write a `Lotto()` function that takes two arguments. The first is the number of spots on a lottery card and the second the number of spots selected at random. The function returns a `vector<int>` object containing, in sorted order, the numbers selected at random. For example, you could use the function as follows:

```
vector<int> winners;
winners = Lotto(51,6);
```

This would assign to `winners` a vector containing six numbers selected randomly from the range 1 through 51. Note that simply using `rand()` doesn't quite do the job because it may produce duplicate values. Suggestion: Have the function create a vector containing all the possible values, use `random_shuffle()`, and then use the beginning of the shuffled vector to obtain the values. Also write a short program that lets you test the function.

7. Mat and Pat want to invite their friends to a party. They ask you to write a program that does the following:

Allows Mat to enter a list of his friends' names. The names are stored in a container and then displayed in sorted order.

Allows Pat to enter a list of her friends' names. The names are stored in a second container and then displayed in sorted order.

Creates a third container that merges the two lists, eliminating duplicates, and displays the contents of this container.

CHAPTER 17

INPUT, OUTPUT, AND FILES

You will learn about the following in this chapter:

- The C++ view of input and output
- The `iostream` family of classes
- Redirection
- `ostream` class methods
- Formatting output
- `istream` class methods
- Stream states
- File I/O

- Using the `ifstream` class for input from files
- Using the `ofstream` class for output to files
- Using the `fstream` class file input and output
- Command-line processing
- Binary files
- Random file access
- Incore formatting

*D*iscussing C++ input and output (I/O, for short) poses a problem. On the one hand, practically every program uses input and output, and learning how to use them is one of the first tasks facing someone learning a computer language. On the other hand, C++ uses many of its more advanced language features to implement input and output, including classes, derived classes, function overloading, virtual functions, templates, and multiple inheritance. Thus, to really understand C++ I/O, you must know a lot of C++. To get you started, the early chapters outlined the basic ways for using the `istream` class object `cin` and the `ostream` class object `cout` for input and output. Now we'll take a longer look at C++'s input and output classes, seeing how they are designed and learning how to control the output format. (If you've skipped a few chapters just to learn advanced formatting, you can skim the sections on that topic, noting the techniques and ignoring the explanations.)

The C++ facilities for file input and output are based on the same basic class definitions that `cin` and `cout` are based on, so this chapter uses the discussion of console I/O (keyboard and screen) as a springboard to investigating file I/O.

The ANSI/ISO C++ standards committee has worked to make C++ I/O more compatible with existing C I/O, and this has produced some changes from traditional C++ practices.

An Overview of C++ Input and Output

Most computer languages build input and output into the language itself. For example, if you look through the lists of keywords for languages like BASIC or Pascal, you'll see that PRINT statements, writeln statements, and the like, are part of the language vocabulary. But neither C nor C++ have built input and output into the language. If you look through the keywords for these languages, you find for and if, but nothing relating to I/O. C originally left I/O to compiler implementers. One reason for this was to give implementers the freedom to design I/O functions that best fit the hardware requirements of the target computer. In practice, most implementers based I/O on a set of library functions originally developed for the UNIX environment. ANSI C formalized recognition of this I/O package, called the Standard Input/Output package, by making it a mandatory component of the standard C library. C++ also recognizes this package, so if you're familiar with the family of C functions declared in the stdio.h file, you can use them in C++ programs. (Newer implementations use the cstdio header file to support these functions.)

C++, however, relies upon a C++ solution rather than a C solution to I/O, and that solution is a set of classes defined in the iostream (formerly iostream.h) and fstream (formerly fstream.h) header files. This class library is not part of the formal language definition (cin and istream are not keywords); after all, a computer language defines rules for how to do things, such as create classes, and doesn't define what you should create following those rules. But, just as C implementations come with a standard library of functions, C++ comes with a standard library of classes. At first, that standard class library was an informal standard consisting solely of the classes defined in the iostream and fstream header files. The ANSI/ISO C++ committee decided to formalize this library as a standard class library and to add a few more standard classes, such as those discussed in Chapter 16, "The string Class and the Standard Template Library." This chapter discusses standard C++ I/O. But first, let's examine the conceptual framework for C++ I/O.

Streams and Buffers

A C++ program views input or output as a stream of bytes. On input, a program extracts bytes from an input stream, and on output, a program inserts bytes into the output stream. For a text-oriented program, each byte can represent a character. More generally, the bytes can form a binary representation of character or numeric data. The bytes in an input stream can come from the keyboard, but they also can come from a storage device, such as a hard disk, or from another program. Similarly, the bytes in an output stream can flow to the screen, to a printer, to a storage device, or to another program. A stream acts as an intermediary between the program and the stream's source or destination. This approach enables a C++ program to treat input from a keyboard in the same manner it treats input from a file; the C++ program merely examines the stream of bytes without needing to know from where the bytes come. Similarly, by using streams, a C++ program can process output in a manner independent of where the bytes are going. Managing input, then, involves two stages:

- Associating a stream with an input to a program
- Connecting the stream to a file

In other words, an input stream needs two connections, one at each end. The file-end connection provides a source for the stream, and the program-end connection dumps the stream outflow into the program. (The file-end connection can be a file, but it also can be a device, such as a keyboard.) Similarly, managing output involves connecting an output stream to the program and associating some output destination with the stream. It's like plumbing with bytes instead of water (see Figure 17.1).

FIGURE 17.1

C++ input and output.

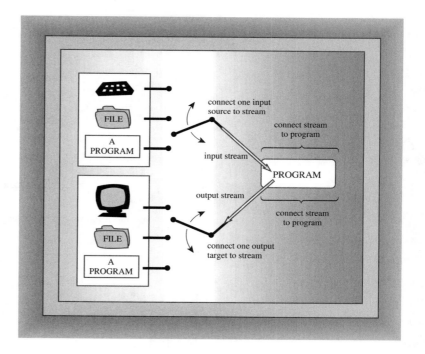

Usually, input and output can be handled more efficiently by using a *buffer*. A buffer is a block of memory used as an intermediate, temporary storage facility for the transfer of information from a device to a program or from a program to a device. Typically, devices like disk drives transfer information in blocks of 512 bytes or more, while programs often process information one byte at a time. The buffer helps match these two disparate rates of information transfer. For example, assume a program is supposed to count the number of dollar signs in a hard-disk file. The program could read one character from the file, process it, read the next character from the file, and so on. Reading a file a character at a time from a disk requires a lot of hardware activity and is slow. The buffered approach is to read a large chunk from the disk, store the chunk in the buffer, and read the buffer one character at a time. Because it is much quicker to read individual bytes of data from memory than from a hard disk, this approach is much faster as well as easier on the hardware. Of course, after the program reaches the end of the buffer, the program then should read another chunk of data from the disk. The principle is similar to that of a water reservoir that collects megagallons of runoff water during a big storm, then feeds water to your home at a more civilized rate of flow (see Figure 17.2). Similarly, on output a program can first fill the buffer, then transfer the entire block of data to a hard disk, clearing the buffer for the next batch of output. This is called *flushing the buffer*. Perhaps you can come up with your own plumbing-based analogy for that process.

FIGURE 17.2

A stream with a buffer.

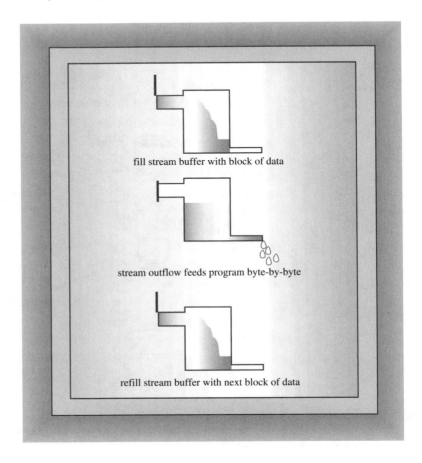

fill stream buffer with block of data

stream outflow feeds program byte-by-byte

refill stream buffer with next block of data

Keyboard input provides one character at a time, so in that case a program doesn't need a buffer to help match different data transfer rates. However, buffered keyboard input allows the user to back up and correct input before transmitting it to a program. A C++ program normally flushes the input buffer when you press <Enter>. That's why the examples in this book don't begin processing input until you press <Enter>. For output to the screen, a C++ program normally flushes the output buffer when you transmit a newline character. Depending upon the implementation, a program may flush input on other occasions, too, such as impending input. That is, when a program reaches an input statement, it flushes any output currently in the output buffer. C++ implementations that are consistent with ANSI C should behave in that manner.

Streams, Buffers, and the `iostream` File

The business of managing streams and buffers can get a bit complicated, but including the `iostream` (formerly `iostream.h`) file brings in several classes designed to implement and manage streams and buffers for you. The newest version of C++ I/O actually defines class templates in order to support both `char` and `wchar_t` data. By using the `typedef` facility, C++ makes the `char` specializations of these templates mimic the traditional non-template I/O implementation. Here are some of those classes (see Figure 17.3):

- The `streambuf` class provides memory for a buffer along with class methods for filling the buffer, accessing buffer contents, flushing the buffer, and managing the buffer memory.

- The `ios_base` class represents general properties of a stream, such as whether it's open for reading and whether it's a binary or a text stream.

- The `ios` class is based on `ios_base`, and it includes a pointer member to a `streambuf` object.

- The `ostream` class derives from the `ios` class and provides output methods.

- The `istream` class also derives from the `ios` class and provides input methods.

- The `iostream` class is based on the `istream` and `ostream` classes and thus inherits both input and output methods.

FIGURE 17.3

Some I/O classes.

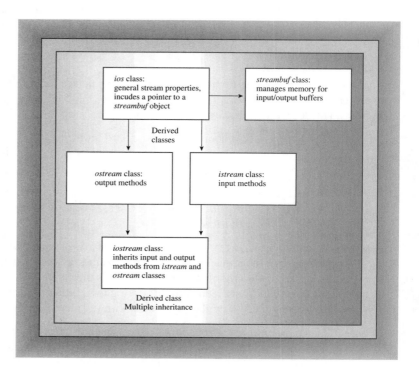

To use these facilities, you use objects of the appropriate classes. For example, use an `ostream` object such as `cout` to handle output. Creating such an object opens a stream, automatically creates a buffer, and associates it with the stream. It also makes the class member functions available to you.

Redefining I/O

The ISO/ANSI C++ standard has revised I/O a couple of ways. First, there's the change from `ostream.h` to `ostream`, with `ostream` placing the classes in the `std` namespace. Second, the I/O classes have been rewritten. To be an international language, C++ had to be able to handle international character sets that require a 16-bit or wider character type. So the language added the `wchar_t` (or "wide") character type to the traditional 8-bit `char` (or "narrow") type. Each type needs its own I/O facilities. Rather than develop two separate sets of classes, the standards committee developed a template set of I/O classes, including `basic_istream<charT, traits<charT> >` and `basic_ostream<charT, traits<charT> >`. The `traits<charT>` template, in turn, is a template class defining particular traits for a character type, such as how to compare for equality and its EOF value. The standard provides `char` and `wchar_t` specializations of the I/O classes. For example, `istream` and `ostream` are `typedef`s for `char` specializations. Similarly, `wistream` and `wostream` are `wchar_t` specializations. For example, there is a `wcout` object for outputting wide character streams. The `ostream` header file contains these definitions.

Certain type-independent information that used to be kept in the `ios` base class has been moved to the new `ios_base` class. This includes the various formatting constants such as `ios::fixed`, which now is `ios_base::fixed`. Also, `ios_base` contains some options that weren't available in the old `ios`.

In some cases, the change in the filename corresponds with the change in class definitions. In Microsoft Visual C++ 6.0, for example, you can include `iostream.h` and get the old class definitions or include `iostream` and get the new class definitions. However, dual versions like this are not the general rule.

The C++ `iostream` class library takes care of many details for you. For example, including the `iostream` file in a program creates eight stream objects (four for narrow characters stream and four for wide character streams) automatically:

- The `cin` object corresponds to the standard input stream. By default, this stream is associated with the standard input device, typically a keyboard. The `wcin` object is similar, but works with the `wchar_t` type.

- The `cout` object corresponds to the standard output stream. By default, this stream is associated with the standard output device, typically a monitor. The `wcout` object is similar, but works with the `wchar_t` type.

- The `cerr` object corresponds to the standard error stream, which you can use for displaying error messages. By default, this stream is associated with the standard output device, typically a monitor, and the stream is unbuffered. This means that information is sent directly to the screen without waiting for a buffer to fill or for a newline character. The `wcerr` object is similar, but works with the `wchar_t` type.

- The `clog` object also corresponds to the standard error stream. By default, this stream is associated with the standard output device, typically a monitor, and the stream is buffered. The `wclog` object is similar, but works with the `wchar_t` type.

What does it mean to say an object represents a stream? Well, for example, when the `iostream` file declares a `cout` object for your program, that object will have data members holding information relating to output, such as the field widths to be used in displaying data, the number of places after the decimal to use, what number base to use for displaying integers, and the address of a `streambuf` object describing the buffer used to handle the output flow. A statement such as

```
cout << "Bjarne free";
```

places the characters from the string `"Bjarne free"` into the buffer managed by `cout` via the pointed-to `streambuf` object. The `ostream` class defines the `operator<<()` function used in this statement, and the `ostream` class also supports the `cout` data members with a variety of other class methods, such as the ones this chapter discusses later. Furthermore, C++ sees to it that the output from the buffer is directed to the standard output, usually a monitor, provided by the operating system. In short, one end of a stream is connected to your program, the other end is connected to the standard output, and the `cout` object, with the help of a type `streambuf` object, manages the flow of bytes through the stream.

Redirection

The standard input and output streams normally connect to the keyboard and the screen. But many operating systems, including Unix, Linux, and MS-DOS, support redirection, a facility that lets you change the associations for the standard input and the standard output. Suppose, for example, you have an executable DOS C++ program called **counter.exe** that counts the number of characters in its input and reports the result. (From various versions of Windows you can go to Start, click Programs, then click the MS-DOS Command Prompt icon or Command Prompt icon to start an MD-DOS window.) A sample run might look like this:

```
C>counter
Hello
and goodbye!
Control-Z           ¬ simulated end-of-file
Input contained 19 characters.
C>
```

Here, input came from the keyboard, and output went to the screen.

With input redirection (`<`) and output redirection (`>`), you can use the same program to count the number of characters in the **oklahoma** file and to place the results in the **cow_cnt** file:

```
C>counter <oklahoma >cow_cnt
C>
```

The `<oklahoma` part of the command line associates the standard input with the **oklahoma** file, causing `cin` to read input from that file instead of the keyboard. In other words, the operating system changes the connection at the inflow end of the input stream, while the outflow end remains connected to the program. The `>cow_cnt` part of the command line associates the standard output with the **cow_cnt** file, causing `cout` to send output to that file instead of to the screen. That is, the operating system changes the outflow end connection of the output stream, leaving its inflow end still connected to the program. DOS (2.0 and later), Linux, and Unix automatically recognize this redirection syntax. (Unix, Linux, and DOS 3.0 and later also permit optional space characters between the redirection operators and the filenames.)

The standard output stream, represented by `cout`, is the normal channel for program output. The standard error streams (represented by `cerr` and `clog`) are intended for a program's error messages. By default, all three typically are sent to the monitor. But redirecting the standard output doesn't affect `cerr` or `clog`; thus, if you use one of these objects to print an error message, a program will display the error message on the screen even if the regular `cout` output is redirected elsewhere. For example, consider this code fragment:

```
if (success)
    cout << "Here come the goodies!\n";
else
{
    cerr << "Something horrible has happened.\n";
    exit(1);
}
```

If redirection is not in effect, whichever message is selected is displayed onscreen. If, however, the program output has been redirected to a file, the first message, if selected, would go to the file but the second message, if selected, would go to the screen. By the way, some operating systems permit redirecting the standard error, too. In Unix and Linux, for example, the `2>` operator redirects the standard error.

Output with `cout`

C++, we've said, considers output to be a stream of bytes. (Depending on the implementation and platform, these may be 16-bit or 32-bit bytes, but bytes nonetheless.) But many kinds of data in a program are organized into larger units than a single byte. An `int` type, for example, may be represented by a 16-bit or 32-bit binary value. And a `double` value may be represented by 64 bits of binary data. But when you send a stream of bytes to a screen, you want each byte to represent a character value. That is, to display the number -2.34 on the screen, you should send the five characters -, 2, ., 3, and 4 to the screen, and not the internal 64-bit floating-point representation of that value. Therefore, one of the most important tasks facing the `ostream` class is converting numeric types, such as `int` or `float`, into a stream of characters that represents the values in text form. That is, the `ostream` class translates the internal representation of data as binary bit patterns to an output stream of character bytes. (Some day we may have bionic implants to enable us to interpret binary data directly. We leave that development as an exercise for the reader.) To perform these translation tasks, the `ostream` class provides several class methods. We'll look at them now, summarizing methods used throughout the book and describing additional methods that provide a finer control over the appearance of the output.

The Overloaded << Operator

Most often, this book has used `cout` with the << operator, also called the *insertion* operator:

```
int clients = 22;
cout << clients;
```

In C++, as in C, the default meaning for the << operator is the bitwise left-shift operator (see Appendix E, "Other Operators"). An expression such as x<<3 means to take the binary representation of x and shift all the bits 3 units to the left. Obviously, this doesn't have a lot to do with output. But the ostream class redefines the << operator through overloading to output for the ostream class. In this guise, the << operator is called the insertion operator instead of the left-shift operator. (The left-shift operator earned this new role through its visual aspect, which suggests a flow of information to the left.) The insertion operator is overloaded to recognize all the basic C++ types:

- unsigned char

- signed char

- char

- short

- unsigned short

- int

- unsigned int

- long

- unsigned long

- float

- double

- long double

The ostream class provides a definition for the operator<<() function for each of the previous types. (Functions incorporating operator into the name are used to overload operators, as discussed in Chapter 11, "Working with Classes.") Thus, if you use a statement of the form

```
cout << value;
```

and if value is one of the preceding types, a C++ program can match it to an operator function with the corresponding signature. For example, the expression cout << 88 matches the following method prototype:

```
ostream & operator<<(int);
```

Recall that this prototype indicates that the operator<<() function takes one type int argument. That's the part that matches the 88 in the previous statement. The prototype also indicates that the function returns a reference to an ostream object. That property makes it possible to concatenate output, as in the following old rock hit:

```
cout << "I'm feeling sedimental over " << boundary << "\n";
```

If you're a C programmer who has suffered through C's multitudinous % type specifiers and the problems that arise when you mismatch a specifier type to a value, using cout is almost sinfully easy. (And C++ input, of course, *is* c*in*fully easy.)

Output and Pointers

The `ostream` class also defines insertion operator functions for the following pointer types:

- `const signed char *`

- `const unsigned char *`

- `const char *`

- `void *`

C++ represents a string, don't forget, by using a pointer to the location of the string. The pointer can take the form of the name of an array of `char` or of an explicit `pointer-to-char` or of a quoted string. Thus, all of the following `cout` statements display strings:

```
char name[20] = "Dudly Diddlemore";
char * pn = "Violet D'Amore";
cout << "Hello!";
cout << name;
cout << pn;
```

The methods use the terminating null character in the string to determine when to stop displaying characters.

C++ matches a pointer of any other type with type `void *` and prints a numerical representation of the address. If you want the address of the string, you have to type cast it to another type.

```
int eggs = 12;
char * amount = "dozen";
cout << &eggs;            // prints address of eggs variable
cout << amount;           // prints the string "dozen"
cout << (void *) amount;  // prints the address of the "dozen" string
```

Note

Not all current C++ implementations have a prototype with the `void *` argument. In that case, you have to type cast a pointer to `unsigned` or, perhaps, `unsigned long`, if you want to print the value of the address.

Output Concatenation

All the incarnations of the insertion operator are defined to return type `ostream &`. That is, the prototypes have this form:

```
ostream & operator<<(type);
```

(Here, *type* is the type to be displayed.) The `ostream &` return type means that using this operator returns a reference to an `ostream` object. Which object? The function definitions say that the reference is to the object used to evoke the operator. In other words, an operator function's return value is the same object that evokes the operator. For example, cout << "potluck" returns the cout object. That's the feature that lets you concatenate output using insertion. For example, consider the following statement:

```
cout << "We have " << count << " unhatched chickens.\n";
```

The expression cout << "We have " displays the string and returns the cout object, reducing the statement to the following:

```
cout << count << " unhatched chickens.\n";
```

Then the expression cout << count displays the value of the count variable and returns cout, which then can handle the final argument in the statement (see Figure 17.4). This design technique really is a nice feature, which is why our examples of overloading the << operator in the previous chapters shamelessly imitate it.

FIGURE 17.4

Output concatenation.

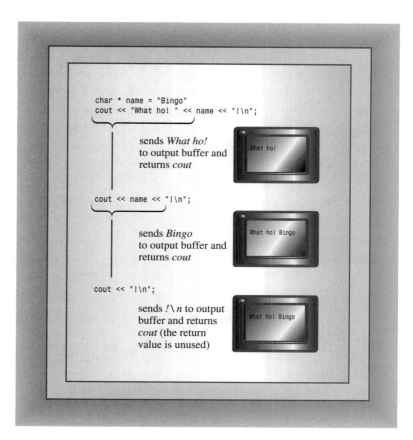

The Other ostream Methods

Besides the various operator<<() functions, the ostream class provides the put() method for displaying characters and the write() method for displaying strings.

Some compilers don't implement the `put()` method correctly. Traditionally, it had the following prototype:

```
ostream & put(char);
```

The current standard is equivalent, except it's templated to allow for `wchar_t`. You invoke it using the usual class method notation:

```
cout.put('W');      // display the W character
```

Here `cout` is the invoking object and `put()` is the class member function. Like the `<<` operator functions, this function returns a reference to the invoking object, so you can concatenate output with it:

```
cout.put('I').put('t'); // displaying It with two put() calls
```

The function call `cout.put('I')` returns `cout`, which then acts as the invoking object for the `put('t')` call.

Given the proper prototype, you can use `put()` with arguments of numeric types other than `char`, such as `int`, and let function prototyping automatically convert the argument to the correct type `char` value. For example, you could do the following:

```
cout.put(65);       // display the A character
cout.put(66.3);     // display the B character
```

The first statement converted the `int` value **65** to a `char` value and then displayed the character having **65** as its ASCII code. Similarly, the second statement converted the type **double** value **66.3** to a type `char` value **66** and displayed the corresponding character.

This behavior came in handy prior to Release 2.0 C++; at that time the language represented character constants with type `int` values. Thus, a statement such as

```
cout << 'W';
```

would have interpreted `'W'` as an `int` value, and hence displayed it as the integer **87**, the ASCII value for the character. But the statement

```
cout.put('W');
```

worked fine. Because current C++ represents `char` constants as type `char`, you now can use either method.

The implementation problem is that some compilers overload `put()` for three argument types: `char`, `unsigned char`, and `signed char`. This makes using `put()` with an `int` argument ambiguous, for an `int` could be converted to any one of those three types.

The `write()` method writes an entire string and has the following template prototype:

```
basic_ostream<charT,traits>& write(const char_type* s, streamsize n);
```

The first argument to `write()` provides the address of the string to be displayed, and the second argument indicates how many characters to display. Using `cout` to invoke `write()` invokes the `char` specialization, so the return type is `ostream &`. Listing 17.1 shows how the `write()` method works.

LISTING 17.1   write.cpp

```
// write.cpp -- use cout.write()
#include <iostream>
using namespace std;
#include <cstring>  // or else string.h

int main()
{
    const char * state1 = "Florida";
    const char * state2 = "Kansas";
    const char * state3 = "Euphoria";
    int len = strlen(state2);
    cout << "Increasing loop index:\n";
    int i;
    for (i = 1; i <= len; i++)
    {
        cout.write(state2,i);
        cout << "\n";
    }

// concatenate output
    cout << "Decreasing loop index:\n";
    for (i = len; i > 0; i--)
        cout.write(state2,i) << "\n";

// exceed string length
    cout << "Exceeding string length:\n";
    cout.write(state2, len + 5) << "\n";

    return 0;
}
```

Here is the output:

```
Increasing loop index:
K
Ka
Kan
Kans
Kansa
Kansas
Decreasing loop index:
Kansas
Kansa
Kans
Kan
Ka
K
Exceeding string length:
Kansas Euph
```

Note that the `cout.write()` call returns the `cout` object. This is because the `write()` method returns a reference to the object that invokes it, and in this case, the `cout` object invokes it. This makes it possible to concatenate output, for `cout.write()` is replaced by its return value, `cout`:

```
cout.write(state2,i) << "\n";
```

Also, note that the `write()` method doesn't stop printing characters automatically when it reaches the null character. It simply prints how many characters you tell it to, even if that goes beyond the bounds of a particular string! In this case, the program brackets the string `"Kansas"` with two other strings so that adjacent memory locations would contain data. Compilers differ in the order in which they store data in memory and in how they align memory. For example, "Kansas" occupies six bytes, but this particular compiler appears to align strings using multiples of four bytes, so "Kansas" is padded out to eight bytes. Because of compiler differences, you may get a different result for the final line of output.

The `write()` method can also be used with numeric data. It doesn't translate a number to the correct characters; instead, it transmits the bit representation as stored in memory. For example, a 4-byte `long` value such as 560031841 would be transmitted as four separate bytes. An output device such as a monitor would then try to interpret each byte as if it were ASCII (or whatever) code. So 560031841 would appear onscreen as some 4-character combination, most likely gibberish. (But maybe not; try it, and see.) However, `write()` does provide a compact, accurate way to store numeric data in a file. We'll return to this possibility later in this chapter.

Flushing the Output Buffer

Consider what happens as a program uses `cout` to send bytes on to the standard output. Because the `ostream` class buffers output handled by the `cout` object, output isn't sent to its destination immediately. Instead, it accumulates in the buffer until the buffer is full. Then the program *flushes* the buffer, sending the contents on and clearing the buffer for new data. Typically, a buffer is 512 bytes or an integral multiple thereof. Buffering is a great time-saver when the standard output is connected to a file on a hard disk. After all, you don't want a program to access the hard disk 512 times to send 512 bytes. It's much more effective to collect 512 bytes in a buffer and write them to a hard disk in a single disk operation.

For screen output, however, filling the buffer first is less critical. Indeed, it would be inconvenient if you had to reword the message "Press any key to continue" so that it consumed the prerequisite 512 bytes to fill a buffer. Fortunately, in the case of screen output, the program doesn't necessarily wait until the buffer is full. Sending a newline character to the buffer, for example, normally flushes the buffer. Also, as mentioned before, most implementations flush the buffer when input is pending. That is, suppose you have the following code:

```
cout << "Enter a number: ";
float num;
cin >> num;
```

The fact that the program expects input causes it to display the `cout` message (that is, flush the `"Enter a number:  "` message) immediately, even though the output string lacks a newline. Without this feature, the program would wait for input without having prompted the user with the `cout` message.

If your implementation doesn't flush output when you want it to, you can force flushing by using one of two manipulators. The `flush` manipulator flushes the buffer, and the `endl` manipulator flushes the buffer and inserts a newline. You use these manipulators the way you would use a variable name:

```
cout << "Hello, good-looking! " << flush;
cout << "Wait just a moment, please." << endl;
```

Manipulators are, in fact, functions. For example, you can flush the `cout` buffer by calling the `flush()` function directly:

```
flush(cout);
```

However, the `ostream` class overloads the `<<` insertion operator in such a way that the expression

```
cout << flush
```

gets replaced with the `flush(cout)` function call. Thus, you can use the more convenient insertion notation to flush with success.

Formatting with `cout`

The `ostream` insertion operators convert values to text form. By default, they format values as follows:

- A type `char` value, if it represents a printable character, is displayed as a character in a field one character wide.

- Numerical integer types are displayed as decimal integers in a field just wide enough to hold the number and, if present, a minus sign.

- Strings are displayed in a field equal in width to the length of the string.

The default behavior for floating-point has changed. The following list details the differences between older and newer implementations:

- (New Style) Floating-point types are displayed with a total of six digits, except that trailing zeros aren't displayed. (Note that the number of digits displayed has no connection with the precision to which the number is stored.) The number is displayed in fixed-point notation or else in E notation (see Chapter 3, "Dealing with Data"), depending upon the value of the number. In particular, E notation is used if the exponent is 6 or larger or -5 or smaller. Again, the field is just wide enough to hold the number and, if present, a minus sign. The default behavior corresponds to using the standard C library function `fprintf()` with a `%g` specifier.

- (Old Style) Floating-point types are displayed with six places to the right of the decimal, except that trailing zeros aren't displayed. (Note that the number of digits displayed has no connection with the precision to which the number is stored.) The number is displayed in fixed-point notation or else in E notation (see Chapter 3), depending upon the value of the number. Again, the field is just wide enough to hold the number and, if present, a minus sign.

Because each value is displayed in a width equal to its size, you have to provide spaces between values explicitly; otherwise, consecutive values would run together.

There are several small differences between early C++ formatting and the current standard; we'll summarize them in Table 17.3 later in this chapter.

Listing 17.2 illustrates the output defaults. It displays a colon (:) after each value so you can see the width field used in each case. The program uses the expression 1.0/9.0 to generate a nonterminating fraction so you can see how many places get printed.

Compatibility Note

Not all compilers generate output formatted in accordance with the current standard. Also, the current standard allows for regional variations. For example, a European implementation can follow the continental fashion of using a comma instead of a period for displacing decimal fractions. That is, it may write 2,54 instead of 2.54. The locale library (header file `locale`) provides a mechanism for *imbuing* an input or output stream with a particular style, so a single compiler can offer more than one locale choice. This chapter will use the U.S. locale.

LISTING 17.2   defaults.cpp

```cpp
// defaults.cpp -- cout default formats
#include <iostream>
using namespace std;

int main()
{
    cout << "12345678901234567890\n";
    char ch = 'K';
    int t = 273;
    cout << ch << ":\n";
    cout << t << ":\n";
    cout << -t <<":\n";

    double f1 = 1.200;
    cout << f1 << ":\n";
    cout << (f1 + 1.0 / 9.0) << ":\n";

    double f2 = 1.67E2;
    cout << f2 << ":\n";
    f2 += 1.0 / 9.0;
    cout << f2 << ":\n";
    cout << (f2 * 1.0e4) << ":\n";
```

LISTING 17.2   Continued

```
        double f3 = 2.3e-4;
        cout << f3 << ":\n";
        cout << f3 / 10 << ":\n";

        return 0;
}
```

Here is the output:

```
12345678901234567890
K:
273:
-273:
1.2:
1.31111:
167:
167.111:
1.67111e+006:
0.00023:
2.3e-005:
```

Each value fills its field. Note that the trailing zeros of 1.200 are not displayed but that floating-point values without terminating zeros have six places to the right of the decimal displayed. Also, this particular implementation displays three digits in the exponent; others might use two.

Changing the Number Base Used for Display

The `ostream` class inherits from the `ios` class, which inherits from the `ios_base` class. The `ios_base` class stores information describing the format state. For example, certain bits in one class member determine the number base used, while another member determines the field width. By using *manipulators*, you can control the number base used to display integers. By using `ios_base` member functions, you can control the field width and the number of places displayed to the right of the decimal. Because the `ios_base` class is an indirect base class for `ostream`, you can use its methods with `ostream` objects (or descendants), such as `cout`.

Note

The members and methods found in the `ios_base` class formerly were found in the `ios` class. Now `ios_base` is a base class to `ios`. In the new system, `ios` is a template class with `char` and `wchar_t` specializations, while `ios_base` contains the non-template features.

Let's see how to set the number base to be used in displaying integers. To control whether integers are displayed in base 10, base 16, or base 8, you can use the `dec`, `hex`, and `oct` manipulators. For example, the function call

```
hex(cout);
```

sets the number base format state for the **cout** object to hexadecimal. Once you do this, a program will print integer values in hexadecimal form until you set the format state to another choice. Note that the manipulators are not member functions, hence they don't have to be invoked by an object.

Although the manipulators really are functions, you normally see them used this way:

```
cout << hex;
```

The **ostream** class overloads the << operator to make this usage equivalent to the function call **hex(cout)**. Listing 17.3 illustrates using these manipulators. It shows the value of an integer and its square in three different number bases. Note that you can use a manipulator separately or as part of a series of insertions.

LISTING 17.3   manip.cpp

```cpp
// manip.cpp -- using format manipulators
#include <iostream>
using namespace std;
int main()
{
    cout << "Enter an integer: ";
    int n;
    cin >> n;

    cout << "n      n*n\n";
    cout << n << "      " << n * n << " (decimal)\n";
// set to hex mode
    cout << hex;
    cout << n << "      ";
    cout << n * n << " (hexadecimal)\n";

// set to octal mode
    cout << oct << n << "      " << n * n << " (octal)\n";

// alternative way to call a manipulator
    dec(cout);
    cout << n << "      " << n * n << " (decimal)\n";

    return 0;
}
```

Here is some sample output:

```
Enter an integer: 13
n      n*n
13       169 (decimal)
d       a9 (hexadecimal)
15       251 (octal)
13       169 (decimal)
```

Adjusting Field Widths

You probably noticed that the columns in the preceding example don't line up; that's because the numbers have different field widths. You can use the width member function to place differently sized numbers in fields having equal widths. The method has these prototypes:

```
int width();
int width(int i);
```

The first form returns the current setting for field width. The second sets the field width to i spaces and returns the previous field width value. This allows you to save the previous value in case you want to restore the width to that value later.

The width() method affects only the next item displayed, and the field width reverts to the default value afterwards. For example, consider the following statements:

```
cout << '#';
cout.width(12);
cout << 12 << "#" <<   24 << "#\n";
```

Because width() is a member function, you have to use an object (cout, in this case) to invoke it. The output statement produces the following display:

```
#           12#24#
```

The 12 is placed in a field 12 characters wide at the right end of the field. This is called right-justification. After that, the field width reverts to the default, and the two # characters and the 24 are printed in fields equal to their own size.

Remember

The width() method affects only the next item displayed, and the field width reverts to the default value afterwards.

C++ never truncates data, so if you attempt to print a seven-digit value in a field width of 2, C++ expands the field to fit the data. (Some languages just fill the field with asterisks if the data doesn't fit. The C/C++ philosophy is that showing all the data is more important than keeping the columns neat; C++ puts substance before form.) Listing 17.4 shows how the width() member function works.

LISTING 17.4   width.cpp

```cpp
// width.cpp -- use the width method
#include <iostream>
using namespace std;

int main()
{
    int w = cout.width(30);
    cout << "default field width = " << w << ":\n";
```

LISTING 17.4   *Continued*

```
      cout.width(5);
      cout << "N" <<':';
      cout.width(8);
      cout << "N * N" << ":\n";

      for (long i = 1; i <= 100; i *= 10)
      {
          cout.width(5);
          cout << i <<':';
          cout.width(8);
          cout << i * i << ":\n";
      }

      return 0;
}
```

Here is the output:

```
      default field width = 0:
  N:    N * N:
  1:        1:
 10:      100:
100:    10000:
```

The output displays values right-justified in their fields. The output is padded with spaces. That is, `cout` achieves the full field width by adding spaces. With right-justification, the spaces are inserted to the left of the values. The character used for padding is termed the *fill character*. Right-justification is the default.

Note that the program applies the field width of 30 to the string displayed by the first `cout` statement but not to the value of w. This is because the `width()` method affects only the next single item displayed. Also, note that w has the value **0**. This is because `cout.width(30)` returns the previous field width, not the one to which it was just set. The fact that w is zero means that zero is the default field width. Because C++ always expands a field to fit the data, this one size fits all. Finally, the program uses `width()` to align column headings and data by using a width of five characters for the first column and a width of eight characters for the second column.

Fill Characters

By default, `cout` fills unused parts of a field with spaces. You can use the `fill()` member function to change that. For example, the call

```
cout.fill('*');
```

changes the fill character to an asterisk. That can be handy for, say, printing checks so that recipients can't easily add a digit or two. Listing 17.5 illustrates using this member function.

LISTING 17.5   fill.cpp

```
// fill.cpp -- change fill character for fields
#include <iostream>
using namespace std;

int main()
{
    cout.fill('*');
    char * staff[2] = { "Waldo Whipsnade", "Wilmarie Wooper"};
    long bonus[2] = {900, 1350};

    for (int i = 0; i < 2; i++)
    {
        cout << staff[i] << ": $";
        cout.width(7);
        cout << bonus[i] << "\n";
    }

    return 0;
}
```

Here's the output:

```
Waldo Whipsnade: $****900
Wilmarie Wooper: $***1350
```

Note that, unlike the field width, the new fill character stays in effect until you change it.

Setting Floating-Point Display Precision

The meaning of floating-point precision depends upon the output mode. In the default mode, it means the total number of digits displayed. In the fixed and scientific modes, to be discussed soon, the precision means the number of digits displayed to the right of the decimal place. The precision default for C++, as you've seen, is 6. (Recall, however, that trailing zeros are dropped.) The `precision()` member function lets you select other values. For example, the statement

```
cout.precision(2);
```

causes `cout` to set the precision to 2. Unlike the case with `width()`, but like the case for `fill()`, a new precision setting stays in effect until reset. Listing 17.6 demonstrates precisely this point.

LISTING 17.6   precise.cpp

```
// precise.cpp -- set the precision
#include <iostream>
using namespace std;

int main()
{
    float price1 = 20.40;
    float price2 = 1.9 + 8.0 / 9.0;
```

LISTING 17.6   Continued

```
cout << "\"Furry Friends\" is $" << price1 << "!\n";
cout << "\"Fiery Fiends\" is $" << price2 << "!\n";

cout.precision(2);
cout << "\"Furry Friends\" is $" << price1 << "!\n";
cout << "\"Fiery Fiends\" is $" << price2 << "!\n";

return 0;
}
```

Compatibility Note

Older versions of C++ interpret the precision for the default mode as the number of digits to the right of the decimal instead of as the total number of digits.

Here is the output:

```
"Furry Friends" is $20.4!
"Fiery Fiends" is $2.78889!
"Furry Friends" is $20!
"Fiery Fiends" is $2.8!
```

Note that the third line doesn't print a trailing decimal point. Also, the fourth line displays a total of two digits.

Printing Trailing Zeros and Decimal Points

Certain forms of output, such as prices or numbers in columns, look better if trailing zeros are retained. For example, the output to Listing 17.6 would look better as $20.40 than as $20.4. The `iostream` family of classes doesn't provide a function whose sole purpose is accomplishing that. However, the `ios_base` class provides a `setf()` (for *set flag*) function that controls several formatting features. The class also defines several constants that can be used as arguments to this function. For example, the function call

```
cout.setf(ios_base::showpoint);
```

causes `cout` to display trailing decimal points. Formerly, but not currently, it also causes trailing zeros to be displayed. That is, instead of displaying 2.00 as 2, `cout` will display it as 2.000000 (old C++ formatting) or 2. (current formatting) if the default precision of 6 is in effect. Listing 17.7 adds this statement to Listing 17.6.

Caution

If your compiler uses the `iostream.h` header file instead of `iostream`, you most likely will have to use `ios` instead of `ios_base` in `setf()` arguments.

In case you're wondering about the notation `ios_base::showpoint`, `showpoint` is a class scope static constant defined in the `ios_base` class declaration. Class scope means that you have to use the scope operator (`::`) with the constant name if you use the name outside a member function definition. So `ios_base::showpoint` names a constant defined in the `ios_base` class.

LISTING 17.7   `showpt.cpp`

```
// showpt.cpp -- set the precision, show trailing point
#include <iostream>
using namespace std;

int main()
{
    float price1 = 20.40;
    float price2 = 1.9 + 8.0 / 9.0;

    cout.setf(ios_base::showpoint);
    cout << "\"Furry Friends\" is $" << price1 << "!\n";
    cout << "\"Fiery Fiends\" is $" << price2 << "!\n";

    cout.precision(2);
    cout << "\"Furry Friends\" is $" << price1 << "!\n";
    cout << "\"Fiery Fiends\" is $" << price2 << "!\n";

    return 0;
}
```

Here is the output using the current formatting. Note that trailing zeros are not shown, but the trailing decimal point for the third line is shown.

```
"Furry Friends" is $20.4!
"Fiery Fiends" is $2.78889!
"Furry Friends" is $20.!
"Fiery Fiends" is $2.8!
```

How, then, can you display trailing zeros? To answer that question, we have to discuss the `setf()` function in more detail.

More About `setf()`

The `setf()` method controls several other formatting choices, so let's take a closer look at it. The `ios_base` class has a protected data member in which individual bits (called *flags* in this context) control different formatting aspects such as the number base or whether trailing zeros are displayed. Turning a flag on is called *setting the flag* (or bit) and means setting the bit to 1. (If you've ever had to set DIP switches to configure computer hardware, bit flags are the programming equivalent.) The `hex`, `dec`, and `oct` manipulators, for example, adjust the three flag bits that control the number base. The `setf()` function provides another means of adjusting flag bits.

The `setf()` function has two prototypes. The first is this:

```
fmtflags setf(fmtflags);
```

Here `fmtflags` is a `typedef` name for a *bitmask* type (see Note) used to hold the format flags. The name is defined in the `ios_base` class. This version of `setf()` is used for setting format information controlled by a single bit. The argument is a `fmtflags` value indicating which bit to set. The return value is a type `fmtflags` number indicating the former setting of all the flags. You then can save that value if you later want to restore the original settings. What value do you pass to `setf()`? If you want to set bit number 11 to 1, you pass a number having its number 11 bit set to 1. The return value would have its number 11 bit assigned the prior value for that bit. Keeping track of bits sounds (and is) tedious. However, you don't have to do that job; the `ios_base` class defines constants representing the bit values. Table 17.1 shows some of these definitions.

Note

A bitmask type is a type used to store individual bit values. It could be an integer type, an `enum`, or an STL `bitset` container. The main idea is that each bit is individually accessible and has its own meaning. The `iostream` package uses bitmask types to store state information.

TABLE 17.1   Formatting Constants

Constant	Meaning
ios_base::boolalpha	Input and output `bool` values as `true` and `false`
ios_base::showbase	Use C++ base prefixes (0,0x) on output
ios_base::showpoint	Show trailing decimal point
ios_base::uppercase	Use uppercase letters for hex output, E notation
ios_base::showpos	Use + before positive numbers

Because these formatting constants are defined within the `ios_base` class, you must use the scope resolution operator with them. That is, use `ios_base::uppercase`, not just `uppercase`. Changes remain in effect until overridden. Listing 17.8 illustrates using some of these constants.

LISTING 17.8   setf.cpp

```
// setf.cpp -- use setf() to control formatting
#include <iostream>
using namespace std;
```

LISTING 17.8   Continued

```
int main()
{
    int temperature = 63;

    cout << "Today's water temperature: ";
        cout.setf(ios_base::showpos);      // show plus sign
      cout << temperature << "\n";

        cout << "For our programming friends, that's\n";
    cout << hex << temperature << "\n"; // use hex
        cout.setf(ios_base::uppercase);       // use uppercase in hex
        cout.setf(ios_base::showbase);        // use 0X prefix for hex
    cout << "or\n";
        cout << temperature << "\n";
    cout << "How " << true << "!  oops -- How ";
    cout.setf(ios_base::boolalpha);
    cout << true << "!\n";

    return 0;
}
```

Compatibility Note

Some implementations may use ios instead of ios_base, and they may fail to provide a boolalpha choice.

Here is the output:

```
Today's water temperature: +63
For our programming friends, that's
3f
or
0X3F
How 0X1!  oops -- How true!
```

Note that the plus sign is used only with the base 10 version. C++ treats hexadecimal and octal values as unsigned, hence no sign is needed for them. (However, some implementations may still display a plus sign.)

The second `setf()` prototype takes two arguments and returns the prior setting:

```
fmtflags setf(fmtflags , fmtflags );
```

This overloaded form of the function is used for format choices controlled by more than one bit. The first argument, as before, is a `fmtflags` value containing the desired setting. The second argument is a value that first clears the appropriate bits. For example, suppose setting bit 3 to 1 means base 10, setting bit 4 to 1 means base 8, and setting bit 5 to 1 means base 16. Suppose output is in base 10 and you want to set it to base 16. Not only do you have to set bit 5 to 1, you also have to set bit 3 to 0—this is called *clearing the bit*. The clever hex manipulator does both tasks automatically. The `setf()` requires a bit more work, because you use the second argument to indicate which bits to clear and then use the first argument to indicate which bit to set. This is not as complicated as it sounds, for the `ios_base` class defines constants (shown in Table 17.2) for this purpose. In particular, you should use the constant `ios_base::basefield` as the second argument and `ios_base::hex` as the first argument if you're changing bases. That is, the function call

```
cout.setf(ios_base::hex, ios_base::basefield);
```

has the same effect as using the hex manipulator.

TABLE 17.2   Arguments for `setf(long, long)`

Second Argument	First Argument	Meaning
ios_base::basefield	ios_base::dec	Use base 10
	ios_base::oct	Use base 8
	ios_base::hex	Use base 16
ios_base::floatfield	ios_base::fixed	Use fixed-point notation
	ios_base::scientific	Use scientific notation
ios_base::adjustfield	ios_base::left	Use left-justification
	ios_base::right	Use right-justification
	ios_base::internal	Left-justify sign or base prefix, right-justify value

The `ios_base` class defines three sets of formatting flags that can be handled this way. Each set consists of one constant to be used as the second argument and two to three constants to be used as a first argument. The second argument clears a batch of related bits; then the first argument sets one of those bits to 1. Table 17.2 shows the names of the constants used for the second `setf()` argument, the associated choice of constants for the first argument, and their meanings. For example, to select left-justification, use `ios_base::adjustfield` for the second argument and `ios_base::left` as the first argument. Left-justification means starting a value at the left end of the field, and right-justification means ending a value at the right end of the field. Internal justification means placing any signs or base prefixes at the left of the field and the rest of the number at the right of the field. (Unfortunately, C++ does not provide a self-justification mode.)

Fixed-point notation means using the 123.4 style for floating-point values regardless of the size of the number, and scientific notation means using the 1.23e04 style regardless of the size of the number.

Under the Standard, both fixed and scientific notation have the following two properties:

- Precision means the number of digits to the right of the decimal rather than the total number of digits.

- Trailing zeros are displayed.

Under the older usage, trailing zeros are not shown unless **ios::showpoint** is set. Also, under older usage, precision always meant the number of digits to the right of the decimal, even in the default mode.

The **setf()** function is a member function of the **ios_base** class. Because that's a base class for the **ostream** class, you can invoke the function using the **cout** object. For example, to request left-justification, use this call:

```
ios_base::fmtflags old = cout.setf(ios::left, ios::adjustfield);
```

To restore the previous setting, do this:

```
cout.setf(old, ios::adjustfield);
```

Listing 17.9 illustrates further examples of using **setf()** with two arguments.

Compatibility Note

This program uses a math function, and some C++ systems don't automatically search the math library. For example, some UNIX systems require that you do the following:

```
$ CC setf2.C -lm
```

The -lm option instructs the linker to search the math library.

LISTING 17.9   setf2.cpp

```cpp
// setf2.cpp -- use setf() with 2 arguments to control formatting
#include <iostream>
using namespace std;
#include <cmath>

int main()
{
    // use left justification, show the plus sign, show trailing
    // zeros, with a precision of 3
    cout.setf(ios_base::left, ios_base::adjustfield);
    cout.setf(ios_base::showpos);
    cout.setf(ios_base::showpoint);
    cout.precision(3);
    // use e-notation and save old format setting
    ios_base::fmtflags old = cout.setf(ios_base::scientific,
        ios_base::floatfield);
    cout << "Left Justification:\n";
    long n;
```

LISTING 17.9 *Continued*

```
    for (n = 1; n <= 41; n+= 10)
    {
        cout.width(4);
        cout << n << "|";
        cout.width(12);
        cout << sqrt(n) << "|\n";
    }

    // change to internal justification
    cout.setf(ios_base::internal, ios_base::adjustfield);
    // restore default floating-point display style
    cout.setf(old, ios_base::floatfield);

    cout << "Internal Justification:\n";
    for (n = 1; n <= 41; n+= 10)
    {
        cout.width(4);
        cout << n << "|";
        cout.width(12);
        cout << sqrt(n) << "|\n";
    }

    // use right justification, fixed notation
    cout.setf(ios_base::right, ios_base::adjustfield);
    cout.setf(ios_base::fixed, ios_base::floatfield);
    cout << "Right Justification:\n";
    for (n = 1; n <= 41; n+= 10)
    {
        cout.width(4);
        cout << n << "|";
        cout.width(12);
        cout << sqrt(n) << "|\n";
    }

    return 0;
}
```

Here is the output:

```
Left Justification:
+1  |+1.000e+00  |
+11 |+3.317e+00  |
+21 |+4.583e+00  |
+31 |+5.568e+00  |
+41 |+6.403e+00  |
Internal Justification:
+  1|+       1.00|
+ 11|+       3.32|
+ 21|+       4.58|
+ 31|+       5.57|
+ 41|+       6.40|
```

```
Right Justification:
  +1|       +1.000|
 +11|       +3.317|
 +21|       +4.583|
 +31|       +5.568|
 +41|       +6.403|
```

Note how a precision of 3 causes the default floating-point display (used for internal justification in this program) to display a total of three digits, while the fixed and scientific modes display three digits to the right of the decimal. (The number of digits displayed in the exponent for e-notation depends upon the implementation.)

The effects of calling `setf()` can be undone with `unsetf()`, which has the following prototype:

```
void unsetf(fmtflags mask);
```

Here `mask` is a bit pattern. All bits set to 1 in `mask` cause the corresponding bits to be unset. That is, `setf()` sets bits to 1 and `unsetf()` sets bits back to 0. For example:

```
cout.setf(ios_base::showpoint);    // show trailing decimal point
cout.unsetf(ios_base::boolalpha);  // don't show trailing decimal point
cout.setf(ios_base::boolalpha);    // display true, false
cout.unsetf(ios_base::boolalpha);  // display 1, 0
```

Standard Manipulators

Using `setf()` is not the most user-friendly approach to formatting, so C++ offers several manipulators to invoke `setf()` for you, automatically supplying the right arguments. You've already seen `dec`, `hex`, and `oct`. These manipulators, most of which are not available to older implementations, work like `hex`. For example, the statement

```
cout << left << fixed;
```

turns on left justification and the fixed decimal point option. Table 17.3 lists these along with several other manipulators.

Tip
If your system supports these manipulators, take advantage of them; if it doesn't, you still have the option of using `setf()`.

TABLE 17.3 Some Standard Manipulators

Manipulator	Calls
boolalpha	setf(ios_base::boolalpha)
noboolalpha	unset(ios_base::noboolalpha)

TABLE 17.3   Continued

Manipulator	Calls
showbase	setf(ios_base::showbase)
noshowbase	unsetf(ios_base::showbase)
showpoint	setf(ios_base::showpoint)
noshowpoint	unsetf(ios_base::showpoint)
showpos	setf(ios_base::showpos)
noshowpos	unsetf(ios_base::showpos)
uppercase	setf(ios_base::uppercase)
nouppercase	unsetf(ios_base::uppercase)
internal	setf(ios_base::internal, ios_base::adjustfield)
left	setf(ios_base::left, ios_base::adjustfield)
right	setf(ios_base::right, ios_base::adjustfield)
dec	setf(ios_base::dec, ios_base::basefield)
hex	setf(ios_base::hex, ios_base::basefield)
oct	setf(ios_base::oct, ios_base::basefield)
fixed	setf(ios_base::fixed, ios_base::floatfield)
scientific	setf(ios_base::scientific, ios_base::floatfield)

The iomanip Header File

Setting some format values, such as the field width, can be awkward using the iostream tools. To make life easier, C++ supplies additional manipulators in the iomanip header file. They provide the same services we've discussed, but in a notationally more convenient manner. The three most commonly used are setprecision() for setting the precision, setfill() for setting the fill character, and setw() for setting the field width. Unlike the manipulators discussed previously, these take arguments. The setprecision() manipulator takes an integer argument specifying the precision, the setfill() takes a char argument indicating the fill character, and the setw() manipulator takes an integer argument specifying the field width. Because they are manipulators, they can be concatenated in a cout statement. This makes the setw() manipulator particularly convenient when displaying several columns of values. Listing 17.10 illustrates this by changing the field width and fill character several times for one output line. It also uses some of the newer standard manipulators.

Compatibility Note

This program uses a math function, and some C++ systems don't automatically search the math library. For example, some UNIX systems require that you do the following:

```
$ CC iomanip.C -lm
```

The `-lm` option instructs the linker to search the math library. Also, older compilers may not recognize the new standard manipulators such as `showpoint`. In that case, you can use the `setf()` equivalents.

LISTING 17.10   `iomanip.cpp`

```cpp
// iomanip.cpp -- use manipulators from iomanip
// some systems require explicitly linking the math library
#include <iostream>
using namespace std;
#include <iomanip>
#include <cmath>

int main()
{
    // use new standard manipulators
    cout << showpoint << fixed << right;

    // use iomanip manipulators
    cout << setw(6) << "N" << setw(14) << "square root"
         << setw(15) << "fourth root\n";

    double root;
    for (int n = 10; n <=100; n += 10)
    {
        root = sqrt(n);
        cout << setw(6) << setfill('.') << n << setfill(' ')
             << setw(12) << setprecision(3) << root
             << setw(14) << setprecision(4) << sqrt(root)
             << "\n";
    }

    return 0;
}
```

Here is the output:

```
    N  square root    fourth root
....10       3.162        1.7783
....20       4.472        2.1147
....30       5.477        2.3403
....40       6.325        2.5149
....50       7.071        2.6591
....60       7.746        2.7832
....70       8.367        2.8925
```

```
....80      8.944       2.9907
....90      9.487       3.0801
...100     10.000       3.1623
```

Now you can produce neatly aligned columns. Note that this program produces the same formatting with either the older or current implementations. Using the `showpoint` manipulator causes trailing zeros to be displayed in older implementations, and using the `fixed` manipulator causes trailing zeros to be displayed in current implementations. Using `fixed` makes the display fixed-point in either system, and in current systems it makes precision refer to the number of digits to the right of the decimal. In older systems, precision always has that meaning, regardless of the floating-point display mode.

Table 17.4 summarizes some of the differences between older C++ formatting and the current state. One moral of this table is that you shouldn't feel baffled if you run an example program you've seen somewhere and the output format doesn't match what is shown for the example.

TABLE 17.4 Formatting Changes

Feature	Older C++	Current C++
`precision(n)`	Display n digits to the right of the decimal point	Display a total of n digits in the default mode, and display n digits to the right of the decimal point in fixed and scientific modes
`ios::showpoint`	Display trailing decimal point and trailing zeros	Display trailing decimal point
`ios::fixed,` `ios::scientific`		Show trailing zeros (also see comments under `precision()`)

Input with `cin`

Now it's time to turn to input and getting data into a program. The `cin` object represents the standard input as a stream of bytes. Normally, you generate that stream of characters at the keyboard. If you type the character sequence 2002, the `cin` object extracts those characters from the input stream. You may intend that input to be part of a string, to be an `int` value, to be a `float` value, or to be some other type. Thus, extraction also involves type conversion. The `cin` object, guided by the type of variable designated to receive the value, must use its methods to convert that character sequence into the intended type of value.

Typically, you use `cin` as follows:

```
cin >> value_holder;
```

Here `value_holder` identifies the memory location in which to store the input. It can be the name of a variable, a reference, a dereferenced pointer, or a member of a structure or of a class. How `cin` interprets the input depends on the data type for `value_holder`. The `istream` class, defined in the `iostream` header file, overloads the `>>` extraction operator to recognize the following basic types:

- `signed char &`

- `unsigned char &`

- `char &`

- `short &`

- `unsigned short &`

- `int &`

- `unsigned int &`

- `long &`

- `unsigned long &`

- `float &`

- `double &`

- `long double &`

These are referred to as *formatted input functions* because they convert the input data to the format indicated by the target.

A typical operator function has a prototype like the following:

```
istream & operator>>(int &);
```

Both the argument and the return value are references. A reference argument (see Chapter 8, "Adventures in Functions") means that a statement such as

```
cin >> staff_size;
```

causes the `operator>>()` function to work with the variable `staff_size` itself rather than with a copy, as would be the case with a regular argument. Because the argument type is a reference, `cin` is able to modify directly the value of a variable used as an argument. The preceding statement, for example, directly modifies the value of the `staff_size` variable. We'll get to the significance of a reference return value in a moment. First, let's examine the type conversion aspect of the extraction operator. For arguments of each type in the preceding list of types, the extraction operator converts the character input to the indicated type of value. For example, suppose `staff_size` is type `int`. Then the compiler matches the

```
cin >> staff_size;
```

to the following prototype:

```
istream & operator>>(int &);
```

The function corresponding to that prototype then reads the stream of characters being sent to the program, say, the characters 2, 3, 1, 8, and 4. For a system using a 2-byte `int`, the function then converts these characters to the 2-byte binary representation of the integer 23184. If, on the other hand, `staff_size` had been type `double`, `cin` would use the `operator>>(double &)` to convert the same input into the 8-byte floating-point representation of the value 23184.0.

Incidentally, you can use the `hex`, `oct`, and `dec` manipulators with `cin` to specify that integer input is to be interpreted as hexadecimal, octal, or decimal format. For example, the statement

```
cin >> hex;
```

causes an input of **12** or **0x12** to be read as hexadecimal **12**, or decimal **18**, and **ff** or **FF** to be read as decimal **255**.

The `istream` class also overloads the `>>` extraction operator for character pointer types:

- `signed char *`
- `char *`
- `unsigned char *`

For this type of argument, the extraction operator reads the next word from input and places it at the indicated address, adding a null character to make a string. For example, suppose you have this code:

```
cout << "Enter your first name:\n";
char name[20];
cin >> name;
```

If you respond to the request by typing **Liz**, the extraction operator places the characters **Liz\0** in the `name` array. (As usual, **\0** represents the terminating null character.) The `name` identifier, being the name of a `char` array, acts as the address of the array's first element, making `name` type `char *` (pointer-to-`char`).

The fact that each extraction operator returns a reference to the invoking object lets you concatenate input, just as you can concatenate output:

```
char name[20];
float fee;
int group;
cin >> name >> fee >> group;
```

Here, for example, the `cin` object returned by `cin >> name` becomes the object handling `fee`.

How `cin >>` Views Input

The various versions of the extraction operator share a common way of looking at the input stream. They skip over white space (blanks, newlines, and tabs) until they encounter a nonwhite-space character. This is true even for the single-character modes (those in which the argument is type `char`, `unsigned char`, or `signed char`), which is not true of C's character input functions (see Figure 17.5). In the single-character modes, the `>>` operator reads that character and assigns it to the indicated location. In the other modes, the operator reads in one unit of the indicated type. That is, it reads everything from the initial nonwhite-space character up to the first character that doesn't match the destination type.

FIGURE 17.5

`cin >>` skips over whitespace.

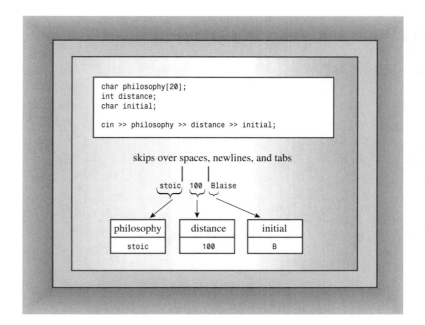

For example, consider the following code:

```
int elevation;
cin >> elevation;
```

Suppose you type the following characters:

`-123Z`

The operator will read the `-`, `1`, `2`, and `3` characters, because they are all valid parts of an integer. But the `Z` character isn't valid, so the last character accepted for input is the `3`. The `Z` remains in the input stream, and the next `cin` statement will start reading at that point. Meanwhile, the operator converts the character sequence -123 to an integer value and assigns it to `elevation`.

It can happen that input fails to meet a program's expectation. For example, suppose you entered `Zcar` instead of `-123Z`. In that case, the extraction operator leaves the value of `elevation` unchanged and returns the value zero. (More technically, an `if` or `while` statement evaluates an `istream` object as `false` if it's had an error state set—we'll discuss this in more depth later in this chapter.) The **false** return value allows a program to check whether input meets the program requirements, as Listing 17.11 shows.

LISTING 17.11   check_it.cpp

```
// check_it.cpp
#include <iostream>
using namespace std;

int main()
{
    cout.precision(2);
    cout << showpoint << fixed;
    cout << "Enter numbers: ";

    double sum = 0.0;
    double input;
    while (cin >> input)
    {
        sum += input;
    }

    cout << "Last value entered = " << input << "\n";
    cout << "Sum = " << sum << "\n";
    return 0;
}
```

Compatibility Note

If your compiler doesn't support the **showpoint** and **fixed** manipulators, use the **setf()** equivalents.

Here's the output when some inappropriate input (-123Z) sneaks into the input stream:

```
Enter numbers: 200.0
1.0E1 -50 -123Z 60
Last value entered = -123.00
Sum = 37.00
```

Because input is buffered, the second line of keyboard input values didn't get sent to the program until we typed <Enter> at the end of the line. But the loop quit processing input at the Z character, because it didn't match any of the floating-point formats. The failure of input to match the expected format, in turn, caused the expression `cin>> input` to evaluate to **false**, thus terminating the **while** loop.

Stream States

Let's take a closer look at what happens for inappropriate input. A **cin** or **cout** object contains a data member (inherited from the **ios_base** class) that describes the *stream state*. A stream state (defined as type **iostate**, which, in turn, is a bitmask type, such as described earlier) consists of the three `ios_base` elements: `eofbit`, `badbit`, or `failbit`. Each element is a single bit that can be 1 (*set*) or 0 (*cleared*). When a `cin` operation reaches the end of a file, it sets the `eofbit`. When a `cin` operation fails to read the expected characters, as in the earlier example, it sets the `failbit`. I/O failures, such as trying to read a non-accessible file or trying to write to a write-protected diskette, also can set `failbit` to 1. The `badbit` element is set when some undiagnosed failure may have corrupted the stream. (Implementations don't necessarily agree about which events set `failbit` and which set `badbit`.) When all three of these state bits are set to 0, everything is fine. Programs can check the stream state and use that information to decide what to do next. Table 17.5 lists these bits along with some `ios_base` methods that report or alter the stream state. (Older compilers don't provide the two `exceptions()` methods.)

TABLE 17.5   Stream States

Member	Description
`eofbit`	Set to 1 if end-of-file reached.
`badbit`	Set to 1 if the stream may be corrupted; for example, there could have been a file read error.
`failbit`	Set to 1 if an input operation failed to read the expected characters or an output operation failed to write the expected characters.
`goodbit`	Just another way of saying 0.
`good()`	Returns `true` if the stream can be used (all bits are cleared).
`eof()`	Returns `true` if `eofbit` is set.
`bad()`	Returns `true` if `badbit` is set.
`fail()`	Returns `true` if `badbit` or `failbit` is set.
`rdstate()`	Returns the stream state.
`exceptions()`	Returns a bit mask identifying which flags cause an exception to be thrown.
`exceptions(iostate ex)`	Sets which states will cause `clear()` to throw an exception; for example, if `ex` is `eofbit`, then `clear()` will throw an exception if `eofbit` is set.
`clear(iostate s)`	Sets the stream state to `s`; the default for `s` is 0 (`goodbit`); throws a `basic_ios::failure` exception if `rdstate() & exceptions())` != `0`.
`setstate (iostate s)`	Calls `clear(rdstate()	s)`. This sets stream state bits corresponding to those bits set in `s`; other stream state bits are left unchanged.

Setting States

Two of the methods in Table 17.5, `clear()` and `setstate()`, are similar. Both reset the state, but in a different fashion. The `clear()` method sets the state to its argument. Thus, the call

```
clear();
```

uses the default argument of 0, which clears all three state bits (`eofbit`, `badbit`, and `failbit`). Similarly, the call

```
clear(eofbit);
```

makes the state equal to `eofbit`; that is, the `eofbit` is set and the other two state bits are cleared.

The `setstate()` method, however, affects only those bits that are set in its argument. Thus, the call

```
setstate(eofbit);
```

sets `eofbit` without affecting the other bits. So if `failbit` were already set, it stays set.

Why would you reset the stream state? For a program writer, the most common reason is to use `clear()` with no argument to reopen input after encountering mismatched input or end-of-file; whether or not doing so makes sense depends on what the program is trying to accomplish. You'll see some examples shortly. The main purpose for `setstate()` is to provide a means for input and output functions to change the state. For example, if num is an `int`, the call

```
cin >> num;  // read an int
```

can result in `operator>>(int &)` using `setstate()` to set `failbit` or `eofbit`.

I/O and Exceptions

Suppose, say, an input function sets `eofbit`. Does this cause an exception to be thrown? By default, the answer is no. However, you can use the `exceptions()` method to control how exceptions are handled.

First, here's some background. The `exceptions()` method returns a bitfield with three bits corresponding to `eofbit`, `failbit`, and `badbit`. Changing the stream state involves either `clear()` or `setstate()`, which uses `clear()`. After changing the stream state, the `clear()` method compares the current stream state to the value returned by `exceptions()`. If a bit is set in the return value and the corresponding bit is set in the current state, `clear()` throws an `ios_base::failure` exception. This would happen, for example, if both values had `badbit` set. It follows that if `exceptions()` returns `goodbit`, no exceptions are thrown. The `ios_base::failure` exception class derives from the `std::exception` class and thus has a `what()` method.

The default setting for `exceptions()` is `goodbit`, that is, no exceptions thrown. However, the overloaded `exceptions(iostate)` function gives you control over the behavior:

```
cin.exceptions(badbit);  // setting badbit causes exception to be thrown
```

The bitwise OR operator (|), as discussed in Appendix E, allows you to specify more than one bit. For example, the statement

```
cin.exceptions(badbit | eofbit);
```

results in an exception being thrown if either **badbit** or **eofbit** subsequently is set.

Listing 17.12 modifies Listing 17.11 so that the program throws and catches an exception if **failbit** is set.

LISTING 17.12   cinexcp.cpp

```
// cinexcp.cpp
#include <iostream>
#include <exception>
using namespace std;

int main()
{
    // have failbit cause an exception to be thown
    cin.exceptions(ios_base::failbit);
    cout.precision(2);
    cout << showpoint << fixed;
    cout << "Enter numbers: ";
    double sum = 0.0;
    double input;
    try {
        while (cin >> input)
        {
            sum += input;
        }
    } catch(ios_base::failure & bf)
    {
        cout << bf.what() << endl;
        cout << "O! the horror!\n";
    }

    cout << "Last value entered = " << input << "\n";
    cout << "Sum = " << sum << "\n";
    return 0;
}
```

Here is a sample run; the **what()** message depends upon the implementation:

```
Enter numbers: 20 30 40 pi 6
ios_base failure in clear
O! the horror!
Last value entered = 40.00
Sum = 90.00
```

Stream State Effects

An `if` or `while` test such as

```
while (cin >> input)
```

tests as `true` only if the stream state is good (all bits cleared). If a test fails, you can use the member functions in Table 17.5 to discriminate among possible causes. For example, you could modify the central part of Listing 17.11 to look like this:

```
while (cin >> input)
{
    sum += input;
}
if (cin.eof())
    cout << "Loop terminated because EOF encountered\n";
```

Setting a stream state bit has a very important consequence: The stream is closed for further input or output until the bit is cleared. For example, the following code won't work:

```
while (cin >> input)
{
    sum += input;
}
cout << "Last value entered = " << input << "\n";
cout << "Sum = " << sum << "\n";
cout << "Now enter a new number: ";
cin >> input;    // won't work
```

If you want a program to read further input after a stream state bit has been set, you have to reset the stream state to good. This can be done by calling the `clear()` method:

```
while (cin >> input)
{
    sum += input;
}
cout << "Last value entered = " << input << "\n";
cout << "Sum = " << sum << "\n";
cout << "Now enter a new number: ";
cin.clear();            // reset stream state
while (!isspace(cin.get()))
    continue;       // get rid of bad input
cin >> input;           // will work now
```

Note that it is not enough to reset the stream state. The mismatched input that terminated the input loop still is in the input queue, and the program has to get past it. One way is to keep reading characters until reaching white space. The `isspace()` function (see Chapter 6, "Branching Statements and Logical Operators") is a `cctype` function that returns `true` if its argument is a white space character. Or you can discard the rest of the line instead of just the next word:

```
while (cin.get() != '\n')
    continue;  // get rid rest of line
```

This example assumes that the loop terminated because of inappropriate input. Suppose, instead, the loop terminated because of end-of-file or because of a hardware failure. Then the new code disposing of bad input makes no sense. You can fix matters by using the `fail()` method to test whether the assumption was correct. Because, for historical reasons, `fail()` returns `true` if either `failbit` or `badbit` is set, the code has to exclude the latter case.

```
while (cin >> input)
{
    sum += input;
}
cout << "Last value entered = " << input << "\n";
cout << "Sum = " << sum << "\n";
if (cin.fail() && !cin.bad() ) // failed because of mismatched input
{

        cin.clear();       // reset stream state
        while (!isspace(cin.get()))
            continue;      // get rid of bad input
}
else // else bail out
{
        cout << "I cannot go on!\n";
        exit(1);
}
cout << "Now enter a new number: ";
cin >> input;  // will work now
```

Other `istream` Class Methods

Chapters 3, 4, "Compound Types," and 5, "Loops and Relational Expressions," discuss the `get()` and `getline()` methods. As you may recall, they provide the following additional input capabilities:

- The `get(char &)` and `get(void)` methods provide single-character input that doesn't skip over white space.

- The `get(char *, int, char)` and `getline(char *, int, char)` functions read entire lines by default rather than single words.

These are termed *unformatted input functions* because they simply read character input as it is without skipping over whitespace and without performing data conversions.

Let's look at these two groups of `istream` class member functions.

Single-Character Input

When used with a *char* argument or no argument at all, the `get()` methods fetch the next input character, even if it is a space, tab, or newline character. The `get(char & ch)` version assigns the input character to its argument, while the `get(void)` version uses the input character, converted to an integer type, typically `int`, as its return value.

Let's try `get(char &)` first. Suppose you have the following loop in a program:

```
int ct = 0;
char ch;
cin.get(ch);
while (ch != '\n')
{
    cout << ch;
    ct++;
    cin.get(ch);
}
cout << ct << '\n';
```

Next, suppose you type the following optimistic input:

```
I C++ clearly.<Enter>
```

Pressing the `<Enter>` key sends this input line to the program. The program fragment will first read the `I` character, display it with `cout`, and increment `ct` to 1. Next, it will read the space character following the `I`, display it, and increment `ct` to 2. This continues until the program processes the `<Enter>` key as a newline character and terminates the loop. The main point here is that, by using `get(ch)`, the code reads, displays, and counts the spaces as well as the printing characters.

Suppose, instead, that the program had tried to use `>>`:

```
int ct = 0;
char ch;
cin >> ch;
while (ch != '\n')      // FAILS
{
    cout << ch;
    ct++;
    cin >> ch;
}
cout << ct << '\n';
```

First, the code would skip the spaces, thus not counting them and compressing the corresponding output to this:

```
IC++clearly.
```

Worse, the loop would never terminate! Because the extraction operator skips newlines, the code would never assign the newline character to `ch`, so the `while` loop test would never terminate the loop.

The `get(char &)` member function returns a reference to the `istream` object used to invoke it. This means you can concatenate other extractions following `get(char &)`:

```
char c1, c2, c3;
cin.get(c1).get(c2) >> c3;
```

First, `cin.get(c1)` assigns the first input character to `c1` and returns the invoking object, which is `cin`. This reduces the code to `cin.get(c2) >> c3`, which assigns the second input character to `c2`. The function call returns `cin`, reducing the code to `cin >> c3`. This, in turn, assigns the next nonwhite-space character to c3. Note that c1 and c2 could wind up being assigned white space, but c3 couldn't.

If cin.get(char &) encounters the end of a file, either real or simulated from the keyboard (<Ctrl>-<Z> for DOS, <Ctrl>-<D> at the beginning of a line for UNIX), it does not assign a value to its argument. This is quite right, for if the program has reached the end of the file, there is no value to be assigned. Furthermore, the method calls setstate(failbit), which causes cin to test as false:

```cpp
char ch;
while (cin.get(ch))
{
    // process input
}
```

As long as there's valid input, the return value for cin.get(ch) is cin, which evaluates as true, so the loop continues. Upon reaching end-of-file, the return value evaluates as false, terminating the loop.

The get(void) member function also reads white space, but it uses its return value to communicate input to a program. So you would use it this way:

```cpp
int ct = 0;
char ch;
ch = cin.get();        // use return value
while (ch != '\n')
{
    cout << ch;
    ct++;
    ch = cin.get();
}
cout << ct << '\n';
```

Some older C++ implementation functions don't provide this member function.

The get(void) member function returns type int (or some larger integer type, depending upon the character set and locale). This makes the following invalid:

```cpp
char c1, c2, c3;
cin.get().get() >> c3;   // not valid
```

Here cin.get() returns a type int value. Because that return value is not a class object, you can't apply the membership operator to it. Thus, you get a syntax error. However, you can use get() at the end of an extraction sequence:

```cpp
char c1;
cin.get(c1).get();    // valid
```

The fact that get(void) returns type int means you can't follow it with an extraction operator. But, because cin.get(c1) returns cin, it makes it a suitable prefix to get(). This particular code would read the first input character, assign it to c1, then read the second input character and discard it.

Upon reaching the end-of-file, real or simulated, `cin.get(void)` returns the value `EOF`, which is a symbolic constant provided by the `iostream` header file. This design feature allows the following construction for reading input:

```
int ch;
while ((ch = cin.get()) != EOF)
{
    // process input
}
```

You should use type `int` for `ch` instead of type `char` here because the value `EOF` may not be expressed as a `char` type.

Chapter 5 describes these functions in a bit more detail, and Table 17.6 summarizes the features of the single-character input functions.

TABLE 17.6   `cin.get(ch)` Versus `cin.get()`

Property	cin.get(ch)	ch = cin.get()
Method for conveying input character	Assign to argument ch	Use function return value to assign to ch
Function return value for character input	Reference to a class istream object	Code for character as type int value
Function return value at end-of-file	Converts to false	EOF

Which Form of Single-Character Input?

Given the choice of `>>`, `get(char &)`, and `get(void)`, which should you use? First, decide whether you want input to skip over white space or not. If skipping white space is more convenient, use the extraction operator `>>`. For example, skipping white space is convenient for offering menu choices:

```
cout  << "a. annoy client     b. bill client\n"
      << "c. calm client      d. deceive client\n"
      << "q.\n";
cout  << "Enter a, b, c, d, or q: ";
char ch;
cin >> ch;
while (ch != 'q')
{
    switch(ch)
    {
        ...
    }
    cout << "Enter a, b, c, d, or q: ";
    cin >> ch;
}
```

To enter, say, a b response, you type b and press <Enter>, generating the two-character response of b\n. If you used either form of get(), you would have to add code to process that \n character each loop cycle, but the extraction operator conveniently skips it. (If you've programmed in C, you've probably encountered the situation in which the newline appears to the program as an invalid response. It's an easy problem to fix, but it is a nuisance.)

If you want a program to examine every character, use one of the get() methods. For example, a word-counting program could use white space to determine when a word came to an end. Of the two get() methods, the get(char &) method has the classier interface. The main advantage of the get(void) method is that it closely resembles the standard C getchar() function, letting you convert a C to a C++ program by including iostream instead of stdio.h, globally replacing getchar() with cin.get(), and globally replacing C's putchar(ch) with cout.put(ch).

String Input: getline(), get(), and ignore()

Next, let's review the string input member functions introduced in Chapter 4. The getline() member function and the third version of get() both read strings, and both have the same function signature (here simplified from the more general template declaration):

```
istream & get(char *, int, char = '\n');
istream & getline(char *, int, char = '\n');
```

The first argument, recall, is the address of the location to place the input string. The second argument is one greater than the maximum number of characters to be read. (The additional character leaves space for the terminating null character used in storing the input as a string.) If you omit the third argument, each function reads up to the maximum characters or until it encounters a newline character, whichever comes first.

For example, the code

```
char line[50];
cin.get(line, 50);
```

reads character input into the character array line. The cin.get() function quits reading input into the array after encountering 49 characters or, by default, after encountering a newline character, whichever comes first. The chief difference between get() and getline() is that get() leaves the newline character in the input stream, making it the first character seen by the next input operation, while getline() extracts and discards the newline character from the input stream.

Chapter 4 illustrated using the default form for these two member functions. Now let's look at the final argument, which modifies the function's default behavior. The third argument, which has a default value of '\n', is the termination character. Encountering the termination character causes input to cease even if the maximum number of characters hasn't been reached. So, by default, both methods quit reading input if they reach the end of a line before reading the allotted number of characters. Just as in the default case, get() leaves the termination character in the input queue, while getline() does not.

Listing 17.13 demonstrates how getline() and get() work. It also introduces the ignore() member function. It takes two arguments: a number specifying a maximum number of characters to read and a character that acts as a terminating character for input. For example, the function call

```
cin.ignore(255, '\n');
```

reads and discards the next 255 characters or up through the first newline character, whichever comes first. The prototype provides defaults of 1 and EOF for the two arguments, and the function return type is istream &:

```
istream & ignore(int = 1, int = EOF);
```

The function returns the invoking object. This lets you concatenate function calls, as in the following:

```
cin.ignore(255, '\n').ignore(8255, '\n');
```

Here the first ignore() method reads and discards one line, and the second call reads and discards the second line. Together the two functions read through two lines.

Now check out Listing 17.13.

LISTING 17.13   get_fun.cpp

```cpp
// get_fun.cpp -- using get() and getline()
#include <iostream>
using namespace std;
const int Limit = 255;

int main()
{
    char input[Limit];

    cout << "Enter a string for getline() processing:\n";
    cin.getline(input, Limit, '#');
    cout << "Here is your input:\n";
    cout << input << "\nDone with phase 1\n";

    char ch;
    cin.get(ch);
    cout << "The next input character is " << ch << "\n";

    if (ch != '\n')
        cin.ignore(Limit, '\n');     // discard rest of line

    cout << "Enter a string for get() processing:\n";
    cin.get(input, Limit, '#');
    cout << "Here is your input:\n";
    cout << input << "\nDone with phase 2\n";

    cin.get(ch);
    cout << "The next input character is " << ch << "\n";

    return 0;
}
```

Here is a sample program run:

```
Enter a string for getline() processing:
Please pass
me a #3 melon!
Here is your input:
Please pass
me a
Done with phase 1
The next input character is 3
Enter a string for get() processing:
I still
want my #3 melon!
Here is your input:
I still
want my
Done with phase 2
The next input character is #
```

Note that the `getline()` function discards the # termination character in the input, while the `get()` function does not.

Unexpected String Input

Some forms of input for `get(char *, int)` and `getline()` affect the stream state. As with the other input functions, encountering end-of-file sets `eofbit`, and anything that corrupts the stream, such as device failure, sets `badbit`. Two other special cases are no input and input that meets or exceeds the maximum number of characters specified by the function call. Let's look at those cases now.

If either method fails to extract any characters, the method places a null character into the input string and uses `setstate()` to set `failbit`. (Older C++ implementations don't set `failbit` if no characters are read.) When would a method fail to extract any characters? One possibility is if an input method immediately encounters end-of-file. For `get(char *, int)`, another possibility is if you enter an empty line:

```
char temp[80];
while (cin.get(temp,80))   // terminates on empty line
    ...
```

Interestingly, an empty line does not cause `getline()` to set `failbit`. That's because `getline()` still extracts the newline character, even if it doesn't store it. If you want a `getline()` loop to terminate on an empty line, you can write it this way:

```
char temp[80];
while (cin.getline(temp,80) && temp[0] != '\0') // terminates on empty line
```

Now suppose the number of characters in the input queue meets or exceeds the maximum specified by the input method. First, consider `getline()` and the following code:

```
char temp[30];
while (cin.getline(temp,30))
```

The `getline()` method will read consecutive characters from the input queue, placing them in successive elements of the `temp` array, until (in order of testing) EOF is encountered, the next character to be read is the newline character, or until 29 characters have been stored. If EOF is encountered, `eofbit` is set. If the next character to be read is a newline character, that character is read and discarded. And if 29 characters were read, `failbit` is set, unless the next character is a newline. Thus, an input line of 30 characters or more will terminate input.

Now consider the `get(char *, int)` method. It tests the number of characters first, end-of-file second, and for the next character being a newline third. It does not set the `failbit` flag if it reads the maximum number of characters. Nonetheless, you can tell if too many input characters caused the method to quit reading. You can use `peek()` (see the next section) to examine the next input character. If it's a newline, then `get()` must have read the entire line. If it's not a newline, then `get()` must have stopped before reaching the end. This technique doesn't necessarily work with `getline()` because `getline()` reads and discards the newline, so looking at the next character doesn't tell you anything. But if you use `get()`, you have the option of doing something if less than an entire line is read. The next section includes an example of this approach. Meanwhile, Table 17.7 summarizes some of the differences between older C++ input methods and the current standard.

TABLE 17.7 Changes in Input Behavior

Method	Older C++	Current C++
getline()	Doesn't set `failbit` if no characters are read.	Sets `failbit` if no characters are read (but newline counts as a character read).
	Doesn't set `failbit` if maximum number of characters are read.	Sets `failbit` if maximum number of characters read and more are still left in the line.
get(char *, int)	Doesn't set `failbit` if no characters are read.	Sets `failbit` if no characters are read.

Other `istream` Methods

Other `istream` methods include `read()`, `peek()`, `gcount()`, and `putback()`. The `read()` function reads a given number of bytes, storing them in the specified location. For example, the statement

```
char gross[144];
cin.read(gross, 144);
```

reads 144 characters from the standard input and places them in the **gross** array. Unlike **get-line()** and **get()**, **read()** does not append a null character to input, so it doesn't convert input to string form. The **read()** method is not primarily intended for keyboard input. Instead, it most often is used in conjunction with the **ostream write()** function for file input and output. The method's return type is **istream &**, so it can be concatenated as follows:

```
char gross[144];
char score[20];
cin.read(gross, 144).read(score, 20);
```

The **peek()** function returns the next character from input without extracting from the input stream. That is, it lets you peek at the next character. Suppose you wanted to read input up to the first newline or period, whichever comes first. You can use **peek()** to peek at the next character in the input stream in order to judge whether to continue or not:

```
char great_input[80];
char ch;
int i = 0;
while ((ch = cin.peek()) != '.' && ch != '\n')
    cin.get(great_input[i++]);
great_input [i] = '\0';
```

The call to **cin.peek()** peeks at the next input character and assigns its value to **ch**. Then the **while** loop test condition checks that **ch** is neither a period nor a newline. If this is the case, the loop reads the character into the array, and updates the array index. When the loop terminates, the period or newline character remains in the input stream, positioned to be the first character read by the next input operation. Then the code appends a null character to the array, making it a string.

The **gcount()** method returns the number of characters read by the last unformatted extraction method. That means characters read by a **get()**, **getline()**, **ignore()**, or **read()** method but not by the extraction operator (>>), which formats input to fit particular data types. For example, suppose you've just used **cin.get(myarray, 80)** to read a line into the **myarray** array and want to know how many characters were read. You could use the **strlen()** function to count the characters in the array, but it would be quicker to use **cin.gcount()** to report how many characters were just read from the input stream.

The **putback()** function inserts a character back in the input string. The inserted character then becomes the first character read by the next input statement. The **putback()** method takes one **char** argument, which is the character to be inserted, and it returns type **istream &**, which allows the call to be concatenated with other **istream** methods. Using **peek()** is like using **get()** to read a character, then using **putback()** to place the character back in the input stream. However, **putback()** gives you the option of putting back a character different from the one just read.

Listing 17.14 uses two approaches to read and echo input up to, but not including, a **#** character. The first approach reads through the **#** character and then uses **putback()** to insert the character back in the input. The second approach uses **peek()** to look ahead before reading input.

LISTING 17.14 peeker.cpp

```cpp
// peeker.cpp -- some istream methods
#include <iostream>
using namespace std;
#include <cstdlib>              // or stdlib.h

int main()
{

// read and echo input up to a # character
    char ch;

    while(cin.get(ch))          // terminates on EOF
    {
        if (ch != '#')
            cout << ch;
        else
        {
            cin.putback(ch);    // reinsert character
            break;
        }
    }

    if (!cin.eof())
    {
        cin.get(ch);
        cout << '\n' << ch << " is next input character.\n";
    }
    else
    {
        cout << "End of file reached.\n";
        exit(0);
    }

    while(cin.peek() != '#')    // look ahead
    {
        cin.get(ch);
        cout << ch;
    }
    if (!cin.eof())
    {
        cin.get(ch);
        cout << '\n' << ch << " is next input character.\n";
    }
    else
        cout << "End of file reached.\n";

    return 0;
}
```

Here is a sample run:

I used a #3 pencil when I should have used a #2.
I used a
is next input character.
3 pencil when I should have used a
is next input character.

Program Notes

Let's look more closely at some of the code. The first approach uses a `while` loop to read input. The expression (`cin.get(ch)`) returns `false` on reaching the end-of-file condition, so simulating end-of-file from the keyboard terminates the loop. If the `#` character shows up first, the program puts the character back in the input stream and uses a break statement to terminate the loop.

```
while(cin.get(ch))              // terminates on EOF
{
    if (ch != '#')
        cout << ch;
    else
    {
        cin.putback(ch);  // reinsert character
        break;
    }
}
```

The second approach is simpler in appearance:

```
while(cin.peek() != '#')     // look ahead
{
    cin.get(ch);
    cout << ch;
}
```

The program peeks at the next character. If it is not the `#` character, the program reads the next character, echoes it, and peeks at the next character. This continues until the terminating character shows up.

Now let's look, as promised, at an example (Listing 17.15) that uses `peek()` to determine whether or not an entire line has been read. If only part of a line fits in the input array, the program discards the rest of the line.

LISTING 17.15   truncate.cpp

```
// truncate.cpp -- use get() to truncate input line, if necessary
#include <iostream>
using namespace std;
const int SLEN = 10;
inline void eatline() { while (cin.get() != '\n') continue; }
int main()
{
```

LISTING 17.15   Continued

```
        char name[SLEN];
        char title[SLEN];
        cout << "Enter your name: ";
        cin.get(name,SLEN);
        if (cin.peek() != '\n')
            cout << "Sorry, we only have enough room for "
                    << name << endl;
        eatline();
        cout << "Dear " << name << ", enter your title: \n";
        cin.get(title,SLEN);
        if (cin.peek() != '\n')
            cout << "We were forced to truncate your title.\n";
        eatline();
        cout << " Name: " << name
                << "\nTitle: " << title << endl;

        return 0;
}
```

Here is a sample run:

```
Enter your name: Stella Starpride
Sorry, we only have enough room for Stella St
Dear Stella St, enter your title:
Astronomer Royal
We were forced to truncate your title.
 Name: Stella St
Title: Astronome
```

Note that the following code makes sense whether or not the first input statement read the entire line:

```
while (cin.get() != '\n') continue;
```

If `get()` reads the whole line, it still leaves the newline in place, and this code reads and discards the newline. If `get()` reads just part of the line, this code reads and discards the rest of the line. If you didn't dispose of the rest of line, the next input statement would begin reading at the beginning of the remaining input on the first input line. With this example, that would have resulted in the program reading the string **arpride** into the **title** array.

File Input and Output

Most computer programs work with files. Word processors create document files. Database programs create and search files of information. Compilers read source code files and generate executable files. A file itself is a bunch of bytes stored on some device, perhaps magnetic tape, perhaps an optical disk, floppy disk, or hard disk. Typically, the operating system manages files, keeping track of their locations, their sizes, when they were created, and so on. Unless you're programming on the operating system level, you normally don't have to worry about those things. What you do need is a way to connect a program to a file, a way to have a program read the contents of a file, and a way to have a program create and write to files. Redirection (as discussed earlier in this chapter) can provide some file support, but it is more limited than explicit file I/O from within a program. Also, redirection comes from the operating system, not from C++, so it isn't available on all systems. We'll look now at how C++ deals with explicit file I/O from within a program.

The C++ I/O class package handles file input and output much as it handles standard input and output. To write to a file, you create a stream object and use the `ostream` methods, such as the `<<` insertion operator or `write()`. To read a file, you create a `stream` object and use the `istream` methods, such as the `>>` extraction operator or `get()`. Files require more management than the standard input and output, however. For example, you have to associate a newly opened file with a stream. You can open a file in read-only mode, write-only mode, or read-and-write mode. If you write to a file, you might want to create a new file, replace an old file, or add to an old file. Or you might want to move back and forth through a file. To help handle these tasks, C++ defines several new classes in the `fstream` (formerly `fstream.h`) header file, including an `ifstream` class for file input and an `ofstream` class for file output. C++ also defines an `fstream` class for simultaneous file I/O. These classes are derived from the classes in the `iostream` header file, so objects of these new classes will be able to use the methods you've already learned.

Simple File I/O

Suppose you want a program to write to a file. You must do the following:

- Create an `ofstream` object to manage the output stream.

- Associate that object with a particular file.

- Use the object the same way you would use `cout`; the only difference is that output goes to the file instead of to the screen.

To accomplish this, begin by including the `fstream` header file. Including this file automatically includes the `iostream` file for most, but not all, implementations, so you may not have to include `iostream` explicitly. Then declare an `ofstream` object:

```
ofstream fout;     // create an ofstream object named fout
```

The object's name can be any valid C++ name, such as `fout`, `outFile`, `cgate`, or `didi`.

Next, you must associate this object with a particular file. You can do so by using the `open()` method. Suppose, for example, you want to open the `cookies` file for output. You would do the following:

```
fout.open("cookies");  // associate fout with cookies
```

You can combine these two steps (creating the object and associating a file) into a single statement by using a different constructor:

```
ofstream fout("cookies");  // create fout object and associate with cookies
```

When you've gotten this far, use `fout` (or whatever name you choose) in the same manner as `cout`. For example, if you want to put the words `Dull Data` into the file, you can do the following:

```
fout << "Dull Data";
```

Indeed, because `ostream` is a base class for the `ofstream` class, you can use all the `ostream` methods, including the various insertion operator definitions and the formatting methods and manipulators. The `ofstream` class uses buffered output, so the program allocates space for an output buffer when it creates an `ofstream` object like `fout`. If you create two `ofstream` objects, the program creates two buffers, one for each object. An `ofstream` object like `fout` collects output byte-by-byte from the program; then, when the buffer is filled, it transfers the buffer contents en masse to the destination file. Because disk drives are designed to transfer data in larger chunks, not byte-by-byte, the buffered approach greatly speeds up the transfer rate of data from a program to a file.

Opening a file for output this way creates a new file if there is no file of that name. If a file by that name exists prior to opening it for output, the act of opening it truncates it so that output starts with a clean file. Later you'll see how to open an existing file and retain its contents.

Caution

Opening a file for output in the default mode automatically truncates the file to zero size, in effect disposing of the prior contents.

The requirements for reading a file are much like those for writing to a file:

1. Create an `ifstream` object to manage the input stream.
2. Associate that object with a particular file.
3. Use the object the same way you would use `cin`.

The steps for doing so are similar to those for writing to a file. First, of course, include the `fstream` header file. Then declare an `ifstream` object, and associate it with the filename. You can do so in two statements or one:

```
// two statements
ifstream fin;              // create ifstream object called fin
fin.open("jellyjar.dat");  // open jellyjar.dat for reading
// one statement
ifstream fis("jamjar.dat"); // create fis and associate with jamjar.dat
```

You now can use `fin` or `fis` much like `cin`. For example, you can do the following:

```
char ch;
fin >> ch;              // read a character from the jellyjar.dat file
char buf[80];
fin >> buf;             // read a word from the file
fin.getline(buf, 80);   // read a line from the file
```

Input, like output, is buffered, so creating an `ifstream` object like `fin` creates an input buffer which the `fin` object manages. As with output, buffering moves data much faster than byte-by-byte transfer.

The connections with a file are closed automatically when the input and output stream objects expire—for example, when the program terminates. Also, you can close a connection with a file explicitly by using the `close()` method:

```
fout.close();      // close output connection to file
fin.close();       // close input connection to file
```

Closing such a connection does not eliminate the stream; it just disconnects it from the file. However, the stream management apparatus remains in place. For example, the `fin` object still exists along with the input buffer it manages. As you'll see later, you can reconnect the stream to the same file or to another file.

Meanwhile, let's look at a short example. The program in Listing 17.16 asks you for a filename. It creates a file having that name, writes some information to it, and closes the file. Closing the file flushes the buffer, guaranteeing that the file is updated. Then the program opens the same file for reading and displays its contents. Note that the program uses `fin` and `fout` in the same manner as `cin` and `cout`.

LISTING 17.16 file.cpp

```cpp
// file.cpp -- save to a file
#include <iostream> // not needed for many systems
#include <fstream>
using namespace std;

int main()
{
    char filename[20];

    cout << "Enter name for new file: ";
    cin >> filename;

// create output stream object for new file and call it fout
    ofstream fout(filename);

    fout << "For your eyes only!\n";      // write to file
    cout << "Enter your secret number: "; // write to screen
    float secret;
    cin >> secret;
    fout << "Your secret number is " << secret << "\n";
    fout.close();            // close file

// create input stream object for new file and call it fin
    ifstream fin(filename);
    cout << "Here are the contents of " << filename << ":\n";
    char ch;
    while (fin.get(ch))      // read character from file and
        cout << ch;          // write it to screen
```

LISTING 17.16   Continued

```
        cout << "Done\n";
        fin.close();

        return 0;
    }
```

Here is a sample run:

```
Enter name for new file: pythag
Enter your secret number: 3.14159
Here are the contents of pythag:
For your eyes only!
Your secret number is 3.14159
Done
```

If you check the directory containing your program, you should find a file named `pythag`, and any text editor should show the same contents that the program output displayed.

Opening Multiple Files

You might require that a program open more than one file. The strategy for opening multiple files depends upon how they will be used. If you need two files open simultaneously, you must create a separate stream for each file. For example, a program that collates two sorted files into a third file would create two `ifstream` objects for the two input files and an `ofstream` object for the output file. The number of files you can open simultaneously depends on the operating system, but it typically is on the order of 20.

However, you may plan to process a group of files sequentially. For example, you might want to count how many times a name appears in a set of ten files. Then you can open a single stream and associate it with each file in turn. This conserves computer resources more effectively than opening a separate stream for each file. To use this approach, declare a `stream` object without initializing it and then use the `open()` method to associate the stream with a file. For example, this is how you could handle reading two files in succession:

```
ifstream fin;             // create stream using default constructor
fin.open("fat.dat");      // associate stream with fat.dat file
...                       // do stuff
fin.close();              // terminate association with fat.dat
fin.clear();              // reset fin (may not be needed)
fin.open("rat.dat");      // associate stream with rat.dat file
...
fin.close();
```

We'll look at an example shortly, but first, let's examine a technique for feeding a list of files to a program in a manner that allows the program to use a loop to process them.

Command-Line Processing

File-processing programs often use command-line arguments to identify files. Command-line arguments are arguments that appear on the command line when you type a command. For example, to count the number of words in some files on a Unix or Linux system, you would type this command at the command-line prompt:

```
wc report1 report2 report3
```

Here `wc` is the program name, and `report1`, `report2`, and `report3` are filenames passed to the program as command-line arguments.

C++ has a mechanism for letting a program access command-line arguments. Use the following alternative function heading for `main()`:

```
int main(int argc, char *argv[])
```

The `argc` argument represents the number of arguments on the command line. The count includes the command name itself. The `argv` variable is a pointer to a pointer to a `char`. This sounds a bit abstract, but you can treat `argv` as if it were an array of pointers to the command-line arguments, with `argv[0]` being a pointer to the first character of a string holding the command name, `argv[1]` being a pointer to the first character of a string holding the first command-line argument, and so on. That is, `argv[0]` is the first string from the command line, and so on. For example, suppose you have the following command line:

```
wc report1 report2 report3
```

Then `argc` would be `4`, `argv[0]` would be `wc`, `argv[1]` would be `report1`, and so on. The following loop would print each command-line argument on a separate line:

```
for (int i = 1; i < argc; i++)
        cout << argv[i] << endl;
```

Starting with `i` = `1` just prints the command-line arguments; starting with `i` = `0` would also print the command name.

Command-line arguments, of course, go hand-in-hand with command-line operating systems like DOS, Unix, and Linux. Other setups may still allow you to use command-line arguments:

- Many DOS and Windows IDEs (integrated development environments) have an option for providing command-line arguments. Typically, you have to navigate through a series of menu choices leading to a box into which you can type the command-line arguments. The exact set of steps varies from vendor to vendor and from upgrade to upgrade, so check your documentation.

- DOS IDEs and many Windows IDEs can produce executable files that run under DOS or in a DOS window in the usual DOS command-line mode.

- Under Metrowerks CodeWarrior for the Macintosh, you can simulate command-line arguments by placing the following code in your program:

```
...
#include <console.h> // for emulating command-line arguments
int main(int argc, char * argv[])
{
    argc = ccommand(&argv); // yes, ccommand, not command
    ...
```

When you run the program, the ccommand() function places a dialog box onscreen with a box in which you can type the command-line arguments. It also lets you simulate redirection.

Listing 17.17 combines the command-line technique with file stream techniques to count characters in those files listed on the command line.

LISTING 17.17   count.cpp

```cpp
// count.cpp -- count characters in a list of files
#include <iostream>
using namespace std;
#include <fstream>
#include <cstdlib>            // or stdlib.h
// #include <console.h>       // for Macintosh
int main(int argc, char * argv[])
{
    // argc = ccommand(&argv);        // for Macintosh
    if (argc == 1)            // quit if no arguments
    {
        cerr << "Usage: " << argv[0] << " filename[s]\n";
        exit(1);
    }

    ifstream fin;             // open stream
    long count;
    long total = 0;
    char ch;

    for (int file = 1; file < argc; file++)
    {
        fin.open(argv[file]);  // connect stream to argv[file]
        count = 0;
        while (fin.get(ch))
            count++;
        cout << count << " characters in " << argv[file] << "\n";
        total += count;
        fin.clear();           // needed for some implementations
        fin.close();           // disconnect file
    }
    cout << total << " characters in all files\n";

    return 0;
}
```

Compatibility Note

Some implementations require using fin.clear() while others do not. It depends on whether associating a new file with the fstream object automatically resets the stream state or not. In does no harm to use fin.clear() even if it isn't needed.

On a DOS system, for example, you could compile Listing 17.17 to an executable file called `count.exe`. Then sample runs could look like this:

```
C>count
Usage: c:\count.exe filename[s]
C>count paris rome
3580 characters in paris
4886 characters in rome
8466 characters in all files
C>
```

Note that the program uses `cerr` for the error message. A minor point is that the message uses `argv[0]` instead of `count.exe`:

```
cerr << "Usage: " << argv[0] << " filename[s]\n";
```

This way, if you change the name of the executable file, the program will automatically use the new name.

Suppose you pass a bogus filename to the count program. Then the input statement `fin.get(ch)` will fail, terminating the `while` loop immediately, and the program will report 0 characters. But you can modify the program to test whether it succeeded in linking the stream to a file. That's one of the matters we'll take up next.

Stream Checking and `is_open()`

The C++ file stream classes inherit a stream-state member from the `ios_base` class. This member, as discussed earlier, stores information reflecting the stream status: all is well, end-of-file has been reached, I/O operation failed, and so on. If all is well, the stream state is zero (no news is good news). The various other states are recorded by setting particular bits to 1. The file stream classes also inherit the `ios_base` methods that report about the stream state and that were summarized earlier in Table 17.5. You can monitor conditions with these stream-state methods. For example, you can use the `good()` method to see that all the stream state bits are clear. However, newer C++ implementations have a better way to check if a file has been opened—the `is_open()` method. You can modify the program in Listing 17.17 so that it reports bogus filenames and then skips to the next file by adding a call to `fin.is_open()` to the `for` loop as follows:

```
for (int file = 1; file < argc; file++)
{
    fin.open(argv[file]);

// Add this
    if (!fin.is_open())
    {
        cerr << "Couldn't open file " << argv[file] << "\n";
        fin.clear();    // reset failbit
        continue;
    }
// End of addition
    count = 0;
```

```
    while (fin.get(ch))
        count++;
    cout << count << " characters in " << argv[file] << "\n";
    total += count;
    fin.clear();
    fin.close();    // disconnect file
}
```

The `fin.is_open()` call returns `false` if the `fin.open()` call fails. In that case, the program warns you of its problem, and the `continue` statement causes the program to skip the rest of the `for` loop cycle and start with the next cycle.

Caution

In the past, the usual tests for successful opening of a file were the following:

```
if(!fin.good()) ... // failed to open
if (!fin) ...       // failed to open
```

The `fin` object, when used in a test condition, is converted to `false` if `fin.good()` is `false` and to `true` otherwise, so the two forms are equivalent. However, these tests fail to detect one circumstance, which is attempting to open a file using an inappropriate file mode (see the File Modes section). The `is_open()` method catches this form of error along with those caught by the `good()` method. However, older implementations do not have `is_open()`.

File Modes

The file mode describes how a file is to be used: read it, write to it, append it, and so on. When you associate a stream with a file, either by initializing a file stream object with a filename or by using the `open()` method, you can provide a second argument specifying the file mode:

```
ifstream fin("banjo", mode1);   // constructor with mode argument
ofstream fout();
fout.open("harp", mode2);       // open() with mode arguments
```

The `ios_base` class defines an `openmode` type to represent the mode; like the `fmtflags` and `iostate` types, it is a `bitmask` type. (In the old days, it was type `int`.) You can choose from several constants defined in the `ios_base` class to specify the mode. Table 17.8 lists the constants and their meanings. C++ file I/O has undergone several changes to make it compatible with ANSI C file I/O.

TABLE 17.8   File Mode Constants

Constant	Meaning
ios_base::in	Open file for reading.
ios_base::out	Open file for writing.

TABLE 17.8   Continued

Constant	Meaning
`ios_base::ate`	Seek to end-of-file upon opening file.
`ios_base::app`	Append to end-of-file.
`ios_base::trunc`	Truncate file if it exists.
`ios_base::binary`	Binary file.

If the `ifstream` and `ofstream` constructors and the `open()` methods each take two arguments, how have we gotten by using just one in the previous examples? As you probably have guessed, the prototypes for these class member functions provide default values for the second argument (the file mode argument). For example, the `ifstream open()` method and constructor use `ios_base::in` (open for reading) as the default value for the mode argument, while the `ofstream open()` method and constructor use `ios_base::out | ios_base::trunc` (open for writing and truncate the file) as the default. The bitwise OR operator (`|`) is used to combine two bit-values into a single value that can be used to set both bits. The `fstream` class doesn't provide a mode default, so you have to provide a mode explicitly when creating an object of that class.

Note that the `ios_base::trunc` flag means an existing file is truncated when opened to receive program output; that is, its previous contents are discarded. While this behavior commendably minimizes the danger of running out of disk space, you probably can imagine situations in which you don't want to wipe out a file when you open it. C++, of course, provides other choices. If, for example, you want to preserve the file contents and add (append) new material to the end of the file, you can use the `ios_base::app` mode:

```
ofstream fout("bagels", ios_base::out | ios_base::app);
```

Again, the code uses the | operator to combine modes. So `ios_base::out | ios_base::app` means to invoke both the **out** mode and the **app** mode (see Figure 17.6).

Expect to find some differences among older implementations. For example, some allow you to omit the `ios_base::out` in the previous example, and some don't. If you aren't using the default mode, the safest approach is to provide all the mode elements explicitly. Some compilers don't support all the choices in Table 17.7, and some may offer choices beyond those in the table. One consequence of these differences is that you may have to make some alterations in the following examples to do them on your system. The good news is that the development of the C++ standard is providing greater uniformity.

Standard C++ defines parts of file I/O in terms of ANSI C standard I/O equivalents. A C++ statement like

```
ifstream fin(filename, c++mode);
```

is implemented as if it uses the C `fopen()` function:

```
fopen(filename, cmode);
```

FIGURE 17.6

Some file-opening modes.

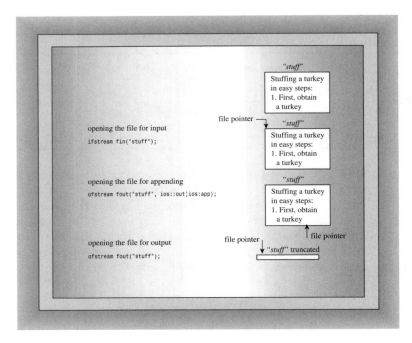

Here *c++mode* is a type `openmode` value, such as `ios_base::in`, and *cmode* is the corresponding C mode string, such as `"r"`. Table 17.9 shows the correspondence between C++ modes and C modes. Note that `ios_base::out` by itself causes truncation but that it doesn't cause truncation when combined with `ios_base::in`. Unlisted combinations, such as `ios_base::in` [vn] `ios_base::trunc`, prevent the file from being opened. The `is_open()` method detects this failure.

TABLE 17.9 C++ and C File-Opening Modes

C++ mode	C mode	Meaning
`ios_base::in`	`"r"`	Open for reading.
`ios_base::out`	`"w"`	(Same as `ios_base::out` | `ios_base::trunc`).
`ios_base::out | ios_base::trunc`	`"w"`	Open for writing, truncating file if it already exists.
`ios_base::out | ios_base::app`	`"a"`	Open for writing, append only.
`ios_base::in | ios_base::out`	`"r+"`	Open for reading and writing, with writing permitted anywhere in the file.

TABLE 17.9   Continued

C++ mode	C mode	Meaning
ios_base::in | ios_base ::out | ios_base::trunc	"w+"	Open for reading and writing, first truncating file if it already exists.
c++mode | ios_base::binary	"cmodeb"	Open in c++mode or corresponding cmode and in binary mode; for example, ios_base::in | ios_base::binary becomes "rb".
c++mode | ios_base::ate	"cmode"	Open in indicated mode and go to end of file. C uses a separate function call instead of a mode code. For example, ios_base::in | ios_base::ate translates to the mode and the C function call fseek(file, 0, SEEK_END).

Note that both `ios_base::ate` and `ios_base::app` place you (or, more precisely, a file pointer) at the end of the file just opened. The difference between the two is that the `ios_base::app` mode allows you to add data to the end of the file only, while the `ios_base::ate` mode merely positions the pointer at the end of the file.

Clearly, there are many possible combinations of modes. We'll look at a few representative ones.

Appending to a File

Let's begin with a program that appends data to the end of a file. The program will maintain a file containing a guest list. When the program begins, it will display the current contents of the file, if it exists. It can use the `is_open()` method after attempting to open the file to check if the file exists. Next, the program will open the file for output using the `ios_base::app` mode. Then it will solicit input from the keyboard to add to the file. Finally, the program will display the revised file contents. Listing 17.18 illustrates how to accomplish these goals. Note how the program uses the `is_open()` method to test if the file has been opened successfully.

Compatibility Note

File I/O was perhaps the least standardized aspect of C++ in its earlier days, and many older compilers don't quite conform to the current standard. Some, for example, used modes such as `nocreate` that are not part of the current standard. Also, only some compilers require the `fin.clear()` call before opening the same file a second time for reading.

LISTING 17.18 append.cpp

```cpp
// append.cpp -- append information to a file
#include <iostream>
using namespace std;
#include <fstream>
#include <cstdlib>        // (or stdlib.h) for exit()

const char * file = "guests.dat";
const int Len = 40;
int main()
{
    char ch;

// show initial contents
    ifstream fin;
    fin.open(file);

    if (fin.is_open())
    {
        cout << "Here are the current contents of the "
            << file << " file:\n";
        while (fin.get(ch))
            cout << ch;
    }
    fin.close();

// add new names
    ofstream fout(file, ios::out | ios::app);
    if (!fout.is_open())
    {
        cerr << "Can't open " << file << " file for output.\n";
        exit(1);
    }

    cout << "Enter guest names (enter a blank line to quit):\n";
    char name[Len];
    cin.get(name, Len);
    while (name[0] != '\0')
    {
        while (cin.get() != '\n')
            continue;    // get rid of \n and long lines
        fout << name << "\n";
        cin.get(name, Len);
    }
    fout.close();

// show revised file
    fin.clear();    // not necessary for some compilers
    fin.open(file);
    if (fin.is_open())
    {
        cout << "Here are the new contents of the "
            << file << " file:\n";
```

LISTING 17.18   Continued

```
            while (fin.get(ch))
                cout << ch;
        }
        fin.close();
        cout << "Done.\n";
        return 0;
    }
```

Here's a sample first run. At this point the `guests.dat` file hasn't been created, so the program doesn't preview the file.

```
Enter guest names (enter a blank line to quit):
Sylvester Ballone
Phil Kates
Bill Ghan

Here are the new contents of the guests.dat file:
Sylvester Ballone
Phil Kates
Bill Ghan
Done.
```

Next time the program is run, however, the `guests.dat` file does exist, so the program does preview the file. Also, note that the new data are appended to the old file contents rather than replacing them.

```
Here are the current contents of the guests.dat file:
Sylvester Ballone
Phil Kates
Bill Ghan
Enter guest names (enter a blank line to quit):
Greta Greppo
LaDonna Mobile
Fannie Mae

Here are the new contents of the guests.dat file:
Sylvester Ballone
Phil Kates
Bill Ghan
Greta Greppo
LaDonna Mobile
Fannie Mae
Done.
```

You should be able to read the contents of `guest.dat` with any text editor, including the editor you use to write your source code.

Binary Files

When you store data in a file, you can store the data in text form or in binary format. Text form means you store everything as text, even numbers. For example, storing the value -2.324216e+07 in text form means storing the 13 characters used to write this number. That requires converting the computer's internal representation of a floating-point number to character form, and that's exactly what the << insertion operator does. Binary format, however, means storing the computer's internal representation of a value. That is, instead of storing characters, store the (typically) 64-bit **double** representation of the value. For a character, the binary representation is the same as the text representation—the binary representation of the character's ASCII code (or equivalent). For numbers, however, the binary representation is much different from the text representation (see Figure 17.7).

FIGURE 17.7

Binary and text representation of a floating-point number.

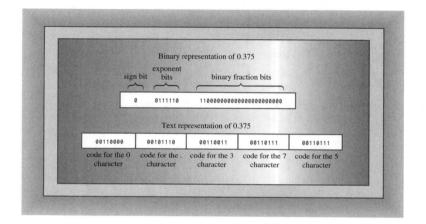

Each format has its advantages. The text format is easy to read. You can use an ordinary editor or word processor to read and edit a text file. You easily can transfer a text file from one computer system to another. The binary format is more accurate for numbers, because it stores the exact internal representation of a value. There are no conversion errors or round-off errors. Saving data in binary format can be faster because there is no conversion and because you may be able to save data in larger chunks. And the binary format usually takes less space, depending upon the nature of the data. Transferring to another system can be a problem, however, if the new system uses a different internal representation for values. Even different compilers on the same system may use different internal representations. In these cases, you (or someone) may have to write a program to translate one data format to another.

Let's look at a more concrete example. Consider the following structure definition and declaration:

```
struct planet
{
    char name[20];        // name of planet
    double population;    // its population
    double g;             // its acceleration of gravity
};
planet pl;
```

To save the contents of the structure pl in text form, you can do this:

```
ofstream fout("planets.dat", ios_base::app);
fout << pl.name << " " << pl.population << " " << pl.g << "\n";
```

Note that you have to provide each structure member explicitly by using the membership operator, and you have to separate adjacent data for legibility. If the structure contained, say, 30 members, this could get tedious.

To save the same information in binary format, you can do this:

```
ofstream fout("planets.dat", ios_base::app | ios_base::binary);
fout.write( (char *) &pl, sizeof pl);
```

This code saves the entire structure as a single unit, using the computer's internal representation of data. You won't be able to read the file as text, but the information will be stored more compactly and precisely than as text. And it certainly is easier to type the code. This approach made two changes:

- It used a binary file mode.

- It used the write() member function.

Let's examine these changes more closely.

Some systems, such as DOS, support two file formats: text and binary. If you want to save data in binary form, you'd best use the binary file format. In C++ you do so by using the ios_base::binary constant in the file mode. If you want to know why you should do this on a DOS system, check the discussion in the following note on Binary Files and Text Files.

Binary Files and Text Files

Using a binary file mode causes a program to transfer data from memory to a file, or vice versa, without any hidden translation taking place. Such is not necessarily the case for the default text mode. For example, consider DOS text files. They represent a newline with a two-character combination: carriage return, linefeed. Macintosh text files represent a newline with a carriage return. Unix and Linux files represent a newline with a linefeed. C++, which grew up on Unix, also represents a newline with a linefeed. For portability, a DOS C++ program automatically translates the C++ newline to a carriage return, linefeed when writing to a text mode file; and a Macintosh C++ program translates the newline to a carriage return when writing to a file. When reading a text file, these programs convert the local newline back to the C++ form. The text format can cause problems with binary data, for a byte in the middle of a **double** value could have the same bit pattern as the ASCII code for the newline character. Also there are differences in how end-of-file is detected. So you should use the binary file mode when saving data in binary format. (Unix systems have just one file mode, so on them the binary mode is the same as the text mode.)

To save data in binary form instead of text form, you can use the write() member function. This method, recall, copies a specified number of bytes from memory to a file. We used it earlier to copy text, but it will copy any type data byte-by-byte with no conversion. For example, if you pass it the address of a long variable and tell it to copy 4 bytes, it will copy the 4 bytes constituting the long value verbatim to a file and not convert it to text. The only awkwardness is that you have to type cast the address to type pointer-to-`char`. You can use the same approach to copy an entire `planet` structure. To get the number of bytes, use the `sizeof` operator:

```
fout.write( (char *) &pl, sizeof pl);
```

This statement goes to the address of the `pl` structure and copies the 36 bytes (the value of `sizeof pl` expression) beginning at this address to the file connected to `fout`.

To recover the information from a file, use the corresponding `read()` method with an `ifstream` object:

```
ifstream fin("planets.dat", ios_base::binary);
fin.read((char *) &pl, sizeof pl);
```

This copies `sizeof pl` bytes from the file to the `pl` structure. This same approach can be used with classes that don't use virtual functions. In that case, just the data members are saved, not the methods. If the class does have virtual methods, then a hidden pointer to a table of pointers to virtual functions also is copied. Because the next time you run the program it might locate the virtual function table at a different location, copying old pointer information into objects from a file can create havoc. (Also, see the note in Programming Exercise 6.)

Tip

The `read()` and `write()` member functions complement each other. Use `read()` to recover data that has been written to a file with `write()`.

Listing 17.19 uses these methods to create and read a binary file. In form, the program is similar to Listing 17.18, but it uses `write()` and `read()` instead of the insertion operator and the `get()` method. It also uses manipulators to format the screen output.

Compatibility Note

Although the binary file concept is part of ANSI C, some C and C++ implementations do not provide support for the binary file mode. The reason for this oversight is that some systems only have one file type in the first place, so you can use binary operations such as `read()` and `write()` with the standard file format. Therefore, if your implementation rejects `ios_base::binary` as a valid constant, just omit it from your program. If your implementation doesn't support the `fixed` and `right` manipulators, you can use `cout.setf(ios_base::fixed, ios_base::floatfield)` and `cout.setf(ios_base::right, ios_base::adjustfield)`. Also, you may have to substitute `ios` for `ios_base`. Other compilers, particularly older ones, may have other idiosyncrasies.

LISTING 17.19 binary.cpp

```
// binary.cpp -- binary file I/O
#include <iostream> // not required by most systems
using namespace std;
#include <fstream>
```

LISTING 17.19 Continued

```cpp
#include <iomanip>
#include <cstdlib>  // (or stdlib.h) for exit()

inline void eatline() { while (cin.get() != '\n') continue; }
struct planet
{
    char name[20];      // name of planet
    double population;  // its population
    double g;           // its acceleration of gravity
};

const char * file = "planets.dat";

int main()
{
    planet pl;
    cout << fixed << right;

// show initial contents
    ifstream fin;
    fin.open(file, ios::in |ios::binary);   // binary file
    //NOTE: some systems don't accept the ios::binary mode
    if (fin.is_open())
    {
    cout << "Here are the current contents of the "
        << file << " file:\n";
    while (fin.read((char *) &pl, sizeof pl))
        {
        cout << setw(20) << pl.name << ": "
                << setprecision(0) << setw(12) << pl.population
                << setprecision(2) << setw(6) << pl.g << "\n";
        }
    }
    fin.close();

// add new data
    ofstream fout(file, ios::out | ios::app | ios::binary);
    //NOTE: some systems don't accept the ios::binary mode
    if (!fout.is_open())
    {
        cerr << "Can't open " << file << " file for output:\n";
        exit(1);
    }

    cout << "Enter planet name (enter a blank line to quit):\n";
    cin.get(pl.name, 20);
    while (pl.name[0] != '\0')
    {
        eatline();
        cout << "Enter planetary population: ";
        cin >> pl.population;
        cout << "Enter planet's acceleration of gravity: ";
```

LISTING 17.19   Continued

```
            cin >> pl.g;
            eatline();
            fout.write((char *) &pl, sizeof pl);
            cout << "Enter planet name (enter a blank line "
                    "to quit):\n";
            cin.get(pl.name, 20);
        }
        fout.close();

// show revised file
        fin.clear();     // not required for some implementations, but won't hurt
        fin.open(file, ios::in | ios::binary);
        if (fin.is_open())
        {
        cout << "Here are the new contents of the "
            << file << " file:\n";
        while (fin.read((char *) &pl, sizeof pl))
            {
            cout << setw(20) << pl.name << ": "
                    << setprecision(0) << setw(12) << pl.population
                    << setprecision(2) << setw(6) << pl.g << "\n";
            }
        }
        fin.close();
        cout << "Done.\n";
        return 0;
}
```

Here is a sample initial run:

```
Enter planet name (enter a blank line to quit):
Earth
Enter planetary population: 5962000000
Enter planet's acceleration of gravity: 9.81
Enter planet name (enter a blank line to quit):

Here are the new contents of the planets.dat file:
            Earth:   5932000000  9.81
Done.
```

And here is a sample follow-up run:

```
Here are the current contents of the planets.dat file:
            Earth:   5932000000  9.81
Enter planet name (enter a blank line to quit):
Bill's Planet
Enter planetary population: 23020020
Enter planet's acceleration of gravity: 8.82
Enter planet name (enter a blank line to quit):

Here are the new contents of the planets.dat file:
            Earth:   5932000000    9.81
    Bill's Planet:   23020020      8.82
Done.
```

You've already seen the major features of the program, but let's reexamine an old point. The program uses this code (in the form of the inline `eatline()` function) after reading the planet's g value:

```
while (cin.get() != '\n') continue;
```

This reads and discards input up through the newline character. Consider the next input statement in the loop:

```
cin.get(pl.name, 20);
```

If the newline had been left in place, this statement would read the newline as an empty line, terminating the loop.

Random Access

For our last example, let's look at random access. This means moving directly to any location in the file instead of moving through it sequentially. The random access approach is often used with database files. A program will maintain a separate index file giving the location of data in the main data file. Then it can jump directly to that location, read the data there, and perhaps modify it. This approach is done most simply if the file consists of a collection of equal-sized records. Each record represents a related collection of data. For example, in the preceding example, each file record would represent all the data about a particular planet. A file record corresponds rather naturally to a program structure or class.

We'll base the example on the binary file program in Listing 17.19, taking advantage of the fact that the `planet` structure provides a pattern for a file record. To add to the creative tension of programming, the example will open the file in a read-and-write mode so that it can both read and modify a record. You can do this by creating an `fstream` object. The `fstream` class derives from the `iostream` class, which, in turn, is based on both `istream` and `ostream` classes, so it inherits the methods of both. It also inherits two buffers, one for input and one for output, and synchronizes the handling of the two buffers. That is, as the program reads the file or writes to it, it moves both an input pointer in the input buffer and an output pointer in the output buffer in tandem.

The example will do the following:

1. Display the current contents of the `planets.dat` file.

2. Ask which record you want to modify.

3. Modify that record.

4. Show the revised file.

A more ambitious program would use a menu and a loop to let you select from this list of actions indefinitely, but this version will perform each action just once. This simplified approach allows you to examine several aspects of read-write files without getting bogged down in matters of program design.

Caution

This program assumes that the `planets.dat` file already exists and was created by the `binary.cpp` program.

The first question to answer is what file mode to use. In order to read the file, you need the `ios_base::in` mode. For binary I/O, you need the `ios_base::binary` mode. (Again, on some non-standard systems you can omit, indeed, you may have to omit, this mode.) In order to write to the file, you need the `ios_base::out` or the `ios_base::app` mode. However, the append mode allows a program to add data to the end of the file only. The rest of the file is read-only; that is, you can read the original data, but not modify it—so you have to use `ios_base::out`. As Table 17.9 indicates, using the in and out modes simultaneously provided a read/write mode, so you just have to add the binary element. As mentioned earlier, you use the | operator to combine modes. Thus, you need the following statement to set up business:

```
finout.open(file,ios_base::in | ios_base::out | ios_base::binary);
```

Next, you need a way to move through a file. The `fstream` class inherits two methods for this: `seekg()` moves the input pointer to a given file location, and `seekp()` moves the output pointer to a given file location. (Actually, because the `fstream` class uses buffers for intermediate storage of data, the pointers point to locations in the buffers, not in the actual file.) You also can use `seekg()` with an `ifstream` object and `seekp()` with an `ostream` object. Here are the `seekg()` prototypes:

```
basic_istream<charT,traits>& seekg(off_type, ios_base::seekdir);
basic_istream<charT,traits>& seekg(pos_type);
```

As you can see, they are templates. This chapter will use a template specialization for the `char` type. For the `char` specialization, the two prototypes are equivalent to the following:

```
istream & seekg(streamoff, ios_base::seekdir);
istream & seekg(streampos);
```

The first prototype represents locating a file position measured, in bytes, as an offset from a file location specified by the second argument. The second prototype represents locating a file position measured in bytes from the beginning of a file.

Type Escalation

When C++ was young, life was simpler for the `seekg()` methods. The `streamoff` and `streampos` types were `typedefs` for some standard integer type, such as `long`. However, the quest for creating a portable standard had to deal with the realization that an integer argument might not provide enough information for some file systems, so `streamoff` and `streampos` were allowed to be structure or class types so long as they allowed some basic operations, such as using an integer value as an initialization value. Next, the old `istream` class was replaced with the `basic_istream` template, and `streampos` and `streamoff` were replaced with template-based types `pos_type` and `off_type`. However, `streampos` and `streamoff` continue to exist as `char` specializations of `pos_type` and `off_type`. Similarly, you can use `wstreampos` and `wstreamoff` types if you use `seekg()` with a `wistream` object.

Let's take a look at the arguments to the first prototype of `seekg()`. Values of the `streamoff` type are used to measure offsets, in bytes, from a particular location in a file. The `streamoff` argument represents the file position in bytes measured as an offset from one of three locations. (The type may be defined as an integral type or as a class.) The `seek_dir` argument is another integer type defined, along with three possible values, in the `ios_base` class. The constant `ios_base::beg` means measure the offset from the beginning of the file. The constant `ios_base::cur` means measure the offset from the current position. The constant `ios_base::end` means measure the offset from the end of the file. Here are some sample calls, assuming `fin` is an `ifstream` object:

```
fin.seekg(30, ios_base::beg);      // 30 bytes beyond the beginning
fin.seekg(-1, ios_base::cur);      // back up one byte
fin.seekg(0, ios_base::end);       // go to the end of the file
```

Now let's look at the second prototype. Values of the `streampos` type locate a position in a file. It can be a class, but, if so, the class includes a constructor with a `streamoff` argument and a constructor with an integer argument, providing a path to convert both types to `streampos` values. A `streampos` value represents an absolute location in a file measured from the beginning of the file. You can treat a `streampos` position as if it measures a file location in bytes from the beginning of a file, with the first byte being byte 0. So the statement

```
fin.seekg(112);
```

locates the file pointer at byte 112, which would be the 113th byte in the file. If you want to check the current position of a file pointer, you can use the `tellg()` method for input streams and the `tellp()` methods for output streams. Each returns a `streampos` value representing the current position, in bytes, measured from the beginning of the file. When you create an `fstream` object, the input and output pointers move in tandem, so `tellg()` and `tellp()` return the same value. But if you use an `istream` object to manage the input stream and an `ostream` object to manage the output stream to the same file, the input and output pointers move independently of one another, and `tellg()` and `tellp()` can return different values.

You can then use `seekg()` to go to the file beginning. Here is a section of code that opens the file, goes to the beginning, and displays the file contents:

```
fstream finout;     // read and write streams
finout.open(file,ios::in | ios::out |ios::binary);
//NOTE: Some UNIX systems require omitting | ios::binary
int ct = 0;
if (finout.is_open())
{
    finout.seekg(0);    // go to beginning
    cout << "Here are the current contents of the "
         << file << " file:\n";
    while (finout.read((char *) &pl, sizeof pl))
    {
        cout << ct++ << ": " << setw(20) << pl.name << ": "
        << setprecision(0) << setw(12) << pl.population
        << setprecision(2) << setw(6) << pl.g << "\n";
    }
    if (finout.eof())
        finout.clear(); // clear eof flag
```

```
        else
        {
            cerr << "Error in reading " << file << ".\n";
            exit(1);
        }
    }
    else
    {
        cerr << file << " could not be opened -- bye.\n";
        exit(2);
    }
```

This is similar to the start of Listing 17.19, but there are some changes and additions. First, as just described, the program uses an `fstream` object with a read-write mode, and it uses `seekg()` to position the file pointer at the start of the file. (This isn't really needed for this example, but it shows how `seekg()` is used.) Next, the program makes the minor change of numbering the records as they are displayed. Then it makes the following important addition:

```
if (finout.eof())
    finout.clear(); // clear eof flag
else
{
    cerr << "Error in reading " << file << ".\n";
    exit(1);
}
```

The problem is that once the program reads and displays the entire file, it sets the `eofbit` element. This convinces the program that it's finished with the file and disables any further reading of or writing to the file. Using the `clear()` method resets the stream state, turning off `eofbit`. Now the program can once again access the file. The `else` part handles the possibility that the program quit reading the file for some reason other than reaching the end-of-file, such as a hardware failure.

The next step is to identify the record to be changed and then change it. To do this, the program asks the user to enter a record number. Multiplying the number by the number of bytes in a record yields the byte number for the beginning of the record. If `record` is the record number, the desired byte number is `record * sizeof pl`:

```
cout << "Enter the record number you wish to change: ";
long rec;
cin >> rec;
eatline();              // get rid of newline
if (rec < 0 || rec >= ct)
{
    cerr << "Invalid record number -- bye\n";
    exit(3);
}
streampos place = rec * sizeof pl;  // convert to streampos type
finout.seekg(place);    // random access
```

The variable `ct` represents the number of records; the program exits if you try to go beyond the limits of the file.

Next, the program displays the current record:

```
finout.read((char *) &pl, sizeof pl);
cout << "Your selection:\n";
cout << rec << ": " << setw(20) << pl.name << ": "
<< setprecision(0) << setw(12) << pl.population
<< setprecision(2) << setw(6) << pl.g << "\n";
if (finout.eof())
    finout.clear();      // clear eof flag
```

After displaying the record, the program lets you change the record:

```
cout << "Enter planet name: ";
cin.get(pl.name, 20);
eatline();
cout << "Enter planetary population: ";
cin >> pl.population;
cout << "Enter planet's acceleration of gravity: ";
cin >> pl.g;
finout.seekp(place);     // go back
finout.write((char *) &pl, sizeof pl) << flush;

if (finout.fail())
{
    cerr << "Error on attempted write\n";
    exit(5);
}
```

The program flushes the output to guarantee that the file is updated before proceeding to the next stage.

Finally, to display the revised file, the program uses **seekg()** to reset the file pointer to the beginning. Listing 17.20 shows the complete program. Don't forget that it assumes that a **planets.dat** file created using the **binary.cpp** program is available.

Compatibility Note

The older the implementation, the more likely it is to run afoul of the standard. Some systems don't recognize the binary flag, the **fixed** and **right** manipulators, and **ios_base**. Symantec C++ appends the new input instead of replacing the indicated record. Also, Symantec C++ requires replacing (twice)

```
while (fin.read((char *) &pl, sizeof pl))
```

with the following:

```
while (fin.read((char *) &pl, sizeof pl) && !fin.eof())
```

LISTING 17.20   random.cpp

```
// random.cpp -- random access to a binary file
#include <iostream>      // not required by most systems
using namespace std;
#include <fstream>
```

LISTING 17.20 Continued

```cpp
#include <iomanip>
#include <cstdlib>        // (or stdlib.h) for exit()

struct planet
{
    char name[20];       // name of planet
    double population;   // its population
    double g;            // its acceleration of gravity
};

const char * file = "planets.dat";  // ASSUMED TO EXIST (binary.cpp example)
inline void eatline() { while (cin.get() != '\n') continue; }

int main()
{
    planet pl;
    cout << fixed;

// show initial contents
    fstream finout;      // read and write streams
    finout.open(file,ios::in | ios::out |ios::binary);
    //NOTE: Some UNIX systems require omitting | ios::binary
    int ct = 0;
    if (finout.is_open())
    {
        finout.seekg(0);     // go to beginning
        cout << "Here are the current contents of the "
             << file << " file:\n";
        while (finout.read((char *) &pl, sizeof pl))
        {
            cout << ct++ << ": " << setw(20) << pl.name << ": "
                 << setprecision(0) << setw(12) << pl.population
                 << setprecision(2) << setw(6) << pl.g << "\n";
        }
        if (finout.eof())
            finout.clear(); // clear eof flag
        else
        {
            cerr << "Error in reading " << file << ".\n";
            exit(1);
        }
    }
    else
    {
        cerr << file << " could not be opened -- bye.\n";
        exit(2);
    }

// change a record
    cout << "Enter the record number you wish to change: ";
    long rec;
    cin >> rec;
```

LISTING 17.20   Continued

```
    eatline();                     // get rid of newline
    if (rec < 0 || rec >= ct)
    {
        cerr << "Invalid record number -- bye\n";
        exit(3);
    }
    streampos place = rec * sizeof pl;  // convert to streampos type
    finout.seekg(place);    // random access
    if (finout.fail())
    {
        cerr << "Error on attempted seek\n";
        exit(4);
    }

    finout.read((char *) &pl, sizeof pl);
    cout << "Your selection:\n";
    cout << rec << ": " << setw(20) << pl.name << ": "
    << setprecision(0) << setw(12) << pl.population
    << setprecision(2) << setw(6) << pl.g << "\n";
    if (finout.eof())
        finout.clear();      // clear eof flag

    cout << "Enter planet name: ";
    cin.get(pl.name, 20);
    eatline();
    cout << "Enter planetary population: ";
    cin >> pl.population;
    cout << "Enter planet's acceleration of gravity: ";
    cin >> pl.g;
    finout.seekp(place);     // go back
    finout.write((char *) &pl, sizeof pl) << flush;
    if (finout.fail())
    {
        cerr << "Error on attempted write\n";
        exit(5);
    }

// show revised file
    ct = 0;
    finout.seekg(0);                 // go to beginning of file
    cout << "Here are the new contents of the " << file
        << " file:\n";
    while (finout.read((char *) &pl, sizeof pl))
    {
        cout << ct++ << ": " << setw(20) << pl.name << ": "
            << setprecision(0) << setw(12) << pl.population
            << setprecision(2) << setw(6) << pl.g << "\n";
    }
    finout.close();
    cout << "Done.\n";
    return 0;
}
```

Here's a sample run based on a `planets.dat` file that has had a few more entries added since you last saw it:

```
Here are the current contents of the planets.dat File:
0:      Earth:          5333000000      9.81
1:      Bill's Planet:  23020020        8.82
2:      Trantor:        58000000000     15.03
3:      Trellan:        4256000         9.62
4:      Freestone:      3845120000      8.68
5:      Taanagoot:      350000002       10.23
6:      Marin:          232000          9.79
Enter the record number you wish to change: 2
Your selection:
2:      Trantor:        58000000000     15.03
Enter planet name: Trantor
Enter planetary population: 59500000000
Enter planet's acceleration of gravity:  10.53
Here are the new contents of the planets.dat file:
0:      Earth:          5333000000      9.81
1:      Bill's Planet:  23020020        8.82
2:      Trantor:        59500000000     10.53
3:      Trellan:        4256000         9.62
4:      Freestone:      3845120000      8.68
5:      Taanagoot:      350000002       10.23
6:      Marin:          232000          9.79
Done.
```

Using the techniques in this program, you can extend it to allow you to add new material and delete records. If you were to expand the program, it would be a good idea to reorganize it by using classes and functions. For example, you could convert the `planet` structure to a class definition; then overload the `<<` insertion operator so that `cout << pl` displays the class data members formatted as in the example.

Real World Note: Working with Temporary Files

Developing applications oftentimes requires the use of temporary files whose lifetimes are transient and must be controlled by the program. Have you ever thought about how to go about this in C++? Well it's really quite easy to create a temporary file, copy the contents of another file, and delete the file. First of all, you will need to come up with a naming scheme for your temporary file(s), but wait, how can you ensure that each file is assigned a unique name. Well, the `tmpnam()` standard function declared in `cstdio` has got you covered.

```
char* tmpnam( char* pszName );
```

The `tmpnam()` function creates a temporary name and places it in the C-style string pointed to by `pszName`. The constants `L_tmpnam` and `TMP_MAX`, both defined in `cstdio`, limit the number characters in the filename and the maximum number of times `tmpnam()` can be called without generating a duplicate filename in the current directory. The following sample generates ten temporary names.

```
#include <cstdio>
#include <iostream>
```

```
using namespace std;

int main()
{
  cout << "This system can generate up to " << TMP_MAX
       << " temporary names of up to " << L_tmpnam
       << " characters.\n";
  char pszName[ L_tmpnam ] = {'\0'};
  cout << "Here are ten names:\n";
  for( int i=0; 10 > i; i++ )
  {
    tmpnam( pszName );
    cout << pszName << endl;
  }
  return 0;
}
```

More generally, using `tmpnam()`, we can now generate `TMP_NAM` unique filenames with up to `L_tmpnam` characters per name.

Incore Formatting

The `iostream` family supports I/O between the program and a terminal. The `fstream` family uses the same interface to provide I/O between a program and a file. The C++ library also provides an `sstream` family that uses the same interface to provide I/O between a program and a `string` object. That is, you can use the same `ostream` methods you've used with `cout` to write formatted information into a `string` object, and you can use `istream` methods such as `getline()` to read information from a `string` object. The process of reading formatted information from a `string` object or of writing formatted information to a `string` object is termed *incore* formatting. Let's take a brief look at these facilities. (The `sstream` family of `string` support supersedes a `strstream.h` family of `char`-array support.)

The `sstream` header file defines an `ostringstream` class derived from the `ostream` class. (There also is a `wostringstream` class based on `wostream` for wide character sets.) If you create an `ostringstream` object, you can write information to it, which it stores. You can use the same methods with an `ostringstream` object that you can with `cout`. That is, you can do something like the following:

```
ostringstream outstr;
double price = 55.00;
char * ps = " for a copy of the draft C++ standard!";
outstr.precision(2);
outstr << fixed;
outstr << "Pay only $" << price << ps << end;
```

The formatted text goes into a buffer, and the object uses dynamic memory allocation to expand the buffer size as needed. The `ostringstream` class has a member function, called `str()`, which returns a string object initialized to the buffer's contents:

```
string mesg = outstr.str();    // returns string with formatted information
```

Using the `str()` method "freezes" the object, and you no longer can write to it.

Listing 17.21 provides a short example.

LISTING 17.21   strout.cpp

```cpp
// strout.cpp -- incore formatting (output)
#include <iostream>
using namespace std;
#include <sstream>
#include <string>
int main()
{
    ostringstream outstr;    // manages a string stream

    string hdisk;
    cout << "What's the name of your hard disk? ";
    getline(cin, hdisk);
    int cap;
    cout << "What's its capacity in GB? ";
    cin >> cap;
    // write formatted information to string stream
    outstr << "The hard disk " << hdisk << " has a capacity of "
            << cap << " megabytes.\n";
    string result = outstr.str();    // save result
    cout << result;                  // show contents

    return 0;
}
```

Here's a sample run:

```
What's the name of your hard disk? Spinar
What's its capacity in GB? 72
The hard disk Spinar has a capacity of 72 megabytes.
```

The `istringstream` class lets you use the `istream` family of methods to read data from an `istringstream` object, which can be initialized from a `string` object. Suppose `facts` is a `string` object. To create an `istringstream` object associated with this string, do the following:

```cpp
istringstream instr(facts);    // use facts to initialize stream
```

Then you use `istream` methods to read data from `instr`. For example, if `instr` contained a bunch of integers in character format, you could read them as follows:

```cpp
int n;
int sum = 0;
while (instr << n)
    sum += num;
```

Listing 17.22 uses the overloaded `>>` operator to read the contents of a string one word at a time.

LISTING 17.22   strin.cpp

```cpp
// strin.cpp -- formatted reading from a char array
#include <iostream>
using namespace std;
#include <sstream>
#include <string>
int main()
{
    string lit = "It was a dark and stormy day, and "
                 " the full moon glowed brilliantly. ";
    istringstream instr(lit);    // use buf for input
    string word;;
    while (instr >> word)         // read a word a time
        cout << word << endl;
    return 0;
}
```

Here is the program output:

```
It
was
a
dark
and
stormy
day,
and
the
full
moon
glowed
brilliantly.
```

In short, `istringstream` and `ostringstream` classes give you the power of the `istream` and `ostream` class methods to manage character data stored in strings.

What Now?

If you have worked your way through this book, you should have a good grasp of the rules of C++. However, that's just the beginning in learning this language. The second stage is learning to use the language effectively, and that is the longer journey. The best situation to be in is a work or learning environment that brings you into contact with good C++ code and programmers. Also, now that you know C++, you can read books that concentrate on more advanced topics and upon object-oriented programming. Appendix H, "Selected Readings," lists some of these resources.

One promise of OOP is to facilitate the development and enhance the reliability of large projects. One of the essential activities of the OOP approach is to invent the classes that represent the situation (called the *problem domain*) that you are modeling. Because real problems often are complex, finding a suitable set of classes can be challenging. Creating a complex system from scratch usually doesn't work; instead, it's best to take an iterative, evolutionary approach. Toward this end, practitioners in the field have developed several techniques and strategies. In particular, it's important to do as much of the iteration and evolution in the analysis and design stages as possible instead of writing and rewriting actual code.

Two common techniques are *use-case analysis* and *CRC cards*. In use-case analysis, the development team lists the common ways, or scenarios, in which they expect the final system to be used, identifying elements, actions, and responsibilities that suggest possible classes and class features. CRC (short for Class/Responsibilities/Collaborators) cards are a simple way to analyze such scenarios. The development team creates an index card for each class. On the card are the class name, class responsibilities, such as data represented and actions performed, and class collaborators, such as other classes with which the class must interact. Then the team can walk through a scenario, using the interface provided by the CRC cards. This can lead to suggesting new classes, shifts of responsibility, and so on.

On a larger scale are the systematic methods for working on entire projects. The most recent of these is the *Unified Modeling Language*, or *UML*. This is not a programming language; rather, it is a language for representing the analysis and design of a programming project. It was developed by Grady Booch, Jim Rumbaugh, and Ivar Jacobson, who had been the primary developers of three earlier modeling languages: the Booch Method, OMT (Object Modeling Technique), and OOSE (Object-Oriented Software Engineering), respectively. UML is the evolutionary successor of these three.

In addition to increasing your understanding of C++ in general, you might want to learn about specific class libraries. Microsoft, Borland, and Metrowerks, for example, offer extensive class libraries to facilitate programming for the Windows environment, and Metrowerks offers similar facilities for Macintosh programming.

Summary

A stream is a flow of bytes into or out of a program. A buffer is a temporary holding area in memory that acts as an intermediary between a program and a file or other I/O devices. Information can be transferred between a buffer and a file using large chunks of data of the size most efficiently handled by devices like disk drives. And information can be transferred between a buffer and a program in a byte-by-byte flow that often is more convenient for the processing done in a program. C++ handles input by connecting a buffered stream to a program and to its source of input. Similarly, C++ handles output by connecting a buffered stream to a program and to its output target. The `iostream` and `fstream` files constitute an I/O class library that defines a rich set of classes for managing streams. C++ programs that include the `iostream` file automatically open eight streams, managing them with eight objects. The `cin` object manages the standard input stream, which, by default, connects to the standard input device, typically a keyboard. The `cout` object manages the standard output stream, which, by default, connects to the standard output device, typically a monitor. The `cerr` and `clog` objects manage unbuffered and buffered streams connected to the standard error device, typically a monitor. These four objects have four wide character counterparts named `wcin`, `wcout`, `wcerr`, and `wclog`.

The I/O class library provides a variety of useful methods. The `istream` class defines versions of the extraction operator (`>>`) that recognize all the basic C++ types and that convert character input to those types. The `get()` family of methods and the `getline()` method provide further support for single-character input and for string input. Similarly, the `ostream` class defines versions of the insertion operator (`<<`) that recognize all the basic C++ types and that convert them to suitable character output. The `put()` method provides further support for single-character output. The `wistream` and `wostream` classes follow similar support for wide characters.

You can control how a program formats output by using `ios_base` class methods and by using manipulators (functions that can be concatenated with insertion) defined in the `iostream` and `iomanip` files. These methods and manipulators let you control the number base, the field width, the number of decimal places displayed, the system used to display floating-point values, and other elements.

The `fstream` file provides class definitions that extend the `iostream` methods to file I/O. The `ifstream` class derives from the `istream` class. By associating an `ifstream` object with a file, you can use all the `istream` methods for reading the file. Similarly, associating an `ofstream` object with a file lets you use the `ostream` methods to write to a file. And associating an `fstream` object with a file lets you employ both input and output methods with the file.

To associate a file with a stream, you can provide the filename when initializing a file stream object or you can first create a file stream object and then use the `open()` method to associate the stream with a file. The `close()` method terminates the connection between a stream and a file. The class constructors and the `open()` method take an optional second argument that provides the file mode. The file mode determines such things as whether the file is to be read and/or written to, whether opening a file for writing truncates it or not, whether attempting to open a nonexistent file is an error or not, and whether to use the binary or text mode.

A text file stores all information in character form. For example, numeric values are converted to character representations. The usual insertion and extraction operators, along with `get()` and `getline()`, support this mode. A binary file stores all information using the same binary representation the computer uses internally. Binary files store data, particularly floating-point values, more accurately and compactly than text files, but they are less portable. The `read()` and `write()` methods support binary input and output.

The `seekg()` and `seekp()` functions provide C++ random access for files. These class methods let you position a file pointer relative to the beginning of a file, relative to the end, or relative to the current position. The `tellg()` and `tellp()` methods report the current file position.

The `sstream` header file defines `istringstream` and `ostringstream` classes that let you use `istream` and `ostream` methods to extract information from a string and to format information placed into a string.

Review Questions

1. What role does the `iostream` file play in C++ I/O?

2. Why does typing a number such as 121 as input require a program to make a conversion?

3. What's the difference between the standard output and the standard error?

4. Why is **cout** able to display various C++ types without being provided explicit instructions for each type?

5. What feature of the output method definitions allows you to concatenate output?

6. Write a program that requests an integer and then displays it in decimal, octal, and hexadecimal form. Display each form on the same line in fields that are 15 characters wide, and use the C++ number base prefixes.

7. Write a program that requests the information shown below and that formats it as shown:

```
Enter your name: Billy Gruff
Enter your hourly wages: 12
Enter number of hours worked: 7.5
First format:
                    Billy Gruff: $      12.00:  7.5
Second format:
Billy Gruff                   : $12.00     :7.5
```

8. Consider the following program:

```cpp
//rq17-8.cpp
#include <iostream>
using namespace std;

int main()
{
    char ch;
    int ct1 = 0;

    cin >> ch;
    while (ch != 'q')
    {
        ct1++;
        cin >> ch;
    }

    int ct2 = 0;
    cin.get(ch);
    while (ch != 'q')
    {
        ct2++;
        cin.get(ch);
    }
    cout << "ct1 = " << ct1 << "; ct2 = " << ct2 << "\n";

    return 0;
}
```

What does it print, given the following input:

```
I see a q<Enter>
I see a q<Enter>
```

Here `<Enter>` signifies pressing the Enter key.

9. Both of the following statements read and discard characters up to and including the end of a line. In what way does the behavior of one differ from that of the other?

```
while (cin.get() != '\n')
    continue;
cin.ignore(80, '\n');
```

Programming Exercises

1. Write a program that counts the number of characters up to the first `$` in input and that leaves the `$` in the input stream.

2. Write a program that copies your keyboard input (up to simulated end-of-file) to a file named on the command line.

3. Write a program that copies one file to another. Have the program take the filenames from the command line. Have the program report if it cannot open a file.

4. Write a program that opens two text files for input and one for output. The program concatenates the corresponding lines of the input files, using a space as a separator, and writing the results to the output file. If one file is shorter than the other, the remaining lines in the longer file are also copied to the output file. For example, suppose the first input file has these contents:

```
eggs kites donuts
balloons hammers
stones
```

And suppose the second input file has these contents:

```
zero lassitude
finance drama
```

Then the resulting file would have these contents:

```
eggs kites donuts zero lassitude
balloons hammers finance drama
stones
```

5. Mat and Pat want to invite their friends to a party, much as they did in Chapter 15, "Friends, Exceptions, and More," Programming Exercise 5, except now they want a program that uses files. They ask you to write a program that does the following:

   • Reads a list of Mat's friends' names from a text file called `mat.dat`, which lists one friend per line. The names are stored in a container and then displayed in sorted order.

- Reads a list of Pat's friends' names from a text file called **pat.dat**, which lists one friend per line. The names are stored in a container and then displayed in sorted order.

- Merges the two lists, eliminating duplicates, and stores the result in the file **mat-npat.dat**, one friend per line.

6. Consider the class definitions of Programming Exercise 13.5. If you haven't yet done that exercise, do so now. Then do the following:

Write a program that uses standard C++ I/O and file I/O in conjunction with data of types **employee**, **manager**, **fink**, and **highfink**, as defined in Programming Exercise 13.5. The program should be along the general lines of Listing 17.17 in that it should let you add new data to a file. The first time through, the program should solicit data from the user, then show all the entries, then save the information in a file. On subsequent uses, the program should first read and display the file data, then let the user add data, then show all the data. One difference is that data should be handled by an array of pointers to type employee. That way, a pointer can point to an employee object or to objects of any of the three derived types. Keep the array small to facilitate checking the program:

```
const int MAX = 10;      // no more than 10 objects
...
employee * pc[MAX];
```

For keyboard entry, the program should use a menu to offer the user the choice of which type of object to create. The menu will use a switch to use **new** to create an object of the desired type and to assign the object's address to a pointer in the **pc** array. Then that object can use the virtual **setall()** function to elicit the appropriate data from the user:

```
pc[i]->setall();   // invokes function corresponding to type of object
```

To save the data to a file, devise a virtual **writeall()** function for that purpose:

```
for (i = 0; i < index; i++)
    pc[i]->writeall(fout);// fout ofstream connected to output file
```

Note

Use text I/O, not binary I/O, for this exercise. (Unfortunately, virtual objects include pointers to tables of pointers to virtual functions, and **write()** copies this information to a file. An object filled by using **read()** from the file gets weird values for the function pointers, which really messes up the behavior of virtual functions.) Use a newline to separate each data field from the next; this makes it easier to identify fields on input. Or you could still use binary I/O, but not write objects as a whole. Instead, you could provide class methods that apply the **write()** and **read()** functions to each class member individually rather than to the object as a whole. That way, the program can save just the intended data to a file.

utt 17 • INPUT, OUTPUT, AND FILES** **949**

The tricky part is recovering the data from the file. The problem is, how can the program know whether the next item to be recovered is an **employee** object, a **manager** object, a **fink** type, or a **highfink** type? One approach is, when writing the data for an object to a file, precede the data with an integer indicating the type of object to follow. Then, on file input, the program can read the integer, then use a **switch** to create the appropriate object to receive the data:

```
enum classkind{Employee, Manager, Fink, Highfink}; // in class header
...
int classtype;
while((fin >> classtype).get(ch)){ // newline separates int from data
    switch(classtype) {
        case Employee  : pc[i] = new employee;
                       : break;
```

Then you can use the pointer to invoke a virtual **getall()** function to read the information:

```
pc[i++]->getall();
```

APPENDIX A

NUMBER BASES

Our method for writing numbers is based on powers of 10. For example, consider the number 2468. The 2 represents 2 thousands, the 4 represents 4 hundreds, the 6 represents 6 tens, and the 8 represents 8 ones:

2468 = 2×1000 + 4×100 + 6×10 + 8×1

One thousand is 10×10×10, which can be written as 10[3], or 10 to the 3rd power. Using this notation, we can write the preceding relationship this way:

2468 = 2×10[3] + 4×10[2] + 6×10[1] + 8×10[0]

Because our number notation is based on powers of 10, we refer to it as base 10, or decimal, notation. One can just as easily pick another number as a base. C++ lets you use base 8 (octal) and base 16 (hexadecimal) notation for writing integer numbers. (Note: 10[0] is 1, as is any nonzero number to the zero power.)

Octal Integers

Octal numbers are based on powers of 8, so base 8 notation uses the digits 0–7 in writing numbers. C++ uses a 0 prefix to indicate octal notation. Thus, 0177 is an octal value. You can use powers of 8 to find the equivalent base 10 value:

0177 (octal)	= 1×8[2] + 7×8[1] + 7×8[0]
	= 1× 64 + 7×8 + 7×1
	= 127 (decimal)

The UNIX operating system often uses octal representation of values, which is why C++ and C provide octal notation.

Hexadecimal Numbers

Hexadecimal numbers are based on powers of 16. That means 10 in hexadecimal represents the value 16 + 0, or 16. To represent the values between 9 and hexadecimal 16, you need a few more digits. Standard hexadecimal notation uses the letters a–f for that purpose. C++ accepts either lowercase or uppercase versions of these characters, as shown in Table A.1.

TABLE A.1   Hexadecimal Digits

Hexadecimal digits	Decimal value	Hexadecimal digits	Decimal value
a or A	10	d or D	13
b or B	11	e or E	14
c or C	12	f or F	15

C++ uses a 0x or 0X notation to indicate hexadecimal notation. Thus, 0x2B3 is a hexadecimal value. To find its decimal equivalent, you can evaluate the powers of 16:

0x2B3 (hex)	$= 2 \times 16[2] + 11 \times 16[1] + 3 \times 16[0]$
	$= 2 \times 256 + 11 \times 16 + 3 \times 1$
	$= 691$ (decimal)

Hardware documentation often uses hexadecimal notation to represent values such as memory locations and port numbers.

Binary Numbers

Whether you use decimal, octal, or hexadecimal notation for writing an integer, the computer stores it as a binary, or base 2, value. Binary notation uses just two digits, 0 and 1. As an example, 10011011 is a binary number. Note, however, that C++ doesn't provide for writing a number in binary notation. Binary numbers are based on powers of 2:

10011011	$= 1 \times 2[7] + 0 \times 2[6] + 0 \times 2[5] + 1 \times 2[4] + 1 \times 2[3]$
	$+ 0 \times 2[2] + 1 \times 2[1] + 1 \times 2[0]$
	$= 128 + 0 + 0 + 16 + 8 + 0 + 2 + 1$
	$= 155$

Binary notation makes a nice match to computer memory, in which each individual unit, called a bit, can be set to off or on. Just identify the off setting with 0 and the on setting with 1. Memory commonly is organized in units called bytes, with each byte being 8 bits. The bits in a byte are numbered corresponding to the associated power of 2. Thus, the rightmost bit is bit number 0, the next bit is bit 1, and so on. Figure A.1, for example, represents a 2-byte integer.

FIGURE A.1
A two-byte integer value.

Binary and Hex

Hex notation often is used to provide a more convenient view of binary data, such as memory addresses or integers holding bit-flag settings. The reason is that each hexadecimal digit corresponds to a four-bit unit. Table A.2 shows this correspondence.

TABLE A.2   Hexadecimal Digits and Binary Equivalents

Hexadecimal digit	Binary equivalent	Hexadecimal digit	Binary equivalent
0	0000	8	1000
1	0001	9	1001
2	0010	A	1010
3	0011	B	1011
4	0100	C	1100
5	0101	D	1101
6	0110	E	1110
7	0111	F	1111

To convert a hex value to binary, just replace each hex digit by the corresponding binary equivalent. For example, the hex number 0xA4 corresponds to binary 1010 0100. Similarly, you easily can convert binary values to hex notation by converting each 4-bit unit into the equivalent hex digit. For example, the binary value 1001 0101 becomes 0x95.

Real World Note: What Are Big Endian and Little Endian?

Oddly enough, two computing platforms that both use binary representation of integers might not represent the same number identically. Intel machines, for example, store bytes using the Little Endian architecture, while Motorola, RISC-based MIPS computers, and the DEC Alpha computers employ the Big Endian scheme. (However, the last two systems can be configured to use either scheme.)

The terms Big Endian and Little Endian are derived from "Big End In" and "Little End In"—a reference to the order of bytes in a word (typically a two-byte unit) of memory. On an Intel computer (Little Endian), the low-order byte is stored first. This means a hex value such as 0xABCD would be stored in memory as (0xCD 0xAB). A Motorola (Big Endian) machine would store the same value in the reverse, so 0xABCD would be stored in memory as (0xAB 0xCD).

You, as a software engineer, should understand the word order of the platform you are targeting. Among other things, it affects the interpretation of data transmitted over a network and how data are stored in binary files. In the example above, the two-byte memory pattern 0xABCD would represent the decimal value 52,651 on a Little Endian machine and the decimal 43,981 on a Big Endian machine.

C++ KEYWORDS

K eywords are identifiers that form the vocabulary of a programming language. They may not be used for other purposes, such as serving as a variable name. The following list shows C++'s keywords; not all of them are currently implemented. Keywords shown in boldface are also keywords in the ANSI C99 standard.

asm	**auto**	bool	**break**	**case**
catch	**char**	class	**const**	const_cast
continue	**default**	delete	**do**	double
dynamic_cast	**else**	**enum**	explicit	export
extern	false	**float**	**for**	friend
goto	**if**	**inline**	**int**	**long**
mutable	namespace	new	operator	private
protected	public	**register**	reinterpret_cast	**return**
short	**signed**	**sizeof**	**static**	static_cast
struct	**switch**	template	this	throw
true	try	**typedef**	typeid	typename
union	**unsigned**	using	virtual	**void**
volatile	wchar_t	**while**		

THE ASCII CHARACTER SET

C omputers store characters using a numeric code. The ASCII code (American Standard Code for Information Interchange) is the most commonly used code in the United States. C++ lets you represent most single characters directly, by including the character in single quotation marks, as in `'A'` for the A character. You can also represent a single character by using the octal or hex code preceded by a backslash; for example, `'\012'` and `'\0xa'` both represent the linefeed (LF) character. Such escape sequences can also be part of a string, as in `"Hello,\012my dear"`.

When used as a prefix in the following table, the ^ character denotes using a Ctrl key.

Decimal	Octal	Hex	Binary	Character	ASCII Name
0	0	0	00000000	^@	NUL
1	01	0x1	00000001	^A	SOH
2	02	0x2	00000010	^B	STX
3	03	0x3	00000011	^C	ETX
4	04	0x4	00000100	^D	EOT
5	05	0x5	00000101	^E	ENQ
6	06	0x6	00000110	^F	ACK
7	07	0x7	00000111	^G	BEL
8	010	0x8	00001000	^H	BS
9	011	0x9	00001001	^I, tab	HT
10	012	0xa	00001010	^J	LF
11	013	0xb	00001011	^K	VT
12	014	0xc	00001100	^L	FF
13	015	0xd	00001101	^M	CR
14	016	0xe	00001110	^N	SO
15	017	0xf	00001111	^O	SI

Decimal	Octal	Hex	Binary	Character	ASCII Name
16	020	0x10	00010000	^P	DLE
17	021	0x11	00010001	^Q	DC1
18	022	0x12	00010010	^R	DC2
19	023	0x13	00010011	^S	DC3
20	024	0x14	00010100	^T	DC4
21	025	0x15	00010101	^U	NAK
22	026	0x16	00010110	^V	SYN
23	027	0x17	00010111	^W	ETB
24	030	0x18	00011000	^X	CAN
25	031	0x19	00011001	^Y	EM
26	032	0x1a	00011010	^Z	SUB
27	033	0x1b	00011011	^[, esc	ESC
28	034	0x1c	00011100	^\	FS
29	035	0x1d	00011101	^]	GS
30	036	0x1e	00011110	^^	RS
31	037	0x1f	00011111	^_	US
32	040	0x20	00100000	space	SP
33	041	0x21	00100001	!	
34	042	0x22	00100010	"	
35	043	0x23	00100011	#	
36	044	0x24	00100100	$	
37	045	0x25	00100101	%	
38	046	0x26	00100110	&	
39	047	0x27	00100111	'	
40	050	0x28	00101000	(	
41	051	0x29	00101001	)	
42	052	0x2a	00101010	*	
43	053	0x2b	00101011	+	
44	054	0x2c	00101100	'	

Decimal	Octal	Hex	Binary	Character	ASCII Name
45	055	0x2d	00101101	-	
46	056	0x2e	00101110	.	
47	057	0x2f	00101111	/	
48	060	0x30	00110000	0	
49	061	0x31	00110001	1	
50	062	0x32	00110010	2	
51	063	0x33	00110011	3	
52	064	0x34	00110100	4	
53	065	0x35	00110101	5	
54	066	0x36	00110110	6	
55	067	0x37	00110111	7	
56	070	0x38	00111000	8	
57	071	0x39	00111001	9	
58	072	0x3a	00111010	:	
59	073	0x3b	00111011	;	
60	074	0x3c	00111100	<	
61	075	0x3d	00111101	=	
62	076	0x3e	00111110	>	
63	077	0x3f	00111111	?	
64	0100	0x40	01000000	@	
65	0101	0x41	01000001	A	
66	0102	0x42	01000010	B	
67	0103	0x43	01000011	C	
68	0104	0x44	01000100	D	
69	0105	0x45	01000101	E	
70	0106	0x46	01000110	F	
71	0107	0x47	01000111	G	
72	0110	0x48	01001000	H	

Decimal	Octal	Hex	Binary	Character	ASCII Name
73	0111	0x49	01001001	I	
74	0112	0x4a	01001010	J	
75	0113	0x4b	01001011	K	
76	0114	0x4c	01001100	L	
77	0115	0x4d	01001101	M	
78	0116	0x4e	01001110	N	
79	0117	0x4f	01001111	O	
80	0120	0x50	01010000	P	
81	0121	0x51	01010001	Q	
82	0122	0x52	01010010	R	
83	0123	0x53	01010011	S	
84	0124	0x54	01010100	T	
85	0125	0x55	01010101	U	
86	0126	0x56	01010110	V	
87	0127	0x57	01010111	W	
88	0130	0x58	01011000	X	
89	0131	0x59	01011001	Y	
90	0132	0x5a	01011010	Z	
91	0133	0x5b	01011011	[	
92	0134	0x5c	01011100	\	
93	0135	0x5d	01011101	]	
94	0136	0x5e	01011110	^	
95	0137	0x5f	01011111	_	
96	0140	0x60	01100000	'	
97	0141	0x61	01100001	a	
98	0142	0x62	01100010	b	
99	0143	0x63	01100011	c	
100	0144	0x64	01100100	d	

Decimal	Octal	Hex	Binary	Character	ASCII Name
101	0145	0x65	01100101	e	
102	0146	0x66	01100110	f	
103	0147	0x67	01100111	g	
104	0150	0x68	01101000	h	
105	0151	0x69	01101001	i	
106	0152	0x6a	01101010	j	
107	0153	0x6b	01101011	k	
108	0154	0x6c	01101100	l	
109	0155	0x6d	01101101	m	
110	0156	0x6e	01101110	n	
111	0157	0x6f	01101111	o	
112	0160	0x70	01110000	p	
113	0161	0x71	01110001	q	
114	0162	0x72	01110010	r	
115	0163	0x73	01110011	s	
116	0164	0x74	01110100	t	
117	0165	0x75	01110101	u	
118	0166	0x76	01110110	v	
119	0167	0x77	01110111	w	
120	0170	0x78	01111000	x	
121	0171	0x79	01111001	y	
122	0172	0x7a	01111010	z	
123	0173	0x7b	01111011	{	
124	0174	0x7c	01111100	l	
125	0175	0x7d	01111101	}	
126	0176	0x7e	01111110	~	
127	0177	0x7f	01111111	del, rubout	

APPENDIX D

OPERATOR PRECEDENCE

*O*perator precedence determines the order in which operators are applied to a value. C++ operators come in 18 precedence groups, which are presented in Table D.1. Those in group 1 have the highest precedence, and so on. If two operators apply to the same operand (something upon which an operator operates), the operator with the higher precedence applies first. If the two operators have the same precedence, C++ uses associativity rules to determine which operator binds more tightly. All operators in the same group have the same precedence and the same associativity, which is either left to right (L–R in the table) or right to left (R–L in the table). Left-to-right associativity means to apply the left-hand operator first, while right-to-left associativity means to apply the right-hand operator first.

Some symbols, such as * and &, are used for more than one operator. In such cases, one form is *unary* (one operand) and the other form is *binary* (two operands), and the compiler uses the context to determine which is meant. The table labels operator groups unary or binary for those cases in which the same symbol is used two ways.

Here are some examples of precedence and associativity:

```
3 + 5 * 6
```

The * operator has higher precedence than the + operator, so it is applied to the 5 first, making the expression 3 + 30, or 33.

```
120 / 6 * 5
```

Both / and * have the same precedence, but these operators associate from left to right. That means the operator to the left of the shared operand (6) is applied first, so the expression becomes 20 * 5, or 100.

```
char * str = "Whoa";
char ch = *str++;
```

The postfix ++ operator has higher precedence than the unary * operator. This means the increment operator operates upon str and not *str. That is, the operation increments the pointer, making it point to the next character, rather than altering the character pointed to. However, because ++ is the postfix form, the pointer is incremented after the original value of *str is assigned to ch. Therefore, this expression assigns the character W to ch and then moves str to point to the h character.

```
char * str = "Whoa";
char ch = *++str;
```

The prefix ++ operator and the unary * operator have the same precedence, but they associate right-to-left. So, again, str and not *str is incremented. Because the ++ operator is in prefix form, first str is incremented, then the resulting pointer is dereferenced. Thus, str moves to point to the h character, and the h character is assigned to ch.

Note that the table uses binary or unary in the Precedence column to distinguish between two operators that use the same symbol, such as the unary address operator and the binary bitwise AND operator.

TABLE D.1   C++ Operator Precedence and Associativity

Precedence	Operator	Assoc.	Meaning
1	::		Scope resolution operator
	(*expression*)		Grouping
2	()	L–R	Function call
	()		Value construction, that is, *type* (*expr*)
	[]		Array subscript
	->		Indirect membership operator
	.		Direct membership operator
	const_cast		Specialized type cast
	dynamic_cast		Specialized type cast
	reinterpret_cast		Specialized type cast
	static_cast		Specialized type cast
	typeid		Type identification
	++		Increment operator, postfix
	--		Decrement operator, postfix
3 (all unary)	!	R–L	Logical negation
	~		Bitwise negation
	+		Unary plus (positive sign)
	-		Unary minus (negative sign)
	++		Increment operator, prefix
	--		Decrement operator, prefix

TABLE D.1 Continued

Precedence	Operator	Assoc.	Meaning
	&		Address
	*		Dereference (indirect value)
	( )		Type cast, that is, (*type*) *expr*
	sizeof		Size in bytes
	new		Dynamically allocate storage
	new []		Dynamically allocate array
	delete		Dynamically free storage
	delete []		Dynamically free array
4	.*	L–R	Member dereference
	->*		Indirect member dereference
5 (all binary)	*	L–R	Multiply
	/		Divide
	^		Modulus (remainder)
6 (all binary)	+	L–R	Addition
	-		Subtraction
7	<<	L–R	Left shift
	>>		Right shift
8	<	L–R	Less than
	<=		Less than or equal to
	>=		Greater than or equal to
	>		Greater than
9	==	L–R	Equal to
	!=		Not equal to
10 (binary)	&	L–R	Bitwise AND
11	^	L–R	Bitwise XOR (exclusive OR)
12	|	L–R	Bitwise OR
13	&&	L–R	Logical AND

TABLE D.1 Continued

Precedence	Operator	Assoc.	Meaning
14	||	L–R	Logical OR
15	=	R–L	Simple assignment
	*=		Multiply and assign
	/=		Divide and assign
	%=		Take remainder and assign
	+=		Add and assign
	-=		Subtract and assign
	&=		Bitwise AND and assign
	^=		Bitwise XOR and assign
	|=		Bitwise OR and assign
	<<=		Left shift and assign
	>>=		Right shift and assign
16	:?	R–L	Conditional
17	throw	L–R	Throw exception
18	,	L–R	Combine two expressions into one

APPENDIX E

OTHER OPERATORS

*I*n order to avoid terminal obesity, the main text of this book doesn't cover two groups of operators. The first group consists of the bitwise operators, which let you manipulate individual bits in a value; these operators were inherited from C. The second group consists of two-member dereferencing operators; they are C++ additions. This appendix briefly summarizes these operators.

Bitwise Operators

The bitwise operators operate upon the bits of integer values. For example, the left-shift operator moves bits to the left, and the bitwise negation operator turns each one to a zero, and each zero to a one. Altogether, C++ has six such operators: <<, >>, ~, &, |, and ^.

The Shift Operators

The left-shift operator has the following syntax:

value << *shift*

Here *value* is the integer value to be shifted, and *shift* is the number of bits to shift. For example:

`13 << 3`

means shift all the bits in the value 13 three places to the left. The vacated places are filled with zeros, and bits shifted past the end are discarded (see Figure E.1).

Because each bit position represents a value twice that of the bit to the right (see Appendix A, "Number Bases"), shifting one bit position is equivalent to multiplying the value by 2. Similarly, shifting two bit positions is equivalent to multiplying by 2[2], and shifting n positions is equivalent to multiplying by 2[n]. Thus, the value of 13 << 3 is 13 × 2[3], or 104.

FIGURE E.1

The left-shift operator.

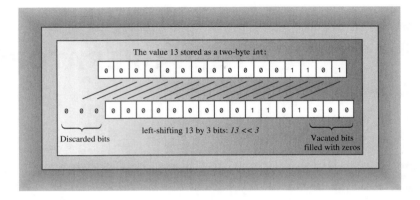

The left-shift operator provides a capability often found in assembly languages. However, an assembly left-shift operator directly alters the contents of a register, while the C++ operator produces a new value without altering existing values. For example, consider the following:

```
int x = 20;
int y = x << 3;
```

This code doesn't change the value of x. The expression x << 3 uses the value of x to produce a new value, much as x + 3 produces a new value without altering x.

If you want to use the left-shift operator to change the value of a variable, you also must use assignment. You can use regular assignment or the <<= operator, which combines shifting with assignment.

```
x = x << 4;          // regular assignment
y <<= 2;             // shift and assign
```

The right-shift operator (>>), as you might expect, shifts bits to the right. It has the following syntax:

```
value >> shift
```

Here *value* is the integer value to be shifted, and *shift* is the number of bits to shift. For example:

```
17 >> 2
```

means shift all the bits in the value 17 two places to the right. For unsigned integers, the vacated places are filled with zeros, and bits shifted past the end are discarded. For signed integers, vacated places may be filled with zeros or else with the value of the original leftmost bit. The choice depends upon the implementation (see Figure E.2 for an example illustrating filling with zeros).

FIGURE E.2
Right-shift operator.

Shifting one place to the right is equivalent to integer division by 2. In general, shifting n places to the right is equivalent to integer division by 2[n].

C++ also defines a right-shift-and-assign operator if you want to replace the value of a variable by the shifted value:

```
int q = 43;
q >>= 2;              // replace 43 by 43 >> 2, or 10
```

On some systems, using left- and right-shift operators may produce faster integer multiplication and division by 2 than using the division operator, but as compilers get better at optimizing code, such differences are fading.

The Logical Bitwise Operators

The logical bitwise operators are analogous to the regular logical operators, except they apply to a value on a bit-by-bit basis rather than to the whole. For example, consider the regular negation operator (!) and the bitwise negation (or complement) operator (~). The ! operator converts a **true** (or nonzero) value to **false** and a **false** value to **true**. The ~ operator converts each individual bit to its opposite (1 to 0 and 0 to 1). For example, consider the **unsigned char** value of 3:

```
unsigned char x = 3;
```

The expression !x has the value 0. To see the value of ~x, write it in binary form: 00000011. Then convert each 0 to 1 and each 1 to 0. This produces the value 11111100, or in base 10, the value 252 (see Figure E.3 for a 16-bit example). The new value is termed the complement of the original value.

FIGURE E.3
Bitwise negation operator.

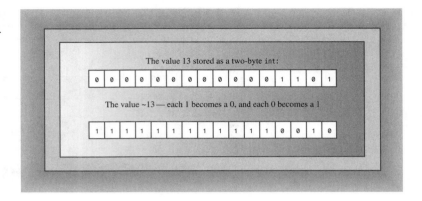

The bitwise OR operator (|) combines two integer values to produce a new integer value. Each bit in the new value is set to 1 if one or the other, or both, of the corresponding bits in the original values is set to 1. If both corresponding bits are 0, then the final bit is set to 0 (see Figure E.4).

FIGURE E.4
The bitwise OR operator.

Table E.1 summarizes how the | operator combines bits.

TABLE E.1 Value of b1 | b2

Bit values	b1 = 0	b1 = 1
b2 = 0	0	1
b2 = 1	1	1

The |= operator combines the bitwise OR operator with assignment:

```
a |= b;  // set a to a | b
```

The bitwise XOR operator (^) combines two integer values to produce a new integer value. Each bit in the new value is set to 1 if one or the other, but not both, of the corresponding bits in the original values is set to 1. If both corresponding bits are 0 or both are 1, the final bit is set to 0 (see Figure E.5).

FIGURE E.5
The bitwise XOR operator.

Table E.2 summarizes how the ^ operator combines bits.

TABLE E.2   Value of b1 ^ b2

Bit values	b1 = 0	b1 = 1
b2 = 0	0	1
b2 = 1	1	0

The ^= operator combines the bitwise XOR operator with assignment:

```
a ^= b;  // set a to a ^ b
```

The bitwise AND operator (&) combines two integer values to produce a new integer value. Each bit in the new value is set to 1 only if both of the corresponding bits in the original values are set to 1. If either or both corresponding bits are 0, the final bit is set to 0 (see Figure E.6).

FIGURE E.6
The bitwise AND
operator.

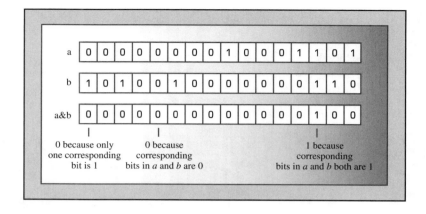

Table E.3 summarizes how the **&** operator combines bits.

TABLE E.3 Value of b1 & b2

Bit values	b1 = 0	b1 = 1
b2 = 0	0	0
b2 = 1	0	1

The **&=** operator combines the bitwise AND operator with assignment:

```
a &= b;  // set a to a & b
```

Alternative Representations

C++ provides alternative representations of several bitwise operators, as shown in Table E.4. They are provided for locales that do not have the traditional bitwise operators as part of their character sets.

TABLE E.4 Bitwise Operator Representations

Standard Representation	Alternative Representation
&	bitand
&=	and_eq
|	bitor
|=	or_eq

TABLE E.4 Continued

Standard Representation	Alternative Representation
~	compl
^	xor
^=	xor_eq

These alternative forms let you write statements like the following:

```
b = compl a bitand b;    // same as b = ~a & b;
c = a xor b;             // same as c = a ^ c;
```

A Few Common Bitwise Techniques

Often, controlling hardware involves turning particular bits on or off or checking their status. The bitwise operators provide the means to perform such actions. We'll go through the methods quickly.

In the following examples, **lottabits** represents a general value, and **bit** represents the value corresponding to a particular bit. Bits are numbered from right to left, beginning with bit 0, so the value corresponding to bit position n is 2[n]. For example, an integer with only bit number 3 set to 1 has the value 2[3] or 8. In general, each individual bit corresponds to a power of 2, as described for binary numbers in Appendix A. So we'll use the term *bit* to represent a power of 2; this corresponds to a particular bit being set to 1 and all other bits set to 0.

Turning a Bit On

The following two operations each turn on the bit in **lottabits** corresponding to the bit represented by **bit**:

```
lottabits = lottabits | bit;
lottabits |= bit;
```

Each sets the corresponding bit to 1 regardless of the former value of the bit. That's because ORing 1 with either 0 or 1 produces a 1. All other bits in **lottabits** remain unaltered. That's because ORing 0 with 0 produces a 0, and ORing 0 with 1 produces a 1.

Toggling a Bit

The following two operations each toggle the bit in **lottabits** corresponding to the bit represented by **bit**. That is, they turn the bit on if it is off, and they turn it off if it is on:

```
lottabits = lottabits ^ bit;
lottabits ^= bit;
```

XORing 1 with 0 produces 1, turning an off bit on, and XORing 1 with 1 produces 0, turning an on bit off. All other bits in **lottabits** remain unaltered. That's because XORing 0 with 0 produces a 0, and XORing 0 with 1 produces a 1.

Turning a Bit Off

The following operation turns off the bit in `lottabits` corresponding to the bit represented by `bit`:

```
lottabits = lottabits & ~bit;
```

These statements turn the bit off regardless of its prior state. First, the operator `~bit` produces an integer with all its bits set to 1 *except* the bit that originally was set to 1; that bit becomes a 0. ANDing a 0 with any bit results in 0, thus turning that bit off. All other bits in `lottabits` are unchanged. That's because ANDing a 1 with any bit produces the value that bit had before.

Here's a briefer way of doing the same thing:

```
lottabits &= ~bit;
```

Testing a Bit Value

Suppose you want to determine whether the bit corresponding to `bit` is set to 1 in `lottabits`. The following test does not necessarily work:

```
if (lottabits == bit)              // no good
```

That's because even if the corresponding bit in `lottabits` is set to 1, so might other bits be set to 1. The equality above is true *only* when the corresponding bit is 1. The fix is to first AND `lottabits` with `bit`. This produces a value that is 0 in all the other bit positions, because 0 AND any value is 0. Only the bit corresponding to the bit value is left unchanged, because 1 AND any value is that value. Thus the proper test is this:

```
if (lottabits & bit == bit)        // testing a bit
```

Real-world programmers often simplify this test to the following:

```
if (lottabits & bit)         // testing a bit
```

Because `bit` consists of one bit set to 1 and the rest set to 0, the value of `lottabits & bit` is either `0` (which tests as `false`) or `bit`, which being non-zero, tests as `true`.

Member Dereferencing Operators

C++ lets you define pointers to members of a class. These pointers involve special notations to declare them and to dereference them. To see what's involved, let's start with a sample class:

```
class Example
{
private:
    int feet;
    int inches;
public:
    Example();
    Example(int ft);
    ~Example();
```

```
    void show_in() const;
    void show_ft() const;
    void use_ptr() const;
};
```

Consider the `inches` member. Without a specific object, inches is a label. That is, the class defines `inches` as a member identifier, but you need an object before you actually have memory allocated:

```
Example ob;  // now ob.inches exists
```

Thus, you specify an actual memory location by using the identifier `inches` in conjunction with a specific object. (In a member function, you can omit the name of the object, but then the object is understood to be the one pointed to by the pointer.)

C++ lets you define a member pointer to the identifier `inches` like this:

```
int Example::*pt = &Example::inches;
```

This pointer is a bit different from a regular pointer. A regular pointer points to a specific memory location. But the `pt` pointer doesn't point to a specific memory location, for the declaration doesn't identify a specific object. Instead, the pointer `pt` identifies the location of `inches` member within any `Example` object. Like the identifier `inches`, `pt` is designed to be used in conjunction with an object identifier. In essence, the expression `*pt` assumes the role of the identifier `inches`. Therefore, you can use an object identifier to specify which object to access and the `pt` pointer to specify the `inches` member of that object. For example, a class method could use this code:

```
int Example::*pt = &Example::inches;
Example ob1;
Example ob2;
Example *pq = new Example;
cout << ob1.*pt << endl; // display inches member of ob1
cout << ob2.*pt << endl; // display inches member of ob2
cout << po->pt << endl;  // display inches member of *po
```

Here `.*` and `->*` are *member dereferencing operators*. Once you have a particular object, such as ob1, then ob1.*pi identifies the `inches` member of the ob1 object. Similarly, pq->*pt identifies the `inches` member of an object pointed to by `pq`.

Changing the object in the above example changes which `inches` member is used. But you also can change the pt pointer itself. Because `feet` is of the same type as `inches`, you can reset `pt` to point to the `feet` member instead of the `inches` member; then `ob1.*pt` will refer to the feet member of `ob1`:

```
pt = &Example::feet;     // reset pt
cout << ob1.*pt << endl; // display feet member of ob1
```

In essence, the combination `*pt` takes the place of a member name and can be used to identify different member names (of the same type).

You also can use member pointers to identify member functions. The syntax is a bit more involved. Recall that declaring a pointer to an ordinary type `void` function with no arguments looks like this:

```
void (*pf)();   // pf points to a function
```

Declaring a pointer to a member function has to indicate that the function belongs to a particular class. Here, for instance, is how to declare a pointer to an `Example` class method:

```
void (Example::*pf)() const;   // pf points to an Example member function
```

This indicates that `pf` can be used the same places an `Example` method can be used. Note that the term `Example::*pf` has to be in parentheses. You can assign the address of a particular member function to this pointer:

```
pf = &Example::show_inches;
```

Note that, unlike the case for ordinary function pointer assignment, that you use the address operator. Having made this assignment, you then can use an object to invoke the member function:

```
Example ob3(20);
(ob3.*pf)();       // invoke show_inches() using the ob3 object
```

You need to enclose the entire `ob3.*pf` construction in parentheses in order to clearly identify the expression as representing a function name.

Because `show_feet()` has the same prototype form as `show_inches()`, you can use `pf` to access the `show_feet()` method, too:

```
pf = &Example::show_feet;
(ob3.*pf)();       // apply show_feet() to the ob3 object
```

The class definition presented in Listing E.1 has a `use_ptr()` method that uses member pointers to access both data members and function members of the `Example` class.

LISTING E.1   memb_pt.cpp

```cpp
// memb_pt.cpp -- dereferencing pointers to class members
#include <iostream>
using namespace std;

class Example
{
private:
    int feet;
    int inches;
public:
    Example();
    Example(int ft);
    ~Example();
    void show_in() const;
    void show_ft() const;
    void use_ptr() const;
};
```

LISTING E.1   Continued

```
Example::Example()
{
    feet = 0;
    inches = 0;
}

Example::Example(int ft)
{
    feet = ft;
    inches = 12 * feet;
}

Example::~Example()
{
}

void Example::show_in() const
{
    cout << inches << " inches\n";
}

void Example::show_ft() const
{
    cout << feet << " feet\n";
}

void Example::use_ptr() const
{
    Example yard(3);
    int Example::*pt;
    pt = &Example::inches;
    cout << "Set pt to &Example::inches:\n";
    cout << "this->pt: " << this->*pt << endl;
    cout << "yard.*pt: " << yard.*pt << endl;
    pt = &Example::feet;
    cout << "Set pt to &Example::feet:\n";
    cout << "this->pt: " << this->*pt << endl;
    cout << "yard.*pt: " << yard.*pt << endl;
    void (Example::*pf)() const;
    pf = &Example::show_in;
    cout << "Set pf to &Example::show_in:\n";
    cout << "Using (this->*pf)(): ";
    (this->*pf)();
    cout << "Using (yard.*pf)(): ";
    (yard.*pf)();
}

int main()
{
    Example car(15);
    Example van(20);
    Example garage;
```

LISTING E.1   Continued

```
        cout << "car.use_ptr() output:\n";
        car.use_ptr();
        cout << "\nvan.use_ptr() output:\n";
        van.use_ptr();

        return 0;
}
```

Here is a sample run:

```
car.use_ptr() output:
Set pt to &Example::inches:
this->pt: 180
yard.*pt: 36
Set pt to &Example::feet:
this->pt: 15
yard.*pt: 3
Set pf to &Example::show_in:
Using (this->*pf)(): 180 inches
Using (yard.*pf)(): 36 inches

van.use_ptr() output:
Set pt to &Example::inches:
this->pt: 240
yard.*pt: 36
Set pt to &Example::feet:
this->pt: 20
yard.*pt: 3
Set pf to &Example::show_in:
Using (this->*pf)(): 240 inches
Using (yard.*pf)(): 36 inches
```

This example assigned pointer values during compile time. In a more sophisticated class, you can use member pointers to data members and methods for which the exact member associated with the pointer is determined during runtime.

APPENDIX F

THE string TEMPLATE CLASS

The string class is based on a template definition:

```
template<class charT, class traits = char_traits<charT>,
                class Allocator = allocator<charT> >
class basic_string {...};
```

Here charT represents the type stored in the string. The traits parameter represents a class that defines necessary properties a type must possess to be represented as a string. For example, it should have a length() method that returns the length of a string represented as an array of type charT. The end of such an array is indicated by the value charT(0), the generalization of the null character. (The expression charT(0) is a type cast of 0 to type charT. It could be just a 0, as it is for type char, or, more generally, it could be an object created by a charT constructor.) The class also includes methods for comparing values, and so on. The Allocator parameter represents a class to handle memory allocation for the string. The default allocator<charT> template uses new and delete in the standard ways.

There are two predefined specializations:

```
typedef basic_string<char> string;
typedef basic_string<wchar_t> wstring;
```

These specializations, in turn, use the following specializations:

```
char_traits<char>
allocator<char>
char_traits<wchar_t>
allocator<wchar_t>
```

You can create a string class for some type other than char or wchar_t by defining a traits class and using the basic_string template.

Thirteen Types and a Constant

The basic_string template defines several types that are used later in defining the methods:

```
typedef traits                        traits_type;
typedef typename traits::char_type    value_type;
typedef Allocator                     allocator_type;
typedef typename Allocator::size_type size_type;
```

```
typedef typename Allocator::difference_type    difference_type;
typedef typename Allocator::reference           reference;
typedef typename Allocator::const_reference     const_reference;
typedef typename Allocator::pointer             pointer;
typedef typename Allocator::const_pointer       const_pointer;
```

Note that **traits** is a template parameter that will correspond to some specific type, such as **char_traits<char>**; **traits_type** will become a **typedef** for that specific type. The notation:

```
typedef typename traits::char_type             value_type;
```

means that **char_type** is a type name defined in the class represented by **traits**. The keyword **typename** is used to tell the compiler that the expression **traits::char_type** is a type. For the string specialization, for example, **value_type** will be **char**.

The **size_type** is used like **size_of**, except that it returns the size of a string in terms of the stored type. For the **string** specialization, that would be in terms of **char**, in which case **size_type** is the same as **size_of**. It is an unsigned type.

The **difference_type** is used to measure the distance between two elements of a string, again in units corresponding to the size of a single element. Typically, it would be a signed version of the type underlying **size_type**.

For the **char** specialization, **pointer** will be type **char ***, and **reference** will be type **char &**. However, if you create a specialization for a type of your own design, these types (**pointer** and **reference**) could refer to classes that have the same properties as the more basic pointers and references.

To allow STL algorithms to be used with strings, the template defines some iterator types:

```
typedef (models random access iterator)        iterator;
typedef (models random access iterator)        const_iterator;
typedef std::reverse_iterator<iterator>        reverse_iterator;
typedef std::reverse_iterator<const_iterator>  const_reverse_iterator;
```

The template defines a static constant:

```
static const size_type npos = -1;
```

Because **size_type** is unsigned, assigning a value of -1 actually amounts to assigning the largest possible unsigned value to **npos**. This value corresponds to 1 greater than the largest possible array index.

Data Information, Constructors, and So On

Constructors can be described in terms of the effects they have. Because the private portions of a class can be implementation-dependent, these effects should be described in terms of information available as part of the public interface. Table F.1 lists several methods whose return values can be used to describe the effects of constructors and of other methods. Note that much of the terminology is from the STL.

TABLE F.1   Some string Data Methods

Method	Returns
begin()	An iterator to the first character in a string (also available in a const version, which returns a const iterator).
end()	An iterator that is the past-the-end value (also available in a const version).
rbegin()	A reverse iterator that is the past-the-end value (also available in a const version).
rend()	A reverse iterator that refers to the first character (also available in a const version).
size()	The number of elements in a string, equal to the distance from begin() to end().
length()	The same as size().
capacity()	The allocated number of elements in a string.
max_size()	The maximum allowable size of a string.
data()	A pointer of type const charT* to the first element of an array whose first size() elements equal the corresponding elements in the string controlled by *this. The pointer should not be assumed to be valid after the string object itself has been modified.
c_str()	A pointer of type const charT* to the first element of an array whose first size() elements equal the corresponding elements in the string controlled by *this and whose next element is the charT(0) character (end-of-string marker) for the charT type. The pointer should not be assumed to be valid after the string object itself has been modified.
get_allocator()	A copy of the allocator object used to allocate memory for the string object.

Be careful of the differences among begin(), rend(), data(), and c_str(). All relate to the first character in a string, but in different ways. The begin() and rend() methods return iterators, which are generalizations of pointers, as described in the Chapter 16, "The string Class and the Standard Template Library," discussion of the STL. In particular, begin() returns a model of a forward iterator, and rend() a copy of a reverse iterator. Both refer to the actual string managed by the string object. (Because the string class uses dynamic memory allocation, the actual string contents need not be inside the object, so we use the term *manage* to describe the relationship between object and string.) You can use the methods that return iterators with the iterator-based algorithms of the STL. For example, you can use the STL reverse() function to reverse the contents of a string:

```
string word;
cin >> word;
reverse(word.begin(), word.end());
```

The `data()` and `c_str()` methods, on the other hand, do return ordinary pointers. Furthermore, the returned pointers point to the first element of an *array* holding the string characters. This array can be, but need not be, a copy of the original string managed by the `string` object. (The internal representation used by the `string` object can be an array, but it doesn't have to be.) Because it is possible that the returned pointers do point to the original data, they are `const`, so they can't be used to alter the data. Also, the pointers are not guaranteed to be valid after the string is modified; this reflects that they may point to the original data. The difference between `data()` and `c_str()` is that the array `c_str()` points to is terminated with a null character (or equivalent), while `data()` just guarantees the actual string characters are present. Thus, the `c_str()` method can be used, for example, as an argument to a function expecting a C-style string:

```
string file("tofu.man");
ofstream outFile(file.c_str());
```

Similarly, `data()` and `size()` could be used with a function that expects to receive a pointer to an array element and a value representing the number of elements to process:

```
string vampire("Do not stake me, oh my darling!");
int vlad = byte_check(vampire.data(), vampire.size());
```

An implementation could choose to represent a `string` object's string as a dynamically allocated C-style string and to implement the forward iterator as a `char *` pointer. In that case, the implementation could choose to have `begin()`, `data()`, and `c_str()` all return the same pointer. But it could just as legitimately (if not as easily) return references to three different data objects.

Table F.2 lists the six constructors and one destructor for the `basic_string` template class. Note that all six constructors have an argument of the following form:

```
const Allocator& a = Allocator()
```

Recall that the term `Allocator` is the template parameter name for an `allocator` class to manage memory. The term `Allocator()` is the default constructor for that class. Thus, the constructors, by default, use the default version of the `allocator` object, but they give you the option of using some other version of the `allocator` object. Let's examine the constructors individually.

TABLE F.2   String Constructors

Constructor and Destructor Prototypes

```explicit basic_string(const Allocator& a = Allocator());```
```basic_string(const charT* s, const Allocator& a = Allocator());```
```basic_string(const basic_string& str, size_type pos = 0,```
```   size_type n = npos, const Allocator& a = Allocator());```
```basic_string(const charT* s, size_type n,```
```   const Allocator& a = Allocator());```
```basic_string(size_type n, charT c, const Allocator& a = Allocator());```

TABLE F.2   Continued

Constructor and Destructor Prototypes

```
template<class InputIterator>
basic_string(InputIterator begin, InputIterator end,
    const Allocator& a = Allocator());

~basic_string();
```

Default Constructor

This is the default constructor:

```
explicit basic_string(const Allocator& a = Allocator());
```

Typically, you would accept the default argument for the `allocator` class and would use the constructor to create empty strings:

```
string bean;
wstring theory;
```

The following relations hold after the constructor is called:

- The `data()` method returns a non-null pointer to which 0 can be added.

- The `size()` method returns 0.

- The return value for `capacity()` is not specified.

Suppose you assign the value returned by `data()` to a pointer `str`. Then the first condition means `str + 0` is valid, which, in turn, means the expression `str[0]` is valid.

Constructor Using an Array

The next constructor lets you initialize a `string` object from a C-style string; more generally, it lets you initialize a `charT` specialization from an array of `charT` values:

```
basic_string(const charT* s, const Allocator& a = Allocator());
```

To determine how many characters to copy, the constructor applies the `traits::length()` method to the array pointed to by `s`. (The pointer `s` shall not be a null pointer.) For example, the statement

```
string toast("Here's looking at you, kid.");
```

initializes the `toast` object using the indicated character string. The `traits::length()` method for type `char` will use the null character to determine how many characters to copy.

The following relations hold after the constructor is called:

- The `data()` method returns a pointer to the first element of a copy of the array `s`.

- The `size()` method returns a value equal to `traits::length()`.

- The `capacity()` method returns a value at least as large as `size()`.

Constructor Using Part of an Array

The next constructor lets you initialize a **string** object from part of a C-style string; more generally, it lets you initialize a **charT** specialization from part of an array of **charT** values:

```
basic_string(const charT* s, size_type n, const Allocator& a = Allocator());
```

This constructor copies a total of n characters from the array pointed to by **s** to the constructed object. Note that it doesn't stop copying if **s** has fewer characters than n. If n exceeds the length of **s**, the constructor will interpret the contents of memory following the string as if they held data of type **charT**.

The constructor requires that **s** is not a null pointer and that **n < npos**. (Recall that **npos** is a static class constant equal to the maximum possible number of elements in a string.) If **n** equals **npos**, the constructor throws an **out_of_range** exception. (Because n is of type **size_type** and **npos** is the maximum **size_type** value, n cannot be greater than **npos**.) Otherwise, the following relations hold after the constructor is called:

- The **data()** method returns a pointer to the first element of a copy of the array **s**.
- The **size()** method returns n.
- The **capacity()** method returns a value at least as large as **size()**.

Copy Constructor

The copy constructor provides several arguments with default values:

```
basic_string(const basic_string& str, size_type pos = 0, size_type n = npos,
    const Allocator& a = Allocator());
```

Calling it with only a **basic_string** argument initializes the new object to the **string** argument:

```
string mel("I'm ok!");
string ida(mel);
```

Here **ida** would get a copy of the string managed by **mel**.

The optional second argument **pos** specifies a location in the source string from which to begin the copying:

```
string att("Telephone home.");
string et(att, 4);
```

Position numbers begin with 0, so position 4 is the **p** character. Thus, **et** is initialized to "phone home.".

The optional third argument n specifies the maximum number of characters to copy. Thus,

```
string att("Telephone home.");
string pt(att, 4, 5);
```

will initialize pt to the string "phone". However, this constructor will not go past the end of the source string; for example,

```
string pt(att, 4, 200)
```

will stop after copying the period. Thus, the constructor actually copies a number of characters equal to the lesser of n and of str.size() - pos.

This constructor requires that pos <= str.size(), that is, that the initial position copied to is inside the source string; if this is not the case, it throws an out_of_range exception. Otherwise, letting copy_len represent the lesser of n and of str.size() - pos, the following relations hold after the constructor is called:

- The data() method returns a pointer to a copy of copy_len elements copied from the string str, starting with position pos in str.
- The size() method returns copy_len.
- The capacity() method returns a value at least as large as size().

Constructor Using n Copies of a Character

The next constructor creates a string object consisting of n consecutive characters all having the value c:

```
basic_string(size_type n, charT c, const Allocator& a = Allocator());
```

The constructor requires that n < npos. If n equals npos, the constructor throws an out_of_range exception. Otherwise, the following relations hold after the constructor is called:

- The data() method returns a pointer to the first element of a string of n elements, each set to c.
- The size() method returns n.
- The capacity() method returns a value at least as large as size().

Constructor Using a Range

The final constructor uses an iterator-defined range in the style of the STL:

```
template<class InputIterator>
basic_string(InputIterator begin, InputIterator end,
             const Allocator& a = Allocator());
```

The begin iterator points to the element in the source at which copying begins, and end points to one past the last location to be copied.

You can use this form with arrays, strings, or STL containers:

```
char cole[40] = "Old King Cole was a merry old soul.";
string title(cole + 4, cole + 8);
vector<char> input;
char ch;
```

```
while (cin.get(ch) && ch != '\n')
    input.push_back(ch);
string str_input(input.begin(), input.end());
```

In the first use, `InputIterator` is evaluated to type `const char *`. In the second use, `InputIterator` is evaluated to type `vector<char>::iterator`.

The following relations hold after the constructor is called:

- The `data()` method returns a pointer to the first element of a string formed from copying elements from the range [`begin`, `end`).

- The `size()` method returns the distance between `begin` and `end`. (The distance is measured in units equal to the size of data type obtained when the iterator is dereferenced.)

- The `capacity()` method returns a value at least as large as `size()`.

Memory Miscellany

Several methods deal with memory; for example, clearing memory contents, resizing a string, adjusting the capacity of a string. Table F.3 lists some memory-related methods.

TABLE F.3   Some Memory-Related Methods

Method	Effect
`void resize(size_type n)`	Throws an `out_of_range` exception if n > npos. Otherwise, changes size of string to n, truncating the end of the string if n < `size()` and padding the string with `charT(0)` characters if n > `size()`.
`void resize(size_type n, charT c)`	Throws an `out_of_range` exception if n > npos. Otherwise, changes size of string to n, truncating the end of the string if n < `size()` and padding the string with the character c if n > `size()`.
`void reserve(size_type res_arg = 0)`	Sets `capacity()` to greater than or equal to res_arg. Because this reallocates the string, it voids previous references, iterators, and pointers into the string.
`void clear()`	Removes all characters from a string.
`bool empty() const`	Returns `true` if `size()` == 0.

String Access

There are four methods for accessing individual characters, two using the [ ] operator, and two using the at() method:

```
reference operator[](size_type pos);
const_reference operator[](size_type pos) const;
reference at(size_type n);
const_reference at(size_type n) const;
```

The first operator[]() method allows you to access an individual element of a string using array notation; it can be used to retrieve or alter the value. The second operator[]() method can be used with const objects, and it can be used only to retrieve the value:

```
string word("tack");
cout << word[0];    // display the t
word[3] = 't';      // overwrite the k with a t
const ward("garlic");
cout << ward[2];    // display the r
```

The at() methods provide similar access, except the index is provided in function argument notation:

```
string word("tack");
cout << word.at(0);    // display the t
```

The difference (besides that of syntax) is that the at() methods provide bounds checking and throw an out_of_range exception if pos >= size(). Note that pos is type size_type, which is unsigned; therefore, a negative value is impossible for pos. The operator[]() methods don't do bounds checking, so the behavior is undefined if pos >= size(), except that the const version returns the null character equivalent if pos == size().

Thus, you get a choice between safety (using at() and testing for exceptions) or execution speed (using array notation).

There also is a function that returns a new string that is a substring of the original:

```
basic_string substr(size_type pos = 0, size_type n = npos) const;
```

It returns a string that's a copy of the string starting at position pos and going for n characters or to the end of the string, whichever comes first. For example, the following initializes pet to "donkey":

```
string message("Maybe the donkey will learn to sing.");
string pet(message.substr(10, 6));
```

Basic Assignment

There are three overloaded assignment methods:

```
basic_string& operator=(const basic_string& str);
basic_string& operator=(const charT* s);
basic_string& operator=(charT c);
```

The first assigns one **string** object to another, the second assigns a C-style string to a **string** object, and the third assigns a single character to a **string** object. Thus, all of the following operations are possible:

```
string name("George Wash");
string pres, veep, source;
pres = name;
veep = "Road Runner";
source = 'X';
```

String Searching

The **string** class provides six search functions, each with four prototypes. Let's describe them briefly.

The find() Family

Here are the **find()** prototypes:

```
size_type find (const basic_string& str, size_type pos = 0) const;
size_type find (const charT* s, size_type pos = 0) const;
size_type find (const charT* s, size_type pos, size_type n) const;
size_type find (charT c, size_type pos = 0) const;
```

The first member returns the position of the beginning of the first occurrence of the substring **str** in the invoking object; with the search beginning at position **pos**. If the substring is not found, the method returns **npos**.

```
string longer("That is a funny hat.");
string shorter("hat");
size_type loc1 = longer.find(shorter);          // sets loc1 to 1
size_type loc2 = longer.find(shorter, loc1 + 1); // sets loc2 to 16
```

Because the second search begins at position 2 (the **a** in **That**), the first occurrence of **hat** it finds is near the end of the string. To test for failure, use the **string::npos** value:

```
if (loc1 == string::npos)
    cout << "Not found\n";
```

The second method does the same thing except it uses an array of characters instead of a **string** object as the substring:

```
size_type loc3 = longer.find("is");             //sets loc3 to 5
```

The third method does the same as the second, except it uses only the first **n** characters of the string **s**. The effect is the same as using the **basic_string(const charT* s, size_type n)** constructor and using the resulting object as the **string** argument to the first form of **find()**. For example, the following searches for the substring **"fun"**:

```
size_type loc4 = longer.find("funds", 3);       //sets loc4 to 10
```

The fourth method does the same as the first except it uses a single character instead of a `string` object as the substring:

```
size_type loc5 = longer.find('a');                //sets loc5 to 2
```

The rfind() Family

The `rfind()` methods have these prototypes:

```
size_type rfind(const basic_string& str, size_type pos = npos) const;
size_type rfind(const charT* s, size_type pos = npos) const;
size_type rfind(const charT* s, size_type pos, size_type n) const;
size_type rfind(charT c, size_type pos = npos) const;
```

These methods work like the analogous `find()` methods, except they find the last occurrence of a string or character that starts at or before position `pos`. If the substring is not found, the method returns `npos`.

```
string longer("That is a funny hat.");
string shorter("hat");
size_type loc1 = longer.rfind(shorter);          // sets loc1 to 16
size_type loc2 = longer.rfind(shorter, loc1 - 1); // sets loc2 to 1
```

The find_first_of() Family

The `find_first_of()` methods have these prototypes:

```
size_type find_first_of(const basic_string& str, size_type pos = 0) const;
size_type find_first_of(const charT* s, size_type pos, size_type n) const;
size_type find_first_of(const charT* s, size_type pos = 0) const;
size_type find_first_of(charT c, size_type pos = 0) const;
```

These methods work like the corresponding `find()` methods except instead of looking for a match of the entire substring, they look for the first match for any single character in the substring.

```
string longer("That is a funny hat.");
string shorter("fluke");
size_type loc1 = longer.find_first_of(shorter);  // sets loc1 to 10
size_type loc2 = longer.find_first_of("fat");    // sets loc2 to 2
```

The first occurrence of any of the five characters of `fluke`, in `longer` is the `f` in `funny`. The first occurrence of any of three characters of `fat` in `longer` is the `a` in `That`.

The find_last_of() Family

The `find_last_of()` methods have these prototypes:

```
size_type find_last_of (const basic_string& str,
                        size_type pos = npos) const;
size_type find_last_of (const charT* s, size_type pos, size_type n) const;
size_type find_last_of (const charT* s, size_type pos = npos) const;
size_type find_last_of (charT c, size_type pos = npos) const;
```

These methods work like the corresponding `rfind()` methods except instead of looking for a match of the entire substring, they look for the last match for any single character in the substring.

```
string longer("That is a funny hat.");
string shorter("hat");
size_type loc1 = longer.find_last_of(shorter);  // sets loc1 to 18
size_type loc2 = longer.find_last_of("any");    // sets loc2 to 17
```

The last occurrence of any of the three letters of **hat** in **longer** is the **t** in **hat**. The last occurrence of any of the three characters of **any** in **longer** is the **a** in **hat**.

The `find_first_not_of()` Family

The `find_first_not_of()` methods have these prototypes:

```
size_type find_first_not_of(const basic_string& str,
                            size_type pos = 0) const;
size_type find_first_not_of(const charT* s, size_type pos,
                            size_type n) const;
size_type find_first_not_of(const charT* s, size_type pos = 0) const;
size_type find_first_not_of(charT c, size_type pos = 0) const;
```

These methods work like the corresponding `find_first_of()` methods, except they search for the first occurrence of any character not in the substring.

```
string longer("That is a funny hat.");
string shorter("This");
size_type loc1 = longer.find_first_not_of(shorter);    // sets loc1 to 2
size_type loc2 = longer.find_first_not_of("Thatch");   // sets loc2 to 4
```

The **a** in **That** is the first character in **longer** that does not appear in **This**. The first space in the **longer** string is the first character not present in **Thatch**.

The `find_last_not_of()` Family

The `find_last_not_of()` methods have these prototypes:

```
size_type find_last_not_of (const basic_string& str,
                            size_type pos = npos) const;
size_type find_last_not_of (const charT* s, size_type pos,
                            size_type n) const;
size_type find_last_not_of (const charT* s, size_type pos = npos) const;
size_type find_last_not_of (charT c, size_type pos = npos) const;
```

These methods work like the corresponding `find_last_of()` methods, except they search for the last occurrence of any character not in the substring.

```
string longer("That is a funny hat.");
string shorter("That.");
size_type loc1 = longer.find_last_not_of(shorter);     // sets loc1 to 15
size_type loc2 = longer.find_last_not_of(shorter, 10); // sets loc2 to 10
```

The last space in **longer** is the last character in **longer** that does not appear in **shorter**. The **f** in the **longer** string is the last character not present in **shorter** found up through position 10.

Comparison Methods and Functions

The string class offers methods and functions for comparing two strings. First, here are the method prototypes:

```
int compare(const basic_string& str) const;
int compare(size_type pos1, size_type n1,
            const basic_string& str) const;
int compare(size_type pos1, size_type n1,
            const basic_string& str,
            size_type pos2, size_type n2) const;
int compare(const charT* s) const;
int compare(size_type pos1, size_type n1,
            const charT* s, size_type n2 = npos) const;
```

These methods use a traits::compare() method defined for the particular character type used for the string. The first method returns a value less than 0 if the first string precedes the second string according to the ordering supplied by traits::compare(). It returns 0 if the two strings are the same, and it returns a value greater than 0 if the first string follows the second. If two string are identical to the end of the shorter of the two strings, the shorter string precedes the longer string.

```
string s1("bellflower");
string s2("bell");
string s3("cat");
int a13 = s1.compare(s3); // a13 is < 0
int a12 = s1.compare(s2); // a12 is> 0
```

The second method is like the first, except that it just uses n1 characters starting from position pos1 in the first string for the comparison.

```
string s1("bellflower");
string s2("bell");
int a2 = s1.compare(0, 4, s2); // a2 is 0
```

The third method is like the first, except that it just uses n1 characters starting from position pos1 in the first string and n2 characters starting from position pos2 in the second string for the comparison. For example, the following compares the out in stout to the out in about:

```
string st1("stout boar");
string st2("mad about ewe");
int a3 = st1.compare(2, 3, st2, 6, 3);  // a3 is 0
```

The fourth method is like the first, except it uses a string array instead of a string object for the second string.

The fifth method is like the third, except it uses a string array instead of a string object for the second string.

The non-member comparison functions are overloaded relational operators:

```
operator==()
operator<()
operator<=()
```

```
operator>()
operator>=()
operator!=()
```

Each operator is overloaded so that it can compare a **string** object to a **string** object, a **string** object to a string array, and a string array to a **string** object. They are defined in terms of the **compare()** method, so they provide a notationally more convenient way of making comparisons.

String Modifiers

The **string** class provides several methods for modifying strings. Most come with an abundance of overloaded versions so that they can be used with **string** objects, string arrays, individual characters, and iterator ranges.

Appending and Adding

You can append one string to another by using the overloaded **+=** operator or by using an **append()** method. All throw a **length_error** exception if the result would be longer than the maximum string size. The **+=** operators let you append a **string** object, a string array, or an individual character to another string:

```
basic_string& operator+=(const basic_string& str);
basic_string& operator+=(const charT* s);
basic_string& operator+=(charT c);
```

The **append()** methods also let you append a **string** object, a string array, or an individual character to another string. In addition, they let you append part of a **string** object by specifying an initial position and a number of characters to append or else by specifying a range. You can append part of a string by specifying how many characters of the string to use. The version for appending a character lets you specify how many instances of that character to copy.

```
basic_string& append(const basic_string& str);
basic_string& append(const basic_string& str, size_type pos,
                     size_type n);
template<class InputIterator>
  basic_string& append(InputIterator first, InputIterator last);
basic_string& append(const charT* s);
basic_string& append(const charT* s, size_type n);
basic_string& append(size_type n, charT c);  // append n copies of c
```

Here are a couple of examples:

```
string test("The");
test.append("ory");  // test is "Theory"
test.append(3,'!');  // test is "Theory!!!"
```

The **operator+()** function is overloaded to enable string concatenation. The overloaded functions don't modify a string; instead, they create a new string consisting of one string appended to a second. The addition functions are not member functions, and they allow you to add a string object to a string object, a string array to a string object, a string object to a string array, a character to a string object, and a string object to a character. Here are some examples:

```
string st1("red");
string st2("rain");
string st3 = st1 + "uce";  // st3 is "reduce"
string st4 = 't' + st2;    // st4 is "train"
string st5 = st1 + st2;    // st5 is "redrain"
```

More Assignment

In addition to the basic assignment operator, the string class provides assign() methods, which allow you to assign a whole string or a part of a string or a sequence of identical characters to a string object.

```
basic_string& assign(const basic_string&);
basic_string& assign(const basic_string& str, size_type pos,
                     size_type n);
basic_string& assign(const charT* s, size_type n);
basic_string& assign(const charT* s);
basic_string& assign(size_type n, charT c); // assign n copies of c
template<class InputIterator>
  basic_string& assign(InputIterator first, InputIterator last);
```

Here are a couple of examples:

```
string test;
string stuff("set tubs clones ducks");
test.assign(stuff, 1, 5);  // test is "et tu"
test.assign(6, '#');       // test is "######"
```

Insertion Methods

The insert() methods let you insert a string object, string array, character, or several characters into a string object. The methods are similar to the append() methods, except they take an additional argument indicating where to insert the new material. This argument may be a position or an iterator. The material is inserted before the insertion point. Several of the methods return a reference to the resulting string. If pos1 is beyond the end of the target string or if pos2 is beyond the end of the string to be inserted, a method throws an out_of_range exception. If the resulting string will be larger than the maximum size, a method throws a length_error exception.

```
basic_string& insert(size_type pos1, const basic_string& str);
basic_string& insert(size_type pos1, const basic_string& str,
                     size_type pos2, size_type n);
basic_string& insert(size_type pos, const charT* s, size_type n);
basic_string& insert(size_type pos, const charT* s);
basic_string& insert(size_type pos, size_type n, charT c);
iterator insert(iterator p, charT c = charT());
void insert(iterator p, size_type n, charT c);
template<class InputIterator>
  void insert(iterator p, InputIterator first, InputIterator last);
```

For example, the following code inserts the string `"former "` before the b in `"The banker."`:

```
string st3("The banker.");
st3.insert(4, "former ");
```

Then the following code inserts the string `" waltzed"` (not including the !, which would be the ninth character, just before the period at the end of `"The former banker."`:

```
st3.insert(st3.size() - 1, " waltzed!", 8);
```

Erase Methods

The `erase()` methods remove characters from a string. Here are the prototypes:

```
basic_string& erase(size_type pos = 0, size_type n = npos);
iterator erase(iterator position);
iterator erase(iterator first, iterator last);
```

The first form removes the character from position **pos** to n characters later, or the end of the string, whichever comes first. The second removes the single character referenced by the iterator position and returns an iterator to the next element, or, if there are no more elements, returns **end()**. The third removes the characters in the range [**first**, **last**); that is, including **first** and up to but not including **last**). The method returns an iterator to the element following the last element erased.

Replacement Methods

The various `replace()` methods identify part of a string to be replaced and identify the replacement. The part to be replaced can be identified by an initial position and a character count or by an iterator range. The replacement can be a **string** object, a string array, or a particular character duplicated several times. Replacement **string** objects and arrays can further be modified by indicating a particular portion, using a position and a count, just a count, or an iterator range.

```
basic_string& replace(size_type pos1, size_type n1, const basic_string& str);
basic_string& replace(size_type pos1, size_type n1, const basic_string& str,
                      size_type pos2, size_type n2);
basic_string& replace(size_type pos, size_type n1, const charT* s,
                      size_type n2);
basic_string& replace(size_type pos, size_type n1, const charT* s);
basic_string& replace(size_type pos, size_type n1, size_type n2, charT c);
basic_string& replace(iterator i1, iterator i2, const basic_string& str);
basic_string& replace(iterator i1, iterator i2, const charT* s, size_type n);
basic_string& replace(iterator i1, iterator i2, const charT* s);
basic_string& replace(iterator i1, iterator i2,
                      size_type n, charT c);
template<class InputIterator>
  basic_string& replace(iterator i1, iterator i2,
                        InputIterator j1, InputIterator j2);
```

Here is an example:

```
string test("Take a right turn at Main Street.");
test.replace(7,5,"left"); // replace right with left
```

Other Modifying Methods: copy() and swap()

The copy() method copies a string object, or part thereof, to a designated string array:

```
size_type copy(charT* s, size_type n, size_type pos = 0) const;
```

Here s points to the destination array, n indicates the number of characters to copy, and pos indicates the position in the string object from which copying begins. Copying proceeds for n characters or until the last character in the string object, whichever comes first. The function returns the number of characters copied. The method does not append a null character, and it is up to the programmer to see that the array is large enough to hold the copy.

Caution

The copy() method does not append a null character nor does it check that the destination array is large enough.

The swap() method swaps the contents of two string objects using a constant time algorithm:

```
void swap(basic_string<charT,traits,Allocator>&);
```

Output and Input

The string class overloads the << operator to display string objects. It returns a reference to the istream object so that output can be concatenated:

```
string claim("The string class has many features.");
cout << claim << endl;
```

The string class overloads the >> operator so that you can read input into a string:

```
string who;
cin >> who;
```

Input terminates on end-of-file, reading the maximum number of characters allowed in a string, or on reaching a whitespace character. (The definition of whitespace will depend on the character set and upon the type charT represents.)

There are two getline() functions. The first has this prototype:

```
template<class charT, class traits, class Allocator>
basic_istream<charT,traits>& getline(basic_istream<charT,traits>& is,
            basic_string<charT,traits,Allocator>& str, charT delim);
```

It reads characters from the input stream **is** into the string **str** until encountering the **delim** delimiter character, reaching the maximum size of the string, or encountering end-of-file. The **delim** character is read (removed from the input stream), but not stored. The second version lacks the third argument and uses the newline character (or its generalization) instead of **delim**:

```
string str1, str2;
getline(cin, str1);        // read to end-of-line
getline(cin, str2, '.');   // read to period
```

APPENDIX G

THE STL METHODS AND FUNCTIONS

T he STL aims to provide efficient implementations of common algorithms. It expresses these algorithms in general functions that can be used with any container satisfying the requirements for the particular algorithm and in methods that can be used with instantiations of particular container classes. This appendix assumes that you have some familiarity with the STL, such as might be gained from reading Chapter 16, "The `string` Class and the Standard Template Library." For example, this chapter assumes you know about iterators and constructors.

Members Common to All Containers

All containers define the types in Table G.1. In this table, `X` is a container type, such as `vector<int>`, and `T` is the type stored in the container, such as `int`.

TABLE G.1 Types Defined for All Containers

Type	Value
X::value_type	T, the element type
X::reference	Behaves like T &
X::const_reference	Behaves like const T &
X::iterator	Iterator type pointing to T, behaves like T *
X::const_iterator	Iterator type pointing to const T, behaves like const T *
X::difference_type	Signed integral type used to represent the distance from one iterator to another; for example, the difference between two pointers
X::size_type	Unsigned integral type size_type can represent size of data objects, number of elements, and subscripts

The class definition will use a `typedef` to define these members. You can use these types, to declare suitable variables. For example, the following takes a roundabout way to replace the first occurrence of `"bonus"` in a vector of `string` objects with `"bogus"` in order to show how you can use member types to declare variables.

```
vector<string> input;
string temp;
while (cin >> temp && temp != "quit")
    input.push_back(temp);
vector<string>::iterator want=
    find(input.begin(), input.end(), string("bonus"));
if (want != input.end())
{
    vector<string>::reference r = *want;
    r = "bogus";
}
```

This code makes r a reference to the element in input to which want points.

These types also can be used in more general code in which the type of container and element are generic. For example, suppose you want a min() function that takes as its argument a reference to a container and returns the smallest item in the container. This assumes that the < operator is defined for the value type and that you don't want to use the STL min_element() algorithm, which uses an iterator interface. Because the argument could be vector<int> or list<string> or deque<double>, use a template with a template parameter, such as Bag, to represent the container. So the argument type for the function will be const Bag & b. What about the return type? It should be the value type for the container, that is, Bag::value_type. However, at this point, Bag is just a template parameter, and the compiler has no way of knowing that the value_type member is actually a type. But you can use the typename keyword to clarify that a class member is a typedef:

```
vector<string>::value_type st;    // vector<string> a defined class
typename Bag::value_type m;       // Bag an as yet undefined type
```

For the first definition, the compiler has access to the vector template definition, which states that value_type is a typedef. For the second definition, the typename keyword promises that the combination Bag::value_type is a typedef. These considerations lead to the following definition:

```
template<typename Bag>
typename Bag::value_type min(const Bag & b)
{
    typename Bag::const_iterator it;
    typename Bag::value_type m = *b.begin();
    for (it = b.begin(); it != b.end(); ++it)
        if (*it < m)
            m = *it;
    return m;
}
```

You then could use this template function as follows:

```
vector<int> temperatures;
// input temperature values into the vector
int coldest = min(temperatures);
```

The temperatures parameter would cause Bag to be evaluated as vector<int> and typename Bag::value_type to be evaluated as int.

All containers also contain the member functions or operations listed in Table G.2. Again, X is a container type, such as vector<int>, and T is the type stored in the container, such as int. Also, a and b are values of type X.

TABLE G.2   Methods Defined for All Containers

Method/Operation	Description
begin()	Returns an iterator to the first element
end()	Returns an iterator to past-the-end
rbegin()	Returns a reverse iterator to past-the-end
rend()	Returns a reverse iterator to first element
size()	Returns number of elements
maxsize()	Returns the size of the largest possible container
empty()	Returns true if the container is empty
swap()	Swaps the contents of two containers
==	Returns true if two containers are the same size and have the same elements in the same order
!=	a != b is the same as !(a == b)
<	Returns true if a lexicographically precedes b
> operator>>	a > b is the same as b < a
<=	a <= b is the same as !(a > b)
>== operator>=>	a >= b is the same as !(a < b)

The > operator for a container assumes that the > operator is defined for the value type. A lexicographical comparison is a generalization of alphabetical sorting. It compares two containers element by element until encountering an element in one container that doesn't equal the corresponding element in the other container. In that case, the containers are considered to be in the same order as the non-corresponding pair of elements. For example, if two containers are identical through the first ten elements, but the eleventh element in the first container is less than the eleventh element in the second container, the first container precedes the second. If two containers compare equal until one runs out of elements, the shorter container precedes the longer.

Additional Members for Vectors, Lists, and Deques

Vectors, lists, and deques are all sequences, and they all have the methods listed in Table G.3. Again, X is a container type, such as `vector<int>`, and T is the type stored in the container, such as `int`, a is a value of type X, t is a value of `type X::value_type`, i and j are input iterators, q2 and p are iterators, q and q1 are dereferenceable iterators (you can apply the * operator to them), and n is an integer of `X::size_type`.

TABLE G.3   Methods Defined for Vectors, Lists, and Deques

Method	Description
`a.insert(p,t)`	Inserts a copy of t before p; returns an iterator pointing to the inserted copy of t. The default value for t is `T()`, that is, the value used for type T in the absence of explicit initialization.
`a.insert(p,n,t)`	Inserts n copies of t before p; no return value.
`a.insert(p,i,j)`	Inserts copies of the elements in range `[i,j)` before p, no return value.
`a.resize(n,t)`	If n > `a.size()`, inserts n - `a.size()` copies of t before `a.end()`; t has a default value of `T()`, that is, the value used for type T in the absence of explicit initialization. If n < `a.size()`, the elements following the nth element are erased.
`a.assign(i,j)`	Replaces the current contents of a with copies of the elements in range `[i,j)`.
`a.assign(n,t)`	Replaces the current contents of a with n copies of t. The default value for t is `T()`, the value used for type T in the absence of explicit initialization.
`a.erase(q)`	Erases the element pointed to by q; returns an iterator to the element that had followed q.
`a.erase(q1,q2)`	Erases the elements in the range `[q1,q2)`; returns an iterator pointing to the element q2 originally pointed to.
`a.clear()`	Same as `erase(a.begin(), a.end())`.
`a.front()`	Returns `*a.begin()` (the first element).
`a.back()`	Returns `*--a.end()` (the last element).
`a.push_back(t)`	Inserts t before `a.end()`.
`a.pop_back()`	Erases the last element.

Table G.4 lists methods common to two out of the three sequence classes.

TABLE G.4   Methods Defined for Some Sequences

Method	Description	Container
`a.push_front(t)`	Inserts a copy of `t` before the first element.	`list, deque`
`a.pop_front()`	Erases the first element.	`list, deque`
`a[n]`	Returns `*(a.begin() + n)`.	`vector, deque`
`a.at(n)`	Returns `*(a.begin() + n)`, throws `out_of_range` exception if n > `a.size()`.	`vector, deque`

The `vector` template additionally has the methods in Table G.5. Here, `a` is a `vector` container and `n` is an integer of `X::size_type`.

TABLE G.5   Additional Methods for Vectors

Method	Description
`a.capacity()`	Returns the total number of elements the vector can hold without requiring reallocation.
`a.reserve(n)`	Alerts object `a` that memory for at least n elements is needed. After the method call, the capacity will be at least n elements. Reallocation occurs if n is greater than the current capacity. If n is greater than `a.max_size()`, the method throws a `length_error` exception.

The `list` template additionally has the methods in Table G.6. Here, `a` and `b` are `list` containers, and `T` is the type stored in the list, such as `int`, `t` is a value of type `T`, `i` and `j` are input iterators, `q2` and `p` are iterators, `q` and `q1` are dereferenceable iterators, and `n` is an integer of `X::size_type`. The table uses the standard STL notation of [i, j) meaning the range from `i` up to, but not including `j`.

TABLE G.6   Additional Methods for Lists

Method	Description
`a.splice(p,b)`	Moves the contents of list **b** to list **a**, inserting them before p.
`a.splice(p,b,i)`	Moves the element in list **b** pointed to by **i** to before position **p** in list **a**.
`a.splice(p,b,i,j)`	Moves the elements in range [i,j) of list **b** to before position **p** in list **a**.
`a.remove(const T& t)`	Erases all elements in list **a** having the value **t**.
`a.remove_if(Predicate pred)`	Given that **i** is an iterator into the list **a**, erases all values for which `pred(*i)` is **true**. (A **Predicate** is a Boolean function or function object, as discussed in Chapter 15, "Friends, Exceptions, and More.")
`a.unique()`	Erases all but the first element from each group of consecutive equal elements.
`a.unique(BinaryPredicate bin_pred)`	Erases all but the first element from each group of consecutive elements for which `bin_pred(*i, *(i - 1))` is **true**. (A **BinaryPredicate** is a Boolean function or function object, as discussed in Chapter 15.)
`a.merge(b)`	Merges the contents of list **b** with list **a** using the < operator defined for the value type. If an element in **a** is equivalent to an element in **b**, the element from **a** is placed first. List **b** is empty after the merge.
`a.merge(b, Compare comp)`	Merges the contents of list **b** with list **a** using the **comp** function or function object. If an element in **a** is equivalent to an element in **b**, the element from **a** is placed first. List **b** is empty after the merge.
`a.sort()`	Sorts list **a** using the < operator.
`a.sort(Compare comp)`	Sorts list **a** using the **comp** function or function object.
`a.reverse()`	Reverses the order of the elements in list **a**.

Additional Members for Sets and Maps

Associative containers, of which sets and maps are models, have a **Key** template parameter and a **Compare** template parameter indicating, respectively, the type of the **key** used to order the contents and the function object, termed a *comparison object*, used to compare key values. For the `set` and `multiset` containers, the stored keys are the stored values, so the key type is the same as the value type. For the `map` and `multimap` containers, the stored values of one type (template parameter `T`) are associated with a key type (template parameter `Key`), and the value type is `pair<const Key, T>`. Associative containers introduce additional members to describe these features, as listed in Table G.7.

TABLE G.7 Types Defined for Associative Containers

Type	Value
`X::key_type`	`Key`, the key type
`X::key_compare`	`Compare`, which has a default value of `less<key_type>`
`X::value_compare`	A binary predicate type that is the same as `key_compare` for `set` and `multiset` and which supplies ordering for the `pair<const Key, T>` values in a `map` or `multimap`.
`X::mapped_type`	`T`, the type of the associated data (`map` and `multimap` only)

Associative containers provide the methods listed in Table G.8. In general, the comparison object need not require that values with the same key are identical; the term *equivalent keys* means that two values, which may or may not be equal, have the same key. In the table, `X` is a container class, `a` is an object of type `X`. If `X` uses unique keys (that is, is a `set` or `map`), `a_uniq` is an object of type `X`. If `X` uses multiple keys (that is, is a `multiset` or `multimap`), `a_eq` is an object of type `X`. As before, `i` and `j` are input iterators referring to elements of `value_type`, [i, j) is a valid range, `p` and `q2` are iterators to `a`, `q` and `q1` are dereferenceable iterators to `a`, [q1, q2) is a valid range, `t` is a value of `X::value_type` (which may be a pair). Also, `k` is a value of `X::key_type`.

TABLE G.8 Methods Defined for Sets, Multisets, Maps, and Multimaps

Method	Description
`a.key_comp()`	Returns the comparison object used in constructing `a`.
`a.value_comp()`	Returns an object of the `value_compare` type.
`a_uniq.insert(t)`	Inserts the value `t` into the container `a` if and only if `a` does not yet contain a value with an equivalent key. The method returns a value of type `pair<iterator,bool>`. The `bool` component is `true` if insertion occurred and `false` otherwise. The iterator component points to the element whose key is equivalent to the key of `t`.
`a_eq.insert(t)`	Inserts `t` and returns an iterator pointing to its location.

TABLE G.8   Continued

Method	Description
a.insert(p,t)	Inserts t using p as a hint to where insert() should begin its search. If a is a container with unique keys, insertion takes place if and only if a doesn't contain an element with an equivalent key; otherwise, insertion takes place. Whether or not insertion takes place, the method returns an iterator pointing to the location with an equivalent key.
a.insert(i,j)	Inserts elements from the range [i,j) into a.
a.erase(k)	Erases all elements in a whose keys are equivalent to k and returns the number of elements erased.
a.erase(q)	Erases the element pointed to by q.
a.erase(q1,q2)	Erases the elements in the range [q1,q2).
a.clear()	Same as erase(a.begin(), a.end()).
a.find(k)	Returns an iterator pointing to an element whose key is equivalent to k; returns a.end() if no such element is found.
a.count(k)	Returns the number of elements having keys equivalent to k.
a.lower_bound(k)	Returns an iterator to the first element with a key not less than k.
a.upper_bound(k)	Returns an iterator to the first element with a key greater than k.
a.equal_range(k)	Returns a pair whose first member is a.lower_bound(k) and whose second member is a.upper_bound(k).
a.operator[](k)	Returns a reference to the value associated with the key k (map containers only).

STL Functions

The STL algorithm library, supported by the `algorithm` and `numeric` header files, provides a large number of non-member, iterator-based template functions. As discussed in Chapter 16, the template parameter names are chosen to indicate what concept particular parameters should model. For example, `ForwardIterator` is used to indicate that a parameter should, at the minimum, model the requirements of a forward iterator, and `Predicate` is used to indicate a parameter that should be a function object with one argument and a `bool` return value. The standard divides the algorithms into four groups: non-modifying sequence operations, mutating sequence operations, sorting and related operators, and numeric operations. The term *sequence operation* indicates the function takes a pair of iterators as arguments to define a range, or sequence, to be operated upon. The term **mutating** means the function is allowed to alter the container.

Non-Modifying Sequence Operations

Table G.9 summarizes the non-modifying sequence operations. Arguments are not shown, and overloaded functions are listed just once. A fuller description including the prototypes follows the table. Thus, you can scan the table to get an idea of what a function does and then look up the details if you find the function appealing.

TABLE G.9   Non-Modifying Sequence Operations

Function	Description
`for_each()`	Applies a non-modifying function object to each element in a range.
`find()`	Finds the first occurrence of a value in a range.
`find_if()`	Finds the first value satisfying a predicate test criterion in a range.
`find_end()`	Finds the last occurrence of a subsequence whose values match the values of a second sequence. Matching may be by equality or by applying a binary predicate.
`find_first_of()`	Finds the first occurrence of any element of a second sequence that matches a value in the first sequence. Matching may be by equality or be evaluated with a binary predicate.
`adjacent_find()`	Finds the first element that matches the element immediately following it. Matching may be by equality or be evaluated with a binary predicate.
`count()`	Returns the number of times a given value occurs in a range.
`count_if()`	Returns the number of times a given value matches values in a range, with a match determined by using a binary predicate.
`mismatch()`	Finds the first element in one range that does not match the corresponding element in a second range and returns iterators to both. Matching may be by equality or be evaluated with a binary predicate.
`equal()`	Returns **true** if each element in one range matches the corresponding element in a second range. Matching may be by equality or be evaluated with a binary predicate.
`search()`	Finds the first occurrence of a subsequence whose values match the values of a second sequence. Matching may be by equality or by applying a binary predicate.
`search_n()`	Finds the first subsequence of *n* elements that each match a given value. Matching may be by equality or by applying a binary predicate.

Now let's look at the prototypes. Pairs of iterators indicate ranges, with the chosen template parameter name indicating the type of iterator. As usual a range of the form [first, last) goes from first up to, but not including last. Some functions take two ranges, which need not be in the same kind of container. For example, you can use equal() to compare a list to a vector. Functions passed as arguments are function objects, which can be pointers (of which function names are an example) or objects for which the () operation is defined. As in Chapter 16, a predicate is a Boolean function with one argument, and a binary predicate is a Boolean function with two arguments. (The functions need not be type bool as long as they return a 0 value for false and a non-zero for true.)

```
template<class InputIterator, class Function>
Function for_each(InputIterator first, InputIterator last, Function f);
```

The for_each() function applies function object f to each element in the range [first, last). It also returns f.

```
template<class InputIterator, class T>
InputIterator find(InputIterator first, InputIterator last, const T& value);
```

The find() function returns an iterator to the first element in the range [first, last) that has the value value; it returns last if the item is not found.

```
template<class InputIterator, class Predicate>
InputIterator find_if(InputIterator first, InputIterator last,
                  Predicate pred);
```

The find_if() function returns an iterator it to the first element in the range [first, last) for which the function object call pred(*i) is true; it returns last if the item is not found.

```
template<class ForwardIterator1, class ForwardIterator2>
ForwardIterator1 find_end(ForwardIterator1 first1, ForwardIterator1 last1,
                     ForwardIterator2 first2, ForwardIterator2 last2);

template<class ForwardIterator1, class ForwardIterator2,
    class BinaryPredicate>
ForwardIterator1 find_end(ForwardIterator1 first1, ForwardIterator1 last1,
                     ForwardIterator2 first2, ForwardIterator2 last2,
                     BinaryPredicate pred);
```

The find_end() function returns an iterator it to the last element in the range [first1, last1) that marks the beginning of a subsequence that matches the contents of the range [first2, last2). The first version uses the == operator for the value type to compare elements. The second version uses the binary predicate function object pred to compare elements. That is, elements pointed to by it1 and it2 match if pred(*it1, *it2) is true. Both return last1 if the item is not found.

```
template<class ForwardIterator1, class ForwardIterator2>
ForwardIterator1 find_first_of(
                ForwardIterator1 first1, ForwardIterator1 last1,
                ForwardIterator2 first2, ForwardIterator2 last2);

template<class ForwardIterator1, class ForwardIterator2,
        class BinaryPredicate>
```

```
ForwardIterator1 find_first_of(
                ForwardIterator1 first1, ForwardIterator1 last1,
                ForwardIterator2 first2, ForwardIterator2 last2,
                BinaryPredicate pred);
```

The `find_first_of()` function returns an iterator `it` to the first element in the range
[`first1`, `last1`) that matches any element of the range [`first2`, `last2`). The first version uses
the == operator for the value type to compare elements. The second version uses the binary
predicate function object `pred` to compare elements. That is, elements pointed to by `it1` and
`it2` match if `pred(*it1, *it2)` is `true`. Both return `last1` if the item is not found.

```
template<class ForwardIterator>
ForwardIterator adjacent_find(ForwardIterator first, ForwardIterator last);
```

```
template<class ForwardIterator, class BinaryPredicate>
ForwardIterator adjacent_find(ForwardIterator first, ForwardIterator last,
                        BinaryPredicate pred);
```

The `adjacent_find()` function returns an iterator `it` to the first element in the range
[`first1`, `last1`) such that the element matches the following element. The function returns
`last` if no such pair is found. The first version uses the == operator for the value type to compare elements. The second version uses the binary predicate function object `pred` to compare
elements. That is, elements pointed to by `it1` and `it2` match if `pred(*it1, *it2)` is `true`.

```
template<class InputIterator, class T>
iterator_traits<InputIterator>::difference_type count(
                InputIterator first, InputIterator last, const T& value);
```

The `count()` function returns the number of elements in the range [`first`, `last`) that match
the value `value`. The == operator for the value type is used to compare values. The return type
is an integer type large enough to contain the maximum number of items the container can
hold.

```
template<class InputIterator, class Predicate>
iterator_traits<InputIterator>::difference_type count_if(
                InputIterator first, InputIterator last, Predicate pred);
```

The `count if()` function returns the number of elements in the range [`first`, `last`) for
which the function object `pred` returns a `true` value when passed the element as an argument.

```
template<class InputIterator1, class InputIterator2>
pair<InputIterator1, InputIterator2> mismatch(InputIterator1 first1,
                    InputIterator1 last1, InputIterator2 first2);
```

```
template<class InputIterator1, class InputIterator2, class BinaryPredicate>
pair<InputIterator1, InputIterator2> mismatch(InputIterator1 first1,
                    InputIterator1 last1, InputIterator2 first2,
                    BinaryPredicate pred);
```

Each of the `mismatch()` functions finds the first element in range [`first1`, `last1`) that doesn't
match the corresponding element in the range beginning at `first2` and returns a pair holding
iterators to the two mismatching elements. If no mismatch is found, the return value is
`pair<last1, first2 + (last1 - first1)>`. The first version uses the == operator to test

matching. The second version uses the binary predicate function object **pred** to compare elements. That is, elements pointed to by **it1** and **it2** don't match if **pred(*it1, *it2)** is **false**.

```
template<class InputIterator1, class InputIterator2>
bool equal(InputIterator1 first1, InputIterator1 last1,
          InputIterator2 first2);

template<class InputIterator1, class InputIterator2, class BinaryPredicate>
bool equal(InputIterator1 first1, InputIterator1 last1,
          InputIterator2 first2, BinaryPredicate pred);
```

The **equal()** function returns **true** if each element in the range [**first1**, **last1**) matches the corresponding element in the sequence beginning at **first2** and **false** otherwise. The first version uses the **==** operator for the value type to compare elements. The second version uses the binary predicate function object **pred** to compare elements. That is, elements pointed to by **it1** and **it2** match if **pred(*it1, *it2)** is **true**.

```
template<class ForwardIterator1, class ForwardIterator2>
ForwardIterator1 search(ForwardIterator1 first1, ForwardIterator1 last1,
                   ForwardIterator2 first2, ForwardIterator2 last2);

template<class ForwardIterator1, class ForwardIterator2,
       class BinaryPredicate>
ForwardIterator1 search(ForwardIterator1 first1, ForwardIterator1 last1,
                   ForwardIterator2 first2, ForwardIterator2 last2,
                   BinaryPredicate pred);
```

The **search()** function finds the first occurrence in the range [**first1**, **last1**) that matches the corresponding sequence found in range [**first2**, **last2**). It returns **last1** if no such sequence is found. The first version uses the **==** operator for the value type to compare elements. The second version uses the binary predicate function object **pred** to compare elements. That is, elements pointed to by **it1** and **it2** match if **pred(*it1, *it2)** is **true**.

```
template<class ForwardIterator, class Size, class T>
ForwardIterator  search_n(ForwardIterator first, ForwardIterator last,
                     Size count, const T& value);

template<class ForwardIterator, class Size, class T, class BinaryPredicate>
ForwardIterator search_n(ForwardIterator first, ForwardIterator last,
                     Size count, const T& value, BinaryPredicate pred);
```

The **search_n()** function finds the first occurrence in the range [**first1**, **last1**) that matches the sequence consisting of **count** consecutive occurrences of **value**. It returns **last1** if no such sequence is found. The first version uses the **==** operator for the value type to compare elements. The second version uses the binary predicate function object **pred** to compare elements. That is, elements pointed to by **it1** and **it2** match if **pred(*it1, *it2)** is **true**.

Mutating Sequence Operations

Table G.10 summarizes the mutating sequence operations. Arguments are not shown, and overloaded functions are listed just once. A fuller description including the prototypes follows the table. Thus, you can scan the table to get an idea of what a function does; then look up the details if you find the function appealing.

TABLE G.10   Mutating Sequence Operations

Function	Description
copy()	Copies elements from a range to a location identified by an iterator.
copy_backward()	Copies elements from a range to a location identified by an iterator. Copying begins at the end of the range and proceeds backwards.
swap()	Exchanges two values stored at locations specified by references.
swap_ranges()	Exchanges corresponding values in two ranges.
iter_swap()	Exchanges two values stored at locations specified by iterators.
transform()	Applies a function object to each element in a range (or to each pair of elements in a pair of ranges), copying the return value to the corresponding location of another range.
replace()	Replaces each occurrence of a value in a range with another value.
replace_if()	Replaces each occurrence of a value in a range with another value if a predicate function object applied to the original value returns true.
replace_copy()	Copies one range to another, replacing each occurrence of a specified value with another value.
replace_copy_if()	Copies one range to another, replacing each value for which a predicate function object is true with an indicated value.
fill()	Sets each value in a range to an indicated value.
fill_n()	Sets n consecutive elements to a value.
generate()	Sets each value in a range to the return value of a generator, which is a function object that takes no arguments.
generate_n()	Sets the first n values in a range to the return value of a generator, which is a function object that takes no arguments.
remove()	Removes all occurrences of an indicated value from a range and returns a past-the-end iterator for the resulting range.
remove_if()	Removes all occurrences of values for which a predicate object returns true from a range and returns a past-the-end iterator for the resulting range.
remove_copy()	Copies elements from one range to another, omitting elements that equal a specified value.
remove_copy_if()	Copies elements from one range to another, omitting elements for which a predicate function object returns true.
unique()	Reduces each sequence of two or more equivalent elements in a range to a single element.

TABLE G.10   Continued

Function	Description
unique_copy()	Copies elements from one range to another, reducing each sequence of two or more equivalent elements to one.
reverse()	Reverses the elements in a range.
reverse_copy()	Copies a range in reverse order to a second range.
rotate()	Treats a range as a circular ordering and rotates the elements left.
rotate_copy()	Copies one range to another in a rotated order.
random_shuffle()	Randomly rearranges the elements in a range.
partition()	Places all the elements that satisfy a predicate function object before all elements that don't.
stable_partition()	Places all the elements that satisfy a predicate function object before all elements that don't. The relative order of elements in each group is preserved.

Now let's go to the prototypes. As you saw earlier, pairs of iterators indicate ranges, with the chosen template parameter name indicating the type of iterator. As usual a range of the form [first, last) goes from first up to, but not including last. Functions passed as arguments are function objects, which can be function pointers or objects for which the () operation is defined. As in Chapter 16, a predicate is a Boolean function with one argument, and a binary predicate is a Boolean function with two arguments. (The functions need not be type bool as long as they return a 0 value for false and a non-zero for true.) Also, as in Chapter 15, a unary function object is one taking a single argument, and a binary function object is one taking two arguments.

```
template<class InputIterator, class OutputIterator>
OutputIterator copy(InputIterator first, InputIterator last,
                OutputIterator result);
```

The copy() function copies the elements in the range [first, last) into the range [result, result + (last - first)). It returns result + (last - first), that is, an iterator pointing one past the last copied-to location. The function requires that result not be in the range [first, last), that is, the target can't overlap the source.

```
template<class BidirectionalIterator1, class BidirectionalIterator2>
BidirectionalIterator2 copy_backward(BidirectionalIterator1 first,
        BidirectionalIterator1 last, BidirectionalIterator2 result);
```

The copy_backward() function copies the elements in the range [first, last) into the range [result -(last - first), result). Copying begins with the element at last -1 being copied to location result - 1, and proceeds backwards from there to first. It returns result - (last - first), that is, an iterator pointing one past the last copied-to location.

The function requires that `result` not be in the range [`first`, `last`). However, because copying is done backwards, it is possible for the target and source to overlap.

```
template<class T> void swap(T& a, T& b);
```

The `swap()` function exchanges values stored at two locations specified by references.

```
template<class ForwardIterator1, class ForwardIterator2>
ForwardIterator2 swap_ranges(
                ForwardIterator1 first1, ForwardIterator1 last1,
                ForwardIterator2 first2);
```

The `swap_ranges()` function exchanges values in the range [`first1`, `last1`) with the corresponding values in the range beginning at `first2`. The two ranges should not overlap.

```
template<class ForwardIterator1, class ForwardIterator2>
void iter_swap(ForwardIterator1 a, ForwardIterator2 b);
```

The `iter_swap()` function exchanges values stored at two locations specified by iterators.

```
template<class InputIterator, class OutputIterator, class UnaryOperation>
OutputIterator transform(InputIterator first, InputIterator last,
OutputIterator result, UnaryOperation op);
```

This version of `transform()` applies the unary function object `op` to each element in the range [`first`, `last`) and assigns the return value to the corresponding element in the range beginning at `result`. So `*result` is set to `op(*first)`, and so on. It returns `result + (last - first)`, that is, the past-the-end value for the target range.

```
template<class InputIterator1, class InputIterator2, class OutputIterator,
         class BinaryOperation>
OutputIterator transform(InputIterator1 first1, InputIterator1 last1,
                InputIterator2 first2, OutputIterator result,
                BinaryOperation binary_op);
```

This version of `transform()` applies the binary function object `op` to each element in the range [`first1`, `last1`) and to each element in the range [`first2`, `last2`) and assigns the return value to the corresponding element in the range beginning at `result`. So `*result` is set to `op(*first1, *first2)`, and so on. It returns `result + (last - first)`, the past-the-end value for the target range.

```
template<class ForwardIterator, class T>
void replace(ForwardIterator first, ForwardIterator last,
          const T& old_value, const T& new_value);
```

The `replace()` function replaces each occurrence of the value `old_value` in the range [`first`, `last`) with the value `new_value`.

```
template<class ForwardIterator, class Predicate, class T>
void replace_if(ForwardIterator first, ForwardIterator last,
                Predicate pred, const T& new_value);
```

The `replace()_if` function replaces each value `old` in the range [`first`, `last`) for which `pred(old)` is `true` with the value `new_value`.

```
template<class InputIterator, class OutputIterator, class T>
OutputIterator replace_copy(InputIterator first, InputIterator last,
    OutputIterator result,const T& old_ value, const T& new_ value);
```

The `replace_copy()` function copies the elements in the range [`first`, `last`) to a range beginning at result, but substituting `new_value` for each occurrence of `old_value`. It returns `result + (last - first)`, the past-the-end value for the target range.

```
template<class Iterator, class OutputIterator, class Predicate, class T>
OutputIterator replace_copy_if(Iterator first, Iterator last,
    OutputIterator result, Predicate pred, const T& new_ value);
```

The `replace_copy_if()` function copies the elements in the range [`first`, `last`) to a range beginning at result, but substituting `new_value` for each value `old` for which `pred(old)` is true. It returns `result + (last - first)`, the past-the-end value for the target range.

```
template<class ForwardIterator, class T>
void fill(ForwardIterator first, ForwardIterator last, const T& value);
```

The `fill()` function sets each element in the range [`first`, `last`) to `value`.

```
template<class OutputIterator, class Size, class T>
void fill_n(OutputIterator first, Size n, const T& value);
```

The `fill_n()` function sets each of the first n elements beginning at location `first` to `value`.

```
template<class ForwardIterator, class Generator>
void generate(ForwardIterator first, ForwardIterator last, Generator gen);
```

The `generator()` function sets each element in the range [`first`, `last`) to `gen()`, where `gen` is a generator function object, that is, one that takes no arguments. For example, `gen` can be a pointer to `rand()`.

```
template<class OutputIterator, class Size, class Generator>
void generate_n(OutputIterator first, Size n, Generator gen);
```

The `generator_n()` function sets each of the first n elements in the range beginning at `first` to `gen()`, where `gen` is a generator function object, that is, one that takes no arguments. For example, `gen` can be a pointer to `rand()`.

```
template<class ForwardIterator, class T>
ForwardIterator remove(ForwardIterator first, ForwardIterator last,
                    const T& value);
```

The `remove()` function removes all occurrences of value from the range [`first`, `last`) and returns a past-the-end iterator for the resulting range. The function is stable, meaning the order of the unremoved elements is unaltered.

Note

Because the various `remove()` and `unique()` functions are not member functions, and also because they aren't restricted to STL containers, they can't reset the size of a container. Instead, they return an iterator indicating the new past-the-end location. Typically, the removed items simply are shifted to the end of the container. However, for STL containers you can use the returned iterator and one of the `erase()` methods to reset `end()`.

```
template<class ForwardIterator, class Predicate>
ForwardIterator remove_if(ForwardIterator first, ForwardIterator last,
                   Predicate pred);
```

The `remove_if()` function removes all occurrences of values `val` for which `pred(val)` is `true` from the range [`first`, `last`) and returns a past-the-end iterator for the resulting range. The function is stable, meaning the order of the unremoved elements is unaltered.

```
template<class InputIterator, class OutputIterator, class T>
OutputIterator remove_copy(InputIterator first, InputIterator last,
                   OutputIterator result, const T& value);
```

The `remove_copy()` function copies values from the range [`first`, `last`) to the range beginning at `result`, skipping instances of `value` as it copies. It returns a past-the-end iterator for the resulting range. The function is stable, meaning the order of the unremoved elements is unaltered.

```
template<class InputIterator, class OutputIterator, class Predicate>
OutputIterator remove_copy_if(InputIterator first, InputIterator last,
                   OutputIterator result, Predicate pred);
```

The `remove_copy_if()` function copies values from the range [`first`, `last`) to the range beginning at `result`, but skipping instances of `val` for which `pred(val)` is `true` as it copies. It returns a past-the-end iterator for the resulting range. The function is stable, meaning the order of the unremoved elements is unaltered.

```
template<class ForwardIterator>
ForwardIterator unique(ForwardIterator first, ForwardIterator last);
```

```
template<class ForwardIterator, class BinaryPredicate>
ForwardIterator unique(ForwardIterator first, ForwardIterator last,
                   BinaryPredicate pred);
```

The `unique()` function reduces each sequence of two or more equivalent elements in a range [`first`, `last`) to a single element and returns a past-the-end iterator for the new range. The first version uses the `==` operator for the value type to compare elements. The second version uses the binary predicate function object `pred` to compare elements. That is, elements pointed to by `it1` and `it2` match if `pred(*it1, *it2)` is `true`.

```
template<class InputIterator, class OutputIterator>
OutputIterator unique_copy(InputIterator first, InputIterator last,
                   OutputIterator result);
```

```
template<class InputIterator, class OutputIterator, class BinaryPredicate>
OutputIterator unique_copy(InputIterator first, InputIterator last,
                   OutputIterator result, BinaryPredicate pred);
```

The `unique_copy()` function copies elements from a range [`first`, `last`) to the range beginning at `result`, reducing each sequence of two or more identical elements to a single element. It returns a past-the-end iterator for the new range. The first version uses the == operator for the value type to compare elements. The second version uses the binary predicate function object `pred` to compare elements. That is, elements pointed to by `it1` and `it2` match if `pred(*it1, *it2)` is true.

```
template<class BidirectionalIterator>
void reverse(BidirectionalIterator first, BidirectionalIterator last);
```

The `reverse()` function reverses the elements in the range [`first`, `last`) by invoking `swap(first, last - 1)`, and so on.

```
template<class BidirectionalIterator, class OutputIterator>
OutputIterator reverse_copy(BidirectionalIterator first,
                            BidirectionalIterator last,
                            OutputIterator result);
```

The `reverse copy()` function copies the elements in the range [`first`, `last`) to the range beginning at `result` in reverse order. The two ranges should not overlap.

```
template<class ForwardIterator>
void rotate(ForwardIterator first, ForwardIterator middle,
            ForwardIterator last);
```

The `rotate()` function performs a left-rotate on the elements in the range [`first`, `last`). The element at `middle` is moved to `first`, the element at `middle + 1` to `first + 1`, and so on. The elements preceding `middle` are wrapped around to the end of the container so that the element at `first` follows that formerly at `last - 1`.

```
template<class ForwardIterator, class OutputIterator>
OutputIterator rotate_copy(ForwardIterator first, ForwardIterator middle,
                           ForwardIterator last, OutputIterator result);
```

The `rotate_copy()` function copies the elements in the range [`first`, `last`) to the range beginning at `result` using the rotated sequence described for `rotate()`.

```
template<class RandomAccessIterator>
void random_shuffle(RandomAccessIterator first, RandomAccessIterator last);
```

This version of the `random_shuffle()` function shuffles the elements in the range [`first`, `last`). The distribution is uniform; that is, each possible permutation of the original order is equally likely.

```
template<class RandomAccessIterator, class RandomNumberGenerator>
void random_shuffle(RandomAccessIterator first, RandomAccessIterator last,
                    RandomNumberGenerator& random);
```

This version of the `random_shuffle()` function shuffles the elements in the range [`first`, `last`). The function object `random` determines the distribution. Given n elements, the expression `random(n)` should return a value in the range [0,n).

```
template<class BidirectionalIterator, class Predicate>
BidirectionalIterator partition(BidirectionalIterator first,
                                BidirectionalIterator last,
                                Predicate pred);
```

The `partition()` function places each element whose value `val` is such that `pred(val)` is `true` before all elements that don't meet that test. It returns an iterator to the position following that last position holding a value for which the predicate object function was `true`.

```
template<class BidirectionalIterator, class Predicate>
BidirectionalIterator stable_partition(BidirectionalIterator first,
                                        BidirectionalIterator last,
                                        Predicate pred);
```

The `stable_partition()` function places each element whose value `val` is such that `pred(val)` is `true` before all elements that don't meet that test. The function preserves the relative ordering within each of the two groups. It returns an iterator to the position following that last position holding a value for which the predicate object function was `true`.

Sorting and Related Operations

Table G.11 summarizes the sorting and related operations. Arguments are not shown, and overloaded functions are listed just once. Each function has a version that uses < for ordering elements and a version that uses a comparison function object for ordering elements. A fuller description including the prototypes follows the table. Thus, you can scan the table to get an idea of what a function does, then look up the details if you find the function appealing.

TABLE G.11   Sorting and Related Operations

Function	Description
`sort()`	Sorts a range.
`stable_sort()`	Sorts a range, preserving the relative order of equivalent elements.
`partial_sort()`	Partially sorts a range, providing the first *n* elements of a full sort.
`partial_sort_copy()`	Copies a partially sorted range to another range.
`nth_element()`	Given an iterator into a range, finds the element that would be there if the range were sorted, and places that element there.
`lower_bound()`	Given a value, finds the first position in a sorted range before which the value can be inserted while maintaining the ordering.
`upper_bound()`	Given a value, finds the last position in a sorted range before which the value can be inserted while maintaining the ordering.
`equal_range()`	Given a value, finds the largest subrange of a sorted range such that the value can be inserted before any element in the subrange without violating the ordering.
`binary_search()`	Returns `true` if a sorted range contains a value equivalent to a given value, and `false` otherwise.
`merge()`	Merges two sorted ranges into a third range.

TABLE G.11   Continued

Function	Description
inplace_merge()	Merges two consecutive sorted ranges in place.
includes()	Returns true if every element in one set also is found in another set.
set_union()	Constructs the union of two sets, which is a set containing all elements present in either set.
set_intersection()	Constructs the intersection of two sets, which is a set containing only those elements found in both sets.
set_difference()	Constructs the difference of two sets, which is a set containing only those elements found in the first set but not the second.
set_symmetric_difference()	Constructs a set consisting of elements found in one set or the other, but not both.
make_heap	Converts a range to heap.
push_heap()	Adds an element to a heap.
pop_heap()	Removes the largest element from a heap.
sort_heap()	Sorts a heap.
min()	Returns the lesser of two values.
max()	Returns the greater of two values.
min_element()	Finds the first occurrence of the smallest value in a range.
max_element()	Finds the first occurrence of the largest value in a range.
lexicographic_compare()	Compares two sequences lexicographically, returning true if the first sequence is lexicographically less than the second, and false otherwise.
next_permutation()	Generates the next permutation in a sequence.
previous_permutation()	Generates the preceding permutation in a sequence.

The functions in this section determine the order of two elements by using the < operator defined for the elements or by using a comparison object designated by the template type Compare. If comp is an object of type Compare, then comp(a,b) is a generalization of a < b and returns true if a precedes b in the ordering scheme. If a < b is false and b < a also is false, a and b are equivalent. A comparison object must provide at least *strict weak ordering*. This means the following:

- The expression comp(a,a) must be false, a generalization of the fact that a value can't be less than itself. (This is the strict part.)

- If comp(a,b) is true and comp(b,c) is true, then comp(a,c) is true (that is, comparison is a transitive relationship).

- If a is equivalent to b, and b is equivalent to c, then a is equivalent to c (that is, equivalency is a transitive relationship).

If you think of applying < to integers, then equivalency implies equality, but this doesn't have to hold for more general cases. For example, you could define a structure with several members describing a mailing address and define a comp comparison object that orders the structures according to ZIP code. Then any two addresses with the same ZIP code would be equivalent but not equal.

Now let's go to the prototypes. We'll divide this section into several subsections. As you saw earlier, pairs of iterators indicate ranges, with the chosen template parameter name indicating the type of iterator. As usual a range of the form [first, last) goes from first up to, but not including, last. Functions passed as arguments are function objects, which can be pointers or objects for which the () operation is defined. As you learned in Chapter 16, a predicate is a Boolean function with one argument, and a binary predicate is a Boolean function with two arguments. (The functions need not be type bool as long as they return a 0 value for false and a non-zero for true.) Also, as in Chapter 16, a unary function object is one taking a single argument, and a binary function object is one taking two arguments.

Sorting

First, let's examine the sorting algorithms.

```
template<class RandomAccessIterator>
void sort(RandomAccessIterator first, RandomAccessIterator last);

template<class RandomAccessIterator, class Compare>
void sort(RandomAccessIterator first, RandomAccessIterator last,
          Compare comp);
```

The sort() function sorts the range [first, last) in increasing order, using the value type < operator for comparison. The first version uses < and the second uses the comparison object comp to determine the order.

```
template<class RandomAccessIterator>
void stable_sort(RandomAccessIterator first, RandomAccessIterator last);

template<class RandomAccessIterator, class Compare>
void stable_sort(RandomAccessIterator first, RandomAccessIterator last,
                 Compare comp);
```

The stable_sort() function sorts the range [first, last) preserving the relative order of equivalent elements. The first version uses < and the second uses the comparison object comp to determine the order.

```
template<class RandomAccessIterator>
void partial_sort(RandomAccessIterator first, RandomAccessIterator middle,
                  RandomAccessIterator last);
```

```
template<class RandomAccessIterator, class Compare>
void partial_sort(RandomAccessIterator first, RandomAccessIterator middle,
RandomAccessIterator last, Compare comp);
```

The `partial_sort()` function partially sorts the range [`first`, `last`). The first `middle` - `first` elements of the sorted range are placed in the range [`first`, `middle`), and the remaining elements are unsorted. The first version uses < and the second uses the comparison object `comp` to determine the order.

```
template<class InputIterator, class RandomAccessIterator>
RandomAccessIterator partial_sort_copy(InputIterator first,
                    InputIterator last,
                    RandomAccessIterator result_first,
                    RandomAccessIterator result_last);
```

```
template<class InputIterator, class RandomAccessIterator, class Compare>
RandomAccessIterator
partial_sort_copy(InputIterator first, InputIterator last,
                RandomAccessIterator result_first,
                RandomAccessIterator result_last,
                Compare comp);
```

The `partial_sort_copy()` function copies the first *n* elements of the sorted range [`first`, `last`) to the range [`result_first`, `result_first` + n). The value of *n* is the lesser of `last` - `first` and `result_last` - `result_first`. The function returns `result_first` + n. The first version uses < and the second uses the comparison object `comp` to determine the order.

```
template<class RandomAccessIterator>
void nth_element(RandomAccessIterator first, RandomAccessIterator nth,
                RandomAccessIterator last);
```

```
template<class RandomAccessIterator, class Compare>
void nth_element(RandomAccessIterator first, RandomAccessIterator nth,
RandomAccessIterator last, Compare comp);
```

The `nth_element()` function finds the element in range [`first`, `last`) that would be at position `nth` were the range sorted, and it places that element at position `nth`. The first version uses < and the second uses the comparison object `comp` to determine the order.

Binary Search

The algorithms in the binary search group assume the range is sorted. They only require a forward iterator but are most efficient for random iterators.

```
template<class ForwardIterator, class T>
ForwardIterator lower_bound(ForwardIterator first, ForwardIterator last,
                        const T& value);
```

```
template<class ForwardIterator, class T, class Compare>
ForwardIterator lower_bound(ForwardIterator first, ForwardIterator last,
                        const T& value, Compare comp);
```

The `lower_bound()` function finds the first position in a sorted range [`first`, `last`) in front of which `value` can be inserted without violating the order. It returns an iterator pointing to this position. The first version uses < and the second uses the comparison object `comp` to determine the order.

```
template<class ForwardIterator, class T>
ForwardIterator upper_bound(ForwardIterator first, ForwardIterator last,
                        const T& value);
```

```
template<class ForwardIterator, class T, class Compare>
ForwardIterator upper_bound(ForwardIterator first, ForwardIterator last,
const T& value, Compare comp);
```

The `upper_bound()` function finds the last position in a sorted range [`first`, `last`) in front of which `value` can be inserted without violating the order. It returns an iterator pointing to this position. The first version uses < and the second uses the comparison object `comp` to determine the order.

```
template<class ForwardIterator, class T>
pair<ForwardIterator, ForwardIterator> equal_range(
    ForwardIterator first, ForwardIterator last, const T& value);
```

```
template<class ForwardIterator, class T, class Compare>
pair<ForwardIterator, ForwardIterator> equal_range(
    ForwardIterator first, ForwardIterator last, const T& value,
    Compare comp);
```

The `equal_range()` function finds the largest subrange [`it1`, `it2`) in a sorted range [`first`, `last`) such that `value` can be inserted in front of any iterator in this range without violating the order. The function returns a `pair` formed of `it1` and `it2`. The first version uses < and the second uses the comparison object `comp` to determine the order.

```
template<class ForwardIterator, class T>
bool binary_search(ForwardIterator first, ForwardIterator last,
                const T& value);
```

```
template<class ForwardIterator, class T, class Compare>
bool binary_search(ForwardIterator first, ForwardIterator last,
                const T& value, Compare comp);
```

The `binary_search()` function returns `true` if the equivalent of `value` is found in the sorted range [`first`, `last`) and `false` otherwise. The first version uses < and the second uses the comparison object `comp` to determine the order.

Note

Recall that if < is used for ordering, values a and b are equivalent if both a < b and b < a are `false`. For ordinary numbers, equivalency implies equality, but this is not the case for structures sorted on the basis of just one member. Thus, there may be more than one location where a new value can be inserted and still keep the data ordered. Similarly, if the comparison object `comp` is used for ordering, equivalency means both `comp(a,b)` and `comp(b,a)` are `false`. (This is a generalization of the statement that a and b are equivalent if a is not less than b and b is not less than a.)

Merging

The merging functions assume ranges are sorted.

```
template<class InputIterator1, class InputIterator2, class OutputIterator>
OutputIterator merge(InputIterator1 first1, InputIterator1 last1,
                     InputIterator2 first2, InputIterator2 last2,
                     OutputIterator result);

template<class InputIterator1, class InputIterator2, class OutputIterator,
class Compare>
OutputIterator merge(InputIterator1 first1, InputIterator1 last1,
                     InputIterator2 first2, InputIterator2 last2,
                     OutputIterator result, Compare comp);
```

The merge() function merges elements from sorted range [first1, last1) and from sorted range [first2, last2), placing the result in the range starting at result. The target range should not overlap either of the merged ranges. When equivalent elements are found in both ranges, elements from the first range precede elements of the second. The return value is the past-the-end iterator for the resulting merge. The first version uses < and the second uses the comparison object comp to determine the order.

```
template<class BidirectionalIterator>
void inplace_merge(BidirectionalIterator first,
        BidirectionalIterator middle, BidirectionalIterator last);

template<class BidirectionalIterator, class Compare>
void inplace_merge(BidirectionalIterator first,
        BidirectionalIterator middle, BidirectionalIterator last,
        Compare comp);
```

The inplace_merge() function merges two consecutive sorted ranges—[first, middle) and [middle, last)—into a single sorted sequence stored in the range [first, last). Elements from the first range will precede equivalent elements from the second range. The first version uses < and the second uses the comparison object comp to determine the order.

Set Operations

Set operations work with all sorted sequences, including set and multiset. For containers holding more than one instance of a value, such as multiset, definitions are generalized. A union of two multisets contains the larger number of occurrences of each element, and an intersection contains the lesser number of occurrences of each element. For example, suppose multiset A contains the string "apple" seven times and multiset B contains the same string four times. Then the union of A and B will contain seven instances of "apple" and the intersection will contain four instances.

```
template<class InputIterator1, class InputIterator2>
bool includes(InputIterator1 first1, InputIterator1 last1,
        InputIterator2 first2, InputIterator2 last2);

template<class InputIterator1, class InputIterator2, class Compare>
bool includes(InputIterator1 first1, InputIterator1 last1,
        InputIterator2 first2, InputIterator2 last2, Compare comp);
```

The `includes()` function returns `true` if every element in range [`first2`, `last2`) also is found in the range [`first1`, `last1`) and `false` otherwise. The first version uses < and the second uses the comparison object `comp` to determine the order.

```
template<class InputIterator1, class InputIterator2, class OutputIterator>
OutputIterator set_union(InputIterator1 first1, InputIterator1 last1,
                         InputIterator2 first2, InputIterator2 last2,
                         OutputIterator result);

template<class InputIterator1, class InputIterator2, class OutputIterator,
         class Compare>
OutputIterator set_union(InputIterator1 first1, InputIterator1 last1,
                         InputIterator2 first2, InputIterator2 last2,
                         OutputIterator result, Compare comp);
```

The `set_union()` function constructs the set that is the union of the ranges [`first1`, `last1`) and [`first2`, `last2`) and copies the result to the location pointed to by `result`. The resulting range should not overlap either of the original ranges. The function returns a past-the-end iterator for the constructed range. The union is the set containing all elements found in either or both sets. The first version uses < and the second uses the comparison object `comp` to determine the order.

```
template<class InputIterator1, class InputIterator2, class OutputIterator>
OutputIterator set_intersection(InputIterator1 first1, InputIterator1 last1,
                         InputIterator2 first2, InputIterator2 last2,
                         OutputIterator result);

template<class InputIterator1, class InputIterator2, class OutputIterator,
         class Compare>
OutputIterator set_intersection(InputIterator1 first1, InputIterator1 last1,
                         InputIterator2 first2, InputIterator2 last2,
                         OutputIterator result, Compare comp);
```

The `set_intersection()` function constructs the set that is the intersection of the ranges [`first1`, `last1`) and [`first2`, `last2`) and copies the result to the location pointed to by `result`. The resulting range should not overlap either of the original ranges. The function returns a past-the-end iterator for the constructed range. The intersection is the set containing those elements common to both sets. The first version uses < and the second uses the comparison object `comp` to determine the order.

```
template<class InputIterator1, class InputIterator2, class OutputIterator>
OutputIterator set_difference(InputIterator1 first1, InputIterator1 last1,
                         InputIterator2 first2, InputIterator2 last2,
                         OutputIterator result);

template<class InputIterator1, class InputIterator2, class OutputIterator,
         class Compare>
OutputIterator set_difference(InputIterator1 first1, InputIterator1 last1,
                         InputIterator2 first2, InputIterator2 last2,
                         OutputIterator result, Compare comp);
```

The `set_difference()` function constructs the set that is the difference of the ranges [`first1`, `last1`) and [`first2`, `last2`) and copies the result to the location pointed to by `result`. The resulting range should not overlap either of the original ranges. The function returns a past-the-end iterator for the constructed range. The difference is the set containing those elements found in the first set but not in the second. The first version uses < and the second uses the comparison object `comp` to determine the order.

```
template<class InputIterator1, class InputIterator2, class OutputIterator>
OutputIterator set_symmetric_difference(
                    InputIterator1 first1, InputIterator1 last1,
                    InputIterator2 first2, InputIterator2 last2,
                    OutputIterator result);

template<class InputIterator1, class InputIterator2, class OutputIterator,
        class Compare>
OutputIterator set_symmetric_difference(
                    InputIterator1 first1, InputIterator1 last1,
                    InputIterator2 first2, InputIterator2 last2,
                    OutputIterator result, Compare comp);
```

The `set_symmetric_difference()` function constructs the set that is the symmetric difference of the ranges [`first1`, `last1`) and [`first2`, `last2`) and copies the result to the location pointed to by `result`. The resulting range should not overlap either of the original ranges. The function returns a past-the-end iterator for the constructed range. The symmetric difference is the set containing those elements found in the first set but not in the second and those elements found in the second set but not the first. It's the same as the difference between the union and the intersection. The first version uses < and the second uses the comparison object `comp` to determine the order.

Heap Operations

A *heap* is a common data form with the property that the first element in a heap is the largest. Whenever the first element is removed or any element is added, the heap may have to be rearranged to maintain that property. A heap is designed so that these two operations are done efficiently.

```
template<class RandomAccessIterator>
void make_heap(RandomAccessIterator first, RandomAccessIterator last);

template<class RandomAccessIterator, class Compare>
void make_heap(RandomAccessIterator first, RandomAccessIterator last,
                Compare comp);
```

The `make_heap()` function makes a heap of the range [`first`, `last`). The first version use < to determine the ordering, while the second version uses the `comp` comparison object.

```
template<class RandomAccessIterator>
void push_heap(RandomAccessIterator first, RandomAccessIterator last);

template<class RandomAccessIterator, class Compare>
void push_heap(RandomAccessIterator first, RandomAccessIterator last,
                Compare comp);
```

The `push_heap()` function assumes that the range [`first`, `last` - 1) is a valid heap, and it adds the value at location `last` - 1 (that is, one past the end of the assumed valid heap) into the heap, making [`first`, `last`) a valid heap. The first version use < to determine the ordering, while the second version uses the `comp` comparison object.

```
template<class RandomAccessIterator>
void pop_heap(RandomAccessIterator first, RandomAccessIterator last);
```

```
template<class RandomAccessIterator, class Compare>
void pop_heap(RandomAccessIterator first, RandomAccessIterator last,
              Compare comp);
```

The `pop_heap()` function assumes that the range [`first`, `last`) is a valid heap. It swaps the value at location `last` - 1 with the value at `first` and makes the range [`first`, `last` - 1) a valid heap. The first version uses < to determine the ordering, while the second version uses the `comp` comparison object.

```
template<class RandomAccessIterator>
void sort_heap(RandomAccessIterator first, RandomAccessIterator last);
```

```
template<class RandomAccessIterator, class Compare>
void sort_heap(RandomAccessIterator first, RandomAccessIterator last,
               Compare comp);
```

The `sort_heap()` function assumes the range [`first`, `last`) is a heap and sorts it. The first version uses < to determine the ordering, while the second version uses the `comp` comparison object.

Minimum and Maximum

The minimum and maximum functions return the minimum and maximum values of pairs of values and of sequences of values.

```
template<class T> const T& min(const T& a, const T& b);
```

```
template<class T, class Compare>
const T& min(const T& a, const T& b, Compare comp);
```

The `min()` function returns the lesser of two values. If the two values are equivalent, it returns the first value. The first version uses < to determine the ordering, while the second version uses the `comp` comparison object.

```
template<class T> const T& max(const T& a, const T& b);
```

```
template<class T, class Compare>
const T& max(const T& a, const T& b, Compare comp);
```

The `max()` function returns the greater of two values. If the two values are equivalent, it returns the first value. The first version uses < to determine the ordering, while the second version uses the `comp` comparison object.

```
template<class ForwardIterator>
ForwardIterator min_element(ForwardIterator first, ForwardIterator last);
```

```
template<class ForwardIterator, class Compare>
ForwardIterator min_element(ForwardIterator first, ForwardIterator last,
Compare comp);
```

The `min_element()` function returns the first iterator `it` in the range [`first`, `last`) such that no element in the range is less than `*it`. The first version uses `<` to determine the ordering, while the second version uses the `comp` comparison object.

```
template<class ForwardIterator>
ForwardIterator max_element(ForwardIterator first, ForwardIterator last);
```

```
template<class ForwardIterator, class Compare>
ForwardIterator max_element(ForwardIterator first, ForwardIterator last,
Compare comp);
```

The `max_element()` function returns the first iterator `it` in the range [`first`, `last`) such that there is no element that `*it` is less than. The first version uses `<` to determine the ordering, while the second version uses the `comp` comparison object.

```
template<class InputIterator1, class InputIterator2>
bool lexicographical_compare(InputIterator1 first1, InputIterator1 last1,
                    InputIterator2 first2, InputIterator2 last2);
```

```
template<class InputIterator1, class InputIterator2, class Compare>
bool lexicographical_compare(InputIterator1 first1, InputIterator1 last1,
                    InputIterator2 first2, InputIterator2 last2,
                    Compare comp);
```

The `lexicographical_compare()` function returns `true` if the sequence of elements in range [`first1`, `last1`) is lexicographically less than the sequence of elements in range [`first2`, `last2`) and `false` otherwise. A lexicographical comparison compares the first element of one sequence to the first of the second, that is, it compares `*first1` to `*first2`. If `*first1` is less than `*first2`, the function returns `true`. If `*first2` is less than `*first1`, the function returns `false`. If the two are equivalent, comparison proceeds to the next element in each sequence. This process continues until two corresponding elements are not equivalent or until the end of a sequence is reached. If two sequences are equivalent until the end of one is reached, the shorter sequence is less. If the two sequences are equivalent and of the same length, neither is less, so the function returns `false`. The first version of the function uses `<` to compare elements and the second version uses the `comp` comparison object. The lexicographic comparison is a generalization of an alphabetic comparison.

Permutations

A permutation of a sequence is a reordering of the elements. For example, a sequence of three elements has six possible orderings, because you have a choice of three elements for the first element. Choosing a particular element for the first position leaves a choice of two for the second, and one for the third. For example, the six permutations of the digits 1, 3, and 5 are as follows:

123 132 213 232 312 321

In general, a sequence of n elements has $n * (n-1) * \ldots * 1$, or $n!$ possible permutations.

The permutation functions assume that the set of all possible permutations can be arranged in lexicographical order, as in the previous example of six permutations. That means, in general, that there is a specific permutation that precedes and follows each permutation. For example, 213 immediately precedes 232, and 312 immediately follows it. However, the first permutation (123 in the example) has no predecessor, and the last permutation (321) has no follower.

```
template<class BidirectionalIterator>
bool next_permutation(BidirectionalIterator first,
                      BidirectionalIterator last);

template<class BidirectionalIterator, class Compare>
bool next_permutation(BidirectionalIterator first,
                      BidirectionalIterator last, Compare comp);
```

The next_permutation() function transforms the sequence in range [first, last) to the next permutation in lexicographic order. If the next permutation exists, the function returns true. If it doesn't exist (that is, the range contains the last permutation in lexicographic order), the function returns false and transforms the range to the first permutation in lexicographic order. The first version uses < to determine the ordering, while the second version uses the comp comparison object.

```
template<class BidirectionalIterator>
bool prev_permutation(BidirectionalIterator first,
                      BidirectionalIterator last);

template<class BidirectionalIterator, class Compare>
bool prev_permutation(BidirectionalIterator first,
                      BidirectionalIterator last, Compare comp);
```

The previous_permutation() function transforms the sequence in range [first, last) to the previous permutation in lexicographic order. If the previous permutation exists, the function returns true. If it doesn't exist (that is, the range contains the first permutation in lexicographic order), the function returns false and transforms the range to the last permutation in lexicographic order. The first version uses < to determine the ordering, while the second version uses the comp comparison object.

Numeric Operations

Table G.12 summarizes the numeric operations, which are described by the numeric header file. Arguments are not shown, and overloaded functions are listed just once. Each function has a version that uses < for ordering elements and a version that uses a comparison function object for ordering elements. A fuller description including the prototypes follows the table. Thus, you can scan the table to get an idea of what a function does; then look up the details if you find the function appealing.

TABLE G.12 Sorting and Related Operations

Function	Description
accumulate()	Calculates a cumulative total for values in a range.
inner_product()	Calculates the inner product of two ranges.
partial_sum()	Copies partial sums calculated from one range into a second range.
adjacent_difference()	Copies adjacent differences calculated from elements in one range to a second range.

```
template <class InputIterator, class T>
T accumulate(InputIterator first, InputIterator last, T init);

template <class InputIterator, class T, class BinaryOperation>
T accumulate(InputIterator first, InputIterator last, T init,
             BinaryOperation binary_op);
```

The accumulate() function initializes a value acc to init; then it performs the operation acc = acc + *i (first version) or acc = binary_op(acc, *i) (second version) for each iterator i in the range [first, last) in order. It then returns the resulting value of acc.

```
template <class InputIterator1, class InputIterator2, class T>
T inner_product(InputIterator1 first1, InputIterator1 last1,
                InputIterator2 first2, T init);

template <class InputIterator1, class InputIterator2, class T,
class BinaryOperation1, class BinaryOperation2>
T inner_product(InputIterator1 first1, InputIterator1 last1,
                InputIterator2 first2, T init,
                BinaryOperation1 binary_op1, BinaryOperation2 binary_op2);
```

The inner_product() function initializes a value acc to init; then it performs the operation acc = *i * *j (first version) or acc = binary_op(*i, *j) (second version) for each iterator i in the range [first1, last1) in order and each corresponding iterator j in the range [first2, first2 + (last1 - first1)). That is, it calculates a value from the first elements from each sequence, then from the second elements of each sequence, and so on, until it reaches the end of the first sequence. (Hence the second sequence should be at least as long as the first.) The function then returns the resulting value of acc.

```
template <class InputIterator, class OutputIterator>
OutputIterator partial_sum(InputIterator first, InputIterator last,
                           OutputIterator result);

template <class InputIterator, class OutputIterator, class BinaryOperation>
OutputIterator partial_sum(InputIterator first, InputIterator last,
                           OutputIterator result,
                           BinaryOperation binary_op);
```

The `partial_sum()` function assigns `*first` to `*result`, `*first + *(first + 1)` to `*(result + 1)`, (first version) or `binary_op(*first, *(first + 1))` to `*(result + 1)` (second version, and so on. That is, the nth element of the sequence beginning at `result` contains the sum (or `binary_op` equivalent) of the first n elements of the sequence beginning at `first`. The function returns the past-the-end iterator for the result. The algorithm allows `result` to be `first`, that is, it allows the result to be copied over the original sequence, if desired.

```
template <class InputIterator, class OutputIterator>
OutputIterator adjacent_difference(InputIterator first, InputIterator last,
                         OutputIterator result);

template <class InputIterator, class OutputIterator, class BinaryOperation>
OutputIterator adjacent_difference(InputIterator first, InputIterator last,
                         OutputIterator result,
                         BinaryOperation binary_op);
```

The `adjacent_difference()` function assigns `*first` to the location `result` (`*result = *first`). Subsequent locations in the target range are assigned the differences (or `binary_op` equivalent) of adjacent locations in the source range. That is, the next location in the target range (`result + 1`) is assigned `*(first + 1) - *first` (first version) or `binary_op(*(first + 1), *first)` (second version, and so on. The function returns the past-the-end iterator for the result. The algorithm allows `result` to be `first`, that is, it allows the result to be copied over the original sequence, if desired.

APPENDIX H

SELECTED READINGS

Booch, Grady. *Object-Oriented Analysis and Design*. Reading, MA: Addison-Wesley, 1993.

This book presents the concepts behind OOP, discusses OOP methods, and presents sample applications. The examples are in C++.

Booch, Grady, Jim Rumbaugh, and Ivar Jacobson. *Unified Modeling Language User Guide*. Reading, MA: Addison-Wesley, 1998.

This book by the creators of the Unified Modeling Language presents the core of UML along with many examples of its use.

Cline, Marshall, Greg Lomow, and Mike Girou. *C++ FAQs, Second Edition*. Reading, MA: Addison-Wesley, 1999.

This book addresses a great number of frequently asked questions about the C++ language.

Jacobson, Ivar. *Object-Oriented Software Engineering: A Use Case Driven Approach*. Reading, MA: Addison-Wesley, 1994.

This book describes successful guidelines and methods (Object-Oriented Software Engineering, or OOSE) for developing large-scale software systems.

Josuttis, Nicolai M. *The C++ Standard Library: A Tutorial and Reference*. Reading, MA: Addison-Wesley, 1999.

This book describes the STL as well as other C++ library features, such as complex number support, locales, and input/output streams.

Lee, Richard C and William M. Tepfenhart. *UML and C++, Second Edition*. Upper Saddle River, New Jersey: Prentice Hall, 2001.

This book is a self-teaching guide to the Unified Modeling Language, and it includes a review of C++ fundamentals.

Meyers, Scott. *Effective C++: 50 Specific Ways to Improve Your Programs and Designs*, Second Edition. Reading, MA: Addison-Wesley, 1998.

This book is aimed at programmers who already know C++, and it provides 50 rules and guidelines. Some are technical, such as explaining when you should define copy constructors and assignment operators. Others are more general, such as discussing *is-a* and *has-a* relationships.

Meyers, Scott. *Effective STL: 50 Specific Ways to Improve Your Use of the Standard Template Library*. Reading, MA: Addison-Wesley, 2001.

This book provides guidance in choosing containers and algorithms and in other facets of using the STL.

Meyers, Scott. *More Effective C++: 35 New Ways to Improve Your Programs and Designs*. Reading, MA: Addison-Wesley, 1996.

This book continues in the tradition of *Effective C++,* clarifying some of the more obscure aspects of the language and showing how to accomplish various goals, such as designing smart pointers. It reflects the additional experience C++ programmers have gained the last few years.

Rumbaugh, James, Michael Blaha, William Premerlani, Frederick Eddy, Bill Lorensen, William Lorenson. *Object-Oriented Modeling and Design*. Englewood Cliffs, Prentice Hall, 1991.

This book presents and explores the Object Modeling Technique (OMT), a method for breaking problems into suitable objects.

Rumbaugh, James, Ivar Jacobson, and Grady Booch. *Unified Modeling Reference Manual*. Reading, MA: Addison-Wesley, 1998.

This book by the creators of the Unified Modeling Language presents the complete description, in reference manual format, of the UML.

Stroustrup, Bjarne. *The C++ Programming Language*. Third Edition. Reading, MA: Addison-Wesley, 1997.

Stroustrup created C++, so this is the definitive text. However, it is most easily digested if you already have some knowledge of C++. It not only describes the language, it also provides many examples of how to use it, as well as discussions of OOP methodology. Successive editions of this book have grown with the language, and this edition includes a discussion of standard library elements such as the STL and strings.

Stroustrup, Bjarne. *The Design and Evolution of C++*. Reading, MA: Addison-Wesley, 1994.

If you're interested in learning how C++ evolved and why it is the way it is, read this book.

The ISO/ANSI standard (ISO/IEC 14882:1998):

A printed version of the standard is available for $231 from

Global Engineering Documents, Inc.
15 Inverness Way East
Englewood, CO 80122-5704

You can order from its Web site:

`http://global.ihs.com`

A downloadable electronic version (`pdf` format) is available for $18 from the American National Standards Institute Web site:

`http://www.ansi.org`

Internet Resources:

The C++ FAQ Lite site for frequently asked questions (in English, Chinese, French, Russian, and Portuguese) is a slimmed down version of the book by Cline, et al. Currently it has the following URL:

`http://www.parashift.com/c++-faq-lite/`

You can find a moderated discussion of C++ questions in the following newsgroup:

`comp.lang.c++.moderated`

CONVERTING TO ANSI/ISO STANDARD C++

Y ou might have programs (or programming habits) developed in C or in older versions of C++ that you want to convert to Standard C++. This appendix provides some guidelines. Some pertain to moving from C to C++, others from older C++ to Standard C++.

Preprocessor Directives

The C/C++ preprocessor provides an array of directives. In general, C++ practice is to use those directives designed to manage the compilation process and to avoid using directives as a substitute for code. For example, the `#include` directive is an essential component for managing program files. Other directives, such as `#ifndef` and `#endif`, let you control whether particular blocks of code get compiled. The `#pragma` directive lets you control compiler-specific compilation options. These all are useful, sometimes necessary, tools. You should exert caution, however, when it comes to the `#define` directive.

Use `const` Instead of `#define` to Define Constants

Symbolic constants make code more readable and maintainable. The constant's name indicates its meaning, and if you need to change the value, you just have to change the value once, in the definition, then recompile. C used the preprocessor for this purpose:

```
#define MAX_LENGTH 100
```

The preprocessor then does a text substitution in your source code, replacing occurrences of `MAX_LENGTH` with 100 prior to compilation.

The C++ approach is to apply the `const` modifier to a variable declaration:

```
const int MAX_LENGTH = 100;
```

This treats `MAX_LENGTH` as a read-only `int`.

There are several advantages to the `const` approach. First, the declaration explicitly names the type. For `#define`, you must use various suffixes to a number to indicate types other than `char`, `int`, or `double`; for example, using `100L` to indicate a `long` type or `3.14F` to indicate a `float` type. More importantly, the `const` approach can just as easily be used with derived types:

```
const int base_vals[5] = {1000, 2000, 3500, 6000, 10000};
const string ans[3] = {"yes", "no", "maybe"};
```

Finally, **const** identifiers obey the same scope rules as variables. Thus, you can create constants with global scope, named namespace scope, and block scope. If, say, you define a constant in a particular function, you don't have to worry about the definition conflicting with a global constant used elsewhere in a program. For example, consider the following:

```
#define n 5
const int dz = 12;
...
void fizzle()
{
    int n;
    int dz;
    ...
}
```

The preprocessor will replace

```
int n;
```

with

```
int 5;
```

and induce a compilation error. The **dz** defined in **fizzle()**, however, will be a local variable. Also, **fizzle()**, if necessary, can use the scope resolution operator and access the constant as **::dz**.

C has borrowed the **const** keyword from C++, but the C++ version is more useful. For example, the C++ version has internal linkage for external **const** values rather than the default external linkage used by variables and by the C **const**. This means that each file in a program using a **const** needs that **const** defined in that particular file. This might sound like extra work, but, in fact, it makes life easier. With internal linkage, you can place **const** definitions in a header file used by various files in a project. That is a compiler error for external linkage but not for internal linkage. Also, because a **const** must be defined in the file using it (being in a header file used by that file satisfies the requirement), you can use **const** values as array size arguments:

```
const int MAX_LENGTH = 100;
...
double loads[MAX_LENGTH];
for (int i = 0; i < MAX_LENGTH; i++)
    loads[i] = 50;
```

This won't work in C because the defining declaration for **MAX_LENGTH** could be in a separate file and not be available when this particular file is compiled. In fairness, it should be added that, in C, you could use the **static** modifier to create constants with internal linkage. It's just that C++, by making **static** the default, requires one less thing for you to remember.

Incidentally, the revised C standard (C99) does allow you to use a `const` as an array size, but the array is treated as a new form of array, called a variable array, that is not part of the C++ standard.

The `#define` directive, however, still is useful as part of the standard idiom for controlling when a header file is compiled:

```
// blooper.h
#ifndef _BLOOPER_H_
#define _BLOOPER_H_
// code goes here
#endif
```

For typical symbolic constants, however, get into the habit of using `const` instead of `#define`. Another good alternative, particularly when you have a set of related integer constants, is to use `enum`:

```
enum {LEVEL1 = 1, LEVEL2 = 2, LEVEL3 = 4, LEVEL4 = 8};
```

Use `inline` Instead of `#define` to Define Short Functions

The traditional C way to create the near-equivalent of an inline function was to use a `#define` macro definition:

```
#define Cube(X) X*X*X
```

This lead the preprocessor to do text substitution, with `X` being replaced by the corresponding argument to `Cube()`:

```
y = Cube(x);       // replaced with y = x*x*x;
y = Cube(x + z++); // replaced with x + z++*x + z++*x + z++;
```

Because the preprocessor uses text substitution instead of true passing of arguments, using such macros can lead to unexpected and incorrect results. Such error can be reduced by using lots of parentheses in the macro to ensure the correct order of operations:

```
#define Cube(X) ((X)*(X)*(X))
```

Even this, however, doesn't deal with cases such as using values like `z++`.

The C++ approach of using the keyword `inline` to identify inline functions is much more dependable because it uses true argument passing. Furthermore, C++ inline functions can be regular functions or class methods.

One positive feature of the `#define` macro is that it is typeless so it can be used with any type for which the operation makes sense. In C++ you can create inline templates to achieve type-independent functions while retaining argument passing.

In short, use C++ inlining instead of C `#define` macros.

Use Function Prototypes

Actually, you don't have a choice. Although prototyping is optional in C, it is mandatory in C++. Note that a function that is defined before its first use, such as an inline function, serves as its own prototype.

Do use `const` in function prototypes and headers when appropriate. In particular, use `const` with pointer parameters and reference parameters representing data that is not to be altered. Not only does this allow the compiler to catch errors that change data, it also makes a function more general. That is, a function with a `const` pointer or reference can process both `const` and non-`const` data, while a function that fails to use `const` with a pointer or reference only can process non-`const` data.

Type Casts

One of Stroustrup's pet peeves about C is its undisciplined type cast operator. True, type casts often are necessary, but the standard type cast is too unrestrictive. For example, consider the following code:

```
struct Doof
{
    double feeb;
    double steeb;
    char sgif[10];
};
Doof leam;
short * ps = (short *) & leam;   // old syntax
int * pi = int * (&leam);        // new syntax
```

Nothing in the language prevents you from casting a pointer of one type to a pointer to a totally unrelated type.

In a way, the situation is similar to that of the `goto` statement. The problem with the `goto` statement was that it was too flexible, leading to twisted code. The solution was to provide more limited, structured versions of `goto` to handle the most common tasks for which `goto` was needed. This was the genesis of language elements such as `for` and `while` loops and `if else` statements. Standard C++ provides a similar solution for the problem of the undisciplined type cast, namely, restricted type casts to handle the most common situations requiring type casts. These are the type cast operators discussed in Chapter 15, "Friends, Exceptions, and More":

```
dynamic_cast
static_cast
const_cast
reinterpret_cast
```

So, if you are doing a type cast involving pointers, use one of these operators if possible. Doing so both documents the intent of the cast and provides checking that the cast is being used as intended.

Become Familiar with C++ Features

If you've been using `malloc()` and `free()`, switch to using `new` and `delete` instead. If you've been using `setjmp()` and `longjmp()` for error handling, use `try`, `throw`, and `catch` instead. Try using the `bool` type for values representing `true` and `false`.

Use the New Header Organization

The Standard specifies new names for the header files, as described in Chapter 2, "Setting Out to C++." If you've been using the old-style header files, you should change over to using the new-style names. This is not just a cosmetic change because the new versions might add new features. For example, the `ostream` header file provides support for wide-character input and output. It also provides new manipulators such as `boolalpha` and `fixed` (as described in Chapter 17, "Input, Output, and Files"). These offer a simpler interface than using `setf()` or the `iomanip` functions for setting many formatting options. If you do use `setf()`, use `ios_base` instead of `ios` when specifying constants; that is, use `ios_base::fixed` instead of `ios::fixed`. Also, the new header files incorporate namespaces.

Use Namespaces

Namespaces help organize identifiers used in a program in order to avoid name conflicts. Because the standard library, as implemented with the new header file organization, places names in the `std` namespace, using these header files requires that you deal with namespaces.

The examples in this book, for simplicity, utilize a using directive to make all the names from the `std` namespace available:

```
#include <iostream>
#include <string>
#include <vector>
using namespace std;              // a using-directive
```

However, the wholesale exporting of all the names in a namespace, whether needed or not, runs counter to the goals of namespaces.

Instead, the recommended approach is to use either using declarations or the scope resolution operator (`::`) to make available just those names a program needs. For example,

```
#include <iostream>
using std::cin;                   // a using-declaration
using std::cout;
using std::endl;
```

makes `cin`, `cout`, and `endl` available for the rest of the file. Using the scope resolution operator, however, makes a name available just in the expression using the operator:

```
cout << std::fixed << x << endl;     //using the scope resolution operator
```

This could get wearisome, but you can collect your common using declarations in a header file:

```
// mynames -- a header file
#include <iostream>
using std::cin;                      // a using-declaration
using std::cout;
using std::endl;
```

Going a step further, you could collect using declarations in namespaces:

```
// mynames -- a header file
#include <iostream>

namespace io
{
    using std::cin;
    using std::cout;
    using std::endl;
}

namespace formats
{
    using std::fixed;
....using std::scientific;
    using std:boolalpha;
}
```

Then a program could include this file and use the namespaces it needs:

```
#include "mynames"
using namespace io;
```

Use the `autoptr` Template

Each use of **new** should be paired with a use of **delete**. This can lead to problems if a function in which **new** is used terminates early via an exception being thrown. As discussed in Chapter 15, using an **autoptr** object to keep track of an object created by **new** automates the activation of **delete**.

Use the `string` Class

The traditional C-style string suffers from not being a real type. You can store a string in a character array, you can initialize a character array to a string. But you can't use the assignment operator to assign a string to a character array; instead, you must remember to use **strcpy()** or **strncpy()**. You can't use the relational operators to compare C-style strings; instead, you must remember to use `strcmp()`. (And if you forget and use, say, the > operator, you don't get a syntax error; instead, the program compares string addresses instead of string contents.)

The `string` class (Chapter 16, "The `string` Class and the Standard Template Library," and Appendix F, "The `string` Template Class"), on the other hand, lets you use objects to represent strings. Assignment, relational operators, and the addition operator (for concatenation) all are defined. Furthermore, the `string` class provides automatic memory management so that you normally don't have to worry about someone entering a string that either overruns an array or gets truncated before being stored.

The `string` class provides many convenience methods. For example, you can append one `string` object to another, but you also can append a C-style string or even a `char` value to a `string` object. For functions that require a C-style string argument, you can use the `c_str()` method to return a suitable pointer-to-`char`.

Not only does the `string` class provide a well-designed set of methods for handling string-related tasks, such as finding substrings, but it also features a design that is compatible with the STL so that you can use STL algorithms with `string` objects.

Use the STL

The Standard Template Library (Chapter 16 and Appendix G, "The STL Methods and Functions") provides ready-made solutions to many programming needs, so use it. For example, instead of declaring an array of `double` or of `string` objects, you can create a `vector<double>` object or a `vector<string>` object. The advantages are similar to those of using `string` objects instead of C-style strings. Assignment is defined, so you can use the assignment operator to assign one `vector` object to another. You can pass a `vector` object by reference, and a function receiving such an object can use the `size()` method to determine the number of elements in the `vector` object. Built-in memory management allows for automatic resizing when you use the `pushback()` method to add elements to a `vector` object. And, of course, several useful class methods and general algorithms are at your service.

If you need a list, a double-ended queue (or deque), a stack, a regular queue, a set, or a map, the STL provides useful container templates. The algorithm library is designed so that you easily copy the contents of a vector to a list or compare the contents of a set to a vector. This design makes the STL into a toolkit providing basic units that you can assemble as needed.

The extensive algorithm library was designed with efficiency as one of the main design goals, so you can get top-flight results with relatively little programming effort on your part. And the iterator concept used to implement the algorithms means that they aren't limited to being used with STL containers. In particular, they can be applied to traditional arrays, too.

ANSWERS TO REVIEW QUESTIONS

Chapter 2

1. They are called functions.

2. It causes the contents of the **iostream** file to be substituted for this directive before final compilation.

3. It makes definitions made in the **std** namespace available to a program.

4. ```
   cout << "Hello, world\n";
   ```
   or
   ```
   cout << "Hello, world" << endl;
   ```

5. ```
   int cheeses;
   ```

6. ```
   cheeses = 32;
   ```

7. ```
   cin >> cheeses;
   ```

8. ```
   cout << "We have " << cheeses << " varieties of cheese\n";
   ```

9. It tells us that the function **froop()** expects to be called with one argument, which will be type **double**, and that the function will return a type **int** value.

10. You don't have to use **return** in a function when the function has return type **void**. However, you can use it providing you don't give a return value:
    ```
    return;
    ```

Chapter 3

1. Having more than one integer type lets you choose the type best suited to a particular need. For example, you could use **short** to conserve space, **long** to guarantee storage capacity, or find that a particular type speeds up a particular calculation.
    ```

2.

```
short rbis = 80;            // or short int rbis = 80;
unsigned int q = 42110;     // or unsigned q = 42110;
unsigned long ants = 3000000000;
```

Note

Don't count on `int` being large enough to hold 3000000000.

3. C++ provides no automatic safeguards to keep you from exceeding integer limits; you can use the `climits` header file to determine what the limits are.

4. The constant **33L** is type `long`, whereas the constant **33** is type `int`.

5. The two statements are not really equivalent, although they have the same effect on some systems. Most important, the first statement assigns the letter A to grade only on a system using the ASCII code, while the second statement also works for other codes. Second, 65 is a type `int` constant, while `'A'` is a type `char` constant.

6. Here are four ways:

```
char c = 88;
cout << c << "\n";          // char type prints as character

cout.put(char(88));         // put() prints char as character

cout << char(88) << "\n";   // new-style type cast value to char

cout << (char)88 << "\n";   // old-style type cast value to char
```

7. The answer depends on how large the two types are. If `long` is 4 bytes, there is no loss. That's because the largest `long` value would be about 2 billion, which is 10 digits. Because `double` provides at least 13 significant figures, no rounding would be needed.

8. a. 8 * 9 + 2 is 72 + 2 is 74

   b. 6 * 3 / 4 is 18 / 4 is 4

   c. 3 / 4 * 6 is 0 * 6 is 0

   d. 6.0 * 3 / 4 is 18.0 / 4 is 4.5

   e. 15 % 4 is 3

9. Either of the following work:

```
int pos = (int) x1 + (int) x2;
int pos = int(x1) + int(x2);
```

Chapter 4

1. a. `char actors[30];`

   b. `short betsie[100];`

   c. `float chuck[13];`

   d. `long double dipsea[64];`

2. `int oddly[5] = {1, 3, 5, 7, 9};`

3. `int even = oddly[0] + oddly[4];`

4. `cout << ideas[1] << "\n";  // or << endl;`

5. `char lunch[13] = "cheeseburger"; // number of characters + 1`

   or

   `char lunch[] = "cheeseburger";  // let the compiler count elements`

6.
   ```
   struct fish {
       char kind[20];
       int weight;
       float length;
   };
   ```

7.
   ```
   fish petes =
   {
       "trout",
       13,
       12.25
   };
   ```

8. `enum Response {No, Yes, Maybe};`

9.
   ```
   double * pd = &ted;
   cout << *pd << "\n";
   ```

10.
   ```
   float * pf = treacle;    // or = &treacle[0]
   cout << pf[0] << " " << pf[9] << "\n";
               // or use *pf and *(pf + 9)
   ```

11.
   ```
   unsigned int size;
   cout << "Enter a positive integer: ";
   cin >> size;
   int * dyn = new int [size];
   ```

12. Yes, it is valid. The expression `"Home of the jolly bytes"` is a string constant, hence it evaluates as the address of the beginning of the string. The `cout` object interprets the address of a `char` as an invitation to print a string, but the type cast `(int *)` converts the address to type pointer-to-`int`, which is then printed as an address. In short, the statement prints the address of the string.

13.

```
struct fish
{
    char kind[20];
    int weight;
    float length;
};

fish * pole = new fish;
cout << "Enter kind of fish: ";
cin >> pole->kind;
```

14. Using `cin >> address` causes a program to skip over whitespace until it finds non-whitespace. It then reads characters until it encounters whitespace again. Thus, it will skip over the newline following the numeric input, avoiding that problem. On the other hand, it will read just a single word, not an entire line.

Chapter 5

1. An entry-condition loop evaluates a test expression before entering the body of the loop. If the condition initially is `false`, the loop never executes its body. An exit-condition loop evaluates a test expression after processing the body of the loop. Thus, the loop body is executed once even if the test expression initially is `false`. The `for` and `while` loops are entry-condition loops, and the `do while` loop is an exit-condition loop.

2. It would print the following:

   ```
   01234
   ```

   Note that the cout `<< "\n";` is not part of the loop body (no braces).

3. It would print the following:

   ```
   0369
   12
   ```

4. It would print the following:

   ```
   6
   8
   ```

5. It would print the following:

   ```
   k = 8
   ```

6. It's simplest to use the `*=` operator:

```
for (int num = 1; num <= 64; num *= 2)
    cout << num << " ";
```

7. You enclose the statements within paired braces to form a single compound statement, or block.

8. Yes, the first statement is valid. The expression 1,024 consists of two expressions—1 and 024—joined by a comma operator. The value is the value of the right-hand expression. This is 024, which is octal for 20, so the declaration assigns the value 20 to x. The second statement also is valid. However, operator precedence causes it to be evaluated as follows:

```
(y = 1), 024;
```

That is, the left expression sets y to 1, and the value of the entire expression, which isn't used, is 024, or 20.

9. The `cin >> ch` form skips over spaces, newlines, and tabs when it encounters them. The other two forms read these characters.

Chapter 6

1. Both versions give the same answers, but the `if else` version is more efficient. Consider what happens, for example, when ch is a space. Version 1, after incrementing spaces, tests to see whether the character is a newline. This wastes time because the program already has established that ch is a space and hence could not be a newline. Version 2, in the same situation, skips the newline test.

2. Both `++ch` and `ch + 1` have the same numerical value. But `++ch` is type char and prints as a character, while `ch + 1`, because it adds a char to an int, is type int and prints as a number.

3. Because the program uses `ch = '$'` instead of `ch == '$'`, the combined input and output looks like this:

```
Hi!
H$i$!$
$Send $10 or $20 now!
S$e$n$d$ $ct1 = 9, ct = 9
```

Each character is converted to the $ character before being printed the second time. Also, the value of the expression `ch = $` is the code for the $ character, hence nonzero, hence true; so ct2 is incremented each time.

4. a. `weight >= 115 && weight < 125`

   b. `ch == 'q' || ch == 'Q'`

c. x % 2 == 0 && x != 26

d. x % 2 == 0 && !(x % 26 == 0)

e. donation >= 1000 && donation <= 2000 || guest == 1

f. (ch >= 'a' && ch <= 'z') ||(ch >= 'A' && ch <= 'Z')

5. Not necessarily. For example, if x is 10, then !x is 0 and !!x is 1. However, if x is a **bool** variable, then !!x is x.

6. (x < 0)? -x : x

or

(x >= 0)? x : -x;

7.

```
switch (ch)
{
    case 'A': a_grade++;
            break;
    case 'B': b_grade++;
            break;
    case 'C': c_grade++;
            break;
    case 'D': d_grade++;
            break;
    default:  f_grade++;
            break;
}
```

8. If you use integer labels and the user types a noninteger such as q, the program hangs up because integer input can't process a character. But if you use character labels and the user types an integer such as 5, character input will process 5 as a character. Then the default part of the switch can suggest entering another character.

9. Here is one version:

```
int line = 0;
char ch;
while (cin.get(ch) && ch != 'Q')
{
    if (ch == '\n')
        line++;
}
```

Chapter 7

1. The three steps are defining the function, providing a prototype, and calling the function.

2. a. `void igor(void);    // or void igor()`

   b. `float tofu(int n);  // or  float tofu(int);`

   c. `double mpg(double miles, double gallons);`

   d. `long summation(long harray[], int size);`

   e. `double doctor(const char * str);`

   f. `void ofcourse(boss dude);`

   g. `char * plot(map *pmap);`

3.

```
void set_array(int arr[], int size, int value)
{
    for (int i = 0; i < size; i++)
        arr[i] = value;
}
```

4.

```
void set_array(int * begin, int * end, int value)
{
    for (int * pt = begin; pt != end; pt++)
        pt* = value;
}
```

5.

```
double biggest (const double foot[], int size)
{
    double max;
    if (size < 1)
    {
        cout << "Invalid array size of " << size << "\n";
        cout << "Returning a value of 0\n";
        return 0;
    }
    else      // not necessary because return terminates program
    {
        max = foot[0];
        for (int i = 1; i < size; i++)
            if (foot[i] > max)
                max = foot[i];
        return max;
    }
}
```

6. We use the **const** qualifier with pointers to protect the original pointed-to data from being altered. When a program passes a fundamental type such as an **int** or **double**, it passes it by value so that the function works with a copy. Thus, the original data is already protected.

7. A string can be stored in a `char` array, it can be represented by a string constant in double quotation marks, and it can be represented by a pointer pointing to the first character of a string.

8.

```
int replace(char * str, char c1, char c2)
{
    int count = 0;
    while (*str)        // while not at end of string
    {
        if (*str == c1)
        {
            *str = c2;
            count++;
        }
        str++;          // advance to next character
    }
    return count;
}
```

9. Because C++ interprets `"pizza"` as the address of its first element, applying the `*` operator yields the value of that first element, which is the character `p`. Because C++ interprets `"taco"` as the address of its first element, it interprets `"taco"[2]` as the value of the element two positions down the line, that is, as the character `c`. In other words, the string constant acts the same as an array name.

10. To pass it by value, just pass the structure name `glitz`. To pass its address, use the address operator `&glitz`. Passing by value automatically protects the original data, but it takes time and memory. Passing by address saves time and memory but doesn't protect the original data unless you use the `const` modifier for the function parameter. Also, passing by value means you can use ordinary structure member notation, but passing a pointer means you have to remember to use the indirect membership operator.

11. `int judge (int (*pf)(const char *));`

Chapter 8

1. Short, non-recursive functions that can fit in one line of code.

2. a. `void song(char * name, int times = 1);`

   b. None. Only prototypes contain the default value information.

   c. Yes, providing you retain the default value for `times`:

   `void song(char * name = "O, My Papa", int times = 1);`

3. You can use either the string `"\""` or the character `'"'` to print a quotation mark. The following functions show both methods.

   `#include <iostream.h>`

```cpp
void iquote(int n)
{
    cout << "\"" << n << "\"";
}

void iquote(double x)
{
    cout << '"' << x << '"';
}

void iquote(const char * str)
{
    cout << "\"" << str << "\"";
}
```

4. a. This function shouldn't alter the structure members, so use the **const** qualifier.

```cpp
void show_box(const box & container)
{
    cout << "Made by " << container. maker << "\n";
    cout << "Height = " << container.height << "\n";
    cout << "Width = " << container.width << "\n";
    cout << "Length = " << container.length << "\n";
    cout << "Volume = " << container.volume << "\n";
}
```

b.

```cpp
void set_volume(box & crate)
{
    crate.volume = crate.height * crate.width * crate.length;
}
```

5. a. This can be done using a default value for the second argument:

```cpp
double mass(double d, double v = 1.0);
```

It can also be done by overloading:

```cpp
double mass(double d, double v);
double mass(double d);
```

b. You can't use a default for the repeat value because you have to provide default values from right to left. You can use overloading:

```cpp
void repeat(int times, const char * str);
void repeat(const char * str);
```

c. You can use function overloading:

```cpp
int average(int a, int b);
double average(double x, double y);
```

d. You can't do this one because both versions would have the same signature.

6.

```
template<class T>
T max(T t1, T t2)   // or T max(const T & t1, const T & t2)
{
    return t1 > t2? t1 : t2;
}
```

7.

```
template<> box max(box b1, box b2)
{
    return b1.volume > b2.volume? b1 : b2;
}
```

Chapter 9

1. a. homer is automatically an automatic variable.

   b. secret should be defined as an external variable in one file and declared using extern in the second file.

   c. topsecret could be defined as a static variable with internal linkage by prefacing the external definition with the keyword static. Or it could be defined in an unnamed namespace.

   d. beencalled should be defined as a local static variable by prefacing a declaration in the function with the keyword static.

2. A using declaration makes a single name from a namespace available, and it has the scope corresponding to the declarative region in which the using declaration occurs. A using directive makes all the names in a namespace available. When you use a using directive, it is as if you declared the names in the smallest declarative region containing both the using declaration and the namespace itself.

3.

```
#include <iostream>
using namespace std;
int main()
{
    double x;
    std::cout << "Enter value: ";
    while (! (std::cin >> x) )
    {
        std::cout << "Bad input. Please enter a number: ";
        std::cin.clear();
        while (std::cin.get() != '\n')
            continue;
    }
    std::cout << "Value = " << x << std::endl;
    return 0;
}
```

4. Rewrite the following so that it uses using declarations instead of the using directive.

```cpp
#include <iostream>
int main()
{
    using std::cin;
    using std::cout;
    using std::endl;
    double x;
    cout << "Enter value: ";
    while (! (cin >> x) )
    {
        cout << "Bad input. Please enter a number: ";
        cin.clear();
        while (cin.get() != '\n')
            continue;
    }
    cout << "Value = " << x << endl;
    return 0;
}
```

5. You could have separate static function definitions in each file. Or each file could define the appropriate average() function in an unnamed namespace.

6.

```
10
4
0
Other: 10, 1
another(): 10, -4
```

7.

```
1
4, 1, 2
2
2
4, 1, 2
2
```

Chapter 10

1. A class is a definition of a user-defined type. A class declaration specifies how data is to be stored, and it specifies the methods (class member functions) that can be used to access and manipulate that data.

2. A class represents the operations one can perform on a class object with a public interface of class methods; this is abstraction. The class can use private visibility (the default) for data members, meaning that the data can be accessed only through the member

functions; this is data hiding. Details of the implementation, such as data representation and method code, are hidden; this is encapsulation.

3. The class defines a type, including how it can be used. An object is a variable or other data object, such as that produced by **new**, created and used according to the class definition. The relationship is the same as that between a standard type and a variable of that type.

4. If you create several objects of a given class, each object comes with storage for its own set of data. But all the objects use the one set of member functions. (Typically, methods are public and data members are private, but that's a matter of policy, not of class requirements.)

Note

The program uses `cin.get(char *, int)` instead of `cin >>` to read names because `cin.get()` reads a whole line instead of just one word (see Chapter 4).

5.

```
#include <iostream>
using namespace std;

// class definition
class BankAccount
{
private:
    char name[40];
    char acctnum[25];
    double balance;
public:
    BankAccount(const char * client = "X", const char * num = "X",
        double bal = 0;)
    void show(void) const;
    void deposit(double cash);
    void withdraw(double cash);
};
```

6. A class constructor is called when you create an object of that class or when you explicitly call the constructor. The class destructor is called when the object expires.

7. Note that you must include **cstring** or **string.h** in order to use **strncpy()**.

```
BankAccount::BankAccount(const char * client, const char * num, double bal)
{
    strncpy(name, client, 39);
    name[39] = '\0';
    strncpy(acctnum, num, 24);
    acctnum[24] = '\0';
    balance = bal;
}
```

Keep in mind that default arguments go in the prototype, not in the function definition.

8. A default constructor is one with no arguments or else with defaults for all the arguments. Having one enables you to declare objects without initializing them, even if you've already defined an initializing constructor. It also allows you to declare arrays.

9.

```
// stock3.h
#ifndef STOCK3_H_
#define STOCK3_H_

class Stock
{
private:
    char company[30];
    int shares;
    double share_val;
    double total_val;
    void set_tot() { total_val = shares * share_val; }
public:
    Stock();                // default constructor
    Stock(const char * co, int n, double pr);
    ~Stock() {}             // do-nothing destructor
    void buy(int num, double price);
    void sell(int num, double price);
    void update(double price);
    void show() const;
    const Stock & topval(const Stock & s) const;
    int numshares() const { return shares; }
    double shareval() const { return share_val; }
    double totalval() const { return total_val; }
    const char * co_name() const { return company; }
};
```

10. The `this` pointer is a pointer available to class methods. It points to the object used to invoke the method. Thus, `this` is the address of the object, and `*this` represents the object itself.

Chapter 11

1. Here's a prototype for the class definition file and a function definition for the methods file:

```
// prototype
Stonewt operator*(double mult);

// definition -- let constructor do the work
Stonewt Stonewt::operator*(double mult)
{
    return Stonewt(mult * pounds);
}
```

2. A member function is part of a class definition and is invoked by a particular object. The member function can access members of the invoking object implicitly, without using the membership operator. A friend function is not part of a class, so it's called as a straight function call. It can't access class members implicitly, so it must use the membership operator applied to an object passed as an argument. Compare, for instance, the answer to Review Question 1 with the answer to Review Question 4.

3. It must be a friend to access private members, but it doesn't have to be a friend to access public members.

4. Here's a prototype for the class definition file and a function definition for the methods file:

```
// prototype
friend Stonewt operator*(double mult, const Stonewt & s);

// definition -- let constructor do the work
Stonewt operator*(double mult, const Stonewt & s)
{
    return Stonewt(mult * s.pounds);
}
```

5. The following five operators cannot be overloaded:

```
sizeof   .   .*   ::   ? :
```

6. These operators must be defined by using a member function.

7. Here is a possible prototype and definition:

```
// prototype and inline definition
operator double () {return mag;}
```

Note, however, that it makes better sense to use the `magval()` method than to define this conversion function.

Chapter 12

1. a. The syntax is fine, but this constructor leaves the `str` pointer uninitialized. The constructor should either set the pointer to `NULL` or use `new []` to initialize the pointer.

   b. This constructor does not create a new string; it merely copies the address of the old string. It should use `new []` and `strcpy()`.

   c. It copies the string without allocating the space to store it. It should use `new char[len + 1]` to allocate the proper amount of memory.

2. First, when an object of that type expires, the data pointed to by the object's member pointer remains in memory, using space and remaining inaccessible because the pointer has been lost. That can be fixed by having the class destructor delete memory allocated by `new` in the constructor functions. Second, once the destructor deletes such memory, it

may wind up trying to delete it twice if a program initialized one such object to another. That's because the default initialization of one object to another copies pointer values but does not copy the pointed-to data, producing two pointers to the same data. The solution is to define a class copy constructor that causes initialization to copy the pointed-to data. Third, assigning one object to another can produce the same situation of two pointers pointing to the same data. The solution is to overload the assignment operator so that it copies the data, not the pointers.

3. C++ automatically provides the following member functions:

   - A default constructor if you define no constructors

   - A copy constructor if you don't define one

   - An assignment operator if you don't define one

   - A default destructor if you don't define one

   - An address operator if you don't define one

   The default constructor does nothing, but it allows you to declare arrays and uninitialized objects. The default copy constructor and the default assignment operator use memberwise assignment. The default destructor does nothing. The implicit address operator returns the address of the invoking object (that is, the value of the `this` pointer).

4. The `personality` member should be declared either as a character array or as a pointer-to-char. Or you could make it a `String` object. Here are two possible solutions, with changes (other than deletions) in boldface.

```
#include <iostream>
#include <cstring>
using namespace std;
class nifty
{
private: // optional
    char personality[40];     // provide array size
    int talents;
public: // needed
// methods
    nifty();
    nifty(const char * s);
    friend ostream & operator<<(ostream & os, const nifty & n);
};    // note closing semicolon

nifty::nifty()
{
    personality[0] = '\0';
    talents = 0;
}

nifty::nifty(const char * s)
{
```

```
    strcpy(personality, s);
    talents = 0;
}

ostream & operator<<(ostream & os, const nifty & n)
{
    os << n.personality << '\n';
    os << n.talent << '\n';
    return os;
}
```

Or you could do this:

```
#include <iostream>
#include <cstring>
using namespace std;
class nifty
{
private: // optional
    char * personality;     // create a pointer
    int talents;
public: // needed
// methods
    nifty();
    nifty(const char * s);
    nifty(const nifty & n);
    ~nifty() { delete personality; }
    nifty & operator=(const nifty & n) const;
    friend ostream & operator<<(ostream & os, const nifty & n);
};     // note closing semicolon

nifty::nifty()
{
    personality = NULL;
    talents = 0;
}

nifty::nifty(const char * s)
{
    personality = new char [strlen(s) + 1];
    strcpy(personality, s);
    talents = 0;
}

ostream & operator<<(ostream & os, const nifty & n)
{
    os << n.personality << '\n';
    os << n.talent << '\n';
    return os;
}
```

5. a.

```
Golfer nancy; // default constructor
Golfer lulu("Little Lulu"); // Golfer(const char * name, int g)
Golfer roy("Roy Hobbs", 12); // Golfer(const char * name, int g)
Golfer * par = new Golfer; // default constructor
Golfer next = lulu; // Golfer(const Golfer &g)
Golfer hazard = "Weed Thwacker"; // Golfer(const char * name, int g)
*par = nancy; // default assignment operator
nancy = "Nancy Putter";// Golfer(const char * name, int g), then
                        // the default assignment operator
```

Note

Some compilers will additionally call the default assignment operator for statements #5 and #6.

b. The class should define an assignment operator that copies data rather than addresses.

Chapter 13

1. The public members of the base class become public members of the derived class. The protected members of the base class become protected members of the derived class. The private members of the base class are inherited, but cannot be accessed directly. The answer to review question 2 provides the exceptions to these general rules.

2. The constructor methods are not inherited, the destructor is not inherited, the assignment operator is not inherited, and friends are not inherited.

3. If the return type were **void**, you would still be able to use single assignment but not chain assignment:

```
baseDMA magazine("Pandering to Glitz", 1);
baseDMA gift1, gift2, gift3;
gift1 = magazine;        // ok
gift 2 = gift3 = gift1;  // no longer valid
```

If the method returned an object instead of a reference, the method execution would be slowed a bit because the return statement would involve copying the object.

4. Constructors are called in the order of derivation, with the most ancestral constructor called first. Destructors are called in the opposite order.

5. Yes, every class requires its own constructors. If the derived class adds no new members, the constructor can have an empty body, but it must exist.

6. Only the derived class method is called. It supersedes the base class definition. A base class method is called only if the derived class does not redefine the method or if you use the scope resolution operator. However, you really should declare as virtual any functions that will be redefined.

7. The derived class should define an assignment operator if the derived class constructors use the `new` or `new []` operator to initialize pointers that are members of that class. More generally, the derived class should define an assignment operator if the default assignment is incorrect for derived class members.

8. Yes, you can assign the address of an object of a derived class to a pointer to the base class. You can assign the address of a base object to a pointer to a derived class (downcasting) only by making an explicit type cast, and it is not necessarily safe to use such a pointer.

9. Yes, you can assign an object of a derived class to an object of the base class. Any data members new to the derived type are not passed to the base type, however. The program will use the base class assignment operator. Assignment in the opposite direction (base to derived) is possible only if the derived class defines a conversion operator, which is a constructor having a reference to the base type as its sole argument, or else defines an assignment operator with a base-class parameter.

10. It can do so because C++ allows a reference to a base type to refer to any type derived from that base.

11. Passing an object by value invokes the copy constructor. Since the formal argument is a base class object, the base class copy constructor is invoked. The copy constructor has as its argument a reference to the base class, and this reference can refer to the derived object passed as an argument. The net result is producing a new base class object whose members correspond to the base class portion of the derived object.

12. Passing an object by reference instead of by value enables the function to avail itself of virtual functions. Also, passing an object by reference instead of value may use less memory and time, particularly for large objects. The main advantage of passing by value is that it protects the original data, but you can accomplish the same end by passing the reference as a `const` type.

13. If `head()` is a regular method, then `ph->head()` invokes `Corporation::head()`. If `head()` is a virtual function, then `ph->head()` invokes `PublicCorporation::head()`.

14. First, the situation does not fit the *is-a* model, so public inheritance is not appropriate. Second, the definition of `area()` in `House` hides the `Kitchen` version of `area()` because the two methods have different signatures.

Chapter 14

1.

class Bear	class PolarBear	Public, a polar bear is a kind of bear
class Kitchen	class Home	Private, a home has a kitchen
class Person	class Programmer	Public, a programmer is a kind of person
class Person	class HorseAndJockey	Private, a horse and jockey team contains aperson
class Person, class	class Driver Automobile	Person public because a driver is a person; Automobile private because a driver has an automobile

2.

```
Gloam::Gloam(int g, const char * s) : glip(g), fb(s) { }
Gloam::Gloam(int g, const Frabjous & f) : glip(g), fb(f) { }
// note: the above uses the default Frabjous copy constructor
void Gloam::tell()
{
    fb.tell();
    cout << glip << '\n';
}
```

3.

```
Gloam::Gloam(int g, const char * s)
            : glip(g), Frabjous(s) { }
Gloam::Gloam(int g, const Frabjous & f)
            : glip(g), Frabjous(f) { }
// note: the above uses the default Frabjous copy constructor
void Gloam::tell()
{
    Frabjous::tell();
    cout << glip << '\n';
}
```

4.

```
class Stack<Worker *>
{
private:
    enum {MAX = 10};        // constant specific to class
    Worker * items[MAX];    // holds stack items
    int top;                // index for top stack item
public:
    Stack();
    Boolean isempty();
    Boolean isfull();
```

```
        Boolean push(const Worker * & item); // add item to stack
        Boolean pop(Worker * & item);         // pop top into item
    };
```

5.

```
    ArrayTP<String> sa;
    StackTP< ArrayTP<double> > stck_arr_db;
    ArrayTp< StackTP<Worker *> > arr_stk_wpr;
```

6. If two lines of inheritance for a class share a common ancestor, the class winds up with two copies of the ancestor's members. Making the ancestor class a virtual base class to its immediate descendants solves that problem.

Chapter 15

1. a. The friend declaration should be as follows:

```
    friend class clasp;
```

b. This needs a forward declaration so that the compiler can interpret `void snip(muff &)`:

```
    class muff;     // forward declaration
    class cuff {
    public:
        void snip(muff &) { ... }
        ...
    };
    class muff {
        friend void cuff::snip(muff &);
        ...
    };
```

c. First, the `cuff` class declaration should precede the `muff` class so that the compiler can understand the term `cuff::snip()`. Second, the compiler needs a forward declaration of `muff` so that it can understand `snip(muff &)`.

```
    class muff;     // forward declaration
    class cuff {
    public:
        void snip(muff &) { ... }
        ...
    };
    class muff {
        friend void cuff::snip(muff &);
        ...
    };
```

2. No. For A to have a friend that's a member function of B, the B declaration must precede the A declaration. A forward declaration is not enough, for it would tell A that B is a class, but it wouldn't reveal the names of the class members. Similarly, if B has a friend that's a

member function of A, the complete A declaration must precede the B declaration. These two requirements are mutually exclusive.

3. The only access to a class is through its public interface, which means the only thing you can do with a `Sauce` object is call the constructor to create one. The other members (`soy` and `sugar`) are private by default.

4. Suppose function `f1()` calls function `f2()`. A return statement in `f2()` causes program execution to resume at the next statement following the `f2()` function call in function `f1()`. A throw statement causes the program to back up through the current sequence of function calls until it finds a try block that directly or indirectly contains the call to `f2()`. This might be in `f1()` or in a function that called `f1()`, and so on. Once there, execution goes to the next matching catch block, not to the first statement after the function call.

5. You should arrange the catch blocks in the order of most derived class to least derived.

6. For sample #1, the `if` condition is `true` if `pg` points to a `Superb` object or to an object of any class descended from `Superb`. In particular, it is also `true` if `pg` points to a `Magnificent` object. In sample #2, the `if` condition is `true` only for a `Superb` object, not for objects derived from `Superb`.

7. The `dynamic_cast` operator only allows upcasting in a class hierarchy, while a `static_cast` operator allows both upcasting and downcasting. The `static_cast` operator also allows conversions from enumeration types to integer types, and vice versa, and between various numeric types.

Chapter 16

1.

```cpp
#include <string>
using namespace std;
class RQ1
{
private:
    string st;        // a string object
public:
    RQ1() : st("") {}
    RQ1(const char * s) : st(s) {}
    ~RQ1() {};
// more stuff
};
```

The explicit copy constructor, destructor, and assignment operator no longer are needed because the `string` object provides its own memory management.

2. You can assign one `string` object to another. A `string` object provides its own memory management so that you normally don't have to worry about a string exceeding the capacity of its holder.

3.

```
#include <string>
#include <cctype>
using namespace std;
void ToUpper(string & str)
{
    for (int i = 0; i < str.size(); i++)
        str[i] = toupper(str[i]);
}
```

4.

```
auto_ptr<int> pia= new int[20];    // wrong, use with new, not new[]
auto_ptr<str>(new string);         // wrong, no name for pointer
int rigue = 7;
auto_ptr<int>(&rigue);             // wrong, memory not allocated by new
auto_ptr dbl (new double);         // wrong, omits <double>
```

5. The LIFO aspect of a stack means you might have to remove a lot of clubs before reaching the one you need.

6. The set will store just one copy of each value, so, say, five scores of 5 would be stored as a single 5.

7. Using iterators allows one to use objects with a pointer-like interface to move through data organized in fashions other than an array; for example, data in a doubly linked list.

8. The STL approach lets STL functions be used with ordinary pointers to ordinary arrays as well as with iterators to STL container classes, thus increasing generality.

9. You can assign one **vector** object to another. A **vector** manages its own memory, so you can insert items into a vector and have it resize itself automatically. By using the **at()** method, you can get automatic bounds checking.

10. The two **sort()** functions and the **random_shuffle()** function require a random-access iterator, while a **list** object just has a bidirectional iterator. You can use the list template class **sort()** member functions instead of the general purpose functions to do the sorting, but there is no member function equivalent to **random_shuffle()**. However, you could copy the list to a vector, shuffle the vector, and copy the results back to the list. (At the time of this writing, most compilers have not yet implemented the **sort()** member function that takes a **Compare** object as its argument. Also, the Microsoft Visual C++ 6.0 implementation of the **list** class has some bugs that prevent making the suggested conversions.)

Chapter 17

1. The **iostream** file defines the classes, constants, and manipulators used to manage input and output. These objects manage the streams and buffers used to handle I/O. The file also creates standard objects (**cin**, **cout**, **cerr**, and **clog** and their wide-character

equivalents) used to handle the standard input and output streams connected to every program.

2. Keyboard entry generates a series of characters. Typing 121 generates three characters, each represented by a 1-byte binary code. If the value is to be stored as type `int`, these three characters have to be converted to a single binary representation of the value 121.

3. By default, both the standard output and the standard error send output to the standard output device, typically a monitor. If you have the operating system redirect output to a file, however, the standard output connects to the file instead of to the screen, but the standard error continues to be connected to the screen.

4. The `ostream` class defines a version of the `operator<<()` function for each basic C++ type. The compiler interprets an expression like

```
cout << spot
```

as the following:

```
cout.operator<<(spot)
```

It then can match this method call to the function prototype having the same argument type.

5. You can concatenate output methods that return type `ostream &`. This causes the invoking of a method with an object to return that object. The returned object can then invoke the next method in a sequence.

6.

```
//rq17-6.cpp
#include <iostream>
#include <iomanip>
using namespace std;

int main()
{
    cout << "Enter an integer: ";
    int n;
    cin >> n;
    cout << setw(15) << "base ten" << setw(15)
          << "base sixteen" << setw(15) << "base eight" << "\n";
    cout.setf(ios::showbase);      // or cout << showbase;
    cout << setw(15) << n << hex << setw(15) << n
          << oct << setw(15) << n << "\n";

    return 0;
}
```

7.

```
//rq17-7.cpp
#include <iostream>
#include <iomanip>
```

```
using namespace std;

int main()
{
    char name[20];
    float hourly;
    float hours;

    cout << "Enter your name: ";
    cin.get(name, 20).get();
    cout << "Enter your hourly wages: ";
    cin >> hourly;
    cout << "Enter number of hours worked: ";
    cin >> hours;

    cout.setf(ios::showpoint);
    cout.setf(ios::fixed, ios::floatfield);
    cout.setf(ios::right, ios::adjustfield);
// or cout << showpoint << fixed << right;
    cout << "First format:\n";
    cout << setw(30) << name << ": $" << setprecision(2)
         << setw(10) << hourly << ":" << setprecision(1)
         << setw(5) << hours << "\n";
    cout << "Second format:\n";
    cout.setf(ios::left, ios::adjustfield);
    cout << setw(30) << name << ": $" << setprecision(2)
         << setw(10) << hourly << ":" << setprecision(1)
         << setw(5) << hours << "\n";

    return 0;
}
```

8. Here is the output:

   ```
   ct1 = 5; ct2 = 9
   ```

   The first part of the program ignores spaces and newlines; the second part doesn't. Note that the second part of the program begins reading at the newline character following the first **q**, and it counts that newline as part of its total.

9. The `ignore()` form falters if the input line exceeds 80 characters. In that case it only skips the first 80 characters.

INDEX

Symbols

&& (AND) logical operator, 215-219
= assignment operator, 175-177
& (bitwise AND operator), 971
! (bitwise negation operator), 969
| (bitwise OR operator), 970
^ (bitwise XOR operator), 971
, (comma) operators, 171-174
? conditional operator, 225-227
-- (decrement operators), 167-168
#define statements, 61, 75
(*) dereferencing operator, 138-139
// (double slash) comments, 24-25
== equal to relational operator, 174-177
#ifndef directive, 350-351
++ (increment operators), 167-168
<< insertion operator
    concatenation, 872-873
    data types recognized, 870-871
    pointers, 872
!= is not equal to relational operator, 175
< less than relational operator, 174-175
<= less than or equal to relational operator, 174-175
-lm option (CC command), 12
\n newline character, 29-30
! (NOT) logical operator, 220-221
! operator, 999
< operator, 999
<= operator, 999
== operator, 999
<< operator, 461-466, 995
|| (OR) logical operator, 214-215
= overloaded operator, string classes, 781-783
<< overloaded operator, string classes, 781-783
+= overloaded operator, string classes, 781-783
0 pointers, 532
& (reference) operator, 303-304

A

ABCs (abstract base classes), 605-610
    interface rules, 610
abort() function, 757, 759
abstract base classes. *See* ABCs
abstract classes, 623
abstract data types. *See* ADTs (abstract data types)
abstraction, classes, 395
access control
    class members, 398
    nested classes, 727
access methods, 987
accessing
    characters, bracket notation, 523-525
    class members, protected access, 601-603
accumulate() function, 1026
acquire() function, 403-404
actual argument/parameter, 250
adaptable,
    binary functions, 847-849
    binary predicate, 847-849
    functors, 847
    generators, 847-849
    predicate, 847-849
    unary functions, 847-849
adapters, 820
addition arithmetic operator, 82-83
    precedence rules, 83-84
addition operators
    combined with assignment operators, 168-169
    operator+(), 450-453
addresses, variables, 122
adjacent_difference() function, 1026-1027
adjacent_find() function, 1005-1007
ADTs (abstract data types), 436-439

G

K

L

M

P

T

W-Z

Other Related Titles